PACIFIC
MEXICO
HANDBOOK

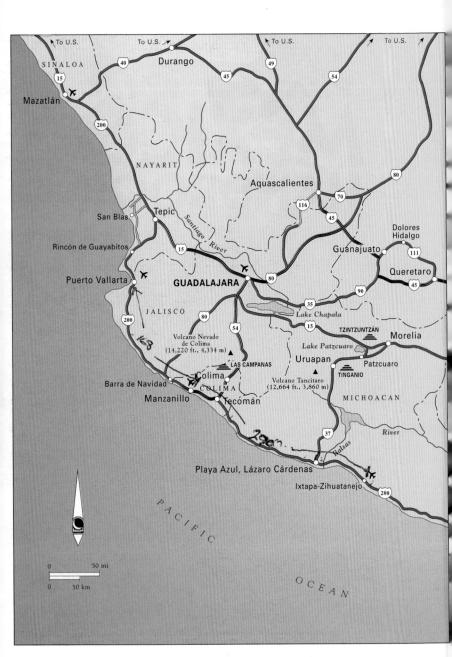

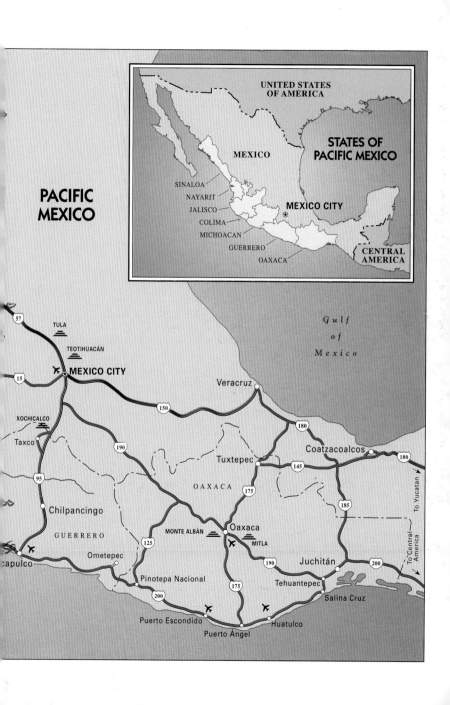

PACIFIC
MEXICO
HANDBOOK

**INCLUDING ACAPULCO, PUERTO VALLARTA
OAXACA, GUADALAJARA & MAZATLÁN**

FOURTH EDITION

BRUCE WHIPPERMAN

MOON
TRAVEL
HANDBOOKS

PACIFIC MEXICO HANDBOOK
FOURTH EDITION

Published by
Moon Publications, Inc.
5855 Beaudry St.
Emeryville, CA 94608, USA

Printed by
Colorcraft Ltd.

ISBN: 1-56691-167-2
ISSN: 1082-488X

Editors: Emily Kendrick, Deana Corbitt Shields
Production & Design: Karen McKinley, David Hurst
Cartography: Brian Bardwell, Allen Leech
Index: Marion Harmon

Front cover photo: Huatulco; © Steven McBride/Picturesque, 1999.

All photos by Bruce Whipperman unless otherwise noted.
All illustrations by Bob Race unless otherwise noted.

Distributed in the United States and Canada by Publishers Group West

Printed in China

Please send all comments,
corrections, additions,
amendments, and critiques to:

**PACIFIC MEXICO HANDBOOK
MOON TRAVEL HANDBOOKS
5855 Beaudry St.
Emeryville, CA 94608
e-mail: travel@moon.com
www.moon.com**

Printing History
1st edition—1993
4th edition—January 2000

5 4 3 2 1 0

To Mom, Dad, and Hilda,
Peter, Sara and Kent,
and Linda

CONTENTS

History; Sights; Beaches; Day Trips; Accommodations; Food;
Entertainment and Events; Sports and Recreation; Shopping; Services;
Information; Getting There and Away

   Playa Caimanero; Concordia, Copala, and Rosario; Teacapán; Novillero;
   Mexcaltitán; Santiago Ixcuintla
   History; Sights and Activities; Accommodations; Food; Entertainment;
   Sports and Recreation; Shopping; Services; Information; Getting There
   and Away; Around the Bay of Matanchén
   History; Sights; Accommodations; Food; Shopping; Services; Information;
   Getting There and Away
   History; Sights; Accommodations; Food; Entertainment and Events;
   Sports; Shopping; Services and Information; Getting There and Away
   Playa Chacala and Mar de Jade
   Sights; Beaches and Activities; Accommodations; Food; Sports and
   Entertainment; Services and Information; Getting There and Away
   Playa Lo de Marco; Playa San Francisco; Sayulita

CHARTS

ABBREVIATIONS

a/c	—	air-conditioned
Av.	—	Avenida
Blv.	—	Búlevar (boulevard)
C	—	Celsius
Calz.	—	*Calzada* (thoroughfare, main road)
d	—	double occupancy
Fracc.	—	Fra iccionimiento (subdivision)
Fco.	—	Francisco (proper name, as in "Fco. Villa")
Hwy.	—	Highway
IAMAT	—	International Association for Medical Assistance to Travelers
km	—	kilometer
Km	—	kilometer marker
kph	—	kilometers per hour
Nte.	—	Norte (north)
Ote.	—	Oriente (east)
Pte.	—	Poniente (west)
s	—	single occupancy
s/n	—	*sin número* (no street number)
t	—	triple occupancy
tel.	—	telephone number

MAPS

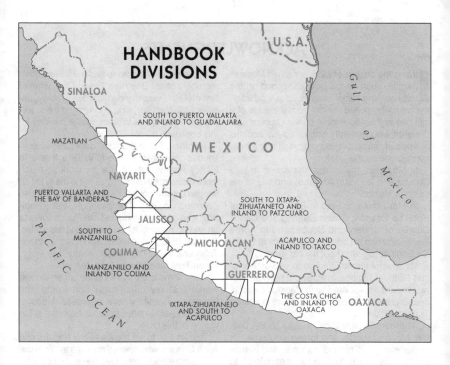

HANDBOOK DIVISIONS

U.S.A.

Gulf of Mexico

SINALOA

MAZATLAN

SOUTH TO PUERTO VALLARTA
AND INLAND TO GUADALAJARA

M E X I C O

NAYARIT

PUERTO VALLARTA AND
THE BAY OF BANDERAS

JALISCO

SOUTH TO IXTAPA-
ZIHUATANETO AND
INLAND TO PATZCUARO

SOUTH TO
MANZANILLO

MICHOACAN

ACAPULCO AND
INLAND TO TAXCO

COLIMA

PACIFIC

MANZANILLO AND
INLAND TO COLIMA

GUERRERO

THE COSTA CHICA
AND INLAND TO
OAXACA

OCEAN

IXTAPA-ZIHUATANEJO
AND SOUTH TO
ACAPULCO

OAXACA

MAP SYMBOLS

═══	Superhighway	⊛	Capitol City	✕	International Airport
═══	Primary Road	○	City	♣	Golf Course
───	Secondary Road	○	Town	⋀	Campground
┄┄┄	Unpaved Road	★	Point of Interest	≜	Archaeological Zone
┄┄┄	Trail	•	Accommodation	▲	Mountain
◯	Mexico Route	▾	Restaurant/Bar	☊	Waterfall
◯	Mexico State Route	▪	Other Location	✛	Unique Natural Feature
Gas		▲	Church	⁙	Mangrove

ACKNOWLEDGMENTS

I thank the dozens of kind, unnamed Mexican people, such as the boy who stood on the road warning trucks away as I changed a tire, the men who pulled my car from the edge of a cliff one night atop a mountain in Oaxaca, and the staff who patiently answered my endless queries at many *turismo* offices. They all deserve credit for this book.

In Mazatlán, my special thanks go to Luis Chavez and Augustín Arellano, who taught me much of Mexico.

In Manzanillo, thanks to Bart Varelman of Hotel La Posada, Susan Dearing and Carlos Cuellar of Underworld Scuba, and to Alfred Hasler and and his tireless mechanics at SIMP-SA Engineering who kept my car running.

My special thanks also go to eco-ornithologist Michael Malone in Puerto Escondido for helping me appreciate Pacific Mexico's wildlife treasury, and to his excellent partners in agency Turismo Rodemar.

At Moon Publications, thanks to Bill Dalton, Moon's founder and former publisher, for undertaking this project with me, and to present publisher Bill Newlin for continuing it to the present. Also thanks to my original editors Mark Morris (who coined the name "Pacific Mexico"), Beth Rhudy, and to editors Pauli Galin and Deana Corbitt Shields for their ton of work, kind encouragement, and hundreds of suggestions that saved my manuscript. Thanks also to Bob Race and Brian Bardwell for their excellent illustrations and maps.

I owe a load of thanks to Susan Hall and other members of the Bay Area Travel Club, where I first met Bill Dalton; and to Gordon Barbery, another Club member, who encouraged me to join the Bay Area Travel Writers, where the idea for this book was born.

To others I owe a unique debt for their continuous generosity. In Puerto Vallarta, thanks to Nancy Adams, who made my work so much more pleasant by gracefully allowing me to set up shop in a corner of her lovely Cafe Sierra. I also owe much to Gary Thompson, of Galería Pacífico, who introduced me to both Puerto Vallarta art and his many gracious friends and associates. For their helpful kindness, I also specially thank John and Nancy Erickson, Kathy von Rohr, Diana Turn, and María Elena Zermeño.

In my home town, thanks to the understanding workers at my office-away-from-home, the Espresso Roma, where espresso Maestro Miguel's luscious lattes became essential to the writing of this book.

Thanks also to my friends Akemi Nagafuji and Anne Shapiro, who opened my eyes to the world.

This book could not have been written if not for Halcea Valdes, my friend and business partner, to whom I am grateful for managing without me while I was on the road for nine months in Pacific Mexico.

Finally, a heap of credit is due to my wife, Linda, who kept the home fires burning while I was away, came and nursed me when I got sick in Oaxaca, and was patient about everything I had to neglect back home while finishing this book.

LET US HEAR FROM YOU

We're especially interested in hearing from female travelers, handicapped travelers, people who've traveled with children, RVers, hikers, campers, and residents, both foreign and Mexican. We welcome the comments of business and professional people—hotel and restaurant owners, travel agents, government tourism staff—who serve Pacific Mexico travelers.

We welcome submissions of unusually good photos and drawings for possible use in future editions. If photos, send duplicate slides or slides from negatives; if drawings, send clear photocopies. Please include a self-addressed stamped envelope if you'd like your material returned. If we use it, we'll cite your contribution and give you a free new edition. Please address your responses to:

Pacific Mexico Handbook
c/o Moon Travel Handbooks
5855 Beaudry St.
Emeryville, CA 94608 USA
e-mail: travel@moon.com

PREFACE

*S*carcely a generation ago, Mexico's tropical Pacific coast was dotted with a few sleepy, isolated towns and fishing villages, reachable only by sea or tortuous mountain roads from the interior. That gradually began to change until, in 1984, the last link of Mexico's Pacific Coast Highway 200 was completed, a palmy thousand-mile path for exploring Mexico and the new tourist region of Pacific Mexico.

The choices seem endless. You can enjoy numerous resorts, some glittering and luxurious and others quiet and homey. In between the resorts stretch jungle-clad headlands, interspersed with palm-shaded, pearly strands where the fishing is good and the living easy.

When weary of lazing in the sun, visitors can enjoy a trove of ocean sports. Pacific Mexico's water is always balmy and fine to fish, swim, surf, windsurf, kayak, water-ski, snorkel, and scuba dive. For nature enthusiasts, dozens of lush jungle-fringed coastal lagoons are ripe for wildlife viewing and photography.

The coastal strip would be enough but Pacific Mexico offers more: Within a hour's flight or a day's drive of the tropical shore rise the cool oak- and pine-tufted highland valleys. Here, colonial cities—Guadalajara, Tepic, Colima, Pátzcuaro, Uruapan, Taxco, Oaxaca—offer fine crafts, colorful festivals, baroque monuments, traditional peoples, and the barely explored ruins of long-forgotten kingdoms.

In short, Pacific Mexico is an exotic, tropical land, easy to visit, enjoy, and appreciate, whether you prefer glamourous luxury, backcountry adventure, or a little bit of both. This book will show you the way.

INTRODUCTION

LAND AND SEA

On the map of North America, Mexico appears as a grand horn of plenty, spreading and spilling to its northern border with the United States. Mexico encompasses a vast landscape, sprawling over an area as large as France, Germany, England, and Italy combined. Besides its size, Mexico is high country, where most people live in mountain valleys within sight of towering, snow-capped peaks.

Travelers heading south of the Río Grande do not realize the rise in elevation, however. Instead, brushy, cactus-pocked plains spread to mountain ranges on the far blue horizon. Northern Mexico is nevertheless a tableland—the *altiplano*—that rises gradually from the Río Grande to its climax at the very heart of the country: the mile-high Bajio (BAH-heeoh) Valley around Guadalajara and the even loftier Valley of Mexico.

Here, in these fertile vales, untold generations of Mexicans have gazed southward at an awesome rampart of smoking mountains, a grand volcanic seam stretching westward from the Gulf of Mexico to the Pacific. In a continuous line along the 19th parallel, more than a dozen volcanoes have puffed sulfurous gas and spewed red-hot rock for an eon, building themselves into some of the mightiest peaks in the Americas. Most easterly and grandest of them all is Orizaba (Citlaltépetl, the "Mountain of the Star"), rising 18,856 feet (5,747 meters) directly above the Gulf. Then, in proud succession, the giants march westward: Malinche, 14,640 feet (4,462 meters); Popocatépetl, 17,888 feet (5,452 meters); Nevado de Toluca, 15,016 feet (4,577 meters); until finally the most active of all—the 13,087-foot (3,989-meter) Volcán de Fuego (Volcano of Fire)—fumes next to its serene twin, the Nevado de Colima (14,220 feet, 4,334 meters) above the long, plumy shoreline of Pacific Mexico.

PACIFIC MEXICO

This sun-drenched western coastland stretches along a thousand miles of sandy beaches, palm-strewn headlands, and blue lagoons, from

Mazatlán in the north and curving to the southeast past Acapulco to the new vacation land of Bahías de Huatulco in Oaxaca.

Pacific Mexico is a land washed by the ocean and sheltered by the western mountains: Sierra Madre Occidental and its southern extension, the Sierra Madre del Sur. Everywhere, except in the north where the coastal plain is broad, these green jungle-clad sierras rise quickly, sometimes precipitously, above a narrow coastal strip. Few rivers and roads breach these ramparts, and where roads do, they wind through deep *barrancas,* over lofty passes to temperate, oak-studded highland valleys.

Climate
Elevation rules the climate of Pacific Mexico. The entire coastal strip (including the mountain slopes and plateaus up to four or five thousand feet) basks in the tropics, never feeling the bite of frost. The seashore is truly a land of perpetual summer. Winter days are typically warm and rainless, peaking at 80-85° F (26-28° C) and dropping to 60-70° F (16-21° C) by midnight. The north-to-south variation on this theme is typically small: Mazatlán will be a few degrees cooler; Acapulco, a few degrees warmer.

Summers on the Pacific Mexico beaches are warmer and wetter. July, August, and September forenoons are typically bright and warm, heating to the high 80s (around 30° C) with afternoon clouding and short, sometimes heavy, showers. By late afternoon, clouds part, the sun dries the pavements, and the breeze is often balmy and just right to enjoy a sparkling Pacific Mexico sunset.

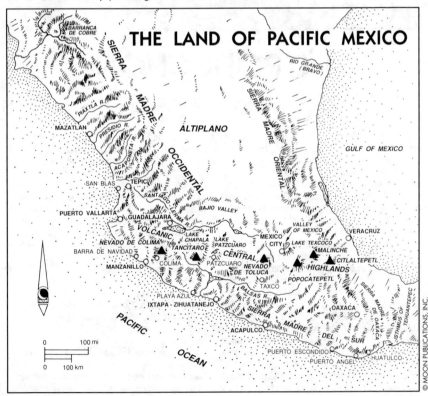

THE LAND OF PACIFIC MEXICO

CLIMATE REGIONS
OF
PACIFIC MEXICO

☐ = TEMPERATE (SUBJECT TO WINTER FROST)

▨ = TROPICAL (FROST - FREE)

0   100mi

0   100km

© MOON PUBLICATIONS, INC.

The highlands around Guadalajara, Pátzcuaro, Taxco, and Oaxaca experience similar, but more temperate seasons. Midwinter days are mild, typically peaking around 70° F (21° C). Expect cool, but frost-free, winter nights between 40 and 50° F (9-14° C). Highland summers are delightful, with afternoons in the 80s (27-32° C) and pleasant evenings in the mid-70s (21-26° C), perfect for strolling. May, before the rains, is often the warmest, with June, July, and August highs being moderated by afternoon showers. Many Guadalajara, Pátzcuaro, Taxco, and Oaxaca residents enjoy the best of all possible worlds: balmy summers at home and similarly balmy winters in vacation homes along the Pacific Mexico coast.

FLORA AND FAUNA

Fascinating hothouse verdure—from delicate orchids and bulbous, fuzzy succulents to giant hanging philodendrons—luxuriates at some roadside spots of Pacific Mexico, as if beckoning admirers. Now and then visitors stop, attracted by something remarkable, such as a riot of flowers blooming from apparently dead branches, or what looks like grapefruit sprouting from the trunk of a roadside tree. More often, travelers pass long stretches of thorny thickets, viny jungles, and broad, mangrove-edged marshes. A little advance knowledge of what to expect can

stunning view over beautiful Acapulco

blossom into recognition and discovery, transforming the humdrum into something quite extraordinary, even exotic.

VEGETATION ZONES

Mexico's diverse landscape and fickle rainfall have sculpted its wide range of plant forms. Botanists recognize at least 14 major Mexican vegetation zones, eight of which occur in Pacific Mexico.

Directly along the coastal highway, you often pass long sections of three of these zones: savanna, thorn forest, and tropical deciduous forest. The other five are less accessible.

Savanna
Great swaths of pasturelike savanna stretch along the roadside south of Mazatlán to Tepic. In its natural state, savanna often appears as a palm-dotted sea of grass—green and marshy during the rainy summer, dry and brown by late winter.

Although grass rules the savanna, palms give it character. Most familiar is the **coconut**—the *cocotero*—used for everything from lumber to candy. Coconut palms line the beaches and climb the hillsides—drooping, slanting, rustling, and swaying in the breeze like troupes of hula dancers. Less familiar, but with as much personality, is the Mexican **fan palm**, or *palma real,* festooned with black fruit and spread flat like a señorita's fan.

The savanna's list goes on: the grapefruitlike fruit on the trunk and branches identify the **gourd tree,** or *calabaza.* The mature gourds, brown and hard, have been carved into *jícaros* (cups for drinking chocolate) for millennia.

Orange-size, pumpkinlike gourds both mark and name the **sandbox tree,** or *jabillo,* because they once served as desktop boxes full of sand for drying ink. The Aztecs, however, called it the exploding tree, because its ripe fruits burst their seeds forth with a bang like a firecracker.

The waterlogged seaward edge of the savanna nurtures forests of the **red mangrove,** or *mangle colorado,* short trees that seem to stand in the water on stilts. Their new roots grow downward from above; a time-lapse photo would show them marching, as if on stilts, into the lagoon.

Thorn Forest
Lower rainfall leads to the hardier growth of the thorn forest, the domain of the pea family—the **acacias** and their cousins, the **mimosas.** Among the most common is the **long spine acacia,** with fluffy, yellow flower balls, ferny leaves, and long,

Lotus blossoms frequently decorate pond and lagoon edges of Pacific Mexico savannahs.

VEGETATION ZONES
OF PACIFIC MEXICO

GULF OF MEXICO

MAZATLAN

TEPIC
SAN BLAS
PUERTO
VALLARTA
GUADALAJARA
BAJIO
VALLEY
PARQUE
NATURAL
NEVADO
DE COLIMA
PARQUE
NACIONAL
TANCITARO
BARRA DE NAVIDAD
COLIMA
PATZCUARO
MEXICO CITY
MANZANILLO
TAXCO
CUERNAVACA
BALSAS RIVER
BASIN

TEMPERATE
= MESQUITE GRASSLAND
= PINE - OAK FOREST
= HIGH CONIFEROUS FOREST

TROPICAL
= SAVANNAH
= THORN FOREST
= ARID TROPICAL SCRUB
= TROPICAL DECIDUOUS FOREST
= CLOUD FOREST

IXTAPA-ZIHUATANEJO
PARQUE
NATURAL
DE GUERRERO
CHILPANCINGO
OAXACA
ACAPULCO

PUERTO ESCONDIDO
HUATULCO
PUERTO ANGEL

PACIFIC

OCEAN

0   100mi
0   100km

© MOON PUBLICATIONS, INC.

narrow pods; less common, but more useful, is the **fishfuddle,** with pink pea-flowers and long pods, a source of fish-stunning poison. Take care around the acacias; some of the long-thorned varieties harbor nectar-feeding, biting ants.

Perhaps the most spectacular and famous member of the thorn forest community is the **morning glory tree,** which announces the winter dry season's end by blooming a festoon of white trumpets atop its crown of seemingly dead branches. Its gruesome Mexican name, *palo del muerto* (tree of the dead), is exceeded only around Taxco, where folks call it *palo bobo* (fool tree), because they believe if you take a drink from a stream near its foot, you will go crazy.

The cactuses are among the thorn forest's sturdiest and most spectacular inhabitants. In the dry Río Balsas basin (along Hwy. 95 inland

from Acapulco) the spectacular **candelabra cactus** *(cordón espinosa)* spreads as much as 60 feet tall and wide.

Tropical Deciduous Forest
In rainier areas, the thorn forest grades into tropical deciduous forest. This is the "friendly" or "short-tree" forest, blanketed by a tangle of summer-green leaves that fall in the dry winter, revealing thickets of dry branches. Some trees show bright fall reds and yellows, later blossoming with brilliant flowers—spider lily, cardinal sage, pink trumpet, poppylike yellowsilk *(pomposhuti),* and mouse-killer *(mala ratón),* which swirl in the spring wind like cherry-blossom blizzards.

The tropical deciduous forest is the lush jungle coat that swathes much of coastal Pacific Mexico. And often, where the mountains rush direct-

CATHY CARLSON

Yellow blooms of the rosa amarilla *(yellow rose) sometimes adorn forest roadsides during the winter dry season. Despite its name, its brown pods mark it as a member of the cochlospermum (shell seed) family.*

ly down to the sea, the forest likewise spills right over the headland into the ocean. Vine-strewn thickets often overhang the highway, like the edge of some lost prehistoric world, where you might expect a last remnant dinosaur to rear up at any moment.

However, biological realities here are nearly as exotic: a four-foot-long green iguana, looking every bit as primitive as a dinosaur, slithers across the pavement; or at roadside, a spreading, solitary **strangler fig** stands, draped with hairy, hanging air roots (which, in time, plant themselves into the ground and support the branches). The Mexican name, *matapalo* (killer tree), is gruesomely accurate, for strangler figs often entwine themselves in a death embrace with some other, less aggressive, victim tree.

Much more benign, however, is my favorite of the tropical deciduous forest: the *guaycoyul, cohune,* or **Colima palm.** *Cohune* in Pacific Mexico means "magnificent." Capped by a proud cock-plume, it presides over the forest singly or

in great, gracefully swaying groves atop the headlands. Its nuts, harvested like small coconuts, yield oil and animal fodder.

Excursions by jeep or on foot along shaded, off-highway tracks through the tropical deciduous forest can yield delightful jungle scenes; unwary travelers must watch out, however, for the poison-oak-like **mala mujer,** the "bad woman" tree. The oil on its large five-fingered leaves can cause an itchy rash.

Pine-Oak Forest

A couple of hours drive inland (especially on the mountain roads from the coast to Guadalajara, Taxco, and Oaxaca), the tropics give way to the temperate pine-oak forest, Pacific Mexico's most extensive vegetation zone. Here, most of Mexico's 112 oak and 39 pine species thrive. At the lower elevations, bushy, nut-yielding piñon pines sometimes cover the slope; then come the tall pines, often Chihuahua pine and Montezuma pine, both yellow varieties, similar to the ponderosa pine of the western United States.

Interspersed with them are oaks, in two broad classifications—*encino* (evergreen, small-leafed) and *roble* (deciduous, large-leafed)—both much like the oaks that dot California hills and valleys. Clustered in their branches and scattered in the shade are the *bellota* (acorns) that irrevocably mark them as oaks.

Mesquite Grassland

Although much of Pacific Mexico's mesquite grassland has been tamed for agriculture, outlying districts, notably in the valleys around Guadalajara, still exhibit its typical landscape, similar to the semi-arid plateau land of the U.S. southwest.

Despite its seemingly monotonous roadside aspect, the mesquite grassland nurtures surprisingly exotic and unusual plants. Among the most intriguing is the **maguey** (mah-GAY), or century plant, so-called because it's said to bloom once, then die, after 100 years of growth, although its lifetime is usually closer to 50 years. The *maguey* and its cactus-like relatives—such as the very useful **mescal, *lechuguilla,*** and **sisal,** all of the genus *Agave*—each grow as a roselike cluster of leathery, long, pointed gray-green leaves, out from which a single flower stalk eventually blooms.

Century plants themselves, which can grow several feet tall and equally wide, thrive either wild or in cultivated ranks and files like a botanical army on parade. These fields, prominently visible from National Hwy. 15 west of Guadalajara, are eventually harvested, the leaves crushed, fermented, and distilled into fiery 80-proof tequila, the most renowned of which comes from the town of Tequila near Hwy. 15.

Watch for the mesquite grassland's **candelilla** *(Euphorbia antisyphillitica),* an odd cousin of the poinsettia, also a Mexico native. In contrast to the poinsettia, the *candelilla* resembles a tall (two- to three-foot) candle, decorated with small white flowers scattered upward along its single vertical stem. Abundant wax on the many pencil-sized stalks that curve upward from the base is useful for anything from polishing your shoes to lubricating your car's distributor.

Equally exotic is the **sangre de drago,** "blood of the dragon," *(Japtropha dioica),* which also grows in a single meaty stem producing two-inch long lobed leaves with small white flowers. Break off a leaf and out oozes a clear sap, which soon turns blood-red.

High Coniferous Forest
Pacific Mexico's least accessible vegetation zone is the high coniferous forest, above about 9,000 feet, which swathes the slopes of the area's tallest peaks, notably the Nevado de Colima, elev. 14,220 feet (4,334 meters), and Tancitaro, elev. 12,665 feet (3,860 meters), in Michoacán. These pristine green alpine islands, accessible only on horseback or by foot, nurture stands of magnificent pines and spruce and grassy meadows, similar to the higher Rocky Mountain slopes in the U.S. and Canada. Reigning over the lesser species is the regal **Montezuma pine,** *Pinus montezumae,* distinguished by its long, pendulous cones and rough, ruddy bark, reminiscent of the sugar pine of the western U.S.

Arid Tropical Scrub and Cloud Forest
Pacific Mexico's two rarest and exotic vegetation zones are far from the coastal tourist centers. You can conveniently see the great cactus forests of the arid tropical scrub habitat (which occupies the wild, dry canyonland of the Río Balsas intermountain basin) either along Hwy. 95 inland from Acapulco, or along Hwy. 37 between Playa Azul and Pátzcuaro. Finally, travelers who drive to high, dewy mountainsides, beginning around 7,000 feet, can explore the plant and wildlife community of the cloud forest. The Parque Natural de Guerrero (around Corral Bravo, 50 miles west of Chilpancingo, Guerrero) and Sierra de Manatlán (in the roadless de facto wilderness 40 miles northeast of Barra de Navidad) preserve such habitats. There, abundant cool fog nourishes forests of tree ferns, lichen-draped pines, and oaks above a mossy carpet of orchids, bromeliads, and begonias. For more details, consult M. Walter Pesman's delightful *Meet Flora Mexicana* (which, unfortunately, is out of print, but major libraries often have a copy). Also informative is the popular paperback *Handbook of Mexican Roadside Flora,* by Charles T. Mason Jr. and Patricia B. Mason. (See the Booklist.)

WILDLIFE

Despite continued habitat destruction—logging of forests, filling wetlands, and plowing savannas—Pacific Mexico still abounds with wildlife. In the temperate pine-oak forest zone of Pacific Mexico live most of the familiar birds and mammals—mountain lion, coyote, jackrabbit, dove, quail—of the American Southwest.

The tropical coastal forests and savannas, however, are home to species seen only in zoos north of the border.

KAREN McKINLEY

Jaguars still hunt in remote mangrove wetlands and mountain jungles of Pacific Mexico.

CATHY CARLSON

Spider monkeys, once common, are now rarely seen in the wild in Pacific Mexico.

The reality of this often first dawns on travelers when they glimpse something exotic, such as raucous, screeching swarms of small green parrots rising from the roadside, or an armadillo or coati nosing in the sand just a few feet away at the forested edge of some isolated Pacific Mexico beach.

Armadillos, Coatis, Spider Monkeys, and Tapirs

Armadillos are cat-size mammals that act and look like opossums but carry reptilianlike shells. If you see one, remain still, and it may walk right up and sniff your foot before it recognizes you and scuttles back into the woods.

A common inhabitant of the tropics is the raccoonlike coati *(tejon, pisote)*. In the wild, coatis like shady stream banks, often congregating in large troops. They are identified by their short brown or tan fur, small round ears, long nose, and straight, vertically held tail. They make endearing pets; the first coati you see may be one on a string offered for sale at a local market.

If you are lucky, you may glimpse a band of now-rare brownish-black spider monkeys *(monos)* raiding a forest-edge orchard. And deep in the mountain fastness of Guerrero or Oaxaca, you may find a tracker who can lead you to a view of the endangered tapir. On such an ex-

cursion, if you are really fortunate, you may even hear the chesty cry of, or even see, a jaguar, the fabled *tigre*.

El Tigre

"Each hill has its own *tigre*," a Mexican proverb says. With black spots spread over a tan coat, stretching five feet (1.5 meters) and weighing about 200 pounds (90 kilograms), the typical jaguar resembles a muscular spotted leopard. Although hunted since prehistory, and now endangered, the jaguar still lives throughout Pacific Mexico, where it hunts along thickly forested stream bottoms and foothills. Unlike the mountain lion *(puma)*, the jaguar will eat any game. They have even been known to wait patiently for fish in rivers and stalk beaches for turtle and egg dinners. If they have a favorite food, it is probably the piglike wild peccary *(jabalí)*. Experienced hunters agree that no two jaguars will, when examined, have the same prey in their stomachs.

Although humans have died of wounds inflicted by cornered jaguars, there is little or no hard evidence they are man-eaters, despite legends to the contrary.

BIRDS

The coastal lagoons of Pacific Mexico lie astride the Pacific flyway, one of the Americas' major north-south paths for migrating waterfowl. Many of the familiar American and Canadian species, including pintail, gadwall, baldpate, shoveler, redhead, and scaup, arrive from October until January, when their numbers will swell into the millions. They settle near food and cover—sometimes, to the frustration of farmers—even at the borders of cornfields. Among the best places to see their spectacle is the **Marismas Nacionales** marsh complex around the Sinaloa-Nayarit border, west of coast Hwy. 15 between Mazatlán and Acaponeta.

Besides the migrants, swarms of resident species—herons, egrets, cormorants, anhingas, lily-walkers, and hundreds more—stalk, nest, and preen in the same lagoons.

Few spots are better for observing seabirds than the beaches of Pacific Mexico. Brown pelicans and huge black-and-white frigate birds are among the prime actors. When a flock of pelicans spots a school of their favorite fish, they go about their routine deliberately: singly or in pairs they circle and plummet into the waves and come up, more often than not, with fish in their gullets. They bob and float over the swells for a minute or two, seemingly waiting for their dozen or so fellow pelicans to take their turns. This goes on until they've bagged a big dinner of 10-15 fish apiece.

Frigate birds, the scavengers par excellence of Pacific Mexico, often profit by the labor of the teams of fisherfolk who haul in fish right on village beaches by the netful. After the fishermen auction off the choice morsels—perch, tuna, red snapper, octopus, shrimp—to merchants, and the villagers have scavenged everything else edible, the motley residue of small fish, sea snakes, skates, squids, slugs, and sharks is often thrown to a screeching flock of frigate birds.

For more details of Mexico's mammals and birds in general, check out Starker Leopold's very readable classic, *Wildlife of Mexico,* and other works in the Booklist.

REPTILES AND AMPHIBIANS

Snakes and Gila Monsters

Mexico has 460-odd snake species, the vast majority shy and nonpoisonous; they will generally get out of your way if you give plenty of warning. In Mexico, as everywhere, poisonous snakes have been largely eradicated in city and tourist areas. In brush or jungle areas, carry a stick or a machete and beat the bushes ahead of you, while watching where you put your feet. When hiking or rock-climbing in the country, don't put your hand in niches you can't see.

You might even see a snake underwater while swimming offshore at an isolated Bay of Banderas beach. The **yellow-bellied sea snake,** *Pelamis platurus* (to about two feet), although shy, can inflict fatal bites. If you see a yellow and black snake underwater, get away pronto.

Some eels, which resemble snakes but have gills like fish and inhabit rocky crevices, can inflict nonpoisonous bites and should also be avoided.

The Mexican land counterpart of the *pelamis platurus* is the **coral snake** *(coralillo),* which occurs as about two dozen species, all with multi-colored bright bands that always include red. Although relatively rare, small, and shy, coral snakes occasionally inflict serious, sometimes fatal bites.

More aggressive and generally more dangerous is the Mexican **rattlesnake** *(cascabel)* and its viper-relative, the **fer-de-lance** *(Bothrops atrox).* About the same size (to six feet) and general appearance as the rattlesnake, the fer-de-lance is known by various local names, such as *nauyaca, cuatro narices, palanca,* and *barba amarilla.* It is potentially more hazardous than the rattlesnake because it lacks a rattle to give warning.

The Gila monster (confined in Mexico to northern Sonora) and its southern tropical relative, black-with-yellow-spots *escorpión (Heloderma horridum),* are the world's only poisonous lizards. Despite its beaded skin and menacing, fleshy appearance, the *escorpión* only bites when severely provoked; even then, its venom is rarely, if ever, fatal.

Crocodiles

The crocodile, *cocodrilo* or *caimán,* once prized for its meat and hide, came close to vanishing in Mexican Pacific lagoons until the government took steps to ensure its survival. Now officially protected, a few isolated breeding populations live in the wild, while government and private hatcheries are breeding more for the eventual repopulation of lagoons where they once were common. Hatcheries open for touring are located in San Blas and Lagunas de Chacagua.

Two crocodile species occur in the region. True crocodile *Crocodilus acutus* has a narrower snout than its local cousin, *Caiman crocodilus fuscus,* a type of alligator *(lagarto).* Although past individuals have been recorded up to 15 feet long (see the stuffed specimen at the Tepic anthropology and history museum or the live ones at the Mazatlán aquarium), wild native crocodiles are usually young and two feet or less in length.

Turtles

The story of Mexican sea turtles is similar: they once swarmed ashore on Pacific Mexico beaches to lay their eggs. Prized for their meat, eggs, hide, and shell, the turtle population was severely devastated. Now officially protected, sea turtles come ashore in numbers at a few isolated locations. Of the three locally occurring species, the green turtle, *tortuga verde,* is by far the most common. From tour boats, it can often be seen grazing on sea grass offshore in the Bay of Banderas. For more sea turtle details, see the special topic Saving Turtles.

FISH AND MARINE MAMMALS

Shoals of fish abound in Pacific Mexico waters. Four billfish species are found in deep-sea grounds several miles offshore: **swordfish, sailfish,** and **blue** and **black marlin.** All are spirited fighters, though the sailfish and marlin are generally the toughest to bring in. The blue marlin is the biggest of the four; in the past, 10-foot specimens weighing more than a thousand pounds were brought in at Pacific coast marinas. Lately, four feet, 200 pounds for a marlin, and 100 pounds for a sailfish are more typical. Progressive captains now encourage victorious anglers to return these magnificent "tigers of the sea" (especially the sinewy, poor-eating sailfish and blue marlin) to the deep after they've won the battle.

Billfish are not the only prizes of the sea. Serious fish lovers also seek varieties of tunalike **jack,** such as **yellowtail, Pacific amberjack, pompano, jack crevalle,** and the tenacious **roosterfish,** named for the "comb" atop its head. These, and the **yellowfin tuna, mackerel,** and *dorado,* which Hawaiians call mahimahi, are among the delicacies sought in Pacific Mexican waters.

Accessible from small boats offshore and by casting from shoreline rocks are varieties of **snapper** *(huachinango, pargo)* and **sea bass** *(cabrilla).* Closer to shore, **croaker, mullet,** and **jewfish** often can be found foraging along sandy bottoms and in rocky crevices.

Sharks and **rays** inhabit nearly all depths, with smaller fry venturing into beach shallows and lagoons. Huge **Pacific manta rays** appear to be frolicking, their great wings flapping like birds, not far off Pacific Mexico shores. Just beyond the waves, local fisherfolk bring in **hammerhead, thresher,** and **leopard sharks.**

Also common is the **stingray,** which can inflict a painful wound with its barbed tail. Experienced swimmers and waders avoid injury by both shuffling (rather than stepping) and watching their feet in shallow, sandy bottoms. (For more on **fishing** and a chart of species encountered in Pacific Mexico waters, turn to the On the Road chapter.)

Seals, Sea Lions, Porpoises, and Whales

Although seen in much greater numbers in Baja California's colder waters, fur-bearing species, such as seals and sea lions, do occasionally hunt in the tropical waters and bask on the sands of island beaches off the Pacific Mexico coast. With the rigid government protections that have been in force for a generation, their numbers appear to be increasing.

The **California Gulf porpoise**—*delfín,* or *vaquita* (little cow)—is much more numerous. The smallest member of the whale family, it rarely exceeds five feet. Its playful diving and jumping antics can occasionally be observed from Puerto Vallarta-based tour and fishing boats, and even sometimes right from Bay of Banderas beaches.

Although the **California gray whale's** migration extends only to the southern tip of Baja California, occasional pods stray farther south, where deep-sea fishers and cruise and tour boat passengers occasionally see them in deep waters offshore.

Larger whale *(ballena)* species, such as the **humpback** and **blue whales,** appear to enjoy tropical waters even more, ranging the north Pacific tropics, from Puerto Vallarta west to Hawaii and beyond.

Offshore islands, such as the nearby Marietas and María Isabel (accessible from San Blas), and the Revillagigedo (ray-vee-yah-hee-HAY-doh) Islands, 300 miles due west of Puerto Vallarta, offer prime viewing grounds for Mexico's aquatic fauna.

HISTORY

Once upon a time, perhaps as early as 50,000 years ago, the first bands of hunters, following great game herds, crossed from Siberia to the American continent. For thousands of years they drifted southward, eventually settling in the rich valleys and plains of North and South America.

Many thousands of years later, around 10,000 B.C., and in what would later be called Mexico, people began gathering and grinding the seeds of a hardy grass that required only the summer rains to thrive. By selecting and planting the larger seeds, their grain eventually yielded tall plants with long ears and many large kernels. This grain, which they eventually called *teocentli,* the "sacred seed" (maize or corn), led to prosperity.

EARLY CIVILIZATIONS

Plentiful food gave rise to leisure classes—artists, architects, warriors, and ruler-priests—who had time to think and create. With a calendar, they harnessed the constant wheel of the firmament to life on earth, defining the days to plant, to harvest, to feast, to travel, and to trade. Eventually, grand cities arose.

Teotihuacán

Teotihuacán, with a population of perhaps 250,000 around the time of Christ, was one of the world's great metropolises, on a par with Rome, Babylon, and Chang'an. Its epic monuments still stand not far north of Mexico City: the towering Pyramid of the Sun at the terminal of a grand, 150-foot-wide ceremonial avenue faces a great Pyramid of the Moon. Along the avenue sprawls a monumental temple-court surrounded by scowling, ruby-eyed effigies of Quetzalcoatl, the feathered serpent god of gods.

Teotihuacán crumbled mysteriously around A.D. 650, leaving a host of former vassal states from what would be the Yucatán to Pacific Mexico free to tussle among themselves. These included Xochicalco, not far from present-day Taxco, and the great Zapotec center of Monte Albán farther southwest in Oaxaca. From its regal hilltop complex of stone pyramids, palaces, and ceremonial ball courts, Monte Albán reigned all-powerful until it, too, was abandoned around A.D. 1000.

The Living Quetzalcoatl

Xochicalco, however, was flourishing; its wise men tutored a young noble who was to become a living legend. In A.D. 947, Topiltzín (literally,

Mexican mothers still teach their daughters to weave with the backstrap loom exactly as did countless generations of their pre-Columbian forebears.

"Our Prince") was born. Records recite Topiltzín's achievements. He advanced astronomy, agriculture, and architecture and founded the city-state of Tula in A.D. 968, north of old Teotihuacán.

Contrary to the times, Topiltzín opposed human sacrifice; he taught that tortillas and butterflies, not human hearts, were the food of Quetzalcoatl. After ruling benignly for a generation, Topiltzín's name became so revered that the people began to know him as the living Quetzalcoatl, the plumed serpent-god incarnate.

Quetzalcoatl was not universally loved, however. Bloodthirsty local priests, desperate for human victims, tricked him with alcohol; he awoke, groggily, one morning in bed with his sister. Devastated by shame, Quetzalcoatl banished himself from Tula with a band of retainers. In A.D. 987, they headed east, toward Yucatán, leaving arrows shot through saplings, appearing like crosses, along their trail.

Although Quetzalcoatl sent word he would reclaim his kingdom during the 52-year cyclical calendar year of his birth, Ce Acatl, he never returned. Legends say that he sailed east and rose to heaven as the morning star.

The Aztecs

The civilization that Topiltzín founded, known to historians as the Toltec (People of Tula), was eventually eclipsed by others. These included the Aztecs, a collection of seven aggressive immigrant subtribes. Migrating from a mysterious western land of Aztlán ("Place of the Herons"; see the special topic **Aztlán**) into the lake-filled valley that Mexico City now occupies, around 1250, the Aztecs survived by being forced to fight for every piece of ground they occupied. Within a century, the Aztecs' dominant tribe, whose members called themselves the México, had clawed its way to dominion over the Valley of Mexico. With the tribute labor that their emperors extracted from local vassal tribes, the México founded a magnificent capital, Tenochtitlán, on an island in the middle of the valley-lake. From there, Aztec armies, like Roman legions, marched out and subdued kingdoms for hundreds of miles in all directions. They returned with the spoils of conquest: gold, brilliant feathers, precious jewels, and captives, whom they sacrificed by the thousands as food for their gods.

Among those gods they feared was Quetzalcoatl, who, legends said, was bearded and fair-skinned. It was a remarkable coincidence, therefore, that the bearded, fair-skinned Castilian Hernán Cortés landed on Mexico's eastern coast on 22 April 1519, during the year of Ce Acatl, exactly when Topiltzín, the Living Quetzalcoatl, had vowed he would return.

THE CONQUEST

Although a generation had elapsed since Columbus founded Spain's West Indian colonies, returns had been meager. Scarcity of gold and of native workers, most of whom had fallen victim to European diseases, turned adventurous Spanish eyes westward once again, toward rumored riches beyond the setting sun. Cortés, then only 34, had left Cuba in February with an expedition of 11 small ships, 550 men, 16 horses, and a few small cannon. By the time he landed in Mexico, he was burdened by a mutinous crew. His men, mostly soldiers of fortune hearing stories of the great Aztec empire west beyond the mountains, realized the impossible odds they faced and became restive.

Cortés, however, cut short any thoughts of mutiny by burning his ships. As he led his grumbling but resigned band of adventurers toward

---

MALINCHE

I f it hadn't been for Doña Marina (whom he received as a gift from a local chief), Hernán Cortés may have become a mere historical footnote. Clever and opportunistic, Doña Marina was a crucial strategist in Cortés's deadly game of divide and conquer. She eventually bore Cortés a son and lived in honor and riches for many years, profiting greatly from the Spaniards' exploitation of the Mexicans.

Latter-day Mexicans do not honor her by the gentle title of Doña Marina, however. They call her Malinche, after the volcano—the ugly, treacherous scar on the Mexican landscape—and curse her as the female Judas who betrayed her country to the Spanish. *Malinchismo* has become known as the tendency to love things foreign and hate things Mexican.

the Aztec capital of Tenochtitlán, Cortés played Quetzalcoatl to the hilt, awing local chiefs. Coaxed by Doña Marina, Cortés's wily native translator/mistress/confidante, local chiefs began to add their armies to Cortés's march against their Aztec overlords.

Moctezuma

While Cortés looked down upon the shimmering Valley of Mexico from the great divide between the volcanoes, Moctezuma, the emperor of the Aztecs, fretted about the returned "Quetzalcoatl." It is no wonder that the Spanish, approaching on horseback in their glittering, clanking armor, seemed divine to people who had never known steel, draft animals, or the wheel.

Inside the gates of the Venice-like island-city it was the Spaniards' turn to be dazzled: by gardens full of animals, gold and palaces, and a great pyramid-enclosed square where tens of thousands of people bartered goods gathered from all over the empire. Tenochtitlán, with perhaps a quarter of a million people, was the great capital of an empire larger and richer than any in Europe.

Moctezuma, the lord of that empire, was frozen by fear and foreboding, however. He quickly surrendered himself to Cortés's custody. After a few months his subjects, enraged by Spanish brutality and Moctezuma's timidity, rioted and mortally wounded the emperor with a stone. With Moctezuma dead, the riot turned into a counterattack against the Spanish. On 1 July 1520, Cortés and his men, forced by the sheer numbers of rebellious Aztecs, retreated along a lake causeway from Tenochtitlán while carrying Moctezuma's treasure with them. Many of them drowned beneath their burdens of stolen Aztec gold, while others hacked a bloody path through thousands of screaming Aztec warriors to safety on the lakeshore.

That infamous night is now known as Noche Triste ("Sad Night"). Cortés, with half of his men dead, collapsed and wept beneath a great *ahuehuete* cypress tree (which still stands) in Mexico City.

A year later, reinforced by fresh soldiers, horses, a small fleet of armed sailboats, and 100,000 Indian allies, Cortés retook Tenochtitlán. The stubborn defenders, led by Cuauhtémoc, Moctezuma's nephew, fell by the tens of thousands be-

Guerrero wooden mask of Malinche

neath a smoking hail of Spanish grapeshot. The Aztecs, although weakened by smallpox, refused to surrender. Cortés found, to his dismay, that he had to destroy the city to take it.

The triumphant conquistador soon rebuilt it in the Spanish image: Cortés's cathedral and main public buildings—the present *zócalo,* central square of Mexico City—still rest upon the foundations of Moctezuma's pyramids.

NEW SPAIN

With the Valley of Mexico firmly in his grip, Cortés sent his lieutenants south, north, and west to extend the limits of a domain that eventually expanded to more than a dozenfold the size of old Spain. He wrote his king, Charles V, ". . . the most suitable name for it would be New Spain of the Ocean Sea, and thus in the name of your Majesty I have christened it."

The Missionaries

While the conquistadores subjugated the local people, missionaries began arriving to teach, heal, and baptize them. A dozen Franciscan brothers impressed Indians and conquistadores alike by trekking the entire 300-mile stony path from Veracruz to Mexico City in 1523.

The missionaries were a slightly more humane counterbalance to the brutal conquistadores. Missionary authorities generally enjoyed a sympathetic ear from Charles V and his successors, who earnestly pursued Spain's Christian mission, especially when it dovetailed with their political and economic goals.

The King Takes Control

After 1525, the crown, through the Council of the Indies, began to wrest power away from Cortés and his conquistador lieutenants. Many of them had been granted rights of *encomienda:* taxes and labor of an Indian district. In exchange, the *encomendero,* who often enjoyed the status of feudal lord, pledged to look after the welfare and souls of his Indian charges.

From the king's point of view, though, tribute pesos collected by *encomenderos* translated into losses to the crown. Moreover, many *encomenderos* callously exploited their Indian wards for quick profit, sometimes selling them as slave labor in mines and on plantations. Such abuses, coupled with European-introduced diseases, began to reduce the Indian population at an alarming rate.

After 1530, the king and his councilors began to realize that the Indians were in peril, and without their labor, New Spain would vanish. They acted decisively: new laws would be instituted by a powerful new viceroy.

Don Antonio de Mendoza, the Count of Tendilla, arrived in 1535. He set the precedent for an unbroken line of more than 60 viceroys who, with few exceptions, served with distinction until independence in 1821. Village after village along Mendoza's winding route to Mexico City tried to outdo each other with flowers, music, bullfights, and feasts in his honor.

Mendoza wasted no time. He first got rid of the renegade opportunist (and Cortés's enemy) Nuño de Guzmán, whose private army, under the banner of conquest, had been laying waste to a broad western belt of Pacific Mexico, now Jalisco, Michoacán, Nayarit, and Sinaloa. (Guzmán, during his rapacious five years in Pacific Mexico, did, however, manage to found several towns: Guadalajara, Tepic, and Culiacán, among others.)

Cortés, the Marqués del Valle de Oaxaca

Cortés, meanwhile, had done very well for himself. He was one of Spain's richest men, with the title of Marqués del Valle de Oaxaca. He received 80,000 gold pesos a year from hundreds of thousands of Indian subjects on 25,000 square miles from the Valley of Mexico through the present states of Morelos, Guerrero, and Oaxaca.

Cortés continued on a dozen projects: an expedition to Honduras, a young wife whom he brought back from Spain, a palace (which still stands) in Cuernavaca, sugar mills, and dozens of churches, city halls, and presidios. He supervised the exploits of his lieutenants in Pacific Mexico: Francisco Orozco subdued the Zapotecs in Oaxaca, while Pedro de Alvarado accomplished the same with the Mixtecs, then continued south to conquer Guatemala. Meanwhile, Cristóbal de Olid subjugated the Tarascans in Michoacán, then moved down the Pacific coast to Zacatula on the mouth of the Río Balsas. There (and at Acapulco and Tehuantepec), Cortés built ships to explore the Pacific. In 1535, he led an expedition to the Gulf of California (hence the Sea of Cortez) in a dreary six-month search for treasure along the Baja California coast.

Cortés's Monument

Disgusted with Mendoza's meddling and discouraged by his failures, Cortés returned to Spain, where he got mired in lawsuits, a minor war, and his daughter's marital troubles, all of which led to his illness and death in 1547. Cortés's remains, according to his will, were eventually laid to rest in a vault at Hospital de Jesús, which he founded in Mexico City.

Since latter-day Mexican politics preclude memorials to the Spanish conquest, no monument nor statue marks his achievements. Cortés's monument, historians note, is Mexico itself.

COLONIAL MEXICO

In 1542, the Council of the Indies, through Viceroy Mendoza, promulgated its liberal New Laws of the Indies. The New Laws rested on high moral ground: the only Christian justification for New Spain was the souls and welfare of the Indians. Colonists had no right to exploit the Indians. Slavery, therefore, was outlawed and *encomienda* rights were to revert to the crown at the death of the original grantees.

Despite uproar and near-rebellion by the colonists, Mendoza (and his successor in 1550, Don Luis Velasco) kept the lid on New Spain. Although some *encomenderos* held on to their rights into the 18th century, chattel slavery was abolished in Mexico—300 years before Abraham Lincoln's Emancipation Proclamation.

Peace reigned in Mexico for 10 generations. Viceroys came and conscientiously served, new settlers arrived and put down roots, friars preached and built country churches, and the conquistadores' rich sons and daughters played while the Indians worked.

The Role of the Church
The church somewhat moderated the Indians' toil. Feast days came when they would dress up and parade their patron saint through the streets and later eat their fill, drink *pulque,* and ooh and aah at the fireworks.

The church profited from the status quo, however. The biblical tithe—one-tenth of everything, from crops and livestock to rents and mining profits—filled church coffers. By 1800, the church owned half of Mexico. Moreover, the clergy (including lay church officers) and the military were doubly privileged. They enjoyed right of *fuero* (exemption from civil law) and could be prosecuted by ecclesiastical or military courts only.

Trade and Commerce
In trade and commerce, New Spain existed for the benefit of the mother country. Spaniards enjoyed absolute monopolies by virtue of the complete prohibition of foreign traders and goods. Colonists, as a result, paid dearly for oft-shoddy Spanish manufactures. The Casa de Contratación, the royal trade regulators, always ensured the colony's yearly balance of payments would result in deficit, which would be made up by bullion shipments from New Spain mines (from which the crown raked 10% off the top).

Despite its faults, New Spain lasted three times longer than the Aztec empire. By most

POPULATION CHANGES IN NEW SPAIN

	EARLY COLONIAL (1570)	LATE COLONIAL (1810)
peninsulares	6,600	15,000
criollos	11,000	1,100,000
mestizos	2,400	704,000
indígenas	3,340,000	3,700,000
negros	22,000	630,000

contemporary measures, New Spain was prospering in 1800. The Indian labor force was completely subjugated and increasing, and the galleon fleets were carrying home increasing tonnage of silver and gold worth millions. The authorities, however, failed to recognize that Mexico had changed in 300 years.

Criollos, the New Mexicans
Nearly three centuries of colonial rule gave rise to a burgeoning population of more than a million criollos—Mexican-born European descendants of Spanish colonists, many rich and educated—to whom power was denied.

High government, church, and military office had always been the preserve of a tiny but powerful minority of *peninsulares*—whites born in Spain. Criollos could only watch in disgust as unlettered, unskilled *peninsulares* (derisively called *gachupines*—"wearers of spurs") were boosted to authority over them.

Although the criollos stood high above the *mestizo,* Indian, and *negro* underclasses, that seemed little compensation for the false smiles, the deep bows, and the costly bribes that *gachupines* demanded.

Mestizos, *Indígenas,* and *Negros*
Upper-class luxury existed by virtue of the sweat of Mexico's mestizo, *indígena,* and *negro* laborers and servants. African slaves were imported in large numbers during the 17th century after typhus, smallpox, and measles epidemics had wiped out most of the Indian population. Although the African-Mexicans contributed significantly (crafts, healing arts, dance, music, drums, and marimba), they had arrived last and experienced discrimination from everyone.

INDEPENDENCE

The chance for change came during the aftermath of the French invasion of Spain in 1808, when Napoléon Bonaparte replaced King Ferdinand VII with his brother Joseph on the Spanish throne. Most *peninsulares* backed the king; most criollos, however, inspired by the example of the recent American and French revolutions, talked and dreamed of independence. One such group, urged on by a firebrand parish priest, acted.

El Grito de Dolores
"¡Viva México! Death to the Gachupines!" Father **Miguel Hidalgo's** impassioned *grito* from the church balcony in the Guanajuato town of Dolores on 16 September 1810 ignited action. A mostly *indígena,* machete-wielding army of 20,000 coalesced around Hidalgo and his compatriots, Ignacio Allende and Juan Aldama. Their ragtag mob raged out of control through the Bajío, massacring hated *gachupines* and pillaging their homes.

Hidalgo advanced on Mexico City but, unnerved by stiff royalist resistance, retreated and regrouped around Guadalajara. His rebels, whose numbers had swollen to 80,000, were no match for a disciplined, 6,000-strong royalist force. Hidalgo (now "Generalisimo") fled north but was soon apprehended, defrocked, and executed. His head and those of his comrades—Aldama, Allende, and Mariano Jiménez—were hung from the walls of the Guanajuato granary (site of the slaughter of 138 *gachupines* by Hidalgo's army) for 10 years as grim reminders of the consequences of rebellion.

The Ten-Year Struggle
Others carried on, however. A former mestizo student of Hidalgo, **José María Morelos,** led a revolutionary shadow government in the present states of Guerrero and Oaxaca for four years until he was apprehended and executed in December 1815.

Morelos's compatriot **Vicente Guerrero** continued the fight, joining forces with criollo royalist Brigadier Agustín de Iturbide. Their Plan de Iguala promised "Three Guarantees"—the renowned Trigarantes: Independence, Catholi-

cism, and Equality—which their army (commanded by Iturbide, of course) would enforce. On 21 September 1821, Iturbide rode triumphantly into Mexico City at the head of his army of Trigarantes. Mexico was independent at last.

Independence, however, solved little except to expel the *peninsulares.* With an illiterate populace and no experience in self-government, Mexicans began a tragic 40-year love affair with a fantasy: the general on the white horse, the gold-braided hero who could save them from themselves.

The Rise and Fall of Agustín I
Iturbide—crowned Agustín I by the bishop of Guadalajara on 21 July 1822—soon lost his charisma. In a pattern that became sadly predictable for generations of topsy-turvy Mexican politics, an ambitious garrison commander issued a *pronunciamiento,* a declaration against the government. Supporting *pronunciamientos* followed, and old revolutionary heroes Guerrero, Guadalupe Victoria, and Nicolás Bravo endorsed a "plan"—the Plan of Casa Mata (not unlike Iturbide's previous Plan de Iguala)—dethroning Iturbide in favor of a republic. Iturbide, his braid tattered and brass tarnished, abdicated in February 1823.

Antonio López de Santa Anna, the eager 28-year-old military commander of Veracruz, whose *pronunciamiento* had pushed Iturbide from his white horse, maneuvered to gradually replace him. Throughout the late 1820s the government teetered on the edge of disaster as the presidency bounced between liberal and conservative hands six times in three years. During the last of these upheavals, Santa Anna jumped to prominence by defeating an abortive Spanish attempt at counterrevolution at Tampico in 1829. "The Victor of Tampico," people called Santa Anna.

The Disastrous Era of Santa Anna
In 1833, the government was bankrupt; mobs demanded the ouster of conservative President Anastasio Bustamante, who had executed the rebellious old revolutionary hero, Vicente Guerrero. Santa Anna issued a *pronunciamiento* against Bustamante; Congress obliged, elevating Santa Anna to "Liberator of the Republic"

and "Conqueror of the Spaniards," and naming him president in March 1833.

Santa Anna would pop in and out the presidency like a jack-in-the-box 10 more times before 1855. First, he foolishly lost Texas to rebellious Anglo settlers in 1836. He later lost his leg (which was buried with full military honors) fighting the emperor of France.

Santa Anna's greatest debacle, however, was to declare war on the United States with just 1,839 pesos in the treasury. With his forces poised to defend Mexico City against a relatively small 10,000-man American invasion force, Santa Anna inexplicably withdrew. United States Marines surged into the "Halls of Montezuma," Chapultepec Castle, where Mexico's six beloved Niños Héroes cadets fell in the losing cause on 13 September 1847.

In the subsequent treaty of Guadalupe Hidalgo, Mexico lost two-fifths of its territory—the present states of New Mexico, Arizona, California, Nevada, Utah, and Colorado—to the United States. Mexicans have never forgotten; they have looked upon gringos with a combination of awe, envy, admiration, and disgust ever since.

For Santa Anna, however, enough was not enough. Called back as president for the last and 11th time in 1853, Santa Anna, now "His Most Serene Highness," financed his extravagances by selling off a part of southern New Mexico and Arizona, known as the Gadsden Purchase, for $10 million.

REFORM, CIVIL WAR, AND INTERVENTION

Mexican leaders finally saw the light and exiled Santa Anna forever. While conservatives searched for a king to replace Santa Anna, liberals (whom Santa Anna had kept in jail) plunged ahead with three controversial reform laws: the Ley Juárez, Ley Lerdo, and Ley Iglesias. These *reformas,* augmented by a new Constitution of 1857, directly attacked the privilege and power of Mexico's landlords, clergy, and generals: Ley Juárez abolished *fueros,* the separate military and church courts; Ley Lerdo forbade excess corporate (read: church) landholdings, and Ley Iglesias reduced or transferred most church power to the state.

Conservative generals, priests, and *hacendados* (landholders), along with their mestizo and *indígena* followers, revolted. The resulting War of the Reform (not unlike the U.S. Civil War) ravaged the countryside for three long years until the victorious liberal army paraded triumphantly in Mexico City on New Year's Day, 1861.

Juárez and Maximilian

Benito Juárez, the leading *reformista,* had won the day. Juárez's similarity to his contemporary, Abraham Lincoln, is legend: Juárez had risen from humble Zapotec origins to become a lawyer, a champion of justice, and the president who held his country together during a terrible civil war. Like Lincoln, Juárez's triumph didn't last long.

Imperial France invaded Mexico in January 1862, initiating a bloody five-year imperialist struggle, infamously known as the **French Interven-**

President Benito Juárez, like his contemporary Abraham Lincoln, was a lawyer of humble origin who kept his country united through years of civil war.

tion. After two costly years, the French army pushed Juárez's liberal army into the hills and installed the king whom Mexican conservatives thought the country needed. Austrian Archduke Maximilian and his wife Carlota, the very models of modern Catholic monarchs, were crowned emperor and empress of Mexico in June 1864.

The naive Emperor Maximilian I was surprised that some of his subjects resented his presence. Meanwhile, Juárez refused to yield, stubbornly performing his constitutional duties in a somber black carriage one jump ahead of the French occupying army. The climax came in May 1867, when liberal forces besieged and defeated Maximilian at Querétaro. Juárez, giving no quarter, sternly ordered Maximilian's execution by firing squad on 19 June.

RECONSTRUCTION AND THE PORFIRIANA

Juárez worked day and night at the double task of reconstruction and reform. He won reelection but died, exhausted, in 1871. The death of Juárez, the stoic partisan of reform, signaled hope to Mexico's conservatives. They soon got their wish: General Don Porfirio Díaz, the "Coming Man," was elected president in 1876.

Pax Porfiriana
Don Porfirio is often remembered wistfully, as old Italians remember Mussolini: "He was a bit rough, but, dammit, at least he made the trains run on time."

Although Porfirio Díaz's humble Oaxaca mestizo origins were not unlike Juárez's, Díaz was not a democrat: when he was a general, his officers often took no captives; when he was president, his country police, the *rurales,* shot prisoners in the act of "trying to escape."

Order and progress, in that sequence, ruled Mexico for 34 years. Foreign investment flowed into the country; new railroads brought the products of shiny factories, mines, and farms to modernized Gulf and Pacific ports. Mexico balanced its budget, repaid foreign debt, and became a respected member of the family of nations.

The human price was high. Don Porfirio allowed more than 100 million acres—one-fifth of Mexico's land area (including most of the arable land)—to be acquired by wealthy Mexicans and foreigners. Poor Mexicans suffered the most. By 1910, 90% of the *indígenas* had lost their traditional communal land. In the spring of 1910, a smug, now-cultured and elderly Don Porfirio anticipated with relish the centennial of Hidalgo's Grito de Dolores.

REVOLUTION AND STABILIZATION

¡No Reelección!
Porfirio Díaz himself had first campaigned on the slogan. It expressed the idea that the president should step down after one term. Although Díaz had stepped down once in 1880, he had gotten himself elected for 26 consecutive years. In 1910, Francisco I. Madero, a short, squeaky-voiced son of rich landowners, opposed Díaz under the same banner.

Although Díaz had jailed him before the election, Madero refused to quit campaigning. From a safe platform in the U.S., he called for a revolution to begin on 20 November.

¡No Reelección!, after all, is not much of a platform. But millions of poor Mexicans were going to bed hungry, and Díaz hadn't listened to them for years.

Villa and Zapata
Not much happened, but soon the millions of poor Mexicans who were going to bed hungry began to stir. In Chihuahua, followers of Francisco (Pancho) Villa, an erstwhile ranch hand, miner, peddler, and cattle rustler, began attacking the *rurales,* dynamiting railroads, and raiding towns. Meanwhile, in the south, horse trader, farmer, and minor official Emiliano Zapata and his *indígena* guerrillas were terrorizing rich *hacendados* and forcibly recovering stolen ancestral village lands. Zapata's movement gained steam and by May had taken the Morelos state capital, Cuernavaca. Meanwhile, Madero crossed the Río Grande and joined with Villa's forces, who took Ciudad Juárez.

The *federales,* government army troops, began deserting in droves, and on 25 May 1911, Díaz submitted his resignation.

As Madero's deputy, General Victoriano Huerta, put Díaz on his ship of exile in Veracruz, Díaz confided: "Madero has unleashed a tiger. Now let's see if he can control it."

The Fighting Continues

Emiliano Zapata, it turned out, was the very tiger whom Madero had unleashed. Meeting with Madero in Mexico City, Zapata fumed over Madero's go-slow approach to the "agrarian problem," as Madero termed it. By November, Zapata had denounced Madero. *"¡Tierra y Libertad!"* ("Land and Liberty") the Zapatistas cried, as Madero's support faded. The army in Mexico City rebelled; Huerta forced Madero to resign on 18 February 1913, then murdered him four days later.

The rum-swilling Huerta ruled like a Chicago mobster; general rebellion, led by the "Big Four"—Villa, Alvaro Obregón, and Venustiano Carranza in the north, and Zapata in the south—soon broke out. Pressed by the rebels and refused U.S. recognition, Huerta fled into exile in July 1914.

The Constitution of 1917

Fighting sputtered on for three years as authority see-sawed between revolutionary factions. Finally, Carranza, who controlled most of the country by 1917, got a convention together in Querétaro to formulate political and social goals. The resulting Constitution of 1917, while restating most ideas of the *reformistas*' 1857 constitution, additionally prescribed a single four-year presidential term, labor reform, and subordinated private ownership to public interest. Every village had a right to communal *ejido* land, and subsoil wealth could never be sold away to the highest bidder.

The Constitution of 1917 was a revolutionary expression of national aspirations, and, in retrospect, represented a social and political agenda for the entire 20th century. In modified form, it has lasted to the present day.

Obregón Stabilizes Mexico

On 1 December 1920, General Alvaro Obregón legally assumed the presidency of a Mexico still bleeding from 10 years of civil war. Although a seasoned revolutionary, Obregón was also a negotiator who recognized peace was necessary to implement the goals of the revolution. In four years, his government pacified local uprisings, disarmed a swarm of warlords, executed hundreds of *bandidos*, obtained U.S. diplomatic recognition, assuaged the worst fears of the clergy and landowners, and began land reform.

All this set the stage for the work of Plutarco Elías Calles, Obregón's Minister of Gobernación (Interior) and handpicked successor, who won the 1924 election. Aided by peace, Mexico returned to a semblance of prosperity. Calles brought the army under civilian control, balanced the budget, and shifted Mexico's revolution into high gear. New clinics vaccinated millions against smallpox, new dams irrigated thousands of previously dry acres, and campesinos received millions of acres of redistributed land.

By single-mindedly enforcing the pro-agrarian, pro-labor, and anti-clerical articles of the 1917 constitution, Calles made many influential enemies. Infuriated by the government's confiscation of church property, closing of monasteries, and deportation of hundreds of foreign priests and nuns, the clergy refused to perform marriages, baptisms, and last rites. As members of the Cristero movement, militant Catholics crying *"¡Viva Cristo Rey!"* armed themselves, torching public schools and government property and murdering hundreds of innocent bystanders.

Simultaneously, Calles threatened foreign oil companies, demanding they exchange their titles for 50-year leases. A moderate Mexican supreme court decision over the oil issue and the skillful arbitration of U.S. Ambassador Dwight Morrow smoothed over both the oil and church troubles by the end of Calles's term.

Calles, who started out brimming with revolutionary fervor and populist zeal, became increasingly conservative and dictatorial. Although he bowed out peaceably in favor of Obregón (the constitution had been amended to allow one six-year nonsuccessive term), Obregón was assassinated two weeks after his election in 1928. Calles continued to rule for six more years through three puppet-presidents: Emilio Portes Gil (1928-30), Pascual Ortíz Rubio (1930-32), and Abelardo Rodríguez (1932-34).

For the 14 years since 1920, the revolution had first waxed, then waned. With a cash surplus in 1930, Mexico, skidded into debt as the Great Depression deepened and Calles and his cronies lined their pockets. In blessing his Minister of

War, General Lázaro Cárdenas, for the 1934 presidential election, Calles expected more of the same.

Lázaro Cárdenas, President of the People
The 40-year-old former governor of Michoacán immediately set his own agenda, however. Cárdenas worked tirelessly to fulfill the social prescriptions of the revolution. As morning-coated diplomats and cabinet ministers fretted in his outer office, Cárdenas ushered in delegations of campesinos and factory workers and sympathetically listened to their problems.

In his six years of rule, Cárdenas moved public education and health forward on a broad front, supported strong labor unions, and redistributed 49 million acres of farmland, more than any president before or since.

Cárdenas's resolute enforcement of the constitution's Artículo 123 brought him the most renown. Under this pro-labor law, the government turned over a host of private companies to employee ownership and, on 18 March 1938, expropriated all foreign oil corporations.

In retrospect the oil corporations, most of which were British, were not blameless. They had sorely neglected the wages, health, and welfare of their workers while ruthlessly taking the law into their own hands with private police forces. Although Standard Oil cried foul, U.S. government did not intervene. Through negotiation and due process, the U.S. companies eventually were compensated with $24 million plus three percent interest. In the wake of the expropriation, President Cárdenas created Petróleos Mexicanos (Pemex), the national oil corporation that continues to run all Mexican oil and gas operations to the present day.

Manuel Avila Camacho
Manuel Avila Camacho, elected in 1940, was the last general to be president of Mexico. His administration ushered in a gradual shift of Mexican politics, government, and foreign policy as Mexico allied itself with the U.S. cause during WW II. Foreign tourism, initially promoted by the Cárdenas administration, ballooned. Good feelings surged as Franklin Roosevelt became the first U.S. president to officially cross the Río Grande when he met with Camacho in Monterrey in April 1943.

In both word and deed, moderation and evolution guided President Camacho's policies. *"Soy creente"* ("I am a believer"), he declared to the Catholics of Mexico as he worked earnestly to bridge Mexico's serious church-state schism. Land policy emphasis shifted from redistribution to utilization as new dams and canals irrigated hundreds of thousands of previously arid acres. On one hand, Camacho established IMSS (Instituto Mexicano de Seguro Social), and on the other trimmed the power of labor unions.

As WW II moved toward its 1945 conclusion, both the U.S. and Mexico were enjoying the benefits of four years of governmental and military cooperation and mutual trade in the form of a mountain of strategic minerals, which had moved north in exchange for a similar mountain of U.S. manufactures that moved south.

CONTEMPORARY MEXICO

The Mature Revolution
During the decades after WW II, beginning with moderate President **Miguel Alemán** (1946-52), Mexican politicians gradually honed their skills of consensus and compromise as their middle-age revolution bubbled along under liberal presidents and sputtered haltingly under conservatives. Doctrine required of all politicians, regardless of stripe, that they be "revolutionary" enough to be included beneath the banner of the PRI (Partido Revolucionario Institucional—the Institutional Revolutionary Party), Mexico's dominant political party.

Mexico's revolution hasn't been very revolutionary about women's rights, however. The PRI didn't get around to giving Mexican women, millions of whom fought and died alongside their men during the revolution, the right to vote until 1953.

Adolfo Ruíz Cortínes, Alemán's secretary of the interior, was elected overwhelmingly in 1952. He fought the corruption that had crept into government under his successor, continued land reform, increased agricultural production, built new ports, eradicated malaria, and opened a dozen automobile assembly plants.

Women, voting for the first time in a national election, kept the PRI in power by electing liberal **Adolfo López Mateos** in 1958. Resembling

Lázaro Cárdenas in social policy, López Mateos redistributed 40 million acres of farmland, forced automakers to use 60% domestic components, built thousands of new schools, and distributed hundreds of millions of new textbooks. *"La electricidad es nuestra"* ("Electricity is ours"), Mateos declared as he nationalized foreign power companies in 1962.

Despite his left-leaning social agenda, unions were restive under López Mateos. Protesting inflation, workers struck; the government retaliated, arresting Demetrios Vallejo, the railway union head, and renowned muralist David Siqueiros, former communist party secretary.

Despite the troubles, López Mateos climaxed his presidency gracefully in 1964 as he opened the celebrated National Museum of Anthropology, appropriately located in Chapultepec Park, where the Aztecs had first settled 20 generations earlier.

In 1964, as several times before, the outgoing president's interior secretary succeeded his former chief. Dour, conservative **Gustavo Díaz Ordaz** immediately clashed with liberals, labor, and students. The pot boiled over just before the 1968 Mexico City Olympics. Reacting to a student rebellion, the army occupied the National University; shortly afterward, on 2 October, government forces opened fire with machine guns on a downtown protest, killing and wounding hundreds of demonstrators.

Maquiladoras

Despite its serious internal troubles, Mexico's relations with the U.S. were cordial. President Lyndon Johnson visited and unveiled a statue of Abraham Lincoln in Mexico City. Later, Díaz Ordaz met with President Richard Nixon in Puerto Vallarta.

Meanwhile, bilateral negotiations produced the **Border Industrialization Program.** Within a 12-mile strip south of the U.S.-Mexico border, foreign companies could assemble duty-free parts into finished goods and export them without any duties on either side. Within a dozen years, a swarm of such plants, called maquiladoras, were humming as hundreds of thousands of Mexican workers assembled and exported billions of dollars worth of shiny consumer goods—electronics, clothes, furniture, pharmaceuticals, and toys—worldwide.

Concurrently, in Mexico's interior, Díaz Ordaz pushed Mexico's industrialization ahead full steam. Foreign money financed hundreds of new plants and factories. Primary among these was the giant Las Truchas steel plant at the new industrial port and town of Lázaro Cárdenas at the Pacific mouth of the Río Balsas.

Discovery, in 1974, of gigantic new oil and gas reserves along Mexico's Gulf coast added fuel to Mexico's already rapid industrial expansion. During the late 1970s and early 1980s billions in foreign investment, lured by Mexico's oil earnings, financed other major developments—factories, hotels, power plants, roads, airports—all over the country.

Economic Trouble of the 1980s

The negative side to these expensive projects was the huge dollar debt required to finance them. President **Luis Echeverría Alvarez** (1970-76), diverted by his interest in international affairs, passed Mexico's burgeoning balance of payments deficit to his successor, **José López Portillo.** As feared by some experts, a world petroleum glut during the early 1980s burst Mexico's ballooning oil bubble and plunged the country into financial crisis. When the 1982 interest came due on its foreign debt, Mexico's largest holding company couldn't pay the $2.3 billion owed. The peso plummeted more than fivefold, to 150 per U.S. dollar. At the same time, prices doubled every year.

But by the mid-1980s, President **Miguel de la Madrid** (1982-88) was straining to get Mexico's economic house in order. He sliced government and raised taxes, asking rich and poor alike to tighten their belts. Despite getting foreign bankers to reschedule Mexico's debt, de la Madrid couldn't stop inflation. Prices skyrocketed as the peso deflated to 2,500 per U.S. dollar, becoming one of the world's most devalued currencies by 1988.

Salinas de Gortari and NAFTA

Public disgust led to significant opposition during the 1988 presidential election. Billionaire PAN candidate Michael Clothier and liberal National Democratic Front candidate Cuauhtémoc Cárdenas ran against the PRI's Harvard-educated technocrat Carlos Salinas de Gortari. The vote was split so evenly that all three candidates claimed victory. Although Salinas eventually won the election, his showing, barely half of the vote, was the worst ever for a PRI president.

Salinas, however, became Mexico's "Coming Man" of the '90s. He was serious about democracy, sympathetic to the *indígenas* and the poor, and sensitive to women's issues. His major achievement, despite significant national opposition, was the North American Free Trade Agreement (NAFTA), which he, U.S. President George Bush, and Canadian Prime Minister Brian Mulrooney negotiated in 1992.

Incoming U.S. President Bill Clinton continued the drama by pushing NAFTA through the U.S. Congress in November 1993, and the Mexican legislature followed suit two weeks later. However, on the very day in January 1994 that NAFTA took effect, rebellion broke out in the poor, remote state of Chiapas. A small but well-disciplined campesino force, calling itself Ejército Zapatista Liberación Nacional ("Zapatista National Liberation Army"; EZLN), or "Zapatistas," captured a number of provincial towns and held the former governor of Chiapas hostage. Although PRI officials minimized the uprising, and President Clinton expressed confidence in the Mexican government, many thoughtful observers wondered if Mexico was ready for NAFTA.

To further complicate matters, Mexico's already tense drama veered toward tragedy. While Salinas de Gortari's chief negotiator, Manuel Camacho Solis, was attempting to iron out a settlement with the Zapatista rebels, Luis Donaldo Colosio, Salinas's handpicked successor, was gunned down just months before the August balloting. However, instead of disintegrating, the nation united in grief; opposition candidates eulogized their fallen former opponent and later earnestly endorsed his replacement, stolid technocrat Ernesto Zedillo, in Mexico's first presidential election debate.

In a closely watched election relatively unmarred by irregularities, Zedillo piled up a solid plurality against his PAN and PRD opponents. By perpetuating the PRI's 65-year hold on the presidency, the electorate had again opted for the PRI's familiar although imperfect middle-aged revolution.

New Crises, New Recovery

Zedillo, however, had little time to savor his victory. The peso, long propped up by Salinas' fiscal policies, lost one-third of its value in the few days before Christmas in 1994. A month later Mexican financial institutions, their dollar debt having nearly doubled in a month, were in danger of defaulting on their obligations to international investors. To stave off a worldwide financial panic, U.S. President Clinton, in February 1995, secured an unprecedented multibillion dollar loan package for Mexico, guaranteed by U.S. and international institutions.

Although disaster was temporarily averted and Mexico became an overnight bargain for dollar-spending travelers, the cure for the country's ills required another painful round of inflation and belt-tightening for poor Mexicans. During 1995, inflation soared by 52%, pushing already-meager wages down an additional 20%. More and more families became unable to purchase staple foods and basic medicines. Malnutrition soared sixfold and third world diseases, such as cholera and dengue fever, resurged in the countryside.

At the same time, Mexico's equally serious political ills seemed to defy cure. Raul Salinas de Gortari, an important PRI party official and the former president's brother, was arrested for money laundering and political assassination. As popular sentiment began to implicate Carlos Salinas de Gortari himself, the former president fled Mexico to an undisclosed location.

Meanwhile, as negotiations with the rebel Zapatistas sputtered on and off in Chiapas, popular discontent erupted in Guerrero, leading to the massacre of 17 unarmed campesinos at Aguas Blancas, in the hills west of Acapulco, by state police in June 1995. One year later, at a demonstration protesting the massacre, a new, well-armed revolutionary group, **Ejército Popular Revolucionario** (People's Revolutionary Army, or EPR), appeared. A few months later, EPR guerrillas killed two dozen police and soldiers at several locations, mostly in southwestern Mexico. Although President Zedillo's immediate reaction was moderate, platoons of soldiers were soon scouring rural Guerrero, Oaxaca, Michoacán and other states, searching homes and arresting suspected dissidents. Public response was mostly negative, though some locals felt that they were far better off in the hands of the army rather than state or federal police.

Mexican democracy, however, got a boost when notorious Guerrero governor Ruben Figueroa, who had tried to cover up the Aguas Blancas massacre with a bogus videotape, was forced from office. At the same time, the Zedillo government gained momentum in addressing the Zapatistas' grievances in Chiapas, even as it decreased federal military presence, built new rural electrification networks, and refurbished health clinics.

The Political Cauldron Bubbles On
Nevertheless, continued federal military presence, especially in Guerrero, Oaxaca, and Chiapas, seemed to trigger violent incidents. Worst was the massacre of 45 indigenous *campesinos,* including women and children, at Acteal, Chiapas, in late December 1997, by paramilitary gunmen. Federal investigators later linked the perpetrators to local PRI officials. In mid-1998, the EPR appeared in Ayutla, Guerrero, passing out leaflets to villagers and giving impromptu speeches. Government soldiers responded with repression, violent searches, and torture. Finally, federal troops cornered and killed 11 suspected EPR members in a schoolhouse 50 miles east of Acapulco.

The rough federal army and police searches, arrests, and jailings have energized a flurry of political action. Local human rights groups are protesting unpunished violence, including dozens of homicides over land disputes and bitter local political, economic, and ecological conflicts, especially in rural areas of southern Pacific Mexico.

Fortunately, foreign visitors have been unaffected by such disputes. Along well-traveled highways, in resorts, towns, and sites of tourist interest, foreign visitors to Pacific Mexico are generally much safer than in their home cities in the United States, Canada, or Europe.

Economic Recovery and Political Reforms
The best news for which the government could justly claim credit was the dramatically improving national economy. By 1999, annual inflation had dropped below 15%, investment dollars were flowing back into Mexico, the peso had stabilized at about eight to the U.S. dollar, and Mexico had paid back every penny of its borrowed U.S. bailout money.

Moreover, in the political arena, although the justice system left much to be desired, a pair of unprecedented events signaled an increasingly open political system. In the 1997 congressional elections, voters elected a host of opposition candidates, depriving the PRI of an absolute congressional majority for the first time since 1929. A year later, in early 1998, Mexicans were participating in their country's first primary elections—in which voters, instead of political bosses, chose party candidates.

So, in 1999, the last year of his term, a bruised but not beaten President Zedillo seemed to be guiding Mexico along a difficult but steady path toward prosperity and democracy. If future presidents follow his example and continue to control inflation, increase employment, press for police and legal reforms, and build bridges with their political opposition, they may lead Mexico into a 21st century of unprecedented prosperity and political maturity.

ECONOMY AND GOVERNMENT

THE MEXICAN ECONOMY

Post-Revolutionary Gains
By many measures, Mexico's 20th-century revolution appears to have succeeded. Since 1910, illiteracy has plunged from 80% to 10%, life expectancy has risen from 30 years to nearly 70, infant mortality has dropped from a whopping 40% to about two percent, and, in terms of caloric intake, Mexicans are on average eating about twice as much as their turn-of-the-century forebears.

Decades of near-continuous economic growth account for rising Mexican living standards. The Mexican economy has rebounded from its last two recessions due to plentiful natural resources, notably oil and metals; diversified manufacturing, such as cars, steel, and petrochemicals; steadily increasing tourism; exports of fruits, vegetables, and cattle; and its large, willing, low-wage workforce.

Recent Mexican governments, moreover, have skillfully exploited Mexico's economic strengths. The Border Industrialization Program has led to millions of jobs in thousands of border maquiladora factories, from Tijuana to the mouth of the Rio Grande. Dependency on oil exports, which lead to the 1980s peso collapse, has been reduced from 75% in 1982 to around 10% by 1999. Foreign trade, a strong source for new Mexican jobs, has burgeoned since the 1980s, due to liberalized tariffs as Mexico joined General Agreement on Tariffs and Trade (GATT) in 1986 and NAFTA in 1994. As a result, Mexico has become a net exporter of goods and services to the United States, its largest trading partner. Although Mexico suffered a peso collapse of about 50% (in relation to the U.S. dollar) in 1995, the Zedillo administration acted quickly. Belt-tightening measures brought inflation, which had initially surged, down to 15% per year, and foreign investment flowed back into Mexico. Although some factory and business closures led to increased unemployment in 1995, benefits from the devalued peso, such as increased tourism and burgeoning exports, have contributed to an improving economy since 1997.

Late 20th-Century Economic Challenges

Despite huge gains, Mexico's Revolution of 1910 is nevertheless incomplete. Improved public health, education, income, and opportunity have barely outdistanced Mexico's population, which has increased nearly sevenfold—from 15 million to 100 million—between 1910 and 2000. For example, although the illiteracy rate has decreased, the actual number of Mexican people who can't read, some 10 million, has remained about constant since 1910.

Moreover, the land reform program, once thought to be a Mexican cure-all, has long been a disappointment. The *ejidos* of which Emiliano Zapata dreamed have become mostly symbolic. The communal fields are typically small and unirrigated. *Ejido* land, constitutionally prohibited from being sold, cannot serve as collateral for bank loans. Capital for irrigation networks, fertilizers, and harvesting machines is consequently lacking. Communal farms are typically inefficient; the average Mexican field produces about *one-quarter* as much corn per acre as a U.S. farm. Mexico must accordingly use its precious oil dollar surplus to import millions of tons of corn—originally indigenous to Mexico—annually.

The triple scourge of overpopulation, lack of arable land, and low farm income has driven millions of campesino families to seek better lives in Mexico's cities. Since 1910, Mexico has evolved from a largely rural country, where 70% of the population lived on farms, to an urban nation where 70% of the population lives in cities. Fully one-fifth of Mexico's people now live in Mexico City.

Nevertheless, the future appears bright for many privately owned and managed Mexican farms, concentrated largely in the northern border states. Exceptionally productive, they typically work hundreds or thousands of irrigated acres of crops, such as tomatoes, lettuce, chiles, wheat, corn, tobacco, cotton, fruits, alfalfa, chickens, and cattle, just like their counterparts across the border in California, New Mexico, Arizona, and Texas.

Staples—wheat for bread, corn for tortillas, milk, and cooking oil—are all imported and consequently expensive for the typical working-class Mexican family, which must spend half or more of its income (typically $500 per month) for food.

Although average gross domestic product figures for Mexico—about $8,000 per capita compared to about $30,000 for the U.S.—place it above nearly all other third world countries, averages, when applied to Mexico, mean little. A primary socioeconomic reality of Mexican history remains: the richest one-fifth of Mexican families earns about 10 times the income of the poorest one-fifth. A relative handful of people own a large hunk of Mexico, and they don't seem inclined to share any of it with the less fortunate. As for the poor, the typical bottom-half Mexican family often owns neither car nor refrigerator; the children do not finish elementary school, nor do their parents practice birth control.

GOVERNMENT AND POLITICS

The Constitution of 1917

Mexico's governmental system is rooted in the Constitution of 1917, which incorporated many of the features of its reformist predecessor of 1857. The 1917 document, with amendments, remains in force. Although drafted at the behest of conservative revolutionary Venustiano Carranza by his hand-picked Querétaro "Constitucionalista" congress, it was greatly influenced by Alvaro Obregón and generally ignored by Carranza during his subsequent three-year presidential term.

Although many articles resemble those of its United States model, the Constitution of 1917 contains provisions developed directly from Mexican experience. Article 27 addresses the question of land. Private property rights are qualified by societal need; subsoil rights are public property, and foreigners and corporations are severely restricted in land ownership. Although the 1917 constitution declared *ejido* (communal) land inviolate, recent 1994 amendments allow, under certain circumstances, the sale or use of communal land as loan security.

Article 23 severely restricts church powers. In declaring that "places of worship are the property of the nation," it stripped churches of all title to real estate, without compensation. Article 5 and Article 130 banned religious orders, expelled foreign clergy, and denied priests and ministers all political rights, including voting, holding office, and even criticizing the government.

Article 123 establishes the rights of labor: to organize, bargain collectively, strike, work a maximum eight-hour-day, and receive a minimum wage. Women are to receive equal pay for equal work and be given a month's paid leave for childbearing. Article 123 also establishes social security plans for sickness, unemployment, pensions, and death.

On paper, Mexico's constitutional government structures appear much like their U.S. prototypes: a federal presidency, a two-house congress, and a supreme court, with their counterparts in each of the 32 states. Political parties field candidates, and all citizens vote by secret ballot.

Mexico's presidents, however, enjoy greater powers than their U.S. counterparts. They need not seek legislative approval for cabinet appointments, can suspend constitutional rights under a state of siege, can initiate legislation, veto all or parts of bills, refuse to execute laws, and replace state officers. The federal government, moreover, retains nearly all taxing authority, relegating the states to a role of merely administering federal programs.

Although ideally providing for separation of powers, the Constitution of 1917 subordinates both the legislative and judicial branches, with the courts being the weakest of all. The supreme court, for example, can only, with repeated deliberation, decide upon the constitutionality of legislation. Five separate individuals must file successful petitions for writs *amparo* ("protection") on a single point of law in order to affect constitutional precedent.

Strong President: Strong PRI

Mexican presidents have successively built upon their potent constitutional mandate for three generations. The **Institutional Revolutionary Party (PRI)**, whose hand-picked candidates have held the presidency continuously for decades, has become an extralegal parallel government, as or more powerful than the formal constitutional government. The PRI is organized hierarchically, in three separate labor, farmer, and "popular" (this last mostly government, business, and professional workers) columns, which send delegates from local committees to state and, ultimately, national-level conventions.

The Mexican president, as head of the PRI, has traditionally reigned at the top of the party apparatus, sending orders through the national PRI delegates, who in turn look after their respective state delegations. The delegates report on the performance of the state and local PRI committees to get out the vote and carry out party mandates. If the local committee's performance is satisfactory, then federal subsidies, public works projects, election funds, and federal jobs flow from government coffers to the state and local level through PRI organizations. In your home town, if you're not in the PRI or don't know someone who is, you might find it difficult to get a small business loan, crop subsidy, government apartment, teaching job, road-repair contract, or government scholarship.

Democratizing Mexican Politics

Reforms in Mexico's stable but top-heavy "Institutional Revolution" have only come gradually. Characteristically, street protests have been brutally put down at first, with officials only later working to address grievances. Dominance by the PRI has led to widespread cynicism and citizen apathy. Regardless of who gets elected, the typical person on the street will tell you that the office-holder is bound to retire with his or her pockets full.

Movement toward more justice and pluralism may nevertheless be in store for Mexico. Minority parties increasingly are electing candidates to state and federal office. Although none have captured a majority of any state legislature, the strongest non-PRI parties, such as the conservative pro-Catholic **Partido Acción Nacional** or National Action Party (PAN) and the liberal-left **Partido Revolucionario Democratico (PRD),** have elected governors. In 1986, minority parties were given federal legislative seats, up to a maximum of 20, for winning a minimum of 2.5% of the national presidential vote. In the 1994 election, minority parties received public campaign financing, depending upon their fraction of the vote.

Following his 1994 inaugural address, in which he called loudly and clearly for more reforms, President Zedillo quickly began to produce results. He immediately appointed a respected member of the PAN opposition party as attorney general—the first non-PRI cabinet appointment in Mexican history. Other Zedillo firsts were federal Senate confirmation of both supreme court nominees and the attorney general, multiparty participation in the Chiapas peace negotiations, and congressional approval of the 1995 financial assistance package received from the United States. Zedillo, moreover, has organized a series of precedent-setting meetings with opposition leaders which led to a written pact for political reform and the establishment of permanent working groups to discuss political and economic questions.

Perhaps most important is Zedillo's campaign and inaugural vow to separate both his government and himself from PRI decision-making. If he keeps this promise, Ernesto Zedillo may become the first Mexican president, in as long as anyone can remember, who did not choose his successor.

But, whatever future candidates—liberal PRD, conservative PAN, or PRI—are chosen to lead the country into the 21st century, they will inherit both Mexico's problems and promise. The fact that the major parties are talking, and maybe even partly agreeing, about the problems may indicate a revitalized Mexican revolution, this time both economic and political, in which broad opportunity—in education, health, employment, and justice under the law—will allow the Mexican nation to achieve its immense but yet unfulfilled human potential.

PEOPLE

Let a broad wooden chopping block represent the high plain, the *altiplano* of Mexico; imagine hacking at one side of it with a sharp cleaver until it is grooved and pocked. That fractured surface resembles Mexico's central highlands, where most Mexicans, divided from each other by high mountains and yawning *barrancas,* have lived for millennia.

The Mexicans' deep divisions, in large measure, led to their downfall at the hands of the Spanish conquistadores. The Aztec empire that Hernán Cortés conquered was a vast but fragmented collection of tribes. Speaking more than a hundred mutually alien languages, those original Mexicans viewed each other suspiciously, as barely human barbarians from strange lands beyond the mountains. And even today the lines that Mexicans still draw between themselves—of caste, class, race, and wealth—are the result, to a significant degree, of the realities of their mutual isolation.

POPULATION

The Spanish colonial government and the Roman Catholic religion provided the glue that over 400 years has welded Mexico's fragmented people into a nation. Mexico's population, officially estimated to reach 100 million by 2000, is exploding. This was not always so. Historians estimate that European diseases, largely measles and smallpox, probably wiped out as many as 20 million—perhaps 95%—of the *indígena* population within a few generations after Cortés stepped ashore in 1519. The Mexican population dwindled to a mere one million inhabitants by 1600. It wasn't until 1950, more than four centuries after Cortés, that Mexico's population recovered to its pre-Cortesian level of 25 million.

Mestizos, *Indígenas,* Criollos, and *Negros*
Although by 1950 Mexico's population had re-

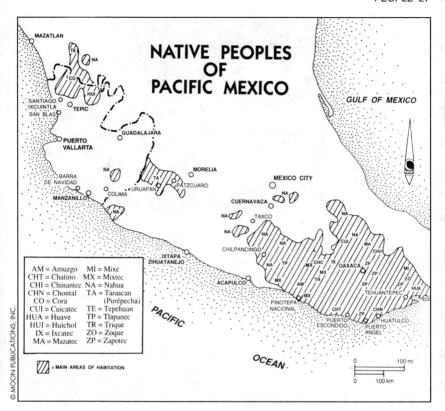

NATIVE PEOPLES OF PACIFIC MEXICO

AM = Amuzgo
CHT = Chatino
CHI = Chinantec
CHN = Chontal
CO = Cora
CUI = Cuicatec
HUA = Huave
HUI = Huichol
IX = Ixcatec
MA = Mazatec
MI = Mixe
MX = Mixtec
NA = Nahua
TA = Tarascan
(Purépecha)
TE = Tepehuan
TP = Tlapanec
TR = Trique
ZO = Zoque
ZP = Zapotec

⫽ = MAIN AREAS OF HABITATION

© MOON PUBLICATIONS, INC.

covered, it was completely transformed. The mestizo, a Spanish-speaking person of mixed blood, had replaced the pure Native American, the *indígena* (een-DEE-hay-nah), as the typical Mexican.

The trend continues. Perhaps three of four Mexicans would identify themselves as mestizo: that class whose part-European blood elevates them, in the Mexican mind, to the level of *gente de razón*—people of "reason" or "right." And there's the rub. The *indígenas* (or, mistakenly but commonly, Indians), by the usual measurements of income, health, or education, squat at the bottom of the Mexican social ladder.

The typical *indígena* family lives in a small adobe house in a remote valley, subsisting on corn, beans, and vegetables from their small, unirrigated *milpa* (cornfield). They usually have chickens, a few pigs, and sometimes a cow, but no electricity; their few hundred dollars a year cash income isn't enough to buy even a small refrigerator, much less a truck.

The typical mestizo family, on the other hand, enjoys most of the benefits of the 20th century. They typically own a modest concrete house in town. Their furnishings, simple by developed-world standards, will often include an electric refrigerator, washing machine, propane stove, television, and a car or truck. The children go to school every day, and the eldest son sometimes even looks forward to college.

Sizable *negro* communities, descendants of 18th-century African slaves, live in the Gulf states and along the Guerrero-Oaxaca coastline. Last to arrive, the *negros* experience discrimination at the hands of everyone else and are integrating very slowly into the mestizo mainstream.

weaving reeds for
petates *(straw mats)*

Above the mestizos, a tiny criollo (Mexican-born white) minority, a few percent of the total population, inherits the privileges—wealth, education, and political power—of their colonial Spanish ancestors.

THE *INDÍGENAS*

Although anthropologists and census takers classify them according to language groups (such as Nahuatl, Mixtec, and Zapotec), *indígenas* typically identify themselves as residents of a particular locality rather than by language or ethnic grouping. And although as a group they are referred to as *indígenas* (native, or aboriginal), individuals are generally made uncomfortable (or may even feel insulted) by being labeled as such.

While the mestizos are the emergent self-conscious majority class, the *indígenas,* as during colonial times, remain the invisible people of Mexico. They are politically conservative, socially traditional, and tied to the land. On market day, the typical *indígena* family might make the trip into town. They bag up some tomatoes, squash, or peppers, and tie up a few chickens or a pig. The rickety country bus will often be full, and the mestizo driver may wave them away, giving preference to his friends, leaving them to trudge stoically along the road.

Their lot, nevertheless, has been slowly improving. *Indígena* families now almost always have access to a local school and a clinic. Improved health has led to a large increase in their population. Official census figures, however, are probably low. *Indígenas* are traditionally suspicious of government people, and census takers, however conscientious, seldom speak the local language.

Recent figures nevertheless indicate that about eight percent of Mexicans are *indígenas*—that is, they speak one of Mexico's 50-odd native languages. Of these, about a quarter speak no Spanish at all. These fractions, moreover, are changing slowly. Many *indígenas* prefer the old ways. If present trends continue, 500 years after the conquest, about the year 2019 will mark the return of the Mexican indigenous population to the preconquest level of roughly 25 million.

Indígena Language Groups
The Maya speakers of Yucatán and the aggregate of the Nahuatl (Aztec language) speakers of the central plateau are Mexico's most numerous *indígena* groups, totaling roughly three million (one million Maya, two million Nahuatl).

Indigenous population centers, relatively scattered in the north of Pacific Mexico, concentrate in the southern states of Guerrero and Oaxaca. The groups are not evenly spread, however. The language map of Oaxaca, for example, looks like a crazy quilt, with important Zapotec, Mixtec, and other centers scattered along the coast and through the mountains surrounding Oaxaca city.

INDIGENOUS POPULATIONS OF PACIFIC MEXICO

STATE	INDIGENOUS POPULATION (OVER FIVE YEARS OF AGE)	TOTAL POPULATION (OVER FIVE YEARS OF AGE)	PERCENT OF TOTAL
Oaxaca	1,307,000	2,603,000	50.2%
Guerrero	299,000	2,228,000	13.4%
Michoacán	106,000	3,037,000	3.4%
Nayarit	24,000	712,000	3.4%
Sinaloa	31,000	1,924,000	1.6%
Jalisco	25,000	4,585,000	0.5%
Colima	1,500	372,000	0.4%

The same government sources tabulate indigenous peoples by language groupings. Although such figures are probably low, the 1990 census figures revealed significant populations in many areas:

LANGUAGE GROUPING	POPULATION (1990)	IMPORTANT CENTERS
Zapotec	402,000	Central, East, and South Oaxaca (Tlacolula, Tehunatepec)
Mixtec	387,000	Northwest, West, and Southwest Oaxaca (Huajuapan, Tlaxiaco, Jamiltepec)
Mazatec	168,000	North Oaxaca (Huatla de Jiménez, Jalapa de Díaz)
Nahua	105,000	Widely dispersed over parts of Jalisco, Colima, Michoacan, Guerrero and Oaxaca
Chinantec	104,000	Northeast Oaxaca (Valle Nacional)
Purépecha (Tarascan)	95,000	Pátzcuaro and Uruapan in Michoacan
Mixe	95,000	Northeast Oaxaca (Ayutla, Santiago Choapan)
Tlapanec	69,000	East Guerrero (Tlapa de Comonfort)
Chatino	29,000	South Oaxaca (Nopala, Juquila)
Amusgo	28,000	Oaxaca-Guerrero (San Pedro Amusgos)
Chontal	24,000	Southeast Oaxaca (Santiago Astata)
Huichol	20,000	Nayarit-Jalisco (Santiago Ixcuintla)
Trique	15,000	West Oaxaca (Tilapa)
Chocho	13,000	Northwest Oaxaca (Coixtlahuaca)
Cuicatec	13,000	North Oaxaca (Cuicatlán)
Cora	12,000	Nayarit (Acaponeta)
Huave	12,000	Southeast Oaxaca (Rincón Juárez, San Mateo del Mar)
Tepuan	5,000	Sinaloa Sierra Madre
Zoque	5,000	Southeast Oaxaca (San Miguel Chimalapa)
Ixcatec	1,000	North Oaxaca (Ixcatlán)

Dress

Maps and figures, however, cannot describe the color of a fiesta or market day. Many country people, especially in Oaxaca, still wear the traditional cottons that blend the Spanish and native styles. Men usually wear the Spanish-origin straw sombrero (literally, "shade-maker") on their heads, baggy white cotton shirt and pants, and leather *huaraches* on their feet. Women's dress is often more colorful. It can include a *huipil* (long, sleeveless dress), often embroidered in bright floral and animal motifs, and a handwoven *enredo* (wraparound skirt that identifies the wearer with a particular locality). A *faja* (waist sash) and, in the winter, a *quechquémitl* (shoulder cape) complete the costume.

RELIGION

"God and Gold" was the two-pronged mission of the conquistadores. Most of them concentrated on gold, while missionaries tried to shift the emphasis to God. They were famously successful: more than 90% of Mexicans profess to be Catholics.

Catholicism, spreading its doctrine of equality of all persons before God and incorporating native gods into the church rituals, eventually brought the *indígenas* into the fold. Within a hundred years, nearly all native Mexicans had accepted the new religion, which raised the universal God of all humankind over local tribal deities.

The Virgin of Guadalupe

Conversion of the *indígenas* was sparked by the vision of Juan Diego, a poor farmer. On the hill of Tepeyac north of Mexico City in 1531, Juan Diego saw a brown-skinned Virgin Mary enclosed in a dazzling aura of light. She told him to build a shrine in her memory on that spot, where the Aztecs had long worshipped their earth mother, Tonantzín. Juan Diego's brown Virgin told him to go to the cathedral and relay her instruction to Archbishop Zumárraga.

The archbishop, as expected, turned his nose up at Juan Diego's story. The vision returned, however, and this time Juan Diego's brown Virgin realized that a miracle was necessary. She ordered him to pick some roses at the spot where she had first appeared to him (a true miracle, since roses had been previously unknown in the vicinity) and take them to the archbishop. Juan Diego wrapped the roses in his rude fiber cape, returned to the cathedral, and placed the wrapped roses at the archbishop's feet. When he opened the offering, Zumárraga gasped: imprinted on the cape was an image of the Virgin herself—proof positive of a genuine miracle.

In the centuries since Juan Diego, the brown Virgin—La Virgen Morena, or Nuestra Señora La Virgen de Guadalupe—has blended native and Catholic elements into something uniquely Mexican. In doing so, she has become the virtual patroness of Mexico, the beloved symbol of Mexico for *indígenas,* mestizos, *negros,* and criollos alike.

Every Mexican city, town, and village celebrates the cherished memory of their Virgin of Guadalupe on 12 December. This celebration, however joyful, is but one of the many fiestas that Mexicans, especially the *indígenas,* live for. Each village holds its local fiesta in honor of their patron saint, who is often a thinly veiled sit-in for some local pre-Cortesian deity. Themes appear Spanish—Christians vs. Moors, devils vs. priests—but the native element is strong, sometimes dominant. During Semana Santa (Holy Week) at Pinotepa Nacional in coastal Oaxaca, for example, Mixtec people, costumed as Jews, shoot arrows skyward, simultaneously reciting traditional Mixtec prayers.

crouching man and suns motif

ON THE ROAD

SPORTS AND RECREATION

BEACHES

It's easy to understand why many vacationers stay right at the beach. And not just at the famous crystalline stretches of Mazatlán, Puerto Vallarta, Manzanillo, Ixtapa, Acapulco, and Puerto Escondido. Many flee the big resorts and spread out along the whole coast—gathering at small beach resorts such as San Blas, Rincón de Guayabitos, Playa Azul, and Puerto Ángel—while others set up camp and enjoy the solitude and rich wildlife of hundreds of miles of even more pristine strands. Shorelines vary from mangrove-edged lagoons and algae-decorated tidepools to shoals of pebbles and sand of dozens of colors and consistencies.

Sand makes the beach, and Pacific Mexico has plenty, from warm, black mica dust to cool, velvety white coral. Some beaches drop steeply to turbulent, close-in surf, fine for fishing. Others are level, with gentle, rolling breakers, made for surfing and swimming.

Beaches are fascinating for the surprises they yield. Pacific Mexico's beaches, especially the hidden strands near resorts and the hundreds of miles of wilderness beaches and tidepools, yield troves of shells and treasures of flotsam and jetsam for those who enjoy looking for them. **Beachcombing** is more rewarding during the summer storm season, when big waves deposit acres of fresh shells—among them conch, scallop, clams, combs of Venus, whelks, limpets, olives, cowries, starfish, and sand dollars.

During the summer-fall rainy season beaches near river mouths are often fantastic outdoor galleries of wind- and water-sculpted snags and giant logs deposited by the downstream flood.

Viewing Wildlife
Wildlife watchers should keep quiet and always be on the alert. Animal survival depends on them

seeing you first. Occasional spectacular offshore sights, such as whales, porpoises, and manta rays, or an onshore giant constrictor, beached squid or octopus, crocodile, or even a jaguar looking for turtle eggs are the reward of those prepared to recognize them. Don't forget your binoculars and your *Field Guide to Mexican Birds* (see the Booklist).

For extensive notes on good hiking, tidepooling, wildlife viewing, and shell-browsing spots, see the destination chapters.

WATER SPORTS

Swimming, surfing, windsurfing, snorkeling, scuba diving, kayaking, sailing, and jet skiing are Pacific Mexico's water sports of choice. For details on local favorite spots, conditions, rental shops, equipment, see the destination chapters.

Safety First
As viewed from Pacific Mexico beaches, the Pacific Ocean usually lives up to its name. Many protected inlets, safe for child's play, dot the coastline. Unsheltered shorelines, on the other hand, can be deceiving. Smooth water in the calm forenoon often changes to choppy in the afternoon; calm ripples lapping the shore in March can grow to hurricane-driven walls of water in November. Such storms can wash away sand, changing a wide, gently sloping beach into a

steep one plagued by turbulent waves and treacherous currents.

Undertow, whirlpools, crosscurrents, and occasional oversized waves can make ocean swimming a fast-lane adventure. Getting unexpectedly swept out to sea or hammered onto the beach bottom by a surprise breaker are potential hazards.

Never attempt serious swimming when tipsy or full of food; never swim alone where someone can't see you. Always swim beyond the breakers (which come in sets of several, climaxed by a big one, which breaks highest and farthest from the beach). If you happen to get caught in the path of such a breaker, avoid it by diving under and letting it roll harmlessly over you. If you do get caught by a serious breaker, try to roll and tumble with it (as football players tumble) to avoid injury.

Now and then swimmers get a nettlelike jellyfish sting. Be careful around coral reefs and beds of sea urchins; corals can sting (like jellyfish) and you can get infections from coral cuts and sea-urchin spines. Shuffle along sandy bottoms to scare away stingrays before stepping on one. If you're unlucky, its venomous tailspines may inflict a painful wound. (See **health** for first-aid measures.)

Snorkeling and Scuba Diving
Many exciting clear-water sites, such as Puerto Vallarta's Los Arcos, Zihuatanejo's Playa Las Gatas, Isla Roqueta at Acapulco, and Playa Es-

Balmy water and gentle conditions make afternoon sailing a breeze in many of Pacific Mexico's protected coves and bays.

tacahuite at Puerto Ángel await both beginner and expert skin divers. Veteran Pacific Mexico divers usually arrive during the dry winter and early spring when river outflows are mere trickles, leaving offshore waters clear. In the major tourist centers, professional dive shops rent equipment, provide lessons and guides, and transport divers to choice sites.

While convenient, rented equipment is often less than satisfactory. To be sure, serious divers bring their own gear. This should probably include wet suits in the winter, when many swimmers begin to feel cold after an unprotected half-hour in the water.

Surfing, Sailing, Windsurfing, and Kayaking
In addition to several well-known surfing beaches, such as Matanchén at San Blas, Puerto Vallarta's Punta Mita, Barra de Nexpa south of Manzanillo, Pacific Mexico has the country's acknowledged best surfing beach—the Playa Zicatela "pipeline," at Puerto Escondido.

The surf everywhere is highest and best during the July-Nov. hurricane season, when big swells from storms far out at sea attract platoons of surfers to favored beaches (except at crowded Acapulco Bay, where surfing is off-limits).

Windsurfers, sailboaters, and kayakers—who, by contrast, require more tranquil waters—do best in the Pacific Mexico winter or early spring. Then they gather to enjoy the near-ideal conditions at many coves and inlets near the big resorts.

While beginners can have fun with the equipment available from rental shops, serious surfers, windsurfers, sailboaters, and kayakers should pack their own gear.

POWER SPORTS

Acapulco and other big resorts have long been centers for water-skiing, parasailing, and jet skiing. In parasailing, a motorboat pulls, while a parachute lifts you, like a soaring gull, high over the ocean. After 10 minutes they deposit you (usually gently) back on the sand. Jet-ski boats are like snowmobiles except they operate on water, where, with a little practice, even beginners can quickly learn to whiz over the waves.

Although the luxury resorts generally provide experienced crews and equipment, crowded con-

ditions increase the hazard to both participants and swimmers. You, as the paying patron, have a right to expect that your providers and crew are well-equipped, sober, and cautious.

Beach Buggies and ATVs
Some visitors enjoy racing along the beach and rolling over dunes with beach buggies and ATVs (all-terrain vehicles—*motos* in Mexico), balloon-tired, three-wheeled motor scooters. While certain resort rental agencies cater to the growing use of such vehicles, limits are in order. Of all the proliferating high-horsepower beach pastimes, these are the most intrusive. Noise, exhaust and gasoline pollution, injuries to operators and bystanders, scattering of wildlife and destruction of their habitats has led (and I hope will continue to lead) to the restriction of dune buggies and ATVs on beaches.

TENNIS AND GOLF

Most Mexicans are working too hard to be playing much tennis and golf. Although there are almost no public courses or courts, Pacific Mexico's resort centers enjoy excellent private facilities. If you are planning on a lot of golf and tennis, check into one of the many hotels with these facilities. Use of hotel tennis courts is often, but not always, included in your hotel tariff. If not, fees will run about $10 per hour or more. Golf greens fees, which begin at about $50 for 18 holes, are always extra.

See the destination chapters for plenty of golf and tennis listings.

FISHING AND HUNTING

Experts agree Pacific Mexico is a world-class deep-sea and surf fishing ground. Sportspersons routinely bring in dozens of species from among the more than 600 that have been hooked in Pacific Mexico waters.

Surf Fishing
Most good fishing beaches away from the immediate resort areas will typically have only a few locals (mostly with nets) and fewer visitors. Mexicans typically do little sportfishing. Most ei-

FISH

A bounty of fish dart, swarm, jump, and wriggle in Pacific Mexico's surf, reefs, lagoons, and offshore depths. While many make delicious dinners (albacore, red snapper, pompano), others are tough (sailfish), bony (bonefish), and even poisonous (puffers). Some grow to half-ton giants (marlin, jewfish), while others are diminutive reef-grazers (parrot fish, damselfish, angelfish) whose bright colors delight snorkelers and divers. Here's a sampling of what you might find underwater or on your dinner plate.

albacore *(albacora, atún):* two to four feet in size; blue; found in deep waters; excellent taste

angelfish *(ángel):* one foot; yellow, orange, blue; reef fish*

barracuda *(barracuda, picuda):* two feet; brown; deep waters; good taste

black marlin *(marlin negro):* six feet; blue-black; deep waters; good taste

blue marlin *(marlin azul):* eight feet; blue; deep waters; poor taste

bobo *(barbudo):* one foot; blue, yellow; found in surf; fair taste

bonefish *(macabi):* one foot; blue or silver; found inshore; poor taste

bonito *(bonito):* two feet; black; deep waters; good taste

bonito

butterfly fish *(muñeca):* six inches; black, yellow; reef fish*

chub *(chopa):* one foot; gray; reef fish; good taste

croaker *(corvina):* two feet; brownish; found along inshore bottoms; rare and protected

damselfish *(castañeta):* four inches; brown, blue, orange; reef fish*

dolphinfish, mahimahi *(dorado):* three feet; green, gold; deep waters; good taste

grouper *(garropa):* three feet; brown, rust; found offshore and in reefs; good taste

grunt *(burro):* eight inches; black, gray; found in rocks, reefs*

jack *(toro):* one to two feet; bluish-gray; offshore; good taste

barracuda

ther make their living from fishing, or they do none at all. Consequently, few shops sell sportfishing equipment in Mexico; plan to bring your own surf-fishing equipment, including hooks, lures, line, and weights.

Your best general information source before you leave home is a good local bait-and-tackle shop. Tell them where you're going, and they'll often know the best lures and bait to use and what fish you can expect to catch with them.

In any case, the cleaner the water, the more interesting your catch. On a good day, your reward might be *sierras, cabrillas,* porgies, or pompanos pulled from the Pacific Mexico surf.

You can't have everything, however. Foreigners cannot legally take Mexican abalone, coral, lobster, pismo clams, rock bass, sea fans, shrimp, turtles, or seashells. Neither are they supposed to buy them directly from fishermen.

Deep-Sea Fishing

Mazatlán and Manzanillo are renowned spots for the big prize marlin and sailfish, while Zihuatanejo, Puerto Vallarta, and Acapulco run close behind.

A deep-sea boat charter generally includes the boat and crew for a full or half day, plus equipment and bait for two to six persons, not in-

mackerel *(sierra):* two feet; gray with gold spots; offshore; good taste

mullet *(lisa):* two feet; gray; found in sandy bays; good taste

needlefish *(agujón):* three feet; blue-black; deep waters; good taste

Pacific porgy *(pez de pluma):* one to two feet; tan; found along sandy shores; good taste

parrot fish *(perico, pez loro):* one foot; green, pink, blue, orange; reef fish

pompano *(pómpano):* one foot; gray; inshore bottoms; excellent taste

puffer *(botete):* eight inches; brown; inshore; poisonous

red snapper *(huachinango, pargo):* one to two feet; reddish pink; deep waters; excellent taste

roosterfish *(pez gallo):* three feet; black, blue; deep waters; excellent taste

sailfish *(pez vela):* five feet; blue-black; deep waters; poor taste

sardine *(sardina):* eight inches; blue-black; offshore; good taste

sailfish

ERIN DWYER

sea bass *(cabrilla):* one to two feet; brown, ruddy; reef and rock crevices; good taste

shark *(tiburón):* 2-10 feet; black to blue; in- and offshore; good taste

snook *(robalo):* two to three feet; black-brown; found in brackish lagoons; excellent taste

spadefish *(chambo):* one foot; black-silver; found along sandy bottoms; reef fish*

swordfish *(pez espada):* five feet; black to blue; deep waters; good taste

triggerfish *(pez puerco):* one to two feet; blue, rust, brown, black; reef fish; excellent taste

wahoo *(peto, guahu):* two to five feet; green to blue; deep waters; excellent taste

yellowfin tuna *(atún amarilla):* two to five feet; blue, yellow; deep waters; excellent taste

yellowtail *(jurel):* two to four feet; blue, yellow; offshore; excellent taste

*fish that are generally too small to be considered edible

ERIC SCHNITTGER

damselfish

cluding food or drinks. The full-day price depends upon the season. Around Christmas and New Year and before Easter (when advance reservations will be mandatory) a boat can run $400 at Mazatlán or Manzanillo. At lesser-known resorts, or even at the big resorts during low season, you might be able to bargain a captain down to as low as $200.

Renting an entire big boat is not the only choice. Winter business is sometimes so brisk at resorts that agencies can make reservations for individuals for about $60 per person per day.

Pangas, outboard launches seating two to six passengers, are available for as little $50, depending on the season. Once in Barra de Navidad six of my friends hired a *panga* for $50, had a great time, and came back with a boatload of big tuna, jack, and mackerel. A restaurant cooked them up as a banquet for a dozen of us in exchange for the extra fish, and I discovered for the first time how heavenly fresh *sierra veracruzana* can taste.

Bringing Your Own Boat

If you're going to be doing lots of fishing, your own boat may be your most flexible and economical option. One big advantage is you can go to the many excellent fishing grounds the charter

FIESTAS

The following calendar lists national and notable regional and local holidays and festivals. If you happen to be where one of these is going on, get out of your car or bus and join in!

1 Jan.: **¡Feliz Año Nuevo!** ("Happy New Year!"; national holiday)

1-5 Jan.: **Inauguration** of the Cora governor in Jesús María, Nayarit (Cora indigenous dances and ceremonies)

6 Jan.: **Día de los Reyes** ("Day of the Kings"; traditional gift exchange)

12 Jan.: **Día de Nuestra Señora de Guadalupe** in El Tuito, Jalisco, an hour's drive south of Puerto Vallarta ("Festival of the Virgin of Guadalupe"; parade, music, evening mass, and carnival)

13-17 Jan.: **Fiesta of the Sweet Name of Jesus** ("Dulce Nombre de Jesús"), in Santa Ana del Valle, Tlacolula and Zimatlán, Oaxaca. Troupes perform many traditional dances, including the Dance of the Feathers.

17 Jan.: **Día de San Antonio Abad** (decorating and blessing animals)

20-21 Jan.: **Fiesta de San Sebastián,** especially in San Pedro y San Pablo Tequixtepec, Pinotepa Don Luis, and Jalapa de Díaz, Oaxaca.

20 Jan.-2 Feb.: **Fiesta of the Virgin of Candlemas,** in San Juan de los Lagos, Jalisco. (Millions, from all over Mexico, honor the Virgin with parades, dances depicting Christians vs. Moors, rodeos, cockfights, fireworks, and much more.)

23 Jan.- 2 Feb.: **Fiesta de la Virgen de la Salud** in Colima, Colima (processions, food, dancing, and fireworks)

1-3 Feb.: **Festival of the Sea** in San Blas, Nayarit (dancing, horse races, and competitions)

2 Feb.: **Día de Candelaria** (plants, seeds, and candles blessed; procession, and bullfights)

5 Feb.: **Constitution Day** (national holiday commemorating the constitutions of 1857 and 1917)

7 - 23 Feb.: **Fiesta de Villa Alvarez** in Colima, Colima (bullfights, rodeos, and carnivals)

24 Feb.: **Flag Day** (national holiday)

February: During the four days before Ash Wednesday, usually in late February, many towns stage **Carnaval**—Mardi Gras—extravaganzas.

Second Friday of Lent (nine days after Ash Wednesday): **Fiesta del Señor del Perdón** ("Lord of Forgiveness"), a big pilgrimage festival in San Pedro and San Pablo Tequixtepec

10-17 March: **Fiesta de San Patricio** at San Patricio-Melaque, Jalisco (St. Patrick's day festival; processions, boat regatta, dances, food, and carnival)

11-19 March: Week before the **Day of St. Joseph** in Talpa, Jalisco (food, edible crafts made of colored *chicle* chewing gum, dancing, bands, and mariachi serenades to the Virgin)

Fourth Friday before Easter Sunday: **Fiesta of Jesus the Nazarene** in Huaxpaltepec, Oaxaca (native Dance of the Conquest; big native country fair)

18 March-4 April: **Ceramics and handicrafts fair,** in Tonalá (Guadalajara), Jalisco

19 March: **Día de San José** ("Day of St. Joseph")

21 Mar.: **Birthday of Benito Juárez,** the "Hero of the Americas" (national holiday), especially in Benito Juárez's birthplace, Guelatao, with a whirl of traditional dances

1-19 April: **Fiesta de Ramos,** in Sayula, Jalisco (on Hwy. 54 south of Guadalajara; local area crafts fair, food, dancing, mariachis)

Good Friday, two days before Easter Sunday: **Fiesta de la Santa Cruz de Huatulco** ("Holy Cross of Huatulco") in Santa María Huatulco, Oaxaca.

April: **Semana Santa** (pre-Easter Holy Week, culminating in Domingo Gloria, Easter Sunday national holiday)

1 May: **Labor Day** (national holiday)May (first and third Wednesdays): **Fiesta of the Virgin of Ocotlán,** in Ocotlán, Jalisco (on Lake Chapala, religious processions, dancing, fireworks, regional food)

3 May: **Fiesta de la Santa Cruz** ("Holy Cross") in many places, especially Salina Cruz and Tehuantepec, Oaxaca, and Mascota, Jalisco

3-15 May: **Fiesta of St. Isador the Farmer,** in Tepic, Nayarit (blessing of seeds, animals, and water; agricultural displays, competitions, and dancing)

5 May: **Cinco de Mayo** (defeat of the French at Puebla in 1862; national holiday)

10 May: **Mothers' Day** (national holiday)

10-12 May: **Fiesta of the Coronation of the Virgin of the Rosary** in Talpa, Jalisco (processions, fireworks, regional food, crafts, and dances)

10-24 May: **Book fair** in Guadalajara (readings, concerts, and international book exposition)

15-30 May **Velas (Fiestas) de San Vicente Ferrer** in Juchitán, Oaxaca (Chontal and Huave dances and fair)

15 June-14 July: **National Ceramics Fair** in the Tlaquepaque district, Guadalajara (huge crafts fair; exhibits, competitions, and market of crafts from all over the country)

24 June: **Día de San Juan Bautista** ("Day of St. John the Baptist"; fairs and religious festivals, playful dunking of people in water)

28-29 June: **Regatta** in Mexcaltitán, Nayarit (friendly rivalry between boats carrying images of St. Peter and St. Paul to celebrate opening of the shrimp season)

29 June: **Día de San Pablo y San Pedro** ("Day of St. Peter and St. Paul")

1-15 July: **Fiesta of the Precious Blood of Christ** in Teotitlán del Valle, Oaxaca (featuring the Danza de la Pluma—"Dance of the Feather")

July: **Lunes del Cerro** in Oaxaca (a two-week extravaganza of native dances, events and fairs, beginning on the first Monday after 16 July; among Mexico's most colorful)

20-30 July: **Fiesta de Santiago Apóstol** ("St. James the Apostle") in Santiago Laollaga, Suchilquitongo, Jamiltepec, Pinotepa Nacional, and Juxtlahuaca, Oaxaca

August: **Copper Fair** in Santa Clara del Cobre, Michoacán

14 Aug.: **Fiesta de la Virgen de la Asunción** ("Virgin of the Assumption") in Tlaxiaco, Oaxaca;15 Aug. in Nochixtlán, Oaxaca; and 13-16 Aug. in Huazolotitlán, Oaxaca.

14 Sept.: **Charro Day** ("Cowboy Day" all over Mexico; rodeos)

15-16 Sept.: **Independence Day** (national holiday; mayors everywhere reenact Father Hidalgo's 1810 Grito de Dolores from city hall balconies on the night of 15 September)

27-29 Sept.: **Fiesta de San Miguel** in San Miguel Tequixtepec and Teotitlán del Camino, Oaxaca (Dance of the "Cristianos y Moros"—Christians and Moors).

1-2 Oct.: **Fiesta de San Miguel Arcangel** in Puerto Ángel, Oaxaca

4 Oct.: **Día de San Francisco** ("Day of St. Francis"; traditional dances, especially in Uruapan, Michoacán)

12 Oct.: **Día de la Raza** ("Columbus Day," national holiday that commemorates the union of the races)

October, second Sunday: **Fiesta del Santa Cristo de Tlacolula** ("Holy Christ of Tlacolula") in Tlacolula, Oaxaca.

12 Oct.: **Fiesta of the Virgin of Zapopan** in Guadalajara (procession carries the Virgin home to the Zapopan cathedral from Guadalajara; regional food, crafts fair, mariachis, and dancing)

October (last Sunday): **Día de Cristo Rey** in Ixtlán del Río, Nayarit ("Day of Christ the King," with Quetzal y Azteca and La Pluma *indígena* dances, horse races, processions, and food)

1 Nov.: **Día de Todos Santos** ("All Souls' Day," in honor of the souls of children. The departed descend from heaven to eat sugar skeletons, skulls, and treats on family altars.)

2 Nov.: **Día de los Muertos** ("Day of the Dead," in honor of ancestors. Families visit cemeteries and decorate graves with flowers and favorite food of the deceased.) Especially colorful in around Pátzcuaro, Michoacán, and in Oaxaca.

7-30 Nov.: **Fería de la Nao de China** in Acapulco (a fair celebrating the galleon trade that linked colonial Acapulco with the Orient)

continues on next page

FIESTAS
(continued)

20 Nov.: **Revolution Day** (anniversary of the revolution of 1910-17; national holiday)

28 Nov.-5 Dec.: **National Silver Fair** in Taxco, Guerrero. Mexico's most skilled silversmiths compete for prizes amidst a whirl of concerts, dances, and fireworks.

1 Dec.: **Inauguration Day** (national government changes hands every six years: 2000, 2006, 2012 . . .)

8 Dec.: **Día de la Purísima Concepción** ("Day of the Immaculate Conception")

late Nov.-8 Dec.: **Fiesta de la Virgen de Juquila** (Oaxaca's biggest fiesta; national pilgrimage in Santa Catarina Juquila)

12 Dec.: **Día de Nuestra Señora de Guadalupe** ("Festival of the Virgin of Guadalupe," pa-troness of Mexico; processions, music, and dancing nationwide, especially in downtown Manzanillo and Puerto Vallarta)

16-18 Dec.: **Fiesta de la Virgen de Soledad** in Oaxaca

16-24 Dec.: **Christmas Week** (week of *posadas* and piñatas; midnight mass on Christmas Eve)

23 Dec.: **Fiesta de los Rábanos** (Radish sculpture competition on the main plaza in Oaxaca)

25 Dec.: **Christmas Day** ("¡Feliz Navidad!"; Christmas trees and gift exchange; national holiday)

26 Dec.: **Vela Tehuantepec** (in Tehunatepec, Oaxaca; everyone in town dances to the lovely melody of the *Sandunga*)

31 Dec.: **New Year's Eve**

---

boats do not frequent. Keep your equipment simple, scout around, and keep your eyes peeled and ears open for local regulations and customs, plus tide, wind, and fish-edibility information.

Fishing Licenses and Boat Permits
Anyone 16 or older who is either fishing or riding in a fishing boat in Mexico is required to have a fishing license. Although Mexican fishing licenses are obtainable from certain travel and insurance agents or at government fishing offices everywhere along the coast, save yourself time and trouble by getting both your fishing licenses and boat permits by mail ahead of time from the Mexican Department of Fisheries. Call at least a month before departure (tel. 619-233-6956, fax 233-0344) and ask for applications and the fees (which are reasonable, but depend upon the period of validity and the fluctuating exchange rate). On the application, fill in the names (exactly as they appear on passports) of the persons requesting licenses. Include a cashier's check or a money order for the exact amount, along with a stamped, self-addressed envelope. Address the application to the Mexican Department of Fisheries, 2550 Fifth Ave., Suite 101, San Diego, CA 92103-6622.

Hunting and Freshwater Fishing
Much game, especially winter-season waterfowl and doves, is customarily hunted in freshwater reservoirs and coastal brackish marshes in Sinaloa, Pacific Mexico's northernmost state. Some of the most popular hunting and fishing reservoirs are **Dominguez** and **Hidalgo,** near colonial El Fuerte town (an hour northeast of Los Mochis). Farther south, just north of Culiacán, is reservoir **López Mateos,** while farther south is lake **Comedero,** about two hours by car north of Mazatlán, or six hours north of Tepic.

Bag limits and seasons for game are carefully controlled by the government Secretary of Social Development (Secretaría de Desarrollo Social), SEDESOL. They and the Mexican consular service jointly issue the various required permits through a time-consuming and costly procedure, which, at minimum, runs months and hundreds of dollars. For more details on Mexican hunting regulations and permits, consult the AAA (American Automobile Association) *Mexico Travelbook* (see the Booklist).

Private fee agencies are a must to complete the mountain of required paperwork. Among the most experienced are the **Mexican Hunting Association,** 3302 Josie Ave., Long Beach, CA 90808 (tel. 562-421-6215, fax 496-2412), and

Wildlife Advisory Service, P.O. Box 76132, Los Angeles, CA 90076 (tel. 213-385-9311, fax 385-0782). The Mexican Hunting Association, operated by veteran sportsman Jim Cauley, also offers books, guides, and accommodations. For many useful hunting and fishing details, including many sites and lodges throughout Northern Mexico, get a copy of Sanborn's *Mexico Recreational Guide,* published by Sanborn's insurance agency ($15.95, plus postage and handling). Order with credit card by calling (800) 222-0158 or by writing P.O. Box 310, McAllen, TX 78502.

BULLFIGHTING

It is said there are two occasions for which Mexicans arrive on time: funerals and bullfights.

Bullfighting is a recreation, not a sport. The bull is outnumbered seven to one and the outcome is never in doubt. Even if the matador (literally, "killer") fails in his duty, his assistants will entice the bull away and slaughter him in private beneath the stands.

La Corrida de Toros

Mexicans don't call it a "bullfight"; it's the *corrida de toros,* during which six bulls are customarily slaughtered, beginning at 5 p.m. (4 in the winter). After the beginning parade, the first bull rushes into the ring in a cloud of dust. Three clockwork *tercios* (thirds) define the ritual: the first, the *puyazos,* or "stabs," requires that two *picadores* on horseback thrust lances into the bull's shoulders, weakening him. During the second *tercio,* the bandilleras dodge the bull's horns to stick three long, streamered darts into his shoulders.

Trumpets announce the third *tercio* and the appearance of the matador. The bull—weak, confused, and angry—is ready for the finish. The matador struts, holding the red cape, daring the bull to charge. Form now becomes everything. The expert matador takes complete control of the bull, who rushes at the cape, past his ramrod-erect opponent. For charge after charge, the matador works the bull to exactly the right spot in the ring—in front of the judges, a lovely señorita, or perhaps the governor—where the matador mercifully delivers the precision *estocada* (killing sword thrust) deep into the drooping neck of the defeated bull.

Benito Juárez, as governor during the 1850s, outlawed bullfights in Oaxaca. In his honor, they remain so, making Oaxaca unique among Mexican states.

FESTIVALS AND EVENTS

Mexicans love a party. Urban families watch the calendar for midweek national holidays that create a *puente* or "bridge" to the weekend and allow them to squeeze in a three- to five-day mini-vacation. Visitors should likewise watch the calendar. Such holidays (especially Christmas and Semana Santa, pre-Easter week) mean packed buses, roads, and hotels, especially around the Puerto Vallarta region's beach resorts.

Country people, on the other hand, await their local saint's or holy day. The name of the locality often provides the clue. For example, in Santa

Skirts whirl and heels click in Guadalajara's renowned "Jarabe Tapatío" courtship dance, also known as the "Mexican Hat Dance."

Cruz del Miramar near San Blas, expect a celebration on May 3, El Día de la Santa Cruz ("Day of the Holy Cross"). People dress up in their traditional best, sell their wares and produce in a street fair, join a procession, get tipsy, and dance in the plaza.

ARTS AND CRAFTS

Mexico is so stuffed with lovely, reasonably priced handicrafts that many crafts devotees, if given the option, might choose Mexico over heaven. A sizable fraction of Mexican families still depend upon homespun items—clothing, utensils, furniture, native herbal remedies, religious offerings, adornments, toys, musical instruments—which either they or their neighbors craft at home. Many such traditions reach back thousands of years, to the beginnings of Mexican civilization. The accumulated knowledge of manifold generations of artisans has, in many instances, resulted in finery so prized that whole villages devote themselves to the manufacture of a certain class of goods.

In Pacific Mexico, handicrafts (*artesanías,* pronounced "ar-tay-sah-NEE-ahs") shoppers who venture away from the coastal resorts to the source towns and villages will most likely benefit from lower prices, wider choices, and, most important, the privilege of encountering the artisans themselves. There, perhaps in a patio-shop on a dusty Tonalá side street or above a breezy Pátzcuaro lakeshore, you might meet the people and view the painstaking process by which they fashion humble materials—clay, wool, cotton, wood, metal, straw, leaves, bark, paper, leather—into irresistible works of art.

BASKETRY AND WOVEN CRAFTS

Weaving straw, leaves, and reeds is among the oldest of Mexican crafts traditions. Mat- and basketweaving methods and designs 5,000 years old survive to the present day. All over Mexico, people weave *petates* (straw mats) upon which vacationers stretch out on the beach and which local folks use for everything, from keeping tortillas warm to shielding babies from the sun. Around Acapulco and along the Oaxaca coast, you might even see a woman or a child waiting for a bus or even walking down the street while weaving creamy white palm leaf strands into a coiled basket. Later, you may see a similar basket, embellished with a bright animal—parrot, burro, or even Snoopy—for sale in the market.

Like the origami paper-folders of Japan, folks who live around Lake Pátzcuaro have taken basketweaving to its ultimate by crafting virtually everything—from toy turtles and Christmas bells to butterfly mobiles and serving spoons—from the reeds they gather along the lakeshore.

Hat-making has likewise attained high refinement in Mexico. Workers in Sahuayo, Michoacán (near the southeast shore of Lake Chapala), craft especially fine sombreros. Due east across Mexico, in Becal, Campeche, workers craft Panama hats (*jipis,* pronounced "HEE-pees") so fine, soft, and flexible that you can stuff one into your pants pocket without damage.

Although Huichol men in the states of Nayarit and Jalisco do not actually manufacture their headwear, they do decorate them. They take ordinary sombreros and embellish them into Mexico's most flamboyant hats, flowing with bright ribbons, feathers, and fringes of colorful wool balls.

CLOTHING AND EMBROIDERY

Although ***traje*** (ancestral tribal dress) has vanished in urban Mexico, significant numbers of Mexican women, especially in remote districts of Michoacán, Guerrero, Oaxaca, Chiapas, and Yucatán, make and wear *traje*. Most common is the ***huipil,*** a full, square-shouldered, short- to mid-sleeved dress, often hand-embroidered with animal and floral designs. *Huipiles* from Oaxaca include designs from San Pedro de Amusgos (Amusgo tribe: white cotton, embroidered with abstract colored animal and floral motifs); San Andrés Chicahuaxtla (Trique tribe: white cotton, richly embroidered red stripes, interwoven with green, blue, and yellow, and hung with colored ribbons); Yalalag (Zapotec tribe: white cotton, with bright flowers embroidered along two or four vertical seams and distinctive colored tassels hanging down the back). Beyond Oaxaca, Yucatán Maya *huipiles* are among the most prized. They are of white cotton, embellished with big, brilliant machine-embroidered flowers around the neck and shoulders.

Shoppers sometimes can buy other, less common types of *traje,* such as a **quechquémitl** (shoulder cape), often made of wool and worn as an overgarment in winter. The **enredo,** a full-length skirt, wraps around the waist and legs like a Hawaiian sarong. Mixtec women in Oaxaca's warm south coast region around Pinotepa Nacional commonly wear the *enredo,* known locally as the *pozahuanco* (poh-sah-oo-AHN-koh) below the waist, and when at home, go barebreasted. When wearing their *pozahuancos* in public, they usually tie a **mandil,** a wide calico apron, around their front side. Women weave the best *pozahuancos,* using cotton thread dyed a light purple with secretions of tidepool-harvested snails, *Purpura patula pansa,* and silk dyed deep red with cochineal, extracted from the dried bodies of a locally cultivated beetle, *Dactylopius coccus.* On a typical day, two or three women will be selling handmade *pozahuancos* at the Pinotepa Nacional market.

Colonial-era Spanish styles have blended with native *traje,* producing a wider class of dress, known generally as **ropa típica.** Lovely embroidered blouses *(blusas),* shawls *(rebozos),* and dresses *(vestidos)* fill boutique racks and market stalls all over Pacific Mexico. Among the most popular is the so-called **Oaxaca wedding dress,** made of cotton with a crochet-trimmed riot of diminutive flowers hand-stitched about the neck and yoke. Some of the finest examples are made in San Antonino Castillo, just north of Ocotlán in the Valley of Oaxaca.

In contrast to women, only a small fraction of Mexican men—members of remote groups, such as Huichol, Cora, and Tarahumara in the northwest, and Maya and Lacandon in the southeast—wear *traje.* Nevertheless, shops offer some fine men's *ropa típica,* such as wool jackets and serapes for northern or highland winter

KAREN McKINLEY

wear, and *guayaberas,* hip-length, pleated tropical dress shirts.

Fine embroidery *(bordado)* embellishes much traditional Mexican clothing, tablecloths *(manteles),* and napkins *(servilletas).* As everywhere, women define the art of embroidery. Although some still work by hand at home, cheaper machine-made factory lace and needlework is more commonly available in shops.

Leather

Pacific Mexico shops offer an abundance of leather goods, which, if not manufactured locally, are shipped from the renowned leather centers. These include Guadalajara, Mazatlán, and Oaxaca (sandals and huaraches), and Leon (shoes, boots, and saddles). For unique and custom-designed articles you'll probably have to confine your shopping to the expensive tourist resort shops. For the more usual though still attractive leather items such as purses, wallets, belts, coats, boots, veteran shoppers go to local city markets. Most notable among these is Guadalajara's Libertad Market, where an acre of stalls offer the broadest leather selection at reasonable prices (with bargaining) in Pacific Mexico.

FURNITURE

Although furniture is usually too bulky to carry back home with your airline luggage, low Mexican prices allow you to ship your purchases home and enjoy beautiful, unusual pieces for a fraction of what you would pay, if you could get them, at home.

A number classes of furniture (*muebles,* pronounced "moo-AY-blays") are crafted in villages near the sources of raw materials—either wood, reeds, bamboo, or wrought iron.

Sometimes it seems as if every house in Mexico is furnished with wood **colonial-style furniture.** The basic design of much of it dates at least back to the middle ages. Although variations exist, most colonial-style furniture is heavily built. Table and chair legs are massive, often lathe-turned; chair backs are usually straight and vertical. Although usually varnished, colonial-style tables, chairs, and chests sometimes shine with inlaid wood or tile, or animal and flower designs. Family shops turn out good furniture, usually in the highlands, where suitable wood is available. Products from shops in and around Guadalajara, Lake Pátzcuaro (especially Tzintzuntzan), Taxco, and Olinalá, Guerrero are among the best known.

A second, very distinctive class of Mexican furniture is *equipal,* usually roundish tables, chairs, and sofas, made of brown pigskin or cowhide stretched over wooden frames. Factories are mostly in Guadalajara and nearby villages.

It is intriguing that **lacquered furniture,** in both process and design, has much in common with lacquerware produced half a world away in China. Moreover, Mexican lacquerware tradition both predated the conquest and was originally practiced only on the Pacific, where legends persist of pre-Cortesian contact with Chinese traders. Consequently, a number of experts believe that the Mexicans learned the craft of lacquerware from Chinese artists many centuries before the conquest.

Today, artisan families in and around Pátzcuaro, Michoacán, and Olinalá, Guerrero, carry on the tradition. The process, which at its finest resembles cloisonné manufacture, involves carving and painting intricate floral and animal designs, followed by repeated layerings of lacquer, clay, and sometimes gold and silver to produce satiny, jewel-like surfaces.

A few villages produce furniture made of plant fiber, such reeds, raffia, and bamboo. In some cases, entire communities, such as Ihuatzio (near Pátzcuaro), and Villa Victoria (in Mexico state, west of Toluca), have long harvested the bounty of local lakes and marshes as the basis for their products.

Wrought iron, produced and worked according to Spanish custom, is used to produce tables, chairs, and benches. Ruggedly fashioned in a riot of baroque scrollwork,

pieces often decorate garden, patio, and park settings. Many colonial cities, notably, San Miguel de Allende, Toluca, and Guanajuato, are wrought-iron manufacturing centers.

GLASS AND STONEWORK

Glass manufacture, unknown in pre-Columbian times, was introduced by the Spanish. Today, factories scattered all over the country turn out mountains of **burbuja** (boor-BOO-hah) bubbled glass tumblers, goblets, plates, and pitchers, usually in blue, green, or red. Finer glass is manufactured in Guadalajara; in suburban Tlaquepaque village, you can watch artisans blow glass into a number of shapes, notably, paper-thin balls in red, green, or blue.

Artisans work stone, usually near sources of supply. Puebla, Mexico's main source of onyx (*onix,* pronounced "OH-neeks"), is the manufacturing center for the galaxy of mostly rough-hewn, cream-colored items, from animal charms and chess pieces to beads and desk sets, which crowd curio shop shelves throughout the country. *Cantera,* a volcanic tufa stone occurring in pastel shades from pink to green, quarried near Pátzcuaro and Oaxaca, is used similarly.

For a keepsake from a truly ancient Mexican tradition, don't forget the hollowed-out stone *metate* (may-TAH-tay), a corn-grinding basin, and the three-legged *molcajete* (mohl-kah-HAY-tay), a mortar for grinding chiles.

HUICHOL ART

Growing demand, especially around Puerto Vallarta, has greatly stimulated the supply of Huichol art. Originally produced by shamans for ritual purposes, pieces such as beaded masks, *cuadras* (yarn paintings), gourd rattles, arrows, and yarn *cicuri* (God's eyes) have a ritual symbolism. Eerie beaded masks of wood nearly always represent the Huichols' mother earth, Tatei Urianaka. The larger *cuadras,* of colored acrylic yarn painstakingly glued in intermeshing patterns to a plywood

KAREN McKINLEY

KAREN McKINLEY

base, customarily depict the drama of life being played out between the main actors of the Huichol pantheon. For example, as Tayau ("Father Sun") radiates down over the land, alive with stylized cactus, flowers, peyote buds, snakes, and birds, antlered "Brother Deer" Kauyumari heroically battles the evil sorcerer Kieri, while nearby, Tatei Urianaka gives birth.

JEWELRY

Gold and silver were once the basis for Mexico's wealth. Spanish conquerors plundered a mountain of gold—ritual offerings, necklaces, pendants, rings, plates—masterfully crafted by a legion of indigenous jewelers. Unfortunately, much of that native tradition was lost as the colonial Spanish denied Mexicans access to precious metals and introduced Spanish methods. Nevertheless, a small native gold-working tradition survived the dislocations of the 1810-21 War of Independence and the 1910-17 revolution. Meanwhile, silver-crafting, moribund during the 1800s, was revived in Taxco, Guerrero, during the 1920s, principally through the joint efforts of architect-artist William Spratling and the local community.

Today, spurred by the tourist boom, jewelry-making is thriving in Mexico. Taxco, where guilds, families, and cooperatives produce sparkling silver and gold adornments, is the acknowledged center. Scores of Taxco shops display the results—shimmering ornamental butterflies, birds, jaguars, serpents, turtles, and fish from the pre-Cortesian tradition. Pieces, mostly in silver, vary from humble but attractive trinkets to glittering necklaces, silver candelabras, and place settings for a dozen, sometimes embellished with precious stones.

Other subsidiary jewelry-crafting centers include Oaxaca (preconquest replicas and gold and silver filigree), Pátzcuaro (silver filigree and earrings), Puebla (sand-cast gold and silver), and Guanajuato (gold and silver, especially earrings.)

WOODCARVING AND MUSICAL INSTRUMENTS

Masks

Spanish and Native Mexican traditions have blended to produce a multitude of masks—some strange, some lovely, some scary, some endearing, all interesting. The tradition flourishes in the strongly indigenous southern Pacific states of Michoacán, Guerrero, Oaxaca, and Chiapas, where campesinos gear up all year for the village festivals—especially Semana Santa (Easter week), early December (Virgin of Guadalupe), and of the local patron, whether it be San José, San Pedro, San Pablo, Santa María, Santa Barbara, or one of a host of others. Every local fair has its favored dances, such as the Dance of the Conquest, the Christians and Moors, the Old Men, or the Tiger, in which masked villagers act out age-old allegories of fidelity, sacrifice, faith, struggle, sin, and redemption.

Although masks are made of many materials—from stone and ebony to coconut husks and paper—wood, where available, is the medium of choice. For the entire year, carvers cut, carve, sand, and paint to ensure that each participant will be properly disguised for the festival.

The popularity of masks has led to an entire made-for-tourist mask industry, which has led to mass-produced duplicates, many cleverly antiqued. Examine the goods carefully; if the price is high, don't buy unless you're convinced it's a real antique.

Tourist demand has made zany wooden animals *(alebrijes)* a Oaxaca growth industry. Virtually every family in certain Valley of Oaxaca villages—notably Arrazola and San Martin Tilcajete—runs a factory studio. There, piles of *copal* wood, which men carve and women finish and intricately paint, become whimsical giraffes, dogs, cats, iguanas, gargoyles, dragons, including most of the possible permutations in between. The farther from the source you get, the higher the *alebrije* price becomes; in Arrazola, what costs $5 will probably run about $10 in Puerto Vallarta and $30 in the U.S. or Canada.

Others commonly available are the charming colorfully painted wooden fish carved mainly in the Pacific coastal state of Guerrero, and the burnished, dark hardwood animal and fish sculptures of desert ironwood from the state of Sonora.

Musical Instruments

Virtually all of Mexico's guitars are made in Paracho, Michoacán (southeast of Lake Chapala, 50 miles north of Uruapan). There, scores of cottage factories turn out guitars, violins, mandolins, *viruelas,* ukuleles, and a dozen more variations every day. They vary widely in quality, so look carefully before you buy. Make sure that the wood is well cured and dry; damp, unripe wood instruments are more susceptible to warping and cracking.

METALWORK

Bright copper, brass, and tinware, sturdy ironwork, and razor-sharp knives and machetes are made in a number of regional centers. **Copperware,** from jugs, cups, and plates to candlesticks—and even the town lampposts and bandstand—all comes from Santa Clara del Cobre, a few miles south of Pátzcuaro, Michoacán.

Although not the source of brass itself, Tonalá, in the Guadalajara eastern suburb, is the place where brass is most abundant and beautiful, appearing as menageries of brilliant, fetching birds and animals, sometimes embellished with shiny nickel highlights.

A host of Oaxaca family factories turn out fine knives and machetes, scrolled cast-iron grillwork, and a swarm of bright tinware mirror frames, masks, and glittering Christmas decorations.

Be sure not to miss the tiny *milagros,* one of Mexico's most charming forms of metalwork. Usually of brass, they are of homely shapes—a horse, dog, or baby, or an arm, head, or foot—which, accompanied by a prayer, the faithful pin to the garment of their favorite saint whom they hope will intercede to cure an ailment or fulfill a wish.

PAPER AND PAPIER-MÂCHÉ

Papier-mâché has become a high art in Tonalá, Jalisco, where a swarm of birds, cats, frogs, giraffes, and other animal figurines are meticulously crafted by building up repeated layers of glued paper. The result—sanded, brilliantly varnished, and polished—resemble fine sculptures rather than the humble newspaper from which they were fashioned.

Other paper goods you shouldn't overlook include **piñatas** (durable, inexpensive, and as Mexican as you can get) available in every town market; colorful decorative cutout-banners (string overhead at your home fiesta) from San Salvador Huixcolotla, Puebla; and *amate,* wild fig tree bark paintings in animal and flower motifs, from Xalitla and Ameyaltepec, Guerrero.

POTTERY AND CERAMICS

Although Mexican pottery tradition is as diverse as the country itself, some varieties stand out. Among the most prized is the so-called Talavera (or Majolica), the best of which is made by a few family-run shops in Puebla. The names Talavera and Majolica derive from Talavera, the Spanish town from which the tradition migrated to Mexico; prior to that it originated on the Spanish Mediterranean island of Mayorca, from a combination of still older Arabic, Chinese, and African ceramic styles. Shapes include plates, bowls, jugs, and pitchers, hand-painted and hard-fired in intricate bright yellow, orange, blue, and green floral designs. So few shops make true Talavera these days that other, cheaper look-alike grades, made around Guanajuato, are more common, selling for one-half to one-third the price of the genuine article.

More practical and nearly as prized is hand-painted **stoneware** from Tlaquepaque and Tonalá, Jalisco. Although made in many shapes and sizes, such stoneware is often sold as complete dinner place settings. Decorations are usually in abstract floral and animal designs, hand-painted over a reddish clay base.

From the same tradition come the famous *bruñido* pottery animals of Tonalá. Round, smooth, and cuddly as ceramic can be, the Tonalá animals—very commonly doves and ducks, but also cats and dogs, and sometimes even armadillos, frogs, and snakes—each seem to embody the essence of its species.

Some of the most charming Mexican pottery, made from a ruddy low-fired clay and crafted following pre-Columbian traditions, comes from western Mexico, especially Colima. Fetching figurines in timeless human poses—flute-playing musicians, dozing grandmothers, fidgeting babies, loving couples—and animals, especially Colima's famous, playful dogs, decorate the shelves of a sprinkling of shops.

The southern states of Guerrero and Oaxaca are both centers of a vibrant pottery tradition. Humble but very attractive are the unglazed brightly painted animals—cats, ducks, fish, and many others—that folks bring to resort centers from their family village workshops.

Pottery making is a time-honored Pacific Mexico pastime. Here a potter of Copala, near Mazatlán, works in his family shop.

Much more acclaimed are certain types of pottery from the valley surrounding the city of Oaxaca. The village of Atzompa is famous for its tan, green-glazed clay pots, dishes, and bowls. Nearby San Bártolo Coyotepec village has acquired even more renown for its **black pottery,** sold all over the world. Doña Rosa, now deceased, pioneered the crafting of big round pots without using a potter's wheel. Now made in many more shapes by Doña Rosa's descendants, the pottery's exquisite silvery black sheen is produced by the reduction (reduced air) method of firing, which removes oxygen from the clay's red (ferric) iron oxide, converting it to black ferrous oxide.

Although most latter-day Mexican potters have become aware of the health dangers of lead pigments, some for-sale pottery may still contain lead. The hazard comes from low-fired pottery in which the lead has not been firmly melted into the glaze. Acids in foods such as lemons, vinegar, and tomatoes dissolve the lead pigments, which, when ingested, eventually results in lead poisoning. In general, the shiniest pottery, which has been twice fired—such as the high-quality Tlaquepaque stoneware used for dishes—is the safest.

WOOLEN WOVEN GOODS

Mexico's finest wool weavings come from Teotitlán del Valle, in the Valley of Oaxaca, less than an hour's drive east of Oaxaca. The weaving tradition, carried on by Teotitlán's Zapotec-speaking families, dates back at least 2,000 years. Most families still carry on the arduous process, making everything from scratch. They gather the dyes from wild plants and the bodies of insects and sea snails. They hand-wash, card, spin, and dye the wool and even travel to remote mountain springs to gather water. The results, they say, *vale la pena,* are "worth the pain": intensely colored, tightly woven carpets, rugs, and wall-hangings that retain their brilliance for generations.

Rougher, more loosely woven blankets, jackets, and serapes come from other parts, notably mountain regions, especially around San Cristóbal Las Casas, in Chiapas, and Lake Pátzcuaro in Michoacán.

ACCOMMODATIONS

Pacific Mexico has thousands of lodgings to suit every style and pocketbook: world-class resorts, small beachside hotels, homey *casas de huéspedes* (guesthouses), palm-shaded trailer parks, and hundreds of miles of pristine camping beaches. The high seasons, when reservations are generally recommended, are mid-December through March, during pre-Easter week, and the month of August.

The hundreds of accommodations described in this book are positive recommendations— checked out in detail—good choices, from which you can pick, according to your own taste and purse.

Hotel Rates

The rates listed in this book are U.S. dollar equivalents of peso prices, taxes included, as quoted by the hotel management at the time of writing. Low- and high-season rates are quoted whenever possible. They are intended as a general guide only, and probably will only approximate the asking rate when you arrive. Some readers, unfortunately, try to bargain by telling desk clerks that, for example, the rate should be $20 because they read it in this book. This is unwise, because it makes hotel managers and clerks reluctant to quote rates for fear readers might hold their hotel responsible for such quotes a few years later.

In Pacific Mexico, hotel rates depend strongly upon inflation and season. To cancel the effect of relatively steep Mexican inflation, rates are reported in U.S. dollars. However, when settling your hotel bill, you should always insist on paying in pesos.

Saving Money

The hotel prices quoted here are rack rates, the maximum tariff, exclusive of packages and promotions, that you would pay if you walked in and rented an unreserved room for one day. Savvy travelers seldom pay the maximum. Always inquire if there are any discounts or packages (*discuentos o paquetes,* pronounced "dees-koo-AYN-tohs OH pah-KAY-tays"). At any time other than the super-high Christmas and Easter seasons, you can get at least one or two free days for a one-week stay. Promotional packages available during slack seasons usually include free extras such as breakfast, a car rental, a boat tour, or a sports rental. A travel agent can be of great help in shopping around for such bargains.

You will often save additional money if you deal in pesos only. Insist on both booking your lodging for an agreed price in pesos and paying the resulting hotel bill in the same pesos, rather than dollars. The reason is that dollar rates quoted by big resorts are often based on the hotel

Guests commonly enjoy swimming pools, even in modest Pacific Mexico lodgings.

desk exchange rate, which is customarily about 10%, or even as much 25%, less than bank rates. For example, if the clerk tells you your hotel bill is $1,000, instead of handing over the dollars, or having him mark $1,000 on your credit card slip, ask him how much it is in pesos. Using the desk conversion rate, he might say something like 9,000 pesos (considerably less than the 10,000 pesos that the bank might give for your $1,000.) Pay the 9,000 pesos or have the clerk mark 9,000 pesos on your credit card slip, and save yourself $100.

For stays of more than two weeks, you'll save money and add comfort with an apartment or condominium rental. Monthly rates range $500-1,000 (less than half the comparable hotel per diem rate) for comfortable one-bedroom furnished kitchenette units, often including resort amenities such as pool and sundeck, beach club, and private view balcony.

Airlines regularly offer air/hotel packages, which, by combining your hotel and air fees, may save you lots of pesos. These deals require that you depart for Pacific Mexico through certain gateway cities, which depend on the airline. Accommodations are usually, but not exclusively, in luxury resorts. If you live near one of these gateways, it may pay to contact the airlines for more information.

GUESTHOUSES AND LOCAL HOTELS

Most coastal resorts began with an old town, which expanded to a new *zona hotelera* (hotel strip) where big hostelries rise along a golden strand. In the old town, near the piquant smells, sights, and sounds of traditional Mexico, are the *casas de huéspedes* and smaller hotels where rooms are often arranged around their plant-decorated patio.

Such lodgings vary from scruffy to spic-and-span, and humble to luxurious. At minimum, you can expect a plain room, a shared toilet and hot-water shower, and plenty of atmosphere for your money. High-season rates, depending on the resort, average between $10 and $20 for two, depending upon amenities. Discounts are often available for long-term stays. *Casas de huéspedes* will rarely be near the beach, unlike many local hotels.

RESORT 800 NUMBERS AND INTERNET SITES

These hotel chains have branches (** = outstanding, * = recommended) at Mazatlán (MZ), Guadalajara (GD), Puerto Vallarta (PV), Nuevo Vallarta (NV), Manzanillo (MN), Ixtapa (IX), Acapulco (AC), Bahías de Huatulco (HU), Oaxaca (OA), and other Pacific Mexico locations:

Bel-Air, tel. (800) 457-7676; info@mtmcorp .com (PV, Playa Carecitos**, Bahía Tenacatita*)

Best Western, tel. (800) 528-1234 (MZ*, GD*, Pátzcuaro*, IX*)

Blue Bay, tel. (800) BLUEBAY (258-3229), e-mail: pvr@bluebayresorts.com (PV*, Bahía Tenacatita*)

Camino Real, tel. (800) 7-CAMINO (722-6466), Web site: www.caminoreal.com (MZ, GD**, PV**, MN*, AC, HU**, OA**)

Calinda (Quality Inn), tel. (800) 221-2222, Web site: www.hotelchoice.com (GD*, AC)

Club Med, tel. (800) CLUBMED (258-2633), Web site: www.clubmed.com (Playa Blanca*, IX, HU*)

Club Maeva, tel. (800) GOMAEVA (466-2382) (MN*, HU**)

Days Inn, tel. (800) 325-2525, Web site: www.daysinn.com (MZ, AC*)

Fiesta Americana, tel. (800) FIESTA-1 (343-7821) (GD*, PV**, AC*, OA)

Holiday Inn, tel. (800) 465-4329, Web site: www.holiday-inn.com (MZ, GD*, PV)

Hyatt, tel. (800) 233-1234, Web site: www.hyatt.com (AC*)

Krystal, tel. (800) 231-9860 (PV**, IX*)

Marriott, tel. (800) 228-9290, Web site: www.marriot.com (PV)

Presidente Intercontinental, tel. (800) 327-0200 (GD, IX, AC)

Sheraton, tel. (800) 325-3535, Web site: www.sheraton.com (PV, IX*, AC, BH*)

Sierra, tel. (800) 457-7676, e-mail: info@mtmcorp.com (NV*, MN**)

Westin, tel. (800) 228-3000, Web site: www.westin.com (PV, IX**)

Medium and Larger Older-Style Hotels

Locally owned and operated hotels make up the most of the recommendations of this book. Many veteran travelers find it hard to understand why people come to Mexico and spend $200 a day for a hotel room when good alternatives average between $20 and $50, high season, depending upon the resort.

Many locally run hostelries are right on the beach, sharing the same velvety sand and golden sunsets as their much more expensive international-class neighbors. Local hotels, which depend as much on Mexican tourists as foreigners, generally have clean, large rooms, often with private view balconies, ceiling fans, and toilet and hot-water bath or shower. What they often lack are the plush extras—air-conditioning, cable TV, phones, tennis courts, exercise gyms, and golf courses—of the luxury resort hotels.

Booking these hotels is straightforward. All can be dialed direct (dial 011-52, then the local area code and number) for information and reservations; and, like the big resorts, many even have U.S. and Canada toll-free 800 information numbers. Always ask about money-saving packages and promotions when reserving.

INTERNATIONAL-CLASS RESORTS

Pacific Mexico has many beautiful, well-managed international-class resort hotels. They spread along the pearly strands of Mazatlán, Puerto Vallarta, Manzanillo, Ixtapa, Acapulco, and Bahías de Huatulco. Their super-deluxe amenities, moreover, need not be overly expensive. During the right time of year you can vacation at many of the big-name spots—Sheraton, Westin, Camino Real, Fiesta Americana, Hyatt, Holiday Inn—for surprisingly little. While high-season room tariffs ordinarily run $120-300, low-season (May-Nov., and to a lesser degree, Jan.-Feb.) prices to as low as $80 or $90. Shop around for savings via your Sunday newspaper travel section, travel agents, and by calling the hotels directly through their toll-free 800 numbers or Internet sites.

APARTMENTS, BUNGALOWS, CONDOMINIUMS, AND VILLAS

For longer stays, many visitors prefer the convenience and economy of an apartment or condominium or the luxurious comfort of a villa vacation rental. Choices vary, from spartan studios to deluxe beachfront suites and rambling, view homes big enough for entire extended families. Prices depend strongly upon season and amenities, from $400 per month for the cheapest, to at least 10 times that for the most luxurious.

A Mexican variation on the apartment style of accommodation is called a bungalow, although, in contrast to English-language usage, it does not usually imply a detached dwelling. Common in the smaller beach resorts, such as Bucerías, Rincón de Guayabitos, Barra de Navidad, and Zihuatanejo, a bungalow accommodation generally means a motel-type kitchenette-suite with less service, but with more space and beds. For families or for long stays by the beach, where you want to save money by cooking your own meals, such an accommodation might be ideal.

At the low end, you can expect a clean, furnished apartment within a block or two of the beach, with kitchen and regular maid service. More luxurious condos (which usually rent for $500 per week and up) are typically high-rise ocean-view suites with hotel-style desk services and resort amenities, such as a pool, jacuzzi, sundeck, and beach-level restaurant.

Higher up the scale, villas vary from moderately luxurious homes to sky's-the-limit beach-view mansions, blooming with built-in designer luxuries, private pools and beaches, tennis courts, and gardeners, cooks, and maids.

Shopping Around

You'll generally find the most economical apartment rental deals through on-the-spot local contacts, such as the tourist newspaper want ad section, neighborhood "for rent" signs, or local listing agents.

If you prefer making rental arrangements prior to arrival, you can usually write, fax, e-mail, or telephone managers—many of whom speak English—directly, using the numbers given in this book. Additional rentals are available through

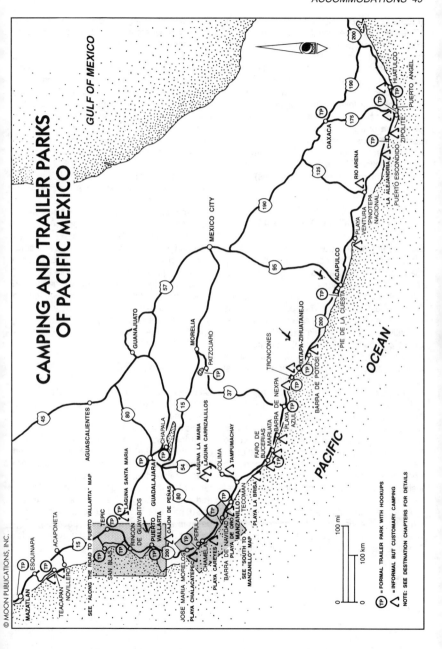

© MOON PUBLICATIONS, INC.

CAMPING AND TRAILER PARKS
OF PACIFIC MEXICO

TP = FORMAL TRAILER PARK WITH HOOKUPS

∧ = INFORMAL BUT CUSTOMARY CAMPING

NOTE: SEE DESTINATION CHAPTERS FOR DETAILS

agents (see the Mazatlán, Puerto Vallarta, Bucerías, Barra de Navidad, Manzanillo, and Ixtapa-Zihuatanejo sections) who will make long-distance rental agreements.

Additionally, a number of U.S.- and Canada-based agencies list some of the more expensive Pacific Mexico vacation rentals. You can often find their toll-free information and reservations numbers in the want ads or Sunday travel section of a metropolitan daily newspaper, such as the *Los Angeles Times*. Also, local real estate agents, such as Century 21, who specialize in nationwide and foreign contacts, sometimes list (or know someone who does) Pacific Mexico vacation rentals.

CAMPING AND *PALAPAS*

Beach camping is popular among middle-class Mexican families, especially during the Christmas-New Year week and during Semana Santa, the week before Easter.

Other times, tenters and RV campers usually find beaches uncrowded. The best spots (see the destination chapter maps and text for details) typically have a shady palm grove for camping and a *palapa* (palm-thatched) restaurant that serves drinks and fresh seafood. (Heads up for falling coconuts, especially in the wind.) Cost for parking and tenting is often minimal; typically only the price of food at the restaurant.

Days are often perfect for swimming, strolling, and fishing; nights are usually balmy—too warm for a sleeping bag, but fine for a hammock (which allows more air circulation than a tent). Good tents, however, keep out mosquitoes and other pests, which may be further discouraged with good bug repellent. Tents are generally warm inside, requiring only a sheet or very light blanket for cover.

As for camping on isolated beaches, opinions vary, from dire warnings of *bandidos* to bland assurances that all is peaceful along the coast. The truth is probably somewhere in between.

Trouble is most likely to occur in the vicinity of resort towns, where a few local thugs sometimes harass isolated campers.

When scouting out a campsite, a good general rule is to arrive early enough in the day to get a feel for the place. Buy a soda at the *palapa* or store and take a stroll up the beach. Say "buenos dias," to the people along the way; ask if the fishing is good: *"¿Pesca buena?"* Use your common sense. If the people seem friendly, ask if it's *seguro* (safe). If so, ask permission: *"¿Es bueno acampar aca?"* ("Is it okay to camp around here?"). You'll rarely be refused. For an informative and entertaining discussion of camping in Mexico, check out *The People's Guide to Mexico.* (See the Booklist.)

Some *palapas* (thatched beach houses) are still rented in small coastal resorts. Amenities typically include beds or hammocks, a shady thatched porch, cold running water, a kerosene stove, and shared toilets and showers. You usually walk right out your front door onto the sand, where surf, shells, and seabirds will be there to entertain you. *Palapa* rentals are available in Maruata and Barra de Nexpa (Michoacán coast, not far north of Playa Azul), Puerto Escondido, and Zipolite (near Puerto Ángel).

TRAILER PARKS

Campers who prefer company to isolation usually stay in trailer parks. Dozens of them dot Pacific Mexico's beaches and inland cities, towns, and scenic mountain spots. The most luxurious have electricity, water, sewer hookups, and many amenities, including restaurants, recreation rooms, and swimming pools; the humblest are simple palm-edged lots beside the beach. Virtually all of them have good swimming, fishing, and beachcombing. Prices run from a maximum of $16 per night, including air-conditioning power, down to a few dollars for tent space only. Significant discounts are generally available for weekly and monthly rentals.

FOOD AND DRINK

Some travel to Pacific Mexico for the food. True Mexican food is old-fashioned, home-style fare requiring many hours of loving preparation. Such food is short on meat and long on corn, beans, rice, tomatoes, onions, eggs, and cheese.

Mexican food is the unique end-product of thousands of years of native tradition. It is based on corn—*teocentli*, the Aztec "holy food"—called *maíz* (mah-EES) by present-day Mexicans. In the past, a Mexican woman spent much of her time grinding and preparing corn: soaking the grain in limewater (which swells the kernels and removes the tough seed-coat) and grinding the bloated seeds into meal on a stone *metate*. Finally, she would pat the meal into tortillas and cook them on a hot, baked-mud griddle.

Sages (men, no doubt) have wistfully imagined the gentle pat-pat-pat of women all over Mexico to be the heartbeat of Mexico, which they feared would someday cease. Fewer women these days make tortillas by hand. The gentle pat-pat-pat has been replaced by the whir and rattle of automatic tortilla-making machines in myriad *tortillerías*, where women and girls line up for their family's daily kilo-stack of tortillas.

Tortillas are to the Mexicans as rice is to the Chinese and bread to the French. Mexican food is invariably some mixture of sauce, meat, beans, cheese, and vegetables wrapped in a tortilla, which becomes the culinary be-all: the food, the dish, and the utensil all wrapped into one. If a Mexican man has nothing to wrap in his tortilla,

---

MEXICAN FOOD

Chiles rellenos: fresh roasted green chiles, stuffed usually with cheese but sometimes with fish or meat, coated with batter, and fried. They provide a piquant, tantalizing contrast to tortillas.

Enchiladas and **tostadas:** variations on the filled-tortilla theme. Enchiladas are stuffed with meat, cheese, olives, or beans and covered with sauce and baked, while tostadas consist of toppings served on crisp, open-faced tortillas.

Guacamole: This luscious avocado, onion, tomato, lime, and salsa mixture remains the delight it must have seemed to its Aztec inventors centuries ago. Anywhere in Mexico except tourist resorts, guacamole is sparingly as a garnish, rather than in appetizer bowls as is common in the U.S. Southwest.

Moles (MOH-lays): uniquely Mexican specialties. *Mole poblano*, a spicy-sweet mixture of chocolate, chiles, and a dozen other ingredients, is cooked to a smooth sauce, then baked with chicken (or turkey, a combination called *mole de pavo*). So *típica* it's widely regarded as the national dish.

Quesadillas: Made from soft flour tortillas, rather than corn, quesadillas resemble tostadas and always contain melted cheese.

Sopas: Soups consist of vegetables in a savory chicken broth, and are an important part of both *comida* (afternoon) and *cena* (evening) Mexican meals. *Pozole*, a rich steaming stew of hominy, vegetables, and pork or chicken, often constitutes the prime evening offering of small side street shops. *Sopa de taco*, an ever-popular country favorite, is a medium-spicy cheese-topped thick chile broth served with ripe corn tortillas.

Tacos or **taquitos:** tortillas served open or wrapped around any ingredient

Tamales (singular: *"tamal"*): as Mexican as apple pie is American. This savory mixture of meat and sauce imbedded in a shell of corn dough and baked in a wrapping of corn husks is rarely known by the singular, however. They're so yummy that one *tamal* invariably leads to more tamales.

Tortas: the Mexican sandwich, usually hot meat with fresh tomato and avocado, stuffed between two halves of a crisp *bolillo* (boh-LEE-yoh) or Mexican bun

Tortillas y frijoles refritos: cooked brown or black beans, mashed and fried in pork fat, and rolled into tortillas with a dash of vitamin-C-rich salsa to form a near-complete combination of carbohydrate, fat, and balanced protein

CATCH OF THE DAY

Ceviche (say-VEE-chay): a chopped raw fish appetizer as popular on Puerto Vallarta beaches as sushi is on Tokyo side streets. Although it can contain anything from conch to octopus, the best ceviche consists of diced young shark *(tiburón)* or mackerel *(sierra)* fillet and plenty of fresh tomatoes, onions, garlic, and chiles, all doused with lime juice.

Filete de pescado: fish fillet sautéed *al mojo* (ahl-MOH-hoh)—with butter and garlic

Pescado frito (pays-KAH-doh FREE-toh): fish, pan-fried whole; if you don't specify that it be cooked lightly *(a medio),* the fish may arrive well done, like a big, crunchy french fry.

Pescado veracruzana: a favorite everywhere. It's best with red snapper *(huachinango),* smothered in a savory tomato, onion, chile, and garlic sauce. *Pargo* (snapper), *mero* (grouper), and *cabrilla* (sea bass) are also popularly used in this and other specialties.

Shellfish abound: *ostiones* (oysters) and *almejas* (clams) by the dozen; *langosta* (lobster) and *langostina* (crayfish) *asado* (broiled), *al vapor* (steamed), or fried. Pots of fresh-boiled *camarones* (shrimp) are sold on the street by the kilo; cafés will make them into *cóctel,* or prepare them *en gabardinas* (breaded) at your request.

he will content himself by rolling a thin filling of salsa (chile sauce) into his lunchtime tortilla.

Hot or Not?
Much food served in Mexico is not "Mexican." Eating habits, as most other Mexican customs, depend upon social class. Upwardly mobile Mexicans typically shun the corn-based Indian fare in favor of the European-style food of the Spanish colonial elite: chops, steaks, cutlets, fish, clams, omelettes, soups, pasta, rice, and potatoes.

Such fare is often as bland as Des Moines on a summer Sunday afternoon. "No picante"—not spicy—is how the Mexicans describe bland food. *Caliente,* the Spanish adjective for "hot" weather or water, does not, in contrast to English usage, also imply spicy, or *picante.*

Vegetarian Food
Strictly vegetarian cooking is the exception in Mexico, as are macrobiotic restaurants, health-food stores, and organic produce. Meat is such a delicacy for most Mexicans they can't understand why people would give it up voluntarily. If vegetable-lovers can manage with corn, beans, cheese, eggs, *legumbres* (vegetables), and fruit and

not be bothered by a bit of pork fat *(manteca de cerdo),* Mexican cooking will suit them fine.

Seafood
Early chroniclers wrote that Moctezuma employed a platoon of runners to bring fresh fish 300 miles every day to his court from the sea. In Pacific Mexico, fresh seafood is fortunately much more available from thousands of shoreline establishments, ranging from thatched beach *palapas* to five-star hotel restaurants.

Pacific Mexico seafood is literally there for the taking. When strolling on the beach, I have often seen well-fed, middle-class local vacationers breaking and eating oysters and mussels right off the rocks. In the summer on the beach at Puerto Vallarta, fish and squid sometimes swarm so thickly in the surf tourists can pull them out by hand. Villagers up and down the coast use small nets (or bare hands) to retrieve a few fish for supper, while communal teams haul in big netfuls of silvery, wriggling fish for sale right on the beach.

Despite the plenty, Pacific Mexico seafood prices reflect high worldwide demand, even at the humblest seaside *palapa.* The freshness and variety, however, make even the typical dishes seem bargains at any price.

Fruits and Juices

Squeezed vegetable and fruit juices (jugos, pronounced "HOO-gohs") are among the widely available delights of Pacific Mexico. Among the many establishments—restaurants, cafés, and loncherías—willing to supply you with your favorite jugo, the juice bars (jugerías) are often the most fun. Colorful fruit piles usually mark jugerías; if you don't immediately spot your favorite fruit, ask anyway; it might be hidden in the refrigerator.

Besides your choice of pure juice, a jugería will often serve licuados. Into the juice, they whip powdered milk, your favorite fruit, and sugar to taste for a creamy afternoon pick-me-up or evening dessert. One big favorite is a cool banana-chocolate licuado, which comes out tasting like a milk shake minus the calories.

Alcoholic Drinks

The Aztecs usually sacrificed anyone caught

A TROVE OF FRUITS AND NUTS

Besides carrying the usual temperate fruits, jugerías, and especially markets, are seasonal sources of a number of exotic (followed by an *) varieties:

avocado (aguacate, pronounced "ah-wah-KAH-tay"): Aztec aphrodisiac

banana (platano): many kinds—big and small, red and yellow

chirimoya* (chirimoya): green scales, white pulp; sometimes called an anona.

coconut (coco): coconut "milk" is called agua coco

grapes (uvas): Aug.-Nov. season

guanabana* (guanabana): looks, but doesn't taste, like a green mango

guava (guava): delicious juice, widely available canned

lemon (limón, pronounced "lee-MOHN"): uncommon and expensive; use lime instead

lime (lima pronounced "LEE-mah"): douse salads with it

mamey* (mamey, pronounced "mah-MAY"): yellow, juicy fruit; excellent for jellies and preserves.

mango (mango): king of fruit, in a hundred varieties June-Nov.

orange (naranja, pronounced "nah-RAHN-ha"): greenish skin but sweet and juicy

papaya (papaya): said to aid digestion and healing

peach (durazno, pronounced "doo-RAHS-noh"): delicious and widely available as canned juice

peanut (cacahuate, pronounced "kah-kah-WAH-tay"): home roasted and cheap

pear (pera): fall season

pecan (nuez): for a treat, try freshly ground pecan butter

piña anona* (piña anona): looks like an ear of corn without the husk; tastes like pineapple

pineapple (piña): huge, luscious, and cheap

strawberry (fresa, pronounced "FRAY-sah"): local favorite

tangerine (mandarina): common around Christmas

watermelon (sandía, pronounced "sahn-DEE-ah"): perfect on a hot day

zapote* (zapote, pronounced "sah-POH-tay"): yellow, fleshy fruit; said to induce sleep

zapote colorado* (zapote colorado): brown skin, red, puckery fruit, like persimmon; incorrectly called (mamey)

chirimoya

drinking alcohol without permission. The later, more lenient, Spanish attitude toward getting *borracho* (soused) has led to a thriving Mexican renaissance of native alcoholic beverages: tequila, mescal, Kahlúa, *pulque,* and *aguardiente.* Tequila and mescal, distilled from the fermented juice of the maguey (century) plant, originated in Oaxaca, where the best are still made. Quality tequila and mescal come 76 proof (38% alcohol) and up. A small white worm, endemic to the maguey plant, is added to each bottle of factory mescal for authenticity.

Pulque, although also made from the sap of the maguey, is locally brewed to a small alcohol content, between beer and wine. The brewing houses are sacrosanct preserves, circumscribed by traditions that exclude both women and outsiders. The brew, said to be full of nutrients, is sold to local *pulquerías* and drunk immediately. If you are ever invited into a *pulquería,* it will be an honor you cannot refuse.

Aguardiente, by contrast, is the notorious fiery Mexican "white lightning," a locally distilled, dirt-cheap ticket to oblivion for poor Mexican men.

While *pulque* comes from an age-old Indian tradition, beer is the beverage of modern mestizo Mexico. Full-bodied and tastier than "light" U.S. counterparts, Mexican beer enjoys an enviable reputation.

Those visitors who indulge usually know their favorite among the many brands, from light to dark: Superior, Corona, Pacífico, Tecate (served with lime), Carta Blanca, Modelo, Dos Equis, Bohemia, Tres Equis, and Negra Modelo. Nochebuena, a flavorful dark brew, becomes available only around Christmas.

Mexicans have yet to develop much of a taste for *vino* (wine), although some domestic wines, such as the Baja California labels Cetto and Domecq, are quite drinkable.

Bread and Pastries

Excellent locally baked bread is a delightful surprise to many first-time visitors to Pacific Mexico. Small bakeries everywhere put out trays of hot, crispy-crusted *bolillos* (rolls) and sweet *pans dulces* (pastries). They range from simple cakes, muffins, cookies, and doughnuts to fancy fruit-filled turnovers and puffs. Half the fun occurs before the eating: grab a tray and tongs, peruse the goodies, and pick out the most scrumptious. With your favorite dozen finally selected, you take your tray to the cashier, who deftly bags everything up and collects a few pesos (two or three dollars) for your whole mouthwatering selection.

Restaurant Price Key

In the destination chapters, restaurants that serve dinner are described as budget, moderate, expensive, or a combination thereof, at the end of each restaurant description. **Budget** means that the entrées cost under $7; **moderate,** $7-14; **expensive,** over $14.

GETTING THERE

BY AIR

From the U.S. and Canada

The vast majority of travelers reach Pacific Mexico by air. Flights are frequent and reasonably priced. Competition sometimes shaves prices down as low as $250 or less for a Mazatlán or Puerto Vallarta roundtrip from Los Angeles, Denver, or Dallas.

Travelers can save even more money by shopping around. Don't be bashful about trying for the best price. Make it clear to the airline or travel agent you're interested in a bargain. Ask the right questions: Are there special incentive, advance-payment, night, midweek, tour-package, or charter fares? Peruse the ads in your Sunday newspaper travel section for bargain-oriented travel agencies. An agent costs you no money, although some don't like discounted tickets because their fee depends on a percentage of ticket price. Nevertheless, many agents will work to get you a bargain.

Although few scheduled flights go directly to Pacific Mexico from the northern U.S. and Canada, many charters do. In locales near Vancouver, Calgary, Ottawa, Toronto, Montreal, Minneapolis, Detroit, Cleveland, and New York, consult a travel agent for charter flight options. Be aware that charter reservations, which often require fixed departure and return dates and provide minimal cancellation refunds, decrease your flexibility. If available charter choices are too rigid, then you might choose to begin your vacation with a connecting flight to one of the Pacific Mexico gateways of San Francisco, Los Angeles, Denver, Chicago, Dallas, or Houston.

You may be able to save money by booking an air/hotel package. A number of airlines routinely offer Pacific Mexico air/hotel packages through certain gateway cities:

Mexicana: from Los Angeles, Denver and Chicago, tel. (800) 539-7321

Alaska: from Seattle, San Francisco, Los Angeles and Phoenix, tel. (800) 468-2248

American: from Dallas, tel. (800) 321-2121

Aeroméxico: from Los Angeles and San Diego, tel. (800) 245-8585

Continental: from Houston, tel. (800) 634-5555

Delta: from Los Angeles, tel. (800) 872-7786

Canadian World of Vacations: winter charter flights from Toronto, Winnipeg, Calgary-Edmonton and Vancouver, tel. (800) 661-8881 or contact a travel agent

From Europe, Australasia, and Latin America

Few airlines fly across the Atlantic or Pacific directly to Mexico. Travelers from Australasia and Europe generally transfer at New York, Chicago, Dallas, San Francisco, or Los Angeles for Pacific Mexico destinations.

A number of Latin American flag carriers fly directly to Mexico City. From there, easy connections are available via Mexicana, Aeroméxico, Aerocalifornia, and Taesa Airlines to Pacific Mexico destinations.

Baggage, Insurance, "Bumping," and In-Flight Meals

Tropical and temperate Pacific Mexico makes it easy to pack light. Veteran tropical travelers often condense their luggage to carry-ons only. Airlines routinely allow a carry-on (not exceeding 45 inches in combined length, width, and girth) and a small book bag and purse. Thus relieved of heavy burdens, your trip will become much simpler. You'll avoid possible luggage loss and long baggage-check-in lines by being able to check in

directly at the boarding gate.

Even if you can't avoid having to check luggage, loss of it needn't ruin your vacation. Always carry your nonreplaceable items in the cabin with you. These should include all money, credit cards, traveler's checks, keys, tickets, cameras, passport, prescription drugs, and eyeglasses.

At the X-ray security check, insist your film and cameras be hand-inspected. Regardless of what attendants claim, repeated X-ray scanning will fog any film, especially the sensitive ASA 400 and 1,000 high-speed varieties.

Travelers packing lots of expensive baggage, or who (because of illness, for example) may have to cancel a nonrefundable flight or tour might consider buying **travel insurance.** Travel agents routinely sell packages that include baggage, trip cancellation, and default insurance. Baggage insurance covers you beyond the conventional $1,250 domestic, $400 international baggage liability limits, but check with your carrier. Trip cancellation insurance pays if you must cancel your prepaid trip, while default insurance protects you if your carrier or tour agent does not perform as agreed. Travel insurance, however, can be expensive. Traveler's Insurance Company, for example, offers $1,000 of baggage insurance per person for two weeks for about $50. Carefully weigh both your options and the cost against benefits before putting your money down.

It's wise to **reconfirm** both departure and return flight reservations, especially during the busy Christmas and Easter seasons. This is a useful strategy, as is prompt arrival at check-in, against getting "bumped" (losing your seat) because of the tendency of airlines to overbook the rush of high-season vacationers. For further protection, always get your **seat assignment and boarding pass included with your ticket.**

Airlines generally try hard to accommodate travelers with dietary or other special needs. When booking your flight, inform your travel agent or carrier of the necessity of a low-sodium, low-cholesterol, vegetarian, lactose-reduced meal or other requirements. Seniors, persons with disabilities, and parents traveling with children, see the Specialty Travel section near the end of this chapter for more information.

AIRLINES

The busiest Pacific Mexico air carriers with direct connections between Pacific Mexico and North American destinations are Mexicana, Aeroméxico, Alaska, American, Aerocalifornia, America West, Continental, Delta, and Canadian World of Vacations charter, with destinations including Mazatlán (MZ), Puerto Vallarta (PV), Manzanillo-Barra de Navidad (MN), Guadalajara (GD), Ixtapa-Zihuatanejo (IX), Acapulco (AC), Mexico City (MX), Morelia (MO), Colima (CO), Huatulco (HU), and Tepic (TP). Other popular Pacific Mexico destinations, such as Oaxaca and Puerto Escondido, are air-accessible via Mexico City.

AIRLINE	ORIGIN	DESTINATIONS
Mexicana		
tel. (800) 531-7921	Los Angeles	MZ, PV, GD, IX, MX, HU
www.mexicana.com.mx	San Francisco	GD, MX
	San Jose	GD
	Tijuana	GD
	Denver	MZ, PV, MX
	Chicago	PV, GD, AC
	Miami	MX
	San Antonio	MX
Aeroméxico		
tel. (800) 237-6639	Los Angeles	PV, MX, GD
www.aeromexico.com	Tijuana	MO, TP, MZ, GD, AC MX
	New York	MX
	Miami	MX
	Houston	MX
	San Diego	MX, PV, GD
	Atlanta	MX
Alaska		
tel. (800) 426-0333	Seattle	MZ, PV, IX
www.alaskaair.com	San Francisco	MZ, PV, GD
	Los Angeles	MZ, PV, GD, IX
	Phoenix	PV

BY BUS

As air travel rules in the U.S., bus travel rules in Mexico. Hundreds of sleek, luxury- and first-class bus lines with names such as Elite, Estrella de Oro (Star of Gold), and Estrella Blanca (White Star) roar out daily from the border, headed for Pacific Mexico.

Since North American bus lines ordinarily terminate just north of the Mexican border, you must usually disembark, collect your things, and, after having filled out the necessary but very simple paperwork at the immigration booth, proceed on foot across the border to Mexico where you can bargain with one of the local taxis to drive you the few miles to the *camionera central* (central bus station).

First- and luxury-class bus service in Mexico is generally cheaper and at least as good as in the United States. Tickets for comparable trips in Mexico cost a small fraction (as little as $40 for a thousand-mile trip, compared to perhaps $150 in the U.S.).

In Mexico, as on U.S. buses, you often have to take it like you find it. *Asientos reservados* (reserved seats), *boletos* (tickets), and information must generally be obtained in person at the bus station, and credit cards and traveler's checks are sometimes not accepted. Neither are reserved bus tickets typically refundable, so don't miss the bus. On the other hand, plenty of buses roll south almost continuously.

Bus Routes to Pacific Mexico

From California and the west, cross the border to Tijuana, Mexicali, or Nogales, where you can

AIRLINE	ORIGIN	DESTINATIONS
Aerocalifornia		
tel. (800) 237-6225	Los Angeles	MZ GD MN MX TP
	Tijuana	CO, MZ, MX, GD
America West		
tel. (800) 235-9292	Phoenix	MZ, PV, MN, PV, MX, AC
www.americawest.com		
Continental		
tel. (800) 231-0856	Houston	PV, GD, AC, MX, IX, MZ
www.flycontinental.com		
American		
tel. (800) 433-7300	Dallas	HU, PV, GD, AC, MX
www.aa.com	Chicago	MX
Canadian World of Vacations		
charter tel. (800) 661-8881	Toronto	HU, MZ, PV, AC
www.worldofvacations.com	Vancouver	MN, IX, MZ, PV, AC
	Calgary-Edmonton	MN, MZ, PV, AC
	Winnipeg	MN AC MZ IX
Delta		
tel. (800) 221-1212	Los Angeles	GD, MX
www.delta-air.com	Dallas	MX
	Atlanta	MX
	Orlando	MX
	New York	MX
Taesa		
tel. (800) 328-2372	Oakland	GD, MO
	Chicago	GD, MO
Trans World (TWA)		
tel. (800) 892-4141	St. Louis	PV, IX

ride one of several bus lines along the Pacific coast route (National Hwy. 15) to points south: Estrella Blanca subsidiaries (Elite, Turistar, Transportes Norte de Sonora) or independent Transportes del Pacífico.

At Mazatlán or Tepic, depending on the line, you transfer or continue on the same bus, south to Puerto Vallarta and Manzanillo, or west to Guadalajara. Allow a full day and a bit more (about 30 hours), depending upon connections, for the trip. Carry liquids and food (which might only be minimally available en route) with you.

From the midwest, cross the border from El Paso to Ciudad Juárez and ride independent line Omnibus de Mexico or Estrella Blanca subsidiaries (luxury-class Turistar or Transportes Chihuahuenses) via Chihuahua and Durango. Both Transportes Chihuahuenses and Turistar

usually offer one or two daily departures direct to Mazatlán. Otherwise, transfer at Durango to a Mazatlán-bound bus, and continue as above. Similarly, from the U.S. southeast and east, cross the border at Laredo to Nuevo Laredo and ride Estrella Blanca subsidiaries Transportes del Norte, Turistar, or Futura direct to Mazatlán or Durango. If only to Durango, transfer to a Mazatlán bus, where you can continue south, as described above.

Travelers heading directly to Acapulco, Oaxaca, and other Pacific Mexico far southern points should ride from the border directly to Mexico City. Mexico City has four bus terminals: north, east, south, and west. (respectively, Terminal Norte, Terminal Tapo, Terminal Sur, and Terminal Poniente.) You will most likely arrive in the Terminal Norte, although some buses from the west via Guadalajara might arrive at Terminal Poniente.

If you're heading south to the coast, share a taxi across town (don't try it by public transportation) to the main southern Mexico City terminal (Terminal Central del Sur). There, continue south via Flecha Roja, Estrella de Oro, Elite, Estrella Blanca or others to Acapulco, thence Ixtapa-Zihuatanejo or Puerto Escondido-Puerto Ángel.

If you're heading straight for Oaxaca City, taxi across town to the Terminal Tapo and catch a first- or luxury-class Cristóbal Colón or Autobus del Oriente (ADO) bus, via Puebla, to Oaxaca City, via the expressway *("autopista," or "corta")*.

From the U.S. border east, allow two days travel for Acapulco or Oaxaca City, and three days for Puerto Escondido-Puerto Ángel or Ixtapa-Zihuatanejo.

BY TRAIN

Due to privatization, rail passenger service in Mexico has all but disappeared. The only exception is the Chihuahua-Pacific railway, which offers good service along the scenic **Copper Canyon** route. Popular alternatives include flying or busing into either Los Mochis or Chihuahua City, the respective western and eastern terminals of the railroad. Only finished during the early 1960s, this rail route traverses the spectacular canyonland-home of the Tarahumara people. The winding, 406-mile (654-km) route parallels the labyrinthine Copper Canyon (Barranca del Cobre), a gorge so deep its climate varies from Canadian at the top to tropical jungle at the bottom. The railway-stop village of Creel, with a few stores and hotels and a Tarahumara mission, is the major jumping-off point for trips into the canyon. For a treat, reserve a stay en route to Pacific Mexico at the Copper Canyon Lodge in Creel. From there, the canyon beckons: explore the village, enjoy panoramic views, observe mountain wildlife, and breathe pine-scented, mountain air. Farther afield, you can hike to a hot spring, or even spend a few days exploring the canyon bottom itself. For more information, contact Copper Canyon Lodges, 2741 Paldan St., Auburn Hills, MI 48326, tel. (800) 776-3942 or (248) 340-7230, Web site: www.coppercanyonlodges.com.

Some agencies arrange unusually good **Copper Canyon rail tours.** Among the most highly recommended is **Columbus Travel,** 900 Ridge Creek Lane, Bulverde, TX 78163-2872, tel. (800) 843-1060, or Web site: www. canyontravel.com, which employs its own resident ecologically sensitive guides. Trips range from small-group rail-based sightseeing tours to customized wilderness rail-jeep-backpacking adventures.

Another noteworthy agency is the **Mexican American Railway Company,** which specializes in luxury Copper Canyon rail sightseeing tours. Trips begin at either Chihuahua or Los Mochis, at opposite ends of the Copper Canyon Line. Participants can choose the amenities of either special restored 1940s-era first-class or the "South Orient Express," super-deluxe European-class cars that are added to the regular train. In addition to on-board sightseeing, the four- to six-day itineraries typically include short tours from railside points of interest, such as Creel and the Tarahumara Indian mission, Mennonite settlements at Cuauhtémoc, and the colonial town of El Fuerte.

Evenings, participants enjoy meals and comfortable accommodations in first-class hotels and mountain lodges. The South Orient Express service features gourmet fare in opulent turn-of-the-century dining cars as well as expansive mountain vistas from deluxe view dome rail coaches. Tariffs average roughly $150/day for first class and about $300/day for super deluxe class, all-inclusive, per person, double occupancy. For details, call toll-free (800) 659-7602 or write the Mexican American Railway Company, 16800 Greenspoint Park Dr., Suite 245 North, Houston, TX 77060-2308, or e-mail: soetrain@ix .netcom.com. In Mexico, contact them at Paseo Bolivar 405, Colonia Centro, Chihuahua, Chihuahua 31000, tel. (14) 107-570.

BY CAR OR RV

If you're adventurous, like going to out-of-the-way places, but still want to have all the comforts of home, you may enjoy driving your car or RV to Pacific Mexico. On the other hand, consideration of cost, risk, wear on both you and your vehicle, and the congestion hassles in towns may change your mind.

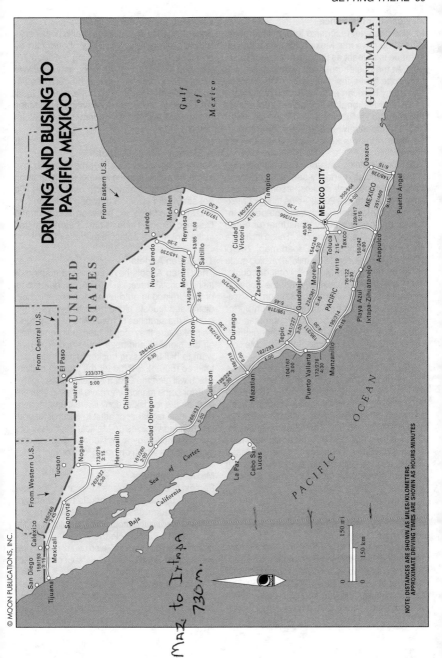

DRIVING AND BUSING TO PACIFIC MEXICO

NOTE: DISTANCES ARE SHOWN AS MILES/KILOMETERS
APPROXIMATE DRIVING TIMES ARE SHOWN AS HOURS:MINUTES

© MOON PUBLICATIONS, INC.

Mexican Car Insurance

Mexico does not recognize foreign insurance. When you drive into Mexico, Mexican auto insurance is at least as important as your passport. At the busier crossings, you can get it at insurance "drive-ins" just south of the border. The many Mexican auto insurance companies (AAA and National Automobile Club agents recommend La Provincial and Tepeyac insurance, respectively) are government-regulated; their numbers keep prices and services competitive.

Sanborn's Mexico insurance, one of the best known agencies, certainly seems to be trying hardest. One of their spokespersons, "Mexico Mike" Nelson, drives 20,000-plus miles of Mexico highway for them each year, gathering information for their lively consumer-oriented newsletter, books, and services. These include a guide to RV campgrounds, road map, *Travel With Health* book, "smile-by-mile" *Travelog* guide to "every highway in Mexico," hotel discounts, and a trip-share newsletter. All of the above is available to members of the "Sanborn's Mexico Club." You can buy insurance, sign up for membership, or order books through their toll-free number, (800) 222-0158. For other queries, call (210) 682-1354 or write Sanborn's Mexico, P.O. Box 310, McAllen, TX 78502.

Mexican car insurance runs from a bare-bones rate of about $2 a day to a more typical $8 a day for more complete coverage ($50,000/$40,000/$80,000 public liability/property damage/medical payments) on a vehicle worth between $10,000-15,000. On the same scale, insurance for a $50,000 RV and equipment runs about $20 a day. These daily rates decrease sharply for six-month or one-year policies, which run from about $150 for the minimum to $400-1,600 for complete coverage.

If you get broken glass, personal effects, and legal expenses coverage with these rates, you're lucky. Mexican policies don't usually cover them.

You should get something for your money. The deductibles should be no more than $300-500, the public liability/medical payments should be about double the ($25,000/$25,000/$50,000) legal minimum, and you should be able to get your car fixed in the U.S. and receive payment in U.S. dollars for losses. If not, shop around.

Crossing the Border

Squeezing through the border traffic bottlenecks during peak holidays and rush hours can be time-consuming. Avoid crossing between 7-9 a.m. and 4:30-6:30 p.m. Also, you may be able to save *mucho* time and sweat by getting all of your car-entry paperwork done at your local AAA-affiliate office prior to leaving home. Many of them will even do it for nonmembers; call for details.

A Sinaloa Note of Caution

Although *bandidos* no longer menace Mexican roads, be cautious in the infamous drug-growing region of Sinaloa state north of Mazatlán. Do not stray from Hwy. 15 between Culiacán and Mazatlán and Hwy. 40 between Mazatlán and Durango. Curious tourists have been assaulted in the hinterlands adjacent to these roads.

The Green Angels

The Green Angels have answered many motoring tourists' prayers in Mexico. Bilingual teams of two, trained in auto repair and first aid, help distressed tourists along main highways. They patrol fixed stretches of road twice daily by truck. To make sure they stop to help, pull completely off the highway and raise your hood. You may want to hail a passing trucker to call them; dial toll-free (800) 903-9200 for the tourism hotline, which will alert the Green Angels for you.

If, for some reason, you have to leave your vehicle on the roadside, don't leave it unattended. Hire a local teenager or adult to watch it for you. Unattended vehicles on Mexican highways are quickly stricken by a mysterious disease, the symptoms of which are rapid loss of vital parts.

Mexican Gasoline

Pemex, short for Petróleos Mexicanos, the government oil monopoly, markets two grades of good unleaded gasoline. **Magna** "Sin" plomo (without lead) is the most widely available and is equivalent to U.S. unleaded regular. Pemex *gasolineras* (gas stations) also usually sell a premium grade, equivalent to U.S. "super unleaded" 89-91 octane gasoline.

In recent years, Pemex has built lots of new stations and franchised a host of private dealers, greatly improving gasoline availability on all major highways. In outlying areas, even though gasoline stations remain generally scarce, humble roadside stores usually sell Magna unleaded, hand-pumped from drums.

Gas Station Thievery

Kids who hang around Pemex gas stations to wash windows are notoriously light-fingered. When stopping at the *gasolinera,* make sure your cameras, purses, and other movable items are out of reach. Also, make sure your car has a lockable gas cap. If not, insist on pumping the gas yourself, or be super-watchful as you pull up to the gas pump. Make certain the pump reads zero before the attendant pumps the gas. Sad, but true, such overcharging for gas and oil is common, especially among teenage male gas-station workers.

A Healthy Car

Preventative measures spell good health for both you and your car. Get that tune-up (or long-delayed overhaul) *before,* rather than after, you leave.

Carry a stock of spare parts, which will probably be both more difficult to get and more expensive in Mexico than at home. Carry an extra tire or two, a few cans of motor oil and octane enhancer, oil and gas filters, fan belts, spark plugs, tune-up kit, points, and fuses. Carry basic tools and supplies, such as screwdrivers, pliers (including Vise-Grip), lug wrench and jack, adjustable wrenches, tire pump and patches, pressure gauge, steel wire, and electrical tape. For breakdowns and emergencies, carry a folding shovel, a husky rope or chain, a gasoline can, and flares.

Car Repairs in Mexico

The American big three—General Motors, Ford, and Chrysler—and Nissan and Volkswagen are well represented by extensive dealer networks in Mexico. Getting your car or truck serviced at such agencies is usually straightforward. While parts will probably be higher, shop rates run about half U.S. prices, so repairs will generally come out cheaper than back home.

The same is not true for repairing other makes. Mexico has few, if any, Toyota or other Japanese car or truck dealers; other than Mercedes-Benz, which has some Mexican agencies, it is generally difficult to find officially certified mechanics for any British and European makes other than Volkswagen.

Many clever Mexican independent mechanics, however, can often fix any car that happens to come their way. Their humble *talleres mecánicos* (tah-YER-ays may-KAH-nee-kohs), or repair shops, dot the town and village roadsides everywhere.

Although most mechanics are honest, beware of unscrupulous operators who try to collect double or triple their original estimate. If you don't speak Spanish, find someone who can assist you in negotiations. **Always** get a cost estimate, including needed parts and labor, in writing, even

ROAD SAFETY

Hundreds of thousands of visitors enjoy safe Mexican auto vacations every year. Their success is due in large part to their frame of mind: drive defensively, anticipate and adjust to danger before it happens, and watch everything—side roads, shoulders, the car in front, and cars far down the road. The following tips will help ensure a safe and enjoyable trip:

Don't drive at night. Range animals, unmarked sand piles, pedestrians, one-lane bridges, cars without lights, and drunk drivers are doubly hazardous at night.

Although **speed limits** are rarely enforced, *don't break them.* Mexican roads are often narrow and shoulderless. Poor markings and macho drivers who pass on curves are best faced at a speed of 40 mph (64 kph) rather than 75 (120).

Don't drive on sand. Even with four-wheel-drive, you'll eventually get stuck if you drive either often or casually on beaches. When the tide comes in, who'll pull your car out?

Slow down at the *topes* (speed bumps) at the edges of towns and for *vados* (dips), which can be dangerously bumpy and full of water.

Extending the **courtesy of the road** goes hand-in-hand with safe driving. Both courtesy and machismo are more infectious in Mexico; on the highway, it's much safer to spread the former than the latter.

if you have to write it yourself. Make sure the mechanic understands, then ask him to sign it before he starts work. Although this may be a hassle, it might save you a much nastier hassle later. Shop labor at small, independent, repair shops should typically run between $10 and $20 per hour. For much more information, and entertaining anecdotes of car and RV travel in Mexico, consult Carl Franz's *The People's Guide to Mexico*. (See the Booklist.)

Highway Routes from the United States

If you've decided to drive to Pacific Mexico, you have your choice of four general routes. At safe highway speeds, each of these routes requires about 24 hours of driving time. For comfort and safety, many folks allow three full south-of-the-border driving days to Pacific Mexico.

From the U.S. Pacific coast and west, follow National Hwy. 15 from the border at Nogales, Sonora, an hour's drive south of Tucson, Arizona. Highway 15 continues southward smoothly, leading you through cactus-studded mountains and valleys, which turn into green lush farmland and tropical coastal plain by the time you arrive in Mazatlán. Peripheral bypasses *(periféricos)* route you past the congested downtowns of Hermosillo, Guaymas, Ciudad Obregón, and Culiacán. Between these centers, you speed along, via *cuota* (toll) expressways virtually all the way to Mazatlán. If you prefer not to pay the high tolls (around $60 total for a passenger car, much more for multiple-wheeled RVs) you should stick to the old *libre* (free) highway. Hazards, bumps, and slow going might force you to reconsider, however.

From Mazatlán, continue along the narrow two-lane route to Tepic, where Hwy. 15 heads east to Guadalajara and Hwy. 200 forks south to Puerto Vallarta. From there you can continue along Hwy. 200 southward along the entire plumy southern coast of Pacific Mexico.

If, however, you're driving to Pacific Mexico from the central U.S., cross the border at El Paso to Ciudad Juárez, Chihuahua. There, National Highway 45, either via the new *cuota* multilane expressway or the old *libre* (free) two-lane highway, leads you southward through high dry plains through the cities of Chihuahua, Jiménez, and Hidalgo del Parral, to Durango.

At Durango, head west along the winding but spectacular trans-Sierra National Hwy. 40, which intersects National Hwy. 15 just south of Mazatlán. From there, continue south as described above.

Folks heading to Pacific Mexico from the eastern and southeastern U.S. should cross the border from Laredo, Texas, to Nuevo Laredo. From there, you can follow either the National Hwy. 85 nontoll *(libre)* route or the new toll *(cuota)* road, which continues all the way to Saltillo. Passenger car tolls total about $25. On the old *libre* Hwy. 85, at the sprawling Monterrey city outskirts, follow the west (Saltillo-direction) bypass, which soon connects with National Hwy. 40. At Saltillo, continue westward on Hwy. 40, via either the two-lane old highway or the new toll expressway, through Torreón to Durango. Continue, via the two-lane Hwy. 40 over the Pacific crest all the way to National Hwy. 15, just south of Mazatlán. Continue southward, as described above.

If you're heading from the midwest or eastern U.S. directly to Pacific Mexico's southern destinations of Acapulco, Ixtapa-Zihuatanejo, or Oaxaca you should cross the border from McAllen, Texas, to Reynosa. From there, head southward to Mexico City, where you continue south via either toll expressway 95 to Acapulco or the toll expressway via Puebla, to Oaxaca.

Bribes *(Mordidas)*

The usual meeting ground between visitors and Mexican police is in their car on the highway or downtown street. To tourists, such cases sometimes appear as mild harassment, accompanied by vague threats of having to go to the police station, or having their car impounded for such-and-such a violation. The tourists often go on to say that "It was all right, though. We paid him $10 and he went away. Mexican cops sure are crooked, aren't they?"

And I suppose, if people want to go bribing their way through Mexico, that's their business. But calling the Mexican cops crooked isn't exactly fair. Police, like most everyone else in Mexico, have to scratch for a living, and they have found many tourists are willing to slip them a $10 bill for nothing. Rather than crooked, I would call them hungry and opportunistic.

BY FERRY

The ferries *(transbordadores)* from La Paz at the tip of Baja California across the Gulf of California to Mazatlán or Topolobampo (Los Mochis) in Sinaloa provide a tempting route option to Pacific Mexico, especially for travelers without cars. However, if you try to take your car during busy times, especially Christmas and Easter holidays, you may get "bumped" by the large volume of commercial traffic, regardless of your reservation.

The ferry system, privatized in the early '90s, has greatly improved service, at the expense of steeply increased fares. Tickets and reservations (apply early) are available at the terminals and may be available through certain travel agents in La Paz, Los Mochis, and Mazatlán.

Passengers are not allowed to remain in their vehicles during the crossing but must purchase a passenger ticket. Options, which include *salón* (reclining coach seats), *turista* (shared cabin with bunks), *cabina* (private cabin with toilet), and *especial* (deluxe private cabin), cost about $15 to $60 per person for the Mazatlán run, a bit less for Topolobampo. To and from Mazatlán, vehicle fees run about $50 for a motorcycle, from $200 for an automobile and upwards of $400 for a motor home or car with big trailer. Corresponding Topolobampo fees run about $30, $130, and $260.

The La Paz-Mazatlán trip takes around 18 hours. Ferries usually depart around 3 p.m. daily, arriving at the opposite shores on the following morning around 9 a.m. The La Paz-Topolobampo trip is shorter, around 10 hours. Ferries depart from each end at about 8 a.m. daily and arrive on opposite shores around 6 p.m.

For more information, usually available in either English or Spanish, contact the La Paz ferry headquarters, tel. (112) 538-33; Mazatlán, tel. (69) 817-020, 817-021, or 817-022; or Topolobampo, tel. (681) 201-04.

BY TOUR, CRUISE, AND SAILBOAT

For travelers on a tight time budget, prearranged tour packages can provide a hassle-free route for sampling the attractions of Pacific Mexico. If, however, you prefer a self-paced vacation, or desire thrift over convenience, you should probably defer tour arrangements until after arrival. Many Pacific Mexico resort agencies, which are as close as your hotel telephone or lobby-front tour desk, can customize a tour for you. Options range from city highlight tours and bay snorkeling adventures to inland colonial cities shopping and sightseeing overnights and boat adventures through wildlife-rich mangrove jungle hinterlands.

By Cruise or Sailboat

Travel agents will typically have a stack of cruise brochures that include Pacific Mexico ports such as Mazatlán, Puerto Vallarta, and Acapulco on their itineraries. People who enjoy being pampered with lots of food and ready-made entertainment (and don't mind paying for it) generally have great fun on cruises. Accommodations on a typical seven-day winter cruise can run as little as $100 per day, per person, double occupancy, to as much as $1,000 or more.

If, however, you want to get to know Mexico and the local people, a cruise is not for you. Onboard, food and entertainment is the main event of a cruise; shore sightseeing excursions, which generally cost extra, are a sideshow.

Sailboats, on the other hand, offer an entirely different kind of sea route to Pacific Mexico. Ocean Voyages, a California-based agency, arranges passage on a number of sail and motor vessels that regularly depart to Pacific Mexico from west coast ports, such as San Diego, Los Angeles, San Francisco, and Vancouver, British Columbia. They offer customized itineraries and flexible arrangements that vary from complete roundtrip voyages to weeklong coastal idylls between palmy Pacific Mexico ports of call. Some captains allow passengers to save money by signing on as crew. For more information, contact Ocean Voyages at 1709 Bridgeway, Sausalito, CA 94965, tel. (800) 299-4444 or (415) 332-4681, fax 332-7460, e-mail: sail@oceanvoyages.com.

Special Tours and Study Options

Some tour programs include in-depth activities centered around arts and crafts, language and culture, wildlife-viewing, ecology, or off-the-beaten-track adventuring.

A number of agencies arrange interesting Copper Canyon tours (see above). Outstanding among them are programs by Elderhostel, the San Diego Natural History Museum, Mexi-Maya Academic Travel, Inc., and the American Association for the Advancement of Science. The **Elderhostel** tour, designed for seniors, is arranged through Geronimo Educational Tours, includes rail-coach sightseeing and scenic canyon-rim nature walks, and nights in rustic but comfortable mountain lodges. For details, ask for the international catalog. Write or call Elderhostel, 75 Federal St., Boston, MA 02110-1941, tel. (877) 426-8056, Web site: www.elderhostel.org. The naturalist-guided **San Diego Natural History Museum** Copper Canyon tour begins at Los Mochis, the western terminus of the Copper Canyon railroad. Highlights include the colonial town of El Fuerte (1564), the Sinaloan thorn forest, the Jesuit Tarahumara Indian mission at the Copper Canyon village of Cerocahui, the Cusarare "Place of Eagles" waterfall, and folklore dances in the colonial city of Chihuahua. For details, contact Betchart Expeditions, Inc., 17050 Montebello Road, Cupertino, CA 95014-5435, tel. (800) 252-4910, fax (408) 252-1444. The nine-day **Mexi-Maya** trip includes visits to Chihuahua Mennonite colonies, the Tarahumara Indian mission in Creel, and climaxes with a Mayo Indian fiesta (or an Easter pageant) near Los Mochis. For details, contact Mexi-Maya Academic Travel, Inc., at 12 South 675 Knoebel Dr., Lemont, IL 60439, tel. (630) 972-9090, fax 972-9393.

The **American Association of the Advancement of Science (AAAS)** also offers noteworthy Pacific Mexico tours through Betchart Expeditions (see above). Among these is the Monarch Butterfly Safari, in the highlands of Michoacán state, half a day's drive east of Lake Pátzcuaro. Itineraries, which customarily begin in Mexico City, include a Mexico City tour and an overnight in Angangueo, an antique mining village. The tour climaxes during two days of on-foot woodland exploring, wondering and delighting at the miracle of the monarch butterflies who, having migrated thousands of miles to roost by the millions, carpet their remote high forest habitat in a fluttering riot of color.

The rich archaeological and cultural heritage of **Oaxaca**, in the Pacific Mexico south, provides a focus for some excellent tour-study programs. Elderhostel, Mexi-Maya Academic Travel (see above), Horizons and Zapotec Tours conduct noteworthy Oaxaca programs. Elderhostel programs, designed for seniors, include Spanish-language instruction, coordinated with Southern Illinois University. All four programs usually include folkloric dance performances and local trips to renowned Valley of Oaxaca crafts villages and archaeological sites. Mexi-Maya tours sometimes extend to the palmy tropical coastal resorts of Puerto Ángel and Puerto Escondido.

Zapotec Tours, based in Chicago, tel. (800) 44-OAXACA (446-2922), Web site: www.oaxacainfo.com, leads three tours: a "Food of the Gods" (beginning of October) gastronomical tour, a crafts and shopping tour (mid-November), and a cultural tour, centering around the famous 1-2 November Day of the Dead festival. You may also contact Zapotec Tours by mail or fax at 5121 N. Ravenswood Ave. Suite B, Chicago, IL 60640, tel. (773) 506-2444, fax 506-2445.

The Horizons program, on the other hand, emphasizes arts and crafts with hands-on study tours. In the past they have offered a pair of tours, one based in Mitla, the famous Valley of Oaxaca archaeological site, offering expert instruction in painting and drawing, woodcarving and sculpture, and ceramics. A second program, usually conducted around the Oct.-Nov. Day of the Dead celebrations, often includes experience in metals and jewelry, ceramics, and baskets and paper arts. Programs customarily last about 10 days and cost about $1,600, including tuition, field trips, and simple room and board. For more details, including an informative brochure, write **Horizons,** 108 North Main St., Sunderland, MA 01375. For phone or fax registration by credit card only, call (413) 665-0300 or fax 665-4141, Web site: www.horizons@horizons-art.org.

Mar de Jade, a holistic-style living center at Playa Chacala, about 50 miles (80 km) north of Puerto Vallarta, offers unique people-to-people work-study opportunities. These include Spanish language, work camps helping local people build houses and teaching practical skills, and assisting at their health clinic in Las Varas town nearby. They also offer accommodations and macrobiotic meals for travelers who would want to do nothing more than stay a few days and enjoy Mar de Jade's lovely tropical ambience.

For more information about the course schedule and fees, contact Mar de Jade's U.S. agent, tel. (415) 281-0164, P.O. Box 1280, Santa Clara, CA 95052-1280. You may also take a look at the Web site, at www.mardejade.com, e-mail info@mardejade.com, or dial them directly from the U.S. or Canada at tel./fax (327) 201-84 or (322) 235-24. In Mexico, write Mar de Jade at Apdo. Postal 81, Las Varas, Nayarit, 63715, Mexico.

Adventurous, physically fit travelers might enjoy the off-the-beaten-path biking, snorkeling, fishing, kayaking, hiking, and sightseeing tours of Seattle-based **Outland Adventures.** The itineraries (typically about $100 per day) run 3-10 days and include lots of local color and food, accommodations in small hotels, and sightseeing in the Puerto Vallarta region of beaches, forest trails, mangrove lagoons, and country roads. Itineraries, besides Puerto Vallarta itself, include villages of Rincón de Guayabitos, San Francisco, and the Costa Azul Adventure Resort, Mismaloya, Chamela, Tenacatita, La Manzanilla, and Barra de Navidad. For more information, contact Outland Adventures, P.O. Box 16343, Seattle, WA 98116, tel./fax (206) 932-7012, or look at the Web site, at www.choice#1.com/villamontana.htm.

A Puerto Vallarta ranch, **Rancho El Charro,** Francisco Villa 895, Fracc. Las Gaviotas, Puerto Vallarta, Jalisco 48300, tel. (322) 401-14, organizes naturalist-led horseback treks in the mountains near Puerto Vallarta. Tours run a minimum of one week, which includes two or three days of guided backcountry horsebacking, exploring idyllic colonial villages, camping out on the trail, swimming and hot-tubbing, and hearty dinners and cozy evenings at luxurious haciendas. Tariffs begin at $900 per person, complete.

The remote lagoons and islands of Baja California, about 200 miles (300 km) due west of Mazatlán, nurture a trove of marine and onshore wildlife. Such sanctuaries are ongoing destinations of winter **Oceanic Society** expedition-tours from La Paz, Baja California. Tours leave from San Diego by boat, customarily cost about $1,800, cover several islands, and include a week of marine mammal watching, snorkeling, birding, and eco-exploring, both on- and off-shore. For details, contact the Oceanic Society, Fort Mason Center, Building E, San Francisco, CA 94123, tel. (800) 326-7491 or (415) 441-1106, fax 474-3395, Web site: www.oceanic-society.org. This trip might make an exciting overture to your Pacific Mexico vacation. You can connect your Pacific Mexico path with the Oceanic Society's Baja California jumping-off-point via Mexicana Airlines' Los Cabos-Mazatlán-Puerto Vallarta flights or Aeroméxico Airlines' La Paz-Mazatlán flight.

GETTING AROUND

Recent privatization has put an end to passenger **train** service in virtually all parts of Pacific Mexico. Drive or take a bus instead.

BY AIR

Mexicana and Aeroméxico, and some smaller carriers, such as Taesa, Aeromorelos, and Aviacsa, connect many of the main destinations of Pacific Mexico. In the north, a scheduled network connects Mazatlán, Puerto Vallarta, Guadalajara, Manzanillo-Barra de Navidad and other Mexican destinations. In the south, the same is true of Ixtapa-Zihuatanejo, Acapulco, Puerto Escondido, Puerto Ángel-Huatulco, and Oaxaca. Although much pricier than first-class bus tickets, domestic airfares are on a par with U.S. prices.

Travelers may book tickets by contacting agencies in the destination cities. (See destina-

WHICH BUSES GO WHERE

DESTINATIONS

Acapulco	EB, EL, EO, FR, TU
Bahías de Huatulco, Oaxaca	CC, EL
Barra de Navidad-Melaque, Jalisco	AC, ACP, EL, ETN, PP, TCN
Chapala, Jalisco	AGC
Colima, Colima	ADO EL, ETN, OM, PP, EL
Guadalajara (new terminal)	ACP, ADO, ATM, EL, ETN, FU, OM, PP, TC, TN, TP
Guadalajara (old terminal)	AGC, AMT
Ixtapa-Zihuatanejo, Guerrero	EB, EL, EO, FR
Las Varas, Nayarit	EL, TNN, TNS, TP
Lázaro Cárdenas, Michoacán	EB, EL, GA, RP, TU
Manzanillo	AC, ADO, ACP, EL, ETN, TU, FA, GA, PP, TNS
Mazatlán	EL, FU, TC, TN, TNS, TP, TU
Oaxaca	AO, CC
Pátzcuaro, Michoacán	ADO, EB, EL, GA, RP
Pinotepa Nacional, Oaxaca	CC, EB, EL, FR
Puerto Ángel, Oaxaca	CC, EB, EL
Puerto Escondido	CC, EL,
Puerto Vallarta	AC, EL, ETN, PP, TCN, TNS, TP, TU
San Blas, Nayarit	TNS, TNN
Rincón de Guayabitos-La Peñita, Nayarit	EL, TNS, TP, TU
Santiago Ixcuintla, Nayarit	TNN
Taxco, Guerrero	EO, FR
Tepic, Nayarit	EL, FU, OM, TC, TNS, TNN, TP, TU
Uruapan, Michoacán	ADO, EL, ETN, GA, RP

BUS KEY

AC	Autobuses Costa Alegre (subsidiary of FA)	FA	Flecha Amarilla
ACP	Autocamiones del Pacífico	FU	Futura, subsidiary of EB
ADO	Autobuses del Occidente	GA	Galeana, subsidiary of FA
AGC	Autotransportes Guadalajara-Chapala	OM	Omnibus de Mexico
AMT	Autobuses Mascota Talpa Guadalajara (blue)	PP	Primera Plus, subsidiary of FA
		RP	Ruta de Paraíso, subsidiary of FA
AO	Autobuses del Oriente	TC	Transportes Chihuahuenses, subsidiary of FA
ATM	Autotransportes Guadalajara-Talpa-Mascota (red)	TCN	Transportes Cihuatlán
		TN	Transportes del Norte, subsidiary of EB
CC	Cristóbal Colón	TNS	Transportes Norte de Sonora, subsidiary of EB
EB	Estrella Blanca		
EL	Elite, subsidiary of EB	TP	Transportes del Pacífico
EO	Estrella de Oro	TU	Turistar, subsidiary of EB
ETN	Enlaces Transportes Nacionales		

See the destination chapters for more detailed bus information.

tion chapters for airlines' local agency phone numbers.)

Local Flying Tips

If you're planning on lots of in-Mexico flying, get the airlines' handy, although rapidly changeable, *itinerarios de vuelo* (flight schedules) booklets at the airport.

Mexican airlines have operating peculiarities that result from their tight budgets: don't miss a flight; you will likely lose half the ticket price. Adjusting your flight date may cost 25% of the ticket price. Get to the airport an hour ahead of time. Last-minute passengers are often "bumped" in favor of early-bird waitees. Conversely, go to the airport and get in line if you must catch a flight that the airlines have claimed to be full. You might get on anyway. Keep your luggage small so you can carry it on. Lost luggage victims receive scant compensation in Mexico.

BY BUS

The bus is the king of the Mexican road. Dozens of lines connect virtually every town in Pacific Mexico. Three distinct levels of service—luxury or super first-class, first-class, and second-class—are generally available. **Super first-class** (usually called something like "Primera Plus," depending upon the line) luxury express coaches speed between major towns, seldom stopping en route. In exchange for relatively high fares (about $50 Puerto Vallarta-Guadalajara, for example), passengers enjoy rapid passage and airline-style amenities: plush reclining seats, air-conditioning, an on-board toilet, video, and aisle attendant.

Although much less luxurious, **first-class** service costs two-thirds less, is frequent, and always includes reserved seating. Additionally, passengers usually enjoy soft reclining seats and air-conditioning (if it is working). Besides their regular stops at or near most towns and villages en route, first-class bus drivers, if requested, will usually stop and let you off anywhere along the road.

Second-class bus seating is unreserved. In outlying parts of Pacific Mexico, there is a class of buses even beneath second-class, but given the condition of many second-class buses, it usually seems as if third-class buses wouldn't run at all. Such buses are the stuff of travelers' legends: the recycled old GMC, Ford, and Dodge school buses that stop everywhere and carry everyone and everything to the smallest villages tucked away in the far mountains. As long as there is any kind of a road to it, such a bus will most likely go there.

Now and then you'll read a newspaper story of a country bus that went over a cliff somewhere in Mexico, killing the driver and a dozen unfortunate souls. The same newspapers never bother to mention the half million safe trips the same bus provided during its 15 years of service prior to the accident.

Second-class buses are not for travelers with weak knees or stomachs. You will often initially have to stand, cramped in the aisle, among a crowd of campesinos. They are warm-hearted, but poor people, so don't tempt them with open, dangling purses or wallets bulging in back pockets. Stow your money safely away. After a while, you will probably be able to sit down. Such privilege, however, comes with obligation, such as holding an old lady's bulging bag of carrots or a toddler on your lap. But if you accept your burden with humor and equanimity, who knows what favors and blessings may flow to you in return.

Tickets, Seating, and Baggage

Mexican bus lines do not usually publish schedules or fares. You have to ask someone (such as your hotel desk clerk) who knows, or call (or have someone call) the bus station. Few travel agents handle bus tickets. If you don't want to spend the time to get a reserved ticket yourself, hire someone trustworthy to do it for you. Another way of doing it all is to get to the bus station early enough on your traveling day to assure you'll get a bus to your destination.

Although some lines accept credit cards and issue computer-printed tickets at their major stations, most reserved bus tickets are sold for cash and handwritten, with a specific seat number *(número de asiento)* on the back. If you miss the bus, you lose your money. Furthermore, airlines-style automated reservations systems have not yet arrived at many Mexican bus stations. Consequently, you can generally buy reserved tickets only at the local departure *(salida local)*

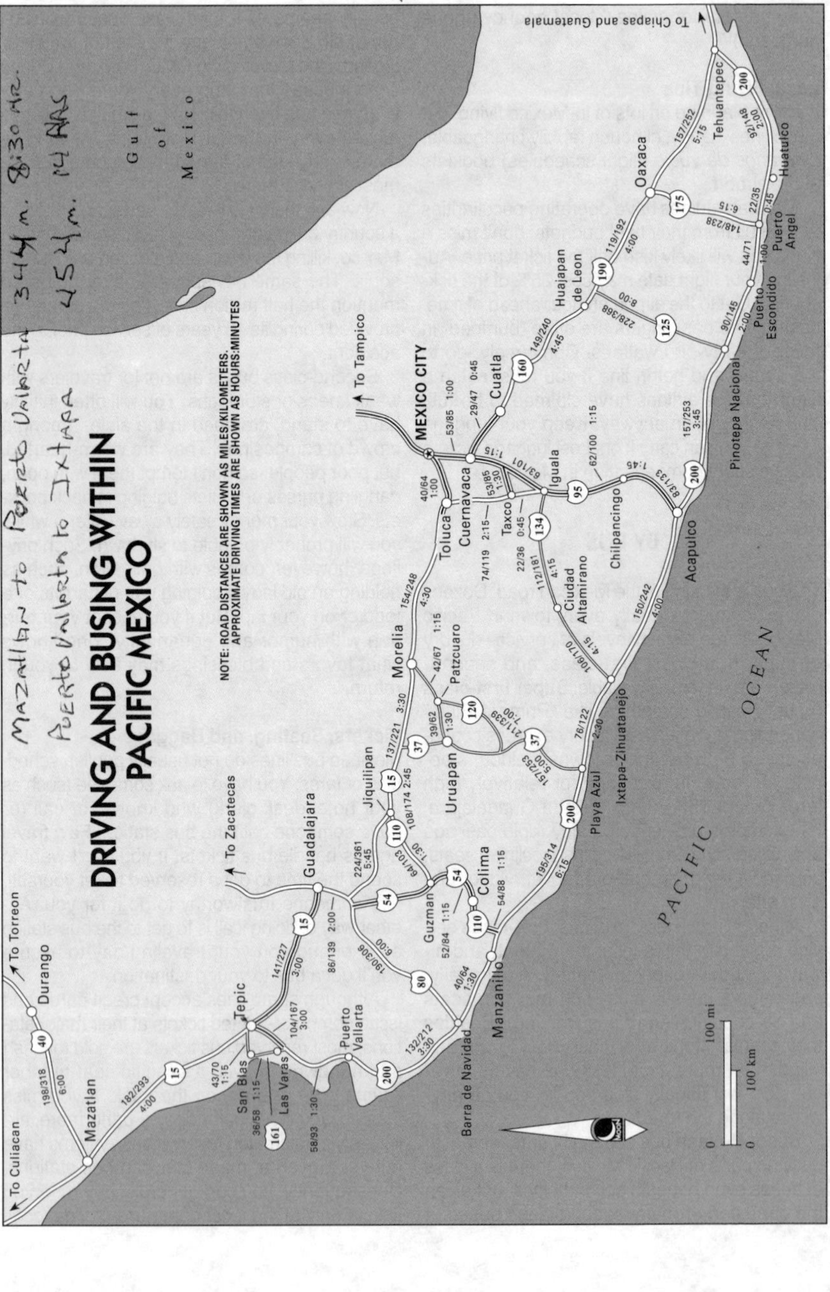
DRIVING AND BUSING WITHIN PACIFIC MEXICO
NOTE: ROAD DISTANCES ARE SHOWN AS MILES/KILOMETERS. APPROXIMATE DRIVING TIMES ARE SHOWN AS HOURS:MINUTES
© MOON PUBLICATIONS, INC.
To Culiacan
To Torreon
To Zacatecas
To Tampico
To Chiapas and Guatemala
Gulf of Mexico
PACIFIC OCEAN
Mazatlan
Durango
Tepic
San Blas
Las Varas
Puerto Vallarta
Barra de Navidad
Manzanillo
Guadalajara
Guzman
Colima
Jiquilipan
Uruapan
Patzcuaro
Morelia
Toluca
MEXICO CITY
Cuernavaca
Cuatla
Taxco
Iguala
Ciudad Altamirano
Chilpancingo
Playa Azul
Ixtapa-Zihuatanejo
Acapulco
Pinotepa Nacional
Puerto Escondido
Puerto Angel
Huatulco
Huajapan de Leon
Oaxaca
Tehuantepec
198/318 6:00
182/293 4:00
36/58 1:15
43/70 1:15
58/93 1:30
104/167 3:00
141/227 3:00
132/212 3:30
40/64 1:30
190/306 6:00
86/139 2:00
224/361 5:45
52/84 1:15
54/88 1:15
64/103 1:30
108/174 2:45
137/221 3:30
195/314 6:15
39/62 1:30
42/67 1:15
154/248 4:30
157/253 5:00
211/339 7:00
76/122 2:30
106/170 4:15
150/242 4:00
40/64 1:00
53/85 1:00
29/47 0:45
74/119 2:15
53/85 1:30
63/101 1:15
22/36 0:45
112/181 4:15
62/100 1:15
83/133 1:45
157/253 3:45
149/240 4:45
228/368 8:00
90/145 2:00
44/71 1:00
22/35 0:45
119/192 4:00
148/238 6:15
157/252 5:15
92/148 2:00
15
40
161
200
80
54
110
37
120
134
95
160
190
125
175
100 mi
100 km
0

station. (An agent in Manzanillo, for example, cannot ordinarily reserve you a ticket on a bus that originates in Zihuatanejo, a day's travel down the road.)

Request a reserved seat number, if possible, from numbers 1 to 25 in the front *(delante)* to middle *(medio)* of the bus. The rear seats are often occupied by smokers, drunks, and general rowdies. At night, you will sleep better on the right side *(lado derecho)* away from the glare of oncoming traffic lights.

Baggage is generally secure on Mexican buses. Label it, however. Overhead racks are often too cramped to accommodate airline-size carry-ons. Carry a small bag of your crucial items on your person; pack clothes and less essentials in your checked luggage. For peace of mind, watch the handler put your checked baggage on the bus and watch to make sure it is not mistakenly taken off the bus at intermediate stops.

If, somehow, your baggage gets misplaced, remain calm. Bus employees are generally competent and conscientious; if you are patient, recovering your luggage will become a matter of honor for many of them. Baggage handlers are at the bottom of the pay scale; a tip for their mostly thankless job would be very much appreciated.

On long trips, carry food, drinks, and toilet paper. Station food may be dubious and the sanitary facilities ill-maintained.

If you are waiting for a first-class bus at an intermediate *salida de paso* (passing station), you often have to trust to luck there will be an empty seat. If not, your best option may be to ride a usually much more frequent second-class bus.

BY RENTAL CAR, TAXI, TOUR, AND HITCHHIKING

Rental Car

Car and jeep rentals are an increasingly popular transportation option for Pacific Mexico travelers. They offer mobility and independence for local sightseeing and beach excursions. In the resorts, the gang's all there: Hertz, National, Dollar, Avis, Budget, and a host of local outfits. They generally require drivers to have a valid driver's license, passport, a major credit card, and may require a minimum age of 25. Some local com-

panies do not accept credit cards, but offer lower rates in return.

Base prices of international agencies, such as Hertz, National, and Avis are not cheap. They run more than in the U.S., with a 17% "value added" tax tacked on. The cheapest possible rental car, usually a vintage stick-shift VW Beetle, runs between $30-60 per day or $200-450 per week, depending on location and season. Prices are steepest during high Christmas and pre-Easter weeks. Before departure, use the international agencies' free 800 numbers to shop around for availability, prices, and reservations (see the chart). During nonpeak seasons, you may save lots of pesos by waiting till arrival and renting a car through a local agency. Shop around, starting with the agent in your hotel

---

CAR RENTAL AGENCY TOLL-FREE NUMBERS

Avis, U.S. and Canada tel. (800) 831-2847: AC, GD, HU, OA, PV

Budget, U.S. tel. (800) 527-0700, Canada tel. (800) 268-8991: AC, GD, HU, IX, MZ, OA, PE, PV

Dollar, U.S. and Canada tel. (800) 800-4000: AC, GD, HU, IX, MN, PV

Hertz, U.S. tel. (800) 654-3001, Canada tel. (800) 263-0600: AC, MZ, GD, OA, PV

National, U.S. and Canada tel. (800) 227-3876: AC, GD, MN, MZ, PV

Thrifty, U.S. and Canada tel. (800) 367-2277: AC, HU, IX, PV

City Key
AC—Acapulco
GD—Guadalajara
HU—Bays of Huatulco
IX—Ixtapa-Zihuatanejo
MN—Manzanillo-Barra de Navidad
MZ—Mazatlán
OA—Oaxaca
PE—Puerto Escondido
PV—Puerto Vallarta

In addition to the international car rental companies listed above, many good local agents rent cars at generally lower rates. See individual destination chapters for more information.

ROAD SIGNS

ALTO
STOP

RAILROAD
CROSSING

CEDA EL PASO
YIELD RIGHT
OF WAY

TOPES
SPEED BUMPS

CIRCULACION
ONE WAY

DOBLE CIRCULACION
TWO WAY

E
PARKING

NO
NO PARKING

DIP (across arroyo)

DIP (across arroyo)

PARADA
BUS STOP

CONSERVE SU DERECHA
KEEP TO THE RIGHT

lobby, or the local Yellow Pages (under *Automoviles, renta de*).

Car insurance that covers property damage, public liability, and medical payments **is an absolute "must"** with your rental car. If you get into an accident without insurance, you will be in deep trouble, probably jail. Driving in Mexico is more hazardous than back home. For important car safety and insurance information, see above.

Taxis
The high prices of rental cars make taxis a viable option for local excursions. Cars are luxuries, not necessities, for most Mexican families. Travelers might profit from the Mexican money-saving practice of piling everyone in a taxi for Sun-

day park, beach, and fishing outings. You may find that an all-day taxi and driver (who, besides relieving you of driving, will become your impromptu guide) will cost less than a rental car.

The magic word for saving money by taxi is *colectivo:* a taxi that you share jointly with other travelers. Your first place to practice getting a taxi will be at the airport, where *colectivo* tickets are routinely sold from booths at the terminal door.

If, however, you want your own private taxi, ask for a *taxi especial,* which will probably run about three or four times the individual tariff for a *colectivo.*

Your airport experience will prepare you for in-town taxis, which rarely have meters. You must establish the price before getting in. Bargaining comes with the territory in Mexico, so don't shrink from it, even though it seems a hassle. If you get into a taxi without an agreed-upon price, you are letting yourself in for a more serious, potentially nasty hassle later. If your driver's price is too high, he'll probably come to his senses as soon as you hail another taxi.

After a few days, getting taxis around town will be a cinch. You'll find you don't have to take the high-ticket taxis lined up in your hotel driveway. If the price isn't right, walk toward the street and hail a regular taxi.

In town, if you can't seem to find a taxi, it may be because they are all hanging around waiting for riders at the local stand, called a taxi *sitio*. Ask someone to direct you to it: Say *"Excúseme. ¿Donde está el sitio taxi, por favor?"* ("Excuse me. Where is the taxi stand, please?")

Tours and Guides

For many Pacific Mexico visitors, locally arranged tours offer a hassle-free alternative to rental car or taxi sightseeing. Hotels and travel agencies, many of whom maintain front-lobby travel and tour desks, offer a bounty of sightseeing, water sports, bay cruise, fishing, and wildlife-viewing tour opportunities. For details, see the destination chapters.

Hitchhiking

Most everyone agrees hitchhiking is not the safest mode of transport. If you're unsure, don't do it. Hitchhiking doesn't make a healthy steady travel diet, nor should you hitchhike at night.

The recipe for trouble-free hitchhiking requires equal measures of luck, savvy, and technique. The best places to catch rides are where people are arriving and leaving anyway, such as bus stops, highway intersections, gas stations, RV parks, and on the highway out of town.

Male-female hitchhiking partnerships seem to net the most rides (although it is technically illegal for women to ride in commercial trucks). The more gear you and your partner have, the

fewer rides you will get. Pickup and flatbed truck owners often pick up passengers for pay. Before hopping onto the truck bed, ask how much the ride will cost.

DISASTER AND RESCUE ON A MEXICAN HIGHWAY

My litany of Mexican driving experiences came to a climax one night when, heading north from Tepic, I hit a cow at 50 mph head on. The cow was knocked about 150 feet down the road, while I and my two friends endured a scary impromptu roller-coaster ride. When the dust settled, we, although in shock, were grateful that we hadn't suffered the fate of the poor cow, who had died instantly from the collision.

From that low point, our fortunes soon began to improve. Two buses stopped and about 40 men got out to move my severely wounded van to the shoulder. The cow's owner, a rancher, arrived to cart off the cow's remains in a jeep. Then the police—a man and his wife in a VW bug—pulled up. *"Pobrecita camioneta,"* "Poor little van," the woman said, gazing at my vehicle, which now resembled an oversized, rumpled accordion. They gave us a ride to Mazatlán, found us a hotel room, and generally made sure we were okay.

If I hadn't had Mexican auto insurance I would have been in deep trouble. Mexican law—based on the Napoleonic Code—presumes guilt and does not bother with juries. It would have kept me in jail until all damages were settled. The insurance agent I saw in the morning took care of everything. He called the police station, where I was excused from paying damages when the cow's owner failed to show. He had my car towed to a repair shop, where the mechanics banged it into good enough shape so I could drive it home a week later. Forced to stay in one place, I and my friends enjoyed the most relaxed time of our entire three months in Mexico. The *pobrecita camioneta,* all fixed up a few months later, lasted 14 more years.

OTHER PRACTICALITIES

TOURIST CARDS AND VISAS

For U.S. and Canadian citizens, entry by air into Mexico for a few weeks could hardly be easier. Airline attendants hand out tourist cards *(tarjetas turísticas)* en route, and officers make them official by glancing at passports and stamping the cards at the immigration gate. Business travel permits for 30 days or less are handled by the same simple procedures.

Although easy, entry to Mexico isn't completely painless. In early spring 1999, the Mexican government announced that, after July 1, 1999, a $15 entry fee would be imposed on all foreign visitors to the interior of Mexico, excluding border zones.

Otherwise, Mexican consulates, Mexican government tourist offices, offices of airlines serving Mexico, border immigration authorities, some auto clubs (AAA and National Auto Club), and certain travel agencies issue free tourist cards to all travelers 15 years old or over who present proper identification. Rules state U.S. citizens must show either birth certificate, valid U.S. passport, or military I.D., while naturalized citizens must show naturalization papers or valid U.S. passport.

Canadian citizens must show a valid passport or birth certificate. Nationals of other countries (especially those, such as Hong Kong, which issue more than one type of passport) may be subject to additional entry regulations. For advice, consult your closest Mexican tourist information office or consulate. See the accompanying chart.

More Options

For more complicated cases, get your tourist card early enough to allow you to consider the options: tourist cards can be issued for multiple entries and a maximum validity of 180 days; photos are often required. If you don't request multiple entry or the maximum time, your card will probably be stamped single entry, valid for some shorter period, such as 90 days. If you are not sure how long you'll stay in Mexico, request the maximum and bring passport photos. The absolute maximum for a tourist card is 180 days; long-term foreign residents routinely make semi-annual "border runs" for new tourist cards.

Student and Extended Business Visas

A visa is a notation stamped and signed into your passport showing the number of days and entries allowable for your trip. Apply for visas at the consulate nearest your home well in advance of your departure. One-year renewable student visas and business visas longer than the routine 30 days are available, though often with considerable red tape. Check with your local Mexican consulate for details; an ordinary 180-day tourist card may be the easiest option, if you can manage it.

Your Passport

Your passport (or birth or naturalization certificate) is your positive proof of national identity; without it, your status in any foreign country is in doubt. Don't leave home without one. United States citizens may obtain passports at local post offices.

Don't Lose Your Tourist Card

If you do, be prepared with a Xeroxed copy of the original, which you should present to the nearest federal Migración (Immigration) office (in most major Pacific Mexico vacation centers) and ask for a duplicate tourist permit. Lacking this, you might present some alternate proof of your date of arrival in Mexico, such as a stamped passport or airline ticket. Savvy travelers carry a copy of their tourist card with them, while leaving the original safe in their hotel room.

Car Permits

If you drive to Mexico, you need to buy a permit for your car. Upon entry into Mexico, be ready with originals and copies of your proof-of-ownership papers (state title certificate and registration, or a notarized bill of sale), current license plates, and a current driver's license. The fee is about $12, payable only by non-Mexican bank MasterCard, Visa, or American Express credit cards. The credit-card-only requirement discourages those who sell or abandon U.S.-reg-

MEXICAN TOURIST INFORMATION OFFICES AND CONSULATES

Dozens of Mexican government tourist information offices and consulates operate in the United States. Consulates generally handle questions of Mexican nationals in the U.S., while tourist information offices service travelers heading for Mexico. For very simple questions and Mexico regional information brochures, dial (800) 44MEXICO from the U.S. or Canada.

Otherwise, contact one of several North American regional or European Mexican government tourist information offices for guidance:

IN NORTH AMERICA

From Alaska, Arizona, California, Colorado, Hawaii, Idaho, Montana, Nevada, New Mexico, Oregon, Utah and Wyoming, contact **Los Angeles:** 2401 W. 6th Street, 5th Floor, Los Angeles, CA 90057, tel. (213) 351-2075, fax 351-2074, e-mail: 104045.3647@compuserve.com

From Washington and the Canadian Provinces of Alberta, British Colombia, and Yukon, contact **Vancouver:** 999 W. Hastings St., Suite 1610, Vancouver, BC V6C 2W2, tel. (604) 669-2845, fax 669-3498, e-mail: mgto@bc.sympatico.ca

From Texas, Oklahoma, and Louisiana, contact **Houston:** 10440 West Office Dr., Houston, TX 77042, tel. (713) 780-8395, fax 780-8362, e-mail: mgtotx@ix.netcom.com

From Alabama, Arkansas, Florida, Georgia, Mississippi, Tennessee, North Carolina and South Carolina, contact **Miami:** 691 Brickell Key Dr., Miami, FL 33131, tel. (305) 381-6996, fax 381-9674, e-mail: mgotmia@netrunner.net

From Illinois, Indiana, Iowa, Kansas, Michigan, Minnesota, Missouri, Nebraska, North Dakota, Ohio, South Dakota, and Wisconsin, contact **Chicago:** 300 N. Michigan Ave., 4th Floor, Chicago, IL 60601, tel. (312) 606-9252, fax 606-9012, e-mail: mgtochi@cis.compuserve.com

From Connecticut, Delaware, Kentucky, Maine, Maryland, Massachusetts, New Hampshire, New Jersey, New York, Pennsylvania, Rhode Island, and Vermont, Virginia, Washington, D.C., and West Virginia, contact **New York:** 21 E. 63rd St., 3rd Floor, New York, NY 10021, tel. (212) 821-0314, fax 821-3067, e-mail: jermgto@interport.net

From Ontario, Manitoba, and Saskatchewan, contact **Toronto:** 2 Bloor St. W, Suite 1502, Toronto, ON M4W 3E2, tel. (416) 925-2753, fax 925-6061, e-mail: mexto3@inforamp.net

From New Brunswick, Newfoundland, Nova Scotia, Prince Edward Island, and Quebec, contact **Montreal:** 1 Place Ville Marie, Suite 1510, Montreal, PQ H3B 2B5, tel. (514) 871-1052, fax 871-3825, e-mail: turimex@cam.org

IN EUROPE

Mexico also maintains tourist information offices throughout Western Europe:

London: 60/61 Trafalgar Square, London WC2N 5DS, England, tel. (171) 734-1058, fax 930-9202, e-mail: mexicanministry@easynet.co.uk

Frankfurt: Weisenhuttenplatz 26, 60329 Frankfurt-am-Main, Deutschland, tel. (69) 25-3509, fax 25-3755, e-mail: 106132.3031@compuserve.com

Paris: 4, Rue Notre-Dame des Victoires, 75002 Paris, France, tel. (1) 428-65620/47/48, fax 428-60580, e-mail: otmex@worldnet.fr

Madrid: Calle Velázquez 126, 28006 Madrid, España, tel. (91) 561-3520, fax 411-0759, e-mail: mexico@lander.es

Rome: Via Barbarini 3-piso 7, 00187 Roma, Italia, tel. (06) 487-2182, fax 487-3630, e-mail: mex.touroffice@agora.stm.it

istered cars in Mexico without paying customs duties. Credit cards must bear the same name as the vehicle proof-of-ownership papers. If you desire to exit Mexico at a border crossing other than your entry point, ask the official who issues your car permit if rules permit this.

The resulting car permit becomes part of the owner's tourist permit and receives the same length of validity. Cars being purchased under finance contracts must be accompanied by a notarized written permission from the finance company. Vehicles registered in the name of an organization or other person must be accompanied by a notarized affidavit authorizing the driver to use the car in Mexico for a specific time.

Border officials generally allow you to carry or tow additional motorized vehicles (motorcycle, another car, a large boat) into Mexico, but will probably require separate documentation and fee for each vehicle. If a border official desires to inspect your trailer or RV, go through it with him.

Accessories, such as a small trailer, boat less than six feet, CB radio, and outboard motor may be noted on the car permit and must leave Mexico with the car.

For many more details on motor vehicle entry and what you may bring in your baggage to Mexico, consult the AAA (American Automobile Association) *Mexico Travelbook* (see the Booklist).

Since Mexico does not recognize foreign automobile insurance, you must purchase Mexican automobile insurance. For more information on this and other details of driving in Mexico, see above.

Entry for Children

Children under 15 can be included on their parents' tourist permit, but complications occur if the children (by reason of illness, for example) cannot leave Mexico with both parents. Parents can avoid such possible red tape by getting a passport and a Mexican tourist card for each of their children.

In addition to a passport or birth certificate, minors (under age 18) entering Mexico without parents or legal guardians must present a notarized letter of permission signed by both parents or legal guardians. Even if accompanied by one parent, a notarized letter from the other must be presented. Divorce or death certificates must also be presented, when applicable.

Pacific Mexico travelers should navigate all such possible delays far ahead of time in the cool calm of their local Mexican consulate rather than the hot, hurried atmosphere of a border or airport immigration station.

Pets

A pile of red tape stalls the entry of many dogs, cats, and other pets into Mexico. Veterinary health and rabies certificates are required to be stamped by a Mexican consul responsible for a specific foreign zone (such as Texas, or Southern California). Contact your closest Mexican Tourist Information Office for assistance

Returning Home

All returning United States citizens are subject to U.S. customs inspection. Rules allow $400 worth of duty-free goods per returnee. This may include no more than one liter of alcoholic spirits, 200 cigarettes, and 100 cigars. A flat 10% duty will be applied to the first $1,000 (fair retail value, save your receipts) in excess of your $400 exemption.

You may, however, mail packages (up to $50 value each) of gifts duty-free to friends and relatives in the United States. Make sure to clearly write "unsolicited gift" and a list of the value and contents on the outside of the package. Perfumes (over $5), alcoholic beverages, and tobacco may not be included in such packages.

Improve the security of such mailed packages by sending them via special **Mexpost** class, similar to U.S. Express Mail service. Even better, send them by **DHL** international courier, which maintains offices in all major Pacific Mexico resort centers. (Consult the local Yellow Pages for phone numbers.)

For more information on customs regulations important to travelers abroad, write for a copy of the useful pamphlet, *Know Before You Go,* from the U.S. Customs Service, P.O. Box 7047, Washington, DC 20044.

Additional U.S. rules prohibit importation of certain fruits, vegetables, and domestic animal and endangered wildlife products. Certain live animal species, such as parrots, may be brought into the U.S., subject to 30-day agricultural quarantine upon arrival, at the owner's expense. For more details on agricultural product and live animal importation, write for the free booklet, *Travelers' Tips,* by the U.S. Department of Agriculture, Washington, DC 20250. For more information on the importation of endangered wildlife products, write the Wildlife Permit Office, U.S. Department of the Interior, Washington, DC 20240.

MONEY

Traveler's checks, besides being refundable, are widely accepted in Pacific Mexico. Before you leave, purchase enough of a well-known brand, such as American Express or Visa, of U.S. dollar traveler's checks to cover your Mexico expenses. Unless you like signing your name or paying lots of per-check commissions, buy denominations of US$50 or more.

On the other hand, nearly all Mexican bank branches have convenient 24-hour automatic teller machines that accept many American and Canadian bank debit cards. Payment is in Mexican pesos at generally favorable exchange rates, and transaction fees are usually modest.

The Peso: Down and Up
Overnight in early 1993, the Mexican government shifted its monetary decimal point three places and created the "new" peso worth about three per U.S. dollar. A later recession pushed the peso down, so that, at the beginning of 1999, the peso was trading at about 10 per dollar.

Mexican coins come in denominations of one, five, and 10 pesos. Bills come in denominations of 10, 20, 50, 100, 200, 500, and 1,000 pesos. Banks like to exchange your traveler's checks for a few crisp large bills, rather than the often-tattered smaller denominations, which are much more useful for everyday purchases. (A 200-peso note, while common at the bank, looks awfully big to a small shopkeeper, who might be hard-pressed to change it.) Ask the bank teller who changes your traveler's checks to break some of those big peso bills into a handful of 20-, 50- or 100-peso notes. Note: Because of the recent rapid inflation of the peso, value is more easily reckoned in U.S. dollars. Accordingly, all prices in this book are given in U.S. dollars.

Since the new peso has acquired respectable value, the centavo (one-hundredth new peso) now appears in coins of five, 10, 20, and 50 centavos. (Incidentally, in Mexico the dollar sign, "$," also marks Mexican pesos.)

Banks and Money Exchange Offices
Mexican banks have lengthened their hours in most locations to Mon.-Fri. 9 a.m.-5 p.m., although money exchange services may be shorter than this. Some banks, notably the Banco Internacional (Bital) are opening longer hours and Saturdays and staffing special after-hours money exchange windows in resort centers. Banks traditionally post the dollar exchange rate in the lobby like this: *Tipo de cambio: venta 10.413, compra 10.502,* which means that they will sell pesos to you at the rate of 10.413 per dollar, and inversely buy them back for 10.502 per dollar. All of which means you get 1,041.30 pesos for each of your $100 traveler's checks.

You don't necessarily have to go to the trouble of changing your money at a bank. Merchants, hotels, and restaurants also change money, but usually at much less favorable rates. Consequently, money-exchange lines (on Monday mornings especially) at Banamex are often long. In such cases, look for a less-crowded (such as Bancomer, Banco Serfín, and Banco Confia) bank around the corner. Small money-exchange offices *(casas de cambio)* are the most convenient, sometimes offering long hours and faster service for a pittance more than the banks (sometimes as little as 25 pennies on $100).

Credit Cards
Credit cards, such as Visa, MasterCard, and to a lesser extent, American Express and Discover, are widely honored in the hotels, restaurants, craft shops, and boutiques that cater to foreign tourists. You will generally get better bargains, however, in shops that depend on local trade and do not so readily accept credit cards. Such shops sometimes offer discounts for cash sales.

Whatever the circumstance, your travel money will usually go much farther in Pacific Mexico than back home. Despite the national 17% ("value added" IVA) sales tax, local lodging, food, and transportation prices will often seem like bargains compared to the developed world. Outside of the pricey high-rise beachfront strips, pleasant, palmy hotel room rates often run $30 or less.

Keeping Your Money Safe

In Pacific Mexico, as everywhere, thieves circulate among the tourists. Keep valuables in your hotel *caja de seguridad* (security box). If you don't particularly like the desk clerk, carry what you cannot afford to lose in a money belt.

Pickpockets love crowded markets, buses, terminals, and airports, where they can slip a wallet out of a back pocket or dangling purse in a wink. Guard against this by carrying your wallet in your front pocket, and your purse, waist pouch, or daypack (which thieves can go so far as to slit open) on your front side.

Don't attract crooks; don't display wads of money or flashy jewelry. Don't get drunk; if so, you may become a pushover for a determined thief.

Don't leave valuables unattended on the beach; share security duties with some of your trustworthy-looking neighbors, or leave a bag with a shopkeeper nearby.

Tipping

Without their droves of foreign visitors, Mexican people would be even poorer. Devaluation of the peso, while it makes prices low for visitors, makes it rough for Mexican families to get by. The help at your hotel typically get paid only a few dollars a day. They depend on tips to make the difference between dire and bearable poverty. For good service, tip 15%. Give your chambermaid *(camarista)* and floor attendant about five pesos every day or two. And whenever uncertain of what to tip, it will probably mean a lot to someone, maybe a whole family, if you err on the generous side.

In restaurants and bars, Mexican tipping customs are similar to U.S., Canada, and Europe: tip waiters, waitresses, and bartenders about 15% for satisfactory service.

SHOPPING

What to Buy

Although bargains abound in Mexico, savvy shoppers are selective. Steep import and luxury taxes drive up the prices of foreign-made goods, such as cameras, computers, sports equipment, and English-language books. Instead, concentrate your shopping on locally made items: leather, jewelry, cotton resort wear, Mexican-made designer clothes, and the galaxy of handicrafts for which Mexico is famous.

Handicrafts

A number of Pacific Mexico regional centers are renowned sources of crafts. A multitude of family shops in Guadalajara and its suburban villages of Tlaquepaque and Tonalá, the Lake Pátzcuaro region, Taxco and its village hinterland, and the Valley of Oaxaca all nurture vibrant traditions with roots in the pre-Columbian past. This rich cornucopia spills over to the Pacific resort centers, where it merges with troves of local offerings to decorate sidewalks, stalls, and shops all over town.

Bargaining

Bargaining will stretch your money even further. It comes with the territory in Mexico and needn't be a hassle. On the contrary, if done with humor and moderation, bargaining can be an enjoyable path to encountering Mexican people and gaining their respect, and even friendship.

The local crafts market is where bargaining is most intense. For starters, try offering half the asking price. From there on, it's all psychology: you have to content yourself with not having to have the item. Otherwise, you're sunk; the vendor will probably sense your need and stand fast. After a few minutes of good-humored bantering, ask for *el último precio* (the "final price"), which, if it's close, you may have a bargain.

Buying Silver and Gold Jewelry

Silver and gold jewelry, the finest of which is crafted in Taxco, Guerrero, and Guanajuato, fills a number of shops in Pacific Mexico. One hundred percent pure silver is rarely sold because it's too soft. Silver (sent from mines all over Mexico to be worked in Taxco shops), is nearly always alloyed with 7.5% copper to increase its durability. Such pieces, identical in composition to sterling silver, should have ".925," together with the initials of the manufacturer, stamped on their back sides. Other, less common grades, such as "800 fine" (80% silver), should also be stamped.

If silver is not stamped with the degree of purity, it probably contains no silver at all and is an alloy of copper, zinc, and nickel, known by the generic label "alpaca," or "Mexican," or "German" silver. Once, after haggling over the purity and prices of his offerings, a street vendor handed me a shiny handful and said, "Go to a jeweler and have them tested. If they're not real, keep them." Calling his bluff, I took them to a jeweler, who applied a dab of hydrochloric acid to each piece. Tiny, tell-tale bubbles revealed the cheapness of the merchandise, which I returned the next day to the vendor.

Some shops price sterling silver jewelry simply by weighing, which typically translates to about $1 per gram. If you want to find out if the price is fair, ask the shopkeeper to weigh it for you.

People prize pure gold partly because, unlike silver, it does not tarnish. Gold, nevertheless, is rarely sold pure (24-karat); for durability, it is alloyed with copper. Typical purities, such as 18-karat (75%) or 14-karat (58%), should be stamped on the pieces. If not, chances are they contain no gold at all.

COMMUNICATIONS

Using Mexican Telephones
Although Mexican phone service has greatly improved, it still can be hit-or-miss. If a number doesn't get through, you may have to redial it more than once. When someone answers (usually *"bueno"*) be especially courteous. If your Spanish is rusty, say *"¿Por favor, habla usted inglés?"* ("POR fah-VOR AH-vlah oos-TAYD een-GLAYS?"). If you want to speak to a particular person (such as María), ask *"¿María se cuentra?"* ("mah-REEAH SAY koo-AYN-trah").

In resort cities and larger towns, direct long-distance dialing is the rule—from private telephones, public phone booths, or your hotel-room phone. Additionally, you can use private *larga distancia* (long distance) offices. Hotels and long distance offices, however, often add expensive surcharges. Public telephone booths, widely available on resort town street corners, are the cheapest way to go. Be ready with coins—one-peso coins for local calls, more for long distance. For long distance within Mexico, dial 01, the national long-distance code, followed by the local Mexican area code *(lada),* followed by the local number. Depending on the telephone, deposit coins *(monedas)* either before you dial or after your party answers.

To call home to the U.S. or Canada station-to-station from a Mexican public phone, you dial *lada* 001, followed by the U.S.-Canada area code and local number. However, to accomplish this, you must either use a Mexican telephone credit card or deposit an impossibly large number of coins. It's more convenient to be prepared with U.S.-Canada telephone credit card numbers, which you can use by first dialing either 001-800-462-4240 for AT&T, 001-800-674-6000 for MCI, or 001-800-877-8000 for Sprint.

Another good way to call home is collect. You can generally do this one of two ways: Simply dial 09 for the local English-speaking international operator, or alternatively, contact the AT&T, MCI, and Sprint long-distance operators by dialing the above-listed numbers.

Beware of certain private "Call Long Distance to the U.S.A. Collect and Credit Card" telephones, installed prominently in airports, tourist hotels, and shops. Tariffs on these phones often run as high as $30 for three minutes. Always ask the operator for the rate, and if it's too high, take your business elsewhere.

In many smaller towns, long-distance phoning is done exclusively in the *larga distancia* (long distance) telephone office. Typically staffed by a young woman and often connected to a café or bus station, the *larga distancia* frequently becomes an informal community social center as people pass the time waiting for their telephone call connection to made.

Calling Mexico
To call Mexico direct from the U.S., first dial 011 (the international access code), then 52 (the country code), followed by the Mexican area code *(lada)* and local number. Consult your local telephone directory or operator for more details.

Post and Telegraph
Mexican *correos* (post offices) operate similarly to their counterparts all over the world. Mail services include *lista de correo* (general delivery; address letters "a/c lista de correo"), *servicios filatélicos* (philatelic services), *por avión* (airmail), *giros* (money orders), and Mexpost fast and secure delivery service, like U.S. Express Mail.

Telégrafos (telegraph offices), usually near the post office, send and receive *telegramas* (telegrams) and *giros* (money orders). *Teleco-*

municaciones, the shiny high-tech offices that have replaced the old *Telégrafos* in larger towns, have added telephone and public fax to the available services.

Electricity and Time

Electric power in Mexico is supplied at U.S.-standard 110-volts, 60-cycles. Plugs and sockets are generally two-pronged, nonpolar, like the old pre-1970s U.S. plugs and sockets. Bring adapters for your appliances with two-pronged polar or three-pronged plugs. (Hint: A two-pronged "polar" plug has different prongs, one of which is generally too large to plug into an old-fashioned nonpolar socket.)

Pacific Mexico operates on central time except for the northwest states of Sinaloa and Nayarit, which operate on mountain time.

STAYING HEALTHY

In Pacific Mexico, as everywhere, prevention is the best remedy for illness. For those visitors who confine their travel to the beaten path, a few basic common sense precautions will ensure vacation enjoyment.

Resist the temptation to dive headlong into Mexico. It's no wonder that some people get sick—broiling in the sun, gobbling peppery food, downing beer and margaritas, then discoing half the night—all in their first 24 hours. Instead, they should give their bodies time to adjust.

Travelers often arrive tired and dehydrated from travel and heat. During the first few days, they should drink plenty of bottled water and juice and take siestas.

Traveler's Diarrhea

Traveler's diarrhea (known in Southeast Asia as "Bali belly" and in Mexico as "turista," or "Moctezuma's revenge") persists even among prudent vacationers. You can even suffer turista for a week after simply traveling from California to New York. Doctors say the familiar symptoms of runny bowels, nausea, and sour stomach result from normal local bacterial strains to which newcomers' systems need time to adjust. Unfortunately, the dehydration and fatigue from heat and travel reduce your body's natural defenses and sometimes lead to a persis-

tent cycle of sickness at a time when you least want it.

Time-tested protective measures can help your body either prevent or break this cycle. Many doctors and veteran travelers swear by Pepto-Bismol for soothing sore stomachs and stopping diarrhea. Acidophilus (yogurt bacteria), widely available in the U.S. in tablets, aids digestion. Warm chamomile *manzanilla* tea, used widely in Mexico (and by Peter Rabbit's mother), provides liquid and calms upset stomachs. Temporarily avoid coffee and alcohol, drink plenty of *manzanilla* tea, and eat bananas and rice for a few meals until your tummy can take regular food.

Although powerful antibiotics and antidiarrhea medications such as Lomotil and Imodium are readily available over *farmacia* counters, they may involve serious side effects and should not be taken in the absence of solid medical advice. If in doubt, see a doctor.

Sunburn

For sunburn protection, use a good sunscreen with a sun protection factor (SPF) rated 15 or more, which will reduce burning rays to one-fifteenth or less of direct sunlight. Better still, take a shady siesta-break from the sun during the most hazardous midday hours. If you do get burned, applying your sunburn lotion (or one of

---

MEDICAL TAGS AND AIR EVACUATION

Travelers with special medical problems might consider wearing a medical identification tag. For a reasonable fee, **Medic Alert** (P.O. Box 1009, Turlock, CA 95381, tel. 800-344-3226) provides such tags, as well as an information hotline that will provide doctors with your vital medical background information.

For life-threatening emergencies, **Critical Air Medicine** (Montgomery Field, 4141 Kearny Villa Rd., San Diego, CA 92123, tel. 619-571-0482; from the U.S. toll-free 800-247-8326, from Mexico 24 hours toll-free 001-800-010-0268) provides high-tech jet ambulance service from any Mexican locale to the United States. For a fee averaging about $10,000, they promise to fly you to the right U.S. hospital in a hurry.

the "caine" creams) after the fact usually decreases the pain and speeds healing.

Safe Water and Food

Although municipalities have made great strides in sanitation, food and water are still major potential sources of germs in Pacific Mexico. Do not drink Mexican tap water. Drink bottled water only. Hotels, whose success depends vitally on their customers' health, generally provide purified bottled water *(agua purificada)*. If, for any reason, water is doubtful, add a few drops of household chlorine bleach *(blanqueador)* or iodine *(yodo* from the *farmacia)* per quart. Iodine crystals or tablets are also readily available in the U.S. from pharmacies or outdoor recreation stores. Polarpure and Aquatabs are two popular brands.

Pure bottled water, soft drinks, beer, and pure fruit juices are so widely available that it is easy to avoid tap water, especially in restaurants. Ice and *paletas* (iced juice-on-a-stick) can be risky, especially in small towns.

Washing hands before eating in a restaurant is a time-honored Mexican ritual, which visitors should religiously follow. The humblest Mexican eatery will generally provide a basin and soap for washing hands *(lavar los manos)*. If it doesn't, don't eat there.

Hot, cooked food is generally safe, as are peeled fruits and vegetables. Milk and cheese these days in Mexico are generally processed under sanitary conditions and sold pasteurized (ask: *"¿pasteurizado?"*) and are typically safe. Mexican ice cream used to be both bad tasting and of dubious safety, but national brands available in supermarkets are so much improved that it's no longer necessary to resist ice cream in resort towns.

In recent years, improved availability of clean water and public hygiene awareness has made salads (once shunned by Mexico travelers) generally safe to eat in tourist-frequented cafés and restaurants in Pacific Mexico. However, lettuce and cabbage, particularly in country villages, is more likely to be contaminated than tomatoes, carrots, cucumbers, onions, and green peppers.

In any case, whenever in doubt, you can obtain some protection by dousing your salad in vinegar *(vinagre)* or the juice of sliced limes *(limas)*, the acidity of which kills bacteria.

Medications and Immunizations

A good physician can recommend the proper preventatives for your Pacific Mexico trip. If you are going to stay pretty much in town, your doctor will probably suggest little more than updating your basic typhoid, diphtheria-tetanus, and polio shots.

For camping or trekking in remote tropical areas—below 4,000 feet or 1,200 meters—doctors often recommend a gamma-globulin shot against hepatitis A and a schedule of chloroquine pills against malaria. While in backcountry areas, you should probably use other measures to discourage mosquitoes—and fleas, flies, ticks, no-see-ums, "kissing bugs" (see below)—and other tropical pests from biting you in the first place. Common precautions include sleeping under mosquito netting, burning mosquito coils *(espirales mosquito)*, and rubbing on plenty of pure DEET (n,n dimethyl-meta-toluamide) "jungle juice," mixed 1:1 with rubbing (70% isopropyl) alcohol (100% DEET, although super-effective, dries and irritates skin).

Chagas' Disease, Scorpions, and Snakes

Chagas' disease, spread by the "kissing" (or, more appropriately, "assassin") bug, is a potential but infrequent hazard in the rural Mexican tropics. Known locally as a *vinchuca*, the triangular-headed three-quarter inch (two centimeter) brown insect, identifiable by its yellow-striped abdomen, often drops upon its sleeping victims from the thatched ceiling of a rural house at night. It bites the victim, while frequently depositing its fecal matter. This may be followed by swelling, fever, and weakness, sometimes leading to heart failure if left untreated. Application of drugs at an early stage, however, can clear the patient of the trypanosome parasites, which infect victims' bloodstreams and vital organs. See a doctor immediately if you believe you're infected.

Also while camping or staying in a *palapa* or other rustic accommodation, watch for scorpions, especially in your shoes (whose contents you should dump out every morning.) Scorpion stings and snakebites are rarely fatal to an adult but are potentially very serious to a child. Get the victim to a doctor calmly but quickly. For precautions against snakes and other venomous reptiles, see **Reptiles and Amphibians** in the Introduction chapter.

Injuries from Sea Creatures

While snorkeling or surfing, you may suffer a coral scratch or jellyfish sting. Experts advise you should wash the afflicted area with ocean (not fresh) water and pour alcohol (rubbing alcohol or a liquor, such as mescal, tequila, or *aguardiente*), if available, over the wound, then apply hydrocortisone cream from your first-aid kit or the *farmacia*.

Injuries from sea urchin spines and sting-ray barbs are both painful and sometimes serious. Physicians recommend similar first aid for both: first remove the spines or barbs by hand or with tweezers, then soak the injury in hot-as-possible fresh water to weaken the toxins and provide relief. Another method is to rinse the area with an antibacterial solution—either rubbing alcohol, vinegar, wine, or ammonia diluted with water. If none are available, the same effect may be achieved by rinsing with urine, either your own or someone else's in your party. Get medical help immediately.

Poisonous sea snakes, although rare and shy, do inhabit Pacific Mexico waters. Much more common, especially around submerged rocks, is the moray eel. Don't stick your fingers or toes in any concealed cracks.

First-Aid Kit

In the tropics, ordinary cuts and insect bites are much more prone to infection and should receive immediate first aid. A first-aid kit (with a minimum of: aspirin; rubbing alcohol; hydrogen peroxide; Potable Aqua brand tablets, iodine, or bleach for water purification; swabs; Band-Aids; gauze; adhesive tape; an Ace bandage; chamomile; Pepto-Bismol; acidophilus tablets; antibiotic ointment; hydrocortisone cream; mosquito repellent; a knife; and tweezers) is a good precaution for any traveler and a top priority for campers.

Medical Care

For medical advice and treatment, let your hotel (or if you're camping, the closest *farmacia*) refer you to a good doctor, clinic, or hospital. Mexican doctors, especially in medium-size and small towns, practice like private doctors in the U.S. and Canada once did before health insurance, liability, and group practice. They will come to you if you request it; they often keep their doors open even after regular hours, and charge reasonable fees.

You will receive generally good treatment at one of the many local hospitals in Pacific Mexico's tourist centers. See individual destination chapters for details. If you must have an English-speaking, American-trained doctor, the **International Association for Medical Assistance to Travelers (IAMAT)** publishes an updated booklet of qualified member physicians, many of whom practice in Pacific Mexico centers. IAMAT also distributes a very detailed "How To Protect Yourself Against Malaria" guide, together with a worldwide malaria risk chart. Contact IAMAT, at 417 Center Street, Lewiston, NY 14092, tel. (716) 754-4883, or in Canada at 40 Regal Road, Guelph, ON N1K 1B5, tel. (519) 836-0102.

For more useful information on health and safety in Mexico, consult Dr. William Forgey's *Traveler's Medical Alert Series: Mexico, A Guide to Health and Safety* (Merrillville, Indiana: ICS Books), or Dirk Schroeder's *Staying Healthy in Asia, Africa, and Latin America* (Chico, California: Moon Publications, Inc., 1999).

CONDUCT AND CUSTOMS

Safe Conduct

Mexico is an old-fashioned country where people value traditional ideals of honesty, fidelity, and piety. Crime rates are low; visitors are often safer in Mexico than in their home cities.

Even though four generations have elapsed since Pancho Villa raided the U.S. border, the image of a Mexico bristling with *bandidos* persists. And similarly for Mexicans: Despite the century and a half since the *yanquis* invaded Mexico City and took half their country, the communal Mexican psyche still views *gringos* (and, by association all white foreigners) with revulsion, jealousy, and wonder.

Fortunately, the Mexican love-hate affair with foreigners does not necessarily apply to individual visitors. Your friendly *"buenos dias"* or *"por favor,"* when appropriate, is always appreciated, whether in the market, the gas station, or the hotel. The shy smile you will most likely receive in return will be your small, but not insignificant, reward.

Women

Your own behavior, despite low crime statistics, largely determines your safety in Mexico. For women traveling solo, it is important to realize the double sexual standard is alive and well in Mexico. Dress and behave modestly and you will most likely avoid embarrassment. Whenever possible, stay in the company of friends or acquaintances; find companions for beach, sightseeing, and shopping excursions. Ignore strange men's solicitations and overtures. A Mexican man on the prowl will invent the sappiest romantic overtures to snare a *gringa*. He will often interpret anything except silence or a firm "no" as a "maybe," and a "maybe" as a "yes."

Men

For male visitors, on the other hand, alcohol often leads to trouble. Avoid bars and cantinas, and if (given Mexico's excellent beers) you can't abstain completely, at least maintain soft-spoken self-control in the face of challenges from macho drunks.

The Law and Police

While Mexican authorities are tolerant of alcohol, they are decidedly intolerant of other substances

MACHISMO

I once met an Acapulco man who wore five gold wristwatches and became angry when I quietly refused his repeated invitations to get drunk with him. Another time, on the beach near San Blas, two drunk campesinos nearly attacked me because I was helping my girlfriend cook a picnic dinner. Outside Taxco I once spent an endless hour in the seat behind a bus driver who insisted on speeding down the middle of the two-laned highway, honking aside oncoming automobiles.

Despite their wide differences (the first was a rich criollo, the campesinos were *indígenas*, and the bus driver, mestizo), the common affliction shared by all four men was machismo, a disease that seems to possess many Mexican men. Machismo is a sometimes reckless obsession to prove one's masculinity, to show how macho you are. Men of many nationalities share the instinct to prove themselves. Japan's *bushido* samarai code is one example. Mexican men, however, often seem to try the hardest.

When confronted by a Mexican braggart, male visitors should remain careful and controlled. If your opponent is yelling, stay cool, speak softly, and withdraw as soon as possible. On the highway, be courteous and unprovocative; don't use your car to spar with a macho driver. Drinking often leads to problems. It's best to stay out of bars or cantinas unless you're prepared to deal with the macho conse-

quences. Polite refusal of a drink may be taken as a challenge. If you visit a bar with Mexican friends or acquaintances, you may be heading for a no-win choice of a drunken all-night *borrachera* (binge) or an insult to the honor of your friends by refusing.

For women, machismo requires even more cautious behavior. In Mexico, women's liberation is long in coming. Few women hold positions of power in business or politics. One woman, Rosa Luz Alegría, did attain the rank of minister of tourism during the former Portillo administration; she was the president's mistress.

Machismo requires that female visitors obey the rules or suffer the consequences. Keep a low profile; wear bathing suits and brief shorts only at the beach. Follow the example of your Mexican sisters: make a habit of going out, especially at night, in the company of friends or acquaintances. Mexican men believe an unaccompanied woman wants to be picked up. Ignore such offers; any response, even refusal, might be taken as a "maybe." If, on the other hand, there is a Mexican man whom you'd genuinely like to meet, the traditional way is an arranged introduction through family or friends.

Mexican families, as a source of protection and friendship, should not be overlooked—especially on the beach or in the park, where, among the gaggle of kids, grandparents, aunts, and cousins, there's room for one more.

such as marijuana, psychedelics, cocaine, and heroin. Getting caught with such drugs in Mexico usually leads to swift and severe results.

Equally swift is the punishment for nude sunbathing, which is both illegal in public and offensive to Mexicans. Confine your nudist colony to very private locations.

Traffic police in Pacific Mexico's resorts often watch foreign cars with eagle eyes. Officers sometimes seem to inhabit busy intersections and one-way streets, waiting for confused tourists to make a wrong move. If they whistle you over, stop immediately or you really will get into hot water. If guilty, say *"lo siento"* (I'm sorry), and be cooperative. Although he probably won't mention it, the officer is usually hoping that you'll cough up a $20 *mordida* (bribe) for the privilege of driving away.

Don't do it. Although he may hint at confiscating your car, calmly ask for an official *boleto* (written traffic ticket, if you're guilty) in exchange for your driver's license (have a copy), which the officer will probably keep if he writes a ticket. If no money appears after a few minutes, the officer will most likely give you back your driver's license rather than go to the trouble of writing the ticket. If not, the worst that will usually happen is you will have to go to the Presidencia Municipal (City Hall) the next morning and pay the $20 to a clerk in exchange for your driver's license.

Pedestrian and Driving Hazards

Although Pacific Mexico's potholed pavements and sidewalks won't land you in jail, they might send you to the hospital if you don't watch your step, especially at night. "Pedestrian beware" is doubly good advice on Mexican streets, where it is rumored that some drivers speed up rather than slow down when they spot a tourist stepping off the curb. **Falling coconuts,** especially frequent on windy days, are a serious hazard to unwary campers and beachgoers.

Cars can get you both in and out of trouble in Mexico. Driving Mexican roads, where slow trucks and carts block lanes, campesinos stroll the shoulders, and horses, burros, and cattle wander at will is more hazardous than back home, and doubly so at night.

Socially Responsible Travel

Latter-day jet travel has brought droves of vacationing tourists to third world countries largely unprepared for the consequences. As the visitors' numbers swell, power grids black out, sewers overflow, and roads crack under the strain of accommodating more and larger hotels, restaurants, cars, buses, and airports.

Worse yet, armies of vacationers drive up local prices and local people begin to lose their long-held values and traditions. While visions of tourists as sources of fast money replace habits of hospitality, television wipes out folk entertainments, Coke and Pepsi replace fruit drinks, and prostitution and drugs flourish.

Some travelers are saying enough is enough, and are forming organizations to encourage visitors to travel with increased sensitivity to native people and customs. They have developed traveler's codes of ethics and guidelines that encourage visitors to stay at local-style accommodations, use local transportation, and seek alternative vacations and tours, such as language and cultural programs and people-to-people work projects.

SPECIALTY TRAVEL

Bringing the Kids

Children are treasured like gifts from heaven in Mexico. Traveling with your kids (or your neighbors' if you don't have any to bring) will ensure your welcome most everywhere. On the beach make sure they are protected from the sun. Children often adjust slowly to Mexican food; fortunately, the familiar choices—eggs, cheese, *hamburguesas,* milk, oatmeal *(avena),* corn flakes, bananas, cakes, and cookies are readily available.

A sick child is no fun for anyone. Luckily, clinics and good doctors are available even in small towns. When in need, ask a storekeeper or a pharmacist, *"¿Dónde hay doctor, por favor?"* ("DOHN-day eye doc-TOHR por fah-VOHR"). In most cases within five minutes you will be in the waiting room of the local physician or hospital.

Your children will have more fun if they are given a little previous knowledge of Mexico and a stake in the trip. For example, help them select some library picture books and magazines, so they'll know where they're going and what to expect; or give them responsibility for packing and carrying their own small travel bag.

Be sure to mention your children's ages when making air reservations; child discounts of one-half or more are often available. Also, if you can arrange to go on an uncrowded flight, you and your kids might be able to stretch out and rest on the empty seats. For many more details of travel with children, check out the excellent *Adventuring With Children,* by Nan Jeffries (see the Booklist).

Travel for People with Disabilities

Mexican airlines and hotels are becoming increasingly aware of the needs of handicapped travelers. Open, street-level lobbies and large, wheelchair-accessible elevators and rooms are available in many Pacific Mexico resort hotels.

United States law forbids travel discrimination against otherwise qualified handicapped persons. As long as your handicap is stable and not liable to deteriorate during passage, you can expect to be treated as any passenger with special needs.

Make reservations far ahead of departure and ask your agent to inform your airline of what you will need, such as boarding wheelchair, or in-flight oxygen. Be early at the gate in order to take advantage of the pre-boarding call.

For many helpful details that might smooth your trip, get a copy of *Traveling Like Everyone Else: A Practical Guide for Disabled Travelers,* by Jaqueline Freeman and Susan Gerstein. It's available at bookstores or from the printer (Lambda Publishing, Inc., 3709 13th Ave., Brooklyn, NY 11218, tel. 718-972-5449). Another useful publication is the IATA (International Air Travel Association) booklet, *Incapacitated Passengers Air Travel Guide,* obtainable from IATA-member airlines and travel agents.

Certain organizations both encourage and provide information about handicapped travel. One with many Mexican connections is **Mobility International USA,** P.O. Box 10767, Eugene, OR 97440, tel. (541) 343-1284 voice/TDD, fax 343-6812. A $35 membership gets you the quarterly newsletter and referrals for international exchanges and homestays. Similarly, **Partners of the Americas,** with chapters in 45 states, works to improve handicapped understanding and facilities in Mexico and Latin America. They maintain lists of local organizations and individuals whom handicapped travelers may contact at their destinations. For more information, contact them at 1424 K St. NW, Suite 700, Washington, DC 20005, tel. (800) 322-7844 or (202) 628-3300.

Travel for Senior Citizens

Age, according to Mark Twain, is a question of mind over matter: if you don't mind, it doesn't matter. Mexico is a country where whole extended families, from babies to great-grandparents, still live together. Elderly travelers will generally benefit from the resulting respect and understanding that Mexicans accord to older people. Besides these encouragements, consider the large numbers of retirees already in Pacific Mexico havens, such as Mazatlán, Puerto Vallarta, Guadalajara, Lake Chapala, Manzanillo, Acapulco, and Oaxaca.

Certain organizations, furthermore, support senior travel. Leading the field is **Elderhostel,** 75 Federal St., 3rd Floor, Boston, MA 02110-1941, tel. (877) 426-8056, which sponsors special study, homestay, and people-to-people travel programs in Mexico. For more details, ask for the international catalog.

A very good newsletter, targeted toward lovers of Mexico, is *Adventures in Mexico,* published six times yearly and filled with pithy hotel, restaurant, touring, and real estate information for independent travelers and retirees seeking the "real" Mexico. For information, address Adventures in Mexico, P.O. Box 31-70, Guadalajara, Jalisco 45050, Mexico. Back issues are $2, one-year subscription, $16, Canadian $19.

Several other books and newsletters publicize senior travel opportunities. *Mature Traveler* is a lively, professional-quality newsletter featuring money-saving tips, discounts, and tours for over-50 active senior and handicapped travelers. Individual copies are $5, a one-year subscription, $29.95. Editor Adele Mallot has compiled years of past newsletters and experience into *Book of Deals,* a 325-page travel tip and opportunity book (included in a *Mature Traveler* subscription or singly for $7.95, plus postage and handling). Order through GEM Publishing Group, 250 E. Riverview Circle, P.O. Box 50400, Reno, NV 89513-0400, tel. (800) 460-6676. Another good buy is the *Complete Guide to Discounts for Travellers 50 And Beyond,* which lists a plethora of hotel, travel club, cruise, air, credit card, single, and off-season discounts. Order

PACKING CHECKLIST

NECESSARY ITEMS

- ❏ camera, film (expensive in Mexico)
- ❏ clothes, hat
- ❏ comb
- ❏ guidebook, reading books
- ❏ inexpensive watch, clock
- ❏ keys, tickets
- ❏ mosquito repellent
- ❏ passport
- ❏ prescription eyeglasses
- ❏ prescription medicines and drugs
- ❏ purse, waist-belt carrying pouch
- ❏ sunglasses
- ❏ sunscreen
- ❏ swimsuit
- ❏ toothbrush, toothpaste
- ❏ tourist card, visa
- ❏ traveler's checks, money
- ❏ windbreaker

USEFUL ITEMS

- ❏ address book
- ❏ birth control
- ❏ checkbook, credit cards
- ❏ contact lenses
- ❏ dental floss
- ❏ earplugs
- ❏ first-aid kit
- ❏ flashlight, batteries
- ❏ immersion heater
- ❏ lightweight binoculars
- ❏ portable radio/cassette player
- ❏ razor
- ❏ travel booklight

- ❏ vaccination certificate

NECESSARY ITEMS FOR CAMPERS

- ❏ collapsible gallon plastic bottle
- ❏ dish soap
- ❏ first-aid kit
- ❏ hammock (buy in Mexico)
- ❏ insect repellent
- ❏ lightweight hiking shoes
- ❏ lightweight tent
- ❏ matches in waterproof case
- ❏ nylon cord
- ❏ plastic bottle, quart
- ❏ pot scrubber/sponge
- ❏ sheet or light blanket
- ❏ Sierra Club cup, fork and spoon
- ❏ single-burner stove with fuel
- ❏ Swiss army knife
- ❏ tarp
- ❏ toilet paper
- ❏ towel, soap
- ❏ two nesting cooking pots
- ❏ water-purifying tablets or iodine

USEFUL ITEMS FOR CAMPERS

- ❏ compass
- ❏ dishcloths
- ❏ hot pad
- ❏ instant coffee, tea, sugar, powdered milk
- ❏ moleskin (Dr. Scholl's)
- ❏ plastic plate
- ❏ poncho
- ❏ short candles
- ❏ whistle

---

for $5, plus postage and handling, from Vacation Publications, Inc., 1502 Augusta, Suite 415, Houston, TX 77057, tel. (713) 974-6903.

WHAT TO TAKE

"Men wear pants, ladies be beautiful" was once the dress code of one of Pacific Mexico's region's classiest hotels. Men in casual Pacific Mexico can get by easily without a jacket, women with simple skirts and blouses.

Loose-fitting, hand-washable, easy-to-dry clothes make for trouble-free tropical vacationing. Synthetic, or cotton-synthetic blend shirts, blouses, pants, socks, and underwear will fit the bill everywhere in the coastal resorts. For breezy nights, bring a lightweight windbreaker. If you're going to the highlands (Guadalajara, Pátzcuaro, Taxco, Oaxaca), add a medium-weight jacket.

In all cases, leave showy, expensive clothes and jewelry at home. Stow items you cannot lose in your hotel safe or carry them with you in a sturdy zipped purse or waist pouch on your front side.

Packing

What you pack depends on how mobile you want to be. If you're staying the whole time at a self-contained resort you can take the two suitcases and one carry-on airlines allow. If, on the other hand, you're going to be moving around a lot, best condense everything down to one easily carryable bag that doubles as luggage and a soft backpack. Experienced travelers routinely accomplish this by packing prudently and tightly, choosing items that will do double or triple duty (such as a Swiss army knife with scissors).

Campers will have to be super-careful to accomplish this. Fortunately, camping along the tropical coast requires no sleeping bag. Simply use a hammock (buy in Mexico), or if sleeping on the ground, a sleeping pad and a sheet for cover. In the winter, at most, you may have to buy a light blanket. A compact tent you and your partner can share is a must against bugs, as is mosquito repellent. Additionally, a first-aid kit is absolutely necessary.

Michoacán ceramic
mother and child

MAZATLÁN

The Pearl of the Pacific

Mazatlán (pop. 500,000) spreads for 15 sun-splashed miles along a thumb of land that extends southward into the Pacific just below the Tropic of Cancer. Mazatlán thus marks the beginning of the Mexican tropics: a palmy land of perpetual summer and a refuge from winter cold for growing numbers of international vacationers.

Mazatlán's beauty is renowned. Its coast sprinkled with beckoning islands and miles of golden beaches and blue lagoons, it aptly deserves its title as "Pearl of the Pacific."

Despite its popularity as a tourist destination, Mazatlán owes its existence to local industry. As well as being a leading manufacturing center in the state of Sinaloa, Mazatlán is home port for a huge commercial and sportfishing fleet, whose annual catch of shrimp, tuna, and swordfish amounts to thousands of tons.

Mazatlán, consequently, lives independently of tourism. The vacationers come and frolic on the beach beside their "Golden Zone" hotels, while in the old town at the tip of the peninsula, life goes on in the old-Mexico style: in the markets, the churches, and the shady plazas scattered throughout the traditional neighborhoods.

HISTORY

Pre-Columbian

For Mexico, Mazatlán is not an old city. Most of its public buildings have stood for less than a hundred years. Evidence of local human settlement dates back before recorded history, however. Scientists reckon petroglyphs found on offshore islands may be as much as 10,000 years old.

During the 1930s archaeologists began uncovering exquisite polychrome pottery, with elaborate black and red designs, indicative of a high culture. Unlike their renowned Tarascan, Aztec, and Toltec highland neighbors, those ancient potters, known as the Totorames, built no pyramids and left no inscriptions. They had been gone a dozen generations before conquistador Nuño de Guzmán burned his way through Sinaloa in 1531.

Colonial

The rapacious Guzmán may have been responsible for the name "Mazatlán," which, curiously, is a name of Nahuatl (Aztec language), rather than local origin. Since Aztecs rarely ventured anywhere near present-day Mazatlán, the name Mazatlán ("Place of the Deer") presents an intriguing mystery. Historians speculate that a Nahuatl-speaking interpreter of Guzmán may have translated the name from the local language.

Mazatlán was first mentioned in 1602 as the name of a small village, San Juan Bautista de Mazatlán (now called Villa Union), 30 miles south of present-day Mazatlán, which was not yet colonized.

English and French pirates, however, soon discovered Mazatlán's benefits. They occasionally used its hill-screened harbor as a lair from which to pounce upon the rich galleons that plied the coast. The colonial government replied by establishing a small *presidio* on the harbor and watchtowers atop the *cerros.* Although the pirates were gone by 1800, legends persist of troves of stolen silver and gold buried in hidden caves and under windswept sands, ripe for chance discovery along the Mazatlán coast.

Independence

Lifting of foreign trade restrictions in 1820 and independence in 1821 seemed to bode well for the port of Mazatlán. However, cholera, yellow fever, and plague epidemics and repeated foreign occupations (the U.S. Navy in 1847, the French in 1864, and the British in 1871) slowed the growth of Mazatlán during the 19th century. It nevertheless served as the capital of Sinaloa from 1859 to 1873, with a population of several thousand.

The "Order and Progress" of dictator/president Porfirio Díaz (1876-1910) gave Mazatlán citizens a much-needed spell of prosperity. The railroad arrived, the port and lighthouse were modernized, and the cathedral was finished. Education, journalism, and the arts blossomed. The Teatro Rubio, completed in the early 1890s, was the grandest opera house between Baja California and Tepic.

The opera company of the renowned diva, Angela Peralta, the "Mexican Nightingale," arrived and gave a number of enthusiastically received recitals in Mazatlán in August 1883. Tragically, Peralta and most of her company fell victim to a disastrous yellow fever epidemic, which claimed more than 2,500 Mazatlán lives.

The revolution of 1910-17 literally rained destruction on Mazatlán. In 1914, the city gained the dubious distinction of being the second city in the world to suffer aerial bombardment. (Tripoli, Libya, was the first.) General (later president) Venustiano Carranza, intent upon taking the city, ordered a biplane to bomb the ammunition magazine atop Nevería Hill, adjacent to downtown Mazatlán. But the pilot missed the target and dropped the crude leather-wrapped package of dynamite and nails onto the city streets instead. Two citizens were killed and several wounded.

Modern Mazatlán

After order was restored in the 1920s, Mazatlán soared to a decade of prosperity, followed by the deflation and depression of the 1930s. Recovery after WW II led to port improvements and new highways, setting the stage for the tourist "discovery" of Mazatlán during the 1960s and '70s. The city limits expanded to include the strand of white sand (Playa Norte) north of the original old port town. High-rise hotels sprouted in a new "Golden Zone" tourist area, which, coupled with Mazatlán's traditional fishing industry, provided thousands of new jobs for an increasingly affluent population, which, by the late '90s, was approaching three-quarters of a million.

SIGHTS

Getting Oriented

Mazatlán owes its life to the sea. The city's main artery, which changes its name five times as it winds northward, never strays far from the shore. From beneath the rugged perch of El Faro ("Lighthouse") at the tip of the Mazatlán peninsula, the *malecón* (seawall) boulevard curves past the venerable hotels and sidewalk cafés of the Olas Altas ("High Waves") neighborhood. From there it snakes along a succession of rocky points and sandy beaches, continuing through the glitzy lineup of Zona Dorada ("Golden Zone") beach hotels and restaurants. Next the boulevard loops inland for a spell, curving around a marina and back to the beach. The hotels thin out as it continues past grassy dunes and venerable groves to a sheltered cove beneath Punta Cerritos hill, 15 miles from where it started.

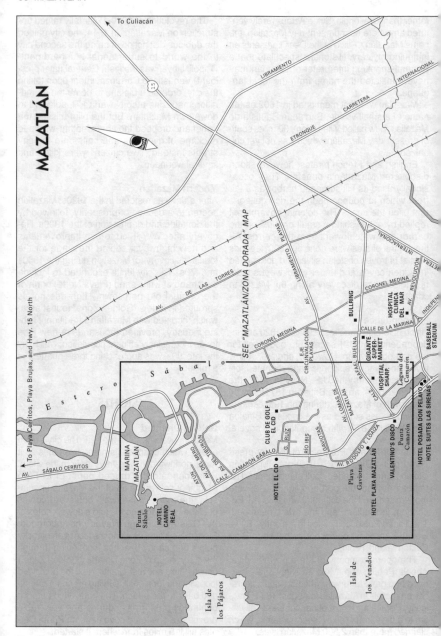

MAZATLÁN

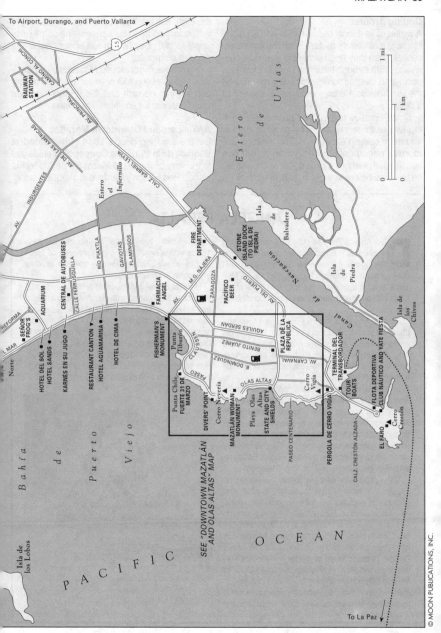

To Airport, Durango, and Puerto Vallarta

15

RAILWAY STATION

CAMINO AL CONCH

AV. PRINCIPAL

Estero de Urias

INSURGENTES

AV.

Estero el Infiernillo

CALZ. GABRIEL LEYVA

REFORMA

AQUARIUM

SEÑOR FROG'S

CENTRAL DE AUTOBUSES

CALLE FERRUSQUILLA

RIO PIAXTLA

GAVIOTAS

FLAMINGOS

M.G. NAJERA

FIRE DEPARTMENT

STONE ISLAND DOCK (TO ISLA DE PIEDRA)

Isla de Balvadere

Isla de Piedra

EL MAR Norte

HOTEL DEL SOL

HOTEL SANDS

KARNES EN SU JUGO

RESTAURANT CANTON

HOTEL AGUAMARINA

HOTEL DE CIMA

FARMACIA ANGEL

I. ZARAGOZA

PACIFICO BEER

AV. DEL PUERTO

Navegación

Canal de

Isla de los Chivos

FISHERMAN'S MONUMENT

Punta Tiburón

CLAUSSEN

AQUILES SERDAN

BENITO JUAREZ

PLAZA DE LA REPUBLICA

TERMINAL DEL TRANSBORDADOR

TOUR BOATS

B. DOMINGUEZ

PASEO

AV. CARNAVAL

Cerro Vigía

FLOTA DEPORTIVA CLUB NAUTICO AND YATE FIESTA

Bahía de Puerto Viejo

Punta Chile

FUERTE 21 DE MARZO

DIVERS' POINT

Cerro Nevería

MAZATLAN WOMAN MONUMENT

OLAS ALTAS

Playa Olas Altas

STATE AND CITY SHIELDS

PASEO CENTENARIO

PERGOLA DE CERRO VIGIA

EL FARO

Cerro Crestón

CALZ. CRESTÓN ALZADA

Isla de Lobos

SEE "DOWNTOWN MAZATLÁN AND OLAS ALTAS" MAP

PACIFIC OCEAN

To La Paz

1 mi

1 km

0

0

Getting Around

A welter of little local buses run to and fro along identical main-artery routes. From the downtown central plaza they head along the *malecón,* continuing north through the Zona Dorada to various north-end destinations, which are marked on the windshields. Fares should run less than half a dollar.

Small, open-air taxis, called **pulmonías,** seating two or three passengers, provide quicker and more convenient service. The average *pulmonía* ("pneumonia," directly translated) ride should total no more than a dollar or two. Agree on the price before you get in, and if you think it's too high, hail another *pulmonía* and your driver will usually come to his senses. The same rules apply to taxi rides, which run about double the price of *pulmonías.*

You can also get around Mazatlán by joining a tour. Hotel travel desks or travel agencies usually can set you up with one. Boat tours offer yet more options; for specifics, see below.

A Walk around Downtown Mazatlán

Let the towering double spire of the **Catedral Basílica de la Purísima Concepción** guide you to the very center of old Mazatlán. Begun by the Bishop Pedro Loza y Pardave in 1856, the cathe-

ANGELA PERALTA

Diva Angela Peralta (1845-83) was thrilling audiences in Europe's great opera houses by the age of 16, when a Spanish journalist dubbed her the "Mexican Nightingale." On 13 May 1863, she brought down the house at La Scala in Milan with an angelic performance of *Lucia de Lammermoor.*

During Angela's second European tour she charmed maestro Guiseppi Verdi into bringing his entire company across the Atlantic so she could sing *Aida* in Mexico City. With Verdi conducting, Angela inaugurated the 1873 Mexico City season on a pinnacle of fame.

Legends abound of the fiercely nationalistic Peralta. She once got the last word in a tête-à-tête with Europe's most famous Italian soprano of the time. In an unforgettable joint recital, Angela courteously extended first bows to the haughty Italian diva, who remarked of her own performance, "That is the way we sing in Italy." Not to be outdone, Angela Peralta rejoined: "Mine was the way we sing in heaven."

Not content with mere performance, Angela Peralta went on to excel as a composer, librettist, and impresario, organizing her own opera companies. Her success and outspoken ways earned her enemies in high places, however. In 1873, Mexico City bluebloods were shocked to find out Angela was having an affair with her lawyer, Julian Montiel y Duarte. (It didn't seem to matter that Peralta was widowed and Montiel single at the time.) Much of Mexico City's high society boycotted her performances; when that didn't work, they sent hecklers to harass her. Liberals, however, defended her, and

Peralta finally regained her audience in the early 1880s with a heartrending performance of *Linda de Chamounix.* She kept her vow, however, to never sing again in Mexico City.

Her star-crossed life came to an early end on 30 August 1883. Touring with her company in western Mexico, a Mazatlán yellow fever epidemic claimed her life and the lives of 76 of her 80-member company. On her deathbed, she married Montiel y Duarte, the only man she ever loved. Later, her remains were removed to Mexico City, where they now lie enshrined at the Rotunda de Hombres Ilustres ("Rotunda of Illustrious Men").

ERIC SCHNITTGER

dral was built on the filled lagoon site of an original Indian temple. Mazatlán's turbulent history delayed its completion until 1899 and final elevation in 1937 to the status of a basilica.

Inside, the image of the city's patron saint, the Virgen de la Purísima Concepción ("Virgin of the Immaculate Conception") stands over the gilded, baroque main altar, while overhead soar rounded Renaissance domes and pious, pointed gothic arches. On the left, as you exit, pause and notice the shrine to the popular Virgin of Guadalupe. The cathedral is open daily 6 a.m.-1 p.m. and 4-8 p.m.

In front of the cathedral, the verdant tropical foliage of the central **Plaza de la Republica** encloses the traditional wrought-iron Porfirian bandstand. To the right is the **Palacio Municipal** ("City Hall"), where on the eve before Independence Day, 16 September, the *presidente municipal* (county mayor) shouts from the balcony the traditional Grito de Dolores above a patriotic and tipsy crowd.

After enjoying the sights and aromas of the colorful **Mercado Central** ("Central Market") two blocks behind the cathedral, reverse your path and head down Juárez. Turn right at Constitución, one block to **Plazuela Machado,** Mazatlán's original central plaza. It was named in honor of Juan Nepomuceno Machado, a founding father of Filipino descent who donated the land. The venerable Porfirian buildings and monuments clustered along the surrounding streets include the **Teatro Angela Peralta,** completed around 1890 and later dedicated to Angela Peralta. At the west end of the Plazuela, along Calle Heriberto Frías, walk beneath the **Portales de Cannobio,** the arcade of the old estate house of apple grower Luis Cannobio, a 19th-century Italian resident.

For a shady break, take a seat at one of the small **sidewalk cafés** on the plaza's north side, or go inside and sample the menu at restaurant **Lola and Pedro** at the plaza's northeast corner, Carnaval and Constitución.

Olas Altas

Continue west a few blocks toward the ocean from Plazuela Machado along Calle Sixto Osuna and step into the small **Museo Arqueologia,** Sixto de Osuna 76, tel. (69) 853-502, to peruse its well-organized exhibits outlining Sinaloan pre-

Children play beneath the monument to the Mazatlán Woman.

history and culture. The displays include case after case of petroglyphs, human and animal figurines, and the distinctive red- and black-glazed ancient polychrome pottery of Sinaloa. Open Tues.-Sun. 10 a.m.-1 p.m. and 4-7 p.m.

Across the street, take a look inside the lovingly restored **Casa de la Cultura.** Its current offerings might include an art exhibit, a literary reading, or a musical or dramatic performance.

Continue west a couple of blocks to the *malecón* and **Av. Olas Altas.** This café-lined stretch of boulevard and adjacent beach was at one time the tourist zone of Mazatlán. It extends several shorefront blocks from the **Monumento al Venado** ("Monument to the Deer") north end, past Hotel Siesta to the **Escudos de Sinaloa y Mazatlán** ("City and State Shields of Sinaloa and Mazatlán") to the south in front of the distinguished 1889 school building at the foot of Cerro Vigía, the steep hill.

Here, you might pause a while and soak up the flavor of old Mazatlán. Take a seat at one of

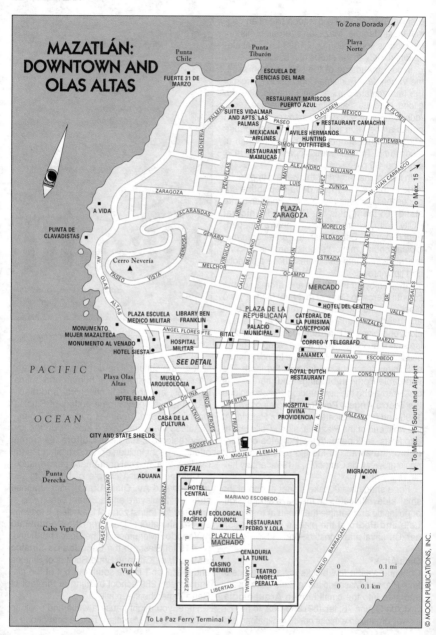

MAZATLÁN:
DOWNTOWN AND
OLAS ALTAS

the sidewalk cafés; later look around the lobby of the old Hotel Belmar. Notice the wall map a few steps inside the entrance door, dated 1948, when the entire state of Sinaloa had a population less than half of present-day Mazatlán, and the whole country had a population equal to Mexico City's today.

Cerro Vigía
Now, unless, you're in the mood for a hike, bargain for a *pulmonía* to take you up Paseo Centenario, the southern extension of Av. Olas Altas, to the Pergola de Cerro Vigía viewpoint at the top of the hill. There, next to the old cannon (stamped by its proud London maker, "Vavaseur no. 830, 1875"), you get the sweep of the whole city.

Cerro Vigía is the spot where, according to tradition, the colonial soldiers of the old Mazatlán presidio maintained their 200-year vigil, scanning the horizon for pirates. Step across the little hilltop plaza and down to the **Cafe El Mirador** and enjoy lunch, a drink, and the view; open daily noon-9 p.m.

Cerro Creston and El Faro
To the south rises Mazatlán's tallest hill, Cerro Creston, topped by the El Faro lighthouse, whose 515-foot (157-meter) elevation qualifies it as the world's highest natural lighthouse. Along the jetty/landfill that connects Cerro Creston to the mainland lie the docks and anchored boats of the several *flotas deportivas* (sport fleets). Every morning they take loads of anglers out in search of big fighting marlin and sailfish.

Boat Tours
Harbor tour boats also depart from the same docks. *Yate Fiesta* leaves regularly at 11 a.m. for a harbor and island cruise, passing the inner harbor shrimp fleet, circling past the lighthouse, sea lion island (winter only) and Mazatlán's offshore islands, Islas Chivos, Pájaros, and Venados. Tickets cost about $12 per person for the three-hour trip. Also, trimaran *Kolonahe* offers a pair of tours, a 9:30 a.m. island tour that includes part of the harbor tour as described above, as well as a landing at Isla Venados for swimming, hiking, lunch, and sunning on the beach, returning in early afternoon. Later in the afternoon, the *Kolonahe* heads seaward again for an open-bar sunset cruise (tariff, about $35). For more infor-

mation and reservations, contact a travel agent or call (69) 852-237 or 852-238 for the *Fiesta,* and (69) 163-468 for the *Kolonahe.*

Across the deep-water harbor entrance looms the bulk of **Isla de Piedra** ("Stone Island"), actually a peninsula. Its southern beach stretches to the horizon in a narrowing white thread, beneath the dark green plumes of Mexico's third-largest coconut grove. If you've a hankering to explore, ride the tour boat **Renegado,** which heads out mornings, first passing the world's biggest shrimp fleet, continuing through the harbor's far mangrove reaches to the Stone Island landing, where, after lunch at a *palapa* restaurant, you can explore the beach and coconut grove by foot, play in the waves, and laze in the sun. Hotel pickup is included in the approximately $25 price. For information and reservations, call a travel agent or contact the *Renegado* directly at (69) 142-477.

For more adventurous tours and activities, such as biking, snorkeling, scuba diving, hiking and wildlife viewing, see **Sports and Recreation** later in this chapter.

Cerro Nevería
The rounded profile of Cerro Nevería ("Icehouse Hill") rises above the patchwork of city streets. Its unique label originated during the mid-1800s, when the tunnels that pock the hill served for storage of ice imported from San Francisco. Now the hilltop holds a number of radio and microwave beacons.

Punta Camarón and Offshore Islands
The curving white ribbon of sand north of the downtown area traces the *malecón* northward to Punta Camarón and the Golden Zone, marked by the cluster of shoreline high-rise hotels. Offshore from Punta Camarón, Mazatlán's three islands—**Chivos** ("Rams") and **Venados** ("Deer"), nearest, and **Pájaros** ("Birds")—on the horizon—seem to float offshore like a trio of sleeping whales.

Along Paseo Claussen
Back downhill on Av. Olas Altas, pass the Statue of the Deer in the middle of the intersection where the *malecón* becomes Paseo Claussen. Named for the rich German immigrant who financed the blasting of the scenic drive, Paseo Claussen continues around the wave-tossed

foot of Cerro Nevería. First, you will pass a striking bronze sculpture, the **Monumento Mujer Mazalteca,** nearly erotic in its intensity. Nearby, a yawning cave (plugged by heavy bars), pierces the hill. Known by local people as the **Caverna del Diablo** ("Devil's Cave"), it served as an escape route for soldiers guarding the ammunition stored in caves farther up the hill.

Not far ahead, a four-story platform at the **Punta de Clavadistas** (Divers' Point) towers above the wave-swept tidepools. The divers—professionals who take their work very seriously, especially at low tide, when their dives must coincide with the arrival of a big swell—perform a number of times daily, more frequently on Sundays and holidays.

Moving north, you'll pass the new **Continuity of Life** sculpture, popular with crowds of local folks who arrive evenings to watch its colored fountains. Continue another block to the 1892 fort turned maritime office, **Fuerte 31 de Marzo,** named in honor of the heroic stand of the local garrison, which repelled a French invasion on 31 March 1864.

BEACHES

Olas Altas to Punta Camarón
Exploration of Mazatlán's beaches can start at Av. Olas Altas, where narrow **Playa Olas Altas** offers some water sports opportunities. The strip is wide and clean enough for wading, sunning, bodysurfing, and boogie boarding. Swimmers take care: the waves often break suddenly and recede strongly. Locally popular intermediate surfing breaks angle shoreward along the north end. Bring your own equipment, since there's rarely any for rent on this largely locals-only beach.

For fly- and bait-casting—although the beach surf is too murky to catch much of interest—casts from the rocks on either end may yield rewards worth the effort.

Continuing north around Paseo Claussen, past the fort, you'll come to a wave-tossed Pinos cove adjacent to the modern Ciencias del Mar ("Marine Sciences") college. Although the narrow strand here is suitable for no more than wading, the rocks provide good casting spots, and the left-breaking swells challenge beginning and intermediate surfers.

Next comes the small boat cove, where **Playa Norte** begins. Unfortunately, the first one-mile stretch is too polluted for much more than strolling (due to the waste from the fleet of fishing *lanchas*) along the beach.

A mile farther north beginning around the oafish **Monumento al Pescador** ("Fisherman's Monument"), where Paseo Claussen becomes Av. del Mar, a relatively wide, clean white strand extends for three miles. This stretch is popular with local families and is uncrowded except during holidays. On calm days the waves break gently and gradually; other times they can be rough. If so, stick by a lifeguard if you see one.

Beginning and intermediate surfers congregate at the north end of this beach, on both flanks of **Punta Camarón** (marked by Valentino's disco), where the swells break gradually left. For fisherfolk, the rocks on the point provide good spots for casting.

Zona Dorada Beaches
At Punta Camarón, Av. del Mar becomes Calz. Camarón Sábalo, which winds northward through the clutter of Zona Dorada streetside eateries, crafts shops, travel agencies, and banks.

The way to enjoy and understand the Zona Dorada is not on the boulevard, but on the beach a few blocks away. The lineup of successful hotels immediately north of Punta Camarón testifies to the beauty of Playa Camarón and Playa Gaviotas. These shining strands—with oft-gentle rolling waves, crystal sand, and glowing, island-silhouetted sunsets—give meaning to the label "Golden Zone": golden memories for visitors and gold in the pockets of the Mazatlán folks lucky enough to own or work in the Zona Dorada. (Sometimes it seems as if half the town *is* trying to work there. During the low-season months of September and October, beachfront crafts and food vendors often outnumber the sunbathers.)

Although the **Playas Camarón** and **Gaviotas** are often lumped together, the beaches themselves contrast sharply. The more southerly Playa Camarón is narrow and steep, with coarse, yellow sand. Its waves often break suddenly and recede strongly. At such times, bodysurfing on Playa Camarón is a thrilling but potentially hazardous pastime.

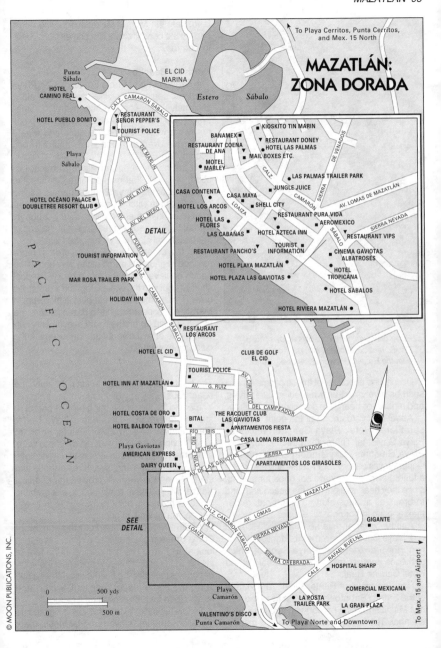

To Playa Cerritos, Punta Cerritos, and Mex. 15 North

MAZATLÁN: ZONA DORADA

Punta Sábalo

EL CID MARINA

Estero   *Sábalo*

HOTEL CAMINO REAL

CALZ CAMARÓN SÁBALO

HOTEL PUEBLO BONITO

RESTAURANT SEÑOR PEPPER'S

TOURIST POLICE

BLVD

DE MARLIN

Playa Sábalo

HOTEL OCÉANO PALACE
DOUBLETREE RESORT CLUB

AV. DEL ATÚN

AV. DEL MERO

AV. DEL PUERTO

DETAIL

DETAIL

BANAMEX

KIOSKITO TIN MARIN

RESTAURANT DONEY
HOTEL LAS PALMAS

RESTAURANT COENA DE ANA

MAIL BOXES ETC.

MOTEL MARLEY

DE VENADOS

CALZ

CAMARÓN

SIERRA

LAS PALMAS TRAILER PARK

JUNGLE JUICE

CASA CONTENTA

CASA MAYA

SHELL CITY

AV. LOMAS DE MAZATLÁN

MOTEL LOS ARCOS

LOAIZA

RESTAURANT PURA VIDA

SIERRA NEVADA

HOTEL LAS FLORES

AEROMEXICO

RESTAURANT VIPS

LAS CABAÑAS

HOTEL AZTECA INN

SÁBALO

RESTAURANT PANCHO'S

TOURIST INFORMATION

CINEMA GAVIOTAS ALBATROSES

HOTEL PLAYA MAZATLÁN

HOTEL TROPICANA

HOTEL PLAZA LAS GAVIOTAS

HOTEL SABALOS

HOTEL RIVIERA MAZATLÁN

TOURIST INFORMATION

MAR ROSA TRAILER PARK

CALZ

CAMARÓN

SÁBALO

HOLIDAY INN

RESTAURANT LOS ARCOS

HOTEL EL CID

CLUB DE GOLF EL CID

TOURIST POLICE

AV. G. RUIZ

AV. CIRCUITO

DEL CAMPEADOR

HOTEL INN AT MAZATLÁN

HOTEL COSTA DE ORO

BITAL

THE RACQUET CLUB LAS GAVIOTAS

HOTEL BALBOA TOWER

RIO IBIS

APARTAMENTOS FIESTA

RIO NILO

CASA LOMA RESTAURANT

Playa Gaviotas
AMERICAN EXPRESS

ALBATROS

AV. DE LAS GAVIOTAS

SIERRA DE VENADOS

DAIRY QUEEN

APARTAMENTOS LOS GIRASOLES

SEE DETAIL

CALZ CAMARÓN SÁBALO

AV. LOMAS

DE MAZATLÁN

GIGANTE

LOAIZA

AV. R.T.

SIERRA NEVADA

SIERRA OREBRADA

RAFAEL BUELNA

HOSPITAL SHARP

COMERCIAL MEXICANA

Playa Camarón

LA POSTA TRAILER PARK

LA GRAN PLAZA

VALENTINO'S DISCO

Punta Camarón

To Playa Norte and Downtown

To Mex. 15 and Airport

0   500 yds

0   500 m

© MOON PUBLICATIONS, INC.

P A C I F I C   O C E A N

Playa Gaviotas, where visitors enjoy some of Pacific Mexico's softest, silkiest sand, curves past the Hotel Cid tower in the background.

Despite the popularity of this strip, small shells, such as lovely rust-brown-mottled little clams, and mother-of-pearl, are sometimes plentiful.

About 500 yards north of the point, near the Las Flores Hotel, Playa Camarón becomes Playa Gaviotas. There, the beach changes to Playa Gaviotas' silky smooth sand and lazy slope. Waves usually roll in gently and always for a long distance. They are not good for surfing, since they head straight into the beach and tend to break all at once along a long front, rather than angling left or right.

Another quarter mile north around Hotel El Cid, Playa Gaviotas becomes its identically lovely northward extension, **Playa Sábalo,** which stretches another mile to Punta Sábalo at the Hotel Camino Real.

Past the rocks of Punta Sábalo, the waters of the **Estero Sábalo** tidal lagoon (now the Marina Mazatlán's outer harbor) ebb through a boat channel. The beach boulevard loops a mile in-

land, past the Marina Mazatlán, curving north, back to the beach, where it becomes Calz. Sábalo Cerritos.

Northern Beaches

The strand north of Punta Sábalo, called **Playa Cerritos,** begins to look like a wild beach along its largely undeveloped northern stretch. Grass sways atop the dunes, flocks of sandpipers probe the wave-washed sand, pelicans and frigate birds glide overhead, and shells and driftwood accumulate.

At the northern end of Playa Cerritos, just south of the hill that marks Punta Cerritos, the beach becomes **Playa Brujas,** named for the *brujas,* female witch doctors, who used to perform their rituals there. If you're thirsty or hungry by that time, a seafood restaurant at the end of the beach will gladly accommodate you.

On the other side of Punta Cerritos, more seafood restaurants perch at the very end of the beach boulevard. On the left, a rocky, tidepool shelf juts out into the waves, forming a protected cove. This, some say, is the best fishing spot in Mazatlán. It appears so; half a dozen *lanchas* are usually pulled up on the rocky beach, while offshore, one or two divers hunt for oysters in the clear, calm waters.

Hikes

The best hike in Mazatlán leads right along the beach. Just walk any of your favorite stretches. You could do the whole thing (or just part of it) starting anywhere—Olas Altas, Playa Norte, Playa Gaviotas—and walking as far north (to avoid having the sun in your eyes) as you want. Other than a hat and sunscreen, you won't have to carry anything along; beach restaurants and stores along the way will provide the goodies. Neither will you have to walk back; just grab the bus or a *pulmonía* back to town whenever you decide you've walked enough.

Another good hike leads to the summit of **Cerro Creston** and provides a close, interesting look at **El Faro.** The trail begins at the foot of the hill, at the end of the pavement past the *flotas deportivas* (sportfishing fleet) docks. Wear a hat, and take some insect repellent, water, and maybe food for a breezy summit picnic.

Follow the initially wide track as it zigzags up the hill. Sometimes overhung by vines, leafy trees, and gnarled cacti, the trail narrows to a rocky path about halfway to the summit. Nearing the top, you wind your way beside rocky outcroppings until you come to the fence around the lighthouse. If your group is small, the keeper may let you in for a look around and to sign his book. He claims the lighthouse is 400 years old.

If you arrive around dusk (bring a flashlight), you will see the beacon in action. The dazzling 1.5-million-watt beacon rotates gradually, like the spokes of a heavenly chariot, with several brilliant wheeling pencils of light focused by the great antique Fresnel lens atop the tower.

At least one local agency offers a city and **hiking tour** that includes a guided climb to the lighthouse summit. It customarily begins at 3 p.m., ending with a sunset view from the hilltop. The $17 tariff includes drinks on the bus and free hotel pickup. Call a travel agent or Vista Tours, tel. (69) 140-187 or 140-188.

DAY TRIPS

Besides restful country ambience, the area around Mazatlán offers interesting history, attractive handicrafts, and rewarding wildlife viewing for the steady flow of visitors to the southern hinterland.

Copala and Concordia
The twin colonial towns of Copala and Concordia, in the lush Sierra Madre foothills, provide the focus for an unhurried day-trip. Concordia, about 12 miles inland along Hwy. 40 (27 miles, 44 km from Mazatlán), offers fine colonial-style furniture and an abundance of attractive pre-Columbian-motif pottery. A short side road leads to a mineral spring, where a number of women make a business of washing clothes. About a dozen miles farther up the road stands Copala (founded 1565), an antique mining town, with hillside lanes winding to a petite plaza and old colonial church. Bring a picnic lunch or stop for refreshment beneath the shady veranda of one of the town's good restaurants.

Get there by tour, car, or bus (ride a Durango-bound first-class Transportes Chihuahenses or a second-class bus from the *central de autobuses*). For a tour (about $30, including lunch) see a travel agent, or call Olé Tours, tel. (69)

166-287 or 166-288, or Vista Tours, tel. (69) 140-187 or 140-188.

Rosario and Teacapán
Rosario and Teacapán likewise provide an inviting, although contrasting day-trip option. Rosario (pop. about 10,000), on Hwy. 15, about 56 miles (90 km) south of Mazatlán, is famed for the towering, solid-gold baroque "Million Dollar Altar" in the town church. You also can visit the home of famous singer Lola Beltrán, on Lola Beltrán street near the church. Beltrán's well-deserved fame flows from her dozens of songs and recordings of Mexican folk-style "Ranchera" music that she popularized during many world tours.

Continue less than an hour (31 miles, 51 km) to Teacapán, where you can enjoy lunch, either at Wayne's Restaurant on the village bayfront, or at hacienda-style Rancho Los Angeles on the beach a few miles north of town. Top your day off by viewing the nesting swarm of pelicans, egrets, and cormorants at Bird Island, via hired launch on Agua Grande Lagoon. Get there by car, bus, or tour along Hwy. 15 south. The tour, sometimes called the "Bird Island" tour, costs about $40, including lunch. See a travel agent, or call Olé Tours, tel. (69) 166-287 or 166-288, or Vista Tours, tel. (69) 140-187 or 140-188.

For more south of Mazatlán tour details, including lodgings, see the South to Puerto Vallarta and Inland to Guadalajara chapter.

ACCOMMODATIONS

You can nearly predict the room price of a hotel by its position on a Mazatlán map. The farther north, away from the old downtown, the newer and more expensive it's likely to be.

Downtown Hotels
At one time, all Mazatlán hotels were downtown. The plush new hotels and condos on the Playa Norte-Zona Dorada luxury beach strip have drawn away practically all the high-ticket vacationers, leaving the old Olas Altas tourist zone to a few old-timers, a handful of budget travelers seeking the charms of traditional Mexico, and Mexican families on holiday outings. The exception to this is the week after Christmas, the week before Easter, and, most of all, Carnaval

(Mardi Gras, in late February or March), when Olas Altas is awash with merrymakers.

The popular **Hotel Siesta,** Av. Olas Altas 11, Mazatlán, Sinaloa 82000, tel. (69) 812-640 or 812-334, fax 137-476, is tops for enjoying the flavor of the Olas Altas neighborhood. The 57 rooms have TV, a/c, and phones. For balcony views of Carnaval or lovely sunsets any time of

---

MAZATLÁN ACCOMMODATIONS

Accommodations (area code 69, postal code 82000 unless otherwise noted) are listed in increasing order of approximate high-season, double-room rates.

DOWNTOWN

Hotel del Centro, Canizales 18, tel. 812-673, $15

Hotel Central, Belisario Dominguez 2 Sur, tel. 821-888, $16

Hotel Belmar, Av. Olas Altas 166, tel. 851-111, fax 813-428, $18

Hotel Siesta, Av. Olas Altas 11, tel. 812-640 or 812-334, fax 137-476, $25

Suites Vidalmar and Apts. Las Palmas, Calle Las Palmas 15, tel. 812-190 or 812-197, $30

PLAYA NORTE

Hotel del Sol, Av. del Mar s/n (P.O. Box 400), tel. 851-103, fax 852-603, $18

Hotel Sands, Av. del Mar 1910 (P.O. Box 309), tel. 820-000, fax 821-025, $22

Hotel de Cima, Av. del Mar 48 (P.O. Box 350), tel. 822-751, $50

Hotel Aguamarina, Av. del Mar 110 (P.O. Box 345), tel. 817-080, 816-909, or (800) 528-1234 from the U.S. and Canada, fax 824-624, $66

ZONA DORADA AND NORTH

Fiesta Apartmentos, Ibis 502 (postal code 82110), tel. 135-355, $15

Los Girasoles, Av. Gaviotas 709 (postal code 82110), tel./fax 135-288 or 113-835, $20

Hotel Plaza Las Gaviotas, Bugambilias 100 (P.O. Box 970, postal code 82110), tel. 134-496, fax 136-685, $27

Bungalows Playa Escondida, Calz. Sábalo Cerritos 999 (P.O. Boxes 682 and 202, postal code 82110), tel. 880-077, $29

Racquet Club Las Gaviotas, Ibis at Bravo (P.O. Box 173), tel. 135-939, $30

Motel Marley, R.T. Loaiza 226 (P.O. Box 214), tel./fax 135-533, $44

Hotel Tropicana, R.T. Loaiza 27 (P.O. Box 501, postal code 82110), tel. 838-000, fax 835-361, $45

Hotel Azteca Inn, R.T. Loaiza 307, tel. 134-477, fax 134-655, $47

Motel Los Arcos, R.T. Loaiza 214 (P.O. Box 132), tel./fax 135-066, $48

Casa Contenta, R.T. Loaiza 224, tel. 134-976, fax 139-986, $53

Hotel Las Flores, R.T. Loaiza 212 (postal code 82110), tel. 135-011 or 135-100, fax 143-422, $52

Hotel Riviera Mazatlán, Camarón Sábalo 51 (P.O. Box 795), tel. 834-722, fax 844-532, $73

Hotel Playa Mazatlán, Av. R.T. Loaiza 202 (P.O. Box 207), postal code 82110, tel. 134-444 or 134-455, fax 140-366, $95

Hotel El Cid, Camarón Sábalo s/n (P.O. Box 335, postal code 82110), tel. 133-333, fax 142-243, $110

Hotel Inn at Mazatlán, Camarón Sábalo 6291 (P.O. Box 1292, postal code 82110), tel. 135-500, fax 134-782, $120

the year, reserve one of the several oceanfront rooms. Another extra is the charming old inner patio, decorated by the colorful umbrellas of the El Shrimp Bucket restaurant and shaded by towering, leafy trees festooned with hanging airroots. A combo plays traditional Latin melodies on the patio (weather permitting) most nights till around 10 p.m. From about $25 d, somewhat higher during holidays; credit cards accepted.

A few blocks south stands the venerable six-story oceanfront **Hotel Belmar,** Av. Olas Altas 166, Mazatlán, Sinaloa 82000, tel. (69) 851-112, fax 813-428, faded but still welcoming the long-timers who remember when it was *the* hotel in Mazatlán. Belmar offers 200 rooms, with a/c, phones, and parking, from about $18 d, credit cards accepted. Although now a bit tattered, its old amenities remain: pool, sidewalk restaurant, and many ocean-view rooms, some carpeted and modern and some so old and makeshift that they're quaint.

About a half mile north, where Paseo Claussen bends around Cerro Nevería, a big sign on the hill above the Ciencias del Mar ("Marine Sciences") college marks **Suites Vidalmar,** Calle Las Palmas 15, Mazatlán, Sinaloa 82000, tel. (69) 812-190 or 812-197. The modern stucco apartment complex clusters artfully above a blue designer swimming pool with a sweeping view of the nearby rocky bay and northward-curving shoreline. Ten one-bedroom suites—all spacious, tastefully furnished, with kitchenettes—can accommodate four in two double beds. One airy, two-story suite accommodates five. Amenities include a/c, phones, parking, pool, kitchenette; high-season rates are about $30 for two, $40 for four, and $60 for the big five-person suite. Corresponding low-season rates run about $27, $36, and $54. This is a place for those who want a restful vacation while enjoying quiet pursuits: cooking, basking in the sun, reading, and watching sunsets from the comfort of their own home in Mazatlán. For the high winter season, be sure to reserve early; credit cards accepted.

The same management operates **Apartmentos las Palmas,** a stack of apartments and a penthouse, across the street. Although not nearly as luxurious as Suites Vidalmar, the apartments are large, modern, and spartan but thoughtfully furnished, and sleep up to four. Residents have access to the pool across the street. Same address and phone as Suites Vidalmar;

the 11 one-bedroom apartments rent, high season, from about $30 d, the penthouse about $50; $27 and $45 low season, with a/c, street parking only, credit cards accepted.

If you want to be near the center of colorful downtown bustle, try the no-frills **Hotel del Centro,** Canizales 18, Mazatlán, Sinaloa 82000, tel. (69) 812-673, within sight of the cathedral, right around the corner from the market. (The hotel's streetfront, although busy, is too narrow for buses, and is consequently not very noisy.) The 24 rooms rent for about $15 d high season, $12 low, with a/c and TV. There's not much in the clean rooms but the basics. No matter; the attraction of this part of town is what's outside the door.

For a little more luxury in the downtown district, walk about four blocks to the opposite and quieter west side of the cathedral to the **Hotel Central,** Calle Belisario Domínguez 2 Sur at Calle Ángel Flores, Mazatlán, Sinaloa 82000, tel. (69) 821-888. Past the upstairs lobby you'll find a small restaurant, a friendly place for meeting other travelers, and three floors of cool, clean, modern-style rooms. Rates for the 40 rooms, with a/c, TV, and phones, are from about $16 d year-round, except for Carnaval, Easter, and Christmas.

Playa Norte Hotels

During the 1960s Mazatlán burst its old city limits at the end of Paseo Claussen and spilled northward along the long sand crescent called Playa Norte. Now, a three-mile string of '60s-style hotels and motels lines the breezy beachfront of Av. del Mar, an extension of Paseo Claussen. Unfortunately, however, the wide, busy thoroughfare intervenes between the hotels (save one) and the beach.

The one exception is the dignified **Hotel de Cima,** a few blocks north of the Fisherman's Monument at Av. del Mar 48, P.O. Box 350, Mazatlán, Sinaloa 82000, tel. (69) 822-751. Its tunnel beneath Av. del Mar leads directly to the hotel's beachfront seafood *palapa* restaurant. Back inside, the staff try hard to live up to the hotel's "We Only Look Expensive" motto, maintaining a cool, relaxed restaurant, pool, nightclub, and bars all while keeping the spacious, comfortable ocean view rooms spotless. The 150 rooms, all with two double beds, run from about $50 high season, with a/c, cable TV, phones, parking, tennis, and limited wheelchair access; credit cards accepted.

About two blocks farther north stands **Hotel Aguamarina,** Best Western's very worthy representative in Mazatlán at Av. del Mar 110, P.O. Box 345, Mazatlán, Sinaloa 82000, tel. (69) 817-080 or 816-909, fax 824-624. With a low-rise stucco motel facade, built around a pool patio, its rooms (either ocean or garden view) are large and gracefully decorated with native-style handmade wood furniture. The wall art hangs tastefully on colonial-style textured white interiors. The 101 rooms rent for about $66 d standard, $77 d deluxe, with a/c, cable TV, phones, parking, an airy, high-ceilinged restaurant, and pool; credit cards accepted. From the U.S. and Canada, reserve through the Best Western toll-free number (800) 528-1234.

Farther north a few blocks (just past the Pizza Hut) appears the smallish facade of the motel-style **Hotel del Sol,** Av. del Mar s/n, P.O. Box 400, Mazatlán, Sinaloa 82000, tel. (69) 851-103, fax 852-603. A few steps from the streetfront reception, you will find that the Motel del Sol is larger than it looks. Its rooms cluster around an inviting pool patio where, on one corner, a comical plaster duck squirts water from his mouth. Inside, tasteful wood furniture, white walls, and spotless tile floors decorate the spacious rooms. Rooms run about $28 d with kitchenette, $18 without, with a/c, phones, some TV, and parking.

Finally, next to the popular Restaurant Señor Frog's, comes the **Hotel Sands,** Av. del Mar 1910, P.O. Box 309, Mazatlán, Sinaloa 82000, tel. (69) 820-000, fax 821-025. It's clean, and if you don't mind a bit of traffic noise from the avenue, has the ingredients for a pleasant beach vacation: sea-view rooms with balconies overlooking an inviting pool patio, a/c, phones, and TV. The 50 rooms usually rent for about $22 d, about $30 during holidays.

Zona Dorada Budget-Moderate Lodgings

Along a six-mile strip of golden sand rise Mazatlán's newest, plushest hotels. But unlike some other world-class resorts, the Zona Dorada is not wall-to-wall high-rises. In the breezy, palm-fringed spaces between the big hotels, there are many excellent moderately priced hotels and apartment complexes.

For one of the most charming budget accommodations in Mazatlán, try **Fiesta Apartmentos,** three blocks directly inland from beachside landmark Balboa Tower, at Calle Ibis 502, Fracc. Gaviotas, Mazatlán, Sinaloa 82110, tel. (69) 135-355. A complex of studios and one-bedroom apartments within a jungle-garden blooming with bushy guavas, hanging vines, squawking parrots, and slinking iguanas. Hardworking owner/manager Yolanda Olivera and her carpenter spouse built the place from the ground up while raising a family during the '60s and '70s. The units are each uniquely furnished with husband-made wooden chairs and tables, toilet, hot shower, and a double bed. Larger units have an additional bed, a sofa or two, and a kitchenette. While you may have to do some initial cleaning up, the price and ambience are certainly right: the 11 studios and one-bedroom apartments rent from about $15/day ($250/month); larger units with kitchenettes go for about $25/day ($450/month). All apartments come with fans and parking; reservations are mandatory during the winter.

Right next door is the less personal, but equally unique, **Racquet Club Las Gaviotas,** on Calle Ibis at Bravo, P.O. Box 173, Mazatlán, Sinaloa 82000, tel. (69) 135-939, a complex of bungalow-type apartments and condominiums spread around a spacious palm-shaded swimming pool and garden. While a good, moderately priced vacation lodging for anyone, this is a paradise for tennis buffs on a budget, with its row of seven well-maintained (three clay and four hard) courts. The bungalows themselves are spacious one- and two-bedroom units with a living room/dining room furnished in Spanish-style tile and wood and equipped with modern kitchenettes. Reservations are mandatory year-round. The 20 units rent from about $450/month for a one-bedroom bungalow and $650/month for two bedrooms (with higher daily and weekly rates, fans and daily cleaning service included). Lower units are wheelchair-accessible.

Even lovelier (but minus the tennis courts) is the nearby **Los Girasoles,** a stucco apartment complex built around an inviting pool patio and spacious garden at Av. Gaviotas 709, Mazatlán, Sinaloa 82110, tel./fax (69) 135-288 or 113-835, five blocks from the beach at the end of Gaviotas, next to Restaurant Casa Loma. When ripe, the fruit of the banana trees that fringe the garden becomes available to guests. Inside, the airy Mexican-style wood and tile kitchenette apartments are comfortably furnished and spotless. The 22 units (both one- and two-bedroom) rent for about $15/day or $300/month low season, $20 and $400 high season. Rental includes fans, parking, and daily cleaning service; credit cards are accepted.

On Mazatlán's most beautiful beach stand a number of small, moderately priced lodgings along Av. R.T. Loaiza, which, about a block north of Valentino's, loops left, one way, away from noisy Calz. Camarón Sábalo. Among the best is **Casa Contenta**, a comfortable two-story complex that lives up to its name at Playa Las Gaviotas, Calz. R.T. Loaiza 224, tel. (69) 134-976, fax 139-986. Step past the off-street parking and you will find seven roomy, tastefully furnished kitchenette apartments tucked behind a luxurious family house, all within a manicured garden. Besides the beach and a small pool in the backyard, Casa Contenta residents can enjoy good restaurants and the entertainment of plush hotels within a few minutes' walk. Reserve early: from about $53/day high season, $37 low for an apartment, $150 high season, $130 low for the house. Approximate 10% discounts are customarily given for a one-month rental. All include daily cleaning service, a/c, and parking. Credit cards are accepted, and lower-level units have limited wheelchair access.

If Casa Contenta is full, you can try its plainer (but nevertheless beautifully located) neighbors, Motel Marley and Motel Los Arcos. Guests at the two-story **Motel Marley**, R.T. Loaiza 226, P.O. Box 214, Mazatlán, Sinaloa 82000, tel./fax (69) 135-533, can choose between upper-or ground-level one- or two-bedroom units, all with living rooms and fully furnished kitchenettes, with daily maid service and air-conditioned bedrooms. Extras include parking and attractive garden grounds that spread from an inviting pool patio. The majority of the apartments are right on the beach. For the most privacy and best of best views, reserve one of the beachfront upper units early. Rates run, year-round, about $44 d for one bedroom (with two double beds), $54 for two bedrooms (four double beds) for four people. Add about $5 per additional person. Credit cards are accepted.

Accommodations at **Motel Los Arcos**, a block south, next to Hotel Las Flores, at R.T. Loaiza 214, P.O. Box 132, tel./fax (69) 135-066, are similar to the Motel Marley. The scruffiness of the grounds and the lack of a pool don't seem to deter the many guests who return yearly to enjoy the sparkling sun, sea, and sand, right from their front doorsteps. The approximately 20 clean, brightly furnished kitchenette view apartments rent, high season, for about $48 d for one bedroom, $60 d for two bedrooms for four people, $44 and $54 low season. Add about $6 per additional person, credit cards accepted.

On the beachfront next door towers the **Hotel Las Flores**, R.T. Loaiza 212, Mazatlán, Sinaloa 82110, tel. (69) 135-011 or 135-100, fax 143-422, very popular with North American winter package vacationers. In the standard-grade (but less than spotless) rooms, bright orange-red bedspreads blend with ruddy brick wall highlights. The deluxe rooms, in contrast, feature soothing blue and white decor and kitchenettes. All units enjoy expansive ocean views. Downstairs, the lobby spreads to an attractive restaurant, pool-bar, and tables beneath thatched-roof beachside *palapas*. During high season, the 119 rooms rent, high season, for about $52 d standard, $69 w/kitchenette, $87 deluxe w/kitchenette; corresponding low season asking rates are about $45, $60 and $76; bargain for a discount. Rentals include a/c, TV, phones, and parking; credit cards are accepted.

The owner of the Hotel Siesta downtown brings similar good management to the **Hotel Azteca Inn**, at R.T. Loaiza 307, Mazatlán, Sinaloa, tel. (69) 134-477, fax 134-655, right in the middle of the Zona Dorada bustle, half a block from the beach. Here, guests enjoy about 40 comfortably furnished, immaculate semi-deluxe rooms, arranged motel-style, in two floors around an inviting inner pool patio. Rentals cost about $47 s or d high season, $35 low, with a/c, TV, parking, and credit cards accepted.

Half a block farther south, the low-rise **Hotel Plaza Las Gaviotas**, Bugambilias 100, P.O. Box 970, Mazatlán, Sinaloa 82110, tel. (69) 134-496, fax 136-685, tucked just off Loaiza, is easy to miss. It nevertheless offers plenty—good management, spacious, tastefully decorated rooms, peace and quiet—for surprisingly little. The petite, attractive lobby leads to a leafy inner patio with a small pool. The surrounding rooms are clean and tiled and decorated in light pastels. They rent for about $27 d, $33 for four, high season. With cable TV, a/c, and lower-floor wheelchair access; credit cards are accepted.

The **Hotel Tropicana,** R.T. Loaiza 27, P.O. Box 501, Mazatlán, Sinaloa 82110, tel. (69) 838-000, fax 835-361, shares virtually everything—beach, shopping, restaurants, and nightlife—with Zona Dorada luxury hotels except prices. For many savvy vacationeers, the hotel's other big pluses—spacious rooms, private ocean-view balconies, big marble baths—far outweigh the sometimes worn furnishings and the half-block walk to the beach. To assure yourself of the best room (top floor, beach side) reserve early. Rooms go for about $45 s or d high season, $27 low. Amenities include a/c, phones, a pool, beach club, restaurant/bar, and full wheelchair access; credit cards accepted.

The mostly young guests at the **Hotel Riviera Mazatlán,** Camarón Sábalo 51, P.O. Box 795, Mazatlán, Sinaloa 82000, tel. (69) 834-722, fax 844-532, enjoy luxurious beachfront amenities at moderate rates. The hotel's design makes the most of its already enviable location. The rooms, in a pair of sunny, breeze-swept tiers, enclose a spacious two-pool patio that looks out on a gorgeous beach, sea, and sunset vista. Upstairs, guest rooms have private balconies and are tiled, clean, and simply but thoughtfully decorated in blues and whites. High-season rates run about $73 d with ocean view, $59 d without, low season $62 and $47. Amenities include nightly rock music in the patio, TV, a/c, parking, and full wheelchair access; credit cards are accepted.

Zona Dorada Luxury Hotels

A few blocks farther north along Loaiza stands the landmark of the Zona Dorada—the first hotel built (despite many doubters) on what was once an isolated sand strip far from the city center. Even during the September and October low-occupancy months (when many Zona Dorada hotels and restaurants are virtually empty) everyone—Mexicans and foreigners alike—still flocks to the **Hotel Playa Mazatlán,** in the heart of the Zona Dorada at Av. R.T. Loaiza 202, P.O. Box 207, Mazatlán, Sinaloa 82110, tel. (69) 134-444 or 134-455, fax 140-366. The band plays every

night, the Fiesta Mexicana buffet show goes on every Saturday, and the fireworks boom and flash above the beach every Sunday night. To enjoy the Playa Mazatlán, you don't have to stay there; just order something at the beachside *palapa* terrace restaurant and enjoy the music, the breeze, and the same ocean view shared by its luxurious rooms. The 425 rooms go for about $95 d for standard grade high season, $85 low; the deluxe one-bedroom suite is $220 high season, and $200 low, with a/c, TV, phones, pool, jacuzzi, tennis, parking, and full wheelchair access; credit cards accepted. Low-season packages and promotional discounts are sometimes available.

For the classiest tropical retreat in town, step northward about a mile to the **Hotel Inn at Mazatlán,** right on silky Playa Camarón at Camarón Sábalo 6291, P.O. Box 1292, Mazatlán, Sinaloa 82110, tel. (69) 135-500, fax 134-782. Although mostly a time share (buy a room for a specified week or two each year), it does rent out the vacant units hotel-style. All guests, furthermore, whether owners or one-time renters, receive the same tender loving service. Every lovely feature of the Inn at Mazatlán shines with care and planning, from the excellent inside-outside beach-view restaurant and the artistically curved pool to the palms' sunset silhouettes and the spacious, luxuriously appointed sea-view rooms. Asking rates for the 126 rooms run about $120 year-round, although you might be able to bargain for a low-season discount. For a bit more, you can have a one-bedroom suite sleeping six including kitchenette. All rentals enjoy a/c, phones, refrigerators, and parking. For recreation there is tennis but no TV. Reservations are generally necessary; credit cards are accepted.

No discussion of Mazatlán hotels would be complete without mention of the **Hotel El Cid** megaresort, the hotel that tries to be everything on Camarón Sábalo s/n, P.O. Box 335, Mazatlán, Sinaloa 82000, tel. (69) 133-333, fax 142-243. The huge complex, which sprawls over the north end of Av. Camarón Sábalo, claims to be the biggest in Mexico—with 1,000 rooms in three separate hotels, 15 separate bars and restaurants, a health club, a giant glittering disco, a country club subdivision, a marina development, and a world-class 18-hole golf course and 17 tennis courts. Size, however, lends El Cid a definite institutional feeling—as if everyone, the 2,000 employees and 2,000 guests alike, were anonymous. The El Cid's saving grace (besides its beachfront), however, may be its huge pool. It meanders among the three hotels, a palm-fringed blue lagoon complete with a fake (albeit very clever fake) rock water slide, waterfall, and diving platform straight from an old Tarzan movie. This doesn't seem to matter, however, to the poolside crowd of guests, from ages four to 90, who enjoy watching each other slipping, sliding, and jumping into the cool water. High-season room rates are from about $110 d, low season, $90, with everything, including complete wheelchair access. El Cid often offers cheaper low-season promotions, obtainable through travel agents or the reservations office.

Beyond the Zona Dorada

Vacationers who hanker for a more rustic beach atmosphere enjoy the **Bungalows Playa Escondida** on palmy Playa Cerritos, about five miles north of the Zona Dorada at Calz. Sábalo Cerritos 999, P.O. Boxes 682 and 202, Mazatlán, Sinaloa 82110, tel. (69) 880-077. Administered by the trailer park office across the boulevard, the 20 whitewashed bungalows laze beneath a swaying coconut palm grove. The clean, spartan, tile-kitchenette units, in parallel rows facing the ocean, sleep two to four. The more heavily used beachfront row enjoys sweeping ocean views, while the others lie sheltered beneath the palms behind the dune. During the winter season you can enjoy plenty of friendly company at the trailer park pool across the street. Stores and restaurants are within a short drive nearby. The bungalows rent for about $29/day d, add about $5 per additional person, with a/c. One-month rentals customarily earn discounts of 30-50% below these rates.

Homestay Program

Besides offering Spanish classes, the privately owned **Centro de Idiomas** ("Language Center") also runs a homestay program. Participants live with a Mexican family (about $150/week, including three meals). The center also offers person-to-person contacts, in which such visiting professionals as teachers, nurses, and doctors meet with and learn from their local counterparts. Contact the downtown school at Belisario Domínguez 1908, upstairs, tel. (69) 822-053, fax 855-606, e-mail: 74174.1340@compuserve.com.

Long-Term Rentals

If you're looking for a long-term apartment, condominium, or house rental, veteran English-speaking realtor **Lupita Bernal** may be able to help. Contact her at (69) 141-753, fax 145-082, or e-mail: bernal@red2000.com.mx.

Alternatively, contact rental agent Carol Sinclair of Walfre Real Estate, tel./fax (69) 830-011 or 835-077, e-mail: walfre@red2000.com.mx.

Another good source of rentals is the classified section of the *Pacific Pearl* tourist newspaper.

RV and Trailer Parks

Mazatlán's beachfront trailer space is an increasingly scarce commodity, victim to rising land values. If you're planning on a Christmas stay, phone or mail in your reservation and deposit by September or you may be out of luck, especially for the choice spaces.

One trailer park owner who is determined never to sell out is Gabriela C. Aguilar van Duyn, of **Mar Rosa Trailer Park,** just north of the Hotel Holiday Inn at Calz. Camarón Sábalo 702, P.O. Box 435, Mazatlán, Sinaloa 82000, tel. (69) 165-967, tel./fax 136-187. Besides being the on-the-spot manager, she's Mazatlán's informal one-woman welcoming committee and information source. "I will never sell. The people who come here are my friends . . . like my family." If you ask if she has a pool, she will probably point to the beach a few feet away, and say, "one big pool." Gabriela offers about 55 spaces, some shaded, with all hookups, for about $17/day, $15/day, and $11/day, depending on location. A three-month winter rental gets a discount of a dollar per day. With toilets, hot showers, a/c power, cable TV; near markets and restaurants; and leashed dogs okay.

Another popular close-in (Zona Dorada, two blocks from the beach) trailer spot is the **Trailer Park Las Palmas,** in a big, palm-shaded lot off Camarón Sábalo, about half a block south of the Dairy Queen at Calz. Camarón Sábalo 333, tel. (69) 135-311. Spaces rent for about $12/day, $270/month, with pool, all hookups, toilets, showers, leashed dogs okay, camping available, and it's near everything.

Nearby (on Calz. R. Buelna, two blocks inland from Valentino's Disco), the **Trailer Park La Posta,** P.O. Box 362, Mazatlán, Sinaloa 82000, tel. (69) 835-310, spreads beneath the shade of a banana, mango, and avocado grove (all-you-can-eat in season). Residents enjoy a plethora of facilities, including all hookups, showers and toilets, a big pool and sundeck, shaded picnic *palapas,* a small store, and the beach two blocks away. The 180 spaces rent for about $13/day or $300/month; add $2 daily for a/c power. Early winter reservations are generally necessary.

In the quieter country a block off north-end Playa Cerritos, the **Playa Escondida Trailer Park,** Calz. Sábalo Cerritos 999, P.O. Box 682 or 202, Mazatlán, Sinaloa 82110, tel. (69) 880-077, spreads for acres beneath a lazy old coconut grove. Residents enjoy direct access to the long, uncrowded beach across the road and to nearby supermarkets and restaurants. They can also stay in the trailer park's Bungalows Playa Escondida (see above) across the street. The 200 spaces are $15/day or $300/month, all hookups, big saltwater pool, rec room, hot showers, toilets, leashed dogs okay.

Mazatlán's most downscale trailer park is **Maravillas,** right on the beach, across the road, not far from Trailer Park Playa Escondida. What it lacks in facilities (bare-bones hookups, toilets, showers) it makes up for in its prime beachfront location and intimate (about 20 spaces), palmy ambience. Drop by and take a look, or call (69) 840-0400 for reservations.

Camping

Although there is no established public campground in Mazatlán, camping is allowed for a fee in all the trailer parks above except Mar Rosa.

If, however, you prefer solitary beach camping, there are plenty of empty grassy dunes on the northerly end of **Playa Cerritos** that appear ripe for tenting. If you are uncertain about the safety or propriety of a likely looking spot, inquire at a local business.

Other, more isolated spots (be sure to bring water) lie along the long curve of sand on the south shore of **Stone Island;** catch a ride on the launch across from the Stone Island dock, at the foot of Av. Gutiérrez Najera on Playa Sur.

Camping is also permitted on **Isla Venados,** a mile off Playa Sábalo. Ride the boat from the El Cid beachfront. On Isla Venados, don't set up your tent on the narrow beach; it's under water at high tide.

For wilderness beach camping, try **Playa Delfín,** the pearly sand crescent north of Punta Cerritos. Get there by taking the right fork toward Hwy. 15 *cuota* about a mile before the northern end of Calz. Sábalo Cerritos. Pass Mazagua water park, continue about another mile and turn left at the gravel road just before the railroad track. This soon leads past the big white El Delfín condo complex, which marks the beginning of Playa Delfín, a 10-mile breezy strip of sand, unused except by occasional local fishermen. There's little of civilization here (not even any trees)—simply sand, surf (steep beach: careful for undertow), seabirds, and a seemingly endless carpet of shells.

FOOD

Mazatlán abounds in good food. The competition is so fierce that bad eateries don't survive. The best are easy to spot because they have customers even during the quiet Sept.-Nov. low season.

Snacks, Stalls, and Market

With care, you can do quite well right on the street downtown. An afternoon cluster of folks around a streetside cart piled with oyster shells and shrimp is your clue that their fare is fresh, tasty, and very reasonably priced. These carts usually occupy the same place every day and, for most of them, the quality of their food is a matter of honor. One of the best is **El Burro Feliz,** which usually occupies a spot at 61 Calle Sixto Osuna, outside of their family house across from the Archaeological Museum. Try the dozen-oyster cocktail, enough for two, for $5.

For dessert, an elderly gentleman runs a shaved—literally, with a hand tool—ice stand across the street, from which he serves the best old-fashioned (safe ice) snow cones in Mazatlán.

If you're cooking your own meals, or simply hanker for some fresh fruit and vegetables, the best place to find the crispest of everything is the **Central Market,** corner of Calles Benito

Juárez and Melchor Ocampo, two short blocks behind the cathedral. Open daily 6 a.m.-6 p.m.

After an hour of hard market bargaining, you may be in the mood for a cool, restful lunch. If so, step upstairs inside the market to the leafy balcony *fonda* over the corner of Juárez and Valle and enjoy the scene. Alternatively, walk one block down Juárez and enter the air-conditioned interior of **Pastelería Panamá,** Av. Juárez, corner of Canizales, tel. (69) 851-853, and try one of the tasty lunch specials or treat yourself to the excellent *helado chocolate* (chocolate ice cream). Open daily 8 a.m.-10 p.m.

Afterward, just outside the door, you may see the *churro* cart that always seems to be parked at that corner. Try three of these uniquely Mexican, foot-long thin sugar doughnuts for $1.

Downtown and Olas Altas Restaurants

The better downtown restaurants are concentrated around Plazuela Machado and the Olas Altas *malecón*. On Plazuela Machado, three stars for food and ambience go to **Restaurant Pedro and Lola,** named after the celebrated Mexican singers Pedro Infante and Lola Beltrán. Here, step into a cool, casual-chic bohemian atmosphere, take a table and choose from a menu long on salads and seafood and short on meat. Find it at the corner of Canalizo and Carnaval, tel. (69) 822-589, open 5 p.m.-midnight, with live jazz and nouveau classical music Thursday, Friday, and Saturday.

Nearby, one block east, **Royal Dutch Restaurant,** at 1307 Juárez, corner of Constitución, tel. (69) 812-007, specializes in breakfast. Besides the usual eggs, pancakes, and French toast, it offers baked-in-house pastries, including croissants, muffins, and brownies. The setting here is especially pleasant: tables around an art-decorated patio, blooming with leafy greenery and tropical birdcalls. Open Mon.-Sat. 8 a.m.-10 p.m. Moderate.

For a special local-style treat, you can return to the same neighborhood for supper and sample the homey fare of the **Cenaduría El Tunel.** Tucked just off the southeast corner of Plazuela Machado at Carnaval 1207 and open daily 6-10 p.m., El Tunel's entry leads you through to a narrow corridor where customers are enjoying the craft of a squad of grandmotherly chefs who carry out their mission at stoves in the interior din-

La Fonda de Don Emiliano

ing room. Their delectable enchiladas, crunchy tacos, rich *pozole* (pork with hominy stew), and creamy refried beans are bound to please all devotees of true Mexican food. Budget.

If you're in a festive mood, **El Shrimp Bucket,** Av. Olas Altas 11, bottom floor of Hotel La Siesta, tel. (69) 816-350, is open daily 6 a.m.-11 p.m., credit cards accepted. The restaurant, hung with a riot of taffeta flowers and balloons inside, with the marimba combo humming away by dinnertime in the tropical patio outside, is a party waiting to happen. This is especially true when you call for the bounteous bucket of shrimp ($16, enough for two or three), which they will fix exactly as you wish—breaded, grilled, steamed, or barbecued. Breakfasts, moreover, are very popular here. Moderate.

Playa Norte Restaurants

It's hard to imagine a restaurant closer to the source than the rough and ready family-style **Restaurant El Camachín,** 97 Paseo Claussen and 5 de Mayo, tel. (69) 850-197, located where the boats bring the fish in every morning. In true Mexican tradition, the restaurant augments many of its dishes with a number of flavorful sauces, which range from a mild salsa Oriental (onions, celery, and a bit of soy) to a peppery salsa ranchero. Pick your favorite and have it served with the recommended catch of the day. Open daily 10 a.m.-10 p.m. Moderate.

Another good seafood bet is **Mamucas,** Mazatlán's "King of Seafood" for 35 years, at 404 Bolivar Pte., two blocks from the Paseo Claussen *malecón,* tel. (69) 813-490. The specialties are *parillada de mariscos*—grilled seafood, you pick which—and *pescado zarandeado en brasero*—fish, toss-broiled in a wood-fired brazier. Open daily 10:30 a.m.-9:30 p.m.

If you're in the mood for Chinese food, you'll find it at **Restaurant Canton,** a legacy of the significant local Chinese community, whose ancestors first migrated to these shores during the 19th century. The food here is pure 1940s-genre Cantonese: almond chicken, pork chow mein, broccoli beef, egg foo yung and about 20 more very recognizable choices, all the way to the fortune cookies at meal's end. Restaurant Canton is a few blocks north of the Fisherman's Monument, just past Hotel Aguamarina, open noon-8 p.m., tel. (69) 851-247, moderate.

Heading a few blocks farther north along the *malecón,* a bright sign marks **Karnes en Su Jugo,** Av. del Mar 550, just south of the Hotel Sands, tel. (69) 821-322. If personable owner Jorge Pérez (who, with his red hair, looks more like a Swede than most Swedes do) is there, let him place your order: bounteous table, likely set with a plate of savory roast beef in juice, hot melted Chihuahua white cheese, refried beans, and enough salsa and hot corn tortillas for a dozen yummy tacos or tostadas. Open daily 1 p.m.-1 a.m.; credit cards not accepted. Moderate-expensive.

A stay in Mazatlán wouldn't be complete without a trip to **Señor Frog's,** Calz. Camarón Sábalo s/n, tel. (69) 821-925, the second (El Shrimp Bucket was the first), and perhaps the best, creation of late owner Carlos Anderson's worldwide chain. Many extreme adjectives—brash, bold, loud, risqué, funny, far-out—have been used to describe the waiters, patrons, and the music at Señor Frog's. Most everyone agrees the ribs are the best and the margaritas the most potent

in town. Open daily noon to past midnight, credit cards accepted. Expensive.

Zona Dorada Restaurants
Despite their Golden Zone locations, Zona Dorada restaurants aren't excessively expensive. When you're in a sweat from shopping, sunburn, and street vendors, and you're ready to escape from Mexico, try Mexico's first **Dairy Queen** instead, Camarón Sábalo 500, corner of R.T. Loaiza, tel. (69) 161-522. The regular hamburgers and the associated soft ice cream goodies will taste better than home. When you emerge, you'll feel like staying another couple of months. Open daily 10 a.m.-11 p.m. Budget.

On the other hand, serious Mexican food devotees needn't look any farther than right across the street, where longtime **Restaurant Doney** has migrated from its former downtown location. Hopefully the owners, Señor and Señora Alfonso T. Velarde, will be able to re-create an atmosphere—cool, airy ambience, towering arched brick ceiling, Victorian chandelier, old Mazatlán photos—as invitingly refined as their old location. The new menu will continue to include the broad selection of home-style dishes, such as chorizo (spiced sausage), various *antojitos* (small tacos, tostadas, tamales), and Mazatlán's regional specialty, *asado* (spicy beef stew), as well as a scrumptious selection of homemade pies and cakes. Open daily 8 a.m.-10 p.m., tel. (69) 165-888; credit cards accepted. Moderate.

For a pleasant surprise, especially for breakfast, walk two blocks south from the Dairy Queen corner to the Zona Dorada branch of the **Pastelería Panamá,** on Camarón Sábalo at Garzas, tel. (69) 140-612. Here, a legion of local middle-to-upper class folks flock for everything from ham and eggs and hamburgers to *enchiladas suizas* and chocolate malts. Open daily 7 a.m.-11 p.m. Moderate.

More of the same, but even fancier, is available at **Restaurant VIPs,** a few blocks farther south on Camarón Sábalo, across from Cinemas Gaviotas y Albatroses, tel. (69) 140-754. Here, the Denny's-modeled food and cool a/c ambience beats Denny's by a mile, with crisp salads, hot entrées, and luscious desserts, appetizingly presented and professionally served. Moreover, the restaurant features a bookstore, where you can browse till midnight over Mazatlán's biggest assortment of English-language magazines. Open daily 7 a.m.-midnight

For good Mexican-style macrobiotic fare, step across to the beach side of Camarón Sábalo, go one short block farther west, to Garzas, and a block north, to **Pura Vida** restaurant, tel. (69) 165-815. Here, in a *palapa*-shaded garden, a bustling cadre of waiters serves from a long list of fresh fruit drinks, veggie-light sandwiches, whole wheat pizza, vegetable and fruit salads, yogurt, granola, omelettes, and much more. Open daily 8 a.m.-10 p.m. Moderate.

Another side-street gem is **La Cocina de Ana** at Laguna 49, near the Dairy Queen corner, behind Banamex, tel. (69) 163-119. Cooking is a labor of love of the friendly owner, and it shows, in her hearty, healthy daily buffet—chili, paella, Chinese, soup, fish—Mon.-Sat. noon-8 p.m.

For a relaxed outdoor resort setting, go to the airy beach-view **Terraza Playa** restaurant at Hotel Playa Mazatlán, R.T Loaiza 202, tel. (69) 134-455, so popular that tables are sometimes hard to get. This is frequently true Sunday nights when families begin to arrive two hours early for the free 8 p.m. fireworks show. The Terraza Playa offers excellent entrées, such as *pescado Veracruzana* for $5-10. Open daily 7 a.m.-11 p.m.; credit cards accepted. Moderate.

A number of worthy open-air *palapa* restaurants cluster along Loaiza across from the Hotel Playa Mazatlán. Among the best in food, service, and friendly, airy ambience is **Tio Juan's.** Here, you can start the day with fruit, coffee, eggs, and toast ($3), return for a big *ensalada de atún* (tuna salad; $3) for lunch, and come back at suppertime for a hearty Mexican plate ($7, enough for two). Open daily 7 a.m.-11 p.m.

Nearby **Lario's,** on side-street Bugambilias, across Loaiza from the Hotel Playa Mazatlán, tel. (69) 141-767, is so popular that, when it moved in 1993, it survived by taking its brigade of loyal customers with it. Customers continue to enjoy gratis happy-hour margaritas, live music nightly, and bountiful, expertly prepared and served meat, fish, and Mexican plates at reasonable prices. Open daily 8 a.m.-10 p.m. Moderate to expensive.

A spectacular beachfront view, cool breezes, snappy service, and fresh salads, sandwiches, and seafood at reasonable prices keep patrons coming to restaurant **Pancho's** year-round, located at the beach end of the small complex across from Shell City, tel. (69) 140-911. During the winter season, when vacationers crowd in, come early. The dozen tables can fill by noon. Open daily 8 a.m.-11 p.m. Moderate.

For impeccable service and tranquil, palm-framed sunsets, **Papagayo** restaurant at the Hotel Inn at Mazatlán is hard to beat. On Camarón Sábalo 6291, a low-rise behind wall and trees between Hotels El Cid and Costa de Oro, tel. (69) 134-151. The menu caters to the tastes of the mostly North American clientele, with salad bar and reasonably priced complete dinner specials, notably a mouthwatering chicken-rib combo. Open daily 7 a.m.-10 p.m.; credit cards accepted. Moderate.

Across the street, at open-air *palapa* **Restaurant Los Arcos,** as at Señor Frog's, the patrons line up during the high season. Los Arcos is situated on Camarón Sábalo s/n (look for the big thatched *palapa* between Holiday Inn and El Cid), tel. (69) 139-577. Los Arcos claims to specialize in "the secret flavor which the sea has confided," meaning piquant sauces, many of them peppery hot. Specify *pica* (spicy) or *no pica* before you order your shrimp, oysters, smoked swordfish, snapper, or other seafood—they'll all be good. Open daily noon-10 p.m.; credit cards accepted. Moderate.

North a few blocks, across from the Holiday Inn, the friendly family management of **Cafeteria Coffee Shop,** tel. (69) 142-200, blends the best of both worlds, with dozens of comfortable American-style breakfasts and lunches (bacon and eggs, hamburgers, and malts), plus tamales, tacos, and enchiladas. Clean and bright; great for breakfast. Open daily 7 a.m.-10 p.m. Moderate.

Zona Dorada Splurge Restaurants

One of the most successfully exclusive restaurants in town is **Casa Loma,** Gaviotas 104, tel. (69) 135-398, which, besides tucking itself behind a wall on a quiet dead-end street, manages to close July to October. The Casa Loma secret: A secluded location, subdued tropical atmosphere, excellent service, and a selection of tasty international specialties continue to attract a clubby list of affluent patrons. Open 1:30-10 p.m.; credit cards accepted, reservations recommended. Expensive.

The low-key facade of **Señor Pepper's,** Camarón Sábalo, north end, across from Hotel Camino Real, tel. (69) 140-101, gives little hint of what's inside: a flight of fancy away from Mexico to some Victorian polished brass, mirror, and wood-paneled miniplanet, more San Francisco than San Francisco ever was. When you sit down at a table and ask for a menu, the tuxedo-attired waiter will probably do a double take, scurry away, and return with a small tray of a few thick steaks, a pork chop huge enough for two, and a big lobster. You choose one of these as the basis for your dinner. The meal proceeds from there like a Mozart symphony, through each delectable course, until dessert served with coffee, which one of your three waiters will rush to your table in polished silver and pour with a determined flourish. You look up at him, convinced that he *believes* in his mission; by the time you exit the front door, comfortably satisfied, you will probably be convinced of his mission, also. Señor Pepper's is open daily 6-11 p.m.; credit cards accepted, reservations recommended. Expensive.

ENTERTAINMENT AND EVENTS

Just Wandering Around
A good morning place to start is the little beach at the beginning of **Playa Norte,** at the north end of Av. 5 de Mayo, where the fishermen sell their daily catches. As the cluster of buyers busily bid for the choicest tuna, shrimp, mahimahi, and mackerel, pelicans and seagulls scurry after the leftovers.

Come back later, around supper time, to enjoy the end product: fresh-cooked seafood (try Restaurant Camachín), accompanied by the tunes of one of many strolling mariachi bands—perhaps even one of the famous Sinaloan-style brass bands. If someone else is paying, just sit back and enjoy, especially the tuba solo. If you are paying, make sure that you agree upon the price, usually around $2 per selection, before the performance begins.

Around noon, the area around the central plaza downtown (Juárez and Ángel Flores) is equally entertaining. Take a seat beneath the shade of the big trees and have your shoes polished for about $1.

Shady Plazas
Downtown Mazatlán has a number of neighborhood squares within strolling distance of the central plaza. Five blocks north along Calle Guillermo Nelson lies **Plaza Zaragoza** and its colorful row of little flower shops.

West of the central plaza, two short blocks behind the Palacio Municipal, is the **Plazuela de Los Leones** (Calles Ángel Flores and Niños Héroes), marked by a pair of brass lions guarding the city library. Upstairs, you can peruse the venerable collection of the all-English **Benjamin Franklin Library.**

In a southerly direction from the cathedral, stroll along Juárez three blocks; at Constitución turn right one block to **Plazuela Machado,** the gem of old Mazatlán. Depending upon the time, you may want to stop for a soda or juice at a sidewalk *refresquería* on the north side of plaza, or a drink and a round of pool at the friendly, elegantly Victorian (or, in Mexico, Porfirian, after former President Porfirio Díaz) Cafe Pacífico at the adjacent corner. Across the square, in the midafternoons on school days, you can take a park bench seat and listen to the sounds of violin lessons that sometimes waft down from the upstairs chambers of the Academia Angela Peralta.

Sidewalk Cafés
A few blocks west, on beachfront Av. Olas Altas, watch the passing parade from a table at one of the shady sidewalk cafés clustered around the old Hotel Belmar. If it's summer and you're lucky, you may get a chance to enjoy a Pacific Mexico rainstorm. It usually starts with a few warm drops on the sidewalk. Then the wind starts the palms swaying. Pretty soon the lightning is crackling and the rain is pouring as if from a million celestial faucets. But no matter; you're comfortably seated, and even if you happen to get a little wet it's so warm you'll dry off right away.

Late afternoons on Olas Altas yield a feast of quiet people-watching delights. Perch yourself on the old *malecón* and watch the sunset, the surfers tackling the high waves *(olas altas)* offshore, and the kids, old folks, and loving couples strolling along the sidewalk.

After dark, stroll a few blocks south along the oceanfront, past the divers' point and join the crowd at streetside enjoying the rainbow flutter and flash of the lights on the *Continuity of Life* fountain.

Old-Fashioned Shops

During your wanderings around old Mazatlán be sure to step into some of the traditional *papelerías, dulcerías,* and *ferreterías* (stationery, candy, and hardware stores) that still sell the quaint dime-store style of goods that only grandparents back home remember. For starters, try the **Dulcería La Fiesta,** two blocks north of the cathedral at Melchor Ocampo 612, for enough candy to fill a truck, plus a delightful selection of huge Minnie Mouse, Donald Duck, and Snow White piñatas.

Fiestas

Mazatlán's century-old **Carnaval** is among the world's renowned Mardi Gras celebrations. The merrymaking begins the week before Ash Wednesday (usually late February or early March, when the faithful ceremoniously receive ash marks on their foreheads), beginning the period of fasting called Lent. Mazatlán Carnaval anticipates all this with a vengeance in a weeklong series of folk dances, balls, ballets, literature readings, beauty contests, and "flower" games. The celebration climaxes on Shrove Tuesday (the day before the beginning of Lent) with a parade of floats and riotous merrymakers, which by this time includes everyone in town, culminating along Av. Olas Altas. If you'd like to join in, reserve your hotel room (streetfront rooms at the Hotels Siesta and Belmar are best located for Carnaval) at least six months in advance.

Fall visitors can enjoy events of the **Festival of the Arts,** which begins in mid-October, continues through November, and concludes mid-December. Find the list of programs, which include classical music and ballet and folkloric dance, in the *Pacific Pearl* tourist newspaper.

Other unique local celebrations include the 8 December **Feast of the Immaculate Conception** and the **Cultural Festival of Sinaloa,** a statewide (but centering in Mazatlán) monthlong feast of concert, sports, and cultural events in November. Check with the tourist information office for details.

Bullfights, Rodeos, and Baseball

Every Sunday from mid-December through Easter, bullfights (not really "fights"), called *corridas de toros,* are held at the big bullring, Plaza Monumental (Av. R. Buelna at Av. de la Marina), about a mile from the beach. The ritual begins at 4 p.m. sharp. Get your tickets through a travel agency or at the bullring.

Once or twice a year the Mazatlán professional association of *charros* (gentleman cowboys) holds a rodeo-like *charreada.* Some events (such as jumping from one racing, unbroken horse to another, or trying to flatten an angry steer by twisting its tail!) make the garden-variety North American rodeo appear tame.

Los Venados ("The Deers"), Mazatlán's entry in the Mexican Pacific Coast Baseball (Béisbol) League (AAA), begins its schedule in early October and continues into the spring. Get your tickets at the stadium (Estadio Teodoro Mariscal), whose night lights are so bright that when the team is home you can't help but see a quarter mile inland from Av. del Mar. Baseball fever locally heats up to epidemic proportions when Culiacán, Los Venados' arch-rival, is in town.

Tourist Shows

While a number of hotels present folkloric song and dance shows, the Hotel Playa Mazatlán's **Fiesta Mexicana** remains the hands-down favorite. The entire three-hour extravaganza, including a sumptuous buffet, begins at 7 p.m. sharp every Tuesday, Thursday, and Saturday during high season (Saturday only during low). Call the hotel (tel. 69-135-320 or 134-174) ticket office or a travel agent for tickets, which run about $25 per person. If you miss Fiesta Mexicana on Saturday, you can get in on the free beach fireworks show the next evening at 8 p.m. It's popular, so arrive an hour early to ensure yourself a seat.

Others are trying harder. Wednesday nights, Hotel El Cid succeeds in capturing the spirit of Mazatlán's pre-Lenten Carnaval with a sumptuous buffet and a Mardi Gras-style song and dance extravaganza. Call the Hotel El Cid (tel. 69-133-333) for information and tickets (about $26, half price for kids).

Movies

A number of Mazatlán cinemas screen first-run Hollywood movies. Try the six-screen **Cinemas Gaviotas y Albatroses,** Camarón Sábalo 218, a few blocks north of Valentino's disco; call (69) 837-545 for programs.

Discos

Dance music is plentiful in Mazatlán. You can start out by enjoying drinks or dinner with the medium-volume bands that play nightly around 8 p.m. at the more popular hotels, especially the **Playa Mazatlán,** tel. (69) 135-340, and others, such as **El Cid,** tel. (69) 133-333; **Los Sábalos,** tel. (69) 835-409 or 838-357; **Costa de Oro,** tel. (69) 135-344; and **La Siesta,** tel. 812-334.

Then, around 11 p.m. or midnight, while the Mazatlán night is still young, you can go out and jump at one of several local discos. **Valentino's,** tel. (69) 841-666, with its jumble of white spires and turrets, perches on Punta Camarón, inspiring intense curiosity, if not wonder, among newcomers. Its three separate dance floors have the requisite flashing lights and speakers varying from loud, louder, and the loudest (with a booming bass audible for a couple of miles up and down the beach).

On the other hand, what **El Caracol,** tel. (69) 133-333, open seasonally Tues.-Sat., at El Cid, lacks on the outside, it makes up on the inside. There is one huge dance floor beneath two upper levels, which patrons can exit to the lower by sliding down a chute or slithering down a brass firehouse pole.

The discos, which charge a cover of about $10 and expect you to dress casually but decently (slacks and shirts, dresses or skirts and blouses, and shoes), open around 10 p.m. and go on until 4 or 5 in the morning.

Bars and Hangouts

Mazatlán has a few romantic, softly lighted piano bars. Besides the suave **Mikonos** piano bar (right next to Valentino's at Camarón Sábalo and Rafael Buelna), you can sample the elegant sophistication of **Señor Pepper's** (tel. 69-141-101) piano bar across from the Hotel Camino Real at the north end of Camarón Sábalo.

For high-volume '70s rock and beer-and-popcorn camaraderie, **Jungle Juice** restaurant's upstairs bar on a side street off R.T Loaiza, one block from Hotel Playa Mazatlán, tel. (69) 133-315, is literally wall-to-wall customers during the high season. The same is true for the disco-style **Pepe Toro** (diagonally across the street) and the open-air cantina **Gringo Lingo,** around the corner, except that, at Gringo Lingo, there's more room and more air.

Child's Play

When your kids get tired of digging in the sand and splashing in the pool, take them to the **Aquarium,** Mexico's largest, with many big, well-maintained fish tanks—of flinty-eyed sharks, clownish wide-bodied box fish, and shoals of luminescent damselfish. It's on Av. de Los Deportes 111, just off Av. del Mar about a mile south of Valentino's (watch for the Acuario sign), tel. (69) 817-816 or 817-817. Admission is about $4 adults, $2 kids; open daily 10 a.m.-6 p.m. Outside, don't miss the exotic tropical botanical garden, where you'll find a pair of monstrously large crocodiles. Time your arrival to take in one of the three daily sea lion shows around 1, 3:30, and 5:30 p.m.

For a different type of frolic, take the kids to **Mazagua** water park, Playa Cerritos s/n, where they'll be able to slip down the 100-foot-long Kamikaze slide, swish along the toboggan, loll in the wave pool, or simply splash in the regular pool. Follow the right fork toward Hwy. 15 near the north end of Calz. Camarón Sábalo and you'll immediately see the water park on the left. Open daily 10 a.m.-6 p.m.; admission is about $10 for everyone over three. The park has a restaurant and snack bar.

During the adult fun and games of Carnaval, there's no reason your kids have to feel left out if you take them to the **"Carnival"** (as known in North America). You'll find it by looking for the Ferris wheel near the bus terminal on Calle Tamazula and the Hwy. 15 downtown boulevard.

SPORTS AND RECREATION

Walking and Jogging

The Mazatlán heat keeps walkers and joggers near the shoreline. On the beaches themselves, the long, flat strands of Playa Norte (along Av. del Mar), Playa Gaviotas (north from about the Hotel Los Flores), and the adjoining Playa Sábalo (north from about El Cid) provide firm stretches for walking and jogging. If you prefer an even firmer surface, the best uncluttered stretch of the *malecón* seaside sidewalk is along Av. del Mar from Valentino's disco south about three miles to the Fisherman's Monument.

Swimming, Boarding, and Sailing

During days of calm water, you can safely swim beyond the gentle breakers, about 50 yards off **Playa Gaviotas** and **Playa Sábalo.** Heed the usual precautions. (See **Water Sports** in the On the Road chapter.)

On rough-water days you'll have to do your laps in a hotel pool, since there is no public pool in Mazatlán. If your hotel has no pool, some of the big hotels, such as El Cid, allow fee day-use by outside guests.

There are several challenging intermediate surfing spots along the Mazatlán shoreline, mostly adjacent to rocky points, such as **Pinos** (next to Ciencias del Mar off Paseo Claussen), **Punta Camarón** (at Valentino's disco), and **Punta Cerritos** at the far north end of the *malecón.*

Bodysurfing and boogie boarding are popular on calm days on Mazatlán's beaches. Boogie boards may be rented for about $3 an hour on

Tough-eating sailfish and black marlin are often discarded after they are brought in. Progressive captains encourage anglers to turn them loose when caught.

the beachfronts of some Zona Dorada hotels, such as Los Sábalos, Playa Mazatlán, El Cid, and Camino Real.

Windsurfing is possible nearly anywhere along Mazatlán's beaches. An especially good, smooth spot is the protected inlet at the north end of Av. Sábalo Cerritos. Bring your own equipment, as there's little windsurfing rental gear available in Mazatlán.

Aqua Sports Center at El Cid and beach shops at other hotels rent Hobie Cats, small catamaran sailboats, for around $25 per hour (three-person limit) to sail from the beach.

Eco-Adventuring

Mazalteco Sports Center on R.T. Loaiza, in front of Las Cabañas shopping center and on the adjacent beach (by Pancho's restaurant), guides a number of local nature adventure tours. Choose from kayaking offshore islands, birdwatching in mangrove wetlands, mountain biking through a thorn forest, snorkeling, scuba diving, sailing, and more. If you prefer, guide yourself via rental kayaks, sailboats, and mountain bikes. For more information, drop by the store, call or fax (69) 165-362 or 165-933, or e-mail: mazalteco@mazalltlan.com.mx.

Snorkeling and Scuba Diving

The water near Mazatlán's beaches is generally too churned up for good visibility. Serious snorkelers and divers head offshore to the outer shoals of Isla Venados and Isla Chivos. A number of shops along the Zona Dorada beaches arrange such trips. The best equipped is **El Cid's Aqua Sports Center,** tel. (69) 133-333, ext. 341, marked by the clutter of equipment on the beach by Hotel El Cid. A three-hour snorkeling or scuba excursion, including equipment and instructor, runs $50 per person, while snorkelers can go along for about $16, including equipment.

Jet Skiing and Parasailing

The highly maneuverable snowmobile-like jet skis have completely replaced water-skiing at Mazatlán. Three or four of them can usually be seen tearing up the water, hotdogging over big waves, gyrating between the swells, and racing each other far offshore. For a not-so-cheap thrill, rent one of them at Aqua Sports Center at El

Cid, tel. (69) 133-333, ext. 341, which has the best and most equipment, for about $35 per half hour for one, $50 for two persons.

Parasailing chutes are continually ballooning high over Zona Dorada beaches. For about $20 for a 10-minute ride, you can fly like a bird through arrangements made at any of the following hotels: El Cid, Playa Mazatlán, or Camino Real.

Tennis and Golf

If you're planning on playing lots of tennis in Mazatlán, best check into one of the several hotels, such as Playa Mazatlán, Inn at Mazatlán, or El Cid (which charges $13/hour even for guests), all of which have courts. If your lodging does not provide courts, you can rent one at **Racquet Club Gaviotas,** tel. (69) 135-939 (three clay, four hard courts, some lighted), for about $10/hour. They're popular and likely to be crowded during the winter season, however.

In-town Mazatlán golf is even more exclusive. The 18-hole course at **El Cid** is the only one within the city limits, and during the high winter-spring season it allows only its guests (and those of a few other deluxe hotels) to play. On the other hand, during low season, outsiders may play for a $75 greens and caddy fee. Carts rent for about $30 for two.

Mazatlán has a pair of more egalitarian, although more pedestrian golf courses. Closest is the nine-hole course at the **Club Campestre,** tel. (69) 800-202, next to the Coca-Cola factory on the airport highway beyond the south edge of town. Fees run a total of about $10 for nine holes. The other, the **Golf Club Estrella del Mar,** is accessible by taxi or car off the airport entrance road. About a quarter mile before the airport terminal, turn right at the signed side road; continue nine miles until the you get to the boat landing, where a launch will take you across to the golf course. Call (69) 823-300 for more information.

Sportfishing

Competent captains and years of experience have placed Mazatlán among the world's leading billfish (marlin, swordfish, and sailfish) ports. The several licensed *flotas deportivas* (sports fleets) line up along the jetty road beneath the El Faro point. They vary, mostly in size of fleet; some have two or three boats, others have a dozen.

Boats generally return with about three big fish—one of them a whopping marlin or sailfish—per day.

The biggest is the **Bill Heimpel Star Fleet,** owned and operated by personable Bill Heimpel, a descendant of a German immigrant family. During the high season he sends out a hundred customers a day. He organizes the groups so you can fish without having to rent a whole boat. One day's fishing runs about $75 per person, complete. Entire boats for about eight passengers (six of whom can fish at a time) rent for around $300 per day, complete. During the May-Oct. low season, reservations only a few days in advance are all that is necessary; for more information, contact the fleet in Mazatlán, tel. (69) 823-878, fax 825-155, P.O. Box 129B, Central Camionera, Mazatlán, Sinaloa 82000. During the high season (Nov.-April) prepaid reservations at Star Fleet's Texas booking office are mandatory. From the U.S. or Canada, contact Star Fleet at (800) CAUGHT-1 (218-4481), or through local number (210) 377-0451, fax 377-8054, or write P.O. Box 290190, San Antonio, TX 78280.

Other operators are equally competent. Heimpel's neighbor is **Mike Maxemin Sportfishing Marina,** whose office is invitingly plastered with yellowing "big catch" photos (Mazatlán's record fish was a half-ton, 13-foot black marlin) beneath huge stuffed marlin and sailfish trophies. Like Heimpel, Maxemin (who has 10 boats) accepts individual reservations. His prices run about $70 per person for a completely supplied fishing outing. Be at the dock at 6 a.m. sharp; expect to return before 3 p.m. Call Mike Maxemin for information and reservations at (69) 812-824 days or 875-988 evenings, or write him at P.O. Box 235, Mazatlán, Sinaloa 82000.

A bit farther down the scale, you can check out some of the more local boats right at the dock, such as **Flota Neptuno,** owned and operated by captain Ricardo Salazar. He rents out a big 42-foot, six person boat with skipper, bait, and poles for billfish for about $160 low season, $200 high. Ask him and he might also be able to furnish a group of four with a launch and skipper, fully equipped for half a day to catch smaller fry, such as 30-pound tuna, or sierra, for around $100.

If price is no object, go to the **El Cid Marina,** located at the north end of Calz. Camarón

Sábalo, where the boulevard bends right around the lagoon, just after the Hotel El Camino. There, the **Aries Fleet,** which "proudly supports the Catch and Release program of the Billfish Foundation," offers either individual reservations in season at about $87 per person, or five elaborately equipped entire boats. Complete charters run from about $300 (28 feet, four lines) to $450 (45 feet, six lines). For information and reservations, call a travel agent or contact Aries Fleet directly, at (69) 163-468, **Naviera Aries,** S.A. de C.V., Marina El Cid, Calz. Camarón Sábalo s/n, Fracc. El Cid C.P., Mazatlán, Sinaloa 82110.

If you're on a tight fishing budget, try negotiating with one of the fishermen on **Playa Norte** (at the foot of 5 de Mayo at Paseo Claussen) to take you and a few friends out in his *panga* for half a day. He can supply lines and bait enough to bring in several big mahimahi and red snapper for a total price of about $50, depending on the season.

Boat Launching

If you have your own boat, you can launch it at at least two official public ramps in Mazatlán. One ramp is at the **Ciencias del Mar** college (on the point just past the boat cove on Paseo Claussen). The school office (tel. 69-828-656) inside sells tickets for about $20 to use the ramp for one day 7 a.m.-6 p.m. The tariff for a one-month permit is only triple that. That would entitle you to anchor your boat, among a dozen neighbors, in the sheltered Playa Norte cove for a month. No facilities are available except the ramp, however.

The other boat ramp is at **Club Náutico,** Explanada del Faro s/n, Mazatlán, Sinaloa 82000, tel./fax (69) 815-195, at the far end of the line of sportfishing docks, below the lighthouse hill. A one-day launching permit runs about $20. The club has a first-class yacht harbor with hoists, a repair shop, and gasoline, but unfortunately no room for outsiders to store boats, either in or out of the water. You may, however, be able to get permission to park your boat and trailer on the road outside the gate.

Hunting Outfitters and Guides

The highest-profile outfitters in town are the **Aviles Hermanos** (Aviles brothers) at 5 de Mayo

2605 at Paseo Claussen. Their business peaks during the winter duck season, when they drive groups about 60 miles south to hunting grounds in the Marismas Nacionales near Esquinapa; their other options include an airplane, which will take you anywhere to legally hunt most anything else. Contact them at their office, 5 de Mayo y Paseo Claussen, P.O. Box 221, Mazatlán, Sinaloa 82000, tel. (69) 813-728, 816-060, or 143-130, fax (69) 146-598, on Paseo Claussen next to Mexicana Airlines.

SHOPPING

Judging from the platoons of racks in the Zona Dorada and in the Mercado Central, T-shirts would seem to be the most popular sale item in Mazatlán. Behind the racks, however, Mazatlán's curio shops stock an amazing bounty of handicrafts from all over the country. The best route to quality purchases at reasonable prices is first to look downtown for the lowest prices, next search the Zona Dorada for the best quality, and then make your choice.

Central Market Shopping

The town *mercado* occupies one square block near the cathedral, between Calles Juárez, Ocampo, Serdan, and Valle. Here, bargaining is both expected and essential unless you don't mind paying $20 for a $5 item. See **Bargaining** in the On the Road chapter.

Although the colorful mélange of meat and vegetable stalls occupies most of the floor space, several small handicrafts shops are tucked inside on the Juárez and Valle sides (west and south) and along all four outside sidewalks.

One of the more unusual of the outside shops is **Artesanías Marina Mercante,** a dusty clutter of handmade accessories, including big Zapatista-style sombreros from Oaxaca, wallets and belts from Guadalajara, and locally made hammocks. Located on the market southeast corner, at Valle and Serdan.

Nothing more typifies Mexico than huaraches. One of Mazatlán's best selections is at **Huarachería Internacional** on the outside market sidewalk at Ocampo and Juárez. Their Michoacán goods are all authentic and, with bargaining, very reasonably priced.

For a big, air-conditioned selection of everything, from hardware and cosmetics to film and groceries, local people and tourists flock to Mexico's Kmart look-alikes, **Gigante,** on R. Buelna, about a mile inland from Valentino's disco, open daily 9 a.m.-9 p.m., and **Comercial Mexicana** at the Gran Plaza mall. Get there by following R. Buelna inland from Valentino's, turn right just past the La Posta trailer park, and continue for a quarter mile to Comercial Mexicana's big orange pelican emblem/sign.

Zona Dorada Shopping

The Zona Dorada presents a bewildering variety of curio shops—in small shopping centers, hotel malls, and at streetside along Av. Camarón Sábalo. Nearly everything you're looking for, however, probably can be found in the concentration of many good and unusual shops along the side street R.T. Loaiza, which forks left, one-way, off of Av. Camarón Sábalo a block north of Valentino's disco. The following are a few highlights, moving north on Loaiza.

One of your first stops should be at a trio of shops in the Hotel Playa Mazatlán shopping center on the beach side of Loaiza. First, on the center's left corner, is **La Carreta,** open daily 9 a.m.-6 p.m., an invitingly arranged museum of fine crafts, including bright Talavera pottery, whimsical Oaxaca wooden animals *(alebrijes),* bright paper flowers, and shining copper and brass chandeliers.

Next door, let the equally attractive selection of **Mexico, Mexico** lead you on, past its racks of colorful women's cotton resort wear, choice Oaxaca wool carpets, eerie Guerrero masks, and shining Tlaquepaque glassware. Open Mon.-Sat. 9 a.m.-6 p.m.

Continue one door uphill to admire the glistening collection of the **Playa** silver store. Virtually all Mexican silver jewelry (see **Shopping** in the On the Road chapter) is crafted far away in Taxco, Guerrero. Without bargaining, Mazatlán silver prices may be a bit steep. You can compare prices against other shops or ask them to weigh the piece. Many shops sell silver jewelry for one U.S. dollar per gram. If your choice is significantly greater than that, you'd better bargain.

Back on the street, head north half a block to the big bargain-basement **Mercado Viejo,** R.T. Loaiza 315, tel. (69) 136-366, open daily 9 a.m.-9 p.m., enclosing a big selection of all-Mexico crafts. If you can name it they probably have it: leather purses, belts, and huaraches, giant ceramic trees of life, onyx animals, painted pottery from Guerrero, carved and gilded wooden fish, shining papier-mâché parrots—the items so common in stores here they seem ordinary—until you take them back home, where on your bookshelf they will become precious mementos.

A block north, step into **Shell City,** Av. R.T. Loaiza 407, tel. (69) 131-301, a de facto museum of shells (and perhaps the reason they've become so scarce on Mazatlán's beaches).

A worker crafts one of dozens of ornaments for sale at Shell City.

Constellations of pearly curios—swirling conches, iridescent abalones, bushy corals, and in one single deviation, whimsical coconut faces—fill Shell City's seeming acres of displays. Open daily 9 a.m.-8 p.m.; credit cards accepted.

After Shell City, move next door to **Centro Comercial Pancho's** and peruse the welter of goods—silver, *huipiles*, ceramics, onyx—for sale. Best here is probably **Arts Sunset**, with its treasury of fetching nativity sets, cuddly Oaxaca dolls, winsome papier-mâché animals, miniature dish sets, glittering pewter, and much more.

Cross the street, toward the beach, and continue your browsing in the intimate beachfront **Cabañas** mall. Some shops stand out: **Garcia's**, with a trove of pewter and fine ceramics; **Mike**, with handsome Taxco silver; and farther back, where the ocean breeze blows through, **La Perla**, with nicely selected ironwood sculptures and papier-mâché.

Pardo Jewelry, 411 Loaiza, tel./fax (69) 143-354, back across the street adjacent to Shell City, specializes in unusually fine gems and jewelry. The glittering silver- and gold-set diamonds, rubies, emeralds, lapis, opals, and amethysts are worth appreciating whether you're buying or not. Open Mon.-Sat. 9:30 a.m.-5:30 p.m.; credit cards accepted.

The **Casa Maya** fine leather store, tel. (69) 167-220, is unmissable because of its replica Mayan pyramid looming above the street. Casa Maya, which specializes in custom boot and leathercraft orders, also offers a fine ready-made selection of boots, coats, jackets, shoes, and purses so original that many are interesting as works of art alone. Lately, Casa Maya has widened its offerings to a fine all-Mexico assortment, including genuine Puebla Talavera ceramics, elaborate censers from Metepec, and Oaxaca *alebrijes* (fanciful wooden animals) and pearly black pottery. Casa Maya is open Mon.-Sat. 10 a.m.-8:30 p.m. and Sunday 10 a.m.- 2 p.m.

For fine graphic art, continue along Loaiza for three blocks and bear left for a long block on Camarón Sábalo to the **Mazatlán Art Gallery**, tel./fax (69) 165-258. The collection focuses on choice impressionist-style Mexican landscapes and folk scenes. Additionally, it sometimes carries the near-surrealistic paintings of artist Paul Modlin. Open Mon.-Sat. 9 a.m.-7 p.m.

SERVICES

Money Exchange

Obtain the most pesos for cash and traveler's checks at **Banamex,** Camarón Sábalo 424, tel. (69) 140-000, 140-001, or 140-002, in the Zona Dorada across the corner, south, from Dairy Queen. Banamex has a special longer-hours cashier outside and to the right of the regular bank, which may be open Mon.-Fri. 8:30 a.m. to as late as 5 p.m. during the high winter season. The downtown main branch at the central plaza, corner of Juárez and Ángel Flores, tel. (69) 823-035 or 824-823, changes both Canadian and U.S. dollars and traveler's checks Mon.-Fri. 8:30 a.m.-2 p.m., closed weekends.

On the other hand, **Banco Internacional** (Bital) offers much longer moneychanging hours: Mon.-Fri. 8 a.m.-7 p.m., Saturday 8 a.m.-2 p.m. Two branches: on Camarón Sábalo, across from Balboa Tower, about three blocks north of Dairy Queen, tel. (69) 163-424 and 163-432, and downtown, corner of Belisario Domínguez and Ángel Flores, tel. (69) 811-595 or 825-579.

After bank hours, change money at one of the many of *casas de cambio* along the Avenidas del Mar and Camarón Sábalo (such as the counter at the north end of R.T. Loaiza, across from Dairy Queen, open daily 9 a.m.-7 p.m., Sunday 10 a.m.-4 p.m., tel. 69-139-209). Also, the **Hotel Playa Mazatlán** reception money-exchange counter, R.T. Loaiza 202, tel. (69) 134-444, services both outside customers and guests daily 6 a.m.-10 p.m.

American Express maintains a full-service Zona Dorada money counter and travel agency on Camarón Sábalo, at Plaza Balboa three blocks north of the Dairy Queen, open Mon.-Fri. 9 a.m.-6 p.m., Saturday 9 a.m.-1 p.m., tel. (69) 130-600, fax 165-908. It gives bank rates for American Express U.S. dollar traveler's checks; no others are accepted, however.

Post Office, Telegraph, and Telephone

For routine mailings, use one of the several post boxes *(buzones)* at the big hotels, such as Los Sábalos, Playa Mazatlán, El Cid, Camino Real, and others.

Otherwise, go to one of the branch post offices. The main branch *(correo)* is adjacent to the central plaza downtown, corner of Juárez and Ángel Flores, tel. (69) 812-121. Open Mon.-Fri. 9 a.m.-7 p.m., Saturday and Sunday 8 a.m.-noon., philatelic services in the morning only. Alternatively, go to the **bus station branch,** open Mon.-Fri. 8 a.m.-6 p.m. (four blocks inland from Playa Norte, behind the Hotel Sands).

Telecomunicaciones (public telephone, fax, and money orders) has two Mazatlán branches, both open Mon.-Fri. 8 a.m.-7 p.m., Sat.-Sun. 8 a.m.-noon. Choose either the downtown branch, in the post office building, tel. (69) 812-220, or the central bus station branch, tel./fax (69) 820-354.

Mail Boxes, Etc., on Calz. Camarón Sábalo, a block south of Dairy Queen, provides many postal services and more, including stamps, mail box, Mexpost express mail, P.O. boxes (with a San Diego, California address), fax, e-mail, and word processing. Hours are Mon.-Sat. 9 a.m.-1 p.m. and 4-7 p.m., tel. (69) 164-009, fax 164-011, e-mail: mailboxes@red2000.com.mx.

Operator-assisted long-distance telephone *(larga distancia)* service is generally available from sidewalk telephones in Mazatlán. For calls within Mexico, dial 020; for international calls, dial 090. (For other hints on using telephones in Mexico, see **Communications** in the On the Road chapter.)

Mazatlán also has **Computel,** an efficient computer-assisted *larga distancia* and fax service: in the Zona Dorada (daily 7 a.m.-9:30 p.m., tel. 69-140-034, fax 140-036) on Camarón Sábalo a few doors north of Dairy Queen, and downtown (tel. 69-853-912, fax 850-108) at Aquiles Serdán 1512. They customarily charge about $2.50 per minute for a daytime call to the U.S.

Beware of the many prominently located but often very expensive "Call U.S. with your Visa or MasterCard" telephones. Ask the operator for the per-minute toll; if it's too high, take your business elsewhere.

Immigration and Customs

If you lose your tourist card, be prepared by having made a copy beforehand; next get a loss report from the tourist police. Then go to **Migración** at the airport or at Aquiles Serdán and Playas Gemelas, on the south side of downtown, near the ferry dock, tel. (69) 813-813. This is also the place to extend your visa (up to 180 days total).

It is open Mon.-Fri. 9 a.m.-3 p.m. for business, closed weekends.

For customs matters, such as leaving your car behind in Mexico while you leave the country temporarily, contact the **aduana** (customs) at the airport, or in the old historic building, at V. Carranza 107, corner of Cruz, in the Olas Altas district, tel. (69) 816-109; open Mon.-Fri. 8 a.m.-3 p.m.

Consulates

The **United States Consular Agent,** Geri Nelson de Gallardo, helps U.S. citizens with legal and other urgent matters in her office, tel./fax (69) 165-889, e-mail: mazagent@red2000.com.mx, open Mon.-Fri. 9:30 a.m.-1 p.m., on R.T. Loaiza, directly across from the Hotel Playa Mazatlán. In emergencies, call the nearest U.S. consulate, in Hermosillo, tel. (62) 172-375 or 172-585.

The **Canadian Consular Office** on Av. R.T. Loaiza, just adjacent to the Hotel Playa Mazatlán, tel. (69) 137-320, fax 146-655, is open Mon.-Fri. 9 a.m.-1 p.m. In an emergency, contact honorary consul Fernando B. Romero through the Canadian Embassy, tel. (5) 724-7900, in Mexico City, or directly to Canada, tel. (800) 123-0200.

Belgium, Finland, Italy, Germany, and France usually also maintain Mazatlán consular officers. See the local telephone Yellow Pages, under *Embajadas, Legaciones, y Consulados,* for contact telephone numbers.

Language Courses and Lessons

The downtown **Centro de Idiomas** ("Language Center"), owned and operated by friendly and very knowledgeable American resident Dixie Davis, offers good beginning and advanced Spanish courses. Registration and all materials run about $105; tuition is about $120/week for small, two-hour daily classes. The center also sponsors homestay and person-to-person programs. For more information, contact the downtown school, two blocks west of the cathedral, at Belisario Domínguez 1908, upstairs, tel. (69) 822-053, fax 855-606, e-mail: 74174.1340@compuserve.com.

Art, Music, and Dance Classes

The **Centro Regional de Bellas Artes Angela Peralta** periodically offers ballet, instrumental and choral music, painting, and other instruction for adults and children. The sessions are conducted in the airy old-world buildings that cluster around the charming downtown Plazuela Machado. For more information, contact the director, Ricardo Urquijo, at Teatro Angela Peralta, tel. (69) 824-447, at the Plazuela Machado.

Nearby, but operating separately, are the **"Free Expression Workshops"** (Talleres de Libre Expression), which invite women of all ages to join the evening classes, which include exercise, yoga, biodance, and relaxation, Mon.-Fri. 6-8 p.m., on Plazuela Machado, south side, second floor, above the Casino Premier restaurant.

Afternoons and evenings, the halls of the **Academia de Artes Centro Francisco Martines Cabrera** echo with the cheerful sounds of students and their violins, guitars, and dancing feet. It offers many semester courses, beginning September and January, including instrumental music, dance, painting, and theater, for children and adults. For more information, drop in and talk to the director, evenings, at 56 Sixto Osuna, two blocks inland from the Av. Olas Altas *malecón*.

Massage

The **Centro de Massage of Mazatlán,** tel. (69) 137-666, open by appointment Mon.-Sat. 10 a.m.-7 p.m., provides massage therapy for around $10 per hour using a variety of techniques, such as shiatsu, neuromuscular, acupressure, Swedish, and cranial vascular, in a studio in the Paraíso Tres Islas shopping center, on R.T. Loaiza, across from Shell City. It advertises itself as the "Land of the Deer Healing Center," quoting a Yaqui proverb: "In gentleness there is great strength." Local hotels refer many customers there.

Photography

Although many big hotel shops develop and sell film, their services are limited and expensive. Competition lowers the prices on "photo row," Calle Ángel Flores downtown, just west of the central plaza. For reasonable one-hour developing and jumbo printing, try **Photo Arauz,** Ángel Flores 607, tel. (69) 822-015, open Mon.-Sat. 8 a.m.-8 p.m., Sunday 9 a.m.-2 p.m. It does 35mm rolls for about $12. Nearby **Photo de Llano,** Ángel Flores 820, tel. (69) 816-277, open Mon.-Sat. 9 a.m.-1:30 p.m. and 4-7 p.m., develops, prints, and enlarges in color on site. They also stock some professional sheet and 120 film, in addition to cameras, photo equipment, and supplies.

INFORMATION

Tourist Information Office

Mazatlán government tourism maintains two information centers. Most convenient is the booth on R.T. Loaiza, across from the Hotel Playa Mazatlán, by the U.S. consular office. If it's not open, go to the main office on Calz. Camarón Sábalo, corner of Tiburón, in the big Banrural building, fourth floor, tel. (69) 165-160 or 165-165, fax 165-166 and 165-167, e-mail: turismo @red2000.com.mx. Office hours are Mon.-Fri. 9 a.m.-3:30 p.m. and 5-7:30 p.m.; Saturday 9 a.m.-1 p.m. by telephone only.

Hospitals and Pharmacies

Its 24-hour duty staff of specialists earns the **Hospital Militar** high recommendations. Despite its exclusive-sounding title, anyone can receive treatment at the Hospital Militar, in the Olas Altas district at Malpica and Venus, tel. (69) 812-079, one block from the Hotel Siesta.

Another good place to be sick is the brand-new, big **Hospital Sharp,** tel. (69) 865-676, at Rafael Buelna and Calz. Jesus Kumate (formerly Calz. Reforma), about a quarter mile along Buelna from Valentino's disco. One of Mexico's newest and best, Sharp Hospital's cadre of highly trained specialists uses its mountain of high-tech equipment to set new Mexican diagnostic and care standards. Prices, however, are generally higher than other Mexican hospitals.

The **Cruz Roja** (private Red Cross), tel. (69) 813-690, operates ambulances and is usually called to auto accidents when the victims are incapacitated. The Cruz Roja hospital is not highly recommended, however. Tell them to take you to Hospital Militar or Sharp, if you can manage it.

If you prefer a bona fide American-trained doctor, try surgeon Dr. Gilberto Robles Guevara's **Clínica Mazatlán** (office tel. 69-812-917, home 851-923) at Zaragoza and 5 de Mayo, on the downtown "doctors' row." Dr. Robles Guevara is the local affiliate of IAMAT, the International Association for Medical Assistance to Travelers.

Farmacias in Mexico are allowed wide latitude to diagnose illnesses and dispense medicines. For a physician and pharmacy all in one right on the *malecón,* try **Farmacia Ángel,** run by friendly Dr. Ángel Avila Tirado, who examines, diagnoses, prescribes, and rings up the sale on the spot, Av. del Mar s/n, one block from the Fisherman's Monument, tel. (69) 824-746 or 816-831, open daily 9 a.m.-11 p.m.

Another good pharmacy is **Farmacia Moderna,** with many Mazatlán branches: downtown, at the corner of 5 de Mayo and 21 Marzo, behind the Palacio Municipal, tel. (69) 810-202 and 816-266; in the Zona Dorada, across from the Hotel Costa de Oro, tel. (69) 140-044, where a doctor is customarily available for advice Mon.-Fri. 6-9 p.m.; also next to Banamex, just south of Dairy Queen, tel. (69) 134-277 or 134-333. After hours, call the 24-hour prescription number, tel. (69) 165-233 or 165-867.

Police and Fire Emergencies

For police emergencies in the Zona Dorada, the special **Policía Turística,** which patrols the Zona Dorada exclusively, can respond quickly. Call (69) 148-444 or go to their headquarters on Gabriel Ruiz, just off Camarón Sábalo, across from the Hotel Inn at Mazatlán.

For downtown police emergencies, contact the *preventiva* police, in the Palacio Municipal on the central plaza, tel. (69) 834-510.

In case of fire, call the *bomberos* (pumpers), tel. (69) 812-769.

Publications

Several stores in the Zona Dorado slake visitors' thirst for English-language books, newspapers and magazines. Perhaps the most bountiful selection is at Restaurant VIPs bookstore, tel. (69) 140-754 or 134-016, open daily 7 a.m.-midnight, across Camarón Sábalo from the Cinemas Gaviotas y Albatroses. It stocks several dozen titles, mostly popular novels and many U.S. popular magazines.

You can also find a supply of U.S. magazines and newspapers, including the *Los Angeles Times, USA Today,* and the Mexico City *News,* plus a rack of used paperback novels, at **Regalos Playa,** on the entrance driveway to the Hotel Playa Mazatlán, open daily 8 a.m.-8 p.m.

Alternatively, trade your old paperbacks for new at **Jean Carmen Book and Gift Shop** nearby, on Loaiza, one door north of the Hotel Playa Mazatlán.

During the November through Easter winter season, you will often find the *Los Angeles Times, USA Today,* and the daily English-language Mexico City *News* at Kioskito Tin Marin, open daily 8:30 a.m.-8:30 p.m., diagonally across Camarón Sábalo from the Dairy Queen.

The unique new-age **Evolución Bookstore** stocks many English-language occult/self-help/meditation/music/astrology titles, along with assorted used paperbacks, cards, Mexico state and city maps, crystals, incense, and oils. Evolución is open daily except Sunday about 10 a.m.-6 p.m. and is located in the Coral shopping center, R.T. Loaiza 204, tel./fax (69) 160-839, e-mail: evol @red2000.com.mx. Find it behind, right side, of Señor Frog's store.

For announcements of local cultural events, tours, restaurants, and interesting feature articles, pick up a copy of *Pacific Pearl,* Mazatlán's visitors' monthly, widely available at tourist shops, restaurants, and hotels. If you can't find one, call or drop by its office, open Mon.-Sat. 9 a.m.-5 p.m., Saturday 9 a.m.- 2 p.m., in shopping Plaza San Jorge, just south of the Dairy Queen corner, tel./fax (69) 130-117, e-mail: webmaster@pacificpearl.com.

Public Library

Mazatlán's respectable public library is downtown, at **Plazuela de Los Leones,** two short blocks behind the Palacio Municipal. Of special interest is the upper-floor **Benjamin Franklin Library:** row upon row of venerable volumes of classic American literature. Open Mon.-Fri. 8 a.m.-8 p.m., Saturday 9 a.m.-noon.

Ecology and Volunteer Work

Mazatlán has a small but growing ecological movement, which has coalesced under the acronym **CEMAZ** (Consejo Ecologico de Mazatlán). Its main focus has been on education by example—cleaning up and restoring Mazatlán's offshore islands and lagoons. Operating out of a small city-financed office on Plazuela Machado, Constitución 511, tel. (69) 852-552, they occasionally need volunteers for projects. Drop in and let them know you're around.

The Mazatlán **Acuario** (Aquarium), Av. de Los Deportes, one block off Av. del Mar about a mile south of Valentino's disco (watch for the signs), tel. (69) 817-815, 817-816, or 817-818, is another center of ecological activity. Mainly through school educational programs, it is trying to save the marine turtles that come ashore to lay eggs along local beaches during the summer and early fall. They may be able to use volunteers to help with such efforts. Check with the public-relations officer or contact the volunteer Friends of the Aquarium: call Kitty, at (69) 839-931 or Vicky, at (69) 166-210 for more details.

Another worthwhile effort is the **Amigos de los Animales,** the local volunteer humane society. For more information, call (69) 880-911.

GETTING THERE AND AWAY

By Air
A number of reliable U.S. and Mexican airlines connect Mazatlán with many destinations in Mexico and the United States.

Alaska Airlines flights connect daily with Los Angeles, San Francisco, and Seattle. The local flight information office is at the airport, tel. (69) 852-730. For reservations and tickets, call the centralized U.S. toll-free booking number, tel. (800) 426-0333.

Mexicana Airlines flights connect daily with Los Angeles, Denver, Miami, Puerto Vallarta (high season), Mexico City, and Los Cabos. The local reservations offices are on the *malecón,* at Paseo Claussen 101B, corner Belisario Domínguez, tel. (69) 827-722. For flight information, call the airport at (69) 825-656 or toll-free (800) 366-5400.

Aeroméxico flights connect daily with Phoenix, Tijuana, Mexico City, Durango, Hermosillo, and Los Mochis. The local reservations/information offices are in the Zona Dorada, at Calz. Camarón Sábalo 310, tel. (69) 141-111 or 141-609, and at the airport, tel. (69) 823-444 or 824-894.

Aero California Airlines flights connect with Los Angeles, Tijuana, La Paz, Guadalajara, and Mexico City. For reservations, call the office at Hotel El Cid, tel. (69) 132-042. For flight information, call the airport office, at (69) 852-557.

America West Airlines flights connect with Phoenix. For reservations in Mexico, call toll-free (800) 235-9292. For flight information, call (69) 811-184.

Canadian World of Vacations charter flights connect with Winnipeg, Vancouver, and Calgary-Edmonton during the winter-spring season. For information, call the agent at the Hotel Playa Mazatlán, tel. (69) 134-444, ext. 221.

Mazatlán Airport Arrival and Departure
For arrivees, the Mazatlán Airport (code-designated MZT, officially the General Rafael Buelna Airport) offers a modicum of services. Although a money exchange office operates daily 9 a.m.-5 p.m., and car-rental agents meet flights, tourist information and hotel booking services are lacking. Travelers should arrive with first-night hotel reservations and guidebook in hand. (Otherwise, they'll be at the mercy of their taxi driver, who will most likely collect a commission from the hotel where he deposits them.)

Local **car rental** agencies include: AGA, tel. (69) 144-405; Price, tel. (69) 866-616; Budget, tel. (69) 132-000, fax (69) 143-611; National, tel. (69) 136-000 or 864-562; Hertz, (69) 136-066 or 134-955, fax 142-525.

Taxi and *colectivo* transportation for the 15-mile (25-km) ride into town is well organized. Booths sell both kinds of tickets: *colectivo* about $5 per person, taxi about $16 per car. No public bus runs from town to the airport.

For departure, *colectivos* are harder to find around hotels than are departing tourists. Share a regular taxi and save on your return to the airport.

The **international airport departure tax** runs $12. If you've lost your tourist card and haven't had time to get a duplicate at immigration, you may be able to avoid the $20 departure fine by presenting a copy of your original tourist card and a police report of your loss. See the Zona Dorada Tourist Police, tel. (69) 148-444, at the corner of Gabriel Ruiz and Santa Monica, across Camarón Sábalo from the Hotel Inn at Mazatlán for such a report.

By Car or RV
Three main highway routes reach Mazatlán: from the U.S. through Nogales and Culiacán; from the northeast, through Durango, and from the southeast, from Guadalajara or Puerto Vallarta through Tepic.

The quickest and safest way to drive to Mazatlán from the U.S. border is by **Mexico National Hwy. 15,** which connects with U.S. Interstate

19 from Tucson, at Nogales, Mexico. A four-lane superhighway for nearly all the 743-mile (1,195-km) route, Hwy. 15 allows a safe, steady 55 mph (90 kph) pace. Although the tolls total about $60 for a car (more for trailers and big RVs) the safety and decreased wear and tear are well worth it. Take it easy and allow yourself at least two full days travel to or from Nogales.

Heading to Mazatlán from the northeast, the winding (but spectacular) two-lane **National Hwy. 40** crosses the Sierra Madre Occidental from Durango. Steep grades over the 7,350-foot (2,235-meter) pass will stretch the trip into a better part of a day, even though it totals only 198 miles (318 km). During the winter, snow can (but rarely) block the summit for a few hours.

From the southeast, heavy traffic slows progress along the mostly two-lane narrow **National Hwy. 15,** which connects with Guadalajara (323 miles, 520 km) via Tepic. Allow at least a full day for this trip.

The same is true of the two-lane route from Puerto Vallarta. Each leg, first National Hwy. 200 (104 miles, 167 km) to Tepic, thence National Hwy. 15 (182 miles, 293 km), is sometimes slowed by heavy traffic and will require at least a full day.

By Bus

The *central de autobuses* (central bus terminal) is at the corner of Hwy. 15 and Calle Chachalulas, about two miles north of downtown and four blocks from Playa Norte behind the Sands Hotel.

Although the terminal is divided into *primera-* (first) and *segunda-clase,* counters on both sides sell both first- and second-class tickets. First class is on the far right, around the terminal corner. Facilities include a kept luggage section (*gurada de equipaje,* about $4 /day), a post office, long distance telephone and public fax, and a number of clean snack stands and stores where travelers can purchase food, pure water, and drinks. Stock up before you leave.

Several well-equipped bus lines provide frequent local departures. Go first or luxury class whenever possible. The service, speed, and reserved seats *(asientos reservados)* of first-class buses far outweigh their small additional cost. Parent company **Estrella Blanca** (which includes Elite, Transportes Chihuahuenses, Transportes Norte de Sonora, Transportes del

Norte, and luxury-class Futura) provides the most departures and the widest range, connecting the entire Pacific corridor, all the way from Acapulco, with border points from California to the Gulf of Mexico. Independent line **Transportes del Pacífico** successfully competes in the northwest, offering both first- and luxury-class departures, connecting Puerto Vallarta with California and Arizona border crossings. All connections listed below are first class and depart locally *(salidas locales)* unless otherwise noted.

First-class **Elite** (EL) buses, tel. (69) 813-811 or 812-335, connect with southeast destinations of Tepic, Guadalajara, Morelia, and Mexico City and intermediate points. *Salidas de paso* (buses passing through) connect en route south to Tepic, Puerto Vallarta, Manzanillo, Zihuatanejo, and Acapulco; in the opposite direction buses connect with northwest destinations of Culiacán and Los Mochis (hourly), Nogales, Agua Prieta, and Tijuana (three per day), including intermediate points.

Several daily **Transportes Norte de Sonora** (TNS) buses, tel. (69) 813-811, connect northwest with Culiacán, Agua Prieta, and Tijuana, northeast with Monterrey, and southeast with Tepic, Guadalajara, Mexico City, San Blas, Puerto Vallarta, Zihuatanejo, Acapulco, and intermediate points.

Transportes Chihuahuenses (TC) buses, tel. (69) 812-335, connect north via Durango, Chihuahua, Juárez, and intermediate points. **Transportes del Norte** buses (TN, operating out of the same office) connect (nine per day) northeast with Durango, Torreón, Monterrey, and Nuevo Laredo.

Luxury-class **Futura** (FU) departures, tel. (69) 812-335, connect northeast with Monterrey, via Durango and Torreón.

Transportes del Pacífico (TP) *salidas de paso* connect hourly en route northwest to Tijuana and southeast to Tepic, Guadalajara, Mexico City, and intermediate points, tel. (69) 820-577. You can change buses at Tepic, however, and continue to Puerto Vallarta.

By Train

Privatization of the Pacific Railroad has put an end to passenger service. Go by bus or airplane instead.

By Ferry

Mazatlán's only ferry connection runs to and from **La Paz**, Baja California, leaving daily at 3 p.m. sharp, from the terminal at the foot of Av. Carnaval. Passengers in cars should get there around 1:30 p.m. to ensure adequate loading time. Vehicle tickets (cars around $200, big RVs and trailers around $400 and up) are sold at the terminal ticket office; information and reservations are available at (69) 817-020, 817-021, or 817-022. Open daily 8 a.m.-noon. You might save yourself *mucho* time, however, by reserving your ferry tickets through a travel agent, such as Marza Tours, in the Galería shopping center across from the Hotel Costa de Oro, tel. (69) 160-896 or 160-897, fax 140-708.

You cannot remain in your vehicle during the 18-hour trip. Passengers can choose from four kinds of accommodations: salon (sitting room, $20/person), tourist (four-person cabin with beds, $33/person), cabin (for four with bath, $54/person), and special (suite, $73/person).

The ferry's increased prices have resulted in greatly improved service. Authorities, especially in La Paz, have reduced the practice of "bumping" private cars and RVs (even with confirmed reservations) in favor of trucks and buses during peak seasons. Hint: If the Mazatlán-La Paz ferry prices are too steep for you, consider crossing via Topolobampo (near Los Mochis, about five hours drive north of Mazatlán) to or from La Paz. It takes only about 10 hours and costs about one-third less.

Mixtec deer motif from pictorial manuscript

SOUTH TO PUERTO VALLARTA AND INLAND TO GUADALAJARA

ALONG THE ROAD TO SAN BLAS

National Hwy. 15 winds southward from Mazatlán through a lush, palm-dotted patchwork of pasture, fields, and jungle-clad hills. To the east rise the sculpted domes of the Sierra Madre Occidental, while on the west, a grand, island-studded marshland stretches to a virtually unbroken barrier of ocean sand.

Although a few scattered fishing villages edge this 150-mile (250-km) coastline, it remains mostly wild, the domain of hosts of shorebirds and waterfowl, and, in the most remote mangrove reaches, jaguars and crocodiles. Its driftwood-strewn beaches invite adventurous trekkers, RV campers, and travelers who enjoy Pacific Mexico beaches at their untouristed best.

PLAYA CAIMANERO

A cluster of beachside *palapa* restaurants marks the southern end of Playa Caimanero, a 20-mile barrier dune that blocks Laguna Caimanero from the sea. (The salinity of Laguna Caimanero, however, is a mystery to local people, who speculate that the salt water migrates under the dune.)

Besides most of the low-key beach pastimes, both Playa Caimanero and its lagoon are a birdwatcher's heaven (bring your bird book, binoculars, and repellent). The broad, shallow **Laguna Caimanero** is less than a mile from the beach along any one of a dozen little tracks through the grove. Local people could probably point you to a boatman who could take you on a birdwatching excursion.

Besides birds, Playa Caimanero is a prime hatching ground for endangered species of sea turtles. They crawl ashore, especially during the later summer and fall, when volunteers patrol the sand, trying to protect the eggs from poachers and predators.

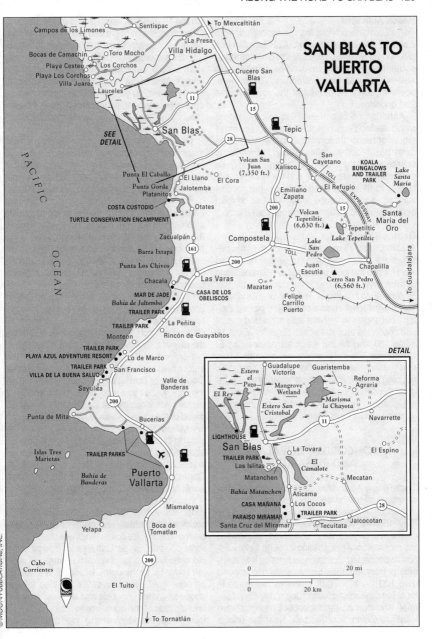

SAN BLAS TO PUERTO VALLARTA

To Mexcaltitán

Campos de los Limones
Sentispac
La Presa
Bocas de Camachin
Toro Mocho
Villa Hidalgo
Playa Cesteo
Los Corchos
Playa Los Corchos
Villa Juárez
Laureles
Crucero San Blas

11

15

SEE DETAIL

San Blas
28
Tepic

Punta El Caballo
El Llano
El Cora
Volcan San Juan (7,350 ft.)
Xalisco
San Cayetano
KOALA BUNGALOWS AND TRAILER PARK
Lake Santa Maria

Punta Gorda
Jalotemba
Platanitos
El Refugio

COSTA CUSTODIO
Otates
Emiliano Zapata
Santa Maria del Oro

TURTLE CONSERVATION ENCAMPMENT

Zacualpán
200
Volcan Tepetiltic (6,630 ft.)
Tepetiltic
Lake Tepetiltic

Barra Ixtapa
161
Compostela
Lake San Pedro

Punta Los Chivos
200
Juan Escutia
Chapalilla

Chacala
Las Varas
Cerro San Pedro (6,560 ft.)

MAR DE JADE
CASA DE LOS OBELISCOS
Mazatan
To Guadalajara

Bahía de Jaltemba
Felipe Carrillo Puerto

TRAILER PARK
La Peñita

TRAILER PARK
Monteon
Rincón de Guayabitos

TRAILER PARK
PLAYA AZUL ADVENTURE RESORT
Lo de Marco

TRAILER PARK
VILLA DE LA BUENA SALUD
San Francisco
Valle de Banderas

Sayulita

200

Punta de Mita
Bucerias

Islas Tres Marietas
TRAILER PARKS

Bahía de Banderas
Puerto Vallarta

Mismaloya

Yelapa
Boca de Tomatlan

Cabo Corrientes

200

El Tuito

To Tornatlán

PACIFIC OCEAN

DETAIL

Estero el Pozo
Guadalupe Victoria
Guaristemba

El Rey
Mangrove Wetland
Reforma Agraria

Estero San Cristobal
Marisma la Chayota

LIGHTHOUSE
San Blas
11
Navarrette

TRAILER PARK
Las Islitas
La Tovara
El Espino

Matanchen
El Camalote
Mecatan

Bahía Matanchen
Aticama

CASA MAÑANA
Los Cocos
28

PARAISO MIRAMAR
TRAILER PARK
Santa Cruz del Miramar
Tecuitata
Jalcocotan

0   20 mi
0   20 km

Beach Activities

Playa Caimanero offers many possibilities, from a scenic, one-day excursion out of Mazatlán or a side loop from Hwy. 15, traveling either north or south, to a weeklong trekking-camping-fishing and wildlife-watching adventure. (Swimmers, however, must be careful of the rough waves and undertow.)

Although no beach facilities exist save the rustic seafood *palapas* at El Caimanero, small stores at two or three villages behind the dune carry basic food supplies. Water, however, is scarce along the beach; campers, bring your purification tablets or filter and some big plastic bottles to fill at the villages. If you get tired of walking, a truck bumps along the beach road every five or 10 minutes; stick out your thumb.

Getting There

At Villa Union, 15 miles (24 km) south of Mazatlán, stock up on gas and supplies. Then head west (or ride the local bus) another 15 miles along Sinaloa Hwy. 5-14 through the dusty little town of El Walamo to beachside Teodoro Beltrán village. The paved road ends a few miles before Beltrán, but improves within a mile to graded gravel and continues atop the beach dune for about 12 miles (20 km) to the seafood *palapas* at El Caimanero. The pavement resumes at the south end (where the road becomes Sinaloa 5-19), heading along the southeastern edge of the lagoon through Agua Verde and rejoining Hwy. 15 at Rosario. The reverse, northbound trip could be done just as easily from Rosario.

CONCORDIA, COPALA, AND ROSARIO

These easily accessible colonial-era towns offer charming off-the-beaten track glimpses of country Mexico. If driving, mark your odometer at the Hwy. 15-Hwy. 40 fork, where you head for Concordia and Copala, east along Hwy. 40, toward the mountains. After winding through lush, wildflower-decorated foothills, you'll notice that roadside pottery factories begin appearing around mile 10 (Km 16). Their offerings, all made in local family workshops, include many floral, animal, and human (some erotic) designs from local pre-Columbian tradition. Near the bridge

at mile 12 (Km 19), which marks the entrance to Concordia, shops make and sell a wealth of sturdy, chestnut-varnished, colonial-style furniture.

For an interesting side excursion, fork sharply right onto a dirt road at the west end of the bridge. After about 100 yards, turn left and continue another 200 yards to a tree-shaded mineral spring (*manantial,* pronounced "mah-NAHN-teeahl"), on the left, where women wash clothes in big collecting basins.

Continue through Concordia. Pass a creek, inviting for picnicking and swimming, at mile 20 (Km 32). Eight miles (13 km) farther, turn right at the signed Copala side road. Copala, an old gold-mining town, founded by conquistador Francisco Ibarra in 1565, continues in the present as a picture-perfect stop for the trickle of tourists who venture out from Mazatlán. However, when the last tour bus departs, at around three in the afternoon, you'll have the place nearly to yourself, save for a few local bench-warmers, a scattering of kids and dogs, and the obligatory chickens scratching around the plaza. The "new" plaza-front church, built in 1624 and dedicated to San José, replaced the original. It presides over the few festivities (Easter, Virgin of Guadalupe 12 December, and Christmas), especially 16 March, the day of San José, when Copala heats up.

For food, try the streetside *taquerías* or the pair of relaxing tourist spots, the **Copala Butter Company** or **Daniel's** restaurant and hotel, on the right, just as you enter town. The friendly expatriate American owner and his wife are justly proud of their Mexican-style fare, which you can enjoy from their airy veranda. They also offer lodging in comfortable hacienda-style rooms for about $20 d. Reserve, especially on weekends and holidays, by writing to Restaurant Daniel's, Copala, Concordia, Sinaloa 82650, or phone Daniel's Mountain Tours, tel. (69) 165-736.

Back on Hwy. 15, continue south to Rosario (pop. about 10,000), about 56 miles (90 km) south of Mazatlán. The dusty town has two claims to fame: its colonial cathedral and its favorite daughter, singer Lola Beltrán. You pass the old church just after the town's entrance arch (off Hwy. 15, to the right). Inside rises the lofty, baroque gold altar, carved as a gilded foliage abode for a choir of angels and cherubs. After the church, stop at the house museum on Lola Beltrán street nearby, where world-renowned

"Ranchera"-style singer Lola Beltrán lived. (Lola's sister, who runs the home as a museum, enjoys company.)

For a restful poolside lunch and/or an overnight lodging in Rosario, try the **Hotel Yuaco** (tel. 69-521-222, about $20 d), on the highway, east side, a couple of blocks south of the entrance arch.

TEACAPÁN

The downscale little beach resorts of Teacapán and Novillero have not yet been "discovered." They remain quiet retreats for lovers of sun, sand, simple lodgings, and super-fresh seafood. Trucks travel from all over Sinaloa and Nayarit to buy their shrimp and fish.

Although Teacapán and Novillero are only a few miles apart, the Río San Pedro estuary that divides Sinaloa from Nayarit also divides Teacapán from Novillero. Novillero's south-side peninsula is identified by Teacapán residents as simply Isla del Otro Lado ("Island on the Other Side").

The small town of Teacapán (pop. 3,000) lies along the sandy northeast edge of the estuary, which most residents know only as *la boca,* the river "mouth." Tambora, Teacapán's broad beach, borders a towering old palm grove on the open ocean a couple of miles north of the town.

Most lodgings and restaurants, however, are on the estuary, a lazy place, where people walk very slowly. Here, a crumbling old dinghy returns to the sand; there, native-style *canoas* lie casually beneath the palms.

Accommodations and Food
A few restaurants line the estuary beach; the best is seafood **Restaurant Mr. Wayne** (from the name of an American friend of the enterprising Mexican owner). He employs his own fisherman to bring the best *pargo, robalo,* and *mero* to the barbecue every afternoon.

The most prominent of Teacapán's hotel accommodations is **Hotel Denisse,** on the main plaza, diagonally adjacent to the church. Enterprising partners Jose Jesús "Pepe" Morales and Carol Snobel revitalized a former private home, and now they have six clean, attractively furnished rooms with bath, spread around an inviting inner patio. The rooms rent for about $18 d with a/c, and $15 with fan only. Although reservations aren't usually necessary, it is best to write or fax the hotel in advance: Hotel Denisse, Calles R. Buelna y Morelos, Teacapán, Sinaloa 82560, fax (695) 452-66.

A few miles back on the road to Teacapán, you may have noticed a sign in passing, advertising the **Hotel Rancho Los Angeles.** If you continue along the side road to the beach, you will find a restaurant, bar, beautiful big pool, and an adjacent trailer park. Upstairs is a luxurious

Wildlife-rich Laguna Caimanero invites exploration by boat.

The shimmering expanse of the Marismas Nacionales (National Marshes) wetlands spreads west from Hwy. 15 south of Mazatlán.

three-room suite that opens to a big deck overlooking a breezy, palm-fringed ocean vista. As the manager says, "The music we have here is the music of the waves." No TV, but plenty of sun, sand, and solitude; the upstairs rents for about $50/day. A three-bedroom cottage beneath the palm grove a short walk away rents for about $100/day. Trailer spaces go for about $15, including all hookups, toilets, showers, and use of the pool. Discounts for longer stays are probably negotiable. For reservations, contact the hotel directly in Teacapán, tel. (695) 325-50, or in Mazatlán, tel./fax (69) 817-867.

Beneath a palm grove on Teacapán's outskirts is the **RV Park Big River,** owned and operated by a friendly refugee from L.A. smog, Hugh Thompson, and his Mexican wife. They, along with many other longtime Teacapán residents, lament the overfishing of the estuary. "When I arrived in the seventies," Hugh reports, "they were pulling big turtles out of the lagoon by the truckloads." There are now no turtles or oysters left from the many acres of original beds, and precious few fish, which the local fishermen must now dive for with spearguns.

Hugh and his wife have 20 shady spaces a quarter mile from Tambora beach that rent for $8.50/day, with all hookups, shower with hot water, a satellite dish available if you have your own lead-in and connectors, discounts available for monthly rentals and self-sufficient units, reservations generally not necessary. Hugh also has a good motorboat, which he likes to use to take

visitors on wildlife-viewing, photography, and fishing excursions in the nearby jungle estuaries. For more information, write them at P.O. Box 22, Teacapán, Sinaloa 82560.

Beach Activities
Fortunately, ocean fishing remains good off Tambora beach. Watch for the sign on the right about two miles before town. You can rent a *lancha* or launch your own boat right on the beach.

Tambora is a very broad silky sand beach where the waves normally roll in gently from about 100 yards out, breaking gradually both left and right for surfing. Windsurfing would also be good here, although the water is too sandy for snorkeling. Various clam, cowrie, and cockle shells turn up at seasonal times. A permanent beachside *palapa* restaurant serves fresh seafood and drinks. Other food and supplies are available in stores back in town.

Camping is customary most anywhere, either on the sand or beneath the big palm grove that edges the shoreline, curving south back to the estuary. To the north, the beach stretches, wild and breeze-swept, for several miles.

Laguna Agua Grande
As it approaches the sea, the Río San Pedro, which forms the Sinaloa-Nayarit border, curves and broadens into a broad brackish lake, Laguna Agua Grande. Fisherfolk traditionally have made their living from the bounty of its waters,

as have a host of waterbirds and myriad other creatures that inhabit its mangrove reaches. Overfishing has unfortunately forced the government to severely limit fish, shrimp, and shellfish catches. The government has to enforce its rules with roadside inspections and military presence.

Since then, an increasing number of boats have begun plying the waters, not hauling fish but eco-tourists and birdwatchers. If you have your own boat, you can do the same, or hire a fisherman to take you. A convenient site for either boat launching or hiring is at the end of Av. Niños Héroes, just one block north of the Teacapán plaza. Follow the gravel road for about a mile and a half to the small fishing camp and improvised boat ramp.

Services
Along the main street back in Teacapán town, residents enjoy the services of a doctor, a pharmacy, a fairly well-stocked grocery, and a long-distance telephone office.

Getting There
Teacapán is accessible from Hwy. 15 by Sinaloa Hwy. 5-23 from Esquinapa. Ride either the local *urbano* or the red-and-blue-striped Transportes Esquinapa buses from in front of the little park adjacent to the plaza cathedral.

Southbound drivers, just before you enter downtown Esquinapa, a diversion funnels through traffic one-way to the right, then left within a block or two. Instead of following left, continue straight ahead for several blocks until you arrive at the asphalt westbound highway out of town, where you should turn right for Teacapán. The all-paved 24 miles (38 km) passes quickly, through bushy thorn forest and past shallow lagoons dotted with waterbirds and rafts of wild lotus. Palm groves and broad fields of chiles, which make Sinaloa one of Mexico's top chile-producing states, line the roadside.

Esquinapa (pop. 40,000), a busy farm town, has a good overnight hotel, the **IQ de Esquinapa** (with restaurant), a block from the downtown plaza at Gabriel Leyva 7 Sur, tel. (695) 304-71 or 307-82. The 30 semideluxe rooms around an enclosed courtyard rent for about $18 d, with TV, a/c, phones, and parking; credit cards accepted.

NOVILLERO

Little Novillero (pop. about 1,000) enjoys one of the longest (55 miles, 90 km), smoothest stretches of sand in Mexico. The waves roll in gently from 100 yards out and swish lazily along a velvety, nearly level beach. Here, all of the ingredients for a perfect beach stay come together: *palapa* seafood restaurants, hotels, a big palm grove for RV or tent camping, ocean fishing, and a broad creamy strand for beachcombers and wilderness campers stretching from both ends of town.

Moreover, Novillero's mangrove hinterland, about a mile or two inland from the beach, is a yet-to-be-discovered wildlife-viewing wonderland. You might be able to enjoy such an opportunity by hiring a local boatman (expect to pay about $15 an hour after bargaining) to take your party on an excursion along pristine jungle waterways. Ask at the hotel, around town, or in the fishing village beneath the estuary bridge (about two miles before town).

Accommodations and Food
Foremost among the several lodgings is the aging, 40-room **Hotel Playa Novillero** beside the palm grove about two blocks from the beach (P.O. Box 56, Tecuala, Nayarit 63440). The hotel encloses a bushy green garden and patio with a spacious, well-maintained pool. The tile-floored rooms are simple but comfortable. Carved dark hardwood doors and tight shutters add a homey touch of class and keep out bugs. A wide, screened-in porch furnished with plants, big wooden rockers, and rustic chairs and tables provides a shady setting for reading and relaxing. Rates run about $10 for one, $20 for two to four; with ceiling fans and seasonal restaurant. It's popular with North Americans and Europeans; best make winter reservations.

If you must stay right on the beach, however, the **Hotel Paraíso de Novillero** can accommodate you (same owner, address, and approximate prices as Hotel Playa Novillero, 24 rooms, a pool, parking, and a restaurant). This lodging's air-conditioned Motel 6-style ambience would appeal most to families busily heading for the pool or beach.

If both of these are full, you can try third-choice **Hotel Miramar** across the street, or fourth-choice

Bungalows on the beach dirt road past the grove on the north edge of town.

For food, Novillero offers a number of choices: a well-stocked country grocery (here called the "mini-super") and half a dozen *palapa* restaurants accustomed to serving a generation of vacationers. Try the big beachside **Hotel Miramar** *palapa,* or look into Lola's **La Gaera,** on the town street two blocks south, where Lola has built a *palapa* furnished with a rainbow assortment of chairs and oilcloth-covered tables. Her son sometimes arrives about 9 p.m. and belts out *gratis* serenades for customers on his guitar.

Getting There

Novillero is about halfway between Tepic and Mazatlán, a two-hour drive either way, plus another half hour (22 miles, 35 km) by paved side road from Hwy. 15. To get there, turn west only a few hundred yards south of the Pemex station (and junction to Acaponeta), at the paved side road signed Tecuala. Continue about eight (13 km) miles and, as you're entering Tecuala, turn right just after the Pemex station. Continue another half mile and turn right at the paved highway, which continues west another 14 (22 km) miles west to Novillero.

MEXCALTITÁN

Mexcaltitán (pop. about 2,000), the "House of the Mexicans," represents much more than just a picturesque little island town. Archaeological evidence indicates that Mexcaltitán may actually be the legendary Aztlán ("Place of the Herons"), where, in 1091, the Aztecs—who called themselves the México (MAY-shi-kah)—began their generations-long migration to the Valley of Mexico.

Each year on 28 and 29 June, the feast days of St. Peter and St. Paul, residents of Mexcaltitán and surrounding villages dress up in feathered headdresses and jaguar robes and breathe life into their tradition. They celebrate the opening of the shrimp season by staging a grand regatta, driven by friendly competition between decorated boats carrying rival images of St. Peter and St. Paul.

Getting There

The southbound Hwy. 15 turnoff for Mexcaltitán is 136 miles (219 km) south of Mazatlán, four miles (six km) after the village of Chilapa. The 25-mile (40-km) southbound side trip passes its last half along a rough (but passable by ordinary automobile) gravel road-dike through the marsh, edged by bushy mangroves and lotus ponds and inhabited by constellations of waterbirds and water-lily-munching cattle.

Northbound from Hwy. 15, follow the signed Santiago Ixcuintla turnoff, 38 miles (60 km) north of Tepic; continue five miles through Santiago Ixcuintla (see below) to the signed and paved Mexcaltitán side road, which continues another 15 miles (25 miles total from Hwy. 15) to the La Batanga *embarcadero* (boat landing).

Mexcaltitán children pose before the town mural, which depicts the traditional story of the migration of their Aztec ancestors to the Valley of Mexico.

AZTLÁN

During their first meeting in imperial Tenochtitlán, the Aztec Emperor Moctezuma informed Hernán Cortés that "from the records which we have long possessed and which are handed down from our ancestors, it is known that no one, neither I nor the others who inhabit this land of Anahuac, are native to it. We are strangers and we came from far outer parts."

Although the Aztecs had forgotten exactly where it was, they agreed on the name and nature of the place from which they came: Aztlán, a magical island with seven allegorical caves, each representing an Aztec subtribe—of which the México, last to complete the migration, had clawed their way to dominion. Aztlán, the Aztecs also knew, lay somewhere vaguely to the northwest, and their migration to Anahuac, the present-day Valley of Mexico, had taken many generations.

For centuries, historians puzzled and argued over the precise location of Aztlán, placing it as far away as Alaska and as near as Lake Chapala. This is curious, for there was an actual Aztlán, a chiefdom, well known at the time of the Spanish Conquest. Renegade conquistador Nuño de Guzmán immediately determined its location and three days before Christmas, in 1529, headed out with a small army of followers, driven by dreams of an Aztec empire in western Mexico. However, when Guzmán arrived at Aztlán—present-day San Felipe Aztatlán village, near Tuxpan in Nayarit—he found no golden city. Others who followed, such as Vásquez de Coronado and Francisco de Ibarra, vainly continued to scour northwestern Mexico, seeking the mythical "Seven Cities of Cíbola" which they confused with the legend of Aztlán's seven caves.

Guzmán probably came closest to the original site. Scarcely a dozen miles due west of his trail through San Felipe Aztatlán is the small island-town of Mexcaltitán, which a number of experts now believe to be the original Aztlán. Many circumstances compel their argument. The spelling common to Mexcaltitán and México is no coincidence, they say. The name Aztlán, furthermore, is probably a contraction of Aztatlán, which translates as "Place of the Herons"—the birds flock in abundance around Mexcaltitán. Moreover, a 1579 map of New Spain by renowned cartographer Ortelius shows an "Aztlán" exactly where Mexcaltitán is today.

The argument goes on: The Codex Boturini, a 16th-century reconstruction of previous Aztec records, reveals a pictogram of Aztecs leaving Aztlán, punting a canoe with an oar. Both the peculiar shape of the canoe and the manner of punting are common to both old Tenochtitlán and present-day Mexcaltitán.

Most compelling, perhaps, is the layout of Mexcaltitán itself. As in a pocket-sized Tenochtitlán, north-south and east-west avenues radiate from a central plaza, dividing the island into four quadrant neighborhoods. A singular, exactly circular plaza-centered street arcs through the avenues, joining the neighborhoods.

If you visit Mexcaltitán, you'll find it's easy to imagine Aztec life as it must have been in Tenochtitlán of old, where many people depended on fishing, rarely left their island, and, especially during the rainy season, navigated their city streets in canoes.

plan view of present-day Mexcaltitán

Sights

From either of the Mexcaltitán road's-end *embarcaderos,* boatmen ferry you across (from the south side, about $4 each way) to Mexcaltitán island-village, some of whose inhabitants have never crossed the channel to the mainland. The town itself is not unlike many Mexican small towns, except more tranquil, due to the absence of motor vehicles.

Mexcaltitán is prepared for visitors. The INAH (Instituto Nacional de Arqueología y Historia) has put together an excellent museum, with several rooms of artifacts, photos, paintings, and maps describing the cultural regions of pre-Columbian México. The displays climax with the museum's centerpiece exhibit, which tells the story of the Aztecs' epic migration to the Valley of México from legendary Aztlán, now believed by experts to be present-day Mexcaltitán.

Outside, the proud village church and city hall preside over the central plaza, from which the town streets radiate to the broad lagoon surrounding the town. In the late afternoons where the watery lagoon meets the end of the streets, village men set out in canoes and boats for the open-ocean fishing grounds, where, armed with kerosene lanterns, they attract shrimp into their nets. Occasionally during the rainy season, water floods the entire town, so that folks must then navigate in boats the streets that become Venice-style canals.

Food and Accommodations

On the town plaza opposite the church stands airy **El Camarón** seafood restaurant, and at the view-edge of the lagoon behind the museum is Mexcaltitán's first official tourist lodging, the **Hotel Ruta Azteca.** More like a guesthouse than a hotel, it has four clean, comfortable, and tiled rooms with bath, some with a/c, that rent from about $20 d. Except for the last week in June, reservations are not usually necessary. You can, however, contact them in advance by writing Hotel Ruta Azteca, Mexcaltitán, via Santiago Ixcuintla, Nayarit.

SANTIAGO IXCUINTLA

If you take the southern approach to Mexcaltitán, you get the added bonus of Santiago Ixcuintla (pop. 20,000, pronounced "eeks-KOOEEN-tlah"), on the north bank of the Río Grande de Santiago, Mexico's longest river. Get there via the signed turnoff from Hwy. 15, 38 miles (60 km) north of Tepic; continue five miles to the town.

Just past the solitary hill that marks the town, turn right at the first opportunity, on to the one-way main street 20 de Noviembre, which in a couple of blocks runs past the picturesque main plaza. Linger a bit to admire the voluptuous Porfirian nymphs who decorate the restored bandstand and the pretty colonial church. Stroll beneath the shaded porticos and visit the colorful market two blocks north of the plaza.

Although its scenic appeal is considerable, the Huichol people are the best reason to come to Santiago Ixcuintla. Hundreds of Huichol families migrate seasonally (late winter and early spring, especially) from their Sierra Madre high-country homeland to work for a few dollars a day in the local tobacco fields. For many Huichol, their migration in search of money includes a serious hidden cost. In the mountains, they have their homes, their friends and relatives around them, and the familiar rituals and ceremonies that they have tenaciously preserved in their centuries-long struggle against Mexicanization. But when the Huichol come to lowland towns and cities, they often encounter the mocking laughter and hostile stares of townspeople, whose Spanish language they do not understand, and whose city ways seem alien. As strangers in a strange land, the pressure for the migrant Huichol to give up their old costumes, language, and ceremonies to become like everyone else is powerful indeed.

Centro Cultural Huichol

Be sure to reserve a portion of your time in Santiago Ixcuintla to stop by the Centro Cultural Huichol, 20 de Noviembre 452, Santiago Ixcuintla, Nayarit 63300, tel. (323) 511-71, fax 510-06. The immediate mission of founders Mariano and Susana Valadez—he a Huichol artist and community leader, and she a U.S.-born anthropologist—is to ensure that the Huichol people enter the 21st century with their traditions intact and growing. Their instrument is the Centro Cultural Huichol—a clinic, dining hall, dormitory, library, crafts-making shop, sale gallery, and interpretive

THE HUICHOL

Because the Huichol have retained more of their traditional religion than perhaps any other group of indigenous Mexicans, they offer a glimpse into the lives and beliefs of dozens of now-vanished Mesoamerican peoples.

The Huichol's natural wariness, plus their isolation in rugged mountain canyons and valleys, has saved them from the ravages of modern Mexico. Despite increased tourist, government, and mestizo contact, prosperity and better health swelled the Huichol population to around 15,000 by the 1990s.

Although many have migrated to coastal farming towns and cities such as Tepic and Guadalajara, several thousand Huichol remain in their ancestral heartland—roughly 50 square miles (80 square km) northeast of Tepic as the crow flies. They cultivate corn and raise cattle on 400 *rancherías* in five municipalities not far from the winding Altengo River valley: Guadalupe Ocotán in Nayarit, and Tuxpan de Bolanos, San Sebastián Teponahuaxtlán, Santa Catarina, and San Andrés Cohamiata in Jalisco.

Although studied by a procession of researchers since Carl Lumholtz's seminal work in the 1890s, the remote Huichol and their religion remain enigmatic. As Lumholtz said, "Religion to them is a personal matter, not an institution and therefore their life is religion—from the cradle to the grave, wrapped up in symbolism."

Hints of what it means to be Huichol come from their art. Huichol art contains representations of the prototype deities—Grandfather Sun, Grandmother Earth, Brother Deer, Mother Maize—that once guided the destinies of many North American peoples. It blooms with tangible religious symbols, from green-faced Mother Earth (Tatei Urianaka) and the dripping Rain Goddess (Tatei Matiniera), to the ray-festooned Father Sun (Tayau) and the antlered folk hero Brother Kauyumari, forever battling the evil sorcerer Kieri.

The Huichol are famous for their use of the hallucinogen peyote, their bridge to the divine. The humble cactus—from which the peyote "buttons" are gathered and eaten—grows in the Huichol's Elysian land of Wirikuta, in the San Luis Potosí desert 300 miles east of their homeland, near the town of Real de Catorce.

To the Huichol, a journey to Wirikuta is a dangerous trip to heaven. Preparations go on for weeks and include innumerable prayers and ceremonies, as well as the crafting of feathered arrows, bowls, gourds, and paintings for the gods who live along the way. Only the chosen—village shamans, temple elders, those fulfilling vows or seeking visions—may make the journey. Each participant in effect becomes a god, whose identity and very life are divined and protected by the shaman en route to Wirikuta.

The fertility goddess symbolically gives birth in a Huichol yarn painting.

center—which provides crucial focus and support for local migratory Huichol people.

Lately, Susana has opened another center high in the mountains (in Huejuquilla, Jalisco, tel. 498-370-54), but Mariano, with the help of their daughter Angélica, continues the original mission in Santiago Ixcuintla. As well as filling vital human needs, the Huichol Cultural Center actively nurtures the vital elements of a nearly vanished heritage. This heritage belongs not only to the Huichol, but to the lost generations of indigenous peoples—Aleut, Yahi, Lacandones, and myriad others—who succumbed to European diseases and were massacred in innumerable fields, from Wounded Knee and the Valley of Mexico all the way to Tierra del Fuego.

Although they concentrate on the immediate needs of people, Mariano, Susana, Angélica, and their volunteer staff also reach out to local, national, and international communities. Their center's entry corridor, for example, is decorated with illustrated Huichol legends in Spanish, especially for Mexican visitors to understand. An adjacent gallery exhibits a treasury of Huichol art for sale —yarn paintings, masks, jewelry, gourds, God's eyes—adorned with the colorful deities and animated heavenly motifs of the Huichol pantheon. Copies of their beautiful coffee table book, *Huichol Indian Sacred Rituals* (published by Amber Lotus Press, 1241 21st St., Oakland, CA 94607), are on sale for about $35. Amber Lotus additionally publishes several gorgeous Huichol art calendars; call (510) 839-3931 for a catalog.

The Centro Cultural Huichol invites volunteers, especially those with secretarial, computer, language, and other skills, to help with projects in the center. If you don't have the time, they also solicit donations of money and equipment (such as a good computer or two) for the center.

Angélica, moreover, enjoys acting as a guide and interpreter, especially for visitors on art-buying trips in towns such as Tepic or Guadalajara. You can contact her, Angélica Valadez, most easily by calling the Huejuquilla center, telephone above.

Get to the Centro Cultural Huichol by heading away from the river along 20 de Noviembre, the main street that borders the central plaza. Within a mile, you'll see the Centro Cultural Huichol, no. 452, on the right.

Services, Accommodations, and Food

Santiago Ixcuintla is an important local business center, offering a number of services. Banks include Banamex (20 de Noviembre and Hidalgo, tel. 323-500-53 or 500-53), Bancomer (20 de Noviembre and Morelos, tel. 323-505-35 or 503-80), and others downtown. There's a *correo* at Allende 23, tel. (323) 502-14. *Telecomunicaciones* including telegraph, long-distance phone, and public fax is available at Zaragoza Ote. 200, tel. (323) 509-89. Magna Sin gasoline is available at the Pemex station on the east-side highway (toward Hwy. 15) as you head out of town.

If you decide to stay overnight in Santiago Ixcuintla, consider the **Hotel Casino** near the plaza downtown, Arteaga and Ocampo, Santiago Ixcuintla, Nayarit, tel./fax (323) 508-50, 508-51, or 508-52. It has a respectable downstairs restaurant/bar and about 35 basic rooms around an inner patio for $20 d, with a/c and parking.

SAN BLAS AND VICINITY

San Blas (pop. about 10,000) is a small town slumbering beneath a big coconut grove. No one seems to care if the clock on the crumbling plaza church remains stuck for months on end. Neither is there anyone who remembers San Blas's glory days, when it was Mexico's burgeoning Pacific military headquarters and port, with a population of 30,000. Ships from Spain's Pacific-rim colonies crowded its harbor, silks and gold filled its counting houses, and noble Spanish officers and their mantilla-graced ladies strolled the plaza on Sunday afternoon.

Times change, however. Politics and San Blas's pesky *jejenes* (pronounced "hey-HEY-nays," invisible "no-see-um" biting gnats) have always conspired to deflate any temporary fortunes of San Blas.

The *jejenes*' breeding ground, a vast hinterland of mangrove marshes, may paradoxically give rise to a new, prosperous San Blas. These thou-

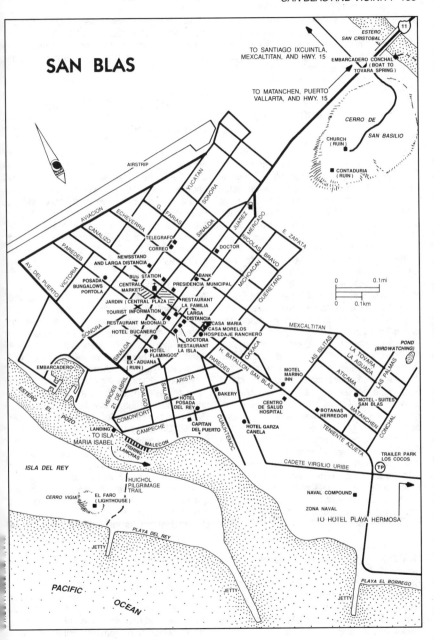

SAN BLAS

TO SANTIAGO IXCUINTLA, MEXCALTITAN, AND HWY. 15

TO MATANCHEN, PUERTO VALLARTA, AND HWY. 15

ESTERO SAN CRISTOBAL

EMBARCADERO CONCHAL (BOAT TO TOVARA SPRING)

CERRO DE SAN BASILIO

CHURCH (RUIN)

CONTADURIA (RUIN)

AIRSTRIP

YUCATAN
SONORA
SINALOA
JUAREZ
MERCADO
E. ZAPATA
AVIACION
ECHEVERRIA
G. FARIAS
NICOLAS BRAVO
CANALIZO
TELEGRAFO
CORREO
DOCTOR
MICHOACAN
PAREDES
NEWSSTAND AND LARGA DISTANCIA
VICTORIA
QUERETARO
AV. DEL PUERTO
BUS STATION
CENTRAL MARKET
BANK
PRESIDENCIA MUNICIPAL
POSADA BUNGALOWS PORTOLA
JARDIN (CENTRAL PLAZA)
RESTAURANT LA FAMILIA
TOURIST INFORMATION
LARGA DISTANCIA
MEXCALTITAN
RESTAURANT McDONALD
CASA MARIA
CASA MORELOS
HOTEL BUCANERO
DOCTORA
HOSPEDAJE RANCHERO
SONORA
HOTEL FLAMINGOS
RESTAURANT LA ISLA
POND (BIRDWATCHING)
SINALOA
EX - ADUANA (RUIN)
H. BATALLON SAN BLAS
OAXACA
LAS ISLITAS
LA TOVARA
LA AGUADA
LAS PALMAS
EMBARCADERO
ARISTA
PAREDES
MOTEL MARINO INN
ATICAMA
ESTERO EL POZO
HEROES 21 DE ABRIL
HIDALGO
SALAS
HOTEL POSADA DEL REY
BAKERY
CENTRO DE SALUD HOSPITAL
MOTEL - SUITES SAN BLAS
MATANCHEN
COMONFORT
CAMPECHE
CAPITAN DEL PUERTO
CUAHTEMOC
HOTEL GARZA CANELA
BOTANAS HERREDOR
CONCHAL
TENIENTE AZUETA
LANDING TO ISLA MARIA ISABEL
MALECON
FISHING LANCHAS
CADETE VIRGILIO URIBE
TRAILER PARK LOS COCOS
TP
ISLA DEL REY
HUICHOL PILGRIMAGE TRAIL
NAVAL COMPOUND
CERRO VIGIA
EL FARO (LIGHTHOUSE)
ZONA NAVAL
TO HOTEL PLAYA HERMOSA
PLAYA DEL REY
JETTY
PACIFIC OCEAN
PLAYA EL BORREGO
JETTY
JETTY

0   0.1 mi
0   0.1 km

sands of acres of waterlogged mangrove jungle and savanna are a nursery-home for dozens of Mexico's endangered species. This rich trove is now protected by ecologically aware governments and admired (not unlike the game parks of Africa) by increasing numbers of eco-tourists.

HISTORY

Conquest and Colonization

San Blas and the neighboring, southward-curving Bay of Matanchén were reconnoitered by gold-hungry conquistador Nuño de Guzmán in May 1530. His expedition noted the protected anchorages in the bay and the Estero El Pozo adjacent to the present town. Occasionally during the 16th and 17th centuries, Spanish explorers in their galleons and the pirates lying in wait for them would drop anchor in the *estero* or the adjacent Bay of Matanchén for rendezvous, resupply, or cargo transfer.

By the latter third of the 18th century, New Spain, reacting to the Russian and English threats in the North Pacific, launched plans for the colonization of California through a new port called San Blas.

The town was officially founded atop the hill of San Basilio in 1768. Streets were surveyed; docks were built. Old documents record more than a hundred pioneer families received a plot of land and "a pick, an adze, an axe, a machete, a plow . . . a pair of oxen, a cow, a mule, four she-goats and a billy, four sheep, a sow, four hens and a rooster."

People and animals multiplied, and soon San Blas became the seat of Spain's eastern Pacific naval command. Meanwhile, simultaneously with the founding of the town, the celebrated Father Junípero Serra set out for California with 14 missionary brothers on *La Concepción,* a sailing vessel built on Matanchén beach just south of San Blas.

Independence

New Spain's glory, however, crumbled in the bloody 1810-21 war for independence, taking San Blas with it. In December 1810, the *insurgente* commander captured the Spanish fort atop San Basilio hill and sent 43 of its cannons to fellow rebel-priest Miguel Hidalgo to use against the loyalists around Guadalajara.

After independence, fewer and fewer ships called at San Blas; the docks fell into disrepair, and the town slipped into somnolence, then complete slumber when President Lerdo de Tejada closed San Blas to foreign commerce in 1872.

SIGHTS AND ACTIVITIES

Getting Oriented

The overlook atop the **Cerro de San Basilio** is the best spot to orient yourself to San Blas. From this breezy point, the palm-shaded grid of streets stretches to the sunset side of **El Pozo** estuary and the lighthouse hill beyond it. Behind you, on the east, the mangrove-lined **San Cristóbal** river-estuary meanders south to the Bay of Matanchén. Along the south shore, the crystalline white line of San Blas's main beach, **Playa El Borrego** ("Sheep Beach"), stretches between the two estuary mouths.

Around Town

While you're atop the hill, take a look around the old *contaduría* counting house and fort (built in 1770), where riches were tallied and stored en route to Mexico City, or to the Philippines and China. Several of the original great cannons still stand guard at the viewpoint like aging sentinels waiting for long-dead adversaries.

Behind and a bit downhill from the weathered stone arches of the *contaduría* stand the gaping portals and towering, moss-stained belfry of the old church of **Nuestra Señora del Rosario,** built in 1769. Undamaged by war, it remained an active church until at least 1872, around the time poet Henry W. Longfellow was inspired by the silencing and removal of its aging bells.

Downhill, historic houses and ruins dot San Blas town. The old hotels **Bucanero** and **Flamingos** on the main street, Juárez, leading past the central plaza, preserve some of their original charm. Just across the street from the Hotel Flamingos, you can admire the crumbling yet monumental brick colonnade of the 19th-century former **Aduana,** now replaced by a nondescript new customhouse at the estuary foot of Av. Juárez.

At that shoreline spot, gaze across El Pozo estuary. This was both the jumping-off point for colonization of the Californias and the anchorage of the silk- and porcelain-laden Manila *galeón* and the bullion ships from the northern mines.

THE BELLS OF SAN BLAS

Renowned Romantic poet Henry Wadsworth Longfellow (1807-82) most likely read about San Blas during the early 1870s, just after the town's door was closed to foreign trade. With the ships gone, and not even the trickle of tourists it now enjoys, the San Blas of Longfellow's time was perhaps even dustier and quieter than it is today.

San Blas must have meant quite a lot to him. Ten years later, ill and dying, Longfellow hastened to complete "The Bells of San Blas," his very last poem, finished nine days before he passed away on 24 March 1882. Longfellow wrote of the silent bells of the old Nuestro Señora del Rosario ("Our Lady of the Rosary") church, which still stands atop the Cerro San Basilio, little changed to this day.

THE BELLS OF SAN BLAS

What say the Bells of San Blas
To the ships that southward pass
From the harbor of Mazatlán?
To them it is nothing more
Than the sound of surf on the shore,—
Nothing more to master or man.

But to me, a dreamer of dreams,
To whom what is and what seems
Are often one and the same,—
The Bells of San Blas to me
Have a strange, wild melody,
And are something more than a name.

For bells are the voice of the church;
They have tones that touch and search
The hearts of young and old;
One sound to all, yet each
Lends a meaning to their speech,
And the meaning is manifold.

They are a voice of the Past,
Of an age that is fading fast,
Of a power austere and grand;
When the flag of Spain unfurled
Its folds o'er this western world,
And the Priest was lord of the land.

The chapel that once looked down
On the little seaport town
Has crumbled into the dust
And on oaken beams below
The bells swing to and fro,
And are green with mould and rust.

"Is then, the old faith dead,"
They say, "and in its stead
Is some new faith proclaimed,
That we are forced to remain

Naked to sun and rain,
Unsheltered and ashamed?

"Once in our tower aloof
We rang over wall and roof
Our warnings and our complaints;
And round about us there
The white doves filled the air,
Like the white souls of the saints.

"The saints! Ah, have they grown
Forgetful of their own?
Are they asleep, or dead,
That open to the sky
Their ruined Missions lie,
No longer tenanted?

"Oh, bring us back once more
The vanished days of yore,
When the world with faith was filled;
Bring back the fervid zeal,
The hearts of fire and steel,
The hands that believe and build.

"Then from our tower again
We will send over land and main
Our voices of command,
Like exiled kings who return
To their thrones, and the people learn
That the Priest is lord of the land!"

O Bells of San Blas, in vain
Ye call back the Past again!
The Past is deaf to your prayer;
Out of the shadows of night
The world rolls into light;
It is daybreak everywhere.

—Henry Wadsworth Longfellow

The palapa restaurant and spring (background) at La Tovara reward visitors with refreshment after the boat tour through the jungle from San Blas.

El Faro (lighthouse) across the estuary marks the top of **Cerro Vigía,** the southern hill-tip of Isla del Rey (actually a peninsula). Here, the first beacon shone during the latter third of the 18th century.

Although only a few local folks ever bother to cross over to the island, it is nevertheless an important pilgrimage site for **Huichol** people from the remote Nayarit and Jalisco mountains. Huichol have been gathering on the Isla del Rey for centuries to make offerings to Aramara, their goddess of the sea. A not-so-coincidental shrine to a Catholic virgin-saint stands on an offshore sea rock, visible from the endpoint of the Huichol pilgrimage a few hundred yards beyond the lighthouse.

A large cave sacred to the Huichol at the foot of Cerro Vigía sadly was demolished by the government during the early 1970s for rock for a breakwater. Fortunately, President Salinas de Gortari partly compensated for the insult by deeding the sacred site to the Huichols during the early '90s.

Two weeks before Easter, people begin arriving by the hundreds, the men decked out in flamboyant feathered hats. On the ocean beach, 10 minutes' walk straight across the island, anyone can respectfully watch them perform their rituals: elaborate marriages, feasts, and offerings of little boats laden with arrows and food, consecrated to the sea goddess to ensure good hunting and crops and many healthy children.

Hotel Playa Hermosa

For a glimpse of a relic from San Blas's recent past, head across town to the crumbling Hotel Playa Hermosa. Here, one evening in 1951, President Miguel Alemán came to dedicate San Blas's first luxury hotel. As the story goes, the *jejenes* descended and bit the president so fiercely the entire entourage cleared out before he even finished his speech. Rumors have circulated around town for years that someone's going to reopen the Playa Hermosa, but—judging from the vines creeping up the walls and the orchids blossoming on the balconies—they'd best hurry or the jungle is going to get the old place first. To get there follow H. Batallón toward the beach and turn left just after the Los Cocos Trailer Park and continue along the jungle road for about half a mile.

La Tovara Jungle River Trip

On the downstream side of the bridge over Estero San Cristóbal, launches for hire will take you up the Tovara River, a side channel that winds about a mile downstream into the jungle.

The channel quickly narrows into a dark tree tunnel, edged by great curtainlike swaths of mangrove roots. Big snowy *garza* (egrets) peer out from leafy branches, startled turtles slip off their soggy perches into the river, while big submerged roots, like gigantic pythons, bulge out of the inky water. Riots of luxuriant plants—white lilies, green ferns, red *romelia* orchids—hang from the trees and line the banks.

Finally you reach Tovara Springs, which well up from the base of a verdant cliffside. On one side, a bamboo-sheltered *palapa* restaurant serves refreshments, while on the other families picnic in a hillside pavilion. In the middle, everyone jumps in and paddles in the clear, cool water.

You can enjoy this trip either of two ways: the longer, three-hour excursion as described ($40 per boatload of six to eight) from El Conchal landing on the estuary, or the shorter version (two hours, $30 per boatload) beginning upriver at road-accessible Las Aguadas near Matanchén village; take the hourly Matanchén bus from the San Blas central plaza. Note: Sometimes a tourist crowd draws all of the boats away from La Conchal to Las Aguadas; go there instead.

The more leisurely three-hour trip allows more chances (especially in the early morning) to spot a jaguar or crocodile, or a giant boa constrictor hanging from a limb (no kidding). Many of the boatmen are very professional; if you want to view wildlife, tell them, and they'll go slower and keep a sharp lookout.

Some boatmen offer more extensive trips to less-disturbed sites deeper in the jungle. These include the Camalota spring, a branch of the Tovara River (where a local *ejido* maintains a crocodile breeding station) and the even more remote and pristine Tepiqueñas, Los Negros, and Zoquipan lagoons in the San Cristóbal Estero's upper reaches.

Compared to the possible wildlife-viewing rewards, trip prices are very reasonable. For example, the very knowledgeable bird specialist Oscar Partida Hernández (Comonfort 134 Pte., San Blas, Nayarit 63740, tel. 328-504-14) will guide a four-person boatload to La Tovara for about $40. If Oscar is busy, call "Chencho," tel. (328) 50-716, for a comparably excellent trip. More extensive options include a combined Camalota-La Tovara trip (allow four to five hours) for about $70, or Tepiqueñas and Los Negros (six hours) for about $90. For each extra person, add about $8, $12, and $16, respectively, to the price of each of these options.

The San Blas tourist information office (see below) has been organizing daily money-saving, collective La Tovara boat tours for visitors. The tariff usually runs about $5 per person.

Isla Isabel

Isla Isabel is a two-mile-square offshore wildlife study area 40 miles (65 km) and three hours north by boat. The cone of an extinct volcano, Isla Isabel is now home to a small government station of eco-scientists and a host of nesting boobies, frigate birds, and white-tailed tropic birds. Fish and sea mammals, especially dolphins, and sometimes whales, abound in the surrounding clear waters. Although it's not a recreational area, local authorities allow serious visitors, accompanied by authorized guides, for a few days of camping, snorkeling, scuba diving, and wildlife viewing. A primitive dormitory can accommodate several persons. Bring everything, including food and bedding. Contact English-speaking Tony Aguayo or Armando Navarrete for arrangements and prices, which typically run $150 per day for parties of up to four persons. Two- and three-day extensions run about $200 and $250, respectively. Rough summer and fall weather limits most Isla Isabel trips to the sunnier, calmer winter-spring season. Their "office" is the little *palapa* to the left of the small floating boat dock at the El Pozo estuary end of Juárez. Armando can also be reached at home, at Sonora 179, in San Blas. Also recommended for the Isla Isabel trip is Antonio Palma, whom you can contact by inquiring at Hotel Garza Canela front desk.

Birdwatching

Although San Blas's extensive mangrove and mountain jungle hinterlands are renowned for their birds and wildlife, rewarding birdwatching can start in the early morning right at the edge of town. Follow Calle Conchal right (southeast) one block from Suites San Blas, then left (northeast) to a small pond. With binoculars, you might get some good views of local species of cormorants, flycatchers, grebes, herons, jacanas, and motmots. A copy of Chalif and Peterson's *Field Guide to Mexican Birds* will assist in further identification.

Rewarding birdwatching is also possible on the **Isla del Rey**. Bargain for a launch (from the foot of Juárez, about $2 roundtrip) across to the opposite shore. Watch for wood, clapper, and Virginia rails, and boat-billed herons near the estuary shore. Then follow the track across the island (looking for warblers and a number of

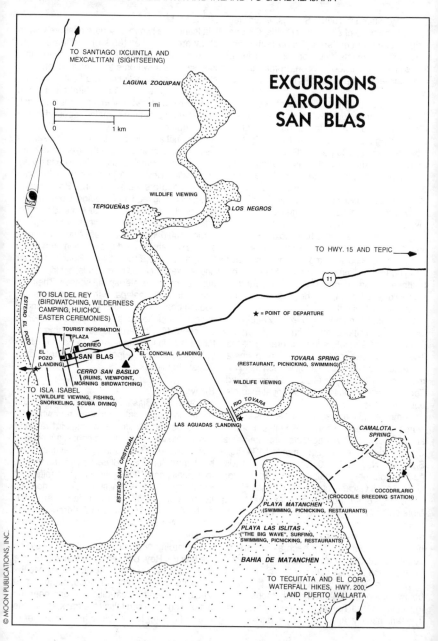

TO SANTIAGO IXCUINTLA AND
MEXCALTITAN (SIGHTSEEING)

LAGUNA ZOQUIPAN

EXCURSIONS
AROUND
SAN BLAS

WILDLIFE VIEWING

TEPIQUEÑAS

LOS NEGROS

TO HWY. 15 AND TEPIC

11

TO ISLA DEL REY
(BIRDWATCHING, WILDERNESS
CAMPING, HUICHOL
EASTER CEREMONIES)

★ = POINT OF DEPARTURE

TOURIST INFORMATION
PLAZA
CORREO
EL POZO
(LANDING)   SAN BLAS   EL CONCHAL (LANDING)

ESTERO EL POZO

CERRO SAN BASILIO
(RUINS, VIEWPOINT,
MORNING BIRDWATCHING)

TOVARA SPRING
(RESTAURANT, PICNICKING, SWIMMING)

WILDLIFE VIEWING

TO ISLA ISABEL
(WILDLIFE VIEWING, FISHING,
SNORKELING, SCUBA DIVING)

RIO TOVARA

CAMALOTA
SPRING

LAS AGUADAS (LANDING)

ESTERO SAN CRISTOBAL

COCODRILARIO
(CROCODILE BREEDING STATION)

PLAYA MATANCHEN
(SWIMMING, PICNICKING, RESTAURANTS)

PLAYA LAS ISLITAS
("THE BIG WAVE", SURFING,
SWIMMING, PICNICKING, RESTAURANTS)

BAHIA DE MATANCHEN

TO TECUITATA AND EL CORA
WATERFALL HIKES, HWY. 200,
AND PUERTO VALLARTA

0   1 mi
0   1 km

species of sparrows) to the beach where you might enjoy good views of plovers, terns, Heerman's gulls, and rafts of pelicans.

Alternatively, look around the hillside cemetery and the ruins atop **Cerro de San Basilio** for good early morning views of hummingbirds, falcons, owls, and American redstarts.

You can include serious birdwatching with your boat trip through the mangrove channels branching from the **Estero San Cristóbal** and **La Tovara River.** This is especially true if you obtain the services of a wildlife-sensitive boatman, such as Oscar Partida Hernández (tel. 328-504-14) or "Chencho" (tel. 328-507-16).

For many more details on birdwatching and hiking around San Blas, get a copy of the booklet *Where to Find Birds in San Blas, Nayarit,* by Rosalind Novick and Lan Sing Wu, at the shop at Garza Canela Hotel ($4). Or order directly from 178 Myrtle Court, Arcata, CA 95521. The American Birding Association Bookstore, P.O. Box 6599, Colorado Springs, CO 80934, and the Los Angeles and Tucson Audubon Society bookstores also stock it.

Waterfall and Birding Hikes

A number of waterfalls decorate the lush jungle foothills above the Bay of Matanchén. Two of these, near Tecuitata and El Cora villages, respectively, are accessible from Hwy. 28 about 10 miles (16 km) south of San Blas. The local white bus *(autobús blanco)* will take you most of the way. It runs south to Santa Cruz del Miramar every two hours 8:30 a.m.-4:30 p.m. from the downtown corner of Juárez and Paredes.

While rugged adventurers may guide themselves to the waterfalls, others rely upon guides Armando Navarrette and Lucio Rodriguez. Lucio works as a volunteer at the tourist information office (on Juárez, just west of the town plaza) or at home (Calle Arista 158, San Blas, Nayarit 63740). His full-day guided hikes by pickup truck cost about $15 per person (minimum of five) or about $50 for two.

Besides the above, Armando Navarette offers birdwatching hikes, especially around Singayta in the foothills, where birders often identify 30 or 40 species in a two-hour adventure. Such an excursion might also include a coffee plantation visit, hiking along the old royal road to Tepic, and plenty of tropical fauna and flora, including butterflies, wildflowers, and giant vines and trees, such as ceiba, *arbolde,* and the peeling, red *papillo* tree. Armando's fee for such a trip, lasting around five hours, runs about $10 per person, plus your own or rented transportation. Armando's "office" is the little *palapa* to the left of the small floating boat dock at the El Pozo estuary end of Juárez. He can also be reached at home, at Sonora 179, in San Blas.

Beach Activities

San Blas's most convenient beach is **Playa El Borrego,** at the south end of Calle Cuauhtémoc about a mile south of town. With a lineup of *palapas* for food and drinks, the mile-long, broad, fine-sand beach is ripe for all beach activities except snorkeling (due to the murky water). The gradually breaking waves provide boogie boarding and intermediate surfing challenges. Bring your own equipment as no one rents on the beach, although the Pato Loco beachware shop on Juárez across the street from Restaurant McDonald in town rents surfboards and boogie boards for about $10 per day.

Shoals of shells—clams, cockles, mother-of-pearl—wash up on Borrego Beach during storms. Fishing is often good, especially when casting from the jetty and rocks at the north and south ends.

ACCOMMODATIONS

Hotels

San Blas has several hotels, none of them huge, but all with personality. They are not likely to be full even during the high winter season (unless, however, the surf off Matanchén Beach runs high for an unusually long spell).

At the low end, the family-run *casa de huéspedes* (guesthouse) **Casa María** makes a reality of the old Spanish saying, *"Mi casa es tu casa."* Located at the corner of Canalizo and Michoacán, three blocks from the plaza, tel. (328) 506-32. With about eight rooms around a homey, cluttered patio, María offers to do everything for the guests except give them baths (which she would probably do if someone got sick). Nowhere near immaculate, but very friendly and with kitchen privileges. Rooms rent for about $10 s, $12 d, with fans, hot water showers, and dinner for $3.

Alternatively, you can try María's original guesthouse, **Casa Morelos,** now operated by her daughter, Magdalena, at Heróico Batallón 108, tel. (328) 506-32, or **Hospedaje Ranchero,** operated by her ex-husband Alfredo, right across the street. They each offer about five rooms around plant-filled patios for about $10 s, $12 d. María, Magdalena and Alfredo all cooperate for the benefit of guests; if one is full, they'll probably be able to find a room next door for you.

Back in the middle of

SAN BLAS ACCOMMODATIONS

Accommodations (area code 328, postal code 63740) are listed in increasing order of approximate high-season, double-room rates.

Casa María, Esquina Canalizo y Michoacán, tel. 506-32, $12

Casa Morelos, Heróico Batallón 108, tel. 506-32, $12

Hospedaje Ranchero, Esquina Batallón y Michoacán, tel. 506-32, $12

Hotel Bucanero, Juárez 75, tel. 501-01, $22

Hotel Posada del Rey, Campeche 10, tel. 501-23, $27

Motel Marino Pacífico Inn, Heróico Batallón s/n, tel. 503-03, $25

Hotel Flamingos, Juárez 105, $30

Motel-Suites San Blas, Aticama and Las Palmas, tel. 505-05, $36

Hotel Garza Canela, Paredes 106 Sur C.P., tel. 501-12 or 504-80, fax 503-08, $69

---

town, **Hotel Flamingos** remains as a reminder of old San Blas. It's at Juárez 105, San Blas, Nayarit 63740, no phone yet, three blocks down Juárez from the plaza. Once the German consulate, it appears from the outside scarcely changed since the day it opened in 1863. A leafy jungle blooms in the patio, enfolded by shaded porticoes. Although it's been recently closed for renovation, a peek through the shutters reveals the best rooms—airy, high ceilinged, and graceful—are being preserved. Rates, with hot water and ceiling fans, will certainly be much higher than they once were. Figure at least $30 d.

Half a block along Juárez, the **Hotel Bucanero** appears to be living up to its name, at Calle Juárez 75, San Blas, Nayarit 63740, a block from the plaza, tel. (328) 501-01. A stanza from the *Song of the Pirate* emblazons one wall, a big stuffed crocodile bares its teeth beside the other, and a crusty sunken anchor and cannons decorate the shady patio. Despite peeling paint the rooms retain a bit of spacious, old-world charm, with high-beamed ceilings under the ruddy roof tile. (High, circular vent windows in some rooms cannot be closed, however. Use repellent or your mosquito net.) Outside, the big pool and leafy old patio/courtyard provide plenty of nooks for daytime snoozing and socializing. A noisy nighttime (winter-spring seasonal) bar, however, keeps most guests without earplugs

jumping till about midnight. The 32 rooms run, low season, about $14 s, $16 d; high season, $18 and $22, with ceiling fans and hot water.

San Blas's more modern hotels are nearer the water. The lively, family-operated **Hotel Posada del Rey,** Calle Campeche 10, San Blas, Nayarit 63740, tel. (328) 501-23, seems to be trying hardest. It encloses a small but inviting pool patio beneath a top-floor viewpoint bar (and high-season-only restaurant) that bubbles with continuous soft rock and salsa tunes. Friendly owner Mike Vasquez, who splits his day between his Pato Loco everything-for-the-beach store and his hotel/bar at night, also arranges tours and fishing, snorkeling, and diving excursions to nearby coastal spots. His hotel rooms, while nothing fancy, are comfortable. Low-season rates for the 13 rooms are about $19 s, $22 d, $23 and $27 high; with a/c, credit cards accepted.

Although the facilities list of the four-star **Motel Marino Pacífico Inn** looks fine on paper, the place is generally unkempt. Its tattered amenities—from the bare-bulb reception and cavernous upstairs disco to the mossy pool patio and mildewy rooms—sorely need scrubbing and a modicum of care. Located at Av. H. Batallón s/n, San Blas, Nayarit 63740, tel. (328) 503-03. The 60 rooms go for about $20 s or d low season, $25 high, all with a/c and private balconies; seasonal restaurant, credit cards accepted.

In the palm-shadowed, country fringe of town not far from Playa Borrego is the **Motel-Suites San Blas,** at Calles Aticama and Las Palmas, San Blas, Nayarit 63740, tel. (328) 505-05, left off H. Batallón a few blocks after the Motel Marino. Its pool patio, playground, game room, and spacious but somewhat worn suites with kitchenettes (dishes and utensils *not* included) are nicely suited for active families. All suites are fan-cooled. The 16 one-bedroom suites accommodate two adults and kids for about $28 low season, $36 high, while the seven two-bedroom suites hold four adults with kids for about $38 low season, $50 high; credit cards accepted.

San Blas's best lodging by far, **Hotel Garza Canela,** Paredes 106 Sur C.P., San Blas, Nayarit 63740, is tucked away at the south end of town, two blocks off H. Batallón, tel. (328) 501-12 or 504-80, fax 503-08. The careful management of its Vásquez family owners (Señorita Josefina Vásquez in charge) shows everywhere: manicured palm-shaded gardens, crystal-blue pool, immaculate sundeck, and centerpiece restaurant. The 60 cool, air-conditioned rooms are tiled, tastefully furnished, and squeaky clean. High winter-season rates run about $54 s, $69 d, with a hearty breakfast included and credit cards accepted; the family runs a travel agency and an excellent gift shop on the premises.

Trailer Park

San Blas's only trailer park, the **Los Cocos,** at H. Batallón s/n, San Blas, Nayarit 63740, tel. (328) 500-55, is a two-minute walk from the wide, yellow sands of Playa El Borrego. Friendly management, spacious, palm-shaded grassy grounds, pull-throughs, unusually clean showers and toilet facilities, a laundry next door, fishing, and a good, air-conditioned bar with satellite TV all make this place a magnet for RVers and tenters from Mazatlán to Puerto Vallarta. The biting *jejenes* require the use of strong repellent for residents to enjoy the balmy evenings. The 100 spaces rent for about $11/day for two persons, $1 for each additional, with all hookups. Monthly rates average about $200 low season, $250 high; pets okay.

Camping

The *jejenes* and occasional local toughs and Peeping Toms make camping on close-in Borrego Beach only a marginal possibility. However, **Isla del Rey** (across Estero El Pozo, accessible by *lancha* from the foot of Calle Juárez) presents possibilities for prepared trekker-tenters. The same is true for eco-sanctuary **Isla Isabel,** three hours by hired boat from San Blas. For those less equipped, the palm-lined strands of **Playa Las Islitas, Playa Matanchén,** and **Playa Cocos** on the Bay of Matanchén appear ripe for camping.

FOOD

Snacks, Stalls, and Market

During the mornings and early afternoons try the fruit stands, groceries, *fondas,* and *jugerías* in and around the **Central Market** (behind the plaza church). Late afternoons and evenings, many semipermanent streetside stands around the plaza, such as the **Taquería Las Cuatas** on the corner of Canalizo and Juárez, offer tasty *antojitos* and drinks.

For sit-down snacks every day till midnight, drop in to the **Lonchería Ledmar** (also at the Canalizo-Juárez corner) for a hot *torta,* hamburger, quesadilla, tostada, or fresh-squeezed *jugo* (juice). For a change of venue, you can enjoy about the same at the **Terraza** café on the opposite side of the plaza.

For basic **groceries** and deli items nearby, try the plaza-front Centro San Blas store, corner of Juárez and H. Batallón San Blas.

Get your fresh cupcakes, cookies, and crispy *bolillos* at the **bakery** at Comonfort and Cuauhtémoc, around the uptown corner from Hotel Posada del Rey, closed Sunday. You can get similar (but not quite so fresh) goodies at the small bakery outlet across from the plaza, corner of Juárez and Canalizo.

Restaurants

Family-managed **Restaurant McDonald,** 36 Juárez, half a block from the plaza, is one of the gathering places of San Blas. The bit-of-everything menu features soups, meat, and seafood in the $5-7 range, besides a hamburger that beats no-relation U.S. McDonald's by a mile. Open daily 7 a.m.-10 p.m. Budget-moderate.

As an option, step across the street to the **Wala Wala** restaurant, for breakfast, lunch, or dinner 8 a.m.-10 p.m. daily except Sunday. The numerous offerings—tasty salads, pastas, seafood, and fillets—crisply prepared and served in a simple but nevertheless clean and inviting setting, will never go out of style. Everything is good; simply pick out your favorite.

For TV with dinner, the **Restaurant La Familia** is just the place at H. Batallón between Juárez and Mercado. American movies, serape-draped walls, and colorful Mexican tile supply the ambience, while a reasonably priced seafood and meat menu furnishes the food. For dessert, step into the luminescent-decor bar next door for giant-screen American baseball or football. Open for lunch and dinner daily except Sunday. Moderate.

For refined marine atmosphere and good fish and shrimp, both local folks and visitors choose **Restaurant La Isla,** at Mercado and Paredes, tel. (328) 504-07. As ceiling fans whir overhead and a guitar strums softly in the background, the net-draped walls display a museum-load of nautical curiosities, from antique Japanese floats and Tahitian shells to New England ship models. Open Tues.-Sun. 2-9 p.m. Moderate.

San Blas's class-act restaurant is the **El Delfín** at the Hotel Garza Canela, Cuauhtémoc 106, tel. (328) 501-12. Potted tropical plants and leafy planter-dividers enhance the genteel atmosphere of this air-conditioned dining room-in-the-round. Meticulous preparation and service, bountiful breakfasts, savory dinner soups, and fresh salad, seafood, and meat entrées keep customers returning year after year. Open daily 8-10:30 a.m. and 1-9 p.m.; credit cards accepted. Moderate to expensive.

ENTERTAINMENT

Sleepy San Blas's entertainment is of the local, informal variety. Visitors content themselves with strolling the beach or riding the waves by day, and reading, watching TV, listening to mariachis, or dancing at a handful of clubs by night.

Nightlife
Owner/manager Mike McDonald works hard to keep **Mike's Place,** Juárez 36, on the second floor of his family's restaurant, the classiest club in town. He keeps the lights flashing and the small dance floor thumping with blues, Latin, and '60s-style rock tunes from his own guitar, accompanied by his equally excellent drum and electronic-piano partners. Listen to live music Friday, Saturday, and Sunday nights and holidays 9 p.m.-midnight. There's a small cover and reasonable drinks.

A few other places require nothing more than your ears to find. During high season music booms out of **Botanas Herredor** (down H. Batallón, a block past the Marino Inn). The same is true seasonally at the bar at the **Hotel Bucanero,** Calle Juárez 75, tel. (328) 501-01.

SPORTS AND RECREATION

Walking and Jogging
The cooling sea breeze and the soft but firm sand of **Playa Borrego** at the south end of H. Batallón make it the best place around town for a walk or jog. Arm yourself against *jejenes* with repellent and long pants, especially around sunset.

Water Sports
Although some intermediate- and beginner-level surf rolls in at Borrego Beach, nearly all of San Blas's action goes on at world-class surfing mecca Matanchén Beach. (See Around the Bay of Matanchén, below.)

The mild offshore currents and gentle, undertow-free slope of Borrego Beach are nearly always safe for good swimming, bodysurfing, and boogie boarding. Conditions are often right for good windsurfing. Bring your own equipment as no rentals are available.

Sediment-fogged water limits snorkeling and scuba diving possibilities around San Blas to the offshore eco-preserve Isla Isabel.

Sportfishing
Tony Aguayo and Abraham "Pipila" Murillo are highly recommended to lead big-game deep-sea fishing excursions. Tony's "office" is the *palapa* shelter to the left of the little dock at the foot of Calle Juárez. You can reach Abraham—distinguished winner of six international tourna-

ment grand prizes—at his home, Comonfort 248, tel. (328) 507-19. Both Tony and Abraham regularly captain big-boat excursions for tough-fighting marlin, *dorado,* and sailfish. The fee will run customarily about $120 for a seven-hour expedition, including boat, tackle, and bait.

On the other hand, a number of other good-eating fish are not so difficult to catch. Check with other captains, such as Antonio Palmas at the Hotel Garza Canela or one of the owners of the many craft docked by the estuary shoreline at the foot of Juárez. For perhaps $80, they'll take three or four of you for a *lancha* outing, which most likely will result in four or five hefty 10-pound snapper, mackerel, tuna, or yellowtail; afterward you can ask your favorite restaurant to cook them up for a feast.

During the latter few days in May, San Blas hosts its long-running (30-plus years) **International Fishing Tournament.** The entrance fee runs around $250; prizes sometimes range from automobiles to Mercury outboards and Penn International fishing rods. For more information, contact the local tourist information office downtown on Juárez, across from Restaurant McDonald.

SHOPPING

San Blas visitors ordinarily spend little of their time shopping. For basics, the stalls at the **Central Market** offer good tropical fruits, meats, and staples. Hours are daily from 6 a.m. till around 2 p.m.

For used clothes and a little bit of everything else, a **flea market** sometimes operates on Calle Canalizo a block past the bus station (away from the *jardín*) Saturday morning and early afternoon.

The plaza-corner store **Comercial de San Blas,** corner of Juárez and H. Batallón, open 9 a.m.-2 p.m. and 5-9 p.m. except Sunday, offers a unique mix of everything from film developing and Hohner harmonicas to fishing poles. Hooks, sinkers, and lines are available.

Handicrafts

Although San Blas has relatively few handicrafts sources, the shop at the **Hotel Garza Canela** has one of the finest for-sale handicrafts collections in Nayarit state. Lovingly selected pieces

from the famous Pacific Mexico crafts centers—Guadalajara, Tlaquepaque, Tonalá, Pátzcuaro, Olinalá, Taxco, Oaxaca, and elsewhere—decorate the shop's cabinets, counters, and shelves.

You'll find a more pedestrian but nevertheless attractive handicraft assortment at the roadside handicrafts and beachwear shop near Playa Borrego, across the street from the naval compound.

Back downtown near the market, two or three small permanent handicrafts shops are scattered along the block (left of the church front) of Calle Sinaloa between Paredes and H. Batallón.

SERVICES

Bank and Moneychanger

Banamex, one block east of the plaza at Juárez 36 Ote., tel. (328) 500-30 or 500-31, exchanges U.S. traveler's checks and cash weekdays 8 a.m.-2 p.m. only. After hours, try your hotel desk or the Pato Loco beach shop across from Restaurant McDonald.

Post Office, Telegraph, and Telephone

The *correo* and *telégrafo* stand side by side at Sonora and Echeverría (one block behind, one block east of the plaza church). The *correo,* tel. (328) 502-95, is open Mon.-Fri. 8 a.m.-2 p.m., Saturday 8 a.m.-noon; *telégrafo,* tel. (328) 501-15, is open Mon.-Fri. 8 a.m.-2 p.m.

In addition to the new long-distance public phone stands that sprinkle the town, there are a number of old-fashioned *larga distancia* stores. Most prominent is the newsstand on Juárez, on the plaza, open daily 8 a.m.-10 p.m. Its rival newsstand, on the opposite side of the plaza (on Canalizo, one block past the bus station), is trying harder, with a fax number (328) 500-01 and longer hours, 8 a.m.-11 p.m. daily.

Immigration and Customs

San Blas no longer has either Migración ("Immigration") or Aduana ("Customs") offices. If you lose your tourist card, you'll have to go to the Secretaría de Gobernación, Oaxaca 220 Sur, in Tepic, or to Migración in Puerto Vallarta. For customs matters, such as having to leave Mexico temporarily without your car, go to the Aduana in Puerto Vallarta for the necessary paperwork.

INFORMATION

Tourist Information Office
The local tourist office is downtown, on Juárez, across from Restaurant McDonald. Although the officer in charge is sometimes out on business, volunteers, such as guide Lucio Rodriguez and Huichol community leader Francisco Pimentel, often staff the office during many of the official hours, Mon.-Fri. 9 a.m.-2 p.m. and 6-10 p.m., Saturday 10 a.m.-2 p.m.

Health and Police
One of San Blas's most highly recommended **physicians** is Dr. Alejandro Davalos, three blocks east of the plaza at Juárez 202 Ote. (corner of Gómez Farías), tel. (328) 502-21 (at his Farmacia Mexicana, on the plaza). If you prefer a female physician, you can go to general practitioner Doctora Dulce María Jácome Camarillo, at her office at Mercado 52 Pte., between Batallón and Paredes; her regular consultation hours are Mon.-Fri. 9 a.m.-1 p.m. and 4-8 p.m.

Alternatively, you can go to San Blas's respectable local hospital, the government **Centro de Salud,** at Yucatán and H. Batallón (across the street from the Motel Marino Inn), tel. (328) 503-32.

For routine advice and medications, the **Farmacia Mexicana** on the plaza, opposite the church, tel. (328) 501-22, stocks a large variety of medicines, along with a bit of everything, including film. Open daily 8:30 a.m.-1:30 p.m. and 5-9 p.m.

For **police** emergencies, contact the headquarters on the left side, behind the Presidencia Municipal ("City Hall"), on Canalizo, east side of the central plaza, tel. (328) 500-28 (or 500-05, the *presidencia*).

Books, News, and Magazines
English-language reading material in San Blas is as scarce as tortillas in Nome. The **newsstand,** on the Juárez side of the plaza, sometimes has *Time, Newsweek,* and *People* magazines. The other newsstand, on the opposite side of the plaza, tries a little harder with *Newsweek, Time, Life,* and *Cosmopolitan.*

As for English-language books, the **tourist information office,** on Juárez, across from Restaurant McDonald, has a shelf of used English and American paperbacks.

GETTING THERE AND AWAY

By Car or RV
To and from Mazatlán and Tepic, National Highway 11 connects San Blas to main-route National Hwy. 15. Highway 11 winds 19 miles (31 km) downhill from its Hwy. 15 junction 161 miles (260 km) south of Mazatlán and 22 miles (35 km) north of Tepic. From the turnoff (marked by a Pemex gas station), the road winds through a forest of vine-draped trees and tall palms. Go slowly; the road lacks a shoulder, and cattle or people may appear unexpectedly around any blind, grass-shrouded bend.

To and from Puerto Vallarta, the new Hwy. 161 cutoff at Las Varas bypasses the slow climb to Tepic, shortening the San Blas-Puerto Vallarta connection to about 94 miles (151 km), or about two and a half hours.

From Tepic, Nayarit Hwy. 28 leaves Hwy. 15 at its signed Miramar turnoff at the northern edge town. The road winds downhill about 3,000 feet (1,000 meters) through a jungly mountain forest to **Santa Cruz del Miramar.** It continues along the **Bahía de Matanchén** shoreline to San Blas, a total of 43 miles (70 km) from Tepic. Although this route generally has more shoulder than Hwy. 11, frequent pedestrians and occasional unexpected cattle necessitate caution.

If your vehicle requires unleaded gas, be sure to fill up with Magna at Las Varas, Tepic, or the Hwy. 11 junction station. Magna may not be available at the San Blas gas station.

By Bus
The San Blas bus terminal stands adjacent to the plaza church, at Calles Sinaloa and Canalizo. First-class **Transportes Norte de Sonora** (TNS) buses, tel. (328) 500-43, connect east several times a day with Tepic, one continuing to Guadalajara. Additionally, a few departures connect north with Mazatlán and south with Puerto Vallarta. One of the Mazatlán departures continues all the way to Tijuana, at the U.S. border.

Four daily second-class navy blue and white **Transportes Noroeste de Nayarit** buses depart about 6 and 8 a.m., noon, and 2 p.m., connecting south with Las Varas, via Bay of Matanchén points of Matanchén, Los Cocos, and Santa Cruz de Miramar. Other departures connect east with Tepic, north with Santiago Ix-cuintla, via intermediate points of Guadalupe Victoria and Villa Hidalgo.

A local white *(autobús blanco)* bus connects San Blas with the Bay of Matanchén points of Las Aguadas, Matanchén, Aticama, Los Cocos, and Santa Cruz del Miramar. It departs from the downtown corner of Paredes and Sinaloa (a block west of the church) four times daily, approximately every two hours, 8:30 a.m.-4:30 p.m.

From Puerto Vallarta, bus travelers have three ways to get to San Blas. Quickest is via one of the four first-class **Transportes Norte de Sonora** departures that connect daily with San Blas. They depart from the new Puerto Vallarta bus station, north of the airport; get your ticket at the Elite-Estrella Blanca desk, tel. (322) 108-48.

On the other hand, many more second-class **Transportes Pacífico** buses connect Puerto Vallarta with Las Varas, on Hwy. 200, where, around 7 and 11 a.m. and 2 and 4 p.m. daily you can transfer to second-class **Transportes Noroeste de Nayarit** navy blue-and-white and white buses that connect with San Blas. If you're too late for that connection, continue to the Tepic bus station, where you might be early enough to catch the last of several daily Transportes Norte de Sonora buses that connect with San Blas.

AROUND THE BAY OF MATANCHÉN

The shoreline of the Bahía de Matanchén sweeps southward from San Blas, lined with an easily accessible, pearly crescent of sand, ripe for beachcombers and tenters. In the luxuriant foothill forest above the bay, trails lead to bubbling waterfalls and idyllic jungle pools, fine for picnicking or wilderness camping. The villages of Matanchén, Aticama, Los Cocos, and Santa Cruz del Miramar dot this strand with *palapa* restaurants and stores offering food and basic supplies. A pair of trailer parks and two good small hotels provide accommodations.

Beaches and Activities

The beaches of **Matanchén** and **Las Islitas** make an inseparable pair. Las Islitas (if heading south, turn right at the Matanchén village junction) is dotted by little outcroppings topped by miniature jungles of swaying palms and spread-

ing trees. One of these is home for a colony of **surfers** waiting for the Big Wave, the Holy Grail of surfing. The Big Wave is one of the occasional gigantic 20-foot breakers that rise off Playa Las Islitas and carry surfers as much as a mile and a quarter—an official Guinness world record—to the soft sand of Playa Matanchén.

About three miles (five km) south of Matanchén village, a sign marks a side road to a *cocodrilario* (crocodile farm). At the end of the two-mile track (truck okay, car-negotiable with caution when dry), you'll arrive at El Tanque, a spring-fed pond, home of the **Ejido de la Palma crocodile farm.** About 50 toothy crocs, large and small, snooze in the sun within several enclosures. Half the fun is the adjacent spring-fed freshwater lagoon, so crystal clear you can see half a dozen big fish wriggling beneath the surface. Nearby, ancient trees swathed in vines and orchids tower overhead, butterflies flutter past, and turtles sun themselves on mossy logs. Bring a picnic lunch, your binoculars, bird book, insect repellent, and bathing suit.

Food and Accommodations

For camping, the intimate, protected curves of sand around Playa Islitas are ideal. Although few facilities exist (save for a few winter-season food *palapas*), the beachcombing, swimming, fishing from the rocks, shell-collecting, and surfing are usually good even without the Big Wave. The water, however, isn't clear enough for good snorkeling. Campers, be prepared with plenty of good insect repellent.

In surfing season (Aug.-Feb.) the Team Banana and other *palapa*-shops open up at Matanchén and Las Islitas to rent surfboards and sell what each of them claims to be the "world's original banana bread."

Getting There

Drive or ride the local *autobús blanco* Santa Cruz del Miramar-bound bus, which departs several times a day from the corner of Paredes and Sinaloa, a block west of the San Blas church. Also, you can ride the second-class navy blue-and-white Noroeste de Nayarit bus, which leaves from the San Blas bus station four times daily.

South from Matanchén

Bending south from Playa Islitas past a lineup of

roadside sign at Matanchén, near San Blas

beachfront *palapa* restaurants, the super-wide and shallow (like a giant kiddie-pool) Playa Matanchén stretches to a palm-fringed ribbon of sand, washed by gentle rollers and frequented only by occasional fisherfolk and a few Sun-

day visitors.

Continuing down the road a mile farther, past the crocodile farm (see above) and a marine sciences school, the beach sand gives way to rocky shoals beneath a jungle headland. The road curves and climbs to shoreline **Aticama** village (small stores and restaurants) and continues along a beachside coconut grove, name-source of the bordering Playa Los Cocos. Unfortunately, the ocean is eroding the beach, leaving a crumbling, 10-foot embankment along a mostly rocky shore.

The place is, nevertheless, balmy and beautiful enough to attract a winter RV colony to **Trailer Park Playa Amor,** overlooking the waves, right in the middle of Playa Los Cocos. Besides excellent fishing, boating, boogie boarding, swimming, and windsurfing prospects, the park offers about 30 grassy spaces for very reasonable prices. Rentals run $7, $8, and $9 for small, medium, and large RVs, respectively, with all hookups, showers, toilets, and pets okay. Write Trailer Park Playa del Amor, c/o gerente Javier López, Playa Los Cocos, San Blas, Nayarit 63740. Although you can expect plenty of friendly company during the winter months, reservations are not usually necessary.

Nestling beneath Playa Los Cocos's venerable palm grove are a few beachfront houses, a couple of very basic lodgings, and a sprinkling of beachside *palapa* restaurants. Outstanding among them is **Mi Restaurant** (open Nov. through May), recently founded by Bernie, the Austrian chef, formerly at Casa Mañana (see below) and super-plush Las Hadas resort in Manzanillo.

Casa Mañana

A mile or two mile farther south, the diminutive shoreline retreat Casa Mañana perches at the south end of breezy Los Cocos beach. Owned and managed by an Austrian man, Reinhardt, and his Mexican wife Lourdes, Casa Mañana's double-storied room tiers rise over a beachfront pool patio and a spic-and-span beach-view restaurant. Very popular with European and North Americans seeking South Seas tranquillity on a budget, Casa Mañana offers fishing, beachcombing, hiking, and swimming right from its palm-adorned front yard. The 26 rooms rent for about $25 with a/c and ocean view, $15 with fan but no view. Add about 15% during the winter high season. Longer-stay discounts negotiable, winter reservations strongly recommended. For reservations, write P.O. Box 49, San Blas, Nayarit 63740; or telephone or fax either the Tepic office at (32) 130-460 or the local cellular phone, (324) 806-10.

Paraíso Miramar

Continue south another two and a half miles and you will pass through rustic Manzanilla village, where a small right-side sign marks the driveway to Paraíso Miramar. The spacious green bay-view park is bedecked by palms and sheltered by what appears to be the grandmother of all banyan trees. Beneath the great tree on a cliff-bottom beach the surf rolls in gently, while the blue bay, crowned by jungle covered ridges, curves gracefully northward toward San Blas.

Paraíso Miramar's owner family, most of whom live in Tepic, and their personable, hard-working manager Porfirio Hernández, offer a little bit for everyone: six simple but clean and comfortable rooms with bath facing the bay; behind that, 12 grassy RV spaces with concrete pads and all hookups, and three kitchenette bungalows sleeping six. A small view restaurant and blue pools—swimming, kiddie, and jacuzzi—complete the lovely picture.

Rooms rent for about $18 s, $21 d; bungalows, about $40. RV spaces go for about $10/day. For a week's stay, they customarily give one day free. If, on the other hand, you'd like to set up a tent, the shady hillside palm grove on the property's south side appears just right. Make reservations by writing Paraíso Miramar directly at Km 1.2 Carretera a San Blas, Playa La Manzanilla, Santa Cruz de Miramar, Nayarit, or calling the family home in Tepic (in Spanish), tel. (32) 120-411.

Waterfall Hikes

A number of pristine creeks tumble down boulder-strewn beds and foam over cliffs as waterfalls (cataratas) in the jungle above the Bay of Matanchén. Some of these are easily accessible and perfect for a day of hiking, picnicking, and swimming. Don't hesitate to ask local directions: say "¿Dónde está el camino a (way to) la catarata, por favor?" If you would like a guide, ask

"¿Hay guia, por favor?" One (or all) of the local crowd of kids may immediately volunteer.

You can get to within walking distance of the waterfall near **Tecuitata** village either by car or by taxi from Santa Cruz de Miramar via Nayarit Hwy. 28 toward Tepic. Half a mile uphill past the village, a sign, Balneario Nuevo Chapultepec, marks a road heading downhill half a mile to a creek and a bridge. Cross over to the other side ($2 entrance), where you'll find a palapa restaurant and a hillside water slide and small swimming pool.

Continue upstream along the right-hand bank of the creek for a much rarer treat, however. Half the fun are the sylvan jungle delights—flashing butterflies, pendulous leafy vines, gurgling little cascades—along the meandering path. The other half is at the end, where the creek spurts through a verdure-framed fissure and splashes into a cool, broad pool, festooned with green, giant-leafed chalata (taro in Hawaii, tapioca in Africa) plants. Both the pool area (known locally as Arroyo Campiste, popular with kids and women who bring their washing) and the trail have several possible campsites. Bring everything, especially your water purification kit and insect repellent.

Another waterfall, the highest in the area, near the village of **El Cora,** is harder to get to, but the reward is even more spectacular. Again, on the west-east Santa Cruz de Miramar-Tepic Hwy. 28, a negotiable dirt road to El Cora branches south just before Tecuitata. At road's end, after about five miles, you can park by a banana loading platform. From there, the walk (less than an hour) climaxes with a steep, rugged descent to the rippling, crystal pool at the bottom of the waterfall. Best ask for a local guide, or go with guides Lucio Rodriguez or Armando Navarrete, who live in San Blas. Lucio can be reached at the tourist information office (on Juárez, just west of the town plaza) or at home (Calle Arista 158, San Blas, Nayarit 63740). Armando's "office" is the little palapa to the left of the small floating boat dock at the El Pozo estuary end of Juárez. He can also be reached at home, at Sonora 179.

Shortcut South to Puerto Vallarta

Newly paved Nayarit Hwy. 161 allows Puerto Vallarta-bound drivers to bypass the old route—

the slow, roundabout climb and descent—via Tepic. Instead, Hwy. 161 forks south from Tepic-bound Hwy. 28 (about 11 miles, 18 km, south of San Blas), just south of Santa Cruz de Miramar village. It continues through lush foothill farms and tropical forest, joining Hwy. 200 at Las Varas, about 53 miles (85 km) north of Puerto Vallarta.

Travelers who wish to explore Tepic, Nayarit's colonial state capital, and its lush, volcano-rimmed valley, should continue uphill along Hwy. 28.

TEPIC

Tepic (elev. 3,001 feet, 915 meters) basks in a lush highland valley beneath a trio of giant, slumbering volcanoes: 7,600-foot (2,316-meter) Sanganguey and 6,630-foot (2,021-meter) Tepeltiltic in the east and south, and the brooding Volcán San Juan (7,350 feet, 2,240 meters) in the west. The waters that trickle from their cool green slopes have nurtured verdant valley fields and gardens for millennia. The city's name reflects its fertile surroundings; it's from the Nahuatl *tepictli,* meaning "land of corn."

Resembling a prosperous U.S. county seat, Tepic (pop. 200,000) is the Nayarit state capital and the service, manufacturing, and governmental center for the entire state. Local people flock to deposit in its banks, shop in its stores, and visit its diminutive main-street state legislature.

The **Huichol** Indians are among the many who come to trade in Tepic. The Huichol fly in from their remote mountain villages, loaded with crafts—yarn paintings, beaded masks, ceremonial gourds, God's eyes—which they sell at local handicrafts stores. Tepic has thus accumulated troves of their intriguing ceremonial art, whose hallucinogenic animal and human forms symbolize the Huichols' animistic world view. (See the special topic on the **Huichol.**)

Beyond the city limits, the Tepic valley offers an unusual bonus for lovers of the outdoors. About 45 minutes from town by car, sylvan mountain-rimmed lake Santa María offers comfortable bungalow lodgings and an RV park and campground, fine for a relaxing day or week of camping, hiking, swimming, kayaking, rowboating, and wildlife viewing.

HISTORY

Scholars believe that, around A.D. 1160, the valley of Tepic may have been a stopping place for a generation of the México (Aztecs) on their way to the Valley of Mexico. By the eve of the conquest, however, Tepic was ruled by the kingdom of Xalisco (whose capital occupied the same ground as the present-day city of Xalisco, a few miles south of Tepic).

In 1524, the expedition headed by the Hernán Cortés' nephew, Francisco Cortés de San Buenaventura, explored the valley in peaceful contrast to those who followed. The renegade conquistador Nuño de Guzmán, bent on accumulating gold and *indígena* slaves, arrived in May 1530 and seized the valley in the name of King Charles V. After building a lodging house for hoped-for future immigrants, Guzmán hurried north, burning a pathway to Sinaloa. He returned a year later and founded a settlement near Tepic, which he named, pretentiously, Espíritu Santo de la Mayor España. In 1532 the king ordered his settlement's name changed to Santiago de Compostela. Today it remains Nayarit's oldest municipality, 23 miles (37 km) south of present-day Tepic.

Immigrants soon began colonizing the countryside of the sprawling new province of Nueva Galicia, which today includes the modern states of Jalisco, Nayarit, and Sinaloa. Guzmán managed to remain as governor until 1536, when the viceroy finally had him arrested and sent back to Spain in chains.

With Guzmán gone, Nueva Galicia began to thrive. The colonists settled down to raising cattle, wheat, and fruit; the padres founded churches, schools, and hospitals. Explorers set out for new lands: Coronado to New Mexico in 1539, Legazpi and Urdaneta across the Pacific in 1563, Vizcaíno to California and Oregon in 1602, and Father Kino to Arizona 1687. Father Junípero Serra stayed in Tepic for several months en route to the Californias in 1767. Excitement rose in Tepic when a column of 200 Spanish dragoons came through, on their way to establishing the new port of San Blas in 1768.

FATHER JUNÍPERO SERRA

His untiring, single-minded drive to found a string of missions and save the souls of native Californians has lifted Junípero Serra to prominence and proposed sainthood. Not long after he was born—on 24 November 1713, to illiterate parents on the Spanish island of Mallorca—he showed a fascination for books and learning. After taking his vows at the Convent of St. Francis in Palma on 15 September 1731, he changed his name to Junípero, after the beloved friend and "merry jester of God" of St. Francis Assisi.

Ordained in 1738 into the Franciscan order, Junípero soon was appointed professor of theology at the age of 30. He made up for his slight five-foot two-inch height with a penetrating intelligence, engaging wit, and cheery disposition. Serra was popular with students, and, in 1748, when he received the missionary call, two of them—Francisco Palóu and Juan Bautista Crespi—accompanied Serra to Mexico, beginning their lifelong sojourn with him.

Serra inspired his followers by example, sometimes to the extreme. On arrival at Veracruz in December 1749, he insisted on walking the rough road all the way to Mexico City. The injuries he suffered led to a serious infection that plagued him the rest of his life. During his association with the Mexico City College of San Fernando (1750-67), which included an extensive mission among the Pames Indians around Jalpan, in Querétero state, he practiced self-flagellation and wore an undercoat woven with sharp bits of wire. Often he would inspire his indigenous flock during Holy Week, as he played the role of Jesus, lugging a ponderous wooden cross through the stations. Afterwards, he would humbly wash his converts' feet.

Serra's later mission to the Californias was triggered by the 24 June 1767 royal decree of King Carlos III, which expelled the Jesuit missionaries from the New World. The king's inspector general of the Indies, José de Galvez, ordered Serra, at age 55, to fulfill a double agenda: organize a Franciscan mission to staff the former Jesuits' several Baja California missions, then push north and found several more in Alta California.

From the summer of 1767 to the spring of 1768, Serra paused in Guadalajara, Tepic, and San Blas with his fellow missionaries en route to the Californias. They sailed north from San Blas in March 1768.

They found the Baja California missions in disarray. The soldiers, left in custody of the missions, were running amok—raping native women, murdering their husbands, and squandering supplies. With the cooperation of military commander and governor Gaspar de Portolá, Serra managed to set things straight within a year and continue northward. On 25 March 1769, Serra, weak with fever, had two men lift him onto his mule, beginning the thousand-mile desert trek from Loreto to San Diego. On 17 May Serra's leg became so infected that Portolá insisted he return to Loreto. Serra refused. ". . . I shall not turn back. . . . I would gladly be left among the pagans if such be the will of God."

Serra, however, was always practical. He asked the mule driver's advice. "Imagine I am one of your mules with a sore on his leg. Give me the same treatment." The mule driver applied the ordinary remedy, a soothing ointment of herbs mixed with lard. Serra resumed the trip and reached San Diego where, on 16 July 1769, he founded San Diego Mission.

The following years would see Serra laboring on, trekking by mule up and down California, founding eight more missions, encouraging the padres whom he assigned, and teaching and caring for the welfare of the Native Americans in his charge. Given the few padres (only two per mission) and the few stores brought by the occasional supply ship from San Blas, it was a monumental, backbreaking task.

In the end, Serra's sacrifices probably shortened his life. On 18 August 1784, at his beloved headquarters mission in Carmel, Serra spent his last days with Palóu, his companion of 40 years. Palóu gave the last sacrament, and two days afterward, Serra, in pain, retraced the stations of the cross with his congregation for the last time. He died peacefully in his cell eight days later.

Regardless of whatever one believes about Spain's colonial role, the fate of the indigenous inhabitants, and sainthood, it is hard not to be awed by this compassionate, gritty little man who would not turn back.

San Blas's glory days were numbered, as were Spain's. Insurgents captured its fort cannons and sent them to defend Guadalajara in 1810, and finally the president closed the port to foreign commerce in 1872.

Now, however, trains, jet airplanes, and a seemingly interminable flow of giant diesel trucks carry mountains of produce and manufactures through Tepic to the Mexican Pacific and the United States. Commerce hums in suburban factories and in banks, stores, and shops around the plaza, where the aging colonial cathedral rises, a brooding reminder of the old days that few have time to remember.

SIGHTS

Getting Oriented

Tepic has two main plazas and two main highways. If you're only passing through, stay on the *libramiento* Hwy. 15 throughway, which efficiently conducts traffic around the city-center congestion. An interchange at the north end of the *libramiento* directs traffic from Hwy. 15 west to Santa Cruz del Miramar and San Blas via Nayarit Hwy. 28, or southeast into town, along Av. Insurgentes. Continue straight ahead on the Hwy. 15 *libramiento* and you reach a second interchange where you can split off, southwest,

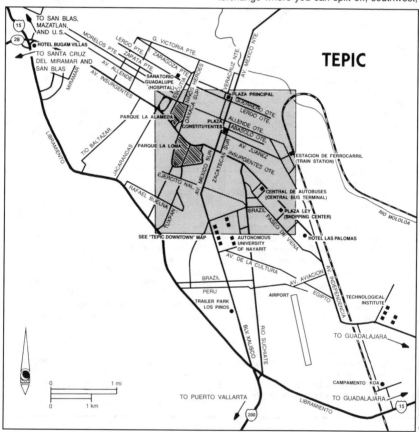

© MOON PUBLICATIONS, INC.

on to Hwy. 200 to Puerto Vallarta, or continue east via Hwy. 15 to Guadalajara.

Av. México, Tepic's main north-south street, crosses Av. Insurgentes just south of big **Parque La Loma** and continues downtown, past the two main plazas: first Plaza Constituyentes, and then Plaza Principal, about a mile farther north.

A Walk around Downtown

The **cathedral,** adjacent to Av. México, at the east side of the Plaza Principal, marks the center of town. Dating from 1750, the cathedral was dedicated to the Purísima Concepción ("Immaculate Conception"). Its twin neo-gothic bell towers rise somberly over everything else in town, while inside, cheerier white walls and neoclassic gilded arches lead toward the main altar. There, the pious, all-forgiving Virgen de la Asunción appears to soar to heaven, borne by a choir of adoring cherubs.

The workaday **Presidencia Municipal** (city and county hall) stands on the plaza opposite the cathedral, while the **municipal tourist information office,** with many good brochures, is just north of it, at the corner of Puebla and Amado Nervo. Back across the plaza, behind the cathedral and a half block to the north at 284 Zacatecas Nte., the **Museo Amado Nervo** occupies the house where the renowned poet was born on 27 August 1870. The four-room permanent exhibition displays photos, original works, a bust of Nervo, and paintings donated by artists J.L. Soto, Sofía Bassi, and Erlinda T. Fuentes. The museum is open Mon.-Fri. 9 a.m.-1 p.m. and 3-7 p.m., Saturday until 1 p.m.

Return back to the plaza and join the shoppers beneath the arches in front of the Hotel Fray Junípero Serra on the plaza's south side, where a platoon of shoe shiners ply their trade.

Head around the corner, south, along Av. México. After about two blocks you will reach the venerable 18th-century former mansion housing the **Regional Anthropology and History Museum,** Av. México 91 Nte., tel. (32) 121-900, open Mon.-Sat. 9 a.m.-6 p.m. The palatial residence was built in 1762 with profits from sugarcane, cattle, and wheat. Since then, the mansion's spacious, high-ceilinged chambers have echoed with the voices of generations of occupants, including the German Consul, Maximiliano Delius, during the 1880s. Now, its down-

stairs rooms house a changing exhibit of charming, earthy, pre-Columbian pottery artifacts from the museum's collection. These have included dancing dogs, a man scaling a fish, a boy riding a turtle, a dog with a corncob in its mouth, and a very unusual explicitly amorous couple. In an upstairs room, displays illustrate the Huichol symbolism hidden in the *cicuri* (eye of God) yarn sculptures, yarn paintings, ceremonial arrows, hats, musical instruments, and other pieces. Also upstairs, don't miss the monstrous 15-foot stuffed crocodile, captured near San Blas and donated by ex-president Carlos Salinas de Gortari in 1989.

If you have time, cross Av. México and continue one block along Hidalgo to take a peek inside a pair of other historic homes, now serving as museums. Within the restored colonial-era house at the southwest corner of Hidalgo and Zacatecas is the **Museo de Los Cuatro Pueblos** ("Museum of the Four Peoples"), which exhibits traditional costumes and crafts of Nayarit's four indigenous peoples—Huichol, Cora, Tepehuan, and México. The museum is open Mon.-Fri. 9 a.m.-2 p.m. and 4-7 p.m., Saturday and Sunday 9 a.m.-2 p.m. Afterward, walk three doors farther on Hidalgo and cross the street, to the **Casa de Juan Escuita,** a colonial house furnished in original style. It's named after a Tepic-born boy who was one of Mexico's beloved six "Niños Héroes"—cadets who fell in the futile defense of Chapultepec Castle (the "Halls of Montezuma") against U.S. Marines in 1846.

Continue south along Av. México; pass the state legislature across the street on the left, and, two blocks farther, on your right, along the west side of the plaza, spreads the straitlaced Spanish classical facade of the State of Nayarit **Palacio de Gobierno.** Inside, in the center, rises a cupola decorated with a 1975 collection of fiery murals by artist José Luis Soto. In a second, rear building, a long, unabashedly biased mural by the same artist portrays the historic struggles of the Mexican people against despotism, corruption, and foreign domination.

Continuing about a mile south of Plaza Constituyentes past Insurgentes, where Av. México crosses Ejército Nacional, you will find the **Templo y Ex-Convento de la Cruz de Zacate** ("Church and Ex-Convent of the Cross of Grass"). This venerable but lately restored monument has two claims to fame: the rooms where Father Junípero Serra stayed for several months in 1767 en route to California, and the miraculous cross that you can see in the open-air enclosure adjacent to the sanctuary. According to chroniclers, the cross-shaped patch of grass has grown for centuries (from either 1540 or 1619, depending upon the account), needing neither water nor cultivation. While you're there, pick up some of the excellent brochures at the **Nayarit State Tourism** desk at the building's front entrance.

Laguna Santa María

Easily accessible by car and about 45 minutes south of town, by either old Hwy. 15 or the new toll *autopista,* Laguna Santa María, tucked into an ancient volcanic caldera, offers near-perfect opportunities for outdoor relaxation. The crater lake itself, reachable via a good paved road, is big, blue, and rimmed by forested, wildlife-rich hills. You can hike trails through shady woods to ridgetop panoramic viewpoints. Afterwards, cool off with a swim in the lake. On another day, row a rental boat across the lake and explore hidden, tree-shaded inlets and sunny, secluded beaches. Afterwards, sit in a palm-fringed grassy park and enjoy the lake view and the orange blossom-scented evening air.

The driving force behind this seemingly too-good-to-be-true scene is Chris French, the personable owner/operator of lakeshore Koala Bungalows and Trailer Park. He's dedicated to preserving the beauty of the lake and its surroundings. It seems a miracle that, lacking any visible government protection, the lake and its forest hinterland remain lovely and pristine. The answer may lie partly in its isolation, the relatively sparse local population, and the enlightened conservation efforts of Chris and his neighbors. For accommodations and access details, see below.

ACCOMMODATIONS

Downtown Hotels

Tepic has a pair of good deluxe and several acceptable moderate downtown hotels. Starting in the north, near the Plaza Principal, the **Hotel Cibrián** is located on Amado Nervo, a block and

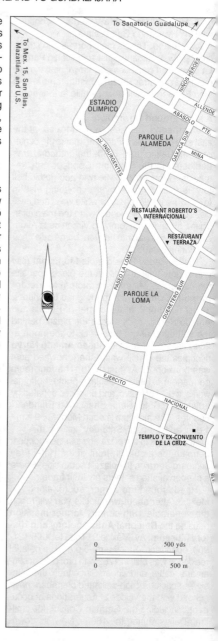

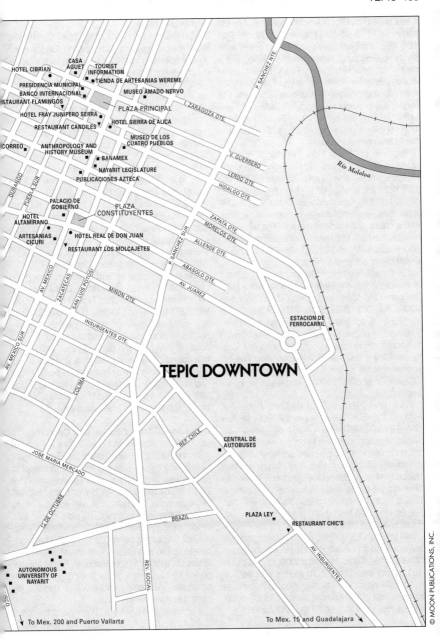

HOTEL CIBRIAN
CASA AGUET
TOURIST INFORMATION
TIENDA DE ARTESANIAS WEREME
PRESIDENCIA MUNICIPAL
BANCO INTERNACIONAL
MUSEO AMADO NERVO
STAURANT FLAMINGOS
HOTEL FRAY JUNIPERO SERRA
PLAZA PRINCIPAL
HOTEL SIERRA DE ALICA
RESTAURANT CANDILES
MUSEO DE LOS CUATRO PUEBLOS
CORREO
ANTHROPOLOGY AND HISTORY MUSEUM
BANAMEX
NAYARIT LEGISLATURE
PUBLICACIONES AZTECA
PALACIO DE GOBIERNO
PLAZA CONSTITUYENTES
HOTEL ALTAMIRANO
ARTESANIAS CICURI
HOTEL REAL DE DON JUAN
RESTAURANT LOS MOLCAJETES

I. ZARAGOZA OTE.
P. SANCHEZ NTE.
V. GUERRERO
LERDO OTE.
HIDALGO OTE.
ZAPATA OTE.
MORELOS OTE.
ALLENDE OTE.
P. SANCHEZ SUR
ABASOLO OTE.
AV. JUAREZ
MINON OTE.
INSURGENTES OTE.

Río Mololoa

DURANGO
PUEBLA SUR
AV. MEXICO
ZACATECAS
SAN LUIS POTOSI
COLIMA
AV. MEXICO SUR

ESTACION DE FERROCARRIL

TEPIC DOWNTOWN

JOSE MARIA MERCADO
REP. CHILE
CENTRAL DE AUTOBUSES

12 DE OCTUBRE
BRAZIL
REV. SOCIAL
PLAZA LEY
RESTAURANT CHIC'S
AV. INSURGENTES

AUTONOMOUS UNIVERSITY OF NAYARIT
TRGO

To Mex. 200 and Puerto Vallarta

To Mex. 15 and Guadalajara

© MOON PUBLICATIONS, INC.

a half behind the Presidencia Municipal, Amado Nervo 163 Pte., Tepic, Nayarit 63000, tel. (32) 128-698. It offers clean, no-frills rooms with baths, ceiling fans, telephones, parking, and a pretty fair local restaurant. The Cibrián's small drawback is the noise that might filter into your room through louvered windows facing the tile (and therefore sound-reflective) hallways. Nevertheless, for the price, it's a Tepic best buy. The 46 rooms go for about $10 s, $11 d; credit cards are not accepted.

Right on the Plaza Principal stands the five-story tower of Tepic's **Hotel Fray Junípero Serra,** Lerdo 23 Pte., Tepic, Nayarit 63000, tel. (32) 122-525, fax 122-051. The hotel offers spacious, tastefully furnished view rooms with deluxe amenities, efficient service, convenient parking, and a cool plaza-front restaurant. The 90 rooms run $30 s and $32 d, and have satellite TV, a/c, phones, parking, and limited wheelchair access; credit cards accepted. No pool.

On Av. México, half a block to the right (south) of the cathedral, the **Hotel Sierra de Alica** (AH-lee-kah), Av. México 180 Nte., Tepic, Nayarit 63000, tel. (32) 120-325, fax 121-309, remains a longtime favorite of Tepic business travelers. Polished wood paneling downstairs and its plain but comfortable rooms upstairs reflect the Sierra de Alica's solid lack of pretension. The 60 rooms rent for $19 s, $22 d with fan and a/c, satellite TV, phones, parking, and credit cards accepted.

The newish **Hotel Real de Don Juan,** Av. México 105 Sur, Tepic, Nayarit 63000, tel./fax (32) 161-820, 161-880, or 161-828, on Plaza Constituyentes, appears to be succeeding in its efforts to become Tepic's class-act hotel. A plush, gleaming lobby and adjoining restaurant/bar match the luxury of the king-size beds, thick carpets, marble baths, and soft pastels of the rooms. Rates for the 48 rooms are $33 s or d, with a/c, TV, parking, and limited wheelchair access; credit cards are accepted.

Nearby on Mina, half a block from the Av. México plaza corner, the **Hotel Altamirano,** Mina 19 Pte., Tepic, Nayarit 63000, tel. (32) 127-131, offers basic bare-bulb rooms with bath at moderate rates. The hotel, although clean, is nondescript to the point of shabbiness. The 31 rooms rent for $11 s or d; fans and parking.

Suburban Motels

If you prefer to stay out of the busy downtown, you have at least two good options. On the north end, three miles from the city center, try the graceful, 50-room **Hotel Bugam Villas,** Insurgentes and Libramiento Pte., Tepic, Nayarit 63000, tel./fax (32) 180-225, 180-226, and 180-227. From the lobby, the grounds extend past lovely, spreading *higuera* (wild fig) trees to the two-story stucco and red-tile-roofed units. Inside, the rooms are clean, high-ceilinged, with huge beds, marble shower baths, TV, a/c, and phone. The restaurant, elegant, cool, and serene within, leads outside to an airy dining veranda that overlooks a manicured shady garden. The food is appealing, professionally presented and served, and moderately priced. The only blot on this near-perfect picture is the noise—which choice of room can moderate considerably—from the trucks on the expressway nearby. Rates run $32 s, $33 d with parking and credit cards accepted.

On the opposite side of town, another good choice is the motel-style **Hotel Las Palomas,** Av. Insurgentes 2100 Ote., Tepic, Nayarit 63000, tel. (32) 140-239 or 140-948, fax 140-953, about two miles southeast of the city center. The two stories of double rooms and suites surround a colonial-chic pool and parking patio. The reception opens into an airy solarium restaurant, which is especially inviting for breakfast. The 67 clean and comfortable Spanish-style, tile-floored rooms rent for $31 s or d, with a/c, satellite TV, and phones; credit cards are accepted.

Bungalows, Trailer Parks, and Camping

On Blvd. Xalisco about a mile before the Puerto Vallarta (Hwy. 200) interchange, the **Trailer Park Los Pinos** offers, besides trailer and camping spaces, six large kitchenette apartments. The 25 pine-shaded concrete trailer pads, with all hookups and good drinkable well water, spread in two rows up a gradual, hillside slope. Los Pinos' mailing address is P.O. Box 329, Tepic, Nayarit 63000, or phone (32) 131-232. The apartments, plain but clean, well-maintained, and spacious, rent for $13 year-round. Trailer spaces go for $9-12 a night, while camping is $6, with discounts for weekly and monthly rentals; includes showers and toilets.

Farther out of town still, RVers and campers used to enjoy the Campamento KOA, but it closed and appears it's going to remain that way, at least until further notice.

RV and tent camping and comfortable rooms are also available at the **Koala Bungalows and Trailer Park** at the gorgeously rural, semitropical mountain lake Santa María (see **Laguna Santa María,** above), about 45 minutes away via Hwy. 15 southeast of Tepic. Owner Chris French maintains a tranquil, palm-studded lakeside park, with bungalow-style rooms, houses, RV and tenting sites, a snack bar, kiddie pool, small swimming pool, and rowboat rentals. For reservations, phone (32) 140-509 or 123-772, or write P.O. Box 493, Tepic, Nayarit 63000. The four spartan but clean and comfortable garden kitchenette apartments, for up to four persons, with bath, rent from about $16 daily, $100 weekly, and $300 monthly. A small house and a larger two-bedroom house are also available for $35 and $44 per day, respectively. About 20 well-maintained shady RV sites rent for $8 daily, $46 weekly, and $170 monthly, with all hookups, and toilets and showers. Add $1 per day for a/c power. Campsites go for about $2 per adult, $1.50 per child, per night. Weekends at Koala Bungalows tend to bustle with local families; weekdays, when the few guests are middle-class European, North American, and Mexican couples, are more tranquil.

Those who yearn for even more serenity and privacy opt for one of the fully furnished semiluxurious **view apartments,** built by Chris's daughter Hayley and her husband on the opposite side of the lake. The apartments' overall plan, on four separate levels, stair-stepping up the hillside among ancient, spreading trees, blends thoughtfully into the pristine lakeside setting. Here, all the ingredients—individual lake-vista *terrazas,* kitchenettes (bring your food), king-sized beds, swimming pool—seem to come together for a perfectly tranquil weekend, week, or month of Sundays. Apartments rent for about $50/day; reserve through the same numbers and address as Koala Bungalows above.

Get there by bus (see below) or by driving, either along Hwy. 15 *libre* (nontoll) or the new toll *(cuota) autopista,* to Guadalajara, which begins at the far southeast suburb. From *libre* Hwy. 15, about 16 miles (26 km) east of Tepic, between roadside kilometer markers 194 and 195, follow the signed turnoff left (north) toward Santa María

del Oro town. Keep on five more miles (eight km) to the town (pop. 3,000). Continue another five miles (eight km), winding downhill to the lake. For a breathtaking lake view, stop at the roadside viewpoint about a mile past the town. At the lakeshore, head left a few hundred yards to Koala Bungalows and Trailer Park. From the *autopista* follow the signed Santa María del Oro exit. Proceed to the town and continue, winding downhill to the lake, as described above.

Laguna Santa María is directly accessible by bus from the second-class bus terminal in downtown Tepic (from the cathedral, walk four blocks north along Av. Mexico; at Victoria, turn east a few steps to no. 9, at the station driveway). The relevant ticket office (*taquilla* of Transportes Noroeste de Nayarit, tel. 32-122-325) is inside at the back. Buses leave for Laguna Santa María three times daily, at 6 a.m., 1 p.m., and 5 p.m. On return, they depart from the lake at 9 a.m., 4 p.m., and 8 p.m.

You can also ride a long-distance Guadalajara-bound bus from the *central camionera* on Insurgentes, southeast of the Tepic town center, to Santa María del Oro town, where you can catch a taxi, local bus, or collective van the remaining five miles downhill to the lake.

FOOD

Traffic noise and exhaust smoke sometimes sully the atmosphere in downtown restaurants. The **Hotel Fray Junípero Serra** restaurant does not suffer such a drawback, however, located in air-conditioned serenity behind its plate glass, plaza-front windows at Lerdo 23 Pte., tel. (32) 122-525. Open daily 7 a.m.-9 p.m., credit cards accepted. Moderate-expensive.

A much humbler but colorful and relatively quiet lunch or supper spot is the downtown favorite **Lonchería Flamingos,** on Puebla Nte., behind and half a block north of the Presidencia Municipal, where a cadre of spirited female chefs puts out a continuous supply of steaming *tortas,* tostadas, tacos, *hamburguesas,* and *chocomiles.* The *tortas,* although tasty, are small. Best try the tostada, which is served on a huge, yummy, crunchy corn tortilla. Open daily except Wednesday, 10 a.m.-10:30 p.m. Inexpensive.

For authentic Mexican cooking, go to Tepic's clean, well-lighted place for tacos, **Tacos Mismaloya,** southwest plaza corner, across from the Banco Internacional. Pick from a long list of tacos in eight styles, as well as *pozole,* enchiladas, tamales, quesadillas, and much more. Open daily 8 a.m.-8 p.m.

Another popular downtown restaurant choice is the **Restaurant Altamirano,** at Av. México 109 Sur, in the big Hotel Real de Don Juan at the southeast corner of Plaza Constituyentes. Here, in a clean rustic-chic atmosphere, businesspeople lunch in the daytime, and middle- and upper-class Tepic families stop for snacks after the movies. The curt but appetizing menu items include a host of Mexican entrées plus a number of international favorites, including spaghetti, hamburgers, omelettes, and pancakes. Open Mon.-Sat. 8 a.m.-8 p.m., Sunday 8 a.m.-4 p.m. Moderate.

Two doors farther down Av. México, the popular evening spot **Restaurant Los Molcajetes** names itself after the *molcajete,* the stone chile mortar in which native Mexican delicacies are often served (and in which they offer *queso fundido,* cheese fondue). Located at México 133 Sur, tel. (32) 146-475. Open Mon.-Sat.1 p.m.-1 a.m. Moderate-expensive.

Tepic has a number of good suburban restaurants. On the north side of town, one of the best is the **Restaurant Higuera** at the Hotel Bugam Villas. In the southeast suburb, **Chic's,** a Mexican version of Denny's, on Av. Insurgentes, by the big Plaza Ley shopping center, about a mile and a half from downtown, offers a bit of everything for the travel-weary: tasty American-style specialties, air-conditioned ambience, and a mini-playground for kids around back. Open daily 7 a.m.-10:30 p.m., tel. (32) 142-810. Moderate.

If Chic's is not to your liking, go into Plaza Ley nearby for about half a dozen more alternative pizzerias, *jugerías, taquerías,* and *loncherías.*

For a deluxe treat, go to **Restaurant Roberto's Internacional,** at Paseo de La Loma 472, at the corner of Av. Insurgentes, west side of La Loma park. Here, tuxedoed waiters, subdued '40s-style decor, attentive service, and good international specialties set a luxurious but relaxing tone. Open nightly until about midnight, tel. (32) 132-085. Moderate.

SHOPPING

Its for-sale collections of Huichol art provide an excellent reason for stopping in Tepic. At least four downtown shops specialize in Huichol goods, acting as agents for more than just the commissions they receive. They have been involved with the Huichol for years, helping them preserve their religion and traditional skills in the face of expanding tourism and development. (See the special topic on the **Huichol.**)

Starting near the Plaza Principal, the **Casa Aguet,** on Nervo, a block behind the Presidencia Municipal (look for the second-story black-and-white Artesanías Huichol sign) has an upstairs attic-museum of Huichol art. It's at 132 Amado Nervo, tel. (32) 124-130; open Mon.-Sat. 9 a.m.-2 p.m. and 4-8 p.m., Sunday 9 a.m.-2 p.m. The founder's son, personable Miguel Aguet, knows the Huichol well. Moreover, he guarantees the "lowest prices in town." His copy of *Art of the Huichol Indians* furnishes authoritative explanations of the intriguing animal and human painting motifs.

The small government handicrafts store, **Tienda de Artesanías Wereme,** corner Nervo and Mérida, next to the Presidencia Municipal, open Mon.-Fri. 9 a.m.-2 p.m. and 4-7 p.m., Saturday until 2 p.m., stocks some Huichol and other handicrafts. The staff, however, does not appear as knowledgeable as the private merchants.

If you can manage only one stop in Tepic, make it one block north of the plaza at **Casa Aguiar,** Zaragoza 100 Pte., corner of Mérida, tel. (32) 206-694, where elderly Alicia and Carmela Aguiar carry on their family tradition of Huichol crafts. There, in the parlor of their graceful old ancestral home, they offer a colorful galaxy of artifacts, both antique and new. Eerie beaded masks, venerable ceremonial hats, votive arrows, God's eyes and huge yarn *cuadras,* blooming like Buddhist *tankas,* fill the cabinets and line the walls. Open Mon.-Sat. 10 a.m.-2 p.m. and 4-7:30 p.m.

Several blocks south on Av. México, at no. 110 Sur, just past Plaza Constituyentes and across from the Hotel Real de Don Juan, **Artesanías Cicuri,** tel. (32) 123-714 or 121-416, names itself after the renowned *cicuri,* the "eye of God" of the Huichol. The collection is both extensive and particularly fine, especially the beaded masks. Open Mon.-Sat. 9 a.m.-2 p.m. and 4-8 p.m.

SERVICES

For best money exchange rates, go to a bank, such as the main **Banamex** branch on Av. México at Zapata. It's open Mon.-Sat. 8:30 a.m.-3 p.m., Saturday 9 a.m.-2 p.m. (although money exchange hours may be shorter) for U.S. dollar only cash and traveler's check exchange. If the lines at Banamex are too long, go to the **Banco Promex** across the street, or **Banco Internacional** (at Mérida 184 Nte., open for U.S. dollar money exchange Mon.-Fri. 8:30 a.m.-5 p.m.) on the main square next to the Presidencia Municipal. After hours, try one of the *casas de cambio* (money exchange counters) nearby, such as the **Serdana** at Av. México 139 Nte., tel. (32) 165-530, near the corner of Hidalgo, open daily 8:30 a.m.-8 p.m.; or **Mololoa,** at 53 Mexico Nte., open Mon.-Fri. 8:30 a.m.-2 p.m. and 4:30-6:30 p.m., Saturday 9 a.m.-2 p.m.

Tepic has two **post offices.** The main branch is downtown at Durango Nte. 27, tel. (32) 120-130, corner of Morelos Pte., open Mon.-Fri. 8 a.m.-7 p.m., Saturday 8:30 a.m.-noon, about two blocks west and three blocks south of the Plaza Principal; the other is at the *central camionera* (central bus terminal) on Av. Insurgentes about a mile east (Guadalajara direction) from downtown, open Mon.-Fri. 8 a.m.-2 p.m., Saturday 7-11 p.m.

Telecomunicaciones, which provides telegraph, telephone, and public fax, likewise has both a downtown branch on Av. México, corner of Morelos, open Mon.-Fri. 8 a.m.-7 p.m., Saturday 8 a.m.-4 p.m., tel./fax (32) 129-655, and a *central camionera* branch, open Mon.-Fri. 8 a.m.-2 p.m., Saturday 8 a.m.-noon, tel./fax (32) 132-327.

Common charms that Huichol pilgrims carry with them include a rattle and a small gourd for collecting peyote.

INFORMATION

Tepic's **municipal tourist information office,** tel. (32) 165-523, 165-661, e-mail: turismo @tepic.gob.mx, is at the plaza principal's northwest corner, just north of the Presidencia Municipal, at the corner of Amado Nervo and Puebla. It dispenses both information and a tableful of excellent brochures, many in English. Hours are 9 a.m.-8 p.m. daily.

Nayarit State Tourism offices, tel./fax (32) 148-071, 148-072, or 148-073, toll-free in Mexico (800) 903-92, are in the Convento de la Cruz (at Av. Mexico and Calzado Ejercito, about a mile south of the cathedral). Stop by the information booth, open Mon.-Fri. 9 a.m.-2 p.m. and 6-8 p.m., Saturday 9 a.m.-2 p.m., which stocks excellent brochures.

English-language books and magazines are scarce in Tepic. **Newsstands** beneath the plaza portals just west of the Hotel Fray Junípero Serra and the bookstore **Publicaciones Azteca** on Av. México, corner Morelos (open daily 7 a.m.-11 p.m.), tel. (32) 160-811, usually have the *News* from Mexico City in the afternoon. Also, the Restaurant Terraza, tel. (32) 132-180, open daily 7 a.m.-11 p.m., on Insurgentes, across from Parque La Loma, between Querétaro and Oaxaca, also generally has the *News* and a couple dozen popular American magazines, such as *Time, Newsweek,* and *National Geographic.*

If you need a doctor, contact the **Sanatorio Guadalupe,** Juan Escuita 68 Nte., tel. (32) 129-401, (32) 122-713, seven blocks west of the Plaza Principal. It has a 24-hour emergency room and a group of specialists on call. A fire-department paramedic squad is also available by calling (32) 131-809.

For **police** emergencies, call the municipal *preventiva* police, tel. (32) 115-850. For **fire** emergencies, call the *bomberos* (firefighters), tel. (32) 131-607.

GETTING THERE AND AWAY

By Car or RV

Main highways connect Tepic with Puerto Vallarta to the south, San Blas to the west, Mazatlán to the north, and Guadalajara to the east.

Two-lane Hwy. 200 from Puerto Vallarta is in good condition for its 104-mile (167-km) length. Curves, traffic, and the 3,000-foot Tepic grade, however, usually slow the northbound trip to about three hours, a bit less southbound.

A pair of routes (both about 43 miles, 70 km) connect Tepic with San Blas. The most scenic, but slower, of the two takes nearly two hours, heading west from the Hwy. 15 interchange at Tepic's north end and descending 3,000 feet along Nayarit Hwy. 28 to Santa Cruz de Miramar on the Bay of Matanchén. From there the route continues north along the bay to San Blas. The quicker route first leads north along Hwy. 15 expressway, descending steeply to its intersection with Hwy. 11, which continues, winding downhill west through the tropical forest to San Blas. Allow about an hour and a half for this route.

To and from Mazatlán, traffic, towns, and rough spots slow progress along the 182-mile (293-km) two-lane stretch of National Hwy. 15. Expect four or five hours of driving time under good conditions.

The same is true of the winding, 141-mile (227-km) continuation of Hwy. 15 eastward over the Sierra Madre Occidental to Guadalajara. Fortunately, a *cuota autopista* (toll superhighway), which begins at Tepic's southeastern edge, eliminates two hours of driving time. Allow about three hours by *autopista,* and at least five hours without.

By Bus

The shiny, modern *central camionera* on Insurgentes Sur about a mile southeast of downtown has many services, including left-luggage lockers, a cafeteria, a post office, long-distance telephone and public fax. Booths *(taquillas)* offering higher class service are generally on the station's left (east) side; the lower class is on the right (west) side as you enter.

Transportes del Pacífico (TP), tel. (32) 132-320 or 132-313, has many local first- and second-class departures, connecting south with Puerto Vallarta, east with Guadalajara and Mexico City, and north with Mazatlán, and the U.S. border at Tijuana and Nogales.

Estrella Blanca (EB), tel. (32) 141-000, operating through its subsidiaries, provides many second-class, first-class and super-first-class direct connections north, east, and south. First-class Elite (EL) departures connect north with the U.S. border (Nogales and Tijuana) via Mazatlán, and south with Acapulco via Puerto Vallarta, Barra de Navidad, Manzanillo (with connections through Colima east to Michoacán and Mexico City), and Zihuatanejo. First-class Transportes del Norte (TN) departures connect, through Guadalajara, north with Saltillo and Monterrey. Super-first-class Futura (FU) connects, through Guadalajara, with Mexico City. First-class Transportes Chihuahuenses (TC) connects north with the U.S. border (Ciudad Juárez) via Aguascalientes, Zacatecas, and Torreón. Second-class Transportes Norte de Sonora (TNS) departures connect north, through Mazatlán, with Nogales, Mexicali and Tijuana, at the U.S. border.

Transportes Norte de Sonora's booths sell tickets for hourly daytime second-class connections with San Blas (tel. 32-143-062, ext. 20) and with Santiago Ixcuintla (tel. 32-143-062, ext. 18), where you can continue by local bus to the Mexcaltitán embarcadero.

Besides providing many first-class connections with Guadalajara, independent **Omnibus de Mexico** (OM) provides a few departures that connect, via Guadalajara, north with Fresnillo, Torreón, and the U.S. border at Ciudad Juárez, and northeast with Aguascalientes, Zacatecas, Saltillo, Monterrey, and the U.S. border at Matamoros.

By Train

The recently privatized Mexican Pacific Railway no longer offers passenger service. Until further notice, trains, which clickety-clacked along the rails for generations, connecting Guadalajara, Tepic, and the U.S. border at Nogales and Mexicali, will be mere fading memories.

GUADALAJARA

Pacific Mexico residents often go to Guadalajara (pop. three million; elev. 5,214 feet, 1,589 meters), the capital of Jalisco, for the same reason Californians frequently go to Los Angeles: to shop and choose from big selections at correspondingly small prices.

But that's only part of the fascination. Although Guadalajarans like to think of themselves as different (calling themselves, uniquely, "Tapatíos"), their city is renowned as the "most Mexican" of cities. Crowds flock to Guadalajara to bask in its mild, springlike sunshine, savor its music, and admire its grand monuments.

HISTORY

Before Columbus

The broad Atemajac Valley, where the Guadalajara metropolis now spreads, has nurtured humans for hundreds of generations. Discovered remains date back at least 10,000 years. The Río Lerma—Mexico's longest river, which meanders across six states—has nourished Atemajac Valley cornfields for at least three millennia.

Although they built no pyramids, high cultures were occupying western Mexico by A.D. 300. They left sophisticated animal- and human-motif pottery in myriad bottle-shaped underground tombs of a style found only in Jalisco, Nayarit, and Colima. Intriguingly, similar tombs are also found in Colombia and Ecuador.

During the next thousand years, waves of migrants swept across the Valley of Atemajac: Toltecs from the northeast, the Aztecs much later from the west. As Toltec power declined during the 13th century, the Tarascan civilization took root in Michoacán to the south and filled the power vacuum left by the Toltecs. On the eve of the Spanish conquest, semi-autonomous local chiefdoms, tributaries of the Tarascan emperor, shared the Atemajac valley.

Conquest and Colonization

The fall of the Aztecs in 1520 and the Taras-cans a few years later made the Valley of Atemajac a plum ripe for the picking. In the late 1520s, while Cortés was absent in Spain, the opportunistic Nuño de Guzmán vaulted himself to power in Mexico City on the backs of the native peoples and at the expense of Cortés's friends and relatives. Suspecting correctly that his glory days in Mexico City were numbered, Guzmán cleared out three days before Christmas, 1529, at the head of a small army of adventurers seeking new conquests in western Mexico. They raped, ravaged, and burned for half a dozen years, inciting dozens of previously pacified tribes to rebellion.

Hostile Mexican attacks repeatedly foiled Guzmán's attempts to establish his western Mexico capital, which he wanted to name after his Spanish hometown, Guadalajara (from the Arabic wad al hadjarah, "river of stones"). Ironically, it wasn't until the year of Guzmán's death in Spain in 1542, six years after his arrest by royal authorities, that the present Guadalajara was founded. At the downtown Plaza de Los Fundadores, a panoramic bronze frieze shows co-founders Doña Beátriz de Hernández and governor Cristóbal de Oñate christening the soon-to-become capital of the "Kingdom of Nueva Galicia."

The city grew; its now-venerable public buildings rose at the edges of sweeping plazas, from which expeditions set out to explore other lands. In 1563, Legazpi and Urdaneta sailed west to conquer the Philippines; 1602 saw Vizcaíno sail for the Californias and the Pacific Northwest. In 1687 Father Kino left for 27 years of mission-building in Sonora and what would be Arizona and New Mexico; finally, during the 1760s, Father Junípero Serra and Captain Gaspar de Portola began their arduous trek to discover San Francisco Bay and found a string of California missions.

During Spain's Mexican twilight, Guadalajara was a virtual imperial city, ruling all of northwest Mexico, plus what would become California, Arizona, New Mexico, and Texas—an empire twice the size of Britain's 13 colonies.

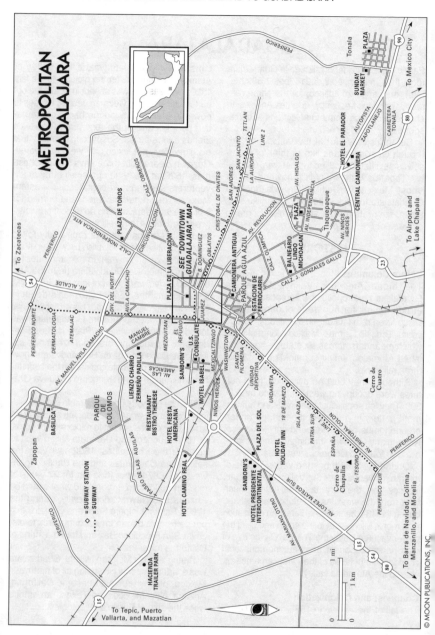

METROPOLITAN GUADALAJARA

© MOON PUBLICATIONS, INC.

Independence

The cry, "Death to the *gachupines,* Viva México" by insurgent priest Miguel Hidalgo ignited rebellion on 16 September 1810. Buoyed by a series of quick victories, Hidalgo advanced on Mexico City in command of a huge ragtag army. But, facing the punishing fusillades of a small but disciplined Spanish force, Hidalgo lost his nerve and decided to occupy Guadalajara instead. Loyalist General Felix Calleja pursued and routed Hidalgo's forces on the bank of the Lerma, not far east of Guadalajara. Although Hidalgo and Allende escaped, they were captured in the north a few months later. It wasn't for another dozen bloody years that others—Iturbide, Guerrero, Morelos—from other parts of Mexico realized Hidalgo's dream of independence.

Guadalajara, its domain reduced by the republican government to the new state of Jalisco, settled down to the production of corn, cattle, and tequila. The railroad came, branched north to the United States and south to the Pacific, and by 1900, Guadalajara's place as a commercial hub and Mexico's second city was secure.

Modern Guadalajara

After the bloodbath of the 1910-17 revolution, Guadalajara's growth far outpaced the country in general. From a population of around 100,000, Guadalajara ballooned to three million by the 1990s. People were drawn from the countryside by jobs in a thousand new factories, making everything from textiles and shoes to chemicals and soda pop.

Handicraft manufacture, always important in Guadalajara, zoomed during the 1960s when waves of jet-riding tourists came, saw, and bought mountains of blown glass, leather, pottery, and metal finery.

During the 1980s, Guadalajara put on a new face while at the same time preserving the best part of its old downtown. An urban-renewal plan of visionary proportions created Plaza Tapatía—acres of shops, stores, and offices beside fountain-studded malls—incorporating Guadalajara's venerable theaters, churches, museums, and government buildings into a single grand open space.

SIGHTS

Getting Oriented

Although Guadalajara sprawls over a hundred square miles, the treasured mile-square heart of the city is easily explorable on foot. The cathedral corner of north-south Av. 16 de Septiembre and Av. Morelos marks the center of town. A few blocks south, another important artery, east-west Av. Juárez, runs above the new metro subway line through the main business district, while a few blocks east, Av. Independencia runs beneath Plaza Tapatía and past the main market to the railway station a couple of miles south.

A Walk around Old Guadalajara

The twin steeples of the **cathedral** serve as an excellent starting point to explore the city-center plazas and monuments. The cathedral, dedicated to the Virgin of the Assumption when it was begun in 1561, was finished about 30 years later. A potpourri of styles—Moorish, Gothic, Renaissance, and Classic—make up its spires, arches, and facades. Although an earthquake demolished its steeples in 1818, they were rebuilt and resurfaced with cheery canary yellow tiles in 1854.

Inside, side altars and white facades climax at the principal altar, built over a tomb containing the remains of several former clergy, including the mummified heart of renowned Bishop Cabañas. One of the main attractions is the **Virgin of Innocence,** in the small chapel to the left just after the entrance. The glass-enclosed figure contains the bones of a 12-year-old girl who was martyred in the third century, forgotten, then rediscovered in the Vatican catacombs in 1786 and shipped to Guadalajara in 1788. The legend claims she died protecting her virginity; it is equally likely that she was martyred for refusing to recant her Christian faith.

Somewhere near the main altar you'll find either a copy of or the authentic **Virgin of Zapopan** (see **Zapopan**). Between sometime in June and October 12, the tiny, adored figure will be the authentic "La Generala," as she's affectionately known; on October 13, a tumultuous crowd of worshippers escorts her back to the cathedral in Zapopan, where she remains until brought back to Guadalajara the next June.

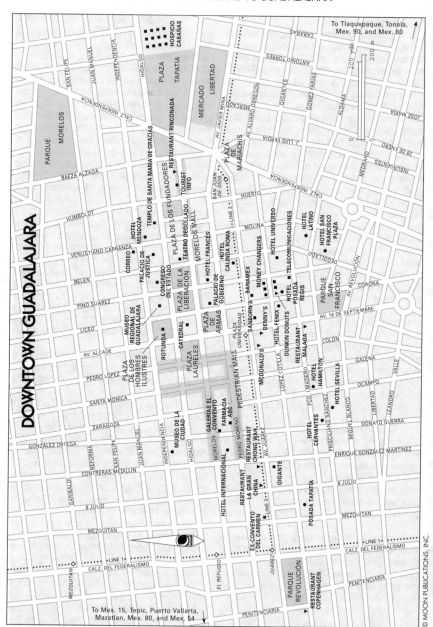

DOWNTOWN GUADALAJARA

To Tlaquepaque, Tonala,
Mex. 90, and Mex. 80

HOSPICIO CABAÑAS

PLAZA TAPATÍA

MERCADO LIBERTAD

CABANAS

ANTONIO TORRES

GIGANTES

GOMEZ FARIAS

ALDAMA

JOSE MARIA

28 DE ENERO

INSURGENTES

MEDRANO

AV. ALVARO OBREGON

AV. LUIS VERDIA

200

200 yds

m

PARQUE MORELOS

PLAZA DE MARIACHIS

AV. JAVIER MINA

MERCADO

J. LUIS MINA

CALZ. INDEPENDENCIA

CALZ. INDEPENDENCIA

RESTAURANT RINCONADA

BAEZA ALZAGA

JUAN MANUEL

INDEPENDENCIA

SAN FELIPE

HIDALGO

HUMBOLDT

PLAZA DE LOS FUNDADORES

TEMPLO DE SANTA MARIA DE GRACIAS

TOURIST INFO

SAN JUAN DE DIOS

HUERTO

Line 2

VENUSTIANO CARRANZA

HOTEL MENDOZA

CORREO

PALACIO DE JUSTICIA

CONGRESO DEL ESTADO

Teatro Degollado

PLAZA DE LA LIBERACIÓN

MORELOS MALL

HOTEL FRANCES

HOTEL CALINDA ROMA

MOLINA

HOTEL UNIVERSO

HOTEL LATINO

HOTEL SAN FRANCISCO PLAZA

BELEN

PINO SUAREZ

LICEO

MUSEO REGIONAL DE GUADALAJARA

PALACIO DE GOBIERNO

BANAMEX

MONEY CHANGERS

HOTEL TELECOMUNICACIONES

DEGOLLADO

AV. REVOLUCION

CORONA

PARQUE SAN FRANCISCO

AV. ALCADE

ROTUNDA

CATEDRAL

PLAZA DE ARMAS

HOTEL POSADA REGIS

HOTEL FENIX

SANBORN'S

DENNY'S

AV. 16 DE SEPTIEMBRE

PEDRO LOPEZ

PLAZA DE LOS HOMBRES ILUSTRES

PLAZA LAURELES

PLAZA UNIVERSIDAD

DUNKIN DONUTS

RESTAURANT MALAGA

COLON

GALENA

SANTA MONICA

McDONALD'S

LOPEZ COTILLA

MADERO

HOTEL HAMILTON

HOTEL SEVILLA

VALLE

OCAMPO

ZARAGOZA

MUSEO DE LA CIUDAD

GALERIAS EL CONVENTO

FARMACIA ABC

PEDRO MORENO

PEDESTRIAN MALL

ECO

PRISCILIANO SANCHEZ

HOTEL CERVANTES

MIGUEL BLANCO

LIBERTAD

LEANDRO

DONATO GUERRA

GONZALEZ ORTEGA

REFORMA

JUAN MANUEL

SAN FELIPE

INDEPENDENCIA

HIDALGO

MORELOS

RESTAURANT CHONG WAH...

AV. JUAREZ

ENRIQUE GONZALEZ MARTINEZ

CONTRERAS MEDILLIN

HOTEL INTERNACIONAL

RESTAURANT LA GRAN CHINA

GIGANTE

Line 2

8 JULIO

GARIBALDI

8 JULIO

MEZQUITAN

EX-CONVENTO DEL CARMEN

Line 2

POSADA TAPATIA

MEZQUITAN

MEZQUITAN

LINE 1

CALZ. DEL FEDERALISMO

LINE 1

JUAREZ

EL REFUGIO

CALZ. DEL FEDERALISMO

PARQUE REVOLUCIÓN

LINE 1

PENITENCIARIA

RESTAURANT COPENHAGEN

PENITENCIARIA

To Mex. 15, Tepic, Puerto Vallarta,
Mazatlan, Mex. 80, and Mex. 54

© MOON PUBLICATIONS, INC.

Outside, broad plazas surround the cathedral: the **Plaza Laureles,** in front (west) of the cathedral, then moving counterclockwise, the **Plaza de Armas** to the south, **Plaza Liberación** to the east (behind), and the **Plaza de los Hombres Ilustres** to the north of the cathedral.

Across Av. Morelos, the block-square Plaza de los Hombres Ilustres is bordered by 15 sculptures of Jalisco's eminent sons. Their remains lie beneath the stone rotunda in the center; their bronze statues line the sidewalk. Right at the corner you'll find the figure of revered Jalisco governor Ignacio Vallarta; a few steps farther north stands the statue of José Clemente Orozco, legally blind when he executed his great works of art.

Adjacent to and east of the Plaza de los Hombres Ilustres, the colonial building behind the lineup of horse-drawn *calandrias* housed the Seminario de San José for the six generations following its construction in 1696. During the 1800s it served variously as a barracks, a public lecture hall, and, since 1918, has housed the **Museo Regional de Guadalajara,** 60 Liceo, tel. (3) 614-6521, open Tues.-Sat. 9 a.m.-6:45 p.m. and Sunday 9 a.m.-3 p.m.

Inside, tiers of rooms surrounding a tree-shaded interior patio illustrate local history. Exhibits depict scenes from as early as the Big Bang and continue with a hulking mastodon skeleton and whimsical animal and human figurines recovered from the bottle-shaped tombs of Jalisco, Nayarit, and Colima. Upstairs rooms contain life-size displays of contemporary but traditional fishing methods at nearby Lake Chapala and costumes and culture of regional Cora, Huichol, Tepehuan, and México peoples.

Back outside, head east two blocks down Av. Hidalgo, paralleling the expansive Plaza Liberación behind the cathedral. On your left you will pass the baroque facades of the *congreso del estado* (state legislature) and the *palacio de justicia* (state supreme court) buildings. Ahead at the east end of the plaza rises the timeless silhouette of the **Teatro Degollado.**

The theater's classic, columned facade climaxes in an epic marble frieze, depicting the allegory of Apollo and the nine muses. Inside, the Degollado's resplendent grand salon is said to rival the gilded refinement of Milan's renowned La Scala. Overhead, its ceiling glows with Gerardo Suárez's panorama of canto IV of Dante's *Divine Comedy,* complete with its immortal cast —Julius Caesar, Homer, Virgil, Saladin—and the robed and wreathed author himself in the middle. Named for the millionaire governor who financed its construction, the theater opened with appropriate fanfare on 13 September 1866, with a production of *Lucia de Lammermoor,* starring Angela Peralta, the renowned "Mexican Nightingale." An ever-changing menu of artists still graces the Degollado's stage, including an excellent local folkloric ballet troupe every Sunday morning.

Walk behind the Degollado, where a modern bronze frieze, the **Frisa de Los Fundadores,** decorates its back side. Appropriately, a mere two blocks from the spot where the city was founded, the 68-foot sculpture shows Guadalajara's cofounders facing each other on opposite sides of a big tree. Governor Cristóbal de Oñate strikes the tree with his sword, while Doña Beátriz de Hernández holds a fighting cock, symbolizing

---

SUBWAY, GUADALAJARA STYLE

Since the early 1990s, Guadalajarans have enjoyed a new underground train system, which they call simply the **Tren Ligero,** or "Light Train." It's nothing fancy, a kind of Motel 6 of subway lines—inexpensive, efficient, and reliable. A pair of intersecting lines, Línea 1 and Línea 2, carry passengers in approximately north-south and east-west directions, along a total of 15 miles (25 km) of track. The station most visitors see first is the Plaza Universidad (on Línea 2), accessible by staircases that descend near the city-center corner of Juárez and Colón. Look for the Denny's restaurant nearby.

Downstairs, if you want to take a ride, deposit coins totaling two pesos in machines, which will give you in exchange a brass *ficha* token, good for one ride and one transfer. If you opt to transfer, you have to do it at Juárez station, the next stop west of Plaza Universidad, where lines 1 and 2 intersect. (Hint: Best begin your Guadalajara subway adventure before 9 p.m.; the Tren Ligero goes to sleep by about 11 p.m.)

An arch on Plaza Laureles frames the glistening yellow tile spires of Guadalajara's downtown cathedral.

her gritty determination (and that of dozens of fellow settlers) that Guadalajara's location should remain put.

Plaza Tapatía

Turn around and face east. The 17 acres of the Plaza Tapatía complex extend ahead for several blocks across sub-plazas, fountains, and malls. Initially wide in the foreground of Plaza de Los Fundadores, the Tapatía narrows between a double row of shiny shops and offices, then widens into a broad esplanade and continues beside a long pool-fountain that leads to the monumental, domed Hospicio Cabañas a third of a mile away. Along the Tapatía's lateral flanks, a pair of long malls—continuations of Avenidas Hidalgo and Morelos—parallel the central Paseo Degollado mall for two blocks.

The eastern end of the Morelos mall climaxes with the striking bronze *escudo* (coat of arms) of Guadalajara. Embodying the essence of the original 16th-century coat of arms authorized by Emperor Charles V, the Escudo shows a pair of lions protecting a pine tree (with leaves, rather than needles, however). The lions represent the warrior's determination and discipline, and the solitary pine symbolizes noble ideals.

Continue east, to where the Plaza Tapatía widens, giving berth for the sculpture-fountain *Imolación de Quetzalcoatl,* designed and executed by Víctor Manuel Contreras in 1982. Four bronze serpent-birds, representing knowledge and the spirit of humankind, stretch toward heaven at the ends of a giant cross. In the center, a towering bronze spiral represents the unquenchable flame of Quetzalcoatl, transforming all that it touches. Locals call the sculpture the "big corkscrew," however.

At this point, Av. Independencia runs directly beneath Plaza Tapatía, past the adjacent sprawling **Mercado Libertad,** built in 1958 on the site of the traditional Guadalajara *tianguis* (open-air market), known since pre-Columbian times. Follow the elevated pedestrian walkway to explore the Libertad's produce, meat, fish, herb, food, and handicrafts stalls.

On Independencia, just beyond the market, musicians at the **Plaza de los Mariachis** continue the second century of a tradition born when mariachi (cowboy troubadour) groups first appeared during the 1860s in Guadalajara. The musical hubbub climaxes Saturday nights and Sunday afternoons, as musicians gather, singing while they wait to be hired for serenades and parties.

Behind the long pool-fountain at the east end of Plaza Tapatía stands the domed neoclassic **Hospicio Cabañas,** the largest and one of the most remarkable colonial buildings in the Americas. Designed and financed by Bishop Juan Ruiz de Cabañas, construction was complete in 1810. The purpose of the "Guadalajara House of Charity and Mercy," as the good bishop originally named it, as a home for the sick, helpless, and homeless, was fulfilled for 170 years. Although still successfully serving as an orphanage during the 1970s, time had taken its toll on the Hospicio Cabañas. The city and state governments built a new orphanage in the suburbs, restored the old building, and changed its purpose. It now houses the **Instituto Cultural Cabañas,** a center for the arts at Cabañas 8, tel. (3) 6540-008 or 6540-129. Open Tues.-Sat. 10 a.m.-6 p.m., Sunday 10 a.m.-3 p.m. Public programs include classes, films, and instrumental, chorale, and dance concerts.

Inside, seemingly endless ranks of corridors pass a host of sculpture-decorated patios. Practice rooms resound with the clatter of dancing feet and the halting strains of apprentice violins, horns, and pianos. Exhibition halls and studios of the **José Clemente Orozco Art Museum** occupy a large fraction of the rooms, while the great muralist's brooding work spreads over a corresponding fraction of the walls. Words such as dark, fiery, nihilistic, even apocalyptic, would not be too strong to describe the panoramas that Orozco executed (1938-39) in the soaring chapel beneath the central dome. On one wall, an Aztec goddess wears a necklace of human hearts; on another, armored, automaton-soldiers menace Indian captives; while in the cupola overhead, Orozco's *Man of Fire*, wreathed in flame, appears to soar into a hellishly red-hot sky.

Out-of-Downtown Sights

The former villages of Zapopan, Tlaquepaque, and Tonalá, now parts of metropolitan Guadalajara, make interesting day-trip destinations from the city center. Although local buses or your own wheels can get you there, crowds of bus commuters and congested city streets increase the desirability of the local tour option. Contact your hotel travel desk, a travel agent, or call a well-equipped agency, such as Panoramex, at Federalismo Sur 944, tel. (3) 810-5057 or 810-5005, which conducts reasonably priced bilingual tours daily from the city center.

Zapopan, about six miles northwest of downtown, is famous for its soaring baroque (1730) basilica, home of the renowned Virgin of Zapopan. The legendary image, one of the beloved "three sisters" virgins of Mexico, has enjoyed generations of popularity so enormous that it must be seen to be believed. Local folks, whenever they happen by, often stop to say a prayer (or at least make the sign of the cross as they pass) in front of the cathedral gate. Inside, the faithful crawl the length of the sanctuary to pay their respects to the diminutive blue and white

MARIACHIS

Mariachis, those thoroughly Mexican troubador bands, have spread from their birthplace in Jalisco throughout Mexico and into much of the United States. The name itself reveals their origin. "Mariachi" originated with the French *mariage,* or marriage. When French influence peaked during the 1864-67 reign of Maximilian, Jaliscans transposed *mariage* to "mariachi," a label they began to identify with the five-piece folk bands that played for weddings.

The original ensembles, consisting of a pair of violins, *vihuela* (large eight-stringed guitar), *jarana* (small guitar), and harp, played exclusively traditional melodies. Song titles such as "Las Moscas" ("The Flies") "El Venado" ("The Stag"), and "La Papaya," thinly disguised their universal themes, mostly concerning love.

Although such all-string folk bands still play in Jalisco, notably in Tecalitlán and other rural areas, they've largely been replaced by droves of trumpet-driven commercial mariachis. The man who

sparked the shift was probably Emilio Azcárraga Vidaurreta, the director of radio station XEW, which began broadcasting in Mexico City in 1930. In those low-fidelity days, the subdued sound of the harp didn't broadcast well, so Azcárraga suggested the trumpet as a replacement. It was so successful the trumpet has become the signature sound of present-day mariachis.

Still, mariachis mostly do what they've always done—serenade sweethearts, play for weddings and parties, even accompany church masses. They seem to be forever strolling around town plazas on Saturday nights and Sunday afternoons, looking for jobs. Their fees, which should be agreed upon before they start, often depend on union scale per song, per serenade, or per hour.

Sometimes mariachis serve as a kind of live jukebox that, for a coin, will play your old favorite. And even if it's a slightly tired but sentimental "Mañanitas" or "Cielito Lindo," you can't help but be moved by the singing violins, bright trumpets, and soothing guitars.

THE THREE SISTERS OF MEXICO

In all of Mexico, only the Virgin of Guadalupe exceeds in adoration the all-Jalisco trio—the "Three Sister" Virgins of Talpa, Zapopan, and San Juan de los Lagos. Yearly they draw millions of humble Mexican pilgrims who bus, walk, hitchhike, or in some cases crawl, to festivals honoring the virgins. Each virgin's popularity springs from some persistent, endearing legend. The Virgin of Talpa defied a haughty bishop's efforts to cage her; the Virgin of Zapopan rescued Guadalajara from war and disaster; the Virgin of San Juan de los Lagos restored a dead child to life.

Talpa, Zapopan, and San Juan de los Lagos townsfolk have built towering basilicas to shelter and honor each virgin. Each small and fragile figurine is draped in fine silk and jewels and worshipped by a continuous stream of penitents. During a virgin festival the image is lifted aloft by a platoon of richly costumed bearers and paraded to the clamor, tumult, and cheers of a million or more of the faithful.

Even if you choose to avoid the crowds and visit Talpa, Zapopan, or San Juan de los Lagos on a nonfestival day, you'll soon see the hubbub continues. Pilgrims come and go, bands and mariachis play, and curio stands stuffed with gilded devotional goods crowd the basilica square.

figure. The adoration climaxes on 12 October when a rollicking crowd of hundreds of thousands accompanies the Virgin of Zapopan from the downtown Guadalajara cathedral home to Zapopan, where she stays from 13 October until June.

Afterward, look over the displays of Huichol Indian handicrafts in the adjacent museum-shop **Artesanías Huichola,** on your left as you exit the basilica; open Mon.-Sat. 10 a.m.-2 p.m. and 4-7 p.m., Sunday 10 a.m.-1 p.m. Sale items include eerie beaded masks, intriguing yarn paintings, and *ojos de dios* (God's eyes) yarn sculptures. Later, browse for bargains among the handicrafts stalls in front of the basilica and in the municipal market in the adjacent plaza on the corner of Av. Hidalgo and Calle Eva Briseño.

Getting There: From downtown Guadalajara, local Zapopan-marked (on the windshield) buses depart from the south-side *camionera antigua* (old bus station) end of Av. Estadio, just

north of Parque Agua Azul), and continue through the downtown, stopping at the corner of López Cotilla and 16 de Septiembre. By car, follow Av. Manuel Avila Camacho, which diagonals northwest for about four miles from the city center to Zapopan, marked by the old baroque arch on the left. After one block, turn left onto Av. Hidalgo, the double main street of Zapopan. Within four blocks you'll see the plaza and the basilica on the left.

Zapopan town is the *cabecera* (headquarters) of the sprawling *municipio* of Zapopan, farm and mountain hinterland, famous for **La Barranca,** the 2,000-foot deep canyon of the Río Grande de Santiago. At the viewpoint past San Isidro, around Km 15, Saltillo Hwy. 54 north of Guadalajara, motorists stop at the viewpoint, **Mirador Dr. Atl,** to admire the canyon vista and the waterfall **Cola del Caballo** ("Horse's Tail") as it plummets hundreds of feet to the river below.

Past that, a small paradise of springs decorates the lush canyonland. First, at Km 17, comes **Los Camachos,** a forest and mountain-framed *balneario* (bathing park) with pools and restaurants; a few miles farther along is the hot spring bathing complex, **Balneario Nuevo Paraíso,** at Km 24. A kilometer farther (follow the left side road from the highway about a half kilometer) you can view the **Geiseres de Ixcatan** ("Ixcatan Geysers") near the village. Get there by car via Hwy. 54, the Saltillo-Zacatecas highway, which heads northward along Av. Alcalde from the city-center cathedral. Bus riders can board the "Los Camachos" bus, which leaves the Glorieta Normal (on Av. Alcalde about a mile north of the downtown cathedral) about every hour from 5 a.m. until the early afternoon. For more information about Zapopan sights, drop by the Zapopan tourist information office at Vicente Guerrero 233, two blocks behind the basilica, or call (3) 636-6727 Mon.-Fri. 9 a.m.-3 p.m.

Tlaquepaque and **Tonalá,** in the southeast suburbs, are among Mexico's renowned handicrafts villages. Tlaquepaque (tlah-kay-PAH-kay), now touristy but still interesting, about five miles from the city center, is famous for fine stoneware and blown glass; Tonalá, another five miles farther, retains plenty of sleepy, colorful country ambience. Shops abound in celebrated ceramic, brass, and papier-mâché animal figurines. The most exciting, but crowded, time to visit is during the Sunday market. (For more Tlaquepaque and Tonalá details, see Shopping, below.)

ACCOMMODATIONS

Downtown Hotels
Several good hotels, ranging from budget to plush, dot the center of Guadalajara, mostly in the Av. Juárez business district, a few blocks from the cathedral and plazas. Many have parking garages, a desirable downtown option for auto travelers. Hotels farthest from the cathedral plazas are generally the most economical.

The **Posada Tapatía,** López Cotilla 619, Guadalajara, Jalisco 44100, tel. (3) 614-9146, one block off Juárez, near the corner of Calle 8 Julio, is about 10 blocks from the cathedral. Its simple but gaily decorated rooms with baths are spread around a light, colorfully restored central patio. Tightly managed by the friendly on-

site owner, the Tapatía's prices are certainly right. Try for a room in the back, away from the noisy street. The 12 rooms rent for $11 s, $16 d, with fans.

Three blocks closer in, at the northeast corner of Prisciliano Sánchez and Donato Guerra, step up from the sidewalk and enter the cool, contemporary-classic interior of the **Hotel Cervantes** at 442 P. Sánchez, tel./fax (3) 613-6686 or 613-6846. Here, everything, from the marble-and-brass lobby, the modern-chic restaurant and bar, pool and exercise room downstairs to the big beds, plush carpets and shiny marble baths of the rooms upstairs seems perfect for the enjoyment of its predominantly business clientele. For such refinement, rates, at about $42 d, are surprisingly moderate. TV, phones, parking, and a/c. Credit cards accepted.

Across the street, on Prisciliano Sánchez between Ocampo and D. Guerra, the old standby **Hotel Sevilla,** Prisciliano Sánchez 413, Guadalajara, Jalisco 44100, tel. (3) 614-9172, 614-9354, or 614-9037, offers basic accommodation at budget prices. Its 80 rooms, furnished in dark brown wood and rugs to match, are plain but comfortable. For more light and quiet, get an upper-story room. Amenities include a lobby with TV, parking, a hotel safe for storing valuables, and a restaurant open daily except Sunday. Rates run $10 s, $11 d, $13 t; fans and telephones included.

One block away, on Madero, the even plainer **Hotel Hamilton,** Madero 381, Guadalajara, Jalisco 44100, tel. (3) 614-6726, offers a rock-bottom alternative. The 32 bare-bulb, not-so-clean rooms border on the dingy; their steel doors seem to enhance the drabness more than increasing security. Store your valuables in the hotel safe. For less noise and more light, get a room in back, away from the street. Rooms rent $6 s, $8 d, and $10 t, with fans but no parking.

Cheerier and closer in, where the pedestrian strolling mall begins on Moreno, stands the big, 110-room **Hotel Internacional,** Pedro Moreno 570, Guadalajara, Jalisco 44100, tel. (3) 613-0330, fax 613-2866. Downstairs, a small lobby with chairs and soft couches adjoins the reception. In the tower upstairs, the '60s-modern rooms, most with city views, are clean, comfortable, and newly renovated. Try for a discount below the asking prices of $35 s, $42 d, which

GUADALAJARA ACCOMMODATIONS

Accommodations (area code 3, postal code 44100 unless otherwise noted) are listed in increasing order of approximate high-season, double-room rates. Toll-free (800) telephone numbers are dialable from the U.S. and Canada.

DOWNTOWN

Hotel Hamilton, F. Madero 381, tel. 614-6726, $8

Hotel Sevilla, P. Sánchez 413, tel. 614-9172, 614-9037, or 614-9354, $11

Hotel Latino, P. Sánchez 74, tel. 614-4484, 614-6214, $12

Hotel Posada Regis, R. Corona 171, tel. 614-8633, fax 613-3026, $15

Posada Tapatía, L. Cotilla 619, tel. 614-9146, $16

Hotel Universo, L. Cotilla 161, tel. 613-2815, fax 613-4734, $24

Hotel San Francisco Plaza, Degollado 267, tel. 613-8954, fax 613-3257, $24

Hotel Frances, Maestranza 35, tel. 613-1190, 613-0936, fax 658-2831, $34

Hotel Cervantes, 442 P. Sánchez, tel./fax 613-6686 or 613-6846, $42

Hotel Internacional, P. Moreno 570, tel. 613-0330, fax 613-2866, $42

Hotel Calinda Roma, Juárez 170, tel. 614-8650, (800) 221-2222, fax 613-0557, $64

Hotel Mendoza, V. Carranza 16, tel. 613-4646, fax 613-7310, $70

Hotel Fénix, R. Corona 160, tel. 614-5714, fax 613-4005, tel. (800) 465-4329, $76

SUBURBAN

Hotel El Parador, Carretera Zapotlanejo 1500, tel. 600-0910, fax 600-0015, $22

Motel Isabel, J. Guadalupe Montenegro 1572, tel. 826-2630, $26

Holiday Inn Crowne Plaza, L. Mateos Sur 2500, postal code 45050, tel. 634-1034, (800) 465-4329, fax 631-9393, $135

Hotel Camino Real, Av. Vallarta 5005, postal code 45040, tel. 121-8000, (800) 7CAMINO (722-6466), fax 121-8070, e-mail: gdl@caminoreal.com, $100

Hotel Holiday Inn Casa Grande, Aeropuerto Internacional, postal code 45640, tel. 678-9001, tel./fax 678-9000, (800) 465-4329, $110

Hotel Fiesta Americana, Aurelio Aceves 225, tel. 825-3434, (800) FIESTA-1 (343-7821), fax 630-3725, $110

---

are high compared to the competition. (They do, however, offer a 15% discount for a one-week rental). Amenities include fans, phones, and TV, and a café, but no parking.

Equally well-located but shinier, **Hotel Fénix,** Corona 160, Guadalajara, Jalisco 44100, tel. (3) 614-5714, fax 613-4005, lies on Corona, smack in the downtown business center, a short walk from everything. The owners have managed to upgrade this rather basic small-lobby hotel into something more elaborate. The some-

what cramped result, while not unattractive, is sometimes noisy and crowded. During the day, tour groups traipse in and out past the reception desk, while at night guests crowd the adjacent lobby bar for drinks and live combo music. Upstairs the 200 air-conditioned rooms are spacious and comfortably furnished with American-standard motel amenities. Walk-in rates, which run about $76 s or d, are high for a hotel with neither pool nor parking. Try for a better deal in advance by booking a package through a travel agent or by calling the toll-free (Holiday Inn) booking number (800) 465-4329 in the U.S. and Canada.

With the same prime location right across the street, the second-floor **Hotel Posada Regis** offers both economy and a bit of old-world charm, at Corona 171, Guadalajara, Jalisco 44100, tel. (3) 614-8633 or tel./fax 613-3026. Its clean and comfortable high-ceilinged rooms enclose a gracious Porfirian-era indoor lobby/atrium. Evening videos, friendly atmosphere, and a good breakfast/lunch café provide opportunities for relaxed exchanges with other travelers. The 19 rooms cost $13 s and $15 d, with phones, fans, optional TV, but no parking; credit cards are accepted.

Central location, comfortable though a bit worn rooms, and moderate prices explain the popularity of the nearby **Hotel Universo**, López Cotilla 161, Guadalajara, Jalisco 44100, tel. (3) 613-2815, fax 613-4734, corner of Cotilla and Degollado, just three blocks from the Teatro Degollado. Guests enjoy carpeted and draped air-conditioned rooms with wood furniture and ceiling-to-floor tiled bathrooms. Some rooms are more tattered than others; inspect more than one before settling in. The 137 rooms and suites rent for $21 s, $24 d, suites from about $28, with TV, phones, and parking; credit cards are accepted.

The Universo's competent owner/managers also run a pair of good-value hotels nearby. Their graceful, authentically colonial **Hotel San Francisco Plaza**, Degollado 267, Guadalajara, Jalisco 44100, tel. (3) 613-8954, fax 613-3257, is replete with traditional charm. The reception area opens to an airy and tranquil inner patio, where big soft chairs invite you to relax amid a leafy garden of potted plants. The venerable stone walls are decorated with a gallery of intriguing etchings depicting Don Quixote's celebrated adventures. Upstairs, the rooms are no less than you would expect: most are high-ceilinged, with plenty of polished wood, handmade furniture, rustic brass lamps by the bed, and sentimental old-Mexico paintings on the walls. Each room has a phone, TV, fan, and a large, modern-standard bathroom with marble sink. You'll find an elegant restaurant downstairs in front and plenty of parking. All this for $22 s, $24 d; credit cards are accepted.

The same owners run the **Hotel Latino,** one of Guadalajara's better cheap hotels, just around the corner at Prisciliano Sánchez 74, Guadalajara, Jalisco 44100, tel. (3) 614-4484 or 614-6214. Although it's a plain hotel with a small lobby, the Latino nevertheless enjoys a modicum of care. The 57 rooms in four stories (no elevator) are clean, carpeted, and thoughtfully furnished, albeit a bit worn around the edges. Baths are modern-standard, with shiny-tile showers and marble sinks. Rates run about $11 s, $12 d, including a/c, TV, parking, and phones; credit cards are not accepted.

Guests at the nearby **Hotel Calinda Roma,** Av. Juárez 170, Guadalajara, Jalisco 44100, tel. (3) 614-8650, fax 613-0557, enjoy luxurious amenities—plush lobby, shiny restaurant/bar, rooftop rose garden and pool—usually available only at pricier hostelries. Owners, however, have upped the tariffs; whether they can make them stick is another question. Try bargaining for discounts below the $60 s, $65 d asking rates. TV, phones, a/c, parking, credit cards, and limited wheelchair access. Some rooms, although clean and comfortable, are small. Look before moving in. From the U.S. and Canada, reserve at the Calinda Roma through the Quality Inn toll-free tel. (800) 221-2222.

The three-story, authentically baroque **Hotel Frances,** Maestranza 35, Guadalajara, Jalisco 44100, tel. (3) 613-1190 or 613-0936, fax 658-2831, rises among its fellow monuments on a quiet side street within sight of the Teatro Degollado. Guadalajara's first hotel, built in 1610, has been restored to its original splendor. The 40-odd rooms, all with bath, glow with polished wood, bright tile, and fancy frosted cut-glass windows. Downstairs, an elegant chandelier illuminates the dignified, plant-decorated interior patio and adjacent restaurant. However, in order to increase business, owners have installed nightly live music downstairs, which, for some, may not fit with hotel's baroque ambience. Rates, however, run a very reasonable $34 s or d, credit cards accepted, fans only, no parking.

The big colonial-facade **Hotel Mendoza,** V. Carranza 16, Guadalajara, Jalisco 44100, tel. (3) 613-4646, fax 613-7310, only a couple of blocks north the Teatro Degollado, is a longtime favorite of Guadalajara repeat visitors. Refined traditional embellishments—neo-Renaissance murals and wall portraits, rich dark paneling, glittering candelabras—grace the lobby, while upstairs, carpeted halls lead to spacious, comfortable rooms furnished with tasteful dark decor, including large baths, thick towels, and many other extras. The 100 rooms and suites rent from $57 s, $70 d, with American cable TV, phones, a/c, a small pool, refined restaurant, parking, credit cards accepted, and limited wheelchair access.

Although not in the immediate downtown area, the **Motel Isabel**, J. Guadalupe Montenegro 1572, Guadalajara, Jalisco 44100, tel. (3) 826-2630, in the affluent west-side embassy neighborhood, offers a flowery garden setting at moderate prices. The Isabel's 1960s-modern amenities—comfortably but not luxuriously furnished rooms with phone, small blue pool, dining room, and parking—have long attracted a loyal following of Guadalajara returnees. Buses (10 minutes to the city center) run nearby. The 50 rooms rent for $22 s, $26 d, with ceiling fans and limited wheelchair access.

West Side Luxury Hotels

During the 1980s the Plaza del Sol, a large American-style hotel, shopping, and entertainment complex, mushroomed on west-side Av. Adolfo López Mateos. The Holiday Inn and its plush neighboring hostelries that anchor the development have drawn many of the high-ticket visitors away from the old city center to the Plaza del Sol's shiny shops, restaurants, and clubs.

The **Holiday Inn Crowne Plaza,** at Av. López Mateos Sur 2500, Guadalajara, Jalisco 45050, tel. (3) 634-1034, fax 631-9393, a quarter mile south on López Mateos (past the traffic circle), offers a relaxed resort setting. The rooms, most with private view balconies, rise in a 10-story tower above the pool and garden. Their luxurious furnishings, in soothing earth tones, include spacious, marble-accented baths. The 285 rooms start at about $135 s or d, with everything; spa, sauna, gym, children's area, miniature golf, tennis courts, and wheelchair access. Besides the local numbers above, you can reserve by e-mail: crowngdbl@acnet.net, or Holiday Inn's toll-free number, (800) 465-4329, in the U.S. and Canada.

About a mile north of Plaza del Sol, the **Hotel Fiesta Americana,** Aurelio Aceves 225, Guadalajara, Jalisco 44100, tel. (3) 825-3434, (800) FIESTA-1 (343-7821) from the U.S. and Canada, fax 630-3725, towering above Av. Vallarta, the Hwy. 15 Blvd. Ingreso, offers another luxury hotel option. From the reception area, a serene, carpeted lobby spreads beneath a lofty, light atrium. The 396 plush view rooms are furnished in pastel tones with soft couches, huge beds, and a host of luxury amenities. Rooms rent from about $110 d, with tennis courts, spa, restaurants, pool, and sundeck.

Along the same boulevard, about a mile farther west, is the **Hotel Camino Real,** Av. Vallarta 5005, Guadalajara, Jalisco 45040, the graceful queen of Guadalajara luxury hotels. In contrast to its high-rise local competitors, the Camino Real spreads through a luxurious park of lawns, pools, and shady tropical verdure. Guests enjoy tastefully appointed bungalow-style units opening onto semiprivate pool patios. Rates run from $100 s or d and include cable TV, phone, four pools, tennis courts, and a nearby golf course. Reserve either through the local numbers, tel. (3) 121-8000, fax 121-8070, or toll-free (800) 7-CAMINO in the U.S. and Canada, or e-mail, at gdl@caminoreal.com.

Hotels El Parador and Holiday Inn Casa Grande

Two hotels on the edge of town offer interesting bus- and air travel-related options, respectively. For bus travelers, the big long-distance *central camionera* bus station is at Guadalajara's far southeast edge, at least 20 minutes by taxi (figure $8) from the center. Some bus travelers find it convenient to stay at the huge, two-pool, moderately priced modern Hotel El Parador and restaurant, Carretera Zapotlanejo 1500, Guadalajara, Jalisco 45625, tel. (3) 600-0910, fax 600-0015. It's adjacent to the sprawling terminal and has a restaurant. Bus and truck noise, however, may be a problem. Ask for a quiet *(tranquilo)* room. The 600 tidy and comfortable rooms, all with bath, rent for about $23 s or d. Rooms vary; look at more than one before moving in.

For air travelers, the deluxe Hotel Holiday Inn Casa Grande is but a block from the airport terminal exit door, at Calle Interior, Aeropuerto Internacional Miguel Hidalgo s/n, Guadalajara, Jalisco 45640, tel./fax (3) 678-9000 or 678-9001. Rates run about $110 for comfortable double room with TV, phone, big bed, a/c, and a pool, restaurant, and bar downstairs.

Trailer Park

Guadalajara's last surviving trailer park, the **Hacienda Trailer Park** is fortunately a good one. About half of the 96 spaces are occupied permanently by the rigs of Canadian and American regulars who return for their annual winter of sunny relaxation. And anyone can see why: In addition to the sparklingly healthful Guadalajara weather, the Hacienda's lavish facilities include, besides the usual concrete pad, all hookups, separate men's and women's toilets and showers, a big blue pool, patio, large clubroom with fireplace, paperback library, pool room, and a/c power. You can even throw in a golf course and Sam's Club shopping center nearby. For all this, rates run $14/day (one free day per week), $270/month, or $225/month on a yearly basis. While summers at La Hacienda are pretty quiet, winter reservations are mandatory. Write, telephone, or fax Hacienda Trailer Park, P.O. Box 5-494, Guadalajara, Mexico, 45000, tel. (3) 627-1724 or 627-1843, fax 627-2832.

Get there from four-lane Hwy. 15 about five miles (eight kilometers) west of the Guadalajara city center. If heading eastbound, from Tepic-Puerto Vallarta direction, pull into the far right lateral lane just after crossing the *periférico* peripheral highway. After about a mile and a half (two km) from the *periférico,* turn right at the Hacienda Trailer Park sign and follow more signs another few hundred yards to the towering entrance gate. In the Hwy. 15 reverse, westbound direction, turn left at the sign about a mile (a kilometer and a half) past Sam's Club.

FOOD

Breakfast and Snacks

Local folks flock to the acres of *fondas* (permanent foodstalls) on the second floor of the **Mercado Libertad,** at the east end of Plaza Tapatía; open daily about 7 a.m.-6 p.m. Hearty home-style fare, including Guadalajara's specialty, *birria*—pork, goat, or lamb in savory, spiced tomato-chicken broth—is at its safest and best here. It's hard to go wrong if you make sure your choices are hot and steaming. Market stalls, furthermore, depend on repeat customers and are generally very careful their offerings are wholesome. Though be sure to douse fresh vegetables with plenty of lime *(lima)* juice.

Downtown Guadalajara is not overloaded with restaurants, and many of them close early. For long-hours breakfast or supper, however, you can always rely on **Sanborn's,** which retains the 1950s' ambience and menu of its former Denny's owners. Find it right in the middle of town, at the corner of Juárez and 16 de Septiembre, open daily 7:30 a.m.-10 p.m.

For a local variation, head directly upstairs to **Restaurant Esquina** on the same corner, open 7 a.m.-10:30 p.m., or to the other **Sanborn's** across the street, open daily 7:30 a.m.-11 p.m. Besides a tranquil, refined North American-style coffee shop, it has a big gift shop upstairs and bookstore, offering English-language paperbacks and magazines, downstairs.

For a light breakfast or snack, try the Guadalajara branch of **Dunkin Donuts** a block away in Bing's ice cream parlor, on the east side of Corona, at López Cotilla, across the street from the Hotel Fénix. Open Mon.-Sat. 7 a.m.-9 p.m., Sunday 8 a.m.-2 p.m.

If you need a little break from Mexico, go to McDonald's for breakfast (at Juárez and Colón, one short block west of Denny's), where you can get an Egg McMuffin with ham, coffee, and hash browns until noon daily for about $3.

Downtown Restaurants

Moving west across downtown, from the Plaza Tapatía, first comes the airy, restored Porfirian **Restaurant Rinconada,** 86 Morelos, across the plaza behind the Teatro Degollado, tel. (3) 613-9914. The mostly tourist and upper-class local customers enjoy Rinconada for its good meat, fish, and fowl entrées plus the mariachis who wander in from the Plaza Mariachi nearby. By 4 p.m. many afternoons, two or three groups are filling the place with their melodies. Moderate-expensive. Open Mon.-Sat. 8 a.m.-9 p.m., Sunday 1-6 p.m.

Nearby, a pair of clean places for good local food stand out. Try **La Chata,** open daily 8 a.m.-11 p.m., on Corona, between Cotilla and Juárez, next to Bancomer. Although plenty good for breakfast, *cena* (supper) is when the cadre of female cooks come into their own. Here you can have it all: tacos, *chiles rellenos,* tostadas, enchiladas, *pozole, moles,* and a dozen other delights you've probably never heard of, all cooked the way *mamacita* used to. Budget-moderate.

One block south and one block west is the no-nonsense but worthy **Restaurant Málaga,** 16 de Septiembre 210, whose hardworking owner really does come from Málaga, Spain. The food shows it: an eclectic feast of hearty breakfasts, which include a fruit plate and good French bread; a bountiful four-course *comida corrida* for around $5; many salads, sandwiches, and desserts; and savory espresso coffee. Besides the food, customers enjoy live semiclassical piano solos 2-4:30 p.m. daily. Open Mon.-Sat. 7 a.m.-9 p.m., Sunday 8 a.m.-9 p.m. Budget-moderate.

A few blocks farther south, at Corona 291, across from Parque San Francisco, you'll find **La Fería** ("The Fair"), which, true to its name, is a party ready to happen: ceilings hung with a rainbow of piñatas and tassels flowing in the breeze of overhead fans, and tables piled high with goodies. Here, vegetarian pretensions must be suspended temporarily, if only for time to sample their enough-in-themselves barbecued appetizers—spicy *chorizo* sausage, tacos, *ahogado* (hot dipped sandwich), ribs, and much more. Actually, vegetarians needn't go hungry—try the mixed salads, guacamole, or soups, for example. Go for it all and share a big *barrillada* specialty of the house appetizer plate with some friends.

By the time the food has gone down, the next course—a mariachi concert, complete with rope tricks, singers, and maybe a juggler or magic act thrown in for good measure, will keep you entertained for hours. Open 1:30 p.m.-midnight daily. The complete show starts around 9 p.m.; tel. (3) 613-7150 or 613-1812. Moderate-expensive.

Return a few blocks west, by the cathedral, to **Sandy's,** at mezzanine level, above the plaza, northeast corner of Colón and P. Moreno, tel. (3) 614-5871. Here, snappy management, service with a flourish and weekend evening live music make their typical but tasty coffee shop menu of soups, salads, meat, pasta, Mexican plates, sandwiches, and desserts seem like an occasion. Open daily 8 a.m.-10:30 p.m. Moderate.

Continue a few blocks west along Juárez to **Restaurant La Gran China,** Juárez 590, be-

tween Martinez and 8 Julio, tel. (3) 613-1447, where the Cantonese owner/chef puts out an authentic and tasty array of dishes. Despite the reality of La Gran China's crisp bok choy, succulent spareribs, and smooth savory noodles, it nevertheless seems a small miracle here, half a world away from Hong Kong. Open daily noon-10 p.m. Budget-moderate.

For a variation, try Gran China's plainer but equally authentic neighboring **Restaurant Chong Wah,** Juárez 558, half a block east, at the corner of E.G. Martinez, tel. (3) 613-9950; open noon-8 p.m. Budget-moderate.

Restaurants West of Downtown

West of the immediate downtown area, about a mile from the cathedral, is **Restaurant Copenhagen 77,** one of Guadalajara's classiest institutions. Its brand of unpretentious elegance—polished 1940s' decor, subdued live jazz, correct attentive service, tasty entrées—will never go out of style. Upstairs at 140 Z. Castellanos; follow Juárez nine blocks west of Av. 16 de Septiembre to the west end of Parque Revolución. Open Mon.-Sat. noon-midnight, Sunday noon-6 p.m.; live jazz afternoons 3-4:30 p.m. and nights 8 p.m.-midnight. Moderate-expensive.

For another interesting diversion, continue approximately another mile west, to **Le Bistro de Therese,** tel. (3) 616-2947, a little bit of Paris in Guadalajara, at Calderón de la Barca 95, between L. Cotilla and I. Vallarta. Here, a gallery of art and antiques and appetizing French-style food and wine turn an ordinary evening into a party, especially Friday and Saturday nights when they feature live music. Open Mon.-Sat. 1:30 p.m.-1 a.m. Expensive.

ENTERTAINMENT AND EVENTS

Just Wandering Around

Afternoons any day, and Sundays in particular, are good for people-watching around Guadalajara's many downtown plazas. Favorite strolling grounds are the broad Plaza Tapatía west of the cathedral and, especially in the evening, the pedestrian mall-streets, such as Colón, Galeana, Morelos, and Moreno, which meander south and west from cathedral-front Plaza Laureles.

In your meanderings, don't forget to stop by the **Plaza de Los Mariachis,** just east of the Plaza Tapatía, adjacent to the Mercado Libertad and the big boulevard, Insurgentes, which runs beneath the Plaza Tapatía. Take a sidewalk table, have a drink or snack, and enjoy the mariachis' sometimes soulful, sometimes bright, but always enjoyable, offerings.

If you time it right you can enjoy the band concert in the Plaza de Armas adjacent to the cathedral (Thursdays and Sundays at 6:30 p.m.), or take in an art film at the Hospicio Cabañas (Mon.-Sat. 4, 6, and 8 p.m.). If you miss these, climb into a *calandria* (horse-drawn carriage) for a ride around town; carriages are available on Liceo between the rotunda and the history museum, just north of the cathedral, for about $15/hour.

Parque Agua Azul

Some sunny afternoon, hire a taxi (about $2 from the city center) and find out why Guadalajara families love Parque Agua Azul. The entrance is on Independencia, about a mile south of Plaza Tapatía. It's a green, shaded place where you *can* walk, roll, sleep, or lie on the grass. When weary of that, head for the bird park, admire the banana-beaked toucans and squawking macaws, and continue into the aviary where free-flying birds flutter overhead. Nearby, duck into the butterfly aviary and enjoy the flickering rainbow hues of a host of *mariposas.* Continue to the orchids in a towering hothouse, festooned with growing blossoms and misted continuously by a rainbow of spray from the center. Before other temptations draw you away, stop for a while at the open-air band or symphony concert in the amphitheater. The park is open Tues.-Sun. 10 a.m.-6 p.m.

Music and Dance Performances

The **Teatro Degollado** hosts world-class opera, symphony, and ballet events. While you're in the Plaza Liberación, drop by the theater box office and ask for a *lista de eventos.* You can also call (or ask your hotel desk clerk to call) the theater box office at (3) 614-4773 (in Spanish only) for reservations and information. Pick up tickets 4-7 p.m. on the day of the performance. For a very typical Mexican treat, attend one of the regular Sunday-morning University of Guadalajara folkloric ballet performances. They're immensely popular; get tickets in advance.

You can also sample the offerings of the **Instituto Cultural Cabañas,** tel. (3) 618-8135 or 618-8132. It sponsors many events, both experimental and traditional, including folkloric ballet performances every Wednesday. For more information, ask at the Hospicio Cabañas admission desk. Open Tues.-Sun. 10 a.m.-5 p.m.

Local jazz mecca **Restaurant Copenhagen 77,** at 140 Z. Castellanos, presents Maestro Carlos de la Torre and his group nightly Mon.-Sat. 8 p.m.-midnight and afternoons 3-4:30 p.m. At the west end of Parque Revolución, about a mile west of the cathedral.

Restaurant/club **Peña Cuicalli** ("House of Song") offers rock music Tuesday evenings and romantic Latin Thurs.-Sun. evenings. It's at westside Av. Niños Héroes 1988, tel. (3) 825-4690, next to the Niños Héroes monument.

For some very typically Mexican great fun, plan a night out for the dinner and the mariachi show at **La Fería** restaurant (see above).

Fiestas

Although Guadalajarans always seem to be celebrating, the town really heats up during its three major annual festivals. Starting the second week in June, the southeast neighborhood, formerly the separate village of **Tlaquepaque,** hosts the **National Ceramics Fair.** Besides its celebrated stoneware, a riot of ceramics and folk crafts from all over Mexico stuff its shops and stalls, while cockfights, regional food, folk dances, fireworks, and mariachis fill its streets.

A few months later, the entire city, Mexican states, and foreign countries get into the **Festival of October.** For a month, everyone contributes something, from ballet performances, plays, and soccer games to selling papier-mâché parrots and sweet corn in the plazas. Concurrently, Guadalajarans celebrate the traditional **Festival of the Virgin of Zapopan.** Church plazas are awash with merrymakers enjoying food, mariachis, dances (don't miss the Dance of the Conquest), and fireworks. The merrymaking peaks on 12 October, when a huge crowd conducts the Virgin from the downtown cathedral to Zapopan. The merrymakers' numbers often swell to a million faithful who escort the Virgin, accompanied by ranks of costumed saints, devils, Spanish conquistadores, and Aztec chiefs.

CHARREADAS

charra

The many Jalisco lovers of *charrera,* the sport of horsemanship, enjoy a long-venerated tradition. Boys and girls, coached by their parents, practice riding skills from the time they learn to mount a horse. Privileged young people become noble *charros* or *charras* or *coronelas*—gentleman cowboys and cowgirls—whose equestrian habits follow old aristocratic Spanish fashion, complete with broad sombrero, brocaded suit or dress, and silver spurs.

The years of long preparation culminate in the *charreada,* which entire communities anticipate with relish. Although superficially similar to an Arizona rodeo, a Jalisco *charreada* differs substantially. The festivities take place in a *lienzo charro,* literally, the passageway through which the bulls, horses, and other animals run from the corral to the ring. First comes the *cala de caballo,* a test of the horse and rider. The *charros* or *charras* must gallop full speed across the ring and make the horse stop on a dime. Next is the *piales de lienzo,* a roping exhibition during which an untamed horse must be halted and held by having its feet roped. Other bold performances include *jineteo de toro* (bull riding and throwing), and the super-hazardous *paso de la muerte,* in which a rider tries to jump upon an untamed bronco from his or her own galloping mount. *Charreadas* often end in a flourish with the *escaramuza charra,* a spectacular show of riding skill by *charras* in full, colorful dress.

Dancing

The big west-side hotels are among the best spots in town for dancing. Moving west from the city center, first comes the **Hotel Fiesta Americana,** about four miles along Avenidas Juárez and Vallarta, on the left side of the Minerva traffic circle. Patrons enjoy dancing both in the lobby bar nightly from about 7 p.m. and in the nightclub Caballo Negro from about 9:30 p.m. Call (3) 825-3434 to double-check the times.

The **Hotel Holiday Inn,** a quarter mile past the Minerva traffic circle, features a live trio for dancing afternoons and evenings in the lobby bar La Cantera (happy hour 5-8 p.m.), and another trio Thurs.-Sat. from about 9 p.m. at the Bar La Fiesta. Additionally, the Da Vinci disco booms away seasonally from about 9 p.m. Call (3) 634-1034 for confirmation.

On the same boulevard, about a mile farther west, the relaxed tropical garden ambience of the **Hotel Camino Real** probably offers Guadalajara's most romantic setting for dancing and dining. Call (3) 121-8000 to verify live music programs and times.

Bullfights and Rodeos

Winter is the main season for **corridas de toros,** or bullfights. The bulls charge and the crowds roar *"Olé"* (oh-LAY) Sunday afternoons at the Guadalajara Plaza de Toros (bullring), on Calz. Independencia about two miles north of the Mercado Libertad.

Local associations of *charros* (gentleman cowboys) stage rodeo-like Sunday **charreadas** at Guadalajara *lienzos charro* (rodeo rings). One oft-used Guadalajara rodeo ring is Lienzo Charro de Jalisco, 477 Calz. Las Palmas, tel. (3) 619-3232, just beyond the southeast side of Parque Agua Azul. Watch for posters, or ask at your hotel desk or the tourist information office, tel. (3) 614-8686, for *corrida de toros* and *charreada* details and dates.

Entertainment and Events Listings

For many more entertainment ideas, pick up the events schedule at the Hospicio Cabañas (see **Plaza Tapatía,** above) or the tourist information office, also in Plaza Tapatía. Another good source of entertaining events is the weekly English-language Guadalajara **Reporter.** If you can't find a newsstand copy, call the paper's office, at Duque de Rivas 254, Guadalajara, tel. (3) 615-2177.

SPORTS

Walking, Jogging, and Exercise Gyms
Walkers and joggers enjoy several spots around Guadalajara. Close in, the **Plaza Liberación** behind the cathedral provides a traffic-free (although concrete) jogging and walking space. Avoid the crowds with morning workouts. If you prefer grass underfoot, try **Parque Agua Azul** (entrance $3) on Calz. Independencia about a mile south of the Libertad Market. An even better jogging-walking space is the **Parque de los Colomos**—hundreds of acres of greenery, laced by special jogging trails—four miles northwest from the center, before Zapopan; take a taxi or bus 51C, which begins at the old bus terminal, near Parque Agua Azul, and continues along Av. 16 de Septiembre, through downtown Guadalajara.

Guadalajara has a number of exercise gyms with the usual machines, plus jacuzzis and steam rooms. For example, try the big **World Gym** fitness center, with a battery of weight machines, indoor pool, squash courts, mixed aerobics area, 250-meter jogging track, and women-only weights area. It's at Jesús Garcia 804, corner of Miguel Ángel de Quevedo, tel. (3) 640-0704 or 640-0576, beside the Cinema Charlie Chaplin.

Tennis, Golf, and Swimming
Although Guadalajara has few, if any, public tennis courts, the west-side Hotel Camino Real, Av. Vallarta 5005, tel. (3) 121-8000, rents its tennis courts to the public, by appointment, for about $8 per hour. Also, the Hotels Fiesta Americana, Aurelio Aceves 225, Glorieta Minerva, tel. (3) 825-3434, and the Holiday Inn, Av. López Mateos Sur 2500, tel. (3) 634-1034, have courts for guests.

The 18-hole **Burgos del Bosque Golf Club** welcomes nonmembers from dawn to dusk Tues.-Sun.; greens fee runs $50 Tues.-Fri. and $60 Saturday and Sunday. Clubs and carts rent for about $14 and $23; a caddy will cost about $12. Get there via Chapala Hwy. 23, the south-of-town extension of Calz. J. Gonzales Gallo. The golf course is at Km 6.5, past the edge of town, near Parque Montenegro.

Nearly all the luxury hotels have swimming pools. One of the prettiest pools (but unheated), however, perches atop the moderately priced Hotel Calinda Roma in the heart of town (corner Juárez and Degollado).

If your hotel doesn't have a pool, try the **World Gym** (above), or go to the very popular public pool and picnic ground at Balneario Lindo Michoacán, Rio Barco 1614, corner Calz. J. Gonzalez Gallo, tel. (3) 635-9399. Find it about two miles along Gallo southeast of Parque Agua Azul. Open daily 9 a.m.-6 p.m.; entrance about $3 adults, $1.50 kids.

Farther out but even prettier are the canyon-country *balnearios* **Los Camachos** and **Nuevo Paraíso** on Hwy. 54 north toward Saltillo.

SHOPPING

Downtown
The sprawling **Mercado Libertad,** at the east end of Plaza Tapatía, has several specialty areas distributed through two main sections. Most of the handicrafts are in the eastern, upper half. While some stalls carry guitars and sombreros, leather predominates—in jackets, belts, saddles, and the most huaraches you'll ever see under one roof. Here, bargaining *es la costumbre.* Competition, furthermore, gives buyers the advantage. If the seller refuses your reasonable offer, simply turning in the direction of another stall will often bring him to his senses. The upper floor also houses an acre of foodstalls, many of them excellent.

A central courtyard leads past a lineup of bird sellers and their caged charges to the Mercado Libertad's lower half, where produce, meat, and spice stalls fill the floor. (Photographers, note the photogenic view of the produce floor from the balcony above.) Downstairs, don't miss browsing intriguing spice and *yerba* (herb) stalls, which feature mounds of curious dried plants, gathered from the wild, often by village *brujos* (shamans or witch doctors). Before you leave, be sure to look over the piñatas, which make colorful, unusual gifts.

Of the few downtown handicrafts shops, a pair stand out. Right near the city center, try the **Galerias El Convento** complex, in a big restored mansion on Donato Guerra, a few blocks away from the cathedral front, between Morelos and Pedro Moreno. Inside, individual shops offer a host of fine arts and handicrafts, from leather furniture and Tlaquepaque glass to baroque religious antiques and fine silver. You might also find what you're looking for at the government **Casa de Artesanías Agua Azul,** by Parque Agua Azul. Here, you can choose from virtually everything—brilliant stoneware, endearing ceramic, brass, and papier-mâché animals, and handsome gold and silver jewelry—short of actually going to Tonalá, Tlaquepaque, and Taxco. Find it at Calz. Gonzales Gallo 20, next to Parque Agua Azul (off of Independencia); hours are Mon.-Sat. 10 a.m.-7 p.m., Sunday 10 a.m.-2 p.m.

Two other promising, but less extensive, downtown handicrafts sources, in the Plaza Tapatía vicinity, are at the **tourist information office,** Morelos 102, and the native vendors in the adjacent alley, called Rincón del Diablo.

Tlaquepaque

Tlaquepaque was once a sleepy village of potters miles from Guadalajara. Attracted by the quiet of the country, rich families built palatial homes during the 19th century. Now, entrepreneurs have moved in and converted them into upscale restaurants, art galleries, and showrooms, stuffed with quality Tonalá and Tlaquepaque ceramics, glass, metalwork, and papier-mâché.

In spite of having been swallowed by the city, Tlaquepaque still has the feel and look of a small colonial town, with its cathedral and central square leading westward onto the mansion-decorated main street, now mall, Av. Independencia.

Although generally pricier than Tonalá, Tlaquepaque still has bargains. Proceed by finding the base prices at the more ordinary crafts stores in the side streets that branch off of the main mall-street Independencia. Then, price out the showier, upscale merchandise in the galleries along Independencia itself. For super-fine examples of Tlaquepaque and Tonalá crafts, be sure to stop by the **Museo Regional de Cerámica y Arte Popular** (237 Independencia, open Tues.-Sat.

10 a.m.-6 p.m., Sunday 10 a.m.-3 p.m.)

From the *museo,* cross the street to the **Sergio Bustamante** store, upscale outlet for the famous sculptor's arresting, whimsical studies in juxtaposition. Bustamante supervises an entire Guadalajara studio-factory of artists who put out hundreds of one-of-a-kind variations on a few human, animal, and vegetable themes. Prices seem to depend mainly on size; rings and bracelets may go for as little as $200, while a two-foot humanoid chicken may run $2,000. Don't miss the restroom. Open Mon.-Sat 10 a.m.-7 p.m., Sunday 10 a.m.-4 p.m., tel. (3) 639-5519.

Next to Bustamante, at 232 Independencia, **La Rosa Cristal** is one of the few spots where (until 2 p.m. daily) visitors may get a chance to see glassblowers practicing their time-honored Tlaquepaque craft. Although the glassblowers do not actually work in the store, ask them to show you (before about 1 p.m.) to the nearby location where they do. The results of their work—clutches of giant red, green, blue, and silver glass balls—are hard to forget. Open Mon.-Sat. 10 a.m.-7 p.m., Sunday 10 a.m.-2 p.m.

Not far west, at the intersection of Independencia and Alfarareros ("Potters"), a pair of regally restored former mansions, now galleries, enjoy a dignified retirement facing each other on opposite sides of the street. **La Casa Canela,** Independencia 258, tel. (3) 657-1343, takes pride in its museum-quality religious art, furniture, paper flowers, pottery, blown glass, and classic, blue-on-white Tlaquepaque stoneware. Open Mon.-Fri. 10 a.m.-2 p.m. and 3-7 p.m., Saturday 10 a.m.-6 p.m., Sunday 11 a.m.-3 p.m. Across the street, **Antigua de Mexico,** Independencia 255, tel. (3) 635-3402, specializes in baroque gilt wood antiques and reproductions, being one of the few studios in Mexico to manufacture fine 17th century-style furniture. Open Mon.-Fri. 10 a.m.-2 p.m. and 3-7 p.m., Saturday 10 a.m.-6 p.m.

Getting to Tlaquepaque: Taxi (about $15 roundtrip) or ride the usually crowded city bus, no. 275, from stops (such as at Madero) along downtown Av. 16 de Septiembre. By car, from the center of town, drive Av. Revolución southeast about four miles to the Niños Héroes traffic circle. From Av. Niños Héroes, the first right off the traffic circle, continue about a mile to the west end of Av. Independencia, on the left.

An ice cream vendor waits for customers on Tlaquepaque's main shopping street, Av. Independencia.

Tonalá

About five miles past Tlaquepaque, Tonalá perches at Guadalajara's country edge. When the Spanish arrived in the 1520s, Tonalá was dominant among the small kingdoms of the Atemajac Valley. Tonalá's widow-queen and her royal court were adorned by the glittering handiwork of an honored class of silver and gold crafters. Although the Spaniards carted off the valuables, the tradition of Tonalá craftsmanship remains today. To the visitor, everyone in Tonalá seems to making something. Whether it be pottery, stoneware, brass, or papier-mâché, Tonalá family patios are piled with their specialties.

Right at the source, bargains couldn't be better. Dozens of shops dot the few blocks around Tonalá's central plaza corner at Av. Hidalgo (north-south) and Av. Juárez (east-west). For super-bargaining opportunities and *mucho* holiday excitement and color, visit the Thursday and Sunday *tianguis* (market), which spreads along the tree-lined *periférico* highway about four blocks west of the Tonalá plaza.

Under any circumstances, make the **Museo Tonallan** your first stop (at Ramón Corona 75, near the corner of Constitución, about two blocks east and two blocks north of the town plaza, open Mon.-Sat. approximately 9 a.m.-2 p.m. and 4-6 p.m.). Although only recently organized, museum staff plan to install exhibits tracing the origins of local crafts in a historical context, working up to modern popular handicrafts. They also plan to eventually have artisans working at the site.

After the musuem, return back down Constitución to Hidalgo, where several shops stand out. Moving south along Hidalgo toward the town plaza from Constitución, **Artesanías Garay,** Hidalgo 86, one of several *fábrica* (factory) shops that retail directly, offers a host of Tonalá motifs. They're especially proud of their fine floral-design stoneware. Open Mon.-Sat. 10 a.m.-3 p.m. and 4-7 p.m., Sunday 10 a.m.-3 p.m., tel. (3) 683-0019; credit cards are accepted.

El Bazar de Sermel, Hidalgo 67, tel. (3) 683-0010, diagonally across the street, has stretched the Tonalá papier-mâché tradition to the ultimate. Stop in and pick out the life-size flamingo, pony, giraffe, or zebra you've always wanted for your living room. Open Mon.-Fri. 9 a.m.-6:30 p.m., Saturday 9 a.m.-2 p.m., Sunday 10 a.m.-3 p.m.

La Mexicanía, at 13 Hidalgo, corner of the plaza, offers an interesting eclectic assortment, both from Tonalá and other parts of Mexico. These include Huichol Indian yarn paintings and God's eyes, painted tin Christmas decorations from Oaxaca, and Guanajuato papier-mâché clowns. Open Mon.-Sat. 10 a.m.-7 p.m., tel. (3) 683-0152.

Around the corner, a few steps west on Juárez, **Artesanías Nuño,** Juárez 59, tel. (3) 683-0011 displays a fetching menagerie, including parrots, monkeys, flamingos, and toucans, in papier-mâché, brass, and ceramics. Open daily 10 a.m.-7 p.m.; bargain for very reasonable buys.

Stalls and shops lining Tonalá's narrow village streets offer a galaxy of papier-mâché and pottery handicrafts.

Continue south past the Juárez plaza corner (where Hidalgo becomes Madero) one block, to **La Antigua Tonalá,** Madero 50, tel. (3) 683-0200. There you'll find a storeful of hand-hewn tables, chairs, and chests all complete with the Tonalá stoneware place settings to go with them. Open Mon.-Sat. 10 a.m.-7 p.m.; they ship.

Getting to Tonalá: Taxi (about $20 roundtrip) or ride the oft-crowded city bus no. 275 from the stops (such as the corner of Madero) on downtown Av. 16 de Septiembre. By car, drive Av. Revolución about six miles southeast of the city-center to the big Plaza Camichines interchange. Continue ahead along the Carretera Tonalá *libre* (free) branch; avoid forking onto the Hwy. 90 Carretera Zaplotanejo *cuota* toll road. The Carretera Tonalá continues due east for about three more miles, passing under the Carretera Zaplotanejo. Continue across the arterial *periférico* (peripheral highway); three blocks farther

turn left and within a few blocks you'll be at the Tonalá central plaza.

Photo, Grocery, Department, and Health Food Stores

The several branches of the **Laboratorios Julio** chain offer quick photofinishing and a big stock of photo supplies and film, including professional 120 transparency and negative rolls. The big downtown branch is at Colón 125 between Juárez and Cotilla, tel. (3) 614-2850. Open Mon.-Sat. 10 a.m.-2 p.m. and 4-8 p.m. The west-side store, at Av. Americas 425, corner of Manuel Acuña, tel. (3) 616-8286, is open daily 8 a.m.-9 p.m.

For convenient, all-in-one shopping, including groceries, try **Gigante,** downtown on Juárez, corner of Martínez, tel. (3) 613-8638. Open daily 8 a.m.-9 p.m. For even more under one air-conditioned roof, try the big **Comercial Mexicana** at Plaza del Sol, Av. López Mateos Sur 2077. Open daily 9 a.m.-9 p.m.

Stock up on health foods and supplements at **Minisuper Naturista Vegetariano,** open Mon.-Sat. 9 a.m.-6 p.m. at Hidalgo 1440, tel. (3) 825-0603. For others, consult the Guadalajara Yellow Pages under *Tiendas Naturistas.*

SERVICES AND INFORMATION

Money Exchange

Change more types of money (U.S., Canadian, German, Japanese, French, Italian, and Swiss) for the best rates at the downtown streetfront **Banamex** office (Juárez, corner of Corona, open Mon.-Fri. 9 a.m.-5 p.m.). After hours, go to one of the dozens of *casas de cambio* (moneychangers) nearby, a block east of Banamex, on Cotilla between Maestranza and Corona.

American Express has two Guadalajara branches: downtown, at the corner of Cotilla and Corona, and on the west side, at Plaza Los Arcos, Av. Vallarta 2440, about three miles west of the city center, tel. (3) 828-2323 and 828-2325. They both provide travel-agency and member financial services, including personal-check and traveler's-check cashing, Mon.-Fri. 9 a.m.-6 p.m., Saturday 9 a.m.-1 p.m.

Consulates

The **U.S. Consulate** is at Progreso 175 (between

Cotilla and Libertad) about a mile west of the town center, open Mon.-Fri. 8 a.m.-4:30 p.m., tel. (3) 825-2700 or 825-2998. The **Canadian Consulate** is in the Hotel Fiesta Americana at Aurelio Aceves 225, local 31, near the intersection of Av. López Mateos and Av. Vallarta, tel. (3) 615-6215, open Mon.-Fri. 8:30 a.m.-4:30 p.m.

Consular agents from many other countries maintain Guadalajara offices. Consult the local Yellow Pages under *Embajadas, Legaciones y Consulados.*

Hospital, Police, and Emergencies

If you need a doctor, the **Hospital Mexico Americano,** Colomos 2110, tel. (3) 641-3141, ambulance emergency (3) 642-7152, has specialists on call. The director, Dr. Carlos Ramírez M., is one of three Guadalajara affiliates of IAMAT, the International Association for Medical Assistance to Travelers English-speaking physicians' organization. Other local members are Dr. Jaime Ramírez Parra, at Tarascos 3514, tel. (3) 813-0440, 813-0700, or 813-1025, and pediatrician Dr. Roberto A. Dumois N., in the Torre La Paz, 5th floor, at Colonias 221, tel. (3) 825-3042.

For ordinary medications, one of the best sources is the Guadalajara chain **Farmacia ABC,** with many branches. You'll find one downtown at 518 P. Moreno between M. Ocampo and D. Guerra, tel. (3) 142-950, open daily 8 a.m.-9 p.m.

For **police** emergencies, call the radio patrol (dial 060) or the police headquarters at (3) 617-6060. In case of **fire,** call the *servicio bomberos* fire station at (3) 619-5241 or 619-0794.

Post Office, Telephone, and Public Fax

The downtown Guadalajara post office is two blocks west of the Teatro Degollado, just past the Hotel Mendoza, at Independencia and V. Carranza. **Telecomunicaciones** offers public telephone and fax in the city center, at Degollado and Madero, below the city *juzgado* "hoosegow" (jail), open Mon.-Fri. 8 a.m.-6 p.m., Saturday 9 a.m.-2 p.m.

Tourist Information Office

The main Guadalajara tourist information office is in the Plaza Tapatía, on Paseo Morelos, the mall extension of Av. Morelos, behind the Teatro Degollado, at Morelos 102, tel. (3) 614-8686 or 658-0049, open Mon.-Fri. 9 a.m.-8 p.m. and Sat.-Sun. 9 a.m.-1 p.m.

Publications

Among the best Guadalajara sources of English-language magazines is **Sanborn's,** a North American-style gift, book, and coffee shop chain. Sanborn's stores are located downtown, corner Juárez and 16 de Septiembre, open 7:30 a.m.-11 p.m.; at Plaza Vallarta, Av. Vallarta 1600, open 7-1 a.m.; and Plaza del Sol, 2718 López Mateos Sur, open 7-1 a.m.

You can usually get the excellent *News* from Mexico City at one of the newsstands edging the Plaza Laureles, across from the cathedral.

While you're at Sanborn's, you might pick up a copy of the informative local weekly, the ***Colony Reporter.*** Its pages are stuffed with valuable items for visitors, including local events calendars, restaurant and performance reviews, meaty feature articles on local customs and excursions, and entertainment, restaurant, hotel, and rental listings. (If Sanborn's is sold out, call the *Reporter,* tel. 3-615-2177, to find out where you can get a copy.)

Additionally, suburban **Librería Sandi,** at Tepeyac 718, Colonia Chapalita, Guadalajara, tel. (3) 121-0863, has one of the best selections of English-language books and magazines in the Guadalajara area.

Language and Cultural Courses

The University of Guadalajara's **Centro de Estudios Para Extranjeros** ("Study Center for Foreigners") conducts an ongoing program of cultural studies for visitors. Besides formal language, history, and art instruction, students may also opt for live-in arrangements with local families. Write the center at Tomás S. V. Gómez 125, P.O. Box 1-2130, Guadalajara, Jalisco 44100, call (3) 616-4399 or 616-4382, fax 616-4013, or e-mail: cepe@corp.udg.mx.

GETTING THERE AND AWAY

By Air

Several air carriers connect the **Guadalajara Airport** (officially, the Miguel Hidalgo International Airport, code-designated GDL) with many U.S. and Mexican destinations.

Mexicana Airlines flights, reservations tel. (3) 678-7676, arrivals and departures (3) 688-5775, connect frequently with U.S. destinations of Los Angeles, San Francisco, San Jose, San Antonio, Denver, and Chicago, and Mexican destinations of Puerto Vallarta, Mazatlán, Manzanillo, Tijuana, and Mexico City.

Aeroméxico flights, tel. (3) 669-0202, connect frequently with U.S. destinations of Los Angeles, San Diego, Houston, Atlanta, Miami, New York, and Mexican destinations of Puerto Vallarta, Acapulco, Culiacán, Monterrey, Tijuana, and Mexico City.

Aerocalifornia, tel. (3) 826-8850, connects with U.S. destinations of Los Angeles and Tucson, and Mexican destinations of Tijuana, Mazatlán, La Paz, Los Cabos, Culiacán, Los Mochis, Puebla, and Mexico City.

Taesa Airlines, reservations in Mexico toll-free (800) 904-6300, local tel. (3) 615-9761, connects with U.S. destinations of Oakland and Chicago, and Mexican destinations of Tijuana, Mexico City, Morelia, Zacatecas, Puerto Vallarta, and Acapulco.

Other carriers include: **American Airlines,** reservations toll-free in Mexico at (800) 904-6000 or local tel. (3) 616-4090, which connects daily with Los Angeles and Dallas; **Delta Air Lines,** reservations toll-free in Mexico tel. (800) 902-2100, or local tel. (3) 630-3530, which connects twice daily with Los Angeles; **Continental Airlines,** reservations toll-free in Mexico tel. (800) 900-5000, local reservations, tel. (3) 647-4251, which connects twice daily with Houston; and **America West Airlines,** which connects with Phoenix. For information and reservations contact a travel agent, such as American Express, tel. (3) 818-2323 or 818-2325.

Airport arrival is simplified by a money exchange counter (daytime hours only) and major car rental (Avis, Hertz, and Optima) booths. Ground transportation is likewise well organized to shuttle arrivees the 12 miles (19 km) along Chapala Hwy. 23 into town. Tickets for *colectivos* (shared VW van taxis, about $12 for one or two persons) and *taxis especiales* (individual taxis, $18 for one to four persons) are sold at a booth just outside the terminal door. No public buses serve the Guadalajara airport.

Airport departure is equally simple, as long as you save enough for your international departure tax of $19 ($12 federal tax, $7 local) cash (no credit cards, no traveler's checks) per person. A post office (inside, right of the entrance), *telecomunicaciones* (telegraph, fax, long-distance phone), newsstand (lobby floor), bookstore (upstairs), and many crafts and gift shops are convenient for last-minute business and purchases.

By Car or RV
Four major routes connect Guadalajara to the rest of Pacific Mexico. From **Tepic-Compostela-Puerto Vallarta** in the west, National Hwy. 15 winds through 141 miles (227 km) over the Sierra Madre Occidental crest. The new *cuota* (toll) expressway, although expensive ($30 for a car, RVs more), greatly increases safety, decreases wear and tear, and cuts the Guadalajara-Tepic driving time to three hours. The *libre* (free) route, by contrast, has two oft-congested lanes that twist steeply up and down the high pass and bump through towns. For safety, allow around five hours to and from Tepic.

To and from Puerto Vallarta, bypass Tepic via the toll *corta* (cutoff) that connects Hwy. 15 (at Chapalilla) with Hwy. 200 (at Compostela). Figure on four hours total if you use the entire toll expressway (about $20), six hours if you don't.

From Barra de Navidad in the southwest, traffic curves and climbs smoothly along two-lane Hwy. 80 for the 190 miles (306 km) to Guadalajara. Allow around five hours.

An easier road connection with Barra de Navidad runs through Manzanillo along *autopistas* (superhighways) 200, 110, and 54. Easy grades allow a leisurely 55 mph (90 kph) most of the way for this 192-mile (311-km) trip. Allow about four hours from Manzanillo; add another hour for the additional smooth (follow the Manzanillo town toll bypass) 38 miles (61 km) of Hwy. 200 to or from Barra de Navidad.

From Lake Chapala in the south, the four level, straight lanes of Hwy. 23 whisk traffic safely the 33 miles (53 km) to Guadalajara in about 45 minutes.

By Bus
The long-distance Guadalajara *camionera central* (central bus terminal) is at least 20 minutes by taxi (about $15) from the city center. The huge modern complex sprawls past the southeast-sector intersection of the old Tonalá Hwy. (Carretera Antigua Tonalá) and the new Zaplotanejo Autopista (Freeway) Hwy. 90. The

camionera central is sandwiched between the two highways. Tell your taxi driver which bus line you want or where you want to go, and he'll drop you at one of the terminal's seven *modulos* (buildings). For arrival and departure convenience, you might consider staying at the adjacent, moderately priced Hotel El Parador.

Each of the *modulos* is self-contained, with restrooms, cafeteria or snack bar, stores offering snack foods (but few fruits or veggies), bottled drinks, common medicines and drugs, and handicrafts. Additionally, *modulos* 2, 5, and 6 have public long-distance telephone and fax service.

Dozens of competing bus lines offer departures. The current king of the heap is **Estrella Blanca,** a holding company that operates a host of subsidiaries, notably Elite, Turistar, Futura, Transportes del Norte, Transportes Norte de Sonora, and Transportes Chihuahenses. Second largest and trying harder is **Flecha Amarilla,** which offers "Servicios Coordinados" through a dozen subsidiaries. Trying even harder are the biggest independents: Enlaces Terrestres Nacionals (ETN, "National Ground Network"), Omnibus de Mexico, Transportes Pacífico, and Autobuses del Occidente, all of whom would very much like to be your bus company.

To **north-central and northeastern destinations** such as Zacatecas, Torreón, Saltillo, Monterrey, and the U.S. border at Ciudad Juárez, Nuevo Laredo, Reynosa, or Matamoros, go to *modulo* 7. Take first-class Transportes Chihuahuenses, tel. (3) 679-0404, via San Juan de Los Lagos, Zacatecas, Torreon, Chihuahua, Juárez; luxury-class Turistar, tel. (3) 679-0404, same route as Transportes Chihuahuenses; or first-class Transportes del Norte, tel. (3) 679-0404, San Juan de los Lagos, Zacatecas, Saltillo, Monterrey, Reynosa, Matamoros.

To and from **Pacific coast** destinations, go to *modulo* 4. Take first-class Elite, tel. (3) 674-

0462, via Tepic, Puerto Vallarta, Mazatlán, to the U.S. border at Nogales, Mexicali, and Tijuana; first-class Transportes Pacífico, tel. (3) 600-0450, virtually the same destinations as Elite; second-class Transportes Pacífico, tel. (3) 600-0450, through small Nayarit coastal towns and villages, such as Las Varas, La Peñita, and Rincón de Guayabitos en route to Puerto Vallarta; or second-class Transportes Norte de Sonora, tel. (3) 679-0463, through smaller northern Nayarit and Sinaloa towns, such as Tepic, San Blas, Santiago Ixcuintla, Mexcaltitán, Acaponeta, Novillero, Esquinapa, and Teacapán.

For far southern Pacific destinations of **Zihuatanejo** and **Acapulco,** you can go by Elite one of two ways: Direct to Acapulco via Mexico City (one or two buses per day) or via Tepic, where you must transfer to the Acapulco-southbound Elite bus. This may necessitate an overnight in Tepic.

Also at *modulo* 4 is first- and second-class Transportes Cihuatlán, tel. (3) 600-0076, which offers service south along Hwy. 80 to the Pacific via Autlán to **Melaque, Barra de Navidad,** and **Manzanillo.** Additionally, at both *modulo* 4 and *modulo* 3, second-class Autotransportes Guadalajara-Talpa-Mascota, tel. (3) 600-0058 or 600-0098, offers connections to the non-touristed western Jalisco mountain towns of **Talpa and Mascota** (where you can connect on to Puerto Vallarta via the hidden old mining village of **San Sebastián**).

The mágica sol, worshipped universally in pre-conquest Mexico, continues as a popular pottery and metalwork motif.

For eastern and southeastern destinations in **Jalisco, Guanajuato, Michoacán,** and **Colima,** go to either *modulo* 6 or *modulo* 1. In *modulo* 6, ride first-class Omnibus de Mexico, tel. (3) 600-0469, which goes through Querétaro, Aguascalientes, Colima, and Manzanillo, or ETN, tel. (3) 600-0501, via Celaya, León, Pátzcuaro, Uruapan, Morelia, Colima, Manzanillo, and Puerto Vallarta. In *modulo* 1, first-class Flecha Amarilla, tel. (3) 600-0398 offers service to a swarm of destinations, including León, Guanajuato, San Miguel de la Allende, Uruapan, Morelia, Puerto Vallarta, Manzanillo, Barra de Navidad, and untouristed villages—El Super, Tomatlán, and El Tuito—on the Jalisco coast.

For many other subsidiary regional destinations, buses arrive and depart from the *camionera antigua* (old bus terminal), at the end of Estadio, off Calz. Independencia downtown. For Lake Chapala, ride one of several daily departures of the second-class red-and-white Autotransportes Guadalajara-Chapala buses. For Talpa, Mascota,

and San Sebastián in the western Jalisco mountains, go by the red second-class Autotransportes Guadalajara-Talpa-Mascota, tel. (3) 619-0708.

By Train

Passenger rail service to and from Guadalajara has been stopped by the privatization of the Mexican Railways' Pacific route. Unless future government subsidies offset private losses, Pacific passenger trains will go the way of buggy whips and Stanley Steamers.

ALONG THE ROAD TO PUERTO VALLARTA

The lush, hundred-mile stretch between Tepic and Puerto Vallarta is a Pacific Eden of flowery tropical forest and pearly palm-shaded beaches, largely unknown to the outside world. The gateway Mexican National Hwy. 200 is still relatively new; the traffic and development that will inevitably follow have barely begun. Only scattered roadside villages, pastures, tobacco fields, and tropical fruit orchards encroach upon the vine-strewn jungle.

PLAYA CHACALA
AND MAR DE JADE

Side roads off Hwy. 200 provide exotic, close-up glimpses of Nayarit's tangled, tropical woodland, but rarely will they lead to such a delightful surprise as the green-tufted golden crescent of Playa Chacala and its diminutive neighbor, Playa Chacalilla.

Nineteen miles (31 km) north of Rincón de Guayabitos, follow the six-mile, newly paved road to the great old palm grove at Chacala. Beyond the line of rustic *palapa* seafood restaurants lies a heavenly curve of sand, enfolded on both sides by palm-tipped headlands.

A mile farther north, past Chacala village on the headland, the road ends at Chacalilla, Chacala's miniature twin, with its own sandy beach, grove, and *palapa*. On Sunday and holidays families crowd in, and someone sells drinks and stokes up a fire to barbecue fish for the picnickers.

Playa Chacala Practicalities

Chacala's gentle surf is good for close-in bodysurfing, boogie boarding, swimming, and beginning-intermediate surfing. Furthermore, the water is generally clear enough for snorkeling off the rocks on either side of the beach. If you bring your equipment, kayaking, windsurfing, and sailing are possible. Moreover, the sheltered north end cove is nearly always tranquil and safe, even for tiny tots. Fishing is so good local people make their living at it. Chacala Bay is so rich and clean that tourists eat oysters right off the rocks.

Supplied by the beachside restaurants and the stores in the village, Playa Chacala is ideal for tent or small RV camping. Now that the road is paved, motor homes and trailers, with care, should be able to get there routinely. Chacalilla would be similarly good for camping, except new development may limit access.

Comfortable accommodation in Chacala is available at **Casa los Obeliscos** ("Hibiscus House"), the life project of local resident Jorge Garcia and his California wife, Margaret. They rent two simply but comfortably furnished tourist rooms in the upper level of their family house, a few steps from the sheltered north-end corner of Chacala's luscious, palm-tufted, sandy crescent. Here, you can enjoy village Mexico at its easygoing best, with super-fresh seafood, a lush, wildlife-rich forest hinterland, a quiet cove, perfect for child's play, and dazzling sunsets.

Rentals run $20 s or d, $25 for three or four; $120 and $150 per week. Reserve through their U.S. agent, Jan Davis, at P.O. Box 151, Santa

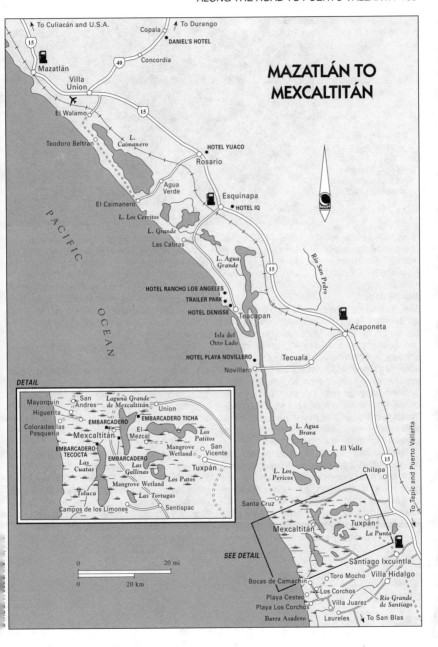

MAZATLÁN TO MEXCALTITÁN

To Culiacán and U.S.A.

Copala

To Durango

DANIEL'S HOTEL

15

Mazatlán

40

Concordia

Villa Union

El Walamo

15

Teodoro Beltran

L. Caimanero

HOTEL YUACO

Rosario

Agua Verde

Esquinapa

El Caimanero

HOTEL IQ

L. Los Cerritos

L. Grande

Las Cabras

L. Agua Grande

15

Río San Pedro

HOTEL RANCHO LOS ANGELES

TRAILER PARK

HOTEL DENISSE

Teacapan

Acaponeta

Isla del Otro Lado

HOTEL PLAYA NOVILLERO

Tecuala

Novillero

PACIFIC

OCEAN

L. Agua Brava

L. El Valle

To Tepic and Puerto Vallarta

15

Chilapa

L. Los Pericos

Santa Cruz

Mexcaltitán

Tuxpán

La Punta

SEE DETAIL

Santiago Ixcuintla

Toro Mocho

Villa Hidalgo

Bocas de Camachin

Los Corchos

Playa Cesteo

Villa Juarez

Río Grande de Santiago

Playa Los Corchos

Barra Asadero

Laureles

To San Blas

0   20 mi

0   20 km

DETAIL

Mayorquin

San Andres

Laguna Grande de Mexcaltitán

Union

Higuerita

EMBARCADERO

EMBARCADERO TICHA

Coloradas las Pesqueria

Mexcaltitán

El Mezcal

Los Patitos

San Vicente

EMBARCADERO TECOCTA

EMBARCADERO

Las Cuatas

Las Gallinas

Mangrove Wetland

Tuxpán

Los Patos

Mangrove Wetland

Toluca

Las Tortugas

Campos de los Limones

Sentispac

Roadside stalls at Las Varas offer a trove of local fruit. Sometimes more exotic varieties, such as guanabanas, shown, are available.

Rosa, CA 95402, tel. (707) 566-0709, e-mail: jan_davis@compuserve.com; or contact Jorge and Margaret directly at P.O. Box 39, Las Varas, Nayarit 63715, fax (327) 203-60.

Mar de Jade

The Mar de Jade, a holistic-style living center at the south end of Playa Chacala, offers unique alternatives. Laura del Valle, Mar de Jade's personable and dynamic physician/founder, has worked hard since the early 1980s, building living facilities and a learning center, while simultaneously establishing a local health clinic. Now, Mar de Jade offers Spanish-language and work-study programs for people who enjoy the tropics but want to do more than laze in the sun. The main thrust is interaction with local people. Spanish, for example, is the preferred language at the dinner table.

The thatched cool and clean adobe and brick cabins and adjacent two-story lodging complex (with concrete floors, showers, restrooms, and good water) nestle among a flowery, palm-shaded garden of fruit trees. Additional units dot a forested, ocean-view hillside nearby. Stone pathways lead to the beachside main center, which consists of a dining room, kitchen, offices, library, and classroom overlooking the sea.

While Mar de Jade's purpose is serious, they have nothing against visitors who *do* want to laze in the sun. Mar de Jade invites travelers to make reservations (or simply drop in) and stay as long as they like, for adults from $70 a day high season (24 Oct.-8 May), per person double occupancy, including three hearty meals. Discounts are available for children.

The core educational program is a three-week Spanish course (fee $80/week), although one- and two-week options are available for those who can't stay the full three weeks. Work-study programs, such as gardening, kitchen assistant, carpentry, and maintenance can possibly be arranged. Sometimes participants join staff in local work, such as at the medical clinic or local construction projects.

For more information about the course schedule and fees, contact Mar de Jade's U.S. agent at P.O. Box 1280, Santa Clara, CA 95052-1280, voice mail (415) 281-0164. You can also contact Mar de Jade directly, at P.O. Box 81, Las Varas, Nayarit, 63715, Mexico, tel./fax (327) 201-84, e-mail: info@mardejade.com, Web site: www.mardejade.com.

RINCÓN DE GUAYABITOS

Rincón de Guayabitos (pop. about 3,000 permanent, maybe 8,000 in winter) lies an hour's drive north of Puerto Vallarta, at the tiny southend *rincón* (wrinkle) of the broad, mountain-rimmed Bay of Jaltemba. The full name of Rincón de Guayabitos's sister town, La Peñita ("Little Rock") de Jaltemba, comes from its perch on the sandy edge of the bay.

Once upon a time, Rincón de Guayabitos (or simply Guayabitos, meaning "Little Guavas") lived up to its diminutive name. During the 1970s, however, the government decided Rincón de Guayabitos would become both a resort and one of three places in the Puerto Vallarta region where foreigners could own property. Today Rincón de Guayabitos is a summer, Christmas, and Easter haven for Mexicans, and a winter retreat for Canadians and Americans weary of glitzy, pricey resorts.

SIGHTS

Getting Oriented
Guayabitos and La Peñita (pop. around 10,000) represent practically a single town. Guayabitos has the hotels and the sleepy scenic ambience, while two miles north La Peñita's main street, Emiliano Zapata, bustles with stores, restaurants, a bank, and a bus station.

Guayabitos's main street, Avenida del Sol Nuevo, curves lazily for about a mile parallel to the beach. From the *avenida,* several short streets and *andandos* (walkways) lead to a line of *retornos* (cul-de-sacs). Most of Guayabitos's community of small hotels, bungalow complexes, and trailer parks lie here within a block of the beach.

Isla Islote
Only a few miles offshore, the rock-studded humpback of Isla Islote may be seen from every spot along the bay. A flotilla of wooden glass-bottomed launches plies the Guayabitos shoreline, ready to whisk visitors across to the island. For $15 an hour parties of up to six or eight can view the fish through the boat bottom and see the colonies of nesting terns, frigate birds, and boobies on Islote's guano-plastered far side. You might see dolphins playing in your boat's wake, or perhaps a pod of whales spouting and diving nearby.

BEACHES AND ACTIVITIES

Playa Guayabitos-La Peñita
The main beach, Playa Guayabitos-La Peñita, curves two miles north from the rocky Guayabitos point, growing wider and steeper at La Peñita. The shallow Guayabitos cove, lined by *palapa* restaurants and dotted with boats, is a favorite of Mexican families on Sunday and holidays. They play in the one-foot surf, ride the boats, and eat barbecued fish. During busy times, the place can get polluted from the people, boats, and fishing.

Farther along toward La Peñita, the beach broadens and becomes much cleaner, with surf good for swimming, bodysurfing, and boogie boarding. Afternoon winds are often brisk enough for sailing and windsurfing, though you must bring your own equipment. Scuba and snorkeling are good near offshore Isla Islote, accessible via rental boat from Guayabitos. Local stores sell inexpensive but serviceable masks, snorkels, and fins.

A mile north of La Peñita, just past the palm-dotted headland, another long, inviting beach begins, offering good chances for beginning and intermediate surfing.

Playa los Muertos
Follow the uphill paved road to Los Ayala, and, just as it reaches its summit, curving around the Guayabitos headland, notice a dirt road forking right, downhill. It continues through a cemetery to Playa los Muertos ("Beach of the Dead"), where the graves come right down to the beach.

Ghosts notwithstanding, this is a scenic little sandy cove. On fair days get your fill of safe swimming, sunning on the beach, or tidepooling amongst the clustered oysters and mussels and the skittering crabs. (The owners of houses

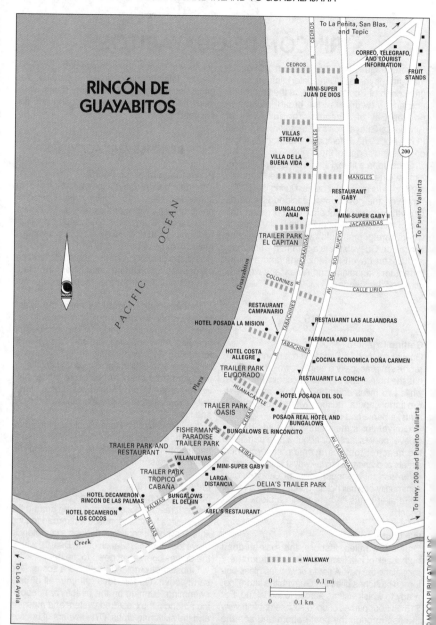

RINCÓN DE
GUAYABITOS

PACIFIC OCEAN

To La Peñita, San Blas,
and Tepic

CORREO, TELEGRAFO,
AND TOURIST
INFORMATION

FRUIT
STANDS

CEDROS

MINI-SUPER
JUAN DE DIOS

200

VILLAS
STEFANY

VILLA DE LA
BUENA VIDA

R. LAURELES

MANGLES

RESTAURANT
GABY

BUNGALOWS
ANAI

MINI-SUPER GABY II

JACARANDAS

To Puerto Vallarta

TRAILER PARK
EL CAPITAN

R. JACARANDAS

AV. DEL SOL NUEVO

Guayabitos

COLORINES

CALLE LIRIO

RESTAURANT
CAMPANARIO

RESTAURANT LAS ALEJANDRAS

HOTEL POSADA LA MISION

R. TABACHINES

FARMACIA AND LAUNDRY

TABACHINES

HOTEL COSTA
ALLEGRE

COCINA ECONOMICA DOÑA CARMEN

TRAILER PARK
EL DORADO

RESTAURANT LA CONCHA

Playa

HUANACAXTLE

HOTEL POSADA DEL SOL

TRAILER PARK
OASIS

POSADA REAL HOTEL AND
BUNGALOWS

R. CEIBAS

FISHERMAN'S
PARADISE
TRAILER PARK

BUNGALOWS EL RINCONCITO

TRAILER PARK AND
RESTAURANT

CEIBAS

AV. GARDENIAS

VILLANUEVAS

MINI-SUPER GABY II

TRAILER PARK
TROPICO
CABAÑA

LARGA
DISTANCIA

DELIA'S TRAILER PARK

HOTEL DECAMERON
RINCON DE LAS PALMAS

BUNGALOWS
EL DELFIN

R. PALMAS

To Hwy. 200 and Puerto Vallarta

HOTEL DECAMERON
LOS COCOS

ABEL'S RESTAURANT

Creek

To Los Ayala

▦▦▦▦▦ = WALKWAY

0   0.1 mi

0   0.1 km

© MOON PUBLICATIONS, INC.

above the beach have placed a gate across the private entrance road to discourage cars. However, they cannot legally bar people from the beach, so, even if you have to hire a launch to drop you off and pick you up there, Playa los Muertos is worth it.)

Playa los Ayala-Playa del Beso

Continue along the road about another mile to the tiny rustic settlement and one-mile yellow strand of Playa los Ayala. With no facilities other than a dusty little store and a lineup of beachside *palapas,* Los Ayala retains its Sunday popularity among local families because of its long, lovely beach. All of the beach sports possible at Guayabitos are possible here, with the added advantage of a much cleaner beach.

Like Guayabitos, Los Ayala has its secluded south-end cove. Follow the path up the beach-end headland. Ten minutes' walk along a tropical forest trail leads you to the romantic little jungle-enfolded sand crescent called Playa del Beso ("Beach of the Kiss"). Except during holidays, for hours on end few if any people come here.

Playa Punta Raza

The road to Playa Punta Raza, while only about three miles long, requires a maneuverable high-clearance vehicle and dry weather. The reward is a long, wild beach perfect for beachcombing and camping. Bring everything, including water.

Three miles south of Guayabitos along Hwy. 200, turn off at El Monteón; pass through the village, turn right at Calle Punta Raza just before the pavement ends. Continue along the rough road through the creek and over the ridge north of town. At the summit, stop and feast your eyes on the valley view below, then continue down through the near-virgin jungle, barely scratched by a few poor cornfields. About a mile downhill from the summit, stop to see if the seasonal hillside restaurant on the right is open. This site has recently been used as headquarters for Campo de Tortugas de Playa Punta Raza, a group of plucky volunteers who camp out on the beach trying to save endangered turtle eggs from poachers.

At the bottom of the steep grade, the track parallels the beach beneath big trees; sandy trails run through the brush to the beach—experienced sand drivers only; it's very easy to get stuck. You have two straight miles of pristine, jungle-backed sand virtually to yourself.

The beach itself slopes steeply, with the resulting close-in crashing waves and undertow. The water would be fine for splashing, but swimmers be careful. Because of the jungle hinterland, birds and other wildlife are plentiful here. Bring your insect repellent, binoculars, and identification books.

Turtles arrive periodically in late summer and fall to lay eggs here. Look for obvious tracks in the sand. The turtles attract predators—cats, iguanas, birds, and human poachers. If you find an egg nest, either report it to the volunteers or keep watch over it; your reward may be to witness the birth and return to the ocean of dozens of baby turtles.

ACCOMMODATIONS

Guayabitos Hotels

Guayabitos has more far more hotels than any other town in Nayarit, including the capital, Tepic. Competition keeps standards high and prices low. During the low season (Sept.-Nov.) most places are less than half full and ready to bargain. During the winter season, the livelier part of town is at the south end, where most of the foreigners, mostly Canadians and Americans, congregate.

Guayabitos has many lodgings that call themselves "bungalows." This generally implies a motel-type suite with kitchenette with less service, but more spacious and more suited to families than a hotel room. For long stays, where you want to save money by cooking your own meals, bungalows can provide a good option.

Perhaps the cheapest good lodging in town is the homey 32-room **Posada Real Hotel and Bungalows,** Retorno Ceibas and Andando Huanacaxtle, Rincón de Guayabitos, Nayarit 63727, tel./fax (327) 401-77, built around a cobbled parking courtyard jungle of squawking parrots and shady palms, mangoes, and bamboo. The bungalow units are on the ground floor in the courtyard; the hotel rooms are stacked in three plant-decorated tiers above the lobby in front. The 26 four-person bungalows with kitchenettes as well as the 20 two-person hotel rooms rent for about $17 low season d, $20 high, with discounts

RINCÓN DE GUAYABITOS ACCOMMODATIONS

Accommodations (area code 327, postal code 63726) are listed in increasing order of approximate high-season, double-room rates.

Posada Real Hotel and Bungalows, Retorno Ceibas s/n, tel./fax 401-77, $20

Hotel Posada La Misión, Retorno Tabachines 6, tel./fax 403-57, $28

Hotel Posada del Sol, Retorno Tabachines s/n, tel. 401-52, $30

Bungalows El Rinconcito, Retorno Ceibas s/n, P.O. Box 19, tel. 402-29, $30

Bungalows El Delfín, Retorno Ceibas s/n, tel. 403-85, $39

Villas Stefany, Retorno Laureles 12 Poniente, tel. 405-36, 405-37, fax 409-63, $42

Hotel Costa Alegre, Retorno Tabachines s/n, tel. 402-41 or 402-42, fax 402-43, $50

Bungalows Anai, Retorno Jacarandas, P.O. Box 44, tel./fax 402-45, $55

Villas de la Buena Vida, Retorno Laureles 2, P.O. Box 62, tel. (327) 40-231, fax 40-756, e-mail: vbv@guayabitos.com.mx, Web site: www.villasbuenavida.com/, $70

Hotel Decameron Rincón de las Palmas, Retorno Palmas s/n, tel. 401-90, fax 401-74, $120 all-inclusive lodging, food, drinks, and in-house entertainment for two

possible for longer-term stays. Amenities include ceiling fans, a small pool and a kiddie pool, water slide, racquetball, and parking; credit cards accepted.

Immediately north, across Andando Huanacaxtle, **Hotel Posada del Sol** (managed by Trailer Park Posada del Sol, see below) offers 14 tastefully furnished bungalows around a palmy garden patio, from about $30/day, $500/month.

One of the most charming off-beach Guayabitos lodgings is **Bungalows El Delfín,** managed by friendly owners Francisco and Delia Orozco at Retorno Ceibas and Andando Cocoteros, Rincón de Guayabitos, P.O. Box 12, Nayarit 63727, tel. (327) 403-85. Amenities include an intimate banana- and palm-fringed pool patio, including recliners and umbrellas for resting and reading. Chairs on the shaded porch and walkways in front of the three room tiers invite quiet relaxation and conversation with neighbors. The pastel-walled four-person suites are large and plainly furnished, with basic stove, refrigerator, and utensils, rear laundry porches, and big, tiled toilet-showers. The 15 bungalows with kitchenettes sleep four and rent for about $33 low season, $39 high. Ceiling fans, pool, and parking; pets okay.

Right-on-the-beach **Bungalows El Rinconcito,** Retorno Ceibas s/n and Calle Ceibas,

P.O. Box 19, Rincón de Guayabitos, Nayarit 63727, tel. (327) 402-29, is one of the best buys in Guayabitos. The smallish whitewashed complex set back from the street offers large, tastefully furnished units with yellow-and-blue tile kitchens and solid, Spanish-style dark-wood chairs and beds. Its oceanside patio opens to a grassy garden overlooking the surf. The three two-bedroom bungalows rent for about $25 low season, $40 high, and seven one-bedroom bungalows for about $20 low season, $30 high, with fans and parking. Discounts are generally available for longer-term stays.

One of the fancier Guayabitos lodgings is the colonial-style **Hotel Posada La Misión,** Retorno Tabachines 6, Rincón de Guayabitos, Nayarit 63727, tel./fax (327) 403-57, whose centerpiece is a beachside restaurant/bar/patio, nestled beneath a spreading, big-leafed *hule* (rubber) tree. Extras include a luxurious shady garden veranda and an inviting azure pool and patio, thoughtfully screened off from the parking. The rooms are high-ceilinged and comfortable except for the unimaginative bare-bulb lighting; bring your favorite bulb-clip lampshades. Doubles rent for about $19 low season, $28 high; quadruples, $26 low season and $40 high; suites sleeping six, $35 and $54. Two kitchenette bungalows go for $38 low season, $58 high. Amenities include a pool, good restaurant, ocean-view bar, ceiling fans, and parking; credit cards are accepted.

Travelers who play tennis and prefer an air-conditioned, modern-style lodging, all drinks, entertainment, and food included, should pick the compact, pool patio ambience of the **Hotel Decameron Rincón de las Palmas,** Retorno Palmas s/n at Calle Palmas, Rincón de Guayabitos, Nayarit 63727, tel. (327) 401-90, fax 401-74, near the south end. With airy beach-view restaurant and bar for sitting and socializing, this is a lodging for those who want company. Guests may often have a hard time *not* getting acquainted. The smallish rooms are packed in two double parallel breezeway tiers around a pool patio above the beach. Right outside your room during the high season you will probably have your pick of around 50 sunbathing bodies to gaze at and meet. This hotel is operated by its big neighbor Hotel Decameron Los Cocos, which handles reservations (in a Bucerías office, tel. 329-811-04, fax 803-33), mandatory in winter. Specifically ask for Hotel Rincón de las Palmas, or they might put you in the oversize Los Cocos. The 40 rooms rent, low season, for about $38 per person, double occupancy, and $60 high, all drinks and food included, with a/c, pool, TV, tennis court, breezy sea-view restaurant/bar, parking; credit cards accepted.

Just as modern but more spacious is the family-oriented **Hotel Costa Alegre,** Retorno Tabachines s/n at Calle Tabachines, Rincón de Guayabitos, Nayarit 63727, tel. (327) 402-41 or 402-42, fax 402-43, where the Guayabitos beach widens out. Its pluses include a big, blue pool patio on the street side and a broad, grassy, ocean-view garden on the beach side. Although the rooms are adequate, the kitchenette bungalows are set away from the beach with no view but the back of neighboring rooms. The best choices are the several upper-tier oceanfront rooms, all with sliding glass doors leading to private sea-view balconies. Some rooms are in better repair than others; look at more than one before paying. The 30 view rooms run about $40 d low season, $50 high; the 43 kitchenette bungalows are $45 and $55 d. With a/c, pool, parking, and restaurant/bar; credit cards accepted.

Most of Guayabitos's newer upscale lodgings are at the north end. For peace and quiet in a luxurious tropical setting, the **Bungalows Anai,** at Calle Jacarandas and Retorno Jacarandas, P.O. Box 44, Rincón de Guayabitos, Nayarit 63727, tel./fax (327) 402-45, is just about the best on the beach. The approximately 15 apartments, in two-story tiers, each with private ocean-view balcony, stand graciously to one side. They overlook a spacious, plant-bedecked garden, shaded by a magnificent grove of drowsy coconut palms. The garden leads to an ocean-view patio where a few guests read, socialize, and take in the beachside scene below. Inside, the two-bedroom suites are simply but thoughtfully furnished in natural wood, bamboo, and tile and come with bath, three double beds, furnished kitchen, fans, a/c, and TV. Rentals run about $45 low season, $55 high for up to four; one-week minimum stay.

About a block farther north, at Retorno Laureles 2, the shiny, deluxe **Villas de la Buena Vida** welcomed guests for the first time in winter 1999. This is Guayabitos's most luxurious lodging, with about 40 tastefully appointed suites with ocean view in five stories above a palm-shaded pool patio right on the beach. For Guayabitos, the high-season asking rates are correspondingly luxurious: two-bed "villa" apartments run $70; junior suites, $94; and master suites $117. Bargain for a discount, especially long-term, midweek, and low season. Reserve at P.O. Box 62, Rincón de Guayabitos, Nayarit 63726, tel. (327) 40-231, fax 40-756, e-mail: vbv@guayabitos.com.mx. Note: The above prices include the hefty 17% "value added" tax, which is omitted in the rates listed on the hotel's Web site, www.villasbuenavida.com/.

Next a few doors north, **Villas Stefany,** Retorno Laureles 12 Poniente, Rincón de Guayabitos, Nayarit 63727, tel. (327) 405-36 or 405-37, fax 409-63, offers another attractive deluxe alternative. Guests in the 34 suites enjoy private balconies overlooking a lush pool-patio garden and ocean vista. The apartments, simply but comfortably furnished in pastels, wood, and tile, have a living room with furnished kitchenette and one bedroom with two double beds and a bath; other extras include cable TV, telephone, and a/c. Rentals run about $32 d low season, $42 high, $50 for four, $60 high, for a one-week minimum stay. With restaurant, pool, and lobby bars, street parking only; credit cards accepted.

Guayabitos Trailer Parks

All but one of the several Guayabitos trailer parks are wall-to-wall RVs most of the winter. Some old-timers have painted and marked out their spaces for years of future occupancy. The best spaces of the bunch are all booked by mid-October. And although the longtime residents are polite enough, some of them are clannish and don't go out of their way to welcome new kids on the block.

This is fortunately not true at **Delia's,** Guayabitos's funkiest trailer park, Retorno Ceibas 4, Rincón de Guayabitos, Nayarit 63727, tel. (327) 403-98. Friendly realtor/owner Delia Bond Valdez and her daughter Rosa Delia have 15 spaces, a good number of which are unfilled even during the high season. Their place, alas, is not right on the beach, nor is it as tidy as some folks would like. On the other hand, Delia offers a little store, insurance, long-distance phone service, and a small *lonchería* right next to the premises. She also rents two bungalows for about $300 a month. Spaces run about $10/night, $250/month high season, $5/night low, with all hookups, room for big rigs, pets okay, showers, toilets.

The rest of Guayabitos's trailer parks line up right along the beachfront. Moving from the south end, first comes **Trailer Park Tropico Cabaña,** built with boats and anglers in mind. One old-timer, a woman, the manager says, has been coming for 20 years running. It must be for the avocados—bulging, delicious three-pounders—that hang from a big shady tree. Other extras are a boat launch and storage right on the beach, with an adjacent fish-cleaning sink and table. This is a prime, very popular spot; get your reservation in early to Retorno Las Palmas, P.O. Box 3, Rincón de Guayabitos, Nayarit 63727. The 28 cramped spaces, six 38-footers and 22 33-footers, rent for about $11/day with all hookups, discounts for longer stays; includes showers, toilets, and barbecue; pets okay.

The single Guayabitos trailer park that celebrates a traditional Christmas-eve *posada* procession is the **Trailer Park Villanuevas,** managed by friendly Lydia Villanuevas, at Retorno Ceibas s/n, P.O. Box 25, Rincón de Guayabitos, Nayarit 63727, tel. (327) 403-91. Allowing for 30 spaces, including three drive-throughs, they can still stuff in some big rigs, although room is at

a premium. Shade, however, is not: lovely palms cover the entire lot. Moreover, their sea-view *palapa* restaurant is very popular with Guayabitos longtimers. Spaces go for $13/daily (or $12/day monthly); add $2/day for a/c power. All hookups, restaurant, showers, toilets, boat ramp, pets okay. There are also four bungalows that rent for about $35 d.

Next door to the north comes **Fisherman's Paradise Trailer Park,** which is also popular as a mango-lover's paradise, Retorno Ceibas s/n, Rincón de Guayabitos, Nayarit 63727, tel./fax (327) 400-14. Several spreading mango trees shade the park's 33 concrete pads, and during the late spring and summer when the mangoes ripen, you'll probably be able to park under your own tree. Winter-season spaces rent for about $13/day (or $11/day for a three-month rental), with all hookups, showers, toilets, pets okay.

Neighboring **Trailer Park Oasis** is among Guayabitos's most deluxe and spacious trailer parks, Retorno Ceibas s/n, Apdo. 42, Rincón de Guayabitos, Nayarit 63727. Its 19 all-concrete partly palm-shaded spaces are wide and long enough for 40-foot rigs. Pluses include green grassy grounds, beautiful blue pool, a designer restaurant, and a luxury ocean-view *palapa* above the beach. Spaces rent for about $16/day, $14/day monthly, with all hookups. Showers, toilets, fish-cleaning facility, boat ramp, pets okay.

Residents of **Trailer Park El Dorado,** Retorno Tabachines s/n, Rincón de Guayabitos, Nayarit 63727, tel. (327) 401-52, enjoy shady, spacious, grass-carpeted spaces beneath a rustling old palm grove, all the result of the tender loving care of the friendly on-site owner/manager. Other extras include a pool and recreation *palapa* across the street in **Hotel Posada Del Sol,** which has 14 tastefully furnished bungalows around a palmy garden/patio, from about $30/day, $500/month. It is managed by the Trailer Park El Dorado. The 21 trailer park spaces rent for about $16/day, with all hookups; add $2 for a/c. Pool, showers, toilets, pets okay. Very popular; get your winter reservations in early.

Three blocks farther north along the beach, newcomer **Trailer Park El Capitán** seems to be trying harder, Retorno Jacarandas at Andando Jacarandas, Rincón de Guayabitos, Nayarit 63727, tel. (327) 403-04. It should have no trouble acquiring a following. The majestic, rustling palm grove provides shade, the rustic *palapa* restaurant supplies food and drinks, while, a few steps nearby, the loveliest part of Playa Guayabitos brims with natural entertainments. The 14 spaces rent for $14/day, with all hookups; larger RVs cost more. Showers, toilets, pets okay.

La Peñita Motel and Trailer Park

It will be good news to many longtime Mexico vacationers that **Motel Russell** remains open and ready for guests. The scene is vintage tropical Mexico—peeling paint, snoozing cats, lazy palms, and a beautiful beach with boats casually pulled onto the sand a few steps from your door—all for rock-bottom prices. Come and populate the place before the octogenarian owner decides to retire. Reserve at Calle Ruben C. Jaramillo no. 24, La Peñita de Jaltemba, Nayarit, tel. (327) 409-59. There are about 15 clean, spartan, one-bedroom kitchenette apartments (most in need of repair) with fans for $10 d, $15 with kitchenette and refrigerator. Great fishing and two blocks from everything in La Peñita. For a small fee, you may also be able to set up a tent or park your RV on one of the old beachfront trailer spaces. Get there by driving to the beach end of La Peñita's main street, Emiliano Zapata. Turn right and parallel the beach for about two blocks.

The big **Trailer Park Hotelera La Peñita,** P.O. Box 22, La Peñita, Nayarit 63727, tel. (327) 409-96, enjoys a breezy ocean-view location one mile north of La Peñita; watch for the big highway sign. The 128 grassy spaces cover a tree-dotted, breezy hillside park overlooking a golden beach and bay. Rates run $12/day ($11/day for three-month rental), with all hookups; closed June, July, and August. The many amenities include a pool, hilltop terrace club, restaurant, showers, and toilets; fine for tenting, surfing, and fishing. Get your winter reservations in early.

FOOD

Fruit Stands and Mini-Supermarkets

The farm country along Hwy. 200 north of Puerto Vallarta offers a feast of tropical fruits. Road-side stands at Guayabitos, La Peñita, and especially at Las Varas, half an hour north, offer mounds of papayas, mangoes, melons, and pineapples in season. Watch out also for more exotic species, such as the *guanabana,* which looks like a spiny mango, but whose pulpy interior looks and smells much like its Asian cousin, the jackfruit.

A number of small Guayabitos mini-supermarkets supply a little bit of everything. Try **Mini-Super Gaby II,** Retorno Ceibas across from Trailer Park Villanueva, on the south end, for vegetables, a small deli, and general groceries. Open daily 7 a.m.-2:30 p.m. and 4-7:30 p.m. Competing next door is **Mini-Super Juan de Dios,** open daily 8 a.m.-8 p.m. On the north end of Av. del Sol Nuevo, second branches of each of these, opposite the church and Hotel Peñamar, respectively, stock more, including fresh baked goods. Both are open daily 8 a.m.-9 p.m.

For larger, fresher selections of everything, go to one of the big main-street *fruterías* or supermarkets in La Peñita, such as **Supermercado Lorena,** tel. (327) 402-55, across from Bancomer, open daily 8 a.m.-2 p.m. and 4-9:30 p.m.

Restaurants

Several Guayabitos restaurants offer good food and service during the busy winter, spring, and August seasons. Hours and menus are often restricted during the midsummer and Sept.-Nov. low seasons.

By location, moving from the Guayabitos south end, first comes spic and span **Abel's Restaurant** *palapa,* at the south end of Av. del Sol Nuevo, behind Bungalows Delfin. Start off your day right, with a home-cooked North American-style breakfast, such as French toast, pancakes, or eggs any style, or finish it in style, with one of Abel's hearty soups, followed by a tasty meat, fish, or chicken plate. Open daily 7 a.m.-9 p.m. in season. Budget.

zapote

Trailer Park Villanueva restaurant, at the beach end of Andando Cocoteros, specializes in caught-in-the-bay fresh seafood. Breakfast here is also relaxing, sitting in the airy *palapa,* enjoying the breeze and the beach scene. Open daily 8 a.m.-9 p.m. in season. Moderate.

For a refreshingly cool and refined indoor atmosphere, go to the new **La Concha,** Guayabitos' only air-conditioned restaurant. Here, skilled chefs specialize in tasty shrimp, fish, and chicken specialties, which patrons enjoy, along with a list of good red and white Cetto-label Baja California wines. On Av. Sol Nuevo, just south of Hotel Posada del Sol, tel. (327) 409-83; open daily 10 a.m.-8 p.m., credit cards accepted.

Right across the street, you can enjoy a more homey option at the family-run **Cocina Económica Doña Carmen.** Here, dedicated cooks put out hearty tacos, enchiladas, spicy *pozole* (shredded pork roast and hominy vegetable stew), and the catch of the day at budget prices. Open every day from early morning till about 10 p.m. year-round.

Across the street, the clean, local-style **Restaurant Las Alejandras,** tel. (327) 404-88, offers good breakfasts and a general Mexican-style menu; on Av. del Sol Nuevo, just north of the pharmacy. Open daily in season 8 a.m.-9 p.m.

Similar good food and service is available at **Restaurant Gaby,** about two blocks north, across from Hotel Peñamar. Open Mon.-Fri. 7:30 a.m.-9:30 p.m. in season.

One of Guayabitos's best, the restaurant **Campanario** in front of the Hotel Posada la Misión, Retorno Tabachines 6 at Calle Tabachines, tel. (327) 403-57, is a longtime favorite of the North American trailer colony. The menu features bountiful fresh seafood, meat, and Mexican plates at reasonable prices. Open 8 a.m.-9 p.m. high season, 2-9 p.m. low; credit cards accepted. Moderate.

For a change of pace or if your preferred Guayabitos restaurants are seasonally closed, try **Chuy's,** La Peñita's local and tourist favorite. It offers a broad, reasonably priced menu within a *típica* Mexican patio setting. Located about five blocks from Hwy. 200, on Calle Bahía Punta Mita, half a block right, off Emiliano Zapata. Open daily till around 9 p.m.

SPORTS AND ENTERTAINMENT

Sports

The aquatic sports center around the south end of Guayabitos beach, where launches ply the waters, offers banana (towed-tube) rides and **snorkeling** at offshore Isla Islote. Rent **sportfishing** launches along the beach. If you want to launch your own boat, ask one of the trailer parks if you can use its ramp.

For **tennis,** you can rent the court (daytime only) in front of the Hotel Decameron Rincón de Las Palmas (at Guayabitos' south end) for about $3 an hour. Inquire at the hotel desk.

Nightlife

Although Guayabitos is a resort for those who mostly love peace and quiet, a few night spots, findable by the noise they emanate, operate along Av. del Sol Nuevo. One of the liveliest is **Hotel Decameron Los Cocos,** the high-rise at the very south end, on Retorno Palmas, tel. (327) 401-90, where a mostly Canadian and American crowd gyrates to rock most winter nights till the wee hours.

SERVICES AND INFORMATION

Nayarit State Tourism maintains an **information office,** tel. (327) 406-93, hours Mon.-Fri. 9 a.m.-7 p.m., in the tree-shaded plaza at the beginning of Av. del Sol Nuevo near the highway. If it's closed, an excellent alternative source is Jorge Castuera, the well informed, personable English-speaking owner of the *farmacia,* on Av. del Sol Nuevo, near the south end, corner of Tabachines.

The *correo* (tel. 327-407-17, open Mon.-Fri. 9 a.m.-1 p.m. and 3-6 p.m.) and *telégrafo* (open Mon.-Fri. 8 a.m.-2 p.m.) are next door. If, however, you just need stamps or a *buzón* (mailbox), they're available at Jorge Castuera's *farmacia* on Av. del Sol Nuevo at Andando Tabachines.

Another possible information source is the **Christopher Travel Agency,** at Km 94, on the highway, east side, about 500 yards north of the Guayabitos entrance, tel. (327) 420-02, fax 407-56.

The La Peñita **correo** and **telecomunicaciones** (telephone, fax, and money orders, open Mon.-Fri. 8 a.m.-2 p.m.) stand side by side, near the beach end of main street Emiliano Zapata.

Guayabitos has no money-exchange agency, although some of the mini-supers may exchange U.S. or Canadian dollars or traveler's checks. More pesos for your cash or traveler's checks are available at the **Bancomer** branch in La Peñita, E. Zapata 22, tel. (327) 402-37; open for both U.S. and Canadian money exchange, Mon.-Fri. 8:30 a.m.-2:30 p.m. and Saturday 10 a.m.-2 p.m.

Although Guayabitos has no hospital, La Peñita does. For medical consultations, go to the highly recommended, small, private 24-hour **Clínica Rentería,** on Calle Valle de Acapulco in La Peñita, tel. (327) 401-40, with a surgeon, gynecologist, and two general practitioners on call. Alternatively, you can drive or taxi 14 miles (22 km) south to the small general hospital in San Francisco (known locally as "San Pancho"). It offers X-ray, laboratory, gynecological, pediatric, and internal medicine consultations and services both during regular office hours, weekdays 10:30 a.m.-noon and 4-6 p.m., and on 24-hour emergency call.

For less urgent medical matters, Jorge Castuera, the well-informed, veterinarian-owner of the **farmacia,** Av. del Sol Nuevo at Tabachines, tel. (327) 404-00, fax 404-46, can recommend medicines or put you in contact with a local doctor. Open daily except Thursday, 8 a.m.-2 p.m. and 4-8 p.m. Jorge and his wife jointly run their enterprise, filling prescriptions, handling their **larga distancia** and **fax** service, selling postage stamps, and running their **laundry** on the same premises.

Another well-used Guayabitos **larga distancia** telephone office (tel. 327-403-97, 403-99, fax 403-98) is next to Mini-Super Gaby II at south-end Retorno Ceibas. Open Mon.-Sat. approximately 9 a.m.-8 p.m., 9 a.m.-noon Sunday during

winter season, but may maintain shorter hours otherwise. It also offers a shelf of used, mostly English paperbacks for purchase or a two-for-one exchange.

GETTING THERE AND AWAY

Puerto Vallarta- and Tepic-bound Transportes Pacífico (TP) second-class buses routinely stop (about once every daylight hour, each direction) on the main highway entrance to Guayabitos's Av. del Sol Nuevo. Additionally, several daily first-class buses pick up Puerto Vallarta- and Tepic-bound passengers at the Transportes Pacífico station, tel. (327) 400-01, at the main street highway corner in La Peñita.

Transportes Norte de Sonora (TNS) and Elite (EL) buses routinely stop at their small La Peñita station, tel. (327) 400-62, just south of the main street highway corner, beach side. Northern destinations include Tepic, San Blas, Mazatlán, and the U.S. border; southern ones include Puerto Vallarta, Manzanillo, Zihuatanejo, and Acapulco.

From Puerto Vallarta, the Guayabitos coast is easily accessible by bus or taxi from the **Puerto Vallarta International Airport,** the busy terminal for flight connections with U.S. and Mexican destinations.

Buses and taxis cover the 39-mile (62 km) distance from the airport to Guayabitos in less than an hour. Across the highway from the airport, hail a green-and-white Transportes Pacífico bus, which will deposit you at the new central bus station (camionera central) a few miles north of the airport. Alternatively, hail a taxi (about $2) to do the same.

If you're driving from Puerto Vallarta, mark your odometer as you pass the Puerto Vallarta airport so you can anticipate the small signs along Hwy. 200 that mark the several turnoffs along the Guayabitos coast.

SOUTH OF GUAYABITOS

PLAYA LO DE MARCO

Follow the signed Lo de Marco ("That of Marco") turnoff 31 miles (49 km) north of the Puerto Vallarta airport (or eight miles, 13 km south of Rincón de Guayabitos). Continue about a mile through the town to the *palapa* restaurants on the beach. Playa Lo de Marco is popular with Mexican families; on Sunday and holidays they dig into the fine golden sand and frolic in the gentle, rolling waves. The surf of the nearly level, very wide Playa Lo de Marco is good for most aquatic sports except surfing, snorkeling, and diving. The south end has a rocky tidepool shelf, fine for bait-casting. Divers and snorkelers can rent boats to go to offshore Isla Islote.

Lo de Marco has a superb trailer park/bungalow complex, **El Caracol**, owned and operated by German expatriate Gunter Maasan and his Mexican wife. Their nine luxuriously large "little bit of Europe in the tropics" motel bungalows sleep four to six people with all the comforts of Hamburg. With a/c, fans, and complete kitchenettes, rents begin at about $35 d low season, $60 high, depending on size and amenities. Add about $8 per extra person.

The trailer park is correspondingly luxurious, with concrete-pad spaces in a palm- and banana-shaded grassy park right on the beach. With pool, all hookups, and immaculate hot-shower and toilet facilities, the 15 spaces rent for $13 per day, $12 per day monthly, or $11 per day for two months; pets okay. Add $4 per extra person. It's popular, so make winter reservations by September. Contact P.O. Box 89, La Peñita de Jaltemba, Nayarit 63726, tel./fax (327) 500-50, Guadalajara tel. (3) 686-0481.

Tent, RV camping, and lodging are available at the trailer park **Pequeño Paraíso** ("Little Paradise") beside the jungle headland at the south end of the beach. Here, the friendly family manager welcomes visitors to the spacious, palm-shaded beachside grove. Basic but clean apartments rent for about $20 d ($35 d with kitchenette), with hot-water showers and fans. RV spaces, with all hookups, rent for about $11/day, $270/month, with showers and toilets. Dozens of grass-carpeted, palm-shaded tent spaces rent for about $3 per person per day. Stores in town nearby can furnish basic supplies. Reserve, especially during the winter, by telephone at (327) 500-89, or in writing to Parque de Trailer Pequeño Paraíso, Carretera Las Miñitas 1938, Lo de Marco, Nayarit.

Continuing south along the Lo de Marco beach road you will soon come to two neighboring pearly sand paradises, **Playa Las Miñitas** and **Playa El Venado.** Bring your swimsuit, picnic lunch, and, if you crave isolation, camping gear.

PLAYA SAN FRANCISCO

The idyllic beach and hotel at the little mango-processing town of San Francisco (San Pancho, locals call it) offer yet another bundle of pleasant surprises. Exit Hwy. 200 at the road sign 25 miles (40 km) north of the Puerto Vallarta airport (or 14 miles, 22 km south of Guayabitos) and continue straight through the town to the beach.

The broad, golden-white sand, enclosed by palm-tipped green headlands, extends for a half mile on both sides of the town. Big, open ocean waves (take care—undertow) pound the beach for nearly its entire length. Offshore, flocks of pelicans dive for fish while frigate birds sail overhead. At night during the rainy months, sea turtles come ashore to lay their egg clutches, which a determined group of volunteers tries to protect from poachers. Beach *palapa* restaurants provide food and drinks. If you're enticed into staying, one of the beachside *palapas* offers basic overnight accommodations.

Accommodations
A sign on the right a couple of blocks before the beach marks the bumpy road to the **Costa Azul Adventure Resort.** In-hotel activity centers around the beach and palm-

shaded pool/bar/restaurant/patio. Farther afield, owner/manager John Cooper and his assistants take guests on kayaking, biking, surfing, snorkeling, and naturalist-guided horseback rides along nearby coves, beaches, and jungle trails. The hotel itself, located on a hillside beneath a magnificent Colima palm grove, offers 20 large, comfortable suites, six one-bedroom villas, and a pair of two-bedroom villas—all with fans only—for $60, $80, and $90 d, respectively. Up to two children 12 and under in rooms stay free. Make reservations through the U.S. booking agent at 224 Avenida del Mar, Room D, San Clemente, CA 92672, tel. (800) 365-7613, fax (969) 498-6300, Web site: www.costa-azul.com, e-mail: getaway@costaazul.com. Reservations are strongly recommended, especially in the winter.

SAYULITA

Little Sayulita, 22 miles (35 km) north of the Puerto Vallarta airport (17 miles, 27 km south of Guayabitos), is the kind of spot romantics hanker for: a drowsy village on a palmy arc of sand, an untouristed retreat for those who enjoy the quiet pleasures and local color of Mexico. Sayulita's clean waters are fine for swimming, bodysurfing, and fishing, while stores, a few restaurants, palm-shadowed bungalows, trailer park and campground, and a lovely bed and breakfast provide food and lodging.

Accommodations

Adrienne Adams, owner/manager of the bed and breakfast **Villa de la Buena Salud**, rents six luxurious upstairs rooms with bath from about $40 d, including breakfast for two, minimum three days. Her airy, art-draped, three-story house is located a few steps from the Sayulita beach. Although her six upper rooms are for adults only, families with children are welcome in a downstairs apartment that sleeps five, with kitchen, VCR, and TV, for about $80 per night. Get your winter reservations in early; Adrienne enjoys dozens of repeat customers. Adrienne's daughter Lynn, at 1754 Caliban Dr., Encinitas, CA 92024, tel. (760) 942-9640, handles reservations year-round. Adrienne

also takes reservations July-Oct. in California, 1495 B San Elijo, Cardiff, CA 92007, tel. (760) 632-7716, fax 632-8585, e-mail: tia@tiaadrianas.com. She returns to Sayulita in November. You can contact her until June at P.O. Box 5, La Peñita de Jaltemba, Nayarit 63727, tel. (327) 501-92. Also, you might take a look at Tía Adriana's Web site at www.tiaadrianas.com.

RV and tent campers love the **Sayulita Trailer Park**, in a big shady, sandy lot, with about 36 hookups (some for rigs up to 40 feet) right on the beach. Guests enjoy just about everything—good clean showers and toilets, electricity, water, a bookshelf, concrete pads, dump station, pets okay—for about $11/day, or $250/month for two persons, discounts available for extended stays. Add $1.50 per extra person and $1.50 for a/c power.

The park also rents out 10 clean, simply but thoughtfully furnished two-bedroom bungalows with kitchen, two of them smack on the beach beneath the palms. Rates begin at $40/day, $250/week, $1,000/month for two; add about $5 per extra person per day. During the two weeks before Easter and 15-31 December, rates run about 20% higher, and reservations must include a minimum seven-day stay and a 50% advance deposit. For reservations, contact the owners, Thies and Cristina Rohlfs, P.O. Box 11, La Peñita de Jaltemba, Nayarit 63727, tel./fax (327) 502-02.

Third choice in Sayulita goes to the very plain, oft-empty **Hotel Sayulita**. Although the asking rate is about $10 double for 33 very basic rooms that surround a cavernous interior courtyard, you might be able to bargain for a better price.

Food

Vegetables, groceries, and baked goods are available at a pair of stores by the town plaza. Local cuisine is supplied by a good plaza taco stand weekend nights, a pair of beachfront *palapa* restaurants, a *lonchería*, and best of all, **Amparo**, an elderly woman who cooks for a few dinner guests a day. Ask for directions (Amparo's house is only a couple of blocks from the plaza) and drop by a day ahead of time to tell her you're coming. (Note: Amparo, over 90, was considering retiring at the time of this writing; consider yourself lucky indeed if she's still active.)

The next day, don't eat much lunch. At dinnertime you will be ready for Amparo's bountiful table of homemade enchiladas, *chiles rellenos,* tacos, perhaps tamales, plus rice, beans, and all of the hot tortillas you can eat for about $10 per person.

Beach Hike

Lovers of the outdoors enjoy the beach and jungle walk from Sayulita to San Francisco, four miles to the north. Besides the birds, flowers, and plants of the forest wilderness and breezy beach, your rewards at trail's end are the pool and restaurant at the Costa Azul Adventure Resort. Wear walking shoes and a hat, and carry insect repellent and water. Allow a full day for strolling both ways and for lingering at the hotel.

Head out north along the beach at Sayulita. After about a mile the beach ends at some rocks, but you can continue along a dirt road above the beach. Then cut to the left, parallel to the beach, across a small meadow to another dirt road that dead-ends at a beachfront house on the left. Follow the palm-shaded jungle track about another mile, bearing left downhill to the beach. Continue beneath the beachside grove of spreading *manzanilla* trees. (Beware: The tree's bark and nuts, which look like little brown or green apples, secrete an irritating sap.) Soon you'll be walking along a driftwood-strewn wild beach beneath a towering jungle headland. Here pelicans, boobies, and cormorants fish just beyond the surf, and occasional manta rays, porpoises, and even whales surface offshore. Swim here with caution, as the rough waves recede with a strong undertow.

Past a cliffside spring—apparently good water in the rainy season, use purifying tablets if you're not sure—you'll see a big, formerly *palapa*-roofed house on a rocky point. This is the former home of once-president Luis Echeverría. At the end of the beach, continue up the stone stairs and straight ahead to San Francisco Beach. In another mile, past the lagoon and *palapa* restaurants, you'll arrive at the hotel. If you prefer not to walk back to Sayulita, hire a taxi in San Francisco.

PUERTO VALLARTA AND THE BAY OF BANDERAS

PUERTO VALLARTA

The town of Puerto Vallarta (pop. 300,000) perches at the most tranquil recess of one of the Pacific Ocean's largest, deepest bays, the Bay of Banderas. The bay's many blessings—golden beaches, sparkling blue waters, and the seafood that they nurture—are magnets for a million seasonal visitors. On the map of Pacific Mexico, the Bay of Banderas looks as if it were gouged from the coast by some vengeful Aztec god (perhaps in retribution for the conquest) with a single 20-mile-wide swipe of his giant hand, just sparing the city of Puerto Vallarta.

Time, however, appears to have healed that great cataclysm. The jagged mountains, Sierra Vallejo on the north and Sierra Cuale on the south, have acquired a green coat of jungle on their slopes, and a broad river, the Ameca, winds serenely through its fertile vale to the bay.

Sand has accumulated on the great arc of the Bay of Banderas, where fisherfolk have built little settlements: Punta Mita, Cruz de Huanacaxtle, and Bucerías north of Puerto Vallarta; and Mismaloya, Boca de Tomatlán, and Yelapa to the south.

Visitors find that Puerto Vallarta is really two cities in one—a new town strung along the hotel strip on its northern beaches, and an old town nestled beneath jungly hills on both sides of a small river, the Río Cuale. Travelers arriving from the north, whether by plane, bus, or car, see the new Puerto Vallarta first—a parade of luxury hotels, condominiums, apartments, and shopping centers. Visitors can stay for a month in a slick new Puerto Vallarta hotel, sun on the beach every day, disco half of every night, and return home, never having experienced the old Puerto Vallarta.

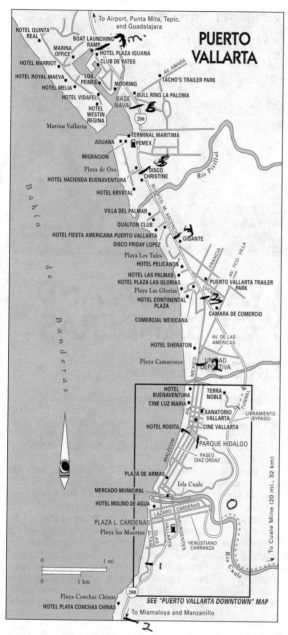

HISTORY

Before Columbus

For centuries prior to the arrival of the Spanish, the coastal region that includes present-day Puerto Vallarta was subject to the indigenous kingdom of Xalisco, centered near the modern Nayarit city of Jalisco. Founded around A.D. 600, the Xalisco civilization was ruled by chiefs who worshipped a trinity of gods: foremost, Naye, a legendary former chief elevated to a fierce god of war, followed by the more benign Teopiltzin, god of rain and fertility, and finally by wise Heri, the god of knowledge.

Recent archaeological evidence indicates another influence: the Aztecs, who probably left Nahuatl-speaking colonies along the southern Nayarit coastal valleys during their centuries-long migration to the Valley of Mexico.

Conquest and Colonization

Some of those villages still remained when the Spanish conquistador Francisco Cortés de Buenaventura, nephew of Hernán Cortés, arrived on the Jalisco-Nayarit coast in 1524.

In a broad mountain-rimmed green valley, an army of 20,000 warriors, their bows decorated by myriad colored cotton banners, temporarily blocked the conquistador's path. So impressive was the assemblage that Cortés called the fertile vale of the Ameca River north of present Puerto Vallarta the Valle de las Banderas ("Valley of the Banners"), and thus the great bay later became known as the Bahía de Banderas.

The first certain record of the Bay of Banderas itself came from the log of conquistador Don Pedro de Alvarado, who sailed into the bay in 1541 and disembarked (probably at Mismaloya) near some massive sea rocks. He named these Las Peñas, undoubtedly the same as the present Los Arcos rocks that draw daily boatloads of snorkelers and divers.

For 300 years the Bay of Banderas slept under the sun. Galleons occasionally watered there; a few pirates hid in wait for them in its jungle-fringed coves.

Independence

The rebellion of 1810-21 freed Mexico, and finally, a generation later, the lure of gold and silver led, as with many of Mexico's cities, to the settlement of Puerto Vallarta. Enterprising merchant Don Guadalupe Sanchez made a fortune (ironically, not from gold, but from salt, for ore processing), which he hauled from the beach to the mines above the headwaters of the Río Cuale. In 1851, Don Guadalupe and his wife built a hut and brought their family. Their tiny trading station grew into a little town, Puerto de Las Peñas, at the mouth of the river.

Later, the local government founded the present municipality, which, on 31 May 1918, officially became Puerto Vallarta, in honor of the celebrated jurist and former governor of Jalisco, Ignacio L. Vallarta.

NIGHT OF THE IGUANA:
THE MAKING OF PUERTO VALLARTA

The idea to film Tennessee Williams's play *Night of the Iguana* in Puerto Vallarta was born in the bar of the Beverly Hills Hotel. In mid-1963, director John Huston, whose movies had earned a raft of Academy Awards, met with Guillermo Wulff, a Mexican architect and engineer. For the film's location Wulff proposed Mismaloya, an isolated cove south of Puerto Vallarta. On leased land, Wulff would build the movie set and cottages for staff housing, which he, Huston, and producer Ray Stark would later sell for a profit as tourist accommodations.

Most directors would have been scared away by the Mismaloya jungle, where they would find no roads, phones, or electricity. But, according to Alex Masden, one of Huston's biographers, Huston loved Mismaloya: "To me, *Night of the Iguana* was a picnic, a gathering of friends, a real vacation."

A "gathering of friends," indeed. The script required most of the cast to be dissolute, mentally ill, or both: A blonde nymphet tries to seduce an alcoholic defrocked minister while his dead friend's love-starved, hard-drinking widow keeps a clutch of vulturous biddies from destroying his last bit of self-respect—all while an iguana roped to a post passively awaits its slaughter.

Huston's casting was perfect. The actors simply played themselves. Richard Burton (the minister) came supplied with plenty of booze. Burton's lover, Elizabeth Taylor, who was not part of the cast and still married to singer Eddie Fisher, accompanied him. Sue Lyon (the nymphet) came with her lovesick boyfriend, whose wife was rooming with Sue's mother; Ava Gardner (the love-starved, hard-drinking widow) became the toast of Puerto Vallarta while romping with her local beach paramour; Tennessee Williams, who was advising the director, came with his lover Freddy; while Deborah Kerr, who acted the only prim lead role, jokingly complained that she was the only one not having an affair.

With so many mercurial personalities isolated together in Mismaloya, the international press flew to Puerto Vallarta in droves to record the expected fireworks. Huston gave each of the six stars, as well as Elizabeth Taylor, a velvet-lined case containing a gold derringer with five bullets, each engraved with the names of the others. Unexpectedly, and partly due to Huston's considerable charm, none of the bullets were used. Bored by the lack of major explosions, the press corps discovered Puerto Vallarta instead.

As Huston explained later to writer Lawrence Grobel: "That was the beginning of its popularity, which was a mixed blessing." Huston nevertheless returned to the area and built a home on the Bay of Banderas, where he lived the last 11 years of his life. Burton and Taylor bought Puerto Vallarta houses, got married, and also stayed for years. Although his Mismaloya tourist accommodations scheme never panned out, Guillermo Wulff became wealthy building for the rich and famous many of the houses and condominiums that now dot Puerto Vallarta's hillsides and golden beaches.

However, the mines eventually petered out, and Puerto Vallarta, isolated, with no road to the outside world, slumbered again.

Modern Puerto Vallarta

But not for long. Passenger planes began arriving sporadically from Tepic and Guadalajara in the 1950s; a gravel road was pushed through from Tepic in the 1960s. The international airport was built, the highway was paved, and tourist hotels sprouted on the beaches. Meanwhile, in 1963, director John Huston, at the peak of his creative genius, arrived with Richard Burton, Elizabeth Taylor, Ava Gardner, and Deborah Kerr to film *Night of the Iguana*. Huston, Burton, and Taylor stayed on for years, waking Puerto Vallarta from its long slumber. It hasn't slept since.

SIGHTS

Getting Oriented

Puerto Vallarta is a long beach town, stretching about five miles from the Riviera-like Conchas Chinas condo headland at the south end. Next, heading north, comes the popular Playa los Muertos beach and the intimate old Río Cuale neighborhood, which join, across the river, with the busy central *malecón* (seawall) shopping and restaurant (but beachless) bayfront. North of there, the beaches resume again at Playa Camarones and continue past the Zona Hotelera string of big resorts to the marina complex, where tour boats and cruise liners depart from the Terminal Marítima dock. In the marina's northern basin lie the Peines (pay-EE-nays) sportfishing and Club de Yates docks. A mile farther north, the city ends at the bustling International Airport.

One basic thoroughfare serves the entire beachfront. Officially Bulevar Francisco Medina Ascencio, but commonly called the **Carretera Aeropuerto** ("Airport Highway") as it conducts express traffic south past the Zona Hotelera, it changes names three times. Narrowing, it becomes the cobbled Av. México, then Paseo Díaz Ordaz along the seafront *malecón* with tourist restaurants, clubs, and shops, changing finally to Av. Morelos before it passes the Presidencia Municipal (city hall) and central plaza.

When southbound traffic reaches Isla Río Cuale, the tree-shaded, midstream island where the city's pioneers built their huts, traffic slows to a crawl and finally dissipates in the colorful old neighborhood on the south side of the river.

There being little traffic south of the Cuale, people walk everywhere, and slowly, because of the heat. Every morning men in sombreros lead burros down to the mouth of the river to gather sand. Little *papelerías, miscelaneas,* and streetside *taquerías* serve the local folks while small restaurants, hotels, and clubs serve the visitors.

Getting Around

Since nearly all through traffic flows along one thoroughfare, Puerto Vallarta transportation is a snap. Simply hop on one of the frequent (but usually crowded) city buses (fare 15-30 cents), virtually all of which end up at Plaza Lázaro Cárdenas on Av. Olas Altas a few blocks south of the river. Northbound, the same buses retrace the route through the Zona Hotelera to one of several destinations scrawled across their windows. Taxis, while much more convenient, are all individual and rather expensive (about $3-4 per trip within the city limits; don't get in until the price is settled).

Drivers who want to quickly travel between the north and the south ends of town often take the *libramiento* bypass and avoid the crowded downtown traffic.

A Walk along Isla Río Cuale

Start at the **Museo Río Cuale,** a joint government-volunteer effort near the very downstream tip of Isla Río Cuale. Inside is a small but fine collection of paintings by local artists as well as locally excavated pre-Columbian artifacts (open Mon.-Sat. when volunteers are available, no phone).

Head upstream beneath the bridge and enjoy the shady *paseo* of shops and restaurants. For fun, stroll out on one of the two quaint suspension bridges over the river. Evenings, these are the coolest spots in Puerto Vallarta. A river of cool night air often funnels down the Cuale valley, creating a refreshing breeze along the length of the clear, tree-draped stream.

The **Río Cuale** was not always so clean. Once upon a time, a few dozen foreign residents, tired of looking down upon the littered riverbank, came out one Sunday and began hauling trash from the riverbed. Embarrassed by the example, a neighborhood crowd pitched in. The river has been clean ever since.

Farther upstream, on the adjacent riverbank, stands the **Mercado Municipal Río Cuale,** a honeycomb of stalls stuffed with crafts from all over Mexico. Continue past the upriver (Av. Insurgentes) bridge to **Plaza John Huston,** marked by a smiling bronze likeness of the renowned Hollywood director who helped put Puerto Vallarta on the map with his filming of Tennessee Williams's *Night of the Iguana* in 1963.

About 50 yards farther on, stop in at the small gallery of the **Centro Cultural Vallartense,** a volunteer organization that conducts art classes, sponsors shows of promising artists, and sometimes invites local artists to meet the public and interested amateurs for informal instruction and idea exchange. Ask the volunteer on duty for more information or see the community events listings in *Vallarta Today,* the local English-language community newspaper.

A few more steps upstream, at a small plaza, stands the round stucco headquarters and practice room of the **Escuela Municipal de Música.** On the left side are the classrooms of the **Instituto de Allende.** They, along with the Centro Cultural Vallartense, offer courses to the general public.

At the boulder-strewn far upstream point of the island, a cadre of women wash clothes. Many of them are professionals who practice their craft on special rocks, perfectly positioned for a day of productive washing. Their clean handiwork stretches out to dry—on rocks, on grass, on bushes—in rainbow arrays beneath the sun.

Gringo Gulch

The steep, villa-dotted hillside above the island's upper end is called Gringo Gulch, for the colony of rich *norteamericanos* who own big homes there. It's an interesting place for a stroll.

Back at the Insurgentes bridge, head right, toward the center of town, bear right to the end of one-block Calle Emilio Carranza, and continue up a steep, bougainvillea-festooned staircase to Calle Zaragoza one block above.

At Zaragoza and the upper level of Emilio Carranza, you are at the gateway to Gringo Gulch. Wander through the winding, hillside lanes and enjoy the picturesque scenes that seem to appear around each rickety-chic corner. For example, note the luxurious *palapas* perched atop the tall villa on Carranza, half a block above Zaragoza.

During your meanderings, don't miss the Gringo Gulch centerpiece mansion at Zaragoza 446, once owned by Elizabeth Taylor. (You'll scarcely be able to miss it, for it has a pink passageway arching over the street.) The house was a gift to Taylor from Richard Burton. After they were married, they also bought the house on the other side of Zaragoza, renovated it, and built a pool; thus the passageway became necessary. The house across the street, no. 446, is now the **Casa Kimberly,** a private Elizabeth Taylor-Richard Burton museum, which offers public tours; call (322) 213-36 for details.

The all-volunteer **Club Internacional de la Amistad** ("International Friendship Club") conducts seasonal tours through some of Puerto Vallarta's showplace homes, beginning at the central plaza around 11 a.m. on Saturday and Thursday. Look for announcement posters or community events listings in *Vallarta Today.* They customarily ask a donation of about $20 per person to further their charitable programs. For more information, call Judy Galena, tel. (322) 309-78.

On the *Malecón*

Head back down Zaragoza, and let the church belfry be your guide. Named **La Parroquia de Nuestra Señora de Guadalupe,** for the city's patron saint, the church is relatively new (1951) and undistinguished except for the very unusual huge crown atop the tower. Curiously, it was modeled after the crown of the tragic 19th-century Empress Carlota, who went insane after her husband was executed. On the church steps, an Indian woman frequently sells textiles, which she weaves on the spot with a traditional backstrap loom (in Spanish, *tela de otate,* loom of bamboo, from the Nahuatl *otlatl,* bamboo).

Continue down Zaragoza past the Presidencia Municipal at one side of the central Plaza de Armas, straight toward the Los Arcos ("The Arches"), right at the water's edge. They form a backdrop for frequent free weekend evening music and dance performances. From there, the *malecón* seawall-walkway stretches north to-

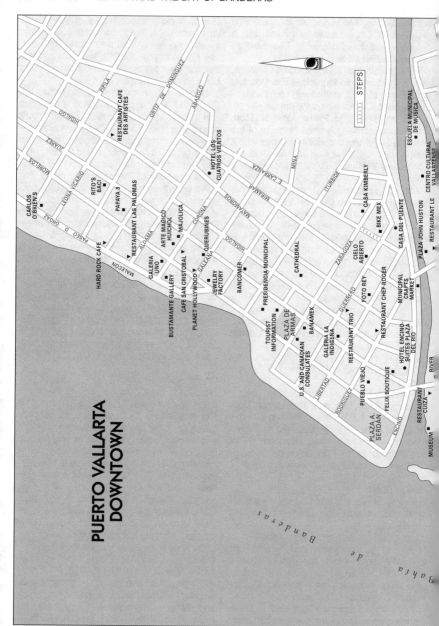

PUERTO VALLARTA
DOWNTOWN

Bahía de Banderas

STEPS

CARLOS O'BRIEN'S
HARD ROCK CAFE
BUSTAMANTE GALLERY
GALERIA UNO
CAFE SAN CRISTOBAL
PLANET HOLLYWOOD
JEWELRY FACTORY
ARTE MAGICO HUICHOL
MAJOLICA
RESTAURANT LAS PALOMAS
PAPAYA 3
RITO'S BACI
RESTAURANT CAFE DES ARTISTES
GALERIA
QUERUBINES
BANCOMER
PRESIDENCIA MUNICIPAL
HOTEL LOS CUATROS VIENTOS
CATHEDRAL
CASA KIMBERLY
BIKE MEX
CASA DEL PUENTE
CIELO ABIERTO
FOTO REY
MUNICIPAL CRAFTS MARKET
PLAZA JOHN HUSTON
RESTAURANT LE
CENTRO CULTURAL VALLARTENSE
ESCUELA MUNICIPAL DE MUSICA
TOURIST INFORMATION
PLAZA DE ARMAS
BANAMEX
GALERIA LA INDIGENA
RESTAURANT TRIO
RESTAURANT CHEF ROGER
HOTEL ENCINO SUITES PLAZA DEL RIO
U.S. AND CANADIAN CONSULATES
LIBERTAD
PUEBLO VIEJO
FELIX BOUTIQUE
RESTAURANT CUIZA
PLAZA A. SERDAN
MUSEUM
RIVER

PIPILA
HIDALGO
JUAREZ
MORELOS
ORTIZ DE DOMINGUEZ
ABASOLO
LEONA VICARIO
PASEO D. ORDAZ
MALECON
ALDAMA
CORONA
HIDALGO
MATAMOROS
E. CARRANZA
MINA
MIRAMAR
ITURBIDE
ZARAGOZA
GUERRERO
RODRIGUEZ
ENCINO

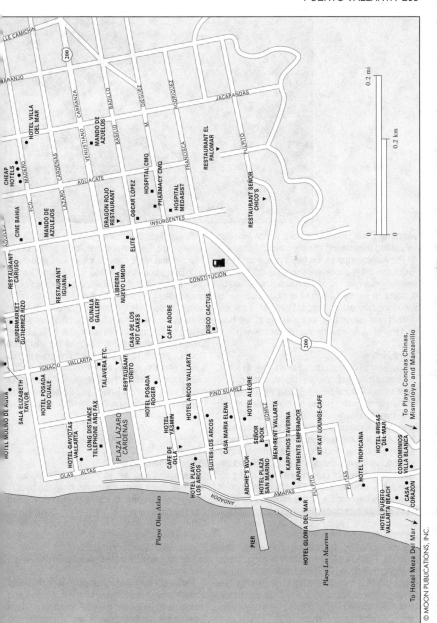

© MOON PUBLICATIONS, INC.

on the malecón

ward the Zona Hotelera hotels, which you can see along the curving northern beachfront.

The *malecón* marks the bay's innermost point. From there the shoreline stretches and curves westerly many miles on both sides, adorned by dozens of sandy beaches until it reaches its wave-washed extremities at Punta Mita (on the distant horizon, at the northwest tip of the bay) and Punta La Iglesia (to the far southwest).

Terra Noble

The dream of owner Jorge Rubio, Terra Noble, on a vista hilltop above the middle of town, is at least unique and at best exhilarating. It's a new age-style retreat, spreading downhill over an airy, breathtakingly scenic tropical deciduous forested hillside, at the western edge of the big Agua Azul Nature Reserve hinterland. The headquarters building is a latter-day interpretation of a traditional Mexican stick and mud wattle house. The inside view, of curving ceilings and passageways dotted with round window-holes, leaves the impression of the interior of a huge hunk of Swiss cheese. For more architectural details, see the Terra Noble feature story in *Architectural Digest* for July 1996.

Besides its singular building and parklike view grounds, Terra Noble is a serious healing center, featuring massage ($45/hour) or an all-day treatment ($145), including massage, sauna-like *temazcal* sweat bath and shamanistic ceremony, tarot reading, and more. It also offers day sculpture and painting workshops.

Regardless of whether you get the full treatment or not, Terra Noble would be worth a visit, if for nothing more than a look around and a picnic. (Bring your own food.) It's generally open daily 8 a.m.-3 p.m., admission about $5. Call ahead, tel. (322) 447-77, fax 240-58, to verify hours; e-mail: terra@zonavirtual.com.mx. Get there by car, taxi, or any local bus that follows the bypass *(libramiento)* through the hills east of town. Follow the side road, signed Par Vial Zona Centro, about 100 yards south of the summit tunnel (not the tunnel at the south end), on the west (ocean) side of the *libramiento*. After about a half mile, curving uphill, you'll see the Terra Noble entrance sign on the view side of the road.

BEACHES

Playa los Muertos

Generations ago, when Puerto Vallarta was a small, isolated town, there was only one beach, Playa los Muertos, the strand of yellow sand that stretches for a mile south of the Cuale River. Old-timers still remember the Sundays and holidays when it seemed as if half the families in Puerto Vallarta had come south of the Río Cuale, to Los Muertos Beach especially, to play in the surf and sand.

This is still largely true, although now droves of winter-season North American vacationers and residents have joined them. Fortunately, Playa los Muertos is much cleaner than during the polluted 1980s. The fish are coming back, as evidenced by the flocks of diving pelicans and the crowd of folks who drop lines every day from the **New Pier** (foot of Francisca Rodríguez).

Fishing is even better off the rocks on the south end of the beach. *Lisa* (mullet), *sierra* (mackerel), *pargo* (snapper), and *torito* are commonly caught anywhere along close-in beaches. On certain unpredictable occasions, fish (and one memorable time even giant 30-pound squids) swarm offshore in such abundance that anyone can pick them out of the water barehanded.

Gentle waves and lack of undertow make Playa Los Muertos generally safe for wading and good for swimming beyond the close-in breakers. The same breakers, however, eliminate Los Muertos for bodysurfing, boogie boarding, or surfing (except occasionally at the far south end).

Playa Conchas Chinas

Playa Conchas Chinas ("Chinese Shells Beach") is not one beach but a series of small sandy coves dotted by rocky outcroppings beneath the condo-clogged hillside that extends for about a mile south of Playa los Muertos. A number of streets and driveways lead to the beach from the Manzanillo Hwy. 200 (the extension of Insurgentes) south of town. Drive—or taxi, or ride one of the many the minibuses marked Mismaloya or Boca that leave the from Olas Altas's Plaza Lázaro Cárdenas, corner Carranza and Suárez—or hike along the tidepools from Los Muertos Beach.

Fishing off the rocks is good here; the water is even clear enough for some snorkeling. Bring your gear, however, as there's none for rent. The usually gentle waves, however, make any kind of surfing very doubtful.

Beach Exploring

Beach lovers can spend many enjoyable days poking around the many little beaches south of town. Drive, taxi, or take a Mismaloya- or Boca-marked minibus from Plaza Lázaro Cárdenas.

Just watch out the window, and when you see a likely spot, ask the driver to stop. Say *"Pare* (PAH-ray) *por favor."* The location will most likely be one of several lovely *playas:* **El Gato** ("The Cat"), **Los Venados** ("The Deers"),

Los Carrizos ("The Reeds"), **Punta Negra** ("Black Point"), **Garza Blanca** ("White Heron"), or **Gemelas** ("Twins").

Although many of these little sand crescents have big hotels and condos, it doesn't matter, because beaches are public in Mexico up to the high-tide line. There is always some path to the beach used by local folks. Just ask *"¿Dónde está el camino* (road, path) *a la playa?"* and someone will probably point the way.

Mismaloya and Los Arcos

If you ride all the way to Playa Mismaloya, you will not be disappointed, despite the oversize Hotel Mismaloya crowding the beach. Follow the dirt road just past the hotel to the intimate little curve of sand and lagoon where the cool, clear Mismaloya stream meets the sea. A rainbow array of fishing *lanchas* lie beached around the lagoon's edges, in front of a line of beachside *palapa* restaurants.

Continue a few hundred yards past the *palapas* to the ruins of the movie set of the *Night of the Iguana.* Besides being built for the actual filming, the rooms behind those now-crumbling stucco walls served as lodging, dining, and working quarters for the hundreds of crew who camped here for those eight busy months in 1963.

North, offshore beyond the Mismaloya cove, rise the green-brushed **Los Arcos** sea rocks, a federal underwater park and eco-preserve. The name comes from the arching grottoes that channel completely through the bases of some of the rocks. Los Arcos is one of the best snorkeling grounds around Puerto Vallarta. Get there by hiring a glass-bottomed boat in the lagoon.

Snorkeling near the wave-washed Los Arcos is a Puerto Vallarta "must do." Swirling bunches of green algae and branching ruddy corals attract schools of grazing parrot, angel, butterfly, and goat fish. Curious pencil-thin cornet fish may sniff you out as they pass, while big croakers and sturgeon will slowly drift, scavenging along the coral-littered depths.

Fishing, especially casting from the rocks beneath the movie set, and every other kind of beach activity are good at Mismaloya, except surfing and boogie boarding, for which the waves are generally too gentle.

Stop for food (big fish fillet plate, any style, with all the trimmings, $6, breakfast eggs from their own hens) or a drink at the **Restaurant Las Gaviotas** *palapas* behind the lagoon.

Alternatively, for food and nostalgia, go to the viewpoint **John Huston Cafe** or the neighboring showplace **Night of the Iguana Restaurant,** off the highway, ocean side, on Mismaloya Bay's south headland. Both are open daily, the restaurant for breakfast, lunch, or dinner, the café for lunch and dinner. Both are designed around the *Night of the Iguana* legend, replete with old Hollywood photos and mementos and a daily video screening of the original film at the restaurant.

For still another treat, visit nearby **Chino's Paradise.** Follow the riverside, lower road that forks upstream at the north end of the bridge across the road from the hotel. Arrive in the late morning (around 11, or around three in the late afternoon) to avoid the tour-bus rush. Chino's streamside *palapas* nestle like big mushrooms

A trove of sleepy tropical havens, such as Boca de Tomatlán, shown, dot the Bay of Banderas' jungly shore.

on a jungle hillside above a cool, cascading creek. Adventurous guests enjoy sliding down the cascades (be careful—some have injured themselves seriously), while others content themselves with lying in the sun or lolling in sandy-bottomed, clear pools. Beneath the *palapas,* they serve respectable but uninspired seafood and steak plates and Mexican *antojitos.* Open daily 11 a.m.-5 p.m.

Beaches Farther South

Three miles south of Mismaloya is the very tranquil, jungle-fringed beach and bay of **Boca de Tomatlán,** where you can rent boats and head out for the pristine paradises of **Las Animas, Quimixto,** and Yelapa farther south. Las Animas has seafood *palapas,* an idyllic beach, and snorkeling; the same is true for Quimixto, which also has a waterfall nearby for splashing.

Yelapa, a settlement nestled beneath verdant, palm-crowned hills beside an aquamarine cove, is home for perhaps a hundred local families and a small colony of foreign expatriates. For visitors, it offers a glimpse of South Seas life as it was before the automobile. Accessible only by sea, Yelapa's residents get around on foot or horseback. A waterfall cascades through the tropical forest above the village, and a string of *palapa* restaurants lines the beach. Lodging is available in the *palapa*-roofed cabañas of the rustic-chic **Hotel Lagunitas.** Rooms run about $45 high season, $25 low. Reserve by calling their agent at (329) 805-54.

North-End (Zona Hotelera) Beaches

These are Puerto Vallarta's cleanest, least crowded, in-town beaches, despite the many hotels that line them. Beginning at the Hotel Rosita at the north end of the *malecón,* **Playas Camarones, Las Glorias, Los Tules,** and **de Oro** form a continuous three-mile strand to the marina. Stubby rock jetties about every quarter mile have succeeded in retaining a 50-yard-wide strip of golden-cream sand most of the way.

The sand is midway between coarse and fine, the waves are gentle, breaking right at the water's edge, and the ocean past the breakers is relatively clear (10- or 20-foot visibility) and blue. Stormy weather occasionally dredges up clam, cockle, limpet, oyster, and other shells from the offshore depths.

Fishing by pole, net, or simply line is common along here. Surfing, bodysurfing, and boogie boarding, however, are not. All other beach sports, especially the high-powered variety, are available at nearly every hotel along the strand (see Sports and Recreation later in this chapter).

Farther north, along the shore past the Maritime Terminal-Marina Harbor entrance, the beach narrows to a seasonally rocky strip at the oceanfronts of a row of big resort hotels.

Beach Hikes

Two good close-in hikes are possible. For either of them don't forget a sun hat, sunscreen, repellent, a shirt, and some light shoes. On the south side, walk from Playa los Muertos about a mile and a half along the little beaches and tidepools to Playa Conchas Chinas. Start at either end and take half a day swimming, snorkeling, sunning, and poking among the rocks.

More ambitiously, you can hike the entire three-mile beach strip from the northern end of the *malecón* to the marina. If you start by 9 a.m. you'll enjoy the cool of the morning with the sun at your back. Stop along the way at the showplace pools and beach restaurants of hotels such as the Sheraton, the Plaza Las Glorias, the Fiesta Americana Vallarta, and Krystal. Walk back, or opt for a return by taxi or city bus.

DAY CRUISES

Most Puerto Vallarta visitors reach these little southern beaches by an alternate route from Boca de Tomatlán. They have two options: fast water taxis or one of several all-day tourist cruises. The water taxis, which allow you more time at your destination, customarily leave the Playa los Muertos New Pier twice in the morning, usually at about 10:30 or 11 a.m., and deposit you back by 4 p.m., allowing about three hours for lunch and swimming at either the Quimixto or Yelapa waterfalls. The roundtrip tariff runs about $12.

The more leisurely tourist cruises leave around 9 a.m. and return by 4 p.m. from the dock at the Puerto Vallarta Maritime Terminal. During the winter high season, a number of these cruises pick up additional passengers at the New Pier on Playa los Muertos downtown.

One of the most popular and least expensive of these excursions is aboard the big **Princess Yelapa,** a triple-decked white steel tub with room for 400. The cruise follows the coastline past Los Arcos, Mismaloya, Las Animas, and Quimixto. Passengers disembark at Yelapa for two hours, just long enough for the short waterfall hike (or by horseback, if desired) and lunch at a beach *palapa*. This no-frills ($18) trip includes a no-host bar and restrooms.

The **Princess Vallarta,** a scaled-down version of the *Princess Yelapa,* offers a more luxurious, all-inclusive cruise ($33), with onboard continental breakfast, live music for dancing, and open bar. The boat heads out, with tourists enjoying views of the town, beaches, and hills, stopping at Los Arcos for snorkeling. Continuing past Mismaloya and Tomatlán, it arrive at Las Animas for lunch, relaxing on the beach, and snorkeling for a couple of hours before returning.

When not being used for eco-excursions to the Islas Marietas, the **Vagabundo,** a smaller but comfortable 50-person sportfishing-type motor yacht, heads straight across the bay, as guests enjoy drinks from the open bar. *Vagabundo* anchors at Yelapa for two hours, enough time for the waterfall hike. On the way back, a modest buffet lunch is served as the cruise continues to Los Arcos for snorkeling. Then it returns, offering views of intimate rocky beaches, green jungle-strewn hills, and a procession of palm-fringed shoreline hotels ($28, includes restrooms).

For information and reservations for all of the above cruises, contact a travel agent, your hotel tour desk, or Princesa Cruises directly at (322) 447-77.

The **Bora Bora,** a 40-foot double-hulled catamaran, offers a deluxe (about $45) cruise, departing from the marina (cruise ship dock) daily at 9:30 a.m. Included en route are open bar, buffet lunch, and stops at Los Arcos for snorkeling, Quimixto to splash in the waterfall, and Las Animas for sunbathing, snoozing, and snorkeling. For reservations, see a travel agent or call directly to the office at Villas Vallarta Mall, local B28, tel./fax (322) 436-80 and 454-84.

If you tend toward seasickness, fortify yourself with Dramamine or similar antinausea medication before these cruises. Destination disembarkation is by motor launch and can be difficult for the physically handicapped.

ACCOMMODATIONS

In Puerto Vallarta you can get any type of lodging you want at nearly any price. The location sets the tone, however. The relaxed, relatively tranquil but interesting neighborhood south of the Río Cuale (especially around Av. Olas Altas) has many budget and moderately priced hotels, apartments, and condos within easy walking distance of restaurants, shopping, and services. Many of them are very close, if not right on, live-

---

PUERTO VALLARTA ACCOMMODATIONS

Accommodations (area code 322; postal code 48300 unless otherwise noted) are listed in increasing order of approximate high-season, double-room rates.

HOTELS~RÍO CUALE AND SOUTH

Hotel Villa del Mar, Fco. I. Madero 440, postal code 48380, tel. 207-85, $20

Hotel Yasmin, Basilio Badillo 168, postal code 48380, tel. 200-87, $18

Hotel Gloria del Mar, Amapas 114, postal code 48380, tel. 251-43, fax 267-37, $32

Hotel Encino-Suites Plaza del Río, Juárez 122, tel. 200-51 or 202-80, fax 225-73, e-mail: encino@go2mexico.com, $36

Hotel Posada Roger, Basilio Badillo 237, postal code 48380, tel. 208-36, fax 304-82, e-mail: pvroger@pvnet.com.mx, $38

Casa del Puente, Puente Av. Insurgentes, postal code 48380, tel. 207-49 or (415) 775-1970, $40

Hotel Posada Río Cuale, A. Serdán 224, P.O. Box 146, tel./fax 204-50 or 211-48, e-mail: legourmet@go2mexico.com, $42

Hotel Gaviotas Vallarta, Fco. I. Madero 154, P.O. Box 497, tel. 255-00, 255-18, fax 255-16, $44

Hotel Brisas del Mar, Privada Abedul 10, tel./fax 218-00 or 218-21, $48

Hotel Alegre, F. Rodríguez 168, postal code 48380, tel./fax 247-93, $48

Hotel Tropicana, Amapas 214, postal code 48380, tel. 209-12 or 209-52, fax 267-37, $50

Hotel Puerto Vallarta Beach, Calle Malecón s/n, P.O. Box 329, tel. 250-40, fax 221-76, $50

Casa Corazón, Amapas 326, P.O. Box 66, tel. 213-71, fax 263-64 or tel./fax (505) 523-4666, $50

Hotel Playa Los Arcos, Olas Altas 380, postal code 48380, tel. 205-83, 215-83, or (800) 648-2403, fax 224-18, e-mail: reservaciones@playalosarcos.com, $63

Hotel Arcos Vallarta, M. Diéguez 171, postal code 48380, tel. 207-12 or (800) 648-2403, e-mail: reservaciones@playalosarcos.com, $66

Suites Los Arcos, M. Diéguez s/n, postal code 48380, tel. 207-17, or (800) 648-2403, fax 224-18, e-mail: reservaciones@playalosarcos.com, $78

Hotel Playa Conchas Chinas, P.O. Box 346, postal code 48390, tel./fax 157-70, $80

Hotel Plaza San Marino, Rudolfo Gómez 111, postal code 48380, tel. 215-55 or 230-50, fax 224-31, $80

Hotel Molino de Agua, I. Vallarta at A. Serdán, postal code 48380, tel. 219-57, fax 260-56, e-mail: molino@acnet.net, $99

Hotel Blue Bay Club Vallarta, Km 4 Carretera a Barra de Navidad, P.O. Box 385, tel. 155-00 or (800) BLUEBAY (258-3229), fax 151-05, e-mail: pvr@bluebayresorts.com, $220 all-inclusive*

Hotel Meza del Mar, Amapas 380, tel. 248-88, fax 223-08, $240 all-inclusive*

Hotel Camino Real, P.O. Box 95, Playa de las Estacas, tel. 150-00 or (800) 7CAMINO (722-6466), fax 160-00, e-mail: pvr@caminoreal.com, $370

ly Playa los Muertos. While no strict dividing line separates the types of available lodgings, hotels (listed first, below) generally offer rooms with maximum service (desk, daily cleaning, restaurant, pool) without kitchens for shorter-term guests, while apartments and condos virtually always offer multiple-room furnished kitchen units for greatly reduced per diem rates for longer term rentals. If you're staying more than two weeks, you'll save money and also enjoy more of the comforts of home in a good apartment or condo rental.

HOTELS~NORTH OF THE RÍO CUALE

Hotel Rosita, Díaz Ordaz 901, P.O. Box 32, tel./fax 320-00, 321-77, 321-51, 321-85, $28

Hotel Los Cuatro Vientos, Matamoros 520, P.O. Box 520, tel. 201-61, fax 228-31, e-mail: fourwinds@pvnet.com.mx, $65

Hotel Buenaventura, México 1301, P.O. Box 8B, postal code 48350, tel. 237-37, fax 235-46, $90

Hotel Hacienda Buenaventura, Paseo de la Marina, P.O. Box 95B, postal code 48310, tel. 466-67 or (800) 223-6764, fax 462-42, e-mail: buenavista@pvnet.com.mx, $111

Hotel Las Palmas Beach, Av. de Ingreso Km 2.5, tel. 406-50, fax 405-43, tel. (800) 876-5278, e-mail: palmaspv@pvnet.com.mx $114

Hotel Pelicanos, Av. de Ingreso, Km 2.5, tel. 410-10, fax 414-14, tel. (800) 342-AMIGO (342-2644), $132

Hotel Continental Plaza, Av. de Ingreso, Km 2.5 Plaza Las Glorias, tel. 401-23, fax 452-36, tel. (800) 88-CONTI (882-6684), e-mail: ncont@pvnet.com.mx, $145

Hotel Fiesta Americana, P.O. Box 270, tel. 420-10 or (800) FIESTA-1 (343-7821), fax 421-08, e-mail: favsale@pvnet.com.mx, $200

Hotel Plaza Las Glorias, Km 2.5, Plaza Las Glorias s/n, tel. 444-44 or (800) 342-AMIGO (342-2644), fax 564-59, $220

Hotel Krystal, Av. de las Garzas s/n, tel. 402-02 or (800) 231-9860, fax 401-11, $260

Hotel Qualton Club and Spa, Km 2.5, Av. de las Palmas s/n, tel. 444-46, fax 444-47, e-mail: qualton@pvnet.com.mx, $480 all-inclusive* for two

APARTMENTS AND CONDOMINIUMS

Prices listed are the approximate high-season monthly rental rate for a studio or one-bedroom unit.

Hotel Villa del Mar, Fco. I. Madero 440, postal code 48380, tel. 207-85, $450

Apartments Emperador, Amapas 114, postal code 48380, tel./fax 233-29, $700

Hotel Gloria del Mar, Amapas 114, postal code 48380, tel. 251-43, fax 267-37, $900

Casa María Elena, F. Rodríguez 163, tel. 201-13, fax 313-80, e-mail: mariazs@acnet.net, $900

Hotel Encino-Suites Plaza del Río, Juárez 122, tel. 200-51 or 208-20, fax 225-73, e-mail: encino@go2mexico.com, $1000

Hotel Brisas del Mar, Privada Abedul 10, tel. 218-00 or 218-21, fax 267-37, $1,000

Hotel Puerto Vallarta Beach, P.O. Box 329, tel. 250-40, fax 221-76, $1,200

Condominios Villa Blanca, Amapas 349, tel./fax 261-90, $1,500

*"All-inclusive" means all lodging, food, drinks, and activities for two persons are included in the listed price.

Hotels—Río Cuale and South

Although landmark **Hotel Molino de Agua** ("Water Mill"), at the corner of Ignacio Vallarta and Aquiles Serdán, Puerto Vallarta 48380, tel. (322) 219-57, fax 260-56, e-mail: molino@acnet.net, occupies two riverfront blocks right on the beach, many visitors miss it completely. Its very tranquil rustic-chic cabañas hide in a jungle-garden of cackling parrots, giant-leafed vines, and gigantic, spreading trees. Most of the cabañas are at ground level and unfortunately don't feel very private inside unless you close the shutters—which seems a shame in a tropical garden. The very popular beachside upstairs units remedy this dilemma. The hotel's 40 garden rooms rent for about $68 d low season, $99 high, while the upstairs beachside rooms go for about $97 d low season, $146 high season; two pools, restaurant, a/c, credit cards accepted.

Adjacent to the Hotel Molino de Agua, as you head south, away from the river, at the corner of I. Vallarta and A. Serdán, the diminutive **Hotel Posada Río Cuale** packs a lot of hotel into a small space. Find it at Av. Aquiles Serdán 242, P.O. Box 146, Puerto Vallarta 48300, tel./fax (322) 204-50 or 211-48, e-mail: legourmet@go2mexico.com. Good management is the key to this picturesque warren of rooms clustered beside its good restaurant/bar and a small but pleasant pool patio. Tasteful brown and brick decor makes the rooms somewhat dark, especially on the ground floor. Artful lighting, however, improves on this. Unless you like diesel-bus noise, try to avoid getting a room on the busy Av. Vallarta side of the hotel. The 41 a/c rooms rent for about $31 d low season, about $42 high season; credit cards accepted.

Nearby, the high-rise but downscale **Hotel Gaviotas Vallarta** is curiously hidden, though nearly right on the beach at Fco. I. Madero 154, P.O. Box 497, Puerto Vallarta, Jalisco 48300, tel. (322) 215-00 or 255-18, fax 255-16. Clean, well managed, and about as Mexican as you can get, the hotel rises in eight tile-and-brick tiers around a pretty, plant-decorated interior pool patio. A small restaurant and snack bar serves guests downstairs, while, upstairs, guests enjoy ocean vistas directly from their room windows, or from arch-framed breezeways just outside their doorways. The 84 nondeluxe but clean and comfortable fan-only rooms rent for about $30 d low season, $44 high; with TV and a/c. A one-week stay earns one free day.

In the opposite direction, north, just across the river bridge from the Molino de Agua, stands the renovated old **Hotel Encino-Suites Plaza del Río,** Av. Juárez 122, Puerto Vallarta, Jalisco 48300, tel. (322) 200-51 or 202-80, fax 225-73, e-mail: encino@go2mexico.com. The entrance lobby opens into a pleasant, tropical fountain patio, enfolded by tiers of rooms. Inside, the rooms are tastefully decorated in blue and white, many with ocean or city-hill views. An adjoining building offers many large, similarly appointed kitchenette suites. The hotel climaxes at the rooftop pool and sundeck, where guests enjoy a panoramic view of the surrounding green jungly hills above the white-stucco-and-tile old town, spreading to the blue, mountain-rimmed bay. The 75 rooms and suites rent for about $28 d low season, $36 high season; one- and two-bedroom kitchenette suites begin at about $35 low season, $40 high season. Phones, a/c, security boxes, restaurant/bar.

Head directly upstream, to the upper (Av. Insurgentes) river bridge, and you'll find **Casa del Puente** tucked uphill behind the sidewalk café by the bridge. The elegant villa-home of Molly Stokes, grandniece of celebrated naturalist John Muir, Casa del Puente is a lovely home-away-from-home. Antiques and art adorn the spacious, beamed-ceiling rooms, while outside its windows and around the decks great trees spread, tropical birds flit and chatter, jungle hills rise, and the river gurgles, hidden from the city hubbub nearby. Molly offers three lodging options: an upstairs river-view room with big bath and double bed for around $40, and a pair of spacious apartments (a one-bedroom, one-bath and a two-bedroom, two bath) for around $50 and $70, respectively. Discounts may be negotiated, depending on season and length of stay. Reserve early for the winter season. For more information contact Molly Stokes, Casa del Puente, Puente Av. Insurgentes, Puerto Vallarta, Jalisco 48380, tel. (322) 207-49. In the U.S. or Canada, reserve through Molly's daughter, tel. (415) 775-1970.

Nearby, across the river and two more blocks upstream, along Avenidas Aquiles Serdán and Fco. I. Madero, are a number of super-economy hotels. These bare-bulb lodgings, with rates averaging less than $10 d, offer tiers of interior rooms with few amenities other than four walls, a bath (check for hot water), and a bed.

One notable exception is the **Hotel Villa del Mar,** Fco. I. Madero 440, corner of Jacarandas, Puerto Vallarta, Jalisco 48300, tel. (322) 207-85, whose longtime loyal patrons swear by it as the one remnant of Puerto Vallarta "like it used to be." The rather austere dark-wood, street corner lobby leads to a double warren of clean upstairs rooms, arranged in a pair of separate "A" and "B" wings. The "A" wing rooms are generally the best, with nondeluxe but comfortable amenities, including queen-size beds, traditional-style dark-wood decor, ceiling fans, and, in some cases, even private street-view balconies. Section "A," with exterior-facing windows, has the triple advantage of more privacy, light, and quiet. "B" rooms, by contrast, have windows that line walkways around a sound-reflective, and therefore oft-noisy, interior tiled atrium, where guests must draw curtains for quiet and privacy. Low season rates for the approximately 30 "A" rooms run about $10 s, $12 d, and $13 t. During the high season, rates rise for the "A" rooms to about $15 s, $20 d, and $23 t. Rooms vary—inspect a few before you decide. No TV, phones, or pool available, and credit cards are not accepted. "B" rooms rent, year-round, for about $7 s, $9 d, $11 t.

Head three blocks farther away from the river and back downstream to Av. I. Vallarta (corner Basilio Badillo) to the longtime favorite **Hotel Posada Roger,** Basilio Badillo 237, Puerto Vallarta, Jalisco 48380, tel. (322) 208-36, fax 304-82, e-mail: pvroger@pvnet.com.mx. Although not the budget bargain it once was, the Hotel Posada Roger's three stories of rooms still enclose an inviting vine-decorated courtyard with plenty of quiet nooks for reading and relaxing. The Tucán, the hotel's breakfast café (open daily 8 a.m.-2 p.m.), provides yet another setting for relaxed exchanges with other travelers. A small pool patio on the roof adds a bit of class to compensate for the increased price of the many smallish rooms that Roger offers. The 50 rooms run about $30 s, $38 d high season, $24 s, $32 d low, three blocks from the beach, with TV and a/c; credit cards accepted.

The **Hotel Yasmin,** nearby at Basilio Badillo 168, at Pino Suárez, Puerto Vallarta, Jalisco 48380, tel. (322) 200-87, offers a viable budget lodging alternative. The Yasmin's main attractions are its two short blocks to the beach, its verdant, plant-festooned inner patio, and Cafe de Olla, a good restaurant next door. The three tiers of fan-only rooms are clean, but small and mostly dreary. Inspect before you pay. You can compensate by renting one of the lighter, more secluded sunny-side upper rooms. Rates for all 30 rooms run about $18 d all year around.

Head downhill toward the beach and left around the Av. Olas Altas corner and you are in the popular Olas Altas neighborhood. At the hub of activity is the **Hotel Playa Los Arcos** (middle of the block between Calles Basilio Badillo and M. Dieguez), a best-buy favorite of a generation of savvy American and Canadian winter vacationers. The Playa Los Arcos is the flagship of a triad that includes the nearby Hotel Arcos Vallarta and the apartments Suites Los Arcos, both of whose guests are welcome to enjoy all of the Playa Los Arcos's leisurely beachfront facilities.

All three of these lodgings have swimming pools and comfortable, tastefully decorated, air-conditioned rooms with TV, phones, and small refrigerators in many rooms. The mecca, however, is the bustling Playa Los Arcos, with its palm- and vine-decorated inner pool-patio sundeck, restaurant with salad bar, live music every night, and beach chairs in the sand beneath shady palms or golden sun. The Hotel Playa Los Arcos is at Olas Altas 380, Puerto Vallarta, Jalisco 48380, tel. (322) 205-83 or 215-83, fax 224-18, or from U.S. and Canada toll-free (800) 648-2403, e-mail: reservaciones@playalosarcos.com. The 183 rooms rent from about $51 d low season, approximately $63 high season, for standard grade rooms. More spacious, some with ocean views, superior-grade rooms run about $65 d low season, $85 high season, with credit cards accepted.

The **Hotel Arcos Vallarta** (formerly Hotel Fontana) is half a block away, around the corner, on a quiet cul-de-sac, at M. Dieguez 171, Puerto Vallarta, Jalisco 48380, tel. (322) 207-12 or (800) 648-2403, same e-mail as the Playa Los Arcos. Its amenities include a rooftop pool patio with a city and hill view. The Arcos Vallarta's 42 thoughtfully furnished pastel-motif rooms, built around a soaring interior atrium, rent from about $54 d low season, $66 d high season; credit cards accepted.

Right across the street, on M. Dieguez (address, telephones and e-mail are the same as the Hotel Arcos Vallarta), is the apartment-style **Suites Los Arcos,** with a long blue pool-/patio and an airy sitting area to one side of the lobby. Upstairs are 15 studio apartments, simply but attractively furnished in tile, wood furniture, and pastel-blue sofas and bedspreads. All have baths, some with tub-shower, king-sized beds, furnished kitchenette, a/c, TV, and private balcony. The apartments rent (daily rate only) for about $63 d, $70 t low season, and $78 d, $88 t high.

The Hotels Playa Los Arcos, Arcos Vallarta, and Suites Los Arcos all accept bookings through travel agents. During times of low occupancy (often May, June, July, September, and October, and sometimes even January), all three may offer special promotions, such as two kids under 12 free when sharing with parents, long-term discounts, or fourth night free. Be sure to ask when you book.

A block farther up Olas Altas, on a quiet uphill side street, at Francisca Rodríguez 168, Puerto Vallarta, Jalisco 48380, tel./fax (322) 247-93, stands the modest but well-managed **Hotel Alegre.** The small lobby leads to an intimate, leafy pool patio, enclosed by three tiers of rooms simply decorated in rustic wood, tile, and stucco, with TV, a/c, and shower bath. Rates are about $33 s or d, $38 d (with two beds) low season, $43 and $48 high, add $4 for a/c and $5 for kitchenette; credit cards are accepted. During low occupancy, Alegre sometimes offers promotions, such as kids free with parents, or fourth day free. Ask before you reserve.

Vacationers who require a bit more space often pick the Playa Los Arcos's beachside neighbor, the **Hotel Plaza San Marino** at Rudolfo Gómez 111, Puerto Vallarta, Jalisco 48380, tel. (322) 215-55 or 230-50, fax 224-31. The San Marino's soaring *palapa* restaurant patio opens to an ocean-view pool and courtyard with a sundeck. Occupants of all of the marble-floored, pastel- and white-decor rooms enjoy city, mountain, or ocean views. The 160 rooms and suites rent for about $59 d low season, about $80 high season; ocean-view suites are $69 low season and $105 high season. Amenities include a/c, TV, phones, and access to the bar and two restaurants. (Inspect two or three rooms, and make sure that everything, such as the a/c, is operating before you pay your money.)

Farther south on Playa los Muertos, the Hotel Tropicana and its nearby brother, condo-style Hotel Gloria del Mar, offer ocean-view lodgings at moderate prices. Although the seven-story beachfront apartments **Hotel Gloria del Mar,** Amapas 114, Puerto Vallarta, Jalisco 48380, tel. (322) 251-43, fax 267-37, has no pool or beach facilities, its prices are certainly right, and its guests are invited to enjoy all of the Tropicana's facilities to boot. The Gloria del Mar has 50 bright kitchenette suites, with either ocean or hill views. For the cheaper hill-view suites, expect to pay $27 low season, $32 high; for ocean view, $40 and $45, with a/c, phones, TV, and credit cards accepted.

The **Hotel Tropicana,** Amapas 214, Puerto Vallarta, Jalisco 48380, tel. (322) 209-12 or 209-52, fax 267-37, although large, is easy to miss, because the beach-level lobby is street-accessible only by an unobtrusive downward staircase. From there the hotel's popular beachfront amenities—pool, sundeck, restaurant, volleyball court, and shady *palapas*—spread all the way to the surf. Upstairs, nearly all of the comfortable but somewhat tattered rooms enjoy private balconies and ocean vistas. The 160 rooms run about $30 d low season, about $50 high; with a/c and security boxes, credit cards accepted.

About a block south along Amapas, the breezy, plant-decorated room tiers of **Casa Corazón** spread down their beachfront hillside at Amapas 326, P.O. Box 66, Puerto Vallarta, Jalisco 48300, tel. (322) 213-71, fax 263-64. Tucked on one of the middle levels, a homey open-air restaurant and adjacent soft-couch lobby with a shelf of used paperbacks invite relaxing, reading, and socializing with fellow guests. No TVs, ringing phones, or buzzing air conditioners disturb the tranquillity; the people and the natural setting—the adjacent lush garden and the boom and swish of the beach waves—set the tone. The 14 rooms, while not deluxe, are varied and comfortably decorated with tile, brick, and colorful native arts and crafts. Guests in some of the most popular rooms enjoy spacious, sunny beach-view patios. Tariffs for smaller rooms run about $30 s, $35 d low season, $50 s or d high; larger run $40 and $45 low season, $60 high.

You may book directly by contacting the hotel above or owner George Tune, P.O. Box 937, Las Cruces, NM 88004, tel./fax (505) 523-4666.

Nearby, on the short beachfront Calle Malecón, stands the neighboring condo-style **Hotel Puerto Vallarta Beach,** P.O. Box 329, Puerto Vallarta, Jalisco 48300, tel. (322) 250-40, fax 221-76. Aptly named for its location right on popular Playa los Muertos, the hotel's five stories of attractively furnished, tile and stucco kitchenette apartments offer all the ingredients for a restful beach vacation: queen-size bed, private sea-view balconies, restaurant, and rooftop pool sundeck with panoramic beach and bay view. During low season, the spacious, one-bedroom suites rent for $50 with kitchenette, $45 without; during high season, $55 and $50. Depending upon occupancy, longer-term and low-season discounts may be available. Cable TV, a/c, phones, and elevator.

The all-inclusive **Hotel Meza del Mar,** Amapas 380, Puerto Vallarta 48300, tel./fax (322) 248-88, fax 223-08, a block farther south, offers a contrasting alternative. A host of longtime returnees swear by the hotel's food, service, and friendly company of fellow guests, who, during the winter, seem to be divided equally between Americans and English- and French-speaking Canadians. The Meza del Mar's 127 rooms and suites are distributed among two adjacent buildings: the Main Tower, a view high-rise overlooking the pool deck, and the Ocean Building, a three-story tier with views right over the beach. Guests in the preferred rooms, most of which are in the Ocean Building, enjoy private balconies and the sound of the waves outside their windows. Other guests are quite happy with the expansive ocean view from the top floors of the Main Tower.

The rooms themselves, while not super-deluxe, are comfortably furnished in the Mexican *equipal* style of handcrafted leather furniture. Although all rooms are clean, details, especially in the cheaper rooms, sometimes appear makeshift. If possible, ask for another room if your assignment isn't satisfactory.

Rates vary sharply according to season and grade of room, and include all food (not gourmet, but good), drinks, and entertainment in the hotels' restaurants, bars, pools, and beachfront club. Rates, quoted per person double occupancy, for a minimum three-night stay, run from about $35/night, low season, for a bare-bones no-view room to $120/night for a choice view suite. All rooms have a/c, no TV nor phones, and limited wheelchair access. Add $7 per person in lieu of tipping. Although it does accept walk-in guests, individual reservations outside of Mexico must be through travel agents, who in turn must work through the Denver-based wholesaler, Tour Express. From U.S. phones, agents should call (800) 525-1948; from Canada, tel. (888) 694-0010; from Colorado, tel. (800) 332-1197, or from the Denver metropolitan area, tel. (303) 694-3466. The above-quoted rates depend on Tour Express issuing the air tickets. If not, add about $18 per person to the minimum first three-night tariff.

Hotels South of Town

Follow the Manzanillo Hwy. 200 (the southward extension of Insurgentes) about a mile south of town and your reward will be the **Hotel Playa Conchas Chinas,** which offers a bit of charm at moderate rates, P.O. Box 346, Puerto Vallarta, Jalisco 48390, tel./fax (322) 157-70. The stucco and brick complex rambles down a palm-shaded hillside several levels to an intimate cove on Conchas Chinas beach. Here, sandy crescents nestle between tidepool-dotted sandstone outcroppings.

Lodgings themselves come in three grades. Standard rooms are spacious, decorated in Mexican traditional tile-brick, and furnished in brown wood with kitchenette and tub bath; most have an ocean view. Deluxe grade adds a bedroom and ocean-view patios/balconies; plushest superior grade comes with all of the above, plus a small private pool with jacuzzi. Very popular—reserve early, especially during high season. Of the 39 rooms, the standard rooms begin at about $60 d low season, $80 high; deluxe, $70 low, $90 high, with a/c, phones, and the romantic El Set sunset restaurant above and a beachfront breakfast café below; sunny pool, but no elevator or wheelchair access; credit cards accepted. It sometimes offers low-season discounts, such as one day free for a four-day stay or two days free for a one-week stay.

Another mile south, you can enjoy the extravagant isolation of the **Hotel Camino Real,** P.O. Box 95, Playa de las Estacas, Puerto Vallarta, Jalisco 48300, tel. (322) 150-00, fax 160-00, tel. (800) 7-CAMINO (722-6466) from the U.S. and Canada, e-mail: pvr@caminoreal.com, at correspondingly extravagant prices. Puerto Vallarta's first world-class hotel, the Camino Real has aged gracefully. It is luxuriously set in a lush tropical valley, with polished wooden walkways that wind along a beachside garden intermingled with blue swimming pools. A totally self-contained resort on a secluded, sometimes seasonally narrow strip of golden-white sand, the twin-towered Camino Real offers every delight: luxury view rooms, all water sports, restaurants, bars, and live music every night. The 250 rooms of the Main tower begin at about $210 d low season, $370 high, while the 150 jacuzzi-equipped rooms of the Royal Beach Club tower go for about $240 d low season, $430 high, with everything, including wheelchair access.

On the other hand, for folks who prefer activity over serenity, the all-inclusive **Hotel Blue Bay Club Puerto Vallarta** (formerly Casa Grande) another mile south may be the right choice for a hassle-free tropical vacation. Find it at Km 4, Carretera a Barra de Navidad, P.O. Box 385, Puerto Vallarta, Jalisco 48300, tel. (322) 155-00, fax 151-05, tel. (800) BLUEBAY in the U.S. and Canada, e-mail: pvr@bluebayresorts.com. Although the hotel's tower rises like a giant space-age beehive sandwiched between the highway and the sea, the beach-level pool deck reveals an entirely different scene: Platoons of guests—reclining, socializing, snoozing, frolicking, and eating—enjoy at no extra charge the hotel's generous menu of activities. These vary from paddleboard, Ping-Pong, scuba

lessons, and exercise machines for the athletic, to Spanish lessons, bingo, and pool-soaking in the airy solarium spa for the more sedentary. With so much going on, the hotel beach hardly seems necessary for an enjoyable week in the sun. A luxurious room with private sea-view balcony with cable TV, a/c, and phone, runs about $70 s, $140 d low season, $110 s, $220 d high, including all food, drinks, and activities. Kids 12 and under get big discounts.

Hotels North of Río Cuale

Hotels generally get more luxurious and expensive the farther north of the Río Cuale you look. The far northern section, on the marina's ocean side, the site of several huge international chain hotels, is both isolated several miles from downtown (and Mexico) and has only a rocky beach, usually with little, if any sand. Most of the central part of town, which stretches for a mile along the *malecón,* has no good beach either and is too noisy and congested for comfortable lodgings.

A notable exception, however, is the **Hotel Los Cuatros Vientos,** Matamoros 520, P.O. Box 83, Puerto Vallarta, Jalisco 48300, tel. (322) 201-61, fax 228-31, e-mail: fourwinds@pvnet.com.mx, perched in the quiet, picturesque hillside neighborhood above and behind the main town church. The 16 rooms and suites are tucked in tiers above a flowery patio and restaurant Chez Elena, and beneath a rooftop panoramic view bar-sundeck. The fan-only units are simply but attractively decorated in colonial style, with tile, brick, and traditional furniture and crafts. Rates (excluding 15 Dec.-5 Jan.) run about $65 s or d 15 Oct.-15 June, lower other times. With continental breakfast and a small pool; credit cards are accepted.

Near the north end of the downtown *malecón,* where the good beach resumes at Playa Camarones, so do the hotels. They continue, dotting the tranquil, golden strands of Playa las Glorias, Playa los Tules, and Playa de Oro. On these beaches are the plush hotels (actually, self-contained resorts) from which you must have wheels to escape to the shopping, restaurants, and the piquant sights and sounds of old Puerto Vallarta.

At the north end of the *malecón* (at 31 de Octubre) stands one of Puerto Vallarta's popular old mainstays, the friendly, beachfront **Hotel Rosita,** Díaz Ordaz 901, P.O. Box 32, Puerto Vallarta, Jalisco 48300, tel./fax (322) 321-85,

320-00, 321-51, or 321-77. The Rosita centers on a grassy, palm-shadowed ocean-view pool patio and restaurant, with plenty of space for relaxing and socializing. About half of the spacious rooms, of *típica* Mexican tile and white stucco and wood, look down upon the tranquil patio scene, while others, to be avoided if possible, border the noisy, smoggy main street. An unfortunate wire security fence mars the ocean view from the patio. Egress to the beach, Playa Camarón, is through a side door. The Rosita's 90 rooms range, depending on location, between $23 and $44 d low season, $28-52 high, including fans or a/c, security boxes, and a bar; credit cards accepted.

The **Hotel Buenaventura,** Av. México 1301, P.O. Box 8B, Puerto Vallarta, Jalisco 48350, tel. (322) 237-37, fax 235-46, on the beach several blocks farther north, where the airport boulevard narrows as it enters old town, is one of Puerto Vallarta's few close-in deluxe hotels. The lobby rises to an airy wood-beamed atrium then opens toward the beach through a jungle walkway festooned with giant hanging leafy philodendrons and exotic palms. At the beachfront Los Tucanes Beach Club, a wide, palm-silhouetted pool patio borders a line of shade *palapas* along the whitish-yellow sand beach. Most of the small rooms, decorated in wood, tile, and earth-tone drapes and bedspreads, open to small, private ocean-facing balconies. The 206 rooms go for about $70 low season, $90 high. Amenities include a/c, phones, restaurant, bar, and live music nightly in season; credit cards accepted.

Zona Hotelera Luxury Hotels

Puerto Vallarta's plush hostelries vary widely, and higher tariffs do not guarantee quality. Nevertheless, some of Pacific Mexico's best-buy luxury gems glitter among the 20-odd hotels lining Puerto Vallarta's north-end Zona Hotelera beaches. The prices listed are "rack rates"—the highest prices paid by walk-in customers. Much cheaper—as much as 50% discount—airfare/lodging packages are often available, especially during low seasons, which are January, May-July, and Sept.-November. Get yourself a good buy by shopping around among travel agents at least several weeks before departure.

Heading north, the **Hotel Continental Plaza,** Av. de Ingreso Km 2.5, Zona Hotelera, Plaza Las Glorias, Puerto Vallarta, Jalisco 48300, tel. (322) 401-23, fax 452-36, tel. (800) 88-CONTI (882-6684) from the U.S. and Canada, e-mail: ncont@pvnet.com.mx, buzzes all day with activities: tennis in the eight-court John Newcombe Tennis Club next door; aerobics, water polo, and volleyball in the big pool; and parasailing, jet skiing, and windsurfing from the golden Playa las Glorias beach. Happy hours brighten every afternoon, and live music fills every balmy evening. The luxurious but not large rooms, decorated in soothing pastels, open to balconies overlooking the broad, palmy patio. The Continental Plaza's 434 room tariffs run about $100 d low season, $145 high; with a/c, some sports, restaurants, bars, sauna, jacuzzi, exercise room, wheelchair access, and parking.

Next door, the **Hotel Plaza Las Glorias,** Plaza Las Glorias s/n, Puerto Vallarta, Jalisco 48300, tel. (322) 444-44, or (800) 342-AMIGO (342-2644) in the U.S. and Canada, fax 465-59, once a Mexican-oriented hotel, now caters to a majority of North American clientele, except during pre-Easter week and August. At the Plaza Las Glorias, a blue swimming pool meanders beneath a manicured patio/grove of rustling palms. The rooms, behind the Spanish-style stucco, brick, and tile facade, overlook the patio and ocean from small view balconies. The South Seas ambience ends, however, in an adjacent jogging track. Inside, the luxurious rooms are tile-floored, in dark wood, white stucco, and blue and pastels. The 237 rooms rent for about $146 d low season, $220 high. All rooms have a/c, cable TV, phone, use of two pools, bars, restaurants, and easy access to the tennis courts next door at John Newcombe Tennis Club, parking, and wheelchair access. Credit cards are accepted.

The hotel's "villa" section, the semi-deluxe **Hotel Pelicanos,** tel. (322) 410-10, fax 414-14, has no ocean view but offers studios with kitchenettes for about $132 d high season, $90 low, with discounts for longer stays.

A quarter mile farther north, the recently enlarged **Hotel Las Palmas Beach,** Av. de Ingreso, Km 2.5, Puerto Vallarta, Jalisco 48300, tel. (322) 406-50, fax 405-43, tel. (800) 876-5278 from U.S. and Canada, e-mail: palmaspv@pvnet.com.mx, is an older, scaled-down, less luxurious version of the Plaza Las Glorias. An airy, rustic *palapa* shel-

SPLENDID ISOLATION

A sprinkling of luxuriously secluded upscale mini-resorts, perfect for a few days of quiet tropical relaxation, have opened in some remote corners of the Puerto Vallarta region. Being hideaways, they are not easily accessible. But for those willing to make a small extra effort, the rewards are rustically luxurious accommodations in lovely natural settings.

In order of accessibility, first comes the **Hotel La Troza,** at pristine Las Animas Beach on the Bay of Banderas, south of Puerto Vallarta. Chico Pérez, owner of Sr. Chico's restaurant, invites adults over 30 to experience his dream come true. He offers 10 rustic-chic thatched native-style cabañas, nestled in the tropical forest overlooking gorgeous Las Animas Beach. Amenities include a seawater pool, jacuzzi, restaurant, and boat excursions to nearby beaches and snorkeling, horseback rides and hiking in the lush surrounding hinterland. Rates run about $90 s, $120 d, breakfast included. Reservations, tel. (322) 242-33 (or Sr. Chico's, tel. 235-70) are recommended. Day guests at the restaurant are also welcome. Get there by hiring a launch from the beach at Boca de Tomatlán, accessible by taxi or bus on Calle Basilio Badillo just below Av. Insurgentes, south end of town.

On the same stretch of Banderas shoreline, even quieter **Majahuitas Resort** is tucked on a diminutive palm-shaded golden strand on the bay between Quimixto and Yelapa. Here, guests have their choice of seven uniquely decorated cabañas, including a honeymoon suite. Solar panels supply electricity and a luxuriously appointed central house serves as dining room and common area. A spring-fed pool, sunning, snorkeling, and horseback and hiking excursions into the surrounding tropical forest provide diversions for guests. Rates run about $200 for two, including all meals. For reservations and information, contact the resort, tel./fax (322) 158-08, e-mail: relax@cruzio.com, Web site: www2cruzio.com/~relax/. Get there by boat from Boca de Tomatlán.

Farther afield but nevertheless car-accessible, **Hotelito Desconocido** ("Undiscovered Little Hotel") basks in luxurious isolation on a pristine lagoon and beach two hours south of Puerto Vallarta. Here, builders have created a colony of thatched designer houses on stilts that appears, from a distance, like a native fishing village. However, inside the houses (called *"palafitos"* by their Italian creator), elegantly simple furnishings—antiques, plush bath towels, and artfully draped mosquito nets—set the tone. Lighting is by candle and oil lantern only. Roof solar panels power ceiling fans and warm showers. Outside, nature blooms, from squadrons of pelicans wheeling above the waves by day to a brilliant overhead carpet of southern stars by night,. In the morning roll over in bed, pull a rope that raises a flag and your morning coffee soon arrives. For the active, a full menu, including volleyball, billiards, birdwatching, kayaking, and mountain biking, can fill the day. Rates, which include all food and activities, begin at about $200 per person during the 15 April-20 Dec. low season and rise to about $300 during the high winter-spring season. For reservations and more information, call (322) 225-46, 225-26, or fax 302-93. Get there via the side road to El Gargantino and Cruz de Loreto, at Km 131 on Hwy. 200 south of Puerto Vallarta. Continue west several miles via good gravel road to Cruz de Loreto village. Follow the signs to Hotel Desconocido from there.

Alternatively, about three hours south of Puerto Vallarta, you can choose holistic retreat **Punta Serena,** perching on a hill overlooking the blue Bay of Tenacatita. Here, guests soak it all in, via meditation, massage, jacuzzi, traditional *temascal* hot bath, and healthy macrobiotic food. Expect to pay about $200-300 per person per day, all included. For more information, call (335) 150-20 or fax 150-13. Get there via the side road signed Hotel Blue Bay, at Km 20 (120 miles south of Puerto Vallarta, 15 miles north of Barra de Navidad). Be sure to call ahead for a reservation or an appointment; otherwise the guard at the gate will, most likely, not let you pass.

---

ters the lobby, which continues to a palm-adorned beachside pool patio. Here, on the wide, sparkling Playa las Glorias, opportunities for aquatic sports are at their best, with the Silent World Diving Center located right on the beachfront. The 240 rooms, most with private ocean-view balconies, are comfortable, but not luxurious. Rates run about $90 d low season, $114 high. Amenities include a/c, phones, TV, restaurant, snack bar, bars, pool, parking; credit cards are accepted.

Another quarter mile north, the **Hotel Fiesta Americana Puerto Vallarta,** P.O. Box 270,

Puerto Vallarta, Jalisco 48300, tel. (322) 420-10 or (800) FIESTA-1 (343-7821), from the U.S. and Canada, fax 421-08, e-mail: favsale@pvnet.com.mx, is, for many, the best hotel in town. The lobby-*palapa,* the world's largest, is an attraction unto itself. Its 10-story palm-thatch chimney draws air upward, creating a continuously cool breeze through the open-air reception. Outside, the high-rise rampart of ocean-view rooms overlooks a pool and garden of earthly delights, complete with a gushing pool fountain, water volleyball, swim-up bar, and in-pool recliners. Beyond spreads a 150-foot-wide strip of wave-washed yellow sand. The 291 super-deluxe view rooms sometimes go for as low as $140 d low season, rising to $200 during the high, with a/c, TV, phones, all sports, three restaurants, huge pool, three bars, disco, wheelchair access, and parking.

Next door, the **Hotel Qualton Club and Spa,** Km 2.5, Av. de las Palmas s/n, Puerto Vallarta, Jalisco 48300, tel. (322) 444-46, fax 444-47, tel. (800) 661-9174 from the U.S. and Canada, e-mail: qualton@pvnet.com.mx, offers an attractive all-inclusive option for vacationers who enjoy lots of food, fun, and company. On a typical day, hundreds of fellow sunbathing guests line the rather cramped poolside, while, a few steps away, dozens more relax beneath shady beachfront *palapas.* Nights glow with beach buffet theme dinners—Italian, Mexican, Chinese, and more—for hundreds, followed by shows where guests often become part of the entertainment. The list goes on—continuous food, open bars, complete gym and spa, tennis by night or day, scuba lessons, volleyball, water sports, free discos, golf privileges, stress therapy, yoga, aerobics galore—all included at no extra charge. If you want relief from the hubbub, you can always escape to the greener, more spacious Fiesta Americana poolside next door. The Qualton Club's 320 rooms, all with private view balconies, are luxuriously decorated in pastels and include a/c, cable TV, and phone. All-inclusive low-season rates run around $150 per person, double occupancy, about $240 high season, with wheelchair access; credit cards accepted.

Another half-mile north, the **Hotel Krystal,** Av. de las Garzas s/n, Puerto Vallarta, Jalisco 48300, tel. (322) 402-02, (800) 231-9860, fax 401-11, is more than a hotel; it's a palmy, manicured resort-village, exactly what a Mexican Walt Disney would have built. The Krystal is one of the few Puerto Vallarta ultraluxury resorts designed by and for Mexicans. Scores of deluxe garden bungalows, opening onto private pool patios, are spread over its 34 beachside acres. A Porfirian bandstand stands proudly at the center, while nearby a colonial-style aqueduct gushes water into a pool at the edge of a serene spacious palm-shaded park. Guests who prefer a more lively environment can have it. Dancing goes on every night in the lobby or beside the huge, meandering beachside pool, where the music is anything but serene. The Krystal's 460 rooms and suites rent from about $185 d low season, $260 high. Amenities include a/c, phones, TV, 44 pools—no joke—six restaurants and all sports.

Next door to the north, the neocolonial **Hotel Hacienda Buenaventura,** Paseo de la Marina, P.O. Box 95B, Puerto Vallarta, Jalisco 48310, tel. (322) 466-67, fax 462-42, e-mail: buenavista@pvnet.com.mx, offers a load of luxurious amenities at moderate rates (for reservations, call a travel agent or 800-223-6764 from the U.S. or Canada). Its 150 low-rise room tiers enfold a quiet patio-garden, graced by a blue free-form pool and a slender, rustic *palapa.* On one side, water spills from a neo-antique aqueduct, while guests linger at the adjacent airy restaurant. The rooms are spacious, with high, hand-hewn beam ceilings, marble floors, and rustic-chic tile and brick baths. The only drawback to all this is guests must walk a couple of short blocks to the beach. Rates run around $88 d low season, $111 d high, with a/c, phones, cable TV, and some wheelchair access. Credit cards accepted.

Apartments and Condominiums— Río Cuale and South

Puerto Vallarta abounds with apartments and condominiums, mostly available for rentals of more than two weeks. A number of U.S.-based agencies specialize in the more luxurious rentals scattered all over the city: Villa de Oro Vacation Rentals, 638 Scotland Dr., Santa Rosa, CA 95409, tel. (800) 638-4552; Villas of Mexico, P.O. Box 3730, Chico, CA 95927, tel. (800) 456-3133; Condo and Villa World, 4230 Orchard Lake Rd., Suite 3, Orchard Lake, MI 48323, tel. (800) 521-2980 from the U.S., (800) 453-8714 from Canada.

The best-buy Puerto Vallarta apartments and condos are concentrated in the colorful Olas Altas-Conchas Chinas south-side district and are generally available only through local owners, managers, or rental agents. Among the helpful local rental agencies is **Mexi-Rent Vallarta,** the brainchild of friendly Dutch expatriate John Dommanschet, who works from his little Olas Altas neighborhood office at R. Gómez 130 across from the Hotel Plaza San Marino, tel./fax (322) 216-55, Web site: www.mexirent.com, e-mail: john@mexirent.com. His rentals, largely confined to the Olas Altas neighborhood, include apartments, condos, and houses rentable by day, week, or month. High-season monthly rates run from about $400 for modest studios to $1,000 and more for three-bedroom houses.

Concentrating on luxury Conchas Chinas house and villa rentals (from around $200/day, high-season) is **Oscar López,** based in his air-conditioned travel agency at 352 B. Badillo, corner of Insurgentes (diagonally opposite the Elite bus ticket station), tel. (322) 300-38 or 323-34, fax 266-36. From the U.S. or Canada, contact his stateside representative, Villa de Oro Vacation Rentals, at (800) 638-4552, 638 Scotland Dr., Santa Rosa, CA 95409. If you hanker to spend a week or a season in luxurious comfort in Puerto Vallarta, whether it be in a deluxe hillside ocean-view home or in a latter-day palace, with pool, tennis court, private beachfront, servants, and enough room for all your living relatives, Oscar can probably get it for you.

Other apartments are rentable directly through local managers. The following listing, by location, moving south from the Río Cuale, includes some of the best-buy Olas Altas apartments and condominiums.

Among the most economical are the top-floor studio apartments at the **Hotel Villa del Mar,** at Fco. I. Madero 440, Puerto Vallarta, Jalisco 48300, tel. (322) 207-85, a block south of the Río Cuale and four blocks uphill from Av. Insurgentes. The several apartments, which cluster around a sunny upstairs patio, are clean and thoughtfully furnished in attractive rustic brick, dark wood, and tile. A living area, with furnished kitchenette in one corner, leads to an airy, city-and-hill private view balcony. A comfortable double bed occupies an adjacent alcove. Four stories (no elevator) above an already quiet street, guests

are likely to enjoy peace and tranquillity here. Rents run about $450 a month high season, $350 low. Get your winter reservations in early.

Downriver several blocks, at the north foot of the Av. I. Vallarta bridge, stands the renovated **Hotel Encino-Suites Plaza del Río,** at Av. Juárez 122, Puerto Vallarta, Jalisco 48300, tel. (322) 200-51 or 202-80, fax 225-73, e-mail: encino@go2mexico.com. The hotel entrance lobby opens into a pleasant, tropical, fountain patio, enfolded by tiers of rooms. The suites are in the adjacent Suites Plaza del Río. You'll find three stories of spacious, comfortable kitchenette units. An additional bonus is the Hotel Encino's rooftop pool and sundeck, where both hotel and suite guests enjoy a panoramic view of the surrounding green jungly hills above the white-stucco-and-tile old town, spreading to the blue, mountain-rimmed bay. The approximately 25 suites rent for a daily rate of about $35 low season, $40 high, with a/c, phones, security boxes, restaurant/bar. Lower weekly and monthly rates are customarily negotiable.

Across the river, on Calle Olas Altas, from the Hotel Playa Los Arcos walk south two short blocks to Francisca Rodríguez, then left a few steps uphill to the **Casa María Elena,** owned and operated by articulate, English-speaking María Elena Zermeño Santana. Her address is Francisca Rodríguez 163, Puerto Vallarta, Jalisco 48380, tel. (322) 201-13, fax 313-80, e-mail: mariazs@acnet.net. The eight attractive fan-only brick-and-tile units stand in a four-story stack on a quiet, cobbled side street just a block and a half from the beach. The immaculate, light, and spacious units have living room with TV, bedroom, and modern kitchenettes (toaster oven and coffee maker) and are all comfortably decorated with folk art chosen by María Elena (who owns a nearby crafts store) herself. Although the units have neither swimming pool nor phones, daily maid service is included. High season rates per apartment run about $50/day, $45/day when rented by the week, and $30/day when rented by the month. Corresponding low-season (May-Nov.) rates are about $40, $35, and $25. An additional discount of up to 10% is sometimes negotiable for rentals of three or more months. Guests also enjoy the option of three weekly hours of free Spanish lessons taught by María Elena herself.

Two blocks farther south and a block toward the beach, the condo-style **Hotel Gloria del Mar** offers ocean-view kitchenette apartments at modest prices. Although the seven-story beachfront complex, at Amapas 114, Puerto Vallarta, Jalisco 48380, tel. (322) 251-43, fax 267-37, has no pool or beach facilities, its prices are certainly right, and its guests are invited to enjoy all of the facilities of the Hotel Tropicana a block away. The Gloria del Mar has 50 bright kitchenette suites, with either ocean or hill views. For the cheaper hill-view suites, expect to pay a daily rate of $27 low season, $32 high; for ocean-view, $40 and $45. Phones, a/c, and TV. Credit cards accepted.

Cheaper rates are available across the street, on Amapas, between Gomez and Pulpito, at the **Apartments Emperador,** tel./fax (322) 233-29. Here, you can get a plainly furnished but clean and comfortable kitchenette studio or one bedroom with phones and a/c from about $500 per month low season, $700 high; credit cards accepted.

Two blocks north on beachfront Calle Malecón stands the condo-style **Hotel Puerto Vallarta Beach,** P.O. Box 329, Puerto Vallarta, Jalisco 48300, tel. (322) 250-40, fax 221-76. Aptly named for its location right on popular Los Muertos Beach, the hotel's five stories of attractively furnished, tile and stucco kitchenette apartments offer all the ingredients for a restful beach vacation: queen-size bed, private sea-view balconies, restaurant, and rooftop pool/sundeck with panoramic beach and bay view. During low season, the spacious, one-bedroom suites with cable TV, phones, and a/c rent daily for $50 with kitchenette, $45 without; during high season, $55 and $50. Depending upon occupancy, lower weekly and monthly and low-season rates may be available.

Three blocks farther south, the path to the 63-unit condo-style **Hotel Brisas del Mar** winds uphill through its view restaurant, across its expansive pool deck to the big white main building perched a short block below the highway. If this place weren't such a climb (although aerobicists might consider it a plus) from the beach, the builders would have sold all the units long ago. Now, however, it's owned and operated by the downhill Hotel Tropicana, whose attractive beachside facilities Brisas del Mar guests are invited to enjoy. The Brisas del Mar, Privada Abedul 10, Puerto Vallarta, Jalisco 48300, tel./fax (322) 218-00 or 218-21, is quite comfortable, with light, comfortable, kitchenette suites with private view balconies. Most units are one-bedroom, with either one king-size bed or a double and twin combination. Rates run from about $35/night or $650/month low season to $48 and $1,000 high season, with a/c, pool, desk service, restaurant, and limited wheelchair access. Credit cards accepted. Book directly or through a travel agent. Get there by car or taxi from the highway, or by climbing from Amapas through the doorway at no. 307, labeled Casa del Tigre.

Back down on Amapas, a half-block farther south, the 10 white designer units of the **Condominios Villa Blanca,** Amapas 349, Puerto Vallarta, Jalisco 48300, tel./fax (322) 261-90, stairstep artfully above the street. These are light, attractive, air-conditioned luxury apartments, rented out for the owners by the friendly manager Jose Luis Alvarez, whose office is at the streetfront. While the apartments vary from studios to two bedrooms, they all have ocean views, modern kitchenettes, and rustic decorator vine-entwined palm trunks adorning the doors and walls. The best apartments occupy the upper levels; the least desirable are the two apartments at the bottom, where a pump buzzes continuously near the complex's small soaking pool. Rentals may be by the day, week, or month. Daily rates for studios run $35 low season, $50 high; for a one bedroom, $45 low, $60 high; two bedrooms, about $70 and $100.

Trailer Parks and Camping

Puerto Vallarta visitors enjoy two good trailer parks, both of them owned and managed by the same family. The smallish, palm-shaded **Puerto Vallarta Trailer Park,** Francia 143, P.O. Box 141, Puerto Vallarta, Jalisco 48300, tel. (322) 428-28, is two blocks off the highway at Francia at Lucerna, a few blocks north of the *libramiento* downtown bypass fork. The 65 spaces four blocks from beach rent for $10 per day, with one free day per week, one free week per month; with all hookups, including showers, toilets, long-distance phone access, laundromat, pets okay. Luxury hotel pools and restaurants are nearby.

Much more spacious **Tacho's Trailer Park** is half a mile from Hwy. 200 on Av. Aramara, the road that branches inland across the airport highway from the cruise ship dock. It offers a large grassy yard, with some palms, bananas, and other trees for shade. Contact Tacho's at P.O. Box 315, Puerto Vallarta, Jalisco 48300, tel. (322) 421-63. Tacho's 100 spaces run $12 per day (one free week on a monthly rental), including all hookups and use of showers, toilets, laundry room, pool and *palapa,* and shuffleboard courts. Pads are paved and pets are okay.

Other than the trailer parks, Puerto Vallarta has precious few campsites within the city limits. Plenty of camping possibilities exist outside the city, however. Especially inviting are the pearly little beaches, such as Las Animas, Quimixto, Caballo, and others that dot the verdant, wild coastline between Boca de Tomatlán and Yelapa. *Colectivo* water taxis regularly head for these beaches for about $3.50 per person from Boca de Tomatlán. Local stores at Quimixto, Las Animas, and Boca de Tomatlán can provide water (bring water purification tablets or filter) and basic supplies.

FOOD

Puerto Vallarta is brimming with good food. Dieters beware: Light or nouvelle cuisine, tasty vegetables, and bountiful salads are the exception, as in all Mexico. In the winter, when the sun-hungry vacationers crowd in, a table at even an average restaurant may require a reservation. During the low season, however, Puerto Vallarta's best eateries are easy to spot. They are the ones with the customers.

Stalls, Snacks, and Breakfast

Good Puerto Vallarta eating is not limited to sit-down restaurants. Many foodstalls offer wholesome, inexpensive meals and snacks to hosts of loyal repeat customers. It's hard to go wrong with hot, prepared-on-the-spot food. Each stand specializes in one type of fare—seafood, *tortas,* tacos, hot dogs—and occupies the same location daily. For example, a number of them concentrate along Avenidas Constitución and Pino Suárez just south of the River Cuale; several others cluster on the side-street corners of Av. Olas Altas a few blocks away.

A number of such foodstalls have graduated to storefronts. **Rickey's Tamales,** 325 Basilio Badil-

lo, capitalizes on the general Mexican belief that tamales (like Chinese food and pizza in the U.S.) are hard to make and must be bought, takeout style. Big rolls of husk-wrapped, lime-soaked cornmeal are stuffed with beef, chicken, or pork and baked; three for $2. Open Mon.-Sat. 6-10 p.m.

If you're lusting for a late-night snack, walk a few doors west toward the beach to either **Cenaduría La Jolla,** open nightly 6 p.m.-midnight, for great *pozole,* or neighboring **Armando's,** open Mon.-Sat. 7 p.m.-3 a.m., for a dozen styles of succulent tacos.

An exceptionally well located late-night burrito stand is at the nightclub crossroads of Avenidas I. Vallarta and Lázaro Cárdenas across from Mariachis Locos. Choose between burritos and *hamburguesas* in a number of styles. Open nightly until around 2 a.m.

Other tasty late-night options are available at many of the eateries along main street Av. Insurgentes, just south of the upstream Río Cuale bridge. For example, drop into the no-name *jugería* a few doors north from the Cine Bahía at Insurgentes 153. Try one of the luscious *tortas de pierna,* roast leg of pork smothered in avocado on a bun, $1.75. Top it off with a banana *licuado,* with a touch of *(un poquito de)* chocolate. Open daily 7 a.m.-midnight.

Similar is **Tuti Fruti,** a good spot for a refreshing snack, especially while sightseeing or shopping around the *malecón.* Find it at the corner of Morelos and Corona, one block from the *malecón;* open Mon.-Sat. 8 a.m.-11 p.m. You could even eat breakfast, lunch, and dinner there, starting with juice and granola or eggs in the morning, a *torta* and a *licuado* during the afternoon, and a *hamburguesa* for an evening snack.

Some of the most colorful, untouristed places to eat in town are, paradoxically, at the tourist-mecca **Mercado Municipal** on the Río Cuale, at the Av. Insurgentes (upstream) bridge. The *fondas* tucked on the upstairs floor (climb the street-side staircase) specialize in steaming, home-style soups, fish, meat, tacos, *moles,* and *chiles rellenos.* Point out your order to the cook and take a seat at the cool, river-view seating area. Open daily 7 a.m.-6 p.m.

For breakfast, **La Casa de Los Hot Cakes,** skillfully orchestrated by personable travel writer-turned-restaurateur Memo Barroso, has become a Puerto Vallarta institution at Basilio Badillo

289, between I. Vallarta and Constitución, tel. (322) 262-72. Breakfast served Tues.-Sun. 8 a.m.-2 p.m. Besides bountiful Mexican- and North American-style breakfasts—orange juice or fruit, eggs, toast, and hash browns for about $4—Memo offers an indulgent list of pancakes. Try his nut-topped, peanut butter-filled "O. Henry" chocolate pancakes, for example. Add his bottomless cup of coffee and you'll be buzzing all day. For lighter eaters, vegetarian and less indulgent options are available.

If Casa de Los Hot Cakes is too crowded, you can get a reasonable facsimile at the **Tucán** restaurant (which Memo inaugurated in the '80s) at Hotel Posada Roger, corner B. Badillo and I. Vallarta, tel. (322) 208-36. Open daily 8 a.m.-2 p.m.

Another good spot for breakfast served 7-11:30 a.m. is the sunny beachfront terrace of the **Hotel Playa Los Arcos** restaurant at 380 Olas Altas. Here the ambience—tour boats arriving and leaving, the passing sidewalk scene, the swishing waves, the swaying palms—is half the fun. The other half is the food, either a hearty $7 buffet, or a briskly served à la carte choice of your heart's desire, from fruit and oatmeal to eggs, bacon, and hash browns.

Coffeehouses

Good coffee has arrived at Puerto Vallarta, where some cafés now roast from their own private sources of beans. Just a block from Playa los Muertos, coffee and book lovers get the best of both worlds at **Page in the Sun,** corner Olas Altas and M. Dieguez, diagonally across from Hotel Playa Olas Altas. There, longtimers sip coffee and play chess while others enjoy their pick of lattes, cappuccinos, ice cream, muffins, and walls of used paperbacks and magazines. Open daily 8 a.m.-9 p.m.

Exactly one block farther up Olas Altas, at the corner of Rodríguez, take a table at the **Cafe San Ángel** and soak up the sidewalk scene. Here, you can enjoy breakfast or a sandwich or dessert and good coffee in a dozen varieties, 8 a.m.-10 p.m.

For similar ambience nearby take your book or newspaper to a shady table at **Señor Book,** at the corner of R. Gómez and Olas Altas, tel. (322) 203-24. Here, you may enjoy all espresso options, plus wines, liquors, pastries, and a very substantial library of new and used paperbacks. Open daily 7:30 a.m.-10:30 p.m.

Restaurants—Río Cuale and South

Archie's Wok, Francisca Rodríguez 130, between Av. Olas Altas and the beach, tel. (322) 204-11, is the founding member of a miniature "gourmet ghetto" that is flourishing in the Olas Altas neighborhood. The owner, now deceased, was John Huston's longtime friend and personal chef. However, Archie's wife, Cindy Alpenia, carries on the culinary mission. A large local following swears by her menu of vegetables, fish, meat, and noodles. Favorites include Thai coconut fish, barbecued ribs Hoi Sin, and spicy fried Thai noodles. Make up a party of three or four, and each order your favorite. Arrive early; there's usually a line by 7:30 p.m. for dinner. Open Mon.-Sat. 2-11 p.m.; Visa accepted. Moderate-expensive.

One block due north, across from the Hotel Plaza San Marino, **Karpathos Taverna,** R. Gomez 110, tel. (322) 315-62, has acquired a considerable local following by creating a little corner of Greece here in Puerto Vallarta. Although the ambience comes, in part, from very correct service and the Greek folk melodies emanating from the sound system, the food—genuine Greek olives, feta cheese, rolled grape leaves, savory moussaka, spicy layered eggplant, piquant roast lamb, garlic-rubbed fish with olive oil—seems a small miracle here, half a world from the source. Open Mon.-Sat. 4-11 p.m. Moderate-expensive.

Head back down Olas Altas to **Cafe Maximilian** at the Hotel Playa Los Arcos, Olas Altas 380B, tel. (322) 307-60, the latest member of the growing roll of Olas Altos gourmet gems. Here, the Austrian expatriate owner skillfully orchestrates a cadre of chefs and waiters to produce a little bit of Vienna with a hint of California cuisine. From his long list of appetizers, consider starting off with prune-stuffed mountain quail in nine-spice sauce with polenta, continue with organic salad greens in vinaigrette, and finish with scalloped *rahmschnitzel* with noodles in a cream mushroom sauce, accompanied by a Monte Xanic Baja California chenin blanc. If you have room, top everything off with Viennese apple strudel. Alas, the only thing seemingly missing at Cafe Maximilian is zither music playing softly in the background. Open daily 4-11 p.m. Reservations strongly recommended. Expensive.

Mexican food is well represented south of Cuale by a trio of good restaurants. Restaurant **Tres Huastecas'** charming, pure-blooded Huastec owner calls himself "El Querreque," while others call him the "Troubadour of Puerto Vallarta." His poetry, together with sentimental Mexican country scenes, covers the walls, while everything from soft-boiled eggs and toast to frog legs and enchiladas Huastecas fills the tables. Find it at Olas Altas, corner of F. Rodríguez, tel. (322) 245-25; open daily 8 a.m.-8 p.m. Moderate.

Nearby, the **Cafe de Olla,** B. Badillo 168, tel. (322) 316-26, a few doors uphill from the Olas Altas corner, draws flocks of evening customers with its bountiful plates of scrumptious local delicacies. It serves Mexican food the way it's supposed to be, starting with enough salsa and *totopes* (chips) to make appetizers irrelevant. Your choice comes next—either chicken, ribs, and steaks from the streetfront grill—or the savory *antojitos* platters piled with either tacos, tostadas, *chiles rellenos,* or enchiladas by themselves, or all together in the unbeatable *plato Mexicano.* Prepare by skipping lunch and arriving for an early dinner to give your tummy time to digest it all before bed. Open daily 8 a.m.-11 p.m. Budget-moderate.

Los Arbolitos, Camino Rivera 184, tel. (322) 310-50 (bear right at the upper end of Av. Lázaro Cárdenas, way upstream along the Río Cuale), remains very popular, despite its untouristed location. Here, home-style Mexican specialties reign supreme. The house pride and joy is the Mexican plate, although they serve dozens of other Mexican and international favorites. Colorful decor, second-floor river-view location, and attentive service spell plenty of satisfied customers. Open daily 8 a.m.-11 p.m. Moderate.

As Archie's Wok did in the Olas Altas neighborhood years ago, Memo Barroso's Casa de Los Hot Cakes has sparked a small restaurant and café renaissance on upper Basilio Badillo (the block between I. Vallarta and Constitución), now so popular it's becoming known as the "Calle de Cafés." One of the originals still going strong is **Restaurant Puerto Nuevo,** at Basilio Badillo 284, tel. (322) 262-10, right across Badillo from the Casa de Los Hot Cakes. Some evening when you're lusting for seafood, take a table with friends and enjoy a no-nonsense gourmet's gourmet seafood feast. Completely without pretension, owner/chef Roberto Castellon brings in the customers with his ingeniously varied list of specialties. For a real party for four, try his guaranteed bottomless seafood special, served course by course, including clams, oysters, lobster, scallops, and red snapper-stuffed *chiles rellenos* thrown in for good measure. For dessert, he recommends either his Kahlúa cheesecake or fried ice cream. Open daily noon-11 p.m. Credit cards accepted. Moderate-expensive.

A few doors downhill, step into the **Cafe Adobe,** at the corner of Basilio Badillo and I. Vallarta, tel. (322) 267-20, and escape from the colorful but insistent Puerto Vallarta street bustle into the Adobe's cool, refined American Southwest ambience. You'll enjoy soft music, flowers, and white table linens while you make your choice from a short but tasty menu of soups, fettuccine, poultry, seafood, and meats. Open Wed.-Mon. 5-11 p.m., closed June, July, and August; reservations recommended. Expensive.

Noisy, smoky bus traffic mars daytime dining at Av. Basilio Badillo sidewalk cafés. Fortunately, this is not true in the evening or any time at both Cafe Adobe and Casa de Los Hot Cakes as both have inside seating.

For atmosphere, the showplace **Le Bistro** is tops, at Isla Río Cuale 16A, just upstream from the Av. Insurgentes bridge. Renovations, with lots of marble and tile, have replaced some of the old bohemian-chic atmosphere with European-elegant. Nevertheless the relaxed, exotic ambience still remains: the river gurgles past outdoor tables, and giant-leafed plants festoon a glass ceiling, while jazz CDs play so realistically that you look in vain for the combo. Hours are Mon.-Sat. 9 a.m.-11:30 p.m.; dinner reservations (tel. 322-202-83) are recommended. Expensive.

The renovated Le Bistro has formidable competition right across the river, at **Restaurant Caruso,** Insurgentes 109, south foot of the river bridge, tel. (322) 227-48, owned and managed by the celebrated Brindisi-born Franco brothers. Here, the refined, airy ambience sets the tone. In the afternoon, sunlight glows warmly through a lofty glass ceiling, while overhead fans spin quietly and the river bubbles downhill just outside the open veranda. Nights, cool air flowing down the river valley swirls refreshing currents past the tables.

The menu provides many choices. You might start with a savory *insalata caprese* (tomato, basil, and mozzarella), continue with *bucatini alla arrabiata* (with a bacon, onion, and tomato sauce), and finish with savory apple strudel for dessert. Enjoy this all with a good wine, such as a Wente California sauvignon blanc, or a Monte Xanic (sha-NEEK) Baja California merlot. Restaurant Caruso is open daily noon-11 p.m.; high season probably earlier, for breakfast. Reservations recommended, especially on weekends. Expensive.

If, on the other hand, you're hungry for Chinese food, go to **Dragon Rojo,** on Insurgentes, uphill side, between V. Carranza and B. Badillo, tel. (322) 201-75. Here, competent chefs put out a respectable line of the usual San Francisco-style Cantonese specialties. Open daily 1-11 p.m. Moderate.

Your stay in Puerto Vallarta would not be complete without sunset cocktails and dinner beneath the stars at one of the Puerto Vallarta's south-of-Cuale hillside view restaurants. Of these, **Señor Chico's,** Púlpito 377, tel. (322) 235-35, remains a longtime favorite, despite its average but nicely presented food. The atmosphere—soft guitar solos, flickering candlelight, pastel-pink tablecloths, balmy night air, and the twinkling lights of the city below—is memorable. Open daily 5-11 p.m.; reservations recommended. Expensive.

Get there by turning left at Púlpito, the first left turn possible uphill past the gasoline station as you head south on Hwy. 200 out of town. After about two winding blocks, you'll see Señor Chico's on the left as the street climaxes atop a rise.

Restaurants North of Río Cuale

Chef Roger, arguably the best restaurant in Puerto Vallarta, is among the least visible at Av. Agustín Rodríguez, between Hidalgo and Juárez, one block downstream from the Río Cuale Market, tel. (322) 259-00. A legion of satisfied customers, however, is the Swiss owner/chef's best advertisement. Heated dinner plates, chilled beer and white wine glasses, candlelight, etchings hung on pastel stucco walls, guitars strumming softly, and an eclectic list of exquisitely executed continental dinner entrées keep the faithful coming year-round. Open Mon.-Sat. 6:30-11 p.m.; reservations mandatory. Expensive.

The success of up-and-coming **Restaurant Trio** at 264 Guerrero, two short blocks exactly behind Chef Roger, flows from an innovative Mediterranean menu and its relaxed, airy, courtyard setting. Imaginative combinations of traditional ingredients, attentive service, and satisfying desserts, all topped off with savory espresso coffee, will keep customers coming back for years. Reservations recommended, tel. (322) 221-96. Moderate-expensive.

Within the bustle of the *malecón* restaurant row stands the longtime favorite **Las Palomas,** *malecón* at Aldama, tel. (322) 236-75. Soothing suppertime live marimba music and graceful colonial decor, all beneath a towering big-beamed ceiling, affords a restful contrast from the sidewalk hubbub just outside the door. Both the breakfasts and the lunch and dinner entrées (nearly all Mexican style) are tasty and bountiful. Open Mon.-Sat. 8 a.m.-10 p.m., Sunday 9 a.m.-5 p.m. Moderate.

A couple of blocks away, **Papaya 3,** Abasolo 169, a block and a half uphill from the Hard Rock Café, tel. (322) 203-03, has achieved success with a dazzlingly varied repertoire for Puerto Vallarta's growing cadre of health-conscious visitors and locals. Its list begins with dozens of creamy tropical fruit *licuados,* which they call "shakes," but which contain no ice cream, and continues through a host of salads, pastas, omelettes, sandwiches, Mexican specialties, and chicken and fish plates. The atmosphere, augmented with plants and soft music, is refined but relaxed. Moderate.

If, however, you hanker for home-cooked Italian food, stop by **Rito's Baci,** tel. (322) 264-48, the labor of love of the sometimes taciturn but warmhearted owner-chef, who stays open seven days a week because his "customers would be disappointed if I closed." His establishment, as plain as Kansas in July, requires no atmosphere other than Rito himself, a member of the Mexican football league hall of fame, to be successful. All of his hearty specialties, from the pestos through the pastas and the eggplant Parmesan, are handmade from traditional family recipes. Rito's Baci is located on the corner of Juárez and Ortíz de Dominguez. Open daily 1-11 p.m. Moderate.

A choice pair of romantic hillside restaurants concludes the list of north-of-Cuale dining options. Highest on the hill is the longtime favorite **Restaurant Chez Elena,** Matamoros 520, tel. (322) 201-61, on a quiet side street a few blocks above and north of the downtown church. Soft live guitar music and flickering candlelight in a colonial garden terrace set the tone, while a brief but solid Mexican-international menu, augmented by an innovative list of daily specialties, provides the food. On a typical evening, you might be able to choose between entrées such as *cochinita pibil* (Yucatecan-style shredded pork in sauce), banana leaf-wrapped Oaxacan tamales, or dorado fillet with cilantro in white sauce. Chez Elena guests often arrive early for sunset cocktails at the rooftop panoramic view bar then continue with dinner downstairs. Open nightly 6-10 p.m.; reservations are recommended. Moderate-expensive.

A few blocks downhill and north, the striking castle-tower of **Restaurant Cafe des Artistes** rises above the surrounding neighborhood at 740 Guadalupe Sanchez at Leona Vicario, tel. (322) 232-28. Only romantics need apply. Candlelit tables, tuxedoed servers, gently whirring ceiling fans, soothing live neoclassical melodies, and gourmet international cuisine all set a luxurious tone. You might start with your pick of soups, such as chilled cream of watercress or cream of prawn and pumpkin, continue with a salad, perhaps the smoked salmon in puff pastry with avocado pine nut dressing. For a finale, choose honey- and soy-glazed roast duck or shrimp sautéed with cheese tortellini and served with a carrot custard and a spinach-basil puree. Open Mon.-Sat. 8 a.m.-4 p.m., 7-11 p.m.; reservations recommended. Expensive.

Supermarkets, Bakeries, and Health Food

The acknowledged best national supermarket chain is **Comercial Mexicana,** Mexico's Kmart with groceries. The quality is generally good to excellent, and the prices match those in the U.S. and Canada. Comercial Mexicana maintains two Puerto Vallarta branches, both in the north-side suburbs: at **Plaza Marina,** Km 6.5, Hwy. 200, just before the airport, beneath the McDonald's sign, tel. (322) 100-53; and three miles closer in, at **Plaza Genovese,** Km 2.5, Hwy. 200, near the John Newcombe Tennis Club, tel. (322) 466-44 or 456-55. Both are open daily 9 a.m.-9 p.m.

Much closer to downtown is the big, locally owned **Supermercado Gutiérrez Rizo,** a remarkably well-organized dynamo of a general store at Constitución and Vallarta, just south of the Río Cuale, tel. (322) 202-22. Besides vegetables, groceries, film, socks, spermicide, and sofas, it stocks one of the largest racks of English-language magazines (some you'd be hard pressed to find back home) outside of Mexico City. Open 6:30 a.m.-10 p.m., 365 days of the year.

Panadería Mungía is nearly worth the trip to Puerto Vallarta all by itself. The two branches are downtown at Juárez and Mina, and south-of-Cuale, corner Insurgentes and A. Serdán. Big, crisp cookies; flaky fruit tarts; hot, fresh rolls; and cool cream cakes tempt the palates of visitors, locals, and resident foreigners alike. Open Mon.-Sat. 7 a.m.-9 p.m.

Rival **Panadería Los Chatos** offers an equally fine selection, also at two locations: downtown, at north-end Plaza Hidalgo, Av. México 995, and in the Hotel Zone, across from the Hotel Sheraton, Fco. Villa 359, tel. (322) 304-85. Both are open Mon.-Sat. 7 a.m.-9 p.m.

If you've run out of *salvado* (oat bran), stock up at the **Vida y Salud** health food store *(tienda naturista),* north end of downtown, at Av. México 1284, tel. (322) 216-52. Its shelves are packed with hundreds of items, such as soy milk, vitamins, aloe vera cream, and tonics purported to cure everything from warts and gallstones to impotence. Open Mon.-Sat. 9 a.m.-2 p.m. and 4-8 p.m.

South of Cuale, health food devotees have at least two choices: **La Panza Es Primero,** at Madero 287, tel. (322) 300-90, and a competing store nearby, on Insurgentes, east side, across from the Elite bus ticket station.

A fourth choice in the hotel zone, north side, is **Tienda Naturista Aguilar,** in Plaza Caracol, local 11, tel. (322) 451-17, on the airport boulevard, east side, by Gigante department store.

ENTERTAINMENT AND EVENTS

Wandering Around

The *malecón,* where the sunsets seem the most beautiful in town, is a perfect place to begin the evening. Make sure you eventually make your way to the downtown central plaza by the Presidencia Municipal. On both weekday and weekend nights, the city often sponsors free music and dance concerts beginning around 8 p.m. at the bayside **Los Arcos** amphitheater. Later, you can join the crowds who watch the impromptu antics of the *mimos* (mimes) on the amphitheater stage and the nearby street artists painting plates, watercolor country scenes, and fanciful, outer-galaxy spray-can spacescapes.

If you miss the Los Arcos concert, you can usually console yourself with a balloon, *palomitas* (popcorn), and sometimes a band concert in the plaza. If you're inconsolable, buy some peanuts, a roasted ear of sweet corn *(elote),* or a hot dog from a vendor. After that, cool down with an *agua* or *jugo* fruit juice from the *juguería* across the bayside plaza corner, or a cone from Baskin-Robbins Ice Cream just north of the city hall.

A tranquil south-of-Cuale spot to cool off evenings is the **Muelle Nuevo** ("New Pier") at the foot of Francisca Rodríguez (beach side of Hotel Playa Los Arcos). On a typical evening you'll find a couple dozen folks—men, women, and kids—enjoying the breeze, the swish of the surf, and, with nets or lines, trying to catch a few fish for sale or dinner.

Special Cultural Events
Puerto Vallarta residents enjoy their share of local fiestas. Preparations for **Semana Santa** (Easter week) begin in February, often with a **Carnaval** parade and dancing on Shrove Tuesday, and continue for the seven weeks before Easter. Each Friday until Easter, you might see processions of people bearing crosses filing through the downtown for special masses at neighborhood churches. This all culminates during Easter week, when Puerto Vallarta is awash with visitors, crowding the hotels, camping on the beaches, and filing in somber processions, which finally brighten to fireworks, dancing, and food on Domingo Gloria (Easter Sunday).

The town quiets down briefly until the May **Fiesta de Mayo,** a countywide celebration of sports contests, music and dance performances, art shows, parades, and beauty pageants.

On the evening of 15 September, the Plaza de Armas (city hall plaza) fills with tipsy merrymakers, who gather to hear the mayor reaffirm Mex-

ican independence by shouting the Grito de Dolores—"Long Live Mexico! Death to the Gachupines!"—under booming, brilliant cascades of fireworks.

Celebration again breaks out seriously during the first 12 days of December, when city groups—businesses, families, neighborhoods—try to outdo each other with music, floats, costumes, and offerings all in honor of Mexico's patron, the Virgin of Guadalupe. The revelry climaxes on 12 December, when people, many in native garb to celebrate their indigenous origins, converge on the downtown church to receive the Virgin's blessing. If you miss the main December Virgin of Guadalupe fiesta, you can still enjoy a similar but smaller-scale celebration in **El Tuito** a month later, on 12 January.

Visitors who miss such real-life fiestas can still enjoy one of several local **Fiesta Mexicana** tourist shows, which are as popular with Mexican tourists as foreigners. The evening typically begins with a sumptuous buffet of salads, tacos, enchiladas, seafood, barbecued meats, and flan and pastries for dessert. Then begins a nonstop program of music and dance from all parts of

Fireworks-stuffed papier-mâché bulls provide exciting finales to local fiestas.

Mexico: a chorus of revolutionary *soldaderas* and their Zapatista male compatriots; raven-haired señoritas in flowing, flowered Tehuantepec silk dresses; rows of dashing Guadalajaran *charros* twirling their fast-stepping *chinas poblanas* sweethearts, climaxing with enough fireworks to swab the sky red, white, and green.

The south-of-Cuale **Restaurant Iguana,** Calle Lázaro Cárdenas 311, between Insurgentes and Constitución, tel. (322) 201-05, stages a very popular and *auténtico* such show Thursday and Sunday (Sunday only in the low season) around 7 p.m. Another safe bet is the **Hotel Krystal** show (tel. 322-402-02), Tuesday and Saturday (Saturday only during the low season) at 7 p.m.

Other such shows are held seasonally at the **Sheraton** on Thursday, tel. (322) 304-04; the **Westin** on Wednesday, tel. (322) 111-00; and the **Playa Los Arcos** on Saturday, tel. (322) 205-83.

The tariff for these shows typically runs $30 per person with open bar—except for the Playa Los Arcos show, which runs about $16, drinks extra. During holidays and the high winter season reservations are generally necessary; it's best to book through a travel or tour desk agent.

Movies

Puerto Vallarta's former "art" movie house, the **Sala Elizabeth Taylor,** 5 de Febrero 19, just south of the River Cuale and a few doors upstream from Av. I. Vallarta, tel. (322) 206-67, has narrowed its offering to mostly hard-core pornographic films. The **Cine Bahía** nearby at Insurgentes 189, between Madero and Serdán, tel. (322) 217-17, however, remains a typical '50s-style small-town movie house, running a mixture of Mexican and American pop horror, comedy, and action, such as *Prince of Egypt* and *Armageddon.* Two similar movie houses on the north side of town are the **Cine Luz María,** at Av. México 227, across the street from the Pemex *gasolinera,* tel. (322) 207-05, and the nearby **Cine Vallarta** at the corner of Uruguay and Peru, tel. (322) 205-07.

Live Music

Cover charges are not generally required at the hotel bars, many of which offer nightly live music and dancing. For example, the band at the **Hotel Krystal,** tel. (322) 402-02, plays Mexican-ro-mantic-pop daily 8 p.m.-midnight, directly adjacent to the hotel reception desk.

The **Hotel Westin Regina,** tel. (322) 111-00, has live guitar music nightly 7-8 p.m., while the **Hotel Fiesta Americana'**s Mexican trio and tropical music groups (nightly 7 p.m.-1 a.m.) are guaranteed to brighten the spirits of any vacationer after a hard day on the beach (tel. 322-420-10).

The **Hotel Playa Los Arcos** combo in the *palapa* restaurant bar, tel. (322) 205-83, offers a little bit of everything nightly from oldies but goodies to including the patrons in the act, nightly 8-10 p.m.

Other hotels with similar, sure-bet nightly offerings are the Sheraton, tel. (322) 304-04; the Westin Regina, tel. (322) 111-00; and the Continental Plaza, tel. (322) 401-23.

Discos

Discos open quietly around 10 p.m., begin revving up around midnight, and usually pound on till about 5 in the morning. They have dress codes requiring shoes, shirts, and long pants for men, and blouses and skirts or pants, or modest shorts for women. Often they serve only (expensive) soft drinks. Discos that cater to tourists (all of the following) generally monitor their front doors very carefully; consequently they are pleasant and, with ordinary precautions, secure places to have a good time. If you use earplugs, even the high-decibel joints needn't keep you from enjoying yourself. Listings below are grouped by Zona Hotelera (north side), *malecón,* and south-of-Cuale locations, in approximate order of increasing volume.

Zona Hotelera: At **Friday López,** tel. (322) 420-10, on the airport boulevard in front of the Hotel Fiesta Americana Puerto Vallarta, a youngish crowd pays an approximate $10 entrance tariff for live, high-volume, mostly Latin rock and rap. Sometimes patrons become part of the action with do-it-yourself-style karaoke. Although the dance floor is small and the room is a bit smoky, it's high-ceilinged and well-lit, and the crowd is congenial.

Another half mile north stands **Christine,** the showplace of Puerto Vallarta discos, in front of Hotel Krystal, tel. (322) 402-02, ext. 878. It entices customers to come and pay the $15 cover charge early (11 p.m.) to see the display of special fogs, spacey gyrating colored lights, and sophisticated woofers and tweeters, which, even when loud as usual, are supposed to leave you with minimal hearing impairment.

Malecón: Many popular *malecón* spots regularly pound out a continuous no-cover repertoire of recorded rap and rock. One of the longtime standouts, popular with all generations, is **Carlos O'Brien's,** *malecón* at Pípila, tel. (322) 214-44. High-volume recorded rock, revolutionary wall-photos, zany mobiles, zingy margaritas, and "loco" waiters often lead patrons to dance on the tables by midnight. Folks who generally shy away from loud music can still have fun at Carlos O'Brien's, since the place is big and the high-volume speakers are confined to one area.

Since most *malecón* discos are trying to imitate the **Hard Rock Café,** you might as well go right to the source at *malecón* at Abasolo, tel. (322) 255-32.

The **Zoo,** however, across Abasolo from the Hard Rock Café, tel. (322) 249-45, appears not to be imitating anyone. While animals—hippos, swooping birds, zebras, even a circulating gorilla —entertain the customers, reggae, rap, and rock thunder from overhead speakers.

South of Cuale: Longtime favorite **Cactus,** south end of I. Vallarta, tel. (322) 260-67, continues to attract youngish crowds with its super lights, sound, and whimsical Disneyland-like decor. Approximately $5 cover charge.

Newcomer **Paco Paco,** one block north at I. Vallarta, between Badillo and Carranza, is trying harder to do the same thing by charging no cover.

Malecón Cafés, Bars, and Hangouts

One of the simplest Puerto Vallarta entertainment formulas is to walk along the *malecón* until you hear the kind of music at the volume you like.

Young film buffs like the glitz and neon of **Planet Hollywood,** at the spot of former Restaurant Brazz, near the *malecón*'s south end, at Morelos 518, at Galeana.

On the other hand, traditionalists enjoy **Restaurant Las Palomas,** which features live marimba music nightly, at the corner of Aldama.

Another block north, the African safari-decorated **Mogambo,** between Ortíz and Abasolo, offers low-volume live music, often piano or jazz, nightly during high season, tel. (322) 234-76.

A few blocks farther north, corner of Allende, **La Dolce Vida** entertains dinner customers with live programs, such as reggae, flamenco, or folk, 9 p.m.-midnight in season, tel. (322) 235-44.

Those who desire a refined, romantic ambience go to **Restaurant Cafe des Artistes,** tel. (322) 232-28, and take a table for dinner or a seat at the bar, where they enjoy soothing neoclassical and jazz piano melodies nightly during high season, Friday and Saturday during low season. Find it by walking three blocks along Leona Vicario inland from the *malecón.*

South-of-Cuale Cafés, Bars, and Hangouts

The increasingly popular small entertainment district along I. Vallarta between V. Carranza and L. Cárdenas has acquired a number of lively spots, among them the **Mariachis Locos** bar/restaurant (corner of L. Cárdenas). Inside, a mostly local clientele enjoys a lively nonstop mariachi show nightly from about 8 p.m. to the wee hours.

Across the street, half a block south, the longtime favorite, friendly **Restaurant Torito,** tel. (322) 237-84, has good ribs, reasonable prices, and seasonal live music from around 10 p.m. to midnight, bar open till around 5 a.m.

Many folks' nights wouldn't be complete without stopping in at the **Andale** Mexican pub, Olas Altas 425, tel. (322) 210-54, whose atmosphere is so amicable and lively that few even bother to watch the nonstop TV. So-so restaurant upstairs; open till around 2 a.m.

Those who desire a more subdued atmosphere head two blocks farther south to **Sí Señor** bar, R. Gómez, corner of Olas Altas, tel. (322) 264-50, for virtuoso jazz and rock until around 1 a.m. nightly in season.

SPORTS AND RECREATION

Jogging and Walking

Puerto Vallarta's cobbled streets, high curbs (towering sometimes to six feet!), and "holey" sidewalks make for tricky walking around town. The exception is the *malecón,* which can provide a good two-mile roundtrip jog when it is not crowded. Otherwise, try the beaches or the big public sports field, Unidad Deportiva, on the airport boulevard across from the Sheraton.

Swimming, Surfing, and Boogie Boarding

While Puerto Vallarta's calm waters are generally safe for swimming, they are often too tranquil for surfing, bodysurfing, and boogie boarding. Sometimes, strong, surfable waves rise along **Playa los Muertos.** Another notable possibility is at the mouth of the Ameca River (north of the airport) where, during the rainy summer season, the large river flow helps create bigger than normal waves. Surfing is also common at **Bucerías** and **Punta Mita.**

Windsurfing and Sailboating

A small but growing nucleus of local windsurfing enthusiasts practice their sport from Puerto Vallarta's beaches. They usually hold a **windsurfing tournament** during the citywide Fiesta de Mayo in the first week in May. **Silent World Diving Center,** headquartered on the Las Palmas Beach Hotel oceanfront, tel. (322) 406-50, also offers windsurfing lessons and equipment and rentals. Additionally, it rents simple-to-operate Hobie Cat sailboats (no lessons required) for $30/hour. Open daily 9 a.m.-5 p.m.

Tropical Sailing, tel. (322) 426-24, which operates from slip E-25 in Marina Vallarta, takes parties out on sailing excursions.

Snorkeling and Scuba Diving

The biggest scuba instructor-outfitter in town is **Chico's Dive Shop,** on the *malecón* at Díaz Ordaz 770, between Pípila and Vicario, tel. (322) 218-95, fax 218-94; open daily 9 a.m.-10 p.m. Chico's offers complete lessons, arranges and leads dive trips, and rents scuba equipment to qualified divers (bring your certificate). A beginning scuba lesson in the pool runs about $15, after which you'll be qualified to dive at Los Arcos. A day boat trip, including one 40-minute dive, costs $58 per person, gear included. Snorkelers on the same trip pay about $25. Chico's takes only certified divers to the **Marietas Islands,** the best site in the bay, for $85, including gear and two dives; snorkelers go for $45. Includes sandwiches and sodas for lunch.

Other smaller shops that offer similar services are **Silent World Diving Center** at the Hotel Las Palmas Beach, and **Paradise Divers** at Av. Olas Altas 443, between Dieguez and F. Rodríguez, tel. (322) 240-04; open daily 9 a.m.-10 p.m.

Jet Skiing, Water-Skiing, and Parasailing

These are available right on the beach at a number of the northside resort hotels, such as the Sheraton, Fiesta Americana Plaza Vallarta, Hotel Las Palmas, Fiesta Americana Puerto Vallarta, and Krystal.

The same sports are also seasonally available south of Cuale on Playa los Muertos, in front of the Hotels Playa Los Arcos and Tropicana.

Expect to pay about $40 per half hour for a jet-ski boat, $70 per hour for water-skiing, and $25 for a 10-minute parasailing ride.

Tennis and Golf

The eight—four outdoor clay, four indoor—courts at the friendly **John Newcombe Tennis Club,** Hotel Continental Plaza, tel. (322) 443-60, ext. 500, rent all day for about $10 an hour. A sign-up board is available for players seeking partners. The club also offers massage, steam baths, equipment sales and rentals, and professional lessons ($30 an hour).

The **Iguana Tennis Club,** adjacent to the airport Hwy. 200, marina side about a block north of the Isla Iguana mock lighthouse, tel. (322) 106-83, rents its three lit Astroturf courts for $7 per hour. Professional lessons run $17 per hour with professional instructor, $12 with a junior instructor. Clients can also use the pool and locker rooms for small additional fees.

The several night-lit courts at the **Hotel Krystal,** tel. (322) 402-02, rent for about $10 an hour. Krystal also offers equipment sales, rentals, and professional lessons. Other clubs, such as the **Sheraton,** tel. (322) 304-04; **Los Tules,** tel. (322) 429-90; and the **Tennis Club Puesta del Sol,** tel. (322) 107-70 or 102-81, also rent their courts to the public.

The 18-hole, par-71 **Marina Vallarta Golf Course,** tel. (322) 105-45, designed by architect Joe Finger, is one of Mexico's best. It is only open, however, to club members and guests of some of the big hotels, such as Vela Vallarta, Camino Real, Plaza Las Glorias, Sheraton, Westin Regina, Vidafel, Krystal, Isla Iguana, and Royal Maeva. The greens fee (about $75) includes caddy and cart. It's open daily 7:30 a.m. to dusk.

The green, palm-shaded 18-hole **Los Flamingos Golf Course,** at Km 145, Hwy. 200, eight

Playa Los Muertos

miles (13 km) north of the airport, tel. (329) 802-80 or 806-06, offers an attractive alternative. Open to the public daily 7 a.m.-4:30 p.m., the Los Flamingos services include carts ($25), caddies ($10), club rentals ($12), a pro shop, restaurant, and locker rooms. The greens fee runs about $40. The pink shuttle bus leaves daily from the Zona Hotelera (front of the Sheraton) at 7:30 and 10 a.m., returning twice in the afternoon, before 5 p.m.

Bicycling

Bike Mex offers mountain bike adventures in surrounding scenic country locations. Trips are tailored from beginning to advanced levels according to individual ability and interests. More advanced trips include such outback spots as Yelapa and mountain destinations of San Sebastián, Mascota, and Talpa. Participants enjoy GT Full Suspension or Rock Hopper mountain bikes (21-gear), helmets, gloves, purified water, and bilingual guides. Contact the downtown office at 361 Guerrero, tel. (322) 316-80, e-mail: bikemex@zonavirtual .com.mex.

Horseback Riding

A pair of nearby ranches give visitors the opportunity to explore scenic tropical forest, river, and mountainside country. Options include either English or Western saddles, and rides range from two hours to a whole day. Contact either Rancho Ojo de Agua, tel. (322) 406-07, or Rancho El Charro, tel. (322) 401-14, e-mail: aguirre@pvnet.com.mx, Web site: www.puerto-vallarta.com\ranchocharro\ for information.

Adventure Tours

A number of nature-oriented tour agencies lead off-the-beaten-track Puerto Vallarta area excursions. **Vallarta Adventures,** tel./fax (322) 106-57 or 106-58, e-mail: adventure@acnet.net, offers boat tours to the Islas Marietas wildlife sanctuary (sea turtles, manta rays, dolphins, whales, seabirds) and a rugged all-day Mercedes-Benz truck ride (canyons, mountains, crystal streams, rustic villages) into the heart of Puerto Vallarta's backyard mountains. Contact Vallarta Adventures or a travel agent for information and reservations.

The offerings of unusually ecologically aware **Expediciones Cielo Abierto** ("Open Sky Expeditions") include sea kayaking in the Marietas Islands, hiking in the Sierra Cuale foothill jungle, snorkeling, birdwatching, and cultural tours. Contact them downtown at 339 Guerrero, two short blocks north of the riverside Municipal Crafts Market, tel.(322) 233-10, fax 324-07, e-mail: openair@vivamexico.com.

Viva Tours, tel. (322) 404-10, 480-26, fax 401-82, e-mail: vivatour@tag01.acnet.net, organizes a number of relaxing adventures, including an excursion to a hot spring on the idyllic Mascota River, just half an hour from downtown Puerto Vallarta. Options include a hike or horseback ride and an overnight at cozy, rustic Rancho Canastilla at the hot spring.

Gyms

Puerto Vallarta has a number of good exercise gyms. The **European Health Spa** (say "ays-PAH") at the marina, Tennis Club Puesta del Sol, tel. (322) 107-70, offers 40 machines, complete weight sets, professional advice, aerobics workouts, and separate men's and women's facilities. Day use runs about $10.

Similar facilities and services are available at the **Hotel Qualton Club and Spa,** tel. (322)

444-46, and the **Hotel Continental Plaza,** tel. (322) 401-23, at Km 2.5, Plaza Las Glorias, in the central hotel zone.

Sportfishing

You can hire a *panga* (outboard launch) with skipper on the beach in front of several hotels, such as Los Arcos on Playa los Muertos; the Buenaventura and Sheraton on Playa los Camarones; the Plaza Las Glorias, Las Palmas, and Fiesta Americana Puerto Vallarta on Playa las Glorias; and Krystal on Playa de Oro. Expect to pay $25/hour for a two- or three-hour trip that might net you and a few friends some five-pound jack, bonito, *toro,* or *dorado* for dinner. Ask your favorite restaurant to fix you a fish banquet.

Another good spot for *panga* rentals is near the **Peines** (pay-EE-nays) docks, where the fishermen keep their boats. You may be able to negotiate a good price, especially if you or a friend speaks Spanish. Access to the Peines is along the dirt road to the left of the Isla Iguana entrance (at the fake roadside lighthouse a mile north of the marina cruise ship terminal). The fishermen, a dozen-odd members of the Cooperativa de Deportes Aquaticos Bahía de Banderas, have their boats lined up along the roadside channel to the left a few hundred yards from the highway.

At the end-of-road dock complex (the actual Peines) lie the big-game sportfishing boats that you can reserve only through agents back in town or at the hotels. Agents, such as American Express (tel. 322-329-10, 329-27, or 329-55, fax 329-26), and Miller Travel Agency, tel. (322) 109-12, customarily book reservations on the big 40-foot boats. They go out mornings at 7:30 and return about eight hours later with an average of one big fish per boat. The tariff averages around $65 per person; food and drinks available but cost extra. Big boats generally have space for 10 passengers, about half of whom can fish at any one time. If not a big sailfish or marlin, most everyone usually gets something.

Another agency that rents big sportfishing boats is the **Sociedad Cooperativa Progreso Turístico,** which has 10 boats, ranging from 32 to 40 feet. Rentals run $200-300 per day for a completely outfitted boat. For more information, drop by or call their office on the north end of the *malecón* at 31 de Octubre, across the street from the Hotel Rosita, tel. (322) 212-02. Best to talk to the manager, Apolinar Arce Palomeres, who is usually there Mon.-Sat. 8 a.m.-noon and 4-8 p.m.

A number of local English-speaking captains regularly take parties out on their well-equipped sportfishing boats. **Mr. Marlin,** record-holder of the biggest marlin catch in Puerto Vallarta, acts as agent for more than 40 experienced captains. Prices begin at about $250 per boat, for a full day, including bait, ice, and fishing tackle. Call (322) 108-09 or 102-62, ext. 10107, at the Tennis Club Puesta del Sol (at the deli) local 16.

Cheforo, a similarly seasoned captain, also offers sportfishing, whalewatching, and snorkeling expeditions on his fully equipped twin-engine diesel boat. For information and reservations, call Candace at (322) 472-50.

If you'd like to enter the Puerto Vallarta **Sailfish Tournament,** held annually in November since 1956, call (322) 154-34 (English) or the Club de Pesca (Spanish), tel./fax (322) 316-65, drop by the office at 874 Morelos, north end of downtown, or write the Puerto Vallarta Torneo de Pez Vela ("Sailfish Tournament"), P.O. Box 212, Puerto Vallarta, Jalisco 48300. The Web site is www .fishvallarta.com. The registration fee runs about $400 per person, which includes the welcome dinner and the closing awards dinner. The five grand prizes include automobiles. The biggest sailfish caught was a 168-pounder in 1957.

At their present rates of attrition, sailfish and marlin will someday disappear from Puerto Vallarta waters. Some captains and participants have fortunately seen the light and are releasing the fish after they're hooked in accordance with IFGA (International Fish and Game Association) guidelines.

Freshwater bass fishing is also an option, at lovely foothill **Cajón de Las Peñas Reservoir** on your own or by **Viva Tours,** at the Terminal Maritima (cruise ship dock), tel. (322) 404-10, fax 401-82, e-mail: vivatour@tag01.acnet.net. For $80 per person, you get all transportation, breakfast and lunch, fishing license, guide and gear. The lake record is 13 pounds.

Boating

The superb 350-berth **Marina Vallarta,** P.O. Box 350-B, Puerto Vallarta, Jalisco 48300, tel.

(322) 102-75, fax 107-22, has all possible hookups, including certified water, metered 110-220 volts, phone, fax, showers, toilets, laundry, dock lockers, trash collection, pump-out, and 24-hour security. With a yacht club and complete repair yard, it is surrounded by luxurious condominiums, tennis courts, a golf course, and dozens of shops and offices. Slip rates run around 70 cents per foot per day for one to six days, 55 cents for 7-29 days, and 45 cents for 30 or more days.

The marina also has a **public boat-launching ramp** where you can float your craft into the marina's sheltered waters for about $2. If the guard isn't available to open the gate, call the marina office for entry permission. To get there, follow the street marked Proa, next to the big pink and white disco, one block south of the main Marina Vallarta entrance.

Sporting Goods Stores

Given the sparse and pricey local sporting goods selection, serious sports enthusiasts should pack their own equipment to Puerto Vallarta. A few stores carry some items. Among the most reliable is **Deportes Gutiérrez Rizo,** corner of south-of-Cuale Avenidas Insurgentes and A. Serdán, tel. (322) 225-95. Although fishing gear—rods, reels, line, sinkers—is its strong suit, it also stocks a general selection including sleeping bags, inflatable boats, tarps, pack frames, wet suits, scuba tanks, and water skis. Open Mon.-Sat. 9 a.m.-2 p.m. and 5-8 p.m.

SHOPPING

Although Puerto Vallarta residents make few folk crafts themselves, they import tons of good—and some very fine—pieces from the places where they *are* made. Furthermore, Puerto Vallarta's scenic beauty has become an inspiration for a growing community of artists and discerning collectors who have opened shops filled with locally crafted sculpture, painting, and museum-grade handicrafts gathered from all over Mexico. And finally, resort wear needn't cost a bundle in Puerto Vallarta, where a number of small boutiques offer racks of stylish, comfortable Mexican-made items for a fraction of stateside prices.

South-of-Cuale Shopping

The couple of blocks of Av. Olas Altas and side streets around the Hotel Playa Los Arcos are alive with a welter of T-shirt and *artesanías* (crafts) stores loaded with the more common items—silver, onyx, papier-mâché, pottery—gathered from all over Mexico.

A few shops stand out, however. **Teté,** tel. (322) 247-97, owned by María Elena Zermeño and run by her daughters Olimpia and Ester, contains a treasury of unusual pre-Columbian reproductions and modern original masks, pottery, human figurines, and bark paintings. Besides such for-sale items, they also display (and if you ask, competently interpret) other pre-Columbian and modern pieces that are not for sale. Located half a block from the beach at 135 F. Rodríguez, across from Restaurant Santos; open Mon.-Sat. 10 a.m.-2 p.m. and 4-10 p.m.

A number of other interesting shops and museum/galleries are sprinkled nearby, on the blocks uphill from Av. Olas Altas. For a treat, head up B. Badillo to **Galería Pyramid,** B. Badillo 272, near the corner of I. Vallarta, tel. (322) 231-61. There, amicable owner J. Jesus Avelar offers a large selection of ceramics, paintings, masks, and Huichol ceremonial objects. These include *cuadras* (yarn paintings), beaded masks, ritual gourds, and animals all colorfully adorned with the spirits of the Huichol pantheon. Periodic public openings feature the works of promising local artists. Open Mon.-Sat. 10 a.m.-2 p.m. and 6-10 p.m., and Sunday 10 a.m.-2 p.m. during high winter season.

A few doors downhill, at the corner of I. Vallarta, admire the eclectic collection of designer **Patti Gallardo,** 250 I. Vallarta, tel./fax (322) 257-12, e-mail: womensnet@acnet.net. Although Patti's creations extend from fine art and jewelry to clothing and metal sculptures, her latest specialty is colorful handmade and designed carpets. The store is open Mon.-Fri. 10 a.m.-2 p.m. low season, Mon.-Sat. 10 a.m.-2 p.m. and 6-10 p.m. high season.

Head north a block and a half along I. Vallarta to **Talavera, Etc.,** 266 I. Vallarta, tel. (322) 241-00, fax 224-13, for an elegant exposition of fine Talavera ceramics. As friendly owner Jackie Kilpatrick explains, the label "Talavera" comes from the town in Spain where the potters, who settled in Puebla in the 16th century, originated. They

The renowned black barra pottery from San Bartolo Coyotepec village near Oaxaca is available in shops all over Pacific Mexico.

brought with them their pottery tradition, an ancient blend of Chinese, Moorish, and Mediterranean styles and methods. Jackie's wares all come from the source at Puebla, where she buys from families expert in the Talavera tradition. "They use no lead," she says, "Only cobalt for blue, copper for green, iron for red, manganese for yellow, and tin for white." Her prices, though not cheap, reflect the quality of her offerings. Open Mon.-Sat. 10 a.m.-2 p.m. and 5-8 p.m. For a more economical but more ordinary selection, continue to **Artesanías San Miguel,** on the adjacent corner, at I. Vallarta 236.

Head half a block up Lázaro Cárdenas for a look around **Olinalá Gallery,** 274 Lázaro Cárdenas, tel. (322) 274-95, Nancy and John Erickson's mini-museum of intriguing masks and fine lacquerware. Although their "Olinalá" name originates from the famed Mexican lacquerware village where they used to get most of their pieces, ceremonial and festival masks—devils, mermaids, goddesses, skulls, crocodiles, horses, and dozens more—crafts from all parts of Mexico now dominate their fascinating selection. Their offerings, moreover, are priced to sell; open Mon.-Sat. 10 a.m.-2 p.m. and 5-9 p.m.

Tucked away on a quiet residential street is **Mando de Azulelos,** at Carranza 374, a few blocks uphill from Insurgentes, tel. (322) 226-75, fax 232-92, offering made-on-site tile and Talavera-style pottery at reasonable prices. Unique, however, are the custom-made tiles—round, square, oval—inscribed and fired as you choose, with which you can adorn your home entryway or facade. Open Mon.-Fri. 9 a.m.-7 p.m., Saturday 9 a.m.-2 p.m.

Shopping along the River: Mercado Municipal and Pueblo Viejo

For the more ordinary, yet attractive, Mexican handicrafts, head any day except Sunday (when most shops are closed) to the Mercado Municipal at the north end of the Av. Insurgentes bridge. Here, most shops begin with prices two to three times higher than the going rate. You should counter with a correspondingly low offer. If you don't get the price you want, always be prepared to find another seller. If your offer is fair, the shopkeeper will often give in as you begin to walk away. Theatrics, incidentally, are less than useful in bargaining, which should merely be a straightforward discussion of the merits, demerits, and price of the article in question.

The Mercado Municipal is a two-story warren of dozens upon dozens of shops filled with jewelry, leather, papier-mâché, T-shirts, and everything in between. The congestion can make the place hot; after a while, take a break at a cool river-view seat at one of the *fonda* permanent foodstalls on the second floor.

One of the most unusual Mercado Municipal stalls is **Cabaña del Tío Tom,** whose menagerie of colorful papier-mâché parrots are priced a peg or two cheaper than at the tonier downtown stores.

It's time to leave when you're too tired to distinguish silver from tin and Tonalá from Tlaquepaque. Head downstream to the Pueblo Viejo complex on Calle Augustín Rodríguez between Juárez and Morelos, near the Av. I. Vallarta lower bridge. This mall, with individual stores rather than stalls, is less crowded but pricier than the Mercado Municipal. Some shopkeepers will turn their noses up if you try to bargain. If they persist, take your business elsewhere.

Downtown Shopping:
Along Juárez and Morelos

A sizable fraction of Puerto Vallarta's best boutiques and arts and crafts stores lie along the six downtown blocks of Av. Juárez, beginning at the Río Cuale. The **Felix Boutique** heads the parade at Juárez 126, half a block north of the river. The friendly, outgoing owner offers reasonably priced women's resort wear of her own design. Open Mon.-Sat. 11 a.m.-2 p.m. and 4-7:30 p.m.

Galería La Indígena, Juárez 270, tel./fax (322) 230-07, in the fourth block of Juárez, features a museum of fine crafts, including Huichol yarn paintings and ceremonial paraphernalia, and religious art. Also prominent is Tarascan art from Ocumicho, Michoacán; Nahua painted coconut faces from Guerrero; a host of masks, both antique originals and new reproductions; pre-Columbian replicas; Oaxaca fanciful wooden *alebrijes* animal figures; and an entire upstairs gallery of contemporary paintings. Open Mon.-Sat. 10 a.m.-3 p.m. and 7-9 p.m., in winter Mon.-Sat. 10 a.m.-9 p.m.

Just across the street from Galería Indígena, at Juárez 263, arts and crafts lovers Barbara and Jean Peters collected so many Mexican handicrafts over the years they had to find a place to store their finds. **Galería Vallarta,** tel./fax (322) 202-90, a small museum of singular paintings, ceremonial masks, lampshades, art-to-wear, and more, is the result. Open Mon.-Sat. 10 a.m.-8 p.m., Sunday 10 a.m.-2 p.m.

A few doors up the street, the store of renowned **Sergio Bustamante** (who lives in Guadalajara), Juárez 275, tel. (322) 211-29, e-mail: marcos@zonavirtual.com.mx, contains so many unique sculptures it's hard to fathom how a single artist could be so prolific. (The answer: He has a factory shop full of workers who execute his fanciful, sometimes unnerving, studies in juxtaposition.) Bustamante's more modest faces on eggs, anthropoid cats, and double-nosed clowns go for as little as $200; the largest, most flamboyant sell for $10,000 or more. Open Mon.-Sat. 10 a.m.-9 p.m.

Back across the street, the government **Instituto de Arte Jaliscense** store, Juárez 284, tel. (322) 213-01, displays examples of nearly every Jalisco folk craft, plus popular items, such as Oaxaca *alebrijes* (ahl-BREE-hays), fanciful wooden animals, from other parts. Hours are Mon.-Sat. 9 a.m.-9 p.m., Sunday 9 a.m.-4 p.m. Since it has a little bit of everything at relatively reasonable prices, this is a good spot for comparison shopping.

A few blocks farther on, at the corner of Galeana, an adjacent pair of stores, the **Querubines** ("Cherubs") and **La Reja** ("Grillwork"), display their excellent traditional merchandise—riots of papier-mâché fruit, exquisite blue pottery vases, gleaming pewter, clay trees of life, rich Oaxaca and Chiapas textiles, shiny Tlaquepaque handpainted pottery—so artfully done they are simply fun to walk through. The stores are at Juárez 501A and 501B. Querubines, tel. (322) 229-88, is open Mon.-Sat. 9 a.m.-9 p.m.; La Reja, tel. (322) 222-72, is open Mon.-Sat. 10 a.m.-2 p.m. and 4-8 p.m., winter season 10 a.m.-6 p.m.

Another block north on the short block of Corona (downhill between Juárez and Morelos) are a number of interesting fine crafts stores. First is the ceramics gallery **Majolica,** 183 Corona, which uses the older name (from the Mediterranean island of Majorca) of where the Talavera pottery style originated, before migrating to Spain and Mexi-

Mexican maskmaking traditions live on, especially in rural areas of Michoacán, Guerrero, and Oaxaca.

ERIN DWYER

ERIN DWYER

Huichol ritual yarn painting depicts a pilgrim praying to the sea gods.

co. The personable owner/manager hand-selects the pieces, all of which come from the Puebla family workshops that carry on the Talavera tradition. Her prices reflect the high demand that the Talavera style of colorful classic elegance has commanded for generations. Open Mon.-Sat. 10 a.m.-2 p.m. and 5-8 p.m.

Downhill a few doors, **Arte Mágico Huichol,** at Corona 179, tel. (322) 230-77, displays an unusually fine collection of Huichol yarn paintings by renowned artists, such as Mariano Valadéz, Hector Ortíz, and María Elena Acosta. Open Mon.-Sat. 10 a.m.-2 p.m. and 4-8 p.m.; winter season also open Sunday 10 a.m.- 2 p.m.

Next door, at the corner of Morelos, you'll find the collection of renowned designer **Billy Moon,** Morelos 558, tel. (322) 301-69, whose best customers are interior decorators. They get their pick from choirs of fine Talavera ceramics, Tlaquepaque colored crystal balls, hand-hewn baroque furniture, sentimental Mexican paintings, and much more. Open Mon.-Sat. 10 a.m.-2 p.m. and 5-8 p.m.

Step across Morelos to **Galería Uno,** one of Puerto Vallarta's longest-established fine art galleries, at Morelos 561, tel. (322) 209-08. The collection—featuring internationally recognized artists with whom the gallery often schedules exhibition openings for the public—tends toward the large, the abstract, and the primitive. Open Mon.-Fri. 10 a.m.-8 p.m. and Saturday 10 a.m.-2 p.m.

For a similarly excellent collection, step one block north and around the uphill corner of Aldama, to newly relocated **Galería Pacífico,** at Aldama 174, tel./fax (322) 219-82, e-mail: gary@artmexico.com, Web site: www.artmexico.com. Here, in an airy upstairs showroom, personable owner Gary Thompson offers a fine collection of paintings, prints, and sculpture of Mexican artists, both renowned and upcoming. The mostly realistic works cover a gamut of styles and feelings, from colorful and sentimental to stark and satirical. Gary often hosts Friday meet-the-artist openings, where visitors are invited to socialize with the local artistic community. Open Mon.-Sat. 10 a.m.-2 p.m. and 5-9 p.m. Low-season hours may be shorter.

Finally, head a few blocks back south along Morelos to the **Jewelry Factory** ("Fábrica de Joyería"), Morelos 434, on the *malecón,* tel. (322) 224-87, for just about the broadest selection and best prices in town. Charges for the seeming acres of gold, silver, and jeweled chains, bracelets, pendants, necklaces, and earrings are usually determined simply by weight; a dollar per gram for silver. Open Mon.-Sat. 10 a.m.-10 p.m.

One more unique store, outside the downtown area, is **Ric** jewelry, which displays the gleaming one-of-a-kind master works of silver artist Erika Hult de Corral, in the Villas Vallarta Shopping Center, Km 2.5, Hwy. 200, local C-8, tel. (322) 445-98, directly across the interior street from the Hotel Continental Plaza.

Department Stores

The best department stores in Puerto Vallarta are the two branches of the big Comercial Mexicana chain and the equally excellent local store, Supermercado Gutiérrez Rizo.

The acknowledged best national supermarket chain is **Comercial Mexicana,** Mexico's Kmart with groceries. The quality is generally good to excellent, and the prices match those in the U.S. and Canada. Comercial Mexicana maintains two Puerto Vallarta branches, both in the north-side suburbs: at **Plaza Marina,** Km 6.5, Hwy. 200, just before the airport, beneath the McDonald's sign, tel. (322) 100-53; and three miles closer in, at **Plaza Genovese,** Km 2.5, Hwy. 200, near the John Newcombe Tennis Club, tel. (322) 466-44 or 456-55. Both are open daily 9 a.m.-9 p.m.

Much closer to downtown is the big, locally owned **Supermercado Gutiérrez Rizo,** a remarkably well-organized dynamo of a general store at Constitución and Vallarta, just south of the Río Cuale, tel. (322) 202-22. Besides vegetables, groceries, film, socks, spermicide, and sofas, it stocks one of the largest racks of English-language magazines (some you'd be hard pressed to find back home) outside of Mexico City. Open 6:30 a.m.-10 p.m., 365 days of the year.

Photofinishing, Cameras, and Film
Although a number of downtown stores do one-hour developing and printing at U.S. prices, **Foto Rey,** Libertad 330, tel. (322) 209-37 (and a second branch a few blocks away, at Morelos 490) is one of the few in town that develops and prints black and whites. Open Mon.-Sat. 9 a.m.-9 p.m., Sunday 9 a.m.-3 p.m.

Right across the street, **Laboratorios Vallarta,** Libertad 335, tel. (322) 250-70, stocks the most cameras, accessories, and film of any Vallarta store: lots of Fuji and Kodak color negative (print) film in many speeds and sizes plus transparency, professional 120 rolls, and black and white. Open Mon.-Sat. 9 a.m.-9 p.m. If it doesn't have what you need, perhaps you'll find it at its second branch, around the corner at Morelos 101.

Cameras are an import item in Mexico and consequently very expensive. Even the simplest point-and-shoot cameras cost half again as much as in the U.S. or Canada. It's best to bring your own.

SERVICES

Money Exchange
Banking has come to the Olas Altas district, with the new branch of **Bancrecer,** on Av. Olas Altas, beach side, near B. Badillo. Hours are Mon.-Sat. 9 a.m.-5 p.m. and Saturday 10 a.m.-2 p.m. After hours, use the automated-teller machine.

Downtown, near the plaza, the **National Bank of Mexico** (Banamex), on Zaragoza, south side of the town plaza, tel. (322) 312-24, changes U.S. and Canadian cash and traveler's checks at the best rates in town. Money exchange hours (go to the special booth at 176 Zaragoza, left of the bank main entrance) are Mon.-Fri. 9 a.m.-5 p.m.

If the lines at Banamex are too long, try **Bancomer,** a block north at Juárez and Mina, tel. (322) 208-78, money exchange hours Mon.-Fri. 9 a.m.-3 p.m.; or **Banco Inverlat,** across the street, tel. (322) 224-45, hours Mon.-Fri. 9 a.m.-3 p.m. After hours, use the banks' ATMs.

Additionally, scores of little *casas de cambio* (exchange booths) dot the old town streets, especially along the *malecón* downtown, and along Av. Olas Altas and Insurgentes south of the Río Cuale. Although they generally offer about $2 per $100 less than the banks, they compensate with long hours, often 9 a.m.-9 p.m. daily. In the big hotels, cashiers will generally exchange your money at rates comparable to the downtown exchange booths.

The local **American Express** agency cashes American Express traveler's checks and offers full member travel services, such as personal-check cashing (up to $1,000, every 21 days; bring your checkbook, your ID or passport, and your American Express card). The office is downtown, at Morelos 160, corner of Abasolo, tel. (322) 276-65 or 329-31, fax 329-26, one block inland from the Hard Rock Café. Business hours are Mon.-Fri. 9 a.m.-6 p.m., Saturday 9 a.m.-1 p.m.

Post Office, Telephone, and Telegraph
Puerto Vallarta has a number of branch post offices. The main *correo* is downtown, two blocks north of the central plaza, just off of Juárez, at Mina 188, tel. (322) 218-88, open Mon.-Fri. 8 a.m.-7:30 p.m., Saturday 8 a.m.-noon. The branch at the Edificio Maritima ("Maritime Building"), near the cruise liner dock, is open Mon.-Fri. 8 a.m.-3 p.m., Saturday 9 a.m.-1 p.m., tel. (322) 472-19. The airport has lost its former post office branch; deposit cards and letters in the airport mailbox *buzón.*

Express mail, telegraph, fax, telex, and money orders *(giros)* are available at the **Mexpost** office, at 584 Juárez, four blocks north of the central plaza, fax (322) 313-60; open Mon.-Fri. 9 a.m.-5:30 p.m., Saturday 9 a.m.-1 p.m.

Nearly all Puerto Vallarta hotels have *larga distancia* telephone service. Lacking this (or if you don't like their extra charges), go to one of the many *casetas de larga distancia,* long-distance telephone offices, sprinkled all over town. For example, **Computel,** the efficient computer-assisted long-distance and public fax service, maintains a number of Puerto Vallarta offices: at Plaza Genovese, Km 2.5 airport highway, on the south side of Comercial Mexicana, tel. (322) 477-73 (open daily 8 a.m.-9 p.m.); and at the marina inner harbor, *puerto interior,* yacht basin, tel. (322) 455-61 (open daily 8 a.m.-9 p.m.)

A number of other offices provide *larga distancia* and public fax in the downtown area. Moving south to north: the Sendetel agency, tel. (322) 329-70, open daily 7 a.m.-10 p.m., at the Elite bus ticket station, corner Insurgentes and B. Badillo; on the north side of Plaza Lázaro Cárdenas, by the Hotel Eloisa, tel. (322) 308-50, fax 235-20; just north of the Río Cuale, at Juárez 136, below the bridge, half a block from the Hotel Encino (open Mon.-Fri. 9 a.m.-2 p.m. and 4-7 p.m., Saturday until 1:30 p.m.); or farther north by the *malecón* at Aldama 180, five blocks north of the central plaza, tel. (322) 301-99 (open Mon.-Sat. 9 a.m.-8 p.m.).

Immigration, Customs, and Consulates

If you need an extension to your tourist card, you can get a total of 180 days at the local branch of **Instituto Nacional de Migración** on the maritime terminal entrance road (cruise ship dock), at 2755 Altos, tel. (322) 477-19, next to the Pemex gas station, open Mon.-Fri. 8 a.m.-2 p.m. If you lose your tourist card (be prepared with a copy), first call the tourist information office, tel. (322) 202-43.

If you have to temporarily leave your car in Mexico, check with the tourist information office or **Aduana** ("Customs") at the airport, tel. (322) 116-59, Mon.-Fri. 8 a.m.- 3 p.m., for the proper procedure to follow.

The small local **United States Consular Office,** P.O. Box 395, Puerto Vallarta, Jalisco 48300, tel. (322) 200-69, fax 300-74, issues passports and does other essential legal work for U.S. citizens at Zaragoza 160, first floor, adjacent to the town plaza, south side, open Mon.-Fri. 10 a.m.-2 p.m.

The **Canadian honorary consul,** Lynn Benoit, tel. (322) 253-98, provides similar services for Canadian citizens Mon-Fri. 9 a.m.-5 p.m., at the same plaza-front address, second floor. In an emergency, after hours call the Canadian Embassy in Mexico City, toll-free at (800) 706-2900.

Arts and Music Courses

The private, volunteer **Centro Cultural Vallartense** periodically sponsors theater, modern dance, painting, sculpture, aerobics, martial arts, and other courses for adults and children. From time to time they stage exhibition openings for local artists, whose works they regularly exhibit at their gallery/information center at Plaza del Arte on Isla Río Cuale. For more information, look for announcements in the "Community Corner" of *Vallarta Today,* or drop by and talk to the volunteer in charge at the Plaza del Arte gallery and information center, at the upstream end of Isla Río Cuale.

Sharing the Plaza de Arte is the round **Escuela Municipal de Música** building, where, late weekday afternoons, you may hear the strains of students practicing the violin, guitar, piano, flute, and pre-Columbian instruments. Such lessons are open to the general public; apply in person during the late afternoons or early evening.

INFORMATION

Tourist Information Offices

Two tourist information offices serve Puerto Vallarta visitors. The downtown branch is on the central plaza, northeast corner (at Juárez), customarily open Mon.-Fri. 9 a.m.-6 p.m., Saturday 9 a.m.-1 p.m., tel. (322) 325-00, extensions 230-232, fax extension 233. The other tourist information office is in the marina shopping plaza (marked by the big McDonald's sign), about the same hours as the plaza branch, tel. (322) 126-46, fax 126-78. Both offices provide assistance and information, dispensing whatever maps, pamphlets, and copies of *Vallarta Today* and *Puerto Vallarta Lifestyles* they happen to have.

Another source of local information (in Spanish) is the Puerto Vallarta branch of the **Cámara Nacional de Comercio** (chamber of commerce), which publishes an excellent *Directorio Comercial Turístico,* a directory to everything you might be likely to need in Puerto Vallarta. Find the chamber at Morelia 138, 2nd floor, tel. (322) 427-08, one block off the *libramiento* downtown bypass boulevard, four blocks from the airport highway. Open Mon.-Fri. 9 a.m.-5 p.m., Saturday 9 a.m.-1 p.m.

Health, Police, and Emergencies

If you need medical advice, ask your hotel desk for assistance, or go to one of Puerto Vallarta's several good small hospital-clinics. One of the most respected is the **Hospital CMQ** (Centro Médico Quirúrgico) south of the Río Cuale at 366 Basilio Badillo, between Insurgentes and Aguacate, tel. (322) 319-19 (ground floor) or (322) 308-78 (second floor).

Right around the corner on Insurgentes, across from the gas station, is the bilingual-staffed **Hospital Medasist,** at M. M. Dieguez 358, tel. (322) 304-44, fax 233-01. The hospital, which advertises that it accepts "all worldwide medical insurance for emergencies," with emergency room, lab, diagnostic equipment, and a staff of specialists, appears to be another good place to go when you're sick.

On the north side, closer to the Hotel Zone, stands the equally well-respected 24-hour hospital clinic of **Servicios Médico de la Bahía,** Km 1 on the airport boulevard across from the Sheraton, tel. (322) 226-27.

If you are more comfortable with an English-speaking doctor, **IAMAT** has two U.S.-trained doctors in Puerto Vallarta. Contact António Sahagún Rodríguez, M.D., downtown, at Corona 234, tel. (322) 213-05, hours Mon.-Sat. 10 a.m.-1 p.m.; or Alfonso Rodríguez L., M.D., at the south-of-Cuale Hospital CMQ, Av. B. Badillo 365, tel. (322) 319-19, hours Mon.-Fri. 6-8 p.m.

For round-the-clock prescription service, call one of the five branches of **Farmacia CMQ;** for example, south of Cuale, at B. Badillo 367, tel. (322) 213-30, 219-40, or on the north side, at Peru 1146, tel. (322) 211-10.

A legion of loyal customers swear by the diagnostic competence of Federico López Casco, of **Farmacia Olas Altas,** Av. Olas Altas 365, two blocks south of Hotel Playa Los Arcos, tel. (322) 223-74, whom they simply know as "Freddy." Although a pharmacist and not a physician, his fans say he is a wizard at recommending remedies for their aches and pains.

For either **police** or **fire** emergencies, dial local emergency number 06.

Publications

New books in English are not particularly common in Puerto Vallarta. However, a number of small stores and stalls, such as the **newsstand** at 420 Olas Altas, beach side, across from Andale restaurant, and **Nuevo Librería Limón,** at 310 Carranza, between Vallarta and Constitución (open Mon.-Sat. 9 a.m.-2 p.m. and 4-8 p.m.), regularly sell newspapers, including Mexico City *News* and sometimes *USA Today* and the *Los Angeles Times.*

Supermercado Gutiérrez Rizo, corner Constitución and F. Madero, offers an excellent American magazine selection and some new paperback novels; open daily 6:30 a.m.-10 p.m. **Señor Book,** on upper Olas Altas, at Gómez, has perhaps the best English-language for-sale book collection in Puerto Vallarta.

Comercial Mexicana and shops at certain big hotels—Camino Real, Sheraton, Continental Plaza, Fiesta Americana, Melia, and Westin Regina—also stock U.S. newspapers, magazines, and paperbacks. Comercial Mexicana maintains two Puerto Vallarta branches, both in the north-side suburbs: at Plaza Marina, Km 6.5, Hwy. 200, tel. (322) 100-53, and at **Plaza Genovese,** Km 2.5, Hwy. 200, tel. (322) 466-44 or 456-55. Both are open daily 9 a.m.-9 p.m.

Vallarta Today, an unusually informative tourist daily, is handed out free at the airport, travel agencies, restaurants and hotels all over town. Besides detailed information on hotels, restaurants, and sports, they include a local events and meetings calendar and interesting historical, cultural, and personality feature articles. Call if you can't find a copy, tel. (322) 429-28, Mon.-Fri. 9 a.m.-8 p.m., at Mérida 118, Colonia Versalles.

Equally excellent is *Puerto Vallarta Lifestyles,* the quarterly English-language tourist magazine, which also features unusually detailed and accurate town maps. If you can't find a free copy at the airport or your hotel, contact the publisher at Calle Timon 1, in the marina, tel./fax (322) 101-06, Mon.-Fri. 9 a.m.-7 p.m.

The local **public library** (actually the "DIF" federally supported library) has a small general collection, including Spanish-language reference books and a dozen shelves of English-language paperbacks, at Parque Hidalgo, one block north of the end of the *malecón,* in front of the church. Open Mon.-Fri. 8 a.m.-8 p.m., Saturday 9 a.m.-5 p.m.

A second **public library,** established and operated by a volunteer committee, has accumulated a sizable English and Spanish book collection, at Francisco Villa 1001, in Colonia Los Mangos. Get there by taxi or car, several blocks along Villa, which diagonals northerly and inland at the sports field across the airport boulevard from the Hotel Sheraton. By bus, take the green and brown Pitillal- and Biblioteca-marked bus.

Women's Network
The Women's Network works for integration of mind, spirit, and ideas of women from different cultures and lifestyles. They also support charitable projects, such as the children's home, Casa Hogar. Look in the "Community Corner" of *Vallarta Today* for more information.

Volunteer Work
A number of local volunteer clubs and groups invite visitors to their meetings and activities. Check with the tourist information office or see the "Community Corner" listing in *Vallarta Today* for current meeting and activity details.

The **Club Internacional de la Amistad** (International Friendship Club), an all-volunteer service club, sponsors a number of health, educational, and cultural projects. They welcome visitors to their (usually second Monday) monthly general membership meeting. For more information, call Judy Galena, tel. (322) 309-78, see the "Community Corner" in *Vallarta Today,* or ask at the tourist information office. One of the best ways to find out about their work is on the popular tour of Puerto Vallarta homes, which begins at the central plaza, near the bandstand, Saturday and Thursday mornings (usually at 11) during the Nov.-April high season. They customarily ask a donation of about $20 per person to further their charitable programs.

The **Ecology Group of Vallarta,** a group of local citizens willing to work for a cleaner Puerto Vallarta, welcomes visitors to their activities and regular meetings. Call Ron Walker, tel. (322) 208-97, for more information.

Amigos de Animales rescues animals from the streets and beaches and finds them homes. Volunteers are needed; dog lovers call Barbara Sands at (322) 262-42, cat lovers, Jhoaranee Mongee at (322) 215-18, and for crocodiles, Ron Walker, at (322) 208-97.

GETTING THERE AND AWAY

By Air
Several major carriers connect Puerto Vallarta by direct flights with United States and Mexican destinations.

Mexicana Airlines flights connect daily with Los Angeles, Denver, Chicago, Mexico City, Mazatlán, Los Cabos, and Guadalajara. In Puerto Vallarta call (322) 112-66 or toll-free (800) 366-5400 for reservations and (322) 489-00 for airport flight information.

Aeroméxico flights connect daily with Los Angeles, San Diego, Tijuana, Guadalajara, Acapulco, León, Aguascalientes, and Mexico City; for reservations and flight information, call (322) 42-777.

Alaska Airlines flights connect with Los Angeles, San Francisco, Portland, Seattle, and Anchorage; for reservations, call a local travel agent or, from Puerto Vallarta, call the U.S. direct toll-free number, tel. (800) 426-0333.

American Airlines flights connect daily with Dallas-Ft. Worth; call (322) 117-99 or 119-27 or toll-free (800) 904-6000 local reservation and information number.

Trans World Airlines charter flights connect seasonally (Dec.-April) with St. Louis; locally, call toll-free (800) 238-1997 for information and reservations.

Continental Airlines flights connect daily with Houston; call (322) 110-96 for reservations.

America West Airlines connects with Phoenix; for reservations and information, call a travel agent, such as American Express, tel. (322) 329-10, 329-27, or 329-55.

Canadian World of Vacations charter flights connect with Toronto, Vancouver, and Calgary-Edmonton (mostly during the winter); for information, call the local agent at (322) 107-36 or a travel agent.

Puerto Vallarta Airport Arrival and Departure
Air arrival at Puerto Vallarta Airport (code-designated PVR, officially the Gustavo Díaz Ordaz International) is generally smooth and simple. After the cursory (if any) customs check, arrivees can avail themselves of: **money-exchange counters,** open daily 9 a.m.-8 p.m. (after hours, use the Banco Internacional automated-teller

machine); a lineup of **car rental booths,** including Budget, National, Avis, Dollar, Advantage, and Hertz.

Transportation to town is easiest by *colectivo* (collective taxi-vans) or *taxi especial* (individual taxi). Booths sell tickets at curbside. The *colectivo* fare runs about $3 per person to the northern hotel zone, $4 to the center of town, and $5 or more to hotels and hamlets south of town. Individual taxis run about $6, $8, and $15 for the same rides.

Taxis to more distant northern destinations, such as Rincón de Guayabitos (39 miles, 62 km) and San Blas or Tepic (100 miles, 160 km), run about $60 and $100, respectively. A much cheaper alternative is to ride one of the second-class **Transportes del Pacífico** green-and-white northbound buses. Wave them down across the highway outside the airport gate. They will deposit you at the new bus terminal north of the airport, where you can continue by very frequent northbound second-class bus. The Bucerías fare should run less than $1; Sayulita, $2; Guayabitos about $3; and Tepic or San Blas (for San Blas, go by Transportes Norte de Sonora or Transportes del Pacífico second class and transfer at Las Varas), $7. They are usually crowded; don't tempt people with a dangling open purse or a bulging wallet pocket.

Airport departure is as simple as arrival. Save by sharing a taxi with departing fellow hotel guests. Agree on the fare with the driver before you get in. If the driver seems too greedy (see airport arrival fares above) hail another taxi. Once at the airport, you can do last-minute shopping at a number of airport shops, or mail a letter at the airport *buzón* (mailbox).

If you've lost your tourist card, be prepared with a copy or pay a fine unless you've gotten a duplicate through the tourist information office. In any case, be sure to save enough pesos or dollars to pay your $12 **departure tax.**

By Car or RV

Three good road routes connect Puerto Vallarta north with Tepic and San Blas, east with Guadalajara, and south via Melaque-Barra de Navidad with Manzanillo. They are all two-lane roads, requiring plenty of caution.

To Tepic, **Mexican National Hwy. 200** is all asphalt and in good condition most of its 104 miles (167 km) from Puerto Vallarta. Traffic is ordinarily light to moderate, except for some slow going around Tepic, over a few low passes about 20 miles hour north of Puerto Vallarta, and a few miles just north of the airport. Allow three hours for the southbound trip and half an hour longer in the reverse direction for the winding 3,000-foot climb to Tepic.

A shortcut connects San Blas directly with Puerto Vallarta, avoiding the oft-congested uphill route through Tepic. Heading north on Hwy. 200, at Las Varas turn off west on to Nayarit Hwy. 161 to Zacualpan and Platanitos, where the road continues through the jungle to Santa Cruz de Miramar on the Bay of Matanchén. From there you can continue along the shoreline to San Blas. In the opposite direction, heading south from San Blas, follow the signed Puerto Vallarta turnoff to the right (south) a few hundred yards after the Santa Cruz de Miramar junction. Allow about three hours, either direction, for the entire San Blas-Puerto Vallarta trip.

The story is similar for Mexican National Hwy. 200 along the 172 miles (276 km) to Manzanillo via Barra de Navidad (134 miles, 214 km). Trucks and potholes may cause slow going while climbing the 2,400-foot Sierra Cuale summit south of Puerto Vallarta, but light traffic should prevail along the other stretches. Allow about four hours to Manzanillo, three from Barra de Navidad, and the same in the opposite direction.

The Guadalajara route is more complicated. From Puerto Vallarta, follow Hwy. 200 as if to Tepic, but, just before Compostela (80 miles, 129 kilometers from Puerto Vallarta) follow the 22-mile (36-kilometer) Guadalajara-bound toll *(cuota)* shortcut east, via Chapalilla. From Chapalilla, continue east via **Mexican National Hwy. 15** toll expressway *autopista*. Although expensive (about $20 per car, much more for motor homes) the expressway is a breeze, compared to the old, narrow and congested *libre* Hwy. 15. Allow around five hours for the entire 214-mile (344 km) Guadalajara-Puerto Vallarta trip, either way.

By Bus

Many bus lines run through Puerto Vallarta, and although some, such as Elite and Transportes Pacífico, still retain their small south-of-Cuale stations as ticket offices on or near Av. Insurgentes, the major long-distance bus action has shifted to the new *camionera central* (central bus station) a few miles north of the airport.

The shiny, new, air-conditioned station resembles an airline terminal, with a cafeteria, juice bars, a travel agency, a long-distance telephone and fax service, luggage storage lockers, a gift shop, and a hotel reservation booth.

Mostly first- and luxury-class departure ticket counters line one long wall. First-class **Elite** (EL) line and its parent **Estrella Blanca** (EB), with other affiliated lines Turistar (TUR), Futura (FU), Transportes Norte de Sonora (TNS), and Transportes Chihuahenses (TC), tel. (322) 108-48 and 108-50, connect the entire northwest-southeast Pacific Coast corridor. Northwesterly destinations include La Peñita (Rincón de Guayabitos), Tepic, San Blas, Mazatlán, all the way to Nogales or Mexicali and Tijuana on the U.S. border. Other departures head north, via Tepic, Durango, Torreón, and Chihuahua to Ciudad Juárez, at the U.S. border. Still others connect northeast, via Guadalajara, Aguascalientes, Zacatecas, Saltillo, with Monterrey. In the opposite direction, other departures connect with the entire southeast Pacific Coast, including Melaque, Manzanillo, Playa Azul, Lázaro Cárdenas, Ixtapa-Zihuatanejo, and Acapulco.

Transportes Pacífico (tel. 322-108-93) first-class departures also travel the northwest Pacific route, via Tepic and Mazatlán to Nogales, Mexicali and Tijuana. Transportes Pacífico has additional first-class connections, east with Guadalajara and Mexico City direct, and others via Guadalajara and Morelia with Mexico City.

Transportes Pacífico also provides second-class daytime connections every 30 minutes, north with Tepic, stopping everywhere, notably, Bucerías, Sayulita, Guayabitos, La Peñita, Las Varas, and Compostela en route.

Affiliated lines Autocamiones del Pacífico and Transportes Cihuatlán (tel. 322-100-21) provide many second-class and some first-class departures along the Jalisco coast. Frequent second-class connections stop at El Tuito, Boca de Tomatlán, El Super, Careyes, Melaque, Barra de Navidad and everywhere in between. They also connect with Guadalajara by the long southern route, via Melaque, Autlán, and San Clemente (a jumping-off point for Talpa and Mascota). Primera Plus, their luxury-class line, provides a few daily express connections southeast with Manzanillo, with stops at Melaque and Barra de Navidad.

A separate luxury-class service, called **Primera Plus**, tel. (322) 100-95, also provides express connections, southeast, with Melaque, Barra de Navidad, Manzanillo, and Colima. Other such Primera Plus departures connect east, with Guadalajara, continuing on to Aguascalientes, Irapuato, Celaya, Querétaro, and León. Affiliated line **Autobuses Costa Alegre** provides frequent second-class connections southeast along the Jalisco coast, via El Tuito, El Super, Careyes, Melaque, and Barra de Navidad and all points in between.

Additionally, ETN (Enlaces Transportes Nacional, tel. 322-104-50) first-class departures connect east with Guadalajara, with continuing connections with many Michoacán destinations.

AROUND THE BAY OF BANDERAS

As a tourist city, Puerto Vallarta is packed with all the services, food, and accommodations a quality resort can supply. What Puerto Vallarta often cannot offer, however, is peace and quiet.

But an out exists. The diadem of rustic retreats—fishing villages, palm-shadowed sandy beaches, diminutive resorts—ringing the Bay of Banderas can provide a day-, week-, or month-long respite from the citified tourist rush.

The Southern Arc—Mismaloya
The southern-arc beach gems of Mismaloya, Boca de Tomatlán, Las Animas, Quimixto, and

Yelapa are described in the Puerto Vallarta section under Sights.

**The Northern Arc—Nuevo Vallarta,
Bucerías, and Punta Mita**
The northern curve of the Bay of Banderas begins as Hwy. 200 crosses the Ameca River and enters the state of Nayarit. Here clocks shift from central to mountain time; heading north, set your watch back one hour. Just after you cross over the bridge, you might want to stop at the **Nayarit tourist information office,** tel./fax (329) 700-18, which regularly supplies several excel-

lent brochures of Nayarit's interesting, but mostly untouristed, destinations.

NUEVO VALLARTA

The Nuevo Vallarta development, just north of the river, is Nayarit's design for a grand resort, comparable to the Zona Hotelera 10 miles south. For years, however, miles of boulevard parkways dotted with streetlights and empty cul-de-sacs remained deserted, waiting for homes, condos, and hotels that were never built. A spurt of activity in the early '90s seemed to promise the potential of Nuevo Vallarta might someday be realized. The **Club de Playa Nuevo Vallarta,** the core of the original development, is indeed a pretty place—perfect for a relaxing beach afternoon. Get there by turning left at Av. Nuevo Vallarta about five miles (eight km) north of the airport at the Jack Tar Village sign (one mile past the north end of the Ameca bridge). At the end of the 1.4-mile driveway entrance you will come to the Club de Playa, with

a parking lot, small regional art and artifacts museum, pool, snack bar, and seemingly endless beach.

The miles-long beach is the main attraction. The nearly level golden white sand is perfect for beachcombing, and the water is excellent for surf fishing, swimming, bodysurfing, and boogie boarding. Beginning or intermediate surfing might be possible for those who bring their own board. Enjoy isolated beach camping during the temperate winter on the endless dune past the north end beach boulevard of Paseo Cocoteros. Bring everything, including water and a tarp for shade.

Accommodations

Adjacent to the Club de Playa is the palmy, Mediterranean-style, French-Canadian-owned **Club Oasis Marival,** which often invites the public to drop in on its continuous party, which includes sports, crafts, games, and food and drink for about $40 per person, per day. If you take a room, the all-inclusive food, lodging, and activities run about $130 per day for two, low season, $200 high. Reservations are available through an agent or at the hotel, Blvd. Nuevo Vallarta, esq. Paseo Cocoteros, Nuevo Vallarta, Nayarit 63573, tel. (329) 701-00, fax 701-60, in Mexico, call toll-free (800) 326-66.

About three miles south of the Club Oasis Marival a cluster of big new hotels woo vacationers with a plethora of facilities and long, velvety beaches. The 344-room **Hotel Sierra Nuevo Vallarta** seems to be the most successful, located at Paseo de Cocoteros 19, Nuevo Vallarta, Nayarit 63732, tel. (329) 713-00, fax 708-00, or Bel Air Hotels U.S. and Canada toll-free tel. (800) 457-7676, e-mail: info@mtmcorp.com. Arriving at the hotel feels like approaching a small, Elysian planet. You drive for miles past uninhabited verdure-lined boulevards, finally pulling up to a huge, apparently deserted structure, where inside, to your surprise, droves of relaxed, well-fed tourists are socializing in half a dozen languages. Above the reception area rises a towering, angular atrium. Nearby, a garden of lovely ceramic fruits decorates white-washed stairsteps leading downstairs. There, a buffet loaded with salads, fruit, poultry, fish, meats, and desserts is spread on one side of an airy, guest-filled dining area. Outside are pools beneath palm trees along the beach, where crowds enjoy nightly dancing and shows. By day, guests lounge, swim, and frolic amid a varied menu of activities, from water aerobics and yoga to beach volleyball, bicycling, and kayaking.

Rates include all food, drinks, activities, and a deluxe ocean-view room with everything. They begin at about $100 s, $145 d low season, about $170 and $225 high. Children under seven stay free; there's a tariff of $25 for those 7-12, and children over 12 are considered adults. If the season is right, a travel agent may be able to secure a reduced-rate package.

Next door the **Allegro Resort,** Paseo de los Cocoteros 18, Nuevo Vallarta, Nayarit 63732, tel. (329) 704-00, fax 706-26, offers a similar all-inclusive vacation package for about $85 s, $150 d low season, $125 and $200 high. Children under seven free, 8-12 half price. Bargain packages may be available during nonpeak seasons; call a travel agent.

BUCERÍAS

The scruffy roadside clutter of Bucerías ("Place of the Divers") is deceiving. Located 12 miles (19 km) north of the Puerto Vallarta airport, Bucerías (pop. 5,000) has the longest, creamiest beach on the Bay of Banderas. Local people flock there on Sunday for beach play, as well as fresh seafood from one of several *palapa* restaurants. (Which, however, may be mostly closed weekdays.)

Bucerías offers a number of options. It is basically a country town of four long streets running for three miles parallel to the beach. The town features small businesses and grocery stores and a sprinkling of local-style restaurants. Bucerías furthermore has lots of old-fashioned local color, especially in the evenings around the lively market at the south end of the business district.

The beach—seemingly endless and nearly flat, with slowly breaking waves and soft, golden-white sand—offers swimming, bodysurfing, boogie boarding, beginning and intermediate surfing, and surf fishing. Tent camping is customary beyond the edges of town, especially during the Christmas and Easter holidays.

at Bucerías on the
Bay of Banderas

Accommodations

At the town's serene north end is the Playas de Huanacaxtle subdivision, with big flower-decorated homes owned by rich Mexicans and North Americans. Sprinkled among the intimate, palm-shaded *retornos* (cul-de-sacs) are a number of good bungalow-style beachside lodgings. Moving southward from the north edge of town, the top accommodations begin with the **Condo-Hotel Vista Vallarta,** Av. de los Picos s/n, Playas de Huanacaxtle, Bucerías, Nayarit 63732, tel. (329) 803-61, fax 803-60 (9 a.m.-7 p.m. only). Here, three stories of stucco and tile apartments cluster intimately around a palm-tufted beachside pool patio. A loyal cadre of longtime guests—mostly U.S. and Canadian retiree-couples—return year after year to enjoy the big blue pool, the *palapa* restaurant, walks along the beach, and the company of fellow vacationers. All enjoy fully furnished two-bedroom suites with dining room, kitchenette, living room, and private ocean-view balconies. Maids clean rooms daily, while downstairs, friendly, English-speaking clerks manage the desk and rent cars, boogie boards, and surf-boards. High-season rates, for up to six persons per suite, run $46/night, $37/night weekly, $33/night monthly; corresponding low season rates (when the place is nearly empty) run $28, $22, and $20.

A block south, the family-style **Bungalows Princess** looks out on the blue Bay of Banderas beneath the rustling fronds of lazy coco-palms. The two-story, detached beachfront bungalows provide all the ingredients for a restful vacation for a family or group of friends. Behind the bungalows, past the swimming pools a stone's throw from the beach, a motel-style lineup of suites fills the economy needs of couples and small families. Reserve in writing or by phone at Retorno Destiladeras, Playas Huanacaxtle, Bucerías, Nayarit 63732, tel. (329) 801-00 or 801-10, fax 800-68. There is a total of 36 bungalows and suites. The big bungalows (ask for a beachfront unit) rent, high season, for about $55 d; off-beach suites, about $45 d. Bargain for discounts and long-term rates, especially during low Jan.-Feb., May-June, and Sept.-Nov. months. All rooms feature TV with HBO, phone, a/c; mini-market, two pools, credit cards accepted.

Continuing south, nearby **Bungalows Pico,** Av. Los Pico and Retorno Pontoque, Playas Huanacaxtle, Bucerías, Nayarit 63732, tel. (329) 804-70, fax 801-31, shares the same palm-shadowed Bucerías beachfront. A rambling, Mexican family-style complex, Bungalows Pico clusters around a big inner pool patio, spreading to a second motel-style bungalow tier beside a breezy beachside pool area. These units, which enjoy ocean views, are the most popular. During low season, the management offers such promotions as three nights for the price of two; discounts for long-term rentals are usually available. Bargain under all conditions. The beachfront, three-bedroom kitchenette bungalows for up to eight run about $87; two-bedroom poolside kitchenette apartments for six, $70. Adjacent smaller, four-person kitchenette suites, $53. Smaller nonkitchenette studios go for about $25. Corresponding low season rates run about $58, $47, $35 and $18. With TV, a/c, snack restaurant, and two pools; credit cards accepted.

Sharing the same beachside a block farther south is **Suites Atlas,** a Spanish-style tile and stucco villa built around a luxurious beachfront pool patio and garden. Located on Retorno Destiladeras, Bucerías, Nayarit 63732, tel. (329) 802-35, fax 800-65, its 11 units rent, high season, for around $72/day, low about $55; a special $1,200/month rate is sometimes available during the low seasons. All rooms are spacious and deluxe, sleeping about six, with fully equipped kitchenettes, all with a/c. Try for one of the choice upstairs front units, which offer private balconies and ocean vistas.

About a mile away, on the opposite, or south, side of town, right across the street from the Bucerías trailer park (see below), is **Bungalows Arroyo,** one of Bucerías's best-buy lodgings at 500 Lázaro Cárdenas, Bucerías, Nayarit 63732, tel. (329) 802-88, fax 800-76. The dozen or so roomy, two-bedroom apartments are clustered beside a verdant, palmy pool and garden half a block from the beach. The units are comfortably furnished, each with king-size bed, private balcony, kitchen, and living and dining room. The friendly, conscientious managers live nearby, at no. 83, half a block south, along the street away from the beach, behind the bungalows. Units rent for about $50 a day, with discounts available for monthly rentals. They're popular; get your winter reservations in months early.

Bucerías Trailer Park

Across the street from Bungalows Arroyo, in a flowery, palm-shaded beachside garden, is **Bucerías Trailer Park,** P.O. Box 148, Bucerías, Nayarit 63732, tel. (329) 802-65, fax 803-00. The property was once owned by Elizabeth Taylor; the present owners, Mayo and Fred, have converted the luxurious living room of the former residence into a homey restaurant and social room, which they call Pira-pa. The 48 spaces rent for about $18/day or $400/month, add $1 a day for a/c power. With all hookups, showers, toilets, pool, nearby boat ramp, and good drinkable well water. Get your winter reservations in early.

Rental Agent

If you can't locate your ideal Bucerías vacation retreat by yourself, try the friendly, reputable and English-speaking real estate team of Carlos and Mina González, who rent a number of deluxe Bucerías beachfront homes and vacation apartments. Drop by their office on the highway, beach side, a few blocks south of town, call (329) 802-65, fax 803-00, or write them at González Real Estate, Héroes de Nacozari 128, Bucerías, Nayarit 63732.

Pie in the Sky

Even if only passing through Bucerías, don't miss Pie in the Sky, the little bakery of entrepreneurs Don and Teri Murray, who've developed a thriving business soothing the collective sweet tooth of Puerto Vallarta's expatriate and retiree colony. Their chocolate-nut cookies have to be tasted to be believed. Watch for their sign on the inland side of the highway just south of town; open Mon.-Fri. 9 a.m.-5 p.m.

PUNTA MITA COUNTRY

A few miles north of Bucerías, you might slow down at the intersection where the Punta Mita Hwy. forks west from Hwy. 200 and stop for information and brochures at the Punta Mita **Nayarit tourist information office.**

Drivers, mark your mileage at the Hwy. 200 turnoff before you head west along the Punta Mita highway. Within a mile (two km), look downhill and you'll see the little drowsy town of **Cruz de Huanacaxtle** above a small fishing harbor. Although the town has stores, a good café, a few simple lodgings, and a protected boat and yacht anchorage, it lacks a decent beach.

Playa Manzanillo

Half a mile (at around Mile 2, Km 3) farther on, a side road to the left leads to beautiful Playa Manzanillo and the **Hotel and Trailer Park Piedra Blanca.** The beach itself, a carpet of fine, golden-white coral sand, stretches along a little cove sheltered by a limestone headland—thus Piedra Blanca, "White Stone." This place was made for peaceful vacationing: snorkeling at nearby **Playa Piedra Blanca** on the opposite side of the headland; fishing from the beach, rocks, or by boat launched on the beach or hired in the Cruz de Huanacaxtle harbor; camping in RV or tent in the trailer park or adjacent open field.

The hotel is a small, friendly, family-managed resort. The best of the big comfortable suites offer upstairs ocean views. All the ingredients— a good tennis court, a shelf of used novels, and a rustic *palapa* restaurant beside an inviting beach-view pool patio—perfectly combine for tranquil relaxation. The 31 suites with kitchenettes and a/c rent from $40 d in the low season ($240 weekly, $700 monthly) to $60 in the high season; credit cards not accepted. Reserve by writing directly to P.O. Box 48, Bucerías, Nayarit 63732, calling the Guadalajara agent at (3) 617-6051 faxing (3) 617-6047, or leaving a message with the long-distance telephone operator in Cruz de Huanacaxtle, tel. (329) 807-53.

The hotel also manages the trailer park in the beachside but largely unshaded lot next door. Although trailer park residents aren't supposed to use the pool, hotel management doesn't seem to mind. This is a popular winter park, so make reservations early. The 26 spaces with all hookups rent for about $12/day, $80/week, $280/month. Showers, toilets, pets okay.

Past Piedra Blanca, the highway winds for 12 miles (19 km) to Punta Mita through the bushy green jungle country at the foot of the Sierra Vallejo, empty except for a few scattered ran-chos. Side roads draw adventurous travelers to hidden beaches for a day—or a week—of tranquil swimming, snorkeling, and beachcombing. You might want to get out and walk before your vehicle bogs down on these side roads. Campers should bring everything, including plenty of drinking water. If in doubt about anything, don't hesitate to inquire locally, or ask Primitivo Navarro in the information office back at Hwy. 200.

Rock coral, the limestone skeleton of living coral, becomes gradually more common on these beaches, thus tinting the water aqua and the sand white. As the highway approaches Punta Mita the living reef offshore becomes intact and continuous.

Playa Destiladeras

A pair of oceanside *palapa* restaurants (at Mile 5, Km 8) mark Playa Destiladeras, a beach-lover's heavenly mile of white sand. Two- to five-foot waves roll in gently, providing good conditions for bodysurfing and boogie boarding. Surfing gets better the closer you get to the end of **Punta el Burro**'s (known also as Punta Veneros) headland, where good left-breaking waves make it popular with local surfers.

The intriguing label *destiladeras* (seepage) originates with the freshwater dripping from the cliffs past Punta el Burro, collecting in freshwater pools right beside the ocean. Campers who happen upon one of these pools may find their water problems solved.

sea cucumbers out to dry at Corral de Riscos, near Punta Mita at the northwest tip of the Bay of Banderas

Los Veneros Beach Club and Rancho Banderas

About a mile past Playa Destiladeras, you'll see the Los Veneros Beach Club entrance. A fee of $8 per person gets you a beach towel and entitles you to enjoy the attractive facilities, which include pools, a beach-view snack bar, and changing rooms. The half-mile-long white coral sand beach, although with waves usually too tranquil for surfing, will most likely be fine for wading, swimming, and boogie boarding. In addition, the resort rents horses and mountain bikes and furnishes guides for beach excursions or along their "archaeological" trail through the nearby tropical deciduous forest.

If you decide to stay overnight, the neighboring Rancho Banderas can put you up in a deluxe suite for perhaps $50 overnight, with bargaining. For more information and reservations, call the Puerto Vallarta office, tel. (322) 203-05.

Playa Pontoque and Restaurant Amapas

The Restaurante Paraíso Escondido sign (Mile 8, Km 13) marks the downhill, vine-draped forest road to Playa Pontoque, an intimate jungle-backed crescent of coral-white sand. Here, the living reef lies offshore, ripe for snorkeling and fishing for red snapper and *toro*. Surfing, boogie boarding, and bodysurfing are possible when snorkeling isn't.

The (seasonally open) restaurant specializes in seafood and steaks, catering to tourist tastes. Relatively few locals come here—the owner says they prefer a continuous shoreline to Pontoque's scenic, outcrop-dotted sand and offshore reef. The people who do come seem to have a great time, strolling, swimming, snorkeling, and tidepooling. Acacia boughs overhang the sand, forming shady nooks perfect for lazing away the day and night. If you want to camp, ask the restaurant owner if it's okay. Bring water; the restaurant has none to spare.

For a treat, stop in at the friendly, family-run **Restaurant Amapas,** across the highway from the Paraíso Escondido road turnoff. Homesteaded when the Punta Mita road was a mere path through the jungle, Restaurant Amapas still retains a country flavor. Ducks waddle around the yard, javelina (wild pigs) snort in their pen, and candles flicker during the evening twilight as the elderly owner recalls her now-deceased husband hunting food for the table: "We ate deer, javelin, ducks, coatimundi, rattlesnake, iguana . . . whatever we could catch." Although local hunters now provide most of the food, she and her daughter-in-law do all the cooking, and their many loyal customers still enjoy the same wild fare. The restaurant is open 9 a.m. to sunset every day.

Trouble at Punta Mita

In the early 1990s, the Mexican government concluded a deal with private interests to build the Four Seasons resort development at Corral de Riscos, at the end of the Punta Mita highway. The idyllic Corral de Riscos inlet, however, was *ejido* (communally owned) land and base of operations for the local fishing and boating cooperative, Cooperativa Corral de Riscos. In 1995 the government moved the people, under protest, into modern housing beside a new anchorage at nearby Playa Anclote.

Although the *ejido* people seem to have grudgingly accepted their new housing and harbor, the road now (hopefully temporarily) ends at Playa Anclote. A private driveway continues to the super-exclusive 18-hole golf course and 100-room Four Seasons Hotel, slated to open August 1999.

Playa Anclote

Head left, downhill, at road's end (Mile 13, Km 21) toward Playa Anclote ("Anchor Beach"), which gets its name from the galleon anchor displayed at one of the beachside *palapa* restaurants. The beach itself is a broad, half-mile-long curving strand of soft, very fine, coral sand. The water is shallow for a long distance out, and the waves are gentle and long-breaking, good for beginning surfing, boogie boarding, and bodysurfing.

A few hundred yards downhill from the highway, at the road "T" before the beach, stands the **Caseta Cooperativa Corral de Riscos Servicios Turísticos,** where friendly Jesús "Chuy" Casilla welcomes tourists daily 9 a.m.-6 p.m. He rents boogie boards, snorkel gear, and surfboards for about $5 per day. Chuy also arranges sportfishing launches (three-hour trip, about $65 complete) and snorkeling, wildlife viewing, and photography boat tours to the pristine offshore wildlife sanctuaries of Islas Marietas. During a typical half-day trip, visitors may glimpse dolphins, sea turtles, and sometimes whales, as well as visit breeding grounds for brown and blue-footed boobies, Heerman's gulls, and other birds.

When he's not working, Chuy follows his love of surfing, which he also teaches. He claims the best surfing in the Bay of Banderas is on the left-breaks off Isla del Mono, off the lighthouse point about a half mile to the west.

Half a block farther west from Chuy's place, you'll find one of Playa Anclote's best seafood restaurants, **El Dorado,** tel. (329) 465-56, open daily 11 a.m. to sunset, run by friendly Hector López. His menu is based on meat, poultry, and the bounty of super-fresh snapper, scallops, oysters, and lobsters that local fisherfolk bring onto the beach.

If you decide to stay, the basic Hotel Punta Mita in the small town of Emiliano Zapata a quarter mile away (commonly known as Punta Mita) can put you up. Don't expect anything but the essentials, however. Reservations are rarely, if ever, necessary.

If you can afford luxury, reserve a room at the **Four Seasons Hotel.** Their airy, exquisitely appointed view rooms run about $350 low season, $425 high, including all the usual resort amenities and activities. For reservations in the U.S. and Canada, call (800) 332-3442, or contact the hotel locally at tel. (329) 160-00, fax (329) 162-07.

Tent camping and RV parking is possible where not prohibited by the government because of local construction. Ask at the Playa Anclote restaurants if it's okay to camp under big trees at either end of the beach. Stores nearby and on the highway in Emiliano Zapata (commonly known as Punta Mita) a quarter-mile away can furnish the necessities, including drinking water.

Corral de Riscos

When the road opens again, visitors will have access to Corral de Riscos, an islet-enfolded aqua lagoon bordered by a long coral-sand beach. Hopefully, kids will again play in gentle waves, and their parents and grandparents will once more be able to relax at beachside seafood restaurants.

Two small bare-rock islands, **Isla del Mono** and **Isla de las Abandonadas,** shelter the scenic lagoon. The name of the former comes from a *mono* (monkey) face people see in one of the outcroppings; the latter label springs from the legend of the fishermen who went out to sea and never returned. Las Abandonadas were their wives, who waited on the islet for years, vainly searching the horizon for their lost husbands.

Getting to Nuevo Vallarta, Bucerías, and Punta Mita

Second-class **Transportes Pacífico** buses, Insurgentes 282, tel. (322) 108-93, leave the Puerto Vallarta central bus station for Tepic via Nuevo Vallarta (highway only) and Bucerías about every half hour. Small local Transportes Pacífico minibuses complete the Punta Mita roundtrip several times daily; the last bus returns from Playa Anclote at around 5:30 p.m.

Autotransportes Medina buses also complete several daily roundtrips between Playa Anclote (Restaurant El Dorado terminal) and their Puerto Vallarta station north of the *malecón.* Stops en route include Bucerías, Cruz de Huanacaxtle, Piedra Blanca, and Destiladeras. The Puerto Vallarta station, tel. (322) 269-43, is at 1279 Brasil, corner of Honduras, one block south of the Buenaventura Hotel and three blocks from the beach.

THE COAST OF JALISCO
THE ROAD TO BARRA DE NAVIDAD

The country between Puerto Vallarta and Barra de Navidad is a landscape ripe for travelers who enjoy getting away from the tourist track. Development has barely begun to penetrate its vast tracts of mountainous jungle, tangled thorny scrub, and pine-clad summit forests. Footprints rarely mark miles of its curving, golden beaches.

Fortunately, everyone who travels south of Puerto Vallarta doesn't have to be a Daniel Boone. The coastal strip within a few miles of the highway has acquired some comforts—stores, trailer parks, campgrounds, hotels, and a scattering of small resorts—enough to become well known to Guadalajara people as the Costa Alegre, the "Happy Coast."

This modicum of amenities makes it easy for all visitors to enjoy what local people have for years: plenty of sun, fresh seafood, clear blue water, and sandy beaches, some of which stretch for miles, while others are tucked away in little rocky coves like pearls in an oyster.

Heading Out

If you're driving, note your odometer mileage (or reset it to zero) as you pass the Pemex gas station at Km 214 on Hwy. 200 at the south edge of Puerto Vallarta. In the open southern country, mileage and roadside kilometer markers are a useful way to remember where your little paradise is hidden.

If you're not driving, simply hop onto one of the many southbound Autocamiones del Pacífico or Transportes Cihuatlán second-class buses just before they pass at the south-end gas station or, alternatively, at their bus terminal, corner Constitución and Madero. Let the driver know a few minutes beforehand where along the road you want to get off.

CHICO'S PARADISE

The last outpost on the Puerto Vallarta tour-bus circuit is Chico's Paradise, 13 miles (22 km, at

Km 192) from the south edge of Puerto Vallarta in the lush jungle country. Here, the clear, cool Río Tuito cascades over a collection of smooth, friendly granite boulders. Chico's restaurant is a big multilevel *palapa* that overlooks the entire beautiful scene—deep green pools for swimming, flat warm rocks for sunning, and gurgling gentle waterfalls for splashing. Although a few homesteads and a humbler rival restaurant, Orchidea Paradise (see below), dot the streamside nearby, the original Chico's still dominates, although its reputation rests mainly on the beauty of the setting rather than the quality of the rather expensive menu.

Orchidea Paradise offers a similarly airy and scenic *palapa* setting upstream from Chico's, at more reasonable prices. Its good soups, salads, and seafood and meat entrées go for $4-8. After refreshment, stroll across the wooden bridge to the rustic view gazebo perched above the beautiful scene.

The forest-perfumed breezes, the gurgling, crystal stream, and the friendly, relaxed ambience are perfect for shedding the cares of the world. Although there are no formal lodgings, a number of potential camping spots border the river, both up- and downstream. Stores at Boca de Tomatlán, three miles downhill, can provide supplies.

Adventurers can hire local guides (ask at Orchidea Paradise) for horseback rides along the river and overnight treks into the green, jungly

Sierra Lagunillas that rises on both sides of the river. If you're quiet and aware, you may be rewarded with views of chattering parrots, dozing iguanas, feisty javelinas (wild pigs), clownish *tejones* (coatimundis), and wary *gatos montaña* (wildcats). If you're especially lucky, you might even get a glimpse of the fabled *tigre* (jaguar).

CABO CORRIENTES COUNTRY

El Tuito

The town of El Tuito, at Km 170 (27 miles, 44 km, from Puerto Vallarta), appears from the highway as nothing more than a bus stop. It doesn't even have a gas station. Most visitors pass by without even giving a second glance. This is a pity, because El Tuito (pop. 5,000) is a friendly little place that spreads along a long main street to a pretty square about a mile from the highway.

El Tuito enjoys at least two claims to fame: besides being the mescal capital of western Jalisco, it's the jumping-off spot for the seldom-visited coastal hinterland of Cabo Corrientes, the southernmost lip of the Bay of Banderas. This is pioneer country, a land of wild beaches and forests, unpenetrated by electricity, phone, and paved roads. Wild creatures still abound: turtles come ashore to lay their eggs, hawks soar, parrots swarm, and the faraway scream of the jaguar can yet be heard in the night.

Flat, friendly rocks decorate the clear River Tuito, which flows beneath the palapa at Chico's Paradise.

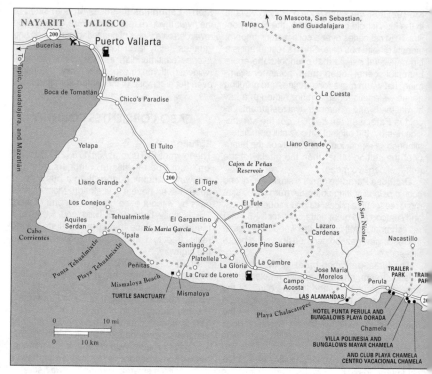

The rush for the **raicilla,** as local connoisseurs call El Tuito mescal, begins on Saturday when men crowd into town and begin upending bottles around noon, without even bothering to sit down. For a given individual, this cannot last too long, so the fallen are continually replaced by fresh arrivals all weekend.

Although El Tuito is famous for the *raicilla,* it is not the source. *Raicilla* comes from the sweet sap of the maguey plants, a close relative of the cactuslike century plant, which blooms once then dies. An *ejido* (cooperative farm) of Cicatan, six miles out along the dirt road as you head to the coast west of town, cultivates the maguey.

Along the Road to Aquiles Serdán

You can get to the coast with or without your own wheels. If you're driving, it should be a strong, high-clearance vehicle (pickup, jeep, very

maneuverable RV, or VW van) filled with gas; if you're not driving, trucks and VW taxi-vans (combis or *colectivos*) make daily trips. Their destinations include the coastal hamlet of Aquiles Serdán, the storied fishing cove of Tehualmixtle, and the agricultural village of Ipala beside the wide Bahía de Tehualmixtle. Fare runs a few dollars per person; inquire at the Hwy. 200 crossing or the west end of the El Tuito central plaza.

Getting there along the bumpy, rutted, sometimes steep 28-mile (45-km) dirt track is half the fun of Aquiles Serdán (pop. 200). About six miles (10 km) from Hwy. 200, you'll pass through the lands of the mescal cooperative, Cicatan, marked only by a whitewash-and-thatch *bodega* (storage house) in front of a tiny school on the right. On the left, you'll soon glimpse a field of maguey in the distance. A few dozen families (who live in the hills past the far side of the field) quietly go

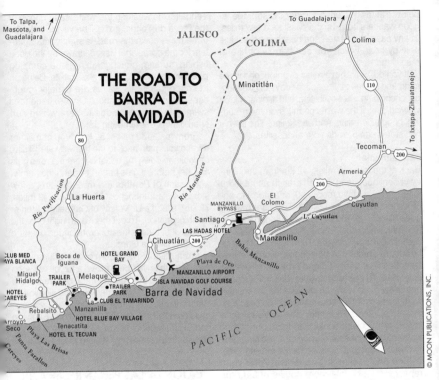

about their business of tending their maguey plants and extracting, fermenting, and distilling the precious sap into their renowned *raicilla*.

The road dips up and down the rest of the way, over sylvan hillsides dotted with oak *(robles),* through intimate stream valleys perfect for parking an RV or setting up a tent, and past the hardscrabble rancho-hamlets of Llano Grande ("Broad Plain," 15 miles, 24 km from the highway, where there's a small store) and Los Conejos ("The Rabbits," 21 miles, 34 km).

You can't get lost, because there's only one route until a few miles past Los Conejos, where a fork (26 miles, 42 km) marks your approach to Aquiles Serdán. The left branch continues south to Maito and Tehualmixtle. A mile and a half to the north along the right branch you will arrive at the Río Tecolotlán. Aquiles Serdán stands on the far bank, across 100 yards of watery sand.

Fortunately the riverbed road is concrete-bottomed, allowing you to drive right across the streambed any time other than after a storm.

Aquiles Serdán

The Aquiles Serdán villagers see so few outsiders you will become their attraction of the week. Wave and say *hola,* buy a *refresco,* stroll around town, and, after a while, the kids will stop crowding around and the adults will stop staring when they've found out you, too, are human. By that time, someone may even have invited you into their tree-branch-walled, clean dirt-floor house for some hot fish-fillet tacos, fresh tomatoes, and beans. Accept, of course.

Aquiles Serdán basks above the lily-edged river lagoon, which during the June-Oct. rainy season usually breaks through the beach-sandbar and drains directly into the surf half a mile below the town. During the dry season, the lagoon wanders lazily up the coast for a few miles. In any case, the white-sand beach is accessible only by boat, which you can borrow or hire at the village.

If you do, you'll have miles of untouched white sand and surf all to yourself for days of camping, beachcombing, shell collecting, surf fishing, wildlife viewing, and, if the waves permit, swimming, surfing, boogie boarding, and snorkeling. The town's two stores can provide your necessities.

Tehualmixtle

Back at the fork (26 miles, 42 km from the highway) continue along the left branch about three miles through Maito (pop. 100, one store) to another fork (29 miles, 47 km). The right branch goes steeply up and then down a rough track to the right, which soon levels out on the cliff above the idyllic fishing cove of Tehualmixtle. Here, a headland shelters a blue nook, where a few launches float, tethered and protected from the open sea. To one side, swells wash over a submerged wreck, while an ancient, moss-stained warehouse crumbles above a rocky little beach. At the end of the road downhill, a beachside *palapa* invites visitors with drinks and fresh-out-of-the-water oysters, lobster, *dorado,* and red snapper.

Owner/operator Candelario is the moving force behind this pocket-size paradise. After your repast, and a couple more bottles of beer for good measure, he might tell you his version of the history of this coast—of legends of sunken galleons, or of the days when the old warehouse stored cocaine for legal shipment to the United States, when Coca-Cola got its name from the cocaine, which, generations ago, was added to produce "the pause that refreshes."

Nowadays, however, Tehualmixtle serves as a resting point for occasional sailboaters, travelers, fisherfolk, and those who enjoy the rewards of clear-water snorkeling and scuba diving around the sunken shrimp trawler and the rocky shoreline nearby. Several level spots beside the cove invite camping or RV parking. Candelario will gladly supply you with your stomach's delight of choice seafood and drinks.

Southeast of Tehualmixtle

Returning back up the road above the cove, glimpse southward toward the azure Bay of Tehualmixtle washing the white-sand ribbon of the Playa de Tehualmixtle. The village of **Ipala,** three miles down the road, is supply headquarters for the occasional visitors drawn by the good fishing, surfing, beachcombing, and camping prospects of the Playa de Tehualmixtle. Being on the open ocean, its waves are usually rough, especially in the afternoon. Only experienced swimmers who can judge undertow and surf should think of swimming here.

From Ipala (32 miles, 52 km), you can either retrace your path back to the highway at El Tuito, or continue down the coast (where the road gets rougher before it gets better) through the hamlet and beach of **Peñitas** (39 miles, 63 km, a few stores, restaurants), past **Mismaloya** (49 miles, 79 km), site of a University of Guadalajara turtle-hatching station. To get there, turn right onto the dirt trail just before the concrete bridge over the broad Río María Garcia.

From Mismaloya, return to the bridge, continue over the river three miles, and you will soon be back to the 20th century at **Cruz de Loreto** (52 miles, 84 km), with many stores, sidewalks, electric lights, and phones. From there, you can head directly to Hwy. 200 (10 miles via Santiago and El Gargantino) at Km 131, just 24 miles (39 km) south of where you started at El Tuito.

CAJON DE LAS PEÑAS RESERVOIR

The lush farms of the Cabo Corrientes region owe much of their success to the Cajón de las Peñas dam, whose waters enable farmers to profit from a year-round growing season. An added bonus is the recreation—boating, fishing, swimming, camping, hiking—which the big blue lake behind the dam makes possible.

With a car, the reservoir is easy to reach. Trucks and cars are frequent, so hikers can easily thumb rides. At Hwy. 200 Km 130, about a mile south of the Cruz de Loreto turnoff, head left (east) at a signed, paved road. After about five miles the road turns to gravel. Continue another four miles to a road fork atop the pair of rock-fill dams, separated by a hill. The left road continues over the smaller of the two dams, where a right fork leads to **El Solitario,** a humble family-run restaurant *palapa* and boat landing. The friendly husband-wife team of Marcos Almanzar and

Eva Olivera maintains their little outpost in hopes of serving the trickle of mostly holiday and weekend visitors. Besides their children, who help with chores, their little settlement consists of two parrots, a brood of turkeys, and a flock of chickens that fly into the nearby forest to roost at night. Eva's cooking, based mostly upon freshly caught *lobina* (largemouth bass), is basic but wholesome. The parking lot above the lake has room for a number of self-contained RVs, while the forested knoll nearby might serve for tent camping. Marcos offers his boat for lake sightseeing and fishing excursions for about $12 an hour. Otherwise, you could swim, kayak, or launch your own motorboat right from the lakeshore below the restaurant.

Head back over the second, larger dam, continuing counterclockwise around the forested, sloping lakeshore. Within three kilometers you'll arrive at the boat-cooperative village, where several downscale *palapa* restaurants and boat landings provide food and recreational services for visitors. For a fee (offer to pay), they usually let you set up a tent or park your RV under a nearby lakeside tree.

PLAYA CHALACATEPEC

Playa Chalacatepec (chah-lah-kah-tay-PEK) lazes in the tropical sun just nine and a half kilometers from the highway at Km 88. Remarkably few people know of its charms except a handful of local youths, a few fisherfolk, and occasional families who come on Sunday outings.

Playa Chalacatepec, with three distinct parts, has something for everyone: on the south side, a wild, arrow-straight, miles-long strand with crashing open-ocean breakers; in the middle, a low, wave-tossed, rocky point; and on the north, a long, tranquil, curving fine-sand beach.

The north beach, shielded by the point, has gently rolling breakers good for surfing, bodysurfing, and safe swimming. Shells seasonally carpet its gradual white slope, and visitors have even left a pair of *palapa* shelters. These seem ready-made for camping by night and barbecuing fish by day with all of the driftwood lying around for the taking.

The point, Punta Chalacatepec, which separates the two beaches, is good for pole fishing on its surf-washed flanks and tidepooling in its rocky crevices.

Folks with RVs can pull off and park either along the approach road just above the beach or along tracks (beware of soft spots) downhill in the tall acacia scrub that borders the sand.

One of the few natural amenities that Playa Chalacatepec lacks is water, however. Bring your own from the town back on the highway.

Getting There

Just as you're entering little José María Morelos (pop. 2,000), a hundred feet past the Km 88 marker turn toward the beach at the corner with the auto-parts store *(refaccionaria)* and grocery Abarrotes Jerez, with a big yellow Bardahl sign. Besides oil and batteries, the store customarily sells a few snack-groceries. Better-stocked stores in the town nearby sell water and more substantial supplies.

The road, although steep in spots, is negotiable by passenger cars in good condition and small-to-medium RVs. Owners of big rigs should do a test run. On foot, the road is an easy two-hour hike—much of which probably won't be necessary because of the many passing farm pickups.

Mark your odometer at the highway. Continue over brushy hills and past fields and pastures, until Mile 5.2 (Km 8.4), where the road forks sharply right. You take the left track and pass a gate (close it after yourself). Atop the dune, glimpse the mangrove lagoon (bring kayak or rubber boat for wildlife-watching) in the distance to the left. Downhill, at Mile 6 (Km 9.7), you will be at Playa Chalacatepec.

LAS ALAMANDAS

After roughing it at Playa Chalacatepec, you can be pampered in the luxurious isolation of Las Alamandas, a deluxe 1,500-acre retreat a few miles down the road.

The small sign at Km 83 gives no hint of the pleasant surprises that Las Alamandas conceals behind its guarded gate. Solitude and simplicity seem to have been the driving concepts in the mind of Isabel Goldsmith when she acquired control of the property in the late 1980s. Although born into wealth (her grandfather was the late tin tycoon Antenor Patiño, who developed Manzanillo's renowned Las Hadas; her father, the late multimillionaire Sir James Goldsmith, bought the small kingdom her family now owns at Cuitzmala, 25 miles south), she was not idle. Isabel converted her dream of paradise—a small, luxuriously isolated resort on an idyllic beach in Puerto Vallarta's sylvan coastal hinterland—into reality. Now, her guests (22 maximum) enjoy accommodations that range from luxuriously simple rooms to entire villas that sleep six. Activities include a health club, tennis, horseback riding, bicycling, fishing, and lagoon and river excursions.

Daily room rates run from $250 to $600 d; entire villas cost $620-2,000, all with full breakfast. Three meals, prepared to your order, cost about $100 additional per day per person. For more information and reservations, call U.S. tel. (800) 223-6510, Canada tel. (800) 424-5500, or contact Las Alamandas in Mexico directly, at Quémaro, Km 83 Carretera Puerto Vallarta-Barra de Navidad, Jalisco 48854, tel. (328) 555-00, fax 550-27. Don't arrive unannounced; the guard will not let you through the gate unless you either have reservation in hand or have made a prior appointment.

CHAMELA BAY

Most longtime visitors know Jalisco's Costa Alegre through Barra de Navidad and two big, beautiful, beach-lined bays: Tenacatita and Chamela. Tranquil Bahía de Chamela, the most northerly of the two, is broad, blue, dotted with islands, and lined with a strip of fine, honey-yellow sand.

Stretching five miles south from the sheltering Punta Rivas headland near Perula village, Chamela Bay is open but calm. A chain of intriguingly labeled rocky *islitas,* such as Cocinas ("Kitchens"), Negrita ("Little Black One"), and Pajarera ("Place of Birds"), scatter the strong Pacific swells into gentle billows by the time they roll onto the beaches.

Besides its natural amenities, Chamela Bay has three bungalow complexes, one mentionable motel, two trailer parks, and an unusual "camping club." The focal point of this low-key resort area is the Km 72 highway corner (88 miles, 142 km from Puerto Vallarta; 46 miles, 74 km

to Barra de Navidad). This spot, marked Chamela on many maps, is known simply as **"El Super"** by local people. Though the supermarket and neighboring bank have closed and are filled with the owner's antique car collection, El Super, nevertheless, lives on in the minds of the local folks.

Beaches and Activities

Chamela Bay's beaches are variations on one continuous strip of sand, from Playa Rosadas in the south through Playa Chamela in the middle to Playas Fortuna and Perula at the north end.

Curving behind the sheltering headland, **Playa Perula** is the broadest and most tranquil beach of Chamela Bay. It is best for children and a snap for boat launching, swimming, and fishing from the rocks nearby. A dozen *pangas* usually line the water's edge, ready to take visitors on fishing excursions (figure $15 per hour, with bargaining) and snorkeling around the offshore islets. A line of seafood *palapas* provides the food and drinks for the fisherfolk and mostly Mexican families who know and enjoy this scenic little village/cove.

Playas Fortuna, Chamela, and Rosadas: Heading south, the beach gradually changes character. The surf roughens, the slope steepens, and the sand narrows from around 200 feet at Perula to perhaps 100 feet at the south end of the bay. Civilization also thins out. The dusty village of stores, small eateries, vacation homes, and beachfront *palapa* restaurants that line Playa Fortuna give way to farmland and scattered houses at Playa Chamela. Two miles farther on, grassy dunes above trackless sand line Playa Rosada.

The gradually varying vigor of the waves and the isolation of the beach determine the place where you can indulge your own favorite pastimes: For bodysurfing and boogie boarding, Rosada and Chamela are best, and while windsurfing is usually possible anywhere on Chamela Bay it will be best beyond the tranquil waves at La Fortuna. For surf fishing, try casting beyond the vigorous, breaking billows of Rosada. And likewise Rosada, being the most isolated, will be the place where you'll most likely find that shell-collection treasure you've been wishing for.

The five-mile curving strand of Chamela Bay is perfect for a morning hike from Rosada Beach.

Accommodations are often available (drop in only) to the public at Centro Vacacional Chamela, the Chamela Bay teachers' resort.

To get there, ride a Transportes Cihuatlán second-class bus to around the Km 65 marker, where a dirt road heads a half mile to the beach. With the sun comfortably at your back, you can walk all the way to Perula if you want, stopping for refreshments at any one of several *palapas* along the way.

The firm sand of Chamela Bay beaches is likewise good for jogging, even for bicycling, provided you don't mind cleaning the sand out of the gears afterwards.

El Super Accommodations

Three accommodations serve travelers near the El Super corner: an emergency-only motel on the highway, some bungalows, and a "camping club." The owners of the "camping club," **Villa Polinesia,** who live in Guadalajara, don't call it a campground because, curiously, in the past their policy has been, instead of allowing campers use their own tents, to rent out their stuffy, concrete, tent-shaped constructions. Unfortunately these have fallen out of repair and are unusable, so they may have to let people put up their own tents after all. It's worth asking them about it, for Villa Polinesia would be a beautiful tenting spot, where the beach and bay set the mood: soft, golden sand, island-silhouetted sunsets, tranquil surf, and abundant birds and fish. Sometimes whales and dolphins, and occasionally great manta rays, leap from the water offshore.

Even without your own tent you can still enjoy staying outdoors by renting one of Villa Poline-sia's several recently renovated open-air ocean-front Swiss Family Robinson-style cabañas, each with cooking-eating area and toilet and shower downstairs, and a pair of thatch-roofed bedrooms with soft, floor sleeping pads upstairs. In addition, you could rent one of the 15 shady spaces in their **trailer park** with all hookups, right next to the communal showers and toilet. Moreover, the lovely, palm-shadowed complex has two tall, elaborate *palapa* restaurant/bars, a minimarket, drinkable water, hot water, communal showers, toilets, and a laundry.

A minor drawback to all this, besides there being no pool, is the somewhat steep rates: the open-air cabañas go for the same price as a moderate hotel room: about $25 for four, $20 for one or two; the trailer spaces go for about $10 per day or $250 per month. Tenting, if they allow it, will probably go for about $5 a day. These prices, however, are subject to bargaining and discounts any time other than peak holidays. For reservations and more information contact the owners: Km 72, Carretera 200, Barra de Navidad a Puerto Vallarta, Chamela, Jalisco, tel. (328) 552-47.

Right across the lane from Villa Polinesia stands the once lovely, now a bit neglected, **Bungalows Mayar Chamela,** Km 72, Carretera Puerto Vallarta, Chamela, Jalisco, tel. (328) 552-52. The 18 spacious kitchenette-bungalows with fans (no a/c) surround a palmy, banana-fringed pool and patio. Although the blue meandering pool and palmy grounds are very inviting, the bungalows themselves are suffering from neglect. Look inside three or four and make sure that everything is in working order before moving in. Given the bungalows' lovely Chamela beach setting, perhaps the owner will soon see the light and restore the interiors. If you're passing through, it might be worthwhile to take a look and see. Rentals run $20 d, $35 for four; monthly discounts are available. For reservations, write or fax the owner, Gabriel Yañez G., at Obregón 1425 S.L., Guadalajara, Jalisco, tel. (3) 644-0044, fax 643-9318.

Note: The summer-fall season is pretty empty on the Chamela Bay beaches. Consequently, food is scarce around Villa Polinesia and Bungalows Mayar Chamela. Meals, however, are available at the restaurant at the El Super corner, and you can buy a few groceries at small stores nearby or in San Mateo a mile south.

Perula Hotels and Trailer Parks

At Km 76, a sign marks a dirt road to Playas Fortuna and Perula. About two miles downhill, right on the beach, you can't miss the bright yellow stucco **Hotel, Bungalows and Trailer Park Playa Dorada,** Perula, Km 76, Carretera 200 Melaque-Puerto Vallarta, Jalisco 48854, tel. (328) 551-32, fax 551-33. More a motel than bungalows, its three tiers of very plain rooms and suites with kitchenettes are nearly empty except on weekends and Mexican holidays.

Playa Dorada's two saving graces, however, are the beach, which curves gracefully to the scenic little fishing nook of Perula, and the motel's inviting palm-shaded pool patio. The best-located rooms are on the top floor, overlooking the ocean. They rent 18 plain rooms sleeping two or three for about $19; 18 kitchenette units sleeping four go for about $36, all with parking. Although they routinely offer a 20% discount for weekly rentals, you might be able to bargain for an even better deal any time other than peak holidays.

Folks who take one of their dozen trailer spaces in the bare lot across the street are welcome to lounge all day beneath the palms of their pool patio. Spaces rent for about $8, with all hookups, and with luxurious, brand-new showers and toilets. Add about $1.50/day for a/c power.

It's easy to miss the low-profile **Hotel Punta Perula,** just one block inland from the Bungalows

Playa Dorada, at Perula, Km 76 Carretera 200, Melaque-Puerto Vallarta, Jalisco 48854, tel. (328) 550-20. This homey place seems like a scene from Old Mexico, with a rustic white stucco tier of rooms enclosing a spacious green garden and venerable tufted grove. The 14 clean, gracefully decorated, colonial-style, fan-equipped rooms go for about $15 d, except for Christmas and Easter holidays. Bargain for lower, long-term rates. No pool.

A few blocks north of the Hotel Playa Dorada is the downscale **Punta Perula Trailer Park,** Perula, Km 76, Carretera 200, Puerto Vallarta, Jalisco 48854. The spare facilities include about 16 usable but shadeless spaces right on the beach, with all hookups, a fish-cleaning sink, and showers and toilets. Playa Perula Trailer Park residents enjoy stores nearby, good fishing, and a lovely beach for a front yard. Rates are low, but indefinite—although one of the residents said he was paying a monthly rate that amounted to about $6 a day.

Centro Vacacional Chamela and Club Playa Chamela

Four miles south of El Super, at Rosada Beach, sharing the same luscious Chamela Bay strand, is the **Centro Vacacional Chamela,** a teachers' vacation retreat that rents its unoccupied units to the general public. The building is a modern, two-story apartment house with a well-maintained pool and patio. An outdoor *palapa* stands by the pool and another open room invites cards and conversation. The units themselves are large, bright, and airy one-bedrooms, sleeping four, with sea views and kitchen. They rent for about $30, drop-in only. Call (328) 552-24 (or arrive) in the morning early, or late afternoon, when "Chuy," the manager, is usually around to check things before going home for the night. On nonholiday weekdays the place is often nearly empty. Have a look by following the upper of two side roads at the big 47 sign near the Km 66 marker. Within a few hundred yards you'll be there. Ask one of the teachers to explain the significance of the 47.

If the teachers' retreat is full, try next door at the **Club Playa Chamela,** perhaps the most downscale time share in Mexico, if not the world. The manager said that, for a one-time fee of about $1,000, you can get one idyllic week for each of 20 years there. In the meantime, while the units are being sold, the owner is renting them out. All 12 of the pink and blue bare bulb cottages have two bedrooms, a kitchenette, and small living room. Although plainly furnished, they're reasonably clean and have ceiling fans and hot water. Outside, beyond a small forest of young palms, is a blue pool, a *palapa* sometimes-restaurant, and a long, pristine, sunset-view beach. The asking rate is about $23/day, $230/week, or $650/month. Try bargaining for a better price anytime other than the popular Christmas, Easter, and August seasons. Contact owner Jose A. Santana Soto at Venezuela 719 (Colonia Moderna), Guadalajara, tel. (3) 610-1103 or 610-3147, for information and reservations.

Camping

For RVs, the best spots are the trailer parks at **Villa Polinesia,** the **Hotel Bungalows and Trailer Park Playa Dorada,** and **Perula Trailer Park** (see preceding).

If you can walk in, you can probably set up a tent anywhere along the bay you like. One of the best places would be the grassy dune along pristine Playa Rosada a few hundred yards north of the Centro Vacacional Chamela (Km 66; see above). Water is available from the manager (offer to pay) at the Centro Vacacional.

Playa Negrito, the pristine little sand crescent that marks the southern end of Chamela Bay, offers still another picnic or camping possibility. Get there by following the dirt road angling downhill from the highway at the south end of the bridge between Km 63 and Km 64. Turn left at the Chamela village stores beneath the bridge, continue about two miles, bearing left to the end of the road, where the *palapa* of an old restaurant stands at beachside. This is the southernmost of two islet-protected coves flanking the low Punta Negro headland. With clear, tranquil waters and golden-sand beaches, both coves are great for fishing from the rocks, snorkeling, windsurfing, and swimming. The south-end beach is unoccupied and has plenty of room for tenting and RV parking; a house sits back from the north-end beach about a quarter-mile away on the far side of the point. If you want to camp around there, ask them if it's okay: *"¿Es bueno acampar acá?"*

Food

Groceries are available at stores near the **El Super** corner (Km 72) or in the villages of **Perula** (on the beach, turn off at Km 76), **San Mateo** (Km 70), and **Chamela** (follow the side road at the south end of the bridge between Km 64 and 63).

Hearty country Mexican food, hospitality, and snack groceries are available at the **Tejaban** truck stop/restaurant at the El Super corner; open daily from breakfast time until 10-11 p.m. Two popular local roadside seafood spots are **La Viuda** ("The Widow," Km 64) and **Don Lupe Mariscos** (Km 63) on opposite ends of the Río Chamela bridge. They both have their own divers who go out daily for fresh fish ($5), octopus *(pulpo)* ($5), conch, clams, oysters, and lobster ($8). Open daily 8 a.m. until around 9 p.m.

Services, Information, and Emergencies

The closest **bank** is 34 miles north at Tomatlán (turnoff at La Cumbre, at Km 116). *Casetas de larga distancia* operate at the Tejeban restaurant at El Super corner, daily 8 a.m.-9 p.m., and at Pueblo Careyes, the village behind the soccer field at Km 52.

Until someone re-opens the **Pemex** *gasolinera* at El Super, the closest Magna Sin gas is 27 miles north at La Cumbre (Km 116) and 50 miles (80 km) south at Melaque (Km 0).

If you get sick, the closest health clinic is in Perula (Km 76, one block north of the town plaza, no phone, but a pharmacy) or at Pueblo Careyes at Km 52 (medical consultations daily 8 a.m.-2 p.m.; doctor on call around the clock in emergencies).

Local special **police,** known as the Policia Auxiliar del Estado, are stationed in a pink roadside house at Km 46, and also in the house above the road at Km 43. The local *preventiva* (municipal police) are at the El Super corner.

HOTEL CAREYES

The Hotel Careyes, one of the little-known gems of Pacific Mexico, is really two hotels in one. After Christmas and before Easter it brims with well-to-do Mexican families letting their hair down. The rest of the year the hotel is a tranquil, tropical retreat basking at the edge of a pristine, craggy cove.

SAVING TURTLES

Sea turtles were once common on Pacific Mexico beaches. Times have changed, however. Now a determined corps of volunteers literally camps out on isolated beaches, trying to save the turtles from extinction. This is a tricky business, because their poacher opponents are invariably poor, determined, and often armed. Since turtle tracks lead right to the eggs, the trick is to get there before the poachers. The turtle-savers dig up the eggs and hatch them themselves, or bury them in secret locations where the eggs hopefully will hatch unmolested. The reward—the sight of hundreds of new hatchlings returning to the sea—is worth the pain for this new generation of Mexican eco-activists.

Once featured on a thousand restaurant menus from Puerto Ángel to Mazatlán, turtle meat, soup, and eggs are now illegal commodities. Though not extinct, Pacific Mexico's three main sea turtle species—green, hawksbill, and leatherback—have dwindled to a tiny fraction of their previous numbers.

The **green turtle** *(Chelonia mydas),* known locally as *tortuga verde* or *caguama,* is named for the color of its fat. Although officially threatened, the prolific green turtle remains relatively numerous. Females can return to shore up to eight times during the year, depositing 500 eggs in a single season. When not mating or migrating, the vegetarian greens can be spotted most often in lagoons and bays, especially the Bay of Banderas, nipping at seaweed with their beaks. Adults, usually three or four feet long and weighing 100-200 pounds, are easily identified out of water by the four big plates on either side of their shells. Green turtle meat was once prized as the main ingredient of turtle soup.

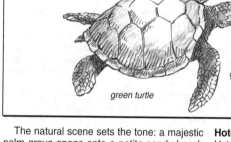

green turtle

The natural scene sets the tone: a majestic palm grove opens onto a petite sandy beach set between rocky cliffs. Offshore, the water, deep and crystal clear, is home for dozens of kinds of fish. Overhead, hawks and frigate birds soar, pelicans dive, and boobies and terns skim the waves. At night nearby, turtles carry out their ancient ritual by silently depositing their precious eggs on nearby beaches where they were born.

As if not to be outdone by nature, the hotel itself is an elegant, tropical retreat. A platoon of gardeners manicure lush spreading grounds that lead to gate and reception. Past the desk, tiers of ochre-hued Mediterranean lodgings enfold an elegant inner courtyard where a blue pool meanders beneath majestic, rustling palms. At night, the grounds glimmer softly with lamps. They illuminate the tufted grove, light the path to a secluded beach, and lead the way up through the cactus-sprinkled hillside thorn forest to a romantic restaurant high above the bay.

Hotel Activities

Hotel guests enjoy a plethora of sports facilities, including tennis courts, riding stables, and a polo field. Aquatic activities include snorkeling, scuba diving, kayaking, sailing, and deep-sea fishing. Boats are additionally available for picnic-excursions to nearby hidden beaches, wildlife-viewing, and observing turtle nesting in season. A luxury spa with view pampers guests with massage, facials, sauna, jacuzzi, and exercise machines. Evenings, live music brightens the cocktail and dinner hours at the elegant beach-view restaurant/bar.

The hotel was named for *carey* (kah-RAY), the native word for an endangered species of sea turtle that used to lay eggs on the little beach of Careyitos that fronts the hotel. Saving the turtles at nearby Playa Teopa, accessible only through hotel property, has now become a major hotel mission. Guards do, however, allow access to serious outside visitors during hatching times; follow the dirt road between Km 49 and

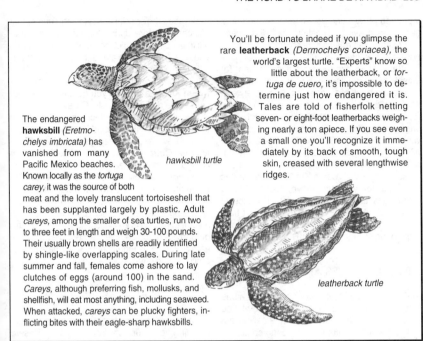

The endangered **hawksbill** (*Eretmochelys imbricata*) has vanished from many Pacific Mexico beaches. Known locally as the *tortuga carey,* it was the source of both meat and the lovely translucent tortoiseshell that has been supplanted largely by plastic. Adult *careys,* among the smaller of sea turtles, run two to three feet in length and weigh 30-100 pounds. Their usually brown shells are readily identified by shingle-like overlapping scales. During late summer and fall, females come ashore to lay clutches of eggs (around 100) in the sand. *Careys,* although preferring fish, mollusks, and shellfish, will eat most anything, including seaweed. When attacked, *careys* can be plucky fighters, inflicting bites with their eagle-sharp hawksbills.

hawksbill turtle

You'll be fortunate indeed if you glimpse the rare **leatherback** (*Dermochelys coriacea*), the world's largest turtle. "Experts" know so little about the leatherback, or *tortuga de cuero,* it's impossible to determine just how endangered it is. Tales are told of fisherfolk netting seven- or eight-foot leatherbacks weighing nearly a ton apiece. If you see even a small one you'll recognize it immediately by its back of smooth, tough skin, creased with several lengthwise ridges.

leatherback turtle

50 to gate and beach; no camping, please. Check with the hotel desk for information and permission.

Hotel Information
For reservations and more information, contact the hotel directly, at (335) 100-00, fax 101-00, or through its North American booking agents, at (800) 525-4800 or (800) 457-7676, e-mail: info@mtmcorp.com. Rooms, standard, superior, and deluxe, run about $150, $180, and $220 low season double, and $200, $250, and $300 high; ocean-view suites run $300 low season and $400 high; all accommodations have a/c, TV, and direct-dial phones. Additional hotel facilities and services include fiber-optic telecommunications, a children's activity center, 100-person meeting room, several shops and boutiques, library, movie theater, babysitters, heliport, private landing strip, boutiques, shops, and many business services.

Getting There
The Hotel Careyes is a few minutes' drive down a cobbled entrance road (bear left all the way) at Km 53.5 (100 miles, 161 km, from Puerto Vallarta; 34 miles, 55 km from Barra de Navidad; and 52 miles, 84 km from the Manzanillo International Airport).

CLUB MED PLAYA BLANCA

The Club Med Playa Blanca basks at the opposite corner of the same little bay as the Hotel Careyes. The Club Med's youngish (mostly 20-40, kids under 12 not allowed) guests enjoy an extensive sports menu, including trampoline, scuba, snorkel, a climbing wall, kayaking, racquetball and volleyball, sailing, and more. Action centers around Playa Blanca, the resort's luxuriously intimate little sand crescent, tucked beneath cactus-decorated tropical headlands. Above the beach, a verdant, tufted grove shades a platoon of reclining vacationers. From there, garden walkways lead past the pool, disco, bars, and restaurants to a hillside colony of 320 luxurious a/c view cabañas.

All meals, drinks, and activities (except for outside tours and deep-sea fishing) are included in a single package price. Rates run between $120 and $250 per day, depending upon season (open approximately November through April only) and promotions. For information and reservations call locally (335) 100-01, 100-02, or 100-03, fax 100-04, or from the U.S. and Canada, call (800) CLUBMED (258-2633).

Get there via the same Km 53.5 side road as the Hotel Careyes (see above). Bear right and follow signs about a mile to the gate. For security reasons, Club Med Playa Blanca doesn't take kindly to outsiders. If you simply want to look around, be sure to arrive with an appointment.

PLAYA CAREYES AND CUITZMALA

At Km 52, just south of a small bridge and a bus stop, a dirt road leads to the lovely honey-tinted crescent of Playa Careyes. Here, a car-accessible track (be careful for soft spots) continues along the dune, where you could enjoy a day or week of beach camping. Beyond the often powerful waves (swim with caution), the intimate, headland-framed bay brims with outdoor possibilities. Birdwatching and wildlife viewing can be quite rewarding; notice the herons, egrets, and cormorants in the lagoon just south of the dune. Fishing is good either from the beach, by boat (launch from the sheltered north end), or from the rocks on either side. Water is generally clear for snorkeling and, beyond the waves, good for either kayaking or windsurfing. If you have no boat, no problem, for the local fishing cooperative (boats beached by the food *palapa* at north end) would be happy to take you on a fishing trip. Figure about $15 per hour, with bargaining. Afterwards, they might even cook up the catch for a big afternoon dinner at their tree-shaded *palapa*. Nearby Pueblo Careyes (behind the soccer field at Km 52) has a store, a **Centro de Salud** (health center), and *larga distancia*.

Access to the neighboring **Playa Teopa** is, by contrast, carefully guarded. The worthy reason is to save the hatchlings of the remaining *carey* turtles (see the special topic Saving Turtles) that still come ashore during the late summer and fall to lay eggs. For a closer look at Playa Teopa, you could walk south along the dune-top track, although guards might eventually stop you. They will let you through (entry gate on dirt road between Km 49 and 50) if you get official permission at the desk of the Hotel Careyes.

The pristine tropical deciduous woodlands that stretch for miles around Km 45 are no accident. They are preserved as part of the **Fideicomiso Cuitzmala** ("Cuitzmala Trust"), the local kingdom of beach, headland, and forest held by the family of late billionaire Sir James Goldsmith. Local officials, many of whom were not privy to Sir James's grand design (which includes a sprawling sea-view mansion complex), say that a team of biologists is conducting research on the property. A ranch complex, accessible through a gate at Km 45, is Fideicomiso Cuitzmala's most obvious highway-visible landmark.

PLAYA LAS BRISAS

For a tranquil day, overnight, or weeklong beach camping adventure consider Playa las Brisas, a few miles by the dirt road (turnoff sign near Km 36) through the village of Arroyo Seco.

About two miles long, Playa las Brisas has two distinct sections: first comes a very broad, white sandy strand decorated by pink-blossomed verbena and pounded by wild, open-ocean waves. For shady tenting or RV parking, a regal coconut grove lines the beach. Before you set up, however, you should offer a little rent to the owner/caretaker, who may soon show up on a horse. Don't be alarmed by his machete; it's for husking and cutting fallen coconuts.

To see the other half of Playa las Brisas, continue along the road past the little beachside vacation home subdivision (with a seasonal store and snack bar). You will soon reach an open-ocean beach and headland, backed by a big, level, grassy dune, perfect for tent or RV camping. Take care not to get stuck in soft spots, however.

The headland borders the El Tecuán Lagoon, part of the Rancho El Tecuán, whose hilltop hotel you can see on the far side of the lagoon. The lagoon is an unusually rich fish and wildlife habitat.

Getting There

You reach the village of Arroyo Seco, where stores can furnish supplies, 2.3 miles (3.7 km) from the highway at Km 36. At the central plaza, turn left, then immediately right at the Conasupo rural store, then left again, heading up the steep dirt road. In the valley on the other side, bear right at the fork at the mango grove, and within another mile you will be in the majestic beach-bordering palm grove.

HOTEL EL TECUÁN

Note: At this writing, Hotel El Tecuán was being renovated and is slated to open by late 1999. By the time you arrive to take a look, hopefully the new managers will have restored it to the former condition as described in an earlier edition of this book:

Little was spared in perching the Hotel El Tecuán above its small kingdom of beach, lagoon, and palm-brushed rangeland. It was to be the centerpiece of a sprawling vacationland, with marina, golf course, and hundreds of houses and condos. Although those plans have yet to materialize, the hotel stands with an ambience more like an African safari lodge than a Mexican beach resort.

Masculinity bulges out of its architecture. Its corridors are lined with massive, polished tree trunks, fixed by brawny master joints to thick, hand-hewn mahogany beams. The view restaurant is patterned after the midships of a Manila Galleon, complete with a pair of varnished tree-trunk masts reaching into inky darkness of the night sky above. If the restaurant could only sway, the illusion would be complete.

The 36 rooms are comfortable and continue the masculine theme. The best have private balconies, which, in addition to a luxurious ocean vista, overlook the hotel's elegantly manicured grounds and blue pool and *palapa* patio a hundred feet below.

Hotel Activities

It is perhaps fortunate the hotel and its surroundings, part of the big **Rancho Tecuán,** may never be developed into a residential community. Being private, public access has always been limited, so the Rancho has become a de facto

habitat-refuge for the rapidly diminishing local animal population. Wildcats, ocelots, small crocodiles, snakes, and turtles hunt in the mangroves edging the lagoon and the tangled forest that climbs the surrounding hills. The lagoon itself nurtures hosts of waterbirds and shoals of *robalo* (snook) and *pargo* (snapper).

Guests can easily enjoy the hotel's fishing and wildlife-viewing opportunities, first by simply walking down to the lagoon, where big white herons and egrets perch and preen in the mangroves. Don't forget your binoculars, sun hat, mosquito repellent, telephoto camera, and identification book. Launch your own boat, canoe, or inflatable raft for an even more rewarding outing.

Hotel El Tecuán offers plenty of jogging and walking opportunities. For starters, stroll along the lagoonside entrance road and back (three miles, 4.8 km) or south along the beach to the Río Purificación and back (four miles, 6.4 km). Take water, mosquito repellent, sunscreen, a hat, and something to carry your beachcombing treasures in. If the tide is right, there are plenty of fish in the river, so you might want to take your fishing rod, too.

Besides swimming in the pool or the lagoon, you can enjoy the hotel's tennis (bring your own racquet and balls) and volleyball courts. If you bring a bicycle you can ride it along miles of beach, lagoon, and ranch roads.

Tecuán Beach

The focal point of the long, wild, white-sand Playa Tecuán is to the north, where, at low tide, the lagoon's waters stream into the sea. Platoons of waterbirds—giant brown herons, snowy egrets, and squads of pelicans, ibises, and grebes—stalk and dive for fish trapped in the shallow, rushing current.

On the beach nearby, the sand curves southward beneath a rocky point, where the waves strew rainbow carpets of limpet, clam, and snail shells. There the billows rise sharply, angling shoreward, often with good intermediate and advanced surfing breaks. Casual swimmers beware; the surf is much too powerful for safety.

Getting There

The Hotel El Tecuán is six miles (10 km) along a paved entrance road marked by a white lighthouse at Km 33 (112 miles, 181 km, from Puerto Vallarta; 22 miles, 35 km, from Barra de Navidad; and 40 miles, 64 km, from the Manzanillo International Airport).

Former rates ran around $60 d, which included a/c, restaurant, bar, and long-distance telephone; low-season discounts were available and credit cards were accepted.

PLAYA TENACATITA

Imagine an ideal tropical paradise: free camping on a long curve of clean white sand, right next to a lovely little coral-bottomed cove, with all the beer you can drink and all the fresh seafood you can eat. That describes Tenacatita, a place that old Mexican Pacific hands refer to with a sigh: Tenacatitaaahhh . . .

Folks usually begin to arrive sometime in November; by Christmas, some years, there's only room for walk-ins. Which anyone who can walk can do: carry in your tent and set it up in one of the many RV-inaccessible spots.

Tenacatita visitors enjoy three distinct beaches: the main one, Playa Tenacatita; the little one, Playa Mora; and Playa la Boca, a breezy, palm-bordered sand ribbon stretching just over three kilometers north to the *boca* (mouth) of the Río Purificación.

Playa Tenacatita's strand of fine white sand curves from the north end of Punta Tenacatita along a long, tall packed dune to **Punta Hermanos,** a total of about two miles. The dune is where most visitors—nearly all Americans and Canadians—park their RVs. The water is clear with gentle waves, fine for swimming and windsurfing. Being so calm, it's easy to launch a boat for fishing—common catches are *huachinango* (red snapper) and *cabrilla* (sea bass)—especially at the very calm north end.

The sheltered north cove is where a village of *palapas* has grown to service the winter camping population. One of the veteran establishments is **El Puercillo,** run by longtimer José Bautista. He and several other neighbors take groups out in his launches ($60 total per half day, complete, bring your own beer) for offshore fishing trips and excursions.

Trouble at Tenacatita

Tenacatita may be headed for changes, however. The federal government has made a deal with private interests to develop a hotel at Tenacatita. The trouble began when the 50-odd squatter-operators of the Tenacatita *palapas* refused to leave. One night in November 1991, after giving the squatters plenty of warning, federal soldiers and police burned and smashed the *palapas.* Nevertheless, the squatters, backed by the Rebalsito *ejido,* the traditional owner of Tenacatita, have vowed to have their day in court. Despite further destruction by an earthquake and 10-foot tidal wave in October 1995, the squatters have tenaciously rebuilt their *palapas.*

Playas Mora and La Boca

Jewel of jewels Playa Mora is accessible by a dirt road running north from Playa Tenacatita, past the *palapas.* Playa Mora itself is salt-and-pepper, black sand dotted with white coral, washed by water sometimes as smooth as glass. Just 15 meters from the beach the reef begins. Corals, like heads of cauliflower, some brown, some green, and some dead white, swarm with fish: iridescent blue, yellow-striped, yellow-tailed, some silvery, and others brown as rocks. (Careful: Moray eels like to hide in rock crannies; they bite. Don't stick your hand anywhere you can't see.)

If you get to Playa Mora by December you may be early enough to snag one of the roughly dozen car-accessible camping spots. If not, plenty of tenting spaces accessible on foot exist; also, a few abandoned *palapa* thatched huts are usually waiting to be resurrected.

Playa la Boca is the overflow campground for Tenacatita. It's not as popular because of its rough surf and steep beach. Its isolation and vigorous surf, however, make Playa la Boca the best for driftwood, beachcombing, shells, and surf fishing.

Wildlife Viewing

Tenacatita's hinterland is a spreading, wildlife-rich mangrove marsh. From a landing behind the Tenacatita dune, you can float a boat, rubber raft, or canoe for a wildlife-viewing excursion. Local guides also furnish boats and lead trips from the same spot. Take your hat, binoculars, camera, telephoto lens, and plenty of repellent.

Tenacatita Bugs

That same marshland is the source for swarms of mosquitoes and **jejenes,** "no-see-um" biting gnats, especially around sunset. At that time no one sane at Tenacatita should be outdoors without having slathered on some good repellent.

Food, Services, and Information

The village of **El Rebalsito,** on the Hwy. 200-Tenacatita road, a mile and a half back from the beach, is Tenacatita's supply and service center. It has two or three fair *abarroterias* (groceries) that carry meat and vegetables, a *caseta de larga distancia,* a *gasolinera* that dispenses gasoline from drums, a water *purificadora* that sells drinking water retail, and even a bus stop. A single Transportes Cihuatlán bus makes one run a day between Rebalsito and Manzanillo, leaving Rebalsito at the crack of dawn (inquire locally) and returning from the Manzanillo central bus station around 3 p.m., arriving at Rebalsito around 6 p.m.

If you want a diversion from the fare of Tenacatita's seafood *palapas* and Rebalsito's single restaurant, you can drive or thumb a ride seven miles (11 km) to **Restaurant Yoly** at roadside Miguel Hidalgo village (Km 30 on Hwy. 200) for some country-style enchiladas, tacos, *chiles rellenos,* tostadas, and beans. Open daily 7 a.m.-8 p.m.

Getting There

Leave Hwy. 200 at the big Tenacatita sign and interchange (at Km 27) half a mile south of the big Río Purificación bridge. Rebalsito is 3.7 miles (six km), Tenacatita 5.4 miles (8.7 km), by a good paved road.

HOTEL BLUE BAY VILLAGE

Despite new owners, who have changed its name to Hotel Blue Bay Village, the former Hotel Los Angeles Locos (which had nothing to do with crazy people from Los Angeles), lives on in minds of local people. Once upon a time, a rich family built an airstrip and a mansion by a lovely little beach on pristine Tenacatita Bay and began coming for vacations by private plane. The local people, who couldn't fathom why their rich neighbors would go to so much trouble and expense to come to such an out-of-the-way place, dubbed them *los angeles locos,* the "crazy angels," because they always seemed to be flying.

The beach is still lovely and Tenacatita Bay, curving around Punta Hermanos south from Tenacatita Beach, is still pristine. Now the Hotel Blue Bay Village makes it possible for droves of sun-seeking vacationers to enjoy it en masse.

Continuous music, open bar, plentiful buffets, and endless activities set the tone at Blue Bay Village—the kind of place for folks who want a hassle-free week of fun in the sun. The guests are typically working-age couples and singles, mostly Mexicans during the summer, Canadians and some Americans during the winter. Very few children (although they are welcome) seem to be among the guests.

Hotel Activities

Although all sports and lessons—including tennis, snorkeling, sailing, windsurfing, horseback riding, volleyball, aerobics, exercises, water-skiing—plus dancing, disco, and games cost nothing extra, guests can, if they want, do nothing but soak up the sun. Hotel Blue Bay Village simply provides the options.

A relaxed attitude will probably allow you to enjoy yourself the most. Don't try to eat, drink, and do too much in order to make sure you get your money's worth. If you do, you're liable to arrive back home in need of a vacation.

Although people don't come to the tropics to stay inside, Blue Bay Village's rooms are quite comfortable—completely private, in pastels and white, air-conditioned, each with cable TV, phone, and private balcony overlooking either the ocean or palmy pool patio.

Hotel Information

For information and reservations, contact a travel agent or the hotel at Km 20, Carretera Federal No. 200, Melaque, Jalisco, tel. (335) 150-02, 150-20, 150-06, fax 155-00, or from the U.S. and Canada, tel. (800) BLUEBAY (258-3229). High-season rates for the 201 rooms and suites run about $80 per person per day, double occupancy, $60 low season. Children under 12 go for about $30 high season, $23 low. For a bigger, better junior suite, add about $20 per room; prices include everything except transportation.

Getting There

The Hotel Blue Bay Village is about four miles (six km) off Hwy. 200 along a signed cobbled entrance road near the Km 20 marker (120 miles, 194 km, from Puerto Vallarta; 14 miles, 23 km, from Barra de Navidad; and 32 miles, 51 km, from the Manzanillo International Airport).

If you want to simply look around the resort, don't drive up to the gate unannounced. The guard won't let you through. Instead, call ahead and make an appointment for a "tour." After your guided look-see, you have to either sign up or mosey along. The Blue Bay doesn't accept day guests.

PLAYA BOCA DE IGUANAS

Plumy Playa Boca de Iguanas curves for six miles along the tranquil inner recess of the Bay of Tenacatita. The cavernous former Hotel Bahía Tenacatita, which slumbered for years beneath the grove, is being reclaimed by the jungle and the animals that live in the nearby mangrove marsh.

The beach, however, is as enjoyable as ever: wide, level, with firm white sand, good for hiking, jogging, and beachcombing. Offshore, the gently rolling waves are equally fine for bodysurfing and boogie boarding. Beds of oysters, free for those who dive for them, lie a few hundred feet offshore. A rocky outcropping at the north end invites fishing and snorkeling while the calm water beyond the breakers invites windsurfing. Bring your own equipment.

Accommodations

The pocket paradise of **Camping and Trailer Park Boca de Iguanas,** Km 16.5, Carretera Melaque-Puerto Vallarta, P.O. Box 93, Melaque, Jalisco 48987, seems to be succeeding where the old hotel failed. Instead of fighting the jungle, the manager is trying to coexist with it. A big crocodile lives in the mangrove-lined lotus marsh at the edge of the trailer park.

"When the crocodile gets too close to my ducks," the manager says, "I drive him back into the mangrove where he belongs. This end of the mangrove is ours, the other side is his."

The trailer park offers 40 sandy, shaded (but smallish) spaces for tents and RVs, including electricity; well water for showering, flushing, and laundry; bottled water for drinking; and a dump station. The manager runs a minimarket that supplies the necessities for a relaxed week or month on the beach. Many American and Canadian regulars stay here all winter. The trailer park includes a funky kitchenette bungalow that sleeps four for $25/day. Reserve by mail (address above) or fax via the long-distance phone operator in La Manzanilla, tel./fax (335) 152-12. To find it, follow the signed gravel road at Km 17 for 1.5 miles, 2.4 km. Reservations are generally needed only during Christmas or Easter week. Rates run about $4 per adult, $1.50 for kids under 10.

The neighboring **Camping Trailer Park Boca Beach** also has about 50 camping and RV spaces shaded beneath a majestic, rustling grove at Km 16.5 Carretera Melaque-Puerto Vallarta, P.O. Box 18, Melaque, Jalisco 48987, tel./fax (335) 152-12, via the long-distance phone operator in La Manzanilla. Although their layout is newer, friendly owners Michel and Bertha Billot (he's French, she's Mexican) are trying harder. Their essentials are in place: electricity, water, showers, toilets, and about 40 spaces with sewer hookups. Much of their five acres is undeveloped and would be fine for tenters who prefer privacy with the convenience of fresh water, a small store, and congenial company at tables beneath a rustic *palapa*. Rates run about $4/day per adult, $1.50 per child, in motor home, trailer, van, or camper, with discounts for weekly or monthly rentals.

A third lodging, the nearby **Hotel and Campamento Entre Palmeras,** offers six plain rooms with fans for one to four persons for about $15. The grounds feature much tent or RV camping space, electricity, showers, toilets, a simple restaurant, and a funky swimming pool. Its location, closer to the mangrove marsh and farther from the beach, is buggier, however.

PLAYA LA MANZANILLA

The little fishing town of La Manzanilla (pop. 2,000) drowses at the opposite end of the same long, curving strip of sand that begins at the Boca de Iguanas trailer parks. Here the beach, Playa La Manzanilla, is as broad and flat and the waves are as gentle, but the sand is several shades darker. Probably no better fishing exists on the entire Costa Alegre than at La Manzanilla. A dozen seafood *palapas* on the beach manage to stay open by virtue of a trickle of foreign visitors and local weekend and holiday patronage.

A pair of basic hotels accommodate guests. Guests at **Hotel Posada del Cazador** ("The Hunter") enjoy friendly husband-wife management, a lobby for sitting and socializing, a shelf of used paperback novels and a long-distance telephone. Find it on the main street on the left, as you enter town, at María Asunción 183, La Manzanilla, Jalisco 48988, tel./fax (335) 150-00. It has seven plain but clean rooms for $7 s, $9 d low season, $11 and $15 high. Kitchenette suites sleeping four rent for $15 low, $20 high; a larger suite, sleeping eight, costs $35 low, $40 high. All have fans and hot-water showers.

On the opposite, even sleepier country edge of town, the **Hotel Puesta de Sol** ("Sunset"), Calle Playa Blanca 94, La Manzanilla, Jalisco, tel. (335) 150-33, offers 17 basic rooms around a cool, leafy central patio. Rates run about $5 s, $10 d, $15 t, with discounts for longer-term rentals.

Get to La Manzanilla by following the signed paved road at Km 13 for one mile. The Hotel Cazador is on the left, one block after you turn left onto the main beachfront street. The Hotel Puesta de Sol is a quarter mile farther along; bear right past the town plaza for a few blocks along the beachfront street, Calle Playa Blanca.

CLUB EL TAMARINDO

The Costa Alegre's newest big development, Club El Tamarindo, occupies the lush, jungly peninsula that forms the southernmost point of Tenacatita Bay. Plans project a giant jungle country club, based on sales of about 100 parcels averaging 20 acres apiece. Owners will have access to extensive resort facilities, including golf course, tennis courts, hotel, restaurants, heliport, skeet range, equestrian paths, beach club, and small marina. Plans apparently include owner commitment to leaving a sizable fraction of the present forest in its original, pristine state.

Many of the resort facilities have been installed, including the golf course, tennis courts, heliport, boat dock, and hotel. Accommodations, at the Hotel Bel Air Tamarindo, are in airy, white stucco and tile, super-deluxe jungle-edge housekeeping villas. Rates run about $600 per day. For information and reservations, call the hotel locally, tel./fax (335) 150-53, 150-56 or 150-52, North America tel. (800) 457-7676, Mexico toll-free tel. (800) 90-229. Camping and RV parking are also available for potential buyers. Get there via the signed side road at Km 8. After about a mile of winding through the sylvan tropical forest, you arrive at the gate, where you must have either a reservation in hand or a prior appointment before the guard will let you through.

BARRA DE NAVIDAD, MELAQUE, AND VICINITY

The little country beach town of Barra de Navidad, Jalisco (pop. 5,000), whose name literally means "Bar of Christmas," has unexpectedly few saloons. In this case, "Bar" has nothing to do with alcohol; it refers to the sandbar upon which the town is built. That lowly spit of sand forms the southern perimeter of the blue Bay of Navidad, which arcs to Barra de Navidad's twin town of San Patricio Melaque (pop. 10,000) a few miles to the west.

Barra and San Patricio Melaque, locally known as "Melaque" (may-LAH-kay), are twin, but dis-

tinct, towns. Barra has the cobbled, shady lanes and friendly country ambience; Melaque is the metropolis of the two, with most of the stores and services.

HISTORY

The sandbar is called "Navidad" because the Viceroy Antonio de Mendoza, the first, and arguably the best, viceroy Mexico ever had, disembarked there on 25 December 1540. The oc-

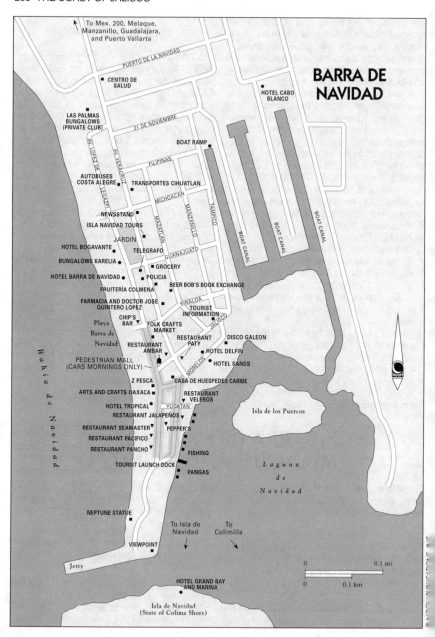

To Mex. 200, Melaque,
Manzanillo, Guadalajara,
and Puerto Vallarta

PUERTO DE LA NAVIDAD

BARRA DE NAVIDAD

CENTRO DE
SALUD

HOTEL CABO
BLANCO

LAS PALMAS
BUNGALOWS
(PRIVATE CLUB)

21 DE NOVIEMBRE

BOAT RAMP

FILIPINAS

AV. LOPEZ (LEGAZPI)

AV. VERACRUZ

AUTOBUSES
COSTA ALEGRE

TRANSPORTES CIHUATLAN

MICHOACAN

MAZATLAN

MANZANILLO

TAMPICO

NEWSSTAND

ISLA NAVIDAD TOURS

JARDIN

HOTEL BOGAVANTE

TELEGRAFO

BUNGALOWS KARELIA

GUANAJUATO

GROCERY

HOTEL BARRA DE NAVIDAD

POLICIA

BEER BOB'S BOOK EXCHANGE

FRUITERÍA COLMENA

FARMACIA AND DOCTOR JOSE
QUINTERO LOPEZ

SINALOA

Playa
Barra de
Navidad

CHIP'S
BAR

FOLK CRAFTS
MARKET

TOURIST
INFORMATION

JALISCO

RESTAURANT
PATY

DISCO GALEON

RESTAURANT
AMBAR

HOTEL DELFIN

PEDESTRIAN MALL
(CARS MORNINGS ONLY)

MORELOS

HOTEL SANDS

Bahía de Navidad

Z PESCA

CASA DE HUESPEDES CARIBE

ARTS AND CRAFTS OAXACA

RESTAURANT
VELEROS

HOTEL TROPICAL

YUCATAN

RESTAURANT JALAPEÑOS

RESTAURANT SEAMASTER

PEPPER'S

RESTAURANT PACIFICO

RESTAURANT PANCHO

FISHING

TOURIST LAUNCH DOCK

PANGAS

Isla de los Puercos

Laguna
de
Navidad

NEPTUNE STATUE

To Isla de
Navidad

To
Colimilla

VIEWPOINT

Jetty

0   0.1 mi

0   0.1 km

HOTEL GRAND BAY
AND MARINA

Isla de Navidad
(State of Colima Shore)

casion was auspicious for two reasons. Besides being Christmas Day, Don Antonio had arrived to personally put down a bloody rebellion raging through western Mexico that threatened to burn New Spain off the map. Unfortunately for the thousands of native people who were torched, hung, or beheaded during the brutal campaign, Don Antonio's prayers on that day were soon answered. The rebellion was smothered, and the lowly sandbar was remembered as Barra de Navidad from that time forward.

A generation later, Barra de Navidad became the springboard for King Philip's efforts to make the Pacific a Spanish lake. Shipyards built on the bar launched the vessels that carried the expedition of conquistador Miguel López de Legazpi and Father André de Urdaneta in search of God and gold in the Philippines. Urdaneta came back a hero one year later, in 1565, having discovered the northern circle route, whose favorable easterly winds propelled a dozen subsequent generations of the fabled treasure-laden Manila Galleon home to Mexico.

By 1600, however, the Manila Galleon was landing in Acapulco, with its much quicker land access to the capital to transport their priceless Asian cargoes. Barra de Navidad went to sleep and didn't wake up for more than three centuries.

Now Barra de Navidad only slumbers occasionally. The townsfolk welcome crowds of beach-going Mexican families during national holidays and a steady procession of North American and European budget vacationers during the winter.

SIGHTS

Exploring Barra and Melaque

Nearly all hotels and the fancier restaurants in Barra lie on one oceanfront street named, uncommonly, after a conquistador, Miguel López de Legazpi. Barra's other main street, Veracruz, one short block inland, has most of the businesses, groceries, and small, family-run eateries.

Head south along Legazpi toward the steep Cerro San Francisco in the distance and you will soon be on the palm-lined walkway that runs atop the famous sandbar of Barra. On the right, ocean side, the Playa Barra de Navidad arcs northwest to the hotels of Melaque, which spread like white pebbles along the far end of the strand.

The great blue water expanse beyond the beach, framed at both ends by jagged, rocky sea stacks, is the **Bahía de Navidad.**

Opposite the ocean, on the other side of the bar, spreads the tranquil, mangrove-bordered expanse of the **Laguna de Navidad,** which forms the border with the state of Colima, whose mountains (including nearby Cerro San Francisco) loom beyond it. The lagoon's calm appearance is deceiving, for it is really an *estero* (estuary), an arm of the sea, which ebbs and flows through the channel beyond the rock jetty at the end of the sandbar. Because of this natural flushing action, local folks still dump fishing waste into the Laguna de Navidad. Fortunately new sewage plants route human waste away from the lagoon, so with care, you can usually swim safely in its inviting waters. Do not, however, venture too close to the lagoon-mouth beyond the jetty or you may get swept out to sea by the strong outgoing current.

On the sandbar's lagoon side, a *panga* (fishing launch) mooring and passenger dock hum with daytime activity. From the dock, launches ferry loads of passengers for about half a dollar to the Colima shore, which is known as **Isla de Navidad,** where the marina and hotel development has risen across the lagoon. Back in town, **minibuses** enter town along Veracruz, turn left at Sinaloa, by the crafts market, and head in the opposite direction, out of town, along Mazatlán, Veracruz, and Hwy. 200, three miles (4.8 km) to Melaque.

The once-distinct villages of San Patricio and Melaque now spread as one along the Bay of Navidad's sandy northwest shore. The business district, still known locally as San Patricio (from the highway, follow a small San Patricio sign two blocks toward the beach), centers around a plaza, market, and church bordering the main shopping street López Mateos.

Continue two blocks to beachfront Calle Gómez Farías, where a lineup of hotels, eateries, and shops cater to the vacation trade. From there, the curving strand extends toward the quiet Melaque west end, where *palapas* line a glassy, sheltered blue cove. Here, a rainbow of colored *pangas* perch upon the sand, sailboats rock gently offshore, pelicans preen and dive, and people enjoy snacks, beer, and the cooling breeze in the deep shade beneath the *palapas.*

MELAQUE

To Barra de Navidad, Manzanillo, and Guadalajara

To Mex. 80, Gas, Puerto Vallarta, and Guadalajara

To Cuastecomate and Hotel Real Costa Sur

200

REVOLUCION

REFORMA

FCO. VILLA

A. OBREGON

M. MORELOS

B. JUAREZ

R. CORONA

GOMEZ FARIAS

C. OROZCO

CORREO

TACOS GUERRERO

VILLAS CAMINO DEL MAR

HOTEL SANTA MARIA

BUNGALOWS AZTECA

BUNGALOWS MALLORCA

ASALGADO VELASCO

PACIFIC BUNGALOWS

M. HIDALGO

LARGA DISTANCIA

LIBRERIA SAFER

LAUNDRY

FONDAS

CENTRO DE SALUD

POSADA PABLO DE TARSO

G. GUZMAN

JARDIN

LOPEZ MATEOS

POLICIAS AND TELEGRAFOS

MUNICIPAL

SUPER FARMACIA PLAZA

C. MARKET

C. PUERTO

TRAILER PARK LA PLAYA

Playa Melaque

V. CARRANZA

AUTOBUSES COSTA ALEGRE

ELITE

MONEY EXCHANGE MELAQUE

BANAMEX

RESTAURANT CESAR AND CHARLEY

BUS TRANSPORTES CIHUATLAN

Bahia de Navidad

L. VALLARTA

RESTAURANT EL DORADO

HOTEL CLUB NAUTICO

DISCO LA TANGA

F.I. MADERO

AV. LAS PALMAS

RESTAURANT VIVA MARIA 1910

RESTAURANT PELICANOS

HOTEL DE LEGAZPI

TRAILER PARK INFORMAL

0.25 mi

0.25 km

0

BEACHES AND ACTIVITIES

Although a continuous strand of medium-fine golden sand joins Barra with Melaque, it changes character and names along its gentle, five-mile arc. At Barra de Navidad, where it's called **Playa de Navidad,** the beach is narrow and steep, and the waves are sometimes very rough. Those powerful swells often provide good intermediate surfing breaks adjacent to the jetty. Fishing by line or pole is also popular from the jetty rocks.

Most mornings are calm enough to make the surf safe for swimming and splashing, which, along with the fresh seafood of beachside *palapa* restaurants, make Barra a popular Sunday and holiday picnic-ground for local Mexican families. The relatively large number of folks walking the beach unfortunately makes for slim pickings for shell collectors and beachcombers.

For a cooling midday break from the sun, drop in to the restaurant of the Hotel Tropical at the south end of Legazpi and enjoy the bay view, the swish of the waves, and the fresh breeze streaming through the lobby.

As the beach curves northwesterly toward Melaque, the restaurants and hotels give way to dunes and pasture. At the outskirts of Melaque, civilization resumes, and the broad beach, now called **Playa Melaque,** billows gently to the west.

Continuing past the town center, a lineup of rustic *palapas* and *pangas* pulled up on the sand decorate the tranquil west-end cove, which is sheltered from the open sea behind a tier of craggy sea stacks. Here, the water clears, making for good fishing from the rocks.

Colimilla and Isla de Navidad

A boat trip across the lagoon for super-fresh seafood at the palm-studded village of Colimilla is a primary Barra pastime. While you sit enjoying a moderately priced oyster cocktail, ceviche, or broiled whole-fish dinner, gaze out on the mangrove-enfolded glassy expanse of the Laguna de Navidad. Far away, a canoe may drift silently, while white herons quietly stalk their prey. Now and then a launch will glide in and deposit its load of visitors, or a fisherman will head out to sea.

One of the most pleasant Colimilla vantage spots is the **Restaurant Susana,** whose broad *palapa* extends out into the lagoon; open daily 8 a.m.-8 p.m. Take mosquito repellent, especially if you're staying for dinner. Launches routinely ferry as many as six passengers to Colimilla from the Barra lagoonside docks for about $5 roundtrip. Tell them when you want to return, and they'll pick you up.

From the same Barra lagoonside dock, launches also shuttle passengers for 50 cents roundtrip across the lagoon to Isla de Navidad and its new Hotel Grand Bay, marina, vacation home development, and golf course.

Playa de Cocos

A trip to wild, breezy Playa de Cocos, hidden just behind the Cerro San Francisco headland south of Barra, makes an interesting afternoon outing, especially when combined with the trip to Colimilla. A wide, golden sand beach curves miles southward, starting beneath a cactus-dotted jungly headland. The beach, although broad, is steep, with strong shorebreakers. Although swimming is hazardous, fishing off the rocks and beachcombing are the delights here. A feast of driftwood and multicolored shells—olives, small conches, purple-striated clams—litters the sand, especially on an intimate, spectacular hidden cove, reachable by scampering past the waves.

There are two ways to get to Playa de Cocos. Through Colimilla, walk uphill to the road above the La Colimilla restaurants. Head left (east) for about a quarter mile. Turn right at the palm-lined boulevard and continue along the golf course about a mile and a quarter to the beach beneath the tip of the Cerro San Francisco headland.

You can also taxi or drive there by turning off Hwy. 200 at the Ejido La Culebra (or Isla Navidad) sign as the highway cuts through the hills at Km 51 a few miles south of Barra. Mark your odometer at the turnoff. Follow the road about three miles (4.8 km) to a bridge, where you enter the state of Colima. From there the road curves right, paralleling the beach. After about two more miles (3.2 km), you pass through the golf course gate. After winding through the golf course another mile, fork left at the intersecting boulevard and traffic circle at the north edge of the golf course. Continue another mile to the end of the road and beach.

Playa Cuastecomate

Playa de Cocos has its exact opposite in Playa Cuastecomate (kooah-stay-koh-MAH-tay), tucked behind the ridge rising beyond the northwest edge of Melaque. The dark, fine-sand beach arcs along a cove on the rampart-rimmed big blue **Bahía de Cuastecomate.** Its very gentle waves and clear waters make for excellent swimming, windsurfing, snorkeling, and fishing from the beach itself or the rocks beneath the adjacent cliffs. A number of *palapa* restaurants along the beach serve seafood and drinks.

The Cuastecomate beachside village itself, home for a number of local fisherfolk and a few North Americans in permanently parked RVs, has a collection of oft-empty bungalows on the hillside, a small store, and about three times as many chickens as people.

To get there, drive, taxi, or bus via the local minibus or Transportes Cihuatlán to the signed Melaque turnoff from Hwy. 200. There, a dirt side road marked Hotel Costa Sur heads into the hills, winding for two miles (3.2 km) over the ridge through pasture and jungle woodland to the village. If you're walking, allow an hour and take your sun hat, insect repellent, and water.

Barra-Melaque Hike

You can do this four-mile stroll either way, but starting from Barra in the morning, with the sun behind you, the sky and the ocean will be at their bluest best. Take insect repellent, sunscreen, and a hat. At either end, enjoy lunch at one of the seaside restaurants. At the Melaque end you can continue walking north to the cove on the far side of town. The trail beneath the cliff leads to spectacular wave-tossed tidepools and rugged sea rocks at the tip of the bay. At the Barra end, you can hire a launch to Colimilla. End your day leisurely by taxiing or busing back from the bus station at either end.

Birdwatching and Wildlife Viewing

The wildlife-rich upper reaches of the Laguna de Navidad stretch for miles and are only a boat ride away. Besides the ordinary varieties of egrets, terns, herons, pelicans, frigate birds, boobies, ducks, and geese, patient birdwatchers can sometimes snare rainbow flash-views of exotic parrots and bright tanagers and orioles.

As for other creatures, quiet, persistent observers are sometimes rewarded with mangrove-edge views of turtles, constrictors, crocodiles, coatimundis, raccoons, skunks, deer, wild pigs, ocelots, wildcats, and, very rarely, a jaguar. The sensitivity and experience of your boatman/guide is, of course, crucial to the success of any nature outing. Ask at the dock-office of the **Sociedad Cooperativa de Servicios Turístico,** 40 Av. Veracruz on the lagoonfront.

You might also ask Tracy Ross at Crazy Cactus (on Jalisco, next door to the church, near the corner of Veracruz) to recommend a good guide, or even a complete wildlife-viewing excursion.

ACCOMMODATIONS

Barra Hotels

Whether on the beach or not, all Barra hotels (except the four-star Cabo Blanco) fall in the budget or moderate category. One of the best, the family-run **Hotel Sands,** offers a bit of class at modest rates at Morelos 24, Barra de Navidad, Jalisco 48987, tel. (335) 550-18. Two tiers of rooms enclose an inner courtyard lined with comfortable sitting areas opening into a lush green garden of leafy vines and graceful coconut palms. A side corridor leads past a small zoo of spider monkeys, raccoons, and squawking macaws to a view of Barra's colorful lineup of fishing launches. On the other side, past the swim-up bar, a big curving pool and outer patio spreads to the placid edge of the mangrove-bordered Laguna de Navidad. The pool bar (happy hour daily 4-6 p.m. in season) and the sitting areas afford inviting places to meet other travelers. The rooms, all with fans (but with sporadic hot water in some rooms—check before moving in) are clean and furnished with dark varnished wood and tile. Light sleepers should wear earplugs or book a room in the wing farthest from the disco down the street, whose music thumps away till around 2 a.m. most nights during the high season. The 43 rooms and bungalows rent from $23 d low season, $48 high (bargain for a better rate); bungalows sleeping four with kitchenette run $53 low season, $90 high; credit cards (with a six percent surcharge) accepted. Parking available.

BARRA AND MELAQUE ACCOMMODATIONS

Accommodations (area code 335) are listed in increasing order of approximate high-season, double-room rates.

BARRA HOTELS (POSTAL CODE 48987)

Casa de Huéspedes Caribe, Sonora 15, tel. 559-52, $12

Hotel Bogavante, Legazpi s/n, tel. 553-84, fax 561-20, $26

Bungalows Karelia, Legazpi s/n, tel. 557-48, $28

Hotel Delfín, Morelos 23, tel. 550-68, fax 560-20, $33

Hotel Barra de Navidad, Legazpi 250, tel. 551-22, fax 553-03, $37

Hotel Tropical, Legazpi 96, tel. 550-20, fax 551-49, $45

Hotel Sands, Morelos 24, tel./fax 550-18, $48

Hotel Cabo Blanco, P.O. Box 31, tel. 551-03, 551-36, fax 564-94, $75

Hotel Grand Bay, P.O. Box 20, tel. 550-50, fax 560-71, $375

MELAQUE HOTELS (POSTAL CODE 48980)

Hotel Santa María, Abel Salgado 85, P.O. Box 188, tel. 556-77, fax 555-53, $18

Posada Pablo de Tarso, Gómez Farías 408, tel. 551-17, fax 552-68, $30

Hotel de Legazpi, Av. de las Palmas s/n, P.O. Box 88, tel. 553-97, $33

Bungalows Azteca, P.O. Box 57, tel. 551-50, $35

Bungalows Mallorca, Abel Salgado 133, P.O. Box 157, tel. 552-19, $35

Hotel Club Náutico, Gómez Farías 1A, tel. 557-70, 557-66, fax 552-39, $36

Hotel Real Costa Sur, P.O. Box 12, tel./fax 550-85, $40

Villas Camino del Mar, P.O. Box 6, tel. 552-07, fax 554-98, $54

Across the street, its loyal international clientele swears by the German family-operated **Hotel Delfín,** Morelos 23, Barra de Navidad, Jalisco 48987, tel. (335) 550-68, fax 560-20. Its four stories of tile-floored, balcony-corridor rooms (where curtains, unfortunately, must be drawn for privacy) are the cleanest and coziest of Barra's moderate hotels. The Delfín's tour de force, however, is the cheery patio buffet where guests linger over the breakfast offered every morning ($3-5, open daily 8:30-10:30 a.m.) to all comers. Overnight guests, like those of the Sands, must put up with the moderate nighttime noise of the disco half a block away. For maximum sun and privacy take one of the top-floor rooms, many of which enjoy lagoon

views. The Delfín's 30 rooms rent $27 d low season, $33 high; with fans, small pool, parking, and credit cards accepted.

One block away and a notch down the economic scale is **Casa de Huéspedes Caribe,** Sonora 15, Barra de Navidad, Jalisco 48987, tel. (335) 559-52, tucked along a side street. Unassuming elderly owner Maximino Oregon offers 11 clean, plain rooms, all with bath and hot water, to a devoted following of long-term customers. Amenities include a secure front door (which Maximino personally locks every night), a homey downstairs garden sitting area, and more chairs and a hammock for snoozing on an upstairs porch. Rates run $8 s, $12 d, and $14 t in rooms with twin, double, or both types of beds.

The longtime **Hotel Tropical,** near the "bar" end of Legazpi, at Av. L. de Legazpi 96, Barra de Navidad, Jalisco 48987, sustained serious damage in the 9 October 1995 earthquake. Alas, at this writing, it is not yet open, but should be by the winter of 1999. It appears as if it will be an improved version of the old hotel, of which, in previous editions, I wrote that "guests in many of its renovated oceanfront tiers of comfortable, high-ceilinged rooms enjoy luxuriously private ocean-view balconies. Downstairs, the natural air-conditioning of an ocean breeze often floods the sea-view lobby-restaurant. The 57 rooms rent for about $30 s, $45 d, with fans, tiny pool, and credit cards accepted." For reservations, write, or, if the phone numbers remain the same, call (335) 550-20, fax 551-49.

Sharing the same beachfront by the town plaza a few blocks away, the white stucco three-story **Hotel Barra de Navidad** encloses a cool, leafy interior courtyard at Av. L. de Legazpi 250, Barra de Navidad, Jalisco 48987, tel. (335) 551-22, fax 553-03. Guests in the seaside upper two floors of comfortable (but not deluxe) rooms enjoy palm-fringed ocean vistas from private balconies. An inviting pool patio on one side and a dependable upstairs restaurant complete the picture. High-season rates for the 57 rooms run $31 s, $37 d, $43 t oceanside ($27, $34, $38 streetside), with fans. Credit cards accepted; subtract about 20% from these rates during the May-July and Sept.-Nov. low season.

The friendly ambience and homey beachside porch of the **Hotel Bogavante** keep a steady stream of mostly North American and European travelers returning year after year to Av. L. de Legazpi s/n, Barra de Navidad, Jalisco 48987, tel. (335) 553-84, fax 561-20. Eight of the 14 accommodations are roomy kitchenette suites, especially handy for groups and families weary of the hassles and expense of eating out. The rooms rent for about $21 s, $26 d, and $32 t high season, the kitchenette units, about $40 s, d, or t. Figure about a 20% low-season discount; monthly rates available, fans, no pool.

Bungalows Karelia, the Bogavante's downscale twin lodging next door, shares the same pleasant beachside porch, Av. L. de Legazpi s/n, Barra de Navidad, Jalisco 48987, tel. (335) 557-48. All the Karelia's rentals are kitchenette bungalows, satisfactory for many young families and travelers who don't mind cleaning up a bit in exchange for more modest rates. The 10 bungalows with fans rent, low season, for $22 s or d, $28 t, $28 and $32, high.

Hint: If considering a beachside room in one of the several Barra oceanfront hotels, listen to the waves before you move in. They may be loud enough to interfere with your sleep. If so, use earplugs or switch to a streetside room or a hotel on the lagoon.

Barra's original deluxe lodging is the peach-hued, stucco-and-tile four-star **Hotel Cabo Blanco,** P.O. Box 31, Barra de Navidad, Jalisco 48987, tel. (335) 551-03, 551-36, or 551-82, fax 564-94. The 125-room complex anchors the vacation home development along the three marina-canals that extend from the lagoon to about

five blocks inland from the town. Within its manicured garden-grounds, Hotel Cabo Blanco offers night-lit tennis courts, restaurants, bars, two pools, kiddie pools, and deluxe sportfishing yachts-for-hire. The deluxe, pastel-decorated rooms run about $47 d low season, $75 high, all with a/c, cable TV, and phones. Available activities include a discotheque and many water sports. Credit cards accepted. Bring your repellent; during late afternoon and evening mosquitoes and gnats from the nearby mangroves seem to especially enjoy the Cabo Blanco's plush ambience.

Barra's plushest accommodation is the class-act **Hotel Grand Bay,** a short boat ride across the lagoon. Builders spared little to create the appearance of a *gran epoch* resort. The 198 rooms are elaborately furnished in marble floors, French provincial furniture, and jade-hued Italian marble bathroom sinks. Accommodations run from spacious "superior" rooms for $200 d low season, $375 high, and master suites ($530 low, $740 high) through grand four-room executive suites that include their own steam rooms, from $2,300. Conveniences include three pools, three elegant restaurants, tennis, volleyball, children's club, marina, and golf course. Reserve by writing P.O. Box 20 Barra de Navidad, Jalisco, 48987, tel. (335) 550-50, fax 560-71. Note: Security is tight at the Hotel Grand Bay. Guards at the lagoonside boat dock allow entrance only to guests and prospective guests. If you want to look around, you have to be accompanied by an in-house guide. Call the desk beforehand for an appointment.

Melaque Hotels

Melaque has a swarm of hotels and bungalows, many of them poorly designed and indifferently managed. They scratch along, nearly empty except during the Christmas and Easter holiday deluges when Mexican middle-class families must accept anything to stay at the beach. There are, nevertheless, several bright exceptions, which can be conveniently divided into "South" and "North of Town" groups:

Hotels South of Town: Classy in its unique way is the **Villas Camino del Mar,** whose owner doesn't believe in advertising. A few signs in the humble beach neighborhood about a quarter mile on the Barra side of the Melaque town center furnish the only clue that this gem of a lodging hides among the Melaque dross at Calle Francisco Villa, corner Abel Salgado, P.O. Box 6, San Patricio-Melaque, Jalisco 48980, tel. (335) 552-07, fax 554-98. Note: Owners have added an annex across the street, which, although inviting, is not as attractive as the original building. Specifically ask for a room in the original building in your written or faxed reservation request.

A five-story white stucco monument draped with fluted, neoclassic columns and hanging pedestals, the original Villas Camino del Mar hotel offers a lodging assortment that varies from simple double rooms through deluxe suites with kitchenettes to a rambling penthouse. The upper three levels have sweeping ocean views, while the lower two overlook an elegant pool patio bar and shady beachside palm grove. The clientele is split between Mexican middle-class families who come for weekends all year around, and quiet Canadian and American couples who come to soak up the winter sun for weeks and months on end. Reserve early, especially for the winter. High-season rates for the 37 rooms and suites run as little as $54 ($51 weekly, $48 monthly) for comfortable ocean-view doubles; $78 ($60 weekly, $48 monthly) for one-bedroom kitchenette suites, and $129 ($116 weekly, $104 monthly) for deluxe two-bedroom, two-bath suites with kitchen; all with fans only. Corresponding low-season rates run about two-thirds the above prices.

If the Camino del Mar is full or not to your liking, you can choose from a trio of acceptable lodgings around the corner that share the same golden sunset-view strand. The plainer but priced-right **Hotel Santa María** offers 46 rooms and kitchenette apartments with bath, close enough to the water for the waves to lull guests to sleep at Abel Salgado 85, P.O. Box 188, San Patricio-Melaque 48980, tel. (335) 556-77 or fax 555-53. Rooms, popular with long-term Canadian and Americans in winter, are arranged in a pair of motel-style stucco tiers around an attractive tropical inner patio. Units vary; look at a few before you move in. High-season prices for the spartan but generally tidy rooms begin at about $18 d per day, $100/week, $300/month; apartments with kitchenettes go for about $24 d per day, $120/week, $400/month. Expect to pay about two-thirds these prices during low summer and fall seasons.

Right next door, the sky-blue and white **Bungalows Azteca** auto court-style cottages line both sides of a cobbled driveway courtyard garden that spreads to a lazy beachfront patio. The 14 spacious kitchenette cottages, in small (one-bedroom) or large (three-bedroom) versions, are plainly furnished but clean. The nine one-bedroom units rent, high season, for about $35/day, $500/month; the four three-bedrooms cost about $600/day, $900/month. Expect a low-season discount of about 25% below these prices. Send your reservation request to P.O. Box 57, San Patricio-Melaque 48980, or call (335) 551-50 in Melaque, or, in Guadalajara, tel. (3) 625-5118, fax 626-1191. Get your reservation in early, especially for the winter.

Less than a block away, the open, parklike grounds, spacious blue pool, and beachside palm garden of the **Bungalows Mallorca** invite unhurried outdoor relaxation. Although its stacked, Motel 6-style layout is about as unimaginative and un-Mexican as you can find south of Anchorage, Alaska, groups and families used to providing their own atmosphere find the kitchens and spacious (but dark) rooms of the Bungalows Mallorca appealing. The 24 two-bedroom bungalows with fans rent from about $35 d ($210/week, $700/month) high season; during low season, negotiate for a lower rate. A pair of beachside units with jacuzzis and view balconies are the best. Reserve directly, at Abel Salgado 133, Colonia Villa Obregón, P.O. Box 157, San Patricio-Melaque, Jalisco 48980, tel. (335) 552-19.

Closer toward town is the well-kept, colonial-chic **Posada Pablo de Tarso** (named after the apostle Paul of Tarsus). This unique label, along with the many classy details, including art-decorated walls, hand-carved bedsteads and doors, and a flowery beachside pool patio, reflect an unusual degree of care and devotion. At Av. Gómez Farías 408, San Patricio-Melaque, Jalisco 48980, tel.(335) 551-17, fax 552-68. The only drawback lies in the motel-style corridor layout, which requires guests to pull the dark drapes for privacy. High season rates for the 27 rooms and bungalows begin at about $30 d; a kitchen raises the tariff to about $43 d, $20 and $26 low season; all with a/c, TV, and phones. You can also reserve through the owner in Guadalajara, tel. (3) 616-4850.

Hotels North of Town: If you prefer hotel high-rise ambience with privacy, a sea-view balcony, and a disco next door, you can have it right on the beach at the in-town **Hotel Club Náutico,** Av. Gómez Farías 1A, San Patricio-Melaque, Jalisco 48980, tel. (335) 557-70 and 557-66, fax 552-39. The 40 deluxe rooms, in blue, pastels, and white, angle toward the ocean in sunset-view tiers above a smallish pool patio. The upper-floor rooms nearest the beach are likely to be quieter with the best views. The hotel also has a good beachside restaurant whose huge *palapa* both captures the cool afternoon sea breeze and frames the blue waters of the Bay of Navidad. The hotel's main drawback is lack of space, being sandwiched into a long, narrow beachfront lot. Rentals run about $36 d, all year around, with a/c, TV, phones, restaurant/bar, and credit cards accepted.

In contrast, the friendly, downscale-modern, white stucco **Hotel de Legazpi** in the drowsy beach-end neighborhood nearby offers a more personal and tranquil ambience, at P.O. Box 88, San Patricio-Melaque, Jalisco 48980, tel. (335) 553-97. A number of the hotel's spacious, clean, and comfortable front-side rooms have balconies with palmy ocean and sunset views. Downstairs, guests enjoy use of a common kitchen and a rear-court pool patio. The hotel's beachside entrance leads through a homey vegetable garden to the idyllic Melaque west-end sand crescent. Here, good times bloom among an informal club of longtime winter returnees beneath the *palapas* of the popular Pelicanos and Viva María restaurants. The hotel's 16 fan-only rooms (two with kitchenette) rent for $27 s, $33 d, and $40 t in the high season; $14 s, $20 d, $25 t low.

The five-star **Hotel Real Costa Sur** on Playa Cuastecomate a few miles north offers a local, Club Med-style alternative at P.O. Box 12, San Patricio Melaque, Jalisco 48980, tel./fax (335) 550-85. The hotel's low-rise view guest cabañas spread like a giant mushroom garden in the jungly palm-forest hillside above the beach. Patrons —mostly Canadians and Americans in winter, Mexicans in summer and holidays—enjoy deluxe air-conditioned view rooms with cable TV, tennis courts, sailing, windsurfing, pedal boats, snorkeling, volleyball, and a broad pool and sundeck right on the beach. Rooms run about $35 d low season, $40 high. All-inclusive lodging, with all meals and drinks, runs about $50 per person, two children under 10 free per couple, children 10 or over $10. During times of low occupancy, the Hotel Real Costa Sur may accept day guests for a set fee. Call for details. (Note: A reader complained that she got sick from musty mildew in her room here. Although new management seems competent and dedicated to correcting such problems, choose a clean, satisfactorily ventilated room before moving in.)

Apartments, Houses, and Long-Term Rentals
If you're planning on a stay longer than a few weeks, you'll get more for your money if you can find a long-term house or apartment rental. Peggy Ross, at Crazy Cactus store in Barra (on Jalisco, corner of Veracruz, next to Restaurant Ambar) specializes in finding local rentals for visitors. Drop by or write her, several weeks in advance, at Tienda Crazy Cactus, Calle Jalisco, esquina Veracruz, Barra de Navidad, Jalisco 48987.

Trailer Parks and Camping
Barra-Melaque has one formal trailer park, **La Playa,** right on the beach in downtown Melaque at P.O. Box 59, Av. Gómez Farías 250, San Patricio-Melaque, Jalisco 48980, tel. (335) 550-65. Although the park is a bit cramped and mostly shadeless, longtimers nevertheless get their winter reservations in early for the choice beach spaces. The better-than-average facilities include a small store, fish-cleaning sinks, showers, toilets, and all hookups. The water is brackish; drink bottled. Boat launching is usually easy on the sheltered beach nearby; otherwise, use the ramp at the Hotel Cabo Blanco. The Trailer Park La Playa's 45 spaces rent for about $10/day, $220/month.

Follow wide, bumpy Av. Las Palmas north past Hotel Club Náutico to its dirt continuation above the west-end Melaque cove. There, you'll find an **informal RV-trailer park-campground** with room for about 50 rigs and tents. The cliff-bottom lot spreads above a calm rocky cove, ripe for swimming, snorkeling, and windsurfing. Other extras include super fishing and a sweeping view of the entire Bay of Navidad. All spaces are usually filled by Christmas and remain that way until March. The people are friendly, the price is certainly right, and the beer and water trucks arrive regularly throughout the winter season. Please, however, dump your waste in sanitary facilities. Continued pollution of the cove by irresponsible occupants has led to complaints, which may force local authorities to close the campground.

Wilderness campers will enjoy **Playa de Cocos,** a miles-long golden-sand beach, accessible by launch from Barra to Colimilla, or by road the long way around. Playa de Cocos has an intimate hidden sandy cove, perfect for an overnight or a few barefoot days of birdwatching, shell collecting, beachcombing, and dreaming around your driftwood campfire. The restaurants at the village of Colimilla or the stores (by launch across the lagoon) in Barra are available for food and water. Mosquitoes come out around sunset. Bring plenty of good repellent and a mosquito-proof tent.

FOOD

Breakfast, Snacks, and Stalls

An excellent way to start your Barra day is at the intimate *palapa*-shaded patio of the **Hotel Delfín,** Av. Morelos 23, tel. (335) 700-68. While you dish yourself fruit and pour your coffee from the little countertop buffet, the cook fixes your choice of breakfast options, from savory eggs and omelettes to French toast and luscious, tender banana pancakes; a complete breakfast costs $3-5, daily 8:30-10:30 a.m.

In Melaque, Club Náutico and Pelicanos (see below) are also good places to start your day.

Plenty of good daytime eating in Melaque goes on at the lineup of small, permanent *fondas* (foodstalls) in the alley that runs south from Av. Hidalgo, half a block toward the beach from the southwest plaza corner. You can't go wrong with *fonda* food, as long as it's made right in front of you and served piping hot.

For evening light meals and snacks, Barra has plenty of options. Here, families seem to fall into two categories: those who sell food to sidewalk passersby, and those who enjoy their offerings. The three blocks of Av. Veracruz from Morelos to the city *jardín* (park) are dotted with tables that residents nightly load with hearty, economical food offerings, from tacos *de lengua* (tongue) and pork tamales to *pozole Guadalajara* and *chiles rellenos.* The wholesomeness of their menus is evidenced by their devoted followings of longtime neighbor and tourist customers.

Restaurants

One such family has built their sidewalk culinary skills into a thriving Barra storefront business, the **Restaurant Paty,** at the corner of Veracruz and Jalisco, tel. (335) 707-43. They offer the traditional menu of Mexican *antojitos*—tacos, quesadillas, tostadas—plus roast beef, chicken, and very tasty *pozole* soup. Open daily 8 a.m.-11 p.m. Budget. For a variation on the same theme, try **Restaurant Chela,** across the street, on the corner.

Seafood palapas await at Colimilla's lagoonside for visitor-filled boats from Barra de Navidad.

Restaurant Ambar, Veracruz 101A, corner Jalisco, one of Barra's most refined eateries, stands beneath a luxuriously airy upstairs *palapa* diagonally across from the Pati. Its unusual menu features lighter fare—eggs, fish, whole-wheat *(harina integral)* tortillas and bread. Besides a large selection of sweet and nonsweet crepes, Ambar also serves a number of seafood and vegetable salads and Mexican plates, including scrumptious *chiles rellenos.* The wine list, which features the good Baja California Cetto label, is the best in town. Open daily 8 a.m.-noon for breakfast, 5-10 p.m. for dinner; American Express accepted. Moderate.

Among Barra's best eateries is the **Restaurant Ramon,** tel. (335) 564-85, tucked beneath its tall *palapa* at 260 Legazpi, across the street from the Hotel Barra de Navidad. Completely without pretension and making the most from the usual list of international and Mexican specialties, friendly owner/chef Ramon and his hardworking staff continue to build their already sizable following. Choose whatever you like—chicken, fish, *chiles rellenos,* guacamole, spaghetti—and you'll most likely be pleased. Extras include gratis salsa and chips to start, hearty portions, and often a healthy side of cooked veggies on your plate. Open daily 7 a.m.-11 p.m. Moderate.

One of Barra's most entertainingly scenic restaurants is **Veleros,** right on the lagoon at Veracruz 64, tel. (335) 558-38. If you happen to visit Barra during the full moon, don't miss watching its shimmering reflection from the restaurant *palapa* as it rises over the mangrove-bordered expanse. An additional Veleros bonus is the fascinating darting, swirling school of fish attracted by the spotlight shining on the water. Finally comes the food, which you can select from a menu of carefully prepared and served shrimp, lobster, octopus, chicken, and steak entrées. The brochettes are especially popular. Open daily noon-10 p.m.; credit cards accepted. Moderate.

Nearby, half a block south, a relative newcomer on the Barra lagoonfront is **Jalapeños,** the brain-child of personable restaurateur Raoul Canet, who built his original Jalapeños in Manzanillo from a solid formula of savory, authentically Mexican-style specialties, professionally served and invitingly presented. Here in Barra, his beachfront *palapa* branch seems destined for the similar success. Closed September and October.

For a change of scene, try **Restaurant Seamaster,** one block away, on the beach side of the sandbar, where guests enjoy a refreshing sea breeze every afternoon and a happy-hour sunset every evening at López de Legazpi 140. Besides super-fresh seafood selections, Seamaster features savory barbecued chicken and rib plates. Open daily 8 a.m.-11 p.m. Moderate.

Restaurant Pancho, three doors away at Legazpi 53, is one of Barra's original *palapas,* which old-timers can remember from the days when *all* Barra restaurants were *palapas.* The original Pancho, who has seen lots of changes in the old sandbar in his 70-odd years, still oversees the operation daily 8 a.m.-8 p.m. Moderate.

Melaque has a scattering of good beachside restaurants. **Restaurant El Dorado,** under the big beachside *palapa* in front of the Hotel Club Náutico, provides a cool breezy place to enjoy the beach scene during breakfast or lunch at Calle Gómez Farías 1A, tel. (335) 557-70. Service is crisp and the specialties are carefully prepared. Open daily 8 a.m.-11 p.m.; credit cards accepted. Moderate-expensive.

Restaurant Pelícanos, a beach *palapa* on the tranquil cove about five blocks northwest of the town-center, remains one of Melaque's most enduring institutions. Although the picture-perfect shoreline and the social scene is half the attraction here, they nevertheless ensure their popularity with respectable hamburgers and very fresh fish. Open daily 8 a.m.-10 p.m. Moderate.

Viva María 1910 next door accomplishes about the same by specializing in good Mexican-style food. The restaurant's name is in honor of the thousands of unsung "Marías," *soldaderas* who fought and died along with their men during the Revolution of 1910-17.

SPORTS AND RECREATION

Swimming, Surfing, and Boogie Boarding

The roughest surf on the Bahía de Navidad shoreline is closer to Barra, the most tranquil closest to Melaque. Swimming is consequently best and safest toward the Melaque end, while, in contrast, the only good surfing spot is where the waves rise and roll in beside the Barra jetty. Bodysurfing and boogie boarding are best somewhere in between. At least one shop in Barra rents surfboards and boogie boards (see below).

Sailing and Windsurfing

Sailing and windsurfing are best near the Melaque end of the Bay of Navidad and in the Bay of Cuastecomate nearby. The only equipment available for use, however, are the windsurfing outfits and Hobie Cats (small catamarans) at the Hotel Real Costa Sur, tel. (335) 550-85. Call about a day membership if you want to participate.

Snorkeling and Scuba Diving

Local snorkeling is often good, especially at **Tenacatita** several miles north. The Crazy Cactus beach shop, near the corner of Jalisco and Veracruz, next to Restaurant Ambar, organizes snorkeling excursions.

Although no commercial dive shops operate out of Barra or Melaque, Susan Dearing, the very professional Manzanillo-based instructor, outfits and leads dives in the Barra-Melaque area. Susan, a veteran certified YMCA-method instructor with a record of many hundreds of accident-free guided dives, and her partner, NAUI-certified instructor Carlos Cuellar, can be contacted at the P.O. Box 295, Santiago, Colima 28860, tel./fax (333) 306-42, e-mail: scubamex@delfin.colimanet.com.

Tennis and Golf

The **Hotel Cabo Blanco** tennis courts, tel. (335) 550-22, 551-82, 551-03, are customarily open for public rental for about $5 per hour. Lessons may also be available. The **Hotel Costa Sur,** tel. (335) 550-85, has tennis courts for guests and day members.

The lovely, breezy 18-hole **Isla de Navidad Golf Course** is available to the public for a fee of around $70 per person. Get there by regular launch from the Barra launch dock on the lagoon (to the Casa Club landing, about $5 roundtrip). By car, turn right from Hwy. 200 at the Ejido La Culebra (or Isla de Navidad) sign as the highway cuts through the hills at Km 51 a few miles south of Barra. Follow the road about three miles (4.8 km) to a bridge, where the road curves right, paralleling the beach. After about two more miles (3.2 km), you pass through the golf course gate. After winding through the golf course another mile (1.6 km), turn right at the traffic circle at the north edge of the golf course. Continue another mile (1.6 km), between the golf course and the adjacent hillside, to the big golf clubhouse on the right.

Sportfishing

Big-game fishing boat rentals are available from friendly Captain Rickey Zuñiga, at his shop, **Z Pesca,** on Legazpi, corner of Jalisco, diagonally across from the church, P.O. Box 45, López de Legazpi 213, Barra de Navidad, Jalisco 48987, tel. (335) 564-64, fax 564-65, e-mail: zpesca@aol.com. Rickey, who grew up in California, has three boats: a launch and two medium-size boats, one with cabin and toilet. His all-day fee runs about $100 (six hours, three people fishing) for the *lancha* and $200 for the biggest boat (six hours, four people fishing) complete with bait, tackle, and soft drinks.

The captains of the Barra Boat Cooperative **Sociedad Cooperativa de Servicios Turístico** routinely take parties on successful marlin and swordfish hunts for about $20 per hour, including bait and tackle. Contact them at their lagoonside office-dock at 40 Av. Veracruz.

There are many other fish in the sea besides deep-sea marlin and swordfish, both of which often make tough eating. Half-day trips (about $20/hour) arranged through Z Pesca or Sociedad Cooperativa de Servicios Turístico and others will typically net several large dorado, albacore, snapper, or other delicious eating fish. Local restaurants will generally cook up a banquet for you and your friends if you give them the extra fish caught during such an outing.

If you'd like to enter one of a pair of annual Barra de Navidad **International Fishing Tournaments** (billfish, tuna, and *dorado* in January and May) and father and son/daughter tournament in August, contact Rickey Zuñiga (above) for information.

Boat Launching

If you plan on mounting your own fishing expedition you can do it from the Barra boat-launching ramp at the end of Av. Filipinas near the Hotel Cabo Blanco. The fee—about $7 per day—covers parking your boat in the canal and is payable either to boatkeeper Señor Alvarez del Castillo (whose headquarters is inside the boatyard adjacent to the ramp, Mon.-Fri. 8 a.m.-4 p.m.) or the Hotel Cabo Blanco desk, tel. (335) 550-22, one block east, past the adjacent boat canal.

The antics of dwarfs, jugglers, and acrobats were common entertainments in pre-conquest Mexico.

Sports Equipment Sales and Rentals

Barra has two sports shops. **Crazy Cactus,** run by friendly, English-speaking Tracy Ross, offers rental snorkels, masks and fins, surfboards, boogie boards, and bicycles. It's on Jalisco, corner of Veracruz, next to (and below) upstairs Restaurant Ambar.

Nearby, personable owner Rickey Zuñiga of **Z Pesca,** on Legazpi, diagonally across from the church, sells snorkels, fins and masks, surfboards, boogie boards, and fishing lures, rods, reels, line, and weights.

EVENTS AND ENTERTAINMENT

Most entertainments in Barra and Melaque are informal and local. *Corridas de toros* (bullfights) are occasionally held during the winter-spring season at the bullring on Hwy. 200 across from the Barra turnoff. Local *vaqueros* (cowboys) sometimes display their pluck in spirited *charreadas* (Mexican-style rodeos) in neighboring country villages. Check with your hotel desk or the Barra tourist information office (see below) for details.

The big local festival occurs in Melaque during the St. Patrick's day week of 10-17 March. Events include blessing of the local fishing fleet, folk dancing, cake eating, and boxing matches.

Nightlife

Folks enjoy the Bahía de Navidad sunset colors nightly at the happy hours at Hotel Tropical and its neighbor, Restaurant Seamaster, a few doors down, or at Chips, the sunset-view bar of friendly ecological spark plug Luis Davila, at the beach end of Sinaloa. The same is true at the beachside Restaurant Dorado at Hotel Club Náutico in Melaque, north end of main street Gómez Farías. You can prepare for this during the afternoons (December, January, and February mostly) at the very congenial 4-6 p.m. happy hour around the swim-up bar at Barra's Hotel Sands.

Lovers of pure tranquillity, on the other hand, enjoy the breeze and sunset view from the end of Barra's rock jetty.

After dinner, huge speakers begin thumping away, lights flash, and the fogs ooze from the ceilings around 10 p.m. at disco **El Galeón** (of the Hotel Sands, young local crowd) and **La Tanga** across the street from Hotel Club Náutico, north end of beachfront street Gómez Farías (entrance $7, mixed young-older local and tourist crowd). Hours vary seasonally; call the Sands, tel. (335) 551-48, or the Tanga, tel. (335) 554-72, for details.

Another popular and friendly dancing hangout is **Peeper's** bar on the sandbar end of Legazpi, across from the Hotel Tropical. Seasonally, from around 9 p.m., couples sway to a live, medium-volume mixed soft rock and tropical music repertoire.

SERVICES AND SHOPPING

Money Exchange
Barra has no bank, but Melaque does: **Banamex,** across the street and half a block north of the main bus station, is open Mon.-Fri. 9 a.m.-2 p.m. for traveler's checks, and until 3 p.m. for cash. Barra's official *casa de cambio,* at Veracruz 214, just north of the plaza, changes both American and Canadian dollars and offers long-distance telephone service; open Mon.-Fri. 9 a.m.-2 p.m. and 4-7 p.m., Sunday 9 a.m.-2 p.m. With even longer hours, the **Liquoría Barra de Navidad,** on Legazpi, across from the Hotel Barra de Navidad, exchanges both Canadian and American traveler's checks and cash; open daily 8:30 a.m.-11 p.m.

After bank hours in Melaque, go to **Money Exchange Melaque,** Gómez Farías 27A across from the bus terminal, tel. (335) 553-43. It exchanges both American and Canadian traveler's checks and cash Mon.-Sat. 9 a.m.-2 p.m. and 4-7 p.m., Sunday 9 a.m.-2 p.m. The tariff, however, often amounts to a steep three dollars per 100 above bank rate.

Post Office, Telephone, and Telegraph
Barra and Melaque each have a small **post office** *(correo)* and a *telégrafo.* The Barra post office is unfortunately far from the town center. From the plaza, head north along Veracruz, continue three blocks past the health clinic, to Calle Nueva España; go right three blocks to the *correo* on the right. Hours are Mon.-Fri. 8 a.m.-3 p.m., Saturday 9 a.m.- 1 p.m. The Melaque post office is three blocks south of the plaza, at 13 Clemente Orozco, between G. Farías and Corona, a block and a half from the beach, tel. (335) 552-30. Open Mon.-Fri. 8 a.m.-3 p.m., Saturday 9 a.m.-1 p.m.

The Barra *telégrafo,* which handles money orders, is right at the Av. Veracruz corner of the *jardín,* tel. (335) 552-62; open Mon.-Fri. 9 a.m.-3 p.m. The Melaque *telégrafo* does the same on Av. López Mateos, behind the *delegación municipal* (municipal agency), northeast corner of the plaza.

In Barra, at the plaza-front municipal agency office, you may use the 24-hour public *larga distancia* telephone. Another long-distance telephone office, tel./fax (335) 556-25, is at Mini-super Hawaii, on Legazpi, across from the Hotel Tropical, open daily noon-11 p.m.

Travel Agent
For airplane tickets and other arrangements in Barra, contact friendly Sandra Kosonoy of **Isla Navidad Tours** at Veracruz 204A (between Sinaloa and Guanajuato), tel./fax (335) 556-67. Open daily 9 a.m.-8 p.m.

Grocery Stores
There are no large markets, traditional or modern, in Barra or Melaque. However, a number of good mini-supers and *fruterías* stock basic supplies. In Barra, your best bet for fruits and vegetables is frutería **La Colmena,** east side of Veracruz, three doors south of the plaza, open daily until around 9 p.m. Three doors north, corner of Veracruz and Guanajuato, the **Mini-super Costa Alegre** stocks basic groceries.

In Melaque, nearly all grocery and fruit shopping takes place at several good stores on main street López Mateos, which runs away from the beach past the west side of central plaza.

Handicrafts
While Melaque has many stores crammed with humdrum commercial tourist curios, Barra sometimes has some unusual sources. For example, a number of Nahua-speaking families from Guerrero operate small individual shops on the bar end of Legazpi, just past the corner of Yucatán. One shop, **Artesanías Nahua** (NAH-waht), run by Oligario Ramírez, is a small museum of delightful folk crafts, made mostly by *indígena* craftspeople in the mountains of Guerrero. Pick what you like from among hundreds of options— lustrous lacquerware trays from Olinalá; winsome painted pottery cats, rabbits, and fish; a battalion of wooden mini-armadillos; and glossy dark-wood swordfish from Sonora. Do bargain, but gently.

You can pick from an equally attractive selection across the street, at **Arts and Crafts of Oaxaca.** Besides a fetching collection of priced-to-sell Oaxacan *alebrijes* (crazy wooden animals), *tapetes* (wool rugs), and masks, you'll also find a host of papier-mâché and pottery from Tlaquepaque and Tonalá, *sombreros* from Zitácuaro in Michoacán, and much more.

Barra's small **folk-crafts market,** on Legazpi, corner of Sinaloa, behind the church, is open daily about 9 a.m.-6 p.m. The vendors, many indigenous, offer handmade items from their own locales, which range along the Pacific from Sinaloa and Nayarit in the north to Guerrero and Oaxaca in the south. The Jalisco items especially—such as sculptures of human figures in local dress and papier-mâché parrots—are bargainable for prices significantly below Puerto Vallarta levels. Don't bargain too hard, however. Many of these folks, far from their country villages, are strangers in a strange land. Their sometimes-meager earnings often support entire extended families back home.

INFORMATION

Tourist Information Office

The small Barra-Melaque regional office of the Jalisco Department of Tourism is tucked in a little office near the east end of Jalisco, at no. 67, across the street from the Terraza upstairs bar, east end of the south end of Veracruz, tel./fax (335) 551-00. The staff distributes maps and literature and answers questions during office hours (Mon.-Fri. 9 a.m.-5 p.m. They also are a good source of information about local civic and ecological issues and organizations.

Health

In Barra, the government **Centro de Salud** clinic, corner Veracruz and Puerto de La Navidad, four blocks from the town square, tel. (335) 562-20, has a doctor 24 hours a day. The Melaque Centro de Salud, Calle Gordiano Guzman 10, no telephone, off main beachside street Gómez Farías two blocks from the trailer park, offers access to a doctor 24 hours a day.

In a medical emergency, dial local number 523-00 for a Red Cross ("Cruz Roja") **ambulance** to whisk you to the well-equipped hospitals in Manzanillo. Melaque's ambulance-equipped *protección civil* paramedic squad is also on call and reachable through the police at (335) 550-80, or directly, at (335) 563-76.

For routine consultations, a number of Barra and Melaque doctors and pharmacists are available long hours at their own pharmacies. For example, in Barra, see Jose Quintero López, M.D., evenings till 10 p.m. at **Farmacia Marcela,** Av. Veracruz 69, near the corner of Sinaloa; 24 hours on call, tel. (335) 554-31. For routine medications in Melaque, go to the **Super Farmacia Plaza,** on López Mateos, northwest corner of the town plaza, tel. (335) 551-67.

Police

The Barra police, tel. (335) 553-99, are on 24-hour duty at the city office at 179 Veracruz, adjacent to the *jardín.*

For the Melaque police, either call (335) 550-80 or go to the headquarters behind the plaza-front *delegación municipal* (municipal agency) at the plaza corner of L. Mateos and Morelos.

Books, Newspapers, and Magazines

The Barra **newsstand,** open daily 7 a.m.-9 p.m., at the corner of Veracruz and Michoacán, regularly stocks the Mexico City *News,* which usually arrives by 4 p.m.

Perhaps the best English-language lending library in all of the Mexican Pacific is **Beer Bob's Book Exchange** on a Barra back street, 61 Mazatlán, near Sinaloa. Thousands of vintage paperbacks, free for borrowing or exchange, fill the shelves. Chief librarian and Scrabble devotee Bob (actually Robert Baham, retired counselor for the California Youth Authority) manages his little gem of an establishment just for the fun of it. It is not a store, he says; just drop your old titles in the box and take away the equivalent from his well-organized collection. If you have nothing to exchange, simply return whatever you borrow before you leave town.

In Melaque, the **Librería Saifer,** open daily 9 a.m.-9 p.m., on the central plaza, southwest corner, also stocks the *News.*

Ecology Groups

The informal community **Grupo Ecobana** accomplishes ecological improvement through practical examples, which include beach-cleaning sessions with schoolchildren and camping out at secluded local beaches in order to discourage turtle egg poachers. For more information, contact Ecobana's personable leader, Luis Davila, who operates the Chips bar, overlooking the beach, a block north of the Barra church.

VOTA

PARTIDO ECOLOGISTA

DE MEXICO

LA VIDA ES PRIMERO
JUSTICIA Y LIBERTAD

Local chapters of Mexico's grassroots Partido Ecologista (Ecology Party) are becoming increasingly influential in municipal elections.

The University of Guadalajara also runs the local **Centro Estudios Ecologíos de la Costa,** which, through research, education, and direct action, is trying to preserve local animal and plant species and habitats. Now and then you may spot one of their white vans on the highway or around town. At the wheel might be the director, Enrique Godinez Domínguez, one of whose better-known efforts is the turtle-hatching station at Mismaloya, about 72 miles (115 km) north of Barra, near Cruz de Loreto. The center's local headquarters is in Melaque at V. Gómez Farías 82, tel. (335) 563-30, fax 563-31, across from the Hotel Pablo de Tarso in Melaque.

GETTING THERE AND AWAY

By Air
Barra de Navidad is air-accessible through airports in Puerto Vallarta and Manzanillo, which is only 19 miles (30 km) south of Barra-Melaque. While the Puerto Vallarta connection has the advantage of many more flights, transfers to the south coast are time-consuming. If you can afford it, the quickest option from Puerto Vallarta is to rent a car. Alternatively, hire a taxi (about $2) from the airport to the nearby new central bus station, north of the airport. There, catch an express bus, preferably Elite (tel. 322-108-48) or Primera Plus (tel. 322-100-95) to Barra-Melaque (three hours).

On the other hand, arrival via the Manzanillo airport, less than an hour from Barra-Melaque, is much more direct, provided that good connections are obtainable through the relatively few carriers that serve the airport.

See the **Puerto Vallarta** and **Manzanillo** sections for more details.

By Car or RV
Three highway routes access Barra de Navidad: from the north via Puerto Vallarta, from the south via Manzanillo, and from the northeast via Guadalajara.

From Puerto Vallarta, **Mexican National Hwy. 200** is all-asphalt and in good condition (except for some potholes, especially at the north end, between El Tuito and the Bay of Banderas) along its 134-mile (216-km) stretch to Barra de Navidad. Traffic is generally light, and there are no long, steep grades. Traffic may slow a bit as the highway climbs the 2,400-foot Sierra Cuale summit near El Tuito south of Puerto Vallarta, but the light traffic and good road make safe passing simple. Allow about three hours for this very scenic trip.

From Manzanillo, the 38-mile (61-km) stretch of Hwy. 200 is nearly all countryside and all level. It's a snap in under an hour.

The same is not true of the winding, 181-mile (291-km) route between Barra de Navidad and Guadalajara. From Plaza del Sol at the center of Guadalajara, follow the signs for Colima that lead along the four-lane combined Mexican National Highways 15, 54, and 80 heading southwest. Nineteen miles from the city center, as Hwy. 15 splits right for Morelia and Mexico City, continue straight ahead, following the signs for Colima and Barra de Navidad. Very soon, follow the Hwy. 80 right fork for Barra de Navidad. Two miles farther, Hwy. 54 branches left to Colima; take the right branch, Hwy. 80 to Barra de Navidad. From there, the narrow, two-lane road continues through a dozen little towns, over mountain grades, and around curves for another 160 miles (258 km) to Melaque and Barra de Navidad. To be safe, allow about six hours' driving time uphill to Guadalajara, five hours in the opposite direction.

An easier Barra de Navidad-Guadalajara road connection runs through Manzanillo along *autopistas* (superhighways) 200 (Manzanillo town bypass), 110 (Manzanillo-Colima), and 54 (Colima-Guadalajara). Easy grades allow a leisurely 55 mph (90 kph) most of the way for this 192-mile (311-km) trip. Allow about four and a half hours, either direction.

By Bus

Various regional bus lines cooperate in connecting Barra and Melaque north with Puerto Vallarta; south with Cihuatlán, Manzanillo, Colima, Playa Azul, Zihuatanejo, and Acapulco; and northeast with Guadalajara, via Hwy. 80. They arrive and leave so often (about every half hour during the day) from the little Barra de Navidad station, on Av. Veracruz a block and a half past the central plaza, tel. (335) 552-65, that they're practically indistinguishable.

Of the various lines, affiliated lines **Transportes Cihuatlán** and **Autocamiones del Pacífico** provide the most options: super-first-class "Primera Plus" buses connect (three per day) with Guadalajara, Manzanillo, and Puerto Vallarta. In addition to this, they offer at least a dozen second-class buses per day in all three directions. These often stop anywhere along the road if passengers wave them down.

Another small line, **Autobuses Costa Alegre,** provides similar services, including a different "Primera Plus" luxury class service out of its separate little station at Veracruz 269, across and half a block up the street, tel. (335) 561-11.

The buses that stop in Barra also stop in Melaque; all Autocamiones del Pacífico and Transportes Cihuatlán buses stop at the Melaque main terminal, *central de autobuses,* on Gómez Farías at V. Carranza, tel. (335) 550-03; open 24 hours daily. Autobuses Costa Alegre maintains its own station two doors south, tel. (335) 561-10.

However, one line, **Elite** (EL), does not stop in Barra. It maintains its own little Melaque station a block south of the main station, across from the Melaque Trailer Park, at Gómez Farías 257, tel. (335) 552-43. From there, Elite connects by first-class express north (two daily departures) all the way to Puerto Vallarta, Mazatlán, and Tijuana, and south (two daily departures) to Manzanillo, Zihuatanejo, and Acapulco.

Note: All Barra de Navidad and Melaque bus departures are *salidas de paso,* meaning they originate somewhere else. Although seating cannot be ascertained until the bus arrives, seats are generally available, except during super-crowded Christmas and Easter beach holidays.

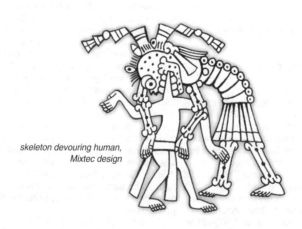

skeleton devouring human, Mixtec design

MIKE WELLINS

MANZANILLO AND INLAND TO COLIMA

MANZANILLO

Manzanillo (pop. 100,000) is a small city tucked at the southern corner of a large bay, so broad that it has room for a pair of five-mile-wide junior bays. From the north spreads the **Bahía de Santiago,** separated by the jutting Peninsula de Santiago from its twin **Bahía de Manzanillo** on the south.

Manzanillo's importance as a port has continued since the conquest. Even its name comes from its fortunate harborfront location, where *manzanillos*—trees whose poisonous yellowish-red fruit resembles a small apple, or *manzanillo*—flourished beside the original wharves.

Splendid local fishing led to an unexpected bonus: flocks of visitors, drawn by Manzanillo's annual International Sailfish Tournament. During three days in 1957, for example, tournament participants brought in 336 sailfish. The word soon got around. The balmy winters and the gold-

en sand beaches drew even more visitors. By the 1980s, a string of small hotels, condos, and resorts lined Manzanillo's long, soft strands, providing jobs and opportunities in the previously sleepy bayside communities of Santiago and Salagua.

HISTORY

Before Columbus
One of the earliest records of Manzanillo comes from a story of Ix, king of ancient Coliman, now the state of Colima. The legend states that Ix received visits from Chinese trader-emissaries at a shore village, which became the present town of Salagua, on Tzalahua Bay (now the Bay of Manzanillo). It's not surprising the dream of riches gained by trade propelled the Chinese across the Pacific hundreds of years before the Spanish

conquest. The same goal drew Columbus across the Atlantic and pushed Hernán Cortés to this gateway to the Orient a generation later.

Conquest and Colonial Times
Cortés heard of the legend of the Chinese at Manzanillo Bay from the emperor of the Tarascan kingdom in Michoacán. With the riches of China tantalizingly within his grasp, Cortés sent his lieutenants to conquer Pacific Mexico, on whose sheltered beaches they would build ships to realize Columbus's elusive quest.

In 1522, Gonzalo de Sandoval, under orders from Cortés, reconnoitered Manzanillo Bay, looking for safe anchorages and good shipbuilding sites. Before he left a year later, Sandoval granted an audience to local chieftains at the tip of the Santiago Peninsula, which to this day retains the name Playa Audiencia.

Cortés himself visited Manzanillo Bay twice, in pursuit of a Portuguese fleet rumored to be somewhere off the coast. Cortés massed his forces at the northern bay of Manzanillo, which he christened Bahía de Santiago on 24 July 1535. Although Cortés's enemy failed to appear, the foreign threat remained. Portuguese, English, and French corsairs menaced Spain's galleons as they repaired, watered, and unloaded their rich cargoes for 10 generations in Manzanillo and other sheltered Pacific harbors.

Independence
The hope generated by independence in 1821 soon dissipated in the turbulent civil conflicts of the next half century. Manzanillo languished until President Porfirio Díaz's orderly but heavy-handed rule (1876-1910) finally brought peace. The railroad arrived in 1889; telephone, electricity, drainage, and potable water soon followed. During the 1950s and '60s the harbor was modernized and deepened, attracting ships from all over the Pacific and capital for new industries. Anticipating the demand, the government built a huge, oil-fueled (but unfortunately smoky) generating plant, which powered a fresh wave of factories. By the 1970s, Manzanillo had become a major Pacific manufacturing center and port, providing thousands of local jobs in dozens of mining, agricultural, and fishing enterprises.

Recent Times
Although Mexican tourists had been coming to Manzanillo for years, international arrivals grew rapidly after the opening of the big Club Maeva and Las Hadas resorts in the 1970s. The new jetport north of town increased the steady flow to a flood; then came the 1980s, with Bo Derek starring in her fabulously successful movie *Ten*, which rocketed Las Hadas and Manzanillo to the stars as an international vacation destination.

SIGHTS

Getting Oriented
Longtimers know two Manzanillos: the old downtown, clustered around the south-end harborfront *jardín* and the rest—greater Manzanillo—spread northerly along the sandy shores of Manzanillo and Santiago Bays. The downtown has the banks, the government services, and the busy market district, while most of the hotels,

Charming reminders of old Mexico await visitors who stroll Manzanillo's downtown lanes.

restaurants, and tourist businesses dot the northern beachfronts.

Everything north of downtown is measured from the **El Tajo** junction (Km 0), marked by the downtown Pemex station. Here, along bayfront **Av. Niños Héroes,** the Barra de Navidad-Puerto Vallarta highway starts north just a few blocks from the *jardín.*

The highway curves past foothills and marshland, crossing the mirror-smooth waters of the **Valle de Las Garzas** ("Valley of the Herons") between Kilometers 5 and 7. The soaring white concrete sailboat sculpture at the traffic circle (Km 7) marks the *crucero* Las Brisas, or "suicide crossing." Here, the **Las Brisas Hwy.** forks left, curving southward, through a quiet neighborhood of condos, homes, and small hotels fronting Playa las Brisas.

Back on the main highway, now the **Boulevard Costera Miguel de la Madrid,** continue north past the hotels and restaurants that dot the long Playa Azul beachfront. Just after the dusty little town *jardín* of **Salagua** around Km 11, a golf course and big white gate mark the Las Hadas *crucero* (crossing) at Km 12. There, **Av. Audiencia** leads uphill along the plush, condo-dotted **Santiago Peninsula,** flanked by the Las Hadas resort on its south side and Hotel Sierra Manzanillo on Playa Audiencia on the north.

Back on the main road, continuing north, you pass the **Pemex** gas station at Km 13. Soon comes the Río Colorado creek bridge, then the **Santiago** town *jardín,* on the right, across from the restaurants, banks, and stores of Plaza Santiago shopping center (Km 13.5) on the left.

From there, traffic thins out, as you pass scattered beachfront condos along Playa Olas Altas (Km 15-16). Soon the **Club Maeva** spreads, like a colony of giant blue-and-white mushrooms, along the hill above Playa de Miramar at Km 17. Finally, another golf course and entrance gate at Km 19 mark the vacation-home community of **Playa Santiago.**

Getting Around

Visitors can easily drive, taxi (share to make it affordable), or bus to their favorite stops along Manzanillo's long shoreline. Dozens of **local buses** run along the highway through Las Brisas, Salagua, and Santiago (destinations marked on the windshields), all eventually returning to the downtown *jardín.* Fares (in pesos) run less than half a dollar. Hop on with a supply of small change and you're in business.

A Walk around Downtown

A pair of busy north-south streets—Av. México and Av. Carrillo Puerto—dominate the downtown. Avenida Carrillo Puerto traffic runs one-way from the *jardín,* while Av. México traffic does the reverse. The corner of Av. México and Av. Juárez, adjacent to the *jardín,* is a colorful slice of old Mexico, crowded with cafés, curio shops, and street vendors. A dignified Porfirian kiosk presides nearby at the *jardín's* center, while, on the far side, bulging rail tank cars queue obediently along dockside Av. Morelos. In the distance, drab gray cutters and destroyer escorts line the **Base Naval** (BAH-say nah-VAHL) wharfs.

Walk a pair of blocks along Av. Juárez (which becomes B. Dávalos) past Av. México to the cathedral, officially the **Parroquia Nuestra Señora de Guadalupe,** after Manzanillo's patron saint. Inside, four shining stained-glass panels flanking the main altar tell the story of Juan Diego and the miracle of the Virgin of Guadalupe.

During the first 12 days of December, a colorful clutter of stalls lines the streetfront, where families bring their children, girls in embroidered *huipiles* and *chinas poblanas,* and boys in sombreros and serapes. After paying their respects to the Virgin, they indulge in their favorite holiday foods and get themselves photographed in front of a portrait of the Virgin. (See **Fiesta de Guadalupe,** below, for more details.)

Town Hills and Market

Steep knolls punctuate Manzanillo's downtown. Residents climb precipitous cobbled alleyways, too narrow for cars, to their small (yet luxuriously perched) homes overlooking the city. For an interesting little detour, climb one of the staircase lanes that angle uphill off Av. Juárez, around the city hall.

An even steeper hill rises behind the cathedral—the brushy slope of **Cerro Vigía Chico**—where colonial soldiers kept a lookout for pirates. Above and beyond that towers the cross-decorated summit of **Cerro Cruz,** the highest point (about 1,000 feet) above the Bay of Man-

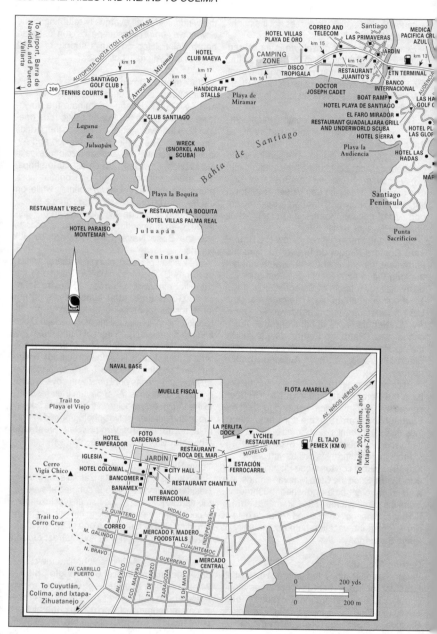

To Airport, Barra de Navidad, and Puerto Vallarta

AUTOPISTA CUOTA (TOLL FWY.) BYPASS

200

km 19

km 18

km 17

km 16

SANTIAGO GOLF CLUB
TENNIS COURTS

Arroyo de Miramar

HOTEL CLUB MAEVA

HANDICRAFT STALLS

CLUB SANTIAGO

Laguna de Juluapán

WRECK (SNORKEL AND SCUBA)

Playa de Miramar

CAMPING ZONE

DISCO TROPIGALA

HOTEL VILLAS PLAYA DE ORO

km 15

CORREO AND TELECOM

LAS PRIMAVERAS

km 14

RESTAURANT JUANITO'S

Santiago

MEDICA PACIFICA CRU AZUL

JARDÍN

km 13

ETN TERMINAL

BANCO INTERNACIONAL

DOCTOR JOSEPH CADET

BOAT RAMP

HOTEL PLAYA DE SANTIAGO

EL FARO MIRADOR

RESTAURANT GUADALAJARA GRILL AND UNDERWORLD SCUBA

HOTEL SIERRA

LAS HA GOLF C

HOTEL PL LAS GLOF

Bahía de Santiago

Playa la Boquita

RESTAURANT L'RECIF

HOTEL PARAISO MONTEMAR

RESTAURANT LA BOQUITA

HOTEL VILLAS PALMA REAL

Juluapán

Peninsula

Playa la Audiencia

HOTEL LAS HADAS

MÁR

Santiago Peninsula

Punta Sacrificios

MOON

NAVAL BASE

MUELLE FISCAL

FLOTA AMARILLA

Trail to Playa el Viejo

LA PERLITA DOCK

AV. NIÑOS HÉROES

FOTO CARDENAS

LYCHEE RESTAURANT

EL TAJO PEMEX (KM 0)

HOTEL EMPERADOR

RESTAURANT ROCA DEL MAR

MORELOS

Cerro Vigía Chico

IGLESIA

JARDÍN

HOTEL COLONIAL

CITY HALL

ESTACIÓN FERROCARRIL

To Mex. 200, Colima, and Ixtapa-Zihuatanejo

BANCOMER

RESTAURANT CHANTILLY

BANAMEX

BANCO INTERNACIONAL

HIDALGO

Trail to Cerro Cruz

T. QUINTERO

CORREO

M. GALINDO

MERCADO F. MADERO FOODSTALLS

INDEPENDENCIA

N. BRAVO

CUAUHTÉMOC

AV. CARRILLO PUERTO

MERCADO CENTRAL

To Cuyutlán, Colima, and Ixtapa-Zihuatanejo

AV. MEXICO

FCO. MADERO

21 DE MARZO

ZARAGOZA

GUERRERO

5 DE MAYO

0   200 yds

0   200 m

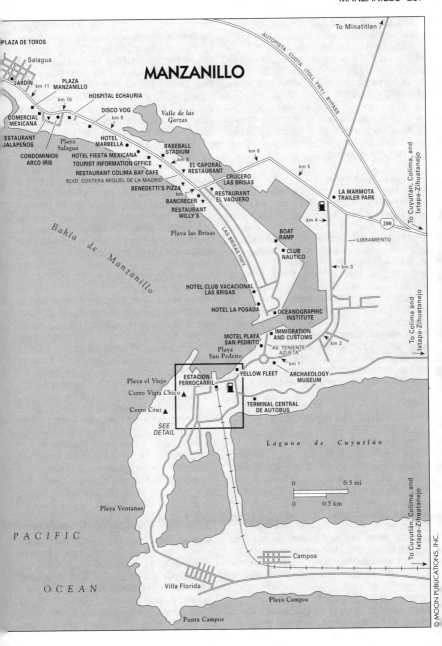

PLAZA DE TOROS

Salagua

MANZANILLO

JARDÍN

km 11

PLAZA MANZANILLO

km 10

HOSPITAL ECHAURIA

DISCO VOG

km 9

COMERCIAL MEXICANA

Valle de las Garzas

ESTAURANT JALAPEÑOS

Playa Salagua

HOTEL MARBELLA

CONDOMINIOS ARCO IRIS

HOTEL FIESTA MEXICANA

TOURIST INFORMATION OFFICE

RESTAURANT COLIMA BAY CAFE

BLVD. COSTERA MIGUEL DE LA MADRID

BENEDETTI'S PIZZA

km 7

BANCRECER

RESTAURANT WILLY'S

BASEBALL STADIUM

km 8

EL CAPORAL RESTAURANT

CRUCERO LAS BRISAS

RESTAURANT EL VAQUERO

km 6

km 5

LA MARMOTA TRAILER PARK

km 4

LIBRAMIENTO

200

To Minatitlan

AUTOPISTA CUOTA (TOLL FWY) BYPASS

To Cuyutlán, Colima, and Ixtapa-Zihuatanejo

Bahía   de   Manzanillo

Playa las Brisas

LAS BRISAS HWY.

BOAT RAMP

CLUB NAUTICO

km 3

HOTEL CLUB VACACIONAL LAS BRISAS

HOTEL LA POSADA

OCEANOGRAPHIC INSTITUTE

MOTEL PLAYA SAN PEDRITO

Playa San Pedrito

IMMIGRATION AND CUSTOMS

AV. TENIENTE AZUETA

km 2

km 1

To Colima and Ixtapa-Zihuatanejo

Playa el Viejo

Cerro Vigía Chico

Cerro Cruz

SEE DETAIL

ESTACION FERROCARRIL

YELLOW FLEET

ARCHAEOLOGY MUSEUM

TERMINAL CENTRAL DE AUTOBUS

Laguna   de   Cuyutlán

0   0.5 mi

0   0.5 km

PACIFIC

Playa Ventanas

OCEAN

Campos

Villa Florida

Playa Campos

Punta Campos

To Cuyutlán, Colima, and Ixtapa-Zihuatanejo

© MOON PUBLICATIONS, INC.

zanillo. Every 3 May, *peregrinos* (pilgrims) climb to its summit.

A Manzanillo downtown walk wouldn't be complete without including a stroll down Av. México, past a dozen old-fashioned little shops—*papelerías, farmacias, dulcerías, panaderías*—to the **Mercado** (turn left at Cuauhtémoc) at Calle 5 de Mayo. Here you can wander among the mounds of bright produce, admire the festoons of piñatas, say a good word to the shrimp-sellers, and stop to listen to the harangue of a sidewalk politician or evangelist.

Archaeology Museum

Manzanillo's new museum, the Museo Universitario de Arqueología, on the waterfront boulevard about a mile, Puerto Vallarta direction, from downtown, displays a wealth of finds from recent investigations, especially around Salagua. Displays include painted ceramic bowls, jars, and a load of decorative shellwork, especially bracelets, earrings, and necklaces, some dating as far back as 2,000 years.

More recent Los Ortices remains, named for the site south of present-day Colima, include charming human and animal figurines—a man with a headache, flutes, dogs, whistles—some masterfully crafted to an alabaster-like stoneware finish.

The museum, tel. (333) 222-56, is on Av. Niños Héroes, near the San Pedrito traffic circle, and is open Tues.-Sat. 10 a.m-2 p.m. and 5-8 p.m.

BEACHES AND HIKES

Playa San Pedrito

Playa San Pedrito is Manzanillo's closest-to-downtown beach, a tranquil little strip of sand right on the harbor along Av. Teniente Azueta (which angles off Niños Héroes half a mile from the El Tajo junction Pemex station). The perfect Mexican Sunday beach, San Pedrito has lots of golden sand, seafood *palapas,* and a few big trees for shade. Although its very gentle waves are fine for swimming and windsurfing (with your own equipment), Playa San Pedrito is too close to the harbor for much good fishing or snorkeling.

Manzanillo Bay Beaches

From either the *jardín* or the Las Brisas *crucero,* ride a Las Brisas-marked bus to end-of-the-line

Hotel La Posada at the southern end of **Playa las Brisas.** From the jetty, which marks the entrance to the Puerto Interior ("Inner Harbor"), a 100-foot-wide sand ribbon seems to curve north without end. It changes its name to **Playa Azul,** then **Playa Salagua** along its five-mile length, ending finally at Las Hadas at the base of the Santiago Peninsula. The beach, while wide, is also steep. The usually gentle waves break suddenly at the sand, allowing little chance for surfing, bodysurfing, or boogie boarding. Windsurfing (bring your own equipment) and surf fishing, however, are popular, as are snorkeling and scuba diving among the fish that swarm around the corals and rocks of the south-end jetty.

A number of restaurants along the beaches provide refreshments. They include the Hotel La Posada, Carlos'n Charlie's, the big adobe-colored Fiesta Mexicana on Playa Azul, and Hotel Marabella on Playa Salagua.

The Santiago Peninsula and Playa Audiencia

One of Manzanillo's loveliest views is from **El Faro,** the white tower atop the Santiago Peninsula. At Las Hadas *crucero* (Km 12) turn onto the cobbled Av. Audiencia. Continue past the golf course to the top of the rise, turn right at Calle La Reyna, and keep winding upward to the summit. Although El Faro is the centerpiece of a serene condominium community atop the hill, residents don't mind if you climb the tower.

The view is unforgettable. From the emerald ridge of the **Juluapan Peninsula** and the 4,000-foot (1,300-meter) Cerro Toro bull's hump on the north, the panorama sweeps past green sierra and the blue bays to the white downtown spread beneath the pyramid-peak of Cerro Cruz on the southern horizon. On the ocean side, due west, the Hotel Sierra Manzanillo rises above the diminutive sand ribbon of Playa Audiencia.

Once an idyllic downscale cove, Playa Audiencia is now dominated by the ultramodern gleaming white tower of the Hotel Sierra Manzanillo. Families nevertheless still come on Sunday to play in the fine golden-black sand, drink coconut milk, eat tacos, and leave everything on the beach. The beach concessionaire, Promociones y Recreaciones del Pacífico, tel. (333) 381-48, rents kayaks, windsurfing boards, water skis, jet skis, banana boats, and boogie boards right on the beach; open daily 9 a.m.-6 p.m. Instructors from the hotel often guide snorkeling and scuba diving parties from the beach to the shoals on either side.

Santiago Bay Beaches

The beaches of Santiago Bay stretch for five golden miles north of the Santiago Peninsula to Playa la Boquita, the lagoon-mouth beneath the Juluapan Peninsula's headland. The beaches are all continuous variations of the same wide carpet of yellow, semi-coarse sand.

First, at around Km 14, **Playa Santiago** reaches the Río Colorado creek, where it becomes **Playa Olas Altas.** Here, although the sand drops steeply into the surf, it levels out offshore, so the waves roll in gradually, providing excellent surfing, bodysurfing, and boogie boarding breaks.

Playa Miramar continues past Club Maeva, marked by the highway pedestrian overpass. The beach itself is popular and cluttered with umbrellas, horses for rent, and vendors. The usually gentle surf is good for bodysurfing and boogie boarding. Concessionaires rent boogie boards for about $2 an hour.

Finally, at Club Santiago, the beach curves past a village of seafood *palapas* and fishing boats called **La Boquita** ("The Little Mouth"). The sand is wide and firm, and the surf is as tranquil as a huge kiddie pool. Offshore, a 200-foot wreck swarms with fish a few feet beneath the surface, excellent for snorkeling and scuba diving. On the other side of the beach, the **Laguna de Juluapan,** a wildlife-rich tidal wetland, winds along miles of forest-edged shallows and grassy marshes.

Hikes

The adventurous can seek out Manzanillo's many hidden corners, beginning right downtown. **Playa Viejo** is often missed, tucked in a little cove over the hill and accessible by path only. Wear walking shoes and a hat, and take your bathing suit, water, and a picnic lunch. Follow Calle Balbino Dávalos past the cathedral. Bear left up the narrow street and climb the steep concrete staircase (on the left) to the hilltop schoolyard. Continue down the other side along a wooded arroyo trail to the beach. The dark sand beach is strewn with shells and surf-rounded rocks. One dry, grassy spot for possible camping perches above the surf.

Also beginning from downtown, the steep trail to Cerro Vigía Chico and Cerro Cruz will challenge fit hikers. It leads to the top of the highest point in Manzanillo for a breezy panoramic view of the city, bay, and ocean below. Allow about an hour and a half roundtrip for Cerro Vigía Chico, about twice that for the very steep continuation to Cerro Cruz. Take plenty of water, and avoid midday heat by going early in the morning or late afternoon.

Cerro Vigía Chico: Head south along Av. Carrillo Puerto from the *jardín.* Notice the *sastrería* (tailor shop) Aguayo at no. 223 on the left-hand side, where the master tailor sews suits by hand. Turn the corner at the *tortillería* at Nícolas Bravo and head along the upward lane, past little hillside-perched houses. Ask the local people if you get lost. Say *"¿A Cerro Vigía, por favor?"* They'll help keep you on the right track.

You'll know you've arrived when you see the white FM radio transmitter station atop the hill.

Cerro Cruz: Extra-fit hikers can gather breath and push ahead, along the steep, forested uphill path from the radio station to the summit of Cerro Cruz. There, a majestic panorama spreads below: from the Gibraltar-like headland of Juluapan in the north, past golden beaches, over the villa-studded Santiago Peninsula, past the white city to the huge expanse of the Laguna de Cuyutlán, where power stanchions leapfrog across the lagoon from the gargantuan, smoke-spewing seaside power plant.

ACCOMMODATIONS

Downtown Hotels

Near cafés, shopping, and transportation, Manzanillo's downtown is colorful and lively, but often noisy.

The **Hotel Colonial,** Bocanegra 28, at Av. México, Manzanillo, Colima 28200, tel./fax (333) 210-80, 211-34, or 212-30, Manzanillo's best downtown hotel, is built around a dignified interior courtyard restaurant. Dating from the 1940s, the Colonial, one block from the *jardín,* is replete with old-fashioned touches—bright-hued tile staircases, stained-glass windows, and sentimental tile wall scenes. The rooms, although

OWNING PARADISE

Droves of repeat visitors have fled their northern winters and bought or permanently rented a part of their favorite Pacific Mexico paradise. They happily reside all or part of the year in beachside developments that have mushroomed, especially in Mazatlán, Puerto Vallarta, Manzanillo, and Acapulco. Deluxe vacation homes, which foreigners can own through special trusts, run upwards from $50,000; condos begin at about half that. Time shares, a type of rental, start at $5,000.

Trusts

In the past, Mexicans have feared, with some justification, that foreigners were out to buy their country. As a consequence, present laws prohibit foreigners from holding direct title to property within 30 miles (50 km) of a beachfront or within 60 miles (100 km) of a national border.

However, Mexican law does permit *fideicomisos* (trusts), which substitute for outright foreign ownership. Trusts allow you, as the beneficiary, all the usual rights to the property, such as use, sale, improvement, and transfer, in exchange for paying an annual fee to a Mexican bank, the trustee, which holds nominal title to the property. Trust ownership has been compared to owning all the shares of a corporation, which in turn owns a factory. While not owning the factory in name, you have legal control over it.

Although some folks have been bilked into buying south-of-the-border equivalents of the Brooklyn Bridge, Mexican trust ownership is a happy reality for growing numbers of American, Canadian, and European beneficiaries who simply love Mexico.

Bienes raíces (real estate) in Mexico works a lot like in the U.S. and Canada. Agents handle multiple listings, show properties, assist negotiations, track paperwork, and earn commissions for sales completed. If you're interested in buying a Mexican property, work with one of the many honest and hardworking Mexican agents, preferably recommended through a reliable firm back home.

Once you find a good property and have a written sales agreement in hand, your agent should recommend a *notaria pública* (notary) who, unlike a U.S. notary public, is an attorney skilled and licensed in property transactions. A Mexican notary, functioning much as a title company does in the U.S., is the most important person in completing your transaction. The notary traces the title, ensuring that your bank-trustee legally receives it, and making sure the agreed-upon amounts of money get transferred between you, seller, bank, agent, and notary.

You and your agent should meet jointly with the notary early on to discuss the deal and get the notary's computation of the closing costs. For a typical trust-sale, closing costs (covering permit, filing, bank, notary, and registry fees) are considerable, typically 8-10% of the sale amount. After that, you will continue to owe property taxes and an approximately one percent annual fee to your bank-trustee.

Time-Sharing

Started in Europe, time-sharing has spread all over the globe. A time share is a prepaid rental of a condo for a specified time period per year. Agreements usually allow you to temporarily exchange your time share rental for similar lodgings throughout the world.

Your first contact with time-sharing will often be someone on a resort street corner who offers you a half-price tour for "an hour of your time." Soon you'll be attending a hard-sell session offering you tempting inducements in exchange for a check written on the spot. The basic appeal is your investment—say $10,000 cash for a two-week annual stay in a deluxe beach condo—will earn you a handsome profit if you decide to sell your rights sometime in the future. What they don't mention is that, in recent years, time shares have become increasingly difficult to sell and the interest you could get for your $10,000 cash would go far toward renting an equally luxurious vacation condo every year without entailing as much risk.

And risk there is, because you would be handing over your cash for a promise only. Read the fine print. Shop around, and don't give away anything until you inspect the condo you would be getting and talk to others who have invested in the same time share. It may be a good deal, but don't let them rush you into paradise.

worn, have traditional high ceilings, hand-hewn leather chairs, and wrought-iron lamp fixtures. They open to shady, street-view corridors, lined with chairs for sitting. Try for a room on the relatively quiet Bocanegra Street side of the hotel. The 38 rooms rent for about $16 s or d, with baths and a/c. Credit cards accepted.

A prime budget stop is the **Hotel Emperador,** at B. Dávalos 69, Manzanillo, Colima 28200, tel. (333) 223-74, a stack of 28 rooms around a dim interior patio, which, at first glance, appears uninviting. Inside, however, the grandmotherly owner, María Trinidad Bautista, and her staff keep the corridors and stairways shining. The rooms too, although very plain, are very clean. Furthermore, the price is certainly right: rates run about $7 s, $10 d, $13 t, with baths, ceiling fans, and a good restaurant downstairs. Located half a block from the *jardín,* on the quiet westward extension of B. Dávalos, just before the church.

If you prefer the beach, to the north the **Motel Playa San Pedrito** offers a homey close-in alternative, right on popular Playa San Pedrito, at Av. Teniente Azueta 3, Manzanillo, Colima 28200, tel. (333) 205-35. This unpretentious Mexican family hotel rambles amidst a flowery garden, edged with colorful tropical plants and centering on a free-form blue swimming pool. A tennis court stands at one side, and beyond that, waves lap the sandy beach. With all those outdoor attractions, the plainness of the rooms and the dust in their corners matter little. Request one of the *piso arriba* (upper-floor) rooms for privacy and sea views from a front balcony-corridor. The 33 fan-only rooms go for about $15 s or d, $20 t, with parking, and credit cards are accepted.

Las Brisas-Playa Azul Hotels

The swish of the waves on the sand, long walks at dusk, and good restaurants nearby summarize the attractions of the "passionate pink" **Hotel La Posada,** a durable jewel among Manzanillo's small hotels, Av. Lázaro Cárdenas 201, P.O. Box 201, Manzanillo, Colima 28200, tel. (333) 318-99, e-mail: posada@bay.net.mx. Every detail—leafy potted plants, rustling palms, brick arches, airy beach-view *sala,* resplendent bayview sunsets—adds to La Posada's romantic

ambience. La Posada's clientele, mostly middle-aged North American winter vacationers, prefer the upstairs rooms, some of which have private balconies and sea views. Get your winter reservations in early. Rates for the 24 comfortable but non-deluxe rooms run about $50 d low season, $75 high, some with a/c, including a big breakfast. The hotel has a bar-cart, snack restaurant, comfortable sitting area, good pool, street parking, and accepts credit cards.

A few doors north along the beach, the **Club Vacacional Las Brisas** likewise enjoys platoons of repeat customers, at Av. L. Cárdenas 207, Fracc. Las Brisas, Manzanillo, Colima 28200, tel. (333) 317-47, fax 400-86. Attentive on-site management keeps the garden manicured, the pool inviting, and the beach beyond the gate clean and golden. The best rooms, white-walled and comfortable but not deluxe, are on the ocean-view upper floors. The 35 rooms and suites, all with kitchenettes, rent, low season, for about $20 s, $27 d, $27 and $35 high, with both fan and a/c; with parking, and credit cards accepted.

The **Hotel Fiesta Mexicana,** Km 8.5, Carretera Manzanillo-Santiago, Blvd. Miguel de la Madrid, P.O. Box 808, Manzanillo, Colima 28200, tel. (333) 321-80, right on Playa Azul, appears as a big adobe box perched on the beach. Inside the rooms rise in tiers, which enclose a lovely patio with a meandering blue pool. On one side is a big restaurant with an ocean-vista veranda. The rooms are smallish but comfortable, with TV, phones, and a/c. The rooms on the ocean side look out on sea views. Although the 190 rooms rent for a pricey $58 d, low-season promotions are sometimes available. With street parking and pool aerobics; credit cards are accepted.

Not far away, the **Motel Marbella,** Km 8.5, Playa Azul, P.O. Box 554, Manzanillo, Colima 28200, tel. (333) 311-03 or 311-05, fax 312-22, offers a breezy beachfront location at moderate prices. All the ingredients seem to be in place—a small pool, rustling palms, a bar/restaurant, sand and surf—for a tranquil Manzanillo week in the sun. The best of the 100 rooms, on the upper floor of the original two-story beachfront wing, have private balconies and sea views. A new wing added many more deluxe, but rather sterile,

TESORO

a/c rooms, most without ocean views. Furthermore, the rates for the a/c rooms (most in the new wing) run $38 d low season and $41 high, while the fan-only rooms in the old beachside wing run a more reasonable $28 d low season, $33 high. If that's your speed, specify reservations in the old wing with an ocean view *(sección vieja con vista del mar).* Parking available, and credit cards are accepted.

The **Condominios Arco Iris,** Km 9.5, P.O. Box 359, Manzanillo, Colima 28200, tel./fax (333) 301-68, half a mile north, is more a garden apartment complex than condominiums. The setting, a spacious, leafy manicured tropical park, with inviting blue pool patio and *palapa,* nicely complements the apartments themselves. The units, all at ground level, with kitchenettes and ei-

MANZANILLO ACCOMMODATIONS

Accommodations (area code is 333, postal code is 28200) are listed in increasing order of approximate high-season, double-room rates. The toll-free 800 numbers are reached from the U.S. and Canada only.

Hotel Emperador, B. Dávalos 69, tel. 223-74, $10

Motel Playa San Pedrito, Teniente Azueta 3, tel. 205-35, $15

Hotel Colonial, Bocanegra 28, tel./fax 210-80, 211-34, or 212-30, $16

Condominios Arco Iris, P.O. Box 359, tel./fax 301-68, $26

Motel Marbella, Km 8.5, Playa Azul (P.O. Box 554), tel. 311-03 or 311-05, fax 312-22, $33

Club Vacacional Las Brisas, L. Cárdenas 207, tel. 317-47, fax 400-86, $35

Hotel Playa de Santiago, P.O. Box 147, Santiago, Colima 28860, tel./fax 300-55 or 302-70, fax 303-44, $38

Hotel Fiesta Mexicana, Km 8.5, Blvd. Miguel de la Madrid (P.O. Box 808), tel./fax 321-80, $58

Hotel La Posada, L. Cárdenas 201, tel. 318-99, e-mail: posada@bay.net.mx, $75

Hotel Villas Palma Real, La Boquita, tel./fax 502-03 or (3) 647-5480, $89

Hotel Las Hadas, P.O. Box 158, tel. 400-00, 420-00, or (800) 7-CAMINO (722-6466), fax 419-50, Web site: www.caminoreal.com, $175

Club Maeva, P.O. Box 440, tel. 505-95 or (800) GO-MAEVA (466-2382), fax 503-95, $180 (two adults, all inclusive, two kids free)

Hotel Sierra Manzanillo, Av. La Audiencia 1, tel./fax 320-00, (800) 457-7676, $400 (two adults, all inclusive, two kids free)

ther one or two bedrooms, are immaculate and tastefully furnished in '70s-modern style. The two-bedroom units, which sleep four, rent for about $53 low or high season; the one-bedrooms cost about $26. Discounts are generally available for monthly (or perhaps even weekly) rentals. A block from the beach and a favorite of many Manzanillo longtimers. Get your winter reservation in early.

Santiago Peninsula Hotels
The Santiago Peninsula's sea-view villas, condo developments, and resorts for the rich and famous are luxuriously isolated, generally requiring a car or taxi to get anywhere.

Hotel Las Hadas, P.O. Box 158, Manzanillo, Colima 28200, tel. (333) 400-00, 420-00, or (800)

7-CAMINO (722-6466) from the U.S. and Canada, reservations fax 419-50, Web site www .caminoreal.com, is a self-contained city with a host of pleasurable amenities. Las Hadas is so large only a fraction of its rooms are near the sand, and most are a small hike to the beach. Furthermore, when guests finally get there, they find no waves on the sheltered Las Hadas cove, and their views are cluttered by the white Arabian-style tents of a regiment of fellow guests.

Las Hadas nevertheless offers plenty of interest, at extra charge: three restaurants, a sportfishing marina, a sunset cruise, horseback riding, a golf course, a squadron of tennis courts, and a dozen aquatic sports. The approximately 300 luxurious white-and-blue motif suites, villas, and standard rooms rent from about $131 d low season, $175 high; larger "Camino Suites" run $175 d low season, $250 high. Breakfast and all amenities included, including complete wheelchair access.

On the other side of the peninsula, the shining white **Hotel Sierra Manzanillo,** Av. La Audiencia 1, Peninsula Santiago, Manzanillo, Colima 28200, tel./fax (333) 320-00, tel. (800) 457-7676 from the U.S. and Canada, towers futuristically above the gemlike Playa Audiencia. The hotel's large size, however, doesn't seem to bother the guests, whose activities focus upon the spreading ocean-view pool patio. There, around the swim-up bar, drinks flow, music bounces, and water volleyball and polo fill the sunny days. No matter if guests tire of pool frolicking; every hotel corner, from the indulgent pastel-appointed rooms (each with sea-view balcony) to **Hidra,** the airy, rustic-chic restaurant-in-the-round, abounds with style. Bars offer nightly live music; fine crafts and designer clothes fill the boutiques, while dozens of books and the latest U.S. magazines line the shop shelves. The all-inclusive rates, which include all in-house lodging, food, and entertainment, for the 350 rooms run about $128 per adult low season, $200 high. One child under 12 per adult free; $26 per teenager under 18. With a/c, color cable TV, phones, minibars, all water sports, tennis, golf, and wheelchair access; credit cards accepted.

Santiago Bay Hotels

The once-grand but now relatively humble '50s-genre **Hotel Playa de Santiago,** Balneario de Santiago s/n, Bahía de Santiago, P.O. Box 147, Santiago, Colima 28860, tel. (333) 300-55 or 302-70, fax 303-44, on the south side of Santiago Bay nevertheless offers much for budget-conscious travelers. Besides spacious, private balcony sea-view rooms overlooking the hotel's placid cove and beach, guests enjoy a palmy, seaside pool and sundeck, a tennis court, a boat ramp, and friendly management. Low-season prices for the 105 rooms and suites run about $32 s or d, $41 t; $38 and $49 high, with phones and fans only; credit cards accepted.

The **Club Maeva,** P.O. Box 440, Manzanillo, Colima 28200, tel. (333) 505-95, or (800) GO-MAEVA (466-2382) from the U.S. and Canada, fax 503-95, Manzanillo's all-inclusive fun-in-the-sun colony, spreads for a whitewashed quarter

mile on the hillside above Santiago Bay. Club Maeva, whose summer clientele is mostly Mexican, while Canadian and American during the winter, demonstrates the power of numbers. Its staff of 700 services upwards of a thousand guests who enjoy a plethora of aquatic, field, court, and gym activities at no extra cost. Months would be needed to take full advantage of the endless sports menu, which includes pool, scuba, snorkeling, tennis, horseback riding, volleyball, softball, aerobics, and basketball.

Besides sports, Club Maeva guests enjoy continuous open bar and restaurant service, nightly theme shows, a disco, a miles-long beach, sunning beside Latin America's largest pool, and a complete water-slide park.

Inclusive rather than exclusive, Club Maeva resembles a huge comfortable summer camp. Children are more than welcome, with a special miniclub for ages 4-12. Club Maeva seems to offer options for everyone, such as table games—cards, backgammon, checkers, and chess—Spanish lessons, and a tranquil adults-only solarium and pool-bar.

The rooms, actually clusters of small villas, are an unusual luxurious-spartan combination, snow white and royal blue with private view balconies and marble floors, but with no movable furniture. With the exception of stoves and refrigerators in some units, all shelves, cabinets, bed platforms, and seats are attractive but indestructible white concrete built-ins. The 550 rooms and suites rent for the all-inclusive rate of about $70 per person, low season double occupancy, about $90 high. One child free per adult; a/c, no phones or room TV; credit cards accepted.

At the sylvan northernmost corner of Santiago Bay, guests at **Hotel Villas Palma Real** enjoy Santiago Bay's entire beach, ocean, and mountain panorama from the comfort of their private, shaded balconies. A 100-unit hybrid condo, time share, and hotel tucked at the foot of a jungly mountain ridge, Villas Palma Real offers luxurious tropical living at relatively modest rates. Apartments range from spacious one-bedroom junior suites without kitchens to huge three-bedroom, three-bath apartments sleeping eight. All suites and apartments are simply but elegantly appointed, with creamy tile floors, decorator pastel sofas and bedspreads, designer lamps, king-size beds, and '90s-standard tiled baths. All but the junior suites have full modern kitchenettes. Here, you can have Las Hadas luxury for half the price. Rates for the one-bedroom junior suites run about $72 low season, $89 high, one-bedroom suites with kitchenette, about $80 low season, $110 high. Two- and three-bedroom apartments run about $160 and $200 low season, $190 and $240 high.

The hotel is adjacent to scenic La Boquita beach and wildlife-rich Laguna de Juluapan; bring your binoculars and bird book. No public transportation is available from the hotel; if you don't have your own wheels, moderately priced taxis are available. Amenities include cable TV, phones, a/c, fans, view balconies, pool, good, open-air *palapa* restaurant, minimarket, and laundry. Reserve through the hotel directly, tel./fax (333) 502-03, or through the Guadalajara office at (3) 647-5480, fax 122-3991.

Trailer Park and Camping

Condos, hotels, and restaurants have crowded out virtually all camping prospects along Manzanillo beaches. However, authorities allow tenting and overnight RV parking in the quarter-mile-long open space on the inland side of the highway (watch for the dirt road angling from the highway), just north of Hotel Villas Playa de Oro between Km 15 and Km 15.5.

If you prefer to park your RV or set up your tent in a trailer park, the downscale **Trailer Park La Marmota,** 100 yards along the highway to Minatitlán (near the Pemex station at Km 4.4), will probably have room to accommodate you. It's nothing special, but it has the basics: all hookups, concrete pads with a bit of shade, parabolic antenna connection, toilets and showers, a pool, and a minimarket. The price, about $8/day, $120/month, is certainly right. Make reservations, generally not necessary except 15 Dec.-2 Jan. and the week before and including Easter, in writing: Trailer Park La Marmota, Kilometer .1, Carretera Minatitlán, Manzanillo, Colima 28200, or by phone, in Spanish, tel. (333) 662-48.

The closest good country campsites are about a dozen miles north, three miles off Hwy. 200, at **Playa de Oro,** accessible by cobbled road from the signed turnoff near Km 31, five miles north of El Naranjo.

A land development turned sour, Playa de Oro has returned to the wild: an endless sandy beach with many drive-in sites, good for RVs and tents. The surf, while often not too rough, has some undertow; don't swim alone. Boogie boarding and surfing are possible for cautious beginners and intermediates. Surf fishing is excellent, and the waves deposit carpets of shells and miles of driftwood, perfect for a week of beach-combing. You'll share the beach with a colony of sand crabs which, like a legion of arthropodic prairie dogs, jealously guard their individual sand holes. Bring everything; the closest stores are in El Naranjo.

Although the Mexican name Playa de Oro ("Beach of Gold") is as common as tacos in Taxco, this particular Playa de Oro is not just another developer's label. The story goes back to 1862, when the paddle-wheeled steamship *Golden Gate*, loaded with 337 passengers and more than a million dollars in California gold, caught fire and sank not far off the beach. Only 80 people were saved and none of the gold. Although a salvage operation two years later netted some of the treasure, most remained until an enterprising American, now a local hotel owner, arrived on the scene. He promoted a powerful suction dredge, brought from the United States, which harvested the lost treasure. Despite the giant underwater vacuum cleaner's efficiency, local folks still tell stories of occasional shiny coins still washing up on the "Beach of Gold."

FOOD

Downtown Snacks and Foodstalls

The cluster of *fondas* (permanent foodstalls) at the **Mercado Francisco Madero** is the downtown mecca for wholesome homestyle cookery. Each *fonda* specializes in a few favorite dishes, which range from rich *pozole* and savory stewed pork, beef, or chicken, to ham and eggs and whole grilled fish.

One of the favorites, the **Menudería Paulita,** open daily 5 a.m.-10 p.m., is tended by a jolly squad of women off Av. México, at the F. Madero and Cuauhtémoc corner, five short blocks from the *jardín*. One of them enjoys the singular job of crafting and baking unending stacks of hot tortillas, which their mostly workingmen customers use to scoop up the last delectable morsels.

Besides sit-down meals, the same downtown neighborhood is a source of on-street desserts. These include *churros* (long doughnuts) and pastries, sold from carts late afternoons along Av. México about four blocks from the *jardín,* and velvety ice cream from the **Bing** ice cream chain's downtown branch on the east end of the *jardín.*

North-End Breakfast and Snacks
No local vacation would be complete without breakfast or lunch at **Juanito's,** Manzanillo's friendly refuge from Mexico, in Santiago, Km 13.5, a few blocks north of Santiago Plaza, tel. (333) 313-88. The longtime American expatriate owner features tasty, modestly priced hometown fare, such as ham and eggs any style, hotcakes, hamburgers, milk shakes, and apple pie. For a generation of repeat customers, Juanito's is home away from home, with satellite TV, a shelf of used paperbacks, a long-distance telephone, and bottomless cups of coffee. Open daily 8 a.m.-10 p.m.

Another excellent spot to start the day is the restaurant at the **Hotel Marbella,** tel. (333) 311-03, at around Km 8.5 on Playa Azul. Here, bright sun streams into the ocean-view bay windows while waitresses bring hearty breakfasts of eggs with potatoes, pancakes with maple syrup, and bottomless cups of coffee.

On the other hand, regulars flock nightly to tiny **Pepe's,** also around Km 8.5, on the beach side, which specializes in mouthwatering barbecued beef, roast chicken, and pork loin tacos; open daily 7 p.m.-1 a.m.

Downtown Restaurants
One of Manzanillo's prime people-watching cafés is the **Restaurant Chantilly** on the *jardín* corner adjacent to city hall, tel. (333) 201-94. The completely unpretentious Chantilly offers its mostly local clientele prompt service, an extensive economical menu, and long moments lingering over several varieties of café espresso. The *comida corrida* (five-course set lunch, $4.50) highlights many patrons' downtown day. Open daily except Saturday 7 a.m.-10 p.m. Budget-moderate.

The dignified, airy ambience of the **El Patio** restaurant of the Hotel Colonial on Av. México,

Doughnutlike deep-fried churros *rank among downtown Manzanillo's most popular street snacks.*

just south of the *jardín,* offers another attractive option. Besides its high-beamed ceiling, softly whirring ceiling fans, and a tranquil adjoining open-air patio, the lunch and dinner menu offers an unusually long selection of seafood, from broiled marlin and tuna to jumbo butterflied shrimp and pan-fried squid. A live duo sometimes adds to the enjoyment with soft guitar music afternoons and evenings. Open daily 7 a.m.-10 p.m. Moderate.

The crowd of midafternoon customers alerts budget-minded eaters to the value and quality of the restaurant at the **Hotel Emperador,** at B. Dávalos 69, half a block west of the *jardín,* tel. (333) 223-74. Although *desayuno, comida,* and *cena* are all good at the Emperador, the favorite is the $3 *comida corrida* set lunch, beginning around 1 p.m. Budget.

A different cadre of loyal customers enjoys the **Cafe Roca del Mar,** at the east end of the *jardín.* With approximately the same menu and prices as the Chantilly, the Roca del Mar, whose tables spread to the shady sidewalk, is perhaps a bit more relaxed. Moderate.

Around the corner, **Restaurant Lychee,** on the dock-front, two blocks east, at Niños Héroes 397, tel. (333) 211-03, serves bountiful plates of tasty Chinese-style specialties. Although their meat and fish dishes are tasty enough, it's the mounds of stir-fried broccoli, bean sprouts, snow peas, and bok choy that you can also order that spell welcome relief for vegetable-hungry palates. Unfortunately, present government plans include demolishing the Lychee and much else along the waterfront to make way for a new Puerto-Vallarta-style *malecón* walkway. Open Tues.-Sun. 2-10 p.m. Moderate.

Las Brisas Restaurants

A number of popular restaurants cluster around the *crucero* Las Brisas intersection (marked by the traffic circle and sculpture) at Km 7. The most modest of them is the Las Brisas branch of the Mexican **Benedetti's Pizza** chain, on the beach side of the highway, just north of the traffic circle, tel. (333) 315-92. The hardworking, friendly staff offers respectable Italian fare, good service, a friendly family atmosphere, and reasonable prices. The cool salad bar plate—carrots, tomato, beets, mushrooms, lettuce, and fresh bread, $3—seems like heaven on a warm afternoon. Open daily 11 a.m.-11 p.m. Budget-moderate. Visit or order pizza from other Benedetti's branches on the *jardín,* tel. (333) 281-99, downtown, and by Comercial Mexicana in Salagua, tel. (333) 315-92.

Half a block but a world away is **Restaurant El Vaquero,** Crucero Las Brisas 19, tel. (333) 316-54, Manzanillo's air-conditioned cowboy B-movie set. Its decor includes checkered tablecloths, wagon wheels, antelope-head wall trophies, and varnish-splashed plywood walls. The impression fits: an 1880s Sonora mining camp saloon-café, where teenage country waiters can manage little more than plopping plates onto your table and picking them up when you're finished. The cook outside hoists the ponderous steak-loaded iron grill to dump great shovels of charcoal into the fire below. You order your Vaquero steak by the kilogram—from two pounds on down. A "petite" half-pound (250-gram) T-bone or sirloin usually suffices. As an impression of the Wild

West, Restaurant El Vaquero seems correct. Historians tell us that the old cowboy joints were both seedy and expensive. Vaqueros represents an improvement, however: it accepts credit cards. Open daily 2-11 p.m. Expensive.

Willy's nearby represents something altogether different. Casual but elegant, Willy's airy, beachside terrace is *the* place to be seen in Manzanillo, two blocks down the Las Brisas Hwy. from the *crucero,* tel. (333) 317-94. Owner Jean François LaRoche features a list of good but pricey designer appetizers, salads, seafood, meats, and desserts. Open daily 7 p.m.-midnight; reservations recommended. Expensive.

Playa Azul-Salagua Restaurants

Restaurants dot the three-mile beach strip north of the *crucero* Las Brisas. One of the renowned is Carlos'n Charlie's **Colima Bay Cafe,** the Manzanillo branch of late owner Carlos Anderson's goofy worldwide chain, Hwy. 200, Km 8, across from the baseball stadium; open Mon.-Sat. 1:30 p.m.-1 a.m. high season, call for low-season hours, tel. (333) 311-50, 318-90. The fun begins at the entrance where a sign announces: "Colima Bay Cafe, since 1800." Inside, the outrageous decorates the ceilings while a riot of photos—romantic, poignant, sentimental, and brutal—covers the walls. Meanwhile, the waiters (who, despite their antics, are gentle sorts) entertain the customers. The menu, with items such as "Moo," "Peep," and "Pemex," cannot be all nonsense, since many of them, such as Oysters 444, TBC Salad, and the tangy barbecued ribs, are delicious. Moderate-expensive.

For a variation on a similar theme, try the **Guadalajara Grill** on Av. Audiencia, across from the Las Hadas golf course, about two blocks west of the Hwy. 200 crossing. Although the eclectic salad, ribs, steak and seafood menu would alone suffice, people flock to the Guadalajara Grill for a good time. "Loco" waiters, zany decorations, and live mariachis in season combine for a good night out on the town. Open daily noon-midnight; call for high-season reservations, tel. (333) 412-72 or 413-91. Moderate-expensive.

A sensational hors d'oeuvre and salsa plate draws customers year-round to **Restaurant Jalapeños,** at Km 10.5, a quarter mile toward downtown from Comercial Mexicana. Don't eat lunch if you want to fully appreciate it: a giant platter piled with hot, fresh chips, a trio of savory salsas, a plate of crisp pickled chiles, and a bowl of scrumptious refried beans. This comes automatically, before all the salads and entrées, and do try the luscious all-fresh cheese *chiles rellenos.* Since you can't possibly have room for dessert, order a Sexy Coffee instead. Open daily 5 p.m.-midnight, tel. (331) 320-75, closed September and October.

ENTERTAINMENT AND EVENTS

Botaneras

One of Manzanillo's unmissable entertainments starts quietly at around 1 p.m. at **El Caporal,** a big *palapa* restaurant/bar specializing in *botanas* (Mexican-style hors d'oeuvres). As soon as you order a drink, the *botanas*—small plates of ceviche, beans, pickled vegetables, and guacamole—begin to flow. By 3 p.m., mariachis begin strumming away, more bottles pop open, and more *botanas* arrive. By 4 p.m., the place is usually packed; if you stay till 6 p.m. you'll probably need someone to stuff you into a taxi home. El Caporal is behind the Superior beer distributor at the Km 8 post across the highway from the beach; open daily noon-7 p.m.

Not far away, crowds have at least as much fun at **Bochos,** another *botanera,* which, for simply the price of drinks, offers gratis snacks and a seasonal "tropical review"—singers, dancers, maybe a juggler and a magician instead of the usual mariachis. Open daily 1-9 p.m., in the big *palapa* around Km 8.5, inland side of the highway, across from Pepe's *taquería.*

Sunsets, Strolling, and Sidewalk Cafés

Playa las Brisas and Playa Azul provide the best vantage for viewing Manzanillo's often spectacular sunsets. For liquid refreshment and atmosphere to augment the natural light show, try one of the romantic beachside spots, such as Hotel La Posada, Restaurant Willy's, Carlos'n Charlie's, Il Navegante, and the Hotel Fiesta Mexicana. (Sunset views from the plush terraces at Santiago Peninsula and Bay hotels, such as Las Hadas, Sierra Manzanillo, and Club Maeva, are unfortunately obstructed by intervening headlands.)

Las Hadas provides an out, however. Its trimaran sloop **Aguamundo** departs daily from the hotel marina (at around 4:30 p.m.) for a *crucero de atardecer* (sunset cruise). The $20 per-person tariff includes drinks. For tickets, contact the hotel, tel. (333) 400-00, or a travel agent, such as Agencia Bahías Gemelas, tel. (333) 310-00.

Early evenings are great for enjoying the passing parade around the downtown *jardín.* Relax over dessert and coffee at bordering sidewalk cafés, such as **Chantilly,** corner Av. México, closed Saturday, or **Roca del Mar,** east side of *jardín,* next to Bing ice cream.

North of downtown, the **Salagua** (Km 11.5) and **Santiago** (Km 14) village plazas offer similar, even more *típica,* sidewalk diversions.

Movies

Television, recession, and the October 1995 earthquake have demolished all but one of Manzanillo's movie houses. Remaining is the **Cine Club Fiesta,** Km 9.5, across from Vog disco, which screens first-run Mexican and U.S. films, $3 beginning around 4 p.m.

Fiestas

Manzanillo's longest yearly party is the **Fiesta de Mayo,** celebrated for two weeks, beginning late April and ending around 10 May. A continuous schedule of events, including sports tournaments, art exhibitions, parades, concerts, folkloric dancing in the *jardín,* and a carnival by the downtown market, brightens Manzanillo days and nights.

The **Fiesta de Guadalupe** honors Manzanillo's—and all Mexico's—patron saint, the **Virgin of Guadalupe.** Shrines to the Virgin, with flower and food offerings beneath her traditional portrait, begin appearing everywhere, especially downtown, by the end of November. For 12 evenings beginning 1 December, floats parade and Indian costumed dancers twirl around the *jardín.* Afternoons, people (women and girls, especially) proudly display their ancestry by dressing up in Indian *huipiles, enredos,* and *fajas* and heading to the cathedral. Nearing their destination, they pass through lanes crowded with stalls offering Indian food, curios, toys, souvenirs of the Virgin, and snapshots of them beside the Virgin's portrait.

Many small shrines to the Virgin of Guadalupe appear in Manzanillo neighborhoods prior to 12 December, the culminating day of the Virgin's fiesta.

Sporting Events

Manzanillo hosts an occasional winter-season *corrida de toros* (bullfight) at either the Salagua or the El Coloma bullring (on Hwy. 200, four miles south of town). Watch for posters. For dates, call a travel agent or the tourist information office, tel. (333) 322-77, fax 314-26.

The renowned Manzanillo **International Sailfish Tournament** kicks off annually during the last half of November (see below).

Maycol

Singer-instrumentalist Maycol (actually Michael, but spelled so that locals pronounce it more or less like a proper English "Michael") wows audiences regularly at big local hotels and clubs, such as La Cueva and the Las Hadas. With fingers flying over half a dozen instruments from the piano to the saxophone and his velvety voice crooning dozens of tunes à la Frank Sinatra, Stevie Wonder, Nat King Cole (and even Dionne

Warwick!), Maycol radiates such charisma that you think he is performing personally for you. In fact, he will: for a private show for you and your friends, contact him or his wife Barbara at P.O. Box 726, Manzanillo 28200, tel. (333) 325-87.

Tourist Shows

The **Club Maeva** seasonally hosts a lively Saturday **Mexican Fiesta,** including swirling dancers, mariachis, rope dance, and rooster fights. Other nights, it stages theme parties where guests become part of the entertainment: International Gala Night, a journey to the world's great cities; Brazilian Night, a glittering Río de Janeiro Carnaval; and Wednesday amateur Night of the Stars, your chance to shine on the stage. Club Maeva parties, open to the public, begin with a big buffet at 8 p.m. and cost about $25 per person, $12 for kids under 12; for reservations, phone the hotel at (333) 505-95, or a travel agency, such as Agencia Bahías Gemelas, tel. (333) 301-00.

Discos

The big hotels, such as Las Hadas, tel. (333) 400-00, or Hotel Sierra, tel. (333) 320-00, nearly always offer no-cover live dance music in their lobby bars and restaurants. Call them for times and programs.

Discomania reigns regularly at a number of clubs along Hwy. 200. Call to verify hours, which vary with season. Bring earplugs, just in case. Some of the longer-lasting spots, moving from south to north:

The very popular **Bar Felix,** Km 9 on Playa Azul, tel. (333) 318-75, has relatively low volume recorded music, soft couches, and no cover, with a two-drink minimum at $3 apiece. Music is much less subdued, however, at its hot new companion supper club, **Disco Vog,** next door, tel. (333) 416-60. There, lights begin gyrating and the woofers begin thumping around 10:30 p.m.; cover is $10.

Nightclub-disco **Buss,** at the hotel Fiesta Mexicana, tel. (333) 321-80, welcomes customers through an entrance resembling the rear of a bus. The music, sometimes live, sometimes recorded, is always loud.

La Cueva, near Salagua at Km 10, tel. (333) 323-33 or 313-03, has live music, often alternating between louder tropical rock and softer Latin-romantic. Beginning around 10, seasonally.

At disco **Tropigala,** in Santiago, Km 15, patrons gather in its soaring black-walled interior to sway to recorded or live salsa "tropical" rock. About $4 cover.

The round, spacey interior of **Disco Solaris,** at Km 15.5, Hotel Villas Playa de Oro, tel. (333) 325-40, feels like a trip in a big flying saucer. Lights begin flashing, colored fogs descend, and music begins booming around 11:30 p.m.; about $3 cover.

SPORTS AND RECREATION

Walking and Jogging
All of the beaches of Manzanillo and Santiago bays are fine for walking. The sand, however, is generally too soft for jogging, except along the wide, firm, north-end Playa de Miramar. On the south side, the last mile of the no-outlet Las Brisas Hwy. asphalt serves as a relatively tranquil and popular jogging course.

Swimming, Surfing, and Bodysurfing
With the usual **safety** precautions, Manzanillo's beaches are generally safe for swimming, except on occasional days of high waves, when all but the most foolhardy avoid the surf. The safest swimming beaches are Playa San Pedrito and Playa de Miramar at the protected south and north ends, respectively.

The best surfing breaks occur along Playa Olas Altas ("High Waves Beach"), where, most any day, a sprinkling of surfers ride the swells a hundred yards offshore.

Bodysurfing and boogie boarding are much more common, especially on Playas Audiencia, Olas Altas, and Miramar, where concessionaires often rent boogie boards.

Sailing, Windsurfing, and Kayaking
Manzanillo's waters are generally tranquil enough for kayaking, but also windy enough for good sailing and windsurfing. A few concessionaires rent equipment at fairly hefty prices. At **Playa Audiencia,** the beach concessionaire, Promociones y Recreaciones del Pacífico, tel. (333) 318-48, rents windsurfers ($10/hour plus $7 lesson) and kayaks ($12/hour) to any able body. At **Las Hadas** beachside, Aguamundo, tel. (333) 400-00, ext. 759, rents windsurfers and kayaks to Las Hadas guests and those of hotels Plaza Las

Glorias, Club Maeva, Sierra Manzanillo, Villa del Palmar, and certain other big hotels.

Snorkeling and Scuba Diving
Manzanillo waters are generally clear. Visibility runs from about 30 feet onshore to 60-80 feet farther out. Manzanillo has three standout shore-accessible spots: the jetty rocks (depth 5-25 feet) at the south end of Playa las Brisas; rocks in mid-bay and shoals on both sides of Playa Audiencia; and the wrecked ('59 hurricane) frigate 200 yards off north-end Playa la Boquita. All of these swarm with schools of sponge- and coral-grazing fish.

The veteran YMCA-method certified dive director Susan Dearing and her NAUI-certified partner, Carlos Cuellar, operate **Underworld Scuba** from both their poolside Hotel Sierra headquarters and their shop on Av. Audiencia (Hotel Sierra Manzanillo-Las Hadas entrance road) next to the big Guadalajara Grill. With thousands of accident-free dives between them, Susan and Carlos rank among Pacific Mexico's best-qualified scuba instructors. They offer all levels and types of certification, including PADI, YMCA, CMAS, NAUI, and SSI.

Susan and Carlos start you out with a free qualifying lesson at the pool. After enough free practice, they'll guide you in onshore dives (for about $50 for a two-hour outing, including one half-hour fully equipped dive). They guide experienced divers (bring your certificate) much farther afield, including super sites such as Roca Elefante at the Juluapan Peninsula's foamy tip. You can also reach them at their Guadalajara Grill office, tel./fax (333) 306-42, cellular phone (335) 803-27, e-mail: scubamex@delfin.colimanet.com, or P.O. Box 295, Santiago, Colima 28860. You can also look at their web site at www.mexonline.com/scubamex.htm.

Although **Aguamundo** at Las Hadas (which also services Club Maeva and guests of other hotels) has boats, scuba equipment, and experienced scuba guides, it has no professionally licensed instructors. Its guided scuba dives (sometimes cluttered with tag-along snorkelers and spectators) are limited to certified scuba divers only.

Jet and Water-Skiing
At Playa Audiencia, Waverunners ($40/half hour) and water-ski towing are available at about $30

per half hour from the beach concessionaire, **Promociones y Recreaciones del Pacífico,** tel. (333) 381-48.

Aguamundo, tel. (333) 400-00, ext. 759, at Las Hadas beach offers similar equipment and services to guests of hotels Las Hadas, Club Maeva, Sierra Manzanillo, Villa del Palmar, and others.

Tennis and Golf

Manzanillo has no free public tennis courts. **Hotel Sierra Manzanillo,** however, rents its six superb courts to outsiders for $6 hourly during the day and $8 at night. The hotel's teaching pro offers lessons for about $20 per hour. Most other large hotels, notably Club Maeva and Las Hadas, have many courts, but do not rent them to the public.

You might also be able to take advantage of the three excellent tennis courts of the **Club Santiago,** tel. (333) 503-70, open about 7 a.m.-6 p.m., about $6/hour. Get there by turning off Hwy. 200 at the side road, signed Canchas de Tenis, just north of the golf course. The nine-hole course (office just inside the Club Santiago gate at Hwy. 200, Km 19) is available for public use daily 8 a.m.-5 p.m. The 18-hole greens fee runs about $24 ($19 for nine holes), clubs rent for about $15 a set, and a golf cart about $24 ($20 for nine holes). Caddies work 18 holes for about $9 ($7 for nine holes).

The renowned 18-hole **Las Hadas** course, at Km 12, Hwy. 200, has lately become available for public use. The greens fee runs about $36 for 18 holes and about $24 for nine holes. Carts cost about $25, clubs $17, and a caddy about $7. Call Las Hadas (tel. 333-400-00, ext. 884) for details and reservations.

Sportfishing

Manzanillo's biggest sportfishing operation is the **Flota Amarilla** ("Yellow Fleet"), whose many captains operate cooperatively through their association, Sociedad Cooperativa de Prestación de Servicios Turísticos Manzanillo. You can see their bright yellow craft anchored off their dockside office on Av. Niños Héroes, a long block east (away from downtown) of the El Tajo Pemex gas station. Their five-person boats run about $110 for a day's billfish (marlin, sailfish) hunting, completely equipped with three fishing lines. Larger,

plusher eight-person, six-line boats go for about $175, complete with ice and no-host bar. All of their boats are insured and equipped with CB radios and toilets. For information and reservations, call (333) 210-31, or write Flota Amarilla-Soc. Coop. de P. de Servicios Turísticos Manzanillo, Niños Héroes frente al 638, Manzanillo, Colima 28200, or drop into their dockside office.

A local Texas-bred couple, Sam and Marilyn Short, offer a trio of highly recommended sportfishing boats. The smaller are the 28-foot *Rosa Elena* and *La Dama;* the larger is the 38-foot *S.F. Marlin.* The captains, Hector and Hugo, veteran trophy-winners in past fishing tournaments, try hard to get their clients big catches. The *Rosa Elena* and *La Dama,* which can handle up to five passengers and three lines, run about $175-190 per day, complete. The *S.F. Marlin* can handle 10 passengers, six lines, and costs about $225. For reservations, call Sam and Marilyn at (333) 407-84, or their cellular number, (335) 707-17, or home number, (335) 506-05.

Other alternatives are available through travel agents, such as the Agencia Bahías Gemelas, tel. (333) 310-00.

Manzanillo sponsors two annual **billfish tournaments** in early February and late November. Competing for automobiles as top prizes, hundreds of contestants ordinarily bring in around 300 big fish in three days. The complete entry fee runs about $500, which includes the farewell awards dinner. For more information, contact Fernando Adachi, prominent Club de Yates ("Yacht Club") officer, at downtown Ferretería Adachi, Av. México 251, tel. (333) 327-70 or 200-73, or write the sponsors, the Deportivo de Pesca Manzanillo, P.O. Box 89, Manzanillo, Colima 28200.

Hopefully, sponsors of such tournaments will soon be able to devise competitions that will preserve, rather than wipe out, the species upon which their sport depends. Some progressive captains have seen the light and encourage their clients to release the caught fish.

Yacht Berthing and Boat Launching

Las Hadas Hotel's excellent marina has about 100 berths (up to 80 feet) rentable for about 50 cents per foot per day, including potable water and 110/220-volt electrical hookup. Reservations recommended, especially during the winter;

write Manager, Las Hadas Marina, P.O. Box 158, Manzanillo, Colima 28200, call (333) 400-00 (ask for the marina), or send your reservation request via fax (333) 419-50.

Las Hadas marina also has a boat ramp, available for a fee. Make arrangements with the marina before you arrive, however, or you might have to do some fast talking to get past the guard at the gate. At Hwy. 200, Km 12, follow Av. Audiencia past the hilltop, turn left at the Las Hadas sign. At the gate, the guard will direct you.

On the south end of Manzanillo Bay, you have a choice of two launching ramps. Use the **Club Náutico** (Yacht Club and sailfish tournament headquarters) boat ramp (inside the cyclone fence) for about $12 for big boats, $6 for medium, and $3 for jet-ski, or the rough impromptu ramp at the road's end for free. Get there at the end of the Las Brisas Hwy.; turn left and follow the road in front of the Oceanographic Institute to the inner harbor. If a naval guard is at the gate, he will let you through; say *"Club de Yates, por favor."* (KLOOB day YAH-tays, por fah-VOR)

On north-side Santiago Bay, you can also use the ramp (smaller boats only) at the **Hotel de Playa Santiago,** tel. (333) 300-55, fax 303-44, for a $3 fee. From Hwy. 200, Km 13.5, just south of the Los Colorados creek bridge, just north of the gas station, follow the side road running behind the ETN bus terminal, along the peninsula's north shore to the hotel at road's end.

SHOPPING

Markets and Downtown

Manzanillo's colorful, untouristed **Mercado Municipal** district clusters around the main market at Cuauhtémoc and Independencia (five short blocks along Av. México from the *jardín,* turn left four blocks). Southbound Mercado-marked buses will take you right there.

Wander through the hubbub of fish stalls, piled with dozens of varieties, such as big, fresh-caught *sierra* (mackerel) or slippery *pulpo* (octopus). Among the mounds of ruby tomatoes, green melons, and golden papayas, watch for the exotic, such as *nopales* (cactus leaves) or spiny green *guanábanas,* the mango-shaped relative of the Asian jackfruit. On your way out, don't miss the spice stalls, with their bundles of freshly gathered aromatic cinnamon bark and mounds of fragrant dried *jamaica* flower petals (for flavoring *aguas* drinks). Be sure to arrive a few hours before 3 p.m., when the inside section shuts down.

Santiago Shopping

Every Saturday morning, folks gather for the **Santiago Market,** beneath *tianguis* (awnings) that spread along Av. V. Carranza, two blocks north of the town plaza. Although merchandise tends toward dime-store-grade clothes and hardware, it's worth a stroll if only for the color and the occasional exotica (wild fruits, antiques, bright for-sale parrots) that may turn up.

For a host of genuine folkcrafts, head to nearby **Centro Artesanal Las Primaveras,** at Juárez 40, tel. (333) 316-99, two blocks from the highway, couple of blocks north of the Santiago town *jardín.* There, scattered amidst a rambling dusty clutter, a warehouse of many attractive handicrafts—blown glass, crepe flowers, pre-Columbian-motif pottery, leatherwork, papier-mâché clowns and parrots—languish, waiting for someone to rescue them. Open Mon.-Sat. 8 a.m.-8 p.m., Sunday 8 a.m.-2 p.m.

Back on the highway, just a few doors north of the Santiago *jardín,* take a look inside **El Palacio de Las Conchas y Caracoles** shell emporium, tel. (333) 302-60. Bring your shell book. Hosts of glistening, museum-quality specimens—iridescent silver nautiluses, luscious rose conches, red and purple corals—line a multitude of shelves. Purchase them (from $1,000 on down) singly or choose from an array of jewelry—necklaces, earrings, brooches, and rings. Open Mon.-Sat. 9 a.m.-2 p.m. and 4-9 p.m., Sunday 9 a.m.-2 p.m.

As you near Club Maeva on the highway, stop about a hundred yards south of the Club Maeva pedestrian overpass and look over the offerings of the **Mercado de Artesanías** on the beach side of the highway. Here, a dozen families sell crafts, many made by family and friends in their native villages in the mountains of Guerrero, Michoacán, Oaxaca, and Chiapas. They're poor but proud people. You should bargain, but gently.

Supermarket, Photo, and Health-Food Stores

The Manzanillo branch of the big **Comercial Mexicana,** tel. (333) 300-05, marked by the orange pelican sign, anchors the American-style Plaza

Shrimp sellers display their fresh offerings near Manzanillo's central market.

Manzanillo shopping center at Km 11.5. It offers everything—from appliances and cosmetics to produce, groceries, and a bakery—spread along shiny, efficient aisles. Open daily 9 a.m.-9 p.m.

At the entrance to the same Plaza Manzanillo complex, drop off your film for quick finishing at up-to-date **Foto Sol,** tel. (333) 318-60. Foto Sol also sells popular films and stocks some camera accessories. Open Mon.-Sat. 9 a.m.-9 p.m., Sunday 9 a.m.- 8 p.m.

Downtown, **Photo Studio Cárdenas** offers three-hour photo finishing, film, and some cameras and accessories on the *jardín,* at Balvino Dávalo 52, tel. (333) 211-60; open 9:30 a.m.-2 p.m. and 4:30-9 p.m., closed Sunday.

Manzanillo's health-food store, **Yacatecuhtli,** located downtown at Av. México 249, urges customers to "watch your health" with yogurt, granola, natural vitamins, ginseng, alfalfa tablets, soy burger, and cheese. Open Mon.-Sat. 8 a.m.-10 p.m., Sunday 8 a.m.-3 p.m. and 5-10 p.m. Its

small branch in Santiago, on the highway, about a block west of the Santiago town *jardín,* open Mon.-Sat. 8 a.m.-2 p.m. and 5-8 p.m., stocks a modest supply of health foods and products.

SERVICES

Money Exchange

The downtown **Banamex** (Banco Nacional de Mexico) exchanges both U.S. and Canadian traveler's checks and cash, Av. México 136, three blocks from the *jardín,* tel. (333) 201-15; open Mon.-Fri. 9 a.m.-5 p.m. The **Bancomer** next door, Av. México 122, tel. (333) 228-88, does the same (Mon.-Fri. 9 a.m.-5 p.m.). If they are both closed or too crowded, the **Banco Internacional,** tel. (333) 208-09, across the street a block toward the *jardín,* changes U.S. traveler's checks and cash and has even longer hours (Mon.-Fri. 8 a.m.-7 p.m., Saturday 9 a.m.-2:30 p.m.). After hours and on Sunday, go to **Casa de Cambio El Puerto,** at Av. Mexico 118, across from Bancomer, tel. (333) 247-59, open Mon.-Sat. 9 a.m.-3 p.m., 4-8 p.m., Sunday 9 a.m.-2 p.m.

Banks along the Hwy. 200 suburbs also change money. At the **Las Brisas Crossing,** Km 7, a small Bancrecer branch, tel. (333) 403-91, is open Mon.-Fri. 9 a.m.-5 p.m. In **Salagua,** try the Banamex, tel. (333) 414-90 (open Mon.-Sat. 9 a.m.- 5 p.m.) in the Manzanillo Plaza shopping center, or the Bancomer, tel. (333) 401-02, across the highway and west a block. In **Santiago,** you have a choice of Banco Internacional, tel. (333) 308-13 (open Mon.-Fri. 8 a.m.-7 p.m., Saturday 9 a.m.-2:30), on the highway, or Banco Santander Mexicano, tel. (333) 302-20 or 307-38 (open Mon.-Fri. 9 a.m.-5 p.m.), on Juárez, two blocks inland from the highway.

American Express Agency

Although it doesn't cash American Express traveler's checks, **Agencia de Viajes Bahías Gemelas,** Hwy. 200 Km 9, next to Chrysler Motor, tel. (333) 310-00 or 310-53, fax 306-49, sells them to card-carrying members for personal checks (usually up to $1,000). As the official Manzanillo American Express office, it also provides the usual membership services and books air tickets, local tours, and hotel reservations. Open Mon.-Sat. 9 a.m.-2 p.m. and 4-6 p.m.

Communication

The downtown combined *correo* and express mail **Mexpost** is on Calle Galindo, between Avenidas Mexico and Carrillo, about four blocks inland from the *jardín*. The *correo,* tel. (333) 200-22, is open Mon.-Fri. 9 a.m.-7 p.m. and Saturday 9 a.m.-1 p.m.; Mexpost, fax (333) 200-32, is open Mon.-Fri. 9 a.m.-2:30 p.m. and 4-7 p.m.

Telecomunicaciones, the new high-tech telegraph office in the Presidencia Municipal on the *jardín,* bottom floor, sends telegrams, telexes, fax messages, and money orders. Open Mon.-Fri. 8 a.m.-6 p.m., Saturday and Sunday 9 a.m.-12:30 p.m. *Giros* (money order) hours are shorter, however: Mon.-Fri. 9 a.m.-1 p.m. and 3-5 p.m. only.

In **Santiago,** the post office, tel. (333) 411-30, and *telecomunicaciones* offices stand side by side on Venustiano Carranza nos. 2 and 4, across Hwy. 200 from Juanito's restaurant. Post office hours are Mon.-Fri. 9 a.m.-1 p.m. and 3-6 p.m., Saturday 9 a.m.-1 p.m., while *telecomunicaciones* hours are Mon.-Fri. 9 a.m.-3 p.m.

Manzanillo's *larga distancia* telephone offices are conveniently spread from the downtown north along Hwy. 200. Everyone's favorite downtown is homey **Lonchería Ríos,** 330 Av. Mexico, about three blocks inland from the *jardín,* where you can enjoy a country-style *enchilada, torta,* or *hamburguesa* while you await your call. Open daily 8 a.m.-9 p.m.

However, if you're in the mood for efficiency, go to computer-assisted **Computel,** with several convenient locations: downtown, at Av. México 302; on the *malecón* at Morelos 196, one block east of the *jardín,* open daily 8 a.m.-9 p.m.; at *crucero* Las Brisas, open daily 8 a.m.-9:30 p.m.; and in Santiago, open Mon.-Sat. 7 a.m.-9:45 p.m., Sunday 9 a.m.-1 p.m., next to Juanito's, which, incidentally, also offers long-distance telephone and fax (tel./fax 333-320-10) service.

Immigration and Customs

Both Migración and the Aduana occupy the upper floors of the **Edificio Federal Portuario** ("Federal Port Building") on San Pedrito Beach, at the foot of Av. Teniente Azueta.

The cooperative, efficient **Migración** staff, third floor, tel. (333) 200-30, can replace a lost tourist card. (Make a copy of it beforehand, just in case.) Open Mon.-Fri. 9 a.m.-2 p.m. for business and around the clock for questions.

Contact the **Aduana,** second floor, tel. (333) 200-87, 211-82, for instructions if you have to leave Mexico temporarily without your car. If your Spanish is rusty, ask your hotel desk clerk or the tourist information office to call for you. Open Mon.-Fri. 8 a.m.-3 p.m.

Both the Aduana and Migración have offices at the Manzanillo airport, and are open daily 11 a.m.-9 p.m. and 24 hours, respectively.

INFORMATION

Tourist Information Office

The combined federal-state-city **Turismo** ("Tourism Office") answers questions and dispenses a small Colima and Manzanillo map. Located on 4960 Blvd. Miguel de la Madrid, across from Mariscos Barra de Navidad, tel. (333) 322-27, fax 314-26; open Mon.-Fri. 8 a.m.-3 p.m.

Hospital, Police, and Emergencies

In a medical emergency, call a taxi or **Cruz Roja** ("Red Cross") at (333) 428-14, and have them take you to either **Centro Médico Quirúrgico Echauri** at Km 9.7, Blvd. Miguel de la Madrid, tel. (333) 400-01, or **Médica Pacífico Cruz Azul,** at Av. Palma Real 10, Km 13, a block off, just south of the gas station, tel. (333) 403-85. Manzanillo's newest and best-equipped private hospitals, they each have round-the-clock service, including a laboratory and several specialists on call you can also visit for routine consultations.

For both medical consultations and a good pharmacy in Santiago, contact French- and English-speaking **Dr. Joseph Cadet Jr.** at his office next to Juanito's at Hwy. 200, Km 14.5 (open Mon.-Sat. 10 a.m.-2 p.m. and 5-8 p.m.), or his adjacent Farmacia Continental, tel. (333) 302-86 (open Mon.-Sat. 9 a.m.-2 p.m. and 4-9 p.m.).

For police emergencies, call the **Preventiva Municipal,** tel. (333) 210-04, in the city hall on the *jardín.*

Although Manzanillo no longer has any foreign consulates, it does have **HELP,** the Manzanillo Foreign Community Association, run by friendly director Bonnie Sumlin, who gives advice and assistance to travelers. Contact her at P.O. Box 65, Santiago, Colima 28860, tel./fax (333) 409-77, e-mail: help@delfin.colimanet.com.

Books, Newspapers, Magazines, and Library
Downtown is **Revistas Saifer,** Av. México 117, across from the Hotel Colonial, and Av. México 207, open daily two blocks down the street from the *jardín,* which stocks the Mexico City *News* and a few American magazines, such as *Time, Life, Newsweek, Computer,* and *Bride;* open daily 9 a.m.-3 p.m. and 5-10 p.m. The same is approximately true for its Plaza Manzanillo shopping center branch in Salagua, Km 11, open daily 8 a.m.-10 p.m.

The *tabaquería* shop at **Hotel Sierra,** tel. (333) 320-00, has the most extensive stock of U.S. newspapers, magazines, and English-language paperbacks in Manzanillo.

The Manzanillo **Biblioteca Municipal** (public library) is open Tues.-Sun. 8 a.m.-1 p.m. and 4-8 p.m. on the third floor of the Presidencia Municipal on the *jardín* downtown.

GETTING THERE AND AWAY

By Air
The **Manzanillo airport,** officially the Playa de Oro International Airport (code ZLO), is 28 easy highway miles (44 km) from downtown Manzanillo, and only about 22 miles (35 km) from most Manzanillo beachside hotels. From the other direction, the airport is 19 miles (30 km) south of Barra de Navidad.

Flights: Aerocalifornia Airlines flights connect with Los Angeles. For local reservations and flight information, call (333) 414-14.

America West Airlines connects with Phoenix during the winter-spring season. For local reservations and flight information, call (333) 411-40.

Aeroméxico Airlines' subsidiary carrier **Aerolitoral** has flights connecting with Guadalajara (where many U.S. connections are available). For reservations, call (333) 412-26 or a travel agent, such as Bahías Gemelas, tel. (333) 310-00; for flight information, contact Aeroméxico's airport office, tel. (333) 324-24 and 419-90.

Mexicana Airlines flights connect daily with Mexico City where many U.S. connections are available. For reservations and flight information, contact the airport office, tel. (333) 323-23, or the national toll-free number, tel. (800) 502-2000 or (800) 501-9900.

Canada World of Vacations charter flights connect with Calgary-Edmonton and Vancouver during the winter-spring season. Contact a travel agent for information and reservations.

Airport Arrival and Departure: The terminal itself is small for an international destination, lacking money exchange, hotel booking, and tourist information booths. The terminal nevertheless has a few gift shops, snack stands, an upstairs restaurant, and a *buzón* (mailbox) just inside the front entrance. Consequently, you should arrive with a day's worth of pesos and a hotel reservation. If not, you'll be at the mercy of taxi drivers who love to collect fat commissions on your first-night hotel tariff. Upon departure, be sure to save enough cash to pay the approximate $12 **departure tax.**

After the usually cursory immigration and customs checks, independent arrivees have their choice of a car rental (see below) or taxi tickets from a booth just outside the arrival gate. *Colectivo* tickets run about $6 per person to any Manzanillo hotel, while a *taxi especial* runs about $15.

Colectivos take passengers to Barra de Navidad and other northern points seasonally only. Taxis, however, will take three passengers to Barra, Melaque, or Hotel Real Coastecomate for about $20 total or to Hotel Blue Bay Village, $30; to hotels El Tecuán and Careyes, $40, or Chamela-El Super, $45, or Las Alamandas, $55.

No public buses service the Manzanillo airport. Strong, mobile travelers on tight budgets could save pesos by hitching or hiking the three miles to Hwy. 200 and flagging down one of the frequent north- or southbound second-class buses (fare about $1 to Barra or Manzanillo). Don't try it at night, however.

As for airport **car rentals,** you have a choice of **National,** tel. (333) 306-11, fax 311-40, and **Dollar,** tel. (333) 314-34. You might save money by contacting some local Manzanillo car rentals, who, even though they don't have booths at the airport, customarily meet passengers with reservations at the airport. Try **Auto Rent de Guadalajara,** at Hotel Villas Playa de Oro, tel. (333) 305-14 or 325-40, or **Odin,** at Ines Parra 28, tel. (333) 311-12. Hint: Unless you don't mind paying upwards of $50 per day, shop around for your car rental by calling Dollar, tel. (800) 800-4000, and National, tel. (800) 227-3876, toll-free numbers at home *before* you leave.

By Car or RV

Three main highway routes connect Manzanillo with the outside world: from the north via Puerto Vallarta and Barra de Navidad; from the northeast via Guadalajara and Colima; and from the southeast via Ixtapa-Zihuatanejo and Playa Azul (Lázaro Cárdenas).

From the north, **Mexico National Hwy. 200** glides 172 smooth asphalt miles (276 km) from Puerto Vallarta via Barra de Navidad. Neither few steep grades nor much traffic slows progress along this foothill-, forest-, and beach-studded route. Allow about four hours to or from Puerto Vallarta, about one hour to or from Barra.

The safety and ease of the new Guadalajara-Colima *autopista* (combined National Highways 15, 54, and 110) more than compensates for the (approximately $10 per car) tolls. Head southwest from the Glorieta Minerva circle in Guadalajara along Hwy. 15 for around 27 miles (45 km) until Acatlán de Juárez, and take the Hwy. 54 fork south for Colima. Later connect with Hwy. 110, bypassing Colima and continuing south to just before Tecomán, where Hwy. 200 splits off right, northwest, to Manzanillo. Figure about four and a half driving hours for this easy, 190-mile (311-km) trip, either way.

The same cannot be said for the winding 238 miles (390 km) of coastline Hwy. 200 between Zihuatanejo and Manzanillo. Keep your gas tank filled; the spectacularly scenic but sparsely populated 150-mile stretch from Playa Azul to the Colima border has no gas stations. Allow a full eight-hour day, in broad daylight, either way. Don't try it at night.

Drivers just passing through who want to avoid the long, sometimes congested Manzanillo Bay beachfront strip should follow the *cuota* (toll) bypass. Southbound, watch for signs around Km 20, at the village of Naranjo. Northbound, do the same. Follow the Cihuatlán sign after you cross the Laguna Cuyutlán bridge on the Hwy. 200 *cuota* freeway.

By Bus

Several bus lines serve Manzanillo from the *central camionera* (central bus terminal) at Hidalgo and Aldama, about a mile from the downtown El Tajo Pemex south along the Colima highway. Unfortunately, the October 1995 earthquake destroyed the terminal building. The bus lines are

operating out of makeshift ticket booths where the old terminal once stood. There is talk of a new terminal, but no one knows when it will be finished. As of this writing the agents and drivers are making do as best they can.

All departures listed below are local *(salidas locales)* unless noted as *salidas de paso*. Choose first class whenever you can; its service, speed, and *asientos reservados* (reserved seats) far outweigh the small additional ticket cost. The bus lines divide roughly into northwest-southeast (coastal) and northeast (Mexico City-Michoacán) categories.

Northwest-Southeast Bus Lines: Elite (EL), tel. (333) 201-35, provides first-class *salidas de paso* service north with Puerto Vallarta, Mazatlán, and Tijuana, and south with Playa Azul junction, Lázaro Cárdenas, Zihuatanejo, and Acapulco. Other first-class departures also connect northeast with Colima, Guadalajara, and Mexico City.

Autocamiones del Pacífico (AP), tel. (333) 205-15, and Transportes Cihuatlán provide Manzanillo's most frequent service northwest and north. Several first-class departures connect with Puerto Vallarta and Guadalajara (via Melaque and Autlán) daily. Many other second-class buses follow the same routes, stopping everywhere.

Autotransportes Sur de Jalisco second-class buses, tel. (333) 210-03, connect half-hourly round the clock during the day with Guadalajara via Colima. Several buses per day also connect south with the Playa Azul junction and Lázaro Cárdenas.

The interurban second-class **Sociedad Cooperativo de Autotransportes** buses connect half-hourly with south Colima destinations of Armería, Cuyutlán, Tecomán, and Colima.

Northeast Buses: More than a dozen **Autobuses del Occidente** (ADO) first-class buses, tel. (333) 201-23, connect round the clock with Mexico City through Michoacán via Morelia and through Guadalajara. At Morelia, you can continue to Pátzcuaro. Many second-class buses connect daily with subsidiary Michoacán destinations of Apatzingan, Zamora, Uruapan, Pátzcuaro, and Morelia.

Also in the same booth as ADO, **Autobuses de Jalisco** connect with Michoacán destinations of Morelia, Uruapan, Nueva Italia and Apatzingan.

Flecha Amarilla, tel. (333) 202-10, and its subsidiary lines combine under the "Servicios Coordinados" blanket to offer a host of departures. Many luxury-class "Primera-plus" buses connect direct with Guadalajara and Mexico City. Other "Primera-plus" connections continue past Guadalajara as far as Aguascalientes. Other departures (about a dozen a day) connect with Mexico City through Colima and Morelia. Others connect with Minatitlán, Colima, Zamora, Salamanca, Irapuato, and Morelia. Another departure connects northwest with Barra de Navidad-Melaque and Puerto Vallarta.

Independent, airline-style luxury **Enlaces Transportes Nacionales** (ETN), tel. (333) 410-60, operates out of its terminal in Santiago, across from the Pemex station. ETN provides frequent connections northwest with Puerto Vallarta, and east, through Colima, Michoacán all the way to Mexico City.

By Train
President Porfirio Díaz's once-plush 19th-century passenger service that carried Guadalajara's elite to frolic on Manzanillo's beaches withered over the years and was finally discontinued in 1998.

COLIMA AND VICINITY

From atop their thrones of fire and ice high above the Valley of Colima, legends say that the gods look down upon their ancient domain. The name "Colima" itself echoes the tradition: from the Nahuatl "Colliman" (*colli:* ancestors or gods, and *maitl:* domain of).

Approaching from Manzanillo, visitors seldom forget their first view of the sacred mountains of Colima: the dignified, snowcapped 14,220-foot (4,334-meter) Nevado de Colima, above his fiery, tempestuous younger brother, the 13,087-foot (3,989-meter) Volcán de Fuego ("Volcano of Fire"). The heat from that heavenly furnace rarely reaches down the green slopes to the spring-fed valley, where the colonial city invites coastal visitors to its more temperate (1,400-foot) heights for a refreshing change of pace.

HISTORY

Although Colima (pop. 180,000) is the smallish capital of a diminutive agricultural state, it is much more than a farm town. Visitors can enjoy the residents' obvious appreciation of their arts and their history—twin traditions whose roots may extend as far south as Ecuador and Peru and as far west as the Gulf coast's mystery-shrouded monument builders, the Olmecs.

Colima's museums display a feast of ceramic treasures left behind by the many peoples—Nahua, Tarascan, Chichimec, Otomi—who have successively occupied the valley of Colima for upwards of 3,000 years. Much more than mere utilitarian objects, the Colima pottery bursts with whimsy and genius. Acrobats, musicians, and dancers frolic, old folks embrace, mothers nurse, and most of all, Colima's famous dogs scratch, roll, snooze, and play in timeless canine style, as if they could come alive at any moment.

Conquest and Colonization
By 1500, the ruler of Colima, in order to deter his aggressive Tarascan neighbors to the north, had united his diminutive kingdom with three neighboring coastal provinces. This union, now known as the Chimalhuacan Confederation, did not prevail against Spanish horses and steel, however. Many local folks take ironic pride that Colima is one of Mexico's earliest provinces. Their ancestors fell to the swords of conquistador Gonzalo de Sandoval and his 145 soldiers, who, in an anticlimax to their bloody campaign, founded the city on 25 July 1523.

Two years later, Cortés appointed his nephew, Francisco Cortés de Buenaventura, mayor and head of a settlement of about 100 Spanish colonists and 6,000 Indian tributaries.

Cortés himself, in search of Chinese treasure in the Pacific, repeatedly visited Colima on his way to and from the Pacific coast during the 1530s, most notably during January 1535, en route to his exploration of Baja California.

Scarcely a generation after the Great Circle route to the Orient was finally discovered in the 1560s, the Spanish king bypassed Colima by designating Acapulco as the prime Pacific port. This, along with a series of disasters—earthquakes,

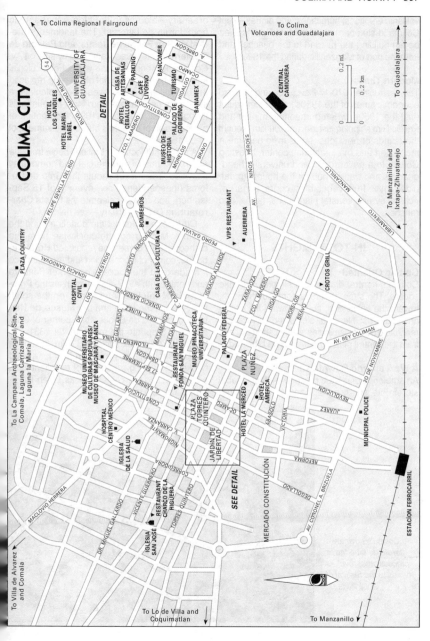

COLIMA CITY

volcanic eruptions, hurricanes, and pirates—kept Colima in slumber until President Porfirio Díaz began building the railroad to the beaches and from the port of Manzanillo during the 1890s.

Modern Times
The destructive 1910-17 Revolution and the hard economic times of the 1930s kept Colima quiet until the 1950s, when burgeoning mining and Pacific Rim shipping, fishing, and tourism brought thousands of new jobs. Manzanillo became a major port and manufacturing center, boosting Colima to a government and university headquarters and trading hub for the bounty (meat, hides, milk, fruit, vegetables, copra, sugar) of rich valley and coastal plantations, farms, and ranches.

IN-TOWN SIGHTS

Getting Oriented
Colima's central district is a simple, one-mile square. The street grid runs north-south (north, toward the volcanoes; south, toward the coast) and east-west. Nearly all sights and services are reachable by a few minutes' walk or short taxi ride from the central plaza, the **Jardín de Libertad.**

A Walk around Downtown
An ambience of refined prosperity—fashionable storefronts, shady portals, and lush, manicured greenery—blooms in the blocks that spread from Jardín de Libertad. The landmark **Catedral de San Felipe de Jesús,** and **Palacio de Gobierno** statehouse stand side by side on Av. Constitución, bordering the *jardín.* For a colonial town, the buildings are not old, having replaced the original earthquake-weakened colonial-era structures generations ago. Most prominent is the cathedral, the latest (1894) incarnation of a succession of churches built on the same spot since 1527.

A number of local celebrations begin from the *jardín,* the hub of commercial and community activities. The mayor shouts the Grito de Dolores (independence cry, evening of 15 September), and crowds celebrate the **Fiesta Charrotaurina** (7-23 February—see below).

Other landmarks dot the portals around the square. Moving counterclockwise from the cathedral, next comes the renovated **Hotel Ceballos,** corner of Constitución and Av. Francisco I. Madero. At the succeeding corner (Madero and north-south Av. V. Carranza) rises the **Presidencia Municipal.** And finally, on the south side, stands the state and city **Museo de Historia** on Av. 16 de Septiembre, corner of Constitución. Step into the museum, tel. (331) 29-228, for excellent examples of Colima's famous pre-Columbian pottery and next door for a good bookstore offering a number of excellent local art, history, and picture-guidebooks. Open Tues.-Sat. 9 a.m.-6 p.m.

At Colima's downtown Jardín de Libertad, a procession of revelers heads to the festival of Villa Alvarez.

Next stroll across the *jardín* corner to the **Palacio de Gobierno** and head through its big, open front door and enjoy the calm, classic elegance of the inner patio. Take a minute or two to admire the stairwell mural, completed in 1953, by muralist Jorge Chaves Carrillo, to commemorate the 200th anniversary of *insurgente* Miguel Hidalgo's birth. Continue out the other side and into Colima's second square, named after Torres Quintero (1866-1934), a beloved Colima teacher whose statue decorates the tree-shaded park.

Back on the Jardín de Libertad, at the cathedral-front, head north across Madero and explore the little block-long **Andando Constitución** pedestrian mall, one of Colima's charming little corners. Here you will find several interesting shops, a good Italian restaurant, and, at the far end, a little doughnut and coffee shop and a good crafts store with a bountiful selection of reasonably priced folk crafts. These include fine ceramic reproductions of Colima's dogs.

Continue one block farther on Constitución to the corner of Guerrero and the University of Colima's **Pinocoteca Universitaria** art museum, tel. (331) 222-28. Besides a permanent collection of historical works by local and nationally noted artists, the museum schedules showings of contemporary painting and photography; open Tues.-Sat. 10 a.m.-2 p.m. and 5-8 p.m., Sunday 10 a.m.-1 p.m.

Two Good Museums
For a look at more excellent regional crafts, continue along Constitución three more blocks north to Gallardo then east a block to G. Barrera to the **Museo de Culturas Populares,** tel. (331) 268-69. Besides a folk-art sales shop (pottery, gourds, baskets, a loom, glassware) and several intriguing displays of masks (don't miss the scary horned crocodile-man) and ceremonial costumes, you can often watch potters and other artisans at work in the little house to the right of the museum entrance on Gallardo. The museum, the full name of which is Museo Universitario de Culturas Populares María Teresa Pomar, is at Avenidas Aldama and 27 de Septiembre; open Mon.-Sat. 10 a.m.-2 p.m. and 4-7 p.m.

The prime repository of Colima's archaeological treasures is the landmark **Museo de Culturas del Occidente** ("Museum of Cultures of the West"). Walk or taxi along the diagonal street

E. Carranza to side street Ejercito Nacional, about a mile from the town center. Inside the modern building, a spiral walkway leads you past artifact-illustrated displays of the history of Colima and surrounding regions. The exposition climaxes on the top floor with choirs of delightful classical Colima figurines: musicians tapping drums and fingering flutes, dancers circling, wrestlers grappling, and hosts of animals, including the all-time favorites, Colima dogs. Open Tues.-Sun. 9 a.m.-6 p.m., tel. (331) 284-31 and 231-55.

OUT-OF-TOWN SIGHTS

The valley and mountainsides surrounding the city offer a variety of scenic diversions, from relaxing in colonial villages and camping on sylvan mountainsides to exploring tombs, examining petroglyphs, and descending into limestone caverns.

La Campana Archaeological Zone
If you're not driving, walk or take a taxi a couple of miles north of the city center to the recently restored La Campana ("The Lookout") Archaeological Zone. Head north about a mile from the city center; at main street Av. Tecnología, turn left and continue about another mile, past the technological institute, to the archaeological zone on the right (north) side of the boulevard.

Although untold generations of local people, especially those of Villa Alvarez, have known that La Campana was a special place, serious studies of the site didn't get underway until about 1920. Engineer José María Gutiérrez first mapped the site in 1917, clearing the way for archaeologist Miguel Galindo, who led the first systematic excavation in 1922. Now, with the perspective of half a century of digging, investigators believe that La Campana reached its heyday around A.D. 800, when it was a complete town with ceremonial platforms, markets and commercial area, schools, priests' and nobles' quarters, and residential zones for several thousand commoners. From physical remains—mainly pottery shards, implements, and small stone sculptures—experts furthermore conclude that the predominant culture of Campana's former inhabitants was Nahua (Aztec-speaking), although signs of other cultures are present.

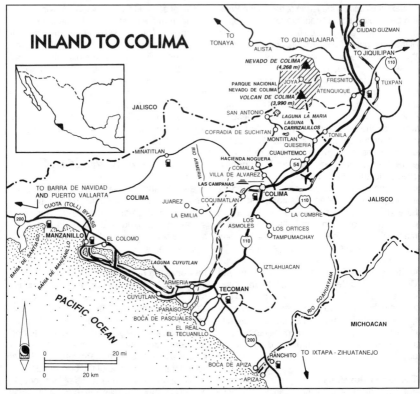

The entire archaeological zone extends over an approximately square area of more than 120 acres, although the restored structures cover only about a tenth of that. The main monument, the Adoritorio Central, is a 15-foot (five-meter) high, 50-foot (six-meter) square-based stone platform. Here, archaeologists uncovered a ritually interred skeleton, apparently a human sacrifice. A pair of secondary (lower, but larger in area) rectangular platform-complexes flank the Adoritorio. Experts believe that all of these platforms supported shrines dedicated to yet unknown gods or goddesses. Earthquakes, most investigators believe, led to the eventual abandonment of La Campana by the time of the conquest.

Plenty is yet to be uncovered here, however. From atop the Adoratorio, between 100 and 300 yards toward the northeast, you might be able to make out the approximately eight additional unexcavated mounds scattered over the archaeological zone.

Northside Foothill Country Tour

Head out the Comala road toward the foothills northwest of the city, where your first reward will be ever-closer views of the volcanoes. **Comala** town, nestling above a lush stream valley about six miles from Colima, has always been a local Sunday favorite.

Just before town, be sure to stop at the roadside stalls of the local woodworkers' cooperative **Cooperativa Artesanal Pueblo.** Their specialty is furniture, adorned with the flower-, bird-, and children-motif decorations of painter Alejandro Rangel Hidalgo.

Continue uphill to the town center, where cares seem to float away in the orange blossom-scented air around the picture-perfect old plaza. Mariachis stroll every afternoon and restaurants (try Los Portales right on the plaza) serve *botanas* free with drinks, which should include at least one obligatory glass of local *ponche* fruit wine.

If you have an extra hour, reverse your path downhill and turn left at the road that heads left (east) just downhill from town. In a few miles, you'll come to the venerable 18th-century **Hacienda Noguera**, where the University of Colima is setting up a new campus, centering on historical, archaeological, and anthropological studies. A small museum, open Tues.-Fri. 10 a.m.-2 p.m. and 4:30-7:30 p.m., tel. (331) 552-80, features artifacts and art from the collection of Comala collector/artist Alejandro Rangel Hidalgo.

Continuing uphill from Comala, the road leads past green pastures and groves, through the village of Cofradia de Suchitán. Soon the road divides. Take the left fork and continue down a jungly, lava-cliffed canyon to ex-hacienda **San Antonio** about 20 miles (32 km) from Colima. Here, water gurgles from the ancient aqueduct, the stone chapel stands intact, and a massive gate and wall, like a medieval keep, still protect the inhabitants from long-forgotten marauders. The owners have recently been renovating the hacienda into a hotel and soon may be receiving guests by the time you read this.

A gravel road continues uphill from San Antonio a few miles farther to the mountainside Shangri-La **Ejido la María.** Past a gate (where you pay a small admission to park), a walking trail downhill leads past tidy vegetable fields to the idyllic shoreline of natural **Laguna la María.** Here, weekend and holiday visitors enjoy creekside picnicking and camping beneath the spreading boughs of a venerable lakeside grove. At other times, walk-in campers often enjoy nearly complete solitude. Bring everything, including water-purifying tablets, insect repellent, and tents for possible rain, especially during the summer. The 4,000-foot (1,200-meter) elevation produces usually balmy days and mild nights.

For noncampers, the *ejido* (communal farm) offers five clean bungalows on the hillside above the lake, with complete kitchens (bring your food), flush toilets, and hot water for about $20 per night. Additionally, self-contained RVs can park hereabouts for a fee. Given the general friendliness of the local *ejido* folks, visitors who enjoy the outdoors by day and mountain stillness by night could spend a very enjoyable few days at Laguna la María.

Centro Turístico Carrizalillos ("Little Reeds Tourist Center") offers yet another outdoor possibility. Back at the fork, two miles uphill past Cofradia de Suchitán, head right. After about two more miles, follow the driveway off to the right. The Carrizalillos campsites spread for about a mile around the circumference of an oak-studded ridge that encloses a small natural lake. The few dozen developed campsites (picnic tables, water, pit toilets), some suitable for small-to-medium RVs, rent for about $3 a day. A rustic view restaurant occupies a lakeside hilltop and a dozen housekeeping cabins overlook the lake. (The cabins may be in usable shape; the tariff is about $10 for two, but take a look before paying.) In season—Easter and Christmas weeks, and August—horses ($10/hour) and boats ($3/hour) are available. Given the magnificent mountain and valley views, the blue lake (if the water level is up), and the fresh air, Carrizalillos might be just right for a cool, restful change of pace.

The Volcanoes

Although taller by about 1,100 feet, Nevado ("Snowy One") de Colima is far quieter than his younger brother, Volcán de Fuego, one of the world's most active volcanoes. The **Volcán de Fuego** has erupted more than a dozen of times since the conquest, continuously belching a stream of smoke and ash and frequently burping up red-hot boulders. The government seals the access road when a serious eruption is imminent.

If you want a close-up look at Volcán de Fuego, check with the state tourism office, at Hidalgo 96, downtown Colima, tel./fax (331) 243-60, for advice, pack everything you're going to need, and head out along Hwy. 54 *libre* (old non-toll route) northeast of Colima. Drive a high-clearance truck or van or ride a second-class bus from the Colima bus station. Pass Tonila (19 miles, 30 km from Colima) to a dirt turnoff road 35 miles (near the Km 56 marker) from Colima. There, at a Teléfonos de Mexico *mi-*

crondas (microwave relay station) sign, take a sharp left toward the mountain. The Volcanic National Park boundary is a bumpy 17 miles (27 km) farther. How far you can go after that depends upon the authorities.

The approach to the much quieter **Nevado de Colima** is considerably more certain. The clear, dry winter months, when the views and the weather are the best, are the Colima climbers' season of choice. This is wilderness mountain country, so you'll need to pack everything—winter sleeping bags, tents, alpine equipment, water, and food—that you'll require.

The ascent, which begins at La Joya hut at around the 11,000-foot level, is not particularly difficult for experienced, fit hikers. The trail starts out leading for an easy hour to the microwave station at the tree line. Then it continues for a few hours of steep walking, except for a bit of scrambling at the end. Ice is a possibility all year-round, however, so carry crampons and ice axes and be prepared to use them. Climbers often sleep overnight at La Joya, get an early morning start, and arrive at the summit before noon.

To get to Nevado de Colima, go by bus or drive a jeep, pickup, or rugged, high-clearance van. Head out northeast along Hwy. 54 *libre,* past Tonila. Continue 39 miles (63 km) from Colima (a couple of miles past the Atequique mining village), where Hwy. 54 *libre* interchanges with the Colima-Guadalajara *cuota* (toll) freeway. Fork left on Hwy. 54 *libre* toward Ciudad Guzmán (rather than straight ahead, toward Jiquilipan). After paralleling the freeway for about four miles, a small sign marks a rough but dry-weather passable uphill track (about six miles) to Fresnito. At Fresnito, head left another 17 very rough miles (27 km) farther to La Joya.

By bus, from the Colima bus station, ride an early Autotransportes Sur de Jalisco or other bus to Ciudad Guzman; transfer to a local bus to Fresnito, where you can continue by truck uphill to La Joya.

Southern Excursion

The valley of Colima has a number of important archaeological sites. One of the most accessible and scenic is at Tampumachay, near the village of **Los Ortices,** eight miles south of Colima city.

The **Centro Turístico Tampumachay,** a shady green miniresort, accommodates visitors with a modest five-room hotel, two swimming pools, a rope bridge, a restaurant, and a camping area. Developed originally by archaeologist Fidencio Perez of Colima, the present owners continue his policy of careful custodianship of the nearby ruins.

The archaeological zone surrounds the hotel, whose grounds perch at the edge of a spectacularly deep, rock-studded gorge. The staff lead visitors on tours of the scenic, cactus-dotted cliffside plateau. Paths wind past intriguing animal- and human-motif petroglyph-sculptures and descend into tombs littered with grave pottery and human bones. Guides point out the remains of an unexcavated ceremonial platform on the opposite side of the canyon. The tombs and petroglyphs are well preserved, since local people, fearing dire ghostly consequences, generally leave the site alone.

Other local excursions include exploration of a limestone cave a couple of miles past the archaeological zone and wildlife-viewing hikes down into the gorge by a trail near the hotel. The Tampumachay resort itself is a lovely, tree-shaded garden, with artifact-dotted paths, a rope bridge, view gazebos, and pool-decks perfect for snoozing.

The five thoughtfully decorated, rustic beamed-ceilinged rooms rent for about $14 d, with hot water shower and fan. A four-room cabin with communal kitchen and campsites for tents and (self-contained) RVs are also available. Reservations are usually not necessary except during holidays; write Centro Turístico Tampumachay, P.O. Box 149, Colima, Colima 28000. You can also contact the center through the Los Ortices local operator, tel. (331) 472-25 (in Spanish), who will forward your message to Tampumachay.

Getting There: Eight miles (13 km) along the Hwy. 110 expressway south of Colima city, just past the gasoline station, follow the Los Ortices turnoff road (signed Los Asmoles), from the east side of the highway. Head uphill toward Los Ortices for 2.5 miles (four km), then turn right at a dirt road just before Los Ortices village. After about 200 yards, a sign directs you left to Tampumachay.

ACCOMMODATIONS

Untouristed Colima has, nevertheless, a sprinkling of good hotels. Some are city-style, downtown near the central plaza, and others are motel-style, in the suburbs. The prices quoted may be subject to discounts, which, under any conditions, you should always ask for: Say *"¿Hay discuento?"*

Downtown Hotels

Many business travelers stay at **Hotel América,** Morelos 162, Colima, Colima 28000, tel. (331) 295-96 or 401-69, fax 444-25, three blocks from the city center. Outside, the facade is colonial; inside a two-story warren of rooms hides among a maze of glass-and-steel tropical terrariums. The rooms are spacious, carpeted, and comfortable. Lack of a pool is partially compensated for y a sauna (use of which is limited to mornings, however). One of Hotel América's pluses is its good restaurant, where patrons enjoy snappy service and tasty food at reasonable prices. The 70 rooms rent for about $30 s or d with TV, a/c, phones, and parking; credit cards are accepted, and there is limited lower-level wheelchair access.

Hotel Ceballos, Portal Medillin 12, Colima, Colima 28000, tel. (331) 244-44, fax 206-45, right on the central plaza, offers a more economical alternative. Although recently renovated, the hotel retains its high ceilings and graceful colonial ambience. Ceballos offers two grades of accommodations: tastefully decorated, clean, and comfortable air-conditioned rooms with TV, and slightly worn fan-only *económico* rooms. During hot weather especially, the a/c rooms are worth the price difference. Rates for the 63 rooms run about $22 economy s or d, $35 deluxe with a/c; credit cards accepted, parking.

Travelers looking for relaxed old-Mexico ambience on a budget might enjoy staying at *posada*-style **Hotel La Merced,** at 188 Hidalgo, tel. (331) 269-69 or 214-21, just off of shady Plaza Nuñes, five blocks west of the city center. Here, travelers have a choice of a dozen plainly furnished high-ceilinged rooms with baths around a homey, traditional inner patio. Rates run about $9 s or d.

Suburban Hotels

Motel-style **Hotel María Isabel,** Blvd. Camino Real at Av. Felipe Sevilla del Río, Colima, Colima 28010, tel./fax (331) 264-62 or 262-64, about two miles northeast of the city-center, appeals to families and RV and car travelers. The double-story room tiers line a long parking lot edged on one side by a lawn and tropical foliage. A large pool and (mediocre) airy restaurant occupy one side near the entrance. The rooms come in economy and deluxe versions. The economy are very plain; the deluxe have tonier decor. Both have air-conditioning and TV. Although the María Isabel is attractive enough at first glance, general cleanliness and service leave something to be desired. The 90 rooms go for about $24 economy s or d, $35 deluxe s or d, $47 junior suite and $52 suite; credit cards accepted, parking.

Neighboring **Hotel Los Candiles,** Blvd. Camino Real 399, Colima, Colima 28010, tel. (331) 232-12, fax 317-07, avoids the usual cluttered motel parking lot atmosphere by putting the swimming pool and patio at the center and the cars off to the side. An attractive tropical garden-style hotel is the result. The rooms, in economy (fan only) and deluxe (with a/c) options are clean, comfortable, and tastefully furnished. The 60 rooms rent for about $27 economy s or d, $38 deluxe, suite $80, with TV, phones, restaurant, and breakfast included; credit cards are accepted.

FOOD

Breakfast and Snacks

A good place to start out the day is the restaurant at the **Hotel América,** Morelos 162, tel. (331) 295-96, open daily at 7 a.m. for breakfast, dinner served till 10 p.m., where the servers greet you with hot coffee and a cheery *"Buenos dias."* The menu affords plenty of familiar fare, from fresh eggs any style to pancakes and fruit, at reasonable prices.

After a few hours among the downtown sights, take a break at one of the sidewalk cafés bordering the Jardín de Libertad. First choice goes to the airy **Cafe de la Plaza,** open daily 7 a.m.-9 p.m., at the Hotel Ceballos on the Jardín de Libertad. Here, high ceilings, graceful arches, and, if you choose, sidewalk tables, add a touch of leisurely refinement to your breakfast or midday lunch break. The relatively short menu—of breakfasts, sandwiches, tacos, *tortas,* juices, desserts, and coffees—is crisply served and reasonably priced.

Alternatively, you can sample the possibilities on the opposite, or south, side of the *jardín,* such as **Restaurant Portales,** where patrons enjoy either shady sidewalk tables or an upstairs balcony perch from which to take in the passing scene.

Restaurants

Starting downtown, by the southwest *jardín* corner (of Degollado and Torres Quintero), the strictly local **Restaurant La Placita** offers hearty breakfasts, lunches, and dinners daily 8 a.m.-8 p.m. Especially popular with the downtown shopping and business crowd is the *comida corrida* (traditional multiple-course set lunch, about $2), served daily from around noon until 3 p.m.

On the diagonally opposite side of the *jardín,* **Livorno's,** tel. (331) 450-30, serves good pizza and other Italian specialties, complete with atmosphere, on Andando Constitución, right off Jardín de Libertad. Livorno's is one of the few spots for a late meal on the *jardín.* Open Tues.-Sat. 11 a.m.-11 p.m.; credit cards accepted. Moderate.

Equally good for breakfast, lunch, or dinner is **Los Naranjos** ("The Orange Trees"), a block away at 34 Gabino Barreda, between Madero and Zaragoza, tel. (331) 273-16. Los Naranjos' relaxed, refined ambience—try the airy back patio—and eclectic menu (salads, sandwiches, tacos, enchiladas, meats, and poultry), professionally prepared and presented, have assured a legion of loyal customers since 1956. Open daily 8 a.m.-11:30 p.m. Moderate.

Nearby, the popularity of **Restaurant Casa Grande** (formerly Fonda San Miguel) is due to its tasty regional specialties, refined ambience, and very correct service, at 129 Av. 27 de Septiembre, near corner of Allende, tel. (331) 448-40. Patrons enjoy shady seating beneath a hacienda roof beside a sun-splashed patio with a fountain. Although Casa Grande serves good breakfasts, the house specialties are Colima regional lunch and early dinner dishes, such as Pepena roast beef in sauce and Tatemado roast pork.

Vegetable lovers, on the other hand, order the excellent tomato, onion, and avocado salad. Open daily 7:30 a.m.-6 p.m., two blocks east, three blocks north, of the *jardín.* Moderate.

Unpretentiously lovely restaurant **El Charco de la Higuera,** tel. (331) 301-92, is a perfect spot for soaking up the charm of traditional Mexico. Its graceful amenities—at the leafy edge of an old church plaza, a bubbling fountain, a shady veranda—and its long list of *típico* Mexican specialties provide all the ingredients for a leisurely breakfast, lunch, or dinner. Located at old San José church, six blocks from the *jardín,* along the westward extension of Madero. Open daily 8 a.m. till midnight.

Crotos Grill, tel. (331) 494-94, near the eastern edge of downtown, is another local favorite, partly due to its airy, tropical setting. Lush vines hang from huge trees nearby, a big-beamed red-tile roof canopy soars overhead, and piano music plays softly in the background. Waiters move briskly about, serving delectable house specialties such as Parrillada (grill) for two, Sopa de Croto, or Ostiones de Chef. Open daily 8-1 a.m., Calzado Pedro A. Galvan 207; follow Av. Morelos from the city center east about a mile to wide Calzado Galvan, where Crotos will be one block south, downhill, across the street. Moderate-expensive.

If, however, you hanker for familiar food in polished, air-conditioned surroundings, head for the local branch of **VIPs,** tel. (331) 306-33, the Mexican (although classier) version of Denny's. Also on east-side Calzado Galvan, just a block downhill from Allende, in front of the big, shiny Auerrera department store. Open Sun.-Thurs. 7 a.m.-11 p.m., Fri.-Sat. 7-2 a.m. Moderate.

ENTERTAINMENT AND EVENTS

Local folks compensate for the lack of nightlife by whooping it up during Colima's three major local festivals. Don't miss them if you happen to be in town.

For nine days beginning 23 January, people celebrate the **Fiesta de La Virgen de La Salud,** which climaxes on 2 February. The church (Iglesia de La Salud) neighborhood near Avenidas Gallardo and Corregidora blooms with colorful processions and food and crafts stalls, and the

Horse-on-a-stick toys appeared among the Mexicans not long after the conquest and the introduction of horses.

church plaza resounds with music, folk dancing, and fireworks.

Ever since 1820 the Villa de Alvarez (a suburb a few miles northwest of the city center) has staged **Fiesta Charrotaurina,** a 10-day combination rodeo/bullfight/carnival. The celebration wouldn't be as much fun if the Villa de Alvarez people stayed to themselves. Every day, however, 7-23 February around noon, a troupe of Villa Alvarez musicians, cowboys, cowgirls, papier-mâché bulls, and a pair of *mojigangos* (giant effigies of the Colima governor and spouse) assemble on Colima's downtown Jardín de Libertad. The music begins, the *mojigangos* start whirling, and a big crowd of bystanders follows them back to Villa de Alvarez.

Visitors who miss the Virgen de La Salud in January can get in on the similar **Fiesta de San José,** which culminates on 19 March in the west-side neighborhood of the Iglesia de San José (corner Quintero and Suárez) with a host of traditional foodstalls, regional folk dancing, and religious processions.

The Casa de Cultura (at the history museum on the Jardín de Libertad downtown) organizes a yearly monthlong (last half of November to first half of December) **fine arts festival.** Performances and exhibits—including classic and folkloric ballet, orchestral and solo music, theater, operas, sculpture, and painting—occur daily. Check with the tourist office, tel. (331) 243-60, or the history museum, tel. (331) 29-228, on the *jardín* for schedule details.

SHOPPING

Two good downtown sources sell reproductions of Colima's charming pre-Columbian animal and human figurines.

The state-operated **Casa de Las Artesanías,** Av. Zaragoza and Andando Constitución, tel. (331) 447-90, near the Jardín de Libertad, stocks a number of locally made figurines, plus shelves of handicrafts gathered from all over Mexico, such as sombreros, *huipiles,* serapes, toys, and Christmas decorations. Other local items include Colima coffee beans, regional cuisine cookbooks, and coconut candy. Open Mon.-Fri. 10 a.m.-2 p.m. and 5-8 p.m., Saturday 10 a.m.-2 p.m.

If you prefer to buy your figurines directly from the artisan, go to the **Museo de Culturas Populares,** Avenidas Gallardo and Barreda, tel. (331) 268-69, four blocks north of the *jardín.* Here, you can see potters reproducing Colima's captivating animal and human figurines. If no artisan is available, the museum shop inside sells their figurines, plus many other folk crafts, both local and national. Open Tues.-Sat. 10 a.m.-2 p.m. and 5-8 p.m., Sunday 10 a.m.-1 p.m.

Among the commercial shops, **Los Volcanes,** at Morelos 167A, across from the Hotel América, offers one of the better local selections, including many shelves of charming pottery curios from both local and nationally imported sources.

SERVICES AND INFORMATION

Money Exchange
The **Banamex** downtown branch, at Hidalgo 90, just two blocks east of the *jardín,* tel. (331) 298-20, exchanges U.S. and Canadian currency and traveler's checks Mon.-Fri. 9 a.m.- 5 p.m. If Banamex lines are too long, walk a block north to **Bancomer,** at Madero 106, corner of Obregón, tel. (331) 468-43, open Mon.-Fri. 9 a.m.-5 p.m.; or another block east to **Banco Internacional,** at Madero 183, tel. (331) 236-23 or 236-24, open Mon.-Fri. 8 a.m.-6 p.m. Saturday 8 a.m.-2 p.m. After bank hours, try one of the nearby *casas de cambio,* on Madero, such as **Agencia de Cambios Su Casa,** at Madero 150, tel. (331) 448-58, or **Casa de Cambio USA-Mex.,** tel. (331) 292-30, at the corner of 27 de Septiembre and Madero.

Communication

The main *correo* (post office) is open Mon.-Fri. 8 a.m.- 6 p.m., Saturday 8 a.m.-noon, tel. (331) 200-33, at Av. Rey Coliman 268, the street that diagonals southeast from Plaza Nuñez (corner Madero and Nuñez) about six blocks east of the Jardín de Libertad.

The Farmacia Colima (on the main *jardín,* northeast corner), across Madero from the cathedral, operates a *larga distancia* telephone Mon.-Sat. 8:30 a.m.-8:30 p.m., Sunday 9 a.m.-2 p.m. On Sunday, you can use the *larga distancia* and fax in the little office (open daily 7 a.m.-10 p.m.) beneath the portal on the south side of the *jardín.*

Tourist Information Office

The efficient and helpful staff of the *oficina de turismo* at Hidalgo 96, across from Banamex, a block east of the Jardín de Libertad, tel. (331) 243-60, fax 283-60, e-mail: turiscol@palmera.colimanet.com, answers questions and offers a Colima map and excellent color brochures. Open Mon.-Fri. 9 a.m.-3 p.m. and 6-8:30 p.m., Saturday 10 a.m.-2 p.m.

Hospital, Police, and Emergencies

The respected private hospital, **Centro Médico,** at Maclovio Herrera 140, a quarter-mile north of Jardín de Libertad, tel. (331) 240-44, 240-45, or 240-46, has emergency service and many specialists on 24-hour call.

The **Farmacia Colima,** tel. (331) 200-31 or 255-37, on the *jardín,* offers a large stock of medicines and drugs. Open Mon.-Sat. 9 a.m.-8:30 p.m., Sunday 9 a.m.-2 p.m.

The **Cabercera Policia** (police headquarters), tel. (331) 314-34 or dial 06, is on the south side of downtown, south side of Av. 20 de Noviembre 235, between Juárez and Revolución.

For **fire** emergencies, call the *bomberos* (fire fighters), tel. (331) 258-58, off of Ejercito Nacional, a block north of the Museum of the Cultures of the West.

Newsstand

English newspapers and magazines are rare in Colima. The newsstand next to the Hotel Ceballos stocks the English-language Mexico City *News,* however; open daily 8 a.m.-9 p.m.

Travel Agency

For tickets, tours, and car rentals, go to the excellent **Vamos A** ("We're Going") travel agency, tel. (331) 496-00 or 497-00, open Mon.-Fri. 9 a.m.-2 p.m. and 4-7:30 p.m., Saturday 9 a.m.-2 p.m., at Independencia 51, two blocks south of the *jardín.*

Photography

Get your film developed in an hour and buy film and basic camera supplies at **Foto Rey,** on the *jardín,* southwest corner of Degollado and Madero, tel. (331) 400-66. Open Mon.-Sat. 9 a.m.-2 p.m. and 4:30-8:30 p.m.

GETTING THERE AND AWAY

By Car or RV

The Manzanillo-Colima combined Highways 200 and 110 *autopista* makes Colima safely accessible from Manzanillo in an hour. From Manzanillo, follow the *cuota* (toll) Hwy. 200 (34 miles, 54 km) southeast to the Hwy. 110 junction near Tecomán. Branch north, continuing on 110 for another 25 miles (40 km) to Colima.

In the reverse direction, ride combined Hwy. 110-toll *autopista* 54D an easy three hours north to Guadalajara.

For southeast coastal destinations, such as Playa Azul and Zihuatanejo, follow Hwy. 200 south at Tecomán southeast along the coast about five hours to Playa Azul (seven to Zihuatanejo). (For more driving details, see the **Manzanillo** section.)

By Bus

The airy, airline-style *nueva central camionera* (new central bus station), on the Hwy. 110 *libramiento* (bypass) east of town, is the Colima point of departure for a number of good first- and luxury-class bus lines. The terminal has a number of services, including a tourist information booth, snack bars, luggage storage, and a Computel long distance telephone (tel. 331-474-23, fax 323-68, open daily 7 a.m.- 10 p.m.)

Elite and its associated lines, tel. (331) 284-99, provide connections northwest, with the U.S. border via Guadalajara, Tepic, and Mazatlán, and northeast with Mexico City via Guadalajara.

First-class **Omnibus de Mexico** buses, tel. (331) 471-99, connect north, with Guadalajara. From there they continue north via Durango to the U.S. border at Ciudad Juárez, or northeast via Aguascalientes and Monterrey, where connections are available with Matamoros and Nuevo Laredo at the U.S. border.

Autobuses del Occidente, tel. (331) 481-79, provides frequent connections with Manzanillo in the southwest, Guadalajara in the north and Mexico City, via Michoacán destinations of Uruapan and Morelia.

Flecha Amarilla, tel. (331) 480-67 or 480-27, and its subsidiary *servicios coordinados* lines provide "Primera-plus" luxury-class and first-class direct connections north with Guadalajara, Aguascalientes, and Leon, northeast with Mexico City, and southwest with Manzanillo, continuing to Puerto Vallarta.

The airline-style, luxury-class buses of **Enlaces Transportes Nacionales** (ETN), tel. (331) 258-99 or 410-60, connect directly north with Guadalajara, southwest with Manzanillo and Puerto Vallarta, and east, with Michoacán destinations of Uruapan and Morelia, continuing to Mexico City.

Autotransportes Sur de Jalisco, tel. (331) 203-16, provides regional second-class connections northeast with Guadalajara via Ciudad Guzman, southwest, with Manzanillo and Cihuatlán, and southeast, with Playa Azul and Lázaro Cárdenas, where you can continue to Zihuatanejo and Acapulco.

Galeana, tel. (331) 347-85, provides second-class connections with Michoacán destinations of Uruapan and Morelia and the southeast coast with Tecomán and San Juan de Lima.

By Train
Privatization has ended Colima passenger train service. Until further notice, drive, fly, or ride the bus.

ceramic mother and child from Colima

SOUTH TO IXTAPA-ZIHUATANEJO AND INLAND TO PÁTZCUARO

ALONG THE ROAD TO PLAYA AZUL

Heading southeast out of Manzanillo, the Mexican Pacific coast highway winds for 200 miles, hugging the shorelines of two states. First, it follows the southern Colima coast, well known for its beaches, surf, and abundant fresh seafood. After that the road pierces the little-traveled wild coast of Michoacán.

That last lonely Michoacán coastal link was completed in 1984. Local people still remember when, if they wanted to travel to Manzanillo, they had to walk half the way. What they saw along the path is still there: mountainsides of great vine-draped trees and seemingly endless pearly, driftwood-strewn beaches, fringed by verdant palm groves and enfolded by golden sandstone cliffs. From ramparts high above the foaming surf, gigantic headlands seem to file in procession along the shore and fade into the sea-mist a thousand miles away. Along the highway, coatimundis peer

from beneath bushes, iguanas scurry along the shoulder, and a rainbow of blossoms—yellow, red, pink, and violet—blooms from the roadside.

HISTORY

Before Columbus

The great Río Balsas, whose watershed includes Michoacán and five other Mexican states, has repeatedly attracted outsiders. Some of the first settlers to the Río Balsas basin came thousands of years ago, from perhaps as far away as Peru. They left remains—pottery, of unmistakable Andean influence—and their language, roots of which remain in the Indian dialects of highland Michoacán.

The major inheritors of this ancient Andean heritage became known as the Tarascans. They founded a powerful Michoacán empire, centered at highland Lake Pátzcuaro, which rivaled the Aztec empire at the time of the conquest.

Conquest and Colonial Era

Although the Tarascans were never subdued by the Aztecs, they quickly fell prey to the Spanish conquistadores, who were also drawn to the River Balsas. In search of the riches of the Southern Sea (as the Pacific was known to him), Hernán Cortés sent his captains Juan Rodríguez and Ximón de Cuenca to the mouth of the Río Balsas, where they founded the Villa de La Concepción de Zacatula in 1523. But, like all the early Pacific ports, Zacatula was abandoned in favor of Acapulco by 1600.

Recent Times

The Michoacán-Colima coast slumbered until the 1880s, when railroad building began at the reawakened port of Manzanillo. By 1887 trains from Manzanillo were stopping at Cuyutlán, a village of salt harvesters, who soon became prosperous by lodging and feeding droves of rich seashore vacationers from Guadalajara.

Neighboring coastal Michoacán had to wait for the dust of the 1910-17 Revolution to settle before getting its own development project. Again the Río Balsas drew outsiders. Dam builders came to harness the river's hydropower to make steel out of a mountain of Michoacán iron ore. In succession came the new port, Lázaro Cárdenas, the railroad, the dam, then finally the huge Las Trucas steel mill. Concurrently, Playa Azul, Michoacán's planned beach resort on the Pacific, was developed nearby.

The new facilities, however, never quite lived up to expectations. Although a few ships and trains still arrive, and some tourists come weekends and holidays, Lázaro Cárdenas and Playa Azul drowse fitfully, dreaming of their long-expected awakening.

CUYUTLÁN

Little Cuyutlán (pop. 2,000) is heaven for lovers of nostalgia and tranquillity. No raucous hangouts clutter its lanes, no rock music bounces from its few cafés. Sun, sand, and gentle surf are its prime amenities. Rickety wooden walkways lead across its hot dark sands to a line of beachfront umbrellas, where you can rent a chair for the day, enjoy the breeze, and feast on the seafood offerings of seaside kitchens.

Most of Cuyutlán's hotels, restaurants, and services lie along a single street: Hidalgo, which runs from the *jardín* (on the Manzanillo-Armería road) a few blocks, crossing Av. Veracruz and ending at the beachfront *malecón*.

The shady, cobbled side streets of Cuyutlán invite impromptu exploring. Near the beach, lanes lead past weathered wooden houses and *palapas* (some for rent). On the inland side of the *jardín* near the rail station, kerosene lamps flicker at night through the walls of bamboo village houses. The station itself is an antique out of the Porfirian age, with cast-iron benches and original filigreed columns still supporting its moss-streaked, gabled platform roof. Nearby, hulking wooden (exotically unusual in Mexico) salt warehouses line an earthen street. Those ancient repositories are reminders of the old tradition of salt harvesting at the edges of nearby Cuyutlán lagoon. Peek through the cracks in the rickety warehouse walls and you'll see the salt—huge white piles, looking exactly like *nieve* (snow) from the heights of the Nevado de Colima.

The Salt Museum

Local authorities have, very appropriately, turned one of those old warehouses into a museum, the **Museo de Sal**, a block north of the *jardín.* Around the walls inside, displays describe the last thousand years of local history, and a model in the middle of the room demonstrates the laborious salt-extraction process. First, workers filled pottery jars with salt-laden brine from *tajos* (shallow wells) near the naturally salty Laguna de Cuyutlán. By hand, they lifted the brine several feet to the top of a *cujete* (leaching bed). After percolating through the *cujete,* the enriched brine gathered in a ground-level *toza* (collection basin). Workers then carried jars full of brine to nearby rectangular salt-diked *planes* (concentration pans) where the sun evaporated the remaining water, leaving pure white sea salt. They sell bags of it in the museum for less than a dollar. A kindly retired salt worker who watches after the museum will gladly explain everything (in Spanish), if you ask. He probably makes a large part of his living off the dona-

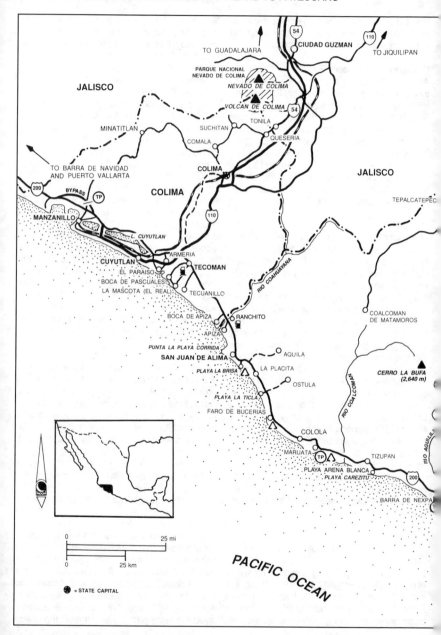

© MOON PUBLICATIONS, INC.

CUYUTLAN

TO EXPRESSWAY MEX. 200 SOUTH

TO MEX 200 NORTH
AND MANZANILLO

TRAIN
STATION

HIGHWAY

SALT
WAREHOUSE

MUSEO DEL SAL
(SALT MUSEUM)
SALT
WAREHOUSE

CENTRO DE SALUD (CLINIC)

JARDIN

ABARROTES BABY
(GROCERY) FARMACIA CARMEN

SAN BLAS

PREVENTIVA (POLICE)

AV. VERACRUZ

AV. HIDALGO

PINO SUAREZ

B. DOMINGUEZ

TO EL PARAISO, ARMERIA,
AND MEX 200 SOUTH

HIGHWAY

MALECON

HOTEL
MORELOS

HOTEL POSADA
SAN MIGUEL

HOTEL
FENIX

HOTEL
CEBALLOS

POSADA
SAN RAFAEL

SEAFOOD STALLS

BEACH UMBRELLAS

0   100 yd

0   100 m

PACIFIC OCEAN

MALECON

TO CAMPAMENTO TORTUGUERO

© MOON PUBLICATIONS, INC.

tions that people leave in the basket on the table by the door.

The Green Wave

Cuyutlán's latter-day claim to fame is the mysterious Green Wave, which is said to occasionally rise offshore and come crashing down from a height of 20, 30, or even 50 feet. (The later at night the story is told, it seems, the greater the height.)

The source of the Green Wave's color is also a mystery, although some local aficionados speculate that an offshore algae bloom might be responsible.

The probable source of the legend is real. On 22 June 1932, a gigantic 60-foot high *maremoto* (tsunami) came close to washing Cuyutlán off the map. The wave reared up from the sea, smashing everything on the beach and flooding the rest of the town.

Although several faithful still apprehensively scan the horizon during the most likely month of May, nothing like the 1932 tidal wave has occurred since. Some suggest that the 1978 local earthquake may have shifted the ocean bottom and quieted the Green Wave (temporarily, at least). The Hotel Morelos, at the corner of Hidalgo and Veracruz, displays, in addition to its lobby gallery of James Dean and Marilyn Monroe photos, a snapshot of an alleged 20-foot Green Wave by local photographer and enthusiast Eduardo Lolo.

Campamento Tortuguero de Cuyutlán

Cuyutlán has its own member of the growing roll of Pacific Mexico turtle-saving encampments. Find it by following main street Av. Veracruz south; after about eight blocks, jog right, then left, and continue for a total of 2.5 miles (four km). At the end of the road you will arrive at the government-sponsored encampment, known officially as the **Centro de Desarrollo, Productivo, Recreativo, y Ecologico de Cuyutlán** ("Cuyutlán Center for Development, Production, Recreation, and Ecology"). It's open Tues.-Sat. 10 a.m.-6 p.m., admission about $1 per person.

Inside the gate, the center staff gladly explains their manifold educational, scientific, economic, and ecological mission. They have made an excellent start. They have been returning more than 50,000 hatchling turtles to the sea annually since the program started in 1995. The turtle hatchery, where they incubate the eggs that they rescue from poachers, is beneath the big tent on the beach.

They also try to educate everyone—most importantly, a steady flow of local schoolchildren and teachers—both about saving turtles specifically and threatened plants and wildlife in general. Animal enclosures and tanks of a (thankfully) few fish, turtles, crocodiles, iguanas, and more serve as examples. Their effort also extends to guiding visitors on wildlife-viewing boat tours in the adjacent lagoon ($2 per person). Moreover, visitors are invited to take a dip in the blue swimming pools, have a *refresco* beneath the *palapa*, and set up tents in the small campground. Crowds often arrive during holidays, and some weekends the place is crowded, so you might leave a campsite reservation message with the local long-distance operator, at (332) 418-10 or 448-71, who will relay it to the Centro Tortuguero.

Beach Activities

Cuyutlán's wide and seemingly endless beach invites a number of activities and sports. The nearly level offshore slope produces little undertow, so wading and swimming conditions are ideal.

The waves, which roll in gradually, are fine for boogie boarding, bodysurfing, and all levels of surfing, depending on the size of the swells. Bring your own surfboard, although boogie board rentals are available on the beach. Shells become more common the farther you stroll away from the few picked-over blocks of beach.

As for fishing, the shallow slope decreases the chances for successful surf-casts. Best hire or launch your boat (easy in calm weather) and head to the happy fishing grounds beyond the waves.

Accommodations

The **Hotel Morelos,** Hidalgo 185, Cuyutlán, Colima 28350, tel. (332) 640-13, founded in the 1890s, continues Cuyutlán's turn-of-the-century tradition with a long (quaintly downhill-sloping) lobby festooned with plastic flowers and green Grecian columns. The hotel has recently added an inviting new patio, built around a designer blue pool. Rooms, moreover, have been redecorated with elegant, hand-carved wooden beds and doors. The family owners top all this off with hearty local-style food, which they serve in the hotel restaurant. Rooms vary; look at more than one before moving in. The Morelos's 40 rooms rent, low season, for about $5 s, $10 d, $10 and $20 high, with hot water and fans.

Across Av. Veracruz stands the equally venerable but second-place (but trying harder) **Hotel Fénix,** Hidalgo 201, Cuyutlán, Colima 28350, tel. (332) 640-82, whose patrons likewise enjoy an open-air street-level restaurant. Although many of the rooms, scattered along upstairs corridors, are clean and airy, they tend toward the scruffy. Take a look before moving in. Rates run about $6 per person low season, $8 high.

Hotel Posada San Miguel, Av. Hidalgo, Cuyutlán, Colima 28350, tel. (332) 640-62, across Hidalgo from the Morelos, has bright, comfortable upstairs rooms that open onto a shady sitting porch overlooking the street. The eight rooms run about $5 per person, low season, $7 high, with hot water and fans.

Last choice goes to Cuyutlán's newest hostelry, the **Hotel Ceballos,** at Veracruz 10, Cuyutlán, Colima 28350, tel. (332) 640-04, fronting the beach at the foot of Hidalgo. Inside, the cavernous atrium-lobby more resembles a bus station than a hotel. But that needn't bother you, especially if you rent one of the many spartan but clean rooms, which, on the oceanfront side, enjoy private, breezy sea-view balconies. The Ceballos is open seasonally, 15 Dec.-31 May only. The 80 rooms rent for about $32 d, with hot water and some fans. Try bargaining for a discount during times of low occupancy, such as weekdays and January and February.

Down the beach, a block south of the Hotel Ceballos, stands the luxuriously located beachfront **Hotel San Rafael,** Av. Veracruz y Piño Suárez, Cuyutlán, Colima 28350, tel. (332) 640-15. Besides its big, blue and inviting swimming pool, the hotel offers 40 comfortably furnished rooms (hand-carved wood, reading lamps), six of which have spacious, breezy semiprivate second- and third-floor ocean-view porches. Downstairs, a roomy open-air restaurant overlooks the beach and waves beyond. Rooms rent for about $15 d—bargain for a longer-term rate—with fans and hot water. Reserve your room *arriba con vista del mar* (upstairs with ocean view).

Camping and RV Parking

Tenters and RVers who desire company stay at the Campamento Tortuguero (see above). Campers who hanker for privacy can follow dirt roads that lead to miles of open beach, good for camping or parking, on both sides of town. (Be careful of soft sand, however.) Cuyutlán, being a generally friendly, upright country place, will ordinarily present no security problem. If in doubt, however, don't hesitate to ask local shopkeepers. Say, *"¿Es bueno acampar acá?"* (EHS boo-WAY-noh ah-kam-PAHR ah-KAH?).

Food

Besides the good restaurants at the Hotels Morelos, Fénix, and Posada San Rafael, the main Cuyutlán eateries are the many seafood vendors, whose semipermanent umbrella-covered establishments do big business on holidays and weekends. Quality of the fare—oyster cocktails, grilled or boiled shrimp and lobster, and fried fish—is generally excellent, since many of them depend on loyal repeat customers.

Shopping, Services, and Information

Most of Cuyutlán's businesses are spread along Hidalgo between the beach and the *jardín*. For groceries, try **Abarrotes Baby,** at the *jardín*, corner Hidalgo. At the same corner is the **Farmacia Carmen,** open daily 9 a.m.-2 p.m. and 4-9 p.m. Up the street, at 144 Hidalgo, the *preventiva* (police) are on duty round the clock. Downhill, a block from the *jardín*, Manzanillo direction, is the **Centro de Salud** ("Health Center"), open routinely till 5 p.m., but only in emergencies after that.

Getting There and Away

By car or RV from Manzanillo, follow the Hwy. 200 *cuota* (toll) branch superhighway 17 miles (28 km) to Cuyutlán. Or, for a more scenic alternative from Manzanillo, follow main street Av. Carrillo Puerto past the *jardín* through downtown Manzanillo and continue along the west end of placid Laguna Cuyutlán. This route curves past the power plant, through miles of *ciruela* orchards, then along a breezy barrier dune and wild beach, eventually joining the toll highway before Cuyutlán. At one point, upon crossing a narrow estuary bridge, the highway asphalt joins with the railroad track. Don't forget to look and listen for the train before starting across.

By car, you can leave Cuyutlán by one of three routes. For Manzanillo, simply head northwest along the local highway-main street that passes the *jardín*. Southeasterly bound drivers not in a hurry simply head in the opposite direction. After a few miles, past lush pastures and palm groves, turn right at the fork for El Paraíso beach (see below), or continue ahead, eventually joining Hwy. 200 at Armería. Alternatively, if you want to get away in a hurry, get on the Hwy. 200 *cuota* (toll) expressway southbound by following the extension of Av. Hidalgo, north, past the *jardín* and over the railroad tracks a few hundred yards to the expressway entrance on the right.

Manzanillo taxis take passengers to and from Cuyutlán for about $20, one way. If this is too expensive, local **buses** make the Manzanillo-Cuyutlán connection approximately every hour until around 8 p.m. via Armería (transfer point on Hwy. 200), half an hour by bus from Manzanillo's *central camionera* bus station.

Although freight trains still run between Cuyutlán and both Manzanillo and Colima, passenger service has, unfortunately, been discontinued until further notice.

SOUTH COLIMA BEACHES

El Paraíso

El Paraíso (pop. 1,000) is just seven miles southeast from Cuyutlán, via the local highway; turn at the right fork, four miles from the Cuyutlán *jardín*. Its beach is especially popular on Sunday and holidays with families, who eat their fill at the dozen shorefront seafood *palapas* lining the bumpy main street. El Paraíso's long strand, which extends for miles on both sides, is similar to Cuyutlán's: warm, dark sand and generally gentle, rolling surf, with little or no undertow, excellent for safe wading, swimming, bodysurfing, boogie boarding, and surfing.

The good beach and seafood account for the success of the **Hotel Paraíso** and restaurant, Playa Paraíso, Armería, Colima 28300, tel. (331) 718-25, which perches above the surf at the south end (left as you arrive) of the beachfront street. Many of the hotel's plain but clean rooms enjoy the same airy oceanfront vista as the popular restaurant. The adjacent pool and sundeck is yet another reason for spending a day or two there. The 54 rooms (none with hot water) rent from about $14 d, $18 t; credit cards are accepted. Reserve, especially during holidays and weekends, by writing or calling the hotel, or contacting its agent in Colima, tel. (331) 210-32.

Boca de Pascuales, El Real, Tecuanillo, and Boca de Apiza

Although none of this quartet of downscale beachside *palapa* heavens has an acceptable hotel, local folks know them well for their gentle surf, abundant seafood, and wide-open spaces for tent and RV camping. Drivers can access them along good paved roads from Hwy. 200. For bus travelers, Tecomán's *camionera central* is the point of departure for local buses, which run frequently until around 6 p.m. After that, you might have to take a taxi.

Boca de Pascuales, eight paved miles (13 km) from Hwy. 200, is literally the *boca* (mouth) of the Armería River, whose waters, which begin on the snowy slope of Nevado de Colima, widen to a broad estuary. Here, they nourish schools of fish and flocks of seabirds—pelicans, cormorants, herons—which dive, swoop, and stalk for fry in the rivermouth lagoon. Fishermen wade in and catch the very same prey with throw-nets.

The beach itself is broad, with semicoarse gray sand. The waves roll gradually shoreward over a near-level, sandy shelf, and recede with little or no undertow. Consequently, swimming, boogie boarding, and bodysurfing are relatively safe, and surfing is not uncommon. A lot of driftwood litters the sandbar, and several rentable fishing *lanchas* lie pulled up along the beach. A quarter-mile lineup of seafood *ramadas* provide shade and food for the local families who crowd in on Sundays and holidays. Find Boca de Pascuales by heading south on Hwy. 200 to just before Tecomán. Follow the signed turnoff road about eight miles to the beach, turn right, and continue a quarter mile past the *ramadas* to the lagoon and sandbar.

For more lovely beach and surf, head from Boca de Pascuales along the two miles of beachfront road to El Real (marked La Mascota on some maps). The paved road passes a file of hurricane-battered shoreline homes, separated by open spaces, good for camping or RV parking (if you don't mind occasional company). Ask if it's okay before setting up camp. Bring all of your supplies, including water; the few stores along this stretch are meagerly stocked.

Three or four restaurants (notably, the popular En Ramada Boca de Río) dot the two miles to El Real. There, a few more rustic seafood *ramadas* crowd the corner where the road heads back about seven miles (11 km) to Hwy. 200 at Tecomán.

For Tecuanillo, head seaward at the paved Hwy. 200 turnoff road about a mile south of the Tecomán (south end) Pemex station. Continue about six miles to the roadside ponds of the La Granja restaurant, open Tues.-Sun. noon-6 p.m., just before the beach. About six acres of ponds supply loads of *langostinas* (prawns) and *pargo* (sea bass) for on-the-spot consumption—broiled, boiled, *ranchera*, garlic, *diabla*, ceviche—any way you prefer, $4-8.

Besides its long, wide beach and good surf fishing, visitors to the hamlet of Tecuanillo enjoy the protection of some of the few official lifeguards on the south Colima coast. The friendly staff of the small road's-end naval detachment volunteer for the duty. They don't mind, since the beach is nearly empty except for weekends and holidays. Tecuanillo is a good tenting or RV parking spot for lovers of seafood and solitude who appreciate the added security of the nearby naval detachment. Beach *palapa* restaurants and a local store can supply food and drinks, and the village has a water supply.

Boca de Apiza, at the mouth of the Coahuayana River (which forms the Colima-Michoacán border), has surfing potential, driftwood, and possible tenting spots next to a wild, mangrove jungle-lined beach. Get there by following Colima Hwy. 185, the signed, paved turnoff road about 21 miles (34 km) south of Tecomán. About three miles from the highway, past a mangrove channel, the road splits. Ahead is a beach with some informal camping spots; left about a mile down the dry-weather-only dirt road dead-ends at a second beach, where powerful surfing waves rise sharply and break both left and right.

Although the fishing hamlet of Apiza is in Michoacán, it's barely so, being just south of the Río Coahuayana. It's reachable by the paved side road about a mile south of the river bridge. A dozen seafood *ramadas,* complete with tables and hammocks, spread along the road's end 2.5 miles from the highway. The long, dark-sand beach spreads seemingly without limit on the south side, while on the other, a bamboo-hut village spreads quaintly along the boat-lined estuary bank. With a store for supplies, tenters and self-contained RV campers could fish, beachcomb, and bodysurf here for a month of Sundays.

TECOMÁN

Tecomán (pop. 50,000), on Hwy. 200, 37 miles (59 km) southeast of Manzanillo, three miles south of the Colima (Hwy. 110) junction, is south Colima's service center. All services are not far from Av. Insurgentes, the Hwy. 200 through-town main boulevard, which splits, diverting city-center traffic into a pair of one-way northbound (Manzanillo-Colima) and southbound (Michoacán) streams.

Accommodations

If you're going to stay overnight, Tecomán offers a pair of good hotels. First choice goes to the refined and comfortable four-star **Real Motel,** on Av. Insurgentes, corner of Lic. M. Gudiño, Tecomán, Colima 28110, tel. (332) 401-00, about eight blocks north of the city center. Rates for the 80 rooms run about $23 s, $28 d, with a/c, phones, satellite TV, pool, and parking.

Alternatively, you'll find approximately the same semi-deluxe amenities at the **Hotel Plaza,** at Insurgentes 502, tel. (332) 435-74, fax 426-75, two blocks closer to town. Here, doubles run about $20, with a/c, TV, parking, restaurant, and phone.

Services and Information

Bital (Banco Internacional), tel. (332) 463-64 or 466-41, with the longest hours (Mon.-Fri. 8 a.m.-6 p.m. and Saturday 8 a.m.-2 p.m.), changes money on the north side of the main plaza. Alternately, try **Banamex,** also on the north side of the plaza, at López Mateos and Hidalgo, tel. (332) 414-13; **Banco Serfin,** on the south side of the main plaza, at 20 de Noviembre 119, tel. (332) 419-96 or 416-88; or **Bancomer,** on Av. Insurgentes, tel. (332) 400-26, about three blocks northwest of the main plaza. For a doctor, go to 24-hour diagnostic **Clínica Centro Médico,** at 592 E. Zapata, a block off Insurgentes, about six blocks north of the main plaza, tel. (332) 435-60.

The ***correo,*** tel. (332) 419-39, is at B. Dávalos 35, two blocks north of the main plaza. **Computel** long-distance telephone and public fax, tel. (332) 438-99, open 7 a.m.-10 p.m., is at the main bus terminal.

Bus Service

A trio of cooperating bus networks operates out of the *camionera central* (central bus terminal), at the Plaza Progreso shopping mall, about four blocks west, and two blocks north of the main plaza.

Autotransportes Sur de Jalisco (ASJ), tel. (332) 407-95, offers many daily first- and second-class departures, connecting north with Colima, Ciudad Guzmán, and Guadalajara, and north-west-southeast, with Manzanillo and Lázaro Cárdenas. Companion line **Autobuses del Occidente** (same phone number) connects north with Mexico City via Morelia, Michoacán, and intermediate destinations.

In an adjacent booth, "Servicios Coordinados" agents, tel. (332) 461-66, sell tickets for first-class Flecha Amarilla (FA) and "Primera-plus" luxury-class departures, which connect, along northern routes, with Manzanillo, Colima, Guadalajara, Celaya, and Querétaro and northeasterly routes, with Michoacán destinations, continuing to Mexico City.

Next door, first-class **Elite** (EL), tel. (332) 402-82, coordinates its services with its Estrella Blanca companion lines. They offer several *salidas de paso* that connect daily along the Hwy. 200 corridor, south with Acapulco (via Playa Azul and Zihuatanejo) and north with the U.S. western border (via Manzanillo, Melaque, Puerto Vallarta, and Mazatlán).

At its own separate Tecomán station, at 125 Cinco de Mayo, tel. (332) 402-32, super-deluxe **Enlaces Transportes Nacionales** (ETN) buses connect northwest with Manzanillo, Melaque, and Puerto Vallarta; north with Colima and Guadalajara; and northeast with Michoacán destinations of Uruapan, Pátzcuaro, and Morelia, continuing to Mexico City.

NORTHERN MICHOACÁN BEACHES

Adventure often draws travelers along the thinly populated, pristine northwestern Michoacán coast. Without telephones and electricity, most people live by natural rhythms. They rise with the sun, tend their livestock, coconuts, and papayas, take shady siestas during the heat of the day, and watch the ocean for what the tides may bring.

Outsiders often begin to enjoy the slow pace. They stop at little beaches, sit down for a soda beneath a *ramada,* ask about the fishing and the waves, and stroll along the beach. They wander, picking up shells and driftwood and saying hello to the kids and fisherfolk along the way. Charmed and fully relaxed, they sometimes linger for months.

On the Road

If driving, best fill up with unleaded Magna Sin gas at the Tecomán (north side) Pemex or the Playa Azul Pemex (if traveling in the opposite direction). The road runs 165 miles (267 km) between them with only one gas station—at Ranchito, just south of the Colima-Michoacán border—and a few stores selling leaded regular from drums. If you're driving south, note your odometer mileage at the Río Coahuayana bridge (Hwy. 200, Km 231) at the Colima-Michoacán border. (The northbound kilometer markers, incidentally, begin with zero at the junction with Hwy. 37 near Playa Azul, thus giving the distance directly from that point.) In such undeveloped country, road mileage will help you find and remember your own favorites among Michoacán's dozens of lovely beach gems.

Bus travelers enjoy the best connections at Manzanillo *central camionera,* Armería, or Tecomán in the northwest, or Lázaro Cárdenas or La Mira (near Playa Azul) in the southeast. Bus lines, such as Autotransportes Sur de Jalisco, Ruta Paraíso, Flecha Amarilla, Elite, and Transportes Norte de Sonora, run a few daily first-class local departures from both Manzanillo and Lázaro Cárdenas. Second-class Autotransportes Galeana buses run from the same terminals approximately hourly during the day, stopping everywhere and giving adventurers the option of getting off wherever they spot the palmy little heaven they've been looking for.

San Juan de Alima

San Juan de Alima appears to be awakening from its slumber. Energized by a growing cadre of visitors, old hotels have added tiers of shiny new rooms, and new hotels are sprouting on the beachfront. The town itself nevertheless remains a scattering of small houses with neither phones nor a well-stocked store, although this is bound to change if the boom continues.

San Juan de Alima's popularity comes from its long, creamy sand beach, framed between a pair of rocky headlands. Very surfable breakers roll in from about 50 yards out and recede with little undertow. All beach sports are relatively safe, except during the fall hurricane season, when the waves are 10 or 15 feet tall and surfers are as common as coconuts.

Fishing is probably best off the rocks at the sheltered north-end beach, **Playa la Punta Corrida,** where the very gentle waves allow easy boat launching. (Be on your guard for soft sand.) The same spot appears ripe for RV or tent camping.

Accommodations: The side-by-side south-end hotels Parador and **Miramar,** each with about 25 rooms and its own sea-view *palapa* restaurant, are open all year. Mutual rivalry keeps their standards and prices on an approximate par. About $10 gets a spartan but clean bare-bulb room for two with toilet and shower (sorry, no hot water).

The **Hotel Parador** (the one on the right) has the largest and most popular *palapa* in town. The family who runs it takes special pride in the cooking, which invariably includes the fresh catch of the day. They're friendly, and the view from their shady tables is blue and breezy.

In third place is the rival motel-style **Hotel San Juan** and beach *palapa* restaurant, which has gained a niche at the north end of town. The 10 simply furnished but clean rooms with (room-temperature-only) baths rent for about $10 d. If you want an advance reservation, call the owner's son in Colima at (332) 416-81.

Getting There: San Juan de Alima is at Km 211, 12 miles (19 km) southeast of the Colima border. Get to the north-end beach by turning off onto the dirt road at Km 212.5 south of town. After a third of a mile (half km), follow the left fork. Continue past the oceanography station at Mile 1.6 (Km 2.6) to the beach a half mile farther.

Playa la Brisa

At Km 207, 16 miles (26 km) south of the Colima line, the highway reaches a breezy vista summit, where a roadside *mirador* (viewpoint) affords a look southeast. Far below, a foam-bordered white strand curves from a little palm grove, past a lagoon to a distant misty headland. This is Playa la Brisa, where, beneath the little grove, the Rentería-Álvarez family members manage their miniature utopia.

Their shady grove is made for either tent or self-contained RV camping. People often ask them how much they charge. "Nothing," they say. "As long as you have a little lunch or dinner in our *palapa* here, stay as long as you like."

On the very broad beach beyond the grove, the waves roll in, breaking gradually both right and left. With little or no undertow, the surf is good for swimming, boogie boarding, and body-surfing. Furthermore, taking your clue from the name "La Brisa," you know that windsurfing is frequently good here, too.

Additionally, the lagoon a mile down the beach affords opportunities for wildlife viewing, aided by your own kayak or portable rubber boat. Fishing is also often rewarding either from the rocks beneath the headland, or by boat (your own or local *panga*) launched from the beach. Get there by following the dirt road at Km 205 at the base of the hill one mile to the palm grove.

Hotel El Paraíso Las Brisas has recently mushroomed on the beach, just north of the Rentería-Álvarez grove. When I arrived it was closed, so I didn't get a look inside. From the outside, it's a big, white stucco place with about 30 rooms around an inner patio with a kiddie pool. Take a look around, and if they're taking care of the place, it might be worth the $30 d they'll probably be asking. If you need air-conditioning on a gorgeous, secluded beach, this may be the place.

La Placita

The dusty town of La Placita (pop. 3,000) sits at Km 199 four miles south of Playa la Brisa. If it's your bedtime, rooms are available in the **Reyna,** a small hotel next to the north-end bridge. A restaurant, the **Zuñiga,** and pharmacies are located on the highway at the central plaza; a government **Centro de Salud** ("Health Center") is on the street that borders the south edge of the plaza; a *larga distancia* phone is on the plaza; and a new *gasolinera,* at the south edge of town, will probably have Magna Sin unleaded gasoline.

Playa La Ticla

The broad, gray-white sands of La Ticla attract visitors—mostly surfers—for one good reason: its big, right-breaking rollers. Besides the surfing waves, a clear, sandy-banked river, fine for freshwater swimming, divides the beach in two. The town has stores and a health center. The beach has plenty of room for RV parking and tents and appears fine for camping. Unfortunately, drugs have led to problems in the past, such as a gunpoint robbery during the early '90s. Lately, however, the situation appears to have improved. Check with a local storekeeper to see if this is still true.

Getting There: Turn off at the signed dirt side road at Km 183, 31 miles from the Colima border. At mile 1.7 (Km 2.7), follow the left, more-traveled fork; at the village basketball-volleyball court, jog right, then left. Continue to the beach at Mile 2.2 (Km 3.5).

Faro de Bucerías

Idyllic perfectly describes Faro de Bucerías: a crystalline yellow-sand crescent and clear blue waters sheltered by offshore islets. The name Bucerías ("Divers") suggests what local people already know: Faro de Bucerías is a top snorkeling location. Favorable conditions, such as minimal local stream runoff and a nearly pure silica-sandstone shoreline, combine to produce unusually clear water. Chance has even intervened to make it better, in the form of a wreck beside the offshore Morro Elefante ("Elephant Islet"), where multicolored fish swarm amongst the corals.

Several petite sandstone bays and beaches dot the coast around the main beach, Playa de Faro de Bucerías, which has all the ingredients for a relaxing stay. The beach itself is a lovely half-mile arc, where the waves rise and crash immediately at the water's edge and recede with strong undertow. Wading is nevertheless generally safe and swimming ideal in a calm south-end nook, protected by a rocky, tidepool-laced outcropping.

For food and accommodations, beachside *palapas* serve seafood during holidays, while the **Parador Turístico** restaurant/campground on the northwest side of the bay serves visitors on a daily basis. You set up your tent or park your RV (motor homes might be a little difficult to get in—do a test run) beneath their beachfront camping *ramada* for $1 per person, per night, freshwater showers included.

This is heaven for fresh seafood lovers. Local divers (their spots marked by their floating offshore inner tubes) bring up daily troves of octopus, conches, clams, oysters, and lobsters, which you can purchase on the spot and have cooked in the restaurant. If you prefer, catch your own from the rocks or hire a local fisherman to take you out for half a day.

For more local diversions, you can poke around in tidepools or climb to the white lighthouse *(faro)* perched atop the southeast rocky point. Another day you can walk in the opposite direction and explore little Playa Manzanilla and other hidden coves beyond the stony northeast headland.

Getting There: A big (southbound-facing) El Faro sign over the highway at Km 173 marks the Faro de Bucerías turnoff, 37 miles (60 km) from the Colima border. Just before the village store (yellow, on the right), at Mile 0.9 (Km 1.4), turn right at the grocery, pass the school, and continue about 300 yards to a "T." Turn left and continue another 200 yards to the Parador Turístico, at the north end of the beach.

Playa Maruata

This unique seaside refuge has formed where a mountain river tries to empty into the sea but is partially blocked by a pair of big rocks. Sand has collected, so the rocks appear as islands in sand rather than water. The ocean has worn away sea tunnels, which surging waves pene-

The lagoon provides a sheltered anchorage and a rest for fishermen at Maruata.

trate, pushing air and water, gushing and spouting onto the shore. At times, a dry sand beach builds up next to the rocks, where campers can build an evening fire and be soothed to sleep by the gurgling, booming, and whistling lullaby of Maruata.

Maruata visitors enjoy three distinctly different beaches. On the northwest, right-side, thunderous, open-ocean breakers (advanced surfing) pound a long, steep beach. A small middle beach, protected between the rocks, has oftswimmable (with caution) water. The southeast, left-side beach is long and sheltered by the sea rocks, enclosing a shallow rivermouth lagoon. Its usually gentle waves are generally safe for wading, swimming, and boat launching. In addition, snorkeling off the rocks is often very good during the winter-spring dry season.

What's even better, the Nahuatl-speaking ejido owners of Playa Maruata, who once fished for turtles for living, have joined the green revolution and now maintain a turtle sanctuary, protecting the turtle from poachers. The local community has organized, under the banner of **Maruata 2000,** with the goal of preserving and protecting local wildlife and habitat into the 21st century and beyond. They back up their ideals with deeds by not allowing Waverunners and other power sports, which, they write, "could alter the view and freedom for swimmers and scuba divers."

As part of their plan, they encourage visitors to stay in their improved facilities. They run a pair of good *palapa* restaurants beneath the sleepy beachfront grove and rent rustic tourist *palapas* ($4 per person). They've developed a campground, where tenters can set up own tent for $1.50 per person per night and motorized folks can set up their self-contained RV for about $1 per person per night. For reservations and more information on Maruata, call Ezequiel Garcia at (332) 503-68.

Community members are also ready with horse rentals ($5 per person), motor *lanchas* for fishing or snorkeling ($30 per trip), and boat tours ($2.50 per person).

Getting There: Playa Maruata is 50 miles (80 km) southeast of the Colima line at Km 150. Just south of a big bridge, a dirt turnoff road descends from the southbound lane. Continue straight across the airstrip to a wide gravel road,

heading through the village. Continue through a stream (low water only) to the palm grove and beach. If, on the other hand, you want to fly in, the airstrip is smooth asphalt at least half a mile long.

Playas Arena Blanca and Carezitu
Near Km 93, the rugged coastal mountains open to a stream valley, where (by a small roadside Conasupo store) a narrow dirt lane winds down from the highway through a small village to Playa Arena Blanca. Here a creamy strand faces a broad blue bay, which arcs gracefully for a mile to a wave-splashed south-end headland. Prospects appear excellent for swimming, beachcombing, and surf- and rock-casting. During calm mornings boat-launching wouldn't be difficult, as evidenced by the *pangas* pulled up on the beach. Seafood lovers are in heaven here, with the fish, octopuses, and oysters that local fisherfolk and divers bring in and sell right on the beach. For water and limited additional supplies, small stores and restaurants in the village and on the highway (a half mile north at the bus stop) are available.

Even prettier and more intimate is neighboring Playa Carezitu, a crescent of yellow sand, enfolded by sandstone cliffs, which is accessible from Playa Arena Blanca, by ducking around the north-end cliff corner. Big rolling surfable breakers rise in the middle of a petite bay, while tranquil billows lap the sand on the sheltered northwest end. The sand curves a few hundred yards past scattered shoreline rocks, where snorkeling and fishing (by either surf or rock casting) appear promising, while shells, driftwood, and even a semipermanent sand volleyball court enrich the beach possibilities. On one side, a food *palapa* appears ready to be renovated to serve holiday visitors.

Playa Carezitu might be good for at least a pleasant afternoon, perhaps more. Temporary palm-thatch *ramadas,* apparently ready for new camper-occupants, stand on the beach.

Barra de Nexpa
While well known as one of Pacific Mexico's best surfing beaches, Barra de Nexpa's appeal is not limited to surfers. Don Gilberto, the grandfatherly founder of this pocket utopia, will gladly tell you all about it (in Spanish, of course). As more people arrived, facilities were added. First,

Rustic beach houses at Barra de Nexpa are popular accommodations, especially during the fall surfing season.

Don Gilberto built *palapas* (now rentable at $2 per person), a well, and showers. Then he built a restaurant, which his son now runs. Next door, another family, the Mendozas, built an informal RV and tenting park along the palmy shoreline of the adjacent freshwater lagoon. Finally, a line of Robinson Crusoe-like rustic beach houses sprouted along the sandbar.

Don Gilberto's enterprise grew, but the natural setting remained unchanged. The breakers (10-footers are common) still roll in, often curling into tubes, to the delight of both surfers and surf-watchers. Nexpa's big waves, however, need not discourage waders and swimmers, who splash and paddle in the freshwater lagoon instead. Beachcombers savor many hours picking through driftwood and shells while birdwatchers enjoy watching dozens of species preen, paddle, stalk, and flap in the lagoon. And finally, when tired of all of these, everyone enjoys the hammocks, which seem to hang from every available Nexpa post and palm.

At the height of the fall-winter season, when lots of surfers and campers crowd in, the atmosphere is generally communal and friendly. At the *palapa* restaurant, on the beach, or in the shade beneath the palms and the *ramadas,* you won't lack company. (Note: Palmy surfing havens such as Barra de Nexpa are sometimes marred by one or two light-fingered individuals. Don't forget to safely stow your valuables.)

Getting There: At Km 56, 109 miles (175 km) southeast of the Colima border, follow the un-marked dirt road, which curves sharply, following an uphill slope. It continues, bumping and winding downhill about half a mile to the beach. The road appears negotiable, when dry, by ordinary cars and RVs, even perhaps big motor homes. If in doubt, do a preliminary run.

Caleta de Campos

Caleta de Campos (pop. 2,000) is at the signed turnoff of Km 50, 112 miles (181 km) southeast of the Colima border. Sometimes called Bahía de Bufadero ("Blowhole"), Caleta de Campos is the metropolis and service center for this corner of Michoacán. Although it has a sandy beach beside a blue bay, the beach is a haven primarily for commercial fishing launches rather than touring visitors. Fishing *pangas* may be rented on the beach. A half-day excursion (about $50) typically returns with 50 pounds of *huachinango* (snapper), *cabrilla* (sea bass), *sierra* (mackerel), *robalo* (snook), and *atún* (tuna). Anyone can launch a boat on the bay's protected northwest end, provided a strong truck is available to lug it up the moderately steep beach-access road; turn right just after the Hotel Yuritzi.

Accommodations, Food, and Services: Caleta's one hotel, the **Hotel Yuritzi,** perches on the hill above the beach. Plain but clean, the Yuritzi is fine for an overnight stay. A big yard within the fenced hotel compound can also accommodate large RVs. Reservations are generally necessary only during Christmas and Easter holidays; contact the hotel at (753) 150-10, fax 150-20, or write the hotel a few weeks in advance, address simply Caleta de Campos, Michoacán. The 19 rooms rent for about $17 s, $20 d, with a/c. They include fans and baths, but lack hot water.

The friendly family owners of Hotel Yuritzi take special pride in their unmissable **home-made ice cream,** which they make in luscious chocolate, vanilla, coconut, and strawberry flavors. If you do nothing else, be sure to stop by for a sample.

The good **Torta and Burger Bahía** *lonchería* occupies the corner across from the hotel. Its *licuados, tortas,* hamburgers, and ham and eggs taste delicious after a hard day riding the waves.

Most of Caleta's stores and institutions are scattered along its single main street, which leads from the highway. A **new pavement,** which replaced the former bumpy, dusty surface, is a source of so much community pride that shopkeepers sweep the new asphalt both morning and night. There you'll find a *larga distancia* telephone office, tel./fax (753) 150-01 through -04, a farmacia, a grocery, and a Centro de Salud on a side street nearby.

Buses stop frequently at either the Hwy. 200 crossing or the small station on the dirt main street a block uphill. Ruta Paraíso first-class and Galeana second-class run between Manzanillo and Lázaro Cárdenas; Elite and Turistar run the entire Pacific coast route, U.S. border to Acapulco; and local microbuses run to and from Lázaro Cárdenas, via La Mira and the Playa Azul junction. Drivers of micro- and second-class buses will generally let you off anywhere along the highway you request.

PLAYA AZUL

It's easy to see how Playa Azul ("Blue Beach") got on the map of Pacific Mexico. The beach is long and level, the sand is yellow and silky. The waves roll in slowly, swish gently, and stop, leaving wet, lazy arcs upon the sand. At sunset, these glow like medallions of liquid gold.

Around Town

Playa Azul (pop. 5,000) is a small town on a big beach with a mile of *palapa* seafood restaurants. Four bumpy streets, Carranza, Madero, Independencia, and Justo Sierra, parallel the beachfront *malecón* walkway. Much of the activity clusters on or near a fifth street (actually a dirt lane), Aquiles Serdán, which bisects the other four and ends at the *malecón*. Here the atmosphere—piquant aromas of steaming *pozole* and hot tacos, the colorful mounds of papayas and tomatoes, the language and laughter of the people—is uniquely and delightfully Mexican.

Beach Activities

The Playa Azul beach is good for just about everything. The waves, big enough for surfing as they break far offshore, roll shoreward, picking up boogie boarders and bodysurfers along the way, finally rippling around the ankles of waders and splashers at the sand's edge. Concessionaires rent chairs, umbrellas, and boogie boards, but few, if any, surfboards. The weekend crowds keep the beach relatively free of shells and driftwood, although pickings will be better farther out along the beach (which stretches many miles in either direction).

Eating is another major Playa Azul beach occupation. Fruit vendors stroll the sand, offering luscious cut pineapple, watermelon, and mangoes-on-a-stick, while semipermanent beach stands and dozens of *malecón* restaurants offer fresh *cóctel de ostión* (oyster cocktail, $4), *langostina al gusto* (prawns any style, $6), and *langosta al vapor* (steamed lobster, $10).

Laguna Pichi

Playa Azul's long, creamy beach is interrupted during the summer rainy season, when the blue Laguna Pichi (follow main street Independencia about a mile south of town) overflows and spills into the ocean. Most of the time, however, it's a big blue freshwater lake, bordered by palms and *palapa* restaurants. The lagoon provides visitors and Sunday families with a variety of diversions, such as super-fresh seafood, wading and swimming, fishing, and viewing the battalion of waterbirds that cackle, paddle, and preen in the clear blue lagoon. The prepared can set up tents for camping along the sandy shore (bring repellent) and venture out in their kayaks and

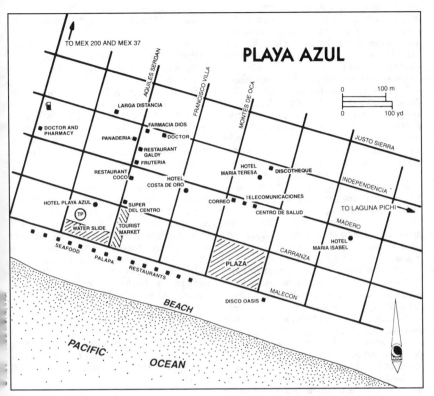

TO MEX 200 AND MEX 37

PLAYA AZUL

AQUILES SERDAN
FRANCISCO VILLA
MONTES DE OCA

0   100 m
0   100 yd

LARGA DISTANCIA

DOCTOR AND PHARMACY

FARMACIA DIOS

PANADERIA

DOCTOR

JUSTO SIERRA

RESTAURANT GALDY

FRUTERIA

RESTAURANT COCO

HOTEL COSTA DE ORO

HOTEL MARIA TERESA

DISCOTHEQUE

INDEPENDENCIA

HOTEL PLAYA AZUL

TP

SUPER DEL CENTRO

CORREO

TELECOMUNICACIONES

TO LAGUNA PICHI

WATER SLIDE

TOURIST MARKET

CENTRO DE SALUD

MADERO

HOTEL MARIA ISABEL

SEAFOOD

PALAPA

RESTAURANTS

CARRANZA

PLAZA

MALECON

DISCO OASIS

BEACH

PACIFIC OCEAN

rubber boats (or lacking those, hire a boat) for birdwatching and wildlife-viewing in the lagoon's mangrove wilderness reaches.

ACCOMMODATIONS

Playa Azul has about half a dozen hotels, one with a trailer park. Three of them stand out. One block from the beach, the triple-tiered main building of the **Hotel Playa Azul and Trailer Park,** Av. V. Carranza s/n, Playa Azul, Michoacán 60982, tel./fax (753) 600-24 or 600-91, fax 600-92, surrounds a lovely pool patio of tall palms, rubber trees, and giant-leafed vines. A spacious blue swimming pool curves artfully in the middle, while the bar and restaurant are tucked beneath a soaring beamed *palapa* on one side. The

shady patio invites quiet relaxation; other rooms offer TV and Ping-Pong. Families especially enjoy the hotel's water-slide minipark (beachside, behind the main building past the trailer park).

The 55 rooms, spacious and comfortable but not luxurious, come in economy and standard versions. Economy rooms (with fan only, on the ground floor by the parking lot) rent for about $19 s or d; standard rooms go for about $27 s or d, with fan only, about $34 with a/c, add $3 per extra person; parking is available, credit cards are accepted, and some ground-level rooms are wheelchair-accessible, with effort.

The trailer park, with about a dozen spaces cramped behind the hotel, is nevertheless popular, since guests have access to hotel facilities. Spaces (up to about 30 feet) rent for about

$10 per day with all hookups, including power for air-conditioning, toilets, and hot showers. Discounts for lower power and weekly and monthly stays are available. Contact the hotel for reservations, which are mandatory for the trailer park during the winter.

The **Hotel María Teresa,** Av. Independencia 626, Playa Azul, Michoacán 60982, tel. (753) 600-05 or 601-50, fax 600-55, three blocks south of Aquiles Serdán and three short blocks from the beach, stands within an airy garden compound, with parking on one side and an attractive *palapa* restaurant and sunny pool patio tucked on the other. Its discotheque, Playa Azul's only one, is usually quiet, but may heat up on the holidays. If this is the case, request a room on the relatively *tranquilo* wing farthest from the disco. The 42 comfortable, near-deluxe rooms, all with TV, phones, and a/c, rent for about $16 s, $19 d, and $23 t; credit cards accepted, limited wheelchair access.

Most of Playa Azul's cheaper accommodations lack hot water, a serious defect for many winter vacationers. One exception is the **Hotel María Isabel,** four blocks south of the center of town, at Av. F. Madero s/n, Playa Azul 60982, Michoacán, tel. (753) 600-16. Its two stories of approximately 20 simply but comfortably furnished motel-modern rooms cluster around an interior pool patio one block from the beach. Rooms rent for about $9 s, $14 d, with fans and hot water.

If the María Isabel is full, fourth choice goes to the closer-in **Hotel Costa de Oro,** a block east of A. Serdán, at Av. F. Madero s/n, Playa Azul, Michoacán 60982, no phone, two blocks from the beach. The 14 spartan rooms rent from about $6 s, $8 d, with fans but no hot water.

FOOD

Avenida Aquiles Serdán (at the Hotel Playa Azul corner) offers several possibilities. The friendly **Super del Centro** grocery has a little bit of everything, from cheese and milk to mops and *espirales mosquitos* (mosquito coils). Open daily 7:30 a.m.-9 p.m.

Evenings, on the adjacent curbside, a squad of taco stalls open up. Their steaming tacos—of *res* (roast beef), *chorizo* (spicy sausage), and

lengua (tongue)—wrapped in hot tortillas and spiced with piquant salsas make perfect appetizers.

Next door, the family owners of the newcomer **Restaurant Coco** next door offer good breakfasts, lunches, and dinners in their shady outdoor patio.

For an equally tasty third course, walk down Serdán past the corner of Madero and take a streetside table at **Restaurant Galdy.** The all-woman cadre of cooks and waitresses tries harder than anyone in town, especially with hearty *pozole* (soup), *pierna* (roast pork), and *platos mexicanos* (combination plates). Open daily 7 a.m.-11 p.m.

For dessert, step back to the Madero corner to **Frutería Berenice** for a succulent selection of fruit. Local mangoes (spring, summer), pineapple, and *platanos* (bananas) will be familiar, but *guanábanas* (green and scaly, like an artichoke) and *ciruelas* (yellow and round, like a plum) probably will not. Open daily 6:30 a.m.-9 p.m.

To top everything off, cross Serdán to the *panadería* and pick up some cake, cookies, or *donas;* open Mon.-Sat. 7 a.m.-10 p.m.

For more elegant dining, go to the fanciest restaurant in town, beneath the big inner-patio *palapa* of the **Hotel Playa Azul.** Your reward will be tasty appetizers, salads, pizza, pasta, meat, seafood, and chicken entrées, professionally prepared and served. Open daily 7:30 a.m.-10 p.m.

ENTERTAINMENT AND SHOPPING

Playa Azul's evening entertainment begins with the sunset, views of which are unobstructed year-round. The effect is doubly beautiful, for the sky's golden glow is reflected from both the ocean and Playa Azul's shoreline swaths of flat wet sand. Sunset is also an excellent time for joggers and walkers to take advantage of the cool sea breeze and Playa Azul's level, firm sand.

The **tourist market,** beneath the awnings stretched over Aquiles Serdán next to the Hotel Playa Azul, has several stands that offer beach balls, T-shirts, and bathing suits. Some of the more common crafts, such as painted ceramic animals and papier-mâché, may be available also.

SERVICES AND INFORMATION

Playa Azul has only a few services. Go to **Lázaro Cárdenas,** 14 miles (22 km) southeast along Hwy. 200, for what Playa Azul lacks.

If you get sick, consult one of the town **doctors,** either Mayolo Martínez Razo, who maintain offices on Independencia, a few doors east of the Farmacia Dios, tel. (753) 601-97, or Dr. Horacio Alcauter, at his pharmacy, next to the *gasolinera* at the entrance to town. Alternatively, hire a taxi to take you to the **Centro de Salud,** tel. (753) 500-04, in La Mira (five miles, at the Hwy. 200 and Hwy. 37 intersection). If they're insufficient, continue to the **General Hospital,** tel. (753) 204-32 or 204-33, in Lázaro Cárdenas.

For routine drugs and medications, go to the **Farmacia Dios,** corner of Independencia and Aquiles Serdán, tel. (753) 601-85; open Mon.-Sat. 9 a.m.-9 p.m., Sunday 9 a.m.-1:30 p.m. and 5:30-9 p.m.

The Playa Azul *correo* (post office) is open Mon.-Fri. 8 a.m.-3 p.m., next to the health center, two blocks from the beach and two blocks from Aquiles Serdán. Next door, *telecomunicaciones,* tel./fax (332) 601-09, provides long-distance telephone, fax, and money order services. If it's closed, go to the private *larga distancia* Cuqui (KOO-kee), on Independencia, one block west of the Farmacia Dios.

GETTING THERE AND AWAY

By car or RV, paved Hwy. 200 connects Playa Azul with Manzanillo in the northwest (195 miles, 314 km). Although the route is in good condition and lightly traveled most of the way, its twists and turns through rugged oceanside canyons and along spectacular shoreline ridges make it considerably slow going. Allow at least six hours for safety. Fill up with gasoline as you start out, since the last available Magna Sin (unleaded) heading southeast is in Tecomán, about 167 miles (269 km) from the Playa Azul Pemex, which also stocks Magna Sin.

Between Playa Azul and Ixtapa-Zihuatanejo in the southeast, the route is relatively short and straight, although trucks sometimes slow progress. Allow two and a half hours for the 76-mile (122-km) trip.

With Pátzcuaro and central Michoacán in the north, Highways 37 and 14 connect with Playa Azul over 191 miles (307 km) of winding mountain highway. Although paved all the way, this route—through fertile valleys and over pine-shadowed crests—is potholed in places and occasionally congested. Allow at least seven hours for safety. Magna unleaded gasoline is only available at Arteaga, Nueva Italia, and Uruapan, so keep filled. As for *bandidos,* stick to the main highway for security. Many mountain folks cultivate marijuana and opium. They're understandably suspicious of wandering strangers.

Just before bus arrival at Playa Azul, ask your driver to drop you at the Hwy. 200-Hwy. 37 Playa Azul junction (three miles from Playa Azul, two miles from La Mira), where a taxi or local minibus can take you the rest of the way.

For long-distance bus departure from Playa Azul, go to La Mira (five miles by local minibus or taxi) and wait at the intersection of Highways 200 and 37. Although most Manzanillo-, Pátzcuaro-, and Zihuatanejo-bound buses stop and pick up passengers frequently at La Mira during daylight hours, reserved seats are only available from the Lázaro Cárdenas stations.

PÁTZCUARO

The high road from Playa Azul leads inland to Pátzcuaro (pop. 70,000), a city brimming with inspirations. Pine- and cedar-brushed mountains ring it, an islet-studded lake borders it. Its air is fresh and clean and the sky always seems blue. Visitors come from all over the world to wander through narrow colonial lanes, buy fine copper and lacquerware, and gaze at grand, mystery-shrouded monuments of long-forgotten emperors.

HISTORY

Before the Conquest

The valley and lake of Pátzcuaro, elev. 7,500 feet (2,280 meters), have nurtured civilizations for millennia. The Tarascans, whose king, Tariácuri, rebuilt the city during the 1370s, were the last and the greatest dynasty. To them the lake and surrounding grounds were sacred: the door to the land of their ancestors. They chose the venerated foundation stones of already-ancient temples as the new city's cornerstones, marking the symbolic door to the land of the dead: *tzacapu-amú-cutin-pátzcuaro*, the "stone door where all changes to blackness." The last part of that original name remains in use today.

The founders of Pátzcuaro did not call themselves Tarascans. This was from the Spanish word, meaning "son-in-law." Before the conquest, Pátzcuaro people called (and still call) themselves the Purépecha (poo-REH-peh-chah). After they arrived in 1521, the Spanish increasingly applied their own label as they intermarried with the Pátzcuaro people.

Prior to the conquest, the Valley of Pátzcuaro was the center of a grand Purépecha empire, which extended beyond the present-day borders of the state of Michoacán. Local folk are still proud that their ancestors were never subjects of the Aztecs, whose armies they defeated and slaughtered by the tens of thousands on the eve of the conquest.

Conquest and Colonization

As Cortés approached the Valley of Mexico, the jittery Aztec emperor Moctezuma sent ambassadors to Tzintzuntzán (seen-soon-SAHN), the Purépecha capital on the shore of the lake a dozen miles northwest of Pátzcuaro. The ambassadors implored King Zuangua, known by his imperial title *caltzonzin,* to send an army to help repel Cortés. The *caltzonzin* refused, hastening Moctezuma's downfall and perhaps his own.

The first Spaniards, a few seemingly harmless travelers, wandered into the Valley of Pátzcuaro in 1521. The smallpox they unwittingly brought, however, was far from harmless. Zuangua soon succumbed to the ugly disease, along with tens of thousands of his subjects.

The Spanish military threat, in the person of conquistador Cristóbal de Olid and 70 mounted cavalry, 200 foot soldiers, and thousands of Indian allies, arrived at Tzintzuntzán in 1522. As the new *caltzonzin,* Tangaxoan II, fled to Uruapan, Olid quickly appropriated the imperial treasure and the gold and jewels from the temples. After a short resistance, Tangaxoan II pledged his homage to Cortés and was soon baptized, accepting the Christian name of Pedro. By 1526, most of his subjects had followed suit.

Peace reigned, but not for long. Cortés was called back to Spain, and the gold-hungry opportunist Nuño de Guzmán took temporary control in Mexico City. In late 1528, Guzmán had the *caltzonzin* tortured and killed. The Spanish royal government, alarmed by Guzmán's excesses, sent an official panel, called the Second Audiencia, to replace him. Guzmán, one jump ahead of them, cleared out in command of a battalion of like-minded adventurers, hellbent to find another Tenochtitlán in western Mexico. They pounced upon the Purépecha, burning, raping, and pillaging the Valley of Pátzcuaro.

Vasco de Quiroga

The Purépecha fortunes began to improve when Father Vasco de Quiroga, a member of the Second Audiencia, arrived in 1533. At the age of 63 he began his life's work on the shore of Lake Pátzcuaro. Through his kindness, compassion, and tireless energy, Don Vasco gained the confidence of the Purépecha. He immediately established a hospital for the care of the poor. Named Santa Fe de la Laguna, it still stands by the lakeshore.

Appointed bishop in 1538, Don Vasco moved the episcopal seat from Tzintzuntzán to Pátzcuaro, which had already become the provincial government headquarters. Pressing ahead, he immediately began the Colegio San Nicolas. Its features became the model for many more: a hospital for the care of the poor, a school to educate young Tarascans, and a seminary for training bilingual Tarascan priests.

Pátzcuaro's rich handicrafts heritage is partly due to Don Vasco. He moderated the Tarascans' *encomienda* obligations so that they had time to become self-sustaining on their communal and individual plots. Entire villages became centers of specific skills and trades. Such tradi-

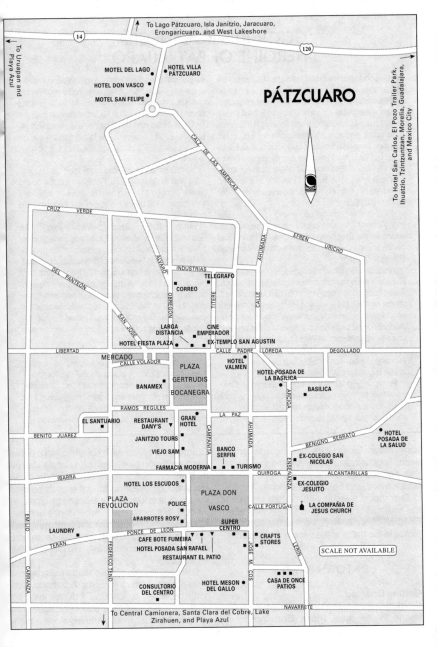

GERTRUDIS BOCANEGRA, HEROINE OF PÁTZCUARO

Independence heroine Gertrudis Bocanegra de Lazo de la Vega was born into a well-to-do Pátzcuaro family on 11 April 1765. Her outspoken nature emerged at an early age. Once, as a young child, on her family balcony overlooking Pátzcuaro's main plaza, she was horrified at the sight of an unruly mob beating a helpless beggar with sticks. She cried out from the top of her lungs, but the crowd took little notice. She retreated inside, sobbing, to her mother's arms. The incident indelibly marked her; from then on, the oppressed had a ready defender in Gertrudis Bocanegra.

As she was growing up, young Gertrudis, like many of her Mexican criollo generation, was inspired by the European liberal ideas of liberty and justice and the daring deeds that led to the American Revolution.

When she arrived at marriageable age, more than just a few young suitors competed for her affections. Pedro Lazo de la Vega, a young criollo second lieutenant of the local army garrison, won Gertrudis's heart with a secret note, declaring his fervent admiration. Soon he proposed marriage, but she imposed one severe condition: she would not marry someone in the service of Mexico's colonial oppressors; in exchange for her consent, her fiancée would have to resign his military commission.

For young Pedro, this was no small matter. Criollos (Mexican-born of pure Spanish descent) such as he had few good professional career options; the most prestigious positions were traditionally reserved for *peninsulares,* Spanish-born colonists, derisively known as *gachupines.* Even after Pedro promised to quit the army, Gertrudis's father refused to give the couple his blessing, citing no better reason than the fact that Pedro had black hair and a swarthy complexion. Finally, however, the father was unable to resist his daughter's pleadings and Pedro's obvious love for her.

Seven children resulted from their union, four sons and three daughters. For 20 years, the young family enjoyed the modicum of success accorded Mexican criollos under the rule of the Spanish-born colonials.

But they chafed under the *peninsular* yoke. On 15 September 1810, when Father Miguel Hidalgo cried "Viva Mexico! Death to the *gachupines!"* he had immediate allies in hundreds of thousands of criollos, including Pedro and Gertrudis. Pedro and their teenage son Manuel quickly joined the insurgent army, which suffered disastrous defeat on 17 January 1811, at the Puente de Calderón, east of Guadalajara. They returned and joined the guerrilla campaign being waged against the Spanish forces in Michoacán.

Meanwhile, Gertrudis never wavered in her support for them and the *insurgente* cause. She made their Pátzcuaro house a secret rebel intelligence, finance, and supply headquarters. She promoted contributions of money and a small mountain of food and ammunition for the *insurgente* fighters. Although authorities suspected her activities, she avoided ar-

---

tions remain: Santa Clara turns out fine copperware; Tzintzuntzán, furniture. Other valley communities produce elaborate baskets, delicate lacquerware, and handsome saddles.

Don Vasco toiled until his death in 1565 at the age of 95. Pátzcuaro people still adore him. Children often leave flowers at the foot of his statue in the plaza at the very heart of the city.

IN-TOWN SIGHTS

Getting Oriented
From the good bishop's tree-shaded bronze image in the main **Plaza Don Vasco de Quiroga,** the city spreads out along half a dozen north-south and east-west main streets. **Avenida Mendoza** runs from the northwest plaza corner one long block north to the city's second square, **Plaza Gertrudis Bocanegra,** named for the city's renowned independence heroine. The **market** spreads from the northwest side of Plaza Bocanegra, while past the south end, Av. La Paz runs uphill (east) two blocks to the **basilica.**

Back at the main plaza's northeast corner, a second main thoroughfare, **Av. Amuhada,** runs north, becoming Av. Lázaro Cárdenas, the main highway-access route. It continues about two miles to the east-west Uruapan-Morelia high-

rest for years as the increasingly bitter war ground on. Rebel guerrillas attacked, killed, and tortured Spanish soldiers and their sympathizers; the royalists responded with equal ferocity. Eventually both Pedro and Manuel died of battle wounds.

Gertrudis nevertheless redoubled her efforts. She traveled tirelessly, gathering support for her compatriots. On one such trip, she left a family friend, a retired sergeant whom she had once saved from the gallows, to watch her house. When she returned, Gertrudis found some valuables missing. She questioned him, and, in retaliation, he denounced her to the authorities.

The local military commander quickly arrived at her house. During a chess party, before her compatriot-guests, he took Bocanegra into custody, placing her under arrest in the house at 14 Calle Ibarra, just around the corner from her childhood home. Her execution was summarily ordered; on 10 October 1817, a military guard escorted her, blindfolded, to the corner square (now Plaza Revolución) in front of San Francisco church. The priest accompanying her asked that she be allowed to stop and pray for a few moments. His request was granted, but she was not allowed to go inside the church to her family altar, for it traditionally had been a place where the persecuted had found refuge from civil authorities.

The guards conducted her to gallows that had been set up in the adjacent small plaza. The streets were empty of passersby; neighbors shut their windows, refusing to witness the execution. Bells rang out in protest from every church tower. At the last moment, the official in charge received an order to take Gertrudis to the main town plaza and execute her by firing squad. There, in front of the jail, she was to become an example for many of her comrades who were being held inside.

First the soldiers tried to rope her to a tree, but she protested such a humiliation. Left standing free, she removed her shawl, then a fine comb from her hair. This, along with a gold watch, Bocanegra handed over to her executioner, requesting that they be given to her three daughters so that they would remember her and not be shamed by their mother, who had been executed for defending the cause of liberty. Then Bocanegra produced a gold peso, saying, "Here's all I have left," as she threw it to the soldiers of her execution squad. She pulled off her blindfold and began addressing the small crowd of friends and compatriots. Her fervent message so stirred the onlookers that the official in charge was forced to disperse the gathering.

A single fusillade ended her life. Her body fell and lay for hours, until her blood caked and crusted in the sun and a swarm of flies gathered on the corpse. Guards finally had to douse it with a bucket of water and cover it with her shawl. The next day, her family was allowed to take her body home for vigil, then burial at the nearby church of the Compañía de Jesús.

The people of Pátzcuaro have never forgotten Bocanegra's sacrifice. During his 1934-40 presidency, Lázaro Cárdenas ordered that a statue of the defiant Gertrudis at her moment of execution be erected in Plaza San Agustín (now Plaza Bocanegra) in Pátzcuaro. Every year, on the 10 October anniversary of her death, the people of Pátzcuaro gather beside her statue and honor Gertrudis Bocanegra's memory with overflowing bouquets of flowers.

---

way and the railroad station. Crossing the railroad tracks at the station, a branch road leads about a mile north to the **Lake Pátzcuaro** embarcadero, where boats depart for Janitzio and other islands.

Getting Around

Virtually everything downtown is within a few blocks of the Plaza Don Vasco de Quiroga. For trips out of the city, hail a taxi or ride a white *colectivo* van of your choice, for about 25 cents (read the destinations on the windows) from in front of the Hotel Los Escudos at the Plaza Don Vasco corner of Ibarra and Mendoza or on the Plaza Bocanegra in front of the market.

A Walk around Old Pátzcuaro

The natural place to start is at the center of the main plaza, beneath the statue of the revered Don Vasco de Quiroga (1470-1565). As first bishop of Pátzcuaro he reversed the despair and destruction wrought by the conquistadores.

Colonial buildings, some dating back to the 17th century, rise behind the portals that spread around the square. The portals are themselves named and localize individual addresses (such as the Hotel Los Escudos, Portal Hidalgo 73).

Walk east, uphill, one block to Pátzcuaro's oldest colonial building, the former **Colegio San Nicolas,** begun by Don Vasco in 1540. Pass inside beneath its quaint three-bell Spanish classic

The facade of the Colegio San Nicolas (1540), a cherished national treasure, graces a quiet Pátzcuaro street corner.

facade to the venerable inner garden. Now called the Museo de Arte Popular, tel. (434) 210-29, its corridors lead past rooms filled with fine regional crafts. In a rear courtyard, be sure to see the stairstep foundations of the original Tarascan temple, exposed on the hillside. Turn around and inspect a wall inscribed with the marks of prisoners counting the days. Open Tues.-Sat. 9 a.m.-7 p.m., Sunday 9 a.m.-3 p.m.

As you exit the museum, glance left at the curious little doorway emerging from the outside uphill lane. Behind that door, Pátzcuaro people say, is an aqueduct that Don Vasco built to supply the poor with water during times of drought.

Walk ahead past the big courtyard and church on the left, a former Jesuit College, now restored as a community cultural center. It maintains an art museum and offers classes in theater, painting, drawing, and music, both instrumental and choral. Watch for posters announcing events. The old church at the far end of the bare courtyard, La Parroquia de la Compañía de Jesús, is the final resting place of renowned Pátzcuaro independence heroine, **Gertrudis Bocanegra,** who was executed on 10 October 1817 for her staunch defense of the *insurgente* cause.

Continue along Calle Enseñanza. After two blocks, turn right, downhill, to the former Dominican Convent of Santa Catarina de Sena, commonly known as the **Casa de Once Patios** ("House of 11 Patios") on the left. Most of its inner labyrinth of gardens, corridors, and rooms are restored and open to the public. Dozens of

artisans have set up display workshops where they paint, weave, polish, and carve handicrafts for sale. Open daily 9 a.m.-2 p.m. and 4-7 p.m.

Return past the former Colegio San Nicolas and continue two blocks along Calle Arciga to the big **Basilica María Inmaculada de la Salud,** begun by Don Vasco during the mid-16th century. In addition to Don Vasco's tomb, the basilica is noted for its four-century-old main altar image of the Virgin, made according to a pre-Columbian recipe of cornstalk paste and orchid glue.

Follow diagonal Av. Buenavista downhill and continue a block along Lloreda to the former monastery, **Ex-Templo San Agustín,** now housing the public library, **Biblioteca Gertrudis Bocanegra,** at the northeast corner of Plaza Bocanegra; open Mon.-Fri. 9 a.m.-7 p.m., Saturday 9 a.m.-1 p.m. The library's main attraction is its huge mural, the first by Juan O'Gorman, completed in 1942. In this panorama of the history of the Valley of Pátzcuaro, O'Gorman is nearly as critical of the Tarascans' slaughter of 30,000 Aztec prisoners as of Nuño de Guzmán (scowling like a demon in armor) as he tortures the last *caltzonzin* (emperor). All is not lost as O'Gorman shows the murdered emperor's niece, Erendira, riding out (and becoming the first Native American to ride a horse) to warn the people. Don Vasco, the savior, appears at the bottom, assuring a happy ending as he brings utopia to Pátzcuaro.

The librarian has a Spanish copy of the mural guide, signed by O'Gorman, who appears with his wife at the mural's left side. Additionally, the librarian will duplicate a copy of a brief but informative Spanish biography of independence heroine Gertrudis Bocanegra, whose statue stands in the adjoining plaza. The library's respectable book collection includes many Spanish-language reference works and several shelves of English-language fiction and nonfiction.

JANITZIO AND YUÑUEN ISLANDS

An excursion to the island of Janitzio (hah-NEET-seeoh) is de rigueur for first-time

Pátzcuaro visitors. The breezy launch trip takes about half an hour. Waves splash, spray, and rock the bow; gulls wheel above the stern as the pyramidal volcanic island-village of Janitzio grows upon the horizon. The Janitzio villagers believe themselves to be the purest of the Purépecha. Only the young speak Spanish; the old—some of whom have never visited the mainland—hold fast to their language and traditional ways.

Fishing for the tasty Pátzcuaro *pescado blanco* (whitefish) used to be the major Janitzio occupation. Overfishing has unfortunately reduced the famous *mariposas* (butterfly nets), which

ERIN DWYER

*Eerie local-style Pátzcuaro (Michoacán) masks
are common sale items in Janitzio shops.*

Don Vasco introduced long ago, to mere ceremonial objects. Long, cumbersome nets are now
needed for the increasingly meager catches.
The price (about $6) of a succulent whitefish
platter—the specialty of the dozen-odd embarcadero restaurants—has inflated beyond the
reach of most Pátzcuaro families.

Fortunately, government and local cooperative
conservation measures show promise of eventually replenishing the whitefish population.
Meanwhile, the *mariposas* come out for display
only during tourist-show regattas on weekends
and holidays.

A steady procession of handicrafts shops lines
the steep lane that winds to the island's summit. Although most items (baskets, masks, papier-mâché, lacquerware, cottons, and woolens)
are cheap and common, some unusual buys
await those willing to look and bargain.

From the hillcrest, you can see the still more
isolated islets of Tecuen, Yuñuen, and La
Pacanda dotting the lake's northern reaches,
while in the opposite direction, the city of
Pátzcuaro basks at the foot of a distant pine-
tufted green sierra. If you have the energy, climb
to the tip-top of the colossal José María Morelos
statue, lined inside with a continuous mural of
scenes from the fiery independence hero's life.

Lake Pátzcuaro's other islands, notably
Yuñuen, also welcome visitors. The community
has built a lovely hilltop cluster of rustic wooden
cabins for guests. Rates run about $30 d, in-
cluding breakfast and transportation. Activities include walks around the island, visits to home
crafts workshops, fishing, traditional dinners,
and Purépecha language lessons. For reservations and more information, contact Jorge
Morales, tel. (434) 210-72 or 244-73.

Getting There: If you're driving, head downhill (north) a couple of miles along Av. Lázaro
Cárdenas and turn left at the Uruapan-Morelia
highway. Within a few hundred yards, turn right
at the road crossing the rail tracks at the rail station. After about half a mile, bear right at a fork,
and soon you'll see the parking lot (about $1). If
you're not driving, taxi or ride the white *colectivo*
VW van (about 40 cents, from the corner by the
Hotel Los Escudos on Plaza Don Vasco, or the
Mercado corner, Plaza Bocanegra) to the embarcadero. Roundtrip boat tickets, available from
a dock-front booth, cost about $2 for Janitzio,
$5 or more for Yuñuen, Pacanda, and Tecuen, in
advance of departure. The last boat returns from
the islands around 5 p.m.

IHUATZIO

Pre-Columbian ruins dot the Pátzcuaro Valley.
Most remain unexcavated grassy mounds except the most famous: Ihuatzio (ee-WAHT-
seeoh) and Tzintzuntzán, both near the
lakeshore northeast of the city.

Pátzcuaro dominated the valley during the
latter-1300s golden-era reign of King Tariácuri.
When he died the valley was divided between his
younger son and his nephews, Hiripan and Tangaxoan (ancestor of Tangaxoan II, the last Tarascan emperor). According to Vasco de Quiroga's
16th-century narrative, *Relación de Michoacán,*

squabbling broke out among the heirs. Hiripan won out, and, by 1400, had concentrated power at Ihuatzio.

Exploring Ihuatzio

The remains of Ihuatzio (literally, "Place of the Coyotes") spread over a rectangular area about half a mile long by a quarter mile wide. Nearly all ruins are mound-dotted unexplored fields, closed to the public. The open part, the so-called **Parade Ground,** is about the size of four football fields and enclosed by a pair of ceremonial stepped-wall raised causeways. These lead toward a pair of hulking truncated pyramids that tower above the Parade Ground's west end. These, Ihuatzio's most prominent structures, lost nearly all of their original stone sheathing to colonial construction projects, although a remnant appears on the right pyramid's face as you approach from the Parade Ground.

Climb carefully (the steps are steep) to the top for a view of the surrounding unexcavated ruins. Along the Parade Ground's north and south sides, notice the **King's Causeways,** a pair of long stepped mounds, presumably used as the *caltzonzin*'s ceremonial approach road.

About a quarter mile due south rises another mound, which marks the **Observatory,** a mysterious 100-foot-wide cylindrical structure whose name merely represents an educated guess about its possible function. In nearly the same direction as the Observatory, but much closer, stands the rubbly mound of the *yácatas,* three half-cylindrical truncated pyramids, whose original forms are unrecognizable due to repeated ransackings. Their shapes, however, are certain, due to a number of other excavated local examples, most notably Tzintzuntzán, five miles to the north. The Ihuatzio site is open daily around 9 a.m.-4 p.m.; entry fee about $2, no facilities except a lavatory; don't forget your hat and drinking water.

Getting There: By car or taxi, take Hwy. 120 from Pátzcuaro northeast (Morelia direction) about five miles (eight kilometers) to the signed Ihuatzio turnoff. Turn left and continue about two more miles to a signed road on the right, which bumps for about another half mile to the site parking lot. By bus, ride one of the blue and white *urbano* buses, which all pass the central bus station front entrance on the south edge of town. Hop on to the bus marked Ihuatzio on the

IHUATZIO ARCHAEOLOGICAL ZONE

WALL-CAUSEWAY

WALL-CAUSEWAY

WALL-CAUSEWAY

OBSERVATORY

RECONSTRUCTED PYRAMIDS

YACATAS

KING'S CAUSEWAYS

PARADE GROUND

AREA OPEN TO THE PUBLIC

PARKING

0   150 yd

0   150 m

TO PATZCUARO

windshield. About 20 minutes later, when the bus turns from the highway on to the Ihuatzio side road, tell the driver *"ruinas, por favor"* and you'll probably get dropped off at the entrance lane about half a mile from the archaeological site. Take a hat and drinking water. The only facilities are a lavatory.

TZINTZUNTZÁN

Ihuatzio's power waned during the 1400s, gradually giving way to nearby Tzintzuntzán ("Place of the Hummingbirds"). Within a generation, Tzintzuntzán (seen-soon-SAHN) became the hub of an expanded Tarascan empire, which included nearly all of present Michoacán and half of Jalisco and Guanajuato. When the Spanish arrived in 1521, authority was concentrated entirely in Tzintzuntzán, an imperial city whose population had swelled to perhaps as much as 100,000.

The present town (pop. 5,000) a dozen miles northeast of Pátzcuaro is a mere shadow of its former glory. The Great Platform, although long abandoned, still towers, in proud relief, on the hill above the dusty modern town.

Exploring the Archaeological Site

The entire archaeological zone—of which the Great Platform occupies a significant but very small area—spreads over nearly three square miles. The excavated part, open to the public, represents only a fiftieth of the total, being confined within a rectangle perhaps 500 yards long and half that in width. The visitor's entrance leads you toward the rear of the Great Platform from the east through a grassy park. You first see the Great Platform spreading from right (north) to left, with the town and lake below the far front side.

The Great Platform is singularly intriguing because of its five side-by-side *yácatas:* massive, semicylindrical ceremonial platforms. The *yácatas* are built of huge cut basalt (lava) stones, like a giant child's neat stacks of black building blocks. When the Spanish arrived, a temple to the legendary god-king Curicaueri perched upon the *yácata* summit.

Although the Great Platform itself was purely ceremonial in function, excavations in outer por-

tions of the zone reveal that imperial Tzintzuntzán was an entire city, housing all classes from kings to slaves. Within the city, people lived and worked according to specialized occupations—farmers, artisans, priests, and warriors. Most experts agree that such urban organization required a high degree of sophistication, including excess wealth, laws and efficient government, and a reliable calendar.

Tzintzuntzán grew through a number of stages from its founding around A.D. 900. Excavations beneath the Great Platform masonry reveal earlier *yácatas* overlaid, like layers of an onion, above earlier constructions with similar, but smaller, features. (Look, for example, at the archaeological test hole between *yácatas* 4 and 5.)

Other intriguing structures dot the Great Platform. **Entrance ramps,** apparently built as boat-traffic terminals, appear beneath the Great Platform's 20-foot-high stepped retaining wall. Records reveal that, at the time of the conquest, lake waters lapped beaches at the foot of these ramps.

The Palace, a group of rooms surrounding an inner patio, stands about a hundred yards northeast of the first *yácata.* Because thousands of human bones and an altar were found here, some archaeologists speculated that it may have been a ceremonial depository for the remains of vanquished enemies.

About 75 yards in front of *yácatas* 4 and 5 is Building E, a puzzling L-shaped group of rooms. Although archaeologists speculate that they may have been storerooms or granaries, excavations, curiously, revealed no entrances.

The site is open daily about 9 a.m.-5 p.m.; facilities include a picnic park and lavatories. Entry fee is about $3; bring your hat and drinking water.

Modern Tzintzuntzán

The buildings the Spanish colonials erected still stand at the far (west) end of the town park, which spreads from the crafts stalls bordering the Hwy. 120 main street. Clustered at the park's far end you will find the **Franciscan monastery and church.** Inside the church are several paintings and murals dedicated to the Señor de Rescate, whose festival the townspeople celebrate with Purépecha music and regional dances. The adjacent monastery, dedicated to Santa Anna, is known for its plateresque facade

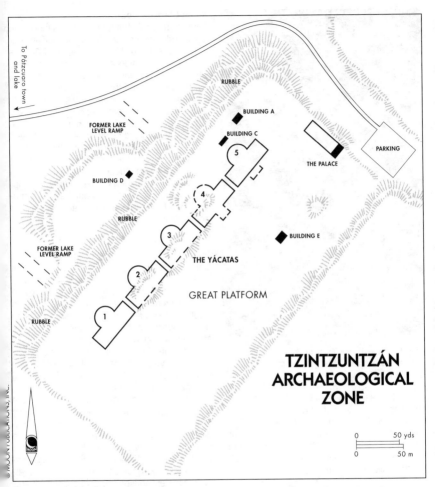

To Pátzcuaro town and lake

RUBBLE

BUILDING A

FORMER LAKE LEVEL RAMP

BUILDING C

5

THE PALACE

PARKING

BUILDING D

4

RUBBLE

3

FORMER LAKE LEVEL RAMP

BUILDING E

2

THE YÁCATAS

GREAT PLATFORM

1

RUBBLE

TZINTZUNTZÁN ARCHAEOLOGICAL ZONE

| 0 | 50 yds |
| 0 | 50 m |

and courtyard, containing some of the world's oldest olive trees (which somehow survived the royal ban on olive trees in Mexico).

Back on the main street, handicrafts stores and shops offer some unusual woodwork. Especially noteworthy are the **Artesanías Colibri** and the warren of shops behind it. Wander among their riots of wooden crafts—giant masks, baskets, headboards, cabinets—where you can select from a potpourri of pre-Columbian, gothic, baroque, and neoclassic motifs.

Even more woodcrafts are available on the road back to Pátzcuaro, a mile or two from Tzintzuntzán, where a village of woodcarvers' shops has sprouted on both sides of the road.

Getting There: By car by head northeast along Hwy. 120, Morelia direction, continuing past the Ihuatzio turnoff about five miles (eight kilometers) to the signed Tzintzuntzán right fork, which leads to the ruins on the hill above the highway. By bus, from the Pátzcuaro *central camionera* (south side of town), ride one of the

A sample of the huge selection of colonial-style woodcrafts for sale at Tzintzuntzán carver's shops.

several Galeana (tel. 434-208-08) second-class bus departures to Tzintzuntzán. A few minutes after the Ihuatzio turnoff (note the road sign), tell the driver *"ruinas, por favor"* and you'll probably get dropped off at the highway fork to the ruins (or, if you're lucky, at the ruins parking lot a quarter mile farther on).

EXCURSIONS SOUTH AND WEST OF PÁTZCUARO

An auto excursion to the copper-crafting town of Santa Clara de Cobre can be conveniently extended into a half-day loop that includes tranquil, storied mountain lake Zirahuén and the mysterious pre-Tarascan ruins at the Tinganio archaeological site.

Santa Clara de Cobre

Santa Clara de Cobre (pop. 5,000) is tucked on a gently sloping mountainside about half an hour (13 miles, 21 km by Hwy. 120) south of Pátzcuaro. The town clusters around an intimate plaza, where most everything you see—the benches, the bandstand, and the lampposts—seems to be made of copper. A look at the shiny contents of the plaza shops—galaxies of gleaming utensils, curios, and art objects—confirms the impression. Although their old mines are all played out, the livelihoods of many Santa Clara families are still based on the fine copperware (made from copper from other parts of Mexico), which they turn out in their workshops/homes. If you decide to linger, attractive colonial-style restaurants and hotels on the plaza can provide food and lodging.

Lake Zirahuén

From Hwy. 120, just past the southern fringe of Santa Clara, a cobbled road forks right about seven miles (12 km) to reed-lined Lake Zirahuén. According to Purépecha legend, the lake resulted from the river of tears that Princess Zirahuén wept after losing her true love. Although Zirahuén died of sorrow, her spirit still lives in the lake. Men who set out upon the water in their canoes must beware, for the spirit appears as a lovely, beckoning young maiden. And alas for the one who cannot resist, for the spirit will take him never to be seen again.

Ghosts notwithstanding, Lake Zirahuén is a jewel set amongst emerald, pine-clad summits and lush communal fields ripe for relaxed exploring, or maybe even renting a local house and soaking in backcountry Michoacán for a week or month. Fisherfolk paddle dugout canoes across Zirahuén's mirror surface; local-style wooden houses known as *trojes* cluster near the lakeshore. Village kids play in the street, old men sit and talk about the "way things used to be." A rough but passable road circles the lake, and excursion boats take parties out from a pair of wharves near sleepy, colonial Zirahuén town (pop. 1,000). **Restaurants** at both wharves offer whitefish dinners for very reasonable prices.

The more upscale of the wharves, Embarcadero Troje Ala, whose signed entrance you pass en route from Santa Clara, has an attractive restaurant/lodge and rustic, clean housekeeping **cabins** sleeping two to six persons. For information and reservations, telephone or fax Operadora Lago de Zirahuén at its office in Morelia, Michoacán, tel. (43) 263-301, 273-624, or call Troje Ala directly, at (434) 227-05. Daily rates run about $47 d, $63 for one to four.

The other route to Lake Zirahuén is via the well-signed turnoff road at Km 17 (10 miles west of Pátzcuaro) on Hwy. 14 to Uruapan. If you go that way, you'll pass the Hotel Zirahuén on the left just as you enter Zirahuén town. For Embarcadero Troje Ala, continue ahead for about 50 yards, then bear left on the cobbled lakeshore road.

Alternatively, take a few minutes to look at the **Hotel Zirahuén,** Av. Vicente Guerrero s/n, Zirahuén, Michoacán 61810, tel./fax (434) 227-05 and 202-72, an unusual family project a couple minutes' walk from the lakeshore. It features 12 deluxe rooms, including a super-deluxe, two-bedroom (king-size) "presidential suite," with a sauna and a grand indoor spa that would accommodate about eight. All this for about $138 for two, three, or four. Smaller but equally luxurious options, all with spa, include a "master" suite, minus the sauna, $95 for up to four; a one-bedroom "junior" suite, about $51 d, and a "super" room, for about $37 d. Regular rooms, still luxurious, but without spa, run about $31 d.

Getting There: Travel to Zirahuén either by car, taxi, or second-class Autobuses del Occidente (ADO), tel. (434) 212-43, which provides several daily Zirahuén departures from the southside bus station.

Tinganio Archaeological Zone

If instead of turning you stay on the same Hwy. 14 you'll arrive at **Tingambato,** at Km 37 (23 miles, 37 km from Pátzcuaro; 16 miles, 26 km from Uruapan). Turn at the small roadside archaeological sign and continue through the town about a mile to the Tinganio archaeological site parking lot.

The excavated section, uncovered during the late 1970s, constitutes a small, albeit very important part of the entire archaeological zone. Modern dating methods show construction occurred in two phases, the first beginning around A.D. 450 and the second continuing between A.D. 600 and A.D. 900. The second stage culminated in the visible reconstructions, which surround a central sunken plaza: on the east side, a 25-foot, six-step pyramid; a tomb complex on the north; and a sunken ball court on the west. The pyramid, accessed by a ritual stairway, is reminiscent of classic Teotihuacán style. Opposite is the ceremonial ball court (see the special topic on *tlatchtli*) in which players tried to bat a solid, natural rubber ball past their opponents with their torsos, shoulders, and heads. Stakes for ritually important contests sometimes ran as high as the lives of the participants.

Although much of the site had been looted before the arrival of the Spanish, excavators discovered an unopened tomb (note the descending staircase) on the north side. Finds included a host of skulls and skeletons—although only one complete, seated at the entrance—and a trove of artifacts, enough for a generation of archaeologists to sort out.

LAKE PÁTZCUARO WEST SHORELINE

The smooth 30-mile (50-km) road that follows Lake Pátzcuaro's rural west shoreline provides a path for a leisurely half-day exploration by car or taxi (or by bus—allow a full day).

Although the folks along this route are accustomed to seeing foreign visitors when they go into the city, the same foreign visitors seldom come to where they live. People are going to wonder why you came. A wave of the hand, a smile, and a simple *"Hola," "Buenos dias,"* or *"Buenos tardes"* on your part will go a long way toward breaking the ice.

Some of the villages en route are known for certain handicrafts. Few, if any, families have formal shops to sell their goods, but people will tell (or lead you) where to find them if you ask.

Get there by either car or bus. By car, the route begins as if you're going to the Janitzio excursion boat dock (see **Janitzio,** above), except that, at the fork past the rail station, instead of heading right to the boat dock, you head left. From the *camionera central,* south side of town, take one of the early, very frequent Autobuses del Occidente (ADO) second-class buses headed for Jarácuaro and/or Erongarícuaro, the biggest towns on the west shore. Hop off at the first likely spot along the way, and continue with a succeeding bus. At Erongarícuaro, if it isn't too late, you can continue by different, but connecting buses, to Quiroga, at the lake's north end, where you can connect with a Galeana bus back to Pátzcuaro, via Tzintzuntzán.

Tócuaro and Jarácuaro

After about five miles (eight km) along the lakeshore from Pátzcuaro, you pass scruffy Tócuaro village on the left, known for its good papier-mâché and masks (*máscaras;* MAHS-cahrahs). About two miles farther you'll see Jarácuaro town, on the offshore island. Head right at the paved fork to the causeway and bridge. Here, you can first visit the rustically serene old Señor San Pedro de Jarácuaro church and garden in the middle of town. Then head around to the back side of town, behind the church, where, instead of the lake, you see a 500-yard-wide grassy "beach" being grazed by a herd of apparently very contented cows. By this time you probably will have noticed what seems to be the townfolks' main occupation: weaving reeds for *petates* (all-purpose straw mats) in their spare time. The whole town—tots, men, women, old folks—do it nimbly, automatically, and often collectively, passing the time of day together.

Erongarícuaro, Opongio, and Chupícuaro

About three miles farther, you'll arrive at the biggest west-shore town, Erongarícuaro (pop. about 3,000), known for its *bordado* (hand embroidery). About two miles (three kilometers) before the town, you might stop for refreshment at the German-owned and operated **Restaurant Campestre Alemán** and try the specialty, trout, German-style. Continue to the town, whose inviting green plaza, grocery stores, and restaurant (one block north, past the plaza) at the roadside, rate at least a stop and a stroll around.

The road winds another five or six miles (8-10 km) past cornfields and pastures to a crest and broad vista point, just before Opongio village. Pause and view the giant arms of the lake spread south and north, separated by a looming, pine-tufted 10,000-foot extinct volcanic peak. On the right, the islands of Pacanda, Yuñuen, Tecuen, and Janitzio appear as a procession of turtles, paddling toward the lake's shallow southern shore. On

the left, Pátzcuaro's deeper northern arm extends to a misty-blue, mountain-rimmed shoreline.

If you want to see the lake close up, you can do so at **Chupícuaro,** several miles farther along. Just before joining the main Zacapu-Quiroga highway, turn right at a paved fork, which leads downhill to a cedar-shaded grassy park right at the lakeshore. A restaurant sells drinks and snacks, and the lake provides plenty of cool water for wading.

Santa Fe de la Laguna

Finally, be sure to leave enough time to stop at Santa Fe de la Laguna, marked by the roadside pottery shops, two miles farther east (toward Quiroga), on the left. Follow the street dividing the shops to the picturesquely restored town plaza, two blocks from the highway. Past the door on the plaza's far side stands the venerable **Iglesia Santa Fe de La Laguna** church and former hospital, behind the church. Built by the singular energy of Bishop Vasco de Quiroga more than four centuries ago, both church and hospital live on in his spirit, even though the hospital has become a library and a soon-to-be museum. Inside, kindly librarian José Luis Bautista shepherds flocks of eager young scholars, while next door in the museum, Don Vasco looks down from his portrait. The good bishop's chair stands sedately on one side, and next to the entrance is the remarkable first page of Don Vasco's rules for the hospital. Loosely translated, the document declares that Hospital Santa Fe de La Laguna is not only for visiting priests, pilgrims, and dignitaries, but for *all* the people. Judging from the devotion that Pátzcuaro people still show for him, Bishop Vasco de Quiroga must have been a man of his word.

PÁTZCUARO ACCOMMODATIONS

Downtown Hotels

Although prices have risen sharply for some Pátzcuaro hotels, visitors can still enjoy some good, reasonably priced colonial-decor hotels clustered near the plazas. Because of the mild, dry climate, rooms generally have neither air-conditioning nor central heating. Fans and *chimeneas* (fireplaces, a cozy winter plus) are sometimes available.

The family-managed **Hotel Los Escudos,** Portal Hidalgo 73, Pátzcuaro, Michoacán 61600, tel. (434) 201-38 and 212-90, fax 206-49, right on the plaza, is a longtime Pátzcuaro favorite. Its rooms rise in three tiers around a cool, serene inner patio, wrapped in wrought iron, tile, and bright greenery. The homey, dark-paneled rooms come with lacy curtains, wood floors, and fireplaces (wood included). The wood-paneled café downstairs, one of Pátzcuaro's favorite meeting places, is a good spot for lingering over dessert with friends or with a good book after a hard day on the lake. The hotel's 30 rooms rent for about $24 s and $33 d, with TV, parking, and credit cards accepted. Reservations, recommended any time, are mandatory weekends and holidays. The hotel has recently acquired an annex *(nueva sección)* next door, which, although authentically colonial and

---

PÁTZCUARO ACCOMMODATIONS

Accommodations (area code 454, postal code 61600) are listed in increasing order of high-season, double-room rates.

DOWNTOWN

Hotel Valmen, Lloreda 34, tel. 211-61, $11

Hotel Posada de la Salud, Av. Serrato 9, tel. 200-58, $17

Hotel Posada San Rafael, Portal Aldama 15, tel. 207-70, $19

Gran Hotel, Portal Regules 6, Plaza Bocanegra, tel. 204-43, fax 230-90, $19

Hotel Los Escudos, Portal Hidalgo 73, tel. 201-38, 212-90, fax 206-49, $33

Hotel Fiesta Plaza, Plaza Bocanegra 24, tel./fax 225-15 or 225-16, $38

Hotel Meson del Gallo, Dr. Coss 20, tel. (434) 214-74, fax 215-11, $40

Posada de la Basilica, Arciga 6, tel. 211-08, fax 206-59, $49

AV. LÁZARO CÁRDENAS

Motel del Lago, L. Cárdenas 509, tel. 214-71, $16

Hotel Villa Pátzcuaro, L. Cárdenas 506, tel. 207-67, fax 229-84, $16

Hotel San Carlos, Calle Caltzonzín s/n, tel. 413-59, $23

Hotel Don Vasco, L. Cárdenas 450, tel. 202-27 or 227-04, fax 202-62, (800) 528-1234 from the U.S. and Canada, $43

Motel San Felipe, L. Cárdenas 321, tel./fax 212-98, $44

---

inviting, lacks the light inner courtyard of the original. When making a reservation, specify "old section" *(sección viejo).*

Hotel Posada San Rafael, Portal Aldama 15, Plaza Vasco de Quiroga, Pátzcuaro, Michoacán 61600, tel. (434) 207-70, on the adjacent plaza-front block, offers an alternative. Greatly expanded during the 1980s from an original colonial mansion core, its 104 rooms spread along three stories of corridors facing a narrow inner parking courtyard. While the parked cars detract, the neocolonial decor—traditional tile, big-beamed ceilings, and hand-carved oak doors—lend a touch of charm. The paneled rooms, with throw rugs, wood floors, and fluffy curtains, if not deluxe, are at least clean and comfortable. Hot-water hours are limited to 7-11 a.m. and 6:30-11 p.m. Rates run about $16 s, $19 d for standard rooms, $19 s and $22 d for superior; no fireplaces, no credit cards accepted.

Once one of Pátzcuaro's beautiful best-buy lodgings, **Hotel Meson del Gallo,** Dr. Coss 20, Pátzcuaro, Michoacán 61600, tel. (434) 214-74, fax 215-11, has lately doubled its prices and been allowed to deteriorate. Located around the corner just a block south of the plaza Don Vasco, guests enjoy many tastefully appointed colonial-decor rooms with bath, and manicured green gardens on both sides of the building. Rooms vary, however, so look before you pay. Other amenities include a (dark) dining room and a sitting room right out of *Don Quixote* with a fireplace that might feel very cozy on a cool Pátzcuaro winter night. The pool, a potential asset, has been out of operation for years. It might be worth checking to see if they've fixed the place up. Asking prices for the 25 rooms and suites rent are about $31 s, $40 d, with parking, limited wheelchair access, and no TV; credit cards are accepted.

The plainer but better-managed, modern-style **Gran Hotel** on Plaza Bocanegra, at Portal Regules 6, Plaza Bocanegra, Pátzcuaro, Michoacán 61600, tel. (434) 204-43, fax 230-90, offers an excellent, economical alternative. Its 20 rooms, stacked in two stories, are clean, comfortable, and thoughtfully decorated in 1960s motel style. For minimum noise, get a room away from the busy street. Rates run about $19 s or d, and $29 t, with restaurant but no phones, parking, or TV.

The **Hotel Fiesta Plaza,** Plaza Bocanegra 24, Pátzcuaro, Michoacán 61600, tel./fax (434) 225-15 or 225-16, on the opposite, north side of Plaza Bocanegra, is a 1990 newcomer among Pátzcuaro hotels. The hotel's three tiers of comfortable rooms enfold a fountain-decorated inner patio. The restaurant, convenient for breakfast, spreads into the patio, while just outside the door the colorful Plaza Bocanegra hubbub—the market, the movie theater, a dozen taco stands, bus and minivan traffic—buzzes from morning to midnight. Guests who require relief should pick an upper-tier room away from the street. Rooms rent for about $31 s, $38 d, and $42 t, with TV, phones, parking, and credit cards accepted.

Hotel Valmen, Lloreda 34, Pátzcuaro, Michoacán 61600, tel. (434) 211-61, on the corner of Lloreda and Ahumada two blocks up the street, offers a budget alternative. Plants, light, and attractive tile soften the Valmen's otherwise spartan ambience. Two upper tiers of plain but tidy rooms, with hot showers, spread around the interior patio. Avoid the street noise by choosing an interior room. Rates run a very reasonable $6 s, $11 d, and $17 t.

Guests at the very popular **Posada de la Basílica,** Arciga 6, Pátzcuaro, Michoacán 61600, tel. (434) 211-08, fax 206-59, one block farther uphill, across from the basilica, enjoy a very attractive view restaurant. The panorama (also visible from the hotel's adjoining patio) of colonial city, lake, and mountains adds a bit of luxury to the hotel's authentically colonial atmosphere. The rooms, furnished in hand-carved, handwoven, and hand-wrought 17th-century chic, add even more. The 11 rooms (seven with fireplaces), all with hot water, run about $39 s, $49 d, and $57 t, with parking; credit cards are accepted. Reservations are generally necessary.

The **Hotel Posada de la Salud,** Av. Serrato 9, Pátzcuaro, Michoacán 61600, tel. (434) 200-58, on the basilica's south side, is especially popular with female basilica visitors. The 15 plain but very clean rooms spread around a sunny, conventlike courtyard. The typical guest, while not saintly, is at least probably in bed reading, by nine at the latest. Rooms rent for about $12 s, $17 d, and $21 t; reservations recommended, especially during religious holidays, such as the Fiesta de la Virgen de La Salud (first two weeks in December) and Semana Santa (week preceding Easter Sunday).

Avenida Lázaro Cárdenas Hotels

A number of acceptable motel-style accommodations cluster along Av. Lázaro Cárdenas, about half a mile from the Uruapan-Morelia Highway. Heading downhill from town, first comes the **Motel San Felipe,** on the left, at Av. L. Cárdenas 321, Pátzcuaro, Michoacán 61600, tel./fax (434) 212-98. Behind the roadside restaurant, 11 motel-style cottages surround a patio parking lot. Clean, comfortable, and carpeted, the units have colonial-style wrought-iron fixtures and brick fireplaces. Room rents have, within the last two years, increased sharply, to about $44 s or d, and $49 t, credit cards accepted. Limited wheelchair access.

A few blocks farther along spreads the 130-room resort-style Best Western **Hotel Don Vasco,** Av. Lázaro Cárdenas 450, Pátzcuaro, Michoacán 61600, tel. (434) 202-27 or 227-04, fax 202-62. Here, guests enjoy old-world decor, comfortable, high-beamed rooms, spreading lawns, quiet patio nooks, a chapel, a big pool, tennis, billiards, bowling, a bar, and a good restaurant with weekend and seasonal folkloric dance shows. Lodgings come in three grades. The colonial-style, high-ceilinged rooms in the older, original building go for about $49 s, $60 d. Large and luxurious modern-decor garden-view balcony rooms in a resort-style wing run about $70 s, and $80 d. Bargain third choice goes to rooms renting for about $37 s, $43 d, in an attractive new colonial-style annex across the boulevard. All lodgings come with TV, phones, central heat, seasonal discotheque, credit cards accepted, parking, and limited wheelchair access to lower floors. From the U.S. and Canada, reserve through the Best Western toll-free number, (800) 528-1234.

Budget travelers head a few blocks farther downhill to the **Motel del Lago,** at Av. L. Cárdenas 509, Pátzcuaro, Michoacán 61600, tel. (434) 214-71. The choice of families with wheels, the del Lago's 12 brick units surround a central parking area garden, bordered by leafy avocado, rubber, and peach trees. Although a bit worn, the clean (although not immaculate), rustic wood-and-tile cottages have fireplaces (wood $2 extra) and hot water. Rooms run a bargain-basement $11 s, $16 d, and $19 t; credit cards not accepted, limited wheelchair access.

Cross Av. Lázaro Cárdenas to **Hotel Villa Pátzcuaro,** Av. L. Cárdenas 506, Pátzcuaro, Michoacán 61600, tel. (434) 207-67, fax 229-84, a homey cluster of a dozen cottages, set half a block back from the road. Owned and operated by longtime lovers of Pátzcuaro, Obdulia and Arturo Pimentel Ramos, the units are attractively furnished in rustic browns, knotty-pine paneling, and brick fireplaces. The grassy grounds spread past a blue swimming pool (not maintained in winter) and a tennis court to an acre of tent and RV (self-contained only) sites on the adjacent gentle hillside. A kitchen is available for use of guests. The cottages rent for a refreshingly moderate $14 s, $16 d, and $24 t. Guests with a big RV pay about $5 per person per night. Tent and small RV guests pay about $4 per person per night. The cottages are often filled; best make reservations. Limited wheelchair access.

Finally, follow Av. Lázaro Cárdenas across the Morelia-Uruapan highway downhill, bear left after the railroad tracks, and continue to road's-end **Hotel San Carlos,** Colonia Morelos, Calle Caltzonzín s/n, Pátzcuaro, Michoacán 61600, tel. (434) 413-59. The 10 rooms are tucked along a long covered veranda adjoining an elegantly tranquil orchard/garden planted with avocado, peach, pear, and fragrant orange and lemon trees. Paths among the trees lead past a graceful, colonial-style restaurant, a big blue (beautiful but unheated) pool and kiddie pool, finally heading, via country lanes, a few blocks to the Janitzio boat dock and the reed-lined lakeshore. Back at the hotel, the simply but thoughtfully furnished beam-ceiling rooms rent for about $23 s or d, $32 t, subject to increases (to about $32 s or d, $43 t) during holidays such as Christmas, Easter, and Day of the Dead (2 November).

RV and Camping Park

Visitors who enjoy RV and tent camping near the lakeside opt for **Trailer Park El Pozo** ("The Well"). Watch for the sign on the highway about a mile in the Morelia direction past the Av. Lázaro Cárdenas intersection. The 20 RV spaces spread downhill in a grassy park about a quarter mile from the reed-lined lakeshore. The friendly, family-run park provides all hookups, a picnic table with each space, some shade, toilets, and hot showers for about $9 per day for two, $13 for three, $14 for four, with one day free per week for weekly and monthly stays. Tenters are also welcome, at about $4 per person. While reservations are generally not necessary, it's best to call or write ahead of time for weekends and holidays: Trailer Park El Pozo, P.O. Box 142, Pátzcuaro, Michoacán 61600, tel. (434) 209-37.

FOOD

Breakfast and Snacks

A good spot to start out your day is **Restaurant Rincón Alemán** ("German Corner") at Mendoza 30 (the street connecting the west sides of Plazas Don Vasco and Bocanegra). Although it serves good food daily 8 a.m.-10 p.m., the American breakfast ($3) in the shiny upstairs section tastes especially good on a crisp Pátzcuaro winter morning.

For quick cooling energy during the heat of the day, try the no-name *nevería* (ice-cream stand) in front of the Hotel Los Escudos on Plaza Vasco de Quiroga. The fruit ices are so popular you may have to wedge your way in. Just point to what you want. Eat without worry—its offerings are pure; the stand depends on repeat customers. Open daily 9 a.m.-6 p.m.

For a hot pick-me-up, go for a cup of freshly ground Michoacán mountain-grown coffee at **Cafeteria Bote Fumeira** ("Smoking Center") beneath Portal Aldama at the adjacent corner of the plaza. It also sells pastries, cookies, and fresh-roasted beans for around $4 per pound ($8 per kilo). Open daily 6 a.m.-10 p.m., if business warrants.

At night at the market corner of Plaza Bocanegra, a very professional lineup of taco stands steams with hearty offerings. Among the best is **Tacos Rápido,** run by Jorge, whose fingers fly as if they could wrap a thousand *chorizo* (spiced sausage), *res* (roast beef), *pastor* (roast lamb, pork or beef), and *lengua* (tongue) tacos a night.

For a late snack, lunch, or early dinner, go to **Hamburguesas Viejo Sam** at Mendoza 15, between Plazas Vasco de Quiroga and Bocanegra. Juicy hamburgers, hot dogs, *tortas,* French fries, and malts plus lots of friendly cheer are the secret to the success of the paradoxically young proprietor Viejo ("Old") Sam. Open daily 10 a.m.-11 p.m.

For tasty late-night Mexican-style fare, try the popular **Charandas'n Pizza Cafe,** open daily 6 p.m. to about midnight, on the north side of Plaza Don Vasco.

Restaurants

Pátzcuaro has a sprinkling of good, moderately priced restaurants, nearly all on or near the Plaza Vasco de Quiroga.

At the **Cafetería Los Escudos** in the Hotel Los Escudos, northwest plaza corner of Mendoza and Ibarra, tel. (434) 201-38, conversation and café espresso sometimes seem as important as the menu. A broad list of regional and international favorites (try the taco soup) keeps customers satisfied. Open daily 8 a.m.-9:30 p.m.; credit cards accepted. Moderate.

Whitefish is the house specialty at the **Restaurant El Patio,** at 19 Plaza Vasco de Quiroga, near the Hotel Posada San Rafael, tel. (434) 204-84, where soft music, muted lighting, and tasteful handicrafts decor set the tone. Despite the mostly tourist clientele, many are longtime repeat customers (who know to start out with the excellent Tarascan soup). Open daily 8 a.m.-9:30 p.m.; credit cards accepted. Moderate.

Romantics congregate at the restaurant of the **Hotel Posada de la Basilica** on Arciga, opposite the basilica, tel. (434) 211-08. They enjoy Pátzcuaro's famous whitefish and wine (ask for Cetto label sauvignon blanc) while feasting on the gleaming view of the old city, the lake, and the mountains beyond. Open daily for breakfast and lunch only, 8 a.m.-5 p.m.; credit cards not accepted. Moderate.

Perhaps the best restaurant on the Plaza Bocanegra is at the **Hotel Fiesta Plaza.** Hearty breakfasts and strong, fragrant espresso head an interestingly varied menu of appetizers, salads, and a number of house specialties such as Tarascan soup, *crema conde,* trout with white wine, and lake whitefish *al gusto.* Open daily 8 a.m.-10 p.m., credit cards accepted. Moderate.

ENTERTAINMENT AND EVENTS

Pátzcuaro's one must-see entertainment is the famous **Viejecitos** ("Little Old Men") dance. Said to have been invented during the early colonial period to mock the conquerors, a troupe of men put on wrinkle-faced masks and campesino-style dress and dance as if every stumbling step were about to send them to the hospital. Hotels, such as the Don Vasco (tel. 434-202-27), often stage regular dance shows in season.

Local people celebrate a number of fiestas and holidays. During the first two weeks in December, dance, music, processions, fireworks, and foodstalls fill Pátzcuaro streets and plazas in celebration of the **Fiesta de La Virgen de La Salud,** the city's patron saint.

Later, Semana Santa festivities climax on **Viernes Santa** (Good Friday), when townsfolk carry big Christ-figures through the packed downtown streets.

Finally, on 2 November, Pátzcuaro (and many neighboring towns) stages Mexico's most spectacular **Día de los Muertos** ("Day of the Dead") festivals. Crowds converge on the *panteón* (cemetery) on the old Morelia road with loads of food offerings and decorations for the graves of their beloved deceased. They keep the candles burning next to the tombstones all night, illuminating their ancestors' return path to feast with the family once again. To get there, walk or ride a taxi a half mile northeast of the basilica.

The big movie house and theater **Cine Emperador** screens Mexican and American movies Sunday and stages occasional concerts and cultural events. Drop by (north end of Plaza Bocanegra, next to the Hotel Fiesta Plaza) and check the schedule.

For after-hours nightlife a couple of café-bars, such as the Charandas'n Pizza and Cafe on the Plaza Don Vasco, offer live music until around midnight seasonally and on weekends.

SHOPPING

The Valley of Pátzcuaro is rich in handicrafts. Visitors need only travel to the **Mercado** (which extends a long block, beginning at the Plaza Bocanegra) to find good examples. Copperware from the village of Santa Clara de Cobre and locally crafted woolens are among the most plentiful and bargainable items.

In the fish stalls, you'll see mounds of pitifully small Pátzcuaro whitefish (at about $5 a pound!) and, farther on, among the piles of produce, unusual fruits from around Uruapan (such as the brown, puckery *mamey* and the greenish-pink *anona,* which is creamy like a Southeast Asian custard apple).

For a uniquely rich selection of fine handicrafts, don't miss the former convent, **Casa de Once Patios,** one block east and one block south of the Plaza Don Vasco de Quiroga. In a dozen separate shops, artisans paint, carve, weave, and polish excellent work for sale. In the *local de paja* (straw shop), for example, workers fashion Christmas decorations—candy canes, trees, wreaths, bells—entirely of strands of colored straw. Nearby, the *local de cobre* (copper shop) displays shelves and cases of brilliant copper and silver plates, vases, cups, and jewelry.

Although other *locales* craft and display fine furniture, textiles, papier-mâché, and masks, the climax comes in the *local de laca,* with lacquerware so fine it rivals the rich cloisonnés of Europe and Asia. In the especially fine shop of the brothers Alozo Meza, artisans finish wares in a myriad of animal, human, and floral motifs in sizes and complexities to fit every pocketbook. Open daily 9 a.m.-2 p.m. and 4-7 p.m.

On your way to or from the Casa de Once Patios, be sure to browse some of the several streetside **handicrafts shops** that have sprouted like mushrooms around the southeast corner of the Plaza Don Vasco.

On Friday, the small plaza, **Jardín Revolución,** blooms with ceramics from all over Michoacán (corner Ponce de Leon and Tena, one block west of the Plaza Don Vasco de Quiroga).

Grocery Stores and Camera Shop

Two old-fashioned grocery stores, **Abarrotes Rosy** and **La Surtidora,** offer very basic gro-

anona fruits (foreground) for sale at the Pátzcuaro market

cery items, including cheese, milk, and deli meats, on opposite ends of Portal Hidalgo, west side of Plaza Don Vasco. You'll find them open Mon.-Sat., about 9 a.m.-2 p.m. and 4-8 p.m. When you enter La Surtidora (near the Hotel Los Escudos), which advertises "since 1916" in its sign, you'll probably agree that it's scarcely changed since then.

The local Kodak dealer, **Foto 30,** is beneath Portal Regules, corner of Mendoza, tel. (434) 219-25, on the Plaza Bocanegra's south side. Besides a fair stock of film (including 120 black-and-white and color negative) and photo equipment, it offers 30-minute color develop and print, three-day transparency, and five-day black-and-white photofinishing services. Open Mon.-Sat. 9:30 a.m.-2 p.m. and 4-8 p.m., Sunday 9:30 a.m.-2 p.m.

SERVICES AND INFORMATION

The helpful **Michoacán Tourism Office,** at Plaza Vasco de Quiroga 50, north side, by the

Banco Serfin, tel./fax (434) 212-14, answers questions and offers a number of excellent brochures, some in English, of colorful out-of-the-way Michoacán towns and scenic points of interest. Hours are Mon.-Sat. 9 a.m.-3 p.m. and 4-7 p.m., Sunday 9 a.m.-3 p.m.

Banamex, on Plaza Bocanegra (Portal Juárez, west side), tel. (434) 215-50 or 210-31, is open Mon.-Fri. 9 a.m.-4 p.m. for changing U.S., Canadian, French, German, Spanish, and Japanese currency and traveler's checks. Alternatively, you have **Bancomer,** tel. (434) 203-34, with approximately the same moneychanging hours, half a block south, at 23 Mendoza, and **Banco Serfin,** around the corner, beneath the north portal on Plaza Don Vasco. A number of small Plaza Bocanegra *casas de cambio* change money after bank hours and Saturdays and Sundays.

For medical advice, go to the very professional **Consultorio Médicos del Centro,** tel. (434) 245-33, at Navarrete 44-A, corner of Nicolas Romero, two blocks south of the southwest corner of Plaza Don Vasco. You'll have the choice of five physicians: Dr. Marlon La Cayo, orthopedist; Dra. Luz María Tirado, gynecologist; Dr. Fidel Orozco, pediatrician; Dra. Norma Gómez, general surgeon; and Dr. Jorge Alberto Ochoa, internal medicine.

Pátzcuaro has many pharmacies; one of the most convenient and best stocked is the **Farmacia Moderna,** which, wryly, has an ancient snake-oil preventative advertisement on the wall outside and shelves filled with old-fashioned apothecary bottles inside. On the Campanito lane-corner, middle of the north side of Plaza Don Vasco, open daily 9 a.m.-3 p.m. and 4-9 p.m., tel. (434) 217-31.

For police emergencies, contact the *preventiva,* tel. (434) 200-04, in the Presidencia Municipal, next to the Clínica San Marcos.

The *correo* (post office), tel. (434) 201-28, is open Mon.-Fri. 8 a.m.-4 p.m., Saturday 9 a.m.-1 p.m., at Obregón 13, one block north of the Plaza Bocanegra.

For computer-assisted *larga distancia* and public fax, go to **Computel,** fax (434) 227-56, on the Plaza Bocanegra next to the Cine Emperador movie house. Alternatively, go to the government *telecomunicaciones,* fax (434) 200-10, open Mon.-Fri. 8 a.m.-6 p.m. and Saturday and Sunday 9 a.m.-1 p.m. at Calle Titere 15, a block north of the Plaza Bocanegra northeast (library) corner.

Among the very few sources of English-language news is the newsstand on the Plaza Bocanegra (at Portal Juárez 30, a few doors north of Banamex), which, around midday, gets the *News* from Mexico City and sometimes stocks *Time* magazine.

GETTING THERE AND AWAY

By Car or RV

North-south National Highways 14 and 37 connect Pátzcuaro with the Pacific coast Hwy. 200 at Playa Azul. The 192-mile (307-km) scenic but winding and sometimes potholed route requires around seven hours of careful driving. Fill with gasoline, especially unleaded. Magna Sin is available only at Uruapan, Nueva Italia, and Arteaga en route.

In the opposite direction, mostly four-lane National Hwy. 120 will connect you with the state capital Morelia (in an hour); from there the winding but very scenic two-lane Hwy. 15 will lead you to Mexico City in about eight hours, or the toll expressway *(autopista cuota)* will do the same in about five hours.

To and from Lake Chapala and Guadalajara, the scenic route is the relatively level, aging Hwy. 15 Lake Chapala south-shore route. Head north 17 miles (27 km) to the Hwy. 15 junction at Quiroga. Turn left (west) onto Hwy. 15, continuing through Zacapu, Sahuayo, the Chapala shore, and Acatlán, to Guadalajara, a total of 210 miles (338 km). Congestion around the several towns en route slows progress. Allow about six hours driving time, either direction. You can cut the Pátzcuaro-Guadalajara driving time to about four hours by picking up the *cuota* (toll) *autopista* near Villa Jiménez, about 10 miles north of Hwy. 15 from Zacapu.

By Bus

The spacious, modern *central camionera,* on the *libramiento* (peripheral boulevard) south of town offers a number of services, including a snack bar, luggage lockers (open 7 a.m.-9 p.m.) and Computel public long-distance telephone and fax (open daily 6 a.m.-9 p.m.).

Several first- and second-class bus lines connect frequently with a host of regional and national destinations. Longest-distance (but infrequent) daily service is provided by **Elite** (EL) and **Transportes del Norte,** tel. (434) 214-60, which offer first-class connections northwest via Guadalajara, continuing north either by the Pacific route to the U.S. border at Mexicali and Tijuana, or by the central route to Monterrey and the U.S. border at Nuevo Laredo or Matamoros.

Several **Autobuses del Occidente** (ADO) buses, tel. (434) 212-243, with first- and second-class departures, connect southwest with Lake Zirahuén and Uruapan, east with Morelia and Mexico City, and locally with Lake Pátzcuaro towns Jarácuaro and Erongarícuaro.

Frequent **Galeana** first- and second-class departures, tel. (434) 208-08, connect with regional destinations: north with Tzintzuntzán and Morelia; south with Uruapan, Apatzingan, Nueva Italia, Playa Azul (La Mira) and Lázaro Cárdenas on the Pacific coast.

Parhikuni first-class and luxury-class departures, tel. (434) 210-60, also connect north, with Quiroga and Morelia.

Flecha Amarilla (FA) first-class and "Primeraplus" luxury-class departures, tel. (434) 209-60, offer broad service east via Morelia to Mexico City; north with Irapuato, León, Querétaro, and San Luis Potosí; west, via the *autopista,* with Guadalajara; and south, with Uruapan, La Mira (Playa Azul) and Lázaro Cárdenas.

By Train

Although Pátzcuaro lies on the rail line connecting Lázaro Cárdenas on the Pacific coast to Morelia, privatization has erased train passenger service from the Pátzcuaro travel menu.

URUAPAN

En route to or from Lake Pátzcuaro, Uruapan (pop. 200,000), Michoacán's second city, is well worth a day or two, if only to bask for a while in its springlike weather and enjoy a stroll through its luxuriantly lovely spring-fed river park.

Uruapan's mile-high (1,610-meter) elevation places it squarely on the delightfully balmy border between the warm tropics and the cool highlands, where a bounty of fruit—citrus, *mamey, chirimoya,* and a million acres of avocados—have earned Uruapan the semi-official title of "avocado capital of the world."

HISTORY

Some of the most important clues to Uruapan's pre-Columbian past have been unearthed beneath the pyramids and platforms in the **Tinganio archaeological zone,** at Tingambato, about 16 miles (26 km) from Uruapan (see above). Here, between A.D. 450 and 950, a highly cultured people built a ceremonial center, with plazas, a ball court, and tombs reminiscent of classic Teotihuacán style. Where those builders originated and why they abandoned their city remains a mystery. Their pyramids were rubble by the time the Tarascans arrived, around A.D. 1200.

The great Tarascan kings Tariácuri, Hiripan, and Tangaxoan, who ruled from the shore of Lake Pátzcuaro, controlled a vast western empire, which included Uruapan (oo-roo-AH-pahn). The name itself comes from the Tarascan (more correctly, Purépecha) language, translating as "Place of Fruit and Flowers."

Although the Purépecha emperors ruled, collecting tribute from the Uruapan tribes, only a small minority of Purépecha-speaking people actually lived in Uruapan; most inhabitants belonged to other indigenous groups—Otomi, Nahua, Chontal, Chichimec, and more—scattered through the mountains and valleys of the Uruapan basin.

In 1522, when conquistador Cristóbal de Olid and his battalion arrived at Lake Pátzcuaro, the last Purépecha emperor, Tangaxoan II, fled to Uruapan. There, after a short resistance, Tangaxoan II was captured and taken to Mexico City, where he pledged fealty to Hernán Cortés. Unfortunately, Cortés had to return to Spain; while he was gone, renegade conquistador Nuño de Guzmán's gold-crazed outlaw army rampaged over all Michoacán—killing, raping, burning—and sending the villagers fleeing into the mountains.

Ruin and desolation confronted Franciscan Father Juan de San Miguel when he arrived in

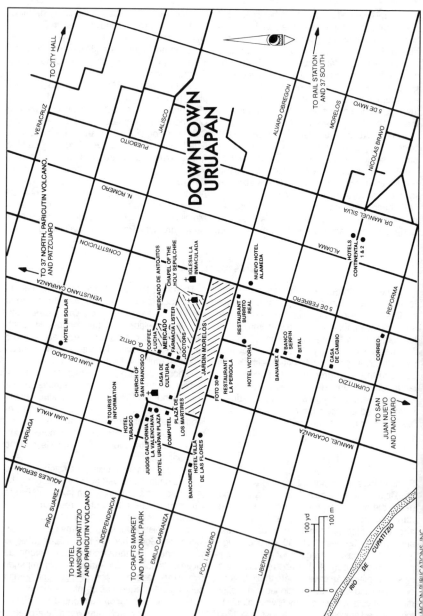

DOWNTOWN URUAPAN

TO CITY HALL

TO RAIL STATION AND 37 SOUTH

TO 37 NORTH, PARICUTIN VOLCANO, AND PÁTZCUARO

VERACRUZ

PUEBOITO

JALISCO

ALVARO OBREGON

MORELOS

5 DE MAYO

NICOLAS BRAVO

N. ROMERO

CONSTITUCION

VENUSTIANO CARRANZA

DR. MANUEL SILVA

MERCADO DE ANTOJITOS
CHAPEL OF THE HOLY SEPULCHRE
IGLESIA LA INMACULADA

ALDAMA

HOTELS CONTINENTAL 1 & 2

NUEVO HOTEL ALAMEDA

5 DE FEBRERO

REFORMA

HOTEL MI SOLAR

COFFEE
LUCHA
MERCADO
FARMACIA LISTER
DOCTORS

RESTAURANT BURRITO REAL

BANCO SERFIN
BITAL

CASA DE CAMBIO

CORREO

Q. ORTIZ

JUAN DELGADO

JARDIN MORELOS

BANAMEX

CUPATITZIO

CHURCH OF SAN FRANCISCO

CASA DE CULTURA

FOTO 30
RESTAURANT LA PERGOLA

HOTEL VICTORIA

TOURIST INFORMATION

JUAN AYALA

HOTEL TARASCO

PLAZA DE LOS MARTIRES

MANUEL OCARANZA

TO SAN JUAN NUEVO AND TANCITARO

I. ARRIAGA

JUGOS CALIFORNIA
LA VALENCIANA
HOTEL URUAPAN PLAZA
COMPUTEL

AQUILES SERDAN

PIÑO SUAREZ

BANCOMER
HOTEL VILLA DE LAS FLORES

INDEPENDENCIA

EMILIO CARRANZA

FCO. I. MADERO

LIBERTAD

TO HOTEL MANSION CUPATITZIO AND PARICUTIN VOLCANO

TO CRAFTS MARKET AND NATIONAL PARK

100 yd
100 m

0

RIO DE CUPATITZIO

© MOON PUBLICATIONS, INC.

Uruapan in early 1532. His first task was to coax those remaining of the original inhabitants to rebuild their homes and return to their fields. Proceeding with care and compassion, much as Father Vasco de Quiroga did in Pátzcuaro, Father Juan gained the confidence of the Uruapan people. He founded the town in December of 1533, organizing it in eight *barrios,* each with its patron saint, church, school, and cemetery. In the center of town, Father Juan laid out the present town plaza, where, in 1533, he began building the Church of San Francisco, the Chapel of the Holy Sepulchre, and the "Huatapera" community hospital, all of which still stand on the plaza.

During succeeding generations, events of historical note occasionally occurred in sleepy Uruapan. During the mid-18th century, local citizens rebelled, refusing to billet Spanish troops without compensation. In retaliation, the Spanish flogged an indigenous chief, igniting a revolt. The local people overran the garrison and were about to massacre the soldiers when a priest interceded; the locals won the day, however, by throwing the soldiers into the river.

During the 1810-21 War of Independence, Uruapan was the seat of the Congress of Anahuac, the insurgent shadow government led by José María Morelos, the father of Mexican independence.

Uruapan briefly served as the Michoacán state capital three times: during the Mexican-American war in 1847, the War of the Reform in 1859, and the French imperialist War of the Intervention in 1863. During the latter, the French army surprised and defeated Mexican troops in a battle at nearby Santa Ana Amatlán. The leading five Mexican officers, including General José Arteaga, were brought to Uruapan and executed on 21 October 1865. They became known as the "Martyrs of Uruapan." A small square and monument in their honor stands in front of the Church of San Francisco on the town plaza.

On 20 February 1943, Mother Nature put Uruapan permanently on the world map by pushing a volcano up through a cornfield near Angahuan town, about 20 miles northwest of Uruapan. The volcano, which the local Purépecha folks call "Parhikútini" ("Paricutín" in Spanish), sent villagers fleeing in fear, buried their church with lava, and blanketed their fields with ash. The fiery mountain roared, smoked, and hissed for years, building up a 1,350-foot (410-meter) cone before going dormant in 1952. Since then, the government has established a national park, which draws thousands of yearly visitors, who hike the cinder-strewn fields, peer inside the lava-choked church, and climb to the top of the Paricutín's gray cone of ash.

SIGHTS

Getting Oriented

Uruapan, walled by mountains on its north and west sides, spreads southeast, down the valley of the **Río Cupatitzio** (koo-pah-TEET-zeeoh). Traveling to or from Pátzcuaro on Highway 37, you can easily miss Uruapan completely by continuing north or south along the highway's main truck route, which skirts Uruapan's eastern suburb. That would be a pity, for a stroll around the shady downtown plaza can provide relaxed glimpses of the charms of old Mexico. The very center of town is at the "T," where north-south Av. Cupatitzio ends at the town plaza, officially **Jardín Morelos.** At the corner of Av. Cupatitzio, face north, toward the *jardín.* The main east-west boulevard, which changes names at Av. Cupatitzio, is called Av. Emilio Carranza on your left and Av. Alvaro Obregón on your right. If you follow Av. Obregón, you'll be heading east, where after about half a mile, you'll reach a traffic circle and the rail station, a block to the south. On the other hand, if you walk west along Carranza in the opposite direction, after about seven blocks you'll arrive at the luxuriantly leafy gorge of the Río Cupatitzio, preserved for public enjoyment as Uruapan's renowned national park.

A Walk around the Plaza

Back at the center of town, at the Av. Cupatitzio corner, look north, directly across the *jardín,* and you'll see a pair of big, old renaissance-style churches on the *jardín's* far side. The right-hand one is the 18th-century **Iglesia La Inmaculada** ("Church of the Immaculate Conception"); on the left stands the **Parroquia de San Francisco** ("Parish Church of San Francisco"), founded by Father Juan de San Miguel in 1533. Step across to the north side of the *jardín,* where, in front of the San Francisco church, a gothic arch leads to a small square, the **Plaza de los Mártires de**

Uruapan. Inside the church, in the *sacristía* (sacristy), you can view a renaissance painting of founder Father Juan de San Miguel.

Next, head east toward La Inmaculada church, along the lane that borders the *jardín*'s north side. Before the first corner, on your left, you pass the **Casa de Cultura,** a modest government-supported museum and performing arts center, open Mon.-Fri. 10 a.m.-2 p.m. and 5-8 p.m. Three exhibit halls display artifacts including an 1899 gold and silver bell, paintings of President Benito Juárez and Father Miguel Hidalgo, pre-Columbian pottery, sculptures, jewelry, stone hatchets and jade masks, and 1910-era revolutionary memorabilia. One of the rooms houses a minimuseum of Michoacán's favorite son, historian Eduardo Ruiz: photos, personal effects, autographed books, and military mementos. The Casa de Cultura, moreover, sponsors occasional films, lectures, art exhibits, and performances; look for posters announcing programs, or stop at the desk for information before you leave.

Outside, continue east across the adjacent lane another 50 yards, where, on the left, a walkway, the Paseo Vasco de Quiroga, leads into an arcade. Along the walkway dozens of stalls offer a multitude of handicrafts—lacquerware, guitars, woolens, sombreros, serapes, copperware, and chocolate stirrers *(molinillos).* Deeper inside, lanes diverge into the main **town market,** a block-square warren of shops displaying a galaxy of everyday items.

Back outside, continue east to the courtyard, just before La Inmaculada church. Here a venerable chapel, La Capilla del Santo Sepulcro ("Chapel of the Holy Sepulchre"), adjoins the picturesque Huatápera former community hospital, founded by Father Juan de San Miguel in 1533. Inside (open Tues.-Sun. 9 a.m.-1:30 p.m. and 3:30-6 p.m.), three spacious rooms gleam with museum-quality Michoacán ceramics, lacquerware, copperware, masks, and textiles.

National Park

For a memorable finale, stroll through Uruapan's lovely **Parque Nacional Lic. Eduardo Ruiz.** Head west to the end of E. Carranza, about seven blocks from the *jardín*, to Av. Fray Juan de San Miguel. At the corner, walk right, uphill, another two blocks to the big curbside crafts market. Across the street, behind the fence, is the leafy ravine of the Río Cupatitzio, a botanist's paradise of bright flowers, twisting vines, and grand spreading trees. Lush trails lead you across bridges and past waterfalls, picnic grounds, and small restaurants nestled beneath the leafy canopy. Along the way, be sure not to miss the **Rodilla del Diablo** ("Devil's Knee") spring, at the top end near the Hotel Mansión Cupatitzio; the **Cascada de Golgota** waterfall, a hundred yards farther downstream; and the **Fuente de Janintzizic** fountain, on the left bank, about a quarter mile farther downstream.

The park has two entrances: the main lower entrance, across Av. Fray Juan de San Miguel from the crafts market, and the upper entrance, at the far end of the parking lot by the **Hotel Mansión Cupatitzio,** about five blocks farther up Av. Fray Juan de San Miguel. Either entrance has its advantages. From the crafts market entrance, you walk gradually uphill, ending at the river's crystal-blue source, the Rodilla del Diablo spring. From there you could continue to the adjacent graceful Hotel Mansion Cupatitzio patio restaurant for a relaxing drink or lunch. From the upper entrance, you could start with lunch at the Hotel de Cupatitzio and begin your downhill stroll at the Rodilla del Diablo spring. In either case, bring along your bathing suit for a swim in the hotel's big blue pool, and/or in the crystal-clear river.

ACCOMMODATIONS AND FOOD

Hotels

Uruapan visitors have their choice of several good budget-moderate hotels, mostly around the central *jardín.* The major exception, in the west suburb, about half a mile from the *jardín*, is the queen of Uruapan lodgings, the **Hotel Mansión Cupatitzio,** adjacent to the lush canyon of the clear, gushing Río Cupatitzio. The hotel's hacienda-style wings enfold a tranquil, flowery pool patio. Tucked on one side, the shady poolside tables of the excellent restaurant lead to an elegant inside dining room. In the hotel, guests enjoy light, spacious rooms, many with patio views, equipped with modern-standard tub baths and furnished with original wall art, hand-painted furniture, fresh flowers, and mints on their pillows. All this for only about $39 s, $52 d, with a/c, cable TV, and telephones. Stay if you possibly can manage it. Be sure to reserve, by writing P.O. Box 63, Uruapan, Michoacán 60000, or calling (452) 321-00, fax 467-72.

Visitors who prefer the livelier downtown atmosphere have many good choices. By location, near the *jardín,* moving from the northwest to the southeast, first comes the budget old-Mexico *posada*-like **Hotel Mi Solar,** two blocks north of the *jardín,* at Juan Delgado 10, Uruapan, Michoacán 60000, tel. (452) 409-12. The hotel's dozen plain but clean rooms encircle a tranquil, homey interior garden patio. Guests also enjoy another, more secluded patio for sitting and sunning in the rear. Prices are certainly right, at about $7 s, $9 d, $11 t.

At the *jardín*'s northwest corner stands the shiny '60s-modern **Hotel Tarasco,** best-buy lodging of local business travelers, at Independencia 2, Uruapan, Michoacán 60000, tel./fax (452) 415-00. Downstairs, guests enjoy an airy lobby, light, lively restaurant, and inviting outside pool patio. Elevators lead upstairs to approximately six stories of clean, modern-standard rooms, comfortably furnished with dark red carpets and bedspreads. Rooms rent for about $25 s, $32 d, with cable TV, a/c, parking, and phones.

Half a block south, on the west side of the *jardín,* is the similar (but without a pool) high-rise **Hotel Plaza Uruapan,** at M. Ocampo 64, Uruapan, Michoacán, 60000, tel. (452) 335-99 or 337-00, fax 339-80. The downstairs reception adjoins an atrium opening to a double level shopping mall that includes a travel agent at lobby level, and a coffee shop and restaurant at the lower level. Upstairs, the 103 rooms are modern, clean, and tastefully decorated with beige carpets, drapes, and bedspreads. Rentals run about $30 s, $36 d, with a/c, TV, phones, bar, disco, live music, and gym.

Villa de las Flores, around the corner and half a block west, at E. Carranza 15, Uruapan, Michoacán, tel. (452) 428-00, offers old-world atmosphere with an unpretentious touch of class. Most rooms surround a spacious, plant-decorated, portal-shaded front patio. Continuing inside, you pass the restaurant, picturesquely tucked to one side. Beyond that is an intimate, bougainvillea-adorned rear patio, enfolded by six or eight rooms in two stories. If you're going to stay, reserve one of these (rooms 23-29). In-side, they're clean and thoughtfully furnished in natural wood and tile. Rates are right, at about $14 s, $18 d, $20 t, with bath, phones, and TV. Private parking is available nearby for about $2 per day. Credit cards are accepted.

For more choices, head east along Carranza; at mid-*jardín,* turn right at Cupatitzio. At midblock on the left rises the modern **Hotel Victoria,** at Cupatitzio 11, Uruapan, Michoacán 60000, tel. (452) 366-11 or 367-00, fax 396-62. Downstairs, guests enjoy a good restaurants and upstairs, very clean modern rooms with bath, tastefully decorated in blues and grays. Rates run about $26 s, $32 d, $37 t, with TV, phones, and parking.

Around the block, spartan business-class high-rise **Nuevo Hotel Alameda,** at 11 Cinco de Febrero, Uruapan, Michoacán 60000, tel. (452) 341-00, fax 336-45, offers 50 rooms at modest rates. Here, what you see is what you get: a clean, smallish, modern, beige-carpeted and draped room, a bargain for about $13 s, $17 d, $21 t, with a/c, TV, telephone, parking, but no restaurant.

Two blocks south, and two blocks east of the southeast *jardín* corner, **Hotels Continental I and II,** at N. Bravo 33 and 34, Uruapan, Michoacán, 60000, tel. (452) 350-28, 373-62, or 397-93, fax 460-55, offer still more moderately priced options. Cheapest is Hotel II, where creative management has upgraded a very plain hotel into something with a bit of charm. Rooms with baths, in a pair of parallel, interior, motel-style two-story tiers, are clean and simply but thoughtfully decorated. Rates, a bit high, run $22 s or d, $25 t. Parking is available, and there's a restaurant in Hotel Continental I, across the street.

Across the street, brother Hotel Continental I offers about the same, except that it's larger, fancier, and the rooms are quite attractively furnished. (If you're a floor person, however, you might be put off by the poorly chosen floor tile in both hotels' rooms, which seemed to need waxing and thus appeared dirty, even though it wasn't.) Rooms at Hotel Continental I cost about $24 s, $32 d, $37 t, with bath, parking, and restaurant in the lobby.

Snacks and Restaurants

Plenty of tasty snacks are available around the *jardín.* The aroma of roasted coffee beans will probably draw you to the coffeehouse **Lucha,** at Garcia Ortíz 20, on the north side of the *jardín,* tel. (452) 403-75, sandwiched between the market and Parroquia de San Francisco. Here, refined atmosphere, quiet conversation, excellent coffee, and good pastries draw customers daily, 9 a.m.-2 p.m. and 4-9 p.m.

Nearby, wholesome homestyle food is the main event at the big **Mercado de Antojitos,** at the interior end of handicrafts lane Paseo de Vasco de Quiroga, in the market, north side of *jardín.*

Late night, you can usually always get a hot dog, hamburger, French fries, or some tacos at stalls and carts around the *jardín,* especially on the south side, corner of Cupatitzio.

A number of restaurants around the *jardín* offer good dining prospects. Among the hotels listed above, customers at both the **Hotel Victoria** (on Cupatitzio south of the *jardín*) and **Hotel Villa de las Flores** (on Carranza, just west of the *jardín*) enjoy good food in refined, relaxing atmospheres.

Perhaps the most successful downtown restaurant is **Restaurant La Pérgola,** south side of the *jardín,* west of Cupatitzio, next to Hotel Concordia, tel. (452) 350-87. Polished dark wood decor, genteel ambience (ask them to turn down the TV), and a good, professionally served menu draw a steady stream of business and professional-class customers. Open daily 8 a.m.-11:30 p.m.

A contrasting but equally worthy spot for good eating, especially for breakfast, is **Restaurant Burrito Real,** facing the *jardín,* a block east of Cupatitzio. Here, in a light, coffee-shop atmosphere, cooks put out a mixed menu of both Mexican and American breakfasts and a little bit of everything else, including hamburgers, milk shakes, juices, and a host of tacos, burritos, *flautas,* enchiladas, and *chiles rellenos.* Open daily 8 a.m.-11 p.m., tel. (452) 468-02.

About the same juice, breakfast, sandwich, and Mexican snack menu is served in the clean *lonchería* atmosphere of **Jugos California,** across the street from Hotel Tarasco, northwest corner of the *jardín,* open daily 7 a.m.-10 p.m.

For a treat, go to one of Uruapan's finest, the **Hotel Mansión Cupatitzio** restaurant, tel. (452) 321-00. Breakfast outside in the shady patio by the pool, and dinner inside, in the elegant, dignified dining room, are equally excellent. On Av. Fray Juan de San Miguel, seven blocks west and five blocks north of the *jardín;* open daily 8 a.m.-10 p.m.

ENTERTAINMENT, EVENTS, AND SHOPPING

In addition to national (especially the 15-16 September Independence and the 12 December Virgin of Guadalupe) fiestas, Uruapan folks celebrate with an abundance of local festivals. Before Easter, around the Sunday of Ramos, usually in late March, campesinos flood into town in their traditional dress. Originally celebrated by artisans of palm-leaf handicrafts, the festival now attracts hundreds of vendors whose stalls mushroom around the *jardín,* filled with an all-Michoacán galaxy of pottery, musical instruments, woolens, baskets, and copperware.

Later, the **Fiesta de Santa María Magdalena** kicks off on 22 July, continuing for eight days of colorful processions of decorated, yoked mules and oxen and climaxing in favorite dances, including Los Viejitos, Cristianos y Moros, and Los Negros. The fiesta centers around the Magdalena church, at the corner of Acapulco and González Ortega, about a mile southeast of the *jardín.*

Other locally important festivals include the 25 July **Día de Santiago Apostíl** ("Day of St. James the Apostle"), with fireworks, carnival, and dances, at Capilla (Chapel) Santiago (end of E. Carranza, about seven blocks west of the *jardín.*

On 4 October, all the townsfolk celebrate the day of **San Francisco,** Uruapan's patron saint, with handicrafts, regional food, and favorite dances, around the Parroquia de San Francisco, on the *jardín.* For three days, 24-26 October, a swarm of local people enjoy the **Fiesta de Coros y Danzas** ("Chorus and Dance"). Performances, limited to folks of native Purépecha blood only, are highlighted by the all-female Danza de las Canacuas.

In addition to Uruapan's yearly fiestas, the government-funded **Casa de Cultura** sponsors cultural events and performances. Stop by Mon.-Fri. 10 a.m.-2 p.m. and 5-8 p.m. (north side of *jardín,* next to Parroquia de San Francisco) for information.

Handicrafts Shopping

Uruapan draws craftspeople from all over Michoacán. Goods made from wood—lacquerware, masks, guitars and other musical instruments, and furniture—are among the most widely available. Also, in addition to lots of wool jackets and sweaters, you'll find woven goods—hats, baskets, mats, and raffia decorations and utensils—and much shiny copperware.

The best place to start shopping is at Uruapan's two main **crafts markets,** one on the Paseo Vasco de Quiroga, in the arcade, north side of the *jardín,* and the other, seven blocks west, on Av. Fray Juan de San Miguel, adjacent to the Río Cupatitzio National Park.

If you can't find everything you want in the markets, continue to the stores around the *jardín,* such as **Artesanías La Valenciana,** which offers plenty of Paracho-made guitars, embroidery, baskets, and lacquerware. Find it on the west side of the *jardín,* a few doors south of the Hotel Plaza Uruapan, open Mon.-Sat. 10 a.m.-2 p.m. and 4-9 p.m., Sunday 10 a.m.-2 p.m.

For an especially fine all-Mexico crafts collection, be sure to visit the shop at the **Hotel Mansión Cupatitzio** before or after you stroll the Río Cupatitzio park.

SERVICES AND INFORMATION

Moneychanging

You can change money at a number of banks near the *jardín,* such as **Banamex,** tel. (452) 349-66, 392-90, or 410-23, at the corner of Cupatitzio, one block south of the *jardín;* or the **Banco Serfin** and **Banco International** (which has very long Mon.-Sat. 8 a.m.-7 p.m. hours), a few steps downhill from Banamex. Additionally, you can go to **Bancomer,** near the southwest *jardín* corner, at 7 E. Carranza, corner 20 de Noviembre, tel. (452) 365-22 or 414-60. On Sunday, try one of the small *casas de cambio* (moneychangers) scattered around the *jardín.*

Travel Agents

For tickets, tours, and information, go to one of the travel agents near the *jardín,* such as **Viajes Titzi,** tel. (452) 334-19 or 334-52, in the Hotel Plaza Uruapan, or **Viajes Cupatitzio,** tel. (452) 411-85, 352-55, or 356-33, fax 416-36, in the

Hotel Tarasco, both on the west side of the *jardín.*

A pair of stores sell photo equipment and develop film on the south side of the *jardín.* Try **Photo 30,** tel. (452) 363-22, open Mon.-Sat. 9 a.m.-2 p.m. and 4-8:30 p.m., Sunday 9 a.m.-2 p.m., on Carranza, a few doors west of the Restaurant Pergola, or **Valencia Foto Express,** on Carranza, at the southwest corner of the *jardín.*

Information

The local state of Michoacán **tourist information office** hands out maps and brochures and answers questions at its downtown office, on Juan Ayala, behind the Hotel Tarasco, adjacent to the hotel parking lot. Hours are Mon.-Sat. 9 a.m.-2 p.m. and 4-7 p.m., Sunday 9 a.m.-2 p.m., tel. (434) 471-99.

English-language reading matter is not easy to find in Uruapan. Nevertheless, the hotel shop at Hotel Plaza Uruapan customarily stocks a few popular American magazines, paperback novels, and a newspaper or two. The newsstand, on the adjacent northwest *jardín* corner, beneath Portal Aldama, across from the Hotel Tarasco, sells the daily English-language *News* from Mexico City, after it arrives around 2 p.m.

Communications

Find the local *correo* (post office), three blocks south of the *jardín,* on Reforma, at the corner of 5 de Febrero. Efficient long-distance telephone and fax is available at the **Computel** office, open daily 6 a.m.-10 p.m., tel. (452) 434-82, at the west side of the *jardín* in front of Hotel Plaza Uruapan.

Emergencies

For police, call the municipal *preventiva,* tel. (452) 406-20 or 327-33; for the firefighters *(bomberos),* call (452) 406-16.

Doctors, Pharmacy, and Hospitals

If you get sick, a pair of good doctors, internist Dr. G. Fernando Hernádez Zarco and pediatrician Dr. Julio Torres Farías, maintain an office, tel. (452) 308-00, at 10 Garcia Ortiz, on the lane just north of the *jardín,* across Ortiz from the Casa de Cultura. A few doors away, at Garcia Ortiz 18, the **Farmacia Lister,** tel. (452) 408-58, offers routine advice and medicines.

Other doctors practicing nearby include general practitioner Dra. Elizabeth Amezcua E., family medicine Dra. Gloria Cornelio, and gynecologist Dr. Rene Zalapo Rios, who maintain joint offices at Juan Delgado 5, behind the San Francisco church, two blocks north of the *jardín*.

If you need hospitalization and/or expert diagnostic services, go to 24-hour emergency **Hospital El Ángel,** tel. (452) 480-30, at the corner of Juan N. López and Hilanderos, about seven blocks east, eight blocks south of the *jardín*. Alternatively, go to the government **Centro de Salud,** tel. (452) 401-56, at 3 M.P. Coronado, in the same southeast neighborhood.

GETTING THERE AND AWAY

By Car or RV

North-south National Highway 37 connects Uruapan with the Pacific coast Hwy. 200 at La Mira (Playa Azul). The 157-mile (253-km) scenic but winding and sometimes potholed route requires around five hours of careful driving. Fill your car with gasoline, especially unleaded; Magna Sin is available only at Nueva Italia and Arteaga en route.

In the opposite direction, the spectacular but curving and sometimes steep 39-mile (62-km) Highway 14 will lead you to Pátzcuaro uphill in about an hour and a half; allow one hour in the opposite direction, downhill.

The scenic route west to Lake Chapala and Guadalajara is the old two-lane, winding but relatively level Lake Chapala south-shore Highway 15. Head north, 48 miles (77 km), via Paracho, to the Hwy. 15 junction at Carapan. Turn left (west) onto Hwy. 15, continuing past Zamora, Sahuayo, along the Chapala shore to Acatlán, then Guadalajara, a total of 232 miles (373 km). Congestion around the towns en route slows progress. Allow about six hours driving time, either direction. You can cut the Uruapan-Guadalajara driving time to about four hours by following Hwy. 37 north, past its Hwy. 15 junction about 20 miles (32 km) to the Churintzio entrance to the toll *autopista* to Guadalajara.

A paved, fairly rapid, and very scenic mountain highway route connects Uruapan southwest with Colima and Manzanillo on the Pacific coast. Head north along Hwy. 37, 48 miles (77 km) to the Hwy. 15 junction. Turn left (west), continuing on Hwy. 15, 22 miles (36 km) to Zamora, then another 38 miles (61 km) to the Hwy. 110 junction at Jiquilpan. Follow Hwy. 110, via Mazamitla, another 116 miles (187 km) to Colima. Allow about six hours for the entire 224-mile (361-km) Uruapan-Colima trip, either way. Add another hour for the extra 54 miles (88 km) via the Hwy. 54 toll expressway to or from Manzanillo.

By Bus

A host of well-equipped long-distance buses connect directly with many western Mexico destinations from the big, modern *camionera central,* on the northeast side Hwy. 37 ingress boulevard. Besides the buses, the station has Computel long-distance telephone and fax (452-345-71) service, left luggage lockers, a snack bar and mini-super for drinks, and canned and packaged foods.

First-class **Elite** and associated first-class **Transportes del Norte,** tel. (452) 344-50 and 344-67, provide service north, either by the Pacific route via Mazatlán to the U.S. border at Mexicali and Tijuana, or by the northeast route to Monterrey and the U.S. border at Nuevo Laredo and Matamoros.

Frequent **Galeana** and **Ruta Paraíso** first- and second-class departures, tel. (452) 303-00 or 441-54, connect with many local and regional destinations: north with Pátzcuaro and Morelia; south with Apatzingan, Nueva Italia, La Mira (Playa Azul), and Lázaro Cárdenas; and southwest with Colima and Manzanillo.

Parhikuni first-class and luxury-class departures, tel. (452) 387-54, also connect north with Morelia and south with Nueva Italia, Playa Azul (La Mira), and Lázaro Cárdenas on the Pacific coast.

Flecha Amarilla first-class and "Primera-plus" luxury-class departures, tel. (452) 439-82, offer broad service east via Morelia to Mexico City; north with Irapuato, León, and San Luis Potosí; and northwest with Guadalajara.

Many **Autobuses del Occidente** first- and second-class departures, tel. (452) 318-71, connect east with Mexico City via Morelia; south with La Mira (Playa Azul) and Lázaro Cárdenas; southwest with Colima and Manzanillo; west with Guadalajara via Jiquilipan along the slow but scenic Hwy. 15 route; and east, via Morelia and Toluca, with Mexico City.

By Train
As with other Mexican railways, privatization has eliminated all passenger service on the rail line

connecting Lázaro Cárdenas on the Pacific coast with Uruapan, Pátzcuaro, Morelia, and Mexico City. As in the U.S. and Canada many years ago, improved highways, cars, airlines, and fast, economical bus service are converting passenger train service all over Mexico to vanishing memory.

WEST OF URUAPAN

Paricutín volcano's spectacular 1943 birth, the world's first volcanic eruption witnessed at its very origin, added to the attraction of its dormant big brother Tancítaro (elev. 12,670 feet, 3,860 meters). The government established a National Park (Parque Nacional Pico Tancítaro); a private volcano visitor center, with cabins, campsites, and a restaurant followed. Now, new paved roads further encourage the adventurous to explore the pine-tufted backcountry of this sylvan, Purépecha Indian heartland, less than an hour's drive northwest of Uruapan.

ANGAHUAN VILLAGE, VOLCÁN PARICUTÍN, AND VICINITY

Before Paricutín there was Angahuan village, about 24 miles (38 km) by road northwest of Uruapan. The name, locals say, was originally "Andanhuan," which means "The Place That the People Reached," or perhaps, simply, "Resting Place." It's also said that the Spanish couldn't pronounce the original name, so it got changed to the present Angahuan (ahn-GAH-wahn).

Although now the gateway to Paricutín, Angahuan (pop. about 3,000) is interesting in its own right. When you arrive, men will probably crowd around, offering to be your guide. Whether you accept their services or not, your first stop should be the main square, by the old plaza church, on the left, at the town center.

Even though the Spanish arrived in 1527, in the person of the rapacious renegade conquistador Nuño de Guzmán, the church, dedicated to Santiago (St. James), wasn't begun until the Franciscan missionaries could gain the confidence of the local folks, who had been victims of Guzmán's reign of terror. By 1577, the church finally was finished, under the guidance of Fa-

ther Jacobo Daciano. He commissioned a Spanish-Moorish stonemason to supervise the work. The flowery patterns, similar to those on the famous Talavera ceramics, that the stonemason executed resulted in the unmistakable Moorish style that blooms, like an ornate Persian carpet, both on the arched front facade and on the nave ceiling inside.

A Stroll around Angahuan

Much of the fun of Angahuan is the old-Mexico scenes—a backyard lumber mill, bright *huipiles* hanging out to dry on a clothesline, kids playing kickball—which you might glimpse while strolling its back lanes. Among the most picturesque of Angahuan sights are the log houses, called *trojes* in the Purépecha tongue. Their steep shake roofs come in two forms: with two slopes, called "two waters," or with four slopes, "four waters."

As you stroll out from the church be sure to look, about 100 yards on and a door or two to the right of the grocery store, across the other side of the plaza from the church front. Eight prize-winning carved panels tell the story of **Volcán Paricutín,** from the moment, one afternoon in 1943, when farmer Dionisio Pulido became the first person in the world to witness a volcano's birth.

If you want to see Paricutín's smoky eruption as it appeared at the time, try to get a video, or catch a cable-TV presentation, of the epic movie ***Captain from Castile*** (1947), starring Tyrone Power, Susan Peters, Lee J. Cobb, and César Romero. It was filmed on location, near Angahuan, with scenes of the erupting Paricutín in the background. The volcano appears during the last 10 minutes of the movie. You might want to record the volcano scenes with a VCR so you can replay them.

DIONISIO PULIDO AND VOLCÁN PARICUTÍN

On the afternoon of 4 March 1943, campesino Dionisio Pulido was the first person to witness the birth of a live volcano and live to tell the tale. He said that, around three in the afternoon, he was plowing his field with his yoke of bullocks, when the earth beneath his feet began to shift, shudder, and roar. Soon steam began rising from the animals' hoofprints. When Dionisio grabbed his hoe and desperately tried to fill the steamy holes, more holes appeared. His wife arrived with a dozen villagers, who worked like demons with sticks, hoes, shovels, and picks, struggling to fill the ever-widening hot fissures. But it was no use; a terrifying fiery explosion blew huge rocks into the air, and most people simply knelt down in the field, weeping and praying.

Over the next few weeks, the smoke and explosions gradually became more violent. People ran for their lives as choking ash blanketed their fields and red-hot boulders rained down for half a mile around. Within six months, lava began oozing from the crater and formed huge flows 10 feet deep that burned the forest and buried the villages of Paricutín and San Juan Parangaricutiro, including their church.

When Volcán Paricutín's fires finally sputtered out on 4 March

1952, a grand 10,000-acre moonscape of burnt embers and hardened lava lay at the foot of a dark cinder mountain nearly a third of a mile in height. The entire displaced population of both villages was resettled in a new town, San Juan Nuevo Parangaricutiro, where the people rebuilt their church, six miles west of Uruapan.

Local resident Simón Lázaro Jiménez heard Dionisio tell his story scarcely two days after the volcano had burst from the ground beneath his feet. Lázaro Jiménez later related the story in his 1993 book, *Paricutín a Cincuenta Años de su Nacimiento* ("Paricutín, Fifty Years After Its Birth"). Guadalajara, Jalisco: Editorial Agata, 1993.

By car, get to Angahuan by heading from Uruapan north along Hwy. 37. After about 19 miles (31 km) turn left at the westbound paved road and continue another 14 miles (23 km) to the Angahuan side road on the left. By bus, go early in the morning by second-class regional bus from the *central camionera,* on the Hwy. 37 ingress boulevard, about a mile northeast of the *jardín.* You can also go by **local tour;** contact Viajes Cupatitzio, tel. (452) 352-55, 356-33, or 411-85, fax 416-36, at the Hotel Tarasco, at 2 Independencia, on the *jardín,* northwest corner.

Centro Turístico Angahuan

Continue from the Angahuan plaza along the main ingress street. After about three blocks,

follow the sign left about another mile, up a low hill, to the private Centro Turístico Angahuan tourist center. An attendant collects a nominal entrance fee at the gate. The office is on the right; after that comes the interpretive center and museum, then the cabins, restaurant, and camping area. Behind the restaurant is the *mirador* (viewpoint), where, above the southern horizon, beyond the lava-choked villages and fields, you can see Paricutín's hulking, truncated cone. On a clear day, more likely during the Dec.-May dry season, you might see the gargantuan, cedar-crested bulk of Tancítaro mountain rising high above the horizon slightly to the right (west) of Paricutín.

Exploring the Paricutín Volcanic Zone

An overnight stay, followed by an early morning start, is the best strategy for exploring Paricutín's ash-strewn wasteland. Along the way you'll pass lava-covered fields, buried village houses and church, a burned forest, and finally dark, forbidding Paricutín and Sapichi, the parasite vent that belched forth the lava that drowned San Juan Parangaricutiro. The 12-mile roundtrip to the top of the volcano requires an entire day. Bring plenty of water, sturdy walking shoes, a hat, and food. The trail is at times vague, and the lava is sharp and pocked with holes. For safety, best hire a guide in Angahuan or at the Centro Turístico. Rental horses are also available to ease your adventure.

Accommodations

Although most of the time the place is largely unoccupied, during the high August season and weekends and holidays reservations are generally needed to spend an overnight in one of the center's dozen rustic family-style cabins or in the men's or women's dormitory. Cabins, which sleep six, have fireplaces, wood included, with bunk beds, attractive locally woven blankets, tile floors and bath with hot shower. They cost about $44. Although not immaculate, the cabins are clean enough for a night or two. Dormitory guests pay $8 tariff per person.

Camping in your own tent costs about $2 plus $1 per person per night. Rain-proof fixed shelters for camping cost about $3, plus $1 per person per night. RVers could probably park their (self-contained) rigs for about the same prices.

As for reservations, the friendly Centro Turístico manager, Guadalupe Amado Bravo, says that, until his phone, tel. (452) 505-83, gets working properly, others are relaying phone reservation messages to him. The best bet seems to be through associate Jesús Angeles, tel. (452) 339-34, in Uruapan. If that fails, try getting a reservation message to him through the state of Michoacán tourism in Morelia, tel./fax (43) 242-944 or 242-372, or in Uruapan, tel./fax (452) 471-99. The surest but slowest method, of course, would be to write him for a reservation, at least a month in advance, Guadalupe Amado Bravo, Gerente, Centro Turístico Angahuan, Camino al Volcán Paricutín, Angahuan, Michoacán.

PARQUE NACIONAL PICO DE TANCÍTARO

The **Parque Nacional Pico de Tancítaro** encompasses the small kingdom of de facto high-country wilderness that climaxes at **Tancítaro Peak,** which rises to its 12,670-foot (3,860-meter) peak just 17 miles (28 km), as the crow flies, due west of downtown Uruapan. Like many Mexican national parks, the 90-square mile (60,000-acre) Tancítaro has little government presence—no campgrounds, no maintained trails, few if any rangers, and no visitor center.

Adventurous travelers nevertheless can safely explore the park and climb the peak, accompanied by a guide. The best—actually the only—time to go is during the clear Dec.-May dry season. Two major routes are customary for Tancítaro climbers, one on the south side, the other on the north. The north-side approach is shortest and easiest, requiring only a rugged high-clearance vehicle, such as a pickup truck, jeep, or other strong sport utility vehicle. Begin at the rugged dirt road that takes off from the south side of the highway, a bit more than a mile (two km) east of Angahuan. Continue about another mile and a half (two km), passing Rancho Choritiro. Another 11 miles (18 km) brings you to Rancho la Escondida ("Hidden Ranch"). Continue three miles (five km) to San Salvador mountain hamlet, where the jeep road ends. The peak is another three hours of rugged walking after that. Light snow (that often soon melts) is possible during the winter. Be prepared with adequate food, water, purification tablets, insect repellent, good boots, layers against the cold, a hat, emergency shelter, and sleeping bags. For a guide, either inquire among the volunteer guides in Angahuan, ask at San Salvador, or (in Spanish) consult the Centro Turístico Angahuan manager, Guadalupe Amado Bravo.

The other route to Tancítaro peak begins on the mountain's south slope, at Tancítaro town (pop. 4,000), about 32 miles (51 km), an hour and a half, by gravel road west of Uruapan.

Around-the-Mountain Excursion

Tancítaro town (pop. 4,000) is a good halfway stopping point on a scenic excursion through the lush foothills around Tancítaro mountain. Start-

AROUND TANCÍTARO NATIONAL PARK

ing early from Uruapan, drivers could do it in one leisurely day. Backpackers could trek, thumb, and bus the same route in a minimum of two days. The clockwise route begins by following Av. Cupatitzio west from the Uruapan *jardín*. Fill up with gas and set your odometer at the Pemex *gasolinera* at the west edge of town. At Mile 5 (Km 8) comes **Nuevo San Juan Parangaricutiro** (pop. about 5,000), the new town built, beginning in 1946, by the villagers displaced by Paricutín. Their pride is the big Templo del Señor de los Milagros, which contains the original patronal image of Jesus, saved from the eruption. Their eight-day patronal fiesta begins on 13 September; they also celebrate the fiesta of the Tres Reyes Magos ("Three Magi Kings") on 7, 8, and 9 January.

After several up-and-down miles through luxuriant foothill avocado groves, the pavement gives way to a graded dirt and gravel road at about Mile 20 (Km 32). Pass Parícuari village (a few stores) at Mile 23.5 (Km 38) and larger Condembaro at Mile 27 (Km 43). You might stop for refreshment and a good word with friendly Dr. Rosendo Zamora Tamaya, who runs his practice out of his pharmacy, on the main side street on the left. Continue as the road bends right (northwest), toward Tancítaro town, at Mile 32 (Km 52).

Tancítaro Town

This is an old colonial-era settlement, with venerable church, town plaza, post and telecommunications offices, and a few restaurants. The **Hotel Saint Louis** (*not* San Luis) is at 35 Morelos, on the main plaza-front thoroughfare, a block uphill from the plaza. At the hotel, you should meet the friendly owner, Dr. Carlos Navarro, who can put you in contact with a reliable mountain trekking guide. His small, new hotel offers eight clean rooms with hot-water showers, television, and phones, for about $11 s, $14 d. Although usually not necessary, you can reserve a room by writing, or better, calling, the hotel (in Spanish) at (459) 150-49.

The customary **climbing route to Tancítaro peak** takes off from Zirimóndiro village, several miles uphill from Tancítaro town. The entire trek requires about 15 hours of hiking and two nights, three days, roundtrip. Net elevation gain is about 6,000 feet (from about 6,500 feet at Zirimóndiro, to the 12,670-foot summit). Although horses are available, most guides do not recommend using them, because of the difficulty of the route. This trek is only for fit, prepared, and preferably experienced hikers. Be equipped with everything—water, purifying tablets or iodine, food, clothing layers against the cold, cooking utensils, small stove with fuel, matches, insect repellent, sleeping bag and pad, a hat, socks, and sturdy, broken-in hiking boots.

Doctor Navarro recommends experienced local mountain man Francisco Mendoza to lead your trek. (If somehow he is unavailable, Mendoza recommends two more: Francisco Monte Longo and Benjamin Mesa). Mendoza will lead a trek to the top, minimum three days, for a fee of about $15 or $20 per day. Although he doesn't expect it, as a courtesy you should carry enough food for him, too. He's a kindly, modest, slender but wiry man of about 50, with a twinkle in his eye. He's probably been to the top a dozen times in a generation of living on the Tancítaro mountainside.

You can usually find Mendoza at his rancho, about two miles uphill, on the road to Zirimóndiro, from town. From Hotel Saint Louis, go two blocks uphill, turn right at Domínguez, go four blocks, turn left at the end of the street, Taria, continue one long block to a white sign at Rayón, and turn right. Continue 1.2 miles (1.9 km) to Mendoza's rancho, where the road bends left.

Back in town, continuing on your round-the-mountain excursion, go uphill from Hotel Saint Louis on Morelos several blocks and turn left on to the paved highway, at Bravo. From there, you'll pass a number of colonial-era towns and villages: Apo del Rosario (stores, *troje* log houses) at Mile 41 (Km 66) and a junction (bear right) at Mile 53 (Km 85) at the farming town Peribán de Ramos (pop. 5,000, has a gas station). Continue through Tzacan village (*troje* log houses) at Mile 65 (Km 105) and Angahuan at Mile 70 (Km 105) and back to Uruapan and Hotel Mansion Cupatitzio at Mile 103 (Km 166).

LÁZARO CÁRDENAS AND ALONG THE ROAD TO IXTAPA-ZIHUATANEJO

The new industrial port city of Lázaro Cárdenas, named for the Michoacán-born president famous for expropriating American oil companies, is Michoacán's Pacific transportation and service hub. Most of its services, including banks, bus stations, post office, hospitals, hotels, and restaurants, are clustered along north-south Av. Lázaro Cárdenas, the main ingress boulevard, about three miles from its Hwy. 200 intersection.

ACCOMMODATIONS AND FOOD

Take a break from the sun beneath the shady streetfront awning of the **Restaurant Las Sombrillas,** open daily 8 a.m.-8 p.m., across from Banamex. If you must stay overnight, a number of nearby hotels offer reasonably priced lodging. Among the most convenient is the **Hotel Delfín,** 1633 L. Cárdenas, Lázaro Cárdenas, Michoacán 60950, tel./fax (753) 214-18. The approximately 20 rooms with baths, in three stories, cluster around an inner pool patio. Rates run about $12 d, fan only, $18 with a/c, with hot water, TV, and telephone.

SERVICES

Money Exchange
Banamex, at Av. L. Cárdenas 1646, tel. (753) 220-20, is open for money exchange Mon.-Fri. 9 a.m.-1 p.m. If it's too crowded, try **Bancomer,** open Mon.-Fri. 8:30 a.m.-5:30 p.m., Saturday

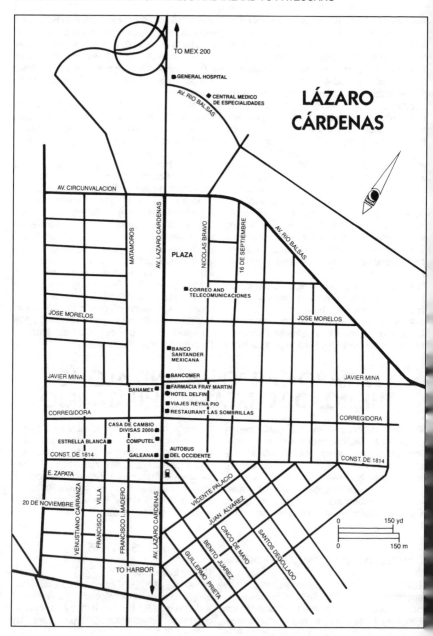

LÁZARO CÁRDENAS

10 a.m.-2 p.m. (money exchange hours may be shorter), a block north and across the street, at 1555 L. Cárdenas, tel. (753) 238-88; or **Banco Santander Mexican,** tel. (753) 200-32, at no. 1681, on the same side, half a block farther south. After hours, try the **Casa de Cambio Divisas 2000,** at L. Cárdenas 1750, a block south of Banamex, tel. (753) 244-37, which changes U.S. money only, open Mon.-Sat. 9 a.m.- 5 p.m.

Hospitals and Pharmacy

The **General Hospital,** known locally as "Seguro Social," tel. (753) 204-32 or 204-33, is on the boulevard into town, left side, corner of Río Balsas, just before the big right-side traffic circle. The private hospital, **Central Médica de Especialidades,** tel. (753) 221-26, is at Río Balsas 80, about a block east of the General Hospital. For routine medicines and drugs, go to **Farmacia Fray Martin,** tel. (753) 724-55, on Av. L. Cárdenas, across the street corner adjacent to Bancomer; or alternatively, **Farmacia Moderna,** tel. (753) 202-46, on the main street, across from the Galeana bus station, open 7:30 a.m.- 9 p.m.

Post Office and Telecommunications

The *correo* (post office), tel. (753) 723-87, is in the middle of the big grassy town plaza; look for it (painted blue) on the left as you arrive at the town center, two long blocks after the big rightside traffic circle. *Telecomunicaciones* (telegraph, money orders, telephone, and public fax), tel. (753) 202-73, is next door to the post office. More expensive, but with more convenient hours, **Computel,** the computer-assisted long-distance telephone and fax agency, operates daily 7 a.m.- 10 p.m., tel./fax (753) 248-06, fax 248-07, next to the Galeana bus terminal, at 1810 L. Cárdenas, corner of Constitución de 1814.

GETTING THERE AND AWAY

Bus Terminals

A trio of long-distance bus terminals serves Lázaro Cárdenas. From the Galeana (officially, "Lineas Unidas del Sur") terminal at 1810 Av. L. Cárdenas, tel. (753) 202-62, **Ruta Paraíso** first- and second-class local-departure buses connect daily north with Uruapan, Pátzcuaro, and Morelia. Additionally, many more first- and second-class departures connect northwest with Manzanillo

and intermediate points. In an adjacent booth (tel. 753-230-06) agents sell tickets for Parhikuni first- and luxury-class buses, connecting north with Michoacán destinations of Apatzingan, Nueva Italia, Uruapan, Pátzcuaro, and Morelia.

Directly across the street, **Autobuses del Occidente** (ADO) and **Autobuses de Jalisco,** tel. (753) 718-50, maintain a small streetfront station. They offer a number of daily first-class departures, connecting north with Tecomán, Manzanillo, Colima, Ciudad Guzmán, and Guadalajara, as well as daily second-class departures, connecting northwest, with Uruapan, Pátzcuaro, Morelia, and Michoacán.

The big **Estrella Blanca** terminal, tel. (753) 211-71, is two short blocks away, on Fco. Villa, directly behind the Galeana terminal, on Fco. Villa, between Constitución de 1814 and Corregidora. From there, first-class buses local departures connect north, with Michoacán destinations of Uruapan, Pátzcuaro, and Morelia. Other luxury-class buses stop, en route southeast to Zihuatanejo, Acapulco, and the Oaxaca coast, and northwest to Manzanillo, Puerto Vallarta, Mazatlán, and the U.S. border. Additionally, many second-class Autotransportes Sur de Cuauhtémoc local departures, tel. (753) 211-71, connect southeast with Zihuatanejo, Acapulco, and intermediate points.

Trains

Privatization has erased passenger service on the Lázaro Cárdenas-Uruapan-Pátzcuaro-Morelia rail line. Ride the bus instead.

Travel Agents

A competent and conveniently located travel agency (and possible information source) is **Viajes Reyna Pio,** on L. Cárdenas, right across from the Galeana bus station and Banamex, tel. (753) 238-68 or 239-35, fax 207-23. Alternatively, try **Chinameca Viajes,** at Javier Mina 278 (at the Bancomer corner, walk a few blocks east from Av. L. Cárdenas), tel. (753) 22-117.

ALONG THE ROAD TO IXTAPA-ZIHUATANEJO

It's hard to remain unimpressed as you cross over the **Río Balsas Dam** for the first time. The dam, which marks the Michoacán-Guerrero state boundary, is huge and hulking. Behind it a grand lake mirrors the Sierra Madre mountains, while on the opposite side, Mexico's greatest river spurts from the turbine exit gates hundreds of feet below. The river's power, converted into enough electric energy for millions of lightbulbs, courses up great looping transmission wires, while the spent river meanders toward the sea.

On the Road
The middle of the dam (Hwy. 200, Km 103 north of Zihuatanejo) is a good point at which to reset your odometer. Your odometer and the roadside kilometer markers may be your best way to find the several little hideaways between the Río Balsas and Zihuatanejo.

As for bus travelers, having gotten aboard at La Mira or Lázaro Cárdenas (or Zihuatanejo, if traveling northwest), ask the driver to let you off at your destination.

Playas Atracadero and Los Llanos
Both of these little havens are especially for shellfish lovers who yearn for their fill of swimming, surfing, splashing, fishing, and beachcombing. Atracadero is the less frequented of the two. The several beach *palapa* restaurants operate only seasonally. Crowds must gather sometimes, however: one of the *palapas* has a five-foot pile of oyster shells! Another thing is certain; the local folks supplement their diet with plenty of iguanas, judging from the ones boys offer for sale along the road.

The beach sand itself is soft and gray. The waves, with good surfing breaks, roll in from far out, arriving gently on the beach. Boat launching would be easy during calm weather. Little undertow menaces casual swimmers, bodysurfers, or boogie boarders. Lots of driftwood and shells—clams, limpets, snails—cover the sand. The beach extends for at least three miles past palm groves on the northwest. A fenced grove and house occupies the southeast. A grassy lot on the northwest side could accommodate some tents and RVs. Bring your own food and water.

To get to Playa Atracadero, turn off at Km 64, 24 miles (39 km) from the Río Balsas and 40 miles from Zihuatanejo. Bear left all the way, 2.1 miles (3.3 km) to the beach.

At Los Llanos (The Plains), the day climaxes when the oyster divers bring in their catches around 2:30 p.m. They combine their catches into big 100-pound (45-kg) bags, which wait for trucks to take them as far as Mazatlán. On the spot, one dozen in a cocktail go for $3-4. On the other hand, if you prefer to shuck your own oysters, you can buy them unshucked $2 a dozen. The divers also bring in octopus and lobsters, which, broiled and served with fixings, sell for about $7 for a one-pounder. You can also do your own fishing via rentable (offer $15/hour) beach *pangas,* which go out daily and routinely return with three or four 20-pound fish.

The beach itself is level far out, with rolling waves fine for surfing, swimming, boogie boarding, and bodysurfing. There's enough driftwood and shells for a season of beachcombing. The beach spreads for hundreds of yards on both sides of the road's end. Permanent *palapa* restaurants supply shade, drinks, and seafood. Beach camping is common and popular, especially during the Christmas and Easter holidays. Other times, you may have the whole place to yourself. A north-end grove provides shade for camping. Bring your own food and water, although the small store at the highway village may help add to your supplies.

To get to Los Llanos, at Km 40, 39 miles (63 km) southeast of the Río Balsas and 25 miles (40 km) northwest of Zihuatanejo, turn off at the village of Los Llanos. (Notice the pharmacy at the highway and the Conasupo store about one-tenth of a mile farther on.) At two-tenths of a mile, turn right, at the church, just before the basketball court, and continue another 3.1 miles (5.1 km) to the beach.

Playa Majagua and Playa Troncones
This pair of palmy nooks basks on a pristine coastal stretch, backed by a jungly, wildlife-rich hinterland. While Playa Troncones has acquired a good beachside restaurant and a sprinkling of restful inns, one with a trailer park, Playa Majagua remains very rustic.

Playa Majagua, at Km 32.5 north of Zihuatanejo, is a fishing hamlet with palmy shade, stick-and-wattle houses, and about half a dozen hammock-equipped *ramadas* scattered along the beach. One of the *ramadas* is competently run by a friendly family who call it Restaurant Los Angeles. Camping is safe and welcomed by local folks (although space, especially for

RVs, is limited). Water is available, but campers should bring purifying tablets and food.

The beach curves from a rocky southeast-end point, past the lagoon of Río Lagunillas, and stretches miles northwest past shoreline palm and acacia forest. The sand is soft and dark yellow, with mounds of driftwood but few shells. Waves break far out and roll in gradually, with little undertow. Fine left-breaking surf rises off the southern point. Boats are easily launchable (several *pangas* lie along the beach) during normal good weather.

Getting There: To get to Playa Majagua, turn off at the sign just south of the Río Lagunillas bridge, at Km 32.5, 44 miles (70 km) southeast of Río Balsas, 20 miles northwest of Zihuatanejo. Continue 2.9 miles to the beach.

Nearby Playa Troncones has a little bit of everything: shady seafood *ramadas* on the left as you enter from the highway; next, a half-mile beach with several spots to pull off and camp. At the southern end, a lagoon spreads beside a pristine coral-sand beach, which curls around a low hill toward a picture-perfect little bay. A small store can supplement your food. Water is available.

But that's just the beginning. Troncones has acquired a small colony of North Americans, some of whom operate small beachside accommodations for lovers of peace, quiet, and the outdoors. First came friendly pioneers Dewey and Karolyn McMillin, who built their **Casa de la Tortuga** during the late 1980s. Now, their guests enjoy a clean room (some with shared bath) and breakfast in their modern beach house, a restful patio with plenty of shade, quiet, and opportunities for delighting in the outdoors. Their six inside rooms rent, low-season, for about $30 s, $35 d and $50 s, $75 d high; a separate guest cottage rents for $40 d low season, $75 d high (with bath); all with breakfast. The entire layout (sleeping a dozen or more) rents, low season, for about $200 per day, $1,200 per week, $450 and $2,800 high. Discounts are negotiable for longer stays. A kitchen is available for guest use. No children under 12, unless you rent the whole place. Write or fax them for reservations (mandatory during the winter) at P.O. Box 37, Zihuatanejo, Guerrero 40880, tel. (755) 707-32, fax (755) 432-96. If business is slow, they close June, July, and August.

Besides lazing in hammocks and sunning on the sand, Casa de La Tortuga guests can swim, surf, bodysurf, and boogie board the waves, jog along the sand, and explore a limestone cave in the adjacent jungle hinterland. Back by the shore, you can beachcomb to your heart's content while enjoying views of the wildlife trove—fish, whales, dolphins, and swarms of herons, boobies, egrets, and cormorants—which abounds in the ocean and in nearby lagoons.

The same bounty of natural amenities is common to all Troncones lodgings. Moving southeast along the shore, next comes **Casa Ki,** the life project of Ed and Ellen Weston, P.O. Box 405, Zihuatanejo, Guerrero 40880, tel. (755) 709-92, fax 324-17, e-mail: casaki@yahoo.com. Casa Ki, (named after the Japanese word for energy and wholeness) offers three immaculate, charmingly rustic cottages, tucked in the Westons' lovingly tended seaside garden compound. Each cottage sleeps approximately two adults and two children and comes with shower, toilet, fans, and a refrigerator. Guests share a shady outside cooking and dining *palapa*. Low-season (1 May-15 Nov.) rentals run $50-60; high season, $75-85 (which includes full breakfast). They also rent a charming two-bedroom, two-bath house that sleeps six, with full kitchen and daily maid service, for about $65 low season. Get your winter reservations in early.

Newest on the beach is the six-room **Eden Beach Hacienda and Garden Restaurant,** which shares the same luscious oceanfront as Casa Ki and Casa de la Tortuga. The amenities include six immaculate rooms, decorated in Talavera tile, with king-size beds and private hot-water bathrooms. With yet no electricity, candles and hurricanes lamps provide romantic old-fashioned illumination. Rates run about $65 d, including breakfast.

Star of the Eden show is chef Christian Shirmer, American graduate of the Baltimore culinary academy, whose menus feature traditional Mexican cuisine with a nouveau flair, focusing on fresh ingredients and seasonal foods. At least, stop in for lunch or dinner and meet Christian and Eva Robbins and Jim Garrity, the builder-owners. For reservations and information, contact the owners directly through their Web site, www.eden-mex.com, or e-mail: evandjim@aol.com, or by mail at 41 Riverview Dr., Oak Ridge, TN 37830.

Bungalows Xochicalli ("House of Flowers"), a few hundred yards farther south along the beach, offers four kitchenette studios in a seafront garden. The apartments are clean and simply but attractively decorated by the owner, amateur archaeologist, eco-activist, and longtime Zihuatanejo resident Anita Rellstab Hahner. For reservations, contact her at Bungalows Pacífico, P.O. Box 12, Zihuatanejo, Guerrero 40880, tel. (755) 421-12.

Farther along, **El Burro Borracho** ("The Drunken Burro") restaurant and inn has become a favorite stopping place for the growing cadre of visitors who are venturing out from Ixtapa and Zihuatanejo. Here, owner Dewey McMillin continues the standard set by former owner/chef Michael Bensal, with spicy shrimp tacos, rum-glazed ribs, jumbo shrimp grilled with coconut-curry sauce, and broiled pork chops with mashed potatoes. Besides the shady ocean-view *palapa* restaurant, Burro Borracho offers six "simply elegant" airy rooms, each with bath, in three stone duplex beachfront cottages. Extras include king-size bed, rustic-chic decor, hot water, and fans. Shared cooking facilities are also available.

Sports and activities include all those listed above, plus kayaks, for use of guests. Room rentals run about $60 d, high season, $30 low, with continental breakfast. Facilities also include five (shadeless) **RV spaces,** with all hookups, adjacent to the cottages for about $10 per night. Discounts are negotiable for long-term rentals. Write, telephone, or fax for reservations (mandatory in winter) at P.O. Box 37, Zihuatanejo, Guerrero 40880, tel. (755) 706-56, fax 432-96.

Getting There: Follow the (signed southbound) paved turnoff to Playa Troncones around Km 30, about 42 miles (73 km) south of the Río Balsas (about 18 miles north of Zihuatanejo). Continue 2.2 miles to the Playa Troncones beachfront *ramadas.* Turn left for the camping spots, the main part of the beach and El Burro Borracho; turn right for Casa de la Tortuga, which is about a mile farther along a beachfront forest road. From there, the car-negotiable dry-weather track continues about a mile and a half along the beach to Playa Majagua.

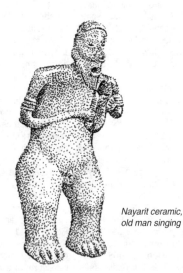

Nayarit ceramic, old man singing

IXTAPA-ZIHUATANEJO AND SOUTH TO ACAPULCO

IXTAPA-ZIHUATANEJO

The Costa Grande, the "Big Coast," of the state of Guerrero angles 200 miles southeast from the Río Balsas to Acapulco. Before the highway came in the 1960s, this was a land of corn, coconuts, fish, and fruit. Although it's still that, the road added a new ingredient: a trickle of visitors seeking paradise in Zihuatanejo, a sleepy fishing village on a beautiful bay.

During the 1970s, planners decided to create the best of all possible worlds by building Ixtapa, a luxurious resort on a pearly beach five miles away. Now, Ixtapa-Zihuatanejo's clear, rich waters, forested eco-sanctuaries, pearly little beaches, pristine offshore islets, good food, comfortable hotels, and friendly local folks offer visitors the ingredients for memorable stays any time of the year.

HISTORY

Zihuatanejo's azure waters attracted attention long before Columbus. Local legend says the Tarascans (whose emperor ruled from now-Michoacán and who was never subject to the Aztecs) built a royal bathing resort on Las Gatas Beach in Zihuatanejo Bay.

That was sometime around 1400. People had been attracted to the Costa Grande much earlier than that: archaic pottery has been uncovered at a number of sites, left by artists who lived and died as long as five thousand years ago. Later, around 1000 B.C., the Olmecs (famous for their monumental Gulf coast sculptures) came and left their unmistakable stamp on local ceramics. After them came waves of set-

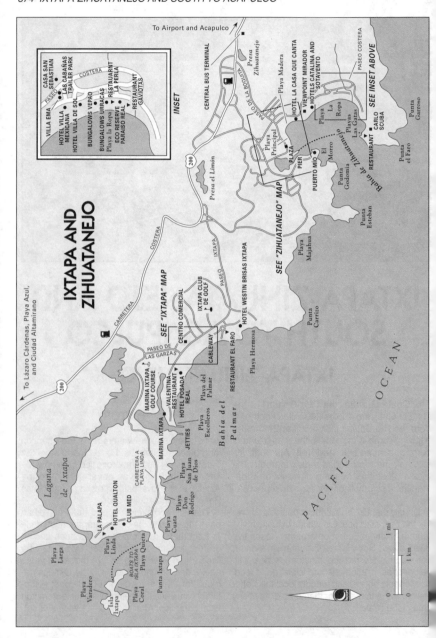

IXTAPA AND ZIHUATANEJO

INSET

To Airport and Acapulco

CENTRAL BUS TERMINAL

Presa Zihuatanejo

Playa Madera

HOTEL LA CASA QUE CANTA
VIEWPOINT MIRADOR
HOTELS CATALINA AND SOTAVENTO

SEE INSET ABOVE

Punta Garroso

PASEO COSTERA

Playa
La
Ropa

Playas
Las Gatas

Punta
el Faro

CARLO
SCUBA

RESTAURANT

Punta
Esteban

INSET:

VILLA EMA
CASA SAN SEBASTIAN
HOTEL VILLA MEXICANA
LAS CABAÑAS TRAILER PARK
HOTEL VILLA DE SOL
COSTERA
BUNGALOWS VEPAO
BUNGALOWS URRACAS
RESTAURANT LA PERLA
Playa la Ropa
ECO RESERVE PARAISO REAL
RESTAURANT GAVIOTAS
PASEO SAN

Presa de la Boquita

Presa el Limón

200

PASEO DE LA BOQUITA

Playa
Principal

PLAZA
PIER

PUERTO MIO

El
Morro

Punta
Godomia

Bahía de Zihuatanejo

SEE "ZIHUATANEJO" MAP

Playa
Majahua

Punta
Curtito

Playa Hermosa

COSTERA

IXTAPA

PASEO

IXTAPA CLUB DE GOLF

SEE "IXTAPA" MAP

CENTRO COMERCIAL

HOTEL WESTIN BRISAS IXTAPA

CABLEWAY

RESTAURANT EL FARO

PASEO DE LAS GARZAS

MARINA IXTAPA GOLF COURSE

VALENTINA RESTAURANT

HOTEL POSADA REAL

Playa del Palmar

Bahía del Palmar

Playa Escolleros

MARINA IXTAPA

JETTIES

Playa San Juan de Dios

CARRETERA A PLAYA LINDA

Playa Don Rodrigo

Playa Cuata

LA PALAPA

HOTEL QUALTON

CLUB MED

Playa Linda

BOATS TO ISLA IXTAPA

Playa Quieta

Playa Larga

Playa Varadero

Isla Ixtapa

Playa Coral

Punta Ixtapa

Laguna de Ixtapa

To Lázaro Cárdenas, Playa Azul, and Ciudad Altamirano

200

CARRETERA

PACIFIC OCEAN

1 mi

1 km

0

0

tlers, including the barbaric Chichimecs ("Drinkers of Blood"), the agricultural Cuitlatecs, and an early invasion of Aztecs, perhaps wandering in search of their eventual homeland in the Valley of Mexico.

None of those peoples were a match for the armies of Tarascan emperor Hiripan, who during the late 1300s invaded the Costa Grande and established a coastal province, headquartered at Coyuca, between Zihuatanejo and present-day Acapulco.

Three generations later the star of the Aztec emperor Tízoc was rising over Mexico. His armies invaded the Costa Grande and pushed out the Tarascans. By 1500 the Aztecs ruled the coast from their provincial town capital at Zihuatlán, the "Place of Women" (so named because the local society was matriarchal), not far from present-day Zihuatanejo.

Conquest and Colonization

Scarcely months after Hernán Cortés conquered the Aztecs, he sent an expedition to explore the "Southern Sea" and hopefully find a route to China. In November 1522 Captain Juan Alvarez Chico set sail with boats built on the Isthmus of Tehuantepec and reconnoitered the coast to the Río Balsas, planting crosses on beaches, claiming the land for Spain.

An oft-told Costa Grande story says that, when Chico was exploring at Zihuatanejo, he looked down on the round tranquil little bay, lined with flocks of seabirds and women washing clothes in a freshwater spring. His Aztec guide told him that this place was called Zihuatlán, the "Place of Women." When Chico described the little bay, Cortés tacked *"nejo"* (little) onto the name, giving birth to "Zihuatlanejo," which later got shortened to the present Zihuatanejo.

Cortés, encouraged by the samples of pearls and gold that Chico brought back, sent out other expeditions. Villafuerte established a shipyard and town at Zacatula at the mouth of the Balsas in 1523. Then, in 1527, Captain Alvaro Saavedra

hieroglyph of Zihuatanejo (the Place of Women)

Cerón set sail for China from Zihuatanejo Bay. Not knowing any details of the Pacific Ocean and its winds and currents, it is not surprising that (although he did arrive in the Philippines) Saavedra Cerón failed to return to Mexico. A number of additional attempts would be necessary until finally, in 1565, Father André de Urdaneta coaxed Pacific winds to give up their secret and returned, in triumph, from the Orient.

By royal decree, Acapulco became Spain's sole port of entry on the Pacific in 1561. Except for an occasional galleon (or pirate caravel) stopping for repairs or supplies, all other Pacific ports, including Zihuatanejo, slumbered for hundreds of years.

Zihuatanejo was one of the last to wake up. The occasion was the arrival of the highway from Acapulco during the 1960s. No longer isolated, Zihuatanejo's headland-rimmed aqua bay attracted a small colony of paradise-seekers.

Zihuatanejo had grown to perhaps 5,000 souls by the late '70s when Fonatur, the government tourism-development agency, decided Ixtapa (which means "White Place," for its brilliant sand beach five miles north of Zihuatanejo) was a perfect site for a world-class resort. Investors agreed, and the infrastructure—drainage, roads, and utilities—was installed. The jetport was built, hotels rose, and by the '90s the distinct but inseparable twin resorts of Ixtapa and Zihuatanejo (combined pop. 70,000) were attracting a steady stream of Mexican and foreign vacationers.

SIGHTS

Getting Oriented

Both Ixtapa and Zihuatanejo are small and easy to know. Zihuatanejo's little Plaza de Armas town square overlooks the main beach, Playa Municipal, just beyond the palm-lined pedestrian walkway, Paseo del Pescador. From the plaza looking out toward the bay, you are facing south. On your right is the *muelle*

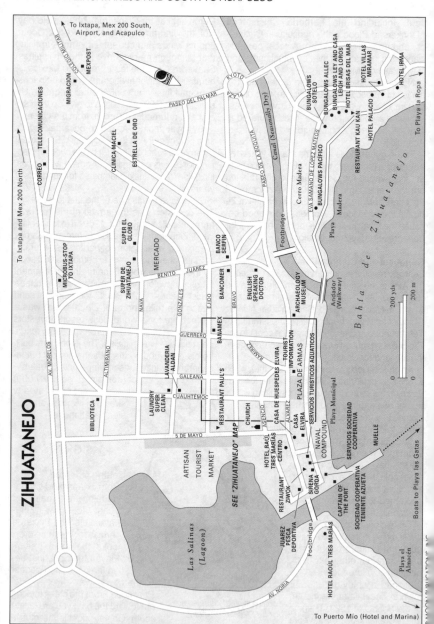

ZIHUATANEJO

To Ixtapa, Mex 200 South, Airport, and Acapulco

To Ixtapa and Mex 200 North

COLEGIO MILITAR
MEXPOST
MIGRACION
TELECOMUNICACIONES
CORREO
ESTRELLA DE ORO
CLINICA MACIEL
PASEO DEL PALMAR
PLAYA
KYOTO
Canal (Seasonally Dry)
PASEO DE LA BOQUITA

BUNGALOWS SOTELO
BUNGALOWS ALLEC
BUNGALOWS LEY AND CASA LEIGH AND LOROS
HOTEL BRISAS DEL MAR
HOTEL VILLAS MIRAMAR
HOTEL IRMA

BUNGALOWS PACIFICO
RESTAURANT KAU KAN
HOTEL PALACIO
To Playa la Ropa

EVA SAMANO DE LÓPEZ MATEOS

Cerro Madera
Playa Madera

Footbridge

MICROBUS-STOP TO IXTAPA
SUPER EL GLOBO
SUPER DE ZIHUATANEJO
MERCADO
BANCO SERFIN
BENITO   JUAREZ
NAVA
GONZALES
BANCOMER
ENGLISH SPEAKING DOCTOR
ARCHAEOLOGY MUSEUM
Andador (Walkway)

AV. MORELOS
ALTIMIRANO
BIBLIOTECA
GUERRERO
BANAMEX
RAMIREZ
BRAVO
EJIDO
TOURIST INFORMATION
SERVICIOS TURISTICOS AQUATICOS

Bahía de Zihuatanejo

200 yds
200 m
0

LAVANDERIA ALDAN
GALEANA
CUAUHTEMOC
LAUNDRY SUPER CLEAN
RESTAURANT PAUL'S
ELVIRA
PLAZA DE ARMAS
CASA DE HUESPEDES ELVIRA
CASA ELVIRA
ASENCIO
ALVAREZ

SEE "ZIHUATANEJO" MAP

CHURCH
5 DE MAYO
HOTEL RAOUL TRES MARIAS CENTRO
Playa Municipal
SERVICIOS SOCIEDAD COOPERATIVA
MUELLE

ARTISAN TOURIST MARKET

Las Salinas (Lagoon)

RESTAURANT ZIWOK
SIRENA GORDA
NAVAL COMPOUND
CAPTAIN OF THE PORT
SOCIEDAD COOPERATIVA TENIENTE AZUETA

Boats to Playa las Gatas

JUAREZ PESCA DEPORTIVA
Footbridge
AV. NORIA
HOTEL RAOUL TRES MARIAS

Playa el Almacén

To Puerto Mío (Hotel and Marina)

MOON PUBLICATIONS, INC.

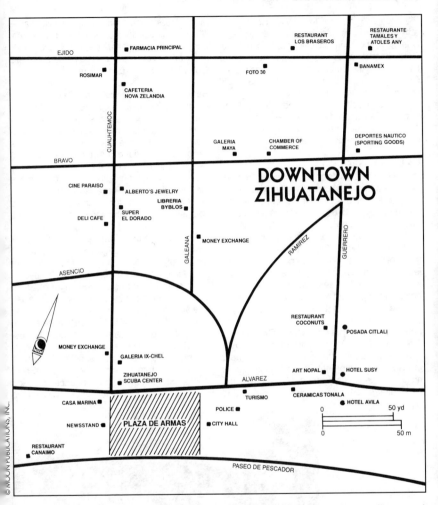

(moo-AY-yay), and on the left, the bay curves along the outer beaches Playas La Ropa, Madera, and finally Las Gatas beneath the far Punta El Faro ("Lighthouse Point").

Turning around and facing inland (north), you see a narrow waterfront street, Juan Alvarez, running parallel to the beach past the plaza, crossing the main business streets (actually tranquil shady lanes) Cuauhtémoc and Guerrero. A third street, busy Benito Juárez, one block to the right of Guerrero, conducts traffic several blocks to and from the shore, passing the market and intersecting a second main street, Av. Morelos. There, a right turn will soon bring you to Hwy. 200 and, within five miles, Ixtapa.

Nearly everything in Ixtapa lies along one three-mile-long boulevard, Paseo Ixtapa, which parallels the main beach, hotel-lined Playa del Palmar. Heading westerly from Zihuatanejo, you first pass the Club de Golf Ixtapa, then the big

Sheraton on the left, followed by a succession of other high-rise hotels. Soon come the Zona Comercial shopping malls and the Paseo de las Garzas corner on the right. Turn right for either Hwy. 200 or the outer beaches, Playas Cuata, Quieta, Linda, and Larga. At Playa Linda, boats continue to heavenly Isla Ixtapa.

If, instead, you had continued straight ahead back at the Paseo de las Garzas corner, you would have soon reached the Marina Ixtapa condo development and yacht harbor.

Getting Around

In downtown Zihuatanejo, shops and restaurants are within a few blocks' walking distance of the plaza. For the beaches, walk along the beachfront *andador* (walkway) to Madera, take a taxi ($2) to La Ropa, and a launch from the pier ($2) to Las Gatas. For Ixtapa or the outer beaches, take a taxi (about $5) or ride one of the very frequent minibuses, labeled by destination, which leave from the east corner of Juárez and Morelos. A taxi ride between central Ixtapa and Zihuatanejo runs about $4. In Ixtapa itself, walk, or ride the minibuses that run along Paseo Ixtapa.

Museo Arqueología de la Costa Grande

The small Museo Arqueología de la Costa Grande on the beachfront side of Alvarez, near the Guerrero corner, details the archaeological history of the Costa Grande. Maps, drawings, small dioramas, and artifacts—many donated by local resident and innkeeper Anita Rellstab—illustrate the development of local cultures, from early hunting and gathering to agriculture and, finally, urbanization by the time of the conquest. Open Tues.-Sun. 9 a.m.-8 p.m.

Beaches around Zihuatanejo Bay

Ringed by forested hills, edged by steep cliffs, and laced by rocky shoals, Zihuatanejo Bay would be beautiful even without its beaches. Five of them line the bay. On the west side is narrow, tranquil **Playa el Almacán** ("Warehouse Beach"), mostly good for fishing from its nearby rocks. Moving past the pier toward town comes the colorful, bustling **Playa Municipal.** Its sheltered waters are fine for wading, swimming, and boat launching (which fishermen, their motors buzzing, regularly do) near the pier end.

For a maximum of sun and serenity, walk away from the pier along Playa Municipal past the usually dry creek outlet where a concrete *andador* winds about 200 yards along the beachfront rocks that mark the beginning of Playa Madera. If you prefer, you can also hire a taxi to take you to Playa Madera, about $1.

Playa Madera ("Wood Beach"), once a loading point for lumber, stretches about 300 yards, decorated with rocky nooks and outcroppings, and backed by the lush hotel-dotted hill, **Cerro Madera.** The beach sand is fine and gray-white. Swells enter the facing bay entrance, breaking suddenly in two- or three-foot waves, which roll in

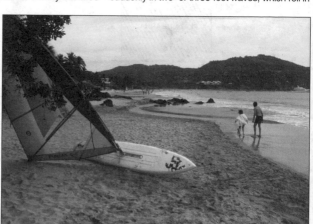

A rental windsurfer rests on Zihuatanejo Bay's Playa la Ropa.

gently and recede with little undertow. Madera's usually calm billows are good for child's play and easy swimming. Bring your mask and snorkel for glimpses of fish in the clear waters. Beachside restaurant/bars Kau Kan, La Bocana, and the Hotel Irma, above the far east end, serve drinks and snacks.

Zihuatanejo Bay's favorite resort beach is **Playa La Ropa** ("Clothes Beach"), a mile-long crescent of yellow-white sand washed by oft-gentle surf. The beach got its name centuries ago from the apparel that once floated in from a galleon wrecked offshore. From the bay's best *mirador* (viewpoint) at the summit of **Paseo Costera,** the La Ropa approach road, the beach sand, relentlessly scooped and redeposited by the waves, appears as an endless line of half-moons.

On the 100-foot-wide beach, vacationers bask in the sun, jet skis buzz beyond the breakers, rental sailboats ply the waves, and windsurf outfits recline on the sand. The waves, generally too gentle and quick-breaking for surf sports, break close-in and recede with little undertow. Joggers come out mornings and evenings. Restaurants at the several beachfront hotels provide food and drinks.

Secluded **Playa Las Gatas** ("Cat Beach"), reachable by very rough shoreline rock-hopping or easily by launch from the town pier, lies sheltered beneath the south-end Punta El Faro headland. Once a walled-in royal Tarascan bathing pool, the beach got its name from a species of locally common, small, whiskered nurse sharks. Generally calm and quiet, often with super-clear offshore waters, Playa Las Gatas is both a snorkeling haven and a jumping-off spot for dive trips headed for prime scuba sites. Beach booths rent gear for beach snorkelers, and a professional dive shop, **Carlos Scuba** right on the beach, instructs and guides both beginner and experienced scuba divers. For many more diving details, see Sports and Recreation later in this chapter.

For a treat, pass the beach restaurant lineup and continue to **Owen's** *palapa* restaurant, visible on **King's Point,** the palm-shaded outcropping past the far curve of the beach. There, enjoy some refreshment, watch the surfers glide around the point, and feast on the luscious beach, bay, and hill view.

Ixtapa Beaches

Ixtapa's 10 distinct beaches lie scattered like pearls along a dozen miles of creamy, azure coastline. Moving from the Zihuatanejo direction, **Playa Hermosa** comes first. The elevators of the super-luxurious clifftop Hotel Westin Brisas Ixtapa make access to the beach very convenient. At the bottom you'll find a few hundred yards of seasonally broad white sand, with open-ocean (but often gentle) waves usually good for most water sports except surfing. Good beach-accessible snorkeling is possible off the shoals at either end of the beach. Extensive rentals are available at the beachfront aquatics shop. A poolside restaurant serves food and drinks. Hotel access is only by car or taxi.

For a sweeping vista of Ixtapa's beaches, bay, and blue waters, ride the *teleférico* (cable tramway, open daily 7 a.m.-noon and 5-7 p.m.) to El Faro restaurant, at the south end of Ixtapa's main beach, Playa del Palmar, tel. 755-310-27. Open daily 8 a.m.-noon and 6-10 p.m.

Long, broad, and yellow-white, **Playa del Palmar** could be called the "Billion-Dollar Beach" for the investment money it attracted to Ixtapa. The confidence seems justified. The broad strand stretches for three gently curving miles. Even though it fronts the open ocean, protective offshore rocks, islands, and shoals keep the surf gentle most of the time. Here, most sports are of the high-powered variety—parasailing ($10), jet and water-skiing ($25), banana-boating ($5)—although boogie boards are rentable for $5 an hour on the beach.

Challenging surfing breaks sometimes roll in consistently off the jetty at **Playa Escolleros,** at Playa del Palmar's far west end. Bring your own board.

Ixtapa Outer Beaches

Ixtapa's outer beaches spread among the coves and inlets a few miles northwest of the Hotel Zone. Drive, taxi, or take a "Playa Linda" minibus along the Paseo de las Garzas (drivers, turn right just past the shopping mall), then fork left again after less than a mile. After the Marina Golf Course, the road turns toward the shoreline, winding past a pair of development-blocked beach gems, Playa San Juan de Dios and Playa Don Rodrigo.

Although automobile access to the entire pristine **Punta Ixtapa** peninsula and its lovely little

MARINA 1 miles

Radison

4 MORE Hotels this way

To Hotel Posada Real
and the Marina Ixtapa

To Ixtapa outer
beaches, Isla Ixtapa,
and Mex 200 North

KRYSTAL
IXTAPA

DORADO
PACIFICO

PASEOS DE LAS GARZAS

IXTAPA

JOY DISCO

GALERIAS
IXTAPA

FOTO IXTAPA

RIVIERA

PARKING

PASEO LAS GAVIOTAS

Nice walking

LAS
PALMAS

BANCOMER

PARKING

CENTRO COMERCIAL

PACIFIC

Playa del

POLICE

PRESIDENTE
INTERCONTINENTAL

TELECOMUNICACIONES

TURISMO

LA
PUERTA

RISTORANTE DA
BAFFONE

RESTAURANT
HACIENDA DE IXTAPA

OCEAN

PASEO IXTAPA

FONTAN

PARKING

PARKING

Palmar

LAS
FUENTES

PLAZA
IXPAMAR

CAFE TOKO TUKAN

GERMAN BAKERY

LOS
PATIOS

ARISTOS

0   100 yds

0   100 m

HANDICRAFTS
MARKET

CAMPO DE GOLF

SHERATON
IXTAPA

To Zihuatanejo Airport and
Mex 200 South

The End!

beaches **Playa Cuata** and **Playa Quieta** has been blocked by condo development, guards do allow pedestrian passage to the Playa Quieta access road. Although Mexican law theoretically allows free public oceanfront access, guards might try to shoo you away from Playa Cuata, on the open-ocean side, even if you arrive by boat. If somehow you manage get there, you will discover a cream-yellow strip of sand, nestled between rocky outcroppings, with oft-gentle waves with correspondingly moderate undertow for good swimming, bodysurfing, and boogie boarding. Snorkeling and fishing are equally good around nearby rocks and shoals.

On the peninsula's sheltered northern flank, Playa Quieta ("Quiet Beach") is a place that lives up to its name. A ribbon of fine yellow sand arcs around a smooth inlet dotted by a regatta of Club Med kayaks and sailboats plying the water. Get there by walking along either the south end access road or the north-end access stairway from the parking lot, signed Azul Ixtapa.

Playa Linda

Playa Linda, an open-ocean yellow-sand beach, extends for miles north from the end of the road. Flocks of sandpipers and plovers skitter at the surf's edge; pelicans and cormorants dive offshore, while gulls, terns, and boobies skim the wavetops. Driftwood and shells decorate the sand beside a green-tufted palm grove that seems to stretch endlessly to the north.

The friendly **La Palapa** beach restaurant, at pavement's end, offers beer, sodas, and seafood, plus showers and free parking and camping beneath their grove. Neighboring stable Rancho Playa Linda, managed by friendly "Spiderman" Jorge, provides horseback rides at about $15 per hour. Despite the stable-associated flies, this informal campground sometimes attracts a small colony of RV- and tent-camping customers.

The flat, wide Playa Linda has powerful rollers often good for surfing. Boogie boarding and bodysurfing—with caution, don't try it alone— are also possible. Surf fishing yields catches, especially of *lisa* (mullet), which locals have much more success netting than hooking.

Isla Ixtapa

Every few minutes a boat heads from the Playa Linda embarcadero to mile-long Ixtapa Island

daily 9 a.m.-5 p.m.; $2 roundtrip. Upon arrival, you soon discover the secret to the preservation of the island's pristine beaches, forests, and natural underwater gardens. "No trash here," the *palapa* proprietors say. "We bag it up and send it back to the mainland."

It shows. Great fleshy green orchids and bromeliads hang from forest branches, multicolored fish dart among offshore rocks, shady native acacias hang lazily over the shell-decorated sands of the island's little beaches. Boats from Playa Linda arrive at **Playa Cuachalatate** (koo-ah-chah-lah-TAH-tay), the island's most popular beach, named for a local tree whose bark relieves liver ailments. Many visitors stay all day, splashing, swimming, and eating fresh fish, shrimp, and clams cooked at any one of a dozen *palapas*. Visitors also enjoy the many sports rentals: water skis, banana rides, boats for fishing, aquatic bicycles ($6/hour), snorkel gear ($3/hour), and kayaks ($4/hour).

For a change of scene, follow the short concrete walkway over the westside (right as you arrive) forested knoll to **Playas Varadero and Coral** on opposite flanks of an intimate little isthmus. Varadero's yellow-white sand is narrow and tree-shaded, its waters are calm and clear. Behind it lies Playa Coral, a steep coral-sand beach fronting a rocky blue bay. Playa Coral is a magnet for beach lovers, snorkelers, and the scuba divers who often arrive by boat to explore the waters around the offshore coral reef.

Scuba diving is so rewarding here the Escuela de Buceos ("Diving School") Oliverio maintains headquarters near the west end of Playa Cuachalatate. Other shops in Zihuatanejo (see Sports and Recreation, below) are better equipped to provide the same services, however.

Isla Ixtapa's fourth and smallest beach, secluded **Playa Carey,** is named for the sea-turtle species (see the special topic Saving Turtles). For access, hire a boat from Playa Cuachalatate.

ACCOMMODATIONS

Ixtapa or Zihuatanejo?

Your choice of local lodging sharply determines the tone of your stay. Zihuatanejo still resembles the colorful seaside village that visitors have enjoyed for years. Fishing *pangas* decorate its beachside, while *panaderías, taquerías,* and *papelerías* line its narrow shady lanes. Many of its hotels—budget to moderate, with spartan but clean fan-only rooms—reflect the tastes of the bargain-conscious travelers who "discovered" Zihuatanejo during the 1960s.

Ixtapa, on the other hand, mirrors the fashion-wise preferences of new-generation Mexican and international vacationers. A broad boulevard fronts your Ixtapa hotel, while on the beach side, thatch-shaded chairs on a wide strand, a palmy garden, blue pool, and serene outdoor restaurant are yours to enjoy. Upstairs, your air-conditioned room—typically in plush pastels, with private sea-view balcony, marble bath, room service, and your favorite TV shows by satellite—brings maximum convenience and comfort to a lush tropical setting.

Actually, you needn't be forced to choose. Split your hotel time between Ixtapa and Zihuatanejo and enjoy both worlds.

Zihuatanejo Downtown Hotels

Zihuatanejo's hotels divide themselves by location and (largely by price) between the budget downtown and more pricey Playas Madera-La Ropa.

Starting on the west side near the beach, begin at the **Hotel Raoul Tres Marias,** across the lagoon-mouth by footbridge from the end of Paseo del Pescador, at Noria 4, Colonia Lázaro Cárdenas, Zihuatanejo, Guerrero 40880, tel. (755) 421-91. Its longtime popularity derives from its low prices and the colorful lagoonfront boat scene, visible from porches outside some of its 25 rooms. Otherwise, facilities are strictly bare-bones, without even hot water. Rooms rent for about $9 s, $13 d, and $16 t, low season, and $14, $17 and $21, high season, with fans.

Guests at the hotel's brother branch, **Hotel Raoul Tres Marias Centro,** Juan Alvarez and Cinco de Mayo, Zihuatanejo, Guerrero 40880, tel./fax (755) 467-06 (owned by brother Raoul,

---

IXTAPA-ZIHUATANEJO ACCOMMODATIONS

Accommodations (area code 755, postal code 40880) are listed in increasing order of approximate high-season, double-room rates. Toll-free (800) telephone numbers are dialable from the U.S. and Canada.

ZIHUATANEJO~DOWNTOWN

Casa de Huéspedes Elvira, Paseo de la Pescador 9, tel. 420-61, $15

Hotel Raoul Tres Marías, Noria 4, Col. Lázaro Cárdenas, tel. 423-91, $17

Hotel Susy, Guerrero and Alvarez, tel. 423-39, $23

Posada Citlali, Guerrero 3, tel. 420-43, $25

Hotel Raoul Tres Marías Centro, Alvarez and Cinco de Mayo, tel./fax 467-06, $36

Hotel Avila, Alvarez 8, tel./fax 420-10, $65

ZIHUATANEJO~PLAYA MADERA

Bungalows El Milagro, Av. Marina Nacional s/n, tel. 430-45, $30

Hotel Palacio, Av. Adelita (P.O. Box 57), tel./fax 420-55, $35

Hotel Brisas del Mar, Cerro Madera, Calle Eva Samano de López Mateos s/n, tel./fax 421-42 or 478-05, $40

Bungalows Allec, Cerro Madera, Calle Eva Samano de López Mateos, tel. 445-10 or 420-02, $45

Bungalows Ley, Cerro Madera, P.O. Box 466, tel./fax 445-63 or 440-87, $47

Bungalows Pacífico, Cerro Madera (P.O. Box 12), tel. 421-12, $50

Hotel Villas Miramar, Av. Adelita (P.O. Box 211), tel. 421-06 or 426-16, fax 421-49, $55

near the end of Alvarez), enjoy a few more amenities and the long-popular Restaurant Garrobos downstairs. Some of the 18 rooms have private balconies looking out on the usually quiet street below. Being close to the pier, the new branch is popular with fishing parties. Newcomers might pick up some local fishing pointers around the tables after dinner. Rooms go for about $30 s or d, $34 t low season, $36 and $43 high, with hot water, a/c, and fans.

Right across the street is **Casa de Huéspedes Elvira,** Paseo del Pescador 9, Zihuatanejo, Guerrero 40880, tel. (755) 420-61, operated since 1956 by its now-elderly founder, Elvira R. Campos. Every day, Elvira looks after her little garden of flowering plants, feeds rice to her birds—both wild and caged—and passes the time of day with friends and guests. She tells of the "way it used to be" when all passengers and supplies arrived from Acapulco by boat, local *almejas* (clams) were as big as cabbages, and

you could pluck fish right out of the bay with your hands. Her petite eight-room lodging divides into an upper section, with more light and privacy, and a lower, with private baths. The leafy, intimate lower patio leads upward, via a pair of quaint, plant-decorated spiral staircases to the airy upper level. The 22 rooms themselves are small, authentically rustic, and clean. The four upper rooms share a bathroom and toilet. Rates run about $5 s, $8 d, $10 t low season, $9, $15, and $20 high. If nighttime noise bothers you, bring earplugs; TV and music from Elvira's adjoining restaurant continues until about 11 p.m. most evenings during the winter season.

A few blocks east, along the beach on Alvarez is the **Hotel Avila,** Juan Alvarez 8, Zihuatanejo, Guerrero 40880, tel./fax (755) 420-10, downtown Zihuatanejo's only beachfront hostelry. Popular for its location rather than its management, which seems to be content with worn curtains and dirt in the corners, the Avila has 27

Hotel Irma, Av. Adelita, tel./fax 437-38, $60

Bungalows Sotelo, Cerro Madera, Calle Eva Samano de López Mateos 13, tel./fax 463-07, $60

Casa Leigh y Loros, Cerro Madera, tel. 437-55 or, in the U.S., tel. (510) 547-2792, $250

La Casa Que Canta, Carretera Escénica a Playa La Ropa, tel. 470-30, U.S. and Canada toll-free (888) 523-5050, fax 470-40, $340

ZIHUATANEJO~PLAYAS LA ROPA AND LAS GATAS

Bungalows Vepao, Playa La Ropa, tel. 420-55 or 426-31, $60

Bungalows Urracas, Playa La Ropa, tel. 420-49, $60

Villas Ema, Playa La Ropa, c/o Posada Citlali, Guerrero 3, tel. 420-43, $65

Hotel Villa Mexicana, tel. 437-76 or 436-36, $84

Hotels Sotavento and Catalina, P.O. Box 2, tel. 420-32 or 420-24, fax 468-70, $85

Casa Sebastián, tel. 437-55 or, in the U.S., tel. (510) 547-2792, $175

Hotel Villa del Sol, Playa La Ropa (P.O. Box 84), tel. 422-39 or 432-39, (800) 223-6510, fax 427-58 and 440-66, $410

IXTAPA

Hotel Posada Real, Paseo Ixtapa s/n, tel. 316-25, 317-45, or (800) 528-1234, fax 318-05, $135

Krystal Ixtapa, Paseo Ixtapa s/n, tel. 303-33, 301-32 or (800) 231-9860, fax 302-16, $205

Hotel Westin Brisas Ixtapa, Paseo de la Roca (P.O. Box 97), tel. 321-21, or (800) 228-3000, fax 307-51, $230

Hotel Dorado Pacífico, Paseo Ixtapa s/n (P.O. Box 15), tel. 320-25, fax 301-26, $280

Hotel Sheraton Ixtapa, Paseo Ixtapa s/n, tel. 318-58, or (800) 325-3535, fax 324-38, $295

rooms, some of which enjoy luxurious private-terrace bay views. Try for an upper-floor beachside room, while avoiding those that front the noisy street. Rooms rent for about $65 s, $70 d high season with view, $60 and $65 without. Low season rates run about $45 s, $50 d with view and $40 s, $45 d without. All rooms have fans, TV, phones, and hot water. Some rooms have a/c at extra cost; credit cards accepted.

Hotel Susy, Guerrero and Alvarez, Zihuatanejo, Guerrero 40880, tel. (755) 423-39, across the street, has three tiers of rooms surrounding a shady inner patio. The seven upper-floor bayside rooms have private view balconies. Inside corridors unfortunately run past room windows, necessitating closing curtains for privacy, a drawback in these fan-only rooms. Avoid traffic noise by requesting an upper-floor room away from the street. The 20 clean but plain rooms go for $15 s, $19 d and $22 t low season, and $18, $23, and $28 high, including fans and hot water.

A better choice, if you don't mind a bit of morning noise from the adjacent school, is the popular **Posada Citlali** ("Star" in Nahuatl), at Guerrero 3, tel. (755) 420-43. The hotel rises in a pair of three-story tiers, around a shady, plant-decorated inner courtyard. The 20 plain, rather small but clean rooms are all thankfully removed from direct street traffic hubbub. Guests on the upper floors have less corridor traffic and consequently enjoy more privacy. Reservations are mandatory during the high winter season and strongly recommended at other times. Rates run about $15 s, $20 d, 22 t low season, $20 s, $25 d and $30 t high, with hot water and fans.

Zihuatanejo Playa Madera Hotels

Another sizable fraction of Zihuatanejo's lodgings spreads along Playa Madera on the east side of the bay, easily reachable during the dry season, by foot from the town plaza, via the scenic beachfront *andador* (walkway). Several hotels cluster on Cerro Madera, the bayside hill just west of town. Due to Zihuatanejo's one-way streets (which fortunately direct most noisy traffic away from downtown), getting to Cerro Madera is a bit tricky. The key is **Plaza Kyoto,** the traffic circle-intersection of Paseo de la Boquita and Paseo del Palmar a quarter mile east of downtown. If you're driving, keep a sharp eye

out and follow the small "Zona Hotelera" signs. At Plaza Kyoto, marked by a big Japanese *torii* gate, bear right across the canal bridge and turn right at the first street. Continue straight ahead for another block to Av. Adelita, the address of several Playa Madera hotels, which runs along the base of Cerro Madera.

By location, moving eastward, start atop Cerro Madera, at **Bungalows Pacífico,** the labor of love of longtime local resident Anita Rellstab Hahner, at Cerro Madera, P.O. Box 12, tel. (755) 421-12. Her guests enjoy six spartan but spacious, art-decorated hillside apartments with broad bay-view patios and complete furnishings, including kitchenettes and daily maid service. Anita, herself an amateur archaeologist, ecologist, birdwatcher, and community leader, is a friendly, forthright, and knowledgeable hostess. She's more than happy to inform other bird and animal-watching enthusiasts of good local viewing spots.

Flower-bedecked and hammock-draped, Anita's retreat is ideal for those seeking quiet relaxation. No matter for lack of a pool; lovely Playa Madera is a short walk down the leafy front slope. Get your reservations in early, especially for winter. The apartments rent for about $50 d, $60 t; with hot water, fans only, and street parking; monthly discount possible during the 1 May-1 Dec. low season; get there via the short street uphill from Av. Adelita.

Several more bungalow complexes cluster a block farther south, along the same rustic-scenic hilltop street. Although their details differ, their basic layouts—which stairstep artfully downhill to private beachfront gardens—are similar. First comes **Bungalows Sotelo,** at Calle Eva Samano de López Mateos 13, Zihuatanejo, Guerrero 40880, tel./fax (755) 463-07. Guests in the clean, thoughtfully designed stucco-and-tile apartments enjoy spacious private or semi-private terraces with deck lounges and sweeping bay views. Rents for the smaller, nonkitchenette units run about $30 d low season, $60 high; larger one- and two-bedroom kitchenette suites rent from about $35 d low season, $70 high. No pool, street parking only, but with a/c; get your winter reservations in early.

Next door but a notch down the economic scale is the aging '60s-modern **Bungalows Allec,** at Cerro Madera, Calle Eva Samano de

The lagoon bridge in Zihuatanejo, though rickety, works just fine.

López Mateos, Zihuatanejo, Guerrero 40880, tel. (755) 445-10 or 420-02. Comfortable, light, and spacious, although a bit tattered, the 12 clean fan-only apartments have hot water and breezy bay views from private balconies. Six of the units are very large, sleeping up to six, with kitchenettes. The others are smaller, nonkitchenette doubles. No pool, but Playa Madera is a few steps downhill. The kitchenette apartments go for about $36 low season, $72 high; the smaller doubles, about $25 low, $45 high. Longer term discounts may be available.

Smaller but similar next door is **Bungalows Ley,** Calle Eva Samano de López Mateos s/n, Playa Madera, P.O. Box 466, Zihuatanejo, Guerrero 40880, tel./fax (755) 445-63 or 440-87, with six white stucco studio apartments that lead directly downhill to heavenly Playa Madera. Although plain and somewhat worn, the furnished apartments, with baths, hot water, basic kitchenettes, and king-size beds, might be just right for your week or month of winter beachside relaxation on a budget. No pool, but the beach is straight down the steps from your door. Fan-only rents run about $33 d, low season and $47 high; with a/c, figure about $45 d low, $70 high.

Perched atop Bungalows Ley, with the same address, but completely separate, is upscale **Casa Leigh y Loros,** the lovely life project of friendly California resident Leigh Roth and her pet parrot, Loros. Casa Leigh y Loros, which Leigh rents when she's away, is a multilevel art-decorated white stucco and tile two-bedroom, two-bath villa, with roof garden, airy bay-view balconies, and '90s-standard kitchen appliances. High winter season (except Christmas) rent runs about $250/day, $1,500/week; during low season, Leigh charges $175/day, $1,150/week. With a/c, fans, TV, daily maid service, and even cooking (at extra charge).

Leigh and her business partner, Oscar Montero, tel./fax (755) 437-17, home 476-26 also rent five smaller but similarly luxurious apartments (from about $95/day, $570/week low season, and $175/day, $1,000/week high) in villa **Casa San Sebastián** on the hillside, a mile away, above Playa La Ropa. For a more economical option, ask Leigh (or Lila as she's known locally) or Oscar about **Casa de Bambu,** which they also rent, across the street from Casa Leigh y Loros. From the U.S., contact Leigh at 2910 Newbury St., Berkeley, CA 94703, tel. (510) 547-2792, or tel. (755) 437-55 in Zihuatanejo.

Two doors away is yet another Cerro Madera option, **Hotel Brisas del Mar,** at Calle Eva Samano de López Mateos s/n, Cerro Madera, Zihuatanejo, Guerrero 40880, tel./fax (755) 421-12 and 478-05. Although the owners have lately brightened the place up with birds, lobby amenities, and potted plants, the bad news is that most of their approximately 20 apartments are each split curiously into a pair of double-bedded alcoves, divided by a swinging door. Amateurishly finished tile floors, tired furnishings, drab shower baths, and very minimal open-air kitchenettes complete the lackluster half of the picture. The bright half is that about eight of the apartments have sweeping bay views overlooking the hotel's lovely beach club, with its shady *palapas,* lounge chairs, and big blue pool adjacent to the excellent Kau Kan beachfront restaurant. This all seems to add to a pretty fair option if you don't plan on spending much time inside. Brisas del Mar rents its apartments for about the same rates as its neighbors: about $35 d with view, $26 d no view low season, $50 and $40 high, with hot water and fans.

Downhill on Av. Adelita is the longtime family-run **Hotel Palacio,** Av. Adelita, Playa Madera, P.O. Box 57, Zihuatanejo, Guerrero 40880, tel. (755) 420-55, fax 431-33, a beachfront maze of rooms connected by meandering, multilevel walkways. Room windows along the two main tiers face corridor walkways, where curtains must be drawn for privacy. Upper units fronting the quiet street avoid this drawback. The rooms themselves are plain, but clean and comfortable, with fans and hot water. Guests enjoy a small but very pleasant bay-view pool and sundeck, which perches above the waves at the hotel beachfront. The 25 rooms rent for about $22 s, $30 d low season, $30 and $35 high; street parking only.

Next door, the **Hotel Villas Miramar,** Playa Madera, Av. Adelita, P.O. Box 211, Zihuatanejo, Guerrero 40880, tel. (755) 421-06 or 426-16, fax 421-49, clusters artfully around gardens of pools, palms, and leafy potted plants. The gorgeous, manicured layout makes maximum use of space, creating both privacy and intimacy in a small setting. The designer rooms have high ceilings, split levels, built-in sofas, and large, comfortable beds. The street divides the hotel into two different but equally lovely sections, each with its own pool. The restaurant, especially convenient for breakfast, is in the shoreside section, but still serves guests who sun and snooze around the luxurious, beach-view pool patio garden on the other side of the street. The 16 rooms rent for about $40 d low season, $55 high; with phones and a/c; credit cards accepted; additional discounts may be available during May-June and Sept.-Oct. low seasons. Reservations strongly recommended during the winter season.

The **Hotel Irma,** Av. Adelita, Playa Madera, Zihuatanejo, Guerrero 40880, tel./fax (755) 437-38, half a block farther uphill, is a favorite for longtime

lovers of Zihuatanejo, if for no reason other than its location. Although details are not the Irma's strong suit, the basics are there: comfortable (although not too clean) rooms, a passably pleasant sunset-view terrace restaurant and bar, and a pair of blue pools perched above the bay. A short walk downhill and you're at beautiful Madera beach. Best of all, most of the simply furnished rooms have private balconies with just about the loveliest view on Playa Madera. (Note: A next-door disco with booming bass pulsates from the Irma's adjacent southside walls weekends till midnight; if this concerns you, best ask if it's still operating before moving in.) The 70 rooms rent, low season, for about $45 s or d with a/c, $40 without, $70 and $60 high season, with TV and hot water.

Nearby, a couple of blocks off the beach, is the downscale but homey **Bungalows El Milagro,** Av. Marina Nacional s/n, P.O. Box 71, Playa Madera, Zihuatanejo, Guerrero 40880, tel. (755) 430-45, the project of local Dr. Niklaus Bührer and his wife Lucina Gomes. A hacienda-like walled compound of cottages and apartments clustering around a shady pool, the Bungalows El Milagro is winter headquarters for a cordial group of German longtime returnees. The friendly atmosphere and the inviting pool/garden account for the El Milagro's success, rather than the plain but clean kitchenette lodgings, which vary in style from rustic to 1940s motel. Look at several before you choose. The 17 units rent, high season, between about $30/day ($500/month) for two for the smaller to about $50/day ($900/month) for the larger, six-person suite. All with kitchenettes, hot water, fans, and parking.

A few hundred yards farther south along the Paseo Costera is **La Casa Que Canta,** Camino Escénico a Playa La Ropa, Zihuatanejo, Guerrero 40880, tel. (755) 470-30, fax 470-40, which is as much a work of art as a hotel. The pageant begins at the lobby, a luxurious soaring *palapa* that angles gracefully down the cliffside to an intimate open air view dining-room. Suite-clusters of natural adobe sheltered by thick *palapa* roofs cling artfully to the craggy precipice decorated with riots of bougainvillea and gardens of cactus. From petite pool terraces perched above foamy shoals, guests enjoy a radiant aqua bay panorama in the morning and brilliant ridge-silhouetted sunsets in the evening.

The 18 art-bedecked, rustic-chic suites, all with private view balconies, come in two grades: spacious "grand suites" and even larger versions with their own small pools. Rentals run about $340 and $550 s or d high season, $265 and $415 low, with a/c, fan, phone, no TV, and no kids under 16. Make winter reservations very early; from the U.S. and Canada, call (888) 523-5050, or from Mexico, (800) 093-45.

Zihuatanejo Playa La Ropa and Playa Las Gatas Hotels

The beginning of luscious Playa La Ropa is marked by the twin **Hotels Sotavento and Catalina,** P.O. Box 2, Zihuatanejo, Guerrero 40880, tel. (755) 420-32 or 420-24, fax 429-75, which perch together on a leafy hillside above the beach. Good management by the owners, a savvy husband-wife team, keeps the rambling complex healthy. The two hotels differ markedly. The Sotavento is a 70-room mod-style warren that stairsteps five stories down the slope. Each floor of rooms opens to a broad, hammock-hung communal terrace overlooking the beach and bay. By contrast, the Hotel Catalina's 30 cabañas lie scattered beneath shady hillside trees all the way down to the beach. A pair of restaurants, a mediocre breakfast-lunch cafeteria at the beach level, and a fancier dinner restaurant upstairs service the guests, many on vacation packages.

The Sotavento's rooms are '60s modern, clean and comfortable, opening onto the view terrace, with king- or queen-size beds and ceiling fans. The Catalina's comfortably appointed tropical-rustic cabañas are more private, being separate units with individual view terraces and hammocks. At the bottom of the hill, the hotel aquatics shop offers sailing, windsurfing, snorkeling, and other rentals; those who want to rest enjoy chairs beneath the shady boughs of a beachside grove. Standard rooms rent during low season for $64 s, $70 d, deluxe terrace suites $72 s, $88 d, and deluxe bungalows $87. A few small "student" units rent for about $53; rates about 20% higher during winter high season; no pool, fans only, parking, credit cards accepted.

A dozen-odd hotels, bungalow complexes, and restaurants spread along La Ropa Beach. The **Hotel Villa Mexicana,** Playa La Ropa, Zihuatanejo, Guerrero 40880, tel. (755) 437-76 or 436-36, seems to be popular for nothing more than its stunning location right in the middle of the sunny beach hubbub. Its 60 rooms, in low-rise stucco clusters, while comfortable and air-conditioned, are (like the entire hotel) neither fancy nor particularly tidy. This, however, doesn't seem to bother the mostly North American winter package-vacation clientele, who jet ski, parasail, and boogie board from the beach, snooze around the pool, and socialize beneath the *palapa* of the beachside restaurant. Asking low season rates for standard rooms are $56 d, $68 for room with private view balcony, $75 for view with jacuzzi; corresponding high season rates are about $84, $102, and $112. With parking; credit cards accepted.

Up the street a few steps, a stone's throw from the beach, **Villas Ema** perches at the top of a homey hillside garden. Here, the enterprising husband-wife owners of downtown Posada Citlali have built six new, simply but thoughtfully furnished apartments adjacent to their family home. Amenities include fans, hot water, and private hill-view balconies and the murmur of the waves on Playa La Ropa a block away. Rates are about $45 d low season, $65 high. For reservations, highly recommended in winter, contact the owners through Posada Citlali, Av. Guerrero 3, Zihuatanejo, Guerrero 40880, tel. (755) 420-43, or at home (in Spanish) tel. 448-80. To avoid confusion, be sure to specify your reservation is for Villas Ema.

German expatriate Helmut Leins sold out in Munich and came to create paradise on Playa La Ropa in 1978. The result is Playa La Ropa's luxury **Hotel Villa del Sol,** Playa La Ropa, P.O. Box 84, Zihuatanejo, Guerrero 40880, tel. (755) 422-39 or 432-39, (800) 223-6510 from the U.S. and Canada, fax 427-58 and 440-66. Here, in Helmut's exquisite beachside mini-Eden, a corps of well-to-do North American, European, and Mexican clients return yearly to enjoy tranquillity and the elegance of the Villa del Sol's crystal-blue pools, palm-draped patios, and classic *palapas.* The lodgings themselves are spacious, with shining floor tile, handcrafted wall art, tropical-canopy beds, and private hammock-hung patios. The plethora of extras includes a restaurant, bars, pools, night tennis courts, a newsstand, boutique, beauty salon, and meeting room for about 30 people. The approximately 50 accommodations begin at $235 s or d, low season, $410 high. Super-plush options include more bedrooms and baths, ocean views, and jacuzzis for $585 and up; with a/c and parking. Credit cards accepted, but no children under 14 are allowed during the winter.

A pair of good housekeeping bungalow-type lodgings share the same luxuriously lovely beachfront as the Hotel Villas del Sol, but at greatly reduced prices. First comes **Bungalows Vepao,** address simply Playa La Ropa, Zihuatanejo, Guerrero 40880; reserve by calling either owner Gonzalo Ramírez, tel. (755) 420-55, or manager Margarita Castro, tel. (755) 426-31. Here they have created your basic clean and pleasant beach lodging, simply but architecturally designed, with floor-to ceiling drapes, modern-standard kitchenettes, tiled floors, shower baths, white stucco walls, and pastel bedspreads and shaded lamps. Guests in each apartment enjoy front patios (upper ones have some bay view) that lead right to the hotel's private beachfront row of *palapas* a few steps away. Rates run about $36 d low season, $60 high, with long-term discounts possible.

Nearby, but as distinct as day from night, is **Bungalows Urracas,** about 15 petite brick houses, like proper rubber planter's bungalows out of Somerset Maugham's *Malaysian Stories,* nestling in a shady jungle of leafy plants, trees, and vines. Inside, the illusion continues: dark, masculine wood furniture, spacious bedrooms, shiny tiled kitchenettes and baths, and overhead, rustic beamed ceilings. From the bungalows, short "jungle" paths lead to the brilliant La Ropa beachfront. Amenities include private, shady front porches (use insect repellent evenings), hot water, and fans. Rentals run about $50 d low season, $60 high. Ask for a long-term discount. Get your winter reservations in early. Write Bungalows Urracas, Playa La Ropa, Zihuatanejo, Guerrero 40880, or call (755) 420-49.

Ixtapa Hotels

Ixtapa's dozen-odd hotels line up in a luxurious strip between the beach and boulevard Paseo Ixtapa. Among the most reasonably priced is the Best Western **Hotel Posada Real,** Paseo Ixtapa s/n, Ixtapa, Guerrero 40880, tel. (755) 316-25, 317-45, fax 318-05, tel. (800) 528-1234 from the U.S. and Canada, at Paseo Ixtapa's far west end. Get there via the street, beach side, just past the Lighthouse Restaurant. With a large grassy football field instead of tennis courts, the hotel attracts a seasonal following of soccer enthusiasts. Other amenities include three restaurants (one of them the attractive Los Cocos), two pools, and a disco. The 110 smallish rooms are clean and comfortable, but lack ocean views. Rooms rent for about $77 d low season, $135 high, often with big discounts for longer stays. Kids under 12 with parents are free; with a/c, satellite TV, phones, and parking; credit cards accepted.

Nearer the middle of the hotel zone, the Mexican-owned **Krystal Ixtapa,** Paseo Ixtapa s/n, Ixtapa, Guerrero 40880, tel. (755) 303-33, 301-32, fax 302-16, tel. (800) 231-9860 from the U.S. and Canada, towers over its spacious garden compound. Its innovative wedge design ensures an ocean view from each room. A continuous round of activities—a Ping-Pong tournament, handicrafts and cooking classes, and aerobics and scuba lessons—fills the days, while buffets, theme parties, and dancing fill the nights. Unscheduled relaxation centers on the blue pool, where guests enjoy watching each other slip from the water slide and duck beneath the waterfall all day. The 260 tastefully appointed deluxe rooms and suites have private view balconies, satellite TV, a/c, and phones. Rooms rent from $175 d low season, about $205 high. Check for additional discounts through extended-stay or other packages. Extras include tennis courts, racquetball, an exercise gym, parking, and wheelchair access; credit cards accepted.

If the Krystal is full, try the nearly-as-good **Hotel Dorado Pacífico,** Paseo Ixtapa s/n, P.O. Box 15, Ixtapa, Guerrero 40880, tel. (755) 320-25, fax 301-26, next door. Although fewer organized activities fill the day, three palm-shaded blue pools, water slides, a swim-up bar, and three restaurant/bars seem to keep guests happy. Upstairs, the rooms, all with sea-view balconies, are pleasingly decorated with sky-blue carpets and earth-tone designer bedspreads. The 285 rooms rent from $140 d low season, $280 high, with a/c, phones, and TV; low season and extended-stay discounts may be available. Extras include tennis courts, parking, and wheelchair access; credit cards accepted.

The **Hotel Sheraton Ixtapa,** Paseo Ixtapa s/n, Ixtapa, Guerrero 40880, tel. (755) 318-58, fax 324-38, (800) 325-3535 from the U.S. and Canada, across from the golf course at the east end of the beach, rises around a soaring lobby/atrium. A worthy member of the worldwide Sheraton chain, the Sheraton Ixtapa serves its mostly American clientele with complete resort facilities, including pools, all sports, an exercise gym, several restaurants and bars, cooking and arts lessons, nightly dancing, and a Fiesta Mexicana. The 332 rooms in standard (which include mountain-view balconies only), ocean view, and junior suite grades, are spacious and tastefully furnished in designer pastels and include a/c, phones, and satellite TV. Standard rooms run about $210 d low season, $295 high; deluxe from $270 d low season, $410 high; with parking, credit cards accepted, and wheelchair access. Low season promotional packages can run as low as $110 d, however.

From the adjacent jungly hilltop, the **Hotel Westin Brisas Ixtapa,** Paseo de la Roca, P.O. Box 97, Ixtapa, Guerrero 40880, tel. (755) 321-21, or (800) 228-3000 from the U.S. and Canada, fax 307-51, slopes downhill to the shore like a latter-day Aztec pyramid. The monumentally stark hilltop lobby, open and unadorned except for a clutch of huge stone balls, contrasts sharply with its surroundings. The hotel's severe lines immediately shift the focus to the adjacent jungle. The fecund forest aroma wafts into the lobby and terrace restaurant, where, at breakfast, during the winter and early spring guests sit watching iguanas munch hibiscus blossoms in the nearby treetops.

The hotel entertains guests with a wealth of luxurious resort facilities, including pools, four tennis courts, a gym, aerobics, an intimate shoal-enfolded beach, restaurants, bars, and nightly live dance music. The standard rooms, each with its own spacious view patio, are luxuriously spartan, floored with big designer tiles, furnished in earth tones and equipped with big TVs, small refrigerators, phones, and a/c. More luxurious options include suites with individual pools and jacuzzis. The 427 rooms begin at about $200 for a standard low-season double, $230 high, and run about twice that for super-luxury suites. June-Oct., bargain packages can run as low as $110 d per night.

Trailer Parks and Camping

Ixtapa-Zihuatanejo has one small, very basic trailer park. At south-end **Trailer Park Las Cabañas,** a block from La Ropa Beach, P.O. Box 197, Zihuatanejo, Guerrero 40880, tel. (755) 447-18, you can find out what it's like to park or camp in someone's shady back yard. Friendly, retired owner-managers María Elena and Hernán Cabañas, in order to make ends meet, decided to rent out their front and back yards. The result is enough space for a dozen tents or four medium-sized RVs in back, and one in front, with electricity, water, showers, and toilets. The price is certainly right: about $7/day for small RVs, tents about $3 per person, and it's only a block from one of the loveliest resort beaches in Pacific Mexico.

If Trailer Park Las Cabañas is too small for you, go to El Burro Borracho at Playa Troncones. See **Playa Majagua and Playa Troncones,** at the end of the preceding chapter.

House, Apartment, and Condo Rentals

Zihuatanejo residents sometimes offer their condos and homes for temporary lease through agents. Among the better known is **Elizabeth Williams,** a longtime local realtor. Contact her at P.O. Box 169, Zihuatanejo, Guerrero 40880, tel. (755) 426-06, fax 447-62, for a list of possible rentals.

Also, **O.J.B. Real Estate,** tel. (755) 426-13 (contact Julia), in Zihuatanejo is helpful in finding rentals.

For other rental options, contact Leigh Roth, who divides her time between her California (tel. 510-547-2792) and Zihuatanejo (tel. 755-437-55) homes.

FOOD

Snacks, Bakeries, and Breakfasts

For something cool in **Zihuatanejo,** stop by the **Paletería y Nevería Michoacana** ice shop across from the plaza. Besides ice cream, popcorn, and safe *nieves* (ices) it offers delicious *aguas* (fruit-flavored drinks, 50 cents), which make nourishing, refreshing Pepsi-free alternatives.

The **Panadería Francesa** bakery, tel. (755) 427-42, four short blocks up Cuauhtémoc from the beach, turns out a daily acre of fresh goodies, from *pan integral* (whole wheat) and black bread loaves to doughnuts and rafts of Mexican-style cakes, cookies, and tarts. It's open daily 7 a.m.-9 p.m., on C. González, corner of Galeana, the lane paralleling Cuauhtémoc.

Tasty, promptly served breakfasts are the specialty of the downtown **Cafetería Nova Zelandia** on Cuauhtémoc, corner of Ejido. Favorites include hotcakes, eggs any style, fruit, juices, and espresso coffee. Nova Zelandia serves lunch and supper also. Open daily 8 a.m.-10 p.m.

For hot sandwiches and good pizza on the downtown beach, try the **Cafe Marina** on Paseo del Pescador, just west of the plaza. The friendly, hardworking owner features a spaghetti party—either bolognesa, pesto, or primavera—Wednesday night and chili Friday. The shelves of books for lending or exchange are nearly as popular as the food. Open Mon.-Sat. noon-10 p.m., closed approximately June to mid-September.

A local vacation wouldn't be complete without dropping in to the **Sirena Gorda** ("Fat Mermaid"), Thurs.-Tues. 7 a.m.-10 p.m., tel. (755) 426-87, near the end of Paseo del Pescador across from the naval compound. Here the fishing crowd relaxes, trading stories after a tough day hauling in the lines. The other unique attractions, besides the well-endowed sea nymphs who decorate the walls, are tempting shrimp-bacon and fish tacos, juicy hamburgers, fish *mole,* and conch and *nopal* (cactus leaves, minus the spines) plates.

In **Ixtapa,** the **Cafe Toko Tucán** offers a refreshing alternative to hotel breakfasts. White cockatoos and bright toucans in a leafy patio add an exotic touch as you enjoy the fare, which, besides the usual juices, eggs, hotcakes, and French toast, includes lots of salads, veggie burgers, and sandwiches. Open daily 9 a.m.-10 p.m., tel. (755) 307-17, on the west front corner of the Los Patios shopping complex, across the boulevard from Hotel Aristos.

The perfume wafting from freshly baked European-style yummies draws dozens of the faithful to the nearby **German Bakery,** tel. (755) 303-10, brainchild of local longtimers Helmut and Esther Walter. He, a German, and she, an East Indian from Singapore, satisfy homesick palates with a continuous supply of scrumptious cinnamon rolls, pies, and hot buns. Open daily 8 a.m.-2 p.m. (closed low season approximately Sept.-

Oct.), on the inner patio, upper floor of the Los Patios shopping complex.

Zihuatanejo Restaurants

Local chefs and restaurateurs, long accustomed to foreign tastes, operate a number of good local restaurants, mostly in Zihuatanejo (where, in contrast to Ixtapa, most of the serious eating occurs *outside* of hotel dining rooms). Note, however, that a number of the best restaurants are closed during low season months of September and October.

All trails seem to lead to the **Deli Cafe,** on Cuauhtémoc a block from the plaza. Here the atmosphere is refined but friendly, and the food—including meatloaf and mashed potatoes, hot dogs, fettuccine, pepper steak, rosemary chicken, omelettes, lots of salads, and a number of veggie options—is worth the price. Open daily 8 a.m.-10 p.m. (closed Sept.-Oct.); credit cards accepted. Moderate.

Zihuatanejo has a pair of good, genuinely local-style restaurants in the downtown area. **Tamales y Atoles "Any,"** tel. (755) 473-03, Zihuatanejo's clean, well-lighted place for Mexican food, is the spot to find out if your favorite Mexican restaurant back home is serving the real thing. Tacos, tamales, quesadillas, enchiladas, *chiles rellenos,* and such goodies are called *antojitos* in Mexico. At Tamales y Atoles "Any," they're savory enough to please even demanding Mexican palates. Open Wed.-Mon. 7 a.m.-10 p.m., corner Guerrero and Ejido. Budget-moderate. Incidentally, "Any" (AH-nee) is the co-owner, whose perch is behind the cash register, while her friendly husband cooks and tends the tables.

Restaurant Los Braseros, half a block along Ejido, at Ejido 21, between Cuauhtémoc and Guerrero, tel. (755) 448-58, is similarly authentic and popular. Waiters are often busy after midnight even during low season serving seven kinds of tacos and specialties such as Gringa, Porky, and Azteca from a menu it would take three months of dinners (followed by a six-month diet) to fully investigate. Open daily 4 p.m.-1 a.m. Moderate.

Casa Elvira, on Paseo del Pescador, by the naval compound, tel. (755) 420-61, founded long ago by now-octogenarian Elvira Campos, is as popular as ever, still satisfying the palates of a battalion of loyal Zihuatanejo longtimers. Elvi-

Fresh fruit is among the big bargains at the Zihuatanejo mercado.

ra's continuing popularity is easy to explain: a palm-studded beachfront, strumming guitars, whirling ceiling fans, and a list of super-fresh salads, soups, fish, meat and Mexican specialties, expertly prepared and professionally served. Open daily 1-10 p.m.; reservations recommended during the high season. Moderate.

If Elvira's is full, a good alternative is relative newcomer **Canaima,** tel. (755) 420-03, which shares the same scenic beach-view *paseo.* Soft music, super fresh fish, and a luscious Mexican plate draw a loyal local and tourist following. Open daily 1-11 p.m. (closed Sept.-Oct.). Moderate.

Walk away from the beach two blocks along the crafts market street, Cinco de Mayo, to **Paul's,** tel. (755) 480-63, where Swiss Chef Paul Karrer has attracted a following with palate-pleasing specialties such as spaghetti with shrimp and mussels, pork chops with new potatoes, artichokes, and quail grilled with wine and herb sauce. Open daily for lunch and dinner (closed Sept.-Oct.). Moderate.

No guide to Zihuatanejo restaurants is complete without mention of **Coconuts** restaurant, on Guerrero, half a block from Alvarez, across from Posada Citlali, tel. (755) 425-18. Here, the food, although good, appears to be of lesser importance than its airy garden setting and good cheer generated among the droves of Zihuatanejo longtimers who return year after year. Open daily in season noon to midnight; closed approximately July-October. Expensive.

Restaurant Kau Kan, right on Playa Madera, tel. (755) 421-42 or 484-46, has become the rage for both its romantic beachside location and its excellent food and service. While guitar music plays softly and waves murmur against the sand, waiters scurry, bringing savory appetizers, romaine Caesar salad, and cooked-to-perfection mahimahi, lobster, steak, and shrimp. Open daily noon-6 p.m. and 7 p.m.-midnight; high-season reservations mandatory, closed Sept.-October. Expensive.

Ixtapa Restaurants

Restaurants in Ixtapa have to be exceptional to compete with the hotels. One such, the **Belle Vista,** tel. (755) 321-21, *is* in a hotel, being the Westin Ixtapa's view-terrace café. Breakfast is the favorite time to watch the antics of the iguanas in the adjacent jungle treetops. These black, green, and white miniature dinosaurs crawl up and down the trunks, munch flowers, and sunbathe on the branches. The food and service, incidentally, are quite good. Open daily 7 a.m.-11 p.m. Call ahead to reserve a terrace-edge table; credit cards accepted. Moderate-expensive.

The **Hacienda de Ixtapa,** tel. (755) 306-02, right on Paseo Ixtapa just south of the police station, offers good food and service in an airy patio setting. Fruit plate, eggs any style, and hotcakes breakfasts run about $2 each, while fish fillet, T-bone, and lobster dinners are similarly reasonable and tasty. Open daily 7 a.m.-11 p.m.; credit cards accepted. Moderate.

Those hankering for Italian-style pastas and seafood head to **Ristorante Da Baffone,** at the back side of the La Puerta shopping complex on Paseo Ixtapa, tel. (755) 311-22. The friendly owner, a native of the Italian isle of Sardinia, claims his restaurant is the oldest establishment in Ixtapa. He's probably right: he served his first meal here in 1978, simultaneous with the opening of Ixtapa's first hotel, right across the boulevard. While Mediterranean-Mex decor covers the walls, marinara-style shrimp and clams with linguini, calamari, ricotta and spinach-stuffed cannelloni, and glasses of Chianti and chardonnay load the tables. Open daily about noon-midnight during high season; call for reservations. Moderate-expensive.

Other Ixtapa restaurants, also popular for their party atmosphere, are described below.

ENTERTAINMENT AND EVENTS

In Zihuatanejo, visitors and residents content themselves mostly with quiet pleasures. Afternoons, they stroll the beachfront or the downtown shady lanes and enjoy coffee or drinks with friends at small cafés and bars. As the sun goes down however, folks head to Ixtapa for its sunset vistas, happy hours, shows, clubs, and dancing.

Sunsets
Sunsets are tranquil and often magnificent from the **Restaurant/Bar El Faro,** tel. (755) 310-27, which even has a cableway, south end of the Ixtapa beach, open 7 a.m.-7 p.m., leading to it. Many visitors stay to enjoy dinner and the relaxing piano bar. Open daily around 5:30-10 p.m.; reservations recommended winter and weekends. Drive or taxi via the uphill road toward the Westin Brisas Ixtapa at the golf course; at the first fork, head right for El Faro.

For equally brilliant sunsets in a lively setting, try either the lobby bar or Belle Vista terrace restaurant at the **Westin Brisas Ixtapa.** Lobby bar happy hour runs 6-7 p.m.; live music begins around 7:30 p.m. Drive or taxi, following the signs, along the uphill road at the golf course, following the signs to the crest of the hill just south of the Ixtapa beach.

The west-side headland blocks most Zihuatanejo sunset views, except for spots at the far end of Playa La Ropa. Here, guests at the longtime favorite **Restaurant La Perla,** open 4-10 p.m., tel. (755) 487-00, and especially **Restaurant Gaviota,** tel. (755) 438-16, at the opposite, inner, end of the beach, delight in Zihuatanejo's most panoramic of sunset vistas.

Sunset and Sunshine Cruises
Those who want to experience a sunset party while at sea ride the trimaran *Tri Star,* which leaves from the Zihuatanejo pier around 5 p.m. daily, returning around 7:30 p.m. The tariff runs about $40 per person, including open bar.

The *Tri Star* also heads out daily on a Sunshine Cruise around 10 a.m., returning around 4:30 p.m. Included are open bar, lunch, and snorkeling, for about $50 per person. Book tickets for both of these cruises, which include transportation to and from your hotel, through a hotel travel agent, such as American Express, tel. (755) 308-53, at Hotel Krystal in Ixtapa. Tickets are also available at the *Tri Star* office, tel. (755) 426-94, at Puerto Mío, the small marina about half a mile across the bay from town. Get there via the road that curves around the western, right-hand shore of Zihuatanejo Bay.

Movies
Head over to the petite **Cine Paraíso,** on Cuauhtémoc, three blocks from the beach in downtown Zihuatanejo, to escape into American pop, romantic comedy, and adventure.

Tourist Shows
Ixtapa hotels regularly stage **Fiesta Mexicana** extravaganzas, which begin with a sumptuous buffet and go on to a whirling skirt-and-sombrero folkloric ballet. Afterward, the audience usually gets involved with piñatas, games, cockfights, dancing, and continuous drinks from an open bar. In the finale, fireworks often boom over the beach, painting the night sky in festoons of reds, blues, and greens.

Entrance runs about $25-35 per person, with kids under 12 usually half price. Shows (seasonally only) at the **Presidente,** tel. (755) 300-18; Tuesdays at the **Dorado Pacífico,** tel. (755) 320-25; and Wednesday at the **Sheraton,** tel. (755) 318-58, are the most reliable and popular.

Usually open to the public; call ahead for confirmation and reservations.

Clubs and Hangouts

Part restaurant and part wacky seasonal nightspot, the **Restaurant-Bar Cocos,** tel. (755) 316-85, at Ixtapa's Hotel Posada Real offers hamburgers and seafood in a Robinson Crusoe-chic setting. Patrons recline in ceiling-hung chairs, while waiters try to outdo each other's zany tricks, and lively tropical music bounces out of the speakers. Open daily 7 a.m.-11 p.m.

Next door, **Carlos'n Charlie's,** tel. (755) 300-85, is as wild and as much fun as all of the other Carlos Anderson restaurants from Puerto Vallarta to Paris. Here in Ixtapa you can have your picture taken on a surfboard in front of a big wave for $3, or have a fireman spray out the flames from the chili sauce on your palate. You can also enjoy the food, which, if not fancy, is innovative and tasty. Loud rock music ($10 minimum) goes on 10 p.m.-4 a.m. during the winter season. The restaurant serves daily noon-midnight. Located on the beachfront about half a block on the driveway road west past the Hotel Posada Real.

Dancing and Discoing

Nearly all Ixtapa hotel lobbies blossom with dance music from around 7 p.m. during the high winter season. Year-round, however, good medium-volume groups usually play for dancing nightly 7:30 p.m.-midnight at the **Westin,** tel. (755) 321-21; the **Sheraton,** tel. (755) 318-58; and the **Krystal,** tel. (755) 303-33, lobby bars.

Christine, Ixtapa's big-league discotheque in the Hotel Krystal, offers fantasy for a mere $6 cover charge. From 10 p.m., the patrons warm up by listening to relatively low-volume rock, watch videos, and talk while they can still hear each other. That stops around 11:30 p.m., when the fogs descend, the lights begin flashing, and the speakers boom forth their 200-decibel equivalent of a fast freight roaring at trackside. Call to verify times, tel. (755) 303-33.

SPORTS AND RECREATION

Walking and Jogging

Zihuatanejo Bay is strollable from the Playa Madera all the way west to Puerto Mío. A relaxing half-day adventure could begin by taxiing to the Hotel Irma, Av. Adelita, on Playa Madera, for breakfast. Don your hats and follow the stairs down to Playa Madera and walk west toward town. At the end of the Playa Madera sand, head left along the **andador** walkway that twists along the rocks, around the bend toward town. Continue along the beachfront Paseo del Pescador; at the west end, cross the lagoon bridge, head left along the bayside road to **Puerto Mío** for a drink at the hotel café and perhaps a dip in the pool. Allow three hours, including breakfast, for this two-mile walk; do the reverse trip during late afternoon for sunset drinks or dinner at the Irma.

Playa del Palmar, Ixtapa's main beach, is good for similar strolls. Start in the morning with breakfast at the Restaurant/Bar El Faro, tel. (755) 310-27, atop the hill at the south end of the beach; open daily 6-11 a.m., 6-10 p.m. Ride the cableway or walk downhill. With the sun at your back stroll the beach, stopping for refreshments at the hotel pool patios en route. The entire beach stretches about three miles to the marina jetty, where you can often watch surfers challenging the waves and where taxis and buses return along Paseo Ixtapa. Allow about four hours, including breakfast. The reverse walk would be equally enjoyable during the afternoon. Time yourself to arrive at the El Faro cableway (call ahead, tel. 755-310-27, to make sure the cableway is running) about half an hour before sundown to enjoy the sunset over drinks or dinner. Get to El Faro by driving or taxiing via Paseo de la Roca, which heads uphill off the Zihuatanejo road at the golf course. Follow the first right fork to El Faro.

Adventurers who enjoy ducking through underbrush and scrambling over rocks might enjoy exploring the acacia forest and pristine beaches of the uninhabited west side of **Isla Ixtapa.** Take water, lunch, and a good pair of walking shoes.

Joggers often practice their art either on the smooth, firm sands of Ixtapa's main beachfront or on Paseo Ixtapa's sidewalks. Best avoid crowds and midday heat by jogging early mornings or late afternoons. For even better beach jogging, try the flat, firm sands of uncrowded Playa Quieta about three miles by car or taxi northwest of Ixtapa. Additionally, mile-long Playa La Ropa can be enjoyed by early morning and late afternoon joggers.

Golf and Tennis

Ixtapa's 18-hole, professionally designed **Campo de Golf** is open to the public. In addition to its manicured, 6,898-yard course, patrons enjoy full facilities, including pool, restaurant, pro shop, lockers, and tennis courts. Greens fee runs $45, cart $25, club rental $20, 18 holes with caddy $16, and golf lessons $20 an hour. Play goes on daily 7 a.m.-7 p.m. The clubhouse, tel. (755) 310-62, is off Paseo Ixtapa, across from the Sheraton. No reservations are accepted; morning golfers, get in line early during the high winter season.

The **Marina Golf Course,** tel. (755) 314-10, 314-24, offers similar services (greens fee $73, cart $68 for two, club rental $25, caddy $20) for higher prices.

Ixtapa has nearly all of the local **tennis** courts, all of them private. The Campo de Golf (see above) has some of the best. Rentals run about $6/hour days, $8 nights. Reservations, tel. (755) 310-62, may be seasonally necessary. A pro shop rents and sells equipment. Teaching professional Luis Valle offers lessons for about $17 per hour.

Several hotels also have tennis courts, equipment, and lessons. Call the **Sheraton,** tel. (755) 318-58); **Dorado Pacífico,** tel. (755) 320-25; **Krystal,** tel. (755) 303-33; and the **Westin,** tel. (755) 321-21, for information.

Horseback Riding

Rancho Playa Linda on Playa Linda rents horses daily for beach riding for about $15 per hour. Travel agencies and hotels offer the same, though for considerably higher prices.

Swimming and Surfing

Calm Zihuatanejo Bay is fine for swimming and sometimes good for boogie boarding and bodysurfing at Playa Madera. On Playa La Ropa, however, waves generally break too near shore for either bodysurfing or boogie boarding. Surfing is generally good at Playa Las Gatas, where swells sweeping around the point give good, rolling left-handed breaks.

Heading northwest to more open coast, waves improve for bodysurfing and boogie boarding along Ixtapa's main beach **Playa del Palmar,** while usually remaining calm and undertow-free enough for swimming beyond the breakers. As for surfing, good breaks sometimes rise off the Playa Escolleros jetty at the west end of Playa del Palmar.

Along Ixtapa's outer beaches, swimming is great along very calm Playa Quieta, while surfing, bodysurfing, and boogie boarding are correspondingly good, but hazardous in the sometimes mountainous surf of farther north Playa Larga.

Snorkeling and Scuba Diving

Clear offshore waters (sometimes up to 100-foot visibility during the Nov.-May dry season) have drawn a steady flow of divers and nurtured professionally staffed and equipped dive shops. Just offshore, good snorkeling and scuba spots, where swarms of multicolored fish graze and glide among rocks and corals, are accessible from **Playa Las Gatas, Playa Hermosa,** and **Playa Carey** (on Isla Ixtapa).

Many boat operators take parties for offshore snorkeling excursions. On Playa La Ropa, contact the aquatics shop at the foot of the hill beneath Hotel Sotavento. Playa Las Gatas, easily accessible by boat for $2 from the Zihuatanejo pier, also has snorkel and excursion boat rentals. In Ixtapa, similar services are available at beachside shops at the Westin Brisas Ixtapa, Sheraton, Krystal, and seasonally at other hotels.

Other even more spectacular offshore sites, such as Morros de Potosí, El Yunque, Bajo de Chato, Bajo de Torresillas, Piedra Soletaria, and Sacramento, are accessible with the help of professional guides and instructors.

A pair of local scuba dive shops stands out. In downtown Zihuatanejo, marine biologist-instructor Juan M. Barnard Avila coordinates his **Zihuatanejo Scuba Center,** at Cuauhtémoc 3, Zihuatanejo, Guerrero 40880, tel./fax (755) 421-47, e-mail: divemexico@mail.com. Licensed for instruction through NAUI (National Association of Underwater Instructors), Avila is among Pacific Mexico's best-qualified professional instructors. Aided by loads of state-of-the-art equipment and several experienced licensed assistants, his shop has accumulated a long list of repeat customers.

Avila's standard resort dive package, including a morning pool instruction session and an afternoon offshore half-hour dive, runs about $70 per person ($60 with your own gear) complete.

Other services for beginners include open-water certification (one week of instruction, $450) and advanced NAUI certification up to assistant instructor. For certified divers (bring your certificate), Avila offers night, shipwreck, deep-water, and marine-biology dives at more than three dozen coastal sites. The dive shop is open Mon.-Sat. 8 a.m.-8 p.m.

Carlo Scuba, at Playa Las Gatas, also offers professional scuba services. The PADI-trained instructors offer a resort course, including one beach dive, for $50; a five-day open-water certification course, $400; and a two-tank dive trip for certified participants, $65, one-tank $45. They also conduct student referral courses and night dives. Contact the manager-owner, friendly Jean-Claude Duran, on Las Gatas beach, tel. (755) 435-70, fax 428-10, e-mail: carloscuba@yahoo.com.

Sailing, Windsurfing, and Kayaking

The tranquil waters of Zihuatanejo Bay, Ixtapa's Playa del Palmar, and the quiet strait off Playa Quieta are good for these low-power aquatic sports. Shops on Playa La Ropa (at Hotel Sotavento and Catalina) in Zihuatanejo Bay and in front of Ixtapa hotels, such as the Westin Brisas Ixtapa, the Sheraton, and the Krystal, rent small sailboats, sailboards, and sea kayaks hourly.

Fishing

Surf or rock casting with bait or lures, depending on conditions, is generally successful in local waters. Have enough line to allow casting beyond the waves (about 50 feet out on Playa La Ropa, 100 feet on Playa del Palmar and Playa Linda).

The rocky ends of Playas La Ropa, Madera, del Palmar, and Cuata on the mainland, and Playa Carey on Isla Ixtapa are also good for casting.

For deep-sea fishing, you can launch your own boat (see below) or rent one. *Pangas* are available for rent from individual fishermen on the beach, the boat cooperative (see below) at Zihuatanejo pier, or aquatics shops of the Hotel Sotavento on Playa La Ropa or the Hotels Westin Brisas Ixtapa, Sheraton, Krystal, and others on the beach in Ixtapa. Rental for a seaworthy *panga,* including tackle and bait, should run $15-

20 per hour, depending upon the season and your bargaining skill. An experienced boatman can help you and your friends hook, typically, six or eight big fish, which local restaurants are often willing to serve as a small banquet for you in return for your extra fish.

Big-Game Sportfishing

Zihuatanejo has long been a center for billfish (marlin, swordfish, and sailfish) hunting. Most local captains have organized themselves into cooperatives, which visitors can contact either directly or through town or hotel travel agents. Trips begin around 7 a.m. and return 2-3 p.m. Fishing success depends on seasonal conditions. If you're not sure of your prospects, go down to the Zihuatanejo pier around 2:30 p.m. and see what the boats are bringing in. During good times they often return with one or more big marlin or swordfish per boat (although captains are increasingly asking that billfish be set free after the battle has been won). Although fierce fighters, the sinewy billfish do not make the best eating and are often discarded after the pictures are taken. On average, boats bring in two or three other large fish, such as *dorado* (dolphinfish or mahimahi), yellowfin tuna, and roosterfish, all more highly prized for the dinner table.

The biggest local sportfishing outfitter is the blue-and-white fleet of the **Sociedad Cooperativa Teniente Azueta,** tel. (755) 420-56, named after the naval hero Lieutenant José Azueta. You can see them adjacent to the Zihuatanejo pier many of their several dozen boats bobbing at anchor. Arrangements for fishing parties can be made through hotel travel desks or at their office, open daily 6 a.m.-6 p.m., at the foot of the pier. The largest 36-foot boats, with four or five lines, go out for a day's fishing for about $250. Twenty-five-foot boats with three lines run about $120 per day.

The smaller (18-boat) **Servicios Sociedad Cooperativa Juárez,** tel. (755) 437-58, tries harder by offering similar boats for lower prices. Their 36-foot boats for six start around $200; their 25-foot for four, about $100. Contact them at their office across from the naval compound near the end of Paseo del Pescador, open daily 9 a.m.-8 p.m.

Next door, the private **Servicios Turísticos Aquaticos,** tel./fax (755) 441-62, also provides boats and captains for similar prices; open daily 9 a.m.-6 p.m.

Prices quoted by providers often (but not necessarily) include fishing licenses, bait, tackle, and amenities such as beer, sodas, ice, and on-board toilets. Such details should be pinned down (ideally by inspecting the boat) before putting your money down.

Sportfishing Tournament

Twice a year, usually in May and January, Zihuatanejo fisherfolk sponsor the **Torneo de Pez Vela,** with prizes for the biggest catches of sailfish, swordfish, marlin, and other varieties. Entrance fee runs around $450, and the prizes usually include a new Dodge pickup, cars, and other goodies. For information, contact the local sportfishing cooperative, Sociedad Cooperativa Teniente José Azueta, Muelle Municipal, Zihuatanejo, Guerrero 40880, tel. (755) 420-56.

Marinas and Boat Launching

Marina Ixtapa, at the north end of Paseo Ixtapa, offers excellent boat facilities. The slip charge runs about 57 cents per foot per day, for one to six days (51 cents for 7-29 days and 46 cents for more than 30 days), subject to a minimum charge per diem. This includes use of the boat ramp, showers, pump-out, electricity, trash collection, mailbox, phone, fax, and satellite TV. For reservations and information, contact the marina Mon.-Fri. 9 a.m.-2 p.m. and 4-7 p.m., Saturday 9 a.m.-2 p.m., at the harbormaster's office in the marina-front white building on the right a block before the big white lighthouse, tel./fax (755) 321-80, or write Harbormaster, Marina Ixtapa, Ixtapa, Guerrero 40880.

The smooth, gradual Marina Ixtapa **boat ramp,** open to the public for an approximately $10 fee, is on the right-hand side street leading to the water, just past the big white lighthouse. Get your ticket beforehand from the harbormaster.

Puerto Mío, Zihuatanejo's small private boat harbor at the end of the western curve of Zihuatanejo Bay, rents boat slips for about $1 per foot, per day. The fee includes toilets, water, electricity, and use of the swimming pool, showers, and adjacent restaurant. The usefulness of Puerto Mío's boat-launching ramp is reduced, however, by its rapid drop-off. Although the owners state that minimum contract slip-rental period is for six months, they may negotiate if they have extra space, Paseo del Morro, Playa del Almacón, Zihuatanejo, Guerrero 40880, tel./fax (755) 427-48.

Sports Equipment Shops

Deportes Náuticos, tel. (755) 444-11, corner of N. Bravo and Guerrero in downtown Zihuatanejo, sells snorkel equipment, boogie boards, tennis racquets, balls, and a load of other general sporting goods. Open Mon.-Sat. 10 a.m.-2 p.m. and 4-9 p.m.

Pesca Deportiva ("Sportfishing"), on the other hand, specializes in fishing rods, reels, lines, weights, and lures. Open Mon.-Sat. 9 a.m.-2 p.m. and 4-7 p.m.

SHOPPING

Zihuatanejo

Every day is market day at the Zihuatanejo **Mercado** on Av. Benito Juárez, four blocks from the beach. Behind the piles of leafy greens, round yellow papayas, and huge gaping sea bass, don't miss the sugar and spice stalls. There you will find big, raw brown sugar cones, thick golden homemade honey, mounds of fragrant *jamaica* petals, crimson dried chiles, and forest-gathered roots, barks, and grasses sold in the same pungent natural forms as they have been for centuries.

For more up-to-date merchandise, go to the nearby **Super El Globo** on the side street next to the market, tel. (755) 469-28. Its well-organized aisles have most of what you'll need, including Choco Krispis, Delaware Punch, Canada Dry soda, Philadelphia cream cheese, spaghetti, a few wines and beers. Open Mon.-Sat. 8 a.m.-7:30 p.m., Sunday 8 a.m.-3 p.m. If you can't get what you want at El Globo, go to **Super de Zihuatanejo,** next door.

For convenience shopping, the **Super El Dorado,** tel. (755) 427-25, one block from the beach, is one of the only stores in downtown Zihuatanejo with much food. Open daily 9 a.m.-2 p.m. and 4-9 p.m.

Ixtapa

Ixtapa's **Centro Comercial** complex stretches along the midsection of Paseo Ixtapa across from the hotels. It has four viable (of about 10 still forthcoming) and attractive subcomplexes, all fronting the boulevard. Moving east to west, first come the Los Patios and Fuentes subcomplexes, where minimarts, T-shirt and trinket shops, and super-expensive designer stores—Bill Blass, Ralph Lauren, and Gucci—occupy the choice boulevard frontages. Behind them, dozens of mostly small and ordinary crafts and jewelry shops languish along back lanes and inside patios. More of the same occupies the La Puerta subcomplex a hundred yards farther on. Next comes the police station, and, after that, the Galerías Ixtapa subcomplex at the corner of Paseo de las Garzas.

Handicrafts Shopping

Although some stores in the Ixtapa Centro Comercial shopping center and the adjacent tourist market (across from the Sheraton) offer handicrafts, Zihuatanejo offers the best selection and prices.

The Zihuatanejo **tourist market** stalls display a flood of crafts brought by families who come from all parts of Pacific Mexico. Their goods—delicate Michoacán lacquerware, bright Tonalá birds, gleaming Taxco silver, whimsical Guerrero masks, rich Guadalajara leather—spread for blocks along Av. Cinco de Mayo on the downtown west side. Compare prices; although bargaining here is customary, the glut of merchandise makes it a one-sided buyer's market, with many sellers barely managing to scrape by. If you err in your bargaining, kindly do it on the generous side.

Prominent among downtown shops nearby is the **Casa Marina,** shopping center, tel. (755) 423-73, a family project of late community leader Helen Krebs Posse. Her adult children and spouses own and manage stores in the two-story complex, just west of the beachfront town plaza.

Their original store, **Embarcadero,** on the lower floor, street-

Guerrero basket

side, has an unusually choice collection of woven and embroidered finery, mostly from Oaxaca. In addition to walls and racks of colorful, museum-quality traditional blankets, flower-embroidered dresses, and elaborate crocheted *huipiles,* she also offers wooden folk-figurines and a collection of intriguing masks.

Other stores in the Casa Marina include **La Zapoteca** on the bottom floor, specializing in weavings from Teotitlán del Valle in Oaxaca. Farther on and upstairs are El Jumil (silver and masks), Latzotil (Mayan art), El Calibria (leather), and the Cafe La Marina (pizza and used paperbacks). Local weavers demonstrate in the Embarcadero and La Zapoteca stores mornings and afternoons. The entire complex is open Mon.-Sat. 10 a.m.-2 p.m. and 5-9 p.m.; credit cards accepted.

A block toward the pier, **La Tienda de Ropa Típica,** on Paseo del Pescador, across from the naval compound, would be easy to pass because of its mounds of ho-hum T-shirts. But if you look inside, you'll find racks of many fetching hand-crocheted *huipiles* and blouses from backcountry Guerrero and Oaxaca. Open daily 8 a.m.-10:30 p.m.

Head back along Alvarez two blocks, past the plaza, to **Cerámicas Tonalá,** 12B Alvarez, beach side, to view one of the finest Tonalá pottery collections outside of the renowned source itself. Here, friendly owner Eduardo López's graceful glazed vases and plates, decorated in traditional plant and animal designs, fill the cabinets, while a menagerie of lovable owls, ducks, fish, armadillos, and frogs, all seemingly poised to spring to life, crowd the shelves. Open Mon.-Sat. 9 a.m.-2 p.m. and 4-8 p.m., tel. (755) 421-61; credit cards accepted.

Step across Alvarez to **Nopal** handicrafts, the labor of love of the owner, who loves things from Oaxaca, especially baskets. Now an organized clutter of unique woven goods, ceramics, and furniture fill his shop. Open Mon.-Sat. 9 a.m.-8 p.m.

A few steps up Cuauhtémoc, **Alberto's** pair of shops, on opposite sides of the street, tel. (755) 421-61, offer an extensive silver jewelry collection. As with gold and precious stones, silver prices can be reckoned approximately by weighing, at about $1 per gram. The cases and cabinets of shiny earrings, chains, bracelets, rings, and much more, are products of a family of artists, taught by a master craftsman, now semiretired, in Puerto Vallarta. Many of the designs are original, and, with bargaining, reasonably priced. Open Mon.-Sat. 9 a.m.-2:30 p.m. and 4-8:30 p.m.; credit cards accepted.

A block farther, at the corner of Ejido, step into **Rosimar,** the creation of Josefina and Manuel Martínez. Manuel's intriguing outside murals lead you inside to their eclectic, priced-to-sell collection of Tonalá and Tlaquepaque pottery, papier-mâché and glassware. You might also take a look inside Manuel's new store, **Arte Mexicano,** nearby, at Cuauhtémoc Ejido 37. Open Mon.-Sat. 9 a.m.-9 p.m. daily.

At **Galería Maya,** a block back down Ejido and around the corner, at N. Bravo 31, tel. (755) 446-06, owner Tania Scales has accumulated a multitude of one-of-a-kind folk curios from many parts of Mexico. Her wide-ranging, carefully selected collection includes masks, necklaces, sculptures, purses, blouses, *huipiles,* ritual objects, and much more. Open Mon.-Sat. 10 a.m.-2 p.m. and 5-9 p.m. Furthermore, be sure not to miss Tania's labor of love, **Ix-chel Maya museum,** which displays several regal sculptures, representing a number of indigenous female deities—Ixta Bay, Mayan jungle goddess; Coyolxauhqui, Aztec moon goddess; Cihuateteo, representing the women of Zihuatanejo—and more. On Cuauhtémoc, a few doors from the plaza; open Mon.-Sat. 10 a.m.-2 p.m. and 6-9 p.m.

Photography

In Zihuatanejo, one-hour photofinishing, popular film varieties, and some photo supplies are available at local Fuji film dealer **Feconde Laboratorio** at the corner of Alvarez and Cuauhtémoc, adjacent to the beachfront plaza, tel. (755) 433-78. Open Mon.-Sat. 10 a.m.-7 p.m.

Foto 30 on Ejido, between Galeana and Guerrero, two blocks from the plaza, tel. (755) 476-10, besides 30-minute develop-and-print service, stocks lots of film and accessories. These include

a host of cameras, including SLRs, and film, including 120 print, 35mm slide, and sheet film, plus filters, tripods, and flashes. Open Mon.-Sat. 9 a.m.-2 p.m. and 4-8 p.m., Sunday 9 a.m.-2 p.m.

SERVICES

Money Exchange

To change money in Zihuatanejo, go to **Banamex,** tel. (755) 472-93 or 472-94, at the corner of Guerrero and Ejido, two blocks from the beach, open for money exchange Mon.-Fri. 9 a.m.-5 p.m. If the Banamex lines are too long, use the teller machine or walk three blocks east, to **Bancomer,** tel. (755) 474-92 or 474-93, open Mon.-Sat. 9 a.m.-5 p.m., or **Banco Serfin,** tel. (755) 439-41, open Mon.-Fri. 9 a.m.-5 p.m., both near the corner of Bravo and Juárez.

After hours, go around the corner to the **Casa de Cambio Guibal,** tel. (755) 435-22, fax 428-00 (with long-distance telephone and fax), at Galeana and Bravo, two blocks from the beach, to change U.S., Canadian, French, German, Swiss, and other currencies and traveler's checks. For the convenience, they offer you significantly less for your money than the banks. Open daily 8 a.m.-9 p.m.

In Ixtapa, change money at your hotel desk; or, for better rates, try **Bancomer** in the Los Portales complex behind the shops across the boulevard from the Hotel Presidente, tel. (755) 321-12, 305-35, or 305-25. For longer moneychanging hours, go to **Banco Internacional,** right on hotel strip Paseo Ixtapa, tel. (755) 306-41, 306-42, or 306-46, open Mon.-Fri. 9 a.m.-6 p.m., Saturday 9 a.m.-2 p.m.

The local **American Express** branch in the Hotel Krystal issues and cashes American Express traveler's checks and provides travel agency services to the public. For card-carrying members, they provide full money services, such as check-cashing. Hours are Mon.-Sat. 9 a.m.-2 p.m. and 4-6 p.m.; money services hours may be shorter. Call for confirmation, tel. (755) 308-53, fax 312-06.

Communication

The only **post office** serving both Zihuatanejo and Ixtapa is in Zihuatanejo at the Centro Federal, in northeast corner of downtown, five blocks from the beach and a couple of blocks east of the Ixtapa minibus stop at Juárez and Morelos. Open Mon.-Fri. 9 a.m.-7 p.m., Saturday 9 a.m.-1 p.m.

Next door is **Telecomunicaciones**, which offers long-distance telephone, public fax (755-421-63), telegrams, and money orders Mon.-Fri. 9 a.m.-3 p.m., Saturday 9 a.m.-noon. Another similar telecommunications office serves Ixtapa, in the La Puerta shopping center (rear side) across Paseo Ixtapa, from the Hotel Presidente.

Also in the northeast section of Zihuatanejo on Av. Colegio Militar (across from the immigration office), a blue building marks the very reliable government **Mexpost** (like U.S. Express Mail) upgraded mail service, tel. (755) 431-65.

Downtown Zihuatanejo's private *larga distancia* telephone and fax office, on Galeana, the lane parallel to Cuauhtémoc, corner of Bravo, tel./fax (755) 435-22, also changes both U.S. and Canadian currency and traveler's checks. Open daily 8 a.m.-9 p.m.

In both Ixtapa and Zihuatanejo, many streetside public phone booths handle international long distance calls. For best rates, call collect or with a credit card. Dial 001-800-462-4240 for the English-speaking AT&T international operator, 001-800-674-6000 for MCI, or 001-800-877-8000 for Sprint.

Beware of certain private "To Call Long Distance to the U.S.A. Collect and Credit Card" telephones installed prominently in airports, tourist hotels, and shops. Tariffs on these phones often run as high as $30 for three minutes. Always ask the operator for the rate, and if it's too high, take your business elsewhere.

Immigration and Customs

If you lose your tourist permit, go to **Migración,** on Colegio Militar, about five blocks northeast of Plaza Kyoto, on the northeast edge of downtown, tel. (755) 427-95; open Mon.-Fri. 9 a.m.-3 p.m. Bring your passport and some proof of the date you arrived in Mexico, such as your airline ticket, stamped passport, or a copy of your lost tourist permit. Although it's not wise to let such a matter go until the last day, you may be able to accomplish the needed paperwork at the airport Migración office (open daily 8 a.m.-6 p.m.). Best call first, however, tel. (755) 484-80.

The **Aduana** ("Customs") office, tel. (755) 432-62, is at the airport, off Hwy. 200 about seven miles south of Zihuatanejo, open daily 9 a.m.-7 p.m. If you have to temporarily leave the country without your car, have someone fluent in Spanish call about the required paperwork.

Laundromat and Dry Cleaner

In Zihuatanejo, take your laundry to **Laundry Super Clean** at Gonzáles and Galeana, just off Cuauhtémoc, four blocks from the plaza, tel. (755) 423-47; open Mon.-Sat. 8 a.m.-8 p.m. If you also need dry-cleaning, take both it and your laundry items to **Lavandería Aldan,** on Cuauhtémoc, a few doors away, open Mon.-Sat. 8:30 a.m.-6 p.m.

INFORMATION

Tourist Information Offices

The helpful staff of the Zihuatanejo municipal office of tourism, tel./fax (755) 420-01, ext. 121, answers questions and hands out maps and brochures at their small office behind the city hall, on the beachfront plaza. Open Mon.-Sat. 9 a.m.-3 p.m. and 6-8 p.m., Saturday 9 a.m.-2 p.m.

The Ixtapa federal office of **Turismo** appears to function more as a regulatory agency rather than an information office. You may do better by seeing the travel agent in your hotel lobby. Open Mon.-Fri. 9 a.m.-3 p.m. in the La Puerta shopping complex, across the boulevard from the Hotel Presidente.

An excellent alternative local information source (in Spanish) is the *cámara de comercio* (chamber of commerce) in downtown Zihuatanejo, on Bravo, near corner of Guerrero, tel. (755) 425-75. Friendly director Gilda Soberanis and her staff are ready and able to answer questions, suggest contacts, and provide whatever local maps and literature they have. Open Mon.-Fri. 9 a.m.-2 p.m. and 4-7 p.m., Saturday 9 a.m.-1 p.m.

Doctors, Hospital, Police, and Emergencies

For medical consultation in English, visitors have a number of options. In Zihuatanejo, contact Dr. Rogelio Grayeb, on Juárez, corner of east-side Paseo de la Boquita, by the canal, a block from the beach, tel. (755) 448-25, 450-12, or 102-34. He's open 8 a.m.-2 p.m. and 4-8 p.m.

Alternatively, visit Swiss-trained Dr. Niklaus Bührer, tel. (755) 430-45, at his pharmacy at

Bungalows El Milagro, at the far east end of Paseo del Palmar, two blocks from Playa Madera. His hours are approximately Mon.-Sat. 9 a.m.-1 p.m. and 4-7 p.m.

Yet another Zihuatanejo option is the very professional **Clínica Maciel,** which has a dentist, pediatrician, gynecologist, surgeon, and general practitioner on 24-hour call, at 12 Palmas, two blocks east, one block north of the market, tel. (755) 423-80.

In Ixtapa, U.S.-trained IAMAT associate, Dr. Carlos Baldwin, offers 24-hour emergency consultations and home visits from his headquarters at the Hotel Presidente, tel. (755) 309-14 or 319-26, fax 302-26.

Neither Ixtapa nor Zihuatanejo has any state-of-the art private hospitals. However, many local people recommend the state of Guerrero *hospital general,* on Av. Morelos, corner of Mar Egeo, just off from Hwy. 200, tel. (755) 439-65, 436-50 and 434-36, for its generally competent, dedicated, and professional staff.

For medicines and drugs in Ixtapa, try your hotel shop, or call Dr. Carlos Baldwin at the Hotel Presidente (above), or call one of the many pharmacies in downtown Zihuatanejo, such as the **Farmacia La Principal,** corner of Cuauhtémoc and Ejido, two blocks from the beachfront plaza, tel. (755) 442-17; open Mon.-Sat. 8:30 a.m.-9:30 p.m.

For police emergencies in Ixtapa and Zihuatanejo, contact the *cabercera de policía* headquarters in Zihuatanejo, on Calle Limón, about five blocks from the beach, tel. (755) 420-40. Usually more accessible is the *caseta de policía* on-duty police booth behind the Zihuatanejo plaza-front city hall, tel. (755) 423-55, or in Ixtapa on the boulevard across from the Hotel Presidente.

Publications

The best local English-language book and magazine selection lines the many shelves of the **Hotel Westin Brisas Ixtapa** *tabaquería.* Besides dozens of new paperback novels and scores of popular U.S. magazines, it stocks *USA Today* and the *News* of Mexico City newspapers and a thoughtful selection of Mexico guides and books of cultural and historical interest. Open daily 9 a.m.-9 p.m.

The newsstand, west side of the Zihuatanejo plaza, is a customary source of popular U.S.

magazines, such as *Vogue, Time,* and *Sports Illustrated,* plus the newspapers *News* of Mexico (around 1 p.m.) and *USA Today.* Open daily 8 a.m.-8 p.m.

The friendly, small Zihuatanejo bookstore **Librería Byblos,** despite its mainly Spanish inventory, does have some used English-language paperbacks. It also stocks English-Spanish dictionaries and a good map of Guerrero. Open Mon.-Sat. 9 a.m.-9 p.m., Sunday 9 a.m.-4 p.m.; on Galeana, between Ejido and Bravo, next to the back entrance of Cafe Nova Zelandia, tel. (755) 422-81.

Many used paperbacks line the walls of friendly **Cafe Marina** adjacent to the beach just west of the plaza; open Mon.-Sat. till 10 p.m., closed June to mid-September.

The small Zihuatanejo **Biblioteca** (public library) also has some shelves of English-language paperbacks. Open Mon.-Fri. 9 a.m.-2 p.m. and 4-8 p.m., Saturday 9 a.m.-1 p.m.; on Cuauhtémoc, five blocks from the beach.

Ecological Association and Humane Society

The grassroots **Asociación de Ecologistas** sponsors local cleanup, tree-planting, save-the-turtles, and other projects. A cadre of community leaders, including the society's president, veterinarian Rafael Lobato, Jorge Luis Reyes, Anita Hahner Rellstab, owner of Bungalows Pacífico, tel. (755) 421-12, and marine biologist Juan M. Barnard Avila, owner of Zihuatanejo Scuba Center, tel. (755) 421-47, are dedicated to preserving the Ixtapa-Zihuatanejo coast. They welcome volunteers to join their efforts.

The family of the late Helen Krebs Posse are the guiding lights of the **Sociedad Protectora de Animales,** which is working hard to educate people about animal issues. Contact them at their shop complex, Casa Marina, just west of the Zihuatanejo plaza, tel. (755) 423-73.

GETTING THERE AND AWAY

By Air

Four major carriers connect Ixtapa-Zihuatanejo directly with U.S. and Mexican destinations year-round; three more operate during the fall-winter season:

Aeroméxico flights connect daily with Los Angeles, Guadalajara, and Mexico City, where quick-transfer connections with Houston and Atlanta may be made. For reservations, call (755) 420-18 or 420-19; for flight information, call (755) 422-37 or 426-34.

Mexicana Airlines flights connect directly with Los Angeles via Guadalajara four times a week. For reservations, call (755) 422-08 or 422-09; for flight information, call (755) 422-27.

Alaska Airlines connects with Los Angeles. Call a travel agent or toll-free (800) 426-0333 for flight information and reservations.

America West Airlines connects with Phoenix. Call a travel agent or toll-free tel. (800) 235-9292 for flight information and reservations.

Trans World Airlines connects with St. Louis seasonally during the fall, winter, and spring. Call a travel agent or toll-free (800) 892-4141 for flight information and reservations.

Continental Airlines connects with Houston seasonally during the fall, winter, and spring. Call a travel agent or toll-free tel. (800) 231-0856 for flight information and reservations.

Canadian World of Vacations charter flights connect with Vancouver and Calgary-Edmonton during the fall, winter, and spring. Call a travel agent, such as American Express, tel. (755) 308-53, for reservations.

Air Arrival and Departure

Ixtapa-Zihuatanejo is quickly accessible, only seven miles (11 km) north of the airport via Hwy. 200. Arrival is generally simple—if you come with a day's worth of pesos and hotel reservations. The terminal has no money exchange, information booth, or hotel-reservation service. It's best not to leave your hotel choice up to your taxi driver, for he will probably deposit you at the hotel that pays him a commission on your first night's lodging.

Transportation to town is usually by *taxi especial* (private taxi) or *colectivo* van. Tickets are available at booths near the terminal exit for $3-6 per person (depending on destination) for a *colectivo*, or $15-20 for three persons in a private taxi. Taxis to Troncones run about $35. Mobile budget travelers can walk the few hundred yards to the highway and flag down one of the frequent daytime Zihuatanejo-bound buses (very few, if any, continue on to Ixtapa, howev-

er). At night, spend the money on *colectivo* or taxi.

Several major **car rentals** staff airport arrival booths. Avoid problems and save money by negotiating your car rental through the agencies' toll-free numbers (see the chart Car Rental Agency Toll-Free Numbers in the On the Road chapter) before departure. U.S. companies with local agents include Hertz, tel. (755) 430-50 or 425-90; Dollar, tel. (755) 430-66; Budget, tel. (755) 448-37; Alamo, tel. (755) 302-06; Quick (755) 318-30; Econo; and Thrifty.

Departure is quick and easy if you have your passport, tourist permit (which was stamped on arrival), and $12 cash (or the equivalent in pesos) international departure tax. Departees who've lost their tourist permits can avoid trouble and a fine by either getting a duplicate at Zihuatanejo Immigration or (perhaps) by having a copy of the lost permit and a police report of the loss.

For last-minute postcards and shopping, the airport has a mailbox and a few gift shops.

By Car or RV

Three routes, two easy and one unsafe and not recommended, connect Ixtapa-Zihuatanejo with Playa Azul and Michoacán to the northwest, Acapulco to the southeast, and Ciudad Altamirano and central Guerrero to the northeast.

Traffic sails smoothly along the 76 miles (122 km) of Hwy. 200, either way, between Zihuatanejo and Lázaro Cárdenas/Playa Azul. The same is true of the 150-mile (242-km) Hwy. 200 southern extension to Acapulco. Allow about two and a half hours to or from Playa Azul, four hours to or from Acapulco.

The story is much different, however, for the winding, sparsely populated, cross-Sierra Hwy. 134 (intersecting with Hwy. 200 nine miles north) from Zihuatanejo to Ciudad Altamirano. Rising along spectacular, jungle-clad ridges, the paved but sometimes potholed road leads over cool, pine-clad heights and descends to the Altamirano high valley after about 100 miles (160 km). The continuing leg to Iguala on the Acapulco-Mexico City highway is longer, about 112 miles (161 km), equally winding, and often busy. Allow about eight hours westbound and nine hours eastbound for the entire trip. Keep filled with gasoline, and be prepared for emergencies, especially along the Altamirano-Zihuatanejo leg, where no hotels and few services exist. Warning: This route, unfortunately, has been plagued by robberies and nasty drug-related incidents. Inquire locally—your hotel, the tourist information office, the bus station—to see if authorities have secured the road before attempting this trip.

By Bus
Zihuatanejo's big, shiny long-distance *central de autobús* is on Hwy. 200, Acapulco-bound side, about a mile south of downtown Zihuatanejo. Travelers enjoy a snack bar, Sendatel public long-distance phone/fax and hotel reservations agency (for certain hotels only), left-luggage lockers, and a snack stand, but no food store. You'd best prepare by stocking up with water and goodies before you depart.

Estrella Blanca (EB), tel. (755) 434-77, the major carrier, computer-coordinates the service of its subsidiaries Flecha Roja (FR), Elite (EL), Futura (FU), and Autotransportes Cuauhtémoc. Tickets are available with cash or credit cards for all departures from computer-assisted agents. In total, they offer luxury class (infrequent, super-first-class, reserved), first class (frequent, reserved), and second class (very frequent, unreserved) service.

Most buses run along the Hwy. 200 corridor, connecting with Lázaro Cárdenas/Playa Azul and northwestern points, and with Acapulco and points south and east.

Several luxury- and first-class buses and many (every half hour) second-class buses connect daily with Acapulco. Several of them continue on to Mexico City. In the opposite direction, many luxury-, first-, and second-class buses (at least one an hour) connect daily with Lázaro Cárdenas, Playa Azul, and northwest points.

A number of departures connect from the same terminal, along the Pacific coast Hwy. 200 corridor, south with Acapulco and the Oaxaca coast, and north via Manzanillo, Puerto Vallarta, and Mazatlán, to the U.S. border at Mexicali and Tijuana. Others departures connect north with Uruapan and Morelia, via Lázaro Cárdenas and La Mira (Playa Azul).

Another major bus carrier, Estrella de Oro, tel. (755) 421-75, offers a few competing long-distance first- and second-class departures (east via Acapulco to Mexico City, northwest to Lázaro Cárdenas) from its station back in town, on Paseo del Palmar, four blocks away from the beach, past Plaza Kyoto.

ALONG THE ROAD TO ACAPULCO

Although the 150-mile (242-km) Zihuatanejo-Acapulco stretch of Hwy. 200 is smooth and easy, resist the temptation to hurry through. Your reward will be a bright string of little pearls—idyllic South Seas villages, miles of strollable, fishable beaches, wildlife-rich *esteros,* lovely small hotels, and a tranquil little beach resort on the hidden edge of Acapulco.

On the Road
If you're driving, mark your odometer at the Zihuatanejo southside Pemex, near Km 240 on Hwy. 200. Or, if driving north, do the same at the Acapulco *zócalo* (old town square) Km 0, and head out on the northbound coast road past Pie de la Cuesta. Road mileages and kilometer markers are helpful in finding the paths to hidden little beaches.

Bus travelers, take a second-class bus from the Zihuatanejo or the Acapulco Estrella Blanca *central de autobús.* Ask the driver to drop you at your chosen haven.

PLAYA LAS POZAS

This surf-fishing paradise is reachable via the Zihuatanejo airport turnoff road. The reward is a lagoon full of bait fish, space for RV or tent camping (be careful of soft sand), a wide beach, and friendly beachside *palapa* restaurants.

The beach itself is 100 yards wide, of yellow-white sand, and extends for miles in both directions. It has driftwood but not many shells. Fish thrive in its thunderous, open-ocean waves. Consequently, casts from the beach can yield five-pound catches by either bait or lures. Local folks catch fish mostly by net, both in the surf and the nearby lagoon. During the June-Sept. rainy season, the lagoon breaks through the bar. Big fish, gobbling prey at the outlet, can be netted or hooked at the same spot themselves.

Camping is popular here on weekends and holidays. Other times you may have the place to yourself. As a courtesy, ask the friendly Netos family, which runs the best of the *palapa* restaurants, if it's okay.

Comfortable rustic accommodations have also arrived at Las Pozas, through the ingenuity of builder Jeffry Meyers, who has erected three rustic tropical cabañas beside a beachside swimming pool. For food, he offers either meals or use of a communal kitchen. Figure about $40-50 per night double. Call him at (755) 482-78 for more information.

Get there by following the well-marked airport turnoff road at Km 230. After one mile, turn right at the cyclone fence just before the terminal and follow the bumpy but easily passable straight level road 1.1 miles (1.8 km) to the beach.

BARRA DE POTOSÍ

At Achotes, nine miles (15 km) south of Zihuatanejo, a Laguna de Potosí sign points right to Barra de Potosí, a picture-perfect fishing hamlet at the sheltered south end of the Bahía de Potosí. After a few miles through green, tufted groves, the road parallels the bayside beach, a crescent of fine white sand, with a scattering of houses and one small hotel.

The **Hotel Resort Barra de Potosí** perches right on the beach. Potentially lovely, with a seaview pool patio, but lately neglected and run down, the place might still be worth a look to see if owners have renovated the place. If they have, it will match my 1993 description, which cited eight tastefully designed air-conditioned kitchenette apartments (with hot water and fans), a pretty beachfront pool, palms, and a bar and restaurant.

The surf is generally tranquil and safe for swimming near the hotel, although the waves, which do not roll but break rather quickly along long fronts, are not good for surfing.

The waves become even more tranquil at the south end, where a sheltering headland rises beyond the village and the lagoon. Beneath its swaying palm grove, the hamlet of Barra de Potosí (pop. 1,000) has the ingredients for weeks of tranquil living. Several broad, hammock-hung *palapa* restaurants (here called *enramadas*) front the bountiful lagoon.

Home for flocks of birds and waterfowl and shoals of fish, the **Laguna de Potosí** stretches for miles to its far mangrove reaches. Adven-

ture out with your own boat or kayak, or go with Orlando, who regularly takes parties out for fishing or wildlife-viewing tours.

Bait fish, caught locally with nets, abound in the lagoon. Fishing is fine for bigger catches (jack, snapper, mullet) by boat or casts beyond the waves. Launch your boat easily in the lagoon, then head, like the local fishermen, past the open sandbar.

Camping is common by RV or tent along the uncrowded edge of the lagoon. Village stores can provide basic supplies.

Get there by taking the signed turnoff road at Km 225, nine miles (14 km) south of Zihuatanejo, just south of the Los Achotes River bridge. Continue along the good (trailer-accessible) dirt road for 5.5 miles (8.9 km) to the hotel and the village half a mile farther south.

PAPANOA

The small town of Papanoa (pop. 3,000) straddles the highway 47 miles (75 km) south of Zihuatanejo and 103 miles (165 km) north of Acapulco. Local folks tell the tongue-in-cheek story of its Hawaiian-sounding name. It seems that there was a flood, and the son of the local headman had to talk fast to save his life by escaping in a *canoa*. Instead of saying "Papa . . . canoa," the swift-talking boy shortened his plea to "Papa . . . noa."

The town itself has a few snack restaurants, a pharmacy, a doctor, groceries, a *gasolinera* that stocks unleaded gas, first-class bus stops, a long-distance telephone, and one resort-style lodging, the **Hotel Club Papanoa,** Papanoa, Guerrero 40907, tel. (742) 201-50.

Near the beach about a mile south of town, the hotel has about 30 large rooms, a restaurant, and a big pool set in spacious ocean-view garden grounds. Intended to be luxurious but now a bit worn around the edges, the hotel is nearly empty most nonholiday times. Rooms rent for about $30 s or d with fan only, $40 with a/c.

The hotel grounds adjoin the beach, **Playa Cayaquitos.** The wide, breezy, yellow-gray strand stretches for two miles, washed by powerful open-ocean rollers with good left and right surfing breaks. Additional attractions include surf fishing beyond the breakers and driftwood along the sand. Beach access is via the off-highway driveway just north of the hotel. At the beach, a parking lot borders a seafood restaurant. Farther on, the road narrows (but is still motor home accessible) through a defunct beachside home development, past several brush-bordered informal RV parking or tenting spots.

PIEDRA TLACOYUNQUE

At Km 150 (56 miles, 90 km from Zihuatanejo, 94 miles, 151 km from Acapulco) a signed Restaurant Las Carabelas side road heads seaward to Piedra Tlacoyunque and the Carabelas Restaurant. About a mile down the paved road, the restaurant appears, perching on a bluff overlooking a monumental sandstone rock, Piedra Tlacoyunque. Below, a wave-tossed strand, ripe for beachcombing and surf fishing, stretches for miles. Powerful breakers with fine right-hand surfing angles roll in and swish up the steep beach. For fishing, buy some bait from the net fishermen on the beach and try some casts be-

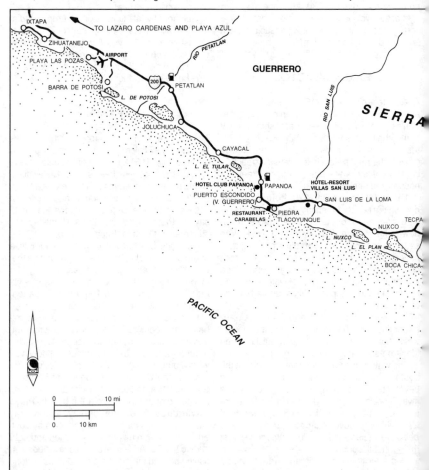

yond the billows crashing into the south side of the Piedra. Later, stroll through the garden of eroded rock sea stacks on the north side. There you can poke among the snails and seaweeds in a big sheltered tidepool, under the watchful guard of the squads of pelicans roosting on the surrounding pinnacles.

The *palapa*-house on the beach is the headquarters of the government-funded **Campamento Playa Piedra de Tlacoyunque,** whose mission is to rescue, incubate, and hatch as many turtle eggs as possible. Several staff patrol the beach with ATVs, especially during the summer-fall hatching (and egg-poaching) season. Although they are dedicated to their task, their vigil is a lonely one, and they generally welcome visitors and contributions of drinks and food.

At the Carabelas Restaurant on the bluff above, you can take in the whole breezy scene while enjoying the recommended catch of the day. The name Carabelas (Caravels) comes

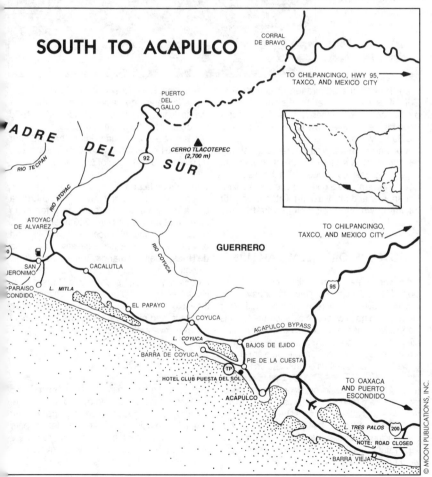

Pelicans, tidepools, a garden of sandstone, and gourmet surf fishing attract adventurers to Playa Piedra Tlacoyunque.

from the owner's admiration of Christopher Columbus. He christened his restaurant's three petite ocean-view gazebos after Columbus's three famous caravels: the Nina, the Pinta, and the Santa María.

For an overnight or a short stay, ask the restaurant owners if it's okay to set up your tent or park your (self-contained) RV in the restaurant lot or in the small beach-level grove down below. For shower and dishwashing water, drop your bucket down into their well, marked by the windmill.

HOTEL RESORT VILLAS SAN LUIS

Little was spared to embellish this pretty hacienda-like corner of a big mango, papaya, and coconut grove. It appears as if the owner, tiring of all work and no play, built a park to entertain his friends. Now, his project blooms with lovely swimming and kiddie pools, a big *palapa* restaurant, a smooth *palapa*-covered dance floor, a small zoo, basketball and volleyball courts, and an immaculate hotel.

Ideal for a lunch/swim break or an overnight or a respite from hard Mexico traveling, the 40 immaculate and attractively furnished hotel rooms rent for about $40 s, $44 d, with a/c and hot water included, credit cards accepted. Add about 10% during holidays. If you'll be arriving on a weekend or holiday, write, phone, or fax for a

reservation: **Hotel Resort Villas San Luis,** Carretera Zihuatanejo-Acapulco, Km 143, Buenavista de Juárez, Guerrero 40906, tel. (742) 703-28 or 702-82, fax 700-08 and 702-35.

It is on the southbound side of the road near Km 142, 61 miles (98 km) south of Zihuatanejo, 89 miles (143 km) north of Acapulco.

San Luis de la Loma

The pleasant little market town of San Luis de la Loma (pop. 5,000) runs along a hilltop main street that angles off Hwy. 200 near Km 140. Besides a number of groceries, fruit stalls, and pharmacies, San Luis has a guesthouse—**Casa de Huespedes Hermanos Ruiz**—a post office, a health center, a *larga distancia,* a dentist, and a doctor, gynecologist José Luis Barrera Garcia, tel. (742) 701-93 and 700-25, on the plaza, three blocks from the highway. First-class buses also stop and pick up passengers at the main street-highway intersection.

BOCA CHICA

For the fun and adventure of it, visit Boca Chica, a beach village accessible by boat only. Here, camping is de rigueur, since even permanent residents are doing it. It makes no sense to pour concrete on a sandbar where palm fronds are free and the next wave may wash everything away anyway.

The jumping-off spot is near Km 98 (88 miles, 142 km south of Zihuatanejo, 61 miles, 98 km north of Acapulco), where a sign marks the dirt road to **Tetitlán** (pop. 2,000). In about three miles, turn left at the "T" at the town plaza (long-distance phone, pharmacy, groceries) and continue a couple more miles along a rough—but negotiable when dry—road to the Laguna Tecpán (which, during the dry season, may have narrowed to a river). Here, launches will ferry you (or you can walk) the mile across to the village on the sandbar. Bargain the *viaje redondo* (return-trip) price with your boatman before you depart (unless of course you have your own kayak or boat).

On the other side, the waves thunder upon the beach and sand crabs guard their holes, while the village's four separate societies—people, dogs, pigs, and chickens—each go about their distinct business. Shells and driftwood decorate the sand, and surf fishing with bait from the lagoon couldn't be better.

Most visitors come for the eating only: super-fresh seafood charcoal-broiled in one of the dozen *palapas* along the beach. If, however,

you plan to camp overnight, bring drinking water, a highly prized Boca Chica commodity.

During the summer rainy season, the Tecpán River, which feeds the lagoon, breaks through the bar. Ocean fish enter the lagoon, and the river current sometimes washes Boca Chica, *palapas* and all, out to sea.

PIE DE LA CUESTA

"Foot of the Hill," the translation of the name Pie (pee-YAY) de la Cuesta, aptly describes this downscale resort village. Tucked around the bend from Acapulco, between a wide beach and placid Laguna Coyuca, Pie de la Cuesta appeals to those who want the excitement the big town offers and the tranquillity it doesn't.

Laguna Coyuca, kept full by the sweet waters of the Río Coyuca, has long been known for its fish, birdlife, and tranquil, palm-lined shores. During the early 1400s, the Tarascans (who ruled from the Michoacán highlands) established a provincial capital near the town of Coyuca. After the Aztecs drove out the Tarascans a cen-

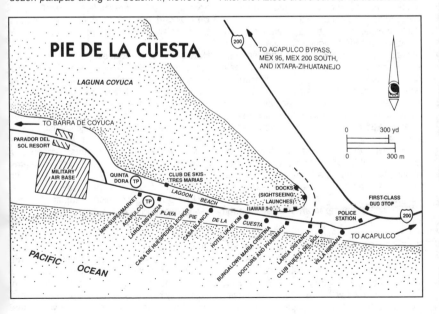

tury later (and the Aztecs in turn were defeated by the Spanish), Pie de la Cuesta and its beautiful Laguna Coyuca slumbered in the shadow of Acapulco.

Sights

Laguna de Coyuca is a large sandy-bottomed lake, lined by palms and laced by mangrove channels. It stretches 10 miles along the shoreline, west from Pie de la Cuesta, which occupies the southeast (Acapulco) side. The barrier sandbar, wide Playa Pie de la Cuesta, separates the lagoon from the ocean. It extends a dozen miles west to the river outlet, which is open to the sea only during the rainy season. A road runs along the beach west the length of Laguna Coyuca to the tourist hamlet of Barra de Coyuca. There, *palapas* line the beach and serve seafood to busloads of Sunday visitors.

Playa Pie de la Cuesta, a seemingly endless, hundred-yard-wide stretch of yellow sand, is fine for surf fishing, beachcombing, jogging, and long sunset walks. However, its powerful open-ocean waves are unsuited for surfing and frequently hazardous for swimming. They often break thunderously near the sand and recede with strong, turbulent undertow.

On the other side of the bar, the tranquil Acapulco (east) end of Laguna Coyuca is an embarkation point for lagoon tours and center for water-skiing and jet skiing. Among the best equipped of the shoreline clubs that offer powerboat services is the **Restaurant and Club de Skis Tres Marias.** Besides a pleasant lake-view shoreline *palapa* restaurant, it offers water-skiing at about $25/hour and jet-ski boats for about $40/hour.

If you want to launch your own boat, you can do so easily at Club Tres Marias and others for about $10. The boat traffic, which confines itself mostly to mid-lagoon, does not deter swimming in the lagoon's clear waters. Slip on your bathing suit and jump in anywhere along the sandy shoreline.

Lagoon tours begin from several landings dotting the Pie de la Cuesta end of the lagoon. Half-day regular excursions (maximum 10 persons, about $6 per person) push off daily around 11 a.m., noon, and 1:30 p.m. Along the way, they pass islands with trees loaded with nesting cormorants, herons, and pelicans. In mid-

lake, gulls dip and sway in the breeze behind your boat while a host of storks, ducks, avocets, and a dozen other varieties paddle, preen, and forage in the water nearby. Other times, your boat passes through winding channels hung with vines and lined with curtains of great mangrove roots. At midpoint, tours usually stop for a bite to eat at Isla Montosa. Here, roosters crow, pigs root, bougainvillea blooms, and a colony of fishing families live, unencumbered by 20th-century conveniences, beneath their majestic shoreline palm grove.

On another day, drive or ride one of the frequent buses that head from Pie de la Cuesta to **Barra de Coyuca** village at the west end of the lagoon. Along the way, you will pass several scruffy hamlets and a parade of fenced lots, some still open meadows where horses graze while others are filled with trees and big houses. Lack of potable water, local residents complain, is a continuing problem on this dry sandbar.

At road's end, 10 miles from Pie de la Cuesta, a few tourist stores, a platoon of T-shirt vendors, and hammock-equipped beach *palapa* restaurants serve holiday crowds. Boats head for tours from lagoonside, where patrons at the **Restaurant Dos Vistas** enjoy a double view of both beach and lagoon.

Hotels and Guesthouses

Approximately a dozen basic bungalows, *casas de huéspedes* (guesthouses), and hotels line the Pie de la Cuesta's single beachside road. Competition keeps cleanliness high, management sharp, and prices low. They all cluster along a one-mile roadfront, enjoying highly visible locations right on the beach. Write for reservations, especially for the winter season and holidays. Most of them have tepid, room-temperature bath water only, and do not accept credit cards; exceptions are noted below.

Note: Some unscrupulous Acapulco taxi drivers are trying to squeeze commissions from Pie de la Cuesta lodgings in return for bringing customers to their doorsteps. Typical tactics include outright refusing to take customers to places that don't pay commissions, or telling customers that the hotel that they request *"no sirve"* ("is not running"). You can combat this on the spot by making sure, before you get into the taxi, that the driver agrees to take you to the hotel of your choice, and, once in Pie de la Cuesta, making sure that he follows through. Daytime taxi fares from Acapulco shouldn't run more than about $5 from old town, $7 from the Costera; nighttime tariffs should be no more than double those amounts. Plenty of daytime buses run there for less than half a dollar. All lodgings recommended below are marked on the Pie de la Cuesta map.

In approximate order of increasing price, first comes **Casa de Huéspedes Playa Leonor,** which is very popular with a loyal cadre of Canadian winter returnees, 63 Carretera Pie de la Cuesta, Guerrero 39900, tel. (74) 600-348. They enjoy camaraderie around the tables of the *palapa* restaurant that occupies the beachside end of a large leafy parking-lot garden. The several breezy, more private upper-floor units are most popular. All 10 rooms have two beds, showers, and fans, and rent for about $14 d low season, $15 high, with approximately 20% discount for monthly rentals.

More picturesque are the **Bungalows María Cristina,** P.O. Box 607, Acapulco, Guerrero 39300, nine units (six rooms, four kitchen-equipped bungalows) set between a streetside parking lot and a palmy beachside restaurant/garden. The very plain rooms, with toilets and showers, rent for about $14 d low season, $21 high. The kitchenettes, most of which face the ocean, run about $36 low season, $46 high, for up to four persons. Negotiate for long-term discounts.

Guests at the nearby **Hotel and Restaurant Casa Blanca,** P.O. Box 370, Acapulco, Guerrero 39300, tel. (74) 600-324, enjoy a tranquil, car-free tropical garden and restaurant and careful feminine management. Their specialty is a four-course daily *comida* for $3. The eight very clean rooms, with toilets, showers, and ruffled bedspreads, are a bargain at about $12 s, $15 d, $20 t all year around. Discounts may be available for monthly or low season (May-Oct,) rentals. American Express cards are accepted.

Husband-wife (she Mexican, he Canadian) owner-managers account for the relaxed atmosphere of the new-age **Villa Nirvana-Villa Rosana,** 302 Playa Pie de la Cuesta, P.O. Box 950, Acapulco, Guerrero 39300. Additional pluses include a big blue pool at the beach end of a lovely high-fenced garden and a *palapa* restau-

rant. Cars park inside the fence. Rooms occupy two-story tiers bordering the garden, upper floors being more private. The 10 rooms (some with hot water) rent for about $20 s or d low season, $30 high. Discounts for monthly rentals run about 15%. The owners are managing their complex amicably in two halves. She operates the Villa Nirvana, tel. (74) 601-631, while he runs the Villa Rosana, tel. (74) 603-252. Guests get to choose which they prefer, between the two equally attractive options.

Among the prettiest of Pie de la Cuesta accommodations is the **Hotel Club Puesta del Sol,** P.O. Box 1264, Acapulco, Guerrero 39300, tel. (74) 600-412, where guests enjoy an airy outside dining area, a blue pool, and a tennis court within spacious, sculpture-decorated garden grounds. Tasty food from the kitchen of the amiable co-managers Juana Ortiz and Josea Hernández and hours spent socializing, relaxing, and reading around the restaurant tables account for the hotel's loyal North American, European, and Mexican clientele. The 24 spartan but clean rooms are spread among two double-story buildings, one at beachfront. Doubles by the beach go for about $16 low season and $20 high; away from the beach, the same run $14 and $17. Kitchen-equipped beachside apartments for six rent for about $30 low season, $40 high. All accommodations come with fans and include parking.

Trying hard to be luxurious is the **Hotel Ukae Kim,** Playa Pie de la Cuesta 336, Pie de la Cuesta, Guerrero 39900, tel./fax (74) 602-187. Unfortunately, the builder crammed the 31 rooms into a small space, rendering them private but generally dark. Amenities include a small, inviting pool patio and *palapa* restaurant at the hotel's beachfront end. The clean, tastefully decorated rooms go for about $55 s or d low season, $58 for ocean view, $60 with ocean view and jacuzzi. Corresponding high season rates are about $65, $67 and $83. With hot water and a/c; credit cards accepted.

Trailer Parks

RV-equipped Pie de la Cuesta vacationers can choose between two trailer parks. First choice goes to the homey **Acapulco Trailer Park,** with about 60 palm-shaded beachfront and lagoon-side spaces, with all hookups, P.O. Box 1, Acapulco, Guerrero 39300, tel. (74) 600-010, fax 602-457. A friendly atmosphere, good management, and many extras, including a secure fence and gate, keep the place full most of the winter. Facilities include a boat ramp, a store, a security guard, and clean restrooms and showers. The choicest beach or lagoonfront spaces rent for about $10; less choice go for $9; one free day per week. Get your winter reservation in early.

The security guard at the Acapulco Trailer Park is a reminder of former times, when muggings and theft were occurring with some frequency on Playa Pie de la Cuesta. Although bright new night lights on the beach and a local police station have greatly reduced the problem, local folks still warn against camping or walking on the beach at night.

Second choice goes to the bare-bones **Quinta Dora Trailer Park,** across the road from the Acapulco Trailer Park. Its main plus is an azure, palm-shaded lagoonfront location; lacking a fence, its main drawback is bad security.

Food

For food, most visitors either do their own cooking, eat at their or each other's Pie de la Cuesta lodgings, or go into Acapulco. Of the few restaurants along the Pie de la Cuesta road, the best is the lake-view *palapa* of the Club de Skis Tres Marias (see above). The open-air dining room of the Hotel Club Puesta de Sol and the poolside beachfront Hotel Ukae Kim are also good prospects for a relaxed light meal.

Entertainment and Events

Pie de la Cuesta's big fiesta honors the local patron, the **Virgin of Guadalupe,** with masses, processions, fireworks, and dances on 10, 11, and 12 December. The fiesta's climax, de rigueur for visitors, is the mass pilgrimage around the lake by boat.

At least one local discotheque, **Hawaii 5-O,** fires up seasonally and occasionally on weekends. Brightly painted signs on the roadside at mid-village make it impossible to miss.

The deluxe **Parador del Sol** all-inclusive resort (about a mile west of Pie de la Cuesta village— turn right at the Barra de Coyuca fork) invites visitors to purchase day and/or evening guest memberships for about $17 per adult (kids 4-11, $7) per seven-hour day (10 a.m.-5 p.m.) and evening (6 p.m.-1 a.m.) sessions. Day guests enjoy breakfast (10-11 a.m.), lunch (1-2 p.m.), open bar, and free use of the pools, beach club, kiddie playground, exercise gym, and basketball, volleyball, nine-hole golf course, and tennis courts. The evening program kicks off at 6, with sports (including night-lit tennis) and swimming, continuing with supper (8:30-9:30 p.m.), open bar, and dancing at the discotheque until after midnight. If after a day you haven't had your fill, you might want to accept their invitation to stay overnight for about $60 per person, double occupancy, low season; $80 high. For details, inquire at the front desk, or call (74) 602-003, 602-004, 602-005, 602-006, or toll-free in Mexico (800) 90-229.

Services

Although most services are concentrated 20 minutes away in Acapulco, Pie de la Cuesta nevertheless provides a few essentials. For medical consultations, see either Doctora Patricia Villalobos or her husband, Doctor Luis Amados Rios, tel. (74) 600-923, at their pharmacy where the lagoon begins, right in the middle of the village. Between them, they understand both English and French.

A scattering of minimarkets supply food. Two public long-distance phones are available, one in front of the Acapulco Trailer Park and the other on the highway by the doctors' pharmacy. In emergencies, go to the *policía,* at the small station near the intersection of the Pie de la Cuesta road and the highway to Acapulco.

Getting There and Away

Pie de la Cuesta is accessible via the fork from Hwy. 200 near Km 10, 144 miles (232 km) southwest of Zihuatanejo. First-class buses drop passengers at the roadside, where they can either walk, taxi, or ride one of the very frequent Acapulco microbuses half a mile to the hotels.

From the same intersection, the Acapulco old town plaza is six miles (10 km) by car, taxi ($5), or local bus.

ACAPULCO AND INLAND TO TAXCO

ACAPULCO

All over Mexico and half the world, Acapulco (pop. 1.5 million) means merrymaking, good food, and palm-shaded beaches. Despite 50 years of continuous development, its reputation is as deserved as ever. The many Acapulcos— the turquoise bay edged by golden sands and emerald hills, the host of hotels, humble and grand, the spontaneous entertainments, the colorful market, and shady old town square—continue to draw millions of yearly visitors from all over the world.

HISTORY

Before Columbus
Despite its modern facade, Acapulco has been well known as a traveler's crossroads for at least a millennium. Its name comes from the Nahuatl (Aztec) words that mean "Place of Dense Reeds."

The earliest discovered local remains, stone metates and pottery utensils, were left behind by seaside residents around 2500 B.C. Much later, sophisticated artisans fashioned curvaceous female figurines, which archaeologists unearthed at Las Sabanas near Acapulco during the mid-20th century. Those unique finds added fuel to speculation of early Polynesian or Asian influences in Pacific Mexico as early as 1,500 years before Columbus.

Other discoveries, however, resemble artifacts found in highland Mexico. Although undoubtedly influenced by Tarascan, Mixtec, Zapotec, and Aztec civilizations and frequented by their traders, Acapulco never came under their direct control, but instead remained subject to local chieftains until the conquest.

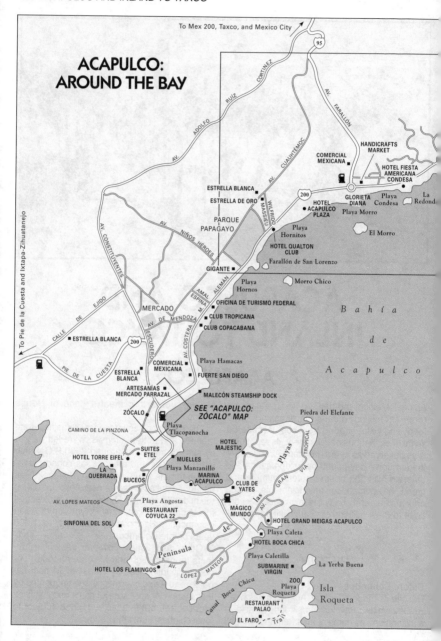

ACAPULCO: AROUND THE BAY

To Mex 200, Taxco, and Mexico City

95

To Pie de la Cuesta and Ixtapa-Zihuatanejo

AV. CORTINEZ

AV. ADOLFO RUIZ

AV. CUAUHTEMOC

AV. FARALLON

AV. NIÑOS HEROES

AV. CONSTITUYENTES

WILFRIDO MASSIEU

HANDICRAFTS MARKET

COMERCIAL MEXICANA

HOTEL FIESTA AMERICANA CONDESA

ESTRELLA BLANCA

ESTRELLA DE ORO

200

GLORIETA DIANA

Playa Condesa

La Redonda

HOTEL ACAPULCO PLAZA

Playa Morro

PARQUE PAPAGAYO

Playa Hornitos

El Morro

HOTEL QUALTON CLUB

GIGANTE

Farallón de San Lorenzo

AMAL ESPINA M. ALEMAN

Playa Hornos

Morro Chico

MERCADO AV. DE MENDOZA

OFICINA DE TURISMO FEDERAL

Bahía

CALLE DE EJIDO

AV. ESCUDERO

CLUB TROPICANA

CLUB COPACABANA

de

ESTRELLA BLANCA

200

AV. COSTERA

Acapulco

PIE DE LA CUESTA

COMERCIAL MEXICANA

Playa Hamacas

ESTRELLA BLANCA

FUERTE SAN DIEGO

ARTESANÍAS MERCADO PARRAZAL

MALECÓN STEAMSHIP DOCK

ZÓCALO

SEE "ACAPULCO: ZÓCALO" MAP

Piedra del Elefante

CAMINO DE LA PINZONA

Playa Tlacopanocha

SUITES ETEL

HOTEL MAJESTIC

Playas

HOTEL TORRE EIFEL

MUELLES

GRAN VIA TROPICAL

LA QUEBRADA

BUCEOS

Playa Manzanillo

MARINA ACAPULCO

CLUB DE YATES

AV. LÓPEZ MATEOS

Playa Angosta

MÁGICO MUNDO

las

RESTAURANT COYUCA 22

HOTEL GRAND MEIGAS ACAPULCO

SINFONIA DEL SOL

de

Playa Caleta

HOTEL BOCA CHICA

Playa Caletilla

Peninsula

SUBMARINE VIRGIN

La Yerba Buena

HOTEL LOS FLAMINGOS

AV. LÓPEZ MATEOS

ZOO

Playa Roqueta

Isla Roqueta

Canal Boca Chica

RESTAURANT PALAO

Trail

EL FARO

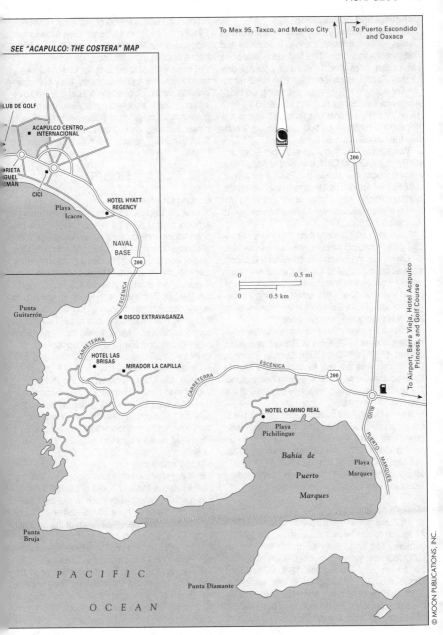

SEE "ACAPULCO: THE COSTERA" MAP

To Mex 95, Taxco, and Mexico City

To Puerto Escondido and Oaxaca

CLUB DE GOLF

ACAPULCO CENTRO INTERNACIONAL

RRIETA
IGUEL
EMÁN

CICI

Playa Icacos

HOTEL HYATT REGENCY

NAVAL BASE

200

Punta Guitarrón

ESCÉNICA

CARRETERRA

DISCO EXTRAVAGANZA

0   0.5 mi

0   0.5 km

HOTEL LAS BRISAS

MIRADOR LA CAPILLA

CARRETERRA

ESCÉNICA

200

To Airport, Barra Vieja, Hotel Acapulco Princess, and Golf Course

HOTEL CAMINO REAL

Playa Pichilingue

BLVD PUERTO MARQUES

Bahía de

Puerto

Marques

Playa Marques

Punta Bruja

PACIFIC

OCEAN

Punta Diamante

© MOON PUBLICATIONS, INC.

Conquest and Colonization

The Aztecs had scarcely surrendered when Cortés sent expeditions south to build ships and find a route to China. The first such explorers sailed out from Zacatula, near present-day Lázaro Cárdenas on the coast 250 miles northwest of Acapulco. They returned, telling Cortés of Acapulco Bay. By a royal decree dated 25 April 1528, "Acapulco and her land . . . where the ships of the south will be built . . ." passed directly into the hands of the Spanish Crown.

Voyages of discovery set sail from Acapulco for Peru, the Gulf of California, and to Asia. None returned from the across the Pacific, however, until Father Andrés de Urdaneta discovered the northern Pacific tradewinds, which propelled him and his ship, loaded with Chinese treasure, to Acapulco in 1565.

From then on, for more than 200 years, a special yearly trading ship, renowned as the Nao de China and in England as the Manila Galleon, set sail from Acapulco for the Orient. Its return sparked an annual merchant fair, swelling Acapulco's population with traders jostling to bargain for the Manila Galleon's shiny trove of silks, porcelain, ivory, and lacquerware.

Acapulco's yearly treasure soon attracted marauders, too. In 1579, Francis Drake threatened, and in 1587, off Cabo San Lucas, Thomas Cavendish was the first to capture the Manila Galleon, the *Santa Anna*. The cash booty alone, 1.2 million gold pesos, severely depressed the London gold market.

After a Dutch fleet invaded Acapulco in 1615, the Spanish rebuilt their fort, which they christened Fort San Diego in 1617. Destroyed by an earthquake in 1776, the fort was rebuilt by 1783. But Mexico's War of Independence (1810-21) stopped the Manila Galleon forever, sending Acapulco into a century-long slumber.

Modern Acapulco

In 1927, the government paved the Mexico City-Acapulco road; the first cars arrived on 11 November. The first luxury hotel, the Mirador, at La Quebrada, went up in 1933; soon airplanes began arriving. During the 1940s President Miguel Alemán (1946-52) fell in love with Acapulco and thought everyone else should have the same opportunity. He built new boulevards, power plants, and a superhighway. Investors responded with a lineup of high-rise hostelries. Finally, in 1959, presidents Eisenhower and Adolfo López Mateos convened their summit conference in a grand Acapulco hotel.

Thousands of Mexicans flocked to fill jobs in the shiny hotels and restaurants. They built shantytowns, which climbed the hills and spilled over into previously sleepy communities nearby. The government responded with streets, drainage, power, housing, and schools. By the 1990s more than a million people were calling Acapulco home.

SIGHTS

Getting Oriented

In one tremendous sweep, Acapulco curves around its dazzling half-moon bay. Face the open ocean and you are looking due south. West will be on your right hand, east on your left. One continuous beachfront boulevard, appropriately named the **Costera Miguel Alemán** (the "Costera," for short), unites old Acapulco, west of the Parque Papagayo amusement zone, with new Acapulco, the lineup of big beach hotels that stretches around the bay to the Las Brisas condo headland. There, during the night, a big cross glows and marks the hilltop lookout, Mirador La Capilla, above the bay's east end.

On the opposite, old-town side of Parque Papagayo, the Costera curves along the palmy, uncluttered *playas* Hornos and Hamacas to the steamship dock. Here the Costera, called the *malecón* as it passes the *zócalo* (town plaza), continues to the mansion-dotted hilly jumble of Peninsula de las Playas.

Getting Around

Buses run nearly continuously along the Costera. Fare averages the equivalent of about 20 cents. Bus routes—indicated by such labels as "Base" (BAH-say, the naval base on the east end), "Centro" *(zócalo),* "Caleta" (the beach, at the far west end), "Cine" (movie theater near the beach before the *zócalo),* "Hornos" (the beach near Parque Papagayo)—run along the Costera.

Taxis, on the other hand, cost between $1 and $5 for any in-town destination. They are not metered, so agree upon the price *before* you get in. If the driver demands too much, hailing another taxi often solves the problem.

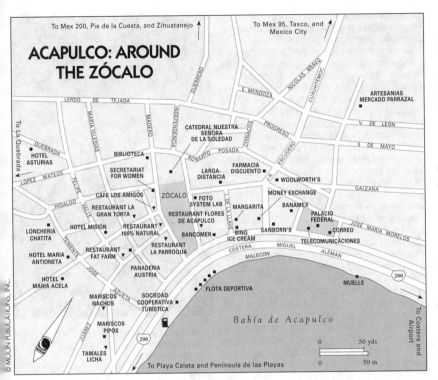

ACAPULCO: AROUND THE ZÓCALO

To Mex 200, Pie de la Cuesta, and Zihuatanejo

To Mex 95, Taxco, and Mexico City

GUERRERO
E. MENDOZA
NICOLAS BRAVO
CUAUHTEMOC

LERDO DE TEJADA
MARIA IGLESIAS
MADERO
INDEPENDENCIA
PROGRESO
ARTESANIAS MERCADO PARRAZAL
V. DE LEÓN

To La Quebrada
QUEBRADA
HOTEL ASTURIAS
BIBLIOTECA
CATEDRAL NUESTRA SEÑORA DE LA SOLEDAD
ROBERTO POSADA
CHINACOS
ESCUDERO
5 DE MAYO

LÓPEZ MATEOS
FELIPE VALLE
SECRETARIAT FOR WOMEN
LARGA-DISTANCIA
FARMACIA DISCUENTO
R.
WOOLWORTH'S
GALEANA

HIDALGO
CAFÉ LOS AMIGOS
ZÓCALO
FOTO SYSTEM LAB
MONEY EXCHANGE
RESTAURANT LA GRAN TORTA
MARGARITA
BANAMEX
PALACIO FEDERAL
JOSÉ MARIA MORELOS

LONCHERIA CHATITA
HOTEL MISIÓN
RESTAURANT 100% NATURAL
RESTAURANT FLORES DE ACAPULCO
BANCOMER
BING ICE CREAM
SANBORN'S
CORREO
TELECOMUNICACIONES

TENIENTE
RESTAURANT FAT FARM
RESTAURANT LA PARROQUA
COSTERA MIGUEL ALEMÁN
MALECON

HOTEL MARIA ANTIONETA
PANADERIA AUSTRIA

HOTEL MARÍA ACELA
JOSÉ AZUETA
SOCIEDAD COOPERATIVA TURÍSTICA
FLOTA DEPORTIVA
MUELLE
200
To Costera and Airport

JUAREZ
MARISCOS NACHOS
Bahía de Acapulco

MARISCOS PIPOS
200
0   50 yds
0   50 m

TAMALES LICHA
To Playa Caleta and Península de las Playas

© MOON PUBLICATIONS, INC.

A Walk around Old Acapulco

In old Acapulco, traffic slows and people return to traditional ways. Couples promenade along the *malecón* dockfront, fishing boats leave and return, while in the adjacent *zócalo,* families stroll past the church, musicians play, and tourists and businessmen sip coffee in the shade of huge banyan trees.

Start your walk beneath those *zócalo* trees. Under their pendulous air roots, browse the bookstalls, relax in one of the cafés; at night, watch the clowns perform, listen to a band concert, or join in a pitch-penny game. Take a look inside the mod-style **cathedral** dedicated to Our Lady of Solitude. Admire its angel-filled sky-blue ceiling and visit the Virgin to the right of the altar.

Outside, cross the boulevard to the *malecón* dockside; in midafternoon, you may see huge marlin and swordfish being hauled up from the boats.

Head out of the *zócalo* and left along the Costera past the steamship dock a few blocks to the 18th-century fort, **Fuerte San Diego,** atop its bayside hill; open Tues.-Sun. 10:30 a.m.-4:30 p.m. Engineer Miguel Costansó completed the massive, five-pointed maze of moats, walls, and battlements in 1783.

Inside, galleries within the original fort storerooms, barracks, chapel, and kitchen illustrate local pre-Columbian, conquest, and colonial history. The excellent, unusually graphic displays include much about pirates (such as Francis Drake and John Hawkins, known as "admirals" to the English-speaking world); Spanish galleons, their history and construction; and famous visitors, notably Japanese Captain Hasekura, who in 1613 built a ship and sailed from Sendai, Japan, to Acapulco; thence he continued overland to Mexico City, by sea to Spain, to the Pope in Rome, and back again through Acapulco to Japan.

La Quebrada

Head back to the *zócalo* and continue past the cathedral. After three short blocks to Av. López Mateos, continue uphill to the La Quebrada diver's point, marked by the big parking lot at the hillcrest. There, Acapulco's energy focuses five times a day (at 1 p.m. and evenings hourly 7:30-10:30 p.m.) as tense crowds watch the divers plummet more than a hundred feet to the waves below. Admission is about $1, collected by the divers' cooperative. Performers average less than $100 per dive from the proceeds. The adjacent Hotel Plaza Las Glorias (the former Hotel Mirador) charges about $5 cover to view the dives from their terrace.

Old Town Beaches

These start not far from the *zócalo*. At the foot of the Fuerte San Diego, the sand of **Playa Hamacas** begins, changing to **Playa Hornos** ("Ovens") and continuing north a mile to a rocky shoal-line called Farallón de San Lorenzo. Hornos is the Sunday favorite of Mexican families, where boats buzz beyond the very tranquil waves and retirees stroll the wide, yellow sand while vendors work the sunbathing crowd.

Moving south past the *zócalo* and the fishing boats, you'll find **Playa Tlacopanocha**, a petite strip of sand beneath some spreading trees. Here, bay-tour launches wait for passengers, and kids play in the glassy water, which would be great for swimming if it weren't for the refuse from nearby fishing boats.

From there, cross the Costera and hop on a bus marked Caleta to gemlike **Playa Caleta** and its twin **Playa Caletilla** on the far side of the hilly peninsula (named, appropriately, Peninsula de las Playas). With medium-coarse yellow sand and blue ripples for waves, Caleta and Caletilla are for people who want company. They are often crowded, sometimes nearly solid on Sunday. Boats offer banana-tube rides, and snorkel gear is rentable from beach concessionaires. Dozens of stalls and restaurants serve refreshments.

Mágico Mundo water park, tel. (74) 831-215—with an aquarium, museum, restaurant, water slides, cascades, and more—perches on the little peninsula between the beaches. Open daily 9 a.m.-5 p.m.; admission $4 adult, $2 child.

Beach palapas *spread like a field of buttons on Playa Hornitos, as seen from the upper floors of the Hotel Qualton Club.*

Isla Roqueta

A Roqueta Island ticket tout will often try to snare you as you get off the Caleta bus. The roundtrip, which runs around $3, is usually in a boat with a glass bottom, through which you can peer at the fish as they peer back from their aqua underwater world. On the other side, you can sunbathe on sunny little Playa Roqueta, have lunch at one of several beachside *palapas,* swim, snorkel, and quench the thirst of the famous Roqueta beer-drinking burros (who are said to prefer Corona).

The burros are the island's sole inhabitants, except for the lighthouse keeper, for whom the burros haul supplies weekly. For those with the energy, the gradual lighthouse trail, only a few hundred yards long, begins at Playa Roqueta. Open Wed.-Mon.; admission $1. Take drinks and a hat.

Other island attractions include a good small zoo in the shady mixed acacia-deciduous hillside forest above Playa Roqueta. Animals include many endangered local varieties, such as howler monkeys, a jaguar, mountain lion, coatimundi, peccary, crocodile, and ocelot. Past the zoo hillcrest, a trail leads steeply downhill to tiny, secluded **Playa Marin,** where you can loll to your heart's content in the waves that funnel into the narrow channel. (Be prepared to avoid sunburn, however.)

A **boat tour** from Playa Tlacopanocha is another way to get to Isla Roqueta. The glass-bottomed boats *Maryvioli, Santa María,* and *Tequila* leave several times daily for 90-minute tours (about $3 per person). Trips include viewing underwater life, shoreline vistas, the *Virgen Submarina* (a statue submerged in the Isla Roqueta channel), a stop on the island, and snorkeling. Beer and soft drinks are sold onboard.

Playa Angosta

Back on the mainland, you can visit another hidden beach nearby, Playa Angosta ("Narrow Beach"), the only Acapulco strand with an unobstructed sunset horizon. A breezy dab of a beach, sandwiched between a pair of sandstone cliffs, Angosta's ocean waves roll in, swishing upon the sand. A food *palapa* occupies one side of the beach and a few fishing launches and nets are on the other. With caution, swimming, bodysurfing, and boogie boarding are sometimes possible here; otherwise, Angosta is best for scenery and picnics.

Just uphill, a few hundred yards along the southbound cliffside boulevard, is **Sinfonia del Sol** sunset amphitheater. Here, local folks gather around 5:30 p.m. daily to watch the sun go down.

Costera Beaches

These are the hotel-lined golden shores where affluent Mexicans and foreign visitors stay and play in the sun. They are variations on one continuous curve of sand. Beginning at the west end with **Playa Hornitos** (also known as Playa Papagayo), they continue, changing names from **Playa Morro** to **Playa Condesa** and finally, **Playa Icacos,** which curves and stretches to its sheltered east end past the naval base. All of the same semicoarse golden silica sand, the beaches begin with fairly broad 200-foot-wide Playas Papagayo and Morro. They narrow

sharply to under 100 feet at Playa Condesa, then broaden again to more than 200 feet along Playa Icacos.

Their surf is mostly very gentle, breaking in one- or two-foot waves and receding with little undertow. This makes for safe swimming within float-enclosed beachside areas, but it's too tranquil for bodysurfing, boogie boarding, or surfing. Beyond the swimming floats, motorboats hurry along, pulling parasailors and banana-tube riders, while jet skis cavort and careen over the swells.

Such motorized hubbub lessens the safety and enjoyment of quieter sports off most new town beaches. Sailboaters and windsurfers with their own equipment might try the remote, more tranquil east end of Playa Icacos, however.

Water-skiing, officially restricted to certain parts of Acapulco Bay, has largely moved to Coyuca Lagoon northwest of the city. Coyuca Lagoon has enough space for many good motorboat-free spots for sailboaters and windsurfers (see **Pie de la Cuesta** in the preceding chapter).

Rocky outcroppings along Playas Papagayo, Morro, and Condesa add interest and intimacy to an already beautiful shoreline. The rocks are good for tidepooling and fishing by pole-casting (or by net, as locals do) above the waves.

Beaches Southeast of Town

Ride a Puerto Marquez- or Lomas-marked bus or drive along the Costera eastward. Past the naval base entrance on the right, the road climbs the hill, passing a number of panoramic bay viewpoints. After the Las Brisas condo-hotel complex, the road curves around the hill shoulder and heads downward past picture-perfect vistas of **Bahía de Puerto Marquez.** At the bottom-of-the-hill intersection and overpass, a road branches right to Puerto Marquez.

The little bayside town is mainly a Sunday seafood and picnicking retreat for Acapulco families. Dozens of *palapa* restaurants line its motorboat-dotted sandy beach. One ramshackle hotel, at the far south end of the single main beachfront street, offers lodgings.

If you're driving, mark your odometer at the hill-bottom intersection and head east toward the airport. If traveling by bus, continue via one of the Lomas buses, which continue east from Acapulco about once an hour. About a mile farther, a turnoff road goes right to the Acapulco Princess and the Pierre Marquez hotels and golf course on Playa Revolcadero.

Beach access is by side roads or by walking directly through the hotel lobbies. If you come by bus, hail a taxi from the highway to the Hotel Princess door for the sake of a good entrance.

Playa Revolcadero, a broad, miles-long, yellow-white strand, has the rolling open-ocean billows that Acapulco Bay doesn't. The sometimes-rough waves are generally good for boogie boarding, bodysurfing, and even surfing near the rocks on the northwest end. Because of the waves and sometimes hazardous currents, the hotel provides lifeguards for safety. The Playa Revolcadero breeze is also brisk enough for sailing and windsurfing with your own boat or board. Some rentals may be available from the hotel beach concession.

Playa Encantada and Barra Vieja

About seven miles (11 km) from the Puerto Marquez traffic intersection, the Barra Vieja road forks right and heads along a breezy wild beach. About two miles from the fork, you will pass the **Hotel Marparaíso Queen.** The 100 two-bedroom luxury apartments surround a spacious pool and garden with beachside restaurant. The luxuriously appointed air-conditioned kitchenette apartments rent for about $130, for one to four persons, mid-December until Easter. Filled with mostly Canadian clients during the winter, the rates are bargainable during slack periods. (Low-season promotions, for example, have run as low as $25 d, including breakfast.) Contact the hotel by phone or fax, tel. (74) 620-518 or 620-348, fax 620-246.

About 18 miles (32 km) from the traffic intersection (11 miles from the fork) a sign marks the former Playa Encantada resort and restaurant, which unfortunately has closed. You might check to see if the owners have restored their little paradise to the condition described in previous editions: an airy downscale beachside restaurant beside a big blue pool, garden, and large parking lot, with camping space along the beach beneath the palms.

Recently a group of volunteers has moved in, maintaining the **Campamento Tortuguero Playa Encantada,** a summer-fall season turtle egg rescue and hatchery encampment. During their lonely July-November vigil the volunteers

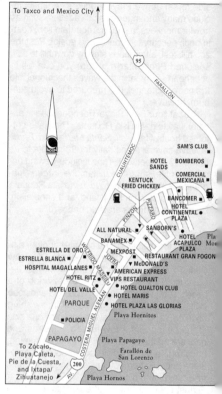

sorely need money and food to sustain their effort. At least, they would probably appreciate some help and sympathetic company in case you decide to also set your tent up beneath the rustling Playa Encantada grove.

If so, you'll be able to share in enjoying the wide, breezy strand, whose rolling waves, with ordinary precautions, appear to be good for boogie boarding, bodysurfing, and possibly surfing. The sun sets on an unobstructed horizon, and the crab-rich beach is good for surf fishing (or by boat if you launch during morning calm). Additionally, the firm, level sand is excellent for jogging, walking, and beachcombing.

About a mile farther on, the stores (groceries and long-distance phone) and modest houses of fishing village Barra Vieja dot the roadside. Many seafood *palapas* line the beachside. The better

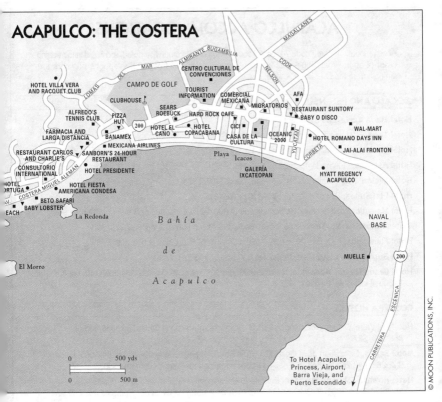

ACAPULCO: THE COSTERA

HOTEL VILLA VERA AND RACQUET CLUB
CAMPO DE GOLF
CENTRO CULTURAL DE CONVENCIONES
CLUBHOUSE
TOURIST INFORMATION
COMERCIAL MEXICANA
AFA
ALFREDO'S TENNIS CLUB
PIZZA HUT
SEARS ROEBUCK
HARD ROCK CAFE
MIGRATORIOS
RESTAURANT SUNTORY
BABY O DISCO
FARMACIA AND LARGA DISTANCIA
BANAMEX
HOTEL EL CANO
HOTEL COPACABANA
CICI
CASA DE LA CULTURA
OCEANIC 2000
WAL-MART
HOTEL ROMANO DAYS INN
RESTAURANT CARLOS AND CHARLIE'S
MEXICANA AIRLINES
Playa Icacos
JAI-ALAI FRONTON
CONSULTORIO INTERNATIONAL
SANBORN'S 24-HOUR RESTAURANT
GALERÍA IXCATEOPAN
HOTEL TORTUGA
HOTEL PRESIDENTE
HOTEL FIESTA AMERICANA CONDESA
HYATT REGENCY ACAPULCO
BETO SAFARI
BABY LOBSTER
BEACH
La Redonda

Bahía de Acapulco

NAVAL BASE

El Morro
MUELLE

To Hotel Acapulco Princess, Airport, Barra Vieja, and Puerto Escondido

0   500 yds
0   500 m

© MOON PUBLICATIONS, INC.

---

among them include Beto's Condesa and Gloria del Mar, both with pools.

Besides the beach, Barra Vieja visitors enjoy access to the vast **Laguna Tres Palos** mangrove wetland from the *estero* at the east end of town before the bridge. From there, boatmen take parties on fishing and wildlife-viewing excursions.

Despite its steady flow of Sunday tourists, this sleepy lagoonside hamlet remains an Acapulco few people know—like a faraway South Seas village—with drowsy palms, rolling waves, pleasant breezes, and fisherfolk who live by the ancient rhythms of sun and tide.

The road (which maps routinely show going through to Hwy. 200) crosses a rickety lagoon bridge and ends about two miles farther east at scruffy Lomas de Chapultepec village.

ACCOMMODATIONS

Location largely determines the price and style of Acapulco hotels. In the old town, most hotels are either clustered around the *zócalo* or perched on the hillsides of Peninsula de las Playas. They are generally not on the beach and are cheaper and less luxurious. Most new town hotels, by contrast, lie mostly along the Costera Miguel Alemán right on the beach. Guests often enjoy a wealth of resort amenities and luxury view rooms at correspondingly luxurious prices.

Many lodgings, however, defy categorization. Acapulco offers numerous choices to suit individual tastes and pocketbooks. In all cases, and especially in the luxury hotels, you can often save money by requesting low-season, pack-

ACAPULCO ACCOMMODATIONS

Accommodations (area code 74, postal code 39300 unless otherwise noted) are listed in increasing order of approximate high-season, double-room rates. Toll-free (800) telephone numbers are dialable from the U.S. and Canada.

ZÓCALO AND PENINSULA DE LAS PLAYAS HOTELS

Hotel María Acela, La Paz 19, tel. 820-661, $10

Hotel Torre Eifel, Inalambrica 110, tel. 821-683, $19

Hotel María Antioneta, Teniente Azueta 17, tel. 825-024, $19

Hotel Asturias, Quebrada 45, tel./fax, 836-548, $20

Hotel Misión, Felipe Valle 12, tel. 823-643, fax 822-076, $36

Hotel Etel Suites, Pinzona 92, tel. 822-240 or 822-241, $42

Hotel Majestic, Pozo del Rey 73, postal code 39390, tel./fax 832-885 or 832-713, 832-032, $55

Suites Alba, Gran Via Tropical 35, postal code 39390, tel. 830-073, fax 838-378, $60

Hotel Flamingos, P.O. Box 70, tel. 820-690, 820-691, or 820-692, fax 839-806, $65

Hotel Boca Chica, Playa Caletilla s/n, tel. 836-601 or 836-741, $110

Hotel Grand Meigas Acapulco, Cerro San Martin 325, tel. 839-334, 839-234, 839-140, fax 839-125, $180 (all inclusive, for two)

COSTERA HOTELS

Hotel del Valle, G. Gomez Espinosa 8 (P.O. Box C-14, postal code 39670), tel. 858-336 or 858-388, $27

Hotel Sands, Calle Juan de la Cosa 178 (P.O. Box 256) postal code 39670, tel. 842-260, 842-261, 842-262, 842-263, or 842-264, fax 841-053, e-mail: sands@sands.com.mx, $50

Hotel Howard Johnson Maralisa, Enrique El Esclavo s/n, postal code 39670, tel. 856-677, fax 859-228, or (800) IGOHOJO (446-4656), e-mail: maralisa@aca.novenet.com.mx, $90

Hotel Days Inn, Costera M. Alemán 130, postal code 39860, tel. 845-332, fax 845-822, tel. (800) DAYSINN (329-7466), $75

Hotel Maris, Costera M. Alemán 59, postal code 39670, tel./fax 858-440 or 858-492, $80

Hotel Villa Vera and Racquet Club, Lomas del Mar 35, P.O. Box 560, postal code 39690, tel. 840-333, 840-334, 840-335, fax 847-479, toll-free tel. (800) 710-9300 in Mexico, $175

Hotel Elcano, Costera M. Alemán 75, postal code 39690, tel. 841-950, $180

Hyatt Regency Acapulco, Costera M. Alemán 1, postal code 39860, tel. 691-234, fax 843-087, or (800) 233-1234, $260

Hotel Fiesta Americana Condesa, Costera M. Alemán 1220, tel. 842-828, 842-355, fax 841-828, or tel. (800) FIESTA-1 (343-7821), e-mail: nsalgado@fiestaamericana.com.mx, $265

Hotel Vidafel Mayan Palace, Av. Costera de las Palmas, Fracc. Playa Diamante, postal code 39900, tel./fax 690-201, tel. (800) VIDAFEL (843-2335) or (800) 996-2926, $312

Hotel Acapulco Princess, Playa Revolcadero, tel. 691-000 or (800) 223-1818, fax 691-015, $365

age, and weekly or monthly discounts. For winter high-season lodgings, call or write for early reservations.

Hotels near the *Zócalo*

A number of clean, economical hotels cluster in the colorful neighborhood between La Quebrada and the *zócalo*. Among the most popular is the colonial-chic **Hotel Misión,** Felipe Valle 12, Acapulco, Guerrero 39300, tel. (74) 823-643, fax 822-076, built in two stories around a plant-decorated patio, shaded by a spreading mango tree, corner of La Paz, two blocks from the *zócalo*. When the mangoes ripen in April guests get their fill of the fragrant fruit. The 24 attractively decorated rooms rent for about $12 per person low season, $18 high. With fans, hot water, and parking.

One block farther along La Paz, the '60s-modern **Hotel María Antioneta** fronts the lively shop- and restaurant-lined Av. Azueta, Teniente Azueta 17, Acapulco, Guerrero 39300, tel. (74) 825-024. The 34 plainly furnished but comfortable rooms are light and pleasant, especially on the upper floor. Most rooms are fortunately recessed along the leafy inner courtyard, away from street noise. Rates run about $17 d low season, $19 high, with hot water and fans.

A block away, on the quiet cul-de-sac end of Av. La Paz, stands the spartan three-story **Hotel María Acela,** Av. La Paz 19, Acapulco, Guerrero 39300, tel. (74) 820-661. Its family management lends a homey atmosphere more like a guest-house than a hotel. The austerely furnished rooms, although clean, lack hot water. The 21 rooms rent for around $5 s, $10 d, with fan.

The **Hotel Asturias,** Quebrada 45, Acapulco, Guerrero 39300, tel./fax (74) 836-548, on Av. Quebrada a few blocks uphill from the *zócalo,* offers a relaxing atmosphere at budget rates. Its two stories of plain but tidy rooms surround a plant-decorated pool patio with chairs for sunning. Get an upper room for more light and privacy. Rates for the 15 rooms are about $10 s, $16 d, and $23 t low season, $20 s or d, $28 t high, with fans; four short blocks from the cathedral, between Ramirez and Ortiz.

A few blocks farther uphill, **Hotel Torre Eifel,** Inalambrica 110, Acapulco, Guerrero 39300, tel. (74) 821-683, rises above its hillside garden overlooking the La Quebrada diver's point tourist

mecca. The 25 simply but comfortably furnished rooms rise in four motel-modern tiers above an inviting pool and patio. Guests in the uppermost rooms enjoy breezy sea views and a sunset horizon. Rooms rent for about $6 s, $12 d, and $18 t low season, and $9, $19, and $28 high, with fans, hot water, and parking; at the corner of Av. Pinzona, one block uphill from the La Quebrada parking lot.

Two more blocks up winding Av. Pinzona, the **Hotel Etel Suites** stands on the hillside above old Acapulco, Av. Pinzona 92, Acapulco, Guerrero 39300, tel. (74) 822-240 or 822-241. Well managed by friendly owner Etel (great-grand-daughter of renowned California pioneer John A. Sutter), the three-building complex stairsteps downhill to a luxurious view garden and pool. Its airy hillside perch lends the Etel Suites a tranquil, luxurious ambience unusual in such an economical lodging. Chairs and sofas in a small street-level lobby invite relaxed conversation with fellow guests. The primly but thoughtfully furnished and well-maintained rooms range from singles to multibedroom view apartments. The dozens of rooms and suites rent from about $30 s or d low season, $42 high, with fans, a/c, and hot water. Completely furnished view apartments with kitchens go for about $42 low season, $54 high, with discounts negotiable for monthly rentals. Some parking, and credit cards are accepted.

Peninsula de las Playas Hotels

Many of these lodgings are spread along one continuous boulevard that winds through this plush hillside neighborhood. The boulevard starts as the Costera Miguel Alemán as it heads past the *zócalo* toward the peninsula. There it veers left as the Gran Via Tropical, rounding the peninsula clockwise. Passing Caleta and Caletilla beaches, the boulevard changes to Av. López Mateos and continues along the peninsula's sunset (southwest) side past Playa Angosta and La Quebrada diver's point before ending back in the *zócalo* neighborhood.

First along that path comes the hillside **Hotel Majestic,** Av. Pozo del Rey 73, Acapulco, Guerrero 39390, tel./fax (74) 832-885 or 832-713, 832-032, winter headquarters for crowds of youthful American, Canadian, and German vacationers. A classy two-year, top-to-bottom renovation has added considerable class to this longtime Acapulco favorite. Now, floors shine with marble, and pleasantly muted hues decorate the lobby, restaurants, and rooms. More than ever, guests will enjoy breezy bay views from the spacious grounds that spread downhill to a bayside beach club. Tennis, beach, and pool sports fill the days, while dining in the restaurants, theme parties, and dancing enliven the nights. The tastefully decorated and comfortable tile-floored rooms, many with panoramic views, come with a/c, cable TV, and telephones. The 210 rooms and suites rent from about $35 d low season, $55 high; credit cards accepted, with parking. Additional sports opportunities include windsurfing, kayaking, a gym, aerobics, and more.

A couple of blocks farther along Gran Via Tropical, the multistory **Suites Alba,** Gran Via Tropical 35, Acapulco, Guerrero 39390, tel. (74) 830-073, fax 838-378, apartment-style complex rambles through its well-kept hilltop garden of palms and pools. The mostly Canadian and American middle-class guests enjoy many facilities, including a pair of pools, a jacuzzi, a restaurant, tennis courts, a minimart, and a downhill bayside beach club with its own saltwater pool. The 292 comfortably furnished apartments have kitchenettes, a/c, and private garden-view balconies. Rentals begin at about $40 d low season, $60 high, with discounts available for monthly rentals; credit cards accepted, parking.

On the opposite side of the peninsula, guests at the **Hotel Boca Chica,** Playa Caletilla s/n, Acapulco, Guerrero 39300, tel. (74) 836-601 or 836-741, enjoy views of Playa Caletilla on one hand and the green Isla Roqueta beyond an azure channel on the other. The hotel perches on a rocky point, invitingly close to the clear aqua water from the pool deck and surrounding garden paths. The light, comfortably furnished rooms vary; if you have the option, look at two or three before you choose. Early reservations year-round are strongly recommended. Rates for the 45 rooms with phones and a/c run about $50 d low season, $110 high, with breakfast; credit cards accepted, parking.

If you like the location but can't get into the Hotel Boca Chica immediately, try the best-buy all-inclusive **Hotel Grand Meigas Acapulco,** Cerro San Martin 225, Playa Caleta, Acapulco, Guerrero 39300, tel. (74) 839-334, 839-234, 839-140, fax 839-125, on the other side of nearby Playa Caleta. Hotel guests enjoy a big blue pool and view sundeck, lush green garden, and deluxe, comfortable rooms, each with private panoramic view balcony. Rates for the 260 rooms run about $60 per person low-season double occupancy, $90 high, including all meals, drinks, and in-house sports and entertainment; with a/c, phones, cable TV, parking, credit cards accepted.

Hotel Flamingos, P.O. Box 70, Acapulco, Guerrero 39300, tel. (74) 820-690, 820-691, or 820-692, fax 839-806, uphill about a mile along Av. López Mateos, is where oldsters reminisce and youngsters find out who John Wayne, Johnny Weissmuller, and Rory Calhoun were. Faded Hollywood photos decorate the open-air lobby walls, while nearby pathways wind through a hilltop jungle of palm, hibiscus, and spreading mangoes. The rooms, several with private, ocean-view balconies, perch on a cliffside that plummets into foaming breakers hundreds of feet below. Soft evening guitar music in an open-air sunset view restaurant and a luxurious cliffside pool patio complete the lovely picture. The 40 rooms, in standard, superior, and junior suite grades, run about $50, $60, and $70 d low season, respectively. Add about $15 for high season, $25 for an extra person. They also rent some bungalows with kitchenettes and a luxurious cliffside view house; with parking, some a/c; credit cards accepted.

Costera Hotels

With few exceptions, these hostelries line both sides of the busy beach boulevard, Costera Miguel Alemán. Hotels are either right on or just a short walk from the beach. By location, moving easterly from the Papagayo amusement park, first comes the economy **Hotel del Valle,** G. Gomez Espinosa 8, P.O. Box C-14, Acapulco, Guerrero 39670, tel. (74) 858-336 and 858-388, which shares its fortunate location with much more luxurious neighbors. Two motel-style tiers of plain but clean rooms border a small but inviting pool patio. On a side street away from the noisy boulevard, the del Valle is a tranquil winter headquarters for retirees and youthful budget travelers. The 20 rooms rent for about $24 s or d low season, $27 high, with hot water; add about $3 for a/c.

Around the corner, high-rise hotels occupy the Costera beachfront. After the towering Plaza Las Glorias Paraíso, inappropriately cramped into a small lot, comes the more comfortably sized **Hotel Maris,** Av. Costera M. Alemán 59, Acapulco, Guerrero 39670, tel./fax (74) 858-440 or 858-492, where guests get spacious rooms with private view balconies for surprisingly reasonable rates. Lobby-level amenities include a small pool above the beach club with bar and restaurant (where you may have to ask them to turn down the TV volume). Street parking only, however. Rates for the 84 rooms run about $40 d low-season, and $80 high season; with a/c, TV, and phones.

Two blocks farther east, the low-rise **Hotel Howard Johnson Maralisa,** Enrique El Esclavo s/n, Acapulco, Guerrero 39670, tel. (74) 856-677, or (800) IGOHOJO (446-4656) from the U.S. and Canada, fax 859-228, e-mail: maralisa @aca.novenet.com.mx, nestles among its big beachside condo neighbors. The Maralisa is a luxuriously simple retreat, where guests, after their fill of sunning beside the palm-lined pool patio, can step down on to the sand for a jog or stroll along the beach. Later, they might enjoy a light meal in the hotel's beachside café and go out for dancing in nearby resort hotels. Several of the Maralisa's 90 comfortable rooms, tastefully decorated in whites and warm pastels, have private balconies. Standard rooms rent for about $80 d low season, $90 high. Up to two kids under 12 stay free; with a/c, TV, phones, and parking; credit cards accepted.

Several blocks farther east the low-rise **Hotel Sands,** Calle Juan de la Cosa 178, P.O. Box 256, Acapulco, Guerrero 39670, tel. (74) 842-260 842-261, 842-262, 842-263, or 842-264, fax 841-053, contrasts sharply with the monumental Hotel Costa Club (formerly Hotel Acapulco Plaza) across the boulevard. In addition to a pool patio and restaurant next to the main '60s-modern building, the deceivingly spacious grounds encompass a shady green park in the rear that leads to an attractive hidden cabaña-enclosed garden. Of the main building rooms, the uppers are best; many have been redecorated with light, comfortable furnishings. Cabaña guests, on the other hand, enjoy tasteful browns, tile decor, and big windows looking out into a leafy garden. Bungalows 1-8 are the most secluded. The 59 rooms

and 34 cabañas run about $38 d low season, $50 high, holidays such as Christmas and Easter even higher. Low-season discounts for longer stays may be available. All with a/c, cable TV, and phones; parking, squash courts, and jeep rental; credit cards accepted. You may also reserve through e-mail: sands@sands.com.mx, Web site: www.sands.com.mx, or in Mexico toll-free tel. (800) 710-9800.

The super-popular luxury **Hotel Fiesta Americana Condesa,** Av. Costera M. Alemán 1220, Acapulco, Guerrero 39690, tel. (74) 842-828, 842-355, fax 841-828, tel. (800) FIESTA-1 (343-7821) from the U.S. and Canada, e-mail: nsalgado@fiestaamericana.com.mx, presides atop its rocky shoreline perch smack in the middle of new Acapulco. Boulevard traffic roars nonstop past the front door and nightclubs rock all night nearby. By day, ranks of middle-class American and Canadian vacationers sun on the hotel's spacious pool/deck and downstairs at its *palapa*-shaded beach club. Resort facilities include multiple restaurants and bars, nightly live music, shops, rentals, tennis, golf, and all aquatic sports. Rooms, most with private bay-view balconies, are furnished in luscious pastels, rattan, and designer lamps. Rooms rent from about $90 d low season, $265 high, with a/c, TV, phones, parking, and full wheelchair access; credit cards accepted.

In exclusive isolation several blocks uphill, guests at the **Hotel Villa Vera and Racquet Club** enjoy what seems like their own Acapulco country club, at Lomas del Mar 35, P.O. Box 560, Acapulco, Guerrero 39690, tel. (74) 840-334, 840-335, fax 847-479, toll-free (800) 710-9300 in Mexico. Overlooking the entire city and bay, the hotel's dozens of bungalows nestle in a manicured garden around an elegant hillside pool and terrace restaurant. The lodgings, which range from one-room doubles to suites, are decorated in creams, pastels, and earth tones and tastefully appointed with handicrafts and one-of-a-kind wall art. No children admitted, however. Rates for the 80 rooms and suites run about $145 d low season, $175 d high for superior grade; $175 and $205, respectively, for suite; with a/c, cable TV, phones, parking, clay tennis courts, massage, and sauna; credit cards accepted. Get there via the street between the Pizza Hut and the golf course, continuing uphill at each fork. The Villa Vera gate will appear on the left after about a quarter mile.

Those who want tranquillity in the middle of Acapulco will likely find it at the recently restored **Hotel Elcano,** which is two blocks removed—and whose rooms also face away—from the Costera traffic hubbub, at Av. Costera Miguel Alemán 75, Acapulco, Guerrero 39690, tel. (74) 841-950. The hotel was named after Ferdinand Magellan's navigator, Sebastián Elcano (who was actually the one who first circumnavigated the globe; Magellan died en route but got the credit). Hotel Elcano is austerely luxurious, hued in shades of nautical blue, from the breezy, gracefully columned lobby and the spacious turquoise beachside pool to the 180 immaculate, marble-tiled view rooms. Unlike some of Acapulco's beachfront hostelries, the Elcano has plenty of space for guests to enjoy its load of extras, which include two restaurants, three bars, poolside jacuzzi, beach club, kiddie pool, gym, nine-hole golf course three blocks away, video games center, and more. Rooms, all with private ocean-view balconies, rent for about $70 d low season, $180 high. Be sure to ask for possible promotional packages, or midweek or weekly rates.

Moving a few blocks farther east along the Costera, where folks who want a bargain-priced view room a block from the beach find it at the **Hotel Days Inn,** Costera M. Alemán 130, Acapulco, Guerrero 39860, tel. (74) 845-332, fax 845-822. The youngish, mostly single clientele also like the lively late-night bar and the big pool/deck where they can rest and recover during the day. The 279 light and comfortable rooms come with a/c, TV, views, and phones. Rooms rent for about $50 d low season, $75 high; parking available, credit cards accepted. From the U.S. and Canada, reserve by toll-free tel. (800) DAYSINN (329-7466).

Two blocks away rises the 20-story tower of the **Hyatt Regency Acapulco,** Costera M. Alemán 1, Acapulco, Guerrero 39860, tel. (74) 691-234, (800) 223-1234 from the U.S. and Canada, fax 843-087, with spacious gardens, blue lagoon swimming pool, a Tarzan jungle waterfall, a squadron of personal beach *palapas*, restaurants, bars, nightly music till midnight, shops, all aquatic sports, and tennis and golf. The 690 rooms, all with private view balconies, are large

and luxurious. Low-season promotional prices, furthermore, can be surprisingly reasonable. Standard rooms rent from about $130 d low season, $260 high, with a/c, cable TV, phones, parking, and full wheelchair access; credit cards accepted.

Out-of-Town Hotels

The sleepy **Pie de la Cuesta** resort village on placid Coyuca Lagoon (about six miles by the oceanfront Hwy. 200 northwest from the Acapulco *zócalo*) has many budget and moderately priced beachside lodgings. Drive, taxi (about $5), or ride a Pie de la Cuesta-marked bus from Av. Escudero in front of Sanborn's and Woolworth's near the *zócalo*. For many more details, see the end of the previous chapter.

Past the southeast end of town near the airport, the showplace **Hotel Acapulco Princess** provides an abundance of resort facilities (including an entire golf course) spreading from luscious beachfront garden grounds at Playa Revolcadero, Acapulco, Guerrero 39300, tel. (74) 691-000, fax 691-015, (800) 223-1818 from the U.S. and Canada. Although the hotel centers on a pair of hulking neopyramids (1,019-room total), the impression from the rooms themselves is of super-luxury; from the garden it is of Eden-like jungle tranquillity—meandering pools, gurgling cascades, strutting flamingos, swaying palms—which guests seem to soak up with no trouble at all. Rooms rent from about $235 d low season, $365 high; all facilities, all sports, full wheelchair access, credit cards accepted.

Alternatively, consider the **Vidafel Mayan Palace** about a mile farther along the beach from the Acapulco Princess. Here, in a palace like the Mayan kings never had, you can have an 18-hole golf course, 12 clay tennis courts, a kilometer-long swimming pool (no kidding), five bars and three restaurants, fountains, waterfalls, and an entire blue lagoon, all overlooking a gorgeous, breezy beach. Rates run from $312 d for a gorgeous, spacious marble and pastel room with everything. Bargain for a discount or promotional package. For information and reservations, contact Vidafel Mayan Palace, Av. Costera del las Palmas, Fracc. Playa Diamante, Acapulco, Guerrero 39900, tel./fax (74) 690-201. From the U.S. and Canada, call either (800) VIDAFEL (843-2335) or (800) 996-2926.

Trailer Parks and Camping

Although condos and hotels have crowded out virtually all of Acapulco's in-town trailer parks, good prospects exist nearby. The best is the **Acapulco Trailer Park,** right on the beach in Pie de la Cuesta resort village, six miles by the coast highway northwest of the *zócalo.* For details, see the **Pie de la Cuesta** section at the end of the preceding chapter.

And although development and urbanization have likewise squeezed out in-town camping, possibilities exist in the trailer parks in Pie de La Cuesta and at Playa Encantada near **Barra Vieja.**

FOOD

Breakfast and Snacks near the *Zócalo*

Eat well for under $3 at **Lonchería Chatita,** Av. Azueta, corner of Hidalgo, open daily 8 a.m.-10 p.m., where a friendly female kitchen squad serves mounds of wholesome, local-style specialties. On a typical day, these may include savory *chiles rellenos,* rich *puerco mole de Uruapan,* *pozole* (savory hominy soup), or potato pancakes.

For something creamy and cool, go to **Bing** ice cream, open daily 9 a.m.-11 p.m., one block from the *zócalo* toward the steamship dock.

Continue another block to **Sanborn's,** *malecón* corner of Escudero, open daily 7:30 a.m.-11 p.m., where you can escape the heat and enjoy home-style ham and eggs, hamburgers, roast beef, and apple pie, although prices are fairly high.

Woolworth's, one block from the Costera, behind Sanborn's, also offers air-conditioned ambience and similar fare at more reasonable prices.

Finally, for dessert, head back over to the other side of the *zócalo* to **Panadería y Pastelería Austria,** for a tasty tart or piece of cake. On Juárez, two doors from the Fat Farm, open Mon.-Sat. 8 a.m.-2 p.m. and 4-8 p.m.

Costera Breakfast and Snacks

Snack food concentrates in Acapulco, as in many places, around **McDonald's,** corner Esclavo and Av. Costera M. Alemán, a few blocks east of the landmark Qualton Club, tel. (74) 860-777. Except for breakfast, which it doesn't serve, you'll find everything from Chicken McNuggets to the Big Mac, priced about a third higher than back home. Open daily 8 a.m.-11 p.m.

For an interesting contrast, visit **Taco Tumbra** across the adjacent street from McDonald's. Here, piquant aromas of barbecued chicken, pork, and beef and strains of Latin music fill the air. For a treat, order three of the delectable tacos, along with a refreshing fruit juice *(jugo)* or fruit-flavored *agua.* Open Sun.-Thurs. 6:30 p.m.-2 a.m., Fri.-Sat. 6:30 p.m.-4 a.m.

About three blocks east, **Gran Fogon** ("Big Stove"), corner Costera M. Alemán and Sandoval, despite its soaring modern canopy, takes pride in its country Mexican cooking, served with a flourish that makes even a bowl of *pozole* seem like a party. If you're hankering for something a bit out of the ordinary, try the house specialty, a *nopales en molcajete* (mohl-kah-HAY-tay)—stone bowl draped with succulent cooked *nopales* (cactus leaves) and filled with big green onions and savory stewed beef, pork, or chicken. Enough for two or three. Open daily about 9 a.m.-midnight.

staff of the Lonchería Chatita

Sanborn's (formerly Denny's) next door provides a blessedly cool, refined, and thoroughly Mexican refuge from the street. Here, 7-1 a.m. daily, you can sample an international menu of either North American favorites (eggs, pancakes, bacon, and bottomless coffee) or hearty Mexican specialties.

100% Natural, in competition directly across the Costera from Sanborn's, offers appropriately contrasting fare: many veggie and fruit drinks (try the Conga—made of papaya, guava, watermelon, pineapple, lime, and spinach), several egg breakfasts, breads, sandwiches, tacos, and enchiladas.

A mile and a half farther along the Costera, past the landmark Hotel Fiesta Americana Costera, **Sanborn's** night owl branch, tel. (74) 841-746, across from the Hotel Presidente, offers the same Sanborn's refined atmosphere, good food, and service 24 hours a day.

Zócalo and Peninsula de las Playas Restaurants

Even though Acapulco has seemingly zillions of restaurants, only a fraction may suit your expectations. Local restaurants come and go like the Acapulco breeze, though a handful of solid longtime eateries continue, depending on a steady flow of repeat customers.

For plain good eating and homey sidewalk atmosphere morning and night, try outdoor **Cafe Los Amigos,** Calle La Paz, a few steps off the *zócalo*. Shady umbrellas beneath a spreading green tree and many familiar favorites, from tuna salad and chili to waffles, T-bone steak, and breaded shrimp, attract a friendly club of Acapulco Canadian and American longtimers. Open daily 9:30 a.m.-10 p.m. Budget-moderate.

Good food and atmosphere keep customers flocking to the German-Mexican **Restaurant La Parroquia,** overlooking the *zócalo,* corner Juárez, tel. (74) 824-728. Not that the plaza views from the restaurant's open-air upper floors aren't interesting, but the old-Europe specialties, such as roast pork Dubrovnik, Wiener schnitzel Vienna, and sauerbraten are too tasty to be ignored. Open daily 8:30 a.m.-midnight. Moderate.

Two blocks from the *zócalo,* along Juárez, the **Fat Farm** (La Granja Pingüe), Juárez 10 at Felipe Valle, tel. (74) 835-339, would be unique even without the name. It's a cooperative, run by graduates of a local orphanage. The relaxed atmosphere, service, and food are made to please. Breakfasts are the high point of many a longtimer's day. Fare also includes several flavors of ice cream and sandwiches (such as the giant tuna, $2.50). Open daily 8 a.m.-11 p.m. Budget.

La Gran Torta at La Paz 6, one block from the *zócalo,* tel. (74) 838-476, is an old town headquarters for hearty local-style food at local-style prices. Specialties here are *tortas* (big sandwiches), often of *pierna* (roast pork), *chorizo,* or *pollo* (chicken) with tomato and avocado stuffed in a *bolillo.* Additional favorites include hearty *pozole* on Thursday and Friday. Open daily 8 a.m.-11 p.m. Budget.

Good, reasonably priced seafood restaurants are unexpectedly hard to come by in Acapulco. An important exception is the lineup of local-style seafood eateries along Av. Azueta three blocks from the *zócalo.* Located right where the boats come in, they get the freshest morsels first. Among the best and friendliest is **Mariscos Nachos,** corner Juárez and Azueta, where continuous patronage assures daily fresh shrimp, prawns, half a dozen kinds of fish, and lobster (big, $14, smaller, $8). Open daily 10 a.m.-9:30 p.m. Moderate.

If you prefer something a bit fancier, head a block farther from the *zócalo* to tourist favorite **Mariscos Pipos,** at 3 Almirante Breton, tel. (74) 822-237. The freshest of everything, cooked and served to please. Open daily around noon-9 p.m. Moderate-expensive.

A few steps away on Costera M. Alemán 322, corner of Almirante Breton, seekers of homestyle Mexican cooking need go no farther than **Tamales Licha,** tel. (74) 822-021. Here, appetizing south-of-the-border specialties—succulent tamales, savory *pozole,* crunchy tostadas, and tangy enchiladas—reign supreme. Portions are generous, ambience is relaxed, and hygiene standards are impeccable. Open nightly 6-11 p.m. Budget.

Many visitors' Acapulco vacations wouldn't be complete without a dinner at the luxurious clifftop *palapa* restaurant at the **Hotel Flamingos,** Av. López Mateos s/n, tel. (74) 820-690, about a mile uphill, west from Playa Caleta. Here all the ingredients for a memorable evening—attentive service, tasty seafood, chicken, and meat entrées, airy sunset view, and soft strumming of guitars—come together. Open daily 8 a.m.-10:30 p.m.; credit cards accepted. Moderate.

Coyuca 22 is both the name and the address of the restaurant so exclusive and popular it manages to close half the year. The setting is a spacious hilltop garden, where tables spread down an open-air bay- and city-view terrace. Arrive early (around 6:45 p.m.) to enjoy the sunset sky lighting up and painting the city ever-deepening colors, ending in a deep rose as finally the myriad lights shimmer and stars twinkle overhead. After that, the food (specialties, such as prime rib and lobster tails) and wines seem like dessert. Open daily 7-10:30 p.m. 1 Nov.-30 April; credit cards accepted. Expensive; entrées run about $30. Reservations are required, tel. (74) 823-468 or 835-030. Dress is elegant resort wear, coat not necessary.

Costera Restaurants

At **VIPs,** on the Costera, a block from Papagayo Amusement Park, tel. (74) 868-574, you can glimpse the Mexico of the future. Here, Mexican middle-class families flock to a south-of-the-border-style Denny's that beats Denny's at its own game. Inside, the air is as fresh as a spring breeze; the windows, water glasses, and utensils shine like silver; the food is tasty and reasonably priced; and the staff is both amiable and professional. Open Sun.-Thurs. 7-midnight, Friday and Saturday 7-2 a.m.; credit cards accepted. Moderate.

One of Acapulco's most atmospheric and palate-pleasing Italian restaurants is **Dino's,** nearby on the Costera a block west of the Fiesta Americana Condesa, on Costera M. Alemán next to Hotel Tortuga, tel. (74) 840-037. Guests can choose to sit on a bay-view terrace in front or an intimate fountain patio in back. From the menu, select among antipastos, salads, meats, and many seafood and meat pastas smothered in sauces, made with a flourish right at the table. Open daily 6-11:30 p.m.; credit cards accepted. Moderate-expensive.

No tour of Acapulco restaurants would be complete without a stop at **Carlos'n Charlie's,** which, like all of the late Carlos Anderson's worldwide chain, specializes in the zany. On the Costera, across and a block east of the Hotel Fiesta Americana Condesa, tel. (74) 840-039.

The fun begins with the screwy decor, continues via the good-natured, tongue-in-cheek antics of the staff, and climaxes with the food and drink, which is organized by categories, such as "Slurp," "Munch," "Peep," "Moo," and "Zurts," and is very tasty. Open daily 6 a.m.-midnight; credit cards accepted. Moderate-expensive.

Another successful culinary experiment is the Acapulco branch of the worldwide **Suntory** Japanese restaurant chain, across from the Oceanic 2000 building, east end of the Costera, tel. (74) 848-088. Although a Japanese restaurant in Mexico is as difficult to create as a Mexican restaurant in Japan, Suntory, the giant beer, whiskey, and wine manufacturer, carries it off with aplomb. From the outside, the clean-lined wooden structure appears authentically classic Japanese, seemingly lifted right out of 18th-century Kyoto. The impression continues in the cool interior, where patrons enjoy a picture-perfect tropical Zen garden, complete with moss, a stony brook, sago palm, and feathery festoons of bamboo. Finally comes the food, from a host of choices—vegetables, rice, fish, and meat—which chefs (who, although Mexican, soon begin to look Japanese) individually prepare for you on the grill built into your table. Open daily 2-11 p.m.; credit cards accepted. Moderate-expensive.

The Acapulco bent for restaurant fantasy continues right across the street, at **El Embarcadero.** Inside, you enter a dim, Disney-esque world. A jungle waterfall cascades behind you while a rickety bridge leads you over a misty lagoon, where, at any moment, you fear that a crocodile or a pirate is going to grab you. If you cross over safely your reward will be a cool salad bar and a choice of several intriguing specialties, such as Siamese chicken, Blackbeard's shrimp, or alligator steak. Credit cards accepted. Open 7 p.m.-midnight.

ENTERTAINMENT AND EVENTS

Strolling and Sidewalk Cafés

The old *zócalo* is the best place for strolling and people-watching. Bookstalls, vendors, band concerts, and, on weekend nights especially, pitch-penny games, mimes, and clowns are constant sources of entertainment. When you're tired of walking, take a seat at a sidewalk café, such as

La Parroquia, La Flor de Acapulco, or Cafe Los Amigos, and let the scene pass *you* by for a change.

Movies

A number of cinemas dot the Costera. The movies usually begin around 4 or 4:30 p.m. The second screening generally starts around 8:30 p.m. and finishes around midnight. From lower-brow to high, first comes the **Cine Tropical,** admission about $2, at 5 de Mayo 10, near the *zócalo,* tel. (74) 82-26-80, where visitors can enjoy viewing a double-whammy bill of Mexican and American action potboilers.

Farther up the scale is the **Cine Hornos,** admission $2, Nuñez de Balboa 10, tel. (74) 852-646, on the Costera, corner of de Ulloa, which shows mostly American first-run action flicks. Topping the list is the **Cine Plaza Bahía,** admission $3, in the Plaza Bahía shopping center, next to the Hotel Costa Club, tel. (74) 855-124, which screens first-run American action and comedy, such as *Armageddon* and *Something About Mary.* You'll get about the same at the newest *cine* in town, tel. (74) 810-646, at the Oceanic 2000 plaza, across from Baby O disco.

Tourist Shows

The **Mexican Fiesta,** Acapulco's dance performance extravaganza, goes on two, three, or four days a week, depending on the season, at the sprawling Centro Cultural de Convenciones convention center just east of the golf course. The all-Mexico sombrero and whirling-skirt folkloric dance show is highlighted by a replica performance of the wheeling Papantla flyers. Tickets, available from travel agents, can include the show only ($15), the show and two drinks ($20), or the show, drinks, and buffet ($34, kids half price). The buffet customarily begins around 7 p.m., followed by the performance at 8:15. Book your tickets through a travel or tour agent, or call Mexican Fiesta box office directly, at (74) 843-218.

Sunsets

West-side hills block Acapulco Bay's sunset horizon. Sunset connoisseurs remedy the problem by gathering at certain points on the Peninsula de las Playas, such as the Sinfonia del Sol sunset amphitheater (see **Playa Angosta,** above), La

Quebrada, Playa Angosta, and the cliffside restaurant and gazebo/bar of the Hotel Flamingos before sunset.

Bay Cruise Parties

One popular way to enjoy the sunset and a party at the same time is on a cruise aboard either of the steel excursion ships *Bonanza* or *Hawaiano.* They leave from the pair of bayside docks on the Costera half a mile (toward the Peninsula de las Playas) from the *zócalo.* Although cruise schedules vary seasonally, offerings can include mid-day (11 a.m.-2 p.m.), sunset (4:30-7 p.m.), and moonlight (10:30 p.m.-1 a.m.) cruises. Tickets are available from hotels, travel agents, or at the dock. Both *Bonanza,* tel. (74) 831-803, and *Hawaiano,* tel. (74) 822-199, tickets run about $11 per person, kids half price.

Bullfights

Bullfights are staged every Sunday at 4:30 p.m. seasonally, usually beginning in January, at the arena near Playa Caletilla. Avoid congestion and parking hassles by taking a taxi. Get tickets (about $25) through a travel agent or the ticket office, tel. (74) 839-561.

Jai-Alai, Bingo, and Offtrack Betting

About $10 gains you entrance to Acapulco's big jai-alai *frontón,* an indoor stadium, on the Costera, east end, across from the Hyatt Regency, open Tues.-Sun. 9 p.m.-1 a.m. Here, it's hard not to ooh and aah at the skill of players competing in the ancient Basque game of jai-alai. With a long narrow, curved basket tied to one arm, players fling a hard rubber ball, at lethal speeds, to the far end of the court, where it rebounds like a pistol shot and must be returned by an opposing player. You can place wagers on your favorite player, or, downstairs, bet on horse races and other sports events taking place far away.

Dancing and Discoing

Several of the Costera hotels have live music for dancing at their lobby bars. Moving east along the Costera, the better possibilities are: the **Hotel Costa Club,** tel. (74) 859-050; the **Fiesta Americana Condesa,** tel. (74) 842-828; the **Presidente,** tel. (74) 841-700; and the **Hyatt Regency,** tel. (74) 691-234. Call to verify times.

Many restaurant/bars along the Costera have nightly dance music, both recorded and live. A pair of favorites of both longtime tourists and local people are the **Tropicana** (on beach side, across the Costera from Cine Hornos) and the **Copacabana** (on beach side, near corner of Amal Espina). Both have cocktails and live Latin (sometimes called "tropical") music for dancing till around 3 a.m. Call ahead—Tropicana tel. (74) 853-050, Copacabana tel. (74) 851-051—to verify times.

A lively band also plays nightly during the high season (Friday, Saturday, and Sunday 3-10 p.m., low season) at the restaurant/club **Paradise** (across from the Hotel Romano), on the Costera beachside entertainment strip (see below) west of the Hotel Fiesta Americana Condesa. Zany waiters, a lively, varied musical repertoire, and good-enough food all spell happy times at the Paradise, tel. (74) 845-988.

Discotheques usually monitor their entrances carefully and are consequently safe and pleasant places for a night's entertainment (provided you either are either immune to the noise or bring earplugs). They open their doors around 10 p.m. and play relatively low-volume music and videos for starters until around 11 p.m., when fogs descend, lights flash, and the thumping begins, continuing sometimes till dawn. Admission runs about $7 to $15 or more for the tonier joints.

Acapulco's discos and dance hangouts concentrate in two major east-side spots. Moving east, between the Diana Circle and the Fiesta Americana Condesa, a solid lineup of clubs, hangouts, and discos occupies the Costera's beach side. During peak seasons, the dancing crowds spill onto the street. Stroll along and pick out the style and volume that you like.

Of the bunch, **Beach** disco is the loudest, brashest, and among the most popular. For the entrance fee of $5, the music and the lights go till dawn. Other neighboring discos, such as Mammy's, Baby Lobster, Blackbeard's, Crazy Lobster, and Beto Safari, while sometimes loud, are nevertheless subdued in comparison.

Another mile east, Planet Hollywood and Hard Rock Café, both of which actually serve food, signal the beginning of a second lineup on both sides of the street of about a dozen live-music or disco clubs. The energy they put out, trying to outdo each other (with brighter lights, louder music, and larger and flashier facades) is exceeded only by the frequency at which they seem to go in and out of business. More or less permanently fixed are **Planet Hollywood,** with recorded music and videos, 10 p.m.-2 a.m., no cover, tel. (74) 840-717; **Hard Rock Café,** "Save the Planet," live music, 10:30 p.m.-2 a.m., no cover, tel. (74) 840-047; **Baby O** disco and concert hall, "There's only one Acapulco and only one Baby O," 10 p.m.-4 a.m., $12 cover, tel. (74) 847-474; and **Andromeda's** concert and night club, "From the underseas world emerge one of the newest universe of fun," 10 p.m.-4 a.m., cover, tel. (74) 842-828.

Reigning above all of these lesser centers of discomania is **Enigma,** visible everywhere around the bay as the pink neon glow on the east-side Las Brisas hill. Go there, if only to look, though call for a reservation beforehand, tel. (74) 847-164, or they might not let you in. Inside, the impression is of ultramodern fantasy—a giant spaceship window facing outward on a galactic star carpet—while the music explodes, propelling you, the dancing traveler, through inner space. A mere $10 cover (women $8) gets you through the door; inside, drinks are $5-10, while French champagne runs $300 a bottle.

Child's Play

CICI (short for Centro Internacional de Convivencia Infantil) is the biggest of Acapulco's water parks. An aquatic paradise for families, CICI has acres of liquid games, where you can swish along a slippery toboggan run, plummet down a towering kamikaze slide, or loll in a gentle wave pool. Other pools contain performing whales, dolphins, and sea lions. Sea mammal performances occur at 12:30, 3:30, and 5:30 p.m. Patrons also enjoy a restaurant, a beach club, and much more. CICI is on the east end of the Costera between the golf course and the Hyatt Regency; open daily 10 a.m.-6 p.m., adult admission $5, kids $3.

Mágico Mundo, tel. (74) 831-215, Acapulco's other water park, is on the opposite side of town at Playa Caleta. Includes an aquarium, museum, restaurant, water slides, cascades, and more; open daily 9 a.m.-5 p.m., admission $3 adult, $2 child.

SPORTS AND RECREATION

Walking and Jogging

The most interesting beach walking in Acapulco is along the two-mile stretch of beach between the Hotel Fiesta Americana Condesa and the rocky point at Parque Papagayo. Avoid the midday heat by starting early for breakfast along the Costera (one option is the Hotel Fiesta Americana Condesa, tel. 74-842-828) and walking west along the beach with the sun to your back. Besides the beach itself, you'll pass rocky outcroppings to climb on, tidepools to poke through, plenty of fruit vendors, and *palapas* to rest in from the sun. Bring a hat, shirt, and sunscreen and allow two or three hours. If you get tired, ride a taxi or bus back. You can do the reverse walk just as easily in the afternoon after about 3 p.m. from Playa Hamacas just past the steamship dock after lunch on the *zócalo* (try the Cafe Los Amigos).

Soft sand and steep slopes spoil most jogging prospects on Acapulco Bay beaches. However, the green open spaces surrounding the Centro Cultural de Convenciones, just east of the golf course, provide a good in-town substitute.

Tennis and Golf

Acapulco's tennis courts are all private and mostly at the hotels. Try the Hotel Costa Club, tel. (74) 859-050, Fiesta Americana Condesa, tel. (74) 842-828, Villa Vera, tel. (74) 840-333, Presidente, tel. (74) 841-700, and the Hyatt Regency, tel. (74) 841-225. The Hyatt, for example, has five night-lit hard courts, which, for visitors, rent for $10 per hour during the day and $16 at night. If, however, you live in Acapulco, or play with someone who does, court rentals are customarily cheaper. Lessons by the in-house teaching pro cost about $20 an hour.

Clay courts are also available. The **Hotel Villa Vera and Racquet Club,** Lomas del Mar 35, tel. (74) 840-333, has three of them for about $14 per hour by day and $18 by night.

One of the coziest places for tennis in town is **Alfredo's Tennis Club,** the home of the late former tennis champion Alfredo Millet. His family continues the tradition, renting their two night-lit courts for $6 per hour during the day, $9 at night, including towel, refreshment, and use of their swimming pool. Lessons run about $5 extra per hour. At Av. Prado 29, tel. (74) 840-004 or 847-070 (call first); get there via Av. Deportes, next to the Pizza Hut. Go uphill one block, then left another to Alfredo's, at the corner of Prado.

If Alfredo's is all booked up and you can't afford $16 an hour for a tennis court, call some of the less plush hotels with courts, such as the Gran Motel Acapulco, $7 an hour days, $12 nights, on the Costera near the Hotel Costa Club, tel. (74) 855-437; Majestic, tel. (74) 832-713; and Suites Alba, tel. (74) 830-073.

The Acapulco **Campo de Golf** course, tel. (74) 840-781 or 840-782, right on the Costera, is open to the public on a first-come, first-served basis, daily 6:30 a.m.-5:30 p.m. Exceptions are Wednesday and Saturday after 1 p.m., when the course is limited to foursomes. Weekend greens fee is about $35 for nine holes and $42 for 18 holes; weekdays, $30 and $35. Caddy costs $5, club rental $10.

Much more exclusive and better maintained are the fairways at the **Club de Golf** of hotels Acapulco Princess and Pierre Marques (tel. 74-691-000), about five miles past the southeast edge of town. Here, the 18-hole greens fee runs $60 if you're a hotel guest and $80 if you're not. Caddies, carts, and club rentals are correspondingly priced.

Swimming, Surfing, and Boogie Boarding

Acapulco Bay's tranquil (if not pristine) waters usually allow safe swimming from hotel-front beaches. The water is often too tranquil for surf sports, however. Strong waves off open-ocean Playa Revolcadero southeast of the city often give good rides. Be aware, the waves can be dangerous. The Acapulco Princess on the beach provides lifeguards. Check with them before venturing in. Bring your own equipment; rentals may not be available.

Snorkeling and Scuba Diving

The best local snorkeling is off **Isla Roqueta.** Closest access point is by boat from the docks at Playa Caleta and Playa Tlacopanocha. Such trips usually run about $20 per person for two hours, equipment included. Snorkel trips can also be arranged through beachfront aquatics shops at hotels such as the Ritz, Hotel Costa Club, Fiesta Americana Condesa, and the Hyatt Regency.

Although local water clarity is often not ideal, especially during the summer-fall rainy season, Acapulco does have some professional dive instructors. NAUI-licensed diver Mario Murrieta, who works out of his shop in front of the Hotel San Francisco, at 450 Costera M. Alemán (about three blocks west of the *Hawaiano* dock), tel. (74) 831-108, offers everything from brief resort courses and beginning dives to complete NAUI open-water certification and advanced dives to choice local spots. Figure on paying about $40 for beginning training, including an easy local dive. Open-water certification averages about five days and costs around $400.

Another dive shop, **Acapulco Scuba Center** at open-ocean Playa Angosta, tel. (74) 859-937 and (74) 829-474, offers approximately the same services.

Sailing and Windsurfing

Close-in Acapulco Bay waters are too congested with motorboats for tranquil sailing or windsurfing. Nevertheless, some beach concessionaires at the big hotels, such as the Hotel Costa Club and Hyatt Regency do rent (or take people sailing in) simple boats from $15 per hour.

Limited windsurfing is also possible at the Hotel Majestic beach club in the little sub-bay sheltered by the Peninsula de las Playas.

Outside of town, tranquil **Laguna Coyuca,** on the coast about 20 minutes' drive northwest of the *zócalo,* offers good windsurfing and sailing

prospects (see the last section of the previous chapter).

Jet Skiing, Water-Skiing, and Parasailing

Power sports are very popular on Costera hotel beaches. Concessionaires—recognized by their lineup of beached mini-motorboats—operate from most big hotel beaches, notably around the Qualton Club, Hotel Costa Club, Fiesta Americana Condesa, and the Hyatt Regency. Prices run about $50 per hour for jet skis, $40 per hour for water-skiing, and $15 for a 10-minute parasailing ride.

Sportfishing

Fishing boats line the *malecón* dockside across the boulevard from the *zócalo.* Activity centers on the dockside office of the 20-boat blue-and-white fleet run by fishing boat cooperative **Sociedad Cooperativa Servicios Turística,** whose dozens of licensed captains regularly take visitors for big-game fishing trips. Although some travel agents may book you individually during high season, the Sociedad Cooperativa Turísticas office, open daily 8 a.m.-6 p.m., tel. (74) 831-257, rents only entire boats, including captain, equipment, and bait.

Rental prices and catches depend on the season. Drop by the dock after 2 p.m. to see what they are bringing in. During good times, boats might average one big marlin or sailfish apiece. Best months for sailfish *(pez vela)* are said to

Sailfish, which sportfishing boats frequently bring in at Acapulco's zócalo-front malecón, *make tough eating and should be released when caught.*

be November, December, and January; for marlin, February and March.

Big 40-foot boats with five or six fishing lines rent from $150 per day. Smaller boats, with three or four lines and holding five or six passengers, rent from $120 or less. All of the Cooperativa boats are radio-equipped, with toilet, life preservers, tackle, bait, and ice. Customers usually supply their own food and drinks. Although the Cooperativa is generally competent, look over the boat and check its equipment before putting your money down.

You can also arrange fishing trips through a travel agent or your hotel lobby tour desk.

Sailfish and marlin are neither the only nor necessarily the most desirable fish in the sea. Competently captained *pangas* can typically haul in three or four large 15- or 20-pound excellent-eating *robalo* (snook), *huachinango* (snapper), or *atún* (tuna) in two hours just outside Acapulco Bay.

Such lighter boats are rentable from the cooperative for about $20 per hour from individual fishermen on Playa Las Hamacas (past the steamship dock at the foot of Fort San Diego).

Marina and Boat Docking

A safe place to dock your boat is the 150-slip **Marina Acapulco** on the Peninsula de las Playas' sheltered inner shoreline, Av. Costera M. Alemán 215, Fracc. Las Playas, Acapulco, Guerrero 39300, tel. (74) 837-498, tel./fax 831-026. Boat launching (30-foot maximum) runs about $35 per day. The slip rate is around 80 cents per foot per day, including 110/220-volt power, potable water, pump-out, satellite disk TV connection, toilets, showers, ice, and access to the marina pool, restaurant, hotel, and repair facilities. Get there via the driveway past the suspension bridge over the Costera about a mile southeast of the *zócalo*.

SHOPPING

Market

Acapulco, despite its modern glitz, has a very colorful traditional market, which is fun for strolling through even without buying anything. It is open daily, dawn to dusk. Vendors arrive here with grand intentions: mounds of neon-red tomatoes,

buckets of *nopales* (cactus leaves), towers of toilet paper, and mountains of soap bars. As you wander through the sunlight-dappled aisles, past big gaping fish, bulging rounds of cheese, and festoons of huaraches, don't miss **Piñatas Amanda,** one of the market's friendliest shops. You may even end up buying one of her charming paper Donald Ducks, Snow Whites, or Porky Pigs. The market is at the corner of Mendoza and Constituyentes, a quarter mile inland from Hornos Beach. Ride a Mercado-marked bus or take a taxi.

Supermarkets and Department Stores

In the *zócalo* area, **Woolworth's** is a good source of a little bit of everything at reasonable prices, on Escudero, corner of Morelos, behind Sanborn's; open daily 9:30 a.m.-8:30 p.m. Its lunch counter, furthermore, provides a welcome refuge from the midday heat.

Comercial Mexicana, with three Acapulco branches, is a big Mexican Kmart, which, besides the expected film, medicines, cosmetics, and housewares, also includes groceries and a bakery. Its locations are: on the Costera, at Cinco de Mayo, just east of the Fort San Diego; on Farallones, a couple of blocks uphill from the Costera's Diana Circle; and two miles farther, across from CICI water park. All open daily 9 a.m.-9 p.m.

If you can't find what you want at Comercial Mexicana, try the huge **Sam's Club,** just uphill from the Farallones Comercial Mexicana, and the giant **Wal-Mart,** at the far east end, across from the Hyatt Regency.

Photography

Acapulco is not overloaded with photography stores. On the Costera, several outlets have come and gone during the past few years. However, **Foto System Lab,** tel. (74) 822-112, seems to be fixed on the *zócalo,* supplying photofinishing, a few cameras and accessories, and several popular film varieties. Open daily 8 a.m.-9 p.m. on the corner of J. Carranza, right side as you enter the *zócalo* from the Costera.

Cuauhtémoc, the street that runs parallel to the Costera, a quarter mile inland, has a cluster of stores not far from the *zócalo* end, a block or two from the Acapulco market. Best supplied of all appears to be **Foto Regalos de Acapulco,** at Cuauhtémoc 68 A, tel. (74) 830-537 and 820-422, with a pretty fair stock of film, point and shoot cameras and accessories, plus most photofinishing services.

Handicrafts

Despite much competition, asking prices for Acapulco handicrafts are relatively high. Bargaining, furthermore, seldom brings them down to size. **Sanborn's,** tel. (74) 824-095, two blocks from the *zócalo,* at Costera M. Alemán and Escudero, is open daily 7:30 a.m.-11 p.m., with bookstore and restaurant. Sanborn's all-Mexico selection includes, notably, black Oaxaca *barra* pottery, painted gourds from Uruapan, Guadalajara leather, Taxco silver jewelry, colorful plates from Puebla, and Tlaquepaque pottery and glass.

With Sanborn's prices in mind, head one block toward the *zócalo* to **Margarita,** where, in the basement of the big old Edificio Oviedo, glitters an eclectic fiesta of Mexican jewelry. Find it at I. de la Llave and Costera M. Alemán, local 1, tel. (74) 820-590 or 825-240; open Mon.-Sat. 9 a.m.-8 p.m., Sunday 9 a.m.-3 p.m. Never mind if the place is empty; cruise-line passengers regularly fill the aisles. Here you'll be able to see artisans adding to the acre of gleaming silver, gold, copper, brass, fine carving, and lacquerware around you. Don't forget to get your free margarita (or soft drink) before you leave.

Another bountiful handicrafts source near the *zócalo* is the artisans' market **Mercado de Parrazal.** From Sanborn's, head away from the Costera a few short blocks to Vasquez de Leon and turn right one block. There, a big plaza of semipermanent stalls offers a galaxy of Mexican handicrafts: Tonalá and Tlaquepaque papier-mâché, brass, and pottery animals; Bustamante-replica eggs, masks, and humanoids; Oaxaca wooden animals and black pottery; Guerrero masks; and Taxco jewelry. Sharp bargaining is necessary, however, to cut the excessive asking prices down to size.

Local artist Blanca Silviera has built a thriving business fashioning *alebrijes* (ahl-BREE-hays), fanciful painted animals. Stop by her handicrafts shop, **Alebrijes,** local 13, main floor, tel. (74) 850-409, in the shopping Plaza Bahía, just west of the Hotel Costa Club.

The biggest crafts store in Acapulco, **AFA** (Artesanías Finas de Acapulco), is tucked a block off the Costera near the Hyatt Regency on Horacio Nelson, corner of James Cook, tel. (74) 848-039 or 848-040, fax 842-448; open Mon.-Sat. 9 a.m.-7:30 p.m., Sunday 9 a.m.-2 p.m. Although jewelry is its strong suit, it has plenty more from most everywhere in Mexico. Items include pottery, papier-mâché, lacquerware, onyx, and much leather, including purses, belts, and saddles.

SERVICES

Money Exchange

In the *zócalo* neighborhood, go to the **Bancomer,** fronting the Costera, tel. (74) 848-055, to change U.S. cash or traveler's checks only (9 a.m.-5 p.m.). Although the lines at **Banamex,** tel. (74) 836-425, nearby, two blocks from *zócalo* next to Sanborn's, are usually longer, it exchanges major currencies (Canadian, French, Spanish, British, German, Swiss, and Japanese) Mon.-Fri. 9 a.m.-3 p.m. Of course, you can avoid the lines by using the bank **ATM machines,** which are routinely connected with international networks.

On the new side of town, change money at **Banamex** across from McDonald's, tel. (74) 859-020, open Mon.-Fri. 9 a.m.-3 p.m.; or at the **Bancomer,** Glorieta Diana ("Diana Circle") office, tel. (74) 847-245, open Mon.-Fri. 9 a.m.-2 p.m. for U.S. currency and traveler's checks and 10:30 a.m.-2 p.m. for Canadian.

After hours on the Costera, the **Consultorio International** (tel. 74-843-108) in Galería Picuda shopping center, across the street and west from the Hotel Fiesta Americana Condesa, exchanges currency and traveler's checks Mon.-Sat. 9 a.m.-8 p.m., Sunday 10 a.m.-5 p.m.

American Express Office

The only Acapulco American Express branch, at Costera M. Alemán 1628, tel. (74) 691-121, 691-122, 691-123, or 691-124, west end, across from McDonald's, cashes American Express traveler's checks at near-bank rates and provides member financial services and travel agency services. It's open Mon.-Sat. 10 a.m.-7 p.m., although check-cashing hours may be shorter.

Post and Telecommunications

The Acapulco main *correo* is in the Palacio Federal across the Costera from the steamer dock three blocks from the *zócalo*. It provides Mexpost fast, secure mail and philatelic services, Mon.-Sat. 8 a.m.-8 p.m., tel. (74) 822-083. A branch **post and telegraph office** at the Estrella de Oro bus terminal, Cuauhtémoc and Massieu, is open Mon.-Fri. 9 a.m.-8 p.m., Saturday 9 a.m.-noon. Mexpost maintains another branch on the Costera, west end, a few doors east of McDonald's and Taco Tumbra.

Telecomunicaciones, tel. (74) 822-622 or 822-621, next to the main post office, provides money order, telegram, telex, and fax services, Mon.-Fri. 9 a.m.-6 p.m. and Saturday 9 a.m.-noon.

Near the *zócalo,* you can call *larga distancia* daily 8 a.m.-10 p.m. from either the small office on J. Carranza at Calle de la Llave, or on the *zócalo*'s other side, next to Restaurant Los Amigos, Mon.-Fri. 9 a.m.-9 p.m., Saturday and Sunday 9 a.m.-2 p.m. and 4-9 p.m.

Be aware of certain private "To Call Long Distance to the U.S.A. Collect and Credit Card" telephones installed prominently in airports, tourist hotels, and shops. Tariffs on these phones often run as high as $30 for three minutes. Always ask the operator for the rate, and if it's too high, take your business elsewhere.

Immigration and Customs

If you lose your tourist card go to **Migración,** on the Costera, across the traffic circle from Comercial Mexicana, same side of the Costera, tel. (74) 844-349, open Mon.-Fri. 8 a.m.-2 p.m. Bring proof of your identity and some proof (such as your stamped passport, airline ticket, or a copy of your lost tourist card) of your arrival date in Mexico. If you try to leave Mexico without your tourist card, you may face trouble and a fine. Also report to Migración if you arrive in Acapulco by yacht.

The **Aduana** ("Customs"), tel. (74) 820-931, is in the Palacio Federal, third floor, on the Costera, *zócalo* area, next to Sanborn's, open Mon.-Fri. 8 a.m.-5 p.m. If you have to temporarily leave your car in Mexico, check to see what paperwork, if any, must be completed.

Consulates

Acapulco has several consulates. The offices of the U.S. consular officer, Joyce Anderson, tel. (74) 811-699 or 695-605, fax 840-300, are in the Hotel Continental Plaza. She's a busy woman, and asks that you kindly have your problem written down, together with a specific request for information or action.

The **Canadian** consul, Diane McLean de Huerta, tel. (74) 841-305, fax 841-306, holds office hours Mon.-Fri. 9 a.m.-5 p.m., at the Centro Comercial Marbella. After hours, in emergency, call toll-free (800) 706-2900.

For the **British** consul, Derek Gore, call (74) 841-650, Mon.-Fri. 1-3 p.m. and 5-7 p.m., at the Hotel Las Brisas.

Call the **German** consul, Mario Wichtendahl, at Antone de Alamino 26, tel. (74) 841-860.

The **Netherlands** consul, Ángel Diaz Acosta, is at (74) 868-350, fax 868-324.

The **French** consul, Vidal Mendoza, is at Av. Costa Grande 235, tel. (74) 823-394; and **Spanish** consul Tomas Lagar Alonso may be reached at (74) 857-205.

For additional information and assistance, the consulates maintain a joint **Consular Corps** office, in the Centro Cultural de Convenciones convention center just west of the golf course, tel. (74) 812-533.

INFORMATION

Tourist Information Office

The helpful federal **Turismo** information office staff answers questions and gives out maps and written materials at their office on the beach side of the Costera, corner of Amal Espina, across from Banamex, at Av. M. Alemán 187, tel. (74) 811-152, 811-156, or 811-160; open Mon.-Fri. 9 a.m.-2 p.m. and 4-7 p.m., Saturday 10 a.m.-2 p.m.

Medical, Police, and Emergencies

If you get sick, see your hotel doctor or go to the **Hospital Magellanes,** one of Acapulco's most respected private hospitals, for either office calls or round-the-clock emergencies. Facilities include a lab, 24-hour **pharmacy,** and an emergency room with many specialists on call, at W. Massieu 2, corner of Colón, one block from the Costera and the Hotel Qualton Club; tel. (74) 856-544 or 856-597, ext. 119 for the pharmacy.

A group of American-trained IAMAT (International Association for Medical Assistance to Travelers) physicians offers medical consultations in English. Contact them at the medical department, Hotel Acapulco Princess, tel. (74) 691-000, ext. 1309.

For routine medications near the *zócalo,* go to one of many pharmacies, such as at Sanborn's, corner of Escudero and the Costera, tel. (74) 826-167, or the big **Farmacia Discuento** (discount pharmacy), tel. (74) 820-804, open daily 8 a.m.-10 p.m., at Escudero and Carranza, across the street from Woolworth's.

For police emergencies, contact one of the many **tourist police,** tel. (74) 850-490 (on the Costera, in safari pith helmets), or call the **Policia Preventiva** station, tel. (74) 850-862 or 850-650, at the end of Av. Camino Sonora, on the inland side of Papagayo Park.

In case of fire, call the *bomberos,* tel. (74) 844-122, on Av. Farallón, behind Comercial Mexicana, two blocks off the Costera from the Glorieta Diana.

Publications

One of the best book sources in town is **Sanborn's** on the Costera, tel. (74) 842-035, open daily 7:30-1 a.m., ground floor of the Oceanic 2000 shopping plaza, beach side of the Costera, a few blocks from the east end. Alternatively, try Sanborn's *zócalo* branch, tel. (74) 824-095, open daily 7 a.m.-11 p.m., on the Costera across from the steamship dock, which stocks a similar, but smaller assortment.

English-language international newspapers, such as the Mexico City *News,* the *Los Angeles Times,* and *USA Today,* are often available in the large hotel bookshops, especially the Hotel Costa Club, Fiesta Americana Condesa, and the Hyatt Regency. In old town, newsstands around the *zócalo* regularly sell the *News* from Mexico City.

A local English-language newspaper, the Acapulco *Heat,* specializes in social events, Mexico travel, and restaurants, and lists houses and apartments for sale or rent. Pick up a copy at their office, tel./fax (74) 812-623, or other spots around town, such as the Fat Farm restaurant or Sanborn's.

Public Library

The small, friendly Acapulco *biblioteca* is near the *zócalo* adjacent to the cathedral, at Madero 5, corner of Quebrada, tel. (74) 820-388. Its collection, used mostly by college and high school students in their airy reading room, is nearly all in Spanish. Open Mon.-Fri. 9 a.m.-9 p.m., Saturday 9 a.m.-2 p.m.

Language Instruction

If you're interested in Spanish lessons, the Guerrero tourism office recommends instructor Dolores Gonzales, tel. (74) 856-166, 862-975, home 822-098.

Alternatively, take a Spanish language course at the reputable private **Universidad Americana** on the Costera, approximately across from the Hotel Costa Club. For more information, contact coordinator Elba Molina, at the University at Costera Miguel Alemán 1756, Fracc. Magellanes, Acapulco 39670, tel. (74) 865-641 or 865-642, fax 865-761, e-mail: uamerica@aca.uamericana.mx, Web site: www.uaa.edu.mx.

Service Club and Women's Meeting

The **Friends of Acapulco** charitable club holds fund-raising fiestas and fashion shows to support the Acapulco Children's home and other local good works. For information, write P.O. Box C-54, Acapulco, Guerrero 39300.

The Guerrero state **Secretaría de Mujer** provides counseling and help for problems such as rape, domestic abuse, abandonment, and birth control at their small Acapulco office at Hidalgo 1, at the *zócalo,* open Mon.-Fri. 9 a.m.-3 p.m. and 6-9 p.m., tel. (74) 826-311, fax 822-525.

The Sub Secretaría also sponsors a public meeting, customarily on the first Thursday (verify by calling) of each month in the evening at the small auditorium in the parklike grounds of the **Centro Cultural,** on the Costera, a block or two west of CICI water park.

GETTING THERE AND AWAY

By Air

Several airlines connect the **Acapulco airport** (code-designated ACA, officially the Juan N. Alvarez International Airport) with U.S. and Mexican destinations.

Aeroméxico flights connect directly with Houston via Mexico City and Tijuana via Guadalajara. For reservations, contact the Aeroméxico Hotel Nikko office, tel. (74) 811-766 or 811-767. For flight information, call the airport at (74) 669-296 or 660-991.

Mexicana Airlines flights connect with Chicago, Oaxaca, and five times daily with Mexico City. For reservations, call (74) 867-586 or 867-587; for flight information, call the airport at (74) 669-136 or 669-138.

MEXICO CITY DRIVING RESTRICTIONS

In order to reduce smog and traffic gridlock, authorities have limited which cars can drive in Mexico City, depending upon the last digit of their license plates. If you violate these rules, you risk getting an expensive ticket. On Monday, no vehicle may be driven with final digits 5 or 6; Tuesday, 7 or 8; Wednesday, 3 or 4; Thursday, 1 or 2; Friday, 9 or 0. Weekends, all vehicles may be driven.

America West Airlines flights connect with Phoenix; for reservations and information, call a local travel agent, such as American Express, tel. (74) 691-124 or toll-free (800) 235-9292.

Continental Airlines flights connect with Houston. For reservations, call a travel agent or (800) 900-5000; for flight information, call (74) 669-063.

Delta Air Lines flights connect with Los Angeles, Portland, and Dallas during the winter season. For reservations, call a travel agent, or toll-free (800) 902-2100.

American Airlines flights connect with Dallas during the winter season. For reservations, call a travel agent, or toll-free (800) 904-6000; for flight information, call the airport at (74) 669-227.

Taesa Airlines flights connect with Mexico City and with Tijuana via Guadalajara, tel. (74) 844-867 for reservations; for flight information call the airport, tel. (74) 669-066.

Canadian **World of Vacations** charter flights connect with Winnipeg and Toronto during the winter-spring season. For reservations, call a travel agent, such as American Express, tel. (74) 691-124, or the local Canadian agent, tel. (74) 465-716.

Air Arrival and Departure

After the usually perfunctory immigration and customs checks, Acapulco arrivees enjoy airport car rentals, efficient transportation for the 15-mile trip to town, and money exchange service (U.S. and Canadian cash and traveler's checks) daily 10 a.m.-1 p.m. and 2-5 p.m. (low season) or 9 a.m.-7 p.m. (high season). If you'll be arriving after money-exchange hours or on weekends, change a day's worth of money before arrival.

Local car rental agents often available for arriving flights include **Hertz**, tel. (74) 858-947 or 856-889; **Avis**, tel. (74) 620-075, 669-039; **Alamo**, tel. (74) 669-444 or 843-305; **Thrifty**, tel. (74) 669-115 or 621-115; **Dollar**, tel. (74) 669-493 or 843-066; **Budget**, tel. (74) 868-551 or 868-955; **Quick**, tel. (74) 863-420, 862-197; and **SAAD** jeep rentals, tel. (74) 843-445 or 845-325. You can ensure availability and often save money by bargaining for a reservation with agencies via their national toll-free numbers (see chart Car Rental Agency Toll-Free Numbers in the On the Road chapter).

Tickets for **ground transport** to town are sold by agents near the terminal exit. Options include collective GMC Suburban station wagon (about $5, kids half price) or microbus (about $2.50, kids half price), both of which deposit passengers at individual hotels. *Taxis especiales* run about $15 to a $26 maximum, depending on distance. GMC Suburbans can be hired *"especial"* as private taxis for $18-28 for up to seven passengers.

On your departure day, save money by sharing a taxi with fellow departees. Don't get into the taxi until you settle the fare. Having already arrived, you know what the airport ride should cost. If the driver insists on greed, hail another taxi.

Simplify your departure by having $17 or its peso equivalent (they might not take traveler's checks or credit cards) for your international (or $12 national) departure tax. If you lost your tourist permit (which immigration stamped upon your arrival) either go to Migración (see Services above) prior to your departure date, or arrive early enough at the airport to iron out the problem with airport Migración officials before departure. Bring some proof of your date of arrival, either stamped passport, airline ticket copy, or a copy of your lost tourist permit.

The Acapulco air terminal building has a number of shops for last-minute handicrafts purchases, a *buzón* (mailbox), stamp vending machine, long-distance telephones (be sure to ask the operator for the price before completing call) and a restaurant.

By Bus

Major competitors Estrella Blanca and Estrella Oro operate separate long-distance *central de autobús* (central bus terminals) on opposite sides of town.

Estrella Blanca, tel. (74) 692-028, 692-029, or 692-030, coordinates the service of its subsidiary lines Elite, Flecha Roja, Autotransportes Cuauhté-moc, Turistar, Futura, and Gacela at three separate terminals. Most first- or luxury-class departures use the big northwest-side terminal at Av. Ejido 47. The airy station is so clean you could sleep on the polished onyx floor and not get dirty; bring an air mattress and blanket. Other conveniences include inexpensive left-luggage lockers, food stores across the street, and a 24-hour *larga distancia* and fax office (Sendatel, fax 74-829-117) open daily 7 a.m.-11 p.m.

Scores of Estrella Blanca *salidas locales* (local departures) connect with destinations in three directions: northern interior, Costa Grande (northwest), and Costa Chica (southeast) coastal destinations.

Most connections are first-class or luxury-class Turistar and Futura. Specific northern interior connections include Mexico City (dozens daily, some via Taxco), Toluca, Morelia via Chilpancingo and Altimirano (six daily), and Guadalajara (three daily).

Many first- (about 10 per day) and second-class (hourly) departures connect northwest with Costa Grande destinations of Zihuatanejo and Lázaro Cárdenas. Southeast Costa Chica connections, terminating in Puerto Escondido, include four first-class daily (one via Ometepec) and approximately one second-class connection per hour.

Also from the Av. Ejido Estrella Blanca terminal, a few daily arrivals and departures connect with the U.S. border (Mexicali and Tijuana) via the entire Pacific coast route, from Salina Cruz and Puerto Ángel, Oaxaca through Zihuatanejo, Manzanillo, Puerto Vallarta, and Mazatlán.

More first- and luxury-class buses depart from Estrella Blanca's separate **Papagayo terminal,** tel. (74) 692-028 or 692-029, across Av. Cuauhtémoc and about a block west of the Estrella de Oro terminal (see below). From there, luxury-class Futura buses connect with northeast Mexico and the U.S. border, via Mexico City Norte station and Querétaro, San Luis Potosí, Monterrey and Nuevo Laredo. Other departures connect northwest, with Guadalajara, Puebla, and Zihuatanejo.

Estrella Blanca also maintains a **second-class terminal** at Cuauhtémoc 101, tel. (74) 822-285, 852-265, 852-252; from Sanborn's near the *zócalo,* walk or taxi about seven blocks along Escudero, which becomes Cuauhtémoc. Many regional departures head to Guerrero, ranging east as far as San Marcos, north to Chilpancingo, and west to Pie de la Cuesta and Tecpán.

The busy, modern **Estrella de Oro** bus terminal on the east side of town, at Cuauhtémoc and Massieu, tel. (74) 858-705 or 859-360, provides connections with Mexico City corridor (Chilpancingo, Iguala, Taxco, Cuernavaca) and northwest (via Zihuatanejo to Lázaro Cárdenas) Costa Grande destinations. Services include left-luggage lockers ($4 per day), snack bars, food stores, restaurant, and *correo* (post) and *telégrafo* offices (on the outside upstairs walkway, west end; open Mon.-Fri. 9 a.m.-8 p.m., Saturday 9 a.m.-noon.)

Estrella de Oro connections include dozens of first- and luxury-class with Mexico City and intermediate points. Only a few, however, connect directly with Taxco. Four departures connect daily with Costa Grande (three with Zihuatanejo, one only with Lázaro Cárdenas). Estrella de Oro offers no Costa Chica (Puerto Escondido) connections southeast.

By Car or RV
Good highways connect Acapulco north with Mexico City, northwest with the Costa Grande and Michoacán, and southeast with the Costa Chica and Oaxaca.

The Mexico City Hwy. 95 *cuota* (toll) superhighway would make the connection via Chilpancingo easy (83 miles, 133 km, about two hours) if it weren't for the Acapulco congestion (see below). The uncluttered extension (125 miles, 201 km) to Cuernavaca via Iguala is a breeze in two and a half hours. For **Taxco,** leave the superhighway at Iguala and follow the winding but scenic old Hwy. 95 cutoff 22 miles (35 km) northwest. From Cuernavaca, the over-the-mountain leg to Mexico City (53 miles, 85 km) would be simple except for Mexico City gridlock, which might lengthen it to two hours. Better allow a minimum of around five and a half driving hours for the entire 261-mile (420-km) Acapulco-Mexico City trip.

The Costa Grande section of Hwy. 200 northwest toward Zihuatanejo is generally uncluttered and smooth (except for some potholes). Allow about four hours for the 150-mile (242-km) trip.

The same is true for the Costa Chica stretch of Hwy. 200 southeast to Pinotepa Nacional (157 miles, 253 km) and Puerto Escondido (247 miles, 398 km total). Allow about four driving hours to Pinotepa, six and a half total to Puerto Escondido.

Acapulco's most congested ingress-egress bottleneck used to be the over-the-hill leg of Hwy. 95 from the middle of town. Although this route has been improved by a tunnel, the scenery is much prettier if you drive east along the Costera past Hotel Las Brisas as if you were heading to the airport. At the big cloverleaf intersection downhill, near Puerto Marques, head north. When you reach Hwy. 200, head right for the Costa Chica, or left for Hwy. 95 and northern points.

TAXCO

As Acapulco thrives on what's new, Taxco (pop. 150,000) luxuriates in what's old. Nestling among forest-crowned mountains and decorated with monuments of its silver-rich past, Taxco now enjoys an equally rich flood of visitors who stop en route to or from Acapulco. They come to enjoy its fiestas and clear, pine-scented air and to stroll the cobbled hillside lanes and bargain for world-renowned silver jewelry.

And despite the acclaim, Taxco preserves its diminutive colonial charm *because* of its visitors, who come to enjoy what Taxco offers. They stay in venerable, family-owned lodgings, walk to the colorful little *zócalo*, where they admire the famous baroque cathedral, and wander among the awning-festooned market lanes just downhill.

HISTORY

The traditional hieroglyph representing Taxco shows athletes in a court competing in a game of *tlatchtli* (still locally played) with a solid, natural rubber *(hule)* ball. "Tlachco," the Nahuatl name representing that place that had become a small Aztec garrison settlement by the eve of the conquest, literally translates as "Place of the Ball Game." The Spanish, more interested in local minerals than in linguistic details, shifted the name to Taxco.

Colonization

In 1524, Hernán Cortés, looking for tin to alloy with copper to make bronze cannon, heard that people around Taxco were using bits of metal for money. Prospectors hurried out, and within a few years they struck rich silver veins in Tetelcingo, now known as Taxco Viejo ("Old Taxco"), seven miles downhill from present-day Taxco. The Spanish Crown appropriated the mines and worked them with generations of Indian forced labor.

Eighteenth-century enlightenment came to Taxco in the person of José Borda, who, arriving from Spain in 1716, modernized the mine franchise his brother had been operating. José improved conditions and began paying the miners, thereby increasing productivity and profits. In contrast to past operators, Borda returned the proceeds to Taxco, building the monuments that still grace the town. His fortune built streets, bridges, fountains, arches, and his masterpiece, the church of Santa Prisca, which included a special chapel for the miners, who before had not been allowed to enter the church.

Independence and Modern Times

The 1810-21 War of Independence and the subsequent civil strife, within a generation, reduced the mines to but a memory. They were nearly forgotten when William Spratling, an American artist and architect, moved to Taxco in 1929 and began reviving Taxco's ancient but moribund silversmithing tradition. Working with local artisans, Spratling opened the first cooperative shop, Las Delicias.

Spurred by the trickle of tourists along the new Acapulco highway, more shops opened, increasing the demand for silver, which in turn led to the reopening of the mines. Soon silver demand outpaced the supply. Silver began streaming in from other parts of Mexico to the workbenches of thousands of artisans in hun-

hieroglyph of Taxco (Place of the Ball Game)

dreds of family- and cooperatively owned shops dotting the still-quaint hillsides of a new, prosperous Taxco.

SIGHTS

Getting Oriented

Although the present city, elev. 5,850 feet (1,780 meters), spreads much farther, the center of town encompasses the city's original seven hills, wrinkles in the slope of a towering mountain.

For most visitors, the downhill town limit is the Carretera Nacional ("National Highway"), named after John F. Kennedy. It contours along the hillside from **Los Arcos** ("The Arches") on the north, Mexico City, end of town about two miles, passing the Calle Pilita intersection on the south, Acapulco, edge of town. Along the *carretera*, immediately accessible to a steady stream of tour buses, lie the town's plusher hotels and many silver shops.

The rest of the town is fortunately insulated from tour buses by its narrow winding streets. From the *carretera*, the most important of them climb and converge, like bent spokes of a wheel, to the *zócalo* (main plaza). Beginning with the most northerly, the main streets (and the directions they run) are La Garita (uphill), Alarcón (downhill), Veracruz (downhill), Santa Ana (downhill), Salubridad (uphill), Morelos (downhill), and Pilita (downhill).

Getting Around

Although walking is Taxco's most common mode of transport, taxis go anywhere within the city limits for about $2. White combi collective vans (fare about 30 cents) follow designated routes, marked on the windshields. Simply tell your specific destination to the driver. For side trips to nearby towns and villages, a fleet of **Flecha Roja** second-class local buses leave frequently from their *carretera* terminal near the corner of Veracruz.

Around the *Zócalo*

All roads in Taxco begin and end on the *zócalo* at **Santa Prisca church.** French architect D. Diego Durán designed and built the church between 1751 and 1758 with money from the fortune of silver king Don José Borda. The facade, decorated with pedestaled saints, arches, and spiraled columns, follows the baroque churrigueresque style (after Jose Churriguera, 1665-1725, the "Spanish Michelangelo"). Interior furnishings include an elegant pipe organ, brought from Germany by muleback in 1751, and several gilded side altars. The riot of interior elaboration climaxes in the towering gold-leaf main altar, which seems to drip with ornamentation in tribute to Santa Prisca, the Virgin of Guadalupe, and the Virgin of the Rosary, who piously preside above all.

Dreamy Bible-story paintings by Miguel Cabrera decorate a chamber behind the main altar, while in a room to the right, portraits of Pope Benedict IV, who sanctioned all this, and Manuel Borda, Santa Prisca's first priest, hang amongst a solemn gallery of subsequent padres.

Outside, landmarks around the plaza include the **Casa Borda,** visible (as you face away from the church facade) on the right side of the *zócalo.* This former Borda family town house, built concurrently with the church in typical baroque colonial style, now serves as the Taxco Casa de Cultura, featuring exhibitions by local artists and artisans.

Heading from the church steps, you can continue downhill in either of two interesting ways. If you walk left immediately downhill from the church, you reach the lane, Calle Los Arcos, running alongside and below the church. From there, reach the **market** by heading right before the quaint archway over the street, down the winding staircase-lane, where you'll soon be in a warren of awning-covered stalls.

If, however, you head right from the church steps, another immediate right leads you beside

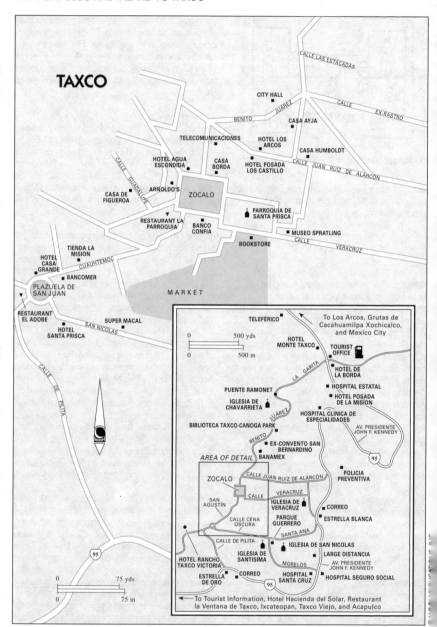

the church along legendary **Calle de los Muertos** ("Street of the Dead"), so named because of the many workers who died constructing the church.

Continuing downhill, you'll find **Museo Guillermo Spratling,** fronting the little plaza behind the church. On the main and upper floors, the National Institute of Archaeology displays intriguing carvings and ceramics (including unusual phallic examples), such as a ball-game ring, animal masks, and a priestly statuette with knife in one hand, human heart in the other. Basement-floor displays interestingly detail local history from the Aztecs through William Spratling. The museum is open seasonally Tues.-Sat. 9 a.m.-6 p.m., Sunday 9 a.m.-5 p.m., although winter hours may be shorter, tel. (762) 216-60.

Back outside, one block down Alarcón (the downhill extension of Calle de los Muertos), stands the **Casa Humboldt,** after the celebrated geographer (who is said to have stayed only one night, however). Now the state maintains it as the Museum of Viceregal (read colonial) Art. Displays feature a permanent collection of historical artifacts, including the Manila Galleon, colonial technology, and colonial religious sculpture and painting. Open Tues.-Sun. 10 a.m.-5 p.m., although winter hours may be shorter, tel. (762) 255-01.

Nearby, the **Museo Platería,** 4 Alarcón, third floor, next door to the Hotel Posada Los Castillo, illustrates a history of Taxco silvercraft and displays outstanding pieces by local artisans. Open daily 10 a.m.-6 p.m.

Other In-Town Sights

A short ride, coupled with a walk circling back to the *zócalo,* provides the basis for an interesting half-day exploration. Taxi or ride a combi to the Hotel Posada de la Misión, where the **Cuauhtémoc Mural** glitters on a wall near the pool. Executed by renowned muralist Juan O'Gorman with a riot of pre-Columbian symbols—yellow sun, pearly rabbit-in-the-moon, snarling jaguar, writhing serpents, fluttering eagle—the mural glorifies Cuauhtémoc, the last Aztec emperor. Cuauhtémoc, unlike his uncle Moctezuma, tenaciously resisted the conquest, but was captured and later executed by Cortés in 1524. His remains were discovered not long ago in **Ixcateopan,** about 24 miles away by local bus or car. (See below.)

Santa Prisca church, built in 1758 with profits from Taxco's silver mines, remains the center of town activities.

Continue your walk a few hundred yards along the *carretera* (Mexico City direction) from the Hotel Posada de la Misión. There, a driveway leading right just before the gas station heads to the Hotel Borda grounds. Turn left on the road just after the gate and you'll come to an antique brick smelter chimney and cable-hung derrick. These mark an inactive **mineshaft** descending to the mine-tunnel honeycomb thousands of feet beneath the town. The mines are still being worked from another entrance, but for lead rather than silver. You can see the present-day works from the hilltop of the Hotel Hacienda del Solar on the south edge of town.

Now, return to the *carretera,* cross over and stroll the **Calle la Garita** about a mile back to the *zócalo.* Of special interest, besides a number of crafts stores and stalls, are the **Iglesia de Chavarrieta,** the **Biblioteca Taxco-Canoga Park** (library, with many English-language novels and reference books, open Mon.-Fri. 10 a.m.-7 p.m., Saturday 10 a.m.-1 p.m.), and the **ex-Convento San Bernardino.**

Farther on, a block before the *zócalo*, pause to decipher the colored stone mosaic of the **Taxco Hieroglyph,** which decorates the pavement in front of the Palacio Municipal ("City Hall").

Cableway to Hotel Monte Taxco

On the north side of town, where the *carretera* passes beneath Los Arcos, a cableway above the highway lifts passengers to soaring vistas of the town on one side and ponderous, pine-studded mesas on the other. Open daily 7:30 a.m.-7:30 p.m.; roundtrip tickets about $3, kids half price; return by taxi if you miss the last car.

The ride ends at the Hotel Monte Taxco, where you can make a day of it golfing, horseback riding, playing tennis, eating lunch, and sunning on the panoramic-view pool deck.

Town Vistas

You needn't go as far afield as the Hotel Monte Taxco to get a good view of the city streets and houses carpeting the mountainside. Vistas depend not only on vantage point but time of day, since the best viewing sunshine (which frees you from squinting) should come generally from *behind.* Consequently, spots along the highway (more or less *east* of town), such as the pool patios of the Hotel Posada de la Misión and the *mirador* atop the Hotel Borda, provide good morning

TLATCHTLI: THE BALL GAME

Basketball fever is probably a mild affliction compared to the enthusiasm pre-Columbian crowds felt for *tlatchtli,* the ball game that was played throughout Mesoamerica and is still played in some places. Contemporary accounts and latter-day scholarship have led to a partial picture of *tlatchtli* as it was played centuries ago. Although details varied locally, the game centered around a hard, natural rubber ball, which players batted back and forth across a center dividing line with leg-, arm-, and torso-blows.

Play and scoring was vaguely similar to tennis. Opponents, either individuals or small teams, tried to smash the ball past their opponents into scoring niches at the opposite ends of an I-shaped, sunken court. Players also could garner points by forcing their opponents to make wild shots that bounced beyond the court's retaining walls.

Courts were often equipped with a pair of stone rings fixed above opposing ends of the center dividing line. One scoring variation awarded immediate victory to the team who could manage to bat the *tlatchtli* through the ring.

Like tennis, players became very adept at smashing the ball at high speed. Unlike tennis, the ball was solid and perhaps as heavy as two or three baseballs. Although protected by helmets and leather, players were usually bloodied, often injured, and sometimes even killed from opponents' punishing *tlatchtli*-inflicted blows. Matches were sometimes decided like a boxing match, with victory going to the opponent left standing on the court.

As with everything in Mesoamerica, tradition and ritual ruled *tlatchtli.* Master teachers subjected initiates to rigorous training, prescribed ritual, and discipline not unlike the ascetic life of a medieval monastic brotherhood.

Potential rewards were enormous, however. Stakes varied in proportion to a contest's ritual significance and the rank of the players and their patrons. Champion players could win fortunes in gold, feathers, or precious stones. Exceptional games could result in riches and honor for the winner, and death for the loser, whose heart, ripped from his chest on the centerline stone, became food for the gods.

views, while afternoon views are best from points west of town, such as the restaurant balcony or the hilltop of the Hotel Rancho Taxco Victoria.

OUT-OF-TOWN SIGHTS

The monumental duo of the Grutas de Cacahuamilpa caves and the ruins of ancient Xochicalco makes for an interesting day-trip. Don't get started too late; the Grutas are 15 miles (25 km) north (Mexico City direction) of town and Xochicalco is 25 miles (40 km) farther.

Grutas de Cacahuamilpa

They're worth the effort. The Grutas de Cacahuamilpa (kah-kah-ooah-MEEL-pah) are one of the world's great cavern complexes. Forests of stalagmites and stalactites, in myriad shapes—Pluto the Pup, the Holy Family, a desert caravan, asparagus stalks, cauliflower heads—festoon a series of gigantic limestone chambers. The finale is a grand, 30-story hall that meanders for half a mile, like a fairyland in stone. The caves are open daily; hourly three-mile, two-hour walking tours in Spanish are included in the $4 admission and begin at 10 a.m. A few gift shops sell souvenirs; snack bars supply food.

Getting There: Combi collective vans leave hourly for the caves, beginning at 8:30 a.m., from just north of the Estrella Blanca bus station on the *carretera*. Watch for Grutas written on the windshields; expect to pay about $3 for a one-way fare. By car, get to the caves via Hwy. 95 north from Taxco; after 10 miles (16 km) from the northside Pemex station, fork left onto Hwy. 55 toward Toluca. Continue five more miles (eight km) and turn right at the signed Cacahuamilpa junction. After a few hundred yards, turn right again into the entrance driveway.

Xochicalco

Xochicalco (soh-shee-KAHL-koh), an hour farther north, although little publicized, is a fountainhead of Mesoamerican legend. The ruin itself spreads over a half dozen terraced pyramid hilltops above a natural lake-valley, which at one time sustained a large population. Xochicalco flowered during the late classic period around A.D. 800, partly filling the vacuum left by the decline of Teotihuacán, the previously dominant Mesoamerican classic city-state. Some archaeologists speculate that Xochicalco at its apex was the great center of learning, known in legend as Tamanchoan, where astronomer-priests derived and maintained calendars and where the Quetzalcoatl legend was born.

Exploring the Site: Walk about 100 yards directly west, uphill, from the parking lot, where the **Pyramid of Quetzalcoatl** ("The Plumed Serpent") rises on the hilltop. Vermilion paint remnants hint of its original appearance, which was perhaps as brilliant as a giant birthday cake. In bas-relief around the entire base a serpent writhes, intertwined with personages, probably representing chiefs or great priests. Above these are warriors, identified by their helmets and *atlatl*, or lance-throwers.

Most notable, however, is one of Mesoamerica's most remarkable sculptures, to the left of the staircase. It shows the 11th week sign, *ozomatli* (monkey), being pulled by a hand (via a rope) to join with the fifth week sign, *calli* (house). Latter-day scholars generally interpret this as describing a calendar correction that resulted from a grand conclave of chiefs and sages from all over Mesoamerica, probably at this very spot.

About 150 feet south rises the **Temple of the Steles,** so named for three large stone tablets found beneath the floor. They narrate the events of the Quetzalcoatl legend, wherein Quetzalcoatl (discoverer of corn and the calendar) was transformed into the morning star (the planet Venus), and who continues to rule the heavens as the brightest star and the Lord of Time.

About 100 yards farther south, the **Main Plaza** was accessible to the common people via roads from below. This is in contrast to the sacrosanct **Ceremonial Plaza** nearby. A faintly visible causeway once connected the yet-to-be explored La Malinche pyramid, 200 yards to the southwest, with the Ceremonial Plaza.

That causeway passed the **Ball Court,** which is strikingly similar to ball courts as far away as Toltec Tula in the north and Mayan Copan, in Honduras far to the south. On the opposite side of the causeway from the Ball Court lies the **Palace,** a complex marked by many rooms with luxury features such as toilet drainage, fireplaces, and steam baths.

On the opposite side of the complex is the **Observatory,** a room hollowed into the hill and

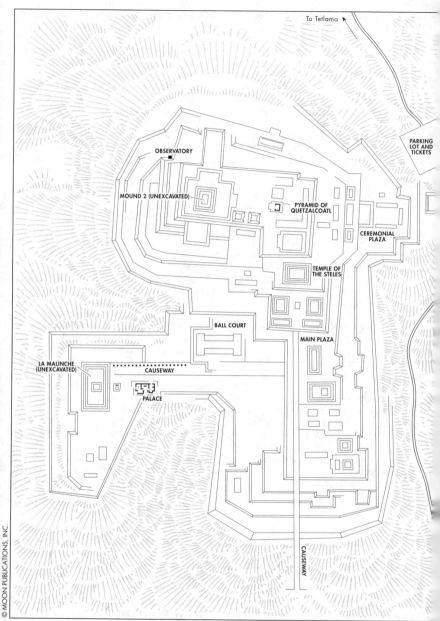

To Tetlama

PARKING LOT AND TICKETS

OBSERVATORY

MOUND 2 (UNEXCAVATED)

PYRAMID OF QUETZALCOATL

CEREMONIAL PLAZA

TEMPLE OF THE STELES

BALL COURT

MAIN PLAZA

LA MALINCHE (UNEXCAVATED)

CAUSEWAY

PALACE

CAUSEWAY

© MOON PUBLICATIONS, INC.

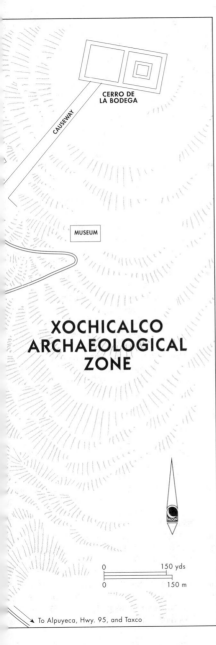

CERRO DE
LA BODEGA

CAUSEWAY

MUSEUM

**XOCHICALCO
ARCHAEOLOGICAL
ZONE**

0   150 yds

0   150 m

▲ To Alpuyeca, Hwy. 95, and Taxco

stuccoed and fitted with a viewing shaft for timing
the sun and star transits essential for an accurate
calendar.

Get to Xochicalco by either tour (for example,
contact Malasia Tours, tel. 762-279-83, on the
Plazuela San Juan, across from the Hotel Casa
Grande) or car. Continue past the *grutas* driveway entrance (see directions above), northeast
via Hwy. 160 toward Alpuyeca. After 25 miles
(40 km) from the caves, a signed road heads
left uphill to the Xochicalco ruins, which are open
daily 10 a.m.-5 p.m. Admission runs about $3.50,
Sunday and holidays free. Since caretakers shoo
all visitors out by 5 p.m., arrive early enough to
allow a couple of hours to explore the ruins.
Bring food, drinks, a hat, and comfortable walking shoes.

Ixcateopan

The picturesque little furniture-making town of
Ixcateopan (eeks-kah-tay-OH-pan) has become
famous for the remains the last Aztec emperor,
Cuauhtémoc, which archaeologists discovered
there on 26 September 1949.

The renown has been beneficial. The town
streets and plaza are smartly cobbled with the
local white marble, and houses and shops are
neatly painted and whitewashed. At the center of
all this stands Cuauhtémoc's resting place, the
venerable **Iglesia de Santa María de la Asunción** church, beside the town plaza. Inside, Jairo
Rodríguez, son of the codiscoverer of Cuauhtémoc's remains and lineal descendant of
Cuauhtémoc himself, devotes his life to maintaining the sanctuary and its small adjoining museum. Cuauhtémoc's relics themselves, which
were subjected to rigorous investigation when
they were unearthed, are undoubtedly authentic.
The bones lie in a glass case directly over the
spot where they were buried beneath the altar
stones more than four centuries ago.

The museum next door details the story of
Cuauhtémoc's heroic defense of the Aztec capital, Tenochtitlán, and his capture, torture, and
subsequent execution by Cortés on 28 February
1525. Copies of pictograms, known as codices,
such as the codex Vatican-Rios (1528), displayed in the museum, represent Cuauhtémoc
(literally, "The Descending Eagle") with an in-
verted, stylized eagle above his head. The sanctuary and museum hours are Mon.-Sat. 9 a.m.-3

p.m. and 4-5 p.m., Sunday 9 a.m.-3 p.m. Jairo sells an excellent booklet ($3) in Spanish, which details the fascinating story of the discovery and authentication of his ancestor's remains.

Besides the historic interest, the town and its environs—the rustic old church and garden, the tranquil plaza, the surrounding lush oak-forested hills—invite lingering. Moreover, the amiable, frankly curious townsfolk—who are definitely not overwhelmed by tourists—are ready for visitors. You'll find some pretty fair plaza-front country restaurants and a homey local hotel.

When asked the name of her hotel, owner Sara Hernández simply gave her name. The **Hotel Hernández** is on the main street, at Calle V. Guerrero 14, Ixcateopán, Guerrero, a block past the plaza, across the street from the church. Señora Hernández offers four very tidy rooms, decorated with handsome wood furniture and frilly feminine bedspreads for about $11 s, d, or t; with private baths and hot water. She'd probably appreciate a call (in Spanish) before you arrive. Dial the local operator, tel. (762) 297-90, then ask for extension 168.

Get to Ixcateopan via *colectivo* Volkswagen van, labeled Ixcateopan. Catch it in front of the Estrella Blanca bus station in Taxco, or at any point on the *carretera* before the south-side, signed, turnoff road to Ixcateopan. Expect to pay about $2 per person, one way. Drivers, follow the signed fork, west (turn right if traveling south) from the *carretera*, past the Pemex *gasolinera* about a mile south of town. Continue about an hour along the very scenic, sometimes roughly paved road for 23 miles (37 km) to the town plaza.

ACCOMMODATIONS

Taxco's inexpensive and moderately priced hotels cluster in the colorful *zócalo* neighborhood, while the deluxe lodgings are scattered mostly along the *carretera*. The dry, temperate local climate relegates air-conditioning, ceiling fans, and central heating to frills offered only in the most expensive hotels. All of the hotel recommendations below have hot water and private baths, however.

Taxco's only *zócalo*-front hostelry, the **Hotel Agua Escondida,** stands on the diagonally op-

posite corner from the church, Calle Guillermo Spratling 4, Taxco, Guerrero 40200, tel. (762) 207-26 or 211-66, fax 213-06. A multilevel maze of hidden patios, rooftop sundecks, and dazzling city views, the Agua Escondida has dozens of clean, comfortable rooms. The name, which translates as "Hidden Water," must refer to its big swimming pool, which is tucked away in a far rooftop corner. Rooms vary; if you have the choice, look at several. Try to avoid the oft-noisy streetfront rooms. If you don't mind climbing, some of the upper-floor rooms have airy, penthouse views. The 76 rooms run about $22 s, $28 d, and $33 t, with limited parking; credit cards accepted.

On Alarcón just downhill behind the Agua Escondida, a pair of former colonial mansions, now popular hotels, face each other across the street. The **Hotel Los Arcos,** J. Ruiz de Alarcón 4, Taxco, Guerrero 40200, tel. (762) 218-36, the homier of the two, has 24 rooms rising in three leafy tiers around an inviting inner patio, replete with reminders of old Mexico. The rooms, with thoughtfully selected handmade polished wooden furniture, tile floors, rustic wall art, and immaculate hand-painted cobalt-on-white tile bathrooms, complete the lovely picture. Rooms rent for about $15 s, $18 d.

The **Hotel Posada Los Castillo,** J. R. Alarcón 7, Taxco, Guerrero 40200, tel. (762) 213-96, across the street, is small and intimate, with plants, carved wood, paintings, and sculptures gracing every wall and corner. Rooms, in neo-colonial decor, are clean and comfortable. The owners also run a nearby silver boutique, whose displays decorate the downstairs lobby. The 14 rooms rent for about $15 s, $19 d, and $24 t, with credit cards accepted.

Heading past the opposite side of the plaza, follow Cuauhtémoc to the Plazuela de San Juan and the adjacent **Hotel Santa Prisca,** Cena Obscura 1, P.O. Box 42, Taxco, Guerrero 40200, tel. (762) 200-80 or 209-80, fax 229-38. A tranquil, dignified old hostelry built around a fragrant garden of orange trees, its off-lobby dining room shines with graceful details, such as beveled glass, a fireplace, blue-white stoneware and ivy-hung portals. Its tile-decorated rooms, in two tiers around the garden just outside, are clean and comfortable. Rooms go for about $16 s and $25 d, with parking; credit cards accepted.

Continue along the hill another two blocks past Plazuela de San Juan to the **Hotel Rancho Taxco Victoria,** Carlos J. Nibbi 5 and 7, Taxco, Guerrero 40200, tel. (762) 202-10 or 200-04, fax 200-10, which rambles, in a picturesque state of decay, along its view hillside. Built sometime back in the 1930s, the hotel usually slumbers on weekdays, reviving on weekends and holidays. (Actually, it's two hotels in one—the Victoria uphill and the Rancho Taxco, neglected and returning to the earth across the road, downhill.) The better-maintained Victoria, however, is brimming with rustic, old-world extras—hand-hewn furniture, whitewashed stucco walls, riots of bougainvillea, a spreading view garden—plus a big pool and a relaxed restaurant and bar where guests enjoy the best afternoon vista in town. Some of the spacious, comfortable rooms have luxurious view balconies. If you prefer peace and quiet, ask for one of the rooms away from the road, numbers 22-28, off the upper *terraza mirador* view patio, where, summer nights, you can enjoy the singing of the tree frogs and watch the lightning flicker in the clouds far away. Standard-grade rooms run about $28 s, $35 d, and $38 t; deluxe junior suites for $38 s, $44 d, with parking; credit cards accepted.

From a distance, the **Hotel Borda,** off the *carretera* downhill, appears to be the luxury hotel it once was, Cerro de Pedregal, P.O. Box 83, Taxco, Guerrero 40200, tel. (762) 200-25 or 202-25, fax 206-17. Lackluster management, however, detracts from the hotel's magnificent assets—grand vistas, spacious garden, and luxurious blue pool patio. Check to see if your room is clean and in working order before you move in. The 110 rooms rent for about $44 s or d, with restaurant, bar, and parking; credit cards accepted.

The **Hotel Posada de la Misión** decorates a hillside nearby, Cerro de la Misión 32, Taxco, Guerrero 40200, tel. (762) 200-63 or 255-19, fax 221-98. Its guests, many on group tours, enjoy cool, quiet patios, green gardens, plant-lined corridors, a sunny pool patio, and a view restaurant. Many of the luxurious rooms have panoramic city views; some have fireplaces. All rooms have color TV and phones. Standard rooms rent for about $69 s, $73 d with breakfast, Christmas-New Year's prices higher; with

parking, credit cards accepted. Just off the *carretera,* uphill side, 200 yards south of the Pemex gas station.

The luxuriously exclusive **Hotel Hacienda del Solar,** P.O. Box 96, Taxco, Guerrero 40200, tel./fax (762) 203-23, spreads over a tranquil hilltop garden on the south edge of town. Guests in many of the 22 airy and spacious rooms enjoy private patios, fireplaces, and panoramic valley and mountain views. Rooms, in standard, deluxe, and junior suite versions, vary individually but are all artfully furnished with appointments including handwoven rugs, colorful tile, paintings, and folk art. The standard rooms share a spacious living area near the lovely view pool patio; deluxe and junior suite rooms have huge beds and deep tile bathtubs. Other amenities include a view restaurant, the Ventana ("Window") de Taxco, and a cocktail lounge. Rooms for two go for about $59 standard, $76 deluxe, and $95 junior suite.

Vacationers who require plenty of activity and resort amenities stay at the **Hotel Monte Taxco,** Lomas de Taxco, Taxco, Guerrero 40200, tel. (762) 213-00 or 213-01, fax 214-28, atop a towering mesa accessible by either a steep road or cableway from the highway just north of town. On weekends, the hotel is often packed with well-heeled Mexico City families, whose kids play organized games while their parents enjoy the panoramic poolside view or play golf and tennis. The 156 deluxe rooms, many with view balconies, rent from about $86 s or d, with a/c, phones, and TV; facilities include restaurants, shops, a piano bar, disco, weekend live music, parking, a gym, pool, sauna, and spa. The adjacent country club offers a nine-hole golf course, tennis courts, and horseback riding; credit cards are accepted.

If you'd like to stay atop Monte Taxco, a more economical alternative to the hotel would be to rent one of the colonial-style two-bedroom apartments of the **Country Club Monte Taxco,** tel./fax (762) 256-09, adjacent to the golf course, 100 yards outside the Hotel Monte Taxco front door. For about $66, for up to four, you get a deluxe, two-bedroom mountain-view apartment with kitchen, use of the country club's pool, and access to the golf course, tennis courts, horseback riding, mountain trails, and the Hotel Monte Taxco's facilities next door.

FOOD

Stalls and Snacks

The numerous *fondas* (foodstalls) atop the *arte-sanías* (ar-tay-sah-NEE-ahs) handicrafts section of the market are Taxco's prime source of wholesome country-style food. The quality of their fare is a matter of honor for the proprietors, since among their local patrons word of a little bad food goes a long way. It's very hard to go wrong, moreover, if your selections are steaming hot and made fresh before your own eyes (in contrast, by the way, to most restaurant and hotel fare).

You can choose from a potpourri that might include steaming bowls of *menudo* or *pozole,* or maybe plates of pork or chicken *mole,* or *molcajetes* (big stone bowls) filled with steaming meat and broth and draped with hot nopal cactus leaves.

Stalls offering other variations appear evenings on the *zócalo.* A family sells tacos and *pozole,* while another, which labels itself La Poblana, sometimes arrives in a truck and offers french-fried bananas, *churros,* and potato chips fried on the spot until about 10:30 p.m., next to the church.

Restaurants

Of the *zócalo* restaurant options, the upstairs **La Parroquia,** tel. (762) 230-96, a half block from the church steps, ranks among the best; open 9 a.m.-11 p.m., credit cards accepted. The front balcony tables are ideal perches for watching the people parade below while enjoying a good breakfast, lunch, or dinner. Moderate.

Another good bet on the *zócalo* is **Pizza Pazza,** at the corner, right side of the cathedral, upstairs, tel. (762) 255-00. Although the menu offers a little bit of everything, the specialty is good pizza, in about 15 varieties. Extras include relaxed ambience, professional service, checkered tablecloths, and airy, plaza-view balcony tables. If the TV bothers you, they won't mind turning it down to low volume, if asked. Open daily noon-midnight. Moderate.

A block from the *zócalo,* along Calle Cuauhtémoc overlooking Plazuela de San Juan, the Mexican-style **Restaurant El Adobe,** Plazuela de San Juan 13, tel. (762) 214-16, is a good place

for breakfast or a lunch break. For breakfast, you can enjoy juice, eggs, and hotcakes; for lunch, hamburgers, tacos, or *tamales Oax-aqueños,* or, for dinner, steak in orange sauce or shrimp brochette. Open daily 8 a.m.-11 p.m. Budget-moderate.

Of the old-town hotel restaurant options, best for old-Mexico ambience is the **Hotel Rancho Victoria** restaurant, especially for lunch and dinner, where, although the food is good enough country fare, the main attraction is the best afternoon view in town. From the *zócalo,* walk west along Cuauhtémoc; continue two blocks past Plazuela de San Juan. Open daily 7:30 a.m.-8 p.m., credit cards accepted. Moderate.

A classy spot where you can enjoy the view, a swim, and lunch after seeing the Cuauhtémoc Mural is the adjacent **Restaurant El Mural,** at the Hotel Posada La Misión on the *carretera;* open daily for breakfast 7-9:30 a.m., lunch 1-3:30 p.m., dinner 7-11 p.m. If the place is packed with tours, have a drink, enjoy the mural, and go somewhere else. Expensive.

For good food in an elegant view setting, go to **Restaurant La Ventana de Taxco,** tel. (762) 205-87, at the Hotel Hacienda del Solar two blocks off the highway, south end of town. Open daily for breakfast 8:30-10:30 a.m., lunch 1-4:30 p.m., and dinner 7-11 p.m., when the whole town appears like a shimmering galaxy through the windows; reservations recommended. The mostly Italian and Mexican specialties include salads, lasagna, scallopini, saltimbocca, *mole* chicken, enchiladas, and wines. Expensive.

ENTERTAINMENT, EVENTS, AND SPORTS

Taxco people mostly entertain each other. Such spontaneous diversions are most likely around the *zócalo,* which often seems like an impromptu festival of typical Mexican scenes. Around the outside stand the monuments of the colonial past, while on the sidewalks sit the Indians who come in from the hills to sell their onions, tamales, and pottery. Kids run between them, their parents and grandparents watching, while young men and women flirt, blush, giggle, and jostle one another until late in the evening.

Three restaurant/bars on the side adjacent to the church provide good perches for viewing the hubbub. Visitors can either join the locals at **Bar Berta,** on the church corner, or take a balcony seat and enjoy the bouncy music with the mostly tourist crowd at **Bar Paco** next door. For more tranquillity, head upstairs to **Restaurant La Parroquia** a few steps farther on.

Later, or another day, continue your Taxco party via the jazzy recorded music pouring out of the speakers at the restaurant/bar **Concha Nostra,** upstairs at Hotel Casa Grande, at Plazuela de San Juan.

For more music, the **Hotel Monte Taxco,** tel. (762) 213-00, 213-01, offers a piano bar and discotheque nightly, and a trio Friday, Saturday, and Sunday evenings. At the Posada de la Misión, tel. (762) 200-63, 255-19, patrons enjoy a roving trio for lunch and a piano bar nightly.

Festivals

An abundance of local fiestas provide the excuses for folks to celebrate, starting on 17 and 18 January with the Festival of Santa Prisca. On the initial day, kids and adults bring their pet animals for blessing at the church. At dawn the next day, pilgrims arrive at the *zócalo* for *mañanitas* (dawn mass) in honor of the saint, then head for folk dancing inside the church.

During the year Taxco's many neighborhood churches celebrate their saints' days (such as Chavarrieta, 4 March; Veracruz, the four weeks before Easter; San Bernardino, 20 May; Santísima Trinidad, 13 June; Santa Ana, 26 July; Asunción, 15 August; San Nicolas, 10 September; San Miguel, 19 September; San Francisco, 4 October; and Guadalupe, 12 December) with food, fireworks, music, and dancing.

Religious fiestas climax during Semana Santa (Easter week), when, on the Thursday and Good Friday before Easter, cloaked penitents proceed through the city,

Taxco people celebrate their festival of the jumil (a type of grasshopper) on the first Monday after the 2 November Day of the Dead.

carrying gilded images and bearing crowns of thorns.

On the Monday after the 2 November Día de los Muertos ("Day of the Dead"), Taxco people head to pine-shaded **Parque Huixteco** atop the Cerro Huixteco behind town to celebrate their unique **Fiesta de los Jumiles.** In a ritual whose roots are lost in pre-Columbian legend, people collect and feast on *jumiles* (small crickets)—raw or roasted—along with music and plenty of beer and fixings. Since so many people go, transportation is easy. Ask a taxi or *zócalo* van driver or your hotel desk clerk for details.

Sports and Recreation

Stay in shape as local folks do, by walking Taxco's winding, picturesque side streets and uphill lanes. And, since all roads return to the *zócalo*, getting lost is rarely a problem.

For more formal sports, the **Monte Taxco Country Club** has horses ready for riding ($9/hour), three good tennis courts ($6/hour), and a nine-hole golf course available for fee use by nonguests for $20 per person. Contact the country club sports desk, tel. 762-213-00, ext. 411, in the little house, about 50 yards directly away from the Hotel Monte Taxco's front entrance. Informal *sendas* (hiking paths; ask directions from the horse-rental man) branch from the horse paths to the surrounding luscious pine- and cedar-forested mesa country. Take sturdy shoes, water, and a hat.

SHOPPING

Market

Taxco's big market day is Sunday, when the town is loaded with people from outlying villages selling produce and live pigs, chickens, and ducks. The market is located just downhill from Los Arcos, the lane that runs below the right side of the *zócalo* church (as you face that church). From the lane, head right before the arch and down the staircase. Soon you'll be descending through a warren of market stalls. Pass the small Baptist church on Sunday and hear the congregation singing like angels floating above the market. Don't miss the spice stall, **Yerbería Castillo,** piled with the intriguing wild remedies collected by owner Elvira Castillo and her son Teodoro.

Farther on you'll pass mostly scruffy meat stalls but also some clean juice stands, such as **Liquados Memo,** open daily 7 a.m.-6 p.m., where you can rest with a delicious fresh *zanahoria* (carrot), *toronja* (grapefruit), or *sandía* (watermelon) juice.

Before leaving the market, be sure to ask for *jumiles* (hoo-MEE-lays), live crickets that sell in bags for about a penny apiece, ready for folks to pop them into their mouths.

If *jumiles* don't suit your taste, you may want to drop in for lunch at one of the *fondas* above the market's *artesanías* (handicrafts) section.

Handicrafts

The submarket **Mercado de Artesanías** (watch for a white sign above an open area by the staircase) offers items for mostly local consumption, such as economical belts, huaraches, wallets, and inexpensive silver chains, necklaces, and earrings.

As you head out for tonier shops, don't miss the common but colorful and charming ceramic cats, turtles, doves, fish, and other figurines that local folk sell very cheaply. If you buy, bargain—but not too hard, for the people are poor and have often traveled far.

Masks are the prime attraction at **Arnoldo,** Palma 1, tel. (762) 212-72, upstairs, across the uphill lane next to Hotel Agua Escondida, where the friendly proprietors, Arnoldo Jacobo and his son Raoul, are more than willing and able to explain every detail about their fascinating array of merchandise. Hundreds of masks from all over Guerrero—stone and wood, antique and new—line the walls like a museum. All of the many motifs, ranging from black men puffing cigarettes and blue-eyed sea goddesses to inscrutable Aztec gods in onyx and grotesque lizard-humanoids, are priced to sell. Open Mon.-Sat. 9 a.m.-8:30 p.m., Sunday 10 a.m.-7:30 p.m.

Other shops nearby have similar offerings. Arnoldo's neighbor, **Celso,** at 4 Palma, just uphill, tel. (762) 228-48, is closed Wednesday, but open other days 10 a.m.-2 p.m. and 4-8 p.m., except

Sunday 10 a.m.-4 p.m. **D'Avila Ofebres'** shop on Plazuela de San Juan just past the end of Cuauhtémoc, Plazuela de San Juan 7, in the entry courtyard of Hotel Casa Grande across from Bancomer, is open daily 9 a.m.-9 p.m.

Silver Shops

Good silver shops cluster around the *zócalo* and downhill on the highway. Perhaps the favorite of all is the family-owned **Los Castillo** in the lobby of the Hotel Posada Los Castillo, downhill from the *zócalo,* to the right of the Hotel Agua Escondida. Run by the industrious and prolific Castillo family, the shop offers all in-house work at reasonable prices. Here you can watch silversmiths at work, and, unlike at many shops, bargain a bit. At J. R. Alarcón 7, tel. (762) 213-96, open daily 9 a.m.-1 p.m. and 3-7 p.m.; credit cards accepted.

One of the more interesting silver shops, if only for a look around, is **David and Saul** (formerly La Gruta) on Cuauhtémoc between the *zócalo* and Plazuela de San Juan, Cuauhtémoc 10, tel. (762) 245-95. They say, with a smile, that the Grutas de Cacahuamilpa were modeled after their shop. Inside, plaster stalagmites hang above small mountains of silver-decorated quartz crystals. Open Mon.-Sat. 10 a.m.-8 p.m., Sunday 10 a.m.-4 p.m.; credit cards accepted.

Enough silver stores for a week of shopping line the *carretera* John F. Kennedy downhill. Although the original shop, Las Delicias, begun by William Spratling in cooperation with local silversmiths in 1931, is long gone, a pair of good shops *(platerías),* **Andre's,** and **Malena,** tel. (762) 232-43, occupy the same premises, at 28 Carretera John F. Kennedy, across from the Hotel Posada de la Misión; open daily 11 a.m.-7 p.m.

Photography Supplies and Grocery Stores

Fairly well-stocked **Tienda la Misión,** half a block from the *zócalo,* offers some cameras and accessories, and Kodak film, including Tri-X Pan, Plus-X, and Ektachrome. Located on Cuauhtémoc 6, tel. (762) 201-16. It also does photocopying, including enlargement and reduction. Open Mon.-Sat. 10 a.m.-8 p.m., Sunday 10 a.m.-2 p.m.

A grocery store, **Casa Ayja,** Benito Juárez 7, tel. (762) 203-64, a rarity in silver-rich Taxco, three blocks down Juárez from the *zócalo,* stocks a bit of everything, including wines, cheeses, and milk on its clean, well-organized shelves and aisles. Open Mon.-Sat. 9 a.m.-10 p.m. If it's closed, go to the similarly efficient **Super Macal,** open daily, on San Nicolas, a blocks downhill from Plazuela de San Juan.

SERVICES AND INFORMATION

Money Exchange

Banks near the *zócalo* are Taxco's cheapest source of pesos. **Banco Confia,** tel. (762) 202-37, at the *zócalo* corner of Cuauhtémoc, changes U.S. currency only, Mon.-Fri. 9 a.m.-3 p.m., Saturday 10 a.m.-2 p.m. A few doors along Cuauhtémoc, the best option, **Banco Santander Mexicano,** tel. (762) 235-36 and 232-70, changes both U.S. currency and traveler's checks Mon.-Fri. 9 a.m.-4:30 p.m. and Canadian, British, French, German, Italian, and other currencies Mon.-Fri. 9 a.m.-2 p.m. For U.S. currency and traveler's check exchange only, go to **Bancomer,** tel. (762) 202-87 or 202-88, Mon.-Fri. 9 a.m.-5 p.m., a few doors farther along Cuauhtémoc.

Communication

The small Taxco **post office,** tel. (762) 205-01, on the highway a half block north of the Estrella de Oro bus station, is open Mon.-Fri. 8 a.m.-7 p.m., Saturday 9 a.m.-1 p.m. **Telecomunicaciones,** downhill, off the *zócalo,* behind Casa Borda, tel. (762) 248-85, fax 200-01, offers telex, money order, and public fax services; open Mon.-Fri. 9 a.m.-3 p.m., Saturday 9 a.m.-noon.

Medical and Police

Taxco has a pair of respected private hospitals, both on the *carretera.* The **Clínica de Especialidades,** 33 Carretera JFK, tel. (762) 211-11 or 245-00, has a 24-hour emergency room, a good pharmacy, and many specialists on call. The similar **Clínica Santa Cruz,** tel. (762) 230-12, offers the same services at the corner of Morelos, across from the government Seguro Social hospital.

For routine drugs and medicines, go to one of many local pharmacies, such as **Farmacia Lourdes,** tel. (762) 210-66, at Cuauhtémoc 8, half a block from the *zócalo;* open 8 a.m.-10 p.m.

For police emergencies, contact the **policía,** either on duty on the *zócalo,* or at the city hall (two blocks downhill, at Juárez 6, tel. 762-200-07), or at the substation on the side street, Calle Fundaciones, one block below the *carretera* near the corner of Alarcón.

Tourist Information Offices

Taxco has at least two tourist information offices, both beside the highway at opposite ends of town, open daily approximately 10 a.m.-6 p.m. The knowledgeable and English-speaking officers readily answer questions and furnish whatever maps and literature they may have. The north office, tel. (762) 207-98, is next to the north-end Pemex gas station; the south office is about a quarter mile south of the south-end Pemex station.

Publications

English-language books and newspapers are hard to find in Taxco. Nevertheless, the bookstore **Agente de Publicaciones Raoul Domínguez,** tel. (762) 201-33, usually has the Mexico City *Times.* He's open daily 9 a.m.-2 p.m. and 4:30-8 p.m. on the Los Arcos lane adjacent and below the church.

The scarcity of English reading matter makes the collection at the small library **Biblioteca Taxco-Canoga Park** even more important. Check out its several shelves of English-language novels, nonfiction, magazines, and reference books Mon.-Fri. 9 a.m.-1 p.m. and 3-7 p.m. Saturday 9 a.m.-1 p.m. Most of the collection was donated by volunteers from Taxco's sister city, Canoga Park, California. The library is a five-minute walk downhill from the city hall on the alley off Juárez, on the right, a half block after Banamex.

GETTING THERE AND AWAY

By Car or RV

National Hwy. 95 provides the main connection south with Acapulco in a total of about 167 miles (269 km) of easy driving via Iguala, accessible to/from Taxco via the winding, 22-mile (36-km) old Hwy. 95 cutoff. From there, sail south via the *cuota* (toll) *autopista.* Allow about four hours' driving time for the entire Taxco-Acapulco trip, either direction.

Highway 95 also connects Taxco north via Cuernavaca with Mexico City, a total of about 106 miles (170 km). The new leg of the Taxco-Mexico City toll *autopista* splits off from old Hwy. 95 about two miles north of town. For those in a hurry, it cuts about half an hour off the driving time. Otherwise, follow the scenic curving old Hwy. 95 about 20 miles (32 km) to its intersection with Hwy. 95 *cuota* (toll) superhighway. Congestion around Mexico City lengthens the driving time to about three hours in either direction. **Authorities limit driving your car in Mexico City** according to the last digit of your license plate. See the special topic Mexico City Driving Limits.

Highway 55 (junction at Cacahuamilpa) gives Michoacán- and Jalisco-bound drivers the desirable option of avoiding Mexico City by connecting Taxco north-south with Toluca. The two-lane Hwy. 55, although paved and in fair-to-good condition for the 74 miles (119 km), is winding and narrow. Fortunately, a straighter, much safer

autopista along the northern half of the stretch improves the Taxco-Toluca driving time by at least half an hour. Northbound, steep grades might stretch this to about two and a half hours; southbound, allow about two hours driving time.

By Bus
Competing lines **Estrella Blanca,** tel. (762) 201-31, and **Estrella de Oro,** tel. (762) 206-48, operate stations on the downhill *carretera* a few blocks apart. Both offer several luxury- and first-class connections north with Mexico City via Cuernavaca and south with Acapulco via Iguala and Chilpancingo. Additionally, Estrella Blanca offers the very useful option for northwest-bound travelers of bypassing Mexico City via the super-scenic Highway 55 route via Ixtapan del Sal (an interesting spa town) to Toluca. There, you can connect via Pátzcuaro, Michoacán, and Guadalajara, Jalisco, to the palmy Pacific Mexico beach destinations of Playa Azul, Manzanillo, Puerto Vallarta, San Blas, and Mazatlán.

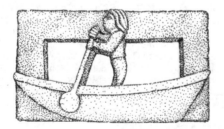

THE COSTA CHICA
AND INLAND TO OAXACA

In reality, the Costa Chica, the "Little Coast," which includes the state of Guerrero south of Acapulco and the adjoining coast of Oaxaca, isn't so small after all. Hwy. 200, heading out of the Acapulco hubbub, requires 300 miles to traverse. Traffic thins out, passing scattered groves, fields, and villages along the Costa Chica southern bulge, where the coast curves, like the belly of a dolphin, to its most southerly point near Puerto Ángel.

In the main resorts of the Costa Chica—Puerto Escondido, Puerto Ángel, and Bahías de Huatulco—the beaches face south, toward the Mar del Sur, the Pacific Ocean. On the other hand, if travelers head inland, they go north, over the verdant, jungle-clad Sierra Madre del Sur and into the Valley of Oaxaca, the Indian heartland of southern Mexico.

To about a million Oaxacan native peoples, Spanish is a foreign language. Many of them—Zapotecs, Mixtecs, and a score of smaller groups—live in remote mountain villages, sub-sisting as they always have on corn and beans, without telephones, sewers, schools, or roads. Those who live near towns often speak the Spanish they have learned by coming to market. In the Costa Chica town markets you will brush shoulders with them—mostly Mixtecs, Amusgos, and Chatinos—men sometimes in pure-white cottons and women in colorful embroidered *huipiles* over wrapped handwoven skirts.

Besides the native people, you will often see African-Mexicans—*morenos,* brown ones—known as *costeños* because their isolated settlements are near the coast. Descendants of African slaves imported hundreds of years ago, the *costeños* subsist on the produce from their village gardens and the fish they catch.

Costa Chica *indígenas* and *costeños* have a reputation for being unfriendly and suspicious. If true in the past (although it's certainly less so in the present), they have had good reason to be suspicious of outsiders, who in their view have been trying to take away their land, gods, and lives for 300 years.

Communication is nevertheless possible. Your arrival, for the residents of a little mountain or shoreline end-of-road village, might be the event of the day. People are going to wonder why you came. Smile and say hello. Buy a soda at the store or *palapa*. If kids gather around, don't be shy. Draw a picture in your notebook. If a child offers to do likewise, you've succeeded.

ALONG THE ROAD TO PUERTO ESCONDIDO

If driving from Acapulco, mark your odometer at the traffic circle where Highways 95 and 200 intersect over the hill from Acapulco. If, on the other hand, you bypass that congested point via the Acapulco airport road, set your odometer to zero at the east-side interchange near Puerto Marquez where the airport highway continues along the overpass—but where you exit to the right, and follow the Hwy. 200 Pinotepa Nacional sign. Mileages and kilometer markers along the road are sometimes the only locators of turnoffs to hidden villages and little beaches.

Fill up with gas before starting out in Acapulco. After that, Magna Sin (unleaded) is available at Cruz Grande (56 miles, 91 km), Pinotepa Nacional (157 miles, 253 km), Puerto Escondido (247 miles, 398 km), and near Puerto Ángel (291 miles, 469 km).

If you're going by bus, ride one of the several daily first-class or second-class buses from the Estrella Blanca terminal in Acapulco.

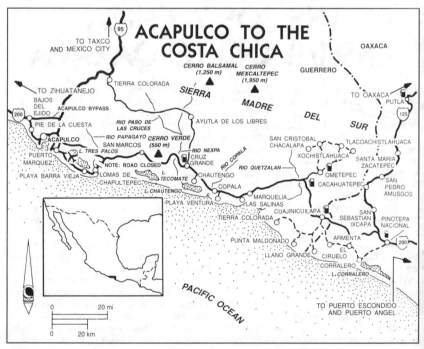

Oxcarts—slow but dependable and cheap—still do their part in rural Pacific Mexico.

PLAYA VENTURA

Three miles east of the small town of Copala, 77 miles (123 km) from Acapulco, a roadside sign points toward Playa Ventura. Four miles down a paved road, which a truck-bus from Copala traverses regularly, you arrive pavement's-end at Ventura village. From there, a mile-long golden-sand beach arcs gently east. Past a lighthouse, the beach leads to a point, topped by a stack of granite rocks, known locally as Casa de Piedra ("House of Stone").

Playa Ventura can provide nearly everything for a restful day or week in the sun. Several good tenting or RV (maneuverable medium rigs, vans, or campers) spots sprinkle the inviting, outcropping-dotted shoreline. Shady *palapas* set up by former campers stand ready for rehabilitation and reuse by new arrivals.

Surf fishing (with net-caught bait fish) is fine from the beach, while *pangas* go out for deep-sea catches. Good surfing breaks angle in from the points, and, during the rainy season, the behind-the-beach lagoon is good for fishing, shrimping, and wildlife viewing. (Bring your kayak or inflatable raft.)

The palm-lined beach stretches southeast for miles. Past the picturesque Casa de Piedra outcropping, an intimate *palapa-* and *panga*-lined sandy cove curves invitingly to yet another palmy point, Pico del Monte. Past that lies still another, even more pristine, cove and beach.

Food and Accommodations

Besides the village stores, food is available at a number of *loncherías* and beach *palapa* restaurants. Accommodations are available at a sprinkling of family *posadas,* the foremost of which is the **Restaurant-Cabañas Perez.** If anyone dispels the rumor that *costeño* folks are unfriendly, it's the hospitable father-son-daughter team of Bulmaro, Luis, and Hortencia Perez, who have put together the modest beginnings of a little resort. Bulmaro and his family invite visitors to park RVs in their small lot, where they offer a friendly word, showers, and a bit of shade for nothing more than the price of a meal at their restaurant. For noncampers, the Perez family offers a pair of modest beach cabañas.

SAN MARCOS, OMETEPEC, AND CUAJINICULAPA

A few larger towns along the road can provide a number of essential services. Thirty-six miles (58 km) east of Acapulco, San Marcos (pop. 10,000) has a bank (Banamex, tel. 745-300-36), Seguro Social (health center, tel. 745-303-39), pharmacies (El Rosario, tel. 745-300-08), a motel (Las Palmas, tel. 745-300-37, 20 rooms around a small pool patio), and post and *telecomunicaciones* (long-distance telephone, money orders and fax, tel. 745-301-30) offices.

THE MIXTECS

Sometime during the 1980s, the Mixtecs regained their pre-conquest population of about 350,000. Of that total, around one-third speak only their own language. Their villages and communal fields spread over tens of thousands of square miles of remote mountain valleys north, west, and southwest of Oaxaca City. Their homeland, the Mixteca, is divided into three distinct regions: Mixteca Alta, Mixteca Baja, and the Costera.

The **Mixteca Alta** centers in the mountains about 100 road miles north of Oaxaca City, in the vicinity of small towns such as San Juan Bautista Cuicatlán, on Hwy. 131, and Jocotipac and Cuyamecalco, several miles along local branch roads from the highway.

Mixteca Baja communities, such as San Miguel El Grande, San Juan Mixtepec, and Santiago Juxtlahuaca, dot the western Oaxaca mountains and valleys in a broad region centering roughly on Tlaxiaco on Hwy. 125.

In the **Costera,** important Mixtec communities exist in or near Pinotepa Nacional, Huaxpaltepec, and Jamiltepec, all on Hwy. 200 in southwestern Oaxaca.

The Aztec-origin name Mixtecos (People of the Clouds) was translated directly from the Mixtecs' name for their own homeland: Aunyuma (Land of

Compare this pre-Columbian Mixtec birth scene with the Huichol birth scene depicted in the special topic "The Huichol."

the Clouds). The Mixtecs' name for themselves, however, is Nyu-u Sabi (People of the Rain).

When the conquistadores arrived in Oaxaca, the Mixtecs were under the thumb of the Aztecs, who, after a long, bitter struggle, had wrested control of Oaxaca from combined Mixtec-Zapotec armies in 1486. The Mixtecs naturally resented the Aztecs, whose domination was transferred to the Spanish during the colonial period, and, in turn, to the mestizos during modern times. The Mixtecs still defer to the town Mexicans, but they don't like it. Consequently, many rural Mixtecs, with little state or national consciousness, have scant interest in becoming Mexicanized.

In isolated Mixtec communities, traditions still rule. Village elders hold final authority, parents arrange marriages through go-betweens, and land is owned communally. Catholic saints are thinly disguised incarnations of old gods such as Tabayukí, ruler of nature, or the capricious and powerful *tono* spirits that lurk everywhere.

In many communities, Mixtec women exercise considerable personal freedom. At home and in villages, they often still work bare breasted. And while their men get drunk and carry on during festivals, women dance and often do a bit of their own carousing. Whom they do it with is their own business.

Ometepec (pop. 15,000), a couple of hours' drive farther east, is accessible via a 10-mile paved road, which branches off Hwy. 200 at a well-marked intersection 110 miles (175 km) from Acapulco. Besides being an important service center, Ometepec (elev. 2,000 feet) enjoys a cooler climate, drawing crowds of native peoples, notably Amusgos, from outlying villages to its big morning market. Many local buses follow dirt and gravel roads from Ometepec to more remote centers, such as **Xochistlahuaca** (so-chees-tlah-hoo-AH-kah, pop. 3,000), the Amusgo town about 30 miles northeast. Not far off the Xochistlahuaca road you can visit **Cochoa-**

pa, the partially excavated archaeological site where a number of very ancient Olmec-style stelae and sculptures have been unearthed. Ask around for a local guide.

In Ometepec itself, banks (Banamex, tel. 741-201-22; Banco Mexicano, tel. 741-201-13), a private hospital (De la Amistad, tel. 741-209-85), a private diagnostic clinic (Clínica de Especialidades Sagrado Corazón, tel. 741-21-40), public Seguro Social clinic (tel. 741-203-92), a pharmacy (Farmacia Hernández, tel. 741-206-66), basic hotels (such as the Montero Mayren, tel. 741-201-00), and telecomunicaciones (tel. 741-203-86) and post office provide essential services.

Back on Hwy. 200, Cuajiniculapa (kwah-hee-nee-kwee-LAH-pah, pop. 10,000), 125 miles (199 km) from Acapulco, also has a travel agent (Viajes Buen Día, tel. 741-404-70), Centro de Salud (tel. 741-401-42), a pharmacy (Santa Isabel, tel. 741-400-17), basic hotels (Alejim, tel. 741-403-10, and Marin, tel. 741-400-21), and post (tel. 741-402-61) and telecomunicaciones (tel. 741-403-37) offices.

Cuajiniculapa is a major market town for the scattering of costeño communities, such as San Nicolas (pop. 5,000, eight miles south), along the beach road (at Km 201) to Punta Maldonado, the local fishing port.

PINOTEPA NACIONAL

Pinotepa Nacional (pop. about 30,000; 157 miles, 253 km, east of Acapulco; 90 miles, 145 km, west of Puerto Escondido) and its neighboring communities represent an important indigenous region. Mixtec, Amusgo, Chatino, and other peoples stream into town for markets and fiestas in their traditional dress, ready to combine business with pleasure. They sell their produce and crafts—pottery, masks, handmade clothes—at the market, then later get tipsy, flirt, and dance.

The Name

So many people have asked the meaning of their city's name that the town fathers wrote the explanation on a wall next to Hwy. 200 on the west side of town. Pinotepa comes from the Aztec-language words pinolli (crumbling) and tepetl (mountain); thus "Crumbling Mountain." The second part of the name came about because, during colonial times, the town was called Pinotepa Real ("Royal"). This wouldn't do after independence, so the name became Pinotepa Nacional, reflecting the national consciousness that emerged during the 1810-21 struggle for liberation.

The Mixtecs, the dominant regional group, disagree with all this, however. To them, Pinotepa has always been Ñí Yu-uku ("Place of Salt"). Only within the town limits do the Mexicans (mestizos), who own most of the town businesses, outnumber the Mixtecs. The farther from town you get, the more likely you are to hear people conversing in the Mixtec language, a complex tongue that relies on many subtle tones to make meanings clear.

Market

Highway 200, called Av. Porfirio Díaz on the west side (B. Juárez on the east) of town, is Pinotepa's one main business street. It passes a block north of the main market, by the big secondary school, on the west side, and continues about a mile to the central plaza.

Despite the Pinotepa market's oft-exotic goods—snakes, iguanas, wild mountain fruits, forest herbs and spices—its people, nearly entirely Mixtec, are its main attraction, especially on the big Wednesday and Sunday market days. Men wear pure-white loose cottons, topped by woven palm-leaf hats. Women wrap themselves in their lovely striped purple, violet, red, and navy blue pozahuanco sarong-like horizontally striped skirts. Many women carry a polished tan ticara gourd bowl atop their heads, which, although it's not supposed to, looks like a whimsical hat. Older women (and younger ones with babies at their breasts) go bare-breasted with only their white huipil draped over their chests as a concession to mestizo custom. Others wear an easily removable mandil, a light cotton apron-halter above their pozahuanco. A number of women can ordinarily be found at any given time selling beautiful handmade pozahuancos.

Festivals

Although the Pinotepa market days are big, they don't compare to the week before Easter (Semana Santa). People get ready for the finale with processions, carrying the dead Christ through town to the church each of the seven Fridays before Easter. The climax comes on Good Friday

POZAHUANCOS

To a coastal Mixtec woman her *pozahuanco* is a lifetime investment symbolizing her maturity and social status, something that she expects to pass on to her daughters. Heirloom *pozahuancos* are wraparound, horizontally striped skirts of hand-spun thread. Women dye them by hand, always including a pair of necessary colors: a light purple *(morada),* from secretions of tidepool-harvested snails, *Purpura patula pansa,* and silk, dyed scarlet red with cochineal, a dye extracted from the beetle *Dactylopius coccus,* cultivated in the Valley of Oaxaca. Increasingly, women are weaving *pozahuancos* with synthetic thread, which has a slippery feel compared to the hand-spun cotton. Consider yourself lucky if you can get a traditionally made *pozahuanco* for as little as $100. If someone offers you a look-alike for $20, you know it's an imitation.

(Viernes Santa), when a platoon of young Mixtec men paint their bodies white to portray Jews, and while intoning ancient Mixtec chants shoot arrows at Christ on the cross. On Saturday, the people mournfully take the Savior down from the cross and bury him, and on Sunday gleefully celebrate his resurrection with a riot of fireworks, food, and folk dancing.

Although not as spectacular as Semana Santa, there's plenty of merrymaking, food, dancing, and processions around the Pinotepa *zócalo* church on 25 July, the day of Pinotepa's patron, Santiago (St. James).

Accommodations and Food

The motel-style **Hotel Carmona,** Av. Porfirio Díaz 127, Pinotepa Nacional, Oaxaca 71600, tel. (954) 322-22, fax 323-22, on Hwy. 200 about three blocks west of the central plaza, offers three stories of clean, not fancy but thoughtfully decorated rooms, a big backyard garden with pool and sundeck, and a passable restaurant. For festival dates, make advance reservations. The 50 rooms run about $10 s, $13 d, $16 t, fan only, $14, $18, and $21 for a/c.

If the Carmona is full, check the two high-profile newer hotels, **Pepe's** and **Las Gaviotas,** tel. (954) 324-02, fax 326-26, beside the highway

on the west side of town. Of the two, Pepe's, at Carretera Pinotepa Nacional-Acapulco Km 1, Pinotepa Nacional, Oaxaca 71600, tel. (954) 343-47, fax 336-42, is probably the better choice, with 35 spacious, immaculate, semideluxe rooms for a very reasonable $8 s, $11 d fan only, $14 and $18 with a/c; with good TV, hot water, restaurant, and parking.

Fourth and fifth choices go to a pair of more basic hotels downtown: **Hotel Marisa,** Av. Juárez 134, tel. (954) 321-01, fax 326-96, and **Hotel Tropical,** Av. 3 Poniente and Progreso, tel. (954) 320-10.

Campers enjoy a tranquil spot (best during the dry late fall-winter-spring season) on the **Río Arena** about two miles east of Pinotepa. Eastbound, turn left just after the big river bridge. Continue a few hundred yards, past a pumphouse on the left, to a track that forks down to the riverbank. Notice the waterfall cascading down the rocky cliff across the river. You will sometimes find neighbors—in RVs or tents—set up on the riverside beneath the abandoned Restaurant La Roca a few hundred yards up the smooth stream, excellent for kayaking (if you have some way of returning back upstream.)

For food, Pinotepa has at least three recommendable restaurants. West of town is **Pepe's Hotel** restaurant, and the relaxed, country-style **Bora Bora,** with *palapa* dining, open daily till about 9 p.m., uphill beyond the arch, just across the street from the west-side Pemex gas station.

For a light lunch or supper, try the very clean and friendly family-run **Burger Bonny,** at the southeast corner of the main plaza, open daily 11 a.m.-10 p.m. Besides six varieties of the best hamburger on the Costa Chica, Burger Bonny offers *tortas,* nachos, tacos, french fries, hot dogs, microwave popcorn, fruit juices, and *refrescos,* at very reasonable prices.

Services

Exchange money at either **Bancomer** (U.S. traveler's checks and cash, open for money exchange Mon.-Fri. 10 a.m.-1:30 p.m., tel. 954-326-44) on main street Porfirio Díaz about two blocks west of the central plaza, or the **Banco Santander Mexicano** (tel. 954-323-63) a block east, around the corner. Alternatively, try the long-hours (open Mon.-Fri. approximately 8 a.m.-6 p.m., Saturday 9 a.m.-3 p.m.) **Banco Inter-**

nacional, tel. (958) 339-49 or 339-79, on the same cross street, Av. Progreso, but across Porfirio Díaz a block from Bancomer.

The **correo** (post office), tel. (954) 322-64, is open Mon.-Fri. 8 a.m.-7 p.m., Saturday 9 a.m.-1 p.m., by the bus station, about two blocks west and across the street from Bancomer. The **telecomunicaciones** (money orders, public telephone and fax) is two blocks north of the Presidencia Municipal and open Mon.-Sat. 8 a.m.-6 p.m., Saturday 9 a.m.-noon at Av. Lic. Alfonso Pérez Gasga. A private **larga distancia** telephone and fax office, on the plaza, is open longer, evening hours.

For a doctor, go to the **Clínica Rodriguez** at 503 Aguirre Palancares, tel. (954) 323-30, one block north, two blocks west of the central plaza. Get routine medications at one of several town pharmacies, such as **Farmacia 24 Horas,** a block north of the central plaza, just north of the church facade.

Getting There and Away

By **car or RV,** Hwy. 200 connects west to Acapulco (160 miles, 258 km) in an easy four and a half hours driving time. The 89-mile (143-km) connection to Puerto Escondido can be done safely in about two and a half hours. Additionally, the 239-mile (385-km) Hwy. 125-Hwy. 190 route connects Oaxaca and Pinotepa Nacional, via Putla de Guerrero and Tlaxiaco (136 miles, 219 km). Although winding most of the way and potholed at times the road is generally uncongested. It's safely driveable with caution from Oaxaca in about seven total hours to Pinotepa, and eight hours, in the reverse, uphill, direction.

Several long-distance **bus** lines connect Pinotepa Nacional with destinations north, northwest, east, and west. **Estrella Blanca** and subsidiaries Elite, Gacela, and Flecha Roja, tel. (954) 322-54, have several daily first- and second-class *salidas de paso* (buses passing through) departures west to Acapulco and east to Puerto Escondido, Pochutla, and Bahías de Huatulco from their station on Porfirio Díaz about three blocks west of the *zócalo*.

Smaller, mostly second-class lines **Fletes y Pasajes, Estrella del Valle,** and **Oaxaca Pacífico** operate out of a pair of small stations one block north of the central plaza on side street

Aguirre Palancares. Fletes y Pasajes, tel. (954) 321-63, connects daily with Oaxaca via Putla, Tlaxiaco and Nochixtlán, by Highways 125 and 190. Estrella del Valle and Oaxaca Pacífico buses, tel. (954) 326-97, also connect with Oaxaca, but in the opposite direction: first east, either to Puerto Escondido to Pochutla (Puerto Ángel), then continuing north over the Sierra to Oaxaca via either Hwy. 131 or 175, respectively.

First-class **Cristóbal Colón** also operates out of a small station on the same street, just around the corner from Banco Santander Mexicano. A few daily departures connect, via Highways 175 and 190, northeast, via Putla and Tlaxiaco, with Oaxaca (by the fast *autopista* via Nochixtlén), and northwest, with Mexico City (via Puebla). Other departures connect east, with Puerto Escondido.

EXCURSIONS NORTH OF PINOTEPA

The local patronal festival year begins early, on 20 January, at **Pinotepa Don Luis** (pop. 5,000), about 15 miles, by back roads, northeast of Pinotepa Nacional, with the uniquely Mixtec festival of San Sebastián. Village bands blare, fireworks pop and hiss, and penitents crawl, until the finale, when dancers whirl the local favorite dance, Las Chilenas.

Yet another exciting time around Pinotepa Nacional is during **Carnaval,** when nearby communities put on big extravaganzas. Pinotepa Don Luis, sometimes known as Pinotepa Chica ("Little Pinotepa"), is famous for wooden masks the people make for their big Carnaval festival. The celebration usually climaxes on the Sunday before Ash Wednesday, when everyone seems to be in costume and a corps of performers gyrates in the traditional dances: Paloma ("Dove"), Tigre ("Jaguar"), Culebra ("Snake"), and Tejón ("Badger").

Pinotepa Don Luis bubbles over again with excitement during Semana Santa, when the faithful carry fruit- and flower-decorated trees to the church on Good Friday, explode Judas effigies on Saturday, and celebrate by dancing most of Easter Sunday.

San Juan Colorado, a few miles north of Pinotepa Don Luis, usually appears as just another dusty little town until Carnaval, when its festival rivals that of its neighbors. Subsequently, on 29 November, droves of Mixtec people come into town to honor their patron, San Andres. After the serious part at the church, they celebrate with a cast of favorite dancing characters such as Malinche, Jaguar, Turtle, and Charros ("Cowboys").

Amusgo Country

Cacahuatepec (pop. about 5,000; on Hwy. 125 about 25 miles north of Pinotepa Nacional) and its neighboring community San Pedro Amusgos are important centers of the Amusgo people. Approximately 20,000 Amusgos live in a roughly 30-mile-square region straddling the Guerrero-Oaxaca state border. Their homeland includes, besides Cacahuatepec and San Pedro Amusgos, Xochistlahuaca, Zacoalpán, and Tlacoachistlahuaca on the Guerrero side.

The Amusgo language is linguistically related to Mixtec, although it's unintelligible to Mixtec speakers. Before the conquest, the Amusgos were subject to the numerically superior Mixtec kingdoms until the Amusgos were conquered by the Aztecs in 1457, and later by the Spanish.

Now, most Amusgos live on as subsistence farmers, supplementing their diet with occasional fowl or small game. Amusgos are best known to the outside world for the lovely animal-, plant-, and human-motif *huipiles,* which Amusgo women always seem to be hand-embroidering on their doorsteps.

Although **Cacahuatepec** enjoys a big market each Sunday, that doesn't diminish the importance of its big Easter weekend festival, the day of Todos Santos ("All Saints' Day"), and Day of the Dead, 2 November, when, at the cemetery, people welcome their ancestors' return to rejoin the family.

San Pedro Amusgos celebrations are among the most popular regional fiestas. On 29 June, the day of San Pedro, people participate in religious processions, and costumed participants dressed as Moors and Christians, bulls, jaguars, and mules dance before crowds of men in traditional whites and women in beautiful heirloom *huipiles.* Later, on the first Sunday of October, folks crowd into town to enjoy the traditional processions, dances, and sweet treats of the fiesta of the Virgen de la Rosario ("Virgin of the Rosary").

Even if you miss the festivals, San Pedro Amusgos is worth a visit to buy *huipiles* alone. Three or four shops sell them along the main street through town. Look for the sign of **Trajes Regionales,** the little store run by Edin Guzmán, tel. (955) 300-45. Besides dozens of beautiful embroidered garments, she stocks a few Amusgo books and offers friendly words of advice and local information.

EXCURSIONS EAST OF PINOTEPA

For 30 or 40 miles east of Pinotepa Nacional, where road kilometer markers begin at zero again near the central plaza, Hwy. 200 stretches through the coastal Mixtec heartland, intriguing to explore, especially during festival times. The population of **San Andres Huaxpaltepec** (oo-wash-pahl-tay-PAYK), about 10 miles east of Pinotepa, sometimes swells from about 4,000 to 20,000 or more during the three or four days before the day of Jesus the Nazarene (the fourth Friday before Good Friday). The entire town becomes a spreading warren of shady stalls, offering everything from TVs to stone metates. (Purchase of a corn-grinding metate, which, including stone roller, sells for about $25, is as important to a Mixtec family as a refrigerator is to an American. Mixtec husband and wife usually examine several of the concave stones, deliberating the pros and cons of each before deciding.)

The Huaxpaltepec Nazarene fair is typical of the larger Oaxaca country expositions. Even the highway becomes a lineup of stalls; whole Indian clans camp under the trees, and mules, cows, and horses wait patiently around the edges of a grassy trading lot as men discuss prices. (The fun begins when a sale is made, and the new owner tries to rope and harness his bargain steed.)

Even sex is for sale within a quarter of very tightly woven no-see-through grass houses, patrolled by armed guards. Walking through, you may notice that, instead of the usual women, one of the houses offers men, dressed in low-cut gowns, lipstick, and high-heeled shoes.

Huazolotitlán

At nearby Santa María Huazolotitlán (pop. 3,000) several resident woodcarvers craft excellent

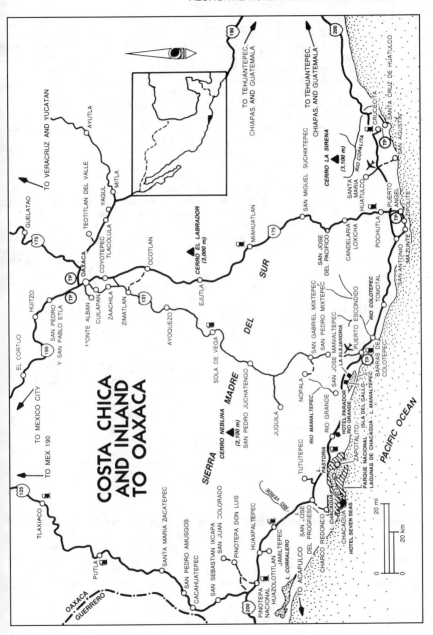

COSTA CHICA AND INLAND TO OAXACA

masks. Local favorites are jaguars, lions, rabbits, bulls, and human faces. Given a photograph (or a sitting), one of them, if asked, might even carve your likeness for a reasonable fee. (Figure perhaps $20-30.) Near the town plaza, ask for José Luna, Lázaro Gómez, or the master Idineo Gómez.

Textiles are also locally important. Look for the colorfully embroidered animal and floral motif *huipiles, manteles,* and *servilletas* (native smocks, tablecloths, and napkins). You might also be able to bargain for a genuine heirloom *pozahuanco* (handwoven wrap-around skirt) for a reasonable price.

Besides all the handicrafts, Huazolotitlán people celebrate the important local **Fiesta de la Virgen de la Asunción** from 13 to 16 August. The celebrations climax on 14 and 15 August, with a number of favorite traditional dances, in which you can see why masks are locally important, especially in the dance of the Tiger and the Turtle on 14 August. The finale comes on 15 August, with the ritual dance of the Chareos, dedicated to the Virgin.

Huazolotitlán (ooah-shoh-loh-teet-LAN) is about two miles via the paved road that forks south uphill from Hwy. 200 in Huaxpaltepec. Get there by driving, hitchhiking (with caution), riding the local bus, or hiring a taxi for about $2.

Santiago Jamiltepec

About 18 miles (at Km 30) east of Pinotepa Nacional is the hilltop town of Santiago Jamiltepec (hah-meel-teh-PAYK, for short). Two-thirds of its 20,000 inhabitants are Mixtec. A grieving Mixtec king named the town in memory of his infant son, Jamilly, who was carried off by an eagle from this very hilltop.

The market, while busy most any day, is biggest and most colorful on Thursday. The town's main fixed-date festivals are celebrated on 1 September, 1 January, and 15 February. In addition, Jamiltepec celebrates its famous pre-Easter (week following Domingo Ramos, or Palm Sunday) festival, featuring neighborhood candlelight processions accompanied by 18th-century music. Hundreds of the faithful bear elaborate wreaths and palm decorations to the foot of their church altars.

Jamiltepec is well worth a stop if only to visit the handicrafts shops **Yu-uku Cha-kuaa** ("Hill of Darkness") of Santiago de la Cruz Velasco. Personable Santiago runs both his home shop and a better stocked one at the Jamiltepec plaza market, because the government cluster of shops (Centro Artesanal de la Costa, on the highway) was closed down, victim of a dispute over control. The local Mixtec artisans wanted to manage their own handicrafts sales, while the regional branch of the INI (Instituto Nacional Indigenista) preferred to manage instead. The Mixtecs stuck together and refused to bring their handicrafts, closing the government operation.

Some of their crafts—masks, *huipiles,* carvings, hats—occupy the shelves and racks in Santiago's two shops. The market shop, signed "Artesanía Yu-uku Cha-kuaa," by the north entrance (ask for Santiago by name) stays open until about 4 p.m.; the home shop stays open until about 8 p.m. each night except Sundays and holidays. His home shop is located on main street Av. Principal at Francisco Madero, by Seguro Social, the government health clinic (turn off at the highway sign). If you don't want to miss him, write Santiago a letter at his shop, Av. Principal, esquina Fco. Madero, Barrio Grande, Sec. 5, Jamiltepec, Oaxaca 71700.

LAGUNAS DE CHACAGUA NATIONAL PARK AND VICINITY

The Lagunas de Chacagua National Park spreads for about 20 miles of open-ocean beach shoreline and islet-studded jungly lagoons midway between Pinotepa Nacional and Puerto Escondido. Tens of thousands of birds typical of a host of Mexican species fish the waters and nest in the mangroves of the two main lagoons, Laguna Pastoría on the east side and Laguna Chacagua on the west.

The fish and wildlife of the lagoons, overfished and overhunted during recent years by local people, are now recovering. Commercial fishing is now strictly licensed. A platoon of Marines patrols access roads, shorelines, and the waters themselves, making sure catches are within legal limits. Crocodiles were hunted out during the 1970s, but the government is trying to restore them with a hatchery on Laguna Chacagua.

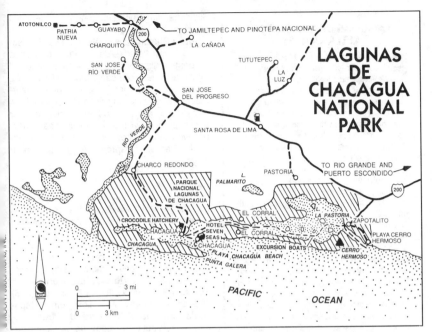

ATOTONILCO
PATRIA NUEVA
GUAYABO
CHARQUITO
SAN JOSE RÍO VERDE
SAN JOSE DEL PROGRESO
200
TO JAMILTEPEC AND PINOTEPA NACIONAL
LA CAÑADA
TUTUTEPEC
LA LUZ
RÍO VERDE
SANTA ROSA DE LIMA

LAGUNAS DE CHACAGUA NATIONAL PARK

CHARCO REDONDO
PARQUE NACIONAL LAGUNAS DE CHACAGUA
L. PALMARITO
PASTORIA
TO RIO GRANDE AND PUERTO ESCONDIDO
200
CROCODILE HATCHERY
CHACAGUA
HOTEL SEVEN SEAS
CHACAGUA
EL CORRAL
EL CORRAL
LA PASTORIA
ZAPOTALITO
PLAYA CERRO HERMOSO
EXCURSION BOATS
CERRO HERMOSO
PLAYA CHACAGUA BEACH
PUNTA GALERA

PACIFIC   OCEAN

0   3 mi
0   3 km

For most visitors, mainly Mexican families on Sunday outings, access is by boat, except for one rugged road. From east-side Zapotalito village, the local fishing cooperative offers full-and half-day boat excursions to the beaches, Playa Hermosa on the east side and Playa Chacagua on the west.

Exploring Lagunas de Chacagua
Zapotalito, on the eastern shore of Laguna Pastoría, is the sole easy access point to the Lagunas de Chacagua. Get there from the Zapotalito turnoff at Km 82, 51 miles from Pinotepa and 41 miles from Puerto Escondido. (Local buses run from Río Grande all the way to Zapotalito on the lagoon, while second class buses from Puerto Escondido and Pinotepa Nacional will drop you on the highway.)

From the Zapotalito landings, the fishing cooperative, Sociedad Cooperativa Turística Escondida, enjoys a monopoly for transporting visitors on the lagoons. The boatmen used to make their livings fishing; now they mostly ferry tourists. Having specialized in fishing, they are generally neither wildlife-sensitive nor wildlife-knowledgeable. Canopied powerboats, seating about 10, make long, full-day trips for about $50 per boat. Cheaper (about $20) half-day excursions take visitors to nearby **Playa Cerro Hermosa** at the mouth of Laguna Pastoría for a couple of hours' beach play and snorkeling—if you bring your own snorkeling gear. On the other hand, you can save yourself $20 and drive or walk the approximately two miles along the shoreline dirt road from Zapotalito to Playa Cerro Hermosa. Here you'll find a lovely open-ocean beach good for surf-fishing and beach sports, camping, a wildlife-rich lagoon mangrove wetland, and several *palapa* restaurants.

The full-day destination, Playa Chacagua, about 14 miles distant, unfortunately seems to necessitate a fast trip across the lagoon. It's difficult to get them to slow down. They roar across broad Laguna Pastoría, scattering flocks of birds ahead of them. They wind among the islands, with names such as Escorpión ("Scorpion"), Venados ("Deer"), or Pinuelas ("Little Pines"), sometimes slowing for viewing multitudes of nesting

LAGUNAS DE CHACAGUA ALTERNATIVES

Few roads penetrate the thick tropical deciduous forest surrounding the lagoons. Well-prepared adventurers can try to thumb a ride or drive a rugged high-clearance vehicle (dry season only) along the very rough 18-mile forest track to Chacagua village from San José del Progreso, which is located on Hwy. 200, 36 miles (58 km) from Pinotepa Nacional. Before setting out, check with local residents or storekeepers about safety and road conditions.

If you have a boat or kayak, you can try launching your own excursion on Laguna Pastoría. The Cooperativa members, being both poor and jealous of their prerogatives, may ask you for a "launching fee," whether they're entitled to it or not.

Some of the islands in Laguna Pastoría are high and forested and might be bug-free enough during the dry Nov.-Feb. months for a relaxing few days of wilderness camping, kayaking, and wildlife-viewing. Another alternative is to pay a boatman to drop you at your choice of islands and pick you up at a specified later time. Take everything, especially drinking water and insect repellent.

pelicans, herons, and cormorants. They pick up speed again in the narrow jungle channel between the lagoons, roaring past idyllic, somnolent El Corral village, and break into open water again on Laguna Chacagua.

The **crocodile hatchery** is at Chacagua village on the west side of the lagoon, home to about two dozen local *costeño* families, a shabby hotel, and a pair of lagoonside *palapa* restaurants. Past the rickety crocodile caretaker's quarters are a few enclosures housing about a hundred crocodiles segregated according to size, from hatchlings to six-foot-long toothy green adults.

The tour climaxes at the west half of Chacagua village across the estuary. Here, palms line the placid lagoon, shading the **Hotel Siete Mares** ("Seven Seas") bamboo tourist cabañas. The hotel, a quiet, rustic tropical resort, offers a small restaurant, showers and toilets, a few cabins (rent negotiable from about

$6, depending upon season), and a beautiful beach a short walk away.

Playa Chacagua is lovely *because* of its isolation. The unlittered golden-white sand, washed by gently rolling waves, seems perfect for all beach activities. You can snorkel off the rocks nearby, fish in the breakers, and surf the intermediate breaks that angle in on the west side. A few *palapas* provide food and drinks, and, for beachcombers, wildlife viewers, and backpackers (who bring their own water), the breezy, jungle-backed beach spreads for 10 miles both ways.

Río Grande

Río Grande (pop. 10,000), five miles east of the Lagunas de Chacagua-Zapotalito access road, is a transportation, supply, and service point for the region. Right on the highway are several *abarroterías* (groceries), pharmacies and doctors, and a *larga distancia* telephone in an office-booth on the left (south) side, at the west edge of town.

The downscale **Hotel Santa Monica,** Av. Puebla, Río Grande, Oaxaca 71830, tel. (958) 260-33, is the big white building off the highway's north side, at the west end of town. It offers 22 plain but clean rooms on two floors, encircling a spacious parking courtyard. With fans, toilets, and hot water, the rooms rent for about $4 s, $7 d.

The friendly, family-run **Restaurant Río Grande,** across the street from the hotel, provides good cheer and hearty meals daily 7 a.m.-10 p.m.

On the east edge of town, the once inviting but now somewhat neglected **Hotel Paraíso Río Grande,** Carretera 200, Río Grande, Oaxaca 71830, tel. (958) 267-96, offers a big swimming pool (if it's in working order) and a kiddie pool in a spreading, grassy patio, plus large brick-and-tile rooms with either fans or a/c. The 20 rooms (check for mildew) rent for about $10 s or d, $13 t with fan, $15 d with a/c.

The hotel's soaring, classically vaulted ceilings and elegant brick arches flow from the expertise of its architect builder. His life project has been to first build, and now extend, the hotel, using unreinforced brick and concrete only, not unlike ancient Roman buildings, but with the addition of innovative new designs.

LAGUNA MANIALTEPEC

Sylvan, mangrove-fringed Laguna Manialtepec, about 10 miles west of Puerto Escondido, is a repository for a trove of Pacific Mexico wildlife. Unlike Lagunas de Chacagua, Laguna Manialtepec is relatively deep and fresh most of the year, except occasionally during the rainy season when its main source, the Río Manialtepec, breaks through its sandbar and the lagoon becomes a tidal estuary. Consequently lacking a continuous supply of ocean fry for sustained fishing, Laguna Manialtepec has been left to local people, a few Sunday visitors, and its wildlife.

Laguna Manialtepec abounds with birds. Of the hundreds of species frequenting the lagoon, 40 or 50 are often spotted in a morning outing. Among the more common are the olivaceous cormorant and its relative, the *anhinga;* and herons, including the tricolored, greenbacked, little blue, and the black-crowned night heron. Other common species include ibis, parrots, egrets, and ducks, such as the Muscovy and the black-bellied whistling duck. Among the most spectacular are the huge great blue herons, while the most entertaining are the northern *jacanas,* or lily walkers, who scoot across lily pads as if they were the kitchen floor.

Lagoon tours are best arranged through travel agencies in Puerto Escondido. Although most of these advertise "ecotours," the most genuine is **Hidden Voyages Ecotours,** led by Canadian ornithologist Michael Malone and arranged through the very competent travel agency Turismo Rodimar, Av. Pérez Gasga 906, P.O. Box 22, Puerto Escondido, Oaxaca 71980, tel./fax (958) 207-34.

La Alejandria and El Gallo

Laguna Manialtepec is ripe for kayaking, boating, and camping along its shoreline. Bring plenty of repellent, however. Alternatively, RV and tent campers can settle in for a few days in one of a number of shady restaurant compounds along the shore. Among the prettiest and quietest of these is the little family-run pocket paradise of La Alejandria, near the Km 125 marker about 10 miles west of Puerto Escondido.

La Alejandria spreads along its hundred yards of lakefront, shaded by palms and great spreading trees. It's so idyllic the *Tarzan* TV series picked La Alejandria for its film setting, adding a rustic lake tree house, complete with rope bridges, to the already gorgeous scene.

La Alejandria rents about six RV spaces with electricity and water for about $5, and four ramshackle thatched cabañas with sink and toilet for about $8 d, $12 t. Camping spaces go for about $4. The homey centerpiece restaurant/bar, screened-in from bugs and embellished with animal trophies, is reminiscent of an old-time East African safari lodge.

A mile or two west of La Alejandria is lakefront restaurant and dock El Gallo, perfect for a day on the lagoon. Stop for lunch at the restaurant, then follow up on more local options, such as snoozing in a hammock, volleyball, swimming or birdwatching along the mangrove-decorated shoreline, launching your own canoe or boat, or hiring one of El Gallo's boatmen to take you on a lagoon excursion from the dock.

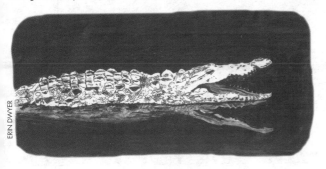

Through public education and the assistance of the government crocodile nursery at Chacagua village, caimanes (crocodiles) may once again hunt in wild Costa Chica lagoons.

PUERTO ESCONDIDO

Decorated by intimate coves, sandy beaches, and washed by jade-tinted surf, Puerto Escondido enjoys its well-deserved popularity. Despite construction of a jet airport in the 1980s, Puerto Escondido remains a place where everything is within walking distance, no high-rise blocks anyone's sunset view, and moderately priced accommodations and good food remain the rule.

Puerto Escondido, "Hidden Port," got its name from the rocky Punta Escondida, which shelters its intimate half-moon cove, which perhaps would have remained hidden if local farmers had not discovered that coffee thrives beneath the cool

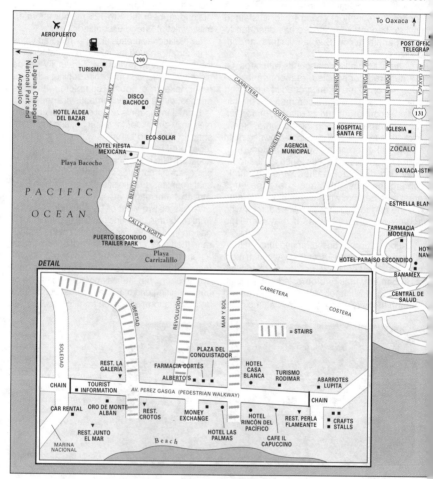

forest canopy of the lush seaward slopes of the Sierra Madre del Sur. They began bringing their precious beans for shipment when the port of Escondido was established in 1928.

When the coast highway was pushed through during the 1970s, Puerto Escondido's then-dwindling coffee trade was replaced by a growing trickle of vacationers, attracted by the splendid isolation, low prices, and high waves. With some of the best surfing breaks in North America, a permanent surfing colony soon got established. This led to more nonsurfing visitors, who, by the 1990s, were enjoying the comfort and food of a string of small hotels and restaurants lining Puerto Escondido's still-beautiful but no longer hidden cove.

AROUND TOWN

Getting Oriented

Puerto Escondido (pop. 35,000) seems like two small towns separated by Hwy. 200, which runs

along the bluff above the beach. The upper town is where most of the local folks live and go about their business, while in the town below the highway, most of the tourist restaurants, hotels, and shops spread along a single, mile-long beachfront street, **Av. Pérez Gasga.**

Avenida Pérez Gasga runs east-west, mainly as a pedestrian mall, where motor traffic is allowed only before noon. Afternoons, the *cadenas* (chains) go up, blocking cars at either end.

Beyond the west-end *cadena,* Pérez Gasga leaves the beach, winding uphill to the highway, where it enters the upper town at the *crucero,* Puerto Escondido's only signaled intersection. From there, Pérez Gasga continues into the upper town as Av. Oaxaca, National Hwy. 131.

Getting Around

In town, walk or take a taxi, which should run no more than $2 to anywhere. For longer local excursions, such as Lagunas Manialtepec and Chacagua (westbound), and as far as Pochutla (near Puerto Ángel) eastbound, ride one of the very frequent *urbano* minibuses that stop at the *crucero.*

BEACHES AND ACTIVITIES

Puerto Escondido's bayfront begins at the sheltered rocky cove beneath the wave-washed lighthouse point, Punta Escondida. The shoreline continues easterly along Playa Principal, the main beach, curving southward at Playa Marineros, and finally straightening into long, open-ocean Playa Zicatela. The sand and surf change drastically, from narrow sand and calm ripples at Playa Principal to a wide beach pounded by gigantic rollers at Zicatela.

Playa Principal

Playa Principal is where Mexican families love to frolic on Sunday and holidays and sun-starved winter vacationers doze in their chairs and hammocks beneath the palms. The sheltered west side is very popular with local people who arrive afternoons with nets and haul in small troves of silvery fish. The water is great for wading and swimming, clear enough for casual snorkeling, but generally too calm for anything else in the cove. However, a few hundred yards east around the bay the waves are generally fine for bodysurfing and boogie boarding, with a minimum of undertow. Although not a particularly windy location, windsurfers do occasionally bring their own equipment and practice their art here. Fishing is fine off the rocks or by small boat, easily launched from the beach. Shells, generally scarce on Playa Principal, are more common on less-crowded Playa Zicatela.

Playa Marineros

As the beach curves toward the south, it increasingly faces the open ocean. Playa Mari-

Playa Principal at Puerto Escondido, the perfect Mexican Sunday beach

LAGUNA MANIALTEPEC

neros begins about 100 yards from the "Marineros," the east-side rocky outcroppings in front of the Hotel Santa Fe. The rocks' jutting forms are supposed to resemble visages of grizzled old sailors. Here the waves can be rough. Swimmers beware; appearances can be deceiving. Intermediate surfers practice here, as do daring boogie boarders and bodysurfers.

Turn around and gaze inland at the giant Mexican flag, waving in the breeze on the hill above the beach. At dawn every day soldiers of the 54th infantry battalion raise the colossal banner, which measures 82 by 59 feet (18 by 25 meters) and is so heavy that it takes 25 of them to do it.

Playa Zicatela

Past the Marineros rocks you enter the hallowed ground of surfing, Playa Zicatela. The wide beach, of fine golden-white sand, stretches south for miles to a distant cliff and point. The powerful Pacific swells arrive unimpeded, crashing to the sand with awesome, thunderous power. Both surfers and nonsurfers congregate year-round, waiting for the renowned Escondido "pipeline," where grand waves curl into whirling liquid tunnels, which expert surfers skim through like trains in a subway. At such times, the watchers on the beach outnumber the surfers by as much as 10 or 20 to one. Don't try surfing or swimming at Zicatela unless you're expert at both.

West-Side Beaches: Playas Puerto Angelito, Carrizalillos, and Bachoco

About a mile west of town, the picture-postcard little blue bays of Puerto Angelito and Carrizalillos nestle beneath the seacliff. Their sheltered gold-and-coral sands are perfect for tranquil picnicking, sunbathing, and swimming. Here, snorkeling and scuba diving are tops, among shoals of bright fish grazing and darting among the close-in coral shelves and submerged rocky outcroppings. Get there by launch from Playa Principal or by taxi. On foot (take a sun hat and water) follow the street that angles from Pérez Gasga uphill across from the Hotel Nayar. Continue a few hundred yards and angle left again at Camino a Puerto Angelito ("Road to Puerto Angelito") and follow the trail down the cliff. Carrizalillos is another quarter mile west, before the trailer park.

Playa Bachoco, a mile farther west, down the bluff from the Hotel Posada Real, is a long, scenic strip of breeze-swept sand, with thunderous waves and correspondingly menacing undertow. Swimming is much safer in the inviting pool of the adjacent Hotel Posada Real beach club.

If you're strong, experienced, and can get past the breaking waves, snorkeling is said to be good around the little surf-dashed islet a hundred yards offshore.

Although Playa Bachoco's rock-sheltered nooks appear inviting for camping, local people don't recommend it, because of occasional *rateros* (thugs and drunks) who roam Puerto Escondido beaches at night.

Trouble in Paradise

Occasional knifepoint robberies and muggings have marred the once-peaceful Puerto Escondido nighttime beach scene. Walk alone and you invite trouble, especially along Playa Bachoco and the unlit stretch of Playa Principal between the east end of Pérez Gasga and the Hotel Santa Fe. If you have dinner alone at the Hotel Santa Fe, avoid the beach by returning by taxi or walking along the highway to Pérez Gasga back to your hotel.

Fortunately, such problems seem to be confined to the beach. Visitors are quite safe on the Puerto Escondido streets themselves, often more so than on their own city streets back home.

Beach Walking

The *andador* concrete walkway, which circles the lighthouse point, provides a pleasant, breezy afternoon (or sunset) diversion. From the west chain, follow the street that heads toward the lighthouse. Soon, on the left, stairs head left down on to the beach cove, where, in front of the Capitania del Puerto building, the *andador* heads left along the rocks. It continues, above the spectacularly splashing surf, for about half a mile. Return by the same route, or loop back through side streets to Pérez Gasga.

For a longer walk, you can stroll as far out of town along on Playa Zicatela as you want, in outings ranging from an hour to a whole day. Best avoid the heat of midday, and bring along a sun hat, shirt, drinks, and snacks (and perhaps sunglasses) if you plan on walking more than a mile past the last restaurant down the beach. Your rewards will be the acrobatics of surfers challenging the waves, swarms of shorebirds, and occasional finds of driftwood and shells.

After about three miles you will reach a cliff and a sea arch, which you can scamper through at low tide to the beach on the other side, **Playa Barra de Colotepec.**

Playa Barra de Colotepec's surf is as thunderous as Zicatela's and the beach even more pristine, being a nesting site for sea turtles. The beach continues for another mile to the jungle-fringed lagoon of the Río Colotepec where, during the dry winter season, a host of birds and wildlife, both common and rare, paddle and preen in the clear, fresh water.

You could break this eight-mile roundtrip into a pair of more leisurely options: Hike A could cover Zicatela only. On Hike B you could explore Barra de Zicatela and the Laguna de Colotepec by driving, taxiing, or busing straight to La Barra, the beach village just west of the Río Colotepec. Access is via the signed side road just before (west of) the Río Colotepec bridge.

Boat Tours

Travel agencies and the local boat cooperative, **Sociedad Cooperativa Punta Escondida,** offer trips for parties of several passengers to beautiful local bays, including Carrizalillo and Puerto Angelito, plus Manzanillo, Puesta del Sol, and Coral. The minimum one-hour trip takes you to a number of sandy little coves east of town, including Carrizalillo ("Little Reeds"), Manzanillo ("Little Apple"), Puerto Angelito, Coral, and Puesto del Sol ("Sunset"). Take drinks, hats, sunscreen, perhaps sunglasses, and don't go unless your boat has a sunroof. Trips can be extended (about $15 per additional hour) to your heart's content of beach picnicking, snoozing, and snorkeling.

SIGHTS OUT OF TOWN

Whether you go escorted or independently, outings away from the Puerto Escondido resort can reveal rewarding glimpses of flora and fauna, local cultures, and idyllic beaches seemingly half a world removed from the Pérez Gasga tourist hubbub.

Farthest afield, to the west of Puerto Escondido, are the festivals, markets, and handicrafts of Mixtec towns and villages around Jamiltepec and Pinotepa Nacional and the crystalline beaches and wildlife-rich mangrove reaches of the Lagunas de Chacagua National Park. To the east lie the hidden beaches of **Mazunte, Zipolite,** and the picture-book **Bay of Puerto Ángel,** with their turtle museum, au naturel sunbathing, and very accessible off-beach snorkeling, respectively. A bit farther are the nine breezy Bays of Huatulco, ripe for swimming, wildlife-viewing, biking, and river rafting. (For details, see the relevant previous and succeeding sections.)

Closer at hand, especially for wildlife lovers and beachgoers, are the jungly lagoons and pristine strands of the **Laguna de Manialtepec** and the nearby hot springs and Chatino sacred site of Atotonilco.

Atotonilco Hot Springs

Also on the west side, the **Aguas Termales Atotonilco** hot springs, a Chatino sacred site, provides an interesting focus for a day's outing. The jumping-off point is the village of San José Manialtepec, about half an hour by bus or car west of Puerto Escondido.

At the village, you should hire someone to show you the way, up the semi-wild canyon of the Río Manialtepec. The trail winds along cornfields, beneath forest canopies and past Chatino Indian villages. Finally you arrive at the hot spring, where a clear bathtub-sized rock basin bubbles with very hot (bearable for the brave), clear, sulfur-smelling water. **Get there** by driving or busing to the Hwy. 200 turnoff for San José Manialtepec, around Km 116, just east of the Río Manialtepec. Village stables provide horses and guides to the hot springs. It's a very easy two-mile walk, except in times of high water on the river, which the trail crosses several times.

Tours

Puerto Escondido agencies conduct outings to all of the above and more. Among the very best are the **Hidden Voyages Ecotours** of the Canadian husband-wife team of Michael Malone and Joan Walker. Working through the competent Turismo Rodimar Travel Agency, Av. Pérez Gasga 906, P.O. Box 22, Puerto Escondido, Oaxaca 71980, tel./fax (958) 207-34, ornithologist Michael and artist/ecologist Joan lead unusually informative beach, lagoon, and mountain tours seasonally, late fall through Easter. In addition, they also offer a sunset lagoon wildlife and beach excursion, plus a two-day trip to Nopala, center of Chatino Indian culture, including a coffee plantation in the cool Sierra Madre del Sur mountain jungle. Their trips ordinarily run $40 per day, per person.

Other Rodimar tours include a full-day jaunt east to the turtle museum at Playa Mazunte, continuing to Playa Zipolite, where you can stop for lunch and an afternoon of snorkeling around Puerto Ángel. The cost runs about $20 per person. Additionally, they offer an all-day hiking, picnic, and swimming excursion at a luxuriously cool mountain river and cascade in the sylvan Sierra Madre foothill jungle above Pochutla for about $15 per person (minimum four persons), or $30 per person for two.

Alternatively, try one of the tours guided by **Ana Marquez,** a highly recommended government-certified tour guide and native of Puerto Escondido. Her itineraries cover the coast, from the renowned blowhole at Huatulco's Maguey Bay to the crocodile nursery at Chacagua National Park. Contact her at home at Futuro Mzna 7 no. 214, Fracc. Costa Chica, Puerto Escondido, Oaxaca 71984, tel. (958) 220-01, or at her office at the Hotel Rincón del Pacífico, tel. (958) 200-56.

ACCOMMODATIONS

Hotels and Bungalows

The successful hotels in Puerto Escondido are appropriate to the town itself: small, reasonably priced, and near the water. They dot the beachfront from Playa Zicatela around the bay and continue up Av. Pérez Gasga to the highway. Most are either on the beach or within a stone's throw of it, which makes sense, because it seems a shame to come all the way to Puerto Escondido and not stay where you can soak up all the scenery.

Downhill along Pérez Gasga from the *crucero* is the **Hotel Paraíso Escondido** on a short side street to the left, Calle Union 1, Puerto Escondido, Oaxaca 71980, tel./fax (958) 204-44. A tranquil colonial-chic refuge, the hotel abounds in unique artistic touches—Mixtec stone glyphs, tiny corner chapels, stained glass, and old-world antiques—blended into the lobby, corridors, and patios. The two levels of rooms nestle around a lovely view pool and restaurant patio. The rooms themselves are large, with view balconies and designer tile bathrooms, wrought-iron fixtures, and handcrafted wooden furniture. Very popular with North American and German winter vacationers; get reservations in early. The 24 rooms rent for about $40 s, $45 d low season, $70 and $80 high, with a/c, pool, kiddie pool, and parking, but *no* credit cards are accepted.

Just downhill is the 1950s' genre **Hotel Nayar,** Pérez Gasga 407, Puerto Escondido, Oaxaca 71980, tel. (958) 201-13, fax 203-19, spreading from its inviting pool patio past the reception to a viewpoint restaurant. Its spacious, spartan but comfortable air-conditioned rooms have private balconies, many with sea views. Improved management has recently cleaned up this nicely located hotel. The Nayar's 36 rooms run about $18 s, $20 d, $25 t, add $3 for a/c, both low and high season.

The popular **Hotel Loren,** Av. Pérez Gasga 507, Puerto Escondido, Oaxaca 71980, tel. (958) 200-57, fax 205-91, downhill half a block farther, is as good as it first appears, from its leafy pool patio and its private balcony view rooms to its rooftop sundeck. Intelligent clerks staff the desk while *camaristas* scrub the rooms spotless every day. (They also assiduously spray with DDT; tell them "no DDT" if you'd prefer they didn't.) The

rooms spread through two three-story buildings; the front building rooms have better views. Reserve a *cuarto con vista* if you want a view room. Reservations are often necessary, especially in the winter. The 24 basic but comfortable rooms rent for about $15 s or d, $20 t low season; $26 s or d, $31 t high, with parking, fans, and some a/c; credit cards accepted.

Right on the beach amid the tourist-mall hullabaloo is the longtime favorite, **Hotel Las Palmas,** Av. Pérez Gasga s/n, Puerto Escondido, Oaxaca 71980, tel. (958) 202-30, fax 203-03. Its main plus is the palmy, vine-strewn patio where you can sit for breakfast every morning, enjoy the breeze, and watch the boats, the birds, and families frolicking in the billows. The big drawback, besides sleepy management and no pool, is lack of privacy. Exterior walkways pass the room windows, which anyone can see through. Closing the curtains unfortunately makes the (fan-only) rooms very dark and hot. This doesn't bother the legions of return customers, however, since they spend little time in their rooms anyway. Tariffs for the 40 smallish rooms run about $14 s or d, $17 t low season, $17, $25, $31 high, with phones, restaurant, no parking, credit cards accepted.

The **Hotel Rincón del Pacífico,** next door to the Hotel Las Palmas, offers about the same,

---

PUERTO ESCONDIDO ACCOMMODATIONS

Accommodations (area code 958, postal code 71980) are listed in increasing order of approximate high-season, double-room rates.

Hotel Rincón del Pacífico, Pérez Gasga 900, tel. 200-56, 201-93, fax 201-01, $18

Casas de Playa Acali, Av. del Morro (P.O. Box 11), tel. 207-54 or 202-78, $18

Rockaway, Av. del Morro, tel. 206-68, $20

Hotel Casa Blanca, Pérez Gasga 905, tel. 201-68, fax 207-37, $22

Hotel Nayar, Pérez Gasga 407, tel. 201-13, fax 203-19, $23

Hotel Las Palmas, Pérez Gasga s/n, tel. 202-30, fax 203-03, $25

Hotel Loren, Pérez Gasga 507, tel. 200-57, fax 205-91, $26

Hotel Arco Iris, Av. del Morro, Colonia Marinero, tel. 223-44, fax 204-32, $30

Beach Hotel Inés, Av. del Morro, P.O. Box 44, tel. 207-92, $30

Hotel Santa Fe, Av. del Morro, P.O. Box 96, tel. 201-70 or 202-66, fax 202-60, $80

Hotel Paraíso Escondido, Calle Union 1, tel./fax 204-44, $80

at Av. Pérez Gasga 900, Puerto Escondido, Oaxaca 71980, tel. (958) 200-56 or 201-93, fax 201-01. The two tiers of clean, comfortable rooms enfold a shady patio that looks out onto the lively beachfront. As at the Hotel Las Palmas above, a stay in one of their glass-front rooms sometimes feels like life in a fishbowl. This is nevertheless a very popular hotel. Reserve early. Rates for the 28 rooms run about $15 s or d, $18 t low season, $18 s or d, $22 t high. Four suites with TV and a/c rent for about $24 s or d low season, $40 high; with a restaurant, but no parking or pool; credit cards accepted (but not American Express).

Although it's not right on the beach like its neighbors across the street, the rooms of the **Hotel Casa Blanca,** Av. Pérez Gasga 905, Puerto Escondido, Oaxaca 71980, tel. (958) 201-68, fax 207-37, are larger, cooler, and much more private. Some rooms even have private balconies, fine for people-watching on the street below. Guests report noise is not a problem since cars and trucks are banned on Gasga noon-7 a.m. Other amenities include hot water, a shelf of used paperback books, and, beyond the graceful arches that border the lobby, a petite, inviting pool patio. The 21 clean, comfortable rooms rent for about $16 s, $22 d, and $26 t all year, with fans. Visa and Mastercard accepted, but no parking.

Puerto Escondido's class-act hostelry is the newish **Hotel Santa Fe,** Av. del Morro, Playa Marinero, Puerto Escondido, P.O. Box 96, Puerto Escondido, Oaxaca 71980, tel. (958) 201-70 or 202-66, fax 202-60, built in graceful neocolonial style, appealing to both Mexican and foreign vacationers. With curving staircases, palm-shaded pool patios, and flower-decorated walkways, the Santa Fe achieves an ambience both intimate and luxuriously private. Its restaurant is outstanding. The rooms are spacious, comfortable, and thoughtfully appointed with handpainted tile, rustic wood furniture, and regional handicrafts. Moreover, the big new room tier that owners added lately has enhanced the hotel's ambience, with an airy, elevated pool patio connecting the new tier with the original section. The 50 rooms rent for about $60 s or d low season, $80 high; with TV, a/c, phones, and parking; credit cards accepted.

A few hundred yards south along the beach is the **Casas de Playa Acali,** Av. del Morro, P.O. Box 11, Puerto Escondido 71980, tel. (958) 202-78 or 207-54, a colony of rustic cabañas clustered around a blue pool in a banana, palm, and mango mini-jungle. The cabañas themselves, like a vision out of a romantic South Seas tale, are built with walls made of sticks (non-see-through) and sturdy plank floors, raised above ground level. Units are clean and equipped with fans, mosquito nets, and good bathrooms. Rentals run about $10 s, $12 d, and $14 t low season; $15, $18, $21 high, with fan, hot water shower, small refrigerator and parking. Additionally, they offer a few rustic sunset-view bungalows perched on their bamboo and mango-decorated hillside. Rentals cost about $25 low season, $35 high, for one to four, with kitchens, and beach-view hammock-hung front porches. Credit cards are accepted.

Farther south on Av. del Morro, which runs along Playa Zicatela, rises the three-story **Hotel Arco Iris,** Av. del Morro s/n, Colonia Marinero, Puerto Escondido, Oaxaca 71980, tel. (958) 223-44, fax 204-32, e-mail: arcoiris@antequera.com. A flowery, shady green garden surrounds the hotel, leading to an attractive pool patio. For those who love sunsets, sand, and waves (and don't mind their sometimes insistent pounding), one of the spacious, simply furnished top-floor view rooms might be just the ticket. The Arco Iris's proximity to the famous Puerto Escondido "pipeline" draws both surfers and surf-watchers to the third-floor restaurant La Galera, which seems equally ideal for wave-watching at breakfast and sky-watching at sunset. Low-season rates for the 26 rooms run about $26 s or d, $30 t; suites with kitchen, about $30 s or d, $32 t (add about 15% high season); with fans and parking.

Next comes **Beach Hotel Inés,** Av. del Morro, P.O. Box 44, Playa Zicatela, Puerto Escondido, Oaxaca 71980, tel. (958) 207-92, fax 223-44, e-mail: pedrovoss@yahoo.com, website: www.hotel-ines.com, the life project of German expatriate Peter Voss and his daughter, Inés. Their 35 units occupy the palmy periphery of a lush, pool-café-garden layout, which climaxes with an attractive, stuccoed, two-story complex of rooms at the back side. At the poolside tables, long-time repeat guests linger for coffee and conversation after late-morning breakfasts, stroll the beach in the afternoon, and return for a balmy sunset happy hour. Other days they sunbathe au naturel or relax in the petite but luxurious health club, which provides massage and jacuzzi.

Most of the rentals are hotel-style rooms, in deluxe and super deluxe grades, with clean, light interiors, comfortable furnishings, and well-maintained bathrooms. Additionally, they rent six downscale second floor (popular with surfers) shared-bath cabañas, and a pair of bungalows with outdoor kitchens, sleeping four to six. Deluxe rooms go for about $20 s or d low season, $30 high; super-deluxe, about $35 low season, $55 high; cabañas, about $10-15 d, and the bunga-lows, about $26 low, $35 high, all with discounts negotiable for long-term rentals.

Farther along Playa Zicatela is the very tidy **Rockaway,** Av. del Morro, Playa Zicatela, Puerto Escondido, Oaxaca 71980, tel. (958) 206-68, a fenced-in cluster of about 15 clean, concrete-floored bamboo-and-thatch cabañas. Spacious and fan-equipped, they sleep about four and have private showers and toilets, mosquito nets, and shady, hammock-hung front porches. An inviting, leafy pool patio occupies the center, while the manager's cabaña, offering water-sport rentals and supplies, stands to one side. Cabaña rentals run about $8 per person low season, $23 per cabaña for up to four; $10 and $40 high season. Weekly or monthly discounts are negotiable, with parking and adjacent pizzeria.

Trailer Park Puerto Escondido

Trailer Park Puerto Escondido, Bahía Carrizalillo, Puerto Escondido, Oaxaca 71980, tel. (958) 200-77, occupies a breezy lot overlooking little blue Carrizalillo Bay on the west side of town. The two acres of around 100 spaces bloom with green grass during the popular winter season, when dozens of Canadians and Americans pull in and stay for two or three months. The congenial company, all hookups, a large swimming pool, clean showers and toilets, some shaded spaces, and good fishing keep them returning. Rentals run about $10 per day, with a 20% discount for monthly rentals paid in advance. **Get there** from Hwy. 200, via Av. Benito Juárez (look for the tourist information sign) a few hundred yards east, past the airport. The Av. Benito Juárez bends left near the Hotel Posada Real, then bends right again at the Hotel Fiesta Mexicana. It ends at Calle 2, which you should follow

by turning left and continuing to the trailer park gate about a hundred yards farther on.

FOOD

Breakfast and Snacks

Mornings you can smell the sweet aroma around Carmen's **La Patisserie** along Playa Marinero, on the little street that heads toward Playa Marinero from Hwy. 200, just past the bridge. Follow the fragrance to the source, a small homey shop with a few tables for savoring the goodies. Before noon you'll usually find owner Carmen Arizmendi in the kitchen or behind the counter; afternoons, however, you'll often glimpse her swimming across the bay. Open Mon.-Sat. 7 a.m.-8 p.m.

You don't have to walk all the way to Carmen's store to enjoy her pastries. She also operates a branch right on Zicatela beach called **Cafecito** (next to Bungalows Acuario), where you can enjoy a cappuccino and one of her goodies as you watch the surfers conquering the waves.

Right in the middle of the Av. Pérez Gasga bustle, **Cafe II Capuchino** is a gathering place for tourists and local folks who enjoy good desserts and coffee with their conversation. Furthermore, the best homesickness remedy in town is their apple pie, a slice of which enables you to endure a minimum of one more hard week on the local beaches. Open daily 8 a.m.-11 p.m.

Also fun for breakfast are the shady, scenic beach-view restaurants **Junto del Mar** and **Restaurant Crotos.** (See the following.)

Restaurants

Most of Puerto Escondido's reliable restaurants line Av. Pérez Gasga. Beginning just outside the west-end chain, first comes the streetside patio of **Restaurant Sardina de la Plata,** Av. Pérez Gasga 512, tel. (958) 203-28, the brainchild of Barcelona-born owner/chef Fernando de Abascal López. His life mission is orchestrating his unique seafood repertoire, such as the Catalan specialty Txanguro de Jaiva (snails, shrimp, and octopus in a white sauce) or Mero a la Sol (a sea bass feast for a party of 4-10). Besides such exotica, he also serves good pasta, steaks, lobster, Mexican plates, and breakfasts.

Open daily 7:30 a.m.-11 p.m.; credit cards accepted. Moderate.

Just inside the chain, on the inland side of Pérez Gasga, **Restaurant La Galería** usually has customers even when most other local eateries are empty. The reason is the excellent Italian fare—crusty, hot pizzas, rich pastas and lasagna, bountiful salads, and satisfying soups—which the European-expatriate owner puts out for her growing battalion of loyal customers. Open daily 8 a.m.-midnight. Moderate.

Across the street, the local rage is the excellent, airy **Restaurant Junto del Mar** ("By the Ocean"), which offers class-act breakfasts—rich coffee, fresh fruit, hotcakes, eggs—and many delectable lunch and dinner options. Specialties include shrimp-stuffed fillets, octopus cooked with garlic, and lobster and shrimp brochettes. Mornings are brightened by the always changing beach scene; evenings the setting turns romantic, with soft candlelight and strumming guitars. Open daily 8 a.m.-11 p.m., tel./fax (958) 212-72. Moderate. Credit cards are accepted.

A block farther east, breakfast patrons at beachfront **Restaurant Crotos,** at shady view tables, enjoy the fascinating morning beachside scene. Later, at lunch and dinner, back beneath the luxuriously breezy, palm-fringed *palapa,* the house specialties—jumbo shrimp, broiled lobster, and super-fresh pompano, attractively presented, competently served, and delicious—seem like an added bonus. Open daily 8 a.m.-11 p.m. Moderate.

Near the east end of the Pérez Gasga mall, the **Restaurant Perla Flameante** offers good food, incense, new-age jazz, and a beach view from beneath a big, cool *palapa.* The friendly, conscientious staff take pride that they make everything in-house, from the mayonnaise to the potato chips that come with their big fish burger. Seafood fillets rule the menu. The varieties, such as sierra, tuna, yellowtail, and mahimahi, are exceeded only by the number of styles—Cajun, teriyaki, wine and herbs, pepper-mustard, butter and garlic, orange—in which they are served. Open daily 7 a.m.-11 p.m.; credit cards accepted.

Devotees of authentic Italian food find paradise at **Restaurant Altro Mundo,** just half a block outside of the east-end chain. Here, white tablecloths and wine glasses set the stage. Start off, perhaps, with Crema Altro Mundo, continue with an Ensalata Mista, share a plate of Lasagna di Calamari, and climax with Fettuccine Flameante and Filete di Dorado. Open for dinner only, daily 6 p.m.-midnight, tel. (958) 214-55.

If you have dinner at the restaurant of the **Hotel Santa Fe,** on Av. del Morro, east side of the bay, tel. (958) 201-70, you may never go anywhere else. Savory food, impeccably served beneath a luxurious *palapa* and accompanied by softly strumming guitars, brings travelers from all over the world. Although everything on the menu is good, they are proudest of their Mexican favorites, such as rich tortilla soup, bountiful plates of *chiles rellenos,* and succulent snapper, Veracruz style. Open daily 7:30 a.m.-11 p.m. Moderate-expensive.

About two blocks farther along the beach, before the Hotel Acuario, the vegetarian restaurant **La Gota de Vida** presents an entirely different option. Here, hearty meat-free fare is king, from delicious soups and crisp salads to fresh fruit and veggie drinks and savory plates of pasta. Open daily 8 a.m.-10 p.m. Budget-moderate.

Farther south along Zicatela beach, **Restaurant Cafecito** (formerly Bruno's) is headquarters for a loyal platoon of local surfers and Canadian and American residents. Breakfasts, hamburgers, and fresh seafood plates are bountiful, tasty, and won't cost you a bundle. Open daily, about 8 a.m.-10 p.m. Budget-moderate.

At the far end of Av. del Morro on Zicatela Beach is friendly **Art and Harry's Surf Inn,** named after the Canadian expatriate owners' grandfathers, open daily noon till about 10 p.m. The restaurant, a big, airy upper-floor *palapa,* is best around sunset when patrons enjoy Frisbee golf and more unobstructed sunsets per year than any other *palapa* in Puerto Escondido. Personable co-owner Patty Mikus keeps customers coming with her fresh salads, soups, and tasty (honey, garlic, teriyaki, Hawaiian, or marinera) fish plates.

ENTERTAINMENT AND EVENTS

Sunsets and Happy Hours

Many bars have sunset happy hours, but not all of them have good sunset views. Since the Oaxaca coast faces south (and the sun sets in the west), bars along eastside Zicatela Beach, such as the Hotel Santa Fe, Hotel Arco Iris, Restaurant Cafecito's, and Art and Harry's, are the only ones that can offer unobstructed sunset horizons.

If, on the other hand, you prefer solitude, stroll the bayfront *andador* walkway to near the lighthouse. Start on the beach side of the Capitán del Puerto office. There, from breezy perches above the waves, you'll enjoy an equally panoramic sunset.

Strolling Pérez Gasga

Strolling the Pérez Gasga mall is Puerto Escondido's prime after-dinner entertainment. By around 9 p.m., however, people get weary of walking and, since there are few benches, begin sitting on the curb and sipping bottles of beer near the west-end chain. Unfortunately, city officials lately have been frowning upon such apparently dissolute behavior and have had a few of the curb-sitters arrested. Meanwhile, people hope that some amiable compromise will be reached.

The main attraction of curb-sitting is watching other people sitting on the curb, while listening to the music blasting nightly from the tiny open-air bars of **Bar Coco, Tubo,** and **Wipe Out,** 50 feet away. The music is so loud little can be gained except hearing impairment by actually taking a seat in the bars themselves.

Those who prefer to dance go to some of the few discotheques in town. On Pérez Gasga, try **Revancha de Moctezuma** ("Montezuma's Revenge"), across from the Hotel Las Palmas; alternatively, try the old standby, **Disco Bachoco** on Av. Gueletao, in the west-side Bachoco suburb.

Festivals

Puerto Escondido pumps up with a series of fiestas during the low-season (but excellent for vacationing) month of November. Scheduled "Fiestas de Noviembre" events invariably include surfing and usually sportfishing, cooking, and beauty contests, and notably, the dance festival, **Fiesta Costeño,** when a flock of troupes—from Pochutla, Pinotepa Nacional, Jamiltepec, Tehuantepec and more—perform regional folk dances.

Visitors who hanker for the old-fashioned color of a traditional fiesta, make sure you arrive in Puerto Escondido before 18 December, when seemingly the whole town takes part in the fiesta of the **Virgen de Soledad.** Besides being the patron saint of the state of Oaxaca, the Virgen de Soledad is also protectress of fishermen. To honor her, the whole town accompanies the Virgin by boat out to the bay's far reach, and then returns with her to the church plaza for dancing, fireworks, and bullfights.

If you can't be in Puerto Escondido in time to honor the Virgin in December, perhaps you may be able to take a day trip one hour west of Puerto Escondido to enjoy a fiesta at one of the small towns around Pinotepa Nacional, or celebrate the Virgin of Juquila with the mountain Chatino folks.

SPORTS AND RECREATION

Walking, Jogging, and Horseback Riding

Playa Zicatela is Puerto Escondido's most interesting walking course. Early mornings, before the heat and crowds, are good for jogging along the level section of Av. Pérez Gasga. Avenida del Morro on Playa Zicatela is good for jogging anytime it isn't too hot.

Ease your hiking by riding horseback along Zicatela beach. Rentals are available on the beach in front of Hotel Santa Fe.

Gym and Tennis

The **Acuario Gym** on Playa Zicatela at the Hotel Acuario has a roomful of standard exercise equipment. Single visits run about $1.50, one-month passes about $15.

One of the only night-lit tennis courts in town available for public rental ($5/hour) is at the **Hotel Fiesta Americana.** Call the hotel at (958) 200-72 for a reservation.

Surfing, Snorkeling, and Scuba Diving

Although surfing is de rigueur for the skilled in Puerto Escondido, beginners often learn by bodysurfing and boogie boarding first. Boogie boards and surfboards are for sale and rent ($7/day) at a number of shops along Pérez Gasga, such as **1000 Hamacas** (next to Hotel Rincón del Pacífico) and at **Central Surf** (by Cafecito) on Playa Zicatela (open daily 9 a.m.-2 p.m. and 4-7 p.m.). **Rockaway,** a few hundred yards farther south along the beach, rents surfboards ($7/day) and boogie boards ($7/day) and sells related supplies.

Beginners practice on the gentler billows of **Playa Principal** and adjacent **Playa Marinero** while advanced surfers go for the powerful waves of **Playa Zicatela,** which regularly slam foolhardy inexperienced surfers onto the sand with backbreaking force.

Clear blue-green waters, coral reefs, and droves of multicolored fish make for good local snorkeling and diving, especially in little **Puerto Angelito** and **Carrizalillo** bays just west of town. A number of Av. Pérez Gasga stores sell serviceable amateur-grade snorkeling equipment.

Although no scuba dive shop currently operates in Puerto Escondido, Huatulco has several options. Contact the professional **Buceos Triton** shop in Santa Cruz de Huatulco, tel./fax (958) 708-44, or **Action Sports,** in Tangolunda, at the Sheraton Hotel, tel. (958) 100-55, ext. 842, fax (958) 705-37, or Leeward Dive Center, across from the Hotel Sheraton, inside the Hotel Club Plaza Huatulco, tel./fax (958) 100-51. (For more details, see the **Bays of Huatulco** section.)

Sportfishing

Puerto Escondido's offshore waters abound with fish. Launches go out mornings from Playa Principal and routinely return with an assortment including big tuna, mackerel, snapper, sea bass, and snook. The sheltered west side of the beach is calm enough to easily launch a mobile boat with the help of usually willing beach hands.

The local **Sociedad Cooperativa Punta Escondida,** which parks its boats right on Playa Principal, regularly takes fishing parties of three or four out for about $15 an hour, including bait and tackle. Check with boatmen right on the beach. Additionally, travel agencies, such as Turismo Rodimar, Av. Pérez Gasga 905, tel. (958) 207-34, arrange such trips at about the same prices.

SHOPPING

Market and Handicrafts

As in most Mexican towns, the place to begin your Puerto Escondido shopping is the local **Mercado,** on Av. 10 Norte one long block west of the electric station on upper Av. Oaxaca. Al-

though produce occupies most of the space, a number of stalls at the south end offer authentic handicrafts. These might include Guerrero painted pottery animals; San Bártolo Coyotepec black pottery; masks from Guerrero and Oaxaca with jaguar, devil, and scary human-animal motifs; the endearing multicolored pottery animals from Iguala and Zitlala in Guerrero; and beautiful crocheted *huipiles* from San Pedro Amusgos and Pinotepa Nacional.

Back downhill on Av. Pérez Gasga, the prices increase along with the selection. Perhaps the most fruitful time and place for handicraft shopping is during the cooler evenings, within the illuminated cluster of crafts stalls just beyond the Gasga east chain.

One shop at that spot, the **Ruiz** textile stand, with genuine handmade rugs and serapes from Teotitlán del Valle near Oaxaca city, stands out. Fine-quality rugs are the most tightly woven—typically about 20 strands per inch.

Another good, authentic shop is **Creaciones Alberto,** next to Farmacia Cortés, tel. (958) 202-84, named for the elderly master craftsman of Puerto Vallarta, whose sons and daughters sell his fine handiwork (and that of associated craftspersons) in a number of Pacific Mexico centers. Open Mon.-Sat. 9 a.m.-2 p.m. and 5-10 p.m. For hints, see the **Shopping** section of the On the Road chapter.

Oaxaca's venerable jewelry tradition is well represented at the very professional Oro de Monte Albán, on Pérez Gasga, ocean side, by the west chain. Here are authentic museumgrade replicas of the celebrated Mixtec-style trove discovered in Monte Albán's tomb 7. Find them open Mon.-Sat. 10 a.m.-2 p.m. and 6:30-10:30 p.m., closed Sunday low season, tel. (958) 205-30.

The Uribe silversmithing family well represents Taxco tradition at their **Platería Taxco,** open Mon.-Sat. 9 a.m.-2 p.m. and 5-10 p.m., Sunday 7-10 p.m., tel. (958) 216-72, a few doors east. Choose from a host of fetching floral, animal, and abstract designs, in silver and turquoise, garnet, jade, and other semiprecious stones.

For unique women's resort wear, look for **Bambaleo,** a gem among the T-shirt clutter, on the beach side, toward the Pérez Gasga east end, open 10 a.m.-10 p.m. Here, a riot of skirts and tops, locally crafted from lovely handpainted cloth from Indonesia, festoon walls and a host of racks.

During the day, if the sun gets too hot for comfort, duck into the shade of the small shopping Plaza del Conquistador, just east of Farmacia Cortés. Here, several stalls offer attractively varied, all-Mexico handicrafts, including masks, *huipiles,* lacquerware, papier-mâché, baskets, black pottery, and much more.

Groceries and Photography

Abarrotes Lupita, a fairly well-stocked grocery, offers meats, milk, ice, and vegetables. In addition, it stocks a few English-language publications, such as the *News* of Mexico City and magazines such as *Time, Life,* and *Newsweek,* on the inland side of Gasga, outside of the east-end chain. Open daily 10 a.m.-11 p.m.

Out on Playa Zicatela, where stores are not nearly so common, the friendly **Abarrotes Merlin** offers a small grocery selection; open daily 9 a.m.-10 p.m., tel. (958) 211-30.

Foto Express Figueroa, tel. (958) 205-26, on Gasga next to Turismo Rodimar, offers fast photofinishing services, Kodak color print and slide film, and a moderate stock of accessories, including point-and-shoot cameras. Open daily 9:30 a.m.-2 p.m. and 4:30-8 p.m.

SERVICES

Money Exchange

Banamex, at Pérez Gasga 314, uphill from the Hotel Nayar, tel. (958) 206-26 or 206-80, changes U.S. and Canadian cash and traveler's checks Mon.-Fri. 9 a.m.-3 p.m., Saturday 9 a.m.-2 p.m.

After hours, the small *casa de cambio* (money exchange) office on Pérez Gasga, a few doors west of Hotel Las Palmas, changes a larger range of foreign currencies for a correspondingly larger fee. Open Mon.-Sat. 9 a.m.-2 p.m. and 5-8 p.m., tel. (958) 205-92. A second *casa de cambio* offers similar services, on Playa Zicatela, by Cafecito, tel. (958) 205-92, open daily 9 a.m.-7 p.m.

Communications

The *correo* and *telégrafo* are side by side on Av. 7 Norte, corner Av. Oaxaca, seven blocks into town from the *crucero.* The post office, tel. (958) 209-59, is open Mon.-Fri. 8 a.m.-7 p.m., Satur-

day 9 a.m.-1 p.m.; the *telégrafo,* which has public fax (tel. 958-202-32), is open Mon.-Fri. 9 a.m.-1 p.m. and 3-7 p.m., Saturday 9 a.m.-noon (Mon.-Fri. 9 a.m.-1 p.m. and 3-5 p.m. for money orders).

More conveniently located on Pérez Gasga, a *larga distancia* offers both telephone and fax service, daily 8 a.m.-11 p.m., tel./fax (958) 204-48, across from Restaurant La Galería. On Playa Zicatela, use the public long-distance telephone at the desk of the Hotel Acuario.

Laundry

Get your laundry done, Mon.-Sat. 8 a.m.-8 p.m., Sunday 8 a.m.-5 p.m., at the **Lavamatico del Centro,** two doors downhill from Banamex, on Pérez Gasga, about two blocks uphill, from the west-end chain.

INFORMATION

Tourist Information Office

During the high winter season, Oaxaca tourism staffs an **information booth** on Pérez Gasga, just inside the west-end chain. Otherwise, you can consult the friendly, well-informed *oficina de turismo,* tel./fax (958) 211-86 or 205-37, which distributes a map of Oaxaca. It's open Mon.-Fri. 8 a.m.-3:30 p.m. and 5-8 p.m. high season, low season (July-Nov.) Mon.-Fri. 8 a.m.-3:30 only, just off of Hwy. 200, in the little office on the beach side of the highway, a couple of blocks east of the airport Pemex gas station.

Ecology Organizations and Projects

Ec Solar, the private Mexican ecological "Peace Corps," maintains its local low-profile headquarters in Puerto Escondido, in a house, tel. (958) 209-50, in Bachoco, at the corner of Huajuapan de León and Tehuantepec. They work quietly with local communities on environmentally appropriate self-help drainage, water, manufacturing and agricultural projects. For more information, contact either Ec Solar (in Spanish) or the national director, Hector Marchelli, in Mexico City, tel. (5) 434-431, at Av. Eugenia 1510, Colonia Narvarte, Mexico City, D.F.

Much more accessible is the local ecological effort, **Eco Escondido,** coordinated by Ramón Acebo, owner of the Restaurant Tigre Azul, beach side, about a block inside the west-end

Pérez Gasga chain, tel. (958) 215-33, 218-71, or 210-23, e-mail: econdido@oax1.telmex.net.mx. Their major project is the recycling plant at the Hotel Acuario on Playa Zicatela.

Another nearby eco-project is the **turtle sanctuary** at Playa Escobilla, about 20 miles (30 km) east of Puerto Escondido. There, a cadre of SE-MARNAT (Secretariat of Marine Natural Resources) professionals and volunteers is rescuing, hatching, and returning tens of thousands of baby turtles to the sea annually.

Travel Agent and Car Rentals

The best travel agent in town is the Turismo Rodimar agency, at the middle of the tourist mall, at Av. Pérez Gasga 906, P.O. Box 22, Puerto Escondido, Oaxaca 71980, tel./fax (958) 207-34.

Rent a car at **Arrendadora Express** at the Pérez Gasga west end chain, beach side, tel. (958) 213-55, or **Budget Rent a Car** on Calle Juárez in the Bachoco suburb, tel. (958) 203-12.

Hospital, Police, and Emergencies

For medical emergencies, go to the 24-hour **Hospital Santa Fe,** tel. (958) 217-67, which has an internist, pediatrician, gynecologist, and a dental surgeon on call. For more routine consultations, office hours are Mon.-Fri. 9 a.m.-2 p.m. and 4-8 p.m., Saturday 9 a.m.-2 p.m. Find the hospital three blocks west of the *crucero*, uphill from the highway on Calle 3 Poniente between Calles 2 and 3 Norte.

Alternatively, see English-speaking general practitioner Dr. Francisco Serrano, tel. (958) 205-48, above the highway, at Calle 1 Norte 205, two blocks west of the main street, across Calle 1 Norte from Bancomer.

You may also go to the 24-hour government health clinic, **Centro de Salud,** no telephone, on Av. Pérez Gasga, just uphill from the Hotel Loren.

Get over-the-counter remedies and prescriptions at either of the two good tourist-zone pharmacies: the 24-hour **Farmacia La Moderna,** tel. (958) 205-49, on Gasga a block below the *crucero*, or **Farmacia Cortés** (open 8 a.m.-2 p.m. and 5-10 p.m.), tel. (958) 201-12, on the Pérez Gasga mall.

For police emergencies, call the **municipal police** at (958) 204-98, or go to the headquarters in the Agencia Municipal on Hwy. 200, about four blocks west of the Pérez Gasga *crucero*.

Meditation and Massage

Healing is the mission of partners Patricia Heuze and Alejandro Villanuevo, who operate **Villa Temazcalli** meditation and massage center, west end of town, on Av. Infragante, two blocks uphill from the highway. Facilities include rustic hot baths, an indigenous-style *temazcalli* hot room, and massage room in an invitingly tranquil tropical garden setting. Prices run about $15 each for massage and the jacuzzi, and about $5 for the *temazcalli*. For more information and appointments, call (958) 210-22 or 210-23.

Publications

One of the few outlets of any English-language newspaper is the Abarrotes Lupita, on Pérez Gasga, just outside the east-end chain. The *News* from Mexico City usually arrives around 3:30 p.m. Prepay to assure yourself a copy. Sometimes there may be a few copies of popular magazines, such as *Time, Newsweek,* and *People.*

The best source of English-language (and French and German) books in town is the **Book Exchange,** at the Restaurant La Gota de Vida, next to the Hotel Acuario on Playa Zicatela.

GETTING THERE AND AWAY

By Air

The small jetport, officially the **Aeropuerto Puerto Escondido** (code-designated PXM), is just off the highway a mile west of town. Only a plain waiting room with check-in desks, the airport has no services save a small snack bar. *Colectivos* to hotels in town run $2 per person. Arrivees with a minimum of luggage, however, can walk a block to the highway and flag down one of the many eastbound local minibuses, which all stop at the main town highway crossing. Arrive with a hotel in mind (better yet a hotel reservation in hand), unless you prefer letting your taxi driver choose one, where he will probably collect a commission for depositing you there.

Although **car rental agents** may not routinely meet flights, they will meet you if you have a reservation in advance. Call **Arrendadora Express,** tel. (958) 213-55, or **Budget Rent a Car,** tel. (958) 203-12.

The international **departure tax** is $12 or its Mexican peso equivalent. If you lose your tourist card, avoid trouble or a fine by going to the *turismo* for help *before* your day of departure.

A few regularly scheduled airlines connect Puerto Escondido with other Mexican destinations:

Aerocaribe Airlines flights connect several times per week with Mexico City and daily with Oaxaca and Huatulco. For reservations or flight information, call (958) 220-24 or 220-25.

If the above flights cannot take you where you want to go fast, try **Aerovega,** the dependable local air-taxi service. See Turismo Rodimar, on Gasga, near Bancomer, tel. (958) 207-34 or 207-37, for information and reservations.

Puerto Escondido is also accessible via the Puerto Ángel-Huatulco airport, one hour away by road. See the **Bays of Huatulco** section later in this chapter.

By Car or RV

National Hwy. 200, although sometimes winding, is generally smooth and uncongested between Puerto Escondido and Pinotepa Nacional (89 miles, 143 km, two and a half hours) to the west. From there, continue another 160 miles (258 km, four and a half hours) to Acapulco. Fill up at Puerto Escondido before you leave, although gasoline is available at several points along the routes.

Traffic sails between Puerto Escondido and Puerto Ángel, 44 miles (71 km) apart, in an easy hour. Actually, Pochutla is immediately on the highway; Puerto Ángel is six miles downhill from the junction, or alternatively accessible via the very scenic paved shortcut, at San Antonio village, Km 198. Santa Cruz de Huatulco is an easy 22 miles (35 km) farther east.

To or from Oaxaca, all-paved National Hwy. 131 connects directly north, along main street Av. Oaxaca, via its winding but spectacular 158-mile (254-km) route over the pine-clad Sierra Madre del Sur. The route, which rises 8,000 feet through Chatino foothill and mountain country, can be chilly in the winter, and has few services along the lonely 100-mile middle stretch between

San Gabriel Mixtepec and Sola de Vega. Take water and blankets, and be prepared for emergencies. Allow about seven hours driving time from Puerto Escondido, six the other way. Fill up with gasoline at the airport Pemex stations on either end before heading out. Unleaded gasoline is only consistently available at the Sola de Vega Pemex *gasolinera* en route.

By Bus

Five long-distance bus lines serve Puerto Escondido; several offer first-class service. **Estrella Blanca** subsidiary lines (first-class Elite, luxury-class Futura, Flecha Roja, Autotransportes Cuauhtémoc and others), from the station on Av. Oaxaca just uphill from the *crucero,* tel. (958) 200-86, travel the Hwy. 200 Acapulco-isthmus route. More than two dozen daily *salidas de paso* come through en route both ways between Acapulco and Pochutla and Huatulco (Crucecita) and Salina Cruz. Other additional buses pass through, connecting with either Ixtapa-Zihuatanejo or Mexico City via Acapulco.

Cristóbal Colón, the other major first-class bus line, on Av. 1 Norte between Av. 4 Oriente and Av. 3 Oriente, about three blocks uphill, two blocks east from the Pérez Gasga highway crossing, tel. (958) 210-73, covers the Oaxaca coast, beginning in Puerto Escondido, connecting all the way to San Cristóbal las Casas in Chiapas. Intermediate destinations include Pochutla, Huatulco (Crucecita), Tehuantepec, and Tapachula, at the Guatemala border. At Pochutla, passengers can transfer to Oaxaca-bound buses. One of these continues, via Puebla, to Mexico City.

Cooperativa Oaxaca-Istmo, on Hidalgo, one block east of Av. Oaxaca, corner of 1 Oriente, tel. (958) 203-92, offers mainly second-class but some first-class service. Several daily local departures connect Puerto Escondido east, with Oaxaca via Tehuantepec. Intermediate destinations include Pochutla and Huatulco (Crucecita). Additionally, first-class "Transol" departures connect with Oaxaca via Hwy. 131.

Cooperating lines **Autobuses Estrella del Valle** and **Autotransportes Oaxaca Pacífico** on Hidalgo, corner of 3 Oriente, tel. (958) 200-50, provide both first- and second-class connections east with Pochutla, Bahías de Huatulco (Crucecita). Also, both first- and second-class buses connect with Oaxaca, both via Hwy. 175 and Pochutla and Hwy. 131.

Other minor mostly second-class bus lines offer departures from the gravel lot, at Calle 10 Norte and Hwy. 131 main street, Av. Oaxaca. From there, **Autobuses Estrella Roja del Sureste** and **Transol** buses connect with Oaxaca via Hwy. 131. Call (958) 208-75 to confirm departures.

PUERTO ÁNGEL AND VICINITY

During his three presidencies, Oaxaca-born Benito Juárez shaped many dreams into reality. One such dream was to better the lot of his native brethren in the isolated south of Oaxaca by developing a port for shipping the lumber and coffee they could harvest in the lush Pacific-slope jungles of the Sierra Madre del Sur. The small bay of Puerto Ángel, directly south of the state capital, was chosen, and by 1870 it had become Oaxaca's busiest port.

Unfortunately, Benito Juárez died two years later. New priorities and Puerto Ángel's isolation soon wilted Juárez's plan and Puerto Ángel lapsed into a generations-long slumber.

In the 1960s, Puerto Ángel was still a sleepy little spot connected by a single frail link—a tortu-ous cross-Sierra dirt road—to the rest of the country. Adventure travelers saw it at the far south of the map and dreamed of a South Seas paradise. They came and were not disappointed. Although that first tourist trickle has grown steadily, it's only enough to support the sprinkling of modest lodgings and restaurants that now dot the beaches and hillsides around Puerto Ángel's tranquil, little blue bay.

BEACHES AND SIGHTS

Getting Oriented
Puerto Ángel is at the southern terminus of Hwy. 175 from Oaxaca, about six miles (nine km)

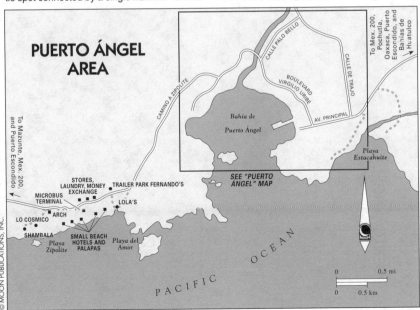

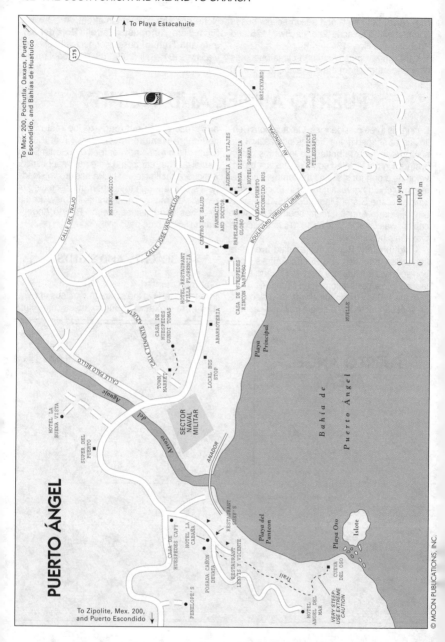

PUERTO ÁNGEL

To Mex. 200, Pochutla, Oaxaca, Puerto Escondido, and Bahías de Huatulco

↑ To Playa Estacahuite

175

Calle del Trajo

METEOROLOGICO

Calle José Vasconcelos

AGENCIA DE VIAJES

LARGA DISTANCIA

HOTEL SORAYA

OAXACA-PUERTO ESCONDIDO BUS

AV. PRINCIPAL

POST OFFICE/ TELEGRAFOS

BRICKYARD

BOULEVARD VIRGILIO URIBE

FARMACIA AND DOCTOR

CENTRO DE SALUD

PAPELERIA EL GLOBO

CASA DE HUESPEDES RINCON SABROSO

HOTEL-RESTAURANT VILLA FLORENCIA

CALLE TENIENTE AZUETA

CASA DE HUESPEDES GUNDI TOMAS

ABARROTERIA

TOWN MARKET

LOCAL BUS STOP

CALLE PALO BELLO

Arroyo del Aguaje

HOTEL LA BUENA VISTA

SUPER DEL PUERTO

SECTOR NAVAL MILITAR

ANDADOR

Playa Principal

MUELLE

Bahía de Puerto Ángel

CASA DE HUESPEDES CAPY

HOTEL LA CABAÑA

POSADA CAÑON DEVATA

RESTAURANT LENYAS Y VICENTE

RESTAURANT SUSY'S

PENELOPE'S

To Zipolite, Mex. 200, and Puerto Escondido ↓

Playa del Panteon

Trail

HOTEL ANGEL DEL MAR

VERY STEEP: USE EXTREME CAUTION

CUEVA DEL OSO

Playa Oso

Islote

0   100 yds
0   100 m

© MOON PUBLICATIONS, INC.

downhill from its intersection with Hwy. 200. It's a small place, where nearly everything is within walking distance along the beach, which a rocky bayfront hill divides into two parts: Playa Principal, the main town beach, and sheltered westside Playa Panteón, the tourist favorite. A scenic boulder-decorated shoreline *andador* connects the two beaches.

A paved road winds west from Puerto Ángel along the coastline a couple of miles to Playa Zipolite, lined by a colony of hammock-and-bamboo beachfront cabañas, popular with an international cadre of budget-minded seekers of heaven on earth. Continuing west, the road passes the former turtle-processing village beaches of Playa San Agustinillo and Playa Mazunte. From there it goes on another four miles, joining with Hwy. 200 (and thence Puerto Escondido) at San Antonio village at Km 198.

The major local service and transportation center is **Pochutla** (pop. 35,000), a mile north along Hwy. 175 from its Hwy. 200 junction.

Getting Around

Local buses run frequently between Pochutla and Puerto Ángel from about 7 a.m. until 9 p.m., stopping at the Hwy. 200 intersection. Some buses continue on to Zipolite and Mazunte from Boulevard Uribe, Puerto Ángel's main bayfront street. Also from Boulevard Uribe, a local shuttle bus connects frequently with Zipolite, San Agustinillo, Mazunte and back about every half hour during daylight hours, stopping everywhere en route. Taxis also routinely make runs between Puerto Ángel and either Zipolite or Pochutla for about $2-3.

You can also get around by boat. Captains routinely take parties of up to eight for sightseeing, snorkeling, and picnicking to a number of nearby beaches. Bargain at the Puerto Ángel pier (rate should run about $15/hour), or contact the local travel agent, **Agencia de Viajes Gambusino**, tel. (958) 430-80 or 430-38.

Playas Principal, Panteón, and Estacahuite

Playa Principal's 400 yards of wide golden sand decorate most of Puerto Ángel's bayfront. Waves can be strong near the pier, where they often surge vigorously onto the beach and recede with some undertow. Swimming is more tranquil at the sheltered west end toward Playa Panteón.

The clear waters are good for casual snorkeling around the rocks, on both sides of the bay.

Sheltered Playa Panteón ("Cemetery Beach") is Puerto Ángel's sunning beach, lined with squadrons of beach chairs and umbrellas in front of beachside restaurants. **Playa Oso** ("Bear Beach") is a little dab of sand beside a rugged seastack of rock beyond Playa Panteón, fun to swim to from Playa Panteón.

Playa Estacahuite, just outside the opposite (east) side of the bay, is actually two beaches in one: a pair of luscious coral-sand nooks teeming with fish grazing the living reef just offshore. (Don't put your hands in crevices; a moray eel may mistake your finger for a fish and bite.) A pair of *palapa* restaurants perched picturesquely above the beaches provide food and drinks. Get there in less than a mile by taxi or on foot via the dirt road that forks right off the highway, about 400 yards uphill from beachfront Boulevard Uribe.

Playa Zipolite

Playa Zipolite is a wide, mile-long strand of yellow-white sand enfolded by headlands and backed by palm groves. It stretches from the intimate little cove and beach of **Playa del Amor** tucked on its east side to towering seacliffs rising behind the new-age Shambala retreat on the west end. The Playa Zipolite surf, although usually tranquil in the mornings (but always with significant undertow), can turn thunderous by the afternoon, especially when offshore storms magnify both the swells and the undertow. Experienced surfers love these times, when everyone but experts should stay out.

Good surfing notwithstanding, Zipolite's renown stems from its status as one of the very few nude beaches in Mexico. Bathing au naturel, practiced nearly entirely by visitors and a few local young men, is tolerated only grudgingly by local people, many of whose livelihoods depend on the nudists. If you're discreet and take off your clothes at the more isolated west end, no one will appear to mind (and women will avoid voyeuristic attentions of Mexican boys and men).

Visitors' nude sunbathing habits may have something to do with the gruffness of some local people. Many of them probably prefer their former occupations in turtle fishing rather than serving tourists, who often seem to be in short supply compared to the battalion of beachfront *palapas* competing for their business.

Most Zipolite visitors stay in the palm-shaded east-end trailer park or in one of the score of hammock-equipped stick-and-thatch beachfront cabaña hotels. Often with fans and outside cold-water showers and privies, cabañas rent for about $6 double per night. Although many are indifferently managed, some, such as Lola's, Lo Cósmico, and Shambala (below), are unique.

Playas San Agustín and Mazunte

About a mile west of Zipolite, a wide, mile-long, yellow-sand beach curves past the village of San Agustín. On the open ocean but partly protected by offshore rocks, its surf is much like that of Zipolite, varying from gentle to rough, depending mostly upon wind and offshore swells. Small village groceries and beachside *palapa* restaurants supply food and drinks to the occasional Zipolite overflow and local families on weekends and holidays. Fishing is excellent, either in the surf, from nearby rocks, by rented *panga*, or your own boat launched from the beach. Beach camping is customary, especially at **El Penasquero,** a five-space, hammock-hung roadside *ramada* at the east (Zipolite) end of the beach.

Remnants of the local turtle industry can be found at the rusting former processing factories on Playa San Agustinillo (west end) and Playa Mazunte two miles farther west.

The half-mile-long, yellow-sand Mazunte Beach, like San Agustinillo, is semisheltered and varies from tranquil to rough. Fishing is likewise good, beach camping is customary (as a courtesy, ask if it's okay), and local stores and seafood *palapa* restaurants sell basic supplies and food.

Mazunte people have also been renovating their houses and building **cabañas** to accommodate an increasing number of visitors. Some have even begun to advertise on the Internet. Signs along the road and at the beach advertise their homespun lodgings and restaurants, such as Cabañas Huerta, Cabañas Don Memo, and Restaurant La Dolce Vita and El Arbol.

Turtle Museum and Cosmetics Factory and Store

The former turtle processing plant at Mazunte lives on as a **turtle museum,** including aquari-um, study center, and turtle hatchery. Here, you can peruse displays illustrating the ongoing turtle research and conservation program and see members of most of Mexico's turtle species paddling in tanks overlooking the beach where their ancestors once swarmed. The center, on the main road, east end of village, is open Tues.-Sat. 10 a.m.-4:30 p.m., Sunday 10 a.m.-2:30 p.m. For more information contact the Centro Mexicano de la Tortuga, P.O. Box 16, Puerto Ángel, Oaxaca 70902, tel. (958) 401-22.

About half a mile farther west along the main road through Mazunte village, stop by the store and works of the **Fábrica Ecológia de Cosmeticos Naturales de Mazunte.** Initially funded mostly by the Body Shop Foundation, spearheaded by the local chapter of **Ec Solar** (see the **Puerto Escondido** section, preceding), and supported by an international government-university consortium, local workers make and sell all-natural shampoo, skin cream, hair conditioner, and more. Staff are working hard to assure that the effort catches on, so that locally grown products, such as coconut, corn and avocado oils, and natural aromatics will form the basis for a thriving cottage cosmetics industry.

Playa La Ventanilla

Continue about a mile and a half west along the main road over the low hill west of Mazunte and turn left at the signed dirt road to pristine wildlife haven Playa and Laguna la Ventanilla. Now protected by local residents, swarms of birds, including pelicans, cormorants, and herons, nest there, and a population of wild *cocodrilos* and *lagartos* is making a comeback in a bushy mangrove wetland. Boatmen headquartered at the *palapa* beach village at road's end guide visitors on a two-hour eco-tour ($10 per boat), which includes a stop for refreshment at a little mid-lagoon island. The boatmen are known for their wildlife-sensitivity and allow no motor vehicles within a hundred yards of their communally owned lagoon-sanctuary.

The Playa La Ventanilla community has also taken responsibility for protecting the turtles that arrive on their beach against poachers. During both February and June through October, hundreds of sea turtles come ashore to lay eggs. If necessary, community volunteers help the exhausted turtles up the steep beach, where they lay their eggs. Volunteers then gather the eggs and rebury them in a secure spot. After the hatchlings emerge about a month and a half later, volunteers nurture them for about three months and release them safely back into the ocean.

ACCOMMODATIONS

Puerto Ángel Hotels and Guesthouses

Although none of Puerto Ángel's dozen or so lodgings is directly on the beach, most of them are within a stone's throw of it. The successful lodgings have given their legion of savvy repeat customers what they want: clean, basic, cool-water accommodations in tranquil, television-free settings where Puerto Ángel's natural isolation and tropical charm set the tone for long, restful holidays.

Moving west around the bay from the pier, first comes the 1960s motel-style **Hotel Soraya,** perched on the bluff above Playa Principal, Priv. José Vasconcelos 2A, Puerto Ángel, Oaxaca 70902, tel./fax (958) 430-09. Well managed by personable owner Hortencia Tanus, the hotel includes a restaurant with an airy bay view, fine for bright morning breakfasts and sunset-glow dinners. Outside, two tiers of spartan but light and comfortable rooms enclose a parking patio. Although some rooms have a/c, the fan-only ones are generally better. Rent on the upper tier for more privacy. The 32 rooms rent for about $11 s, $14 d, and $17 t low season, $20, $25, $27 high.

Although recent hurricane damage put it out of operation, check to see if the splendidly isolated **Casa de Huéspedes Rincón Sabroso,** Puerto Ángel, Oaxaca 70902, tel. (958) 430-95, atop the adjacent bay-vista hill has been restored to its original condition: Here, guests enjoy lodgings that open onto a hammock-hung view breezeway adorned by luscious tropical greenery. Inside, rooms are very clean (but dark), with white walls, tile floors, shiny bathrooms, and natural wood furnishings. Guests have the additional option of good food and each other's company in an airy café, perched above a heavenly bay and sunset panorama. Rates for the eight rooms run about $11 s or d, $14 t low season, $14 and $17 high, with fans.

Equally exceptional nearby is **Casa de Huéspedes Gundi y Tomás,** the life project of friend-ly German expatriate Gundi López, address simply Puerto Ángel, Oaxaca 70902, tel. (958) 630-02. Her homey, rustic-aesthetic complex rambles up a leafy hillside to a breezy bay-view *palapa* where patrons relax, socialize, and enjoy food and drink from Gundi's kitchen. Just above that, guests enjoy a double row of several clean, simply furnished (although dark) rooms, shaded by a hammock-hung communal view porch. Besides all this, Gundi is happy to volunteer information about local sights and activities and arrange excursions for her guests. Another plus on the premises is the gallery-studio of Gundi's brother-in-law, accomplished oil painter Mateo López. Rooms with shared showers and toilets cost about $9 d low season, $11 high; rooms with private shower and toilet run about $12 d low season, $14 high, all with fans. Get there by walking uphill along the little alley adjacent to the town market and just opposite the marine compound.

Another Puerto Ángel gem is **Hotel La Buena Vista,** P.O. Box 48, Puerto Ángel, Oaxaca 70902, tel./fax (958) 431-04, tucked on the hillside just west of the Arroyo del Aguaje. The hotel's four tiers stairstep artfully up the jungly slope. First- and second-level rooms open to shady hammock-hung view porches. On the third level, a luxuriously airy restaurant *palapa* opens to a picture-perfect bay vista. The climax is a pair of large onyx-tile-floored fourth-floor rooms that share an entire private view patio with hammocks. All rooms are immaculate, light, and simply but tastefully furnished, with spotless bathrooms. Low-season rates for the approximately 20 rooms run about $20 s or d for standard, $28 s or d for room with private balcony, and $33 for the top-floor room with double-size onyx bathtub; high season, the same go for about $28, $32, and $38 with fans, and the deluxe rooms have hot water.

Heading around the curve of the bay to the Playa Panteón neighborhood, you'll find one of Puerto Ángel's best cheaper lodgings, **Casa de Huéspedes Capy,** Playa Panteón, P.O. Box 44, Puerto Ángel, Oaxaca 70902, tel./fax (958) 430-02, sitting on the bay-view hillside by the road fork to Zipolite. Rooms, in two tiers with views toward Playa Panteón, are basic but clean with fans and cool-water private baths. Good family management is the Capy's strong suit. This shows in the shady view restaurant, Arcely, where good food in a friendly atmosphere encourages guests to linger, reading or talking, for hours. The family also watches the community TV at night; if it bothers you, ask them to turn it down. The 10 rooms rent for about $6 s, $9 d low season, $7 and $11 high.

Nearby, about 100 yards along the road to Zipolite (watch for the sign at the hilltop driveway on the left), take a look at the guesthouse **Penelope's,** with only a few rooms, but a breezy, quiet hilltop setting, at P.O. Box 49, Puerto Ángel, Oaxaca 70902, tel. (958) 430-73. Here owner Patricia and her husband Steve enjoy sharing their home with guests. Rooms come comfortably furnished with hot water showers, porches with hammocks and fans. Rentals run about $8 s, $10-15 d. Add about $3 per person for breakfast, $5 for dinner.

Downhill, on Playa Panteón, the unusually well-kept **Hotel La Cabaña,** Calle Pedro Sainz de Barada, P.O. Box 22, Puerto Ángel, Oaxaca 70902, tel. (958) 431-05, downhill, is just a few steps from Playa Panteón. Past the lobby is a verdant, plant-decorated patio, while upstairs, guests enjoy chairs and shady tables on a breezy bay-vista sundeck. Marble shines in the baths and the floors of the 23 comfortable, very clean rooms, some with private view balconies. A reader reported a burglary here; store your valuables in the hotel safe. Several beachfront restaurants are conveniently nearby. Rooms rent for about $13 s, $15 d, and $19 t low season, and $16, $20, and $25 high, with fans and hot water.

Hidden in the leafy canyon a hundred yards uphill from the beach is **Posada Cañon Devata,** life project of the ecological pioneer López family, P.O. Box 10, Puerto Ángel, Oaxaca 70902, tel./fax (958) 430-48, e-mail lopezk@spin.com.mx. Artists Mateo and Suzanne López (he's Mexican, she's American) became an example to local people, reforesting their originally denuded canyon property over a period of several years. They gradually added on land, so their now-lush arroyo encompasses an entire watershed-ecosystem. Although Suzanne and Mateo have now retired, their daughter Cali and son Darshave carry on the day-to-day management every bit as skillfully as their parents did.

Their accommodations, a multiroom lodge and several luxury/rustic detached cabins, dot the slopes of their sylvan tropical forest retreat. All are comfortably furnished and thoughtfully decorated with handicrafts and Mateo's expressive primitivist oil paintings. Lodge rooms rent for about $20 d, cabins $30 d low season, $30 and $50 high, with fans and parking.

Their restaurant serves all-organic fruits and vegetables and whole-wheat homemade bread and tortillas, while their gift shop, Sueños de Amusgo, offers one-of-a-kind handicrafts, including many Amusgo indigenous *huipiles* and a gallery of Mateo's paintings.

Atop the hill via the adjacent steep road, the **Hotel Ángel del Mar,** Puerto Ángel, Oaxaca 70902, tel. (958) 430-08, fax 430-14, offers a sharply contrasting style of lodging. Rates for the 42 rooms run about $27 d low season, $31 high; credit cards accepted. Guests enjoy a big, open-air dining room, swimming pool, and large light rooms with private balconies looking down upon a panoramic bay vista. Mornings, guests can enjoy sunrise over the bay and evening sunsets over the ocean. Revitalized management has recently brightened the place up with new paint everywhere and new bedspreads and lampshades to go with the venerable polished wood furniture in the rooms.

Vacationers hankering for splendid isolation can have it at **Bahía de la Luna,** on the coast about three small bays east of Puerto Ángel, at P.O. Box 90, Pochutla, Oaxaca 70900, fax (958) 430-74, e-mail: tomzap@eden.com. Here, friendly builder Tom Penick enjoys sharing his paradise with visitors. His approximately 15 rustic-chic adobe, palm-thatched cabañas cluster on a lovely isolated crescent of golden sand. No phones, TV, or traffic; simply sun, sea, sand, and home-cooked food. Rooms, thoughtfully and comfortably furnished, rent for about $22 s, $27 d low season, $32 and $44 including three meals, with fans, but room temperature only water. Bring your own hammock.

Get there by the jeep road, signed La Boquilla, which forks east about four miles uphill from Puerto Ángel.

Zipolite Accommodations

Zipolite's line of rustic (bring your own towel and soap) lodgings starts at **Lola's** on the east end of the beach, Playa Zipolite, Puerto Ángel, Oaxaca 70902. The friendly, elderly owner continues her decades-long good management of her thatch-shaded restaurant and beach cabañas. For customers who hanker for a bit better lodging, Lola has broken new ground with Zipolite's first modern-standard units, eight new rooms with hot water and ceiling fans. The best are two front, top-floor units overlooking the gorgeous beach and sunset vista.

The scene at Lola's resembles a miniresort, with the restaurant right on the beach, where guests enjoy late breakfasts, stroll out for swims, read thick novels, and kick back and enjoy convivial conversation with their mostly North American and European fellow vacationers. Although the last hurricane wiped out the rustic wood cabañas, they've been rebuilt with modern-standard stucco units that rent for about $10 s or d year-round, with fan, and private room-temperature shower baths.

The **Lo Cósmico** cabañas nestle on a cactus-dotted rocky knoll at the opposite end of the beach, Playa Zipolite, P.O. Box 36, Pochutla, Oaxaca 70900. White spheres perched on their thatched roof peaks lend a mystical Hindu-Buddhist accent to the cabañas' already picturesque appearance. In the restaurant atop the knoll, you're likely to find Regula and Antonio Nadurille, Lo Cósmico's European-Mexican owners. Regula manages the restaurant, specializing in a dozen varieties of tasty crepes, while Antonio supervises the hotel. Their hillside and beach-level cabañas are clean, candle-lit, and equipped with hammocks and concrete floors. Showers and toilets are outside. Cabañas rent for about $7 per person.

Shambala, on the adjacent forested hillside, is as it sounds—a tranquil Buddhist-style retreat, at Puerto Ángel, Playa Zipolite, Oaxaca 70902. Shambala's driving force is the friendly owner/ community leader Gloria Esperanza Johnson, who arrived in Zipolite by accident in 1970 and decided to stay, eventually adopting Mexican citizenship. She built the place from the ground up, gradually adding on until now there are about 50 primitive-rustic cabañas, a macrobiotic beach-view restaurant, and a spiritual center. Shambala is a quiet, alcohol-free haven for lovers of reading, sunbathing, hiking, yoga, and meditation. It sits atop an enviable few acres at the edge of a sylvan hinterland. Adjacent cactus-studded cliffs plummet spectacularly to surf-splashed rocks below, while trails fan out through lush tropical deciduous forest. The very simple

candle-lit thatched concrete-floored cabañas with hammocks rent for about $5 per person. Toilets and showers are shared.

Gloria also welcomes lovers of the outdoors to camp (about $2.50 per person, per day) in Shambala's get-away-from-it-all jungle "El Retiro" retreat, in a pristine mountain river valley about an hour away by car or local bus. For more information and directions, ask Gloria or her staff assistants. (Note: Although the October 1997 hurricane decimated Shambala, Gloria will hopefully have her mini-paradise up and running by the time you read this.)

Get to both Shambala and Lo Cósmico by turning from the main road onto the dirt driveway just west of the arch at Zipolite's west end. Bear right at the first fork, then left at the next for Lo Cósmico, right for Shambala.

Posada Rancho Cerro Largo

Outstandingly innovative Posada Rancho Cerro Largo is the creation of eco-activist Mario Corella, descendant of a longtime Hermosillo, Sonora, hotel family. After knocking around in the hospitality trade for several years, Mario decided to create his own version of utopia. Mario says that he wanted to "be in contact with nature and live among the community with as little impact as possible. I would welcome guests as friends, to share the dinner table with me and the hotel staff."

He's done it, with a reception-restaurant and six rustically charming tile-floored, stick-and-adobe cabañas, furnished with hand-loomed bedspreads and opening to hammock-hung ocean-view verandas. The entire complex nestles in a cactus-dotted leafy hillside forest, linked by a path that meanders, between panoramic ocean viewpoints, to a gorgeously isolated, wave-washed sandy beach below. Rates run a reasonable $50 for two, *including* full breakfast and dinner. For reservations (mandatory in winter, highly recommended anytime), write the Posada Rancho Cerro Largo, P.O. Box 121, Pochutla, Oaxaca 70900, or fax (958) 430-63. Look for the signed driveway on the Puerto Ángel-Mazunte road, four miles (6.4 km) from the Puerto Ángel bus stop.

Trailer Parks and Camping

The rustic **Trailer Park Fernando's** has about 20 parking (big rigs possible) or camping spaces beneath a shady, tufted grove by the road at the east end of Playa Zipolite. Reserve by writing friendly owner Fernando Torres, at Carretera Playa Zipolite-Puerto Ángel, Oaxaca 70902. A spirit of camaraderie often blooms among the tents and assorted RVs of travelers from as far away as the Klondike, Kalispell, and Khabarovsk. About $5 gets you an RV space for two persons, including electricity, shared shower and toilets, and satellite dish (if you have your own hookup). No sewer connections, however. Tent spaces cost $3 for two persons. Bottled drinking water is available in local stores.

If you prefer being nearer the beach, take a look at the very small, simple **Trailer Park Chano,** Playa Zipolite, Puerto Ángel, Oaxaca 70902, by Lola's at Zipolite's east end. Chano, the friendly owner, offers about six spaces, a shower, and a toilet for vans, campers, or tents. Sorry, too cramped for big trailers or rigs. The tariff runs about $3 for RVs, $1.50 per person for tents, including electricity.

One of Zipolite's best tenting spots is the forested hilltop behind Shambala. The friendly owner, Gloria Johnson, will probably allow you to use Shambala's showers and toilets for a small fee. Ask at the Shambala office first for permission to camp.

FOOD

For a country place, Puerto Ángel has surprisingly good food, starting with the **Hotel Villa Florencia,** right on the main beachfront street. The Italian-born owner/chef specializes in antipasti, salads, and meat and seafood pastas. Like a good country Italian restaurant, service is crisp; presentations are attractive. The modest wine list includes some good old-country imports, and the spaghetti al dente and cappuccino are of course the best on the coast. Open daily 8 a.m.-11 p.m. Moderate. (If you're in need of lodging, ask at the hotel desk, in the rear, to see some of clean, comfortable rooms.)

The unpretentiously elegant view *palapa* restaurant at the **Hotel La Buena Vista,** tel. (958) 431-04, is the best spot in town for a leisurely, intimate dinner. Here, the prodigious effort that owner/managers Lourdes and Carrie Díaz have invested in their kitchen and staff

comes together beautifully. The servers, fetchingly attired in colorful Oaxaca *huipiles,* glide gracefully between kitchen and tables with a bounty of crisp salads, savory soups, tender pastas, and fresh broiled fish and meats. It's open 7:30-11 a.m. for breakfast, closed afternoons, then open for supper 6-10 p.m. Moderate.

For a homey change of pace, get in on breakfast or lunch daily 7:30 a.m.-2 p.m. and/or the 7 p.m. family-style dinner at the macrobiotic restaurant at the **Posada Cañon Devata,** tel. (958) 430-48. The fare is all fresh, organic, and high in vegetables and grains and low in meat. Reserve for the dinner by 2 p.m. Moderate.

Four or five restaurants line Playa Panteón. Here, the main attraction is the beach scene rather than the food. **Susy's** and **Leyvis y Vicente** seem to be the best of the bunch. Fish will generally be the best choice; make sure it's fresh. Open seasonally about 8 a.m.-9 p.m. Moderate.

Zipolite also has some good eating places. For hearty macrobiotic-style fare and a breezy beach view, go to the restaurant at **Shambala** at the west end of Playa Zipolite. Personable owner Gloria Johnson runs a very tidy kitchen, which serves good breakfasts, soups, salads, and sandwiches. Open daily 8 a.m.-8 p.m. No alcohol. Budget-moderate.

Regula, the European co-owner of **Lo Cósmico** on the knoll just east of Shambala, cooks from a similar macrobiotic-style menu, although she specializes in several variations of crepes, including egg, meat, cheese, and vegetable. Open daily, high season, from around 8 a.m. to about 7 p.m. Shorter hours and closed Monday during the low season.

For rustic elegance, continue past Zipolite to the view restaurant at **Posada Rancho Cerro Largo.** Here, friendly eco-activist owner Mario Corella invites guests to share a meal with him and the hotel staff.

ENTERTAINMENT AND SPORTS

Puerto Ángel's entertainments are mostly spontaneous. If anything exciting is going to happen, it will most likely be on the beachfront Boulevard Uribe where people tend to congregate during the afternoon and evenings. A small crowd may accumulate in the adjacent restaurant Villa Florencia for coffee, talk, or something from the bar.

The town's major scheduled event is the big **Fiesta de San Miguel Arcangel** on 1 and 2 October. Then the *mascaritas* (masked children) dancers romp, carnival games and rides light up the main streetfront and a regatta of fishing boats parades around the bay.

Sunsets

Sunset-watchers get their best chance from the unobstructed hilltop perch of the Hotel Ángel del Mar, or Lola's, on the beach in Zipolite, where the bar and restaurant at each place can provide something to enliven the occasion even if clouds happen to block the view.

Hotel Ángel del Mar sometimes provides music for dancing during the highest seasons, most likely between Christmas and New Year and the week before Easter.

Another spot for good company around sunset time is **El Cielo,** Posada Cañon Devata's canyonside view perch. Owner-managers Cali and Darshave invite guests and visitors to join them around sunset time (5-7 p.m.) for snacks and liquid refreshments.

For additional diversions, head west to Puerto Escondido or east to Bahías de Huatulco, each about an hour by car, for more and livelier entertainments.

Jogging

Potholed streets, rocky roads, and lack of grass sharply curtail Puerto Ángel jogging prospects. The highway, however, which runs gradually uphill from near the pier, does provide a continuous, more or less smooth surface. Confine your jogging to early morning or late afternoon, and take water along.

Swimming and Surfing

Swimming provides more local exercise opportunities, especially in the sheltered waters off of Playa Panteón. Bodysurfing, boogie boarding, and surfing can be rewarding, depending on wind and swells, off Playa Zipolite. **Be super-careful of undertow,** which is always a threat, even on calm days at Zipolite. If you're inexperienced, don't go out alone. Novice and even experienced swimmers sometimes drown at Zipolite. If you get caught in a current pulling you out

to sea, don't panic. Experts advise that you simply float and paddle parallel to the beach a hundred yards or so, to a spot where the offshore current is not so severe (or may even push you back toward the beach). Alcohol and surf, moreover, don't mix. On rough days, unless you're an expert, forget it. Bring your own board; few, if any, rentals are available.

Sailing and Windsurfing

If you have your own carryable boat or windsurfing gear, sheltered **Playa Panteón** would be a good place to put it into the water, although the neighboring headland may decrease the available wind. Calm mornings at **Playas Zipolite, San Agustín,** or **Mazunte** (see above), with more wind but rougher waves, might also be fruitful.

Snorkeling and Scuba Diving

Rocky shoals at the edges of Puerto Ángel Bay, especially just off **Playa Panteón,** are excellent for casual snorkeling. **Playa Estacahuite,** on the open ocean just beyond the bay's east headland, is even better. Best bring your own equipment. If you don't, you can rent a snorkel and mask from Vicente, at his restaurant, Leyvis y Vicente, on Playa Panteón, for about $3 an hour.

Although Puerto Ángel has no professional dive shop, beginners can contact the well-equipped and certified dive instructors of **Buceos Triton** dive shop, tel./fax (958) 708-44, or **Leeward Dive Center,** tel./fax (958) 100-51, a 45-minute drive east, in Santa Cruz de Huatulco. (See the following **Bays of Huatulco** section.)

Fishing

The bayfront pier is the best place to bargain for a boat and captain to take you and your friends out on a fishing excursion. Prices depend on season, but you can figure on paying about $20 an hour for a boat for four or five persons with bait and two or three good rods and reels. During a three-hour outing a few miles offshore, a competently captained boat will typically bring in three or four big, good-eating *robalo* (snook), *huachinango* (snapper), *atún* (tuna), or pompano. If you're uncertain about what's biting, go down to the dock around 2 or 3 p.m. in the afternoon and see what the boats are bringing in.

Puerto Ángel children use hand power when necessary.

Vicente, of Leyvis y Vicente restaurant on Playa Panteón, takes out fishing parties of up to six persons for around $20 an hour, bait and tackle included. You can also arrange fishing trips through the **Gambusino Travel Agency,** tel. (958) 430-80, 430-38, open Mon.-Sat. 9 a.m.-2 p.m. and 4-8 p.m., in the office across the street from the doctor and pharmacy on Av. Teniente Vasconcelos, just uphill from Uribe.

SHOPPING

Market
The biggest local market is the Monday *tianguis,* which spreads along the Pochutla main street, Hwy. 175, about seven miles from Puerto Ángel, one mile inland from the Hwy. 200 junction. Mostly a place for looking rather than buying, throngs of vendors from the hills line the sidewalks, even crowding into the streets, to sell their piles of onions, mangoes, forest herbs, carrots, cilantro, and jícama.

On other days, vendors confine their displays to the permanent Mercado 5 de Octubre, east side of the main street, between Calles 1 and 2 Sur.

Groceries
The best-stocked Puerto Ángel local store is the **Super Del Puerto** at the west end of beachfront street Uribe, uphill past the arroyo bridge. Also, a few little-bit-of-everything stores in Zipolite and on Uribe in the middle of Puerto Ángel sell cheese, milk, bread, some vegetables, and other essentials.

Handicrafts
Sueños ("Dreams") de Amusgos, at Posada Cañon Devata, is one of the Costa Chica's most interesting handicrafts shops. Owners Suzanne and Mateo López have assembled an authentic collection of Amusgo, Mixtec, and Chatino native crafts, including many fine hand-crocheted *huipiles* from San Pedro de Amusgos.

For fine custom-made hammocks, visit local craftsman Gabino Silva at his country shop, off a jungly stretch of the road between Zipolite and San Agustín. He also rents a cabaña. Watch for the little sign labeled Hamacas and Cabaña on the beach side of the road, 4.2 miles (6.7 km) from the Puerto Ángel bus stop.

Some unique handicrafts are available in Pochutla. **Foto Garcia,** on main street Lázaro Cárdenas 76, west side, offers many whimsical coconut carvings by a local craftsman. It's open Mon.-Sat. 8 a.m.-2 p.m. and 4-8 p.m., tel. (958) 407-35.

Additionally, the *larga distancia,* open daily 7 a.m.-10 p.m., between Calles 1 and 2 Norte, has a varied collection of hand-embroidered purses, *huipiles,* shirts, vests, and 1960s-style tie-dyed apparel.

SERVICES AND INFORMATION

Money Exchange
The only local money exchange is along the road through Zipolite about three miles west of Puerto Ángel. Otherwise, go to **Banco Internacional** (Bital) on the Pochutla main street, Lázaro Cárdenas, tel. (958) 406-96 or 406-97, open Mon.-Fri. 8 a.m.-6 p.m., Saturday 8 a.m.-3 p.m.

Or go to **Bancomer,** corner of Lázaro Cárdenas and Av. 3A Norte, tel. (958) 402-59, open Mon.-Fri. 9 a.m.-3 p.m., Saturday 9 a.m.-noon. Another option is **Bancrecer,** next door to Bancomer, tel. (958) 407-63, open Mon.-Fri. 9:30 a.m.- 5 p.m., Saturday 10 a.m.-2 p.m. Call to confirm moneychanging hours.

Communications and Travel Agent
The Puerto Ángel *correo* and *telecomunicaciones* stand side by side with the Agencia Municipal at the foot of Hwy. 175. Both are open Mon.-Fri. 9 a.m.-3 p.m.

The Puerto Ángel *larga distancia* telephone and fax office (tel. 958-430-46 or 430-54, fax 430-70) is on Calle José Vasconcelos, just uphill from main street Uribe. Hours are daily 7 a.m.-10 p.m.

Puerto Ángel's travel agent, **Agencia de Viajes Gambusino,** tel. (958) 430-80, 430-38, arranges tours and fishing trips and sells reserved air and bus tickets at the small office on Vasconcelos next door, uphill from the *larga distancia.*

Medical and Police
Puerto Ángel's friendly and respected private **doctor,** Dr. Constancio Aparicio Juárez, holds consultation hours (Mon.-Sat. 7 a.m.-2 p.m. and 5-9 p.m.) and also runs the **pharmacy,** tel. (958) 430-58, on Av. Vasconcelos, across from the *larga distancia.* For serious illness requiring diagnostic specialists, Dr. Juárez recommends you go to the government Hospital Regional in Pochutla, tel. (958) 402-04, or the Seguro Social in Crucecita, tel. (958) 701-24 or 702-64.

Another option is to go to the small government **Centro del Salud** health clinic, which concentrates on preventative, rather than diagnostic medicine, on the hill behind the church. Go up Vasconcelos a long curving block, go left at the first corner, and continue another block to the health center.

For police emergencies, call the *policía preventiva* at the Presidencia Municipal, in Pochutla, on the town plaza, one block east of the main north-south town thoroughfare, tel. (958) 431-01.

Ecological Projects
Community leaders, such as Suzanne and Mateo López and their son and daughter Cali and Darshave López, managers of Posada Cañon Devata, and Gloria Esperanza Johnson, owner of Shambala in Zipolite, have awakened local awareness of ecological issues. Suzanne and Mateo and their children, by restoring their entire canyon ecosystem property, and Gloria, by spearheading efforts to prevent the deforestation of coastal lands, have served as examples of the benefits that simple but persistent efforts can yield.

Ecological activism has spread to Mazunte, where the **Asociación de Comuneros de Mazunte** has picked up the green banner. Led by their earnest activist-president Ermilo López Bustamante, the association is building an ecologically correct time-share development and encouraging waste composting and water and forest conservation. Partly as a result of their efforts, cutting trees around Zipolite, San Agustín, and Mazunte has become a definite community no-no. Consequently, the tropical deciduous forest zone between Zipolite and Mazunte is rapidly becoming a luxuriantly healthy eco-preserve.

In parallel but separate action, **Ec Solar,** the private ecological "Peace Corps," works hard and effectively with local campesinos to build environmentally appropriate solutions to village sewage, water, health, and agricultural problems. Its headquarters is in Puerto Escondido, tel. (958) 209-50, in the west-side Bachoco suburb, corner of Calles Huajuapan de León and Tehuantepec.

GETTING THERE AND AWAY

By Air
Scheduled flights to Mexican destinations connect daily with airports at **Huatulco,** 19 miles (30 km) away, or **Puerto Escondido,** 44 miles (71 km) by road from Puerto Ángel. For details see the **Puerto Escondido** and **Bays of Huatulco** sections of this chapter.

By Car or RV
Good roads connect Puerto Ángel to the west with Puerto Escondido and Acapulco, north with Oaxaca, and east with the Bahías de Huatulco and the Isthmus of Tehuantepec.

Highway 200 connects westward with Puerto Escondido in an easy 44 miles (71 km), continuing to Pinotepa Nacional (135 miles, 217 km, three hours) and Acapulco in a total of seven hours (291 miles, 469 km) of driving. In the opposite direction Bahías de Huatulco (actually Crucecita) is a quick 22 miles (35 km). The continuation to Salina Cruz stretches another 92 miles (148 km), or around two and a half additional hours of driving time.

North to Oaxaca, paved but narrow and winding National Hwy. 175 connects 148 miles (238 km) over the Sierra Madre del Sur from its junction with Hwy. 200 at Pochutla. The road climbs to around 9,000 feet through cool (chilly in winter) pine forests and hardscrabble Chatino and Zapotec Indian villages. Fill up with gas in Pochutla. Unleaded gasoline is available at the Pochutla Pemex stations, both on through-town Hwy. 175: about 300 yards toward town from Hwy. 200 and on the north, uphill, edge of town. Carry water and blankets, and be prepared for emergencies. The first gas station is at Miahuatlán, 90 miles north. Allow about seven driving hours from Puerto Ángel to Oaxaca, about six in the opposite direction.

By Bus

One long-distance bus line, second-class Estrella del Valle, connects Puerto Ángel directly to Oaxaca and Pochutla (where travelers may connect to many long-distance destinations). Buses depart from the main-street corner of Uribe and Vasconcelos; the Pochutla bus departs hourly during daylight hours, the Oaxaca bus once, nightly, at 10 p.m. The adjacent Papelería El Globo serves as the information and ticket office.

Many other long-distance buses connect with points west, east, and north from Pochutla. The three separate stations cluster less than a mile from the Hwy. 200 junction along Av. Lázaro Cárdenas, the Hwy. 175 main street into Pochutla (before the town center near the taxi stand).

Many first-class **Estrella Blanca** subsidiary-line buses (such as first-class Elite, luxury-class Turistar, Flecha Roja, and Autotransportes Cuauhtémoc) depart from their station at L. Cárdenas 94, tel. (958) 403-80. They connect west daily with Puerto Escondido, continuing to Acapulco, there connecting with the entire Pacific Coast, all the way to the U.S. border. They also connect east (many per day) with Bahías de Huatulco destinations of Crucecita and Santa Cruz de Huatulco and Salina Cruz on the Isthmus. A few "plus" (say "ploos") luxury-class buses connect daily, all the way to Mexico City.

All first-class **Cristóbal Colón** buses (L. Cárdenas 84, tel. 958-402-74) connect east with Crucecita (several per day). Some also continue east, connecting with Salina Cruz and Tehuantepec, continuing to Chiapas destinations of Tuxtla Gutiérrez San Cristóbal and Tapachula, at the Guatemala border. A few buses connect north with Oaxaca via Tehuantepec; one bus connects daily with Puebla and Mexico City. A few buses also connect daily west with Puerto Escondido.

Frequent second-class and some first-class service is offered by cooperating lines (tel. 958-401-38 or 403-49) **Autobuses Estrella del Valle, Autobuses Oaxaca Pacífico,** and **Fletes y Pasajes.** They connect west with Puerto Escondido and Pinotepa Nacional, north with Oaxaca and Mexico City, and east with Huatulco, Salina Cruz, and the Chiapas border.

BAYS OF HUATULCO AND VICINITY

The nine azure Bahías de Huatulco decorate a couple dozen miles of acacia-plumed rocky coastline east of Puerto Ángel. Between the bays, the ocean joins in battle with jutting, rocky headlands, while in their inner reaches the ocean calms, caressing diminutive crescents of coral sand. Inland, a thick hardwood forest seems to stretch in a continuous carpet to the Sierra.

Ecologists shivered when they heard that these bays were going to be developed. Fonatur, the government tourism development agency, says, however, it has a plan. Relatively few (but all upscale) hotels will occupy the beaches; other development will be confined to a few inland centers. The remaining 70% of the land will be kept as pristine ecological zones and study areas.

Although this story sounds sadly familiar, Fonatur, which developed Ixtapa and Cancún, seems to have learned from its experience. Up-to-date sewage treatment has been installed *ahead of time;* logging and homesteading have been halted, and soldiers patrol the beaches, stopping turtle poachers. If all goes according to the plan, the nine Bahías de Huatulco and their 100,000-acre forest hinterland will be both a tourist and ecological paradise, in addition to employing thousands of local people, when complete in 2020. If this Huatulco dream ends as well as it has started, Mexico should take pride while the rest of the world should take heed.

HISTORY

Long before Columbus, the Huatulco area was well-known to the Aztecs and their predecessors. The name itself, from Aztec words meaning "Land where a Tree (or Wood) Is Worshipped," reflects one of Mexico's most intriguing legends—of the Holy Cross of Huatulco.

When the Spanish arrived on the Huatulco coast, the local native people showed them a huge cross they worshipped at the edge of the sea. A contemporary chronicler, Ignacio Burgoa, conjectured the cross had been left by an ancient saint—maybe even the Apostle Thomas—some 15 centuries earlier. Such speculation notwithstanding, the cross remained as the Spanish colonized the area and established headquarters and a port, which they named San Agustín, at the westernmost of the Bays of Huatulco.

Spanish ports and their treasure-laden galleons from the Orient attracted foreign corsairs—Francis Drake in 1579 and Thomas Cavendish in 1587. Cavendish arrived at the bay now called Bahía Santa Cruz, where he saw the cross the Indians were worshipping. Believing it was the work of the devil, Cavendish and his men tried to chop, saw, and burn it down. Failing at all of these, Cavendish looped his ship's mooring ropes around the cross and with sails unfurled tried using the force of the wind to pull it down. Frustrated, he finally sailed away, leaving the cross of Huatulco still standing beside the shore.

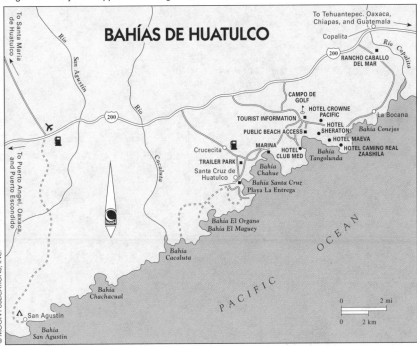

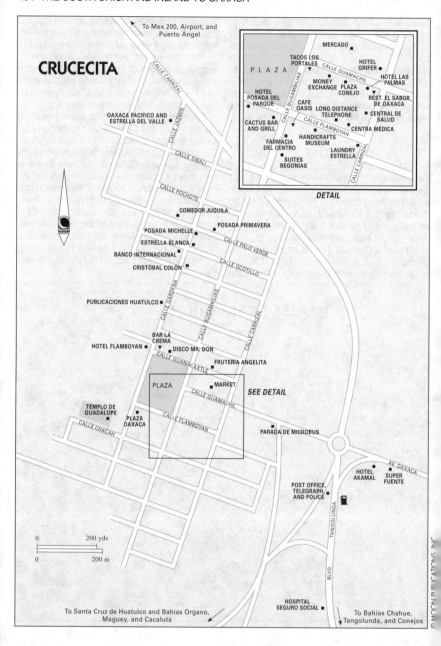

CRUCECITA

To Mex 200, Airport, and
Puerto Ángel

CALLE CARRIZAL

CALLE JAZMIN

OAXACA PACIFICO AND
ESTRELLA DEL VALLE

CALLE SIBALI

CALLE POCHOTE

COMEDOR JUQUILA

POSADA PRIMAVERA

POSADA MICHELLE

CALLE PALO VERDE

ESTRELLA BLANCA

BANCO INTERNACIONAL

CALLE OCOTILLO

CRISTÓBAL COLÓN

PUBLICACIONES HUATULCO

CALLE GARDENIA

CALLE BUGAMBILIAS

CALLE CARRIZAL

BAR LA
CREMA

HOTEL FLAMBOYAN

DISCO MR. DON

FRUTERÍA ANGELITA

CALLE GUANACAXTLE

PLAZA

MARKET

SEE DETAIL

CALLE GUAMACHIL

TEMPLO DE
GUADALUPE

PLAZA
OAXACA

CALLE FLAMBOYAN

CALLE CHACAH

PARADA DE MICROBUS

AV. OAXACA

HOTEL
AKAMAL

SUPER
FUENTE

POST OFFICE,
TELEGRAPH
AND POLICE

TANGOLUNDA

0   200 yds

0   200 m

BLVD.

HOSPITAL
SEGURO SOCIAL

To Santa Cruz de Huatulco and Bahías Organo,
Maguey, and Cacaluta

To Bahías Chahue,
Tangolunda, and Conejos

DETAIL

MERCADO

PLAZA

TACOS LOS
PORTALES

CALLE GUAMACHIL

HOTEL
GRIFER

HOTEL LAS
PALMAS

MONEY
EXCHANGE

PLAZA
CONEJO

CALLE BUGAMBILIAS

HOTEL
POSADA DEL
PARQUE

CAFE
OASIS

LONG DISTANCE
TELEPHONE

REST. EL SABOR
DE OAXACA

CENTRAL DE
SALUD

CACTUS BAR
AND GRILL

CALLE FLAMBOYAN

CENTRA MÉDICA

FARMACIA
DEL CENTRO

HANDICRAFTS
MUSEUM

LAUNDRY
ESTRELLA

CALLE CARRIZAL

SUITES
BEGONIAS

© MOON PUBLICATIONS, INC.

By 1600, a steady trail of pilgrims were chipping pieces from the cross; so much so that in 1612, Bishop Juan de Cervantes had to rescue it. He brought the cross to Oaxaca, where he made four smaller two-foot crosses of it. He sent one specimen to church authorities, respectively, in Mexico City, Rome, and Santa María de Huatulco, head town of the Huatulco *municipio*. Cervantes kept the fourth copy in the cathedral in Oaxaca, where it has remained, venerated and visible in a side chapel, to the present day.

SIGHTS

Getting Oriented

With no road to the outside world, the Bahías de Huatulco remained virtually uninhabited and undeveloped until 1982, about the time that coastal Hwy. 200 was pushed through. A few years later, Huatulco's planned initial kernel of infrastructure was complete, centering on the brand-new residential service town, Crucecita (pop. 10,000), and nearby Santa Cruz de Huatulco boat harbor and hotel village on Bahía Santa Cruz.

The Bays of Huatulco decorate the coastline both east and west of Santa Cruz. To the east, a paved road links Bahías Chahue, Tangolunda, and Conejos. To the west lie Bahías El Organo, El Maguey, and Cacaluta, all accessible by very rough roads from Santa Cruz. Isolated farther west are Bahías Chachacual and San Agustín, with no road from Santa Cruz (although a good dirt road runs to San Agustín from Hwy. 200 near the airport).

Besides Bahía Santa Cruz, the only other bay that has been extensively developed is Tangolunda, five miles east. Its golf course, small restaurant/shopping complex, and five resort hotels (Club Med, Sheraton, Club Maeva, Crown Pacific, and Zaashila) have all been fully operational since the early 1990s.

Getting Around

Frequent public **minibuses** connect Crucecita and Bahías Santa Cruz, Chahue, and Tangolunda. Taxis make the same trips for about $2 by day, $3 at night. No public transportation is available to the other bays. If the roads are passable, taxi drivers might take you for a picnic to west-side bays El Organo, El Maguey, and Cacaluta for about $25 roundtrip from Crucecita or Tangolunda, perhaps $5 to Bahía Conejos.

For an extended day trip to all road-accessible bays, figure on $40-50 for either a taxi or a rental car. Call Dollar at the Sheraton, tel. (958) 100-55, ext. 787; Advantage in Santa Cruz (at Hotel Castillo), tel. (958) 713-79 or 102-92; or Budget in Crucecita at Octillo and Jazmín, tel. (958) 700-10, fax 700-19.

Another option is to go by boat. The local boat cooperative (Sociedad Cooperativa Turístico Tangolunda) runs a daily excursion—around 10:30 a.m., $15 per person, kids half price—to all nine bays. Included is open bar, bilingual guide, and snacks; snorkeling is $4 extra. Reserve directly through their dock office, tel. (958) 700-81, or through a travel agent such as Servicios Turísticos del Sur, at the Sheraton, tel. (958) 100-55, ext. 784; Servicios Turísticos del Sur, in Crucecita, tel./fax (958) 712-11; or Paraíso Huatulco, tel. (958) 701-81, fax 701-90.

The same cooperative also rents entire boats for up to 10 people. Full-day excursions run on the catamaran *Fiesta*, about $60, while drop-off runs to the nearest beach are about $10 per boat roundtrip; to the more remote, around $20-30.

Local travel agents offer other tour options: several hours of sunning, swimming, picnicking, and snorkeling at a couple of Bahías de Huatulco beaches runs around $20 per person. Tours to Puerto Ángel, Puerto Escondido, and wildlife-rich lagoons go for $30-50 per person. For reservations, call Servicios Turísticos del Sur, at the Sheraton, tel. (958) 100-55, ext. 784; Servicios Turísticos del Sur, in Crucecita, tel./fax (958) 712-11; or Paraíso Huatulco, tel. (958) 701-81, fax 701-90.

Crucecita and Santa Cruz

Despite its newness, Crucecita ("Little Cross," pop. 10,000) resembles a traditional Mexican town, with life revolving around a central plaza and market nearby. Crucecita is where the people who work in the Huatulco hotels, businesses, and government offices live. Although pleasant enough for a walk around the square and a meal in a restaurant, it's nothing special—mostly a place whose modest hotels and restaurants accommodate business travelers and weekenders who can't afford the plush hotels near the beach.

While in Crucecita, be sure to step into the church on the plaza's west side to admire the heavenly **ceiling mural** of Mexico's patron, the Virgin of Guadalupe. The mural, the largest of Guadalupe in Mexico, is the work of local artists José Ángel del Signo and Marco Antonio Contreras, whose for-sale art is on display locally. Besides the heavenly Virgin overhead, the muralists have decorated the space above the altar with the miraculous story of Don Diego and the **Virgin of Guadalupe.**

The four deluxe hotels and the few travel-oriented businesses of Santa Cruz de Huatulco (on Bahía Santa Cruz about two miles from Crucecita) cluster near the boat harbor. Fishing and tour boats come and go, vacationers sun themselves on the tranquil yellow-sand Playa Santa Cruz (beyond the restaurants adjacent to the boat harbor), while T-shirt and fruit vendors and boatmen hang around the quay watching for prospective customers. After the sun goes down, tourists quit the beach for their hotels and workers return to their homes in Crucecita, leaving the harbor and streets empty and dark.

Exploring the Bays of Huatulco

Isolation has left the Huatulco waters blue and unpolluted, the beaches white and clean. Generally, the bays are all similar: tropical deciduous (green July-Jan.) forested rocky headlands enclosing yellow-white coral sand crescents. The water is clear and good for snorkeling, scuba diving, sailing, kayaking, and windsurfing during the often-calm weather. Beaches, however, are typically steep, causing waves to break quickly near the sand, unsuitable for bodysurfing, boogie boarding, or surfing.

The six undeveloped Huatulco bays have neither drinking water nor much shade, and since they're so pristine coconut palms haven't even gotten around to sprouting there. When exploring, bring food, drinks, hats, sunscreen, and mosquito repellent. When camping (which is permitted everywhere except Tangolunda), bring everything.

East Side

Bahía Chahue, about a mile from both Crucecita and Santa Cruz, is wide, blue, and forest-tufted, with a steep yellow dune, stretching to the marina jetty at the east end. Chahue is uncrowded even on weekends and holidays and nearly empty the rest of the time.

About four miles farther east is the breezy and broad **Bahía Tangolunda.** Although hotels front much of the beach, a signed Playa Pública public access road borders the western edge of the golf course (turn right just past the creek bridge). Except for its east end, the Tangolunda beach is steep and the waves break quickly right at the sand. *Palapa* restaurants at the beach serve food and drinks; or, if you prefer, stroll a quarter mile for refreshments at the luxurious poolside beach clubs of the Sheraton and Club Maeva resorts.

Bahía Santa Cruz

Over the headland about two miles farther east, **Punta Arena** ("Sand Point"), a forested thumb of land, juts out into wide **Bahía Conejos.** Three separate steep beaches spread along the inner shoreline. The main entrance road arrives at high-duned Playa Punta Arena. Playa Tejoncito ("Little Wild Pig") is beyond the rocks far to the right; Playa Conejos ("Rabbits") is to the left on the other side of Punta Arena. A few palm-frond *ramadas* for shade and a saltwater flush toilet lavatory occupy the Playa Punta Arena dune. Trees behind the dunes provide a few shady spots for RV or tent campers.

Beyond **La Bocana,** near the mouth of the Río Copalita, less than a mile farther on, a long, broad beach with oft-powerful surfing rollers (novices beware) stretches for at least a mile east. Beach *palapas* serve drinks and very fresh seafood. A lagoon above the beach (bring your kayak) appears ripe for wildlife viewing.

After Magallitos, the road bends inland, paralleling the **Río Copalita wildlife sanctuary,** perfect for adventurous exploring. Several operators guide visitors on river eco-tours: José Aussenac, owner of Posada Michelle, tel. (958) 705-35, organizes and guides outdoor adventure-tours. Options include bird- and animal-watching walks along riverine forest trails, kayaking river rapids, and mud baths at a riverside ranch. Very well-equipped **Huatulco Outfitters,** tel. (958) 103-15, offers several river-rafting excursions, from beginning ($25) to advanced ($75) levels.

West Side

Playa Entrega is a little dab of sand slipped into the west side of Bahía Santa Cruz. It is the infamous spot where, on 20 January 1831, Vicente Guerrero, president and independence hero, was brought ashore in custody of arch-villain Francisco Picaluga and sent to be murdered in Oaxaca a few months later.

Quarter-mile-long Playa Entrega is the ideal Sunday beach, with calm, clear water and clean yellow sand. Swimming, kayaking, and often snorkeling, sailing, and windsurfing possibilities are excellent. Some trees provide shady spots for tenting and RV camping. No facilities exist except for seasonal and holiday food and drink stands.

Get there via the main street, Boulevard Benito Juárez, which passes the Santa Cruz boat harbor. Continue west, bearing left, at the "Y," at the Hotel Binneguenda (mark your odometer) on the right. After a few hundred yards, the road bends left and winds uphill, past panoramic viewpoints of Bahía Santa Cruz. Follow the signs and you'll soon be at Playa Entrega.

If, instead of curving left to La Entrega, you follow the rough dirt road that forks right at the same spot, you'll be headed for the Bahías El Organo, El Maguey, and Cacaluta. The roads to these bays have deteriorated in recent years. Until authorities get around to paving them, land access may only be achievable by experienced drivers, preferably in maneuverable, high-clearance vehicles. If in doubt, hire a taxi or take a boat tour.

Bahía El Organo is first; after about half a mile along the dirt road, look for a rough dirt track angling sharply left. The beach is isolated, intimate, and enfolded by rocky shoals on both sides. Some trees behind the dune provide shade.

Continuing straight ahead, the road forks again (about 1.3 miles from the hotel). Continue straight ahead downhill to El Maguey, or fork sharply right to Cacaluta. The sandy crescent of **Bahía El Maguey** is bordered by tidepools tucked beneath forested headlands. Facing a protected fjordlike channel, the Maguey beach is virtually waveless and fine for swimming, snorkeling, diving, windsurfing, and sailing. It would be a snap to launch a boat here for fishing in the bay. During weekends and holidays, picnickers arrive and banana towboats and *aguamotos* (mini-motorboats) buzz the beach and bay. Although camping is possible, room is limited. Bring everything, including water.

Bahía Cacaluta, two miles past the El Maguey fork, spreads along a mile-long, heart-shaped beach, beckoningly close to a cactus-studded offshore islet. Swimmers beware, for waves break powerfully, surging upward and receding with strong undertow. Many shells—limpets and purple- and brown-daubed clams—speckle the beach. Surf fishing prospects, either from the beach itself or from rocks on either end, appear excellent. Although the sand directly behind the beach is too soft for vehicles, space exists farther back for RV parking and camping. Tenters could have their pick anywhere along the dune.

Bahía Chachacual, past the Río Cacaluta about four miles farther west, is a sand-edged azure nook accessible only via forest trails.

Bahía San Agustín, by contrast, is well known and easily reachable by Pochutla-bound bus, then by the good dirt road (taxi $5) just across the highway from the fork to Santa María Huatulco (at Km 236, a mile west of the airport). After about seven miles along a firm track, accessible by all but the bulkiest RVs, bear right to the modest village of *palapas* at the bay's sheltered west end. From there, the beach stretches eastward along a mile of forest-backed dune. Besides good swimming, sailing, windsurfing, shell-collecting, and fishing prospects, San Agustín has a number of behind-the-dune spots (follow the left fork shortly before the road's end) for RV and tent camping. Beachside *palapas* can, at least, supply seafood and drinks and maybe some water and basic groceries.

ACCOMMODATIONS

In Huatulco, as in other resorts, hotels on the beach are the most expensive. Crucecita's hotels are cheapest, Tangolunda's are most expensive, and the Santa Cruz hotels fall in between. All Huatulco lodgings have private baths with hot water.

Crucecita Accommodations

Most of the Crucecita lodgings are near the central plaza. The **Hotel Grifer,** at Guamuchil and Carrizal, a block east of the plaza, would be nothing special in most Mexican resorts, but in hotel-poor Huatulco, it is often full; reserve by writing the hotel, at P.O. Box 159, Crucecita, Oaxaca 70980, tel./fax (958) 700-48. Three stories of nondescript modern rooms enclose a TV-dominated atrium; a passable street-level restaurant is convenient for breakfast. The 16 rooms rent for about $15 s or d, $17 t, with ceiling fans; no credit cards.

Across Guamuchil, half a block back toward the plaza, the **Hotel Las Palmas,** Calle Guamuchil 206, Crucecita, Oaxaca 70980, tel. (958) 700-60, fax 700-57, offers small, plain but clean a/c rooms on the two floors above its good street-level restaurant. The eight rooms rent for about

$18 s, $20 d low season, $26 and $28 high; credit cards are accepted.

The **Hotel Suites Begonias,** at the southeast plaza corner, offers a more deluxe, family-run alternative, Bugambilias 503, Crucecita, Oaxaca 70980, tel. (958) 700-18, fax 713-90. The rooms, although clean and comfortable, have motel-style walkways passing their windows, decreasing privacy. Rates for the 13 rooms run about $19 s or d, $20 t, with fan and TV; credit cards are accepted.

Half a block away, you might consider taking one of the attractive rooms on the very top floor of the **Hotel Posada del Parque,** Flamboyan 306, Crucecita, Oaxaca 70980, tel./fax (958) 702-19, fax 711-98, on the south side of the plaza. Although not especially large, the top-floor rooms have high rustic beamed ceilings, window views, and surround a cheery inner balcony-atrium. An airy sidewalk café downstairs serves breakfast, lunch, and dinner. All 14 rooms rent for about $18 s or d low season, with TV and a/c, $25 high season; $15 s or d with fan only, no TV.

About three blocks east of the Crucecita plaza hubbub, the **Hotel Amakal** offers semideluxe, modern-standard rooms at reasonable prices. A stairway from the small, spartan lobby leads upstairs to about a dozen clean, light, white-tile-floored, tastefully decorated rooms with modern-standard baths. Rates are $17 s, $30 d low season, $22 s, $40 d high, with a/c. Credit cards are accepted. Street parking only. Reserve in writing at Av. Oaxaca 1, Crucecita, Bahías de Huatulco, Oaxaca 79089, or by phone, tel. (958) 715-00 or 715-15, fax 700-36.

A pair of simple but attractive *posadas* near the bus stations on Gardenia, four blocks north of the plaza, offer other options. The **Hotel Posada Michelle,** Gardenia 8, Crucecita, Oaxaca 70980, tel./fax (958) 705-35, run by friendly eco-tour guide José Aussenac, has about a dozen small-ish but clean and comfortable rooms with big beds, baths, and good satellite TV. Some of the rooms are airy and light; others, although dark because of their half-mirrored windows (for privacy), do have white walls and open to a light, breezy second-story walkway that leads to a pleasant, hammock-hung and shady view porch. Rates, for a/c rooms, run about $20 d, low season, $30 high; rooms with fans only cost $15 low season, and $20 high.

Posada Primavera, just around the corner, at Palo Verde 5, Crucecita, Oaxaca 70980, tel. (958) 711-67, fax 706-30, offers six simply furnished but clean, light, high-ceilinged upstairs rooms with bath. Windows look out onto the palmy, bougainvillea-adorned surrounding neighborhood. Rates are about $12 s or d low season, $20 high, with fans.

Santa Cruz Hotels

A block from the beach in Santa Cruz, first choice goes to the **Hotel Binneguenda,** Benito Juárez 5, Santa Cruz de Huatulco, Oaxaca 70900, tel. (958) 700-77, fax 702-84. Neocolonial arches, pastel stucco walls, and copper and ceramics handicrafts decorate the interiors, while in the adjacent leafy patio guests sun themselves around the elaborate cascade pool. In the restaurant, the customers seem as well fed and satisfied as the waiters are well trained and attentive. Upstairs, the colonial/modern-decor rooms are spacious, comfortable, and equipped with phones, TV, and a/c. Rates for the 75 rooms run about $45 d low season, $75 high, with parking and credit cards accepted. Bargain for a discount, especially during times of low occupancy.

Hotel Castillo Huatulco, Benito Juárez, P.O. Box 354, Santa Cruz de Huatulco 70980, tel. (958) 701-35 or 701-44, fax 701-31, east along the street three blocks, amounts to a poor second choice, unless you can get in for prices substantially less than the Binneguenda. Loosely managed, with recorded salsa music often thumping away in the bar, its 106 rooms, although comfortable, are crowded into a smaller space than the Binneguenda's 75. They are nevertheless popular with families on weekends and holidays but nearly empty (and perhaps bargainable) during quieter seasons. Low-season rates run about $80 s or d, $110 high. Bargain for a discount, especially during times of low occupancy. Phones, TV, a/c, pool, and parking; credit cards accepted

Smaller, recently renovated **Hotel Marlin,** a block closer toward the beach, at Paseo Mitla 107, Santa Cruz de Huatulco, Oaxaca 70989, tel. (958) 700-55 or 713-31, fax 705-46, e-mail hmarlin@huatulco.net.mex, is only two blocks from the beach. From street level, the small lobby leads to an appealingly intimate coral-hued inner pool patio and restaurant, enfolded by three sto-

ries of rooms. Upstairs, the three dozen rooms are thoughtfully decorated with coral bedspreads, floor-length drapes, attractive, rustic tile floors, and deluxe '90s-standard bathrooms. Rates run $45 s or d (fourth night free) low season, $95 high, with a/c, cable TV, and phones. One possible drawback (or advantage) to all this is the hotel's adjoining discotheque, which the management swears cannot be heard in the rooms, even at full volume.

Tangolunda Luxury Resorts

Five luxury resort hotels spread along the Tangolunda shoreline. The Club Med dominates the sheltered western side-bay, with four stack-like towers that make the place appear as a big ocean liner. The smaller Sheraton and Club Royal Maeva stand side by side on the bay's inner recess next to the golf course. The Hotel Zaashila spreads gracefully to its east-end cove, while the hot-pink Hotel Crown Pacific (formerly Holiday Inn) stairsteps up the hillside, away from the beach.

The emphasis of all five resorts is on facilities, such as multiple pools, bars, and restaurants, full wheelchair access, live music, discos, shows, and sports such as tennis, golf, sailing, kayaking, windsurfing, snorkeling, diving, and swimming. Other amenities may include shops, baby-sitting, children's clubs, and arts and crafts instruction.

In contrast to the Sheraton and the Zaashila, which operate in usual hotel style, the rates at the Maeva, Club Med, and Crown Pacific include everything—all food, sports, lessons, and entertainment. Their cuisine, although tasty and bountiful, is not fancy. The atmosphere resembles a big upscale summer camp, with hosts of options, even for those who want to do nothing.

The **Sheraton Huatulco** is a generic (but worthy) member of the worldwide chain, Paseo Benito Juárez, Bahía Tangolunda, Oaxaca 70989, tel. (958) 100-55, 100-05, or 100-39, fax 101-13, or toll-free (800) 325-3535 from the U.S. and Canada. Rooms are comfortable, deluxe, and decorated in soothing pastels, with private bayview balconies, phones, cable TV, and a/c. Rates for its 360 rooms and suites begin at about $145 s or d low season, about $200 high.

If the **Hotel Zaashila Resort,** Bahía de Tangolunda Huatulco, Oaxaca 70989, tel. (958) 104-

60, fax 104-61, tel. (800) 7CAMINO (722-6466) from the U.S. and Canada, hasn't yet gotten an architectural award, it should soon. Builders have succeeded in creating a modern luxury hotel that has an intimate feel. This begins right at the reception, a plush round *palapa,* where arriving guests are graciously invited to sit in soft chairs while being attended to by personable clerks, who are also seated, behind rustic, designer desks. Outside, you walk to your room through manicured tropical gardens, replete with gurgling fountains, splashing brooks, and cascading, green lawn terraces.

If the Zaashila has a drawback, it's in some of the 120 rooms, which, although luxurious and comfortable, are entirely tile-floored and could use more color and warmth. However, the arrangement of separate units, nested like a giant child's building blocks, resembles a space-age Hopi Indian pueblo, each unit being uniquely perched among the whole, affording much privacy and light, especially in upper-floor units. Outside, a few steps downhill, past the big, meandering blue pool, comes the superb beachfront: acres of luscious, billow-washed yellow sand, intimately enclosed between wave-sculpted rocks on one side and a jungly headland on the other. Low-season rentals begin at about $110, or about $150 if you must have your own little private pool. Corresponding high-season rates are $200 and $300, with access to water sports, tennis, golf, three restaurants, and nightly live music.

If you're activity-oriented, you'll likely get more for your money at either the Club Med, the Royal Maeva, or the Hotel Crown Pacific. The 300-room Maeva is very well managed and smaller; consequently it's likely to be more personalized than both the sprawling 554-room Club Med or the Crown Pacific (which, although it has relatively few rooms, rambles up the hillside in 10 separate buildings, accessible from below via either shuttle or a funicular elevator).

Of the three hotels, the **Crown Pacific** has the largest rooms. Perhaps this is meant to compensate for the drawback that it's not actually on the beach: guests must either walk or shuttle a couple of blocks to the beach club.

The biggest plus of the Crown Pacific is the price, which, low season, runs only about $70 per person, double occupancy (three kids up to age six with parents go free, $25 for ages seven through 12), including all meals, drinks, sports, kid's mini-club, and in-house entertainment. No fans, all air-conditioned. During high season, the same costs about $100 per person. Reserve directly at Hotel Crown Pacific, Boulevard Benito Juárez 8, Bahía Tangolunda, Bahías de Huatulco, Oaxaca 70989, tel. (958) 100-44 or fax 102-21, e-mail: cvhuatulco@compuserve.com.mx. Save money by paying your hotel bill in pesos, if at all possible.

All-inclusive packages at the **Club Med** vary according to season, but begin at about $1,500 for two, per week ($216 d per day), plus around $100 in "membership" fees. Child (6-11 years) rates run about $600 per week. High season rates often run nearly double that. Call (800) CLUBMED (258-2633) for information and reservations in the U.S. and Canada.

Club Maeva all-inclusive rates run about $200 for two, low season, $300 high; kids, six years or under, with parents, go free, while rates for kids seven through 12 are $40 low season, $60 high. Reserve directly at Club Royal Maeva, P.O. Box 227, Bahías de Huatulco, Oaxaca 70989, tel. (958) 100-00, 100-48, or 100-64, fax 102-20. For information and reservations in the U.S. and Canada, call (800) GOMAEVA (466-2382).

Trailer Parks and Camping

In Santa Cruz, the **Trailer Park Mangos** rents about 30 spaces in a shady mango grove about a quarter mile east (toward Tangolunda) of the Hotel Castillo. The bare-bones scruffy facilities include toilets, showers, and electricity, but no sewer hookup. RVs pay about $5 daily, tenters about $2 per person. They also have some scuzzy rooms, which, if you don't mind cleaning up yourself, go for about $50 per month.

Authorities generally permit **camping** at all of the Bahías de Huatulco except Tangolunda. You might also save time by checking with the government tourist information offices for any access changes or recommendations. In the Tangolunda hotel zone, go to the office on the far inland side, west edge of the hotel-shopping complex, tel. (958) 101-76, open high season Mon.-Fri. 9 a.m.-5 p.m., Saturday 9 a.m.-2 p.m. If it is closed go to Santa Cruz and try the Sedetur (Secretery of Tourism) office on the main boulevard a block east of the banks. Its hours are

Mon.-Sat. 8 a.m.-3:30 p.m. and Saturday 9 a.m.-3 p.m., tel. (958) 715-41.

The soldiers who guard the beaches against turtle poachers and squatters also make camping much more secure. They usually welcome a kind word and maybe a cool drink as a break from their lonely and tedious vigil.

FOOD

Aside from the Tangolunda hotels, nearly all good Huatulco eateries are near the Crucecita plaza.

Breakfast and Snacks

For inexpensive homestyle cooking, try the *fondas* at the Crucecita Mercado ("Market"), between Guamuchil and Guanacastle, half a block off the plaza.

The Mercado stalls are good for fresh fruit during daylight hours, as is the **Frutería Angelita,** open daily 6 a.m.-8 p.m., just across Guanacastle.

Also nearby, the **Panadería San Alejandro,** at the southeast plaza corner of Flamboyan and Bugambilias, tel. (958) 703-17, open 6 a.m.-10 p.m., offers mounds of fresh baked goodies.

The crowds will lead you to Crucecita's best-bet snack shop, **Los Portales Taco and Grill,** corner of Guamuchil and Bugambilias, right on the plaza, tel. (958) 700-70. Breakfasts, a dozen styles of tacos, Texas chili (or, as in Mexico, *frijoles charros*—"cowboy beans"), and barbecued ribs are their specialties. Beer is half a dollar. Open daily 6-2 a.m.

Restaurants

The relaxed, refined sidewalk atmosphere of **Cafe Oasis** has made it Crucecita's plaza-front restaurant of choice. Beneath cooling ceiling fans, customers watch the passing plaza scene while enjoying a full bar and a professionally prepared and served menu of breakfast, good espresso, fruit, salads, hamburgers, Mexican and international specialties, and much more. At the southeast plaza corner (Bugambilias and Flamboyan), open daily 8 a.m.-midnight, tel. (958) 700-45.

Nearly as successful is **Restaurante Sabor de Oaxaca,** on the bottom floor of the Hotel Las Palmas on Guamuchil, half a block from the plaza, tel. (958) 700-60. Wall art, folk crafts, and quiet conversation set the tone, while tasty country specialties fill the tables. Try their Oaxacan-style tamales, or *botanas Oaxaqueños*—cheese, sausage, pork, beef, and guacamole snacks. Open daily 8 a.m.-11 p.m.

Travelers weary of the plaza tourist scene can find authentic Mexican cooking at **Comedor Juquila,** which does quite well on nearly exclusively local patronage. Tasty regional specialties—*moles, pansita, chiles rellenos,* tamales—are its key to success. Open daily 7 a.m.-10 p.m., off of Gardenia, five blocks north of the plaza, corner of Palo Verde.

ENTERTAINMENT

Hangouts and Dancing

Huatulco entertainments center on the Crucecita plaza. Although the hubbub quiets down during low seasons, some spots are reliable amusement sources year-round. The **Cactus Bar and Grill,** on the Flamboyan side of the plaza, livens up with videos and music nightly 7 p.m.-3 a.m.

On the other hand, you can get swept up nightly by the seasonal salsa and Latin rock repertoire of the band at the **Sports Bar Iguana,** next to Tacos Los Portales, Bugambilias side of the plaza. Open about 11 a.m.-2 a.m., in season.

You need only follow your ears to the source at **Mr. Don** bar, at the diagonally opposite plaza corner of Gardenia and Guanacastle, upstairs. Live Latin rock is featured nightly in season and on weekends, 8-2 a.m.

In Santa Cruz, lights flash, fogs descend, and customers gyrate to the boom-boom at **Magic Circus** disco in the Marlin Hotel on Calle Mitla, two blocks behind Banamex off the main boulevard. Admission (from around 10 p.m.) runs about $10. Call (958) 700-55 to confirm.

Nearby, continue your party at **Poison** disco, which offers continuous recorded reggae, salsa, and Latin rock from about 9:30 p.m. At the Marina Hotel and Resort, in Santa Cruz, Calle Tehuantepec 112; call for confirmation, tel. (958) 709-66.

The **Sheraton** in Tangolunda is among the most reliable sources of hotel nightlife. Live music plays before dinner (about 6-8 p.m.) in the lobby bar, guests dance to a live Latin band in the Banquet Salon (about $30 with dinner, $7 without), and decorations overflow at theme-night parties (Italian, French, Mixtec, Chinese; about $25 per person with dinner). Call (958) 100-55, 100-05, or 100-39 for details and reservations. Other hotels, such as the Crown Pacific, Maeva, and Zaashila may also offer similar entertainments, in season.

SPORTS AND RECREATION

Walking, Jogging, Tennis, and Golf
Huatulco's open spaces and smooth roads and sidewalks afford plenty of walking and jogging opportunities. One of the most serene spots is along the Tangolunda Golf Course mornings or evenings. Also, an interesting sea-view forest trail takes off from the stables at Bahía Conejos.

If you're planning on playing lots of tennis, best stay at one of the Tangolunda luxury resorts. Otherwise, the Sheraton, tel. (958) 100-55, 100-05, or 100-39, and the Tangolunda Golf Course, tel. (958) 100-37, fax 100-59, rent tennis courts for about $7/hour. Call for rental information and reservations.

The breezy green **Tangolunda Golf Course,** tel. (958) 100-37, fax 100-39, designed by the late architect Mario Chegnan Danto, stretches for 6,851 yards down Tangolunda Valley to the bay. The course starts from a low building complex (watch for bridge entrance) off the Hwy. 200-Tangolunda highway across from the sewage plant. Greens fee runs about $30, cart $25, club rental $12, caddy $15. The tennis courts, maintained by the same government corporation that owns the golf course, are next to the clubhouse on the knoll at the east side of the golf course.

Horseback Riding,
Bicycle Rentals, and Tours
Rancho Caballo del Mar on the road (east past Tangolunda) to Copalita, about a mile south of Hwy. 200, guides horseback trips along the ocean-view forest trail that stretches from their corral to the eco-preserve zone by the Río Copalita. The four-mile tour, which costs about $25 per person at the ranch (more if through an agent), returns via Bocana shoreline vista point

for lunch. For more information and reservations, contact the horseback tour office, tel. (958) 103-23, at the Punta de Tangolunda shopping center, local no. 7, before the Sheraton, as you enter the Tangolunda hotel zone.

Adventurers can also walk the same four-mile roundtrip in around three hours. Take a hat, water, and a bathing suit, and start early (around 8 a.m.) or late (around 3 p.m.) to avoid the midday heat.

Discover Tours Huatulco, also known as Rent-a-Bike, hires out mountain bikes and leads bicycle tours, ranging from leisurely half-day jaunts for $10 to challenging all-day jungle trail adventures for about $25 per person. Contact either of its two shops, at the southwest corner of the Crucecita plaza (at Flamboyan, corner of Gardenia), tel. (958) 702-54, or in Tangolunda at Plaza Las Conchas, across from Hotel Sheraton, tel. (958) 100-02, tel./fax 706-78.

Río Copalita Eco-Touring and Rafting
José Aussenac, owner of Posada Michelle, organizes and guides outdoor adventure-tours in the east-side Río Copalita wildlife sanctuary. Options include bird- and animal-watching walks along riverine forest trails, kayaking river rapids, and mud baths at a riverside ranch. Call him, tel. (958) 705-35, for more information and reservations.

Very well-equipped **Huatulco Outfitters,** tel. (958) 103-15, at the first shopping complex on the left as you enter Tangolunda, offers several river-rafting excursion, from beginning ($25) to advanced ($75) levels.

Upland Jungle Eco-Touring
and Coffee Farms
Local tour operators guide hiking and bird-watching tours to waterfalls, springs, archaeological zones, pilgrimage and sacred sites, and coffee farms in the jungly foothill hinterland north of Huatulco. One of the most experienced and environmentally sensitive operators is **Turismo Conejo** in Crucecita, at Plaza Conejo, on Guamuchil, half a block east of the town plaza, tel. (958) 700-29 or 700-09, fax 700-54. Turismo Conejo offers a range of options, from one-day walks along the Copalita River (ruins, bird-watching by canoe, mudbath) and jungle jeep safaris and lunch at La Gloria coffee plantation to

jungle overnights (waterfalls, rock hieroglyphic paintings) to complete five-day excursions from Oaxaca city, including all of the above. Other agents may also offer similar tours; contact your hotel tour desk.

Swimming, Surfing, Snorkeling, and Scuba Diving

Swimming is ideal in the calm corners of the Bahías de Huatulco. Especially good swimming beaches are at **Playa Entrega** in Bahía Santa Cruz and **Bahía El Maguey.** A few spots are also good for surfing. **Huatulco Outfitters,** tel. (958) 103-15, at the first shopping complex on the left as you enter Tangolunda, offers completely equipped surfing excursions.

Generally clear water makes for rewarding snorkeling off the rocky shoals of all of the Bays of Huatulco. Local currents and conditions, however, can be hazardous. Novice snorkelers should go on trips accompanied by strong, experienced swimmers or professional guides. Bring your own equipment; gear purchased locally will be expensive at best and unusable at worst.

Huatulco scuba divers enjoy the services of well-equipped and professional **Buceos Triton** dive shop in Santa Cruz de Huatulco, in the small complex between Santa Cruz main beach and boat harbor, tel./fax (958) 708-44. Owner and certified instructor Enrique La Clette has had extensive training in France, the U.S., and Mexico City. He starts novices out with a pool mini-course, followed by a three-hour ($50) trip in a nearby bay. Snorkelers go for about $20, with good equipment furnished. Open Mon.-Sat. 9 a.m.-2 p.m. and 4-7 p.m.

Buceos Triton's PADI open-water certification course takes about five days and runs about $350, complete. After that, you are qualified for more advanced tours, which include local shipwrecks, night dives, and marine flora, fauna, and ecology tours.

La Clette, a marine biologist by training, is a leader in the local ecological association that watchdogs Fonatur's Huatulco development work.

If Buceos Triton is all booked up, try **Action Sports,** at the Sheraton Hotel, tel. (958) 100-55, ext. 842, fax (958) 705-37; or **Leeward Dive Center** (formerly Buceo de Sotavento) across from the Hotel Sheraton, inside the Hotel Club Plaza Huatulco, tel./fax (958) 100-51.

Fishing and Boat Launching

The local boat cooperative **Sociedad Servicios Turísticos Bahía Tangolunda** takes visitors out for fishing excursions from the Santa Cruz boat quay. For a launch with two lines and bait, figure on paying about $40 minimum for a three-hour excursion. For big-game fishing, rent a big 40-foot boat, with lines for several persons, for about $400. More reasonable prices might be obtainable by asking around among the fishermen at the Santa Cruz boat harbor or the village at San Agustín.

On the other hand, you can leave the negotiations up to a travel agent, who will arrange a fishing trip for you and your friends. You can stop afterward at a beachside *palapa,* which will cook up a feast with your catch. Save money by bringing your own tackle. Rates for an approximately three-hour trip for three run about $60 if you supply your own tackle, $120 if you don't. Contact the agent at your hotel travel desk, or an outside agent, such as Servicios Turísticos del Sur, in Crucecita, on south-side Blvd. Santa Cruz, tel./fax (958) 712-11, or Paraíso Huatulco in the Hotel Flamboyan, on the Crucecita plaza, tel. (958) 701-81, fax 701-90.

Some of the Huatulco bays offer easy boat-launching prospects, especially at sites at easily reachable Bahía Chahue marina and Bahía Santa Cruz's Playa la Entrega. Easy launching is also possible at more remote spots, especially at the protected beaches on Bahías El Maguey and San Agustín.

SHOPPING

Market and Handicrafts

Crucecita has a small traditional market (officially the Mercado 3 de Mayo) east of the plaza, between Guanacastle and Guamuchil. Although produce, meats, and clothing occupy most of the stalls, a few offer Oaxaca handicrafts. Items include black *barra* pottery, hand-crocheted Mixtec and Amusgo *huipiles,* wool weavings from Teotitlán del Valle, and whimsical duck-motif wooden bowls carved by an elderly, but sharp-bargaining, local gentleman.

A woodcarver displays his unique wares in the Crucecita market.

Steep rents and lack of business force many local silver, leather, art, and other handicrafts shops to hibernate until tourists arrive in December. The few healthy shops with good selections cluster either around the Crucecita plaza (check out the handicrafts museum—Museo de Artesanías Oaxaqueñas—next to the Cafe Oasis), the Santa Cruz boat quay, or in the Punta Tangolunda shopping complex adjacent to the Sheraton (or shops in the hotel itself).

Don't miss the singularly excellent **gallery** of artist José Ángel del Signo, at Plaza Conejo, Guamuchil 208, just east of the Crucecita town plaza. Besides his own fine works, José also displays the paintings, sculptures, and photography of a number of other local artists. Open daily 10 a.m.-9 p.m.

Supermarket, Laundry, and Photo Supplies
The supermarket **La Fuente** in Crucecita on east-side Av. Oaxaca offers a large stock of groceries, an ice machine, and a little bit of everything else, a block east of the Pemex station, tel. (958) 702-22. Open daily 8 a.m.-10 p.m.

Take your washing to the **Lavandería Estrella,** tel. (958) 705-92, open Mon.-Sat. 8 a.m.-2 p.m. and 4-7 p.m. Find it a block east of the Crucecita plaza, on Flamboyan, corner of Carrizal.

For film and quick develop-and-print, go to **Foto Conejo,** tel. (958) 705-85, just off the Crucecita plaza, across Guamuchil from the market. Besides a photo-portfolio of the Bays of Huatulco, the friendly owner stocks supplies, point-and-shoot cameras, and Kodak, Fuji, and Konica slide and print film. Open Mon.-Sat. 9 a.m.-8 p.m., Sunday 9 a.m.-2 p.m.

SERVICES

Money Exchange
The best place to get money in Crucecita is **Banco Internacional** (Bital), tel. (958) 702-59 or 712-26, open Mon.-Fri. 8 a.m.-7 p.m., Saturday 9 a.m.-3 p.m. (call to verify moneychanging hours), at 1204 Gardenia, corner of Palma Real, five short blocks north of the town plaza. Other banks are in Santa Cruz. **Banamex,** on the main street Av. Benito Juárez, corner of Pochutla, tel. (958) 702-66, exchanges both U.S. and Canadian traveler's checks Mon.-Fri. 9 a.m.-2 p.m.; **Bancomer** across the street, tel. (958) 703-85, does the same Mon.-Fri. 8:30 a.m.-2 p.m. Call to double-check moneychanging hours.

After bank hours, go to the hole-in-the-wall Money Exchange booth on Guamuchil, near the corner, at the east side of the Crucecita plaza, tel. (958) 711-14.

Post and Telecommunications
The Huatulco *correo* and *telecomunicaciones* stand side by side, across from the Pemex gas station on east-side Blvd. Tangolunda. Post office (tel. 958-705-51) hours are Mon.-Fri. 9 a.m.-6 p.m., Saturday 9 a.m.-12:30 p.m.; *telégrafo* (tel. 958-708-94) is open Mon.-Fri. 9 a.m.-1 p.m. and 3-6 p.m., Saturday 9 a.m.-noon.

After hours, go to one of the *larga distancias* on Carrizal, near the Hotel Grifer, such as **Caseta Telefónica Gemenis,** tel. (958) 707-35 or 707-36, or **Servitel,** tel. (958) 708-97 or 710-84.

Immigration and Customs
Both Migración and the Aduana are at the Huatulco airport. If you lose your tourist permit, try to

avoid trouble or a fine at departure by presenting Migración with proof of your date of arrival—stamped passport, an airline ticket, or preferably a copy of your lost tourist permit—a day (or at least a couple of hours) before your scheduled departure.

Medical and Police

Among the better of Huatulco private clinics is **Central Médica,** half a block east of the Crucecita plaza, at Flamboyan 205, tel. (958) 701-04. It has 24-hour emergency service (tel. 958-702-20) and several specialists on call.

For an English-speaking, U.S.-trained doctor, go to IAMAT (International Association for Medical Assistance to Tourists) member and general practitioner Dr. Andrés González Ayvar, at Sabali 403, corner of Gardenia, eight short blocks north of the Crucecita plaza.

Alternatively, go around the corner to the 24-hour government **Centro de Salud** clinic, tel. (958) 714-21, on Carrizal, a block east of the Crucecita plaza, or the big **Seguro Social** hospital, tel. (958) 711-82 or 711-83, in Crucecita, on the boulevard to Tangolunda, a quarter mile south of the Pemex gas station.

For routine medications, Crucecita has many pharmacies, such as **Farmacia del Centro,** plaza corner of Flamboyan and Bugambilias, tel. (958) 702-32, open Mon.-Sat. 8 a.m.-10 p.m., Sunday 9 a.m.-2 p.m. and 5-10 p.m., at street level, below the Hotel Begonias.

For police emergencies, call the Crucecita **policía,** tel. (958) 702-10, in the Agencia Municipal behind the post office, across the Tangolunda boulevard from the Pemex *gasolinera.*

INFORMATION

Tourist Information Offices

Two government tourist information offices serve visitors locally. In the Tangolunda hotel zone, go to the office on the far inland side, west edge of the hotel-shopping complex., tel. (958) 101-76, open high season, Mon.-Fri. 9 a.m.-5 p.m., Saturday 9 a.m.-2 p.m. If it's closed go to Santa Cruz and try the Sedetur (Secretery of Tourism) main office in the San Miguel shopping complex, on the main boulevard, a block east of the banks. Its hours are

Mon.-Sat. 8 a.m.-3:30 and Saturday 9 a.m.-3 p.m., tel. (958) 715-41.

Alternatively, in Crucecita, try the private agent **Space 2000,** tel. (958) 700-27, at the Tourist Information sign on Guamuchil just east of the plaza.

Newspapers, Books, and Magazines

The bookshop at the Sheraton (tel. 958-100-55) in Tangolunda stocks English-language paperback novels, Mexico art and guidebooks, newspapers such as *USA Today,* and many magazines.

In Crucecita, the small **Publicaciones Huatulco** newsstand sells the English-language *News* of Mexico City (which arrives around noon), at the corner of Gardenia and Macuil, three blocks north of the plaza; open daily 6 a.m.-9 p.m. Reserve your copy by paying in advance.

Pick up a copy of **Huatulco Espacio 2000,** the useful and unusually informative commercial tourist booklet, at your hotel or a store or travel agent, or at their office, tel. (958) 700-44 in Huatulco.

Ecology Association

Local ecologists and community leaders monitor Huatulco's development through their **Asociación Pro Desarrollo Sociocultural y Ecologíos de Bahías de Huatulco.** Association president marine biologist Enrique La Clette and his associates are working earnestly to assure the government's plan—that 70% of Huatulco will remain undeveloped—continues in force as development proceeds. One of their initial victories was to dissuade Club Med from dumping its raw sewage into Tangolunda Bay. Enrique, who is friendly and fluent in English, enjoys talking to fellow nature lovers. Drop into his dive shop, Buceos Triton, in Santa Cruz de Huatulco, in the complex between the boat harbor and the beach, tel./fax (958) 708-44.

GETTING THERE AND AWAY

By Air

The **Huatulco airport** (officially the Aeropuerto Internacional Bahías de Huatulco, code-designated HUX) is just off Hwy. 200, eight miles (13 km) west of Crucecita and 19 miles (31 km) east of Puerto Ángel. The terminal is small, with only check-in booths, a few snack bars, and handicrafts and trinket shops.

A few major carriers connect with U.S. and Mexican destinations:

American Airlines connects with Dallas on Saturday during low season, more frequently high season. For reservations, call a travel agent, such as Servicios Turísticos del Sur, in Crucecita, tel./fax (958) 712-11, or Paraíso Huatulco, tel. (958) 701-81, fax 701-90.

Mexicana Airlines flights connect daily with Mexico City. For reservations, call Mexicana's office in the Hotel Castillo, tel. (958) 702-23 or 702-43.

Aeromorelos flights connect daily with Oaxaca and four times a week with Puerto Escondido. For flight information, call (958) 190-22 or 104-44. For reservations, call a travel agent, such as Servicios Turísticos del Sur, at the Sheraton, tel. (958) 100-55, ext. 784.

Aeromar connects daily with Mexico City. For reservations, call (958) 190-01.

Aerocaribe connects with Oaxaca. For reservations, call a travel agent.

United Airlines, Miami Air, Sun Country and **Canada 3000** have seasonal, mostly winter **charter-flight** connections with U.S. and Canadian destinations. For reservations, call a travel agent.

Huatulco **air arrival** is usually simple. Since the terminal has no hotel booking agency or money-exchange counter, come with a hotel reservation and sufficient pesos to last until you can get to the bank in Santa Cruz or Crucecita. After the typically quick immigrations and customs checks, arrivees have a choice of efficient ground transportation to town. Agents sell tickets for collective "ichivan" vans or GMC Suburbans to Crucecita or Santa Cruz (about $6) or the Sheraton, Club Maeva, or Club Med. A private *taxi especial* for three, possibly four passengers, runs about $8. Prices to Puerto Ángel are about double these.

Mobile travelers on a budget can walk the couple of blocks from the terminal to Hwy. 200 and catch one of the frequent public **minibuses** headed either way to Crucecita (east, left) or the Pochutla (Puerto Ángel) junction (west, right).

Car rental agents are usually on duty for flight arrivals. If not, make a reservation ahead of time

and they will meet your flight: **Budget** in Crucecita, tel. (958) 700-10, fax 700-19; **Dollar** in Tangolunda, tel. (958)100-55, ext. 787; **Advantage** in Santa Cruz, tel. (958) 713-79; or local agent **Fast Auto Rent** in Tangolunda (which rents Geo Trackers), opposite the Hotel Sheraton, tel. (958) 100-02. For Budget, U.S. tel. (800) 527-0700, Canada tel. (800) 268-8991, and Dollar, tel. (800) 800-4000, make reservations in the U.S. and Canadian prior to departure.

By Car or RV

Paved highways connect Huatulco east with the Isthmus of Tehuantepec, west with Puerto Ángel and Puerto Escondido, and north with Oaxaca.

Highway 200, the east-west route, runs an easy 100 miles (161 km) to Tehuantepec, where it connects with Hwy. 190. From there, it continues northwest to Oaxaca or east to Chiapas and the Guatemala border. In the opposite direction, the Hwy. 200 route is equally smooth, connecting with Pochutla (Puerto Ángel), 22 miles (35 km) west, and Puerto Escondido, 66 miles (106 km), continuing to Acapulco in a long 322 miles (519 km). Allow about three hours to Tehuantepec, an hour and a half to Puerto Escondido, and to Acapulco, a full nine hours' driving time, either direction.

Highway 175, the cross-Sierra connection north with the city of Oaxaca, although paved, is narrow and winding, with few services in the 80-mile stretch between its junction with Hwy. 200 at Pochutla (22 miles west of Crucecita) and Miahuatlán in the Valley of Oaxaca. The road climbs to 9,000 feet into pine-tufted, winter-chilly Chatino and Zapotec country. Be prepared for emergencies. Allow eight hours northbound, seven hours southbound, for the entire 175-mile (282-km) Huatulco-Oaxaca trip.

By Bus

Several long-distance bus lines connect Huatulco with destinations east, west, and north. They depart from small separate terminals in Crucecita, scattered mostly along Calle Gardenia north of the plaza.

Many daily **Cristóbal Colón** first-class buses, terminal located on the corner of Ocotillo, tel. (958) 702-61, connect west with Pochutla (Puerto Ángel) and Puerto Escondido. Buses also connect east with the Salina Cruz and Tehuantepec on the Isthmus, continuing either east to San Cristóbal las Casas and Tapachula in Chiapas, or northwest to Mexico City via Oaxaca and Puebla.

A few **Estrella Blanca** buses, from their terminal, one block farther up the street at the corner of Palo Verde, tel. (958) 701-03, connect

west with Pinotepa Nacional, via Pochutla and Puerto Escondido, and east with Salina Cruz.

A few second- and first-class **Estrella del Valle** and **Autobuses Oaxaca-Pacífico** buses connect daily with Oaxaca via Pochutla, from Jazmin, corner Sabali, nine blocks north of the plaza, tel. (958) 701-93.

OAXACA

The Valley of Oaxaca is really three valleys, which diverge, like the thumb, index finger, and middle finger of a hand, from a single strategic point. Aztec conquerors called that hilltop spot Huaxyacac (oo-AHSH-yah-kahk, "Point of the Guaje") for a forest of pod-bearing trees that once carpeted its slopes. The Spanish, who founded the city at the foot of the hill, shifted that name to the more-pronounceable Oaxaca (wah-HAH-kah).

The people of the Valley of Oaxaca, walled in by mountains from the rest of Mexico, both benefit and suffer from their long isolation. They are poor but proud inheritors of rich traditions that live on despite 300 years of Spanish occupation.

A large proportion of Oaxacans are pure native Mexicans and speak one of dozens of languages. Significant numbers speak no Spanish at all. Even in the valley around Oaxaca city itself they make up a sizable fraction of the people. Far out in the country, they *are* the people. Mostly speaking dialects of Zapotec or Mixtec, they harvest their corn for tortillas and their maguey for *pulque* and *aguardiente* (fire water). They spin their wool, hoe their vegetables, then go to market and sit beside their piles of blankets and mounds of onions, wondering if their luck is going to change.

HISTORY

Before Columbus
Evidence of human prehistory litters the riverbottoms and hillsides of the Valley of Oaxaca. Cave remains near the ancient city-state of Mitla tell of hunters who lived there as long as 8,000 years ago. Several thousand years later, their descendants, heavily influenced by the mysterious Olmecs of the Gulf coast, were carving gods and glyphs on stone monuments in the Valley of

Oaxaca. Around 600 B.C., people speaking a Zapotec mother tongue, similarly influenced by the Olmecs, founded Monte Albán on a mountaintop above the present city of Oaxaca.

Monte Albán ruled the Valley of Oaxaca for more than a millennium, climaxing as a sophisticated metropolis of perhaps 40,000, controlling a large and populous area of southern Mexico and enjoying diplomatic and trade relations with distant kingdoms. But, for reasons unknown, Monte Albán declined to a shadow of its former glory by A.D. 1000.

Mixtec-speaking people filled the vacuum. They took over Monte Albán, using it mostly as a burial ground. Their chiefs divided up the Valley of Oaxaca and ruled from separate feudalistic city-states, such as Mitla, Yagul, Mazatlán, and Zaachila, for hundreds of years.

The Mixtecs in turn gave way to the Aztecs whose invading warriors crossed the mountains and threatened Oaxaca during the 1440s. In 1456 the Aztecs established a fort on the hill of Huaxyacac (now called Cerro del Fortín), overlooking the present city of Oaxaca, ruling their restive Zapotec and Mixtec subjects for only two generations. On 21 November 1521, conquistador Francisco de Orozco and his soldiers replaced them on the hill of Huaxyacac scarcely four months after the Spanish tide had flooded the Aztecs' Valley of Mexico homeland.

Conquest and Colonization
Spanish settlers began arriving soon after the conquistadores. At the foot of the hill of Huaxyacac, they laid out their town, which they christened Antequera after the old Spanish Roman city. Soon, however, the settlers came into conflict with Cortés, whom the king had named marquis of the Valley of Oaxaca, and whose entire valley domain surrounded the town. Townspeo-

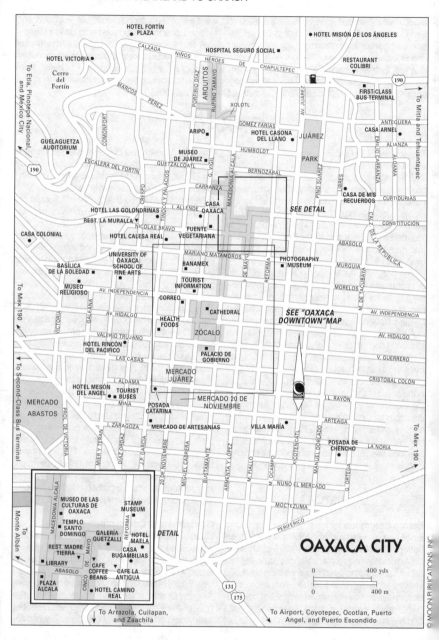

OAXACA CITY

HOTEL FORTÍN PLAZA
HOTEL MISIÓN DE LOS ÁNGELES
HOTEL VICTORIA
CALZADA NIÑOS HÉROES DE CHAPULTEPEC
HOSPITAL SEGURO SOCIAL
RESTAURANT COLIBRI
Cerro del Fortín
PORFIRIO DÍAZ
ARQUITOS
RUFINO TAMAYO
MARCOS PÉREZ
XOLOTL
AV. JUÁREZ
FIRST-CLASS BUS TERMINAL
190
To Etla, Pinotepa Nacional, and México City
COMONFORT
GÓMEZ FARÍAS
ANTEQUERA
CASA ARNEL
190
GUELAGUETZA AUDITORIUM
ARIPO
HOTEL CASONA DEL LLANO
JUÁREZ
ALIANZA
ALDAMA
ESCALERA DEL FORTÍN
MUSEO DE JUÁREZ
HUMBOLDT
PARK
EMILIO CARRANZA
To Mitla and Tehuantepec
QUETZALCOATL
G. VIGIL
BERNOZÁBAL
MACEDONIA ALCALÁ
CASA DE MIS RECUERDOS
LIBRES
PINO SUÁREZ
CRESPO
TINOCO Y PALACIOS
CARRANZA
SEE DETAIL
HOTEL LAS GOLONDRINAS
I. ALLENDE
CASA OAXACA
CONSTITUCIÓN
CASA COLONIAL
REST. LA MURALLA
NICOLAS BRAVO
FUENTE VEGETARIANA
ABASOLO
HOTEL CALESA REAL
UNIVERSITY OF OAXACA SCHOOL OF FINE ARTS
MARIANO MATAMOROS
PHOTOGRAPHY MUSEUM
MURGUIA
CALZ. DE LA REPÚBLICA
BASÍLICA DE LA SOLEDAD
BANAMEX
5 DE MAYO
REFORMA
MORELOS
M. DE TACUBAYA
MUSEO RELIGIOSO
AV. INDEPENDENCIA
TOURIST INFORMATION
AV. INDEPENDENCIA
VICTORIA
GALEANA
AV. HIDALGO
CORREO
SEE "OAXACA DOWNTOWN" MAP
AV. HIDALGO
HEALTH FOODS
CATHEDRAL
To Mex 190
VALERIO TRUJANO
ZÓCALO
V. GUERRERO
HOTEL RINCÓN DEL PACÍFICO
LAS CASAS
PALACIO DE GOBIERNO
CRISTÓBAL COLÓN
To Second-Class Bus Terminal
I. ALDAMA
MERCADO JUÁREZ
HOTEL MESÓN DEL ANGEL
TOURIST BUSES
MINA
MERCADO 20 DE NOVIEMBRE
MooN
J.L. RAYÓN
MERCADO ABASTOS
POSADA CATARINA
ARTEAGA
I. ZARAGOZA
MERCADO DE ARTESANIAS
VILLA MARÍA
XICOTÉNCATL
MANUEL DOBLADO
POSADA DE CHENCHO
LA NORIA
To Mex 190
PROL. DE VICTORIA
MIER Y TERÁN
DÍAZ ORDAZ
J.P. GARCÍA
20 DE NOVIEMBRE
MIGUEL CABRERA
BUSTAMANTE
ARMENTA Y LÓPEZ
M. FIALLO
M. OCAMPO
NUÑO EL MERCADO
G. ORTEGA
MOCTEZUMA
PERIFÉRICO

DETAIL

MACEDONIA ALCALÁ
MUSEO DE LAS CULTURAS DE OAXACA
STAMP MUSEUM
TEMPLO SANTO DOMINGO
GALERÍA QUETZALLI
REFORMA
HOTEL MAELA
REST. MADRE TIERRA
CASA BUGAMBILIAS
DE 5 MAYO
CINCO DE MAYO
LIBRARY
CAFE COFFEE BEANS
CAFE LA ANTIGUA
ABASOLO
PLAZA ALCALÁ
HOTEL CAMINO REAL
To Monte Albán

0   400 yds
0   400 m

To Arrazola, Cuilapan, and Zaachila
131
175
To Airport, Coyotepec, Ocotlan, Puerto Angel, and Puerto Escondido

© MOON PUBLICATIONS, INC.

ple had to petition the queen of Spain for land on which to grow vegetables: they were granted a one-league square in 1532.

For hundreds of years, Cortés's descendants reigned, the church grew fat, the colonists prospered, and the Indians toiled—in cane and corn, in cattle pastures and silk mulberry groves.

Independence, Reform, and the Porfirian Era
In contrast to its neighbors in the state of Guerrero, conservative Oaxaca was a grudging player in the (1810-21) War of Independence. But, as the subsequent republican tide swept the country, local fervor produced a new state constitution, including a state legislature and governmental departments, as well as public instruction and an Institute of Arts and Sciences.

By the 1850s, times had changed. Oaxacans were leading a new national struggle. Benito Juárez, a pure Zapotec native Mexican, was rallying liberal forces in the civil War of the Reforms against the oligarchy that had replaced colonial rule. Born in Guelatao, north of the valley, Juárez at age 12 was an orphan sheepherder. A Catholic priest, struck by the boy's intelligence, brought him to the city as a servant and taught him Spanish in preparation for the priesthood.

Instead, Benito became a lawyer. He hung out his shingle in Oaxaca, first as a defender of the poor, then state legislator, governor, chief justice, and finally the president of Mexico. In his honor, the city's official name was again changed—to Oaxaca de Juárez—in 1872.

In 1861, after winning the three-year civil war, Juárez's Reformista forces had their victory snatched away. France, taking advantage of the United States's preoccupation with its own civil war, invaded Mexico and installed an Austrian Hapsburg prince as Emperor Maximilian of Mexico.

It took Juárez five years to prevail against Maximilian and his conservative Mexican backers. Although Maximilian and Juárez paradoxically shared many of the same liberal ideas, Juárez had Maximilian executed after his defeat and capture in 1867. Juárez bathed Mexico in enlightenment as he promulgated his "Laws of the Reform" (which remain essentially in force). Although the country rewarded him with reelection, he died of exhaustion in 1871.

Another Oaxacan of native Mexican descent, General Porfirio Díaz, vowed to carry Juárez's banner. Díaz, the hero who defeated the French in the battle of Puebla on Cinco de Mayo (5 May) of 1862, was elected president in 1876. *"No Reelección"* was his campaign cry. He subsequently ruled Mexico for 34 years.

Under Díaz's "Order and Progress," Mexico, and to a lesser degree, Oaxaca, was modernized at great human cost. As railroads, factories, and mines mushroomed, property ownership increasingly became concentrated among rich Mexicans and their foreign friends. Smashed protest marches, murdered opposition leaders, and rigged elections returned Díaz to office time and again.

Modern Oaxaca
But Díaz couldn't last forever. The revolution that ousted him in 1911 has, in theory, never ceased. Now, the PRI, the Institutional Revolutionary Party, presides over a uniquely imperfect Mexican form of democracy. Under three generations of PRI rule, the lives of native Oaxacans have improved gradually. Although Indian families have now go to government health centers and more of their children attend government rural schools, the price for doing so is to become less Indian and more Mexican.

Times in the Valley of Oaxaca nevertheless seem to be getting gradually better. In the late 1980s, UNESCO recognized Oaxaca as one of several world sites belonging to the "Cultural Patrimony of Mankind." The government took notice and began preparing Oaxaca for an influx of visitors. Museums were built, monuments refurbished, and the venerable buildings restored. Burgeoning tourism during the 1990s has visibly improved the economic well-being of many Oaxaca families.

Increased international and national awareness seems to have contributed to other improvements. Some longstanding grievances are being recognized. In 1995, moderate PRI governor Diodoro Carrasco Altamirano pushed through an unprecedented "Usos y Costumbres" law, which legalized Oaxacan native rights to their indigenous language and their traditional, town-meeting form of government.

Nevertheless, by developed-world standards, most Oaxaca city families remain very poor. The political system, moreover, is far from perfect. Police brutality, bribes of public officials, vote-buying and murder of opposition community activists still continue to occur, but hopefully, with gradually diminishing frequency.

CITY SIGHTS

Getting Oriented

The streets of Oaxaca (pop. 350,000, elev. 5,110 feet, 1,778 meters) still run along the same simple north-south grid the city fathers laid out in 1529. If you stand at the center of the old *zócalo* and look out toward the *catedral* across the Av. Hidalgo, you will be looking north. Diagonally left, to the northwest, you'll see the smaller plaza, **Alameda de León,** and directly beyond, in the distance, the historic hill of Huaxyacac, now called **Cerro del Fortín.**

Along the base of that hill the Pan American Hwy. (National Hwy. 190) runs generally east-west through the northern suburbs. Turn around and you'll see the porticoed facade of the **Palacio de Gobierno,** where Oaxaca's governor tends to the state's business. Half a mile behind that (although you can't see it from the *zócalo*) the *periférico* peripheral boulevard loops around the town's south end. There it passes the yawning but oft-dry wash of the **Río Atoyac** and the sprawling **Mercado Abastos** market and second-class bus terminal on the southwest. Finally, if you find a clear vantage point you'll see the hill of **Monte Albán** looming 1,000 feet (450 meters) above the southwest horizon.

A Walk around Town

The venerable restored downtown buildings and the streets, some converted to traffic-free malls, make a delightful strolling ground for discovering traditional Mexico at its best. The *zócalo* itself sometimes seems to be a place of slow, leisurely motion, perfect for sitting at one of many sidewalk cafés and watching the world glide by.

Step to the *zócalo*'s south side and give the guards at the front door of the **Palacio de Gobierno** a cheery *buenos dias* or *buenas tardes* and step under the entrance arch. Straight ahead, across the courtyard, you'll see the main mural, by Arturo Bustos, completed during the 1980s. It depicts the struggles of Oaxaca's in-

dependence, reform, and revolutionary heroes. In the center is Oaxaca's favorite son and Mexico's revered *presidente,* Benito Juárez, and his wife, Margarita Maza. Below them is Juárez's *reformista* cabinet (notice the young, restive, General Porfirio Díaz with the sword on the right), which struggled through two bloody wars, finally emerging, with Juárez, triumphant in 1867.

Head to the *zócalo*'s opposite, north side, for a look at the present **cathedral.** It replaced the 1550 original, demolished by an earthquake in 1696. Finished in 1733, with appropriately twin bell towers, the present cathedral is distinguished by its Greek marble main altar, where a polished Italian bronze Virgin of the Assumption is being drawn upward to the cloud-tipped heavenly domain of the Holy Spirit (the dove) and God (the sunburst). Flanking opposite sides of the altar, notice the glass images of noble, bearded St. Peter and St. Paul.

Of considerable historical interest is the **Santa Cruz de Huatulco** ("Holy Cross of Huatulco"), enshrined in a chapel at the middle, south (right) side of the nave. The cross, about two feet high, is one of four made in 1612 by Oaxaca bishop Juan Cervantes from the original mysterious cross worshipped by the natives on the southern Oaxaca coast long before the conquest. (See the **Bays of Huatulco** section of this chapter.) An explanation, in Spanish, gives three versions of the story of the cross, which, the natives reported to the conqueror Pedro Alvarado in 1522, was erected long before by a strange, white-robed holy man, who soon departed and never returned. Bishop Cervantes sent the three other copies, respectively, to authorities at Santa María Huatulco town, Mexico City, and Rome.

Continue behind the cathedral north along the tranquil **Andador de Macedonio Alcalá** pedestrian mall, named after the composer of the Oaxacan hymn "Dios Nunca Muere" ("God Never Dies"). Paved with Oaxaca green stone in 1985 and freed of auto traffic, the mall connects the *zócalo* with a number of distinguished Oaxaca monuments.

Among them is the **Teatro Alcalá,** at 900 Independencia, tel. (951) 629-69 (from the back of the cathedral head right one block along Independencia to the corner of Independencia and 5 de Mayo). Christened by a 1909 opening per-

OAXACA CITY DOWNTOWN

MARIANO MATAMOROS

ARTE DE OAXACA

HOTEL CAMINO REAL

LA MANO MAGICA

MURGUIA

U.S. CONSUL

CASA DE CANTERA

ARTESANIAS DEL PATRÓN

MUSEO RUFINO TAMAYO

BANAMEX

PANADERÍA BAMBY

NATIONAL PAWN SHOP

CASA DE CORTÉS

WOMEN ARTESANS OF THE REGIONS OF OAXACA (M.A.R.O.)

HOTEL PRINCIPAL

AV. MORELOS

BIBLIOTECA

CITY TURISMO

RESTAURANT CATEDRAL

BANCOMER

PALACIO DE LAS GEMAS

TEMPLO SAN FELIPE NERI

FEDERAL-STATE TOURIST INFORMATION

COFFEE BEANS

HOTEL ANTONIO'S

COMPUTEL

BANCO SERFIN

RESTAURANT QUICKLY

PASTELERÍA LA VASCONIA

TELEGRAFO

BANCO SANTANDER MEXICANO

CORREO

AV. INDEPENDENCIA

OAXAKOLOR

PLAZA ALAMEDA DE LEÓN

CATHEDRAL

REST. EL SAGRARIO

TEATRO MACEDONIO ALCALÁ

HOTEL MONTE ALBÁN

LIBRERIA CRYSTAL

FARMACIA HIDALGO

MONEY EXCHANGE

REST. EL MESON

RESTAURANT LOS CHALOTES

FOTO FIGUEROA

REST. MI CASITA

PRIMAVERA

HOTEL MARQUÉS DEL VALLE

BANAMEX

REST. CASA DE LA ABUELA

AMERICAN EXPRESS

AV. HIDALGO

LA CAFETERÍA

HOTEL FRANCIA

HOTEL SEÑORIAL

PLAZA DE ARMAS

CAFÉ AMARANTOS

REST. ASADOR VASCO

HOTEL LAS ROSAS

VALERIO TRUJANO

CAFÉ-BAR DEL JARDÍN

CAFÉ TERRANOVA

RESTAURANT DEL VITRAL

HOSTAL SANTA ROSA

PALACIO DE GOBIERNO

CINE MITLA

V. GUERRERO

LIBRERIA UNIVERSITARIA

TEMPLO SAN AGUSTÍN

LA FLOR DE OAXACA

HOTEL GALA

LAS CASAS

CRISTÓBAL COLÓN

MERCADO JUÁREZ

0   100 yds

0   100 m

I. ALDAMA

TEMPLO SAN JUAN DE DIOS

MERCADO 20 DE NOVIEMBRE

L.L. RAYÓN

© MOON PUBLICATIONS, INC.

formance of *Aida*, the Alcalá houses a treasury of Romantic-era art. Above the foyer, a sumptuous marble staircase rises to a bas-relief medallion allegorizing the triumph of art. Also take a look around the theater's gallery of paintings of Miguel Cabrera (1695-1768), a native Zapotec who rose to become New Spain's renowned baroque painter.

Continuing north along the Alcalá street mall, you soon pass the so-called **Casa de Cortés,** now the **Museo de Arte Contemporaneo de Oaxaca,** Macedonio Alcalá 202, tel. (951) 428-

18, open Wed.-Mon. 10:30 a.m.-8 p.m. Past the bookstore (mostly Spanish but some English-language history, art, and guidebooks), exhibitions feature works of local and nationally known modern artists. Although named popularly for Hernán Cortés, the building is at least a hundred years too new for Cortés to have lived there. The coat of arms on the facade above the door reveals it to have been the 17th-century home of a different Oaxaca family.

Continue uphill and, at Murguia, detour right again, to the **Ex-Convento de Santa Catalina,**

Oaxaca stonemason

the second-oldest convent in New Spain, founded in 1576. Although the quarters of the first initiates were spare, the convent grew into a sprawling chapel and cloister complex decorated by fountains and flower-strewn gardens. Juárez's reforms drove the sisters out in 1862; the building has since served as city hall, school, and movie theater. Now, it stands beautifully restored as the Hotel Camino Real. Note the native-motif original murals that the renovation revealed, on interior walls.

Return to the Alcalá street mall and continue another block uphill to Oaxaca's pride, the **Centro Cultural de Santo Domingo,** which contains two main parts, side by side: the **Museum of the Cultures of Oaxaca** and the **Church and Ex-Convent of Santo Domingo,** both behind the broad Plaza Santo Domingo maguey garden and pedestrian square.

Inside, Santo Domingo church (open daylight hours, except 1-4 p.m.) glows with a wealth of art. Above the antechamber spreads the entire genealogical tree of Santo Domingo de Guzmán, starting with Mother Mary and weaving through a score of noblemen and women to the saint himself over the front door.

Continuing inside, the soaring, Sistine Chapel-like nave glitters with saints, cherubs, and Bible-story paintings. The altar climaxes in a host of cherished symbols—the Last Supper, sheaves of grain, loaves and fishes, Jesus and Peter on the Sea of Galilee—in a riot of gold leaf.

Continue next door, to the museum, open Tues.-Sun. 10 a.m.-8 p.m., which occupies the completely restored convent section of the Santo Domingo church. Exhibitions begin on the bottom floor in rooms adjacent to the massive convent cloister, restored in 1998 to all of its original austere glory. A downstairs highlight is the long-neglected but now safely preserved **Library of Francisco Burgoa,** which you can walk right through and examine some of the more important works on display. The collection, 23,000 titles in all, includes its earliest work, a 1484 commentary on the works of Aristotle by Juan Versor.

A Museo sign points you upstairs, via a glitteringly restored, towering domed chamber, adorned overhead with the Dominican founding fathers, presided over by Santo Domingo de Guzmán himself.

It's hard not to be impressed by the seeming miles of meticulously prepared displays, divided into about a dozen long rooms covering respective historical periods. One room exhibits priceless Monte Albán-era artifacts, including one of the most important of the original so-called *danzantes,* with the typically mutilated sex organs. The climax comes in the Tesoros of Tomb 7 room, where the entire gilded trove discovered at Monte Albán Tomb 7 is on display. Besides a small mountain of gold and turquoise ornaments, notice the small but masterfully executed golden head of Ecéchatl, god of the wind, made eerie by the omission of facial skin over the jaw, to produce a nightmarishly skeletal piece of jewelry.

Back outside, step across Alcalá, a few doors uphill, into the rust-colored old building, now tastefully restored as the museum of the **Instituto de Artes Gráficos de Oaxaca,** tel. (951) 669-80. Inside, displays exhibit mostly contemporary etchings, wood-block prints, and paintings by artists of both national and international renown. Exhibits change approximately monthly; open daily except Tuesday 9:30 a.m.-8 p.m.

Head west one block (along the Plazuela Carmen mall, off Alcalá across from the museum) to 609 Garcia Vigil and the **Casa de Juárez** museum, tel. (951) 618-60. The modest but beautifully restored house was the home of Juárez's benefactor, priest and bookbinder Father Antonio Salanueva. Rooms decorated with homey mid-19th-century furnishings realistically illustrate the life and times of a man as revered in Mexico as is his contemporary, Abraham Lincoln, north of the border. Open Tues.-Sat. 10 a.m.-7 p.m.

Sights West and South of the *Zócalo*

The **Museo Arte Prehispánico de Rufino Tamayo,** 503 Morelos, tel. (951) 647-50, two blocks west and north of the *zócalo,* exhibits the brilliant pre-Columbian artifact collection of celebrated artist Rufino Tamayo (1899-1991). Displays include hosts of animal motifs—Colima dogs, parrots, ducks, snakes—whimsically crafted into polychrome vases, bowls, and urns. Open Monday and Wed.-Sat. 10 a.m.-2 p.m. and 4-7 p.m., Sunday 10 a.m.-3 p.m.

Continue three blocks west, past the University of Oaxaca School of Fine Arts and the airy Plaza of Dances, to the baroque **Basilica de Nuestra Señora de la Soledad.** Inside, the Virgin of Solitude, the patron of Oaxaca, stands atop the altar with her five-pound solid golden crown, encrusted with 600 diamonds.

Step into the **Museo Religioso,** at the downhill side of the church, rear end. A multitude of objects of adornment—shells, paintings, jewelry—crowd cabinets, shelves, and aisles of musty rooms. Large stained-glass panels tell of the images of Jesus and the Virgin that arrived miraculously in 1620, eventually becoming Oaxaca's patron symbols. Open Mon.-Sat. 9 a.m.-2 p.m. and 4-7 p.m., Sunday 9 a.m.-2 p.m.

Return to the vicinity of the *zócalo* and the traditional **Juárez Market,** which occupies the one-block square that begins just one block southwest of the *zócalo.* Stroll around for fun and perhaps a bargain in the honeycomb of traditional leather, textile, and clothing stalls.

ACCOMMODATIONS

Oaxaca offers a wide range of good hotels. Air-conditioning is not particularly necessary in temperate Oaxaca, although hot-water showers (furnished by all lodgings listed below) feel especially comfy during cool winter mornings and evenings. The less expensive hotels, which generally do not accept credit cards, are mostly near the colorful, traffic-free *zócalo.* With one exception, Oaxaca's plush, resort-style hostelries dot the northern edge of town. During holidays and festivals (Easter week, July, August, late Oct.-early Nov., 15 Dec.-4 Jan.) many Oaxaca hotels raise their prices 20-30% above the numbers listed below.

Hotels near the *Zócalo*

Along with an enviable *zócalo* location, the **Hotel Señorial,** Portal de Flores 6, Oaxaca, Oaxaca 68000, tel. (951) 639-33, fax 636-68, provides clean rooms, efficient management, a reliable restaurant, and an inviting (but unheated) swimming pool and patio. The hotel's only drawback is that many of its interior rooms have louvered (non-soundproof) communal air shaft windows and hallway transoms. This, especially during high fiesta seasons, results in noise that can't be shut out. Light sleepers should bring earplugs, especially on weekends and holidays, when the popular Señorial will be brimming with guests. The 107 rooms rent for about $34 s, $41 d, $46 t, with TV, limited wheelchair access, phones, and parking $3 extra; credit cards are *not* accepted.

A number of good budget to moderately priced hotels cluster beside or behind the Hotel Señorial, within a block or two of the *zócalo.* Moving generally clockwise around the *zócalo,* first comes the petite **Hotel Las Rosas,** Trujano 112, Oaxaca, Oaxaca 68000, tel. (951) 422-17, behind the Señorial and half a block from the *zócalo.* Climb a flight of stairs to the small lobby, relatively tranquil by virtue of its second-floor location. Beyond that, a double tier of rooms surrounds a homey inner patio. Adjacent to the lobby is a cheery sitting room with big, beautiful tropical aquarium, and a TV, usually kept at subdued volume. The rooms themselves, although plainly furnished, are clean and tiled (except

OAXACA ACCOMMODATIONS

Accommodations (area code 951, postal code 68000 unless otherwise noted) are listed in increasing order of approximate high-season, double-room rates.

Hotel Monte Albán, Alameda de León 1, tel. 627-77, $22

Hotel Las Rosas, Trujano 112, tel. 422-17, $27

Hotel Las Golondrinas, at Tinoco y Palacios 411, tel. 432-98 or tel./fax 421-26, $27

Hóstal Santa Rosa, Trujano 201, tel. 467-14 or 467-15, $28

Hotel Antonio's, Independencia 601, tel. 672-27, fax 636-72, $28

Hotel Rivera del Ángel, Mina 518, tel. 666-66, fax 454-05, $40

Hotel Señorial, Portal de Flores 6, tel. 639-33, fax 636-68, $41

Hotel Gala, Bustamante 103, tel. 422-51 or 413-05, fax 636-60, $44

Hotel Marques del Valle, Portal Clavería, P.O. Boxes 13 and 35, tel. 406-88 or 634-74, fax 699-61, $50

Hotel Fortín Plaza, Av. Venus 118, Colonia Estrella, Oaxaca 68040, tel. 577-77, fax 513-28, $70

Hotel Victoria, Km 545, Carretera Panamericana, Oaxaca 68070, tel. 526-33, fax 524-11, $85

Hotel Misión de Los Angeles, Calz. Porfirio Díaz 102, Oaxaca 68050, tel. 515-00, fax 516-80, $100

Camino Real, Calle 5 de Mayo 300, tel. 606-11, or (800) 7-CAMINO (722-6466) from the U.S. and Canada, fax 607-32, Web site: www.caminoreal.com, $200

and Monte Albán. Credit cards not accepted.

Return back to the immediate *zócalo* vicinity, to the newly renovated **Hóstal Santa Rosa,** a block from the *zócalo's* southwest corner, at Trujano 201, Oaxaca, Oaxaca 68000, tel. (951) 467-14 or 467-15. The streetside lobby leads past an airy restaurant to the rooms, recessed along a meandering inner passageway and courtyard. Inside, the rooms are very clean, comfortably furnished, and decorated in pastels. Rents, although raised, continue to be reasonable, usually at $22 s, $28 d, except during festivals and holidays, when they might rise as much as 50%. With TV, phones, parking, limited wheelchair access, and an in-house travel-tour agency included, but no credit cards accepted.

Move two and a half blocks farther north to the newly renovated, authentically colonial **Hotel Antonio's,** at the corner of Independencia. Here you'll be in the middle of it all, with colorful streetfront ambience, a restaurant, and more than a bit of old Mexico charm within its quiet inner courtyard. It's at Independencia 601, Oaxaca, Oaxaca 68000, tel. (951) 672-27, fax 636-72. The 15 thoughtfully decorated, comfortable, and clean rooms rent for about $22 s, $28 d, and $33 t; parking not included, and credit cards not accepted.

Head one block east to the southwest corner of leafy Alameda de León square in front of the cathedral and the very popular **Hotel Monte Albán,** Alameda de León 1, Oaxaca, Oaxaca 68000, tel. (951) 627-77. The hotel centers on a big patio/restaurant that hosts folk-dance shows nightly 8:30-10 p.m. During the first evening this could be understandably exciting, but after a week you might feel as if you were living in a

some bathrooms, which could use an extra scrubbing). Prices, moreover, at about $22 s, $27 d, $31 t, are reasonable. No credit cards, parking, or wheelchair access.

Hotel Rivera del Ángel, at Mina 518, Oaxaca, Oaxaca 68000, tel. (951) 666-66, fax 454-05, offers several advantages. Downstairs, an airy, shiny, but busy lobby and restaurant area offers nothing special, but through the lobby windows, feast your eyes on the inviting big blue pool and sunny central patio. Upstairs, moreover, you'll find the rooms semideluxe, clean, spacious, and comfortable, many with private terraces overlooking the pool patio. The hotel's main drawback is street noise, from buses along Mina. Ask for a *tranquilo* off-street room. Rentals run about $20 s, $30 d, low season, $30 and $40 high, with TV, fans, phones, restaurant, parking, travel agency, and tour buses to Mitla

three-ring circus. The 20 rooms, which surround the patio in two tiers, are genuinely colonial, with soaring beamed ceilings, big bedsteads, and the requisite few cockroaches per room. (When a cockroach was pointed out, the bellman promptly crushed it underfoot and nudged it into a corner with the toe of his shoe.) For such a nicely located hotel, rates run a reasonable $17 s, $22 d, and $28 t; credit cards accepted.

For a fancier option, go to the old standby, the **Hotel Marques del Valle** on the north side of the zócalo, Portal Clavería, P.O. Boxes 13 and 35, Oaxaca, Oaxaca 68000, tel. (951) 406-88 or 634-74, fax 699-61. Managers have recently restored the lobby with bright chandeliers, mirrors, and shiny dark wood paneling. Upstairs, however, massive wrought-iron fixtures cast gloomy nighttime shadows through the soaring, balconied central atrium. The 96 rooms, nevertheless, retain their original 1940s polish, with handcrafted cedar furniture and marble-finished baths. Deluxe rooms have TV, carpets, and some balconies looking out on to the zócalo. Rooms rent for about $42 s or $50 d, $63 t, with restaurant/bar, limited wheelchair access, and credit cards accepted.

The '80s-mod **Hotel Gala,** Bustamante 103, Oaxaca, Oaxaca 68000, tel. (951) 422-51 or 413-05, fax 636-60, half a block south of the zócalo's southeast corner, is for those who want comfortable, modern-standard deluxe accommodations at relatively moderate prices. Rooms, although tastefully decorated and carpeted, are small. Get one of the quieter ones away from the street. The 36 rooms rent for about $37 s, $44 d, and $51 for junior suite; credit cards are accepted. With phones, TV, fans, and a restaurant, but parking is not included.

Oaxaca's classiest hotel, the **Camino Real,** Calle 5 de Mayo 300, Oaxaca, Oaxaca 68000, tel. (951) 606-11, or (800) 7-CAMINO (722-6466) from the U.S. and Canada, fax 607-32, occupies the lovingly restored exconvent of Santa Catalina, four blocks north, one block east of the zócalo. Flowery secluded courtyards, massive arched portals, soaring beamed ceilings, a big blue pool and impeccable bar and restaurant service combine to create a refined but relaxed old-world atmosphere. Rooms are large, luxurious, and exquisitely decorated with antiques and folk crafts and furnished with mod-

ern-standard conveniences. If street noise is likely to bother you, get a room away from bustling Calles Abasolo and 5 de Mayo. Rates run about $175 s, $200 d; with phones and TV, but parking not included; credit cards accepted.

Although a six-block walk (four north, two west) away from the zócalo, **Hotel Las Golondrinas,** at Tinoco y Palacios 411, Oaxaca, Oaxaca 68000, tel. (951) 432-98 or tel./fax 421-26, is nearly always full. Step inside and you'll immediately see why. Rooms enfold an intimate garden, lovingly decorated with festoons of hothouse verdure. Leafy bananas, bright bougainvillea, and platoons of potted plants line pathways, which meander past an intimate fountain patio in one corner and lead to an upstairs panoramic vista sundeck on the other. The care also shows in the rooms, which are immaculate and adorned with spartan-chic pastel earthtoned curtains and bedspreads and natural wood furniture. Guests additionally enjoy use of laundry facilities, a TV sitting room, a shelf of paperback books, and a breakfast restaurant 8-10 a.m. All this for only about $22 s, $27 d, and $31 t. In addition to the 27 regular rooms, two honeymoon suites rent for about $30 and $33, respectively.

North-Side Luxury Hotels
Three upscale suburban hostelries dot the north side of Hwy. 190. The **Hotel Victoria,** Km 545, Carretera Panamericana, Oaxaca, Oaxaca 68070, tel. (951) 526-33, fax 524-11, choicest of the three, spreads over a lush hillside garden of panoramic vistas and luxurious resort ambience. The '50s-style lobby extends from an upstairs view bar downhill past a terrace restaurant to a flame tree and jacaranda-decorated pool patio. As for rooms, the best ones are in the newer view wing detached from the lobby building. There, the junior suites are spacious, comfortable, and luxuriously appointed, with double-size bathrooms and private view balconies. The 150 rooms, bungalows, and junior suites rent for about $85, $110, and $130 d, respectively; with TV, phones, a/c, tennis court, nightly live music, handicrafts shop, and parking; credit cards accepted.

The **Hotel Fortín Plaza,** Av. Venus 118, Colonia Estrella, Oaxaca, Oaxaca 68040, tel. (951) 577-77, fax 513-28, next to the highway two blocks downhill, is hard to miss, especially at night. Its blue-lit six-story profile tops everything else in town. The hotel offers the usual modern facilities—restaurant/bar, pool, live music, disco, and parking—in a compact, attractively designed layout. Upstairs, guests enjoy deluxe, clean, and comfortable rooms with private view balconies (whose tranquillity is reduced, however, by considerable highway noise). Room rates run about $55 s and $70 d, with phones, TV, and parking; credit cards accepted. Discounts are sometimes negotiable.

Hotel Misión de Los Angeles, Calz. Porfirio Díaz 102, Oaxaca, Oaxaca 68050, tel. (951) 515-00, fax 516-80, half a mile farther east (on the prolongation of Juárez), rambles like a hacienda through a spreading oak- and acacia-dotted garden-park. After a rough few days on the sightseeing circuit, it's an ideal place to kick back beside the big pool or enjoy a set or two of tennis. The rooms and suites are spacious and comfortable, with big garden-view windows or balconies. Upper rooms are quieter and more private. The 162 rooms and suites rent from about $100 d for standard, $130 d for junior suite; with phones, parking, disco, restaurant, and a folkloric performance; credit cards accepted.

Trailer Parks and Camping

Oaxaca has a pair of longtime trailer and camping parks. First choice goes to the **Oaxaca Trailer Park,** at the far northeast side of town, 900 Av. Violetas, Oaxaca, Oaxaca 68000, tel. (951) 527-96. The 100 all-hookup spaces include showers, toilets, laundromat, recreation hall, a fence, and a night watchman. Spaces rent for about $7 per night without a/c power, $12 with, with discounts for extended stays. Pets okay. Get there by turning left at Violetas, several blocks east of the first-class bus terminal on Hwy. 190. The street is marked by the big green Col Reforma sign over the highway and the red-white-and-blue Pepsi-marked building on the left corner across the street. Continue uphill six long blocks to the trailer park on the left.

The **Rosa Isabel trailer park,** at Km 539, Carretera Nacional, Colonia Loma del Pueblo, Oaxaca, Oaxaca 68000, tel. (951) 272-10 or 607-70, is on Hwy. 190, on the northwest (Mexico City) side of town in the Loma del Pueblo

Nuevo suburb. It features hookups, toilets, showers, and a recreation hall, with the Brenamiel tennis and sports club nearby. The 50 spaces rent for about $10 a night, with discounts for extended stays. Get there, on Hwy. 190, by turning right (heading southeast, into town) about a half mile past the big Hotel Villas Del Sol sign.

FOOD

Snacks, Foodstalls, and Coffeehouses

During fiestas, snack stalls along Hidalgo at the cathedral-front Alameda de León square abound in local delicacies. Choices include *tlayudas,* giant crisp tortillas loaded with avocado, tomato, onions, and cheese, and *empanadas de amarillo,* huge tacos stuffed with cheese and red salsa. For dessert, have a *buñuelo,* a crunchy, honey-soaked wheat tortilla.

At nonfiesta times, you can still fill up on the sizzling fare of taco, *torta,* hamburger, and hot dog (eat 'em only when they are served hot) stands that set up in the same vicinity.

For very economical, wholesome local-style fare, go to the acre of foodstalls inside the **Mercado 20 de Noviembre,** two blocks south of the *zócalo's* southwest corner. Here, adventurous eaters will be in heaven among a wealth of succulent *chiles rellenos;* piquant *moles* (moh-LAYS); fat, banana leaf-wrapped *tamales Oaxaqueños;* and savory *sopas* and *guisados* (soups and stews). Insist, however, that your selection be served hot.

The airy, tranquil interior patio of **Hostería Alcalá** at Alcalá 307 is ideal for a relaxing refreshment or lunch break from sightseeing along Alcalá mall. For coffee and dessert, you have a number of downtown choices, notably **Coffee Beans,** at Cinco de Mayo 114, couple of blocks north of the *zócalo,* and its second location, at Cinco de Mayo 400, five blocks north of the *zócalo.* Alternatively, sample the excellent coffee and baked goods at **Restaurant Madre Tierra,** across the street at 5 de Mayo 411, or **Restaurant La Antigua** a block west, at Reforma 401, just above Abasolo.

For baked goods by themselves, a trio of good carry-out bakeries stand within a stone's throw of the *zócalo.* First, try the sweet offerings of **Pastelería Frances** on Trujano, half a block west from the Del Jardín café *zócalo* corner, open Mon.-Sat. 7 a.m.-8 p.m., Sunday 11:30 a.m.-7 p.m. Continue clockwise, north of the *zócalo* a block, to **Panadería Bamby,** at the northwest corner of G. Vigil and Morelos, open Mon.-Sat. 7 a.m.-9 p.m. Finally, stop by the **Pastelería La Vasconia,** a block east of the *zócalo,* at Independencia 907, between Cinco de Mayo and Reforma, open daily 8 a.m.-9 p.m.

Cafés and Restaurants around the *Zócalo*

Oaxaca visitors enjoy many good eateries right on or near the *zócalo*. In fact, you could spend your entire Oaxaca time enjoying the fare of the several *zócalo*-front sidewalk cafés. Of the seven cafés, five offer recommendable food and service. Moving counterclockwise from the northwest corner, they are: Primavera, La Cafetería, Del Jardín, Terranova, and Amarantos. First place overall goes to the pricier upper-class **Terranova,** at the southeast corner, for its professionally prepared and served lunch and dinner entrées. For the best breakfasts, however, go to **Primavera,** at the diagonally opposite corner. **La Cafetería** and **Del Jardín** (with loud marimba music most nights) rate generally good for food, but their service is spotty. While service at **Amarantos** is usually good, its food is only fair. They all are open long hours, from about 8 a.m.-midnight, and serve from very recognizable menus.

The one drawback of *zócalo*-level eating is the persistent flow of vendors, which can be unnerving. If, however, you refuse (or bargain for) their offerings gently and with humor, you might begin to accept and enjoy them as part of the entire colorful scene. (If they really get to you, best take an inside table, or retreat to the one restaurant that shoos them away, the Terranova.)

Serious-eating longtimers return to **El Asador Vasco** restaurant on the second-floor balcony above the Restaurant Jardín, Portal Flores 11. The menu specializes in hearty Basque-style country cooking: salty, spicy, and served in the decor of a medieval Iberian manor house. Favorites include fondues (bean, sausage, and mushroom), garlic soup, salads, veal tongue, oysters in hot sauce, and the *carnes asadas* (roast meats) house specialties. Open daily 1-11 p.m. Expensive; expect to pay about $20 per person.

Longtimers swear by the Oaxacan specialties at **Casa de la Abuela,** at the *zócalo*'s northwest corner, above the Primavera café. Here, you can enjoy tasty, professionally prepared regional dishes and airy *zócalo* vistas from the balcony. Open daily 9 a.m.-9 p.m. Call (951) 635-44 for reservations and a good view table. Moderate.

For a tasty regional-style meal or snack, try **La Casita** around the corner, upstairs, on Hidalgo, at the plaza Alameda de León, Hidalgo 612, tel. (951) 629-17. You can order either a hearty *comida corrida* multicourse lunch or one of the tasty "mystery" offerings, such as tortilla, "cat," or "nothing" soup. Open daily 11 a.m.-7:30 p.m. Moderate.

For many loyal local upper-class patrons, **Restaurant Catedral,** two blocks north of the *zócalo,* at Garcia Vigil 105, corner of Morelos, tel. (951) 632-85, serves as a tranquil refuge from the street hubbub. Here, the refined ambience—music playing softly in the background, tables set around an airy, intimate fountain patio crowned by the blue Oaxaca sky above—is half the show. The finale is the very correct service and quality food for breakfast, lunch, or supper. The Aguilar family owners are especially proud of their *moles* (MOH-lays), sauces that flavor their house specialties. These include fillets, both meat and fish, and regional dishes such as banana leaf-wrapped *tamales Oaxaqueños*. It's open daily 8 a.m.-midnight. Moderate-expensive.

Back on Hidalgo, just past the *zócalo*'s northeast corner, the spotless little *fonda* **El Mesón** specializes in a lunch buffet, at Hidalgo 805, tel. (951) 627-29. For about $3, you can select your fill of fresh fruit, salads, chili beans, and several entrées, including roast beef and pork, chicken, *moles,* tacos, tamales, and enchiladas. Open daily 8 a.m.-11:30 p.m. Budget.

More good eating, in a genteel but relaxed atmosphere, awaits you at the very popular **Restaurant El Sagrario,** around the corner behind the church at 120 Valdivieso, tel. (951) 403-03. Here, mostly local, youngish upper-class customers enjoy either a club/bar atmosphere (lower level), pizza parlor booths (middle level), or restaurant tables (upper level). At the restaurant level during the evening, you can best take in the whole scene around you—chattering, upbeat crowd, live guitar, flute, or jazz melodies, elegantly restored colonial details. Then, finally, comes the food: beginning, perhaps, with an appetizer, continuing with a soup or salad, then an international or regional specialty, which you top off with a light dessert and a savory espresso coffee. Open daily 8 a.m.-midnight. Music volume goes up later in the evening. Credit cards accepted. Moderate-expensive.

On the other hand, a legion of American, Canadian, and European budget travelers swear by the no-nonsense **Restaurant Quickly,** half a block farther from the *zócalo,* at 100 Alcalá, tel. (951) 470-76, on the Alcalá pedestrian mall. Once you taste the giant hamburgers, chocolate milk shakes, or pancakes (or veggies, if you prefer), you'll understand why. Open daily 8 a.m.-11 p.m. Budget.

For a completely contrasting culinary experience, walk two blocks east from the *zócalo* along Hidalgo to **Restaurant Los Chalotes,** at M. Fiallo 116, tel. (951) 648-97. Once inside, you begin to believe that you're somewhere in France, and as soon as you see the menu, you're convinced. Here, for example, you can start with *pâté d' chef,* continue with *asperges* sauce Tartare, and finish with *caille* sauce Zarní. Otherwise, you can choose from an equally expertly prepared and served list of soups, salads, fish, and vegetables. Open daily 2-11 p.m. Expensive.

Restaurants and Cafés North of the *Zócalo*

Devotees of light, vegetarian-style cuisine get what they're hungering for at **La Fuente Vegetariana,** at G. Vigil 406, just below Allende, four blocks north, uphill, from the *zócalo,* tel. (951) 617-38. The airy patio sets the tone for breakfast, which you can select from juices, vegetable omelettes, fruit, and granola; for lunch, enjoy a good *comida corrida,* or chicken, cheese, crepes, or pasta. For early supper, pick soup and salad. Open daily 9 a.m.-8 p.m.

Although **Restaurant La Muralla** ("The Wall"), tel. (951) 622-68, is a six-block walk (four north, two west) from the *zócalo* to the corner of N. Bravo and Crespo, your effort will be amply rewarded. Again, after a few minutes inside, as in Restaurant Los Chalotes, above, it's not hard to be convinced that you've been transported to a foreign realm. This time, it's somewhere in the country outside Xian or Guangzhou. Beside

the standard but tastily prepared dishes (such as wonton soup, chicken chow mein, barbecued spareribs), you will be entertained by the occupants of a big, midroom tropical aquarium. Open daily 1-8 p.m.; Visa accepted. Moderate.

Restaurants South of the *Zócalo*

Only a few good sit-down restaurants sprinkle the south *zócalo* neighborhoods. A pair of them, well-known for Oaxacan cuisine, shouldn't be missed.

Local folks strongly recommend the refined country-style **La Flor de Oaxaca,** at Armenta y López 311, a block east, half a block south from the *zócalo*'s southeast corner, tel. (951) 655-22. Here, along with spotless linen and very correct service, you'll get the customary bottomless plate of warm corn tortillas to go with your entrée. The *mole*-smothered regional specialties come mostly in four styles: *con tasajo* (with a thin broiled steak), *con pollo* (chicken), *con cesina* (roast pork), or *sola* (without meat). Besides those, you can choose from an extensive menu of equally flavorful items such as *tamales Oaxaqueños* (wrapped in banana leaves), pork chops, several soups, spaghetti, and much more. Vegetable lovers get started right with their crisp *ensalada mixta* (sliced tomato, cucumber, onions, avocado, and lettuce with vinegar and oil dressing). Open Mon.-Sat. 7:30 a.m.-10 p.m., Sunday 7:30 a.m.-3 p.m. Credit cards accepted. Moderate.

If, however, you hanker for some nouveau variations on the Oaxaca regional theme, go to **Restaurant El Naranjo** ("The Orange Tree"), at Trujano 203, two blocks west of the *zócalo*'s southwest corner. Here, the tranquil, genteel patio sets the tone, and the long, inviting menu tempts the palate. Choose among soups, salads, and Oaxaca's seven *moles,* one for each day of the week. Use them to flavor any one of a host of stuffed chiles, tamales, stewed chicken, roast pork, and much, much more. Open Mon.-Sat. 9 a.m.-9 p.m., tel. (951) 418-78. Moderate.

ENTERTAINMENT AND EVENTS

Around the *Zócalo*

The Oaxaca *zócalo,* years ago relieved of traffic, is ideal ground for spontaneous diversions. A concert or performance seems to be going on nearly every evening. When it isn't, you can run like a kid over the plaza, bouncing a 10-foot-long *aeroglobo* into the air. (Get them from vendors in front of the cathedral.) If you're in a sitting mood, watch the world go by from a *zócalo* sidewalk café. Later, take in the folk-dance performance at the Hotel Monte Albán on the adjacent Plaza Alameda de León, nightly 8:30 a.m.-10 p.m., about $3. After that, return to a *zócalo* café and enjoy the musicians who entertain most every evening until midnight.

Fiestas

There seems to be a festival somewhere in the Valley of Oaxaca every week of the year. Oaxaca's wide ethnic diversity explains much of the celebrating. Each of the groups celebrates its own traditions. Sixteen languages, in hundreds of dialects, are spoken within the state. Authorities recognize around 500 distinct regional costumes.

All of this ethnic ferment focuses in the city during the July **Lunes de Cerro** festival. Known in preconquest times as the Guelaguetza (gay-lah-GAY-tzah, "Offering"), tribes reunited for rituals and dancing in honor of Centeotl, the god of corn. The ceremonies, which climaxed with the sacrifice of a virgin who had been fed hallucinogenic mushrooms, were changed to tamer mixed Christian-native rites by the Catholic Church. Lilies replaced marigolds, the flower of death, and saints sat in for the Indian gods.

Now, for the weeks around the two Mondays following 16 July, the Virgin of Carmen day, Oaxaca is awash with native Mexicans in costume from all seven traditional regions of Oaxaca. The festivities, which include a crafts and agricultural fair, climax with dances and ceremonies at the Guelaguetza auditorium on the Cerro del Fortín hill northwest of the city. Entrance to the Guelaguetza dances runs about $30; bring a hat and sunglasses. Make hotel reservations months ahead of time. For more information, contact the local tourist information office, corner of 5 de Mayo and Morelos two blocks north, one block east from the *zócalo*, tel. (951) 648-28.

Note: If the first Monday after 16 July happens to fall on July 18, the anniversary of Benito Juárez's death, the first Lunes del Cerro shifts to the next succeeding Monday, 25 July.

On the Sunday before the first Lunes del Cerro, Oaxacans celebrate their history and culture at the Plaza de Danzas adjacent to the Virgen de la Soledad church. Events include a big sound, light, and dance show and depictions in tableaux of the four periods of Oaxaca history.

Besides the usual national holidays, Oaxacans celebrate a number of other locally important fiestas. The first day of spring, 21 March, kicks off the **Flower Games** ("Juegos Florales"). Festivities go on for 10 days, including crowning of a festival queen at the Teatro de Alcalá, poetry contests, and performances by renowned artists and the National Symphony.

On the second Monday in October, residents of Santa María del Tule venerate their ancient tree in the **Lunes del Tule** festival. Locals in costume celebrate with rites, folk dances, and feats of horsemanship beneath the boughs of their beloved great cypress.

Oaxacans venerate their patron, the Virgin of Solitude, 16-18 December. Festivities, which center on the Virgin's basilica (on Independencia six blocks west of the *zócalo*), include fireworks, dancing, food, and street processions of the faithful bearing the Virgin's gold-crowned image decked out in her fine silks and satins.

For the Fiesta of the Radishes *(rábanos)* on 23 December, celebrants fill the Oaxaca *zócalo*, admiring displays of plants, flowers, and figures crafted of large radishes. Ceremonies and prizes honor the most original designs. Foodstalls nearby serve traditional delicacies, including *buñuelos* (honey-soaked fried tortillas), plates of which are traditionally thrown into the air before the evening is over.

Oaxaca people culminate their Posada week on **Nochebuena** (Christmas Eve) with candle-lit processions from their parishes, accompanied by music, fireworks, and floats. They converge on the *zócalo* in time for a midnight cathedral Mass.

Folkloric Dance Shows

If you miss the Lunes del Cerro festival, some towns and villages stage smaller Guelageutza celebrations year-round. So do a number of hotels, the most reliable of which occurs nightly at 8:30 p.m. at the Hotel Monte Albán, on Plaza de León, tel. (951) 627-77, adjacent to the *zócalo*. At other hotels, days may change, so call ahead to confirm: Hotel Camino Real, tel. (951) 606-11, Friday, $22 show with dinner, not including drinks; Restaurant Casa de Cantera,

Murguia 102, at 8:30 p.m., $6 per person, varied schedule, tel. (951) 806-66, 446-03, or 475-85.

Films, Theater, Music, Dance, and Art Exhibits

Many Oaxaca institutions, such as the **Museo de Arte Contemporaneo de Oaxaca,** the **Teatro Macedonio Alcalá,** the **University of Oaxaca School of Fine Arts** ("Bellas Artes"), and others sponsor many first-rate cultural events. See the excellent monthly calendar of events in the English-language *Oaxaca Times* for details.

Nightlife

When lacking an official fiesta, you can create your own at a number of nightspots around town.

The big hotels are most reliable for live dance music and discotheques. Call to confirm programs: Camino Real, tel. (951) 606-11; San Felipe, tel. (951) 350-50; Fortín Plaza, tel. (951) 501-00; and the Victoria, tel. (951) 526-33.

Besides many of the sidewalk cafés around the *zócalo,* a number of restaurants also offer live music seasonally. Try the El Sagrario, tel. (951) 403-02, evenings, beginning at about 9 p.m., and the Hotel Marques del Valle (tel. 951-634-74) restaurant on the *zócalo.*

Perhaps the most popular in-town nightspot is **Candela,** which jumps with hot salsa and African-Latin rhythms nightly from about 10 p.m., at Murguia 413, corner of Pino Suárez, tel. (951) 420-10.

SPORTS AND RECREATION

Jogging and Walks

For jogging, try the public **Ciudad Deportiva** ("Sports City") fields on the west side of Hwy. 190 about two miles north of the town center.

For an invigorating in-town walk, climb the **Cerro del Fortín** hill. Your reward will be a breezy city, valley, and mountain view. The key to getting there through the maze of city streets is to head to the **Escalera del Fortín** (staircase), which will lead you conveniently to the instep of the hill. For example, from the northeast *zócalo* corner walk north along the Alcalá mall. After five blocks, in front of the Santo Domingo church turn left onto Allende, continue four blocks to Crespo, and turn right. After three blocks, you'll see the staircase on the left. Continue uphill, past the Guelaguetza open-air auditorium, to the road (Nicolas Copernicus) heading north to the **Planetarium.** After that, enjoying the panorama, you can keep walking along the hilltop for at least another mile. Take a hat and water. The roundtrip from the *zócalo* is a minimum of two miles; the hilltop rises only a few hundred feet. Allow at least a couple of hours.

Swimming, Tennis, and Sporting Goods

Swimmers do their thing at **Balneario La Bamba,** tel. (951) 409-25, about 2.5 miles (four km) south of town along Hwy. 175 before the airport. The pool is open Tues.-Sun. 10 a.m.-5 p.m. Serious lap swimmers should choose days and hours in order to avoid crowds, Sunday being the worst.

For tennis, stay at either the **Hotel Victoria** or the **Misión de los Angeles,** which have courts. Otherwise, call the **Club de Tenis Brenamiel,** next to the Hotel Villas del Sol, Km 539.5 on Hwy. 190, about three miles north of the center of town, tel. (951) 268-22, and reserve a court; about $6 an hour.

A good sporting goods and clothing selection is available at **Deportes Ziga,** on the southwest corner of Alcalá and Matamoros, next to La Mano Mágico handicrafts shop. Open Mon.-Sat. 9 a.m.-2 p.m. and 4-8:30 p.m., tel. (951) 416-54.

SHOPPING

The city of Oaxaca is renowned as a handicrafts shopper's paradise. Prices are low, quality is high, and sources—in both large traditional markets and many dozens of private stores and galleries—are manifold. In the city, however, vendors do not ordinarily make the merchandise they sell. They buy wholesale from family shops in town, the surrounding valley, and remote localities all over the state of Oaxaca. If your time is severely limited, best buy from the good in-town sources, many of which are listed below.

If, on the other hand, you have the time to benefit (both because of lower prices and person-to-person contact with the artisans) by going to the villages, consult the succeeding Around the Valley of Oaxaca section for sources of local village handicrafts.

Traditional Markets

The original town market, **Mercado Juárez,** covers the entire square block just one block south and one block west of the *zócalo.* Many dozens of stalls offer everything; cotton and wool items—such as dresses, *huipiles,* woven blankets, and serapes—are among the best buys. Despite the overwhelming festoons of merchandise, bargains are there for those willing to search them out.

Before diving into the Juárez market's cavernous interior, first orient yourself by looking over the lineup of stalls on the market's west side, along the block of 20 de Noviembre, between Las Casas and Trujano. Here, you'll be able to select from a reasonably priced representative assortment—black and green pottery, tinware, *huipiles,* leather goods, *alebrijes* (fanciful wooden animals), pewter, cutlery, filigree jewelry—of much that Oaxaca offers.

After your Juárez market tour, walk a block west, to J.P. Garcia, and three and a half blocks south, between Mina and Zaragoza, for a look inside the **Mercado de Artesanías** handicrafts market. Here, you'll find more of the same—a ton of textiles—*huipiles, camisas* (shirts), *blusas* (blouses), and *tapetes* (carpets)—plus *alfarería* (pottery), *alebrijes,* and some for-tourist masks.

Private Handicrafts Shops

Although pricier, the private shops generally offer the choicest merchandise. Here you can select from the very best: *huipiles* from San Pedro de Amusgos and Yalalag, richly embroidered "wedding" dresses from San Antonino de Castillo, rugs and hangings from Teotitlán del Valle; pottery—black from San Bártolo Coyotepec and green from Atzompa; carved *alebrijes* animals from Arrazola; whimsical figurines by the Aguilar sisters of Ocotlán; mescal from Tlacolula; and masks from Huazolotitlán.

Most of the best individual shops lie scattered along three streets— 5 de Mayo, Macedonio Alcalá, and Garcia Vigil, which run uphill, north of the *zócalo.*

A good place to get prices and selection in perspective is the crafts shop in the federal tourist information center, at 607 Independencia, off the *zócalo,* diagonally north of the cathedral. It's open Mon.-Fri. 8 a.m.-3 p.m. and 5-8 p.m., Saturday 8 a.m.-3 p.m.

Next, head north along the Alcalá mall; two blocks north of Independencia, you'll arrive at a Oaxaca favorite, the **Palacio de las Gemas,** corner of Morelos and Alcalá, tel. (951) 446-03. Although specializing in semiprecious stones and jewelry, it has much more, including a host of charming handpainted tinware Christmas decorations, Guerrero masks, and pre-Columbian reproductions in onyx and turquoise. Open Mon.-Sat. 10 a.m.-2 p.m. and 4-8:30 p.m.

Head a block east to Cinco de Mayo, turn left (north) half a block to the big house on the right, no. 204, headquarters of MARO, **Mujeres Artesanas del las Regiones de Oaxaca.** ("Craftswomen of the Regions of Oaxaca"). Here a remarkable all-Oaxaca grass-roots movement of women artisans has gotten the government to stake them to a building, where they sell their goods and demonstrate their manufacturing techniques. The artisans are virtually pure native Mexicans from all parts of Oaxaca, and their offerings reflect their unique effort. Hosts of gorgeous handicrafts—wooden masks, toys, carvings; cotton *traje* native clothing, such as *huipiles, pozahuancos, quechquémitles;* wool serapes, rugs, and hangings; woven palm hats, mats, and baskets; fine steel knives, swords, and machetes; tinplate mirrors, candlesticks, and ornaments; leather saddles, briefcases, wallets, and belts—fill the shelves of several rooms. It's open daily 9 a.m.-2 p.m. and 4-8 p.m., at 204 Cinco de Mayo, Oaxaca, Oaxaca 68000, tel./fax (951) 606-70. Don't miss them; better still, do a major part of your Oaxaca shopping at this store.

Walk a block west along Murguia back to Alcalá and step into **La Mano Mágico** on the west side, just below the corner of Murguia, at Alcalá 203, tel./fax (951) 642-75. The shop offers both a colorful exposition of crafts from all over Mex-

Rich colors, graceful designs, and fine quality draw streams of visitors to Teotitlán del Valle weaving village near Oaxaca.

ico and a patio workshop, where artisans work, dyeing wool and weaving examples of the lovely, museum-quality rugs and serapes that adorn the walls. Open Mon.-Sat. 10 a.m.-2:30 p.m. and 3:30-6 p.m.

Continue uphill on Alcalá, a block farther north, to the **Plaza Alcalá** complex, west corner of N. Bravo, which has both a tranquil courtyard restaurant and some good shops. Notable among them is **Corazón del Pueblo,** which, besides a select all-Mexico folk crafts assortment on the lower level, offers a discriminating selection of English-language books about Mexico: guides, literature, ethnography, archaeology, history, cookbooks, maps, postcards, and much more upstairs. Located at Alcalá 307, tel. (951) 669-60; open Mon.-Sat. 10:30 a.m.-2:30 p.m. and 3:30-7:30 p.m.

Continue up Alcalá past venerable Santo Domingo church on the right and turn left and stroll a block along the **Plazuela del Carmen** street plaza. There, you can appreciate the offerings of the many local vendors, often including Zapotec and Trique women in traditional dress, weaving on their backstrap looms.

Rewards await shoppers who are willing to walk a few long blocks farther uphill, to the state-run **ARIPO** (Artesanías y Industrias Populares de Oaxaca) at 809 Garcia Vigil, tel. (951) 440-30 or 408-61. There, you can pick from a broad, authentic, and very traditional selection of masks, *huipiles,* wedding dresses, carved animals, ceramics, tinware, and much more. Prices vary: cheap on some items and high on others. Open Mon.-Sat. 9 a.m.-7 p.m.

Fine Arts Galleries
The tourist boom has stimulated a Oaxaca fine arts revival. Several downtown galleries bloom with the sculpture and paintings of masters, such as Rufino Tamayo and Rudolfo Morales, and a host of up-and-coming local artists. Besides La Mano Mágico, listed above, a number of galleries stand out. Foremost among them is **Arte de Oaxaca,** the gallery of the Rudolfo Morales Foundation (see the **Ocotlán** section), at Murguia 105, between Alcalá and 5 de Mayo, open Mon.-Sat. 10 a.m.-2 p.m., 4-8 p.m., tel. (951) 423-24 or 409-10.

Also outstanding is **Galería Quetzalli,** opposite the south side of Santo Domingo church, at Constitución 104, between Reforma and 5 de Mayo, open Mon.-Sat. 10 a.m.-2 p.m. and 5-8 p.m., tel. (951) 426-06, fax 407-37. Also well worth visiting, downhill opposite Santo Domingo church, is **Galeria Arte Mexicano** at Alcalá 407 #16, tel. (951) 438-15, open Mon.-Sat. 10 a.m.-2 p.m. and 4-8 p.m.

Groceries and Natural Food
For fruits and vegetables, the cheapest and freshest are in the Juárez and 20 de Noviembre markets, which take up the two square blocks immediately southwest of the *zócalo.*

For simpler, straightforward grocery shopping, stop by **Abarrotes Lonja** on the *zócalo* next to the Hotel Señorial; open daily 8 a.m.-9:30 p.m.

Local natural food devotees get their heart's content of teas—arnica, anise, manzanilla—and ginseng, organic grains, granola, and soy burgers at **Tienda Naturista Trigo Verde,** two blocks west of the *zócalo,* at J.P. Garcia 207, tel. (951) 623-69. Open Mon.-Sat. 8:30 a.m.-9 p.m., Sunday 9 a.m.-6 p.m.

Camera and Photo

Downtown has some good photo shops, most on 20 de Noviembre, a block west of the *zócalo.* Best of all is **Oaxakolor,** at 20 de Noviembre 108, tel. (951) 634-87, perhaps the best-stocked photo store in Oaxaca. It carries dozens of cameras—35mm point-and-shoot, SLRs, professional medium format—as well as an abundance of film, including popular and professional color, slides, sheet, black and white, and a host of accessories. Open Mon.-Sat. 9 a.m.-9 p.m.

More ordinary, but still well-stocked, is **Foto Figueroa** at Hidalgo 516, corner 20 de Noviembre, tel. (951) 637-66. With plenty of Kodak film and accessories, it offers quick develop-and-print. Open Mon.-Sat. 9 a.m.-8:30 p.m.

Express Kolor, half a block farther down at 20 de Noviembre 225, tel. (951) 614-92, is better stocked, with scores of point-and-shoot cameras and many Minolta, Vivitar, and Olympus accessories. It also stocks Konica, Fuji, Kodak, and Agfa films in color and black and white, both roll and sheet. Open Mon.-Sat. 9 a.m.-8 p.m.

SERVICES

Money Exchange

Several banks dot the downtown area. Two **Banamex** branches, corner Morelos and Díaz, tel. (951) 644-44, and Hidalgo at Cinco de Mayo, tel. (951) 659-00, money exchange hours Mon.-Fri. 9 a.m.-4:30 p.m., usually give the best rates for U.S., Canadian, Japanese, and many European currencies and traveler's checks. If they're too crowded, try **Bancomer** (Mon.-Fri. 9 a.m.-6 p.m., Saturday 10 a.m.-2 p.m.) at Vigil and Morelos, tel. (951) 293-77. Otherwise, go to **Banco Santander Mexicano** (Mon.-Fri. 9 a.m.-5 p.m., Saturday 10 a.m.-2 p.m., U.S. cash and traveler's checks only), just north of the cathedral, at Independencia 605, tel. (951) 625-26; or its neighbor **Banco Serfin** (Mon.-Fri. 9 a.m.-6 p.m., Saturday 10 a.m.-2 p.m.; U.S., Canadian, Japanese, and many European currencies and traveler's checks), tel. (951) 611-00, at the adjacent corner of Garcia Vigil, diagonally across from the *zócalo* cathedral.

After bank hours, go to **Casa de Cambio Internacional de Divisas,** tel. (951) 633-99, on the Alcalá street mall just north of the *zócalo,* behind the cathedral. Although it may pay about a percent less than banks, it changes many major currencies and traveler's checks. Open Mon.-Sat. 8 a.m.-8 p.m., Sunday 9 a.m.-5 p.m.

Travel Agencies and Tour Services

The local **American Express** agency, Viajes Mexico Istmo y Caribe, operates an efficient, full-service office nearby. It both sells and cashes American Express traveler's checks at the best rates in town. Located behind the cathedral, at Valdiviesio 2, tel. (951) 627-00 or 629-19, fax 674-75. Open Mon.-Fri. 9 a.m.-2 p.m. and 4-6 p.m., Saturday 9 a.m.-1 p.m.; money service hours may be a bit shorter.

Although American Express does offer tours, it does not specialize in them. Among the several reliable travel agencies that do is **Oaxaca Tours,** at Garcia Vigil 406 (four blocks uphill from the plaza), tel./fax (951) 610-05, e-mail: oaxaca-tours@oaxaca.infosel.com.mx. Although Oaxaca Tours mostly arranges Oaxaca city and valley destinations, guides (for about $25 per person per day, for guide and exclusive transportation, or $15 shared) can lead you on excursions through the Mixteca regions, the mountains north of Oaxaca, and the southern coast Huatulco-Puerto Escondido region.

Another, more local, less expensive option is to go with longtime **Viajes Turisticos Mitla,** at Hóstal Santa Rosa, Trujano 201 (a block west of the plaza), tel. (951) 478-00 or 478-06. This company offers tours, usually around the Valley of Oaxaca, minimum charge $30, including guide and transportation, for small or medium sized-groups. Its main office is at the Hotel Rivera del Ángel, at F.J. Mina 518 (two blocks south, three blocks west of the plaza), tel. (951) 478-00 or 431-52, fax 661-75.

More vigorous travelers might enjoy the services of **Mountain Bike Tours** at J.P. Garcia

509, east side, between Mina and Aldama, a few blocks west and south of the plaza, tel. (951) 431-44, which both rents bikes and conducts guided bike tours into the nearby countryside.

A Oaxaca regiment of private individual guides also offer tours. Among the most highly recommended is English-fluent **Juan Montes Lara,** backed up by his wife Karin Schutte. Besides cultural sensitivity and extensive local knowledge, they can also provide comfortable transportation in a GMC Suburban wagon. Contact them at their home, at Prol. de Eucaliptos 303, Colonia Reforma, Oaxaca, Oaxaca 68050, tel. (951) 301-26.

Former clients volunteer rave reviews of the tours given by English-speaking expatriate **Susan McGlynn,** who can be reached at (951) 873-44 or by e-mail at terran@antequera.com.

For more recommendations, go to the government tourist information office, north side of the *zócalo,* at Independencia 607, tel. (951) 648-28.

Communications

The Oaxaca *correo* (post office), tel. (951) 626-61, is across from the cathedral at the corner of the Alameda de León square and Independencia. Open Mon.-Fri. 8 a.m.-7 p.m., Saturday 9 a.m.-1 p.m.

Telégrafo, tel. (951) 649-02, at the next corner of Independencia and 20 Noviembre, offers money orders, telephone, and public fax. Hours are Mon.-Fri. 9 a.m.-8 p.m. (money orders 9 a.m.-6 p.m.) and Saturday 9 a.m.-1 p.m. (money orders 9 a.m.-noon).

After hours, you can take advantage of a pair of efficient **Computel** long-distance phone and public fax offices: on Independencia, by Banco Mexicano, across from the Plaza Alameda de León, tel. (951) 480-84, open 7 a.m.-10 p.m.; and at Trujano 204, just off the *zócalo's* southwest corner, tel. (951) 473-19, same hours.

Consulates and Immigration

The U.S. Consul, Mark Leyes, tel./fax (951) 430-54, holds hours Mon.-Fri. 10 a.m.-6 p.m. at Alcalá 201, three blocks north of the *zócalo.* The Canadian Consul does the same for Canadian citizens Mon.-Fri. 11 a.m.-2 p.m., at 700 Pino Suárez, local 11B, tel. (951) 337-77, fax 521-47.

Other consuls available in Oaxaca are the French (tel. 951-419-00) and the British (toll-free tel. 01-800-706-29), and sometimes the Spanish, German, and Italian. Look for their numbers in the *Oaxaca Times* or the telephone directory Yellow Pages, under *Embajadas, Legaciones, y Consulados,* or call the U.S. or Canadian Consuls above for information.

If you lose your tourist permit, make arrangements with **Migración** several hours prior to departure from Mexico. Take proof of arrival date in Mexico—stamped passport, airline ticket, or copy of lost permit—to either one of two offices: Periférico 2724, third floor, tel. (951) 456-74, or the airport office, tel. (951) 157-33.

Language Instruction and Courses

A long list of satisfied clients attests to the competence of the **Becari Language School,** N. Bravo 210, tel./fax (951) 460-76 or 434-99. Offerings include small group Spanish instruction, as well as cooking and dancing classes. If you desire, the school can arrange homestays with local families. Its modest midtown facility includes, besides classrooms, a social area for sitting and getting to know other students.

Similarly highly recommended is the **Vinigulaza Language and Tradition** ("Vinigulaza Idioma y Tradición") school, associated with the local English-language Cambridge Academy, at Abasolo 209 (about two blocks east, four blocks north, of the plaza), tel. (951) 464-26, e-mail: vinigulaza@infosel.net.mx. The star behind the show is the friendly and hospitable director Catherine Kumar. Offerings include instructive (and even fun) small-group Spanish instruction. Schedules are flexible, and prices, at around $35 for 10 hours per week, are very reasonable. Social activities often include no-host dinners at local restaurants and a small on-site café where students can enjoy tea, coffee, and conversation. For more info, take a look at the school's Web site: oaxaca.infosel.com.mx/vinigulaza.

INFORMATION

Tourist Information

The combined state-federal-city tourist information center, 607 Independencia, tel. (951) 601-23, fax 609-84, e-mail: sedetur1@oaxaca.gov.mx, which includes a good handicrafts shop, is conveniently located at the main plaza's northern edge, at the traffic corner, north side of the Cathedral front. It's open daily 9 a.m.-8 p.m.

Medical, Police, and Emergencies
If you get sick, ask your hotel desk to recommend a doctor. Otherwise, go to **Sanatorio Carmen,** one of Oaxaca's best hospitals, at Abasolo 215, tel. (951) 600-27.

For routine medicines and drugs, go to one of many pharmacies, such as the **Farmacias Ahorro** on Cinco de Mayo, near the southwest corner of Independencia, open daily 7 a.m.-10 p.m. After hours, call Farmacia Ahorros' 24-hour free delivery service, tel. (951) 444-00.

For police emergencies, call the **Dirección de Seguridad,** tel. (951) 627-26, at Aldama 108, just north of the *zócalo.* For fire, call the **bomberos,** tel. (951) 622-31.

Publications
One of Oaxaca's best sources of new English-language books about Mexico is the **Corazón del Pueblo** store on the second floor of Plaza Alcalá, Alcalá 307, tel. (951) 669-60; open Mon.-Sat. 10 a.m.-8 p.m.

Another good source is bookstore **Librería Universitaria,** at Guerrero 104, half a block east of the *zócalo,* tel. (951) 642-43. It has English paperbacks, both used and new, a number of indigenous language dictionaries, and guides, cookbooks, art, and history books. Open Mon.-Sat. 9:30 a.m.-2 p.m. and 4-8 p.m.

The daily English-language *News* of Mexico City is usually available late mornings at stands near the southwest corner of the *zócalo.* If not, try the small news shop near the same corner at Trujano 106A, open daily 8 a.m.-9:30 p.m. Besides the *News,* it might also have *Time* and *Newsweek.*

Pick up a copy of the informative tourist monthly, the **Oaxaca Times,** at your hotel, the state or city tourist office, or at the publisher, the Instituto de Comunicación y Cultura, tel. (951) 634-43, at 307 Alcalá, second floor. The newspaper prints cultural and historical features, tourist hints, and a list of local events. Also useful is the commonly available alternative trilingual tourist newspaper **Oaxaca,** published in English, Spanish, and French, at Calz. P. Díaz, 321-7, Colonia Reforma, tel./fax (951) 587-64.

Libraries
The city **biblioteca** (public library), in a lovingly restored exconvent, is worth a visit, if only for its graceful, cloistered Renaissance interiors and patios. At the corner of Morelos and Alcalá, two blocks north of the *zócalo,* tel. (951) 656-81. Open Mon.-Sat. 9 a.m.-8:30 p.m.

Visitors starving for a good read will find satisfaction from at least one of the thousands of volumes at the **Oaxaca Lending Library,** at M. Alcalá 305, corner of Murguia; open Mon.-Fri. 10 a.m.-1 p.m. and 4-7 p.m., Saturday 10 a.m.-1 p.m.

GETTING THERE AND AWAY

By Air
The **Oaxaca Airport** (code-designated OAX) has several daily flights that connect with Mexico City and other Mexican destinations. Many of the Mexico City flights allow same-day connections between Oaxaca and many U.S. gateways.

Mexicana Airlines flights connect three or four times daily with Mexico City. For reservations or flight information, call (951) 684-14 or 472-53.

Aeroméxico flights connect three times daily with Mexico City; one flight continues on to Tijuana. For reservations, call (951) 637-65 or 610-66; for flight information, call (951) 150-55.

Mexicana Airlines affiliate **Aerocaribe** flights connect daily with Huatulco and twice a week with Cancún, via Tuxtla Gutiérrez, Villahermosa, and Mérida. For reservations, call (951) 660-88 or 602-29; for flight information, call (951) 152-47.

Aviacsa airlines connects once daily with Mexico City and once daily with Tijuana (via Tuxtla Gutiérrez, Mexico City, and Monterrey). For information and reservations, call (951) 451-23 or 451-86.

Aeromorelos flights connect daily with Puerto Escondido and Huatulco. For reservations, call (951) 609-74 or 609-75; for arrival and departure information, call (951) 151-00.

The Oaxaca airport is not large, with few services other than a café, several shops, and car rentals. Since there is no money-exchange agency, arrive with enough pesos to last until you can get to a bank.

Arrival transportation for the six-mile trip into town is easy. Fixed-fare collective taxi tickets run about $2 per person ($4 to north-side Hotels Misión de los Angeles, Fortín Plaza, and Victoria). For the same trip, a taxi especial (private taxi) ticket runs about $10 for three persons. No public buses run between the airport and town.

Car rental agents operating at the Oaxaca Airport are **Budget,** tel. (951) 100-52 airport (644-45 downtown); **Hertz,** tel. (951) 624-34 downtown; **Avis,** tel./fax (951) 157-36 airport; and **Advantage,** tel. (951) 468-09 downtown.

On **departure,** save enough dollars or pesos for your $12 international departure tax (which may be collected in Mexico City). If you lose your tourist permit, make arrangements with **Migración** several hours prior to departure from Mexico. Take proof of arrival date in Mexico—stamped passport, airline ticket, or copy of lost permit—to either one of two branch offices: in town, at the Periférico 2724, third floor, tel. (951) 456-74, or the airport office, tel. (951) 157-33.

By Car or RV
Paved (but long, winding, and sometimes potholed) roads connect Oaxaca city with all regions of Oaxaca:

South to the coast via the southern Sierra, narrow **National Hwy. 175** connects along 148 winding miles (238 km) over the Sierra Madre del Sur with its junction with Hwy. 200 at Pochutla (thence six miles to Puerto Ángel). The road climbs to more than 9,000 feet through winter-chilly pine forests and indigenous Chatino and Zapotec villages. Fill up with gas at the last-chance Mihuatlán Pemex heading south and at Pochutla (north edge of town) heading north; carry water and blankets and be prepared for emergencies. Allow about six and a half driving hours south from Oaxaca to Puerto Ángel, about seven and a half in the opposite direction.

About the same is true for the newly paved **National Hwy. 131** route south from Oaxaca, which splits off of Hwy. 175 two miles (three kilometers) south of San Bártolo Coyotepec. On your way out of town, fill up with gasoline at the airport Pemex. Continue, via Zimatlán and Sola de Vega, over the pine-clad Pacific crest, a total of 158 miles (254 kilometers) to Puerto Escondido. Allow about six hours southbound, and seven hours in the opposite direction. Unleaded gasoline is regularly available at Sola de Vega only.

The 229-mile (368-km) **Hwy. 190-Hwy. 125** route connects Oaxaca southwest with coastal Pinotepa Nacional, via the Mixtec country destinations of Yanhuitlán, Teposcolula, and Tlaxiaco. Although winding most of the way, the generally uncongested road is safely driveable (subject to some potholes however) from Oaxaca in about seven driving hours if you use the cuota (toll) Hwy. 190 autopista northwest of Oaxaca city. Add an hour for the 5,000-foot climb in the opposite direction.

The 350-mile (564-km) winding **Hwy. 190-160** from Oaxaca to Cuernavaca and Mexico City via Huajuapan de León requires a long day, or better two, for safety. Under the best of conditions, the Mexico City-Oaxaca driving time runs 10 hours either way. Take it easy and stop overnight en route. (Make sure you arrive in Mexico City on a day when your car is permitted to drive. See the special topic Mexico City Driving Regulations.)

Alternatively, you can cut your the Mexico City-Oaxaca driving time significantly via the **Puebla-Oaxaca autopista** 190 D, which, southbound, takes off from the southeast end of Mexico City's Calz. General Ignacio Zaragoza. Northbound, follow the signs on Hwy. 190 a few miles north of Oaxaca. Allow about six hours driving time at a steady 60 mph (about 100 kph). Tolls, which are worth the increased speed and safety, run about $30 for a car, much more for a big RV.

By Bus
Luxury and First Class: Cristóbal Colón (CC) and Autobuses del Oriente (AO), Oaxaca's major luxury- and first-class carriers, operate out of the big modern terminal on Hwy. 190, Calz. Héroes de Chapultepec 1036, at Carranza, on the north side of town. Here passengers enjoy convenient snack stands, luggage lockers, and a long-distance telephone and fax service.

Cristóbal Colón, tel. (951) 512-14, offers service to most major points in Oaxaca. Buses connect northwest with Mixteca Baja destinations of Nochixtlán, Tamazulapan, and Huajapan de León, continuing to Puebla and Mexico City.

Westerly, they connect with the Mixteca Alta, via Teposcolula, Tlaxiaco, Juxtlahuaca, Putla de Guerrero amd Pinotepa Nacional on the coast. Southerly, they connect with Puerto Escondido, Pochutla, Puerto Ángel, and Huatulco; southeasterly, with Tehuantepec, Chiapas, and Guatemala; and northerly, with Villahermosa.

Moreover, Cristóbal Colón, operating through its agency, **Ticket Bus**, sells tickets for all first-class buses at both the 1036 Héroes de Chapultepec station and a convenient downtown outlet, at 20 de Noviembre 204A, tel. (951) 466-55, a block west of the *zócalo*.

Autobuses del Oriente, tel. (951) 509-03 and 517-03, offers limited Oaxaca connections, mostly along the Hwy. 190 corridor, connecting northwest with Mexico City, via Nochixtlán and Huajuapan de León, and southeast, with Tehuantepec and Salina Cruz. Other departures connect northwest with Veracruz, Coatzacoalcos, Villahermosa, and Mérida.

Second Class: A swarm of long-distance second-class buses runs from the *central camionera segunda clase* southwest of downtown, just north of the Abastos market. Get there by taxi, or by walking due west about eight blocks from the *zócalo*, to the west end of Calle Las Casas. Cross the *periférico* (peripheral boulevard) straight across the railroad tracks; keep walking the same direction, along the four-lane street for two more blocks, where you'll see the terminal gate on the right. Inside, you'll find an orderly array of snack stalls, a cafeteria, luggage lockers, a long-distance telephone and fax, and a squad of *taquillas* (ticket booths).

Autotransportes Oaxaca-Pacífico, tel. (951) 629-08, and **Autobuses Estrella del Valle**, tel. (951) 654-29, travel the Hwy. 175 north-south route between Oaxaca and Pochutla-Puerto

Ángel. Both lines continue, connecting along east-west coastal Hwy. 200 with Bahías de Huatulco, Puerto Escondido and Pinotepa Nacional.

Estrella Roja del Sureste second-class and first-class buses, tel. (951) 606-94, connect along newly paved Hwy. 131 north-south via Sola de Vega and Juquila, directly with Puerto Escondido. From there, you can make coastal connections with Pochutla-Puerto Ángel, Bahías de Huatulco, and Pinotepa Nacional.

Fletes y Pasajes, tel. (951) 474-00, offers very broad second-class service, connecting with nearly everywhere in Oaxaca: westerly, with Mixteca destinations of Nochistlán, Tamazulapan, Huajuapan, and Tlaxiaco, connecting all the way, via Hwy. 125, with Pinotepa Nacional on the coast; northerly, via Teotitlán del Camino and Mazateca destinations around Huatla de Jiménez; easterly, with Mixe destinations of Ayutla, Zacatepec, and Juquila Mixes; and southeasterly, with isthmus destinations of Tehuantepec, Juchitán, and Salina Cruz.

By Train

Although they're sometimes painfully slow, passenger trains still rumble along, connecting Oaxaca (via Puebla) with Mexico City, and thence with a few other Mexican destinations.

One Mexico City-bound train departs daily at 7 p.m. from the station on Calz. Madero about a mile and a half west of downtown. Service, very cheap, is by first- and second-class coach only and includes no restaurant car. Bring food and drinks. Call the station, tel. (951) 622-53 or 625-64, to double-check departure information and prices. Note: Due to railroad privatization, passenger train service is quickly disappearing in Mexico. By the time you read this, it may have vanished completely.

AROUND THE VALLEY OF OAXACA

Oaxaca offers much of interest—archaeological sites, crafts villages, and weekly markets—outside the city. Valley market towns each have their market day, when local color is at a maximum and prices are at a minimum. Among the choices, starting on the east side, are: **Teotitlán del Valle,** half an hour east, Saturday; **Tlacolula,** one hour east, Sunday; **Ocotlán,** half

an hour south, Friday; **Zaachila,** half an hour southwest, Thursday; **Zimatlán,** one hour southwest, Wednesday; and **San Pedro y San Pablo Etla,** half an hour northeast, Wednesday.

These market visits can be conveniently combined with stops at handicrafts villages, ruins (notably Mitla, on the east side, and Monte Albán, west), and other sights along the way.

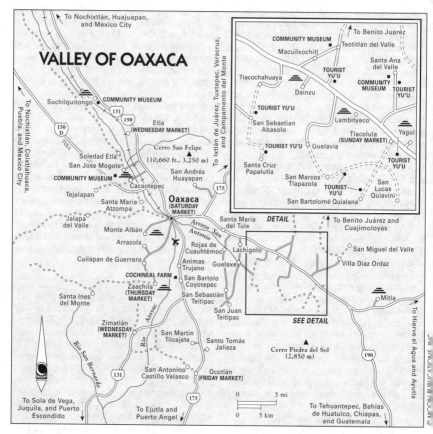

VALLEY OF OAXACA

To Nochixtlán, Huajuapan, and Mexico City

To Nochixtlán, Coixtlahuaca, Puebla, and Mexico City

150 D TOLL

Suchilquitongo — COMMUNITY MUSEUM

131

190

Etla (WEDNESDAY MARKET)

Cerro San Felipe (10,660 ft., 3,250 m)

Soledad Etla
San Jose Mogote
COMMUNITY MUSEUM
Cacaotepec

Tejalapan

Santa Maria Atzompa

Jalapa del Valle

Monte Albán

Arrazola

Cuilapan de Guerrero

Santa Ines del Monte

Zimatlán (WEDNESDAY MARKET)

San Martin Tilcajete

Santo Tomás Jalieza

San Antonino Castillo Velasco

Ocotlán (FRIDAY MARKET)

To Sola de Vega, Juquila, and Puerto Escondido

To Ejutla and Puerto Angel

San Andrés Huayapan

Oaxaca (SATURDAY MARKET)

Santa Maria del Tule

Arroyo San Antonio

Rojas de Cuauhtémoc

Lachigolo

Guelaxe

Animas Trujano

COCHINEAL FARM

San Bartolo Coyotepec

Zaachila (THURSDAY MARKET)

San Sebastián Teitipac

San Juan Teitipac

Cerro Piedra del Sol (2,850 m)

Rio Atoyac

Rio San Bernardo

131

175

DETAIL

To Ixtlán de Juárez, Tuxtepec, Veracruz, and Campamento del Monte

To Benito Juárez and Cuajimoloyas

San Miguel del Valle

Villa Diaz Ordaz

Mitla

To Hierve el Agua and Ayutla

SEE DETAIL

190

To Tehuantepec, Bahías de Huatulco, Chiapas, and Guatemala

0   5 mi
0   5 km

DETAIL

COMMUNITY MUSEUM
Teotitlán del Valle

Macuilxochitl

Tlacochahuaya

Dainzu

Santa Ana del Valle

TOURIST YU'U

COMMUNITY MUSEUM

TOURIST YU'U

TOURIST YU'U

San Sebastian Abasolo

Lambityeco

Tlacolula (SUNDAY MARKET)

Yagul

TOURIST YU'U

Guelavia

Santa Cruz Papalutla

San Marcos Tlapazola

TOURIST YU'U

San Lucas Quiavini

San Bartolomé Quialana

To Benito Juárez

To Benito Juárez and Cuajimoloyas

Getting around the Valley of Oaxaca

Although droves of second-class buses from the Abastos terminal run everywhere in the Valley of Oaxaca, it would take you a month touring that way. It's better to rent a car or ride a tourist bus. For a car, call **Budget,** tel. (951) 100-52 airport (644-45 downtown); **Hertz,** tel. (951) 624-34 downtown; **Avis,** tel./fax (951) 157-36 airport; or **Advantage,** tel. (951) 468-09 downtown.

For tourist buses, ride one of those leaving daily from the **Hotel Rivera del Ángel,** at F.J. Mina 518 (two blocks south, three blocks west of the plaza), tel. (951) 478-00 or 431-52, fax 661-75. The Hotel Señorial (on the *zócalo,* tel. 951-639-33) and other hotels also have such tour arrangements. See your desk clerk.

An excellent alternative is to go with the well-organized **Community Museums of Oaxaca** ("Museos Comunitarios de Oaxaca"), headquartered at Tinoco y Palacios 311, second floor, tel. (951) 657-86, e-mail: muscoax@antequera .com. This company acts as agent for 14 local museums, including five important spots in the Valley of Oaxaca (Teotitlán del Valle, Santa Ana del Valle, San Pablo Huixtepec, San José Mogote, and Santiago Suchilquitongo). The museums offer guided tours of their localities, including ruins, lakes, springs, mountain summits, and artisans' shops, with lunch thrown in, from $15 per person. The headquarters furnishes an English-speaking guide to the museum, via your car or taxi or public bus.

For many more suggestions, see Travel Agencies and Tour Services in the **Oaxaca** section.

EAST SIDE: EL TULE AND TEOTITLÁN DEL VALLE

Enough attractions lie along this route for days of exploring. For example, you could visit El Tule and the Teotitlán market on Saturday, continuing for an overnight at Mitla. Next morning, explore the Mitla ruins for a couple of hours, then return, stopping at the hilltop Yagul ruins and the Sunday market at Tlacolula. In either direction going or coming from the city, you could pause for an hour's exploration of the Dainzu and Lambityeco roadside archaeological sites. One more day would allow more time to venture past Mitla, to the remarkable mountainside springs and mineral deposits at Hierve de Agua.

El Tule is a gargantuan Mexican cypress *(ahuehuete),* probably the largest tree in Latin America and maybe the world. Its gnarled, house-size trunk divides into a forest of elephantine limbs that rise to festoons of bushy branches reaching 15 stories overhead. The small town of Santa María del Tule, nine miles (14 km) east of the city on Hwy. 190, seems built around the tree. A crafts market, a church, and the town plaza, where residents celebrate their El Tule with a fiesta on 7 October, all surround the beloved 2,000-year-old living giant.

Dainzu and Lambityeco Archaeological Sites
Among the dozen-odd Valley of Oaxaca's buried cities, Dainzu and Lambityeco, both beside the highway, are the most accessible. Dainzu comes first, on the right about six miles (nine km) east of El Tule.

Dainzu (in Zapotec, "Hill of the Candelabra Cactus") spreads over an approximate half-mile square, consisting of a partly restored ceremonial center surrounded by clusters of unexcavated mounds. Beyond that, on the west side, a stream runs through fields, which, at Dainzu's apex (around A.D. 300) supported a town of about 1,000 inhabitants.

The major excavation, at the foot of the hill about a hundred yards south of the parking lot, reveals more than 30 bas-reliefs of ball players draped with leather head, arm, and torso protectors. Downhill, to the west, lies the partly re-

constructed complex of courtyards, platforms, and stairways. The northernmost of these was excavated to reveal a tomb, with a carved door supporting a jaguar head on the lintel and arms—note the claws—extending down along the stone door jambs. The jaguar's face, with a pair of curious vampire teeth and curly nostrils, appears so bat-like that some investigators have speculated that it may represent a composite jaguar-bat god.

A couple of hundred yards diagonally southwest you'll find the ball court, running east-west, in the characteristic capital "I" shape, with a pair of "scoring" niches at each end and flanked by a pair of stairstep stone-block grandstand-like "seats." Actually, archaeologists know that these were not seats, because the blocks were once stuccoed over, forming a pair of smooth inclined planes that flanked the central playing area.

Lambityeco, three miles (five km) farther, is on the right, just past the Teotitlán del Valle side road. The excavated portion, only about 100

Weaving is but the climax of the laborious processes that include growing, shearing, washing, carding, spinning, and dyeing wool.

yards square, is a small but significant part of Yegui ("Small Hill" in Zapotec), a large buried town of some 200 mounds, covering about half a square mile.

Salt-making appears to have been the main occupation of Yegui people during the town's heyday, around A.D. 700. The name "Lambityeco" probably derives from the Arabic-Spanish *alambique,* the equivalent of English "alembic," or distillation or evaporation apparatus. This would explain the intriguing presence of the more than 200 local mounds. It's tempting to speculate that they are the remains of *cujetes,* raised leaching beds, still used in Mexico for concentrating brine, which workers subsequently evaporate into salt. (See the **Cuyutlán** section in the South to Zihuatanejo and Inland to Pátzcuaro chapter.)

In the present small restored zone, archaeologists have uncovered, besides the remains of the Valley of Oaxaca's earliest known *temazcal* (ritual steam house), a number of fascinating ceramic sculptures. Next to the parking lot, a platform, mound 195, rises above ground level. If, after entering through the gate, you climb up its partially restored slope and look down into the excavated hollow in the adjacent east courtyard, you'll see stucco friezes of a pair of regal, lifelike faces, one male and one female, presumably of the personages who were found buried in the royal grave (tomb 6) below. Experts believe this to be the case, because the man was depicted with the symbol of his right to rule—a human femur bone, probably taken, as was the custom, from the grave of his chieftain father.

Mound 190, sheltered beneath the adjacent large corrugated roof about 50 yards to the south, contains a restored platform decorated by pair of remarkably lifelike, nearly identical divine stucco masks. These are believed to be of Zapotec rain god Cocijo (see the water flowing from the mouths). Notice also the rays, perhaps lightning, representing power, in one hand, and flowers, for fertility, in the other.

Teotitlán del Valle, Tlacolula, and Yagul Archaeological Zone

Teotitlán del Valle, nine miles east of El Tule, at the foot of the Sierra, means "Place of the Gods" in Nahuatl; before that it was known as Xa Quire, or "Foot of the Mountain," by the Zapotecs who settled it around A.D. 1000. Dominican missionaries introduced the first sheep, whose wool, combined with local skills, results in the fine serapes, carpets, and blankets that seem to fill every shop in town.

Nearly every house is a mini-factory where people card, spin, and dye wool, often using traditional hand-gathered cochineal, indigo, and moss dyes. Every step of wool preparation is laborious; pure water is even a chore—families typically spend two days a week collecting it from mountain springs. The weaving, on traditional hand looms, is the easy part.

In Teotitlán you have many choices. First, visit the weaving shops. Don't miss the shop of friendly master weaver Isaac Vasquez (Hidalgo 30, tel. 951-441-22, open daily 9 a.m.-6 p.m.) and others, such as the Cooperativa Mujeres Tejedoras ("Women Weavers Cooperative"), at Hidalgo 37, two blocks from the town plaza and market. Later, you can select from the hosts of bright displays at the market itself, by the church, end of Hidalgo.

The best weaving is generally the densest, typically packing in about 20 strands per inch; ordinary weaving uses about half that. Please don't bargain too hard. Even the highest prices typically bring the weavers less than a dollar an hour for their labor.

While you're at the Teotitlán market, stop by the local museum, called, in Zapotec, the **Balaa Xtee Guech Gulal** ("House of the Old Town"), open Tues.-Sat. 10 a.m.-6 p.m., in the brick building at the plaza end of Hidalgo. Exhibits detail the Teotitlán weaving tradition, archaeological artifacts, and traditions surrounding the traditional Zapotec marriage ceremony.

The Zapotecs who founded **Tlacolula** (24 miles, 38 km, from Oaxaca) around A.D. 1250 called it Guichiibaa ("Town of Heaven"). Besides its Sunday market, its 1523 chapel, Señor de Tlacolula (with a headless St. Paul), and its adjacent 1531 church, Tlacolula is famous for mescal. Get a good free sample at friendly **Pensamiento** shop, Juárez 9, as you head toward the market. Besides many hand-embroidered Amusgo *huipiles* and Teotitlán weavings, Pensamiento offers mescal in 24 flavors, 17 for women and seven for men.

The **Yagul** (Zapotec for "Old Tree") ruined city stands regally on its volcanic hilltop, 28 miles (45 km) east of Oaxaca city. Although only six miles from Mitla and sharing architectural details, such as Mitla's famous *greca* fretwork, the size and complexity of Yagul's buildings suggests that Yagul was an independent city-state in its own right. Local folks call the present ruin the Pueblo Viejo and remember it as the forerunner of the present town of Tlacolula. Archaeological evidence, which indicates that Yagul was occupied for about a thousand years, until around A.D. 1100 or 1200, bears them out.

One of Yagul's major claims to fame is its **Palace of Six Patios,** actually three nearly identical but separate complexes of two patios each. In each patio, rooms surround a central courtyard. The northerly patio of each complex is more private, and probably was the residence, while the other, more open, patio served administrative functions.

South of the palace sprawls Yagul's huge **ball court,** the second largest in Mesoamerica, shaped in the characteristic Oaxaca "I" configuration. Southeast of the ball court is Patio 4, of four mounds, surrounding a courtyard. A boulder sculpted in the form of a frog lies at the base of the east mound. At the courtyard's center, a tomb was excavated; descend and explore its three *greca*-style fretwork-decorated chambers.

If it's not too hot, gather your energy and climb to the hilltop **citadel** above the parking lot for a fine view of the ruin and the entire Valley of Oaxaca. The name for this prominence probably was accurately descriptive, for Yagul's defenders long ago added rock walls to enhance the hilltop's security.

The airy *palapa* **Restaurant Centeotl,** tel. (951) 661-86, on the Yagul archaeological zone entrance road is worth a stop all by itself. Here, you can quickly double your Mexican food vocabulary by sampling such regional delights as *coloradito* (savory red *mole* chicken or beef stew), *verde de espinazo* (similar ingredients, but stewed in green *mole*), *sopa de guias* (corn and squash soup), and *estofado* (tasty chile-tomato-pork soup). Open daily 11 a.m.-7 p.m.

Besides its gastronomical significance, Centeotl (sayn-tay-OH-tl) is an earnest cultural-ecological endeavor of the friendly elderly owner, who articulately explains his purpose in prose and verse. Ask for his pamphlet, *folleto* (foh-YAY-toh), about Centeotl.

As you leave, take a look at the pre-Columbian ball game ring mounted by the restaurant entrance. Although the ring is interesting all by itself, the cannonball-sized stone sphere perched atop the ring doubles the intrigue, since (if it's authentic as the owner claims) a stone ball is in variance with general archaeological opinion that the pre-Columbian ball game was played with a rubber, rather than a rock ball. (Pity the pre-Columbian ball players who had to bat such a hard, heavy missile around with their arms, shoulders, and torsos.)

MITLA

The ruins at Mitla, about 31 miles (50 km) from Oaxaca city, are a "must" for Valley of Oaxaca sightseers. Mitla ("Lioobaa" in Zapotec, the "Place of the Dead") flowered late, reaching a population of perhaps 10,000 during its apex around A.D. 1350. It remained occupied and in use for generations after the conquest.

During Mitla's heyday, several feudalistic, fortified city-states vied for power in the Valley of Oaxaca. Concurrently, Mixtec-speaking people arrived from the north, perhaps under pressure from Aztecs and others in central Mexico. Evidence suggests that these Mixtec groups, in interacting with the resident Zapotecs, created the unique architectural styles of late cities such as Yagul and Mitla. Archaeologists believe, for example, that the striking *greca* (Greek-like) frets that honeycomb Mitla facades result from the Mixtec influence.

Exploring the Site

In a real sense, Mitla lives on. The ruins coincide with the present town of San Pablo Villa de Mitla, whose main church actually occupies the northernmost of five main groups of monumental ruins. Virtually anywhere archaeologists dig within the town they hit remains of the myriad ancient dwellings, plazas, and tombs that connected the still-visible landmarks.

Get there by forking left from main Oaxaca Highway 190 onto Hwy. 176. Continue about two miles to the Mitla town entrance, on the left. Head straight through town, cross a bridge, and, after about a mile, arrive at the site. Of the five ruins clusters, the best preserved is the fenced-

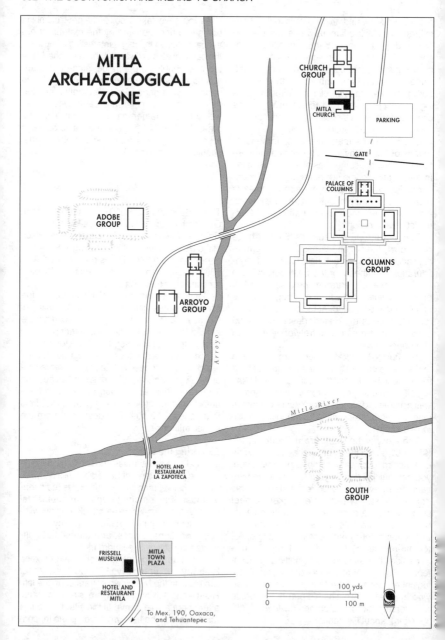

MITLA ARCHAEOLOGICAL ZONE

CHURCH GROUP

MITLA CHURCH

PARKING

GATE

PALACE OF COLUMNS

COLUMNS GROUP

ADOBE GROUP

ARROYO GROUP

Arroyo

Mitla River

HOTEL AND RESTAURANT LA ZAPOTECA

SOUTH GROUP

FRISSELL MUSEUM

MITLA TOWN PLAZA

HOTEL AND RESTAURANT MITLA

To Mex. 190, Oaxaca, and Tehuantepec

0   100 yds
0   100 m

in Columns Group. Its exploration requires about an hour. The others—the Arroyo and Adobe groups beyond an arroyo, and the South Group across the Mitla River—are rubbly, unreconstructed mounds. The North Group has suffered due to past use by the local parish. Evidence indicates the Adobe and South groups were ceremonial compounds, while the Arroyo, North, and Columns groups were palaces.

The public entrance to the Columns Group leads from the parking lot, past a tourist market and through the gate (open daily 9 a.m.-5 p.m., admission $2). Inside, two large patios, joined at one corner, are each surrounded on three sides by elaborate apartments. A shrine occupies the center of the first patio. Just north of this stands the **Palace of Columns,** the most important of Mitla's buildings. It sits atop a staircase, inaccurately reconstructed in 1901.

Inside, a file of six massive monolithic columns supported the roof. A narrow "escape" passage exits out the right rear side to a large patio enclosed by a continuous narrow room. The purely decorative *greca* facades, which required around 100,000 cut stones for the entire complex, embellish the walls. Remnants of the original red and white stucco that lustrously embellished the entire complex hide in niches and corners.

Walk south to the second patio, which has a similar layout. Here, the main palace occupies the east side, where a passage descends to a tomb beneath the front staircase. Both this and another tomb beneath the building at the north side of the patio are intact, preserving their original crucifix shapes. (The guard, although he is not supposed to, may try to collect a tip for letting you descend.) No one knows who and what were buried in these tombs, which were open and empty at the time of the conquest.

The second tomb is similar, except that it contains a stone pillar called the Column of Life; by embracing it, legend says, you will learn how many years you have left.

The Church Group (notice the church domes) on the far side of the Palace of Columns is worth a visit.

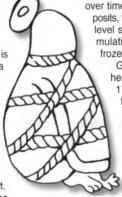

hieroglyph of Mitla (Place of the Dead)

Builders used the original temple stones to erect the church here. On its north side is a patio leading to another interior patio surrounded by another *greca* fret-embellished palace.

Museum, Accommodations, and Food

The University of the Americas (Mexico City) houses an exceptionally fine Oaxaca artifact collection at the **Frissell Museum,** tel. (956) 801-94, just west of (left as you enter) the Mitla town plaza. Displays include a host of finely preserved ceramic figurines, yet-to-be-deciphered Zapotec glyphs, and a Zapotec marriage certificate in stone. Open daily 9 a.m.-5 p.m. For food, a restaurant in the museum serves regional dishes from 9 a.m. to about 4:30 p.m., or, alternatively, go to the homey **Hotel and Restaurant Mitla** across the street from the museum.

A few blocks back toward the ruins, just before the Mitla River bridge, **Hotel La Zapoteca,** 5 de Febrero 12, Mitla, Oaxaca 70430, tel. (956) 800-26, offers both a good restaurant and clean, reasonably priced lodgings, fine for an overnight. The 20 rooms with bath rent for about $11 s, $20 d, $25 t with hot water and parking.

Hierve de Agua Mineral Springs

Although the name of this place translates as "boiling" water, the springs that seep from the side of the limestone mountain less than an hour's drive east of Mitla are not hot. Instead, they are loaded with minerals. These minerals, over time, have built up into rock-hard deposits, forming great algae-painted slabs in level spots and, on steep slopes, accumulating into what appear to be grand frozen waterfalls.

Get there by driving or riding a bus heading east out of Mitla along Hwy. 179, the road that branches east from Hwy. 190, two miles before the town of Mitla. After another approximately 11 miles (18 km), follow the gravel road that branches right, another five miles (eight km), through San Lorenzo village to Hierve de Agua.

Although the road's end may be crowded on weekends and holidays, you'll probably have the place nearly to yourself on

The Yagul archaeological zone, on a valley-view hilltop near Mitla, includes a restored ball court (foreground), ceremonial platforms, and a maze-like palace complex.

weekdays. A tourist Yu'u ("lodging" in Zapotec) offers six newish housekeeping bungalows with baths for about $10 d with pool, and a lineup of snack and curio stalls surrounds the cliffside parking lot. A trail leads downhill to the main spring, which bubbles from the mountain and trickles into a huge basin that the operators have dammed as a swimming pool. Bring your bathing suit.

From the pool, agile walkers can hike farther down the hill, following deposits, curiously accumulated in the shape of limestone mini-dikes that trace the mineral water's downhill path. Soon you'll glimpse the towering limestone formation, like a giant petrified waterfall, appearing to ooze from the cliff on the right.

SOUTH SIDE: SAN BÁRTOLO COYOTEPEC AND OCOTLÁN DE MORELOS

These crafts towns make a nice pair to visit on Ocotlán's Friday market day. **Coyotepec** ("Hill of the Coyote") on Hwy. 175, 14 miles (23 km) south of the Oaxaca, is famous for its pottery and its 24 August festival, when masked villagers, costumed half-man, half-woman in tiaras, blond wigs, tin crowns, and velvet cloaks, dance in honor of their patron, San Bártolo.

Their pottery, the renowned black *barra* sold all over Mexico, is available at a number of cottage factory-shops (watch for signs) off the highway

on (east side) Juárez Street. **Doña Rosa,** who passed away in 1980, pioneered the technique of crafting lovely, big, round jars without a potter's wheel. With their local clay, Doña Rosa's descendants and neighbor families regularly turn out acres of glistening black plates, pots, bowls, trees of life, and fetching animals for very reasonable prices. (Figure on $25 for a pearly three-gallon vase, and perhaps $2 for a cute little black rabbit.)

Ocotlán ("Place of Pines"), 26 miles, 42 km south of Oaxaca, has the equally interesting trio of shops run by the Aguilar sisters, Irene, Guillerma, and Josefina. Watch for the signs about a quarter mile on the Oaxaca side from the town plaza. Their creations include a host of fanciful figures in clay: vendors with big ripe strawberries, green and red cactus, goats in skirts, and bikini-clad blondes.

Your main Ocotlán attraction (unless you're lucky enough to arrive during the 18 May fiesta) will be the big Friday market. Hint: Since markets are best in the morning, make Ocotlán your *first* Friday stop.

SOUTHWEST SIDE: ARRAZOLA, CUILAPAN, AND ZAACHILA

This excursion is best on Thursday, when you can begin fresh in the morning at the big weekly market and ruins in Zaachila, then reverse your path back to the exconvent Santiago Aposto near Cuilapan. On the final reverse leg, stop to see the animals being crafted in Arrazola village.

Get there by tour bus or by car heading toward Monte Albán (look for the big road sign) west over the Atoyac River from the *periférico* at the south edge of town. Just after crossing the bridge, fork left (south) from the Monte Albán road onto the Zaachila road.

Your destination is the Zaachila town plaza-market about 10 miles south of Oaxaca. Like Mitla, **Zaachila** overlies the ruins of its ancient namesake city, which rose to prominence after the decline of Monte Albán. Although excavations have uncovered many Mixtec-style remains, historical records nevertheless list a number of Zapotec kings who ruled Zaachila as a virtual Zapotec capital. On the eve of the conquest, it was a Mixtec noble minority who dominated the Zapotec-speaking inhabitants, whose leaders the Mixtec warriors had sent fleeing for their lives to Tehuantepec.

The big forested hill that rises north of the plaza market is topped by a large, mostly unexplored pyramid. Several unexcavated mounds and courtyards dot the hill's north and south flanks. The site parking lot and entrance gate are adjacent to the colonial church just north of the plaza.

In 1962, archaeologist Roberto Gallegos uncovered a pair of unopened tombs beneath the summit of the Zaachila pyramid. They yielded a trove of polychrome pottery, gold jewelry (including a ring still on a left hand), and jade fan handles. Tomb 1, which is open for public inspection, descends via a steep staircase to an entrance decorated with a pair of cat-motif heads. On the antechamber walls a few steps farther on are depictions of owls and a pair of personages (perhaps former occupants) inscribed respectively with name-dates (month-week) 5 Flower

and 9 Flower. Do not miss the bas-reliefs on the tomb's back wall (take a flashlight), which depict a man whose torso is covered with a turtle shell and another whose head is emerging from a serpent body.

Hint: The narrow tomb staircase is negotiable by only a few persons at a time and often requires an hour for a tour bus crowd to inspect it. Rather than wasting your market time standing in line, go downhill, stroll around the market, and return when the line is smaller. If driving, arrive early, around 9 a.m. on Thursday, to avoid tour bus crowds.

Cuilapan de Guerrero, a few miles back north toward Oaxaca, is known for its elaborate unfinished exconvent of Saint James, or Santiago (visible from the highway), where President Guerrero was executed in 1831. Although begun in 1535, the cost of the basilica and associated monastery began to balloon. In 1550, King Philip demanded humility and moderation of the builders, whose work was finally ended by a 1570 court ruling. The extravagances—soaring, roofless basilica, magnificent baptismal font, splendid Gothic cloister, and elaborate frescoes—remain as national treasures.

Arrazola, a few miles farther north, is the source of the intricately painted *alebrijes* (ah-lay-BREE-hays), fanciful wooden creatures that are increasingly turning up in shops all over Mexico and foreign countries. To get there turn west (left) onto Hwy. 145 a few miles north of Cuilapan, or 3.2 miles (5.1 kilometers) miles south of the Atoyac River Bridge. Pass through San Javier village and continue from the turnoff, a total of three miles (five kilometers), to just before the Arrazola town plaza. Turn right onto E. Zapata, then turn left after one block, at Independencia. After one more block, you will be at Calle Obregón, where everyone seems to be making *alebrijes*. Although every family along the street crafts its own variations, **Pepe Santiago** and his Santa's workshop of craftspersons ap-

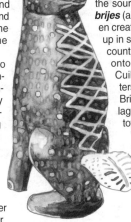

carved wooden rabbit from Arrazola, in the Valley of Oaxaca

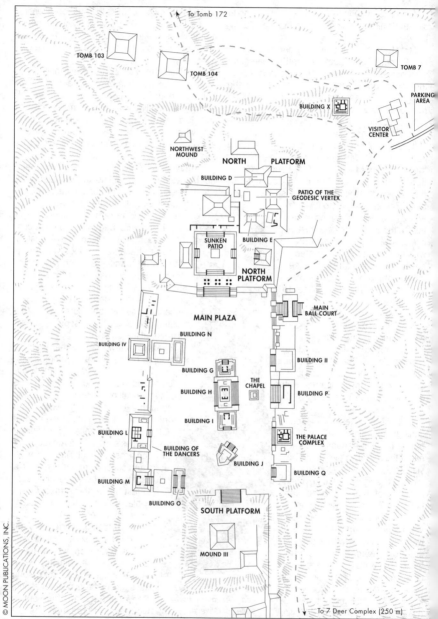

To Tomb 172

TOMB 103

TOMB 104

TOMB 7

PARKING AREA

BUILDING X

VISITOR CENTER

NORTHWEST MOUND

NORTH PLATFORM

BUILDING D

PATIO OF THE GEODESIC VERTEX

BUILDING E

SUNKEN PATIO

NORTH PLATFORM

MAIN BALL COURT

MAIN PLAZA

BUILDING N

BUILDING IV

BUILDING II

BUILDING G

THE CHAPEL

BUILDING H

BUILDING P

BUILDING I

BUILDING L

THE PALACE COMPLEX

BUILDING OF THE DANCERS

BUILDING J

BUILDING Q

BUILDING M

BUILDING O

SOUTH PLATFORM

MOUND III

To 7 Deer Complex (250 m)

© MOON PUBLICATIONS, INC.

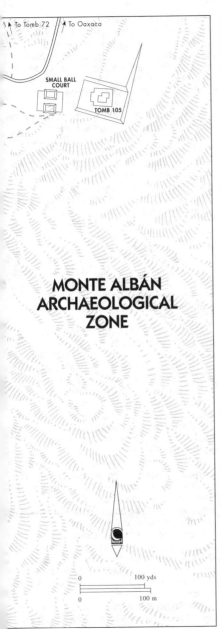

MONTE ALBÁN ARCHAEOLOGICAL ZONE

To Tomb 72 To Oaxaca

SMALL BALL COURT

TOMB 105

0   100 yds
0   100 m

pear to have the edge. Inside the Santiago compound (on the right, just below the hilltop), men saw and carve away, while a cadre of young women painstakingly add riots of painted brocade to whimsical dragons, gargoyles, armadillos, giraffes, rabbits, and everything in between.

NORTHEAST OF TOWN: MONTE ALBÁN AND ETLA

Monte Albán is among Mesoamerica's most regal and spectacular ruined cities. The original name is lost in antiquity. "Monte Albán" was probably coined by a local Spaniard because of its resemblance to a similarly named Italian hill town.

Monte Albán's people cultivated corn, beans, squash, chiles, and fruits on the hillsides and adjacent valleys, occasionally feasting on meat from deer, small game, and perhaps (as did other ancient Mexicans) domesticated dogs. Tribute from surrounding communities directly enriched Monte Albán's ruling classes, and, by extension, its artisans and farmers.

Monte Albán reigned for at least 1,200 years, between 500 B.C. and A.D. 750, as the capital of the Zapotecs and the dominant force between Teotihuacán in the Valley of Mexico and the Maya empires of the south.

Archaeologists have organized the Valley of Oaxaca's history from 500 B.C. to the conquest in five periods, known as Monte Albán I through V. Over those centuries, the hilltop city was repeatedly reconstructed, with new walls, plazas, and staircases, which, like peels of an onion, now overlie earlier construction.

Remains from Monte Albán Period I (500 B.C.-A.D. 0) reveal an already advanced culture, with gods, permanent temples, a priesthood, writing, numerals, and a calendar. Sharply contrasting house styles indicate a differentiated, multilayered society. Monte Albán I ruins abound in graceful polychrome ceramics of uniquely Zapotec style.

Concurrent Olmec influences have also been found, notably in the buildings known as the **Danzantes** ("Dancers"), decorated with unique bas-reliefs, similar to those unearthed along the Veracruz and Tabasco coasts.

Monte Albán II people (A.D. 0-300), by contrast, came under heavy influence from Chiapas and Guatemala in the south. They built strange, ship-shaped buildings, such as Monte Albán's Building J, and left unique remains of their religion, such as the striking jade bat-god now on display in the Anthropology Museum in Mexico City.

Monte Albán reached its apex during Period III (A.D. 300-800), attaining a population of perhaps 40,000 in an urban zone of about three square miles, which spread along hilltops (including the El Gallo and Atzompa archaeological sites) west of the present city of Oaxaca.

Vigorous Period III leaders rebuilt the main hilltop complex as we see it today. Heavily influenced by the grand Teotihuacán styles, the buildings were finished with handsome sloping staircases, corniced walls, monumental carvings, ball courts, and hieroglyph-inscribed stelae depicting gods, kings, and heroic scenes of battle.

By A.D. 750 few foreign influences were continuing to enrich Monte Albán's uniquely Zapotec pottery styles. Quality declined until they seemed like mere factory copies. Concurrently, the Zapotec pantheon expanded to a horde of gods, as if mere numbers could protect the increasingly isolated Valley of Oaxaca from the outside world.

In A.D. 800, Monte Albán, mysteriously cut off from the rest of Mesoamerica, was declining in population and power. By A.D. 1000, the city was nearly abandoned. The reasons—whether drought, disease, or revolt—and the consequent loss of the necessarily imported water, wood, salt, and food supplies, remain an enigma.

During Periods IV and V, Mixtec peoples from the north invaded the Valley of Oaxaca. They warred with valley Zapotecs and, despite their relatively small numbers, became a ruling class in a number of valley city-states. The blend of Mixtec and Zapotec art and architecture sometimes led to new forms, especially visible at the westvalley sites of Yagul and Mitla.

Monte Albán, meanwhile, although abandoned, was not forgotten. It became both a refuge and a venerated burial place. In times of siege, local people retreated within the walls of a fortress built around Monte Albán's South Platform. At other times, Mixtec nobles opened tombs and reused them as burial vaults right down until the eve of the conquest.

Exploring Monte Albán

Visitors to Monte Albán enjoy a panoramic view of green mountains rising above the checkerboard of the Valley of Oaxaca. Monte Albán is fun for a picnic; alternatively, it is an auspicious place to perch atop a pyramid above the grand Main Plaza, etched by lengthening afternoon shadows, and contemplate the ages.

As you enter past the visitor center, north is on your right, marked by the grand **North Platform,** topped by clusters of temples. The **Ball Court** will soon appear below on your left. Twenty-foot-high walkways circumscribe the sunken "I"-shaped playing field. To ensure true bounces, builders spread smooth stucco over all surfaces, including the slopes on opposite sides (which, contrary to appearances, did not seat spectators). This, like all Oaxacan ball courts, had no stone ring (for supposed goals), but rather four mysterious niches at the court's opposite "I"-end corners.

The **Main Plaza,** 1,000 feet long and exactly two-thirds that wide, is aligned along a precise north-south axis. Probably serving as a market and civic-ceremonial ground, the monumentally harmonious Main Plaza was the Zapotec "navel" of the world.

Monte Albán's oldest construction, of the **Danzantes** (surmounted by newer Building L, on the west side of the plaza between Buildings M and IV) dates from Period I. Its walls are graced with a host of personages, known commonly as the *danzantes* (dancers) from their oft-contorted postures—probably chiefs, vanquished by Monte Albán's armies. Their headdresses, earplugs, bracelets, and necklaces mark them among the nobility, while glyphs around their heads identify each individual.

Building J (circa A.D. 0), one of the most remarkable in Mesoamerica, stands nearby in midplaza at the foot of the South Platform. Speculation has raged since excavators unearthed its arrow-shaped base generations ago. It is not surprising that Alfonso Caso, Monte Albán's principal excavator, theorized it was an astronomical observatory. In the mind's eye, it seems like some fantastic ocean (or space?) vessel, being navigated to some mysteriously singular southwest destination by a ghostly crew oblivious of its worldly, earthbound brother monuments.

The **South Platform,** especially during the late afternoon, affords Monte Albán's best van-

Ocotlán's Aguilar sisters specialize in whimsical, one-of-a-kind pottery pieces.

tage point. Starting on the right-hand, palace complex side, **Building II** has a peculiar tunnel on its near side, covertly used by priests for privacy or perhaps some kind of magical effect. To the south stands Building P, an undistinguished albeit multiroom palace.

The South Platform itself is only marginally explored. Looters have riddled the mounds on its top side. Its bottom four corners were embellished by fine bas reliefs, two of which had their engraving intentionally buried from view. You can admire the fine sculpture and yet-undeciphered Zapotec hieroglyphs on one of them, along with others, at the South Platform's plaza-edge west side.

Still atop the South Platform, turn southward, where you can see the 7 Deer complex, a few hundred yards away, labeled for the name-date inscribed on its great lintel.

Turning northward again, look just beyond Building J to Buildings G, H, and I at plaza center, erected mostly to cover a rocky mound impossible to remove without the then-unavailable dynamite. Between these buildings and the palace complex on the right stands the small chapel where the remarkable bat-god jade sculpture was found.

On Monte Albán's northern periphery stand a number of tombs which, when excavated, yielded a trove of artifacts, now mostly housed in museums. Walking west from the Northern Platform's northeast base corner, you will pass Mound X on the right. A few hundred yards farther comes the **Tomb 104** mound, presided over by an elaborate ceramic urn representing Cojico, the Zapotec god of rain. Just north of this is **Tomb 172**, with the skeletons and offerings left intact.

Heading back along the northernmost of the two paths from Tomb 104, you will arrive at **Tomb 7** a few hundred feet behind the visitor center. Here, around 1450, Mixtec nobles removed the original 8th-century contents and reused the tomb, burying a deceased dignitary and two servants for the netherworld. Along with the bodies they left a fabulous treasure in gold, silver, jade, alabaster, and turquoise, now visible in Oaxaca at the regional **Museum of the Cultures of Oaxaca.**

A few hundred feet toward town on the opposite side of the road from the parking lot is a trail, leading past a small ball court to the Cerro de Plumaje ("Hill of Plumage"), site of **Tomb 105.** A magnificent entrance door lintel, reminiscent of those at Mitla, welcomes you inside. Past the patio, descend to the mural-decorated tomb antechamber. Inside the cruciform tomb itself, four figures walk in pairs toward a great glyph, flanked by a god and goddess, identified by their name-dates.

Visitor Center and Getting There

The Monte Albán Visitor Center has an excellent museum, café, information counter, and good store, with many books—guides, histories, art, folklore—on Mesoamerica. One of the most useful archaeological guides is Ignacio Bernal's *Official Guide of the Oaxaca Valley,* which includes Monte Albán, Cuilapan, Zaachila, Dainzu, Lambityeco, Yagul, and Mitla. Also covering the same territory, but in more depth, is *Oaxaca, the Arche-*

ological Record, by archaeologist Marcus Winter.

Get to Monte Albán either by driving yourself (follow the big Monte Albán sign on the *periférico,* end of Cabrera) over the Río Atoyac bridge; bear right after the bridge and continue about four miles (six km), bearing uphill, to the summit. Alternatively, go by tourist bus departing from your hotel or downtown Hotel Señorial (tel. 951-639-33) or Hotel Rivera del Ángel (tel. 951-653-27 or 431-61). Tours leave daily. A third option is to ride one of the very frequent Monte Albán buses from the Abastos terminal, on the *periférico* end of Trujano.

Monte Albán is open daily from 10 a.m., closing promptly at 5 p.m.

Etla

The untouristed, very colorful Wednesday market at Villa de Etla, northeast of Oaxaca, could be visited either separately or in coordination with a visit to Monte Albán. Although Etla's market invariably has stalls overflowing with its famous white cheese, vendors offer much other old-fashioned merchandise. (How would you like, for example, some fresh sheepskins, burro pack-frames, green Atzompa pottery, or red Oaxaca tamales?)

Preferably visit the market in the forenoon and Monte Albán in the midafternoon. Arrive at Monte Albán by 2:30 p.m. to allow enough leisure to tour the ruins before closing at 5 p.m.

Getting to Etla: By car, head north along Hwy. 190 about nine miles (15 km) from the city center and turn left just before the Pemex station. The Etla market is about half a mile from the highway. By bus, ride one of the many Etla-marked buses from the Abastos second-class terminal, or a tour bus.

mask with unusual monkey mascot motif

APPENDIX
GLOSSARY

Many of the following words have a social-historical meaning; others you will not find in the usual English-Spanish dictionary.

abarrotería—grocery store

alcalde—mayor or municipal judge

alfarer—pottery

andando—walkway, or strolling path

antojitos—native Mexican snacks, such as tamales, *chiles rellenos,* tacos, and enchiladas

artesanías—handicrafts, as distinguished from *artesanio,* a person who makes handicrafts

audiencia—one of the royal executive-judicial panels sent to rule Mexico during the 16th century

ayuntamiento—either the town council or the building where it meets

bienes raices—literally "good roots," but popularly, real estate

birria—goat, pork, or lamb stew, in spiced tomato broth, especially typical of Jalisco

boleto—ticket, boarding pass

cabercera—head town of a municipal district, or headquarters in general

cabrón—literally a cuckold, but more commonly, bastard, rat, or S.O.B.; sometimes used affectionately

cacique—chief or boss

calandria—early 1800s-style horse-drawn carriage, common in Guadalajara

camionera—bus station

campesino—country person; farm worker

canasta—basket of woven reeds, with handle

casa de huéspedes—guesthouse, usually operated in a family home

caballero—literally, "horseman," but popularly, gentleman

caudillo—dictator or political chief

charro, charra—gentleman cowboy or cowgirl

chingar—literally, to "rape," but is also the universal Spanish "f" word, the equivalent of "screw" in English

churrigueresque—Spanish baroque architectural style incorporated into many Mexican colonial churches, named after José Churriguera (1665-1725)

científicos—literally, scientists, but applied to President Porfirio Díaz's technocratic advisers

cofradia—Catholic fraternal service association, either male or female, mainly in charge of financing and organizing religous festivals

colectivo—a shared public taxi or minibus that picks up and deposits passengers along a designated route

colegio—preparatory school or junior college

colonia—suburban subdivision-satellite of a larger city

Conasupo—government store that sells basic foods at subsidized prices

correo—post office

criollo—person of all-Spanish descent born in the New World

cuadra—Huichol yarn painting, usually rectangular

Cuaresma—Lent

curandero(a)—indigenous medicine man or woman

damas—ladies, as in "ladies room"

Domingo de Ramos—Palm Sunday

ejido—a consitutional, government-sponsored form of community, with shared land ownership and cooperative decision making

encomienda—colonial award of tribute from a designated indigenous district

estación ferrocarril—railroad station

farmacia—pharmacy, or drugstore

finca—farm

fonda—foodstall or small restaurant, often in a traditional market complex

fraccionamiento—city sector or subdivision

fuero—the former right of clergy to be tried in separate ecclesiastical courts

gachupín—"one who wear spurs"; a derogatory term for a Spanish-born colonial

gasolinera—gasoline station

gente de razón—"people of reason"; whites and mestizos in colonial Mexico

gringo—once-derogatory but now commonly used term for North American whites

grito—impassioned cry, as in Hidalgo's Grito de Dolores

hacienda—large landed estate; also the government treasury

hidalgo—nobleman; called honorifically by "Don" or "Doña"

indígena—indigenous or aboriginal inhabitant of all-native descent who speaks his or her native tongue. Commonly, but incorrectly, an Indian *(indio)*

jejenes—"no-see-um" biting gnats, especially around San Blas, Nayarit

judiciales—the federal "judicial," or investigative police, best known to motorists for their highway checkpoint inspections

jugería—stall or small restaurant providing a large array of squeezed vegetable and fruit *jugos* (juices)

juzgado—the "hoosegow," or jail

larga distancia—long-distance telephone service, or the *caseta* (booth) where it's provided

licencado—academic degree (abbrev. Lic.) approximately equivalent to a bachelor's degree

lonchería—small lunch counter, usually serving juices, sandwiches, and *antojitos* (Mexican snacks)

machismo; macho—exaggerated sense of maleness; person who holds such a sense of himself

mestizo—person of mixed Indian-European descent

mescal—alcoholic beverage distilled from the fermented hearts of maguey (century plant)

milpa—Indian farm plot, usually of corn

mordida—slang for bribe; "little bite"

palapa—thatched-roof structure, often open and shading a restaurant

panga—outboard launch *(lancha)*

papier-mâché—the craft of glued, multilayered paper sculpture, especially in Tonalá, Jalisco, where creations resemble fine pottery or lacquerware

Pemex—acronym for Petróleos Mexicanos, the national oil corporation

peninsulares—the Spanish-born ruling colonial elite

peón—a poor wage-earner, usually a country native

piñata—papier-mâché decoration, usually in animal or human form, filled with treats and broken open during a fiesta

plan—political manifesto, usually by a leader or group consolidating or seeking power

Porfiriata—the 34-year (1876-1910) ruling period of President-dictator Porfirio Díaz

pozole—stew, of hominy in broth, usually topped by shredded pork, cabbage, and diced onion

preventiva—municipal police

presidencia municipal—the headquarters, like a U.S. city or county hall, of a Mexican *municipio*, county-like local governmental unit

pronunciamiento—declaration of rebellion by an insurgent leader

puta—whore, bitch, or slut

pueblo—town or people

quinta—a villa or country house

quinto—the royal "fifth" tax on treasure and precious metals

retorno—cul-de-sac

rurales—former federal country police force created to fight bandidos

Semana Santa—pre-Easter holy week

taxi especial—private taxi, as distinguished from *taxi colectivo*, or collective taxi

telégrafo—telegraph office, lately converting to high-tech **telecomunicaciones**, or *telecom*, offering telegraph, telephone, and public fax services

vaquero—cowboy

vecinidad—neighborhood

yanqui—Yankee

zócalo—town plaza or central square

PRONUNCIATION GUIDE

Your Puerto Vallarta adventure will be more fun if you use a little Spanish. Mexican folks, although they may smile at your funny accent, will appreciate your halting efforts to break the ice and transform yourself from a foreigner to a potential friend.

Spanish commonly uses 30 letters—the familiar English 26, plus four straightforward additions: ch, ll, ñ, and rr, which are explained in "Consonants," below.

Vowels

Once you learn them, Spanish pronunciation rules—in contrast to English—don't change. Spanish vowels generally sound softer than in English. (Note: The capitalized syllables below receive stronger accents.)

Pronounce *a* like ah, as in hah: *agua* AH-gooah (water), *pan* PAHN (bread), and *casa* CAH-sah (house).

Pronounce *e* like ay, as in may: *mesa* MAY-sah (table), *tela* TAY-lah (cloth), and *de* DAY (of, from).

Pronounce *i* like ee, as in need: *diez* dee-AYZ (ten), *comida* ko-MEE-dah (meal), and *fin* FEEN (end).

Pronounce *o* like oh, as in oh: *peso* PAY-soh (weight), *ocho* OH-choh (eight), and *poco* POH-koh (a bit).

Pronounce *u* like oo, as in cool: *uno* OO-noh (one), *cuarto* KOOAHR-toh (room), and *usted* oos-TAYD (you).

Accent

The rule for accent, the relative stress given to syllables within a given word, is straightforward. If a word ends in a vowel, an n, or an s, accent the next-to-last syllable; if not, accent the last syllable.

Pronounce *gracias* GRAH-seeahs (thank you), *orden* OHR-dayn (order), and *carretera* kah-ray-TAY-rah (highway).

Otherwise, accent the last syllable: *venir* vay-NEER (to come), *ferrocarril* fay-roh-cah-REEL (railroad), and *edad* ay-DAHD (age).

For practice, apply the accent ("vowel, n, or s") rule for the vowel-pronunciation examples above. Try to accent the words correctly without looking at the "answers" to the right.

Exceptions to the accent rule are always marked with an accent sign: (á, é, í, ó, or ú), such as *teléfono* tay-LAY-foh-noh (telephone), *jabón* hah-BON (soap), and *rápido* RAH-pee-doh (rapid).

Consonants

Seventeen Spanish consonants, *b, d, f, k, l, m, n, p, q, s, t, v, w, x, y, z,* and *ch,* are pronounced almost as in English; *h* occurs, but is silent—not pronounced at all.

As for the remaining seven *(c, g, j, ll, ñ, r, and rr)* consonants, pronounce *c* "hard," like k as in keep: *cuarto* KOOAR-toh (room), Tepic tay-PEEK (capital of Nayarit state). Exception: Before *e* or *i,* pronounce *c* "soft," like an English s, as in sit: *cerveza* sayr-VAY-sah (beer), *encima* ayn-SEE-mah (atop).

Before *a, o, u,* or a consonant, pronounce *g* "hard," as in gift: *gato* GAH-toh (cat), *hago* AH-goh (I do, make). Otherwise, pronounce *g* like h as in hat: *giro* HEE-roh (money order), *gente* HAYN-tay (people).

Pronounce *j* like an English h, as in has: *jueves* HOOAY-vays (Thursday), *mejor* may-HOR (better).

Pronounce *ll* like y, as in yes: *toalla* toh-AH-yah (towel), *ellos* AY-yohs (they, them).

Pronounce *ñ* like ny, as in canyon: *año* AH-nyo (year), *señor* SAY-nyor (Mr., sir).

The Spanish *r* is lightly trilled, with tongue at the roof of your mouth like the British r in very ("vehdy"). Pronounce *r* like a very light English d, as in ready: *pero* PAY-doh (but), *tres* TDAYS (three), *cuatro* KOOAH-tdoh (four).

Pronounce *rr* like a Spanish r, but with much more emphasis and trill. Let your tongue flap. Practice with *burro* (donkey), *carretera* (highway), and Carrillo (proper name), then really let go with *ferrocarril* (railroad).

ENGLISH-SPANISH PHRASEBOOK

A profitable route to learning Spanish in Mexico is to refuse to speak English. Prepare yourself (instead of watching the in-flight movie) with a basic word list in a pocket notebook. Use it to speak Spanish wherever you go.

Basic and Courteous

Courtesy is very important to Mexican people. They will appreciate your use of basic expressions. (Note: The upside-down Spanish question mark merely warns the reader of the query in advance.)

Hello—*Hola*
How are you?—*¿Cómo está usted?*
Very well, thank you.—*Muy bien, gracias.*
okay, good—*bueno*
not okay, bad—*malo, feo*
and you?—*¿y usted?*
(Note: Pronounce *"y,"* the Spanish "and," like the English "ee," as in "keep.")
Thank you very much.—*Muchas gracias.*
please—*por favor*
You're welcome.—*De nada.*
Just a moment, please.—*Momentito, por favor.*
How do you say . . . in Spanish?—*¿Cómo se dice . . . en español?*
Excuse me, please (when you're trying to get attention).—*Excúseme, con permiso.*
Excuse me (when you've made a boo-boo).—*Lo siento.*
good morning—*buenos días*
good afternoon—*buenas tardes*
good evening—*buenas noches*
Sir (Mr.), Ma'am (Mrs.), Miss—*Señor, Señora, Señorita*
What is your name?—*¿Cómo se llama usted?*
Pleased to meet you.—*Con mucho gusto.*
My name is . . .—*Me llamo . . .*
Would you like . . . ?—*¿Quisiera usted . . . ?*
Let's go to . . .—*Vámonos a . . .*
I would like to introduce my . . .—*Quisiera presentar mi . . .*
wife—*esposa*
husband—*esposo*
friend—*amigo* (male), *amiga* (female)

sweetheart—*novio* (male), *novia* (female)
son, daughter—*hijo, hija*
brother, sister—*hermano, hermana*
father, mother—*padre, madre*
See you later (again).—*Hasta luego (la vista).*
goodbye—*adiós*
yes, no—*sí, no*
I, you, he, she—*yo, usted, él, ella*
we, you (pl.), they—*nosotros, ustedes, ellos*
Do you speak English?—*¿Habla usted inglés?*

Getting Around

If I could use only two Spanish phrases, I would choose *"Excúseme,"* followed by *"¿Dónde está . . . ?"*

Where is . . . ?—*¿Dónde está . . . ?*
the bus station—*la terminal autobús*
the bus stop—*la parada autobús*
the taxi stand—*el sitio taxi*
the train station—*la terminal ferrocarril*
the airport—*el aeropuerto*
the boat—*la barca*
the bathroom, toilet—*el baño, sanitorio*
men's, women's—*el baño de hombres, de mujeres*
the entrance, exit—*la entrada, la salida*
the pharmacy—*la farmacia*
the bank—*el banco*
the police, police officer—*la policía*
the supermarket—*el supermercado*
the grocery store—*la abarrotería*
the laundry—*la lavandería*
the stationery (book) store—*la papelería (librería)*
the hardware store—*la ferretería*
the (long distance) telephone—*el teléfono (larga distancia)*
the post office—*el correo*
the ticket office—*la oficina boletos*
a hotel—*un hotel*

a cafe, a restaurant—*una café, un restaurante*
Where (Which) is the way to . . . ?—*¿Dónde (Cuál) está el camino a . . . ?*
How far to . . . ?—*¿Qué tan lejos a . . . ?*
How many blocks?—*¿Cuántos cuadras?*
(very) near, far—*(muy) cerca, lejos*
to, toward—*a*
by, through—*por*
from—*de*
the right, the left—*la derecha, la izquierda*
straight ahead—*derecho, directo*
in front—*en frente*
beside—*a lado*
behind—*atrás*
the corner—*la esquina*
the stoplight—*la semáforo*
a turn—*una vuelta*
right here—*aquí*
somewhere around here—*acá*
right here—*allí*
somewhere around there—*allá*
street, boulevard, highway—*calle, bólevar, carretera*
bridge, toll—*puente, cuota*
address—*dirección*
north, south—*norte, sur*
east, west—*oriente, poniente (oeste)*

Doing Things

Verbs are the key to getting along in Spanish. They employ mostly predictable forms and come in three classes, which end in ar, er, and ir, respectively:

to buy—*comprar*
I buy, you (he, she, it) buys—*compro, compra*
we buy, you (they) buy—*compramos, compran*

to eat—*comer*
I eat, you (he, she, it) eats—*como, come*
we eat, you (they) eat—*comemos, comen*

to climb—*subir*
I climb, you (he, she, it) climbs—*subo, sube*
we climb, you (they) climb—*subimos, suben*

Got the idea? Here are more (with irregularities marked in bold).

to do or make—*hacer*
I do or make, you (he she, it) does or makes—*hago, hace*
we do or make, you (they) do or make—*hacemos, hacen*

to go—*ir*
I go, you (he, she, it) goes: *voy, va*
we go, you (they) go: *vamos, van*

to love—*amar*
to swim—*nadar*
to walk—*andar*
to work—*trabajar*
to want—*desear*
to read—*leer*
to write—*escribir*
to repair—*reparar*
to arrive—*llegar*
to stay—*quedar*
to look at—*mirar*
to look for—*buscar*
to give—*dar* (regular except for **doy,** I give)
to have—*tener* (irregular but important: *tengo, tiene, tenemos, tienen*)
to come—*venir* (similarly irregular: *vengo, viene, venimos, vienen*)

Spanish has two forms of "to be." Use *estar* when speaking of location: "I am at home." "**Estoy** *en casa.*" Use *ser* for state of being: "I am a doctor." "**Soy** *una doctora.*" *Estar* is regular except for **estoy,** I am. *Ser* is very irregular:

to be—*ser*
I am, you (he, she, it) is—*soy, es*
we are, you (they) are—*somos, son*

At the Station and on the Bus

I'd like a ticket to . . .—*Quisiera un boleto a . . .*
first (second) class—*primera (segunda) clase*
roundtrip—*ida y vuelta*
how much?—*¿cuánto?*
reservation—*reservación*
reserved seat—*asiento reservado*
seat number . . .—*número asiento . . .*
baggage—*equipaje*
Where is this bus going?—*¿Dónde va este autobús?*

What's the name of this place?—*¿Cómo se llama este lugar?*
Stop here, please.—*Pare aquí, por favor.*

Eating Out

A *restaurante* (rays-tah-oo-RAHN-tay) generally implies a fairly fancy joint, with prices to match. The food and atmosphere, however, may be more to your liking at other types of eateries (in approximate order of price): *comedor, café, fonda, lonchería, jugería, taquería.*

I'm hungry (thirsty).—*Tengo hambre (sed).*
menu—*lista, menú*
order—*orden*
soft drink—*refresco*
coffee, cream—*café, crema*
tea—*té*
sugar—*azúcar*
drinking water—*agua pura, agua potable*
bottled carbonated water—*agua mineral*
bottled uncarbonated water—*agua sin gas*
glass—*vaso*
beer—*cerveza*
dark—*obscura*
draft—*de barril*
wine—*vino*
white, red—*blanco, tinto*
dry, sweet—*seco, dulce*
cheese—*queso*
snack—*antojo, botana*
daily lunch special—*comida corrida*
fried—*frito*
roasted—*asada*
barbecue, barbecued—*barbacoa, al carbón*
breakfast—*desayuno*
eggs—*huevos*
boiled—*tibios*
scrambled—*revueltos*
bread—*pan*
roll—*bolillo*
sweet roll—*pan dulce*
toast—*pan tostada*
oatmeal—*avena*
bacon, ham—*tocino, jamón*
salad—*ensalada*
lettuce—*lechuga*
carrot—*zanahoria*
tomato—*tomate*
oil—*aceite*
vinegar—*vinagre*

lime—*limón*
mayonnaise—*mayonesa*
fruit—*fruta*
mango—*mango*
watermelon—*sandía*
papaya—*papaya*
banana—*plátano*
apple—*manzana*
orange—*naranja*
fish—*pescado*
shrimp—*camarones*
oysters—*ostiones*
clams—*almejas*
octopus—*pulpo*
squid—*calamare*
meat (without)—*carne (sin)*
chicken—*pollo*
pork—*puerco*
beef, steak—*res, biftec*
the check—*la cuenta*

At the Hotel

In beach resorts, finding a reasonably priced hotel room presents no problem except during the high-occupancy weeks after Christmas and before Easter.

Is there . . . ?—*¿Hay . . . ?*
an (inexpensive) hotel—*un hotel (económico)*
an inn—*una posada*
a guesthouse—*una casa de huéspedes*
a single (double) room—*un cuarto sencillo (doble)*
with bath—*con baño*
shower—*ducha*
hot water—*agua caliente*
fan—*abanico, ventilador*
air-conditioned—*aire acondicionado*
double bed—*cama matrimonial*
twin beds—*camas gemelas*
How much for the room?—*¿Cuánto cuesta el cuarto?*
dining room—*comedor*
key—*llave*
towels—*toallas*
manager—*gerente*
soap—*jabón*
toilet paper—*papel higiénico*
swimming pool—*alberca, piscina*
the bill, please—*la cuenta, por favor*

At the Bank

El banco's often-long lines, short hours, and minuscule advantage in exchange rate make a nearby private *casa de cambio* a very handy alternative:

money—*dinero*
money-exchange bureau—*casa de cambio*
I would like to exchange traveler's checks.— *Quisiera cambiar cheques de viajero.*
What is the exchange rate?—*¿Cuál es el cambio?*
How much is the commission?—*¿Cuánto cuesta el comisión?*
Do you accept credit cards?—*¿Aceptan tarjetas de crédito?*
money order—*giro*
teller's window—*caja*
signature—*firma*

Shopping

Es la costumbre—it is the custom—in Mexico that the first price is never the last. Bargaining often transforms shopping from a perfunctory chore into an open-ended adventure. Bargain with humor, and be prepared to walk away if the price is not right.

How much does it cost?—*¿Cuánto cuesta?*
too much—*demasiado*
expensive, cheap—*caro, barato (económico)*
too expensive, too cheap—*demasiado caro, demasiado barato*
more, less—*más, menos*
small, big—*chico, grande*
good, bad—*bueno, malo*
smaller, smallest—*más chico, el más chico*
larger, largest—*más grande, el más grande*
cheaper, cheapest—*más barato, el más barato*
What is your final price?—*¿Cuál es su último precio?*
Just right!—*¡Perfecto!*

handicrafts—*artesanías*
craftsman, craftswoman—*artesano, artesana*
fanciful wooden animal—*alebrije*
mask—*máscara*
tinware—*hojalata*
basket (of reeds, with handle)—*canasta*
basket (of palm)—*tenate*

wool rug or hanging—*tapete*
mask—*máscara*
doll—*muñeca*
cutlery—*cuchillería*
knife—*cuchilla*
sword—*espada*
vase—*florera*
cup—*tasa*
bowl—*escudilla*
pot—*olla*
pitcher—*jarro*
furniture—*muebles*
jewelry or gem—*joya*
filigree jewelry—*filigrana*
candlestick—*candelero*
tablecloth—*mantel*
napkin or placemat—*servilleta*
embroidery—*bordado*
skirt—*falda*
blouse—*blusa*
shirt—*camisa*
dress—*vestido*
purse or bag—*bolsa*
wallet—*cartera*
wool—*lana*
maguey fiber—*ixtle*
leather—*cuero, piel*
cotton—*algodón*
copper—*cobre*
silver—*plata*
gold—*oro*
iron—*hierro*
pewter—*peltre*
glass—*vidrio*
wood—*madera*
black clay—*barro negro*
red clay—*barro rojo*
onyx—*onix*
wraparound skirt—*enredo, pozahuanco* (on the coast)
belt—*cinturón*
shawl—*rebozo*

Telephone, Post Office

In smaller Mexican towns, long-distance connections must be made at a central long-distance office, where people sometimes can sit, have coffee or a *refresco,* and socialize while waiting for their *larga distancia* to come through.

long-distance telephone—*teléfono larga*
I would like to call . . .—*Quisiera llamar a . . .*
station to station—*a quien contesta*
person to person—*persona a persona*
credit card—*tarjeta de crédito*
post office—*correo*
general delivery—*lista de correo*
letter—*carta*
stamp—*estampilla*
postcard—*tarjeta*
aerogram—*aerograma*
air mail—*correo aero*
registered—*registrado*
money order—*giro*
package, box—*paquete, caja*
string, tape—*cuerda, cinta*

Formalities

Though many experienced travelers find Mexico among the most exotic of destinations (more so than either India or Japan), crossing the border remains relatively easy.

border—*frontera*
customs—*aduana*
immigration—*migración*
tourist card—*tarjeta de turista*
inspection—*inspección, revisión*
passport—*pasaporte*
profession—*profesión*
marital status—*estado civil*
single—*soltero*
married, divorced—*casado, divorciado*
widowed—*viudado*
insurance—*seguros*
title—*título*
driver's license—*licencia de manejar*
fishing, hunting, gun license—*licencia de pescar, cazar, armas*

At the Pharmacy, Doctor, Hospital

For a third-world country, Mexico provides good health care. Even small Puerto Vallarta regional towns have a basic hospital or clinic.

Help me please.—*Ayúdeme por favor.*
I am ill.—*Estoy enfermo.*
Call a doctor.—*Llame un doctor.*
Take me to . . .—*Lleve me a . . .*
hospital—*hospital, sanatorio*
drugstore—*farmacia*

pain—*dolor*
fever—*fiebre*
headache—*dolor de cabeza*
stomache ache—*dolor de estómago*
burn—*quemadura*
cramp—*calambre*
nausea—*náusea*
vomiting—*vomitar*
medicine—*medicina*
antibiotic—*antibiótico*
pill, tablet—*pastilla*
aspirin—*aspirina*
ointment, cream—*pomada, crema*
bandage—*venda*
cotton—*algodón*
sanitary napkins (use brand name)
birth control pills—*pastillas contraceptivos*
contraceptive foam—*espuma contraceptiva*
diaphragm (best carry an extra)
condoms—*contraceptivas*
toothbrush—*cepilla dental*
dental floss (bring an extra supply)
toothpaste—*crema dental*
dentist—*dentista*
toothache—*dolor demuelas*

At the Gas Station

Some Mexican gas station attendants are experts at shortchanging you in both money and gasoline. If you don't have a locking gas cap, either insist on pumping the gas yourself, or make certain the pump is zeroed before the attendant begins pumping. Furthermore, the kids who hang around gas stations are notoriously light fingered. Stow every loose item—cameras, purses, binoculars—out of sight *before* you pull into the *gasolinera*.

gas station—*gasolinera*
gasoline—*gasolina*
leaded, unleaded—*plomo, sin plomo*
full, please—*lleno, por favor*
gas cap—*tapón*
tire—*llanta*
tire repair shop—*vulcanizadora*
air—*aire*
water—*agua*
oil (change)—*aceite (cambio)*
grease—*grasa*
My . . . doesn't work.—*Mi . . . no sirve.*
battery—*batería*

radiator—*radiador*
alternator, generator—*alternador, generador*
tow truck—*grúa*
repair shop—*taller mecánico*
tune-up—*afinación*
auto parts store—*refaccionería*

Numbers and Time

zero—*cero*
one—*uno*
two—*dos*
three—*tres*
four—*cuatro*
five—*cinco*
six—*seis*
seven—*siete*
eight—*ocho*
nine—*nueve*
10—*diez*
11—*once*
12—*doce*
13—*trece*
14—*catorce*
15—*quince*
16—*dieciseis*
17—*diecisiete*
18—*dieciocho*
19—*diecinueve*
20—*veinte*
21—*veinte y uno*, or *veintiuno*
30—*treinta*
40—*cuarenta*
50—*cincuenta*
60—*sesenta*
70—*setenta*
80—*ochenta*
90—*noventa*
100—*ciento*
101—*ciento y uno*, or *cientiuno*
200—*doscientos*
500—*quinientos*
1,000—*mil*
10,000—*diez mil*
100,000—*cien mil*
1,000,000—*milión*

1997—*mil novecientos noventa y siete*
one-half—*medio*
one-third—*un tercio*
one-fourth—*un quarto*

What time is it?—*¿Qué hora es?*
It's one o'clock.—*Es la una.*
It's three in the afternoon.—*Son las tres de la tarde.*
It's 4 a.m.—*Son las cuatro de la mañana.*
six-thirty—*seis y media*
a quarter till eleven—*un cuarto hasta once*
a quarter past five—*un cuarto después cinco*

Monday—*lunes*
Tuesday—*martes*
Wednesday—*miércoles*
Thursday—*jueves*
Friday—*viernes*
Saturday—*sábado*
Sunday—*domingo*

January—*enero*
February—*febrero*
March—*marzo*
April—*abril*
May—*mayo*
June—*junio*
July—*julio*
August—*agosto*
September—*septiembre*
October—*octubre*
November—*noviembre*
December—*diciembre*

last Sunday—*domingo pasado*
next December—*diciembre próximo*
yesterday—*ayer*
tomorrow—*mañana*
an hour—*una hora*
a week—*una semana*
a month—*un mes*
a week ago—*hace una semana*
after—*después*
before—*antes*

BOOKLIST

Some of these books are informative, others are entertaining, and all of them will increase your understanding of Mexico. Some are easier to find in Mexico than at home, and vice versa. Take a few along on your trip. If you find others which are especially noteworthy, let us know. Happy reading.

HISTORY

Calderón de la Barca, Fanny. *Life in Mexico, with New Material from the Author's Journals.* New York: Doubleday, 1966. Edited by H.T. and M.H. Fisher. An update of the brilliant, humorous, and celebrated original 1913 book by the Scottish wife of the Spanish ambassador to Mexico.

Casasola, Gustavo. *Seis Siglos de Historia Gráfica de Mexico* (Six Centuries of Mexican Graphic History). Mexico City: Editorial Gustavo Casasola, 1978. Six fascinating volumes of Mexican history in pictures, from 1325 to the present.

Cortés, Hernán. *Letters From Mexico.* Translated by Anthony Pagden. New Haven: Yale University Press, 1986. Cortés's five long letters to his king, in which he describes contemporary Mexico in fascinating detail, including, notably, the remarkably sophisticated life of the Aztecs at the time of the conquest.

Díaz del Castillo, Bernal. *The True Story of the Conquest of Mexico.* Translated by Albert Idell. Garden City: Doubleday, 1956. A soldier's still-fresh tale of the conquest from the Spanish viewpoint.

Garfias, Luis. *The Mexican Revolution.* Mexico City: Panorama Editorial, 1985. A concise Mexican version of the 1910-1917 Mexican revolution, the crucible of present-day Mexico.

Gugliotta, Bobette. *Women of Mexico.* Encino CA: Floricanto Press, 1989. Lively legends, tales and biographies of remarkable Mexican women, from Zapotec princesses to Independence heroines.

León-Portilla, Miguel. *The Broken Spears: The Aztec Account of the Conquest of Mexico.* New York: Beacon Press, 1962. Provides an interesting contrast to Díaz del Castillo's account.

Meyer, Michael, and William Sherman. *The Course of Mexican History.* New York: Oxford University Press, 1991. An insightful, 700-plus-page college textbook in paperback. A bargain, especially if you can get it used.

Novas, Himilce. *Everything You Need to Know About Latino History.* New York: Plume Books (Penguin Group), 1994. Chicanos, Latin rhythm, La Raza, the Treaty of Guadalupe Hidalgo, and much more, interpreted from an authoritative Latino point of view.

Reed, John. *Insurgent Mexico.* New York: International Publisher's Co., 1994. Republication of 1914 original. Fast-moving, but not unbiased, description of the 1910 Mexican revolution by the journalist famed for his reporting of the subsequent 1917 Russian revolution. Reed, memorialized by the Soviets, was resurrected in the 1981 film biography *Reds.*

Ruíz, Ramon Eduardo. *Triumphs and Tragedy: A History of the Mexican People.* New York: W.W. Norton, Inc., 1992. A pithy, anecdote-filled history of Mexico from an authoritative Mexican-American perspective.

Simpson, Lesley Bird. *Many Mexicos.* Berkeley: The University of California Press, 1962. A much-reprinted, fascinating broad-brush version of Mexican history.

UNIQUE GUIDE AND TIP BOOKS

American Automobile Association. *Mexico Travelbook.* Heathrow, FL: 1995. Published by the American Automobile Association, offices at 1000 AAA Drive, Heathrow, FL 32746-5063. Short sweet summaries of major Mexican tourist destinations and sights. Also includes information on fiestas, accommodations, restaurants, and a wealth of information relevant to car travel in Mexico. Available in bookstores, or free to AAA members at affiliate offices.

Burton, Tony. *Western Mexico, A Traveller's Treasury.* Guadalajara: Editorial Agata (Juan Manuel 316, Guadalajara 44100). A well-researched and lovingly written and illustrated guide to dozens of fascinating places to visit, both well-known and out of the way, in Michoacán, Jalisco, and Nayarit.

Church, Mike and Terry. *Traveler's Guide to Mexican Camping.* Kirkland, WA: Rolling Homes Press, P.O. Box 2099, Kirkland, WA 98083-2099. This is an unusually thorough guide to trailer parks all over Mexico, with much coverage of the Pacific Coast in general and the Puerto Vallarta Region in particular. Detailed maps guide you accurately to each trailer park cited and clear descriptions tell you what to expect. The book also provides very helpful information on car travel in Mexico, including details of insurance, border crossing, highway safety, car repairs, and much more.

Franz, Carl. *The People's Guide to Mexico.* Santa Fe: John Muir, 10th edition, 1998. An entertaining and insightful A to Z general guide to the joys and pitfalls of independent economy travel in Mexico.

Freedman, Jacqueline, and Susan Gerstein. *Traveling Like Everybody Else.* Brooklyn NY: Lambda Publishing, Inc. Your handicap needn't keep you at home.

Graham, Scott. *Handle With Care.* Chicago: The Noble Press, 1991. Should you accept a meal from a family who lives in a grass house? This insightful guide answers this and hundreds of other tough questions for persons who want to travel responsibly in the third world.

Howells, John, and Don Merwin. *Choose Mexico.* Oakland, CA: Gateway Books (distributed by Publishers Group West, Dept. M, 2023 Clemens Rd., Oakland, CA 94602). A pair of experienced Mexico residents provide a wealth of astute counsel about the important questions —health, finance, home ownership, work, driving, legalities—of long-term travel, residence, and retirement in Mexico. Includes specific sections on Puerto Vallarta, Guadalajara, and Lake Chapala.

Jeffries, Nan. *Adventuring With Children.* San Francisco: Foghorn Press/Avalon House, 1992. This unusually detailed book starts where most travel-with-children books end. It contains, besides a wealth of information and practical strategies for general travel with children, specific chapters on how you can adventure—trek, kayak, river-raft, camp, bicycle, and much more —successfully with the kids in tow.

Rogers, Steve, and Tina Rosa. *The Shopper's Guide to Mexico.* Santa Fe: John Muir, 1989. A well-written guide to shopping in Mexico, with emphasis on handicrafts. Contains inventory details and locations of out-of-the-ordinary shops in towns and cities all over Mexico, including much on the Pacific centers, especially Puerto Vallarta, greater Guadalajara, Mazatlán, Pátzcuaro, and Oaxaca.

Stillman, Alan Eric. *Kwikpoint.* Alexandria VA: GAIA Communications, P.O. Box 238, Alexandria, VA 22313-0238, e-mail: kwikpoint@his.com. Eight dollars by cash or check gets you a super handy, durable color fold-out of pictures to point to when you need something in a foreign country. The pictures, such as a frying pan with fire under it (for "fried"), a compass (for "Which direction?"), a red lobster, and a cauliflower, are imaginative and unmistakable, anywhere between Puerto Vallarta and Pakistan or San Blas and Santander.

Weisbroth, Ericka, and Eric Ellman. *Bicycling Mexico.* New York: Hunter, 1990. These intrepid adventurers describe bike trips from Puerto Vallarta to Acapulco, coastal and highland Oaxaca, and highland Jalisco and Michoacán.

Werner, David. *Where There Is No Doctor.* Palo Alto: Hesperian Foundation (P.O. Box 1692, Palo Alto, CA 94302). How to keep well in the backcountry.

FICTION

Fuentes, Carlos. *Where the Air Is Clear.* New York: Farrar, Straus and Giroux, 1971. The seminal work of Mexico's celebrated novelist.

Jennings, Gary. *Aztec.* New York: Atheneum, 1980. Beautifully researched and written monumental tale of lust, compassion, love, and death in pre-conquest Mexico.

Peters, Daniel. *The Luck of Huemac.* New York: Random House, 1981. An Aztec noble family's tale—of war, famine, sorcery, heroism, treachery, love, and finally disaster and death—in the Valley of Mexico.

Porter, Katherine Ann. *The Collected Stories.* New York: Delacorte, 1970.

Rulfo, Juan. *The Burning Plain.* Austin: University of Texas Press, 1967. Stories of people torn between the old and new in Mexico.

Traven, B. *The Treasure of the Sierra Madre.* New York: Hill and Wang, 1967. Campesinos, *federales,* gringos, and *indígenas* all figure in this modern morality tale set in Mexico's rugged outback. The most famous of the mysterious author's many novels of oppression and justice set in Mexico's jungles.

Villaseñor, Victor. *Rain of Gold.* New York: Delta Books (Bantam, Doubleday, and Dell), 1991. The moving, best-selling epic of the author's family's gritty travails. From humble rural beginnings in the Copper Canyon, they flee revolution and certain death, struggling through parched northern deserts to sprawling border refugee camps. From there they migrate to relative safety and an eventual modicum of happiness in Southern California.

PEOPLE AND CULTURE

Berrin, Kathleen. *The Art of the Huichol Indians.* Lovely, large photographs and text by a symposium of experts provide a good interpretive introduction to Huichol art and culture.

Lewis, Oscar. *Children of Sanchez.* New York: Random House, 1961. Poverty and strength in the Mexican underclass, sympathetically described and interpreted by renowned sociologist Lewis.

Meyerhoff, Barbara. *Peyote Hunt: the Sacred Journey of the Huichol Indians.* Ithaca: Cornell University Press, 1974. A description and interpretation of the Huichol's religious use of mind-bending natural hallucinogens.

Palmer, Colin A. *Slaves of the White God.* Cambridge: Harvard University Press. A scholarly study of why and how Spanish authorities imported African slaves into America and how they were used afterwards. Replete with poignant details, taken from Spanish and Mexican archives, describing how the Africans struggled from bondage to eventual freedom.

Riding, Alan. *Distant Neighbors: A Portrait of the Mexicans.* New York: Random House Vintage Books. Rare insights into Mexico and Mexicans.

Toor, Frances (1890-1956). *A Treasury of Mexican Folkways.* New York: Crown Books, 1947, reprinted by Bonanaza, 1985. An illustrated encyclopedia of vanishing Mexicana—costumes, religion, fiestas, burial practices, customs, legends—compiled during the celebrated author's 35 years' residence in Mexico.

Wauchope, Robert, ed. *Handbook of Middle American Indians.* Vols 7 and 8. Austin: University of Texas Press, 1969. Authoritative surveys of important Indian-speaking groups in northern and central (vol. 8) and southern (vol. 7) Mexico.

FLORA AND FAUNA

Goodson, Gar. *Fishes of the Pacific Coast*. Stanford, California: Stanford University Press, 1988. Over 500 beautifully detailed color drawings highlight this pocket version of all you ever wanted to know about the ocean's fishes (including common Spanish names) from Alaska to Peru.

Leopold, Starker. *Wildlife of Mexico*. Berkeley: University of California Press. Classic, illustrated layperson's survey of common Mexican mammals and birds.

Mason, Jr., Charles T., and Patricia B. Mason. *Handbook of Mexican Roadside Flora*. Tucson: University of Arizona Press, 1987. Authoritative identification guide, with line illustrations, of all the plants you're likely to see in the Puerto Vallarta region.

Morris, Percy A. *A Field Guide to Pacific Coast Shells*. Boston: Houghton Mifflin. The compleat beachcomber's Pacific shell guide.

Novick, Rosalind, and Lan Sing Wu. *Where to Find Birds in San Blas, Nayarit*. Order through the authors at 178 Myrtle Court, Arcata, CA 95521, tel. (707) 822-0790.

Pesman, M. Walter. *Meet Flora Mexicana*. Delightful anecdotes and illustrations of hundreds of common Mexican plants. Published around 1960, now out of print.

Peterson, Roger Tory, and Edward L. Chalif. *Field Guide to Mexican Birds*. Boston: Houghton Mifflin. With hundreds of Peterson's crisp color drawings, this is a must for serious birders and vacationers interested in the life that teems in the Puerto Vallarta region's beaches, jungles, lakes, and lagoons.

Wright, N. Pelham. *A Guide to Mexican Mammals and Reptiles*. Mexico City: Minutiae Mexicana, 1989. Pocket-edition lore, history, descriptions, and pictures of commonly seen Mexican animals.

ART, ARCHITECTURE, AND CRAFTS

Baird, Joseph. *The Churches of Mexico*. Berkeley: University of California Press. Mexican colonial architecture and art, illustrated and interpreted.

Cordrey, Donald, and Dorothy Cordrey. *Mexican Indian Costumes*. Austin: University of Texas Press, 1968. A lovingly photographed, written, and illustrated classic on Mexican Indians and their dress, emphasizing textiles.

Covarrubias, Miguel. *Indian Art of Mexico and Central America*. New York: Knopf, 1957. A timeless work by the renowned interpreter of *indígena* art and design.

Martínez Penaloza, Porfirio. *Popular Arts of Mexico*. Mexico City: Editorial Panorama, 1981. An excellent, authoritative, pocket-sized exposition of Mexican art.

Sayer, Chloë. *Arts and Crafts of Mexico*. San Francisco: Chronicle Books, 1990. All you ever wanted to know about your favorite Mexican crafts, from papier-mâché to pottery and toys and Taxco silver. Beautifully illustrated by traditional etchings and David Lavender's crisp black-and-white and color photographs.

ACCOMMODATIONS INDEX

RESTAURANT INDEX

INDEX

MARKETS

MUSEUMS

ABOUT THE AUTHOR

In the early 1980s, the lure of travel drew Bruce Whipperman away from a 20-year career of teaching physics. The occasion was a trip to Kenya, which included a total solar eclipse and a safari. He hasn't stopped traveling since.

With his family grown, he has been free to let the world's wild, beautiful corners draw him on: to the ice-clawed Karakoram, the Gobi Desert's trellised oases, the pink palaces of Rajasthan, Japan's green wine country, Bali's emerald terraces, and now, the Puerto Vallarta region's golden beaches, wildlife-rich mangrove wetlands, and flower-festooned mountain valleys.

Bruce has always pursued his travel career for the fun of it. He started with slide shows and photo gifts for friends. Others wanted his photos, so he began selling them. Once, stranded in Ethiopia, he began to write. A dozen years later, after scores of magazine and newspaper feature stories, *Pacific Mexico Handbook* became his first book. For him, travel writing heightens his awareness and focuses his own travel experiences. He always remembers what a Nepali Sherpa once said: "Many people come, looking, looking; few people come, see."

Travel, after all, is for returning home, and that coziest of journeys always brings a tired but happy Bruce back to his friends, son, daughter, and wife Linda in Berkeley, California.

Bruce invites *Puerto Vallarta Handbook*'s readers likewise to "come see"—and discover and enjoy—Puerto Vallarta's delights with a fresh eye and renewed compassion.

LOSE YOURSELF IN THE EXPERIENCE, NOT THE CROWD

For more than 25 years, Moon Travel Handbooks have been the guidebooks of choice for adventurous travelers. Our award-winning Handbook series provides focused, comprehensive coverage of distinct destinations all over the world. Each Handbook is like an entire bookcase of cultural insight and introductory information in one portable volume. Our goal at Moon is to give travelers all the background and practical information they'll need for an extraordinary travel experience.

The following pages include a complete list of Handbooks, covering North America and Hawaii, Mexico, Latin America and the Caribbean, and Asia and the Pacific. To purchase Moon Travel Handbooks, check your local bookstore or order c/o Publishers Group West, Attn: Order Department, 1700 Fourth St., Berkeley, CA 94710, or fax to (510) 528-3444.

"An in-depth dunk into the land, the people and their history, arts, and politics."
—*Student Travels*

"I consider these books to be superior to Lonely Planet. When Moon produces a book it is more humorous, incisive, and off-beat."
—*Toronto Sun*

"Outdoor enthusiasts gravitate to the well-written Moon Travel Handbooks. In addition to politically correct historic and cultural features, the series focuses on flora, fauna and outdoor recreation. Maps and meticulous directions also are a trademark of Moon guides."
—*Houston Chronicle*

"Moon [Travel Handbooks] . . . bring a healthy respect to the places they investigate. Best of all, they provide a host of odd nuggets that give a place texture and prod the wary traveler from the beaten path. The finest are written with such care and insight they deserve listing as literature."
—*American Geographical Society*

"Moon Travel Handbooks offer in-depth historical essays and useful maps, enhanced by a sense of humor and a neat, compact format."
—*Swing*

"Perfect for the more adventurous, these are long on history, sightseeing and nitty-gritty information and very price-specific."
—*Columbus Dispatch*

"Moon guides manage to be comprehensive and countercultural at the same time . . . Handbooks are packed with maps, photographs, drawings, and sidebars that constitute a college-level introduction to each country's history, culture, people, and crafts."
—*National Geographic Traveler*

"Few travel guides do a better job helping travelers create their own itineraries than the Moon Travel Handbook series. The authors have a knack for homing in on the essentials."
—**Colorado Springs** *Gazette Telegraph*

MEXICO

"These books will delight the armchair traveler, aid the undecided person in selecting a destination, and guide the seasoned road warrior looking for lesser-known hideaways."
—*Mexican Meanderings* Newsletter

"From tourist traps to off-the-beaten track hideaways, these guides offer consistent, accurate details without pretension."
—*Foreign Service Journal*

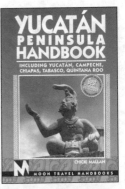

Archaeological Mexico	**$19.95**
Andrew Coe	420 pages, 27 maps
Baja Handbook	**$16.95**
Joe Cummings	540 pages, 46 maps
Cabo Handbook	**$14.95**
Joe Cummings	270 pages, 17 maps
Cancún Handbook	**$14.95**
Chicki Mallan	240 pages, 25 maps
Colonial Mexico	**$18.95**
Chicki Mallan	400 pages, 38 maps
Mexico Handbook	**$21.95**
Joe Cummings and Chicki Mallan	1,200 pages, 201 maps
Northern Mexico Handbook	**$17.95**
Joe Cummings	610 pages, 69 maps
Pacific Mexico Handbook	**$17.95**
Bruce Whipperman	580 pages, 68 maps
Puerto Vallarta Handbook	**$14.95**
Bruce Whipperman	330 pages, 36 maps
Yucatán Handbook	**$16.95**
Chicki Mallan	400 pages, 52 maps

"Beyond question, the most comprehensive Mexican resources available for those who prefer deep travel to shallow tourism. But don't worry, the fiesta-fun stuff's all here too."
—*New York Daily News*

LATIN AMERICA AND THE CARIBBEAN

"Solidly packed with practical information and full of significant cultural asides that will enlighten you on the whys and wherefores of things you might easily see but not easily grasp."

—*Boston Globe*

Belize Handbook	**$15.95**
Chicki Mallan and Patti Lange	390 pages, 45 maps
Caribbean Vacations	**$18.95**
Karl Luntta	910 pages, 64 maps
Costa Rica Handbook	**$19.95**
Christopher P. Baker	780 pages, 73 maps
Cuba Handbook	**$19.95**
Christopher P. Baker	740 pages, 70 maps
Dominican Republic Handbook	**$15.95**
Gaylord Dold	420 pages, 24 maps
Ecuador Handbook	**$16.95**
Julian Smith	450 pages, 43 maps
Honduras Handbook	**$15.95**
Chris Humphrey	330 pages, 40 maps
Jamaica Handbook	**$15.95**
Karl Luntta	330 pages, 17 maps
Virgin Islands Handbook	**$13.95**
Karl Luntta	220 pages, 19 maps

NORTH AMERICA AND HAWAII

"These domestic guides convey the same sense of exoticism that their foreign counterparts do, making home-country travel seem like far-flung adventure."

—*Sierra Magazine*

Alaska-Yukon Handbook	**$17.95**
Deke Castleman and Don Pitcher	530 pages, 92 maps
Alberta and the Northwest Territories Handbook	**$18.95**
Andrew Hempstead	520 pages, 79 maps
Arizona Handbook	**$18.95**
Bill Weir	600 pages, 36 maps
Atlantic Canada Handbook	**$18.95**
Mark Morris	490 pages, 60 maps
Big Island of Hawaii Handbook	**$15.95**
J.D. Bisignani	390 pages, 25 maps
Boston Handbook	**$13.95**
Jeff Perk	200 pages, 20 maps
British Columbia Handbook	**$16.95**
Jane King and Andrew Hempstead	430 pages, 69 maps

Canadian Rockies Handbook	**$14.95**
Andrew Hempstead	220 pages, 22 maps
Colorado Handbook	**$17.95**
Stephen Metzger	480 pages, 46 maps
Georgia Handbook	**$17.95**
Kap Stann	380 pages, 44 maps
Grand Canyon Handbook	**$14.95**
Bill Weir	220 pages, 10 maps
Hawaii Handbook	**$19.95**
J.D. Bisignani	1,030 pages, 88 maps
Honolulu-Waikiki Handbook	**$14.95**
J.D. Bisignani	360 pages, 20 maps
Idaho Handbook	**$18.95**
Don Root	610 pages, 42 maps
Kauai Handbook	**$15.95**
J.D. Bisignani	320 pages, 23 maps
Los Angeles Handbook	**$16.95**
Kim Weir	370 pages, 15 maps
Maine Handbook	**$18.95**
Kathleen M. Brandes	660 pages, 27 maps
Massachusetts Handbook	**$18.95**
Jeff Perk	600 pages, 23 maps
Maui Handbook	**$15.95**
J.D. Bisignani	450 pages, 37 maps
Michigan Handbook	**$15.95**
Tina Lassen	360 pages, 32 maps
Montana Handbook	**$17.95**
Judy Jewell and W.C. McRae	490 pages, 52 maps
Nevada Handbook	**$18.95**
Deke Castleman	530 pages, 40 maps
New Hampshire Handbook	**$18.95**
Steve Lantos	500 pages, 18 maps
New Mexico Handbook	**$15.95**
Stephen Metzger	360 pages, 47 maps
New York Handbook	**$19.95**
Christiane Bird	780 pages, 95 maps
New York City Handbook	**$13.95**
Christiane Bird	300 pages, 20 maps
North Carolina Handbook	**$14.95**
Rob Hirtz and Jenny Daughtry Hirtz	320 pages, 27 maps
Northern California Handbook	**$19.95**
Kim Weir	800 pages, 50 maps
Ohio Handbook	**$15.95**
David K. Wright	340 pages, 18 maps
Oregon Handbook	**$17.95**
Stuart Warren and Ted Long Ishikawa	590 pages, 34 maps

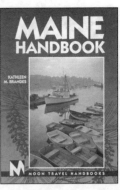

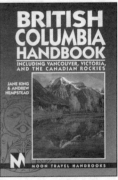

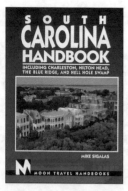

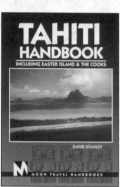

Pennsylvania Handbook	**$18.95**
Joanne Miller	448 pages, 40 maps
Road Trip USA	**$24.00**
Jamie Jensen	940 pages, 175 maps
Road Trip USA Getaways: Chicago	**$9.95**
	60 pages, 1 map
Road Trip USA Getaways: Seattle	**$9.95**
	60 pages, 1 map
Santa Fe-Taos Handbook	**$13.95**
Stephen Metzger	160 pages, 13 maps
South Carolina Handbook	**$16.95**
Mike Sigalas	400 pages, 20 maps
Southern California Handbook	**$19.95**
Kim Weir	720 pages, 26 maps
Tennessee Handbook	**$17.95**
Jeff Bradley	530 pages, 42 maps
Texas Handbook	**$18.95**
Joe Cummings	690 pages, 70 maps
Utah Handbook	**$17.95**
Bill Weir and W.C. McRae	490 pages, 40 maps
Virginia Handbook	**$15.95**
Julian Smith	410 pages, 37 maps
Washington Handbook	**$19.95**
Don Pitcher	840 pages, 111 maps
Wisconsin Handbook	**$18.95**
Thomas Huhti	590 pages, 69 maps
Wyoming Handbook	**$17.95**
Don Pitcher	610 pages, 80 maps

ASIA AND THE PACIFIC

"Scores of maps, detailed practical info down to business hours of small-town libraries. You can't beat the Asian titles for sheer heft. (The) series is sort of an American Lonely Planet, with better writing but fewer titles. (The) individual voice of researchers comes through."

—Travel & Leisure

Australia Handbook	**$21.95**
Marael Johnson, Andrew Hempstead, and Nadina Purdon	940 pages, 141 maps
Bali Handbook	**$19.95**
Bill Dalton	750 pages, 54 maps
Fiji Islands Handbook	**$14.95**
David Stanley	350 pages, 42 maps
Hong Kong Handbook	**$16.95**
Kerry Moran	378 pages, 49 maps

Indonesia Handbook	$25.00
Bill Dalton	1,380 pages, 249 maps
Micronesia Handbook	**$16.95**
Neil M. Levy	340 pages, 70 maps
Nepal Handbook	**$18.95**
Kerry Moran	490 pages, 51 maps
New Zealand Handbook	**$19.95**
Jane King	620 pages, 81 maps
Outback Australia Handbook	**$18.95**
Marael Johnson	450 pages, 57 maps
Philippines Handbook	**$17.95**
Peter Harper and Laurie Fullerton	670 pages, 116 maps
Singapore Handbook	**$15.95**
Carl Parkes	350 pages, 29 maps
South Korea Handbook	**$19.95**
Robert Nilsen	820 pages, 141 maps
South Pacific Handbook	**$24.00**
David Stanley	920 pages, 147 maps
Southeast Asia Handbook	**$21.95**
Carl Parkes	1,080 pages, 204 maps
Tahiti Handbook	**$15.95**
David Stanley	450 pages, 51 maps
Thailand Handbook	**$19.95**
Carl Parkes	860 pages, 142 maps
Vietnam, Cambodia & Laos Handbook	**$18.95**
Michael Buckley	760 pages, 116 maps

OTHER GREAT TITLES FROM MOON

"For hardy wanderers, few guides come more highly
recommended than the Handbooks. They include good
maps, steer clear of fluff and flackery, and offer plenty of
money-saving tips. They also give you the kind of
information that visitors to strange lands—on any budget—
need to survive."

—*US News & World Report*

Moon Handbook	$10.00
Carl Koppeschaar	150 pages, 8 maps
The Practical Nomad: How to Travel Around the World	**$17.95**
Edward Hasbrouck	580 pages
Staying Healthy in Asia, Africa, and Latin America	**$11.95**
Dirk Schroeder	230 pages, 4 maps

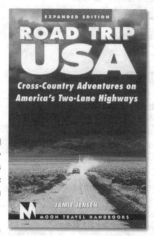

WHERE TO BUY MOON TRAVEL HANDBOOKS

BOOKSTORES AND LIBRARIES: Moon Travel Handbooks are distributed worldwide. Please contact our sales manager at info@moon.com for a list of wholesalers and distributors in your area.

TRAVELERS: We would like to have Moon Travel Handbooks available throughout the world. Please ask your bookstore to contact us for ordering information. If your bookstore will not order our guides for you, please contact us for a free catalog.

Moon Travel Handbooks
c/o Publishers Group West
Attn: Order Department
1700 Fourth Street
Berkeley, CA 94710
fax: (510) 528-3444

IMPORTANT ORDERING INFORMATION

PRICES: All prices are subject to change. We always ship the most current edition. We will let you know if there is a price increase on the book you order.

SHIPPING AND HANDLING OPTIONS: Domestic UPS or USPS priority mail (allow 10 working days for delivery): $6.00 for the first item, $1.00 for each additional item.

UPS 2nd Day Air or Printed Airmail requires a special quote.

International Surface Bookrate 8-12 weeks delivery: $5.00 for the first item, $1.00 for each additional item. Note: We cannot guarantee international surface bookrate shipping. We recommend sending international orders via air mail, which requires a special quote.

FOREIGN ORDERS: Orders that originate outside the U.S.A. must be paid for with an international money order, a check in U.S. currency drawn on a major U.S. bank based in the U.S.A., or Visa, MasterCard, or American Express.

INTERNET ORDERS: Visit our site at: www.moon.com

ORDER FORM

Prices are subject to change without notice. Please check our Web site
at **www.moon.com** for current prices and editions.
(See important ordering information on preceding page.)

Name: _____ Date: _____

Street: _____

City: _____ Daytime Phone: _____

State or Country: _____ Zip Code: _____

QUANTITY	TITLE	PRICE

Taxable Total _____

Sales Tax in CA and NY _____

Shipping & Handling _____

TOTAL _____

Ship: ☐ UPS (no P.O. Boxes) ☐ Priority mail ☐ International surface mail

Ship to: ☐ address above ☐ other _____

_____

Make checks payable to: **PUBLISHERS GROUP WEST**, Attn: Order Department, 1700 Fourth St.,
Berkeley, CA 94710, or fax to (510) 528-3444. We accept Visa, MasterCard, or American Express.
   To Order: Fax in your Visa, MasterCard, or American Express number, or send a written order
with your Visa, MasterCard, or American Express number and expiration date clearly written.

Card Number: ☐ **Visa**   ☐ **MasterCard**   ☐ **American Express**

☐ ☐ ☐ ☐   ☐ ☐ ☐ ☐   ☐ ☐ ☐ ☐   ☐ ☐ ☐ ☐

Exact Name on Card: _____

Expiration date: _____

Signature: _____

Daytime Phone: _____

U.S.~METRIC CONVERSION

1 inch = 2.54 centimeters (cm)
1 foot = .304 meters (m)
1 yard = 0.914 meters
1 mile = 1.6093 kilometers (km)
1 km = .6214 miles
1 fathom = 1.8288 m
1 chain = 20.1168 m
1 furlong = 201.168 m
1 acre = .4047 hectares
1 sq km = 100 hectares
1 sq mile = 2.59 square km
1 ounce = 28.35 grams
1 pound = .4536 kilograms
1 short ton = .90718 metric ton
1 short ton = 2000 pounds
1 long ton = 1.016 metric tons
1 long ton = 2240 pounds
1 metric ton = 1000 kilograms
1 quart = .94635 liters
1 US gallon = 3.7854 liters
1 Imperial gallon = 4.5459 liters
1 nautical mile = 1.852 km

To compute celsius temperatures, subtract 32 from Fahrenheit and divide by 1.8. To go the other way, multiply celsius by 1.8 and add 32.

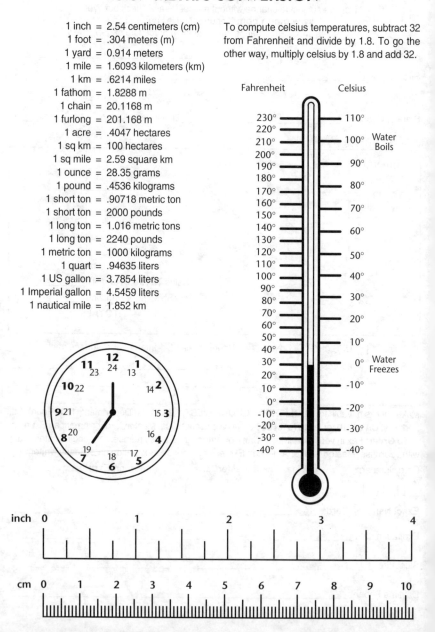